ILLUSTRATED HISTORY OF ROCK & ROLL

THE ROLLING STONE

Gene Laverne of Buffalo, N.Y.

Ersel Hickey, the personification of early rock & roll style.

THE RollingStone ILLUSTRATED HISTORY OF ROCK & ROLL

The Definitive History of the Most Important Artists and Their Music

EDITED BY ANTHONY DeCURTIS AND JAMES HENKE

WITH HOLLY GEORGE-WARREN

ORIGINAL EDITOR: JIM MILLER

RANDOM HOUSE NEW YORK

This work was originally published in 1976
by Random House, Inc., in different form. A
revised and updated edition was published in
1980 by Random House, Inc.

Permission acknowledgments for previously
published material can be found on page 691.

Song lyric credits appear on page 693.

Photo credits appear on page 697.

Library of Congress Cataloging-in-Publication Data

The Rolling Stone illustrated history of rock & roll / edited by
Anthony DeCurtis and James Henke with Holly George-Warren; original
editor, Jim Miller.—[New ed.], 1st ed.
p.   cm.
Includes index.
ISBN 0-679-73728-6
1. Rock music—History and criticism. I. DeCurtis, Anthony.
II. Henke, James. III. George-Warren, Holly. IV. Rolling Stone.
ML3534.R64   1992   781.66'09—dc20   92-6339
CIP
MN

Manufactured in the United States of America
98765
Third Edition
Design by Jo Anne Metsch

CONTENTS

INTRODUCTION

BY ANTHONY DeCURTIS

Could the world of rock & roll possibly have changed more radically than it did between 1980, the year of the first updating of *The* ROLLING STONE *Illustrated History of Rock & Roll* (originally published in 1976), and 1992? In the early Eighties it would have seemed inconceivable that a twenty-four-hour music-video network would become the most significant means by which popular music reached its audience or that vinyl records would become virtually obsolete. Who could have foreseen that songs consisting of intensely rhythmic spoken rhymes over grooves lifted from other records—songs, amazingly, on which no one played an instrument or sang—would become the most vital and popular music of the day?

By the early Nineties all of the cultural forces unleashed during the boom years of the Eighties were contending with one another for the attention of an audience that was more diverse or fragmented—take your pick, depending on your disposition—than ever before. Were the great surviving rock bands of the Sixties lumbering dinosaurs too addled by age to realize that their moment of meaning had passed? Or were they the proud bearers of a classical legacy, battling the current era's barbarism? Were the hip-hop kids stellar examples of popular music's infinite ability to reinvent itself? Or were they offensive no-talents indulged by a cynical industry willing to make a buck on any fad that came down the pike?

Was MTV liberating or soul-deadening? Was lip syncing harmless or criminally fraudulent? Was any contemporary music truly "underground" or "alternative"? Or were those terms most useful as descriptions of marketing strategies? Was the "world music" phenomenon simply an exotic distraction for terminally hip consumers desperate to find the next edge? Or the best hope for the revitalization of a pop scene bled nearly to death by stagnant formulas and stifling commercial imperatives?

And, finally, what can it mean to put forward a history of rock & roll in the face of such questions? Well, as the past two decades have taught, there is no single history of anything, but a variety of histories that blend together at certain points, drift apart at others, intersect and repel, reinforce and contradict. That assumption underlies the third edition of this book. At a time when it is impossible to define in any absolute way what rock & roll even *is*, no other approach will do.

Fifteen new chapters have been added to this book; four chapters have been entirely redone by new writers; three chapters have been deleted; nearly fifty have been substantially revised. If, as editors and researchers, we all did our jobs properly, all matters of historical fact that you encounter will be as true as thorough reporting and verification can make them. And if we all did our jobs properl

critics, you will sometimes be enlightened and sometimes outraged, sometimes overjoyed at having your own feelings expressed in delightfully compelling terms, sometimes upset at having your most cherished notions unsettled. If you read any chapter and come away unaffected, we have failed. I don't believe that will happen.

The discographies that follow each chapter require a bit of explanation. They list singles or albums—and sometimes both—as the editors and authors deemed appropriate. They are selective, not exhaustive, and are meant to demonstrate some combination of historical significance, aesthetic quality and commercial impact. Each single and album is listed chronologically with its original label, the year in which it was released and an indication of how well it did on the *Billboard* charts. Here is a sample entry:

Elvis Presley, "Don't Be Cruel" b/w "Hound Dog" (RCA Victor; r☆1, c☆1, ☆1, 1956)

That entry indicates that Elvis Presley's two-sided hit on RCA reached Number One on the rhythm & blues, country & western and pop charts in 1956.

Many people helped make this third edition of the *Illustrated History* a reality. James Henke and I would like to thank Jann S. Wenner and our colleagues at ROLLING STONE magazine for their encouragement. Acknowledgment is also due to Jim Miller, who oversaw the first two editions and set a standard that simultaneously daunted and inspired us, Sarah Lazin, the literary agent and former director of Rolling Stone Press, who is as responsible as anyone for the existence of this volume, and Patricia Romanowski for her keen editorial insight. Leora Kahn researched the photos for this edition, and Joseph Angio, Brandon Holley, Alison Kalfus, Mick Leland, Steven Mirkin, Laura Nolan and Andrea Odintz provided research support. Kim Neely, Lori Berk, Cara Manning, Beth Cohen, Shawn Dahl, Susan Cole, Eric Marquard and Jude Biersdorfer—all of ROLLING STONE—helped out in many ways and more than deserve our heartfelt appreciation.

A final word of thanks must go to Holly George-Warren, whose editorial and organizational genius saved the day more often than can be thought of comfortably. Both supportive and challenging, she made a staggeringly difficult task a form of pleasure. And, most valuably, in her energy, unstoppable good cheer and sheer love of rock & roll, she provided a constant reminder of why this music and this writing are important.

THE ROLLING STONE

ILLUSTRATED HISTORY OF ROCK & ROLL

ROCK BEGINS

BY ROBERT PALMER

Several dozen black dancers shuffled around the floor of the tiny rural church, stamping out a steady rocking beat on the floorboards and clapping their hands in complex cross-rhythms. A hoarse-voiced leader shouted out one-line phrases in a kind of singsong, the dancers answering with whiplash responses. When the song leader fell back on a bench, overcome by the shuddering rhythms, the heat and the furious pace of the singing, a second leader took over, half-singing, half-gurgling in an unknown tongue.

> O my Lord
> O my Lordy
> Well, well, well
> I've gotta rock
> You gotta rock
> Wah wah ho
> Wah wah wah ho

In a corner of the church two white folklorists, John Lomax and his son Alan, sat transfixed as their bulky portable recording rig transcribed the music onto an aluminum disc. The year was 1934, and the Lomaxes had stumbled upon a survival of one of the oldest varieties of African-American religious songs, a genuine backcountry ring shout. But they had also stumbled upon the future. The rhythmic singing, the hard-driving beat, the bluesy melody and the improvised, stream-of-consciousness words of this particular shout—eventually issued by the Library of Congress as ''Run Old Jeremiah''—all anticipate key aspects of rock & roll as it would emerge some twenty years later.

The Lomaxes were just beginning to record folk music on location in the rural South in 1934, but rock prototypes were already abundant. In Mississippi the sedate spiritual singing of earlier genera-

Backyard blues: Sonny Boy Williamson blows harp to sell flour.

tions was being replaced by a new style, emphasizing the deliberate rhythms of the archaic ring shouts. The style was called "rocking and reeling," and it probably originated in the maverick Sanctified or Holiness churches, where guitars, drums and horns were as acceptable as the piano or the organ, and more easily afforded. Moreover, it was a style that was already beginning to influence secular music. The Graves brothers of Hattiesburg, Mississippi, who had recorded "rocking and reeling" spirituals for Paramount in 1929, made several blues records as the Mississippi Jook Band in 1936. Their "Barbecue Bust" and "Dangerous Woman" featured fully formed rock & roll guitar riffs and a stomping rock & roll beat.

It is possible, with the help of a little hindsight, to find rock roots at almost every stratum of American folk and popular music during the mid-Thirties. In Chicago transplanted Southern bluesmen like Tampa Red and Big Bill Broonzy were taming irregular rural forms to the demands of the urban accompaniment, often including horns, piano, bass and drums. In the Midwest jump bands were keeping their fans dancing with hard-riffing instrumental blues, featuring gruff-toned tenor saxophone solos and a four-to-the-bar walking rhythm that was an urban descendant of the down-home sanctified stomp. In Nashville two white hillbillies named Alton and Rabon Delmore were entertaining radio audiences with their hit "Brown's Ferry Blues," a black-influenced, two-guitar dance tune as redolent of things to come as the music of the Mississippi Jook Band. In Texas and Oklahoma large, white Western swing bands such as Bob Wills and His Texas Playboys and Milton Brown's Musical Brownies were mixing big-band jazz, black blues and white country music into a heady brew.

Rock & roll was an inevitable outgrowth of the social and musical interactions between blacks and whites in the South and Southwest. Its roots are a complex tangle. Bedrock black church music influenced blues, rural blues influenced white folk song, and the black popular music of the Northern ghettos—blues and black pop—influenced jazz and so on. But the single most important process was the influence of black music on white. Rock might not

have developed out of a self-contained African-American tradition, but it certainly would not have developed had there been no African-Americans.

In a very real sense rock was implicit in the music of the first Africans brought to North America. This transplanted African music wasn't exactly boogie-woogie or jazz, but it did have several characteristics that survive in American music today. It was participatory; often a song leader would be pitted against an answering chorus, or a solo instrument against an ensemble, in call-and-response fashion. It sometimes attained remarkable polyrhythmic complexity and always had a kind of percussive directionality or rhythmic drive. Vocal quality tended to be hoarse or grainy by European standards, though there was also considerable use of falsetto. Melodies fell within a relatively narrow range and often incorporated flexible pitch treatment around certain "blue notes." There was some improvisation, but always within the limits of more or less traditional structures.

All these characteristics are evident in quite a few rock & roll records. For example, in "What'd I Say," Ray Charles calls out a lead melody while a chorus responds and riffing horns answer his piano figures. His band's rhythm section drives relentlessly and

Pianist Moon Mullican, who played hillbilly boogie.

Bob Wills and His Texas Playboys taking Western swing seriously.

superimposes fancy accent patterns over the basic beat. His voice has a hoarse, straining quality, with occasional leaps into falsetto. His melody is narrow in range and blueslike, and the improvisations that occur never threaten the continuity of the song's gospel-derived metric and harmonic structure.

One shouldn't conclude from these similarities that pure African music was somehow transformed into rock & roll. Music in Africa was always flexible, ready to accommodate new influences from the next village or from foreign cultures, and in America plantation owners and preachers tried to stamp it out entirely. Accordingly, it adapted. The traits that survived without much alteration tended to be of two kinds. Some were musical imponderables, like vocal quality or rhythmic drive, aspects of style so basic to the culture they were rarely considered consciously and were therefore immune to conscious change. Others—blues scales, call-and-response

forms—were close enough to some varieties of European folk music to be assimilated and perpetuated by whites.

The acculturation of black Americans to mainstream musical values proceeded more and more rapidly as the twentieth century gathered momentum, but pockets of tradition remained. In 1940, when Charlie Christian and T-Bone Walker were already playing modern jazz and blues on electric guitars, a team of interviewers in the Georgia Sea Islands found elderly residents who still knew songs in African languages and knew how to make African drums. Elsewhere, the bedrock African culture persevered most tenaciously in the black church, just as in Africa itself religion, magic and music had been closely linked in a kind of composite cultural focus. This is why the most African-sounding rock & roll has always come from the church, from gospel-inspired blues shouters such as Ray Charles or

Worshipers at the Church of God in Christ, Clarksdale, Mississippi, 1968.

from former gospel singers such as the Isley Brothers, whose "Shout" was an old-fashioned ring shout done up with band accompaniment.

But there is more to rock & roll than this single primordial strain. The roots of "What'd I Say" and "Shout" are not necessarily identical to the roots of Chuck Berry's "Johnny B. Goode" or of Carl Perkins's "Blue Suede Shoes." It would take at least one book, if not a library, to trace these various kinds of rock & roll back through their myriad sources. Here we can only indicate some of the most important contributors and trace a few of the most prominent developmental processes.

The music brought to America by European settlers determined most of the forms in which both old and new song materials would be set. Song stanzas of four and eight bars were a heritage of European epic poetry and narrative ballads; there are examples of such things in some traditional African music, but only as one formal scheme among many. The narrative ballad itself, with its objective performer who comments on but does not become involved in the action, was a European product very foreign to the mainstream of black tradition. A ballad vogue among blacks during the late nineteenth century did produce memorable songs such as "Stagger Lee" and "Frankie and Johnny," several of which were revived by early rockers.

In isolated rural areas, particularly Appalachia and the Ozarks, traditional English, Scotch and Irish dance music survived, along with folk fiddling. But even there the African banjo became as popular as the fiddle. The guitar, which had been derived by the Spanish and Portuguese from the African Moors, came later. During the late nineteenth and early twentieth centuries, white country musicians developed a tradition of virtuosity on all these instruments. Their repertoires retained many old-time folk ballads, dance tunes and hymns, but black-influenced minstrel tunes, blueslike ballads and camp meeting songs were also popular.

African-Americans had developed their own distinctive and diverse body of folk music by 1900 alongside the relatively pure African strains that survived in some church music and in the work songs sung by gang laborers. The black creations that whites knew best were minstrel songs—lively, often humorous tunes that tended to resemble Anglo-American jigs and reels. Many minstrel songs were composed by whites such as Dan Emmett (composer of "Dixie") and Thomas D. Rice ("Jump Jim Crow"), but all of them were inspired ultimately by the black plantation orchestras that had regaled visitors in the antebellum South. Both the black groups and their white imitators consisted of banjos, fiddles (an instrument with numerous West African precedents) and various percussion instruments, notably tambourines, triangles and bone clappers. The earliest plantation orchestras had probably played African dance music like that performed by the lute- and fiddle-playing *griots* of the African savanna today. But by the time we heard of them, they had learned enough European dance tunes to satisfy their white patrons, and the fiddlers were paying some attention to European musical standards. The white minstrels, who copied black playing styles and tunes as closely as they could, became the rage of America and Europe during the years just before the Civil War. For the first time, an essentially black music, albeit in diluted form, had found favor with a large white audience. Oddly enough, many popular minstrel songs were absorbed back into black tradition following the war. They turned up in the repertoires of black banjo- and guitar-playing minstrels, or songsters, well into the twentieth century.

During the first decades of the century a new kind of black secular song emerged. The songs were originally known as "one-verse songs" because they repeated a single line several times. Gradually an *aab* stanza form replaced the older *aaa,* and the songs began to be called blues. They may have represented an attempt by rural blacks to accommodate the demands of guitar accompaniment within the free-flowing strains of their field cries and work songs. In any case, the blues spread rapidly, first through the tent-show performances of such vaudeville singers as Gertrude "Ma" Rainey, then through the polished blues-based compositions of W. C. Handy, and finally, after 1926, through recordings by authentic rural bluesmen such as Blind Lemon Jefferson. Along with blues recordings, which were popular among Northern blacks as well as in the South, came records of singing black preachers and of holy dance music from the Sanctified churches.

W. C. Handy, "Father of the Blues," *(left)* with Nat "King" Cole, 1957. Handy wrote "St. Louis Blues"; Cole motored west on "Route 66."

The rise of the recording industry in the Twenties accelerated musical syntheses. For the first time, white guitar players from Kentucky were able to listen carefully to the music of black bluesmen from Texas, and rural medicine-show entertainers could hear the latest cabaret hits from New York. Early recordings documented musical changes rather than determining them, but by the mid-Thirties records were the primary source of inspiration for many musicians.

In white country music, the largely traditional repertoires of performers like Uncle Dave Macon became outmoded as younger musicians popularized their own hybrid material. Among the most influential of these were Jimmie Rodgers, the "singing brakeman" from Meridian, Mississippi, and the Alabama-born Delmore Brothers. Both acts recorded black-influenced blues and blueslike dance tunes. The Monroe Brothers, Bill and Charlie, popularized a more Anglo-American brand of country music. In a sense they helped preserve white folk traditions by dressing them up with a new vocal intensity and unprecedented instrumental flash. But even mandolinist Bill Monroe, who went on to become the "father of bluegrass," injected a great deal of blues feeling into his playing. Early in his career he had been impressed by a black guitarist and fiddler named Arnold Schultz, who reportedly exercised a

decisive influence on Ike Everly and Merle Travis as well. In the West, Western swing bands combined country music, black-oriented repertoires, horns, drums and hot improvised solos from another black musical source, jazz.

Jazz itself was growing in several different directions, but in the Southwest it was heavily indebted to vocal blues. Bands like Count Basie's ("the band that plays the blues") concentrated on the twelve-bar blues form almost exclusively and often played "head" arrangements: blues riffs developed by the musicians on the spur of the moment. Rhythmically, Basie and the other Southwestern bands played a danceable, even, four-to-the-bar pulse that gradually replaced the jerky 2/4 associated with Dixieland. The bluesiness, the riffing horns, the tough tenor saxophone solos and the driving rhythm of these groups had a profound impact on Western swing—which led in turn to country boogie and rockabilly—and on black popular music, which led to rhythm & blues and rock & roll.

As rural bluesmen moved to urban centers, their music lost much of its delicacy and lilt. In keeping with the pace of city life, rhythms became heavier, more insistent and faster. An indication of this shift came from Memphis as early as the Twenties. There, several two-guitar teams worked out a characteristic differentiation of parts in which one played lead lines while the other provided bass notes and chords. (Earlier country-blues guitar duets had tended toward a more intricate, more democratic counterpoint.) Memphis blues rhythms were already harder and steadier than those of the surrounding countryside.

Chester Arthur Burnett, the "Howlin' Wolf."

From left: Jimmy Rushing, emcee Pee Wee Marquette and Count Basie, at Birdland in New York City, 1953. Basie's riffing blues inspired many of the postwar R&B jump bands.

Big Bill Broonzy, a Mississippian who relocated in Chicago, took these ideas a step further by working with washtub-and-string bassists and with the percussive washboard of Washboard Sam. During the Thirties Broonzy and his Chicago friends, among them Sam and Tampa Red, became America's most popular blues performers. Harmonically, they were increasingly influenced by jazz, while rhythmically they favored the easy, relaxed swing of the Southwestern bands. When horns, drums and piano were added to their accompaniments, these ties to jazz became even more apparent.

Meanwhile, Southwestern blues and jazz musicians were experimenting with a revolutionary new instrument, the electric guitar. Eddie Durham seems to have recorded the first solos on the amplified instrument in 1938 with the Kansas City Five and Six, groups recruited from the Count Basie band. In 1939 Charlie Christian, an Oklahoman, recorded on electric guitar with Benny Goodman. His virtuoso horn-like single-string lines and the deep, bluesy

character of his playing set standards for jazz guitar playing that have yet to be superseded. But Christian was a former country bluesman. As a youngster he performed with an older guitarist, Aaron "T-Bone" Walker, who had recorded country blues (as Oak Cliff T-Bone) as early as 1929.

If Christian invented modern jazz guitar (and helped to invent modern jazz), it was T-Bone Walker who invented modern blues, setting the style that almost all subsequent blues and rock lead guitarists would follow, from B. B. King through Eric Clapton. The jazzy flash of Walker's work was not in itself revolutionary. While the Memphis bluesmen were

luted cry of blues and gospel singers. In addition, he developed a chordal style on fast numbers, a pumping guitar shuffle that led eventually to the archetypal rock & roll guitar style of Chuck Berry.

Jazz, which was a popular music with mass appeal through much of the Thirties, continued to produce black pop hits during the Forties and early Fifties. But slick, sophisticated jazz bands did not appeal to a significant number of urban African-Americans who were either born in the country or only a generation removed from it. To cater to their tastes, a raunchier, more down-home jazz style emerged. Lionel Hampton, vibraharpist who had worked with Benny Goodman, produced the definitive record in the new genre in 1942. It was "Flying Home," a riff-based number with a heavy beat. Hampton, who was also a drummer, is credited with being the first popular jazz percussionist to make a habit of turning the sticks around and hitting the drums with the blunt ends. But "Flying Home" had more than a big beat; it had a grainy, shrieking saxophone solo by the Texas-bred Illinois Jacquet. Hampton now says he was influenced to move in this direction by guitarist Charlie Christian and other Southwestern musicians, and Jacquet was one of a long line of Texas tenors who screamed and honked like sanctified preachers in spiritual paroxysms. There can be little doubt that the new idiom, often called "jump blues," was originally a Texas-Oklahoma phenomenon.

Louis Jordan, an Arkansas-born alto saxophonist and vocalist, played in a lighter, more urbanely humorous style, but his novelty hits of the Forties— "Saturday Night Fish Fry," "Caldonia," "Blue Light Boogie"—moved out to a rocking Southwestern boogie beat, and his alto solos were speech-inflected and gritty. Soon saxophone-dominated-band blues, usually with a boogie rhythm and T-Bone-derived guitar leads, became a dominant strain in black popular music. The headquarters for this music was the West Coast, where war industry jobs attracted thousands of blacks from the southwest and where a number of early jump-blues artists made records that were practically rock & roll—Amos Milburn's "Down the Road Apiece" (1946) and Little Willie Littlefield's "K.C. Loving" (1952, the same Leiber-

developing early lead guitar styles within a relatively simple framework, Eddie Lang and Lonnie Johnson were working in New York City as jazz soloists, playing single-note lines on their acoustic guitars on recordings by Bix Beiderbecke, Duke Ellington and other prominent figures.

Their techniques were exemplary, and necessarily so, for they had to fill with their virtuosity the spaces left by their instrument's rapidly decaying notes and relatively thin sound. Christian continued their style of rapid runs. But it took Walker to really exploit electricity. By using his amplifier's volume control to sustain pitches and combining this technique with the string-bending and finger vibrato practiced by traditional bluesmen, Walker in effect invented a new instrument. He was able to reproduce both the linear urgency of jazz saxophonists and the convo-

Clarence "Gatemouth" Brown *(left)* and T-Bone Walker, two Texas musicians, shake hands after a battle of the blues guitar.

Stoller tune later made famous as "Kansas City") are good examples. But the style's outreach was national. Roy Brown, from New Orleans, made the most seminal of all jump-blues hits, "Good Rockin' Tonight," in 1947, and the Nashville pianist Cecil Gant prefigured the Jerry Lee Lewis piano style in 1950 with "We're Gonna Rock."

Even black vocal harmony groups were affected by the emergence of band blues. Many of these groups had roots in the quartet singing that had been an important part of black religious music since the Twenties, but rather than base their styles on those of the more abandoned sanctified singers, they usually emulated the smooth pop harmonies of the Ink Spots. During the mid-Forties, however, the Spots' popularity waned, and some of the vocal groups adopted a harder approach that was much closer to Southern blues and gospel.

Lionel Hampton at the Band Box, New York City, 1953. His show-stopping bands featured wildly honking saxophonists.

In some cases this was the result of suggestions by white record producers. Independently operated record companies such as Savoy, Aladdin, Atlantic, Modern, Imperial and King recorded a majority of the black music popular after World War II. (For the most part, the ''majors,'' including Columbia and Victor, either concentrated on middle-of-the-road pop or continued to issue ''race'' discs by prewar favorites.) The independents were successful in part because they were run by men who knew black music. Many of the producers were collectors of blues, jazz and gospel records, and even when they were working with Northern musicians and singers they attempted to give their records a Southern flavor.

The increasing prominence of rocking boogie rhythms in black popular music during the Forties and early Fifties was an important but not particularly surprising phenomenon. Old-time Southwestern musicians remember people playing rocking boogies as far back as 1910—Texas pianist Sammy Price recalls Blind Lemon Jefferson referring to the style as ''booger rooger''—and the supercharged ''Pinetop's Boogie Woogie'' by Alabama-born pianist Clarence ''Pinetop'' Smith was a ''race record'' hit in 1928. More interesting, for the purposes of the present study, is the fact that the boogie fever that swept America beginning in the late Thirties and continuing through the early Fifties, right up to the beginnings of rock & roll, was a biracial phenomenon. It began, for all practical purposes, in 1938, when the white jazz collector and entrepreneur John Hammond brought black music to Carnegie Hall for his first ''From Spirituals to Swing'' concert. Featured on the bill were the rotund Kansas City blues shouter Joe Turner and his pianist Pete Johnson (who together made music that rocked as hard as the hits Turner would cut for Atlantic during the Fifties), along with two first-generation Chicago boogie-woogie pianists, Meade Lux Lewis and Albert Ammons. Turner and the three pianists settled in for a five-year run at New York's Cafe Society following the concert, and they made a number of recordings. Before long the infectious boogie-woogie beat was

The original Johnny Otis Band, 1947. Starting out as a postwar bandleader in Los Angeles, Otis became a pioneering R&B talent scout and record producer.

finding its way into the mainstream of white popular music. Tommy Dorsey scored a hit with "Boogie Woogie," a record so kinetic it is still cited as a favorite by one of rock's founding fathers, Sun Records producer Sam Phillips. The Andrews Sisters did "Boogie Woogie Bugle Boy."

Country artists started making boogie records, too. The Delmore Brothers, who were no strangers to black rhythms, set the pace in 1945 with their "Hillbilly Boogie," which lent an entire movement its name. By 1950, when Louis Jordan's "Blue Light Boogie" was a Number One rhythm & blues hit, Tennessee Ernie Ford was hitting the top of the country charts with "Shotgun Boogie." Black country bluesmen made raw, heavily amplified boogie records of their own, especially in Memphis, where guitarists like Joe Hill Louis, Willie Johnson (with the early Howlin' Wolf band) and Pat Hare (with Little Junior Parker) played driving rhythms and scorching, distorted solos that might be counted the distant ancestors of heavy metal.

From left: John Doe, Ira Louvin of the Louvin Brothers, John Doe II, Chet Atkins, Merle Travis, Charlie Louvin—country music stars of the Fifties.

Memphis in the early Fifties was a hotbed of musical activity, and many of the artists who were making a new kind of Southern city blues there—B. B. King, Bobby "Blue" Bland, Roscoe Gordon—would go on to shape the rhythm & blues and soul music of the Sixties. Perhaps the most important and influential record to come out of this ferment was "Rocket '88,'" cut at Sam Phillips's Memphis Recording Service, credited to Jackie Brenston on the Chess label, but actually by the Ike Turner band, with saxophonist Brenston taking the lead vocal. Turner, a pianist and aspiring guitarist from the Mississippi Delta, was acting as talent scout for the Modern and RPM labels of Los Angeles and leading a band, the Delta Rhythm Kings, that took the West Coast jump-blues groups as its models. "Rocket '88'" could almost have been a Wynonie Harris or Amos Milburn jump record, but the saxophone solo (by Raymond Hill) was wilder and rougher than the work of West Coast sax men like Maxwell Davis, and the boogie-woogie beat that kicked the performance along was carried by a fuzzed-out, overamplified electric guitar. (The story behind the guitar sound turns out to be prosaic enough; the amplifier fell off the top of Turner's automobile on the way to Memphis, and Sam Phillips stuffed some paper in the burst speaker cone in order to get on with the session.) These striking characteristics and the song's lyrics, which celebrate the automobile, have led some listeners to credit "Rocket '88,'" a Number One R&B hit in 1951, as "the first rock & roll record."

"Rocket '88'" *was* an unusually accurate indicator of what some early rock & roll would sound like. It was also recorded by Western swing musician Bill Haley and his group the Saddlemen as their first R&B-styled performance, for the small Essex label of Philadelphia. By 1952 Haley and his rechristened Comets were recording full-fledged rockers such as "Rock the Joint" in a similar style. Despite their lingering Western swing touches, these early Haley recordings, which predate both his first national hits and Presley's first Sun records by several years, are authentic rock & roll. So are numerous black records from the same period, 1951 to 1953, and by this time white disc jockeys, including Alan Freed in Cleveland and Dewey Phillips in Memphis, were beginning to program such records for a racially mixed but predominantly teenaged audience. The music was ready and waiting for America to discover it.

But America's musical tastes were changing across the board. Guitarist Les Paul, who had been among the first to use the electric instrument, was beginning to revolutionize pop music with his multitracked guitar overdubs. His wife, Mary Ford, sang sweetly enough, but Paul had been a friend of Charlie Christian's, and his playing was blues and jazz oriented. Johnnie Ray's "Cry," a record so emotionally bluesy it virtually parodied itself, was a pop and R&B hit in 1951. By this time urban R&B had begun to make way for the Southern sound. The 1952 R&B hits included Eddie Boyd's "Five Long

Years'' and Little Walter's ''Juke,'' both Mississippi Delta blues played by musicians who had only recently moved to Chicago. The Caribbean-tinged rhythms of New Orleans were featured on two more R&B hits, Fats Domino's ''Goin' Home'' and Lloyd Price's ''Lawdy Miss Clawdy'' (with Domino on piano). B. B. King, the Beale Street Blues Boy, combined Southern intensity with T-Bone Walker's guitar style on his ''3 O'Clock Blues'' and ''You Know I Love You.'' Many of the hits produced in the North, among them records by Ruth Brown and Willie Mabon, emulated Southern music or had themes and imagery rooted in the South. Billy Ward and the Dominoes' hits, featuring young Clyde McPhatter, were thinly secularized gospel, often with the stomping beat and rasping saxophone style of jump blues.

By 1954 the music on the R&B charts was even rawer. Guitar Slim's ''The Things That I Used to Do'' combined superamplified lead guitar with a vocal so country many urban listeners probably had trouble understanding the diction. The Midnighters' ''Work

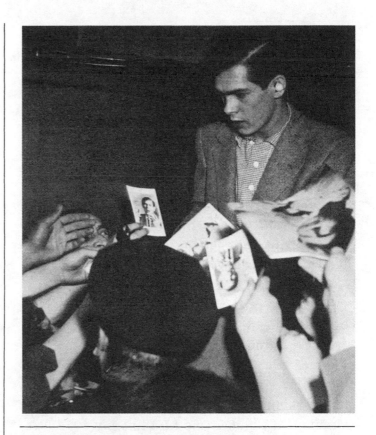

Johnnie Ray, the first and (so far) last pop idol with a hearing aid, signing autographs in 1952.

Etta James, when ''Dance with Me Henry'' was a hit.

with Me Annie'' was a thinly disguised sexual metaphor; Etta James's similar ''Roll with Me Henry'' roared along in a raucous sanctified vein. Both records had followups. James's ''Hey Henry'' resembled its predecessor, while the Midnighters' ''Annie Had a Baby'' left no doubt as to what the ''working'' in their earlier hit had been about. These records were widely attacked by white ministers and disc jockeys. Abandoned singing and suggestive lyrics were nothing new to black listeners, but black music was beginning to reach a sizable audience of white adolescents.

In 1954 the Crew-Cuts' version of the Chords' R&B hit ''Sh-Boom'' was the most successful of many white ''covers'' of black material. A year later Bill Haley and His Comets made Number One on the pop charts with ''Rock Around the Clock,'' which

Les Paul and Mary Ford wishing you their very best.

From left: LaVern Baker, Nat ''King'' Cole, Della Reese and Erskine Hawkins.

was introduced to many Americans through the film *The Blackboard Jungle*. This was the original white rock & roll hit, although the music and group's over-all style were a somewhat crude copy of the Southern-influenced New York R&B sound exemplified by Joe Turner's ''Shake, Rattle and Roll'' (which Haley covered). That same year Elvis Presley scored his first C&W Number One with ''I Forgot to Remember to Forget,'' backed with the black-influenced ''Mystery Train'' on Sun, while Chuck Berry (with his classic automotive epic ''Maybellene'') and Fats Domino had Number One R&B hits. By 1956 Pres-

ley, Berry and Domino, along with newcomer Little Richard, had crossed over to the pop charts. The rock & roll era had begun.

Each of these early rock & rollers was firmly rooted in the music of earlier years. Presley and the other white singers groomed by Sun's Sam Phillips were raised on white country music, hillbilly boogie and black blues. Presley, for one, knew the recordings of Roy Brown and Mississippi bluesman Arthur ''Big Boy'' Crudup well before he began recording; Sam Phillips encouraged him to go ahead and make that kind of music himself. Carl Perkins's classic ''Blue Suede Shoes'' and most of his other work was closer to hillbilly boogie, although his ''Matchbox'' was a twelve-bar blues that had been popularized by Blind Lemon Jefferson. Jerry Lee Lewis's piano style was shaped by the blues and boogie players he heard in Haney's Big

Bill Haley and His Comets in 1955. Pedal steel and accordion didn't become staples of the modern rock band, but this was the beginning.

House, a black nightclub in his native Ferriday, Louisiana, and perhaps by the recordings of white country boogie pianists like Moon Mullican and Merrill Moore.

Chuck Berry's guitar work was redolent of the fast shuffle playing of T-Bone Walker; it was his unique talent as a lyricist that made him one of the most original of the early rock & rollers. Fats Domino had been making R&B records since 1949 and he did little to change his style. It was his astute producer and bandleader, Dave Bartholomew, who added guitar solos and other effects and also wrote many of the songs that Domino made into rock & roll hits. Little Richard, who was backed by Bartholomew's band on many of his early recordings, simply sang novelty blues with the no-holds-barred enthusiasm of a particularly unabashed sanctified vocalist. Bo Diddley, the most primitive of the early black rock & rollers, built his hits on blues and folk materials from backcountry Mississippi and on the Latinlike "hambone" beat.

Without Presley, Berry and the rest rock & roll might have turned out differently. But the music was able to flourish and, eventually, to become the dominant popular music of the Western world precisely because it was firmly rooted in, and sustained by, the fertile soil of the South and Southwest.

Little Junior Parker, whose "Mystery Train" inspired Elvis.

DISCOGRAPHY

SINGLES: NUMBER ONE HITS, 1950 TO 1956

1950
Rhythm & Blues
Roy Brown: "Hard Luck Blues." **Ruth Brown:** "Teardrops from My Eyes." **Lowell Fulson:** "Blue Shadows." **Ivory Joe Hunter:** "I Almost Lost My Mind." **Louis Jordan:** "Blue Light Boogie." **Joe Liggins:** "Pink Champagne." **Percy Mayfield:** "Please Send Me Someone to Love." **Amos Milburn:** "Bad, Bad Whiskey." **Joe Morris:** "Anytime, Anyplace, Anywhere." **Johnny Otis:** "Double Crossing Blues," "Mistrustin' Blues."

Pop
Ames Brothers: "Rag Mop." **Andrews Sisters:** "I Can Dream, Can't I?" **Eileen Barton:** "If I Knew You Were Comin' I'd've Baked a Cake." **Teresa Brewer:** "Music! Music! Music!" **Nat "King" Cole:** "Mona Lisa." **Red Foley:** "Chattanoogie Shoe Shine Boy." **Phil Harris:** "The Thing." **Gordon Jenkin and the Weavers:** "Goodnight Irene." **Anton Karas:** "The Third Man Theme." **Sammy Kaye:** "Harbor Lights." **Patti Page:** "The Tennessee Waltz."

Country & Western
Red Foley: "Chattanoogie Shoe Shine Boy," "Birmingham Bounce." **Tennessee Ernie Ford:** "Shotgun Boogie." **Moon Mullican:** "I'll Sail My Ship Alone." **Hank Snow:** "I'm Movin' On," "Golden Rocket." **Ernest Tubb and Red Foley:** "Goodnight, Irene." **Hank Williams:** "Long Gone Lonesome Blues," "Why Don't You Love Me."

1951
Rhythm & Blues
Earl Bostic: "Flamingo." **Jackie Brenston:** "Rocket '88." **Charles Brown:** "Black Night." **Clovers:** "Don't You Know I Love You," "Fool, Fool, Fool." **Dominoes:** "Sixty Minute Man." **Five Keys:** "Glory of Love." **"Peppermint" Harris:** "I Got Loaded." **Tab Smith:** "Because of You."

Pop
Tony Bennett: "Because of You," "Cold, Cold Heart." **Rosemary Clooney:** "Come On-a My House." **Nat "King" Cole:** "Too Young." **Perry Como:** "If." **Eddy Howard:** "Sin." **Mario Lanza:** "Be My Love." **Les Paul and Mary Ford:** "How High the Moon." **Johnnie Ray:** "Cry."

Country & Western
Eddy Arnold: "There's Been a Change in Me," "Kentucky Waltz," "I Want to Play House with You." **Lefty Frizzell:** "I Want to Be with You Always," "Always Late." **Pee Wee King:** "Slow Poke." **Carl Smith:** "Let Old Mother Nature Have Her Way." **Hank Snow:** "Rhumba Boogie."

1952
Rhythm & Blues
Johnny Ace: "My Song." **Eddy Boyd:** "Five Long Years." **Clovers:** "Ting-a-Ling." **Fats Domino:** "Goin' Home." **Dominoes:** "Have Mercy Baby." **Ruth Brown:** "5-10-15 Hours." **Jimmy Forest:** "Night Train." **Roscoe Gordon:** "Booted." **B. B. King:** "3 O'Clock Blues," "You Know I Love You." **Little Walter:** "Juke." **Willie Mabon:** "I Don't Know." **Lloyd Price:** "Lawdy Miss Clawdy." **Johnnie Ray:** "Cry."

Pop
Leroy Anderson: "Blue Tango." **Jimmy Boyd:** "I Saw Mommy Kissing Santa Claus." **Percy Faith:** "Delicado." **Joni James:** "Why Don't You Believe Me." **Vera Lynn:** "Auf Wiedersch'n Sweetheart." **Al Martino:** "Here in My Heart." **Patti Page:** "I Went to Your Wedding." **Jo Stafford:** "You Belong to Me." **Johnny Standley:** "It's in the Book." **Kay Starr:** "Wheel of Fortune."

Country & Western
Eddy Arnold: "Easy on the Eyes." **Red Foley:** "Midnight." **Webb Pierce:** "Back Street Affair." **Carl Smith:** "Don't Just Stand There." **Hank Thompson:** "Wild Side of Life." **Kitty Wells:** "It Wasn't God Who Made Honky Tonk Angels." **Hank Williams:** "Jambalaya," "I'll Never Get out of This World Alive."

1953
Rhythm & Blues
Johnny Ace: "The Clock." **Faye Adams:** "Shake a Hand." **Ruth Brown:** "(Mama) He Treats Your Daughter Mean." **"5" Royales:** "Baby, Don't Do It," "Help Me Somebody." **Willie Mabon:** "I'm Mad." **Clyde McPhatter and the Drifters:** "Money Honey." **Orioles:** "Crying in the Chapel." **Willie Mae Thornton:** "Hound Dog."

Pop
Tony Bennett: "Rags to Riches." **Teresa Brewer:** "Till I Waltz Again with You." **Perry Como:** "Don't Let the Stars Get in Your Eyes." **Percy Faith:** "Song from Moulin Rouge." **Eddie Fisher:** "I'm Walking Behind You," "Oh! My Pa-pa."

Stan Freberg: "St. George and the Dragonet." Patti Page: "The Doggie in the Window." Les Paul and Mary Ford: "Vaya Con Dios."

Country & Western
Eddy Arnold: "Eddy's Song." Davis Sisters: "I Forgot More Than You'll Ever Know." Webb Pierce: "It's Been So Long," "There Stands the Glass." Jim Reeves: "Mexican Joe." Jean Shepard and Ferlin Husky: "Dear John Letter." Carl Smith: "Hey, Joe." Hank Williams: "Kaw-Liga," "Take These Chains from My Heart."

1954
Rhythm & Blues
Faye Adams: "I'll Be True," "Hurts Me to My Heart." Ruth Brown: "Oh What a Dream," "Mambo Baby." Charms: "Hearts of Stone." Guitar Slim: "The Things That I Used to Do." Roy Hamilton: "You'll Never Walk Alone." Clyde McPhatter and the Drifters: "Honey Love." Midnighters: "Work with Me Annie," "Annie Had a Baby."

Pop
Chordettes: "Mr. Sandman." Rosemary Clooney: "Hey There," "This Ole House." Perry Como: "Wanted." Crew-Cuts: "Sh-Boom." Doris Day: "Secret Love." Eddie Fisher: "I Need You Now." Kitty Kallen: "Little Things Mean a Lot." Jo Stafford: "Make Love to Me!"

Country & Western
Webb Pierce: "Slowly," "More and More." Carl Smith: "Loose Talk." Hank Snow: "I Don't Hurt Anymore."

1955
Rhythm & Blues
Johnny Ace: "Pledging My Love." Chuck Berry: "Maybellene." Fats Domino: "Ain't That a Shame." Roy Hamilton: "Unchained Melody." Little Walter: "My Babe." Jay McShann: "Hands Off." Penguins: "Earth Angel." Platters: "Only You," "The Great Pretender."

Pop
Fontane Sisters: "Hearts of Stone." Tennessee Ernie Ford: "Sixteen Tons." Four Aces: "Love Is a Many Splendored Thing." Bill Haley and His Comets: "Rock Around the Clock." Bill Hayes: "The Ballad of Davy Crockett." Dean

Martin: "Memories Are Made of This." McGuire Sisters: "Sincerely." Mitch Miller: "The Yellow Rose of Texas." Perez Prado: "Cherry Pink and Apple Blossom White." Joan Weber: "Let Me Go Lover." Roger Williams: "Autumn Leaves."

Country & Western
Eddy Arnold: "The Cattle Call." Tennessee Ernie Ford: "Sixteen Tons." Webb Pierce: "In the Jailhouse Now," "I Don't Care," "Love, Love, Love." Elvis Presley: "I Forgot to Remember to Forget" b/w "Mystery Train." Red Sovine and Webb Pierce: "Why, Baby, Why?"

1956
Rhythm & Blues
Bill Doggett: "Honky Tonk." Fats Domino: "I'm in Love Again." Little Willie John: "Fever." Little Richard: "Long Tall Sally," "Rip It Up." Frankie Lymon and the Teenagers: "Why Do Fools Fall in Love." Elvis Presley: "Don't Be Cruel."

Pop
Les Baxter: "The Poor People of Paris." Pat Boone: "I Almost Lost My Mind." Gogi Grant: "The Wayward Wind." Platters: "The Great Pretender," "My Prayer." Elvis Presley: "Heartbreak Hotel," "Don't Be Cruel." Kay Starr: "Rock and Roll Waltz."

Country & Western
Elvis Presley: "Heartbreak Hotel," "I Want You, I Need You, I Love You," "Don't Be Cruel." Ray Price: "Crazy Arms."

ALBUMS
Charlie Christian: *Charlie Christian: The Genius of Electric Guitar* (CBS; 1987). Louis Jordan: *The Best of Louis Jordan* (MCA, 1975). *Atlantic Blues* (Atlantic; 1991). Hank Williams: *Hank Williams: 40 Greatest Hits* (Polydor; 1978). Bob Wills and His Texas Playboys: *Bob Wills and His Texas Playboys* (Rhino; 1991). Anthologies: *From Spirituals to Swing: Carnegie Hall Concerts 1938/39* (Vanguard; 1987).

(Compiled from Joel Whitburn's *Record Research,* based on *Billboard's* Pop, Rhythm & Blues and Country & Western charts.)

RHYTHM & GOSPEL

BY BARRY HANSEN

Early rock & roll derived the lion's share of its energy and inspiration from black music. In the Fifties "rock & roll" was often taken to be simply a new name for "rhythm & blues," or "R&B," the music industry's generic term for any popular music primarily produced and consumed by African-Americans.

The R&B scene of the early Fifties was diverse enough to accommodate the suave stylings of a Charles Brown, the earthy, fiery Chicago blues of a Muddy Waters and everything in between. But when one thinks today of R&B in the early Fifties, it's usually the vocal groups that first come to mind— the Drifters, the Dominoes, the Midnighters, so many more.

During those years, the years just before rock & roll became a worldwide phenomenon, a new energy came into black vocal group music. In the Forties it had been dominated by the Ravens, the Orioles and other groups that sang love songs sweet and low, after the fashion of the Ink Spots, who became world famous just before World War II.

Around 1950, though, certain R&B vocal groups began moving away from the sweet tones of the Ink Spots' Bill Kenny and toward something much closer to the sanctified shouts of such contemporary gospel groups as the Soul Stirrers, the Pilgrim Travelers and the Swan Silvertones.

For some in the black community, this was tantamount to blasphemy. The new mix of gospel-style singing, sensual R&B rhythms and risqué lyrics on such trend-setting records as "Honey Love" by the Drifters and "Work with Me Annie" by the Midnighters was as outrageous to conservatives as the rap excesses of 2 Live Crew would be some thirty-five years later. (When Sam Cooke launched his pop career in 1957 after six years of singing pure gospel with the Soul Stirrers, the schism among his fans was deeper and more permanent even than what happened among Bob Dylan's folk fans after he went electric in 1965.)

For young R&B fans, though—blacks and whites—this was electrifying stuff. This "rhythm & gospel" music (the trend didn't really have a name at the time it was happening) was what first intro-

The Dixie Hummingbirds, one of the greatest pure gospel groups of the postwar period.

duced the world of secular music to the passion of postwar gospel and paved the way for such "soul" giants of the Sixties as Otis Redding, James Brown and Wilson Pickett.

The first "rhythm & gospel" group on records was the Dominoes, organized by Billy Ward. Ward wasn't much of a singer, but he was a good musician and an even better talent manager. In 1950 he organized the Dominoes and had the perspicacity to engage as the group's lead singer the seventeen-year-old Clyde McPhatter, who had been brought up in the church and knew only one way to sing—the gospel way.

Clyde sang lead on one side of the group's first record, "Do Something for Me." Musically, it's a gospel song, the slow tempo allowing for numerous gospel-style melismas (rapid cascades of notes improvised by the singer on a single syllable of lyrics). Lyrically, on the other hand, it's a proposition. McPhatter was conducting a courtship with magical incantations previously reserved for the good Lord.

(The Dominoes weren't entirely given over to the rhythm & gospel idea; the group's biggest hit, later in 1951, featured Ravens-style bass singer Bill Brown on the ribald "Sixty Minute Man," which was straight R&B.)

In 1952, however, the Dominoes produced the definitive fast rhythm & gospel record, "Have Mercy Baby," one of that year's best-selling R&B discs. The title summarizes the whole rhythm & gospel idea: "Baby" is interchangeable with "Lord." In fact, the entire lyric could be transformed back into a gospel prayer with very little effort. Clyde and the other singers trade two-bar phrases throughout the record, echoing the familiar call-and-response device of gospel quartets. Melodically and harmonically, though, it's a straight twelve-bar blues, a form that gospel singers had always avoided.

In the first chorus McPhatter sticks close to the simple melody. From there on he improvises freely, much as a gospel singer might. Often he strings out a phrase so that it overlaps the background singers' response: The melismas are short (due to the fast tempo), but abundant and often spectacular. While Clyde shouts his gospel funk, the backup band takes special care of the rhythm. The tenor sax solo that was de rigueur in those days is here stretched out for two choruses, while screams and the vocalists' most sensual *yeah*s help establish "Have Mercy" as a classic of its time. For the coup de grace, Clyde breaks down in tears during the fadeout.

Indeed, McPhatter wept all the way through his next great record with the Dominoes, "The Bells," cut in late 1952. Here is the absolute apotheosis of sob rock: Clyde's melismas alternate with wrenching wails, while an R&B tenor sax honks rather unsteadily alongside a gospel organ; the accompanying harmonies steer an extremely curious middle course between gospel and blues changes.

By this time the group was being billed on disc labels as "Billy Ward and His Dominoes." Considering Ward's lack of vocal contribution, McPhatter could hardly be blamed for feeling the wrong man's name was being billed above that of the group, so in 1953 he took a little gamble. He left the security of the now prestigious Dominoes (where his place was taken by Jackie Wilson) to join a group just being organized. The new group was to be called the Drifters because (according to an early press release) "the members had done a lot of drifting from one group to another." This might not have seemed like the

Clyde McPhatter, one of the sweetest voices of the Fifties. Originally a member of Billy Ward's Dominoes, he became the lead singer of the original Drifters, and then went on to pop success as a soloist ("A Lover's Question," "Lover Please").

By the time McPhatter left the army in 1956, the barriers between R&B and pop music were breaking down. He went solo (one of the first group members to do so) and enjoyed substantial if intermittent success for the next decade, with "A Lover's Question" (1958) and "Lover Please" (1962) as highlights. His style was prettier and less passionate than it had been, however, and next to an Otis Redding (who might have had a much rougher road to the top without McPhatter's precedent), McPhatter sounded dated and tame. He died, washed up at thirty-eight, on June 13th, 1972. (The Drifters, of course, went on to great success in the early Sixties, but the group's composition—and style—had changed radically by then.)

The Drifters and Dominoes were among the very few groups with the vocal equipment, skill and desire to sing in the true rhythm & gospel style; most preferred the much easier task of imitating the Ink Spots. Several other groups from the early Fifties, however, did achieve popularity singing in a gospel vein. The "5" Royales are best remembered today for such later hits as "Think" and "Dedicated to the One I Love," but their 1953 blazers, "Baby, Don't Do It" (with the inspirational verse "If you leave me pretty baby / I'll have bread without no meat") and "Help Me Somebody," remain fine examples of rhythm & gospel.

And then there are the Royals. After a string of edifying flops on Okeh and Federal, this group struck it rich in 1954 with "Work with Me Annie." Right in the middle of the song's lengthy chart run, the Royals were forced to change their name to avoid confusion with the aforementioned "5" Royales,

The "5" Royales.

most promising premise for a new group, but there was a recording contract waiting for the Drifters at Atlantic Records, which was already established as one of the steadiest ports in the R&B storm thanks to Joe Turner, Ruth Brown and a group called the Clovers, whose early records—"Don't You Know I Love You" and "Fool, Fool, Fool"—nearly matched the Dominoes in terms of successfully synthesizing rhythm & blues with gospel.

Not only that, but Atlantic offered Clyde the glory of having his own name on the label along with the group's. Clyde was destined to make only six singles with the Drifters before he was drafted in 1954, but the first four were all smash hits. First came "Money Honey," later a hit for Elvis, followed by the torrid "Such a Night" and the outrageous "Honey Love," whose gasps, grunts and sighs made radio executives as incensed as rap did a third of a century later. For hit number four, though, the Drifters mended fences with an endearingly strutting version of "White Christmas."

who presumably hadn't noticed the Royals before their hit. The switch might have confused the fans, but there was no confusion about the intent of the lyrics they sang as the newly named Hank Ballard and the Midnighters: "Work with me Annie . . . let's get it while the gettin' is good / Annie please don't cheat . . . gimme all my meat."

Hot on the heels of "Work" came the first of its many sequels, "Annie Had a Baby" ("Can't work no more . . . that's what happens when the gettin' gets good"). Sequels soon flowed in from everywhere, most notably Etta James's "The Wallflower," the record that launched her career. "The Wallflower" was better known as "Roll with Me Henry" (as in Henry Ballard); those outside the range of R&B stations may remember Georgia Gibbs's bowdlerized "Dance with Me Henry," the only song of the "Annie"-"Henry" cycle to penetrate the pop consciousness of 1955.

R&B initiates, meanwhile, smirked at "Annie's Answer" ("I ain't had no baby") by Al Smith's Combo with Hazel McCollum and the El Dorados. Berkeley's Music City label chimed in with "Annie Pulled a Humbug" ("That's not my kid . . . can't be mine 'cause he's got a bald head") by the Midnights. A label note in very small type said: "Not to be confused with the Midnighters recordings." The Midnighters themselves, meanwhile, pursued the idea far past the point of diminishing returns with sequels-to-sequels including "Annie's Aunt Fannie" and "Henry's Got Flat Feet (Can't Dance No More)." One of these followups deserves a morsel of immortality for its title alone: "Switchie Witchie Titchie."

Hank Ballard went on to new fame in the Sixties with such early soul dance hits as "Finger Poppin' Time" and "Let's Go, Let's Go, Let's Go." Dancers remember him best, though, for a simple little tune he composed in 1959 to fill the back side of "Teardrops on Your Letter," something called "The Twist." Chubby Checker's cover of this song, not as nicely sung but more danceably produced and tirelessly promoted, achieved the unique feat of hitting Number One on the pop chart two separate times, more than a year apart.

But Hank Ballard got less credit for "The Twist" than he deserved. With the exception of Jackie Wilson, the other rhythm & gospel pioneers had even less luck in the Sixties, a decade that belonged to a new generation of gospel-influenced black singers. There was one very big difference: The hybrid was no longer nameless. And I sometimes wonder what the course of rock & roll might have been if someone had dreamt up the name "soul music" while Clyde McPhatter was still in his prime.

Hank Ballard and the Midnighters. Ballard, who had hits with "Work with Me Annie" and "Finger Poppin' Time," also wrote and first recorded "The Twist," the song that made Chubby Checker a star.

DISCOGRAPHY

SINGLES
Dominoes: "Do Something for Me" (Federal; r☆6, 1951). "Sixty Minute Man" (Federal; r☆1, 1951). "I Am with You" (Federal; r☆8, 1951). "That's What You're Doing to Me" (Federal; r☆7, 1952). "Have Mercy Baby" (Federal; r☆1, 1952). **Billy Ward and His Dominoes:** "I'd Be Satisfied" (Federal; r☆8, 1952). "The Bells" (Federal; r☆6, 1953). "These Foolish Things Remind Me of You" (Federal; r☆5, 1953). "Rags to Riches" (King; r☆3, 1953). **Drifters:** "Money, Honey" (Atlantic; r☆1, 1953). "Such a Night" b/w "Lucille" (Atlantic; r☆5, 1954). "Honey Love" (Atlantic; r☆1, 1954). "Bip Bam" (Atlantic; r☆7, 1954). "White Christmas" (Atlantic; r☆2, 1954). "What'cha Gonna Do" (Atlantic; r☆3, 1955). **"5" Royales:** "Baby, Don't Do It" (Apollo; r☆1, 1953). "Help Me Somebody" b/w "Crazy, Crazy, Crazy" (Apollo; r☆1, 1953). "Too Much Lovin' " (Apollo; r☆4, 1953). **Midnighters:** "Work with Me Annie" (Federal; r☆1, 1954). "Sexy Ways" (Federal; r☆3, 1954). "Annie Had a Baby" (Federal; r☆1, 1954). "Annie's Aunt Fannie" (Federal; r☆10, 1954).

ALBUMS
Clovers: *The Best of the Clovers* (Atlantic; 1991). **Drifters** *Let the Boogie-Woogie Roll: Drifters' Greatest Hits, 1953–1958* (Atlantic; 1988). **Anthologies:** *Risqué Rhythms* (Rhino; 1991).

(Chart positions compiled from Joel Whitburn's *Record Research,* based on *Billboard*'s Rhythm & Blues chart.)

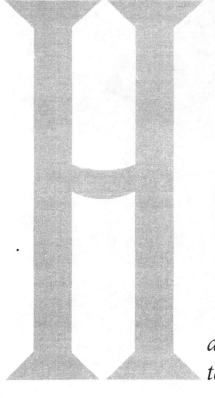

ELVIS PRESLEY

BY PETER GURALNICK

ave you heard the news? . . . There's good rockin' tonight.''

—Elvis Presley, the Hillbilly Cat, in his recording of the Roy Brown song, 1954

"The pure products of America go crazy."
—William Carlos Williams,
"Spring and All," 1923

The world was not prepared for Elvis Presley. The violence of its reaction to him ("unspeakably untalented," a "voodoo of frustration and defiance") more than testified to this. Other rock & rollers had a clearer focus to their music. An egocentric genius like Jerry Lee Lewis may even have had a greater talent. Certainly Chuck Berry or Carl Perkins had a keener wit. But Elvis had the moment. He hit like a Pan American flash, and the reverberations still linger from the shock of his arrival.

In some ways the reaction may seem to have been out of proportion, for Elvis Presley was in retrospect merely one more link in a chain of historical inevitability. His ducktail was already familiar from Tony Curtis, the movie star whose pictures Elvis haunted at the Suzore No. 2 in Memphis; the hurt, truculent expression we had seen before in Marlon Brando's

motorcycle epic, *The Wild One*. His vulnerability was mirrored by James Dean, whose first movie, *East of Eden*, was released in April 1955, just as Elvis's own career was getting under way. ("He knew I was a friend of Jimmy's," said Nicholas Ray, director of Dean's second film, *Rebel Without a Cause*, "so he got down on his knees before me and began to recite whole pages from the script. Elvis must have seen *Rebel* a dozen times by then and remembered every one of Jimmy's lines.") His eponymous sneer and the whole attitude that it exemplified—not derision exactly but a kind of scornful pity, indifference, a pained acceptance of all the dreary details of square reality—was foreshadowed by Brando, John Garfield, the famous picture of Robert Mitchum after his 1948 pot bust. Even his music had its historical parallels, not just in the honky-tonk clatter of Bill Haley

Elvis warming up backstage in his heyday, before he was quarantined in Hollywood.

and His Comets but in the genuine popular success that singers like Frankie Laine and Johnnie Ray— and Al Jolson, Mildred Bailey, even Bing Crosby in an earlier era—had enjoyed in bringing black vocal stylings to the white marketplace.

None of it seemed to matter somehow. To anyone who was alive at the time, Presley was, and remains, a truly revolutionary force. Country singer Bob Luman, a near-contemporary, described in Paul Hemphill's *Nashville Sound* what might almost be considered a typical first reaction. "This cat came out in red pants and a green coat and a pink shirt and socks, and he had this sneer on his face and he stood behind the mike for five minutes, I'll bet, before he made a move. Then he hit his guitar a lick, and he broke two strings. I'd been playing ten years, and I hadn't broken a *total* of two strings. So there he was, these two strings dangling, and he hadn't done anything yet, and these high school girls were screaming and fainting and running up to the stage, and then he started to move his hips real slow like he had

a thing for his guitar. That was Elvis Presley when he was about nineteen, playing Kilgore, Texas. He made chills run up my back, man, like when your hair starts grabbing at your collar. For the next nine days he played one-nighters around Kilgore, and after school every day me and my girl would get in the car and go wherever he was playing that night. That's the last time I tried to sing like Webb Pierce and Lefty Frizzell."

It was the same for countless fans and for other performers, too. To Waylon Jennings he was "like an explosion, really." To Buddy Holly, "Without Elvis none of us could have made it." As for Elvis Presley, the center of the storm, it was something over which he professed to have no control. Over and over again in the course of his life, he refused to speculate on the reasons for his success, putting it down to luck, blind instinct, anything but conscious design. "I don't know what it is," he said to C. Robert Jennings of the *Saturday Evening Post* in 1956. "I just fell into it, really. My daddy and I were laughing about it the other day. He looked at me and said, 'What happened, El? The last thing I can remember is I was working in a can factory, and you

The solid-gold rocker.

were driving a truck.' We all feel the same way about it still. It just . . . caught us up.''

There it all is: the modesty, the deferential charm, the soft-spoken assumption of commonsense virtues (in this version even the tireless twitching and suggestive pelvic action are seen as involuntary reflex) that became the official Elvis. In many ways I am sure that this picture is accurate, and it undoubtedly conforms to the image that Elvis Presley had of himself. It tends to leave something out, however. What it leaves out is the drive and consuming ambition of the nineteen-year-old Elvis Presley, who possessed a sweeping musical intelligence, energies that could barely be contained, and a ferocious determination to escape the mold that had seemingly been set for him at birth. Even more, it ignores the extent to which his rebellion, his surly refusal of responsibility, his reaction to the stifling conformity of the time, could stand for an entire generation, taking in a social base of which he could scarcely have been aware, much less directly known. Most of all, though, this explanation, or lack of it, overlooks the music itself, a music that expressed a kind of pure joyousness, a sense of soaring release that in such self-conscious times as ours seems unlikely ever to be recaptured.

An early photo taken just before the first sessions for Sun.

He was born Elvis Aron Presley on January 8th, 1935, in Tupelo, Mississippi, a child of hard times but an only child, adored and pampered by a mother who would walk him to school until he was in his teens. His twin, Jesse Garon, died at birth, and he was always to be reminded of this absence (''They say when one twin dies, the other grows up with all the quality of the other, too. . . . If I did, I'm lucky.''), as if he were somehow incomplete, even down to his matching name. His first picture shows a little boy in overalls, sober in an oversize soft-brimmed hat similar to his

father's. He is flanked by parents who regard the camera with touching blank-faced looks that reflect neither expectation nor disappointment. His mother's hand rests on his father's shoulder; she is still young and pretty. And the child looks lost, waiflike, with that strange, familiar hurt look in his eyes, that unmistakable, unfathomable curl to his lips.

He grew up, schooled in all the classic virtues of small-town America: diffident, polite, sirring and ma'aming his elders, hungry with an unfocused yearning that would have been impossible for him— or anyone of his background and generation—either to explicitly admit or implicitly deny. ''My daddy was a common laborer,'' he said. ''He didn't have any trade, just like I didn't have. He mostly drove trucks, and when he used to bring the truck home from the wholesale grocery, I used to sit in it by the hour.'' The car radio was his first exposure not to music necessarily but to the world outside.

Sam Phillips, entrepreneur of vision, founder of Sun Records, first to record Elvis, Carl Perkins, Johnny Cash, Jerry Lee Lewis, Roy Orbison. Without him, there would have been no rock & roll.

Music, to begin with, came from the Pentecostal First Assembly of God church. "We were a religious family, going around together to sing at camp meetings and revivals. Since I was two years old all I knew was gospel music; that was music to me. We borrowed the style of our psalm singing from the early Negroes. We used to go to these religious singings all the time. The preachers cut up all over the place, jumping on the piano, moving every which way. The audience liked them. I guess I learned from them. I loved the music. It became such a part of my life it was as natural as dancing, a way to escape from the problems and my way of release."

There is another picture of Elvis and his parents, taken in 1956 after the phenomenal early success. In this picture Elvis is playing the piano; the mouths of all three are open, their eyes half-shut. They hold themselves stiffly and are evidently singing with fervent emotion. Both parents have put on weight; Vernon is still handsome in a beefy sort of way, but Gladys has taken on the bloated, starch-fed appearance of so many poor Southerners. She is forty-four but will die in only two years' time, her son's eternal and heartfelt sorrow. "I think of her nearly every single day," he said nearly five years later. "If I never do anything really wrong, it's all because of her. She wouldn't let me do anything wrong."

I can remember to my embarrassment the reaction that my friends and I had when we first saw the picture. We thought it was a joke. We thought that Elvis was putting us on; it seemed so clearly at odds with Elvis's rebel image and the mythology that, unable to construct from our own lives, we had erected around a pop idol. Today it is easier to recognize that out of this seeming contradiction (newness vs. tradition, rebellion vs. authority, sacred vs. profane) arose the tension that was rock & roll. Such thinking was at the time beyond the scope of our experience—and probably Elvis's as well.

He won a singing prize at ten, when his grammar school principal sponsored his appearance at the Mississippi-Alabama Fair and Dairy Show. The song he sang, "Old Shep," was a bathetic C&W ballad about a boy and his dog that Red Foley had popularized and Elvis would record for RCA some ten years later. It is not difficult to imagine the tow-headed little boy standing on a chair so that he could be seen, and singing, unaccompanied, with that same throbbing emotion for which he would one day become famous. "I wore glasses, no music, and

Elvis with his "copilot," Colonel Tom Parker.

I won, I think it was fifth place. I got a whipping the same day, my mother whipped me for something. I thought she didn't love me."

When he was eleven, his parents got him a guitar ("I wanted a bicycle"). Teachers and relatives remember him carrying the guitar around with him everywhere he went. Elvis later compared his guitar playing to "someone beating on a bucket lid." He listened to the *Grand Ole Opry*, Roy Acuff, Eddy Arnold, Jimmie Rodgers's early records, and Bob Wills. He idolized the Blackwood Brothers and the

Statesmen Quartet, two prominent white gospel groups. Billy Eckstine, Bill Kenny and the Ink Spots were his favorite rhythm & blues performers. And he absorbed the blues from the radio and the pervasive contact that a poor white family like the Presleys, always living on the edge of town and respectability, would necessarily have with blacks. "I dug the real low-down Mississippi singers, mostly Big Bill Broonzy and 'Big Boy' Crudup. Although they would scold me at home for listening to them." When he was thirteen his family moved to Memphis. "We were broke, man, broke, and we left Tupelo overnight. Dad packed all our belongings in boxes and put them on top and in the trunk of a 1939 Plymouth. We just headed for Memphis. Things had to be better."

Memphis in the late Forties and early Fifties was a seedbed of musical activity. Never really much of a center for commercial country music, it had a raw hillbilly style and a distinguished blues tradition that went back to the Twenties. In 1950 Howlin' Wolf and Sonny Boy Williamson were broadcasting on station KWEM from West Memphis; WDIA, the "mother station of the Negroes" and the first black-operated radio outlet in the South, featured B. B. King and Rufus Thomas spinning records and performing daily. On Beale Street and in W. C. Handy Park you could hear all manner of blues singers and entertainers. And at 706 Union Avenue an ex-radio engineer and announcer from Florence, Alabama, named Sam Phillips had opened the Memphis Recording Service for "Negro artists in the South who wanted to make a record [but] just had no place to go."

Elvis in a pensive moment ponders the fate of the less fortunate: *He* was not born to die in a plane crash.

It sounds a little disarming, but Phillips in fact recorded Howlin' Wolf, Walter Horton, Bobby "Blue" Bland, Little Junior Parker and B. B. King, all at the beginning of their careers. To begin with he leased his sides to the Biharis' West Coast RPM label and to the Chess brothers in Chicago. It was not until 1952 that he started his own Sun label. In the meantime, though, a quiet revolution was taking place. Many of the small independent promoters were becoming aware of it, and in Memphis, where there had long been a relaxed social, as well as musical, interchange, it was particularly noticeable. White kids were picking up on black styles—of music, dance, speech and dress. "Cat clothes" were coming in; bebop speech was all the rage; and Elvis Presley, along with Carl Perkins, Jerry Lee Lewis, Charlie Rich and all the other Southern children of the Depression who would one day develop the rockabilly style, was seeking his models in unlikely places.

In other ways Memphis was an oppressively impersonal urban dream for an only child, shy and strangely insecure, living in a city project, working jobs after school, going off by himself to play the guitar. High school was a fog. He went out for football and ROTC but failed to distinguish himself in this or any other way. He majored in shop, grew his hair long, carefully slicked it down and tried to grow sideburns from the time he started shaving, because, he said, he wanted to look like a truck driver. Which may or may not have gotten him kicked off the football team. Dressed anomalously in pink and black, he called attention only to his personal colorlessness and lived out typical adolescent fantasies of rebellion in teenage anonymity. "Nobody knew I sang, I wasn't popular in school, I wasn't dating anybody. In [my senior year] they entered me in another talent show. I came out and did my two songs and heard people kinda rumbling and whispering. It was amazing how popular I was in school after that."

Whether he was in fact popular even then is doubtful. Memories of rejection were inevitably clouded in the aftermath of success. Indeed it is as if in later years he set out deliberately to erase the loneliness of that time by gathering around him all the popular figures—football heroes, high school politicians, well-established Memphians—who would barely even speak to him then. For some twenty years of his life, as the so-called Memphis Mafia, they made up his personal retinue, subject to his every whim, devoted only to their chief. When he graduated from Humes High School in 1953, he was perceived by one schoolmate as an individual with "character, but he had no personality, if you

Elvis considers the proper tempo during one of his first sessions for RCA.

know what I mean. Just acted kind of goofy, sitting in the back of the class, playing his guitar. No one knew that he was ever going to be *anything*." When he got a job working on an assembly line at the Precision Tool Company, it seemed as if his life pattern was set.

One year later he had a record out, and everything was changed.

One of Sam Phillips's sidelights was a custom recording service where anyone could go in and make a record for two dollars a side. Sometime in the summer after graduation Elvis went in and cut two sides, "My Happiness" and "That's When Your Heartaches Begin," stylized ballads that had been popular for Jan and Sandra Steele and the Ink Spots. He came back several times over the next few months to see if Sam Phillips might be interested in recording him professionally for the Sun Records label. Phillips put him off, though Elvis evidently made enough impression for Phillips to hold on to his address and phone number. Elvis was not singing professionally, but he had his mind on music at the time. He was always going to the all-night gospel sings at the Memphis Auditorium and that spring almost joined the Songfellows, a junior division of the renowned Blackwood Brothers Quartet.

In late spring, by Sam Phillips's calculation, he called Elvis to try out a demo on "Without You," still another ballad that met with minimal success. Phillips was more or less undeterred. He put Elvis together with Scotty Moore, a twenty-two-year-old guitar player who had been hanging around the studio and had recently persuaded Phillips to record his own group, Doug Poindexter's Starlite Wranglers, in one of the earliest gropings toward a rockabilly style. Elvis showed up at Scotty's apartment, wearing, says Scotty, "a pink suit, white shoes and the ducktail. I thought my wife was going to go out the back door." Bill Black, the bass player for the Starlite Wranglers, wandered in and out without being overly impressed. Over the next few weeks, as Phil-

Otis Blackwell, one of the greatest R&B songwriters of all time, author of "Don't Be Cruel" and "All Shook Up" for Elvis; "Great Balls of Fire" for Jerry Lee Lewis.

lips recalls (everyone's version of this crucial moment in history is a little bit different), they ran down song after song—country, ballads, blues. What they were looking for no one seemed quite sure of. What they got everybody knows.

"Over and over," said Marion Keisker, Sam Phillips's secretary, "I remember Sam saying, 'If I could find a white man who had the Negro sound and the Negro feel, I could make a billion dollars.' " With Elvis, Phillips apparently found the key.

"That's All Right," a traditional blues by Arthur "Big Boy" Crudup, was the first number that actually jelled in July of 1954. According to legend it was worked out during a break between ballads. According to Scotty Moore the initial recording date took place only days after Scotty first met Elvis. "It wasn't intended to be a session at all. That was the reason only Bill and I were in the studio. Sam just wanted to see what he sounded like on tape. Then we were taking a break, I don't know, we were having Cokes and coffee, and all of a sudden Elvis started singing a song, jumping around and just acting the fool, and then Bill picked up his bass and he started acting the fool, too, and, you know, I started playing with 'em. Sam, I think, had the door to the control room open—I don't know, he was either editing some tape or doing something—and he stuck his head out and said, 'What are you doing?' and we said, 'We don't know.' 'Well, back up,' he said, 'try to find a place to start and do it again.' "

Whatever the evolution of the session, it marked a turning point in the history of American popular music.

Elvis arrives late for a game show, registers shock that it could have begun without him.

"That's All Right" was at first glance an unlikely song to create such a transformation. A conventional blues put out by a very pedestrian blues singer (if any bluesman deserves the charge of monotony, it is Arthur "Big Boy" Crudup, who rarely escaped from one key and possessed a singular ineptitude on guitar), it consists of a string of traditional verses set to a familiar, slightly shopworn blues melody. The copy in this instance bore little resemblance to the original. For if the record was not worked out during a break, but was in fact the product of months of hard work, trial and error, and direct calculation, that isn't the way that it comes across at all.

It sounds easy, unforced, joyous, spontaneous. It sounds as if the singer has broken free for the first time in his life. The voice soars with a purity and innocence. There is a crisp authority to Scotty Moore's lead guitar, Elvis's rhythm is ringing and clear, the bass gallops along in slap-heavy fashion. The record sparkles with a freshness of conception, a sharpness of design, a total lack of pretentiousness, an irrepressible enthusiasm. Like each of the ten sides eventually released on Sun—evenly divided between blues and country—"That's All Right" has a timeless quality that was just as striking and just as far removed from the trends of the day as it is from contemporary fashion. The sound is clean, without affectation or clutter. And there remains in the conventional lyrics, easing their way into a scat verse that was in Crudup's original leaden and pedestrian, a sense of transformation, both diz-

zying and breathtaking, an emotional transcendence, which, if only because of the burden of knowledge, could never happen again.

And yet this is not quite literally true either. It is perhaps another self-sustaining myth, with the reality at once more straightforward and more paradoxical. The B side of "That's All Right" was Bill Monroe's classic bluegrass tune "Blue Moon of Kentucky," recorded at the same session and taken at something like breakneck tempo in the released version. An alternate take exists, however. It indicates that "Blue Moon of Kentucky" at any rate started out its rockabilly life in a slower, bluesier version, more direct emotionally and more ornate vocally, much in the manner of "She's Gone," an alternate interpretation from a later session of the innocuous enough "I'm Left, You're Right, She's Gone." Both contain surprising intimations of what is to come, with hints of the familiar vibrato, the smoky drop to a bass register, the lazy crooning style, all hallmarks, I would have thought, of a later decadent period. In fact it is a style with which Elvis is distinctly more at home than the more frantic rockabilly mold, giving vent to all the smoldering passion that was to be so conspicuously absent from his later efforts. "Fine, fine, man," Sam Phillips declares, as the bluegrass number disintegrates into nervous laughter and edgy chatter. "Hell, that's different. That's a pop song now, nearly about. That's good!"

"That's All Right" was cut on the night of July 5th, 1954. A dub was delivered within days to Dewey Phillips, host of the popular *Red Hot and Blue* show, which was a kind of Memphis Moondog Matinee: rhythm & blues and hipster talk for a mixed black and white audience. Phillips, who enjoyed a close, almost fraternal relationship with his nonrelative Sam, played the record half a dozen times in a row on the first night.

By the time the record came out there was a back order of 5000 copies, and Elvis and Sun Records were well on their way.

Largely on the strength of this success (the record went on to sell 20,000 copies and even made Number One briefly on the Memphis C&W charts) Elvis was named eighth most promising new hillbilly artist in *Billboard*'s annual poll at the end of the year. Almost immediately he began to appear around Memphis, sitting in with the Starlite Wranglers at the Bon Air, playing with Scotty and Bill (very briefly billed as the Blue Moon Boys) at the Eagle's

The King with kissin' cousins.

the edge of the stage, only to leap back from clutching hands. "He threw everything into it," says Bob Neal, his first manager, "trying to break that audience down, trying to get it with him. He'd always react to audience reaction, and in the rare instances where he'd be placed on the show early, I always felt he kind of outdid himself, making it tough for the next guy to follow."

The records followed, one after another, although according to Marion Keisker, "Every session came hard." Each came out sounding like some kind of inspired accident: the unexpected falsetto with which Little Junior Parker's "Mystery Train" trails off, the bubbly hiccuping beginning to "Baby, Let's Play House," the wailing lead-in to "Good Rockin' Tonight," the too-perfect beautiful slow intro to blues singer Kokomo Arnold's "Milkcow Blues Boogie," which Elvis interrupts to declare portentously, "Hold it, fellas. That don't *move* me. Let's get real, real gone for a change."

Well, he got gone. The records picked up in sales, though never on a scale larger than a relatively tiny independent company like Sun could expect. The bookings increased. The cars and the clothes got fancier; the money did, too. A year after his Sun debut, in July of 1955, "Baby, Let's Play House" made the national C&W charts. By the end of the year Elvis Presley was named most promising new C&W artist. But by then, of course, he was a proven commercial commodity, for he had signed with RCA Records.

"He was greatly anxious for success," said Bob Neal, with whom he signed in January 1955, and with whom he went to New York for the first time for an unsuccessful audition with Arthur Godfrey's *Talent Scouts.* "He talked not in terms of being a moderate success. No—his ambition and desire was to be big in movies and so forth. From the very first he had ambition to be nothing in the ordinary but to go all the way. He was impatient. He would say, 'We got to figure out how to do this, we got to get ahead.' "

Sometime early in 1955 Colonel Tom Parker, who claimed to be a scion of the Great Parker Pony Circus though he was really a Dutch immigrant, onetime manager of Eddy Arnold and current manager of Hank Snow, entered the picture. Through Snow,

Nest, debuting at a big country show at the Overton Park Shell, even opening a shopping center. In October he appeared on the *Grand Ole Opry* for a one-shot appearance. He met with more success on the *Louisiana Hayride,* where he signed on as a regular after his second appearance, and where he picked up a drummer, D. J. Fontana. And he began touring, through Texas and Mississippi, performing at schoolhouses and dance halls, traveling in a succession of second-hand Lincolns and Cadillacs that were sometimes driven until they gave out.

Everywhere the reaction was the same—a mixture of shock and wild acclaim. No one knew what to make of him. "I recall one jockey telling me that Elvis Presley was so country he shouldn't be played after 5 A.M.," said Sam Phillips. "And others said he was too black for them."

Nonetheless the records continued to sell ("Good Rockin' Tonight," the second release, cut in September 1954, made Number Three on the Memphis C&W charts); teenagers turned out in droves to hear the so-called Hillbilly Cat, the King of Western Bop (his titles alone betray the cultural schizophrenia with which he was greeted); and they came away with the same dazed reaction as Bob Luman in Kilgore, Texas. He did splits, kneedrops, and crawled to

Elvis at ease in the army.

then one of the nation's top country stars, Parker had developed Hank Snow Jamboree Attractions into one of the major booking agencies in the South, and working through Neal at first, the Colonel began booking Elvis. In November 1955 Bob Neal was eased into a secondary position. On November 22nd Colonel Tom Parker produced a document that entitled him to represent Elvis Presley exclusively and signed a contract with RCA. Sun Records received $35,000 plus $5000 in back royalties for Elvis. It was an unheard-of sum for the time.

There were many cogent reasons for such a move. For Sun Records the deal provided much-needed capital, and Sam Phillips has always staunchly defended his decision, citing the subsequent success of Carl Perkins, Johnny Cash and Jerry Lee Lewis on his label as proof. For Elvis Presley the benefits became obvious immediately. On January 10th, 1956, he entered RCA's Nashville studio and recorded ''Heartbreak Hotel.'' The rest, I think, is history. As for the Colonel, he soon divested himself of all other interests and devoted himself to advancing his boy, a devotion that took such forms as the decline of all presidential and nonremunerative invitations, the hawking and retrieving of souvenir programs at concerts, the personal dispensation of Elvis calendars at the fabled Las Vegas debut in 1970—in short a steadfast refusal to cheapen his product. ''When I first knew Elvis,'' the Colonel once remarked, ''he had a million dollars' worth of talent. Now he has a million dollars.''

I don't know what there is to say about the success. There are, of course, the hits: ''Heartbreak Hotel,'' with its bluesy country feel, metallic guitar and dour bass; ''Hound Dog,'' with its reversed sexual imagery, savage musical ride and spewed-out lyric (''Well, they said you was high class, well that was just a lie''); ''Jailhouse Rock,'' with its frenetic pace and furiously repeated drum roll; ''Love Me Tender,'' ''Love Me,'' ''Loving You''; the scornful ease of ''Don't Be Cruel,'' the mnemonic pop of ''All

Shook Up.'' There was the impact of hit after hit after hit, fourteen consecutive million-sellers, RCA claimed, simultaneously topping pop, country and R&B charts; the phenomenal explosion of both the mode and the music over a period of twenty-seven months until his March 1958 induction into the army; the elevation to socio-mytho-psychosexual status, as Elvis Presley unwittingly became a test of the nation's moral fiber.

Elvis in the mid-Sixties— his debonair look.

The peculiar thing is that in retrospect it is all irrelevant. Not just in the wake of Presley's success but as the inevitable consequence of the almost total acceptance that rock & roll has come to enjoy. When Elvis Presley was first recorded by Sam Phillips, he was an unmarketable commodity, an underground hero on the fringes of society and artistic respectability. Today, like every trend and tidal wave that comes along in our consumer-oriented society, with its voracious appetite for novelty and its pitiless need to reduce what it does not understand, his achievement has been subsumed, his art has been converted to product, and rock & roll itself has become part of the fabric of corporate America. And the music—what of the music?

For some reason Elvis Presley never again recaptured the spirit or the verve of those first Sun sessions. When I say ''never,'' I don't mean to imply that all of the output for his last twenty years was worthless, nor do I mean to set up some arbitrary, pure-minded standard by which to measure, and dismiss, his popular achievement. Many of the

Elvis in the late Sixties, young and beautiful again.

songs he recorded, from "Hound Dog" to such extravagant items as "Don't," "Wear My Ring Around Your Neck," "A Fool Such as I," were still classic performances, despite their musical excesses and pronounced air of self-parody (the clear, hard tenor had yielded to tremulous vibrato, dramatic swoops from high to low, and lighthearted groans). They were also fundamentally silly records, a charge that could never be leveled at the Sun sides, which, whatever else they might appear to be, were seriously, passionately, joyously in earnest. You are left with the inescapable feeling that if he had never recorded again, if Elvis Presley had simply disappeared after leaving the little Sun studio for the last time, his status would be something like that of a latter-day Robert Johnson: lost, vulnerable, eternally youthful, forever on the edge, pure and timeless.

Not that RCA would not have liked to duplicate the Sun sound. At the beginning there is little question that they tried. Still, even RCA was aware of the difference. It was "a new sound," according to Steve Sholes, Elvis's RCA discoverer, because Elvis had evolved so rapidly in the months following his RCA signing. The fact is, I think, that Elvis was too well suited to success. He was intelligent, adaptable, ambitious and sure of his goals. He wanted to break loose, and music was only his vehicle for doing so.

He soon settled in fact on a fairly comfortable and formulaic approach that took advantage of his wide-ranging musical background, facility in a number of styles, real talent as a quick study and almost total lack of taste. With the addition of the Jordanaires, a popular vocal quartet present from the first RCA sessions, the sound quickly took on the trappings of the gospel and pop groups that Elvis had always admired. With the almost inexhaustible demand for material brought on by the unprecedented dimensions of the Presley success, professional songwriters were called in and invited to submit their compositions for approval (and publication, under the Gladys or Elvis Presley Music imprint). Whereas

Elvis, with dad, Vernon, in Las Vegas, 1969.

a song like "Hound Dog," although already part of the stage act, required as many as thirty takes, after a while vocals were merely patterned on the demos that were submitted, and while no session could be complete without the warmups and inevitable gospel sings that always remained a feature of Elvis Presley's musical life, the loose feel of the Sun studio was gone.

Events moved too rapidly even to try to comprehend. Million-sellers, national tours, the triumph over Ed Sullivan's stuffy personal pronouncements (Presley will never appear on my show, said Sullivan, just weeks before he signed Elvis for a $50,000 series of appearances), instant celebrity, the promise of immortality, the rush of success. Record making in fact became something of a subsidiary interest once Elvis went to Hollywood in the summer of 1956. By the time he entered the army in 1958 he was what Sam Phillips had said he would become: a genuine pop singer. A pop singer of real talent, catholic interests, negligent ease and magnificent aplomb, but a pop singer nonetheless.

Elvis with then-wife, Priscilla, at his opening at the International Hotel, Las Vegas, 1969.

I can remember the suspense my friends and I felt when Elvis came out of the army in 1960. By this time we were growing sideburns of our own, and in some ways his fate, like that of any other icon, seemed inextricably linked with ours. What would he be like? Would he declare himself once again? Would he keep the faith? We hadn't long to wait for the answers.

His first release, "Stuck on You," followed the familiar formula of "All Shook Up," "Too Much," "Let Me Be Your Teddy Bear," innocuous enough rock & roll fare but still rock & roll. The second release was the monumental best-seller "It's Now or Never," reputedly Elvis's favorite song and loosely based on the "O Sole Mio" of Mario Lanza, one of Elvis's favorite operatic tenors. The first, and last, paid public appearance was a Frank Sinatra TV special, in tails. Frank Sinatra! After that he retreated from the world for nearly a decade to make movies.

We forgave him his apostasy, just as we forgave him all his lapses and excesses; his self-parodying mannerisms, his negligible gift for, or interest in, acting; his corporeal puffiness; his indifference to the material he recorded; his apparent contempt for his own talent; his continuing commercial success in the face of all these fallings-away. The spectacle itself of the bad boy made good.

Because that is what I think gratified us most of all. Elvis's success, flying as it did not only in the face of reason but of good taste as well, seemed in a way a final judgment on the world that had scorned him and, by the sheer magnitude of his talent, he had transformed. We took it as a cosmic joke. We speculated endlessly on the life that Elvis must be leading, and the laughs he must be having, behind the locked gates of Graceland, his Memphis mansion. Every fact that is presented in this essay was a mystery then, the subject for painstaking detective work, an intricately assembled collage that has since been exploded by knowledge. Most of all we labored happily in the wilderness, self-mocking but earnest, possessors of a secret knowledge shared by only fellow fans: Elvis Presley was to be taken seriously.

There were only two footnotes to this long and continuing saga of perfect decline.

The first was the TV special that ended Presley's eight-year slumber in Hollywood. This came about quite simply because by 1968 Elvis had exhausted his audience, as well as himself, with movies that were no longer drawing, records that, devoid of even a semblance of commitment, were no longer selling. The Beatles, the Rolling Stones and Dylan had eclipsed their onetime mentor. Elvis was beginning to look dated. And so the Colonel, who had always avowed that it was his patriotic duty to keep Elvis in the 90-percent tax bracket, decided that it was time for his boy to step out. Seizing the moment with customary astuteness, he wangled a remarkable financial deal for a special to be shown at Christmastime. What could be more appropriate, the Colonel argued, than the star's appearance in a kind of formal Christmas pageant, singing a medley of Christmas carols and hymns. For the first time in his career Elvis seems to have put his foot down. Or perhaps that is merely what the Colonel would like us to believe. In association with the show's young

producer-director, Steve Binder, he determined to appear in live performance, doing his old songs in taped segments in front of a handpicked but real, live breathing audience. A good chunk of the special was still choreographed, it's true, and some big production numbers remained, but the core of the show was just Elvis, alone on the stage with his guitar and such old musical friends as Scotty Moore and D. J. Fontana.

I'll never forget the anticipation with which we greeted the announcement and then the show itself, having the opportunity to see our idol outside his celluloid wrappings for the very first time, knowing that we were bound to be disappointed. The credits flashed, the camera focused on Elvis, and to our utter disbelief there he was, attired in black leather, his skin glistening, his hair long and greasy, his look forever young and callow. "If you're looking for trouble," he announced, "you've come to the right place."

I don't know if I can convey how transcendent, how thrilling a moment it was. Here were all our fantasies confirmed—the look, the sound, the stance, the remarkable appositeness of the selection. The voice took off, it soared, it strained, and then to our vast surprise Elvis is sweating. He is unsure of himself, he is ill at ease, he is uncertain of our reaction, and it seems clear for the first time that Elvis is trying, and trying very hard, to please us. He needs to have our attention, and it comes as something of a shock after all this time to discover that a hero whom we had set up to feel only existential scorn, a hero who was characterized by a frozen sneer and a look of sullen discontent, should need us in the end.

I say that this is a footnote, but maybe it was more than that. Because to my mind at least it gave rise to the second brief flourishing of the art of Elvis Presley, a flourishing that could not have taken place without all that went before but which can stand on its own nonetheless as a real and significant artistic achievement. On the strength of the success of the

Elvis in 1971 after receiving the rarely granted Bing Crosby Award of the National Academy of Recording Arts and Sciences.
Does he look impressed?

The great comeback: Elvis performs in front of a live audience for the first time in years as part of his December 1968 TV special on NBC. One of the great moments of rock.

TV show, and the subsequent sales of "If I Can Dream," the inspirational single that concluded it, he went back to Memphis to record for the first time in nearly fourteen years. The singles ("Suspicious Minds," "Kentucky Rain," "Don't Cry Daddy") and initial album, *From Elvis in Memphis,* that came out of these sessions are true reflections of the passion and soul which Elvis invested in that rare moment of unease in an otherwise uninterrupted career. There continues to be that same sense of tension, the atmosphere remains nervous and almost self-effacing, there is that strange anxiety to please and constriction in the voice that seems a million years away from the perfect self-assurance of the nineteen-year-old "natural" who first recorded for Sun so very long ago.

What happened after that everybody knows. Amid much hoopla Elvis returned to live performing, first in Las Vegas, where a flock of critics were flown out to the historic opening, to come back with tales of vitality undimmed, robust roots and disarming charm. We are all fans. When it became obvious from the relative unsuccess of *Elvis: That's the Way It Is,* a documentary of the Vegas act, that movies were no longer a viable commercial formula, the Colonel hustled his product back out on the road, where he appeared in coliseums, hockey rinks, the Astrodome and Madison Square Garden. There was a great deal of money made very quickly, and very soon the burst of involvement that had so briefly galvanized Elvis dissipated, the act was reduced to total self-parody and Elvis to practicing his karate kicks onstage. When I finally saw him in person at the Boston Garden in 1971, it was like going to a gathering of the faithful, grown middle-aged, perhaps, in pantsuits and double-knits, but faithful nonetheless. I sat as far away from the stage as you can sit in a big arena, but even from there you could see that he was the perfect artifact, preserved like the great woolly mammoth in a block of ice, suspended, Greil Marcus has suggested, in a perpetual state of grace, all his illusions and mine intact.

After that, sadly, the ice melted. Elvis's final years were a grotesque parade of tabloid headlines (ELVIS AT 40—PAUNCHY, DEPRESSED AND LIVING IN FEAR; IT'S ELVIS THE NIGHTSTALKER) and disturbing personal revelations (*Elvis: What Happened?* written by renegade members of the Memphis Mafia and on the newsstands just days before his death, told a dark tale of drugs, spiritualism and paranoia). His death, in Au-

The 1968 TV special. Elvis could still do it all.

gust 1977, only represented the final violation of a jealously guarded privacy, as we learned of last words, last acts, past sins, both real and imagined. Even in death the waxy image was maintained, with pious tributes and a blurred open-coffin picture, showing Elvis at peace, on the front page of the *National Enquirer.* And life after death? That, too, has come in a triumph of pure plasticity, the enshrinement of the hero as all-purpose product—book, record, liqueur, pewter statuette, dashboard icon, portrait suitable for framing. As the Colonel is reputed to have said, nothing has changed. It's just like when his boy went into the army.

It doesn't matter, none of it matters. For Elvis was merely a prisoner of the same fantasies as we. What he wanted he got. What he didn't he deliberately threw away. There is a moment in *Elvis on Tour,* his final film and yet another documentary, in which Elvis yields the stage to J. D. Sumner and the Stamps, the gospel group in his entourage. He has just finished singing "You Gave Me a Mountain," a Marty Robbins song that tells in a series of dramatic crescendos a tale of separation from an only child. It could just as easily be "My Boy" or "Separate Ways" or even "Mama Liked the Roses," all dramas of broken marriage and separation from loved ones (Elvis's daughter, whom he was said to adore, was

A concert in 1977. By then he was struggling with ill health, drug dependencies and personal problems. In August of that year he died.

is at rest, expression pensive, eyes uplifted, mouthing the words and shaking his head with a smile, carried outside of himself. It is as if it is intended in expiation, and it probably is. Then the music starts up, the show begins again, he launches into "Lawdy Miss Clawdy" without so much as a blink, and Elvis Presley is once again encapsulated in the gauzelike world from which he will never emerge.

It's all right, you want to say to him impertinently. It's all right. You did okay, even if your greatest talent did turn out to be for making money.

Earlier in the same film there are moving images from *The Ed Sullivan Show* of 1956, where youth is forever captured, forever joyous, with a swivel of the hip, a sneer of the lip, and the full confidence and expectation that nothing will ever go wrong. "My daddy knew a lot of guitar players," recalls Elvis in one of the film's interview segments, "and most of them didn't work, so he said, 'You should make your mind up to either be a guitar player or an electrician, but I never saw a guitar player that was worth a damn!' " Elvis smiles. Elvis laughs. His face fills the screen. "When I was a boy," you can hear Elvis Presley saying, "I was the hero in comic books and movies. I grew up believing in that dream. Now I've lived it out. That's all a man can ask for."

Jerry Hopkins's biography, Elvis, *has been an invaluable source of information. Several unattributed quotes have been taken from the book.*

born nine months to the day after his 1967 marriage, which subsequently ended when his wife took up with her karate instructor). These are the only secular songs that he seems able to sing with any real conviction, painful substitutes for self-expression, artful surrogates for real life. In the film he introduces the gospel group, enlists the audience's attention ("I don't sing in this. Just listen to them, please. It's a beautiful song.") and for the first time

Worldly tokens of eternal life, at his grave in Memphis.

DISCOGRAPHY

SINGLES

"That's All Right" b/w "Blue Moon of Kentucky" (Sun; 1954). "Good Rockin' Tonight" b/w "I Don't Care If the Sun Don't Shine" (Sun; 1954). "Milkcow Blues Boogie" b/w "You're a Heartbreaker" (Sun; 1955). "Baby, Let's Play House" b/w "I'm Left, You're Right, She's Gone" (Sun; c☆10, 1955). "Mystery Train" b/w "I Forgot to Remember to Forget" (Sun; c☆1, 1955). "Heartbreak Hotel" b/w "I Was the One" (RCA Victor; r☆5, c☆1, ☆1) 1956). "Blue Suede Shoes" (RCA Victor; ☆24, 1956). "I Want You, I Need You, I Love You" b/w "My Baby Left Me" (RCA Victor; r☆10, c☆1, ☆3, 1956). "Don't Be Cruel" b/w "Hound Dog" (RCA Victor; r☆1, c☆1, ☆1) 1956). "Love Me Tender" b/w "Anyway You Want Me (That's How I Will Be)" (RCA Victor; r☆4, c☆3, ☆1) 1956). "Love Me" b/w "When My Blue Moon Turns to Gold Again" (RCA Victor; ☆6, 1956). "Poor Boy" (RCA Victor; ☆35, 1956). "Old Shep" (RCA Victor; ☆47, 1956). "Too Much" b/w "Playing for Keeps" (RCA Victor; r☆7, c☆5, ☆2, 1957). "All Shook Up" b/w "That's When Your Heartaches Begin" (RCA Victor; r☆1, c☆3, ☆1) 1957). "(There'll Be) Peace in the Valley" (RCA Victor; ☆39, 1957). "Let Me Be Your Teddy Bear" b/w "Loving You" (RCA Victor; r☆1, c☆1, ☆1) 1957). "Jailhouse Rock" b/w "Treat Me Nice" (RCA Victor; r☆1, c☆1, ☆1) 1957). "Don't" b/w "I Beg of You" (RCA Victor; r☆4, c☆2, ☆1) 1958). "Wear My Ring Around Your

Neck" b/w "Doncha' Think It's Time" (RCA Victor; r☆7, c☆3, ☆3, 1958). "Hard Headed Woman" b/w "Don't Ask Me Why" (RCA Victor; r☆2, c☆2, ☆2, 1958). "One Night" b/w "I Got Stung" (RCA Victor; r☆10, c☆24, ☆4, 1958). "(Now and Then There's) A Fool Such as I" b/w "I Need Your Love Tonight" (RCA Victor; r☆16, ☆2, 1959). "A Big Hunk o' Love" b/w "My Wish Came True" (RCA Victor; r☆10, ☆1, 1959). "Stuck on You" b/w "Fame and Fortune" (RCA Victor; r☆6, c☆27, ☆1, 1960). "It's Now or Never" b/w "A Mess of Blues" (RCA Victor; r☆7, ☆1, 1960). "Are You Lonesome Tonight?" b/w "I Gotta Know" (RCA Victor; r☆3, c☆22, ☆1, 1960). "Surrender" b/w "Lonely Man" (RCA Victor; ☆1, 1961). "Flaming Star" (RCA Victor; ☆14, 1961). "I Feel So Bad" b/w "Wild in the Country" (RCA Victor; r☆15, ☆5, 1961). "(Marie's the Name) His Latest Flame" b/w "Little Sister" (RCA Victor; ☆4, 1961). "Can't Help Falling in Love" b/w "Rock-a-Hula Baby" (RCA Victor; ☆2, 1961). "Good Luck Charm" b/w "Anything That's Part of You" (RCA Victor; ☆1, 1962). "Follow That Dream" (RCA Victor; ☆15, 1962). "She's Not You" (RCA Victor; r☆13, ☆5, 1962). "King of the Whole Wide World" (RCA Victor; ☆30, 1962). "Return to Sender" (RCA Victor; r☆5, ☆2, 1962). "One Broken Heart for Sale" (RCA Victor; r☆21, ☆11, 1963). "(You're the) Devil in Disguise" (RCA Victor; r☆9, ☆3, 1963). "Bossa Nova Baby" b/w "Witchcraft" (RCA Victor; r☆20, ☆8, 1963). "Kissin' Cousins" b/w "It Hurts Me" (RCA Victor; ☆12, 1964). "Kiss Me Quick" (RCA Victor; ☆34, 1964). "What'd I Say" b/w "Viva Las Vegas" (RCA Victor; ☆21, 1964). "Such a Night" (RCA Victor; ☆16, 1964). "Ask Me" b/w "Ain't That Loving You Baby" (RCA Victor; ☆12, 1964). "Do the Clam" (RCA Victor; ☆21, 1965). "Crying in the Chapel" (RCA Victor; ☆3, 1965). "(Such an) Easy Question" (RCA Victor; ☆11, 1965). "I'm Yours" (RCA Victor; ☆11, 1965). "Puppet on a String" (RCA Victor; ☆14, 1965). "Tell Me Why" (RCA Victor; ☆33, 1966). "Frankie and Johnny" b/w "Please Don't Stop Loving Me" (RCA Victor; ☆25, 1966). "Love Letters" (RCA Victor; ☆19, 1966). "Spinout" b/w "All That I Am" (RCA Victor; ☆40, 1966). "Indescribably Blue" (RCA Victor; ☆33, 1967). "Big Boss Man" b/w "You Don't Know Me" (RCA Victor; ☆38, 1967). "Guitar Man" (RCA Victor; ☆43, 1968). "U.S. Male" (RCA Victor; ☆28, 1968). "If I Can Dream" (RCA; ☆12, 1968). "Memories" (RCA; ☆35, 1969). "In the Ghetto" (RCA; ☆3, 1969). "Clean Up Your Own Back Yard" (RCA; ☆35, 1969). "Suspicious Minds" (RCA; ☆1, 1969). "Don't Cry Daddy" (RCA; c☆13, ☆6, 1969). "Kentucky Rain" (RCA; ☆16, 1970). "The Wonder of You" (RCA; ☆9, 1970). "I've Lost You" (RCA; ☆32, 1970). "You Don't Have to Say You Love Me" (RCA; ☆11, 1970). "I Really Don't Want to Know" (RCA; c☆9, ☆21, 1970). "Where Did They Go, Lord" (RCA; ☆33, 1971). "I'm Leavin'" (RCA; ☆36, 1971). "Until It's Time for You to Go" (RCA; ☆40, 1972). "Burning Love" (RCA; ☆2, 1972). "Separate Ways" (RCA; ☆20, 1972). "Steamroller Blues" b/w "Fool" (RCA; c☆31, ☆17, 1973). "Raised on Rock" b/w "For Ol' Times Sake" (RCA; c☆42, ☆41, 1973). "I've Got a Thing About You Baby" b/w "Take Good Care of Her" (RCA; c☆4, ☆39, 1974). "If You Talk in Your Sleep" b/w "Help Me" (RCA; c☆6, ☆17, 1974). "Promised Land" b/w "It's Midnight" (RCA; c☆9, ☆14, 1974). "My Boy" (RCA; c☆14, ☆20, 1975). "T-R-O-U-B-L-E" (RCA; c☆11, ☆35, 1975). "Pieces of My Life" (RCA; c☆33, 1975). "Hurt" b/w "For the Heart" (RCA; c☆6, ☆28, 1976). "Moody Blue" b/w "She Thinks I Still Care" (RCA; c☆1, ☆31, 1976). "Way Down" (RCA; c☆1, ☆18, 1977). "My Way" (RCA; c☆2, ☆22, 1977). "Unchained Melody" b/w "Softly, As I Leave You" (RCA; c☆6, 1978). "Puppet on a String" b/w "(Let Me Be Your) Teddy Bear" (RCA; c☆78, 1978).

ALBUMS

The Sun Sessions CD (RCA; 1987). *The Number One Hits* (RCA; 1987). *Essential Elvis* (RCA; 1988). *Stereo '57 (Essential Elvis, Volume 2)* (RCA; 1988). *Elvis: The King of Rock 'n' Roll—The Complete 50's Masters* (RCA; 1992.)

(Chart positions compiled from Joel Whitburn's *Record Research*, based on *Billboard*'s Pop chart, unless otherwise indicated: r☆ = position on *Billboard*'s Rhythm & Blues chart; c☆ = position on *Billboard*'s Country & Western chart.)

THE SOUND OF NEW ORLEANS

BY LANGDON WINNER

Tales from American folklore attach a flattering but totally exaggerated importance to New Orleans as the wellspring of the nation's musical traditions. Schoolchildren are asked to believe that the lovely city on the Gulf of Mexico was the "home of jazz," "gave birth to the blues" and spread the rudiments of black music in great shovelfuls pitched from steamboats chugging up and down the Mississippi. Hollywood filmmakers of the Fifties liked to portray Louis Armstrong and his Dixieland band parading through nightclubs, as if in the middle of some never-ending odyssey, playing "When the Saints Go Marching In"; regardless of plot or context, the action would stop long enough for the actors to pay homage to old Satchmo and the place where it all supposedly began—New Orleans.

In point of fact, there was no one geographical center that served as the origin for the many strands of music that have sprung from this continent during the past century. The wonder of it is that jazz, blues and rock & roll have flourished in many different forms and localities across the land. Nevertheless, though the myth of New Orleans is a distortion, there is no denying the magnificence of the city's actual contributions. Among other things, the place has given us the oldest, richest and most influential continuing tradition of rock & roll playing the music has ever had. A joyous, rambling, uncomplicated feeling for rhythm, melody and lyric ties together the likes of Fats Domino, Huey "Piano" Smith, Little Richard, Lloyd Price, Shirley and Lee, Professor Longhair, Clarence "Frogman" Henry, Ernie K-Doe, Chris Kenner, Lee Dorsey, Dr. John, Allen Toussaint, the Neville Brothers and others as master craftsmen of a special "sound." Within this extraordinary genealogy, other notable families—Motown, Stax/Volt, British rock and reggae—find their ancestry.

New Orlean's vitality as a musical capital reflects the rich diversity of ethnic groups and cultural elements that form its local culture. Founded in 1718 as a French colony, the city was later transferred to Spain, then back to France before it finally became an official part of the United States in the Louisiana Purchase of 1803. Pre–Civil War trade in slaves and cotton brought fabulous wealth to the coffers of this convenient seaport. In its ability to mix elegant high fashion with delights from the haunts of sin and shame, New Orleans soon became notorious as a place where the good life was easily available. Over the years the city became a home for people of remarkably diverse origins: French, African, English, Spanish, Western Indian, Cajun and Creole. From their harmony and conflict arose a distinctive culture, a characteristic food, dress, architecture, language, entertainment and public ritual, which gave New Orleans an exotic atmosphere totally exceptional for an American city.

Rock & roll performers nurtured in this fertile environment had a wealth of musical sources upon which to draw. The fabulous ensemble playing of the black funeral bands, the syncopated "second line" rhythms of Mardi Gras parades, the rugged country blues from the surrounding Mississippi Delta, the raucous chords of barrelhouse piano players, the elegant styles of jazz improvisation—all became underlying elements of New Orleans rock. The first major hit in this genre, Fats Domino's "The Fat Man," is a poorly disguised version of the old barrelhouse standard, "Junker's Blues." Just triple the blues tempo, change the words "Some people call me a junker, because I am loaded all the time," to "They call, they call me the fat man, because I weight two hundred pounds," and you've got it. In mid-career, Shirley and Lee produced a small hit, "Feel So Good," which they proudly took credit for having written. Actually, of course, the tune is a version of an old standard, "It Feels So Good," which the parade bands had been playing for decades. Again and again in this tradition a well-established set of riffs, rhythms, tunes and lyrics is cleverly reworked to provide the basis for new songs and new careers.

Typical of the influence this heady mixture has had on rock & roll is the work of a seminal postwar rhythm & blues player, the legendary Professor Longhair. Born Henry Roeland Byrd in Bogalusa in 1918, Longhair transformed the age-old tradition of barrelhouse playing into the foundations for a bass-centered rhythm & blues. Here it happened that an accident of low-life economics became crucial to musical history. Since whorehouses did not bother to keep their pianos well repaired and well tuned, the great barrelhouse pianists—Drive 'Em Down, Sullivan Rock, Kid Stormy Weather and the latter-day exponent, Champion Jack Dupree—learned how to cover the keyboard with fists and fingers to extort the sound they wanted. Professor Longhair refined this rugged mode of attack, added some Latin rhythms and sang blues lyrics with a raw, gentle voice. In the late Forties he began performing in New Orleans clubs and had an immediate impact on local audiences and musicians; over the next several years he recorded for Star Talent, Mercury, Atlantic and other labels and in 1950 had a minor R&B hit with "Bald Head." But his lasting influence extends far beyond his limited personal fame.

Already evident in Longhair's work is the essential substratum of all New Orleans rock & roll: a rugged rolling bass riff in which piano, string bass, guitar and saxophone chug along together, powerful but completely carefree. If Sun Records created rock's excited treble, New Orleans provided its solid bass foundations. Weaned on blues and boogie, Crescent City musicians have never been afraid to load up the lower end of the scale with more instrumentation than seems reasonable. On top of that foggy rumble it becomes possible to contrast the higher range of a fine tenor sax or the voice of a good R&B shouter and generate a marvelous tension in the music.

Two of the people most responsible for codifying this approach remain to this day relatively unknown and unheralded: Dave Bartholomew and Cosimo Matassa. Bartholomew, trumpet player and leader of the best New Orleans R&B group of the late Forties and Fifties, wrote,

Lloyd Price and father, cresting: He hit the charts with "Lawdy Miss Clawdy," "Stagger Lee," "Personality" and "I'm Gonna Get Married."

arranged and played for Fats Domino and other stars of the period. Son of Louis Bartholomew, a well-known Dixie tuba player, Dave grew up learning how the sounds of a proper New Orleans group were crafted. In two decades after World War II he kept a stable of first-class musicians together blowing in clubs like the Dew Drop Inn and Club Tijuana as well as in countless recording sessions. Earl Palmer, master of bass-drum syncopation and possibly the most inventive drummer rock & roll has ever had, was the mainstay in Bartholomew's organization. Tenor saxophonist Lee Allen, the Lester Young of rock, a superior improviser with a remarkable flair for constructing one-chorus solos precisely appropriate for a given tune, was another continuing presence in the group. Other capable musicians—Alvin ''Red'' Tyler, tenor; Frank Fields, string bass; Ernest McLean, guitar; Herb Hardesty, tenor; Wendell Duconge, alto; Clarence Ford, baritone and tenor; and Justin Adams, guitar—gave Bartholomew a sound that was extremely tight in the best musical sense yet totally relaxed in the accustomed Crescent City fashion. While Bartholomew's name never became widely known outside New Orleans, the truth is that he was one of the most successful tunesmiths of all time (eclipsed in the rock & roll era of the Fifties only by Jerry Leiber and Mike Stoller). The reason was, of course, that teamed with Domino, he had composed dozens of best-selling tunes.

Another unheralded but nonetheless crucial figure was Cosimo Matassa, owner and chief engineer of J&M Studio, where all of the New Orleans groups recorded. Cosimo devised a simple formula for rock recording similar to that used by George Goldner and other early producers: set the dials at some sensible level, turn on the tape machine and let the performers wail. Either one caught the sound live or one did the song over again until it was right. No overdubbing, no electronic manipulation (other than an occasional echo or sound effect) was ever used. In the Fifties performers such as Little Richard and Ray Charles flocked to Cosimo's studio in search of that marvelous sound that came from the New Orleans sessionmen, the acoustics of the room and the simplicity of Cosimo's control board. Attempts in the Seventies by Dr. John and others to employ much more sophisticated techniques to achieve the same effects proved utterly fruitless: The fullness of electronic embellishment sounds completely hollow

Cosimo Matassa, out of whose studios came some of the finest rock & roll ever made.

when compared to the amazing density of the J&M takes.

The New Orleans style first came to national attention in 1948 with the success of Roy Brown's ''Good Rockin' Tonight'' on Deluxe. Although Wynonie Harris's cover version of the song sold more copies, Brown's lugubrious blues vocals and big-band arrangements soon became trendsetters in rhythm & blues. Brown went on to record a series of first-rate minor hits in the early Fifties, and after exerting a profound influence on the vocal styles of B. B. King, Bobby Bland and Jackie Wilson, faded into virtual obscurity.

With the exception of Fats Domino's steadily growing popularity, the early Fifties were fairly modest years for New Orleans performers. Pianists such as Paul Gayten and Archibald recorded very good material that failed to catch on with the rhythm & blues audience. Gravelly-voiced Smiley Lewis, heavily influenced by Fats Domino's singing, made a string of records that in retrospect stand out as small gems. But except for ''The Bells Are Ringing,'' briefly a hit in 1952, and the reflected glory of Gale Storm's smash cover of his ''I Hear You Knocking'' in 1955, Smiley was never able to find listeners for his buzzy, hard-edge singing.

A more successful Domino imitator, Lloyd Price,

claimed a hit with "Lawdy Miss Clawdy" on Speciality in 1952. Price made a series of fine records on Specialty in subsequent years, but none with the popular appeal of his first success. Although a capable blues balladeer, Price was at his best in peppy, uptempo numbers that matched his husky, handsome voice with a hard-charging brass and reed section. Several years later, from 1957 to 1959, he refined this style in a sequence of national hits on ABC: "Stagger Lee," "Personality," "I'm Gonna Get Married" and others were among the most successful commercial adaptations of the New Orleans métier.

Another extraordinary Specialty artist of the early Fifties was Guitar Slim, whose slow blues "The Things That I Used to Do" topped the R&B charts in early 1954. Born Eddie Jones in Greenwood, Mississippi, in 1926, Slim synthesized the essence of country-blues singing and guitar with a rhythm & blues backup. Most importantly, he managed to expand the limits of electric blues guitar playing. Comparing Slim's work to that of Jimi Hendrix, New Orleans songwriter Al Reed told blues historian John Broven: "He had an electric sound like you never heard and they would open the club doors wide so that the sound could just go in and out of the club and he would draw people off the street. Big passing automobiles would stop and just listen to this guy play and watch him walk." As the decade went on, Guitar Slim's star fell into eclipse. Moving to Atco Records in 1957, he was unable to match the sound and success of his early work. Slim died a young man of thirty-two in 1959, the victim of ill health, drink and undeserved neglect.

The great breakthrough year for New Orleans finally came in 1955, the point at which R&B finished its metamorphosis into rock & roll and began to win a huge national audience. It was then that Fats Domino's gentle Creole voice began to be heard by Northern teenagers increasingly able to distinguish the genuine music in songs like "Ain't That a Shame" from Pat Boone's pale, cleaned-up imitations. It was then also that the wonderful, wild Little Richard, backed by a great Crescent City studio band, unleashed "Tutti-Frutti" on an American public that had never heard anything

like it. Over the next five years the first generation of New Orleans rock performers had dozens of national hits that, along with innovations out of New York, Philadelphia, Chicago, Memphis and Texas, totally transformed American popular music.

Most popular of the New Orleans–based performers were, of course, Fats Domino, Little Richard and Lloyd Price, each with his string of best-sellers. But

Bobby Charles, the man who wrote "See You Later Alligator."

other artists of lesser standing had their moments in the spotlight as well. Characteristic of the second-level New Orleans artists of this period was a tendency to sing novelty songs and to employ musical gimmicks. The jokes and goofing on the record are sometimes fun, sometimes totally annoying. New Orleans rock is so fundamentally solid that the layers of nonsense often get in the way of what the listener wants to hear.

One master of this musical mummery, Clarence "Frog Man" Henry, made a tiny dent in the hit parade in 1956 with a catchy tune, "Ain't Got No Home," cut with Paul Gayten's band. In the song Clarence bemoans the modern condition of rootlessness and anomie, using falsettos to mimic a woman's voice and a frog's. Tibetan monks traditionally sang by inhaling rather than exhaling, a technique enabling a single voice to produce as many as three notes at once. As he inhaled to croak the part of the frog, Clarence Henry rediscovered this fruitful but seldom used musical approach. In the early Sixties the Frog Man (minus the frog voice) returned to national prominence with the ballads ''I Don't Know Why, but I Do'' and ''You Always Hurt the One You Love.'' Clarence Henry still performs in New Orleans clubs, one of the most accessible performers of the old school.

Another act in which the tension between pure talent and obvious contrivance played a central role was the male-female duo Shirley and Lee. Plucked off the streets of the Latin Quarter by Aladdin Records' Eddie Mesner in the early Fifties, young teenagers Shirley Goodman and Leonard Lee were billed as the ''Sweethearts of the Blues.'' After their original success in 1952 with a doo-wop song, ''I'm Gone,'' they made a continuing series of records that described the ecstasy and turmoil of a young couple in the throes of first romance: ''Shirley Come Back to Me,'' ''Shirley's Back,'' ''Lee Goofed'' and others with the same theme. Even more important to their success than the convenient boy-girl device, however, was the bizarre, alluring quality of Shirley Goodman's voice. When Shirley sings, her natural voice goes simultaneously sharp and flat. Each note is an average of tones, a half step up and a half step down. There is no strain or contortion of her vocal cords to achieve this effect. It's simply what comes out. ''My voice is a gimmick rather than a singing voice,'' Shirley once commented. ''I've tried to change it many times; I used to go out and scream and scream, trying to force it to go down. But that only made it stronger than before.''

Shirley and Lee soared to national fame in 1956 with ''Let the Good Times Roll.'' A clever merry-go-round riff played by a hot J&M studio band sets the tune in motion. Lee's pleasant, orthodox blues vocal carries the first two choruses solo. Then on the third time around Shirley steps forward. ''Come on, baby, let the good times roll / Come on, baby, let me thrill your soul.'' The listener isn't sure whether to take the record back as defective, have the phonograph repaired or just pay closer attention. Although it reached no higher than Number Twenty-seven on the *Billboard* lists, ''Let the Good Times Roll'' stayed

a hit long enough to sell a million copies and has been remade in countless versions during the three and a half decades since. Unfortunately, Shirley and Lee never were able to find a suitable followup. ''I Feel Good,'' ''That's What I Wanna Do'' and ''Rock All Nite'' were interesting, well-produced songs with a fine groove, but none of them enjoyed the sales of their one smash hit. Perhaps their sound was just a little too ''black,'' a little too rough-hewn to win the permanent favors of the white record-buying public.

Shirley and Lee, the Sweethearts of the Blues, just kids.

Shirley and Lee eventually fell back to the rhythm & blues circuit and continued to perform as a team until 1963. Leonard Lee eventually gave up music altogether and went to work for a U.S. government poverty agency. Shirley's still-incredible voice surfaced again as the lead in the colossal disco hit of 1975, ''Shame, Shame, Shame.'' Few if any of the fans who enjoyed this ebullient dance number realized that the Shirley of Shirley and Company was the same woman whose voice had scandalized popular music two decades earlier.

The ultimate extension of New Orleans music's playful dynamism during this period was achieved by the most wonderful of second-level groups, Huey ''Piano'' Smith and the Clowns. Since the late Forties Smith had been a journeyman keyboard wizard in the bands of Guitar Slim and Earl King and had played on dozens of recording sessions with Smiley Lewis, Shirley and Lee and others. With the founding of Johnny Vincent's Ace Records in Jackson, Mississippi, Huey was given a chance to show his stuff. A lazy, loping ditty called ''Rockin' Pneumonia and the Boogie Woogie Flu'' reached the middle of the Top 100 in August 1957. Several months later the Clowns' fabulous two-sided hit, ''Don't You Just Know It'' b/w ''High Blood Pressure,'' captured Number Nine on the charts.

All of Smith's singles on Ace carry the same basic format. A heavily accented left-hand piano is set against a low, growling saxophone section. Above that, human voices of varying degrees of freakiness wail away as best they can with lyrics containing as little intelligible verbal content as possible. The poignant hook line in ''Don't You Just Know It''— ''gooba, gooba, gooba, gooba''—is about as profound as the message ever gets. Sound, not words, was Huey's forte. His organization featured some of the finest instrumentalists in rock, including Lee Allen, Red Tyler and drummer Charles ''Hungry'' Williams, and a collection of the wildest singers going. Matched with the gruff talking bass of Billy Roosevelt and shrill squeals of Gerri Hall was the elegant master of nasalized lead vocals, Bobby Marchan (whom many fans mistakenly believed to be Huey Smith). The Clowns' ability to mix comic voices, piano and saxophone produced what may have been the most exciting rock & roll band of its time.

Although Smith and his group soon ran short of good material and began to slip from national popularity, they did appear on a record that stands today as the finest example of pure romping, stomping New Orleans rock ever made, Frankie Ford's ''Sea Cruise.'' In this hit of early 1959 all of the elements of a sound that had been evolving for a decade are carried to their logical extremes. The New Orleans horns finally cook like their lives depend on it. The piano prances along, reaching the very essence of boogie-woogie. The lead vocal finally achieves the perfect mix of pure joke and pure hysteria: ''Old man rhythm gets in my shoes / It's no use sitting and singing the blues.'' White pretty boy Frankie Ford—Ace's first attempt to find a teen idol—sings the tune in a style heavily indebted to Bobby Marchan. In the background, overdubbed foghorns add a deranged emphasis. *Bwammmp! Bwammmmmrmmp! Bwammmmmmmmmmmmp!* Completely out of con-

Huey ''Piano'' Smith, boss of the eighty-eights in the New Orleans of the Fifties—he made ''Sea Cruise'' a memorable trip. In the Seventies, as we see here, he turned to loftier pursuits.

trol, threatening to take over the whole damned song, the foghorns are definitely necessary; another version of the song that Huey Smith did without them missed the boat completely. What we have in the foghorns is the perfect embodiment of the sound New Orleans hornmen had been after for years. The *Queen Mary* as the ultimate baritone sax!

As the Fifties drew to a close, it was becoming clear that the music of the first generation of New Orleans performers was wearing dangerously thin. Ace Records' Jimmy Clanton wooed white audiences with sweet pap like ''Just a Dream'' (1958), ''Go, Jimmy, Go'' (1959) and ''Venus in Blue Jeans'' (1962) and became a crashing bore. A host of once-successful artists floundered and were no longer able to discover formulas that could sell records. A sign of the vitality of New Orleans as a rock tradition was its ability at this point to transform its foundations, retain its integrity and advance to a whole new stage. The

Allen Toussaint's first album was strictly instrumental. It wasn't too wild, really, but Al Hirt got a big hit when he recorded one of its tunes, ''Java.''

person most crucial to this remarkable renewal was a young, quiet, almost compulsively shy pianist, writer and producer, Allen Toussaint.

As a teenager Toussaint hung around studios and clubs copying musicians' licks and learning the trade. He idolized Professor Longhair and succeeded in mastering all of the tricks of classic New Orleans piano. After a time he was asked to play in sessions for Fats Domino and other senior performers. Young Toussaint, the word got out, was a ''natural,'' a man who played rhythm & blues as easily as breathing.

In 1960, while still in his early twenties, Toussaint became the producer, arranger and bandleader for the newly formed Minit Records. By the summer of that year he had already scored his first hit, ''Ooh Poo Pah Doo'' by Jessie Hill. The song features Hill's crazed shouting on simple, yes, even idiotic lyrics. In the background the band moves along through an ambling, cleverly syncopated pattern, a deliberate contrast to the vocal's unrestrained madness. Toussaint's trademark, then as now, is a lively but light-handed background riff. The horns enter and leave to punctuate the lyric rather than keep up a sustained, rocking flow. Often the drummer applies the brushes rather than attack with Earl Palmer–style crackling sticks. The hard-edge thrusting of earlier New Orleans bands is completely gone. With a group of fine studio musicians—Roy Montrell, gui-

tar; Chuck Badie, bass; Nat Perrilliat, tenor; Clarence Ford, baritone; James Black, drums—Toussaint chose a much more mellow approach.

Another characteristic of Toussaint's production is the use of ingenious hook lines, often delivered at a pause in the music at the end of a chorus. Two superior examples of this device became hits in spring 1961: Ernie K-Doe's ''Mother-in-Law'' and Chris Kenner's ''I Like It Like That.'' Ernest Kador (K-Doe) has a sharp, sparkling voice, not unlike a latter-day Bobby Marchan. In his only big hit, one of the few New Orleans songs to reach Number One, he complains of the tribulations of domestic life: ''If she'd leave us alone / We could have a happy home / Sent from down below . . .'' The music stops and foggy-voiced Benny Spellman chimes in, ''Mutha-in-law.''

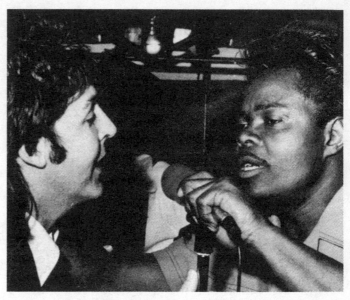

Paul McCartney with New Orleans artiste Ernie K-Doe singing ''I Want to Hold Your Hand.''

''I Like It Like That'' finds a male chorus trading lines with reedy-voiced Chris Kenner, who moans whimsically, ''Come on, come on, let me show you where it's at.'' Kenner: ''The name of the place is . . .'' Chorus: ''I like it like that.'' A little jewel in the Crescent City genre, the tune begins with a brief piano signature, a nod of acknowledgment to Huey Smith.

In the salad days of 1961 to 1963 Toussaint produced dozens of wonderful songs on the Minit, Instant, A.F.O. and Fury labels. ''Ya Ya,'' Number Seven in September 1961, featured the creamy soft tones of Lee Dorsey singing the extraordinarily dumb lines, ''Sittin' in la la / Waitin' for my ya ya.''

Barbara George scored with "I Know" later the same year. Chris Kenner had a second hit with "Land of 1000 Dances" in 1963. With varying degrees of commercial success, Toussaint also worked with Aaron Neville, Irma Thomas, Benny Spellman, Eskew Reeder, Diamond Joe and Allen Orange. Traces of his influence are also evident on the marvelous anthem to rock & roll, "It Will Stand," a small hit by the Showmen in late 1961.

With Toussaint's departure into the army in 1963, New Orleans fell into a musical doldrums. In the following year the best it could muster was the dazzlingly insipid "Chapel of Love" by the Dixie Cups, which climbed, Lord knows how, to Number One. Not until 1965, when Toussaint left uniform and

Dr. John the Night Tripper in full regalia.

Lee Dorsey, not working in the coal mine at this moment.

teamed up again with Lee Dorsey, was the music put back on its feet. With more mature, more complex arrangements than they had employed earlier, Dorsey and Toussaint released a series of hits: "Ride Your Pony" (1965); "Get out of My Life Woman," "Working in the Coal Mine" and "Holy Cow" (all 1966); and "Everything I Do Gonna Be Funky" (1969). These and other less well known songs amount to the New Orleans version of mid-Sixties soul music.

In the late Sixties a self-consciously psychedelic version of the Latin Quarter's weirdness arrived in the form of Dr. John the Night Tripper. The point of many of his amusing songs was that people looking for the best of mind-expanding preparations should turn to old voodoo medicines and rituals. Under his real name, Mac Rebennack, the doctor had been a peripheral figure in some of the less important mo-

Singer Aaron Neville of the Neville Brothers: Perhaps the most prominent figure in the contemporary revival of New Orleans music.

ments in Fifties recordings. *Dr. John's Gumbo* (1972) on Atlantic, and occasional flashes in other performances, recapture some of the tunes and feeling of the old masters. The hits ''Right Place, Wrong Time'' and ''Such a Night'' in 1973 established Dr. John as a pianist and singer-songwriter of national prominence. He continues to perform in concerts and television commercials as a gracious embodiment of the legacy of the late Professor Longhair.

During the past twenty years the tradition of New Orleans rhythm & blues has matured and mellowed. Several of the old performers, including Fats Domino, still travel the oldies circuit, keeping their memories alive. Irma Thomas has enjoyed a revival of her music and now operates a nightclub in the Crescent City. Lee Dorsey gained renewed prominence in the late Seventies touring as the opening act for the Clash and recording some successful albums. Dor-

sey's producer Allen Toussaint has now all but retired into the role of record company executive.

During the Eighties a number of younger bands such as the Dirty Dozen Brass Band, Rebirth Jazz Band and the Radiators cropped up to keep the traditions of New Orleans musicianship alive. Closely associated in public awareness were Cajun and zydeco players from adjacent Louisiana locales—Buckwheat Zydeco, Zachary Richard, Wayne Toups and Rockin' Sydney, whose Creole rocker ''My Toot Toot'' was a surprise hit in 1985.

The most notable sign of New Orleans music's continuing vitality is the growing fame of the Neville Brothers. Founded as the Meters in the late Sixties, the band features the singing of Aaron Neville, a man with the build of a longshoreman and vocal cords capable of the most delicate bel canto flourishes. In addition to Aaron's singing on the Nevilles' *Yellow Moon* (1989), *Brother's Keeper* (1990) and other albums, he accompanied Linda Ronstadt on *Cry Like a Rainstorm, Howl Like the Wind,* which won a Grammy in 1989. His singing on his solo album, *Warm Your Heart* (1991), again reveals what many consider to be the most beautiful and moving voice in all of popular music.

By and large, the music of New Orleans now exists in a kind of continuing time warp, a pleasant backwater that survives despite the direction of musical fashions elsewhere. The New Orleans Jazz and Heritage Festival held each spring has become one of the most important music festivals in the country, attracting major artists from jazz, rhythm & blues and gospel, as well as musicians from all over the world. Its spotlight is always the best of local talent, but the perspective is now global, for the groups are presented in the context of multicultural world music in its various dimensions. Indeed, the most prominent musicians to emerge from the New Orleans nexus in recent years have not been rockers at all, but rather leading jazz artists such as Wynton and Branford Marsalis as well as pop crooner and big-band leader Harry Connick Jr.

New Orleans's great contribution to American music represents the vitality of a local environment where things could grow and blossom at their own speed. Against the forces of an expanding, homogenizing national culture, its players have been able to maintain their integrity and breathe freely. New Orleans rockers arc not so much individual stars as they are master craftsmen within a special indigenous, collective art. Educated in ways of playing passed on from generation to generation, they have enjoyed the special nourishment that only a strong tradition can bring.

DISCOGRAPHY

SINGLES (1950–1965)

Lee Allen and His Band: "Walkin' with Mr. Lee" (Ember; ☆54, 1958). **Elton Anderson:** "Secret of Love" (Mercury; r☆22, ☆88, 1960). **Archibald:** "Stack-a'-Lee" (Imperial; r☆10, 1950). **Joe Barry:** "I'm a Fool to Care" (Smash; r☆15, ☆24, 1961). **James Booker:** "Gonzo" (Peacock; r☆3, ☆43, 1960). **Roy Brown:** "Hard Luck Blues" (Deluxe; r☆1, 1950). "Love Don't Love Nobody" (Deluxe; r☆2, 1950). "Cadillac Baby" b/w "Long About Sundown" (Deluxe; r☆6, 1950). "Big Town" (Deluxe; r☆8, 1951). **Roy Byrd (Professor Longhair):** "Bald

Head" (Mercury; r☆5, 1950). **Jimmy Clanton:** "Just a Dream" (Ace; r☆1, ☆4, 1958). **Larry Darnell:** "I Love My Baby" (Regal; r☆4, 1950). "Oh Babe" (Regal; r☆5, 1950). **Dixie Cups:** "Chapel of Love" (Red Bird; ☆1, 1964). "People Say" (Red Bird; ☆12, 1964). "You Should Have Seen the Way He Looked at Me" (Red Bird; ☆39, 1964). "Iko Iko" (Red Bird; r☆20, ☆20, 1965). **Lee Dorsey:** "Ya Ya" (Fury; r☆1, ☆7, 1961). "Do-Re-Mi" (Fury; r☆22, ☆27, 1962). "Ride Your Pony" (Amy; r☆7, ☆28, 1965). **Frankie Ford:** "Sea Cruise" (Ace; r☆11, ☆14, 1959). "Time After Time" (Ace; ☆75, 1960). **Paul Gayten:** "The Hunch" (Anna; ☆68, 1959). **Paul Gayten and Annie Laurie:** "I'll Never Be Free" (Regal; r☆8, 1950). **Barbara George:** "I Know" (AFO; r☆1, ☆3, 1961). "You Talk About Love" (AFO; ☆46, 1962). **Guitar Slim:** "The Things That I Used to Do" (Specialty; r☆1, 1954). **Betty Harris:** "Cry to Me" (Jubilee; r☆10, ☆23, 1963). **Clarence "Frog Man" Henry:** "Ain't Got No Home" (Argo; r☆3, ☆30, 1956). "I Don't Know Why (but I Do)" (Argo; r☆9, ☆4, 1961). "You Always Hurt the One You Love" (Argo; r☆11, ☆12, 1961). "Lonely Street" (Argo; r☆19, ☆57, 1961). **Jessie Hill:** "Ooh Poo Pah Doo—Part II" (Minit; r☆3, ☆28, 1960). **Jivin' Gene:** "Breaking Up Is Hard to Do" (Mercury; r☆69, 1959). **Joe Jones:** "You Talk Too Much" (Ric; r☆9, ☆3, 1960). "California Sun" (Roulette; ☆89, 1961). **Ernie K-Doe:** "Mother-in-Law" (Minit; r☆1, ☆1, 1961). "Te-Ta-Te-Ta-Ta" (Minit; r☆21, ☆53, 1961). **Chris Kenner:** "I Like It Like That" (Instant; r☆2, ☆2, 1961). "Land of 1000 Dances" (Instant; ☆77, 1963). **Earl King:** "Don't Take It So Hard" (King; r☆13, 1955). "Always a First Time" (Imperial; r☆17, 1962). **Annie Laurie:** "It Hurts to Be in Love" (Deluxe; r☆3, ☆61, 1957). **Smiley Lewis:** "The Bells Are Ringing" (Imperial; r☆10, 1952). "I Hear You Knocking" (Imperial; r☆2, 1955). **Barbara Lynn:** "You'll Lose a Good Thing" (Jamie; r☆1, ☆8, 1962). "You're Gonna Need Me" (Jamie; r☆13, ☆65, 1962). "Oh! Baby" (Jamie; ☆69, 1964). **Bobby Marchan:** "There's Something on Your Mind" (Fire; r☆1, ☆31, 1960). **Aaron Neville:** "Over You" (Minit; r☆21, 1960). **Lloyd Price:** "Lawdy Miss Clawdy" (Specialty; r☆1, 1952). "Oooh-Oooh-Oooh" b/w "Restless Heart" (Specialty; r☆5, 1952). "Ain't It a Shame" (Specialty; r☆7, 1953). "Just Because" (ABC-Paramount; r☆4, ☆29, 1957). "Stagger Lee" (ABC-Paramount; r☆1, ☆1, 1958). "Where Were You (on Our Wedding Day)" (ABC-Paramount; r☆4, ☆23, 1959). "Personality" (ABC-Paramount; r☆1, ☆2, 1959). "I'm Gonna Get Married" (ABC-Paramount; r☆1, ☆3, 1959). "Come into My Heart" b/w "Wont'cha Come Home" (ABC-Paramount; r☆2, ☆20, 1959). "Lady Luck" b/w "Never Let Me Go" (ABC-Paramount; r☆3, ☆14, 1960). "No Ifs—No Ands" (ABC-Paramount; r☆16, ☆40, 1960). "Question" (ABC-Paramount; r☆5, ☆19, 1960). "Misty" (Double-L; r☆11, ☆21, 1963). **Alvin Robinson:** "Something You Got" (Tiger; ☆52, 1964). **Shirley and Lee:** "I'm Gone" (Aladdin; r☆2, 1952). "Feel So Good" (Aladdin; r☆5, 1955). "Let the Good Times Roll" (Aladdin; r☆2, ☆27, 1956). "I Feel Good" (Aladdin; r☆5, ☆38, 1956). "Let the Good Times Roll" (Warwick; ☆48, 1960). **Showmen:** "It Will Stand" (Minit; ☆61, 1961). **Huey "Piano" Smith and the Clowns:** "Rocking Pneumonia and the Boogie Woogie Flu" (Ace; r☆9, ☆52, 1957). "Don't You Just Know It" (Ace; r☆4, ☆9, 1958). "Don't You Know Yockomo" (Ace; ☆56, 1958). "Pop-Eye" (Ace; ☆51, 1962). **Benny Spellman:** "Lipstick Traces" (Minit; r☆28, ☆80, 1962). **Spiders:** "I Didn't Want to Do It" b/w "You're the One" (Imperial; r☆3, 1954). "Witchcraft" (Imperial; r☆7, 1955).

ALBUMS

Neville Brothers: *Treacherous: A History of the Neville Brothers* (Rhino; 1988). **Anthologies:** *The Best of New Orleans Rhythm & Blues, Volumes 1 & 2* (Rhino; 1988). *Lay That New Orleans Rock 'n' Roll Down* (Specialty; 1988). *New Orleans Party Classics* (Rhino; 1992).

(Omitting hits by Fats Domino and Little Richard. Chart positions compiled from Joel Whitburn's *Record Research,* based on *Billboard*'s Pop chart, unless otherwise indicated; r☆ = position on *Billboard*'s Rhythm & Blues chart.)

FATS DOMINO

BY PETER GURALNICK

Christened Antoine Domino upon his birth on February 26th, 1928, in the Crescent City of New Orleans, "Fats" Domino was the most comfortable of the rock & roll founders. He came unequipped with the usual iconography; he was never a sex symbol. He did not threaten the established order. He was neither a herald of the new age, like Elvis Presley, nor a scuffed-up leftover of the old, like Big Joe Turner. He was simply the most consistent, predictable hitmaker of them all over a period of nearly twenty years, selling more than 65 million records, earning—depending on whose claim you believe—more gold records (fifteen, eighteen, twenty-two) than anyone except Elvis and the Beatles. He was a performer of great charm but little charisma, the interpreter, if not the creator, of a music that is instantly recognizable, dominated by a warm vocal style and a thick, chunky, boogie-woogie-based New Orleans–flavored piano. He was a reassuring artist, all of whose records were put across in the same lazily inimitable fashion—a fashion that was undoubtedly informed with stylishness and wit, but that possessed none of the flash, none of the passion and outrageousness of Chuck Berry or Little Richard, Elvis or Jerry Lee Lewis.

The "Fat Man," one of the most prolific hit makers of the Fifties.

It missed this passion, this sense of desperate release, primarily because Fats Domino was not breaking away from a tradition (hillbilly in the case of the white performers, jump blues in the case of the black): He was sustaining it. The New Orleans tradition goes back, of course, to the evolution of jazz in the Vieux Carré at the turn of the century, and carries through the great jazz names as well as celebrated whorehouse pianists like Kid Stormy Weather, Sullivan Rock, Drive 'Em Down. It is a tradition in which distinctions of musical genre are not easily made and one in which the boogie-woogie piano styles of non–New Orleans residents like Pine Top Smith, Jimmy Yancey and Albert Ammons mix with the light, almost whimsical second-line, or syncopated, beat that permeates all of New Orleans music, from funeral marches to traditional jazz to the rhythm & blues with which Fats Domino began his career.

Fats Domino was born into a musical family. His father was a well-known violinist, and his brother-in-law, Harrison Verrett, some twenty years older than Fats, was a familiar figure in the city and mainstay for years in Fats's band on guitar. It was Verrett who taught Fats how to play piano by marking the keys for his nine-year-old brother-in-law and showing him the progressions. Once he learned how to play, music seems to have become the consuming interest in Domino's life, for he quit school at fourteen, went to work in a factory, and began playing the clubs at night. It was in one of those clubs, the Hideaway, that Dave Bartholomew, a trumpet player, bandleader and fledgling entrepreneur, first heard the twenty-one-year-old Fats Domino. He was local A&R man for the West Coast–based Imperial Records, and he soon arranged a session, backing Fats with his own band. The result was "The Fat Man," Fats's first hit and eventually (four years after it was released, in 1953) one of his first million-sellers.

There is nothing so very revolutionary, or even startling, about "The Fat Man." Like its flip side, "Detroit City Blues," it is a conventional enough blues, in this case eight-bar, based on Champion Jack Dupree's 1940 recording of "Junker Blues," which in turn was based on the traditional New Orleans treatment of the "Stag-o-Lee" melodic family (Lloyd Price's landmark 1952 crossover, "Lawdy Miss Clawdy," on which Fats Domino played piano, is another example, as, of course, is Price's Number One rock & roll hit from 1958, "Stagger Lee"). The instrumentation is typical of the period, with riffing saxes, trumpet, full-bodied guitar, bass and drums, and the boogie-woogie piano part could well have been played by any one of the legendary New Orleans pianists (Salvador Doucette, Huey "Piano" Smith, Archibald, Clarence "Frogman" Henry, or even Professor Longhair, the inspiration for them all), each more or less contemporaneous with Fats, all of whom could, and often did, imitate one another's styles almost flawlessly. Dave Bartholomew's charts are clear, punchy and unadventurous. And the vocal, while featuring, it is true, Fats's unique buglelike falsetto waa-waaing, and pitched a little higher than on later Fats Domino recordings, is distinguished most not by any emotional intensity but by a sense of warmth, good humor and an almost disarming simplicity.

In short, "The Fat Man" was a classic Fats Domino record, bringing together not only all the musical elements (instrumentation, blues form, production) but the very musicians, arranger, studio engineer (Cosimo Matassa), and co-writers (Domino and Bartholomew) who were to figure on nearly every one of Fats's hits for the next twenty years. It displayed as well those same qualities of gentle self-deprecation and reassuring familiarity which were to continue to serve Fats well; the setting, while slightly bluesier and rhythmically less regular than his later hits, reflects most of all the personality of the singer. There is no sign of strain, and you can almost picture the young Fats Domino characteristically cocking his head to one side, grinning in that shy ingratiating way and leaning into the microphone to declare with no apparent self-consciousness, "They call, they call me the fat man/Because I weigh two hundred pounds."

It wasn't until 1955 that Fats Domino officially crossed the color line with "Ain't That a Shame," but his records always sold in numbers (between 500,000 and a million) that belied his appeal to a strictly black audience. Perhaps this was because his blues were not very cutting, or perhaps it was because his lyrics, even when they had a serious intent ("Going home tomorrow/I can't stand your evil ways"), were tossed off with such deferential charm, with none of the implicit threat of raw blues singers like Muddy Waters or Howlin' Wolf. In any case it is obvious that Fats Domino had a wider appeal than any R&B artist of the time. According to Dave Bartholomew, "We all thought of him as a country & western singer. Not real downhearted, but he always had that flavor, not the gutbucket sound." It is little wonder, then, that Fats should have crossed over so easily when the new rock & roll market was solidified.

Mr. Domino takes a stand.

"Ain't That a Shame," "I'm in Love Again," "Blueberry Hill," "Blue Monday," "I'm Walkin'," "Whole Lotta Loving," "I'm Gonna Be a Wheel Some Day," "Be My Guest," "Walking to New Orleans," "My Girl Josephine," "Let the Four Winds Blow": That is a familiar litany—and not due to Fats's efforts alone, either. The songs, with their clean arrangements, simple melodies, casual feel and catchy lyrics, were an invitation to white covers, and performers like Ricky Nelson, Pat Boone, even Elvis Presley tried their hand often and successfully at a style that was ready-made for co-optation.

Through the years the Domino-Bartholomew partnership continued, both in the studio and on the authorship of songs. Over the years virtually nothing changed. Strings were added, and Fats surmounted them. Standards were introduced, and "Blueberry Hill" became his biggest hit. The piano was confined mostly to right-hand triplets, the beat was accentuated with hand claps and tighter rhythms, and the feel remained the same. Fats left Imperial and signed with ABC in 1963. The hits slowed down, and Fats switched to Mercury in 1965, enjoying little success but cutting a live album which showed that the sound in any case hadn't altered. Even after fashion had passed him by, he came back with a 1968 hit, the Beatles' "Lady Madonna," and a relatively successful *Fats Is Back* LP. Removed from the trumped-up hysteria of the rock & roll revival, his live shows continued to be a series of genial reunions, in which with a twist of his body, a flash of his chubby jeweled pinky, a shy winsome smile or a discreet upward rolling of the eyes, Fats could evoke the charm of an era, convey his simple pleasure simply to be there and entertain.

Lately you don't hear so much from Fats. Perhaps he is simply played out, with those hundreds of songs, that vast repertoire of absolutely consistent product, forming a weight which makes it impossible to go forward. And, too, they say that the bands he fronts nowadays—after death, retirement and disastrous road accidents have taken their toll—are pale imitations of the old days. Maybe so. But it's hard to believe that Fats will not come ambling back someday, slipping into the charts with another lazy, childlike, softly phrased, boogie-woogie accented,

Mr. Domino eats cake—to honor twenty-five years of performing.

rock-solid hit. Regardless, Cosimo Matassa, the studio owner and engineer who oversaw the rise and fall of the New Orleans sound from the beginning, has long since provided a perfect epitaph. "Domino, he was creative," said Cosimo. "No matter what he does comes through. He could be singing the national anthem, you'd still know by the time he said two words it was him, obviously, unmistakably, and pleasurably him."

DISCOGRAPHY

SINGLES

"The Fat Man" (Imperial; r☆6, 1950). "Every Night About This Time" (Imperial; r☆5, 1950). "Rockin' Chair" (Imperial; r☆9, 1951). "Goin' Home" (Imperial; r☆1, 1952). "How Long" (Imperial; r☆9, 1952). "Goin' to the River" (Imperial; r☆2, 1953). "Please Don't Leave Me" (Imperial; r☆5, 1953). "Rose Mary" (Imperial; r☆10, 1953). "Something's Wrong" (Imperial; r☆6, 1953). "You Done Me Wrong" (Imperial; r☆10, 1954). "Don't You Know" (Imperial; r☆12, 1955). "Ain't That a Shame" (Imperial; r☆1, ☆16, 1955). "All by Myself" (Imperial; r☆3, 1955). "Poor Me" (Imperial; r☆3, 1955). "Bo Weevil" (Imperial; r☆6, ☆35, 1956). "I'm in Love Again" (Imperial; r☆1, ☆5, 1956). "When My Dreamboat Comes Home" (Imperial; r☆6, ☆22, 1956). "Blueberry Hill" (Imperial; r☆1, ☆4, 1956). "Blue Monday" (Imperial; r☆1, ☆9, 1956). "I'm Walkin' " (Imperial; r☆1, ☆5, 1957). "Valley of Tears" (Imperial; r☆4, ☆13, 1957). "Wait and See" (Imperial; r☆14, ☆27, 1957). "Sick and Tired" (Imperial; r☆15, ☆30, 1958). "Little Mary" (Imperial; r☆15, ☆49, 1958). "Whole Lotta Loving" (Imperial; r☆2, ☆6, 1958). "Telling Lies" (Imperial; r☆13, ☆50, 1959). "I'm Ready" (Imperial; r☆7, ☆16, 1959). "I Want to Walk You Home" (Imperial; r☆1, ☆8, 1959). "Be My Guest" (Imperial; r☆2, ☆8, 1959). "Walking to New Orleans" (Imperial; r☆2, ☆6, 1960). "Three Nights a Week" (Imperial; r☆8, ☆15, 1960). "My Girl Josephine" (Imperial; r☆7, ☆14, 1960). "What a Price" (Imperial; r☆7, ☆22, 1961). "It Keeps Rainin' " (Imperial; r☆18, ☆23, 1961). "Let the Four Winds Blow" (Imperial; r☆2, ☆15, 1961). "What a Party" (Imperial; ☆22, 1961). "You Win Again" (Imperial; ☆22, 1962).

ALBUMS

My Blue Heaven: The Best of Fats Domino (EMI; 1990). *They Call Me the Fat Man: Antoine "Fats" Domino, the Legendary Imperial Recordings* (EMI; 1991).

(Chart positions compiled from Joel Whitburn's *Record Research*, based on *Billboard*'s Pop chart, unless otherwise indicated; r☆ = position on *Billboard*'s Rhythm & Blues chart.)

LITTLE RICHARD

BY LANGDON WINNER

As the needle touches the vinyl, there is a brief moment of silence. Then: "A WOP BOP ALU BOP A WOP BAM BOOM!" Has any record ever brought a more outrageous surprise? A scant few voices made the difference in determining how rock & roll sounds, and why it is so powerfully different from other kinds of music. On an autumn day in New Orleans in 1955, an unknown, struggling young blues singer named Richard Penniman suddenly found a voice which set America on its ear. In an unprecedented burst of sighs, moans, screams, whoos and breathless panting, Little Richard opened whole continents of energy and expression for others to explore. Along with that of Elvis, Fats Domino, Chuck Berry and Buddy Holly, Richard's work defined what rock & roll was all about. That he himself was able to lay claim to only a small corner of the territory he helped pioneer makes small difference now. Those who came after—the Beatles, the Rolling Stones, Creedence Clearwater Revival and countless others—carry his legacy in every song. Any list of rock immortals that does not include Little Richard near the top has gotten too sophisticated.

Little Richard, the Georgia Peach, testifies at the altar of Tinseltown.

Six inches of hair in July 1965 and that's not all—the Handsomest Man in Rock & Roll.

Richard Wayne Penniman was born December 5th, 1932, in Macon, Georgia, one of twelve children in his family. According to the story he now tells, his grandfather and two uncles were preachers, his father a bartender and seller of bootleg whiskey. As a boy, Richard sang gospel music and learned to play piano in a neighborhood church. But his growing hunger for music was thwarted by his parents. "I came from a family where my people didn't like rhythm & blues. Bing Crosby, 'Pennies from Heaven,' Ella Fitzgerald, was all I heard. And I knew there was something that could be louder than that, but didn't know where to find it. And I found it was me."

Evidently, he made this discovery at a very young age. As a young teenager he left home to perform as a singer in Doctor Hudson's Medicine Show, one of the small circuses that traveled through the South in that period. Somewhat later he joined B. Brown and His Orchestra, singing songs like "Goodnight Irene" and "Mona Lisa" in small clubs in Georgia and Florida. Billed as "Little Richard," he already displayed the flamboyant six-inch-high pompadour that later became a trademark. But the B. Brown band was far too tame for him. Soon he was em-

ployed in traveling minstrel shows and carnivals—Sugarfoot Sam from Alabam, the Tidy Jolly Stompers and Broadway Follies—where he often appeared in evening gowns, pancake makeup and fake eyelashes, a combination drag queen and emerging R&B singer.

Richard Penniman, his eyes on the prize.

Black music often bestows the name "Little" upon performers who show their style and talent early on. Some who earned this title—Little Esther Phillips and Little Stevie Wonder, for example—later dropped it as they sought a more mature public image. It is significant that Penniman never abandoned his "Little" and that the outrageous figure we saw at the birth of rock & roll and now see well into middle age was already showing his "thing" in the streets, churches, tents and clubs of Georgia in the late Forties.

In 1951, at age eighteen, Richard performed at an audition organized by Daddy Zenas Sears of WGST in Atlanta and won a recording contract with RCA Victor. During the next two years, Richard cut eight sides for RCA. The songs from this period—"Every Hour," "Get Rich Quick," "Ain't Nothin' Happening" and others—are skillfully done small-band jump-blues numbers in the style of Roy Brown and Southern gospel-blues singer Billy Wright. Richard's voice and habit of wavering around a note before hitting it are clearly developed even though there is little particularly original or exciting about the tunes.

About this time Richard met Esquerita, a.k.a. Eskew Reeder, flamboyant R&B pianist and singer, notorious in Southern black, gay circles during the Fifties and Sixties. While Penniman had learned some piano in Macon churches, Esquerita taught him the treble bass licks that would become fundamental in Little Richard's rock & roll piano.

Richard's next recordings were made in Houston in 1953, on Don Robey's Peacock label, with the Tempo Toppers and the Deuces of Rhythm, two backup groups handling vocals and instrumentals. Tunes from this period show Little Richard approaching his later rock & roll breakthrough from the direction of orthodox rhythm & blues. In an easygoing doo-wop swing he croons, "Ain't that good news; I'm wild about the blues." There is a great deal of fun in songs like "Rice, Red Beans and Turnip Greens" and "Fool at the Wheel" but none of the raw power that marks his later work. In early 1955 Penniman went on to record four sides with the Johnny Otis Orchestra, also on the Peacock label. None of these early efforts on RCA and Peacock sold well.

Down on his luck, Penniman made a demo tape of rhythm & blues songs and mailed it to Art Rupe of Specialty Records in Los Angeles. According to one story, he then went back to Macon, washed dishes in a Greyhound bus depot and waited seven months before hearing from Specialty. Rupe found considerable promise in the tapes. He had been scouting the music scene in New Orleans and thought it would be a fine idea to have a voice as sharp as Penniman's backed by a solid Crescent City rhythm section. On September 14th, 1955, the musicians gathered for what was destined to be a crucial turning point in American music.

Along with Elvis Presley's early sides for Sun Records, Little Richard's first day with Specialty gives us the chance to say, "Rock & roll begins right here." Ironically, all the tunes from that first session, with the exception of one, are painfully dull: Richard is still trying to wring mileage out of an uninspiring rhythm & blues idiom. Then, almost as an afterthought, the players turn to a song based on an obscene ditty Richard liked to rail during the breaks. Revised for lyrical purity by New Orleans songwriter Dorothy La Bastrie, "Tutti-Frutti" leaps out as something audacious and new. Suddenly all of the restraints and vanities of imitation are gone from Richard's singing. What we hear is a kind of comic madness that requires a gleeful, bombastic voice, chaotic piano playing and hard-charging drums, guitars and saxophones. "I've got a gal / Named Daisy / She almost drives me crazy / Whoooo-ooo . . ." At long last Little Richard found (or, perhaps more accurately, stumbled into) his groove.

"Tutti-Frutti" was exciting enough to get played on white pop music stations, innocuous enough to prevent it from getting banned. For youngsters who had never heard black performers sing at full throttle, the effect was hypnotizing. Even though the words had been cleaned up, the song's pure sexual excitement came through as plain as day—everyone knew that behind all that foolishness lurked a turn-on somewhere. Parents who might well tolerate Elvis Presley balked at the prospect of having Little Richard on the family phonograph. Yet the record soon sold 500,000 copies and had an impact far beyond its sales. Other black performers of the era like Screamin' Jay Hawkins may have been wilder and more exotic, but Richard succeeded in building strong ties to an audience that included hordes of white as well as black kids.

During his amazing rise to stardom, Little Richard cut about three dozen sides for Specialty, many of which became rock & roll classics. "Long Tall Sally," "Slippin' and Slidin'," "Rip It Up," "Ready Teddy," "The Girl Can't Help It," "Send Me Some Lovin'," "Jenny, Jenny," "Miss Ann," "Keep A Knockin'," "Good Golly, Miss Molly," "Ooh! My Soul" and "True, Fine Mama" were all successful on the pop charts and established Little Richard as one of the leading forces in the revolution that had overtaken American pop music. Some of his songs employed a great New Orleans band—Earl Palmer (drums), Lee Allen (tenor sax), Alvin "Red" Tyler (baritone sax), Frank Fields (bass) and guitarists Edgar Blanchard, Justin Adams or Ernest McLean—other cuts used Los Angeles studio musicians capable of putting down equally hard-rocking sax and guitar riffs. (Whether or not Richard himself played piano on all of his hits is still a subject of controversy; according to his producer, Bumps Blackwell, there were four different piano players—Huey "Piano" Smith, James Booker, Edward Frank and Warren Myles—a suggestion Penniman himself vehemently denies.)

Complementing Richard's recordings from this period is his work in three motion pictures, each of which betrays a different side of the star's ebullient personality. All of them feature Little Richard standing at the piano in front of his band singing (actually lip syncing) his hits. The first, *Don't Knock the Rock*, shows Richard as the Great God Pan, a combination of imp and clown. When he sings "He duck back in the alley," Richard spins away from the piano and

Top this, Elvis.

dives back as if to hit the note right on time. With the saxophonist blowing a chorus while kneeling on the grand piano, Richard puts his foot up on the lid and begins exaggerated hip and body undulations—acceptable in public only under the guise of rock & roll dance.

The Girl Can't Help It, released in December 1956, shows a totally different Richard—a serious, somber, vaguely threatening figure standing at the piano staring out into space. He looms as a great black force seeking his essential contact with the world, the rock & roll equivalent of a blues singer haunted by dark obsessions.

Richard's last film of the period, *Mister Rock 'n' Roll,* adds yet another dimension to our understanding of what the man is about. Here we find him

reeling about the stage, rolling his eyes in a coy, beguiling pose that later fashion would term "gay." He wears a sweet but totally maniacal smile. There's more than a faint hint of something demented in his manner. Then the camera zooms in for a close-up. Can it be? Little Richard is wearing mascara! Those who think that Penniman's camp antics were born of a later period should take a closer look at this intriguing segment.

In 1957, at the very peak of his fame and less than a year and a half after his meteoric rise had begun, Little Richard suddenly quit rock & roll and disappeared from the scene. Specialty Records did its best to conceal the fact and continued to release records from his earlier sessions, including "Keep A Knockin'," which recording engineers pieced together

Richard preaching to a college audience, 1958, and almost unrecognizable from a year earlier.

revelation and God's message for our troubled times. From there he began a career that he hoped would make him a major force on the American evangelical circuit. A song he recorded somewhat later tells the story:

I'm quittin' show business; I want to go straight.
I'm going to serve my Lord, before it's too late.
If I die, while I'm in my sin,
I know that Jesus won't let me in.
I'm quittin' show business, I want to go straight.

Whether or not one believes this story, the fact is that Richard went the better part of a decade without offering a rock & roll song under his own name. In 1960 he appeared anonymously on some lackluster remakes of Fats Domino hits done by his former road band, the Upsetters, on Little Star. But otherwise all of his records and public performances were pure gospel. Moving from one label to another—Coral, End, Crown, Mercury—Richard cut dozens of sides that comprise a rarely heard second Penniman opus. The earliest of these recordings show Richard trying to conceal his rock & roll identity altogether. His voice presents itself in a mood of subdued reverence or in the unrestrained hysteria of a Sunday meeting. While most material from his religious pe-

from a short take Richard and his road band had blasted out at a Washington, D.C., radio station in 1957. But essentially, Richard's career as a rock & roller of the first rank was over. He withdrew into a world of religious study, evengelism and gospel singing, only to reemerge seven years later.

As is true of almost all aspects of Little Richard's career, the story of his decision to retire is shrouded in myth. The most popular account of the circumstances, one that Richard himself tells in widely differing versions, places the turning point at a powerful conversion experience that seized him on tour in Australia. A horrifying dream showed him the Apocalypse and the ugly stain of his own damnation. On an airline flight soon after (which may or may not have been threatened by a fire on board), Richard prayed to God to hold that plane in the air. Evidently, the Lord in His infinite wisdom obliged. When Richard reached safety he threw his jewelry into the harbor at Sydney, Australia, and vowed to cease his evil ways. He quit rock recording and touring and enrolled in Oakwood College, a bible school in Huntsville, Alabama, where he studied prophecy,

He studies the Bible.

57

Little Richard and friend, grits and vestments.

riod is undistinguished at best, there are a few great songs. One of them on Mercury, "He Got What He Wanted (but He Lost What He Had)," contains a doubly ironic commentary on Richard's own conversion experience. As a brassy big band blares in the background, he recites the sins of Judas, Adam and Eve and other Biblical figures and preaches that what is offered in temptation leads us to sacrifice the blessings we had all along. At some level the man obviously believed it.

Lamentably, Little Richard was never able to join Billy Graham and Oral Roberts in the world of evangelical chartbusters. And in 1964, stimulated by the success of the Beatles and other British rockers and more than a little jealous of their liberal use of his licks, Penniman finally returned to the world of pop music. Taking up exactly where he left off, he cut a tune on Specialty Records, "Bama Lama Bama Loo," which has much the same kinetic drive and childlike foolishness of his mid-Fifties work. The song attracted enough attention to put it in the eighties on the *Billboard* Hot 100. But tastes had changed; any continuation of this anachronistic approach seemed ridiculous.

From this point, Little Richard's career became a continuing series of frustrated comeback attempts. Shifting from Vee-Jay to Modern, Okeh and Brunswick, he issued a stream

of dreadful remakes of his own and other people's oldies. Occasionally, there were flashes of brilliance. In 1965 he worked up a powerful new single for Vee-Jay, "I Don't Know What You've Got but It's Got Me," a Don Covay song expressing the desperation of a man whose woman is cheating on him. A slow blues spiced with gospel-style preaching, the song suggests that the Lord's message is ultimately one of betrayal, abandonment and utter loss. Richard's beautifully agonized singing, comparable to the approach that made Otis Redding famous a short while later, suggests the beginning of an interesting new phase. The record, however, fell stillborn from the plastic presses.

It is not as if Richard was never given an adequate second chance. A major recording contract with Reprise in the early Seventies enabled him to release three albums of new material—*The Rill Thing, King of Rock and Roll* and *Second Coming*. Indeed, each of these records had its moments; Richard's extraordinary voice can still belt out a song as well as ever. But the albums ooze a kind of "getting with the kids and their groovy out-of-sight soul beat" overproduction that makes them barely listenable. The solid center of gravity that once held it all together had vanished. Richard's wildness just seemed flaky.

At the same time that the "Georgia Peach" was making his bid on Reprise, he also regained a certain notoriety showing up on late-night talk shows. "They won't forget me," he would tell friends before he went on. He was right about that. Sporting mirror-cloth costumes with long capes, dangling frills and hideous pancake makeup, Penniman made himself a spectacle by whooping it up, talking out of turn and running through the audience screaming, "I am the most beautiful thing in show business!" The crowning moment came when he actually displaced Johnny Carson from behind Carson's sacred little desk. As his former fans watched in dismay, many wondered whether it might not have been better for the man to have protected his legend in the shadows of retirement.

During the mid-Seventies Little Richard performed in occasional club dates and oldies shows around the United States and Europe, making a virtue of *not* having his act together, babbling incoherently between songs (perhaps to catch his breath at the onset of middle age), bawling out his bands for no apparent reason and putting his audiences on edge with a variety of schizy pranks. By his own account, this was also a time in which the excessive use of alcohol, cocaine and other drugs nearly brought his ruin. As the decade drew to a close, Richard Penniman again sought refuge in the church, working as a traveling bible salesman and evangelist. "God wants you to give up rock & roll!" he shouted to a tent revival meeting in North Richmond, California. This time he explicitly linked the music to his involvement with drugs and homosexuality. "I gave up rock & roll for the Rock of Ages. If God can save me, an old homosexual, he can save anybody," he exhorted the crowd.

In recent years Little Richard seems at long last to have found balance in his previously troubled existence. Having survived a near-fatal automobile accident in 1985, he has become a familiar presence in the Hollywood entertainment scene, showing up in frequent cameo spots in movies and television commercials. As a supporting actor in the 1986 film *Down and Out in Beverly Hills,* he won both critical praise and wide popular approval. Spike Lee's amusing TV ad for Nike shoes presented Richard as the smiling, larger-than-life King of Rock & Roll. In a similar light he appears as a manic singing King Cole in the children's movie *Mother Goose Rock 'N' Rhyme,* produced in the late Eighties for the Disney Channel.

The unfortunate feature of Penniman's current persona is that it includes few opportunities to sing rock & roll. While he has finally made peace with the music and no longer denounces it as the devil's workshop, the record industry seems thoroughly uninterested in sponsoring yet another attempted comeback. His lively rendition of "Itsy Bitsy Spider" on the all-star *For Our Children* AIDS benefit album shows he still has plenty of voice and flair. The recent rerelease of his phenomenal Specialty sides in a CD boxed set brought new waves of media acclaim. Now and again he appears as an opening act in rock concerts. But as he approaches the age of (can it be?) sixty, Little Richard seems fated to live out his final years not as a performer with anything new to say, but as a cherished living icon of rock & roll history.

DISCOGRAPHY

SINGLES
"Tutti-Frutti" (Specialty; r☆2, ☆21, 1955). "Long Tall Sally" b/w "Slippin' and Slidin' " (Specialty; r☆1, ☆13, 1956). "Rip It Up" b/w "Reddy Teddy" (Specialty; r☆1, ☆27, 1956). "She's Got It" (Specialty; r☆15, 1956). "The Girl Can't Help It" (Specialty; r☆11, ☆49, 1957). "Lucille" b/w "Send Me Some Lovin' " (Specialty; r☆2, ☆27, 1957). "Jenny, Jenny" b/w "Miss Ann" (Specialty; r☆2, ☆14, 1957). "Keep A Knockin' " (Specialty; r☆5, ☆8, 1957). "Good Golly, Miss Molly" (Specialty; r☆6, ☆10, 1958). "Ooh! My Soul" b/w "True, Fine Mama" (Specialty; r☆15, ☆35, 1958). "Baby Face" (Specialty; r☆12, ☆41, 1958). "I Don't Know What You've Got but It's Got Me" (Vee-Jay; r☆12, ☆92 1965). "Freedom Blues" (Reprise; r☆28, ☆47, 1970).

ALBUMS
Little Richard: 18 Greatest Hits (Rhino; 1985). *The Specialty Sessions* (Fantasy; 1991).

(Chart positions compiled from Joel Whitburn's *Record Research,* based on *Billboard*'s Pop chart, unless otherwise indicated; r☆ = position on *Billboard*'s Rhythm & Blues chart.)

CHUCK BERRY

BY ROBERT CHRISTGAU

I f there was any doubt about it before, Chuck Berry proved himself the greatest of the rock & rollers in the Seventies. Elvis competed first with Frank Sinatra and then with Rudolph Valentino, Little Richard camped his way to self-negation, Fats Domino got old in Las Vegas, and Jerry Lee Lewis faded out gracelessly as a country singer before deigning to hit the oldies circuit. But for a fee—which went up markedly after the freak success of ''My Ding-a-Ling,'' his first certified million-seller, in 1972, and then diminished again—Chuck Berry will hop on a plane with his guitar and go play some rock & roll. He is the symbol of the music—the man invited to come steal the show at the 1975 Grammys, although he has never been nominated for one himself, not even in the rock & roll or rhythm & blues categories. More important, he is also the music's substance—he taught George Harrison and Keith Richards to play guitar long before he met either, and his songs are still claimed as encores by everyone from folkies to heavy-metal kids. But Chuck Berry isn't merely the greatest of the rock & rollers, or rather, there's nothing mere about it. Say rather that unless we can somehow recycle the concept of the great artist so that it supports Chuck Berry as well as it does Marcel Proust, we might as well trash it altogether.

As with Charlie Chaplin or Walt Kelly or the Beatles, Chuck Berry's greatness doesn't depend entirely on the greatness or originality of his oeuvre. The body of his top-quality work isn't exactly vast, comprising three or perhaps four dozen songs that synthesize two related traditions: blues and country & western. Although in some respects Berry's rock & roll is simpler and more vulgar than either of its musical sources, its simplicity and vulgarity are defensible in the snootiest high-art terms—how about ''instinctive minimalism'' or ''demotic voice''? But his case doesn't rest on such defenses. It would be perverse to argue that his songs are in themselves as rich as, say, *Remembrance of Things Past*. Their richness is rather a function of their active relationship with an audience—a complex relationship that shifts every time a song enters a new context, club or album or radio or mass singalong. Where Proust wrote about a dying subculture from a cork-lined room, Berry helped give life to a subculture, and both he and it change every time they confront each other. Even ''My Ding-a-Ling,'' a fourth-grade wee-wee joke that used to mortify true believers at college concerts, permitted a lot of twelve-year-olds new insight into the moribund concept of ''dirty'' when it hit the airwaves; the song changed again when an oldies crowd became as children to shout along with Uncle Chuck the night he received his gold record at Madison Square Garden. And what happened to ''Brown Eyed Handsome Man,'' never a hit among whites, when Berry sang it at interracial rock & roll concerts in Northern cities in the Fifties? How many black kids took ''eyed'' as code for ''skinned''? How many whites? How did that make them feel about each other, and about the song? And did any of that change the song itself?

Berry's own intentions, of course, remain a mystery. Typically, this public artist is an obsessively private person who has been known to drive reporters from his own amusement park, and the sketches of his life overlap and contradict each other. The way I tell it, Berry was born into a lower middle-class colored family in St. Louis in 1926. He was so quick and ambitious that he both served time in reform school on a robbery conviction and acquired a degree in hairdressing and cosmetology before taking a job on an auto assembly line to support a wife and kids. Yet his speed and ambition persisted. By 1953 he was working as a beautician and leading a three-piece blues group on a regular weekend gig.

Chuck Berry, dressed for ''motorvatin','' with guitar to match.

His gimmick was to cut the blues with country-influenced humorous narrative songs. These were rare in the black music of the time, although they had been common enough before phonograph records crystalized the blues form, and although Louis Jordan, a hero of Berry's, had been doing something vaguely similar in front of white audiences for years.

In 1955 Berry recorded two of his songs on a borrowed machine: ''Wee Wee Hours,'' a blues that he and his pianist, Johnnie Johnson, hoped to sell, and an adapted country tune called ''Ida Red.'' He traveled to Chicago and met Muddy Waters, the uncle of the blues, who sent him on to Leonard Chess of Chess Records. Chess liked ''Wee Wee Hours'' but flipped for ''Ida Red,'' which was renamed ''Maybellene,'' a hairdresser's dream, and forwarded to Alan Freed. Having mysteriously acquired a substantial portion of the writer's credit, Freed played ''Maybellene'' quite a lot, and it became one of the first nationwide rock & roll hits.

At that time, any fair-minded person would have judged this process exploitative and pecuniary. A blues musician comes to a blues label to promote a blues song—"It was 'Wee Wee Hours' we was proud of, that was *our* music," says Johnnie Johnson—but the owner of the label decides he wants to push a novelty: "The big beat, cars and young love. It was a trend and we jumped on it," Chess has said. The owner then trades away a third of the blues singer's creative sweat to the symbol of payola, who hypes the novelty song into commercial success and leaves the artist in a quandary. Does he stick with his art, thus forgoing the first real recognition he's ever had, or does he pander to popular taste?

The question is loaded, of course. "Ida Red" was Chuck Berry's music as much as "Wee Wee Hours," which in retrospect seems rather uninspired. In fact, maybe the integrity problem went the other way. Maybe Johnson was afraid that the innovations of "Ida Red"—country guitar lines adapted to blues-style picking, with the ceaseless legato of his own piano adding rhythmic excitement to the steady backbeat—were too far out to sell. What happened instead was that Berry's limited but brilliant vocabulary of guitar riffs quickly came to epitomize rock & roll. Ultimately, every great white guitar group of the early Sixties imitated Berry's style, and Johnson's piano technique was almost as influential. In other words, it turned out that Berry and Johnson weren't basically bluesmen at all. Through some magic combination of inspiration and cultural destiny, they had hit upon something more contemporary than blues, and a young audience, for whom the Depression was one more thing that bugged their parents, understood this better than the musicians themselves. Leonard Chess simply functioned as a music businessman should, though only rarely does one combine the courage and insight (and opportunity) to pull it off, even once. Chess became a surrogate audience, picking up on new music and making sure that it received enough exposure for everyone else to pick up on it, too.

Obviously, Chuck Berry wasn't racked with doubt about artistic compromise. A good blues single usually sold around 10,000 copies and a big rhythm & blues hit might go into the hundreds of thousands, but "Maybellene" probably moved a million, even if Chess never sponsored the audit to prove it. Berry had achieved a grip on the white audience and the solid future it could promise, and, remarkably, he had in no way diluted his genius to do it. On the contrary, that was his genius. He would never have fulfilled himself if he hadn't explored his relationship to the white world—a relationship that was much different for him, an urban black man who was used to machines and had never known brutal poverty, than it was for, say, Muddy Waters.

Berry was the first blues-based performer to successfully reclaim guitar tricks that country & western innovators had appropriated from black people and adapted to their own uses twenty-five or fifty years before. By adding blues tone to some fast country runs, and yoking them to a rhythm & blues beat and some unembarrassed electrification, he created an instrumental style with biracial appeal. Alternating guitar chords augmented the beat while Berry sang in an insouciant tenor that, while recognizably African-American in accent, stayed clear of the melisma and blurred overtones of blues singing, both of which enter only at carefully premeditated moments. His few detractors still complain about the repetitiveness of his style, but they miss the point. Repetition without tedium is the backbone of rock & roll, and the components of Berry's music proved so durable that they still provoke instant excitement at concerts some three and a half decades later. And in any case, the instrumental repetition was counterbalanced by unprecedented and virtually unduplicated verbal variety.

Chuck Berry is the greatest rock lyricist this side of Bob Dylan, and sometimes I prefer him to Dylan. Both communicate an abundance of the childlike delight in linguistic discovery that page poets are supposed to convey and too often don't, but Berry's most ambitious lyrics, unlike Dylan's, never seem pretentious or forced. True, his language is ersatz and barbaric, full of mispronounced foreignisms and advertising coinages, but then, so was Whitman's. Like Whitman, Berry is excessive because he is totally immersed in America—the America of Melville and the Edsel, burlesque and installment-plan funerals, pemmican and pomade. Unlike Whitman, though, he doesn't quite permit you to take him seriously—he can't really think it's pronounced "a la carty," can he? He is a little surreal. How else can a black man as sensitive as Chuck Berry respond

In 1972 he had his first certified million-seller, "My Ding-a-Ling," a silly song about you-know-what. Here he teaches an audience to sing along.

plication, Brown Eyes's sharp sense of life's nettlesome and even oppressive details provided a kind of salvation by humor, especially in "Too Much Monkey Business," a catalog of hassles that included work, school and the army. But the white teenagers who were the only audience with the cultural experience to respond to Berry's art weren't buying this kind of salvation, not en masse. They wanted something more optimistic and more specific to themselves; of the four singles that followed "Maybellene," only "Roll Over Beethoven," which introduced Berry's other half, the rock & roller, achieved any real success. Chuck got the message. His next release, "School Day," was another complaint song, but this time the complaints were explicitly adolescent and were relieved by the direct action of the rock & roller. In fact, the song has been construed as a prophecy of the Free Speech Movement: "Close your books, get out of your seat/ Down the halls and into the street."

It has become a cliché to attribute the rise of rock & roll to a new parallelism between white teenagers and black Americans; a common "alienation" and even "suffering" are often cited. As with most clichés, this one has its basis in fact—teenagers in the Fifties certainly showed an unprecedented consciousness of themselves as a circumscribed group, though how much that had to do with marketing refinements and how much with the Bomb remains unresolved. In any case, Chuck Berry's history points up the limits of this notion. For Berry was closer to white teenagers both economically (that reform school stint suggests a JD exploit, albeit combined with a racist judicial system) and in spirit (he shares his penchant for youthfulness with Satchel Paige but not Henry Aaron, with Leslie Fiedler but not Norman Podhoretz) than the average black man. And even at that, he had to make a conscious (not to say calculated) leap of the imagination to reach them, and sometimes fell short.

Although he scored lots of minor hits, Chuck Berry made only three additional *Billboard* Top Ten singles in the Fifties—"Rock and Roll Music," "Sweet Little Sixteen" and "Johnny B. Goode"— and every one of them ignored Brown Eyes for the assertive, optimistic and somewhat simpleminded rock & roller. In a pattern common among popular artists, his truest and most personal work didn't flop, but it wasn't overwhelmingly popular either. For such artists, the audience can be like a drug. A

to the affluence of white America—an affluence suddenly his for the taking.

Chuck Berry is not only a little surreal but also a little schizy; even after he committed himself to rock & roll story songs, relegating the bluesman in him to B sides and album fillers, he found his persona split in two. In three of the four singles that followed "Maybellene," he amplified the black half of his artistic personality, the brown-eyed handsome man who always came up short in his quest for the small-time hedonism America promises everyone. By im-

little of it is so good for them that they assume a lot of it would be even better, but instead the big dose saps their autonomy, often so subtly that they don't notice it. For Chuck Berry, the craving for overwhelming popularity proved slightly dangerous. At the same time that he was enlivening his best songs with faintly Latin rhythms, which he was convinced were the coming thing, he was also writing silly exercises with titles like "Hey Pedro." Nevertheless, his pursuit of the market also worked a communion with his audience, with whom he continued to have an instinctive rapport remarkable in a thirty-year-old black man. For there is also a sense in which the popular artist is a drug for the audience, and a doctor, too—he has to know how much of his vital essence he can administer at one time, and in what compound.

Berry *(right)* with assorted groupies and Bo Diddley, another giant of early rock & roll.

The reason Berry's rock & roller was capable of such insightful excursions into the teen psyche—"Sweet Little Sixteen," a celebration of everything lovely about fanhood; or "Almost Grown," a basically unalienated first-person expression of teen rebellion that Sixties youth-cult pundits should have taken seriously—was that he shared a crucial American value with the humorous Brown Eyes. That value was fun. Even among rock critics, who ought to know better, fun doesn't have much of a rep, so that they commiserate with someone like LaVern Baker, a second-rate blues and gospel singer who felt she was selling her soul every time she launched into a first-rate whoop of nonsense like "Jim Dandy" or "Bumble Bee." But fun was what adolescent revolt had to be about—inebriated affluence vs. the hangover of the work ethic. It was the only practicable value in the Peter Pan utopia of the American dream. Because black music had always thrived on exuberance—not just the otherworldly transport of gospel, but the candidly physical good times of great pop blues singers like Washboard Sam, who is most often dismissed as a lightweight by the heavy blues critics—it turned into the perfect vehicle for generational convulsion. Black musicians, however, had rarely achieved an optimism that was cultural as well as personal—those few who did, like Louis Armstrong, left themselves open to charges of Tomming. Chuck Berry never Tommed. The trouble he'd seen just made his sly, bad-boy

voice and the splits and waddles of his stage show that much more credible.

Then, late in 1959, fun turned into trouble. Berry had imported a Spanish-speaking Apache prostitute he'd picked up in El Paso to check hats in his St. Louis nightclub, and then fired her. She went to the police, and Berry was indicted under the Mann Act. After two trials, the first so blatantly racist that it was disallowed, he went to prison for two years. When he got out, in 1964, he and his wife had separated, apparently a major tragedy for him. The Beatles and the Rolling Stones had paid him such explicit and appropriate tribute that his career was probably in better shape after his jail term than before, but he couldn't capitalize. He had a few hits—"Nadine" and "No Particular Place to Go" (John Lennon, like many, believed they were written before he went in)—but the well was dry. Between 1965 and 1970 he didn't release one even passable new song, and he died as a recording artist.

In late 1966 Berry left Chess for a big advance from Mercury Records. The legends of his money woes at Chess are numerous, but apparently the Chess brothers knew how to record him; the stuff he produced himself for Mercury was terrible. Working alone with pickup bands, he still performed a great deal, mostly to make money for Berry Park, a recreation haven thirty miles from St. Louis. And as he toured, he found that something had happened to his old audience—it was getting older, with troubles of its own, and it dug blues. At auditoriums like the Fillmore, where he did a disappointing live LP with the Steve Miller Blues Band, Chuck was more than willing to stretch out on a blues. One of his favorites was from Elmore James: "When things go wrong, wrong with you, it hurts me too."

By 1970 he was back home at Chess, and suddenly his new audience called forth a miracle. Berry was a natural head—no drugs, no alcohol—and most of his attempts to cash in on hippie talk had been embarrassments. But "Tulane," one of his greatest story songs, was the perfect fantasy. It was about two dope dealers: "Tulane and Johnny opened a novelty shop / Back under the counter was the cream of the crop." Johnny is nabbed by narcs, but Tulane, his girlfriend, escapes, and Johnny confidently predicts that she will buy off the judge. Apparently she does, for there is a sequel, a blues. In "Have Mercy Judge," Johnny has been caught again, and this time he expects to be sent to "some stony mansion." Berry devotes the last stanza to Tulane, who is "too alive to live alone." The last line makes me wonder just how he felt about his own wife when he went to prison: "Just tell her to live, and I'll forgive her, and even love her more when I come back home."

Taken together, the two songs are Berry's peak, although Leonard Chess would no doubt have vetoed the vocal double track on "Tulane" that blurs its impact a bit. Remarkably, "Have Mercy Judge" is the first important blues Berry ever wrote, and like all his best work it isn't quite traditional, utilizing an *abc* line structure instead of the usual *aab*. Where did it come from? Is it unreasonable to suspect that part of Berry really was a bluesman all along, and that this time, instead of him going to his audience, his audience came to him and provided the juice for one last masterpiece?

Although 1979's *Rockit* was Berry's best album in fifteen years (and his first in four), it was groove rather than songs that made it go. When he was sentenced to a second jail term plus an incredible 1000 hours of benefits for tax evasion, the shock wasn't that a black artist was being robbed of his spirit, but that a black man was being deprived of his livelihood—the object of a persecution recapitulated in his legal battles of 1990, when local cops arrested him on "pornography" charges that were later dropped. A charter member of the Rock & Roll Hall of Fame who won belated recognition from the Na-

tional Academy of Recording Arts and Sciences when he received a Lifetime Achievement Award in 1984, he was plainly a rock & roll monument, a pleasing performer whose days of inspiration were over. Yet two 1987 events proved him muscle and bone. One was the long-promised *Chuck Berry: The Autobiography,* which he'd started writing as long ago as 1959 and begun anew while serving his prison sentence in 1979. Berry claims it's entirely unghosted and that's how it reads. His pleasure in language doesn't have quite the same immediacy when he's not singing, but it's just as untrammeled, and the dirty parts make you wonder what he saved for the sequel, which he says will concentrate on his love life. The other was *Hail! Hail! Rock 'n' Roll,* keyed to an all-star sixtieth-birthday concert that Berry actually rehearsed for—with a crack band organized by Keith Richards and featuring the long-absent Johnnie Johnson. As a record it's only a document—Berry's half-cracked timbre signifies natural bluesman, not perpetual adolescent. But Taylor Hackford's film is a wickedly funny and moving rock-doc classic, exposing Berry the money-grubbing control freak without devaluing his genius in the process. Sometime in the next twenty years Chuck Berry will probably die, and while his songs have already stuck in the public memory a lot longer

By 1970 Berry was courting a new audience, donning paisley duds and writing songs about dealing dope.

than Washboard Sam's, it's likely that most of them will fade away too. So is he, was he, will he be a great artist? It won't be we judging, but perhaps we can think of it this way. Maybe the true measure of his greatness was not whether his songs "lasted"—a term which as of now means persisted through centuries instead of decades—but that he was one of the ones to make us understand that the greatest thing about art is the way it happens between people. I am grateful for aesthetic artifacts, and I suspect that a few of Berry's songs, a few of his recordings, will live on in that way. I only hope that they prove too alive to live alone. If they do, and if by some mishap Berry's name itself is forgotten, that will nevertheless be an entirely apposite kind of triumph for him.

Clark Gable in rock garb, a dapper Chuck Berry shows off the "duck walk," his most famous stunt.

DISCOGRAPHY

SINGLES

"Maybellene" (Chess; r☆1, ☆5, 1955). "Thirty Days" (Chess; r☆8, 1955). "No Money Down" (Chess; r☆11, 1956). "Roll Over Beethoven" (Chess; r☆7, ☆29, 1956). "Too Much Monkey Business" b/w "Brown Eyed Handsome Man" (Chess; r☆7, 1956). "School Day" (Chess; r☆1, ☆5, 1957). "Oh Baby Doll" (Chess; ☆57, 1957). "Rock and Roll Music" (Chess; r☆6, ☆8, 1957). "Sweet Little Sixteen" (Chess; r☆1, ☆2, 1958). "Johnny B. Goode" (Chess; r☆5, ☆8, 1958). "Carol" (Chess; r☆12, ☆18, 1958). "Sweet Little Rock and Roll" (Chess; r☆13, ☆47, 1958). "Anthony Boy" (Chess; ☆60, 1959). "Almost Grown" (Chess; r☆3, ☆32, 1959). "Back in the U.S.A." (Chess; r☆16, ☆37, 1959). "Too Pooped to Pop" (Chess; r☆18, ☆42, 1960). "Nadine" (Chess; ☆23, 1964). "No Particular Place to Go" (Chess; ☆10, 1964). "You Never Can Tell" (Chess; ☆14, 1964). "Little Marie" (Chess; ☆54, 1964). "Promised Land" (Chess; ☆41, 1964). "My Ding-a-Ling" (Chess; ☆1, 1972). "Reelin' and Rockin' " (Chess; ☆27, 1972).

ALBUMS

The Chess Box (Chess/MCA; 1990).

(Chart positions compiled from Joel Whitburn's *Record Research,* based on *Billboard*'s Pop chart, unless otherwise indicated; r☆ = position on *Billboard*'s Rhythm & Blues chart.)

ROCKABILLY

BY PETER GURALNICK

Rockabilly is the purest of all rock & roll genres. That is because it never went anywhere. It is preserved in perfect isolation within an indistinct time period, bounded on the one hand by the July 1954 release of Elvis's first record on the yellow Sun label and on the other by the decline and fall of Elvis (his 1958 induction into the army), Jerry Lee Lewis (his marriage to his fourteen-year-old cousin, Myra, at about the same time), Carl Perkins (his 1956 car crash and long period of convalescence just subsequent to the sales takeoff of "Blue Suede Shoes," the rockabilly anthem) and Gene Vincent (the 1960 London taxi accident that killed Eddie Cochran and made worse a virtually crippling leg injury Vincent had suffered earlier). It was a very brief flourishing, as much of feeling as of talent, during which country music almost died, aging hillbilly stars rushed to record in the new style, the major record companies scrambled to learn how to formulize and market an unknown product, and every up-and-coming young singer in the South beat a path to the Memphis door of Sam Phillips's tiny Sun label, where it all began.

Eddie Cochran, feeling those "Summertime Blues."

The tale of Sun Records is so familiar it hardly needs retelling. How Sam Phillips started out recording the great black blues singers and leasing the results to independents like Chess in Chicago and RPM on the Coast. How Elvis Presley wandered in and paid $3.98, presumably to cut a record for his mother on Phillips's custom recording service. How with the release of "That's All Right," Presley's first record and Sun No. 209, Phillips never looked back, scarcely recorded another black artist and put together a roster that at one time or another included Presley, Carl Perkins, Jerry Lee Lewis, Johnny Cash, Charlie Rich, Roy Orbison, and such lesser lights, and rockabilly luminaries, as Sonny Burgess, Warren Smith, Onie Wheeler and Malcolm Yelvington.

It was a music of almost classical purity and definition. Perhaps that is why, except for the work of its major practitioners, it holds up so poorly today. It was, to begin with, Southern music. Ricky Nelson could emulate it in California, but the only way he could begin to approach the rockabilly sound was through the hot guitar runs of James Burton, his Louisiana-born lead guitarist. It was not just Southern music either, it was white Southern music and, with the almost sole exception of Wanda Jackson, white Southern *male* music. It was blues inspired and bluegrass based, in Carl Perkins's definition, "blues with a country beat." It was "cat music," a secret language for the young seeking to break away

from the adult music of their forebears, which—judging by the hillbilly boogie of Hank Williams and Lefty Frizzell—was not always very staid nor even very adult. It was called rockabilly, because it was not the clankety rock of Bill Haley and His Comets nor the hillbilly sound of Roy Acuff and Ernest Tubb but a fusion of the two.

Every genre has its unique requirements. Rockabilly's, however, were more stringent than most. Its rhythm was nervously uptempo, accented on the offbeat, and propelled by a distinctively slapping bass. Instrumentation took its cue from the original trio of Elvis, Scotty and Bill (rhythm guitar, lead guitar and string bass) with drums added later and the honky-tonk piano of Jerry Lee Lewis establishing an entirely different, if just as vigorous and chaotic a strain. The sound was always clean, never cluttered, with a kind of thinness and manic energy that was filled by the solid lead of Scotty Moore's guitar or Jerry Lee's piano. The sound was further bolstered by generous use of echo, a homemade technique refined independently by Sam Phillips and Leonard Chess in Chicago with sewer pipes and bathroom acoustics. Critics charged that echo was employed to cover up a multitude of vocal sins—and it did in fact sometimes render lyrics indecipherable—but this was of little moment, since the essence of rockabilly lyrics was inspired nonsense and rhythmic patter. Children's games, clothing trends, nursery rhymes, outer-space odysseys—all were legitimate subjects for the spontaneous bop prosody of artists from Carl Perkins ("Put Your Cat Clothes On") to Gene Vincent ("Be-Bop-a-Lula") to Roy Orbison ("Ooby Dooby") to Charlie Feathers ("Tongue Tied Jill") to Billy Lee Riley and the Little Green Men ("Flyin' Saucers Rock 'n' Roll"). Even vocal technique was something of a constant, with a generation of hiccupers, stutterers and vibrato-laden warblers, from Elvis's "Baby, Let's Play House," through Buddy Holly, up to Freddy Fender and Narvel Felts. It was indeed a music of high spirits, wild rebellion and almost rigorous classicism.

Its final quality is one that is not so easily appreciated, however, except by the true devotee of the form. That quality is imitation, most kindly seen as *hommage*, but imitation when you come down to it, mimicry of the most slavish and blatant sort.

For rockabilly started and in a sense ended with Elvis Presley. He was the colossus that bestrode its narrow world. Not that he was its most devoted prac-

Gene Vincent and the Blue Caps, planting the flag at Iwo Jima. His music was secondhand, his guitar a battered prop. Who cared?

Carl Perkins in the days of "Blue Suede Shoes." He didn't have the looks, but along with Elvis he coined the sound.

whole success—deserved though it may have been—was his uncanny resemblance both vocally and visually to a younger, greasier Elvis Presley. Even Ricky Nelson, the only suburban rockabilly (unless you want to count Midwestern-born Californian Eddie Cochran), took his sneer, his stance and some of his repertoire from Elvis Presley. And I'm only speaking of the better known, and more stylistically formed, of the rockabilly artists.

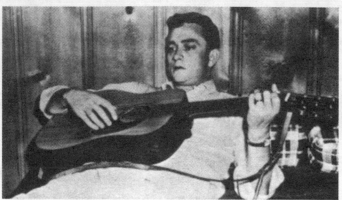

Johnny Cash, glazed over after a hard day's night.

Ray "Caterpillar" Campi, Jackie Lee Waukeen Cochran, Mac Curtis, Peanuts Wilson, Eddie Fontaine, Mack and Ronnie Self, Groovey Joe Poovey, Alvis Wayne, Teddy Reidel, Johnny Spain, Frenchy D., Rudy "Tutti" Grayzell—these are truly names from obscurity, and ones for which I have great personal affection. They cultivated the look, the stance, the sound, the part of their more celebrated colleagues. All they lacked for the most part was the talent. Rockabilly fanatics will tell you that if you could only hear Johnny Carroll's "Wild Wild Women," if you would just take a listen to the Commodores' or Roy Hall's original versions of "Whole Lot of Shakin' Going On," then the doors of perception would open wide for you and you would recognize the true source behind the legend. It's a nice mythology, and one that has its analogue in every field, but in the case of rockabilly anyway most of the cream rose to the top. Carl Perkins's instrumental brilliance, Jerry Lee's vocal and pianistic acrobatics, Elvis's raw energy and Gene Vincent's brash tastelessness ("I'm lookin' for a woman with a one-track mind," he sang in a 1956 echo chamber that wreaked havoc with articulation, "a-fuggin' and a-kissin' and a-smoochin' all the time")—these, together with the Sun sound of Sam Phillips's makeshift studio, are the elements for which rockabilly will be remembered.

titioner by any means, nor even necessarily its most inspired. He was, however, undeniably the first, and the influence he exerted over every one of the singers who followed, either directly or by example, is incalculable.

Carl Perkins was a country boy working low-paying gigs and doing a live radio show in Jackson, Tennessee, playing music much the same as that which Elvis was evolving at the time. When Perkins heard Elvis's first record he headed for Memphis and Sam Phillips's studio, where a little over a year later—after Elvis's contract was sold to RCA—he would record "Blue Suede Shoes." Jerry Lee Lewis sold all the eggs from his father's farm and camped out on the Sun doorstep until given an audition. Roy Orbison's first recordings in Clovis, New Mexico, later duplicated on Sun, were fashioned with Elvis very much in mind. Buddy Holly first saw Elvis perform in Lubbock, Texas, and it changed his life and singing style forever. The basis for Gene Vincent's

Today most of the surviving ex-rockabillies have returned to the establishment fold. Some are pumping gas; some are traveling salesmen; some are bus drivers; many still have dreams of making it in the music business, although the focus may have shifted to the country or gospel field. The echoes of their achievement still linger—on the radio, in nods from everyone from Creedence Clearwater Revival to various ex-Beatles, in the periodic revivals that spring up on either side of the Atlantic from time to time and then steal away again. And I wonder sometimes if rockabilly has died or if, like the blues, it has simply gone underground.

From time to time I go to see my favorite of them all, the one basso profundo in the choir, Arkansas rockabilly Sleepy LaBeef. Sleepy, an imposing figure at six feet six and almost 300 pounds, was, like so many others, inspired to make records upon hearing and seeing Elvis Presley perform at the Magnolia Gardens in Houston in 1955, when both were twenty. "I knew exactly where he was coming from. I thought, This is really something. Here's somebody singing just like we have in church for years. Only he was putting that gospel feeling to blues lyrics—that was what was so different about him."

I first saw Sleepy myself in 1977, after hearing his name for years and wondering to whom such a curious appellation might belong. If my initial visit was prompted by curiosity, however, I was quickly converted to another point of view. In fact, Sleepy challenged many of the assumptions that I had developed about rockabilly, and indeed about music in the abstract, over the years. Music in the abstract is often divided into eras and categories. Music as Sleepy conceived of it and presented it onstage had no divisions. Rockabilly as I had imagined it existed primarily in a time warp. Rockabilly as Sleepy delivered it—in a nonstop barrage in which a song could last thirty seconds or thirty minutes, depending on Sleepy's whim or mood—was "freedom." Rockabilly, like blues or soul or any other kind of music that depends more upon feeling than upon technical expertise, was whatever you wanted it to be.

I suppose I shouldn't have been surprised. As Sleepy says, "You don't ever want to get too scientific. You don't ever want it to sound exactly the same way twice." And indeed anyone who has ever

The battered remains of the car that carried Eddie Cochran to his death in England, April 1960.

Gene Vincent *(left)* and Eddie Cochran *(right),* with Billy Fury *(next to Cochran)* and Joe Brown, leader of the Bruvvers, England, 1960. Rockabilly had a longer life span in Britain than in America. Imports like Vincent prospered there, while local stars like Fury and Brown pointed the way for the Beatles.

seen Sleepy—or, perhaps more pertinently, anyone who has ever played in his band—knows that it never will come out the same way two times in a row, so you had better just watch out. Charlie Feathers's idea for a contemporary (1991) rockabilly album would be to cut ten different versions of "Roll Over Beethoven," and certainly Sleepy could match him note for note. In the end, as in most things, it's feeling that counts. To Sleepy, "The only music that I care about is the kind that makes the goose bumps come out on your skin." And after almost thirty years in the business, what *of* the business? Does he still dream of chart success? "I know I'm good," he told me some years ago with a mixture of self-consciousness and pride. "I wouldn't be honest if I didn't tell you that. I've been around long enough to know that if I get the breaks I can still make it . . . And if I don't get the breaks—well, when I started in this business I didn't even know you could make a dime out of it. And I think I'd still be doing it tomorrow, if there wasn't any money in it at all.'' Which is just the way the music sounds—and the very quality to which rockabilly originally aspired. As Charlie Feathers's piano player for a night once said to the room at large, ''I don't care what you say, you get the best music in the world in these little juke joints and holes in the wall. I'm telling the truth, you better believe it, buddy, this is where they always sing from the heart.''

DISCOGRAPHY

SINGLES

Johnny Cash: ''Cry, Cry, Cry'' (Sun; c☆14, 1955). ''Folsom Prison Blues'' (Sun; c☆5, 1956). ''I Walk the Line'' (Sun; c☆2, ☆19, 1956). ''Home of the Blues'' (Sun; c☆5, ☆88, 1957). ''Ballad of a Teenage Queen'' (Sun; c☆1, ☆16, 1958). ''Guess Things Happen That Way'' b/w ''Come in Stranger'' (Sun; c☆1, ☆11, 1958). ''The Ways of a Woman in Love'' (Sun; c☆2, ☆24, 1958). **Dale Hawkins:** ''Susie-Q'' (Checker; ☆29, 1957). ''La-Do-Dada'' (Checker; ☆32, 1958). ''A House, a Car and a Wedding Ring'' (Checker; ☆88, 1958). ''Class Cutter (Yeah Yeah)'' (Checker; ☆52, 1959). **Ronnie Hawkins:** ''Forty Days'' (Roulette; ☆45, 1959). ''Mary Lou'' (Roulette; r☆7, ☆26, 1959). **Roy Orbison:** ''Ooby Dooby'' (Sun; ☆59, 1956). **Carl Perkins:** ''Blue Suede Shoes'' (Sun; r☆2, c☆2, ☆4, 1956). ''Boppin' the Blues'' (Sun; c☆9, ☆70, 1956). ''Dixie Fried'' b/w ''I'm Sorry, I'm Not Sorry'' (Sun; c☆10, 1956). ''Your True Love'' (Sun; c☆13, 1957). ''Pink Pedal Pushers'' (Columbia; c☆17, ☆91, 1958). **Gene Vincent:** ''Be-Bop-a-Lula'' (Capital; c☆5, ☆9, 1956). ''Race with the Devil'' (Capitol; ☆96, 1956). ''Lotta Lovin' '' (Capitol; r☆7 ,☆14, 1957). ''Dance to the Bop'' (Capitol; ☆43, 1957).

ANTHOLOGIES

The Sun Story (Rhino; 1987). *Rock This Town: Rockabilly Hits, Volumes 1 & 2* (Rhino; 1991).

(Omitting hits by Elvis Presley, Jerry Lee Lewis and Buddy Holly. Chart positions compiled from Joel Whitburn's *Record Research,* based on *Billboard*'s Pop chart, unless otherwise indicated; r☆ = position on *Billboard*'s Rhythm & Blues chart; c☆ = position on *Billboard*'s Country & Western chart.)

JERRY LEE LEWIS

BY JIM MILLER

Jerry Lee Lewis looks surly. It's 9:30 at the county fair in Cedar Rapids, Iowa, and Lewis, the feature attraction at the fair's auditorium, is onstage a half hour late. He surveys the sparse crowd, his lips snarled like his curly blond hair. He is angry at the disappointing turnout.

It is 1963, and Jerry Lee Lewis is up shit creek. For almost six years he's been on the road nonstop, mostly in the South, playing one-nighters, trying to recoup some momentum in a career that skidded to a dead stop in 1958, after it became known he married his fourteen-year-old second cousin. Incest, they said; and Jerry Lee has been fighting a losing battle against high-placed hypocrites ever since.

The crowd is restless. To the majority, Jerry Lee Lewis is at best a memory, at worst a washed-up has-been. Boredom, not interest, has driven them to gawk at this once-upon-at-time rock & roll star.

Lewis prowls over to his piano from stage right, where he has been silently counting empty seats. He pulls out a gigantic comb from his hip pocket and, in a trademark gesture, runs the comb through his hair. He swivels a curious half wiggle of vanity wounded.

The crowd boos. ''Music!'' yells one.

''Queer!'' yells another.

Jerry Lee spins around and glares.

''*Shaaaaaad*dup ya muuthers,'' he bellows. Silence.

''This is the *Killer,* baby, and *nobody* cuts the Killer. *Nobody.*''

He pauses, and turns back to the piano. And then Jerry Lee Lewis lights into one of the nastiest versions of ''Great Balls of Fire'' to taunt human ears.

For more than a quarter century, Jerry Lee Lewis performed his own brand of rock, country and pop anyplace, anytime and anywhere he got the money and the opportunity. Although he scored only three Top Ten hits, all during the Fifties, his personal style helped define the rock tradition. Out of a genre populated by dime-a-dozen Presley imitators, Lewis emerged a giant, an entertainer gifted with intuitive flair, musical brashness and a genius for self-promotion. Despite daunting obstacles, his ego let him persevere—and as long as he's alive, he's not about to let anyone forget it.

The externals of Lewis's career are the stuff of folk

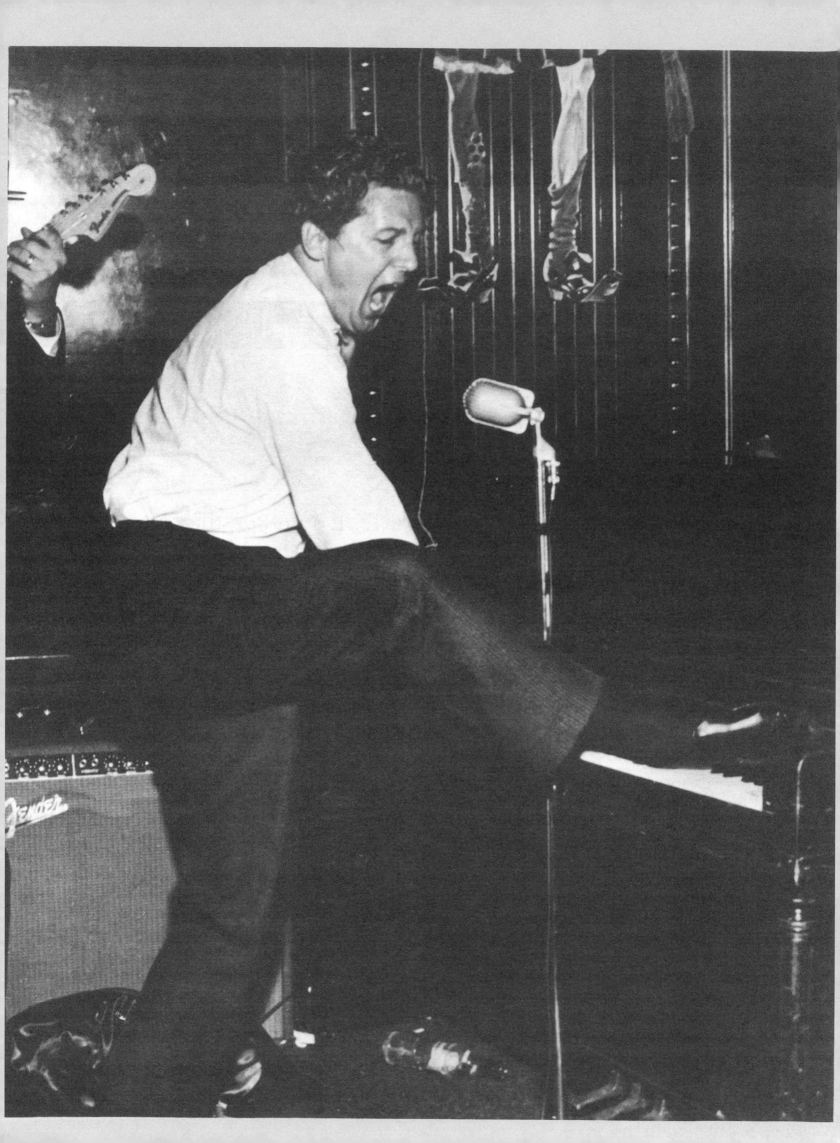

legend. Born in Ferriday, Louisiana, near Natchez, Mississippi, in 1935, Lewis performed music professionally from the age of fifteen. He played what he heard, and what he heard was country swing, rural blues, piano boogies and jump-band R&B. When he decided in 1956 to strike out on his own and seek a recording contract, Lewis headed for Memphis to audition for Sam Phillips at Sun Records.

A collection of classics.

Upon arriving, he found Phillips unavailable, so he cornered Sam's assistant Jack Clement instead. According to Clement, Jerry Lee boasted that "he could play piano like Chet Atkins"—a claim that intrigued Clement (not least, presumably, because Atkins played guitar, not piano). Clement recalled cutting four country tunes that day, although Lewis himself remembers a marathon audition covering "everything from Muddy Waters to 'Silent Night.'"

Whatever the tapes contained, Sam Phillips was duly impressed. Clement had already dispatched Lewis with the standard instructions of the Presley era—"Go learn some rock & roll"—and three weeks later Jerry Lee was back, for a session that yielded a striding treatment of Ray Price's recent country

Mr. Lewis, in the manner of a front-porch grandee, takes his ease.

smash, "Crazy Arms." The song sold well regionally, but didn't dent the national charts.

Lewis's next visit to the studio changed all that. At the tail end of the session during which Lewis had cut "It'll Be Me" as a sequel to "Crazy Arms," Clement told Jerry to play anything he wanted. With the tapes rolling, Jerry Lee and his combo blithely lit into a little ditty called "Whole Lot of Shakin'"—and Lewis and Clement had their followup.

"Whole Lot of Shakin' Going On" went on to sell a million copies; Lewis, catapulted into prominence by television and radio, became an international celebrity.

"Whole Lot of Shakin'" is pure Jerry Lee Lewis from its first pounding chords. The song is delivered over an incessant piano backbeat; Jerry Lee, his voice the very incarnation of nonchalant lust, exploits the lyrics' hints of lewdness to the hilt.

The public loved it. Suddenly Jerry Lee Lewis, the country kid from Ferriday, Louisiana, was crisscrossing the United States on package tours and appearing on Dick Clark's *American Bandstand*, becoming, some said, the successor to Elvis himself. "Whole Lot of Shakin'" went to Number One on both the country & western and rhythm & blues charts, and lingered for twenty-nine weeks on the pop charts, cresting in June of 1957. Subsequent hits, such as "Great Balls of Fire," "Breathless" and "High School Confidential," followed effortlessly.

But in mid-1958, Jerry Lee decided to marry Myra Brown, a sweet young girl who also happened to be his second cousin (it was his third marriage). Industry elders were aghast; no amount of payola, it seemed, could right a taboo once wronged. Overnight, Jerry Lee Lewis's career dried up. Without access to the big tours, the TV shows, the major radio stations, Jerry Lee Lewis became just another entertainer condemned to one-nighters in undreamt-of locales.

There may seem little reason to distinguish Jerry Lee Lewis from a thousand other two-shot hitmakers. But Lewis was different. A natural in an industry filled with calculating mimics, his creativity and consequent impact spilled far beyond the few hits that reached the general public.

Onstage he was a picture of piety dissolved, pounding the piano, scrambling over the instru-

As he appeared in the heyday of ''Whole Lot of Shakin'.''

Just married, 1958.

ment's lid—there, like King Kong with curly locks, assaulting culture by commanding the summit of his very own white piano, shaking his all-too-long blond hair, as if to mock the well-coiffed mane of a Southern aristocrat.

Hauteur incarnate, Jerry Lee was a talented punk who knew he was talented, and his flamboyant antics conveyed a class resentment that any self-avowed outsider could grasp immediately. It was all a show, of course. Carl Perkins claimed that Jerry

Jerry Lee with Myra, the teen-cousin bride that got him blacklisted: ''What's it to ya, punk?''

Lee, on his first tour with Perkins and Johnny Cash after ''Crazy Arms'' had been released, had trouble with shyness. ''John and I told him,'' recalls Perkins, '' 'Turn around so they can see you; make a fuss.' So the next night he carried on, stood up, kicked the stool back, and a new Jerry Lee was born.''

With a vengeance, Jerry Lee leered his way into the annals of American popular culture. As Waylon Jennings once remarked, ''He'll burn a goddamn piano if he has to.''

(And, as legend has it, he did once, too. During his heyday in the late Fifties, Lewis used to demand that he close any package tour he appeared on. As writer John Grissim tells the story, ''One exception came during a concert tour with Chuck Berry, emceed by Alan Freed. Both Berry and Lewis had million-seller hits on the charts at the same time and one night Freed flat-out insisted that Jerry Lee perform first. After a furious argument, Lewis obeyed. The story has it that he blew nonstop rock for a brutal thirty minutes and, during the final ''Whole Lot of Shakin','' poured lighter fluid over the piano and threw a match to it. As he stomped off the stage he hollered to the stage crew: 'I'd like to see *any* son of a bitch follow that!' '')

Lewis often seemed on the verge of exploding. His swagger and phrasing exuded an aura of profound lust, the kind of lust that secretly chastises itself as un-Christian and sinful. Therein lay its power: a magic potion of the repressed, right there before millions of American eyes and ears. Lewis's music represented the ungodly miscegenation Presley and Little Richard had only hinted at. A white man with a black soul? Onstage Lewis, unlike Presley, didn't mess much with ballads and hymns. As he admitted in an argument with Sam Phillips early in his career, Lewis saw himself as playing the devil's music—and a true Christian doesn't mix God's music with the devil's.

Presley's early performances had in any case been fastidiously rehearsed, each inflection properly placed. Jerry Lee by contrast always sang with unquenchable spontaneity, as though he were tapping some primordial wellspring of energy; there are clearly perceptible differences of nuance and phrasing even between two takes of "Great Balls of Fire" cut the same day. His persona, simply, is irrepressible. It emerges on the most benign material, and even in interpretations of songs strongly associated with other performers.

Take "Little Queenie." Originally a sluggish sock-hop send-up by Chuck Berry, the song was later revived in a grinding version by the Rolling Stones (*Get Yer Ya-Ya's Out!*). In the Stones' recording, Mick Jagger minces his words carefully during the song's spoken interlude: "Now if she'll dance, we can make it—come on, Queenie: let's shake it." But a lumbering tempo and the all-too-familiar guile in his voice give the game away.

Jerry Lee doesn't think twice. With utter self-abandon, he sails through the choruses in a charging tempo, and then matter-of-factly executes the spoken bit, which any fool, Jerry Lee seems to imply, can see is a come-on, pure and simple.

In themselves, "off-color" sentiments do not a great rock & roll record make, of course. What makes Jerry Lee Lewis great is rather the tension in

Jerry Lee as Iago in *Catch My Soul,* a Sixties musical version of *Othello.*

his persona between worldly sin and salvation, a battle in which sin seems destined inevitably to win. But that is not all: There is also in Lewis's work a parity of means and ends, and a natural economy of musical expression.

The backbone of Lewis's sound is his piano playing, invariably some elementary boogie figure. His solos have always been sheer flash, punctuated by pointless but exhilarating glissando runs. Avoiding the evenly turned figures of a Fats Domino, or the baroque intricacies of a boogie master like Pete Johnson (the great Kansas City jazz pianist), Lewis is content to play crudely with a jerky bravado that matches his vocal unpredictability. He constructs breaks out of the most outrageous elements, hammering triplet chords against prominent, forceful bass lines with the left hand (on some of his early recordings, Lewis performed without an accompanying bass). His piano playing is undisciplined, intuitive and potentially uncontrollable—just like his singing.

Yet as a singer as well as a pianist, Lewis represents something more than licentious maniac. His voice is tempered, polished, with a rounded fullness that hovers, surrounding notes with a barely frenetic halo before engulfing them. His carefully controlled vibrato conveys tension as well as release: His intonation suggests labor, as if he were holding back a scream. But paradoxically the final impression is one of easy mastery. Through his singing, Lewis effortlessly commands a range of moods that other performers (like Jagger) strain for.

Some years later, demonstrating piano technique.

His Sun-period band, featuring Roland James on guitar, reinforces the impression of natural mastery. In their own way, Lewis's early Sun recordings even swing, not in the mellow way that Fats Domino swings, but rather in the clipped, urgent way that Lewis's own piano swings.

The Sun production enhances this overall texture, with a prominent echo smoothing over any rough edges. Although the early records rarely add saxes or an organ and never use strings or a chorus, Sam Phillips's engineering coaxes a fullness out of Lewis's small band; each of the instruments—usually electric guitar, bass and drums accompanying Jerry Lee's piano and singing—assumes a mysterious resonance of its own. Just as with Leonard Chess's production of Little Walter, the judicious use of echo adds depth and a sheen without sacrificing spontaneity or feeling.

U nlike some of his fellow rockers, Lewis did not burn out young; his pride, talent and impenetrable vanity saved him that humiliation. Although he vanished from public view for almost ten years, Jerry Lee continued to present, as one album billed it, "the greatest live show on earth." Finally, when all hope of a successful recording career seemed gone, he made a last bid for renewed popularity.

It worked—but at a price. In 1967 Lewis and Jerry Kennedy, his producer at Mercury (where Jerry Lee had recorded since 1964), surveyed his spectacularly unsuccessful three-year track record. The de facto blacklist that followed his marriage was still in effect, and Lewis's efforts rarely penetrated even the bottom of the trade charts. Only country DJs showed any enthusiasm at all.

So Jerry Lee struck a bargain. "I decided to cut a country record, and then I talked to a lot of jocks," Lewis has explained to John Grissim. "This time I said, 'Look, man, let's get together and draw a line on this stuff—a peace treaty, you know. I'm gonna do "Great Balls of Fire" and "Whole Lot of Shakin'" and "Breathless" and "High School Confi-

The Killer. Guilty as charged.

dential" and whatever else I wanna do, and I'm also gonna do country stuff onstage. But my records will all be country, not rock. So what do you say we get together and get off this kick.' And they did."

Lewis enjoyed a new career in his reincarnation as a country crooner. Between 1968 and 1973 he scored twelve Top Ten country hits on Mercury/Smash, and when Sun reissued some early Lewis country singles, he added three more Top Ten singles on that label. His country material at Mercury was strong, and Lewis's performance, on tunes such as "What's Made Milwaukee Famous (Has Made a Loser Out of Me)," was undiluted. But then Jerry Lee Lewis probably couldn't sing even the Lord's Prayer straight; his style is too voracious.

Jerry Lee still sang rock, too. In 1973 he even got another taste of pop-chart success, with a remake of "Drinkin' Wine Spo-Dee O'Dee," a 1949 R&B novelty number Lewis first cut at Sun. But his creative days were numbered. In the late Seventies his voice frayed around the edges and his piano playing became ragged. His country career effectively over, his countless nights of drinking and drug abuse finally caught up with him, as did the Internal Revenue Service, in search of back taxes. His health and finances in a shambles, he faded from public view, letting the 1989 movie of his life, Great Balls of Fire, keep his legend alive.

Not that his legend needed Hollywood's help. For his classic Sun recordings have stood the test of time. And as he mulls over his past, Jerry Lee Lewis may find some solace in the knowledge that, after all, he was right all along. In the world of rock & roll, nobody cuts the Killer.

DISCOGRAPHY

SINGLES

"Whole Lot of Shakin' Going On" (Sun; r☆1, c☆1, ☆3, 1957). "Great Balls of Fire" (Sun; r☆3, c☆1, ☆2, 1957). "Breathless" (Sun; r☆6, c☆4, ☆7, 1958). "High School Confidential" (Sun; r☆16, c☆9, ☆21, 1958). "Break-Up" b/w "I'll Make It All Up to You" (Sun; c☆19, ☆52, 1958). "I'll Sail My Ship Alone" (Sun; ☆93, 1959). "What'd I Say" (Sun; r☆26, c☆27, ☆30, 1961). "Cold Cold Heart" (Sun; c☆22, 1961). "Pen and Paper" (Smash; c☆36, 1964). "Another Place, Another Time" (Smash; c☆4, 1968). "What's Made Milwaukee Famous (Has Made a Loser Out of Me)" (Smash; c☆2, 1968). "She Still Comes Around" (Smash; c☆2, 1968). "To Make Love Sweeter for You" (Smash; c☆1, 1968). "One Has My Name" (Smash; c☆3, 1969). "Invitation to Your Party" (Sun; c☆6, 1969). "She Even Woke Me Up to Say Goodbye" (Smash; c☆2, 1969). "One Minute Past Eternity" (Sun; c☆2, 1969). "Once More with Feeling" (Smash; c☆2, 1970). "I Can't Seem to Say Goodbye" (Sun; c☆7, 1970). "There Must Be More to Love Than This" (Mercury; c☆1, 1970). "Waiting for a Train" (Sun; c☆11, 1970). "Touching Home" (Mercury; c☆3, 1971). "When He Walks on You (Like You Walked on Me)" (Mercury; c☆11, 1971). "Would You Take Another Chance on Me" (Mercury; c☆1, 1971). "Drinking Wine Spo-Dee O'Dee" (Mercury; c☆20, ☆41, 1973). "I Can Still Hear the Music in the Restroom" (Mercury; c☆13, 1975). "Boogie Woogie Country Man" (Mercury; c☆24, 1975). "A Damn Good Country Song" (Mercury; c☆68, 1975).

ALBUMS

18 Original Sun Greatest Hits (Rhino; 1984).

(Chart positions compiled from Joel Whitburn's *Record Research,* based on *Billboard*'s Pop chart, unless otherwise indicated; r☆ = position on *Billboard*'s Rhythm & Blues chart; c☆ = position on *Billboard*'s Country & Western chart.)

THE EVERLY BROTHERS

BY KIT RACHLIS

he Everly Brothers were innocents. From their first hit, "Bye Bye Love" in 1957, to their last, "That's Old Fashioned (That's the Way Love Should Be)" five years later, the Everly Brothers sang about love, always love, and always with ingenuous passion and conviction. They never hungered after sex and never sought revenge. Instead, they were dreamers, seeking not the ideal woman, but the ideal—or perhaps more accurately, the idealized—relationship.

The Everly Brothers introduced white country harmony to rock & roll: High tenors with about a third of a note's difference between their voices, they sang in the country duo tradition of the Delmore Brothers and the Louvin Brothers. The children of Ike and Margaret Everly, a highly respected country & western team, Phil and Don, born in 1939 and 1937, respectively, had been weaned on country music, touring with their parents and appearing on their radio show from the time they were nine and seven years old. In fact, it was their potential as a country act that originally brought them to the attention of Cadence Records in 1957.

Archie Bleyer, president of Cadence, had come to Nashville to work with Wesley Rose in establishing a country & western division to bolster Cadence's flagging sales. At the time the small independent label featured pop singer Andy Williams as its only big name. Rose, with country star Roy Acuff, owned and ran the industry's most prestigious publishing-house-management company. Among the many songwriters Rose had under contract were the Everly Brothers. With the exception of "Thou Shalt Not Steal," a song written by Don and transformed into a hit by Kitty Wells, the Everlys had little to show for their two years in Nashville. Their one experience in a studio had produced a single for Columbia Records, "The Sun Keeps Shining," which hadn't even reached the lower depths of the C&W charts. Despite their meager record, Rose urged Bleyer to sign the brothers to a recording contract.

Rose then introduced Bleyer and the Everly Broth-

They brought Appalachian harmony to rock & roll: The Everly Brothers show their guitarist how to play ''Cathy's Clown.''

The cast of the Everly family radio show of the late Forties *(from left):* Don, Ike, Phil; seated, Margaret.

Onstage in the Fifties.

ers to Boudleaux Bryant, a highly successful C&W songwriter in the Acuff-Rose stable. One of the tunes Bryant showed them was ''Bye Bye Love,'' a song already rejected by thirty acts. The Everly Brothers, however, persuaded Bleyer that they should record the song at their first session. Ten days after its release, ''Bye Bye Love'' exploded onto the charts, eventually reaching the Number Two spot on the pop listings and Number One on the country charts.

''Bye Bye Love'' established the model that the Everly Brothers would follow for the rest of their stay on Cadence. With a pair of acoustic guitars leading the way, the rhythm section of bass, drums and piano firmly yet unaggressively propelled the song along. The harmonies floated above it all, lightly charting the melody line. It was an almost seamless gown of sound. The Everly Brothers didn't shout or scream. The echo was almost nonexistent. A lone electric guitar provided the ornamental cross-stitching with brief single-note runs. Simultaneously precise, cohesive and effervescent, ''Bye Bye Love'' had

fused country music's obsession for order with the boundless energy of rock & roll.

It's difficult to ascertain who was responsible for the Everly Brothers' sound because their recording sessions were remarkably collective efforts, with the Everlys, Bryant, Rose, Bleyer and the sessionmen all contributing suggestions. What is known, though, is that the sessions were methodically and meticulously run. The Everly Brothers, practicing with a tape machine, would rehearse their vocals two or three days in advance. All arrangements were carefully worked out before entering the studio. The sessionmen, usually including Chet Atkins on guitar and Floyd Cramer on piano, were among Nashville's finest—consummate professionals able to adapt to any performer without sacrificing their individuality.

With Johnny Otis.

For as long as they remained on Cadence, the Everly Brothers adhered to that sound with few modifications. As they became more comfortable as rock & rollers, they placed greater emphasis on the drums and electric guitar. Both Chet Atkins and Don Everly, who usually played rhythm guitar, admired Bo Diddley, and increasingly they attempted to incorporate his choppy guitar style into their playing. They experimented by adding strings to "Let It Be Me" and the sound of a screwdriver tapped against a Coke bottle to "Take a Message to Mary." Still, for all its restrictions the Everly Brothers' formula was remarkably flexible. They rushed headlong into Little Richard's "Rip It Up" with the same ease as they crooned the mawkish sentiments of "Love of My Life." Crucial to their success was an abundance of strong hooks and catchy melodies—always Bleyer's first priorities. And in Boudleaux Bryant, who wrote many of the Everly Brothers' early hits, Bleyer had a songwriter perfectly suited to the Everlys' skills.

Following the success of "Bye Bye Love," Bryant began tailoring songs specifically to the Everly Brothers' range, harmonies and audience. And what that audience wanted, Bryant presumed, were songs about love. He then proceeded to write some of the most elegantly concise encomiums to romance that rock has ever produced: tender and sensitive, yet rarely yielding to either self-pity or sentimentality. Taken as a whole, the songs created an hermetically sealed world where only love mattered and only parents ("Wake Up Little Susie" and "Poor Jenny") and school ("Problems") interfered. Unquestionably simplistic and adolescent, it assumed that love cured all ills. But what saved the Everly Brothers from becoming purveyors of Tin Pan Alley pablum was not the dream itself, but their faith in its possibility. Even on songs ostensibly about despair— "Bye Bye Love" and "When Will I Be Loved"—they expressed resilience and optimism by singing with unabashed exuberance.

For three years on Cadence the Everly Brothers averaged a Top Ten hit every four months. During the same period (with many of the same songs) they amassed four Number One singles on the country charts. As they progressed, the brothers began to achieve Top Ten success with songs of their own (Don's "['Til] I Kissed You" in 1959 and Phil's "When Will I Be Loved" in 1960). Like their parents, they were troupers and they crisscrossed the

Less than clean cut in the Fifties.

country in a continual series of one-night stands. But in 1960 the team that had constructed the Everly Brothers' sound began to fall apart. The Everlys were unhappy with their low royalty rate, and a bitter fight broke out between them and Bleyer during new contract negotiations. As a result they left Cadence for Warner Bros. Records. A year later they fired Wesley Rose, who had been acting as both their manager and producer, in a dispute over the arrangement of "Temptation," a single released in 1961.

The commercial effects of the switch were, if anything, positive. "Cathy's Clown," the pair's first single for Warner, sold more than two million copies and stands as their all-time best seller. Musically, however, the change in labels and the breakup of their production team marked their decline. Under the stewardship of various producers, their sound became increasingly grandiose. The muted mix and insouciant precision of the Cadence production had always contained the Everly Brothers' maudlin impulses. The hard-edge clarity of their new approach—with horns, piano and backup vocals all competing for attention—magnified their sentimentality, distorted their romanticism. For the first time, their voices began to whine and strain. Without access to Bryant's material (he still worked for Wesley Rose), they resorted to tearjerkers like "Ebony Eyes."

Despite such material, the Everly Brothers continued to produce hits—until the release, in April 1962, of "That's Old Fashioned," which signaled the end. Its very title implied that the Everly Brothers had become an anachronism. Whereas their earlier songs simply assumed their romanticism, "That's

Old Fashioned" justified it as if under attack. They never reached the Top Ten again.

The Sixties were not kind to Fifties rock stars, and the Everly Brothers were no exceptions. Don, thanks to "vitamin" treatments from a New York doctor, became hooked on speed, and for the next few years was in and out of sanitariums; before he finally cured himself in 1966, he had attempted suicide. Phil also received the treatments but the effects weren't as serious. During this period, both Don and Phil were divorced from their wives.

They continued, however, to churn out record after record: a C&W album (*The Everly Brothers Sing Great Country Hits*); a couple of R&B albums (*Rock 'n Soul* and *Beat 'n Soul*); an English album (*Two Yanks in England*). Each one was meant to regain the audience they had lost. Each one failed. They had become prisoners of their past, outstripped by the Beach Boys, the Beatles and the Byrds, all of whom had acknowledged their debt to the Everly Brothers. For reasons that remain unclear, the Everlys never actively pursued a country & western career. Instead, they played in Las Vegas and became encrusted youthful oldies, biding their time for a possible revival. As their careers floundered, the relationship between the two became increasingly tense.

But the Everly Brothers were not through. In 1968 they released *Roots,* their last magnificent hurrah. Reminiscent of *Songs Our Daddy Taught Us,* an album of traditional songs they had recorded while still at Cadence, *Roots* was a self-conscious attempt to retrieve their past. Interjected between the traditional tunes ("Shady Grove," "T for Texas") were snippets of recordings they had made as children on their parents' radio show. Though the album is framed as a documentary, it also revives their Cadence sound and recasts it in contemporary rock & roll terms. One can hear simultaneously how the Everly Brothers influenced such groups as the Byrds, and how, in turn, the Byrds were now affecting the Everly Brothers.

The album's centerpiece is their reworking of "I Wonder If I Care as Much," the second song they recorded on Cadence. The original version is too jaunty. Their harmonies gloss over the lyrics, which seem beyond their capabilities. On *Roots* their voices display an added edge and weight. They slow down the song—changing the tempo several times—and

break it down into pieces, as if they were rolling it around in their hands and carefully examining it. As they sing it now, the song questions their whole career.

> Tears that I have to shed by day
> Give relief and wash away
> The memory of the night before.
> I wonder if I'll suffer more.
> I wonder if I'll care as much as I did before.

It is the Everly Brothers' last great moment, but *Roots* was no more successful in rekindling their career than any of its immediate predecessors. Not long afterward the Everly Brothers left Warners to record for RCA, where they did no better. Tired, their relationship becoming more acrimonious, they performed in July 1973 at the John Wayne Theater in Buena Park, California. Before the concert was over, Phil smashed his guitar on the floor and walked off the stage. Don finished the last two shows by himself. "The Everly Brothers," he said, "died ten years ago."

Only once in the next decade would they speak to each other, and that was at their father's funeral. It was as if having spent their entire lives intertwined and in public, the only way they could separate was to divorce violently—a final and ironic image left by

Gone mod in the Sixties.

the two men who, more than anybody else, had so defined what love and affection meant in rock & roll.

As it turned out, it was an image the Everlys didn't want to let stand. After years of putting out one desultory solo album after another and then not recording altogether, the brothers agreed in 1983 to perform in London's Royal Albert Hall. They were going to reconcile the only way they knew how—onstage. Typical of the Everlys, they produced a reunion concert (which aired on HBO) of great care, dignity and conviction. But the moment was gone. Craft had replaced passion, and neither rock & roll nor the Everly Brothers could sustain the teenagers' faith that love, all-consuming love, could offer salvation.

DISCOGRAPHY

SINGLES 1957–1967

"Bye Bye Love" (Cadence; r☆5, c☆1, ☆2, 1957). "Wake Up Little Susie" (Cadence; r☆2, c☆1, ☆1, 1957). "This Little Girl of Mine" (Cadence; c☆4, ☆28, 1958). "All I Have to Do Is Dream" b/w "Claudette" (Cadence; r☆1, c☆1, ☆1, 1958). "Bird Dog" b/w "Devoted to You" (Cadence; r☆3, c☆1, ☆2, 1958). "Problems" (Cadence; c☆17, ☆2, 1958). "Take a Message to Mary" b/w "Poor Jenny" (Cadence; ☆16, 1959). "('Til) I Kissed You" (Cadence; r☆22, c☆8, ☆4, 1959). "Let It Be Me" (Cadence; ☆7, 1960). "Cathy's Clown" (Warner Bros.; r☆1, ☆1, 1960). "When Will I Be Loved" (Cadence; ☆8, 1960). "So Sad" b/w "Lucille" (Warner Bros.; r☆16, ☆7, 1960). "Walk Right Back" b/w "Ebony Eyes" (Warner Bros.; r☆25, c☆25, ☆7, 1961). "Temptation" (Warner Bros.; ☆27, 1961). "Don't Blame Me" (Warner Bros.; ☆20, 1961). "Crying in the Rain" (Warner Bros.; ☆6, 1962). "That's Old Fashioned (That's the Way Love Should Be)" (Warner Bros.; ☆9, 1962). "Don't Ask Me to Be Friends" (Warner Bros.; ☆48, 1962). "Gone, Gone, Gone" (Warner Bros.; ☆31, 1964). "Bowling Green" (Warner Bros.; ☆40, 1967).

ALBUMS

Cadence Classics (Their 20 Greatest Hits) (Rhino; 1985). The Best of the Everly Brothers (Rhino; 1985).

(Chart positions compiled from Joel Whitburn's Record Research, based on Billboard's Pop chart; r☆ = position on Billboard's Rhythm & Blues chart; c☆ = position on Billboard's Country & Western chart.)

BUDDY HOLLY

BY JONATHAN COTT

ccording to American mythology, psychopaths and rock & roll stars have almost invisible origins, springing parthenogenetically out of the headlines or onto the record charts as if they had no past. "I taught him once," one of Buddy Holly's high school teachers recalls, "but to be honest, it was only after the news was in the paper about his death that I remembered that he had been in my class. He was a quiet kid—wasn't any great student, but didn't cause any trouble either, you understand. So I really don't remember anything about him."

Killed at the age of twenty-two on February 3rd, 1959 ("The day the music died"), in the still-memorialized plane crash that also took the lives of the Big Bopper (J. P. Richardson) and Ritchie Valens, Buddy Holly was born in Lubbock, Texas, on September 7th, 1936. He made his first appearance onstage when he was five years old, at a local talent show, singing "Down the River of Memories"—a song his mother had taught him—and winning a five-dollar prize for the performance. After forming the Western and Bop Band with his high school friends Bob Montgomery and Larry Welborn, he signed with Decca, cut several uncommercial discs, and then, under the supervision of producer Norman Petty in Clovis, New Mexico, made his famous series of recordings, both with his group the Crickets, and as a soloist. Between 1957 and 1958 he enjoyed seven Top Forty hits in the United States, and scored several more in England. Late in 1958 he broke with Petty and the Crickets, moved to a Greenwich Village apartment and married Maria Elena Santagio, a New Yorker whom he proposed to at P. J. Clarke's on their first date.

Buddy Holly was one of the few Fifties rock & roll stars never to be filmed (although he did appear in several home movies and television programs). So

On *The Ed Sullivan Show,* 1957.

we remember his photographs—all variations of the archetypal high school graduation yearbook picture showing the "shy Texan" in his horn-rimmed glasses. And like one of the figures in a Picasso painting, this conventional image became blurred, transformed through his music into forms and colors. And unique and radiant they were and are. For unlike Bo Diddley (who defined and embodied himself in terms of rhythm), Elvis Presley (who adopted and transmogrified the experiences and values of black sexuality and alienation), or Chuck Berry (who took on and extended Walt Whitman's visionary embrace of American geography), Buddy Holly perfectly, almost obsessively, communicated in song

Buddy Holly and the Crickets. With his amazing capacity to synthesize styles, Holly became one of the most creative composers in early rock & roll.

after song his joyful acceptance of "true love ways," his indivertible expectation ("crying, waiting, hoping") of someday finding a love "so rare and true."

Onstage, he came across like a frenetic raver, yet his songs and vocal presentation often belied and went against the grain of this stylized pose. As writer Dave Laing has observed about Holly's rendition of "Rock Around with Ollie Vee": "There is a notable vocal touch on the line 'I'm gonna shake it just a bit *in the middle of the night,*' where the voice suddenly drops an octave for the italicized words. But while Presley manages to get a menacing sexual growl by a similar effect, Buddy Holly comes across here as playful rather than sensual; it is a wink, not a snarl." And it is this playfully ironic, childlike quality that defines and gives the key to Buddy Holly's style.

When adults communicate with infants, they use

the language of baby talk, exaggerating changes in pitch, speaking almost in singsong, uttering their words more slowly, reduplicating syllables and rhymes, and employing simple sentence structures. It is clear that Buddy Holly absorbed, transformed and revitalized this mode of expression in his use of titles and phrases like "Maybe Baby," "Oh Boy," "oops a daisy," "riddle dee pat," and "hey a hey hey"; in his embellished, rollicking six-syllable delivery of the word "well" at the beginning of "Rave On"; in lines like "Pretty, pretty, pretty, pretty Peggy Sue" (reminding you of a child talking to a little animal in order to tame it) or "You know my love not fade away" (telegraphing its message like a Chinese ideogram); and, most obviously, in his famous "hiccup" signature or in the sudden glides from deep bass to falsetto (and back again), revealing the child inside the man, the man inside the child.

It is Buddy Holly's childlike vocal timbre and phrasing, suggesting the insouciance of a choirboy who doesn't realize his voice is changing, that serves to express his almost prayerful expectancy of a love that will surely come his way . . . because it already exists in his heart. "Take your time," he sings in one of his loveliest songs, "And take mine, too." The mood of the song makes it seem as if the young singer has all the time in the world, but he is at the same time actually urging his girl to take (seize) the ripened moment of love.

And in "I'm Gonna Love You Too," Buddy Holly—like a little boy confusing the present and hoped-for future, reality and anticipation—sings: "You're gonna say you've missed me / You're gonna say you'll kiss me." The irrepressible optimism of this song, like the adolescent confidence of "That'll Be the Day" and "Think It Over" or the incantatory trance of "Listen to Me" and "Words of Love," conveys Holly's magical notion that the insistent repetition of one's wishes ("The dreams and wishes you wish / In the night when the lights are low"—"Well All Right") is in fact the fulfillment of the wish itself; and, as in ritual, the rapture of the song becomes the proof of this magic and, in the end, the magic itself.

In an essay entitled "Pop as Ritual in Modern Culture," the English critic Wilfrid Mellers writes about the Australian aborigines who "make a music consisting of isolated words and phrases—invoca-

tions of sun, moon, cloud, and other natural phenomena—yelled against the everlasting drone of the dijiridu and accompanied by the rhythmic beating of sticks. In the silent emptiness the aborigine dramatizes the basic fact of his life: the beating of the pulse, the thudding of the heart." And in today's era of sophisticated production techniques, it is important to remember that Holly's most moving songs—whether accompanied by the Crickets, background vocalists or strings—attest to the fact that he was one of the first white rock & roll musicians to keep alive and draw inspiration from the simplest ritual gestures, phrases and forms of musical expression. (Black musicians such as Washboard Sam, Tampa Red, Lonnie Johnson and Arthur Crudup had earlier created rock & roll out of the barest and most humble instrumental resources. It is also not surprising that the most revelatory "cover" versions of Holly's songs are not by bubblegum Holly imitators or English rock artists [the Beatles' "Words of Love," the Rolling Stones' "Not Fade Away" and Blind Faith's "Well All Right" are the exceptions] but by singers such as Carolyn Hester ["Lonesome Tears"], Tom Rush ["Love's Made a Fool of You"] and Skeeter Davis ["True Love Ways"].)

Several of Holly's friends recall that some of his most memorable playing occurred in 1956 and 1957, when he and fellow Cricket Jerry Allison performed regularly at the Lubbock youth center—Holly's vocals and guitar supported only by Allison's drumming. And even later Holly's rhythm section often consisted of just a tom-tom or jelly. From the slapping-hands-on-knees accompaniment on "Everyday" to the modal plainness and almost shamanistic cymbal drumming on "Well All Right," from the light incantations of "Crying, Waiting, Hoping" to Waylon Jennings's and Slim Corbin's hand-clapping on the original version of "You're the One," Holly's deepest, wisest and seemingly least complicated songs express the unadorned confrontation of beauty and love with time.

The women of Fifties rock & roll—about whom songs were written and to whom they were addressed—almost always fell into two categories: the fast and earthy (Lucille, Fannie Mae, Hank Ballard's Annie) and the slow and

As a sophomore in high school, Holly wrote, "My life has been what you might call an uneventful one, and it seems there is not much of interest to tell. . . ."

dreamy (Donna, Denise, Sheila). In most cases they were like the emblematic and conventional ladies of the courtly and Petrarchan schools—as interchangeable as hurricanes or spring showers, Party Doll ornaments of the song.

With Peggy Sue, however, Buddy Holly created the first rock & roll folk heroine (Chuck Berry's Johnny B. Goode is her male counterpart). And yet it is difficult to say how Holly did it. Unlike the Sad-Eyed Lady of the Lowlands—whom Bob Dylan fills in as he invents and discovers her—Peggy Sue is hardly there at all. Most Fifties singers let it be known that they liked the way their women walked and talked; sometimes they even let on as to the color of their sweethearts' eyes and hair. But Buddy Holly didn't even give you this much information. Instead, he colluded with his listeners, suggesting that they imagine and create Peggy Sue *for* him.

Singing in his characteristically shy, coy, ingenuous tone of voice, Holly seems to let us in on a secret—just as later, in "Peggy Sue Got Married," he continues his complicit arrangement with his listeners, half-pleading with them, and with himself, not to reveal something that he himself must hesitatingly disclose. In this brilliantly constructed equivocation, Holly asks us to suspend disbelief (just as, contrarily, Wendy in *Peter Pan* beseeches the children in the audience to give credence to fairies in order to keep them alive) until that inexorable last stanza when we realize that no longer can Holly sing: "You're the one," but only that "She's the one." He has become one of his own listeners as Peggy Sue vanishes, like Humbert Humbert's Lolita, into the mythology of American Romance.

In his invaluable biography of Buddy Holly, John Goldrosen informs us that Holly originally composed a song called "Cindy Lou," and that Jerry Allison suggested he change the title to the name of Allison's girlfriend (whom Allison married and later divorced). But the Peggy Sue of our hearts continued to live on, making an appearance not only at the living room party in "Splish Splash" but also in Bobby Darin's "Queen of the Hop" and Ritchie Valens's "Ooh My Head"—finally to be scorned and discarded for a younger rival in the insolent "Barbara Ann": "Played our favorite tune / Danced with Betty Lou / Tried Peggy Sue but I knew she wouldn't do—/ Barbara Ann." (Barbara Ann, indeed!)

"Love is not love / Which alters when it alteration finds / Or bends with the remover to remove," wrote William Shakespeare. And some of us would like to

This is how it all began. Rehearsing with the Crickets in Lubbock, Texas, 1955.

think that Peggy Sue is still with us, as we keep alive the vibration of her life—and that of her creator—rediscovering her presence in the coded Personal Column message from the English rock group Buddy Holly influenced so strongly:

P.S. I LOVE YOU

Buddy shortly before his death; that's Waylon Jennings behind the shades.

You recall a girl that's been in nearly every song,'' Buddy Holly sang. And it's tempting to imagine that the *idea* of Peggy Sue permeated all of Holly's compositions. Similarly, it is tempting to view all of Holly's recordings as a synchronic rather than a diachronic structure . . . to see them, in other words, as one long song—all the more tempting in that the early Western and Bop demo tapes made by Holly and Bob Montgomery in 1953 and 1954, as well as the scores of radio and garage tapes that were rediscovered and issued after Holly's death (some untouched, most with overdubbed backings), are among his greatest performances.

His first recordings for Decca—including songs like ''Modern Don Juan,'' ''Midnight Shift,'' ''Girl On My Mind'' and the first version of ''That'll Be the Day''—were either commercial failures or unreleased, and have long been criticized for their poor instrumental balance and overemphasized echo effects. Today they strike oversatiated ears as some of Holly's freshest and most unpretentious work. Likewise, the often-criticized overdubbed recordings of the slow version of ''Slippin' and Slidin' '' (backed by the Fireballs), the string-drenched ''Love Is Strange'' and the version of ''Peggy Sue Got Married'' overdubbed with New York City studio musicians (in contrast to the forced-ebullient Clovis studio arrangement) are sublime masterpieces, achieving a seemingly effortless clarity. The early Holly-Montgomery recordings of songs such as ''I Wanna Play House with You'' and ''Down the Line,'' as well as this duo's later consummate songwriting collaborations (''Wishing'' and ''Love's Made a Fool of You''—both recordings featuring the extraordinary lead guitar work of Tommy Allsup), are still too little known. And no one should overlook ''Because I Love You,'' one of Holly's most haunted and haunting ballads—a song that, along with ''Love's Made a Fool of You,'' represents the darker side of Buddy Holly's emotional world.

All of Holly's compositions and performances reflect his amazing capacity to synthesize musical influences as diverse as Hank Williams, Hank Snow, the Louvin Brothers, Western swing bands, Elvis Presley, Bo Didley, Carl Perkins, Tony Williams, Ray Charles, black gospel and Baptist church tunes. And through Holly, all these musical strands were later taken up and developed in the Sixties.

During the Crickets' first cross-country package tour in 1957 Buddy Holly and Chuck Berry used to spend their time traveling together at the back of the bus, kneeling on the floor and shooting craps with their night's earnings. And on hindsight, it is clear today that it was Holly and Berry who were the major influences on the rock music of the Sixties. But Holly's specific contribution is too often underestimated. He was certainly the main inspiration for the Beatles (think of ''I'll Follow the Sun,'' ''Every Little Thing,'' ''I'll Cry Instead,'' ''Here Comes the Sun'' and ''One After 909''—the last of which is almost an exact imitation of the early Holly-Montgomery recordings), as well as the entire English Mersey school, the Kinks (think of ''I'll Remember'' or ''Starstruck''), the Hollies (he gave them their name) and Eric Clapton. In the States, of course, he directly influenced singers and groups like Bobby Vee, Tommy Roe, the Bobby Fuller Four, the Everly Brothers, Skeeter Davis, Creedence Clearwater Revival, Tom Paxton and Bob Dylan.

In the words of Malcolm Jones, writing in an English rock magazine, Holly "scored with a dazzling series of firsts in an era when everyone followed the flock. He was one of the first white rock stars to rely almost exclusively on his own material. The Crickets were probably the first white group to feature the lead-rhythm-bass-drums lineup. He was the first rock singer to double-track his voice and guitar. He was the first to use strings on a rock & roll record. In addition, he popularized the Fender Stratocaster and was probably the only rock star to wear glasses onstage!"

He made his first appearance onstage when he was five, singing "Down the River of Memories."

These were no mean accomplishments for a twenty-two-year-old who, as an "unmemorable" high school student six years before his death, had written in an autobiography for his sophomore English course: "My life has been what you might call an uneventful one, and it seems there is not much of interest to tell . . . I have many hobbies. Some of these are hunting, fishing, leatherwork, reading, painting, and playing Western music. I have thought about making a career out of Western music if I am good enough but I will just have to wait to see how that turns out . . . Well, that's my life to the present date, and even though it may seem awful and full of calamities, I'd sure be in a bad shape without it."

As Bob Dylan once confessed: "I just carry that other time around with me . . . The music of the late Fifties and early Sixties when music was at that root level—that for me is meaningful music. The singers and musicians I grew up with transcend nostalgia—Buddy Holly and Johnny Ace are just as valid to me today as then."

DISCOGRAPHY

SINGLES
Crickets: "That'll Be the Day" (Brunswick; r☆2, ☆3, 1957). "Oh, Boy!" (Brunswick; r☆15, ☆10, 1957). "Maybe Baby" (Brunswick; r☆8, ☆18, 1958). "Think It Over" (Brunswick; ☆27, 1958). **Buddy Holly:** "Peggy Sue" (Coral; r☆2, ☆3, 1957). "Rave On" (Coral; ☆37, 1958). "Early in the Morning" (Coral; ☆32, 1958). "Heartbeat" (Coral; ☆82, 1959). "It Doesn't Matter Anymore" (Coral; ☆13, 1959).

ALBUMS
The Complete Buddy Holly (MCA; 1979).

Chart positions compiled from Joel Whitburn's *Record Research*, based on *Billboard*'s Pop chart, unless otherwise indicated; r☆ = position on *Billboard*'s Rhythm & Blues chart.)

DOO-WOP

BY BARRY HANSEN

O f all the musical instruments on our planet, the all-time favorite is the only one the human race didn't invent—the larynx. No sax, Synclavier or any other instrument has come close to matching the variety, versatility and impact of the human voice.

The larynx has, however, one terribly frustrating liability: It can sing only one note at a time. This became especially aggravating after moving bass lines and chord changes—what we call harmony—were added to the European musical vocabulary during the early Renaissance.

Though the rest of the world's musicians and singers have managed to get along pretty well without harmony (at least until recently), Europeans and Americans have always found harmony indispensable . . . and that, whatever detractors might say, goes for rock & roll as well. Harmonized group vocals have been part of every stage of rock's development. They were especially prominent in the Fifties, when a couple dozen major vocal groups and more than a thousand obscure ones, comprised chiefly of black singers, created the music that rock & roll connoisseurs still regard as the cream of the cream—at least if one measures the music's worth by the value of the records as collector's items.

No particular name was given to this form of R&B music by the people who made and enjoyed it in the Fifties. Today we call it "doo-wop," after two of the characteristic nonsense syllables invented early in the game by the fellows who didn't get to sing lead and got tired of singing nothing but "aaaaah."

Black vocal harmony is as old as America. Some astonishing examples were recorded in the Twenties by the Norfolk Jazz Quartet, a gospel group doing a little backsliding during the jazz age. Everybody's heard the Mills Brothers. For rock & roll purposes, a more important antecedent would be the equally famous Ink Spots, whose ballads, such as "If I Didn't Care" and "My Prayer," featuring lead singer Bill Kenny and talking bassman Orville "Hoppy" Jones, were among the nation's best-selling records in the late Thirties and early Forties.

The Spots faded after Jones died in 1944, but their incredible success gave rise to innumerable imitations. By 1949 two groups had gained national star-

The Platters welcome you.

Cornel Gunter and the Flairs.

The Ink Spots, influential forerunners of doo-wop.

A 1955 incarnation of the Drifters.

dom, at least among black listeners: the Ravens, whose bass singer Jimmy Ricks virtually created the role of Mr. Bassman, and the Orioles, whose Sonny Til carried on in the tradition of Bill Kenny. The Orioles' ballad recordings such as "Tell Me So" (1949) added something significant to the Ink Spots' pattern: a wordless falsetto doing a kind of obligato to the lead vocal. This device, plus a slightly rougher vocal tone and freer, more prominent background parts, makes "Tell Me So" sound like primeval rock & roll, while the Ink Spots reside securely in rock's *pre*-history.

All three pioneer groups, the Ink Spots, Ravens and Orioles, recorded many fast numbers as well, jive tunes done with a restrained, delicate touch that sounds enchanting four decades later. By the early Fifties, however, they sounded like pussyfeet. The emerging boppers may have been as sentimental as their older sisters and brothers when it came to the slow stuff at evening's end, but when they wanted to get it on, the Ravens' "Ol' Man River" didn't quite fill the bill anymore. They were replaced by such groups as the Dominoes, the Clovers and the Drifters, who combined liberated gospel-style lead singing with a beat far heftier than any previously heard behind a black vocal group.

The next major figure in our story is Alan Freed, who couldn't sing a note. Freed featured black vocal groups on his radio shows. As sales of group records skyrocketed, every R&B label (plus some that had never before given the music a second thought) was

The Rivingtons, of "Papa-Oom-Mow-Mow" fame.

hungry for groups. The bird groups (Orioles, Ravens, Robins, Penguins, Flamingos, Crows) multiplied like rabbits, soon to be joined by flowers (Orchids, Gladiolas), dogs (Spaniels, Rovers) and automobiles (Cadillacs, El Dorados, Edsels).

Few of these new groups could do a ballad as sweetly or as smoothly as the Orioles. Few could sell a sexy song with the verve of the Drifters' lead singer Clyde McPhatter. But there was far more demand in the mid-Fifties than those masters could possibly supply, and the cities were packed with aspiring vocal groups. One writer estimates 15,000 groups eventually cut a record apiece. (I'd be tempted to remove at least one zero from that figure, but for legend's sake, I'll let it pass.)

Typically, the popular groups of the Fifties struck a compromise between the Ink Spots–Orioles ballad style and the fervor of the rhythm & gospelers, coming as close to one or both models as their talents allowed. More often than not, their records had one fast side and one slow side.

The Orioles' "Crying in the Chapel" (1953) is often cited as the first R&B record to win a big white audience. Since it was a cover of a country song, I tend to consider it a fluke, lovely fluke though it is. More seminal was the Crows' early 1954 coupling of "Gee" and "I Love You So." This record provided ample confirmation for the many musicians, writers and comedians (such as Stan Freberg) who considered rock & roll artists hopelessly deficient in the basic techniques of music making. On the uptempo "Gee," the lead singer attempts a Clyde McPhatter gospel shout but can produce little more than a croak (or caw, if you please). The equally well beloved B side, "I Love You So," is a woefully discordant ballad, opening with "I love you so / I want you to

know / I'm telling you darling / I'll never let you go"—and becoming less articulate as the song proceeds.

So much for the Crows, one might say. But a whole generation, including myself, loved that record. Much has been written and said about rock & roll sung on street corners by neighborhood kids in the Fifties, and there's no denying that "Gee" and "I Love You So" have a delicious amateurishness to them. The complexity of recording and performing in recent times has almost driven that spirit from rock, and it's no small loss.

With Alan Freed as the pusher, "Gee" and contemporaneous songs got thousands of teenage Americans hooked on rock & roll, né rhythm & blues. It wasn't yet a majority taste in 1954, but it was getting there very fast. Group records started coming out at the rate of a couple dozen a week. They ranged from splendidly recorded, aggressively promoted products of major independents like Atlantic and King to things thrown together on home tape recorders, promoted from a phone booth and sold from a car trunk.

The Harptones.

The saga of "Earth Angel," the R&B sensation of late 1954, is typical. Often hailed as *the* all-time favorite R&B oldie, "Earth Angel" by the Penguins was originally released early in 1954, by Dootone Records of Los Angeles.

Dootone was owned by a south L.A. producer named Dootsie Williams (who later became prosperous via a long series of raunchy comedy LPs by Redd Foxx). Before the Penguins came along, Dootsie had graduated from the car-trunk and phone-booth league, thanks to "party" records by Billy Mitchell and Hattie Noel; but Dootone in 1954 was by no means a major independent, even by R&B standards.

The Penguins, named after the Kool cigarette

The Ravens.

trademark, were students at L.A.'s Fremont High School when Dootsie heard them. Even though he felt they needed more practice, he booked time in a local garage studio (it really *was* in a garage, in a South L.A. residential neighborhood) and cut eight sides, including ''Earth Angel.''

Dootsie thought it was just about good enough to fill the B side of the group's second single. Fortunately, radio stations sometimes played both sides of the singles in those days, and ''Earth Angel'' gradually became a major request item.

It was murky sounding, distorted, badly balanced and utterly lovable . . . true love, undiluted by any sort of artistic pretense. It was real people's music—you or your lover could have made it—yet it's sublimely beautiful. For the next ten years group after group sought to emulate this distillation of pure rock & roll romanticism, free from all artistic trappings such as complex harmonies and clever lyrics.

And what of the Penguins themselves? Lead singer Cleve Duncan told their story in a 1972 issue of *Record Exchanger*, the biggest and most permanent

The Crew-Cuts, whose whitewash of the Chords' ''Sh-Boom'' helped bring doo-wop onto the pop charts.

of a host of fanzines dealing with rock & roll and R&B oldies. The Penguins' story could be that of any of a hundred doo-wop groups.

''Earth Angel'' hit Number One on the R&B charts and Number Eight on the pop charts, tying for the latter position with a pop ''cover'' by the Crew-Cuts. The Penguins played Harlem's Apollo Theatre, the Brooklyn Paramount (with Alan Freed), the Regal in Chicago and most of the other major R&B venues of the time.

They quickly got into a dispute with Dootone, however, over advances on record royalties. In frustration they turned to Buck Ram, who managed their friends the Platters. Ram was able to get the Penguins released from Dootone, and signed with the Mercury label as part of a package deal with the Platters. For the Penguins, the price was high: In a court case, Dootsie Williams wound up with all rights to ''Earth Angel.''

The Crowns.

On Mercury the Penguins cut some fine sides but failed to produce another big hit. Mercury's enthusiasm waned, and after the first year the company didn't get around to recording the eight sides a year the group's contract called for. The Penguins moved on to Atlantic, but after one unsuccessful Atlantic release they found themselves back in L.A., older, wiser, deep in debt and recording once again for Dootsie Williams.

They remained with Dootsie, hitless, for two years; after one final effort on Sun State Records, the original Penguins disbanded. Since then Cleve has recruited new Penguins on several occasions, one of them a 1963 recording of a song called ''Memories of El Monte,'' written by a young Frank Zappa and Ray Collins. More recently the new Penguins have been heard at rock & roll revival shows, sharing the stage with dozens of other groups, each one with its own bittersweet story to tell about the rush of success and the frustrations of not being able to sustain it.

Of all the doo-wop groups mentioned in this chapter's discography, only two became long-running pop successes: the Platters and the Coasters. Give an honorable mention to Frankie Lymon and the Teenagers. A few others that got into the game early were able to hold loyal R&B audiences for several years without the benefit of a big pop hit: the Spaniels, Moonglows, Five Keys, Charms, Flamingos. For most doo-wop groups, it was one or two hits, boom and bust. Success came much more quickly to a group in the Fifties than it does today, but failure followed even more quickly.

Frankie Lymon *(center)* with the Teenagers, wondering why fools fall in love.

The School Boys, one of the first—and last—prepubescent doo-wop vocal groups.

The Moonglows, ready to sing "Sincerely."

But what glorious one-shots! Here are a few favorites:

"Story Untold" by the Nutmegs. This ballad is totally definitive of doo-wop in mid-1955. Unlike "Earth Angel," it is competently recorded, accompanied by a professional-sounding combo. Like "Angel," though, its aim is the expression of romantic sentiments in a slow dance tempo uncluttered by any pretense to art. While the background voices perform all the standard functions of their craft, the late Leroy Griffin sings a lead part that manages to be expressive while staying very neutral stylistically, attempting neither the power surges of gospel nor the gloss of a Bill Kenny. The Nutmegs were named after their native Connecticut, the Nutmeg State.

"Speedoo" by the Cadillacs. Despite slow dancing's great popularity in the Fifties, about half the doo-wop songs that went pop were uptempo. Here, after a bass-dominated intro, Earl Carroll (that's Mr. Earl, of course; he later joined the Coasters) takes

over this macho manifesto, written by Esther Navarro. The lyrics sound like they were made up on the spot, but the character is well drawn. Did you ever notice that the sax solo is faster than the rest of the record?

"Why Do Fools Fall in Love" by the Teenagers featuring Frankie Lymon. The ill-starred Frankie, who died tragically in 1968, was the premier boy soprano of his time, his rich, round tone dwarfing the bleats of later preteen idols. This song, which Frankie coauthored, is everything you'd expect of the third-prize entry in a junior high poetry contest, but Frankie's pipes and the lively music make it a paean of ecstasy. Bass singer Sherman Garnes opens the side with a resonant "eh toom-ah-ta-toom-ah-ta-toom-ah-toh-doh"—spell it any way you like. (Garnes was also the creator of "oodly pop-a-cow cow.") Before Frankie's voice changed, the Teenagers enjoyed an atypically long string of hits, including "I Want You to Be My Girl" and "The ABCs of Love." Their "I'm Not a Juvenile Delinquent" was as close as doo-wop ever got to social consciousness.

The Five Satins, "In the Still of the Nite."

"In the Still of the Nite" by the Five Satins. A year later than "Story Untold," this makes further progress toward freeing the music from artistic trappings. Most of the vocal counterpoint is abandoned in favor of a simple "shoo-doo-shoo-be-doo" repeated so constantly it becomes a hypnotic hook, while Fred Parris sings the romantic lead in a style even more neutral than Leroy Griffin's. Though this was a relatively modest hit in 1956, it closely rivals "Earth Angel" as the most requested doo-wop oldie today.

"Come Go with Me" by the Dell-Vikings. The first of a long line of racially integrated vocal groups, the Dell-Vikings were with the U.S. Air Force when they recorded "Come Go with Me" in the basement of a Pittsburgh disc jockey's house. After local success on the Fee Bee label the song went national on Dot, the first of several label switches the Dell-Vikings made in what was to be a very confused career. There's nary an original line in the lyrics, as shopworn a satchel of clichés as you could ask for—but the record's best parts are where the fellows sing only syllables, "dum dum dum dum dum-be-oo-bee." A terrific dance disc.

"Silhouettes" by the Rays. Here by contrast is a

The
Medallions.

highly professional affair, the work of a journeyman group coached by songwriter-producers Frank Slay and Bob Crewe. The lyrics to this ballad of mistaken identity are downright fancy by comparison with those we've just encountered, but the music is as simple and artless as any doo-wopper could wish.

"Get a Job" by the Silhouettes. This song is actually about a guy whose woman is nagging him to get a job, an unusually adult subject for doo-wop. I doubt that very many people noticed, for the "background" singers are the whole show, from the first "byip byip byip byip" to the oft-disputed "sha-na-na" or "shad-da-da," whichever you prefer. An awful lot of socks were worn out to "Get a Job" in 1958.

"Book of Love" by the Monotones. Another supreme one-shot. Like the Silhouettes, this group never again had a Top 100 record, though connoisseurs of the bizarre might do well to look up the Monotones' follow-up attempts, "Legend of Sleepy Hollow" and "Zombi." This record has the simplest and catchiest "hook" of the decade: a single bass drum beat happening all by itself right in the middle of the chorus.

"Book of Love" was close to the end of the line for classic doo-wop. By 1958 R&B groups were fighting a losing battle for the young record buyer's 98¢ (up from 89¢ that year) against the young, mostly white artists who were getting saturation exposure on *American Bandstand*.

Two totally dissimilar groups, the Platters and the Coasters, kept the doo-wop tradition going, with modifications. To introduce the first, we go back to 1955, the year "Rock Around the Clock" changed the rock audience from a minority to the majority. Easily the second biggest rock event of that year was the emergence of a doo-wop group called the Platters. The Platters debuted on the charts in 1955, after being brought to Mercury, a national label, by their manager Buck Ram. The Platters were a highly professional group that had been recording for some time on one of the bigger independent labels, Federal. Ram, who had once written songs for the original Ink Spots, had coached the Platters into a modernized reincarnation of the Spots, featuring Tony Williams in the Bill Kenny role. Ram relied on a sturdy rhythm section, with lots of piano triplets, to bring the music up-to-date.

The Platters' last Federal release had been a Ram-composed ballad called "Only You." The group remade it for Mercury, in the highest of fi. It was an across-the-board smash. "The Great Pretender" was even bigger, becoming the first doo-wop record to hit Number One on the pop charts. After another Ram-penned hit, "You've Got the Magic Touch," the Platters paid true tribute to their roots with "My Prayer," an almost literal reproduction of the Ink Spots' 1939 hit. The Platters went on to become the most successful rock & roll vocal group of the Fifties.

Closest contenders to the Platters for consistent commercial supremacy was a group that started on the West Coast (whence their name). The Coasters began as the Robins, part of the troupe of veteran bandleader and showman Johnny Otis. The year 1955 found the Robins recording the spectacular "Riot in Cell Block No. 9" and "Smokey Joe's Cafe" for Spark Records, an L.A. label owned by Jerry Leiber and Mike Stoller, who also had written the songs. These enjoyed enough regional success to interest Atlantic Records, which offered Leiber and Stoller a contract to produce similar records for their Atco subsidiary. (This was an industry milestone: rock & roll's first independent production deal. Before this, nearly all records had been produced by staff members of the labels that released them. Nowadays nearly all rock recordings (and many other kinds as well) are supervised by independent producers.)

The Robins, meanwhile, were splitting up. Half the group retained the Robins' name and quickly flew into obscurity, while the other faction went with Leiber and Stoller and became the nucleus of the Coasters.

Their first Coasters record, "Down in Mexico,"

did well on the R&B market in the spring of '56. The group's real rock & roll fame, however, began with the coupling of "Searchin' " and "Young Blood," which hit the streets in April 1957. Every Top Forty station in America glowed with the sweet funk of these sides. "Young Blood" became the model for a whole series of sly "playlets" (the word is Mike Stoller's) on teenage life and love, all written and produced by Leiber and Stoller.

"Charlie Brown," "Yakety Yak," "Along Came Jones" and "Idol with the Golden Head" are as entertaining today as ever. Though the Coaster's style has no real precedent in the doo-wop mainstream aside from the Robins, the Coasters' records were so often imitated (notably by the Olympics) that they became very much a part of doo-wop's legacy to the Sixties.

The Olympics, who brought you "Western Movies."

The Coasters and the Platters, having in their highly divergent ways established themselves as the fittest, survived into the Sixties. In the meantime, though, classic doo-wop was fading from the airwaves: 1957 was the last great vintage year. Ironically, just as classic doo-wop disappeared, we began hearing from the second generation of rock group-dom—white, black and integrated groups who took their inspiration not from the old masters like Bill Kenny or the great showmen like Clyde McPhatter but from the naive, street-corner sound of records like "Earth Angel" and "I Love You So."

Neo-doo-wop, as I like to call this development, produced some of the most awful records of all time. Nostalgia, however, has given some of them a luster no producer could have imagined: "Oh Julie" by the Crescendos, "You" by the Aquatones, "Sorry (I Ran All the Way Home)" by the Impalas and "You

The Solitaires.

Cheated'' in rival versions by the original Slades and the covering Shields. Most successful of all were the Fleetwoods, two girls and a guy who carried on in rock & roll's Cadillac tradition by crooning, "Come Softly to Me" and "Mr. Blue" in voices as gentle as the drizzles of their native Olympia, Washington.

In 1959 a record from Pittsburgh pointed the way to the future. "Since I Don't Have You" by the Skyliners was one of the first hits to capture the street-corner aura while expanding the music's horizons. In addition to relatively sophisticated harmony, its elaborately orchestrated production supported the singers instead of fighting them. Phil Spector, then just getting his producing feet wet with the Teddy Bears, has cited "Since I Don't Have You" as a major inspiration.

The Flamingos, also-rans on the doo-wop scene since the early Fifties, finally soared in 1959 with a similarly adventurous production of the 1934 standard "I Only Have Eyes for You" (doo-vop-she-bop). Meanwhile, another bird group, the Falcons, debuted with the much funkier "You're So Fine."

The Flamingos, whose version of "I Only Have Eyes for You" sounded like music from another planet.

The Marcels, ready to demolish "Blue Moon."

Together with other 1959–60 black groups such as the Impressions and the Miracles, and such soloists as Sam Cooke, the Falcons marked a beginning of what we now know as soul music: An idiom that owes a lot to the rhythm & gospel style of Clyde McPhatter but differs from basic doo-wop in owing absolutely nothing to the Ink Spots.

After a fallow year in 1960 (a year in which most of the best-selling singles had only the most tenuous connection with rock of any kind) neo-doo-wop produced a bumper crop in 1961. That year saw not only a huge boom in reissued oldies from the Fifties, but a whole new crop of one-shot groups firmly entrenched in neo-doo-wop style, such as the Capris ("There's a Moon Out Tonight," said to have actually been cut in 1958), the Edsels ("Rama Lama Ding Dong"), the Regents ("Barbara-Ann"), the Marcels, who hit Number One on the pop charts with "Blue Moon," and above all Shep and the Limelites, who after making Number Fifty-three on the charts in 1956 with "A Thousand Miles Away," under the name the Heartbeats, came back with a Number Two hit in 1961 with its sequel, "Daddy's Home."

In New York City the neo-doo-wop phenomenon achieved nirvana with the a cappella craze. Groups of young blacks, whites and Latins from all over Gotham vied one another to produce the purest imaginable doo-wop ballads, letting it all hang out with no instrumental accompaniment of any kind. The New York a cappella sound (not to be confused with the later unaccompanied soul stylings of the

Persuasions) was rarely heard outside Fun City, but immortalized itself with hundreds of 45s, some now nearly as valuable as original discs from the Fifties.

Despite such fanaticism, neo-doo-wop did not survive the British Invasion of 1964 (unless we count the Four Seasons, who owe at least a little to the style). Once again, the sweet sounds faded from the airwaves, to live on in the minds of collectors, the bank accounts of rare-record dealers and the hearts of just about everyone who had the fortune (good or bad) to be young in those times.

DISCOGRAPHY

SINGLES

Lee Andrews and the Hearts: "Long Lonely Nights" (Chess; ☆45, 1957). "Tear Drops" (Chess; r☆13, ☆20, 1957). "Try the Impossible" (United Artists; ☆33, 1958). **Belmonts:** "Tell Me Why" (Sabrina; ☆18, 1961). **Joe Bennett and the Sparkletones:** "Black Slacks" (ABC-Paramount; ☆17, 1957). **Blue Jays:** "Lover's Island" (Milestone; ☆31, 1961). **Bobbettes:** "Mr. Lee" (Atlantic; r☆2, ☆6, 1957). **Jerry Butler and the Impressions:** "For Your Precious Love" (Abner; r☆10, ☆11, 1958). **Cadets:** "Stranded in the Jungle" (Modern; r☆4, ☆18, 1956). **Cadillacs:** "Speedoo" (Josie; r☆3, ☆30, 1955). "Peek-a-Boo" (Josie; r☆20, ☆28, 1958). **Capris:** "There's a Moon Out Tonight" (Old Town; r☆11, ☆3, 1961). **Cardinals:** "The Door Is Still Open" (Atlantic; r☆10, 1955). **Chantels:** "Maybe" (End; r☆5, ☆15, 1958). **Chanters:** "No, No, No" (DeLuxe; r☆9, ☆41, 1961). **Charms:** "Hearts of Stone" (DeLuxe; r☆1, ☆15, 1954). "Two Hearts" (DeLuxe; r☆9, 1955). "Ling, Ting, Tong" (DeLuxe; r☆6, ☆26, 1955). **Chimes:** "Once in Awhile" (Tag; ☆11, 1960). **Chords:** "Sh-Boom" (Cat; r☆3, ☆9, 1954). **Cleftones:** "Little Girl of Mine" (Gee; r☆8, 1956). "Heart and Soul" (Gee; r☆10, ☆18, 1961). **Clovers:** "Crawlin'" (Atlantic; r☆3, 1953). "Good Lovin'" (Atlantic; r☆2, 1953). "Lovey Dovey" b/w "Little Mama" (Atlantic; r☆2, 1954). "I've Got My Eyes on You" b/w "Your Cash Ain't Nothin' but Trash" (Atlantic; r☆7, 1954). "Devil or Angel" (Atlantic; r☆4, 1956). "Love, Love, Love" (Atlantic; r☆10, ☆30, 1956). "Love Potion No. 9" (United Artists; r☆23, ☆23, 1959). **Coasters:** "Searchin'" b/w "Young Blood" (Atco; r☆1, ☆5, 1957). "Yakety Yak" (Atco; r☆1, ☆1, 1958). "Charlie Brown" (Atco; r☆2, ☆2, 1959). "Along Came Jones" (Atco; r☆14, ☆9, 1959). "Poison Ivy" (Atco; r☆1, ☆7, 1959). **Corsairs:** "Smoky Places" (Tuff; r☆10, ☆12, 1962). **Crescendos:** "Oh Julie" (Nasco; r☆4, ☆5, 1958). **Crests:** "16 Candles" (Coed; r☆4, ☆2, 1959). **Crows:** "Gee" (Rama; r☆6, ☆17, 1954). **Danleers:** "One Summer Night" (Mercury; r☆11, ☆16, 1958). **Danny and the Juniors:** "At the Hop" (ABC-Paramount; r☆1, ☆1, 1957). "Rock and Roll Is Here to Stay" (ABC-Paramount; r☆16, ☆19, 1958). **Dells:** "Oh What a Nite" (Vee-Jay; r☆4, 1956). **Dell-Vikings:** "Come Go with Me" (Dot; r☆3, ☆5, 1957). "Whispering Bells" (Dot; r☆5, ☆9, 1957). **Diamonds:** "Little Darlin'" (Mercury; r☆3, ☆2, 1957). "The Stroll" (Mercury; r☆7, ☆5, 1958). **Dion and the Belmonts:** "I Wonder Why" (Laurie; ☆22, 1958). "A Teenager in Love" (Laurie; ☆5, 1959). **Don and Juan:** "What's Your Name" (Big Top; ☆7, 1962). **Dovells:** "Bristol Stomp" (Parkway; r☆7, ☆2, 1961). **Dreamlovers:** "When We Get Married" (Heritage; ☆10, 1961). **Drifters:** "Adorable" (Atlantic; r☆5, 1955). "Ruby Baby" (Atlantic; r☆13, 1956). "There Goes My Baby" (Atlantic; r☆1, ☆2, 1959). "Dance with Me" (Atlantic; r☆2, ☆15, 1959). "This Magic Moment" (Atlantic; r☆4, ☆16, 1960). "Save the Last Dance for Me" (Atlantic; r☆1, ☆1, 1960).

"Up on the Roof" (Atlantic; r☆4, ☆5, 1962). **Dubs:** "Could This Be Magic" (Gone; ☆24, 1957). **Du Droppers:** "I Wanna Know" (RCA Victor; r☆3, 1953). **Duprees:** "You Belong to Me" (Coed; ☆7, 1962). **Earls:** "Remember Then" (Old Town; r☆29, ☆24, 1962). **Edsels:** "Rama Lama Ding Dong" (Twin; ☆21, 1961). **El Dorados:** "At My Front Door" (Vee-Jay; r☆2, ☆21, 1955). **Elegants:** "Little Star" (Apt; r☆1, ☆1, 1958). **Falcons:** "You're So Fine" (Unart; r☆2, ☆17, 1959). "I Found a Love" (Lupine; r☆6, 1962). **Fiestas:** "So Fine" (Old Town; r☆3, ☆11, 1959). **Fireflies:** "You Were Mine" (Ribbon; ☆21, 1959). **Five Keys:** "Ling, Ting, Tong" (Capitol; r☆5, ☆28, 1954). "Close Your Eyes" (Capitol; r☆6, 1955). "Out of Sight, Out of Mind" (Capitol; ☆27, 1956). **Five Satins:** "In the Still of the Nite" (Ember; r☆4, ☆29, 1956). "To the Aisle" (Ember; r☆5, ☆25, 1957). **Flairs:** "Foot Stomping—Part I" (Felsted; r☆20, ☆25, 1961). **Flamingos:** "I'll Be Home" (Checker; r☆10, 1956). "Lovers Never Say Goodbye" (End; r☆25, 1959). "I Only Have Eyes for You" (End; r☆3, ☆11, 1959). **Fleetwoods:** "Come Softly to Me" (Dolphin; r☆5, ☆1, 1959). "Mister Blue" (Dolton; r☆3, ☆1, 1959). **Gladiolas:** "Little Darlin'" (Excello; r☆11, ☆41, 1957). **Heartbeats:** "A Thousand Miles Away" (Rama; r☆5, 1956). **Hearts:** "Lonely Nights" (Baton; r☆8, 1955). **Hollywood Flames:** "Buzz-Buzz-Buzz" (Ebb; r☆11, ☆11, 1957). **Impalas:** "Sorry (I Ran All the Way Home)" (Cub; r☆14, ☆2, 1959). **Innocents:** "Gee Whiz" (Indigo; r☆15, ☆28, 1960). **Jacks:** "Why Don't You Write Me?" (RPM; r☆4, 1955). **Jamies:** "Summertime, Summertime" (Epic; ☆26, 1958). **Jarmels:** "A Little Bit of Soap" (Laurie; r☆7, ☆12, 1961). **Jay and the Americans:** "She Cried" (United Artists; ☆5, 1962). **Jive Five:** "My True Story" (Beltone; r☆1, ☆3, 1961). **Johnnie and Joe:** "Over the Mountain; Across the Sea" (Chess; r☆3, ☆8, 1957). **Little Anthony and the Imperials:** "Tears on My Pillow" (End; r☆2, ☆4, 1958). "Shimmy, Shimmy, Ko-Ko Bop" (End; r☆14, ☆24, 1959). **Little Caesar and the Romans:** "Those Oldies but Goodies (Remind Me of You)" (Del Fi; r☆28, ☆9, 1961). **Little Joe and the Thrillers:** "Peanuts" (Okeh; ☆23, 1957). **Frankie Lymon and the Teenagers:** "Why Do Fools Fall in Love" (Gee; r☆1, ☆7, 1956). "I Want You to Be My Girl" (Gee; r☆3, ☆17, 1956). "I Promise to Remember" (Gee; r☆10, 1956). "The ABCs of Love" (Gee; r☆14, 1956). "Goody Goody" (Gee; ☆22, 1957). **Majors:** "A Wonderful Dream" (Imperial; r☆23, ☆22, 1962). **Marcels:** "Blue Moon" (Colpix; r☆1, ☆1, 1961). "Heartaches" (Colpix; r☆19, ☆7, 1961). **Monotones:** "Book of Love" (Argo; r☆4, ☆5, 1958). **Moonglows:** "Sincerely" (Chess; r☆2, 1954). "Most of All" (Chess; r☆11, 1955). "See Saw" (Chess; r☆11, ☆28, 1956). **Harvey and the Moonglows:** "Ten Commandments of Love" (Chess; r☆9, ☆22, 1958). **Mystics:** "Hushabye" (Laurie; ☆20, 1959). **Nutmegs:** "Story Untold" (Herald; r☆2, 1955). **Olympics:** "Western Movies" (Demon; r☆7, ☆8, 1958). "Big Boy Pete" (Arvee; r☆10, ☆50, 1960). **Orioles:** "Crying in the Chapel" (Jubilee; r☆1, ☆11, 1953). **Orlons:** "Wah Watusi" (Cameo; r☆5, ☆2, 1962). "Don't Hang Up" (Cameo; r☆3, ☆4, 1962). **Paradons:** "Diamonds and Pearls" (Milestone; r☆27, ☆18, 1960). **Pastels:** "Been So Long" (Argo; r☆15, ☆24, 1958). **Penguins:** "Earth Angel" (Dootone; r☆1, ☆8, 1954). **Platters:** "Only You" (Mercury; r☆1, ☆5, 1955). "The Great Pretender" (Mercury; r☆1, ☆1, 1955). "(You've Got) The Magic Touch" (Mercury; r☆4, ☆4, 1956). "My Prayer" (Mercury; r☆2, ☆1, 1956). "Twilight Time" (Mercury; r☆1, ☆1, 1958). "Smoke Gets in Your Eyes" (Mercury; r☆3, ☆1, 1958). "Harbor Lights" (Mercury; r☆15, ☆8, 1960). **Playmates:** "Jo-Ann" (Roulette; ☆20, 1958). "Beep Beep" (Roulette; ☆4, 1958). **Quin-Tones:** "Down the Aisle of Love" (Hunt; r☆6, ☆20, 1958). **Rays:** "Silhouettes" (Cameo; r☆3, ☆3, 1957). **Regents:** "Barbara-Ann" (Gee; r☆7, ☆13, 1961). "Runaround" (Gee; r☆30, ☆28, 1961). **Robert and Johnny:** "We Belong Together" (Old Town; r☆18, ☆33, 1958). **Safaris:** "Image of a Girl" (Eldo; ☆6, 1960). **Sensations:** "Let Me In" (Argo; r☆2, ☆4, 1962). **Shells:** "Baby Oh Baby" (Johnson; ☆21, 1960). **Shep and the Limelites:** "Daddy's Home" (Hull; r☆4, ☆2, 1961). "Our Anniversary" (Hull; r☆7, 1962). **Shields:** "You Cheated" (Tender; r☆11, ☆15, 1958). **Silhouettes:** "Get a Job" (Ember; r☆1, ☆1, 1958). **Six Teens:** "A Casual Look" (Flip; r☆7, ☆48, 1956). **Skyliners:**

"Since I Don't Have You" (Calico; r☆3, ☆12, 1959). **Spaniels:** "Baby It's You" (Chance; r☆10, 1953). "Goodnite Sweetheart, Goodnite" (Vee-Jay; r☆5, 1954). **Spiders:** "I Didn't Want to Do It" (Imperial; r☆3, 1954). **Spinners:** "That's What Girls Are Made For" (Tri-Phi; r☆5, ☆27, 1961). **Stereos:** "I Really Love You" (Cub; r☆15, ☆29, 1961). **Teen Queens:** "Eddie My Love" (RPM; r☆3, ☆22, 1956). **Tempos:** "See You in September" (Climax; ☆23, 1959). **Tokens:** "Tonight I Fell in Love" (Warwick; ☆15, 1961). "The Lion Sleeps Tonight" (RCA Victor; r☆7, ☆1) 1962). **Tune Weavers:** "Happy, Happy Birthday Baby" (Checker; r☆4, ☆5, 1957). **Turbans:** "When You Dance" (Herald; r☆12, ☆33, 1955). **Valentinos:** "Lookin' for a Love" (Sar; r☆8, 1962). **Velvets:** "Tonight (Could Be the Night)" (Monument; ☆26, 1961). **Vocaleers:** "Is It a Dream?" (Red Robin; r☆8, 1953). **Volumes:** "I Love You" (Chex; ☆22, 1962). **Billy Ward and His Dominoes:** "Star Dust" (Liberty; r☆5, ☆13, 1957). **Maurice Williams and the Zodiacs:** "Stay" (Herald; r☆3, ☆1, 1960). **Otis Williams and His Charms:** "Ivory Tower" (DeLuxe; r☆9, ☆12, 1956). "United" (DeLuxe; r☆5, 1957). **Willows:** "Church Bells May Ring" (Melba; r☆11, 1956).

ALBUMS

Cadillacs: *The Best of the Cadillacs* (Rhino; 1990). **Flamingos:** *The Best of the Flamingos* (Rhino; 1990). **Frankie Lymon and the Teenagers:** *The Best of Frankie Lymon and the Teenagers* (Rhino; 1989). **Marcels:** *The Best of the Marcels* (Rhino; 1990). **Platters:** *The Magic Touch: Platters Anthology* (Polygram; 1991). **Anthologies:** *The Best of Doo Wop Uptempo* (Rhino; 1989). *The Best of Doo Wop Ballads* (Rhino; 1989).

(Chart positions compiled from Joel Whitburn's *Record Research,* based on *Billboard*'s Pop chart, unless otherwise indicated; r☆ = position on *Billboard*'s Rhythm & Blues chart.)

THE RISE OF TOP FORTY AM

BY JOHN MORTHLAND

t is 1953, and Alan Freed is on the air again for his late night *Moondog Show* on WJW in Cleveland. Over his theme, Todd Rhodes's "Blues for Moon Dog," Freed yips, moans and brays, gearing up for another evening hosting the hottest rhythm & blues show in the land. Slipping on a golf glove, he bangs on a phone book in time to the music—maybe "Money Honey" by the Drifters, or "Shake a Hand" by Faye Adams. Swigging constantly from a trusty bottle of booze, he spins the hits and continues his manic patter throughout the night, spewing forth rhymed jive with the speed and inflections of a Holy Roller at the Pearly Gates.

There had been celebrated disc jockeys before Alan Freed, but never anyone quite so crazed or obsessive. In the early days, the national networks, which dominated radio, programmed live musical broadcasts and adventure and comedy serials; rarely did a mere disc jockey become a star. But in the late Forties, as the networks' attention shifted to television, radio began to open up. While live broadcasts and the serials continued, some listeners interested in drama started watching TV, while the listeners interested in music started flipping the dial to the smaller independent stations—stations too small to afford hiring a live band. The independents had one big advantage over the networks: They usually had a much stronger sense of what music their local audiences liked. As television siphoned off the audience for drama, the independents began to attract audiences for specialized music, from hillbilly to rhythm & blues; whether it was on a record or live didn't much matter.

This was the situation Alan Freed faced when he arrived in Cleveland in 1950. Raised in Ohio by a

Wolfman Jack brings the light to Middle America. Working for a pirate superstation just over the border from Del Rio, Texas, the Wolfman sold snake oil and spun the latest in hard-core rock & roll.

Welsh mother and a Lithuanian-born Jewish father, he had worked on a number of jobs, although in high school his true goal in life was to front a band of his own (he played trombone). An ear infection contracted during the war years eliminated that possibility. He tried his hand at being a disc jockey, first in a succession of small towns, then in Akron where he was a hit with the high school crowd and later on WJW in Cleveland, a ''good music'' station.

That same year Leo Mintz, the biggest local record dealer, hipped Freed to rhythm & blues. Freed was impressed by the number of young people buying these records, so he started programming them. He claims he jumped on rhythm & blues right away; others at his station recall that he approached it cautiously, programming only a little until he was flooded with requests. Freed called the music ''rock & roll,'' eliminating the racial stigma attached to rhythm & blues; though he credited himself with

coining the term, it had been common on ''race'' records for decades—as a metaphor for sexual intercourse. (But Freed *did* apply for a copyright on the term ''rock & roll''—and wanted record companies to pay him in order to so describe their product.)

Playing black music by itself did not make Freed such a revolutionary figure; any number of black DJs—''Professor Bop'' in Shreveport, ''Jocky Jack'' Gibson in Atlanta, ''Sugar Daddy'' in Birmingham—were already doing that. Freed was, however, among the first to program black music for a white audience, and for this he was labeled a ''nigger lover'' and suffered legal harassment well before his fall in the payola hearings. At the same time, his popularity was skyrocketing.

Other white DJs soon followed Freed's lead: Hunter Hancock in Los Angeles, ''Poppa Stoppa'' in New Orleans, Gene Nobles in Nashville, Dewey Phillips in Memphis with his *Red Hot and Blues* show. As they attracted more and more white listeners, the bigger stations were forced either to start bopping themselves or go out of business.

In March 1952 Freed sponsored a Moondog Ball in Cleveland featuring top black acts: A reported six thousand fans crashed the gates, in addition to the several thousand already inside the hall that held 10,000. The show had to be canceled, but it wasn't the sheer numbers that most upset adults; it was the fact that the young crowd was there for rhythm & blues, which had not yet been renamed rock & roll.

In 1954 Freed made a triumphant move to New York's WINS; within a few months he raised WINS to the top of the AM heap. He continued staging shows, now at the Brooklyn Paramount. Opening them himself, he would gyrate onstage in a plaid sports coat, shouting, ''Go man go!'' to the house band, blowing kisses to the audience. Freed had an emphatic retort for those who scorned his style: ''Anyone who says rock & roll is a passing fad or a flash-in-the-pan trend along the music road has *rocks in the head*, dad!''

Freed kept the faith until the bitter end. As rock & roll by whites broke, he programmed it alongside discs by his favorite black artists. And as the record industry began to seize control of the savage new music and tame it down with white ''cover'' versions of the biggest songs, Freed continued to play only the originals. In this endeavor, he was joined by a few others (some of them black) such as Danny ''Cat Man'' Stiles in Newark, George ''Hound Dog''

Alan Freed in 1956, years before the fall, presenting an award to LaVern Baker *(on the left)*. On his left stand two other Atlantic recording artists, Ruth Brown and Clyde McPhatter (then on duty in the army).

Lorenz in Buffalo, "Symphony Sid" Torin in Boston, Tommy "Dr. Jive" Smalls in New York, "John R." in Nashville, Al Benson in Chicago and Peter Potter on the West Coast—to say nothing of Bob "Wolfman Jack" Smith south of the border.

Because he worked for a "pirate" station just across the Mexican border from Del Rio, Texas, the Wolfman didn't have to concern himself with such petty details as wattage limits or sign-off times. On a good night you could hear him all the way north to Canada, and all the way west to California, so powerful were the station's transmitters. The Wolfman played only the finest blues, occasionally a little hillbilly music, and spent the night howling at the moon between (and during) records, advising listeners to "get yo'self nekkid" and dig the music, all the while peddling various snake oils, plastic replicas of Jesus, coffins and inspirational literature. He was assumed to be black, but wasn't; he kept his secret by refusing interviews or public appearances.

The increasing number of white "cover" versions and the popularity of the white teen idols indicated new trends in rock & roll; equally fateful was the upswing in chain ownership of AM stations. Independent stations were on the way out, even as they were providing the most exciting radio on the dial. Ironically, the very same wild men who would soon become ensnared in format radio provided the chains with a paradigm of the pop DJ.

The chain owners made no bones about it: Radio was a business proposition, plain and simple, and the best way to take the guesswork out of profit making was to refine a basic music-and-news format. KOWH in Omaha (a Storz station) began working within that format in 1949, and by the mid-Fifties the approach had caught on. In order to attract and stabilize both a maximum audience and maximum ad revenue, Storz cultivated a distinctive "sound" by using identification jingles at regular intervals, saturation programming for a few hit records, fast-talking DJs for personality and a go-go frenzy punctuated only by the hourly news break.

The concept worked, and by the mid-Fifties other Storz stations in New Orleans, Kansas City and Minneapolis fell into line. Gordon McClendon's stations in Dallas, San Antonio and Houston followed suit. They were joined by stations in the Gerald Bartell chain, and those licensed to the Plough pharmaceutical firm. At first, Top Forty referred to mainstream pop music, but as rock & roll came to dominate the market, the music was fit, successfully, into the same format.

Of course this meant that disc jockeys were no longer playing their favorite records, but instead were following a programming schedule (based on heavily researched "popularity charts") involving just forty songs or less, with the Top Ten of those being played even more frequently. They had to read prepared commercials at a certain time—eighteen minutes of the hour was deemed optimum—and they had to read news off the wire services. While they were often still local stars in their own right, they had to fit themselves into the station's image.

Still, rock & roll radio remained the most vital sound on the airwaves. The DJs shouted with the same intensity as the music they played—they just had to compress their shouts into a shorter time span—and the news itself came off like ampheta-

Murray the K, the "fifth Beatle," still alive in '68.

mine-induced ravings. Perhaps the sense of exhilaration was artificial, but it remained, well . . . exhilarating.

Stations battled each other for ratings, and teenagers had their favorite DJs. Promotion stunts to attract new listeners became valuable tools to the chains. DJs were buried alive; they held contests to see who could stay awake the longest or talk nonstop the longest; they raced down rivers in bathtubs; they sponsored treasure hunts; they threw money off buildings; they hiked barefoot across deserts; they sat on flagpoles.

Many pioneering DJs kept at it even in the chain format, because there were really no alternatives.

Despite their lesser roles, jocks like Jerry Blavatt ("The Geator with the Heator") became stars long after the heyday of the true fire-breathing DJ. Murray the K rode the coattails of the Beatles to stardom, and Wolfman Jack (who never showed his face in public until the Seventies) preserved his outlandish style and his mystique throughout the Sixties, despite a transfer to a southern California pirate.

And while AM Top Forty became ever more conservative, producing such rigid institutions as the Drake chains, the AM dial and Top Forty stations to this day remain a place where sometimes, just sometimes, men can be boys and make a living at it to boot.

THE TEEN IDOLS

BY GREG SHAW

here are few dates that can be clearly pinpointed as turning points in rock & roll. One would be February 3rd, 1959, when Buddy Holly died, and with him, at least symbolically, rock & roll's first rush of breathless innocence.

By a curious coincidence, Holly's death came at a time when several others of equal prominence in the first generation of rockers were also exiting the scene. Within a few years Elvis was in the army, Chuck Berry was in jail, Jerry Lee Lewis had been banned from the airwaves, Eddie Cochran was dead, and Gene Vincent had left the country, his popularity on the wane.

This mass exodus left a void that was instantly filled. From the death of Holly to the arrival of the Beatles, pop music fell into the hands of those same old men of the music industry—promoters, radio programmers, A&R men, record executives—who had long sought a means to remove the unpredictability originally inherent in rock, and to bring the phenomenon (or fad, as they considered it) more into line with their own standards and marketing expertise. From the start, industry elders had been intent on "improving" rock & roll. Young rockabilly singers such as Carl Dobkins, Terry Noland, and, for that matter, Holly and Presley, were given ballad material; their sound was "cleaned up" with orches-

tras and choirs. Many disc jockeys, promoters and TV hosts gave preference to clean-cut singers such as Pat Boone. Thus, while audience demand and the efforts of a few crusading DJs were responsible for occasional hard rock or raunchy R&B hits, the years 1959 to 1963 were, to an overwhelming extent, the Era of the Teen Idol: The music left the streets and moved to the studios.

The results of this shift were not, as has often been claimed, altogether dire. In the hands of such inspired craftsmen as Phil Spector, Bert Berns, Neil Sedaka and Carole King, studio pop rose to truly creative heights. The best records of the era were a product of New York's Brill Building. The worst came out of Philadelphia.

As the home of Dick Clark's *American Bandstand*—at this time the national showcase for rock talent—Philadelphia became the hub of the record business. The city had already spawned its share of doo-wop groups and labels, but it was Clark's move to Philadelphia, and the emergence of record companies geared to grooming teen idols from among the local

Frankie Ford. Would you believe that this is the man who sang ''Sea Cruise''?

Italian populace for exposure on his show, that put Philadelphia on the musical map.

''Philadelphia,'' Phil Spector has recalled, ''was just the most insane, most dynamite, the most beautiful city in the history of rock & roll and the world.'' Its energies ''were just phenomenal. Everyone you met was raging and racing, twenty-four hours a day, seven days a week, and existed for nothing but hype. They existed to pull strokes, conjure deals out of nowhere, juggle hits off nothing. Money was a lot of it, of course, but there was something else as well, a real glee involved; a purist's love of hustle for its own sake.''

Money was, indeed, a lot of it. The machinery was so well constructed that a good-looking teenager could be spotted on the street (as was Fabian, according to legend), cut a record and, aided by a few bribed DJs, within a few weeks have a hit on the national charts—no uncertainties, no risks. It was such a blatant racket that in 1960 it came crashing down under government pressure. But while it flourished, the influence of Philadelphia on the musical tastes of young America was staggering, particularly when compared with the actual musical value of the records being promoted.

The Philadelphia sound was the product chiefly of three companies, Cameo-Parkway, Chancellor and Swan. Each had its house band and arranger, yet the records were virtually interchangeable. Played by bored, middle-aged studio musicians, the music, despite an occasionally tasty saxophone break, at best had an ersatz vivacity. More often, it flaunted the cloying, string-laden blandness that the first rockers had revolted against.

The songs were aimed primarily at teenage girls, the ones in the suburbs who wanted big fluffy candy-colored images of male niceness on which to focus their pubescent dreams. Charming, wholesome dreamboats, the singers were safe and well mannered, perhaps with a teasing tendency toward wildness. The most convincing and successful of the lot were Bobby Rydell, Fabian and Frankie Avalon.

Rydell was a young man with a boyish smile who loved his mother, liked girls a whole lot and wanted someday to be a nightclub entertainer. He was a fairly good singer with a friendly sort of adolescent baritone, and in later years he remained popular with the supper club crowd, although his last Top Forty hit was in 1963. But in five years he had more than twenty chart singles, almost all of them Top Forty. The earliest, such as ''Kissin' Time'' and ''We Got Love,'' were the best, depicting a self-contained world of ponytails and transistor radios, centered around high school, where life's greatest concerns were on the order of who would be going with whom to the dance.

The same set of adolescent themes reappeared on many unbelievably trite hits, but none articulated the high school ethos better than Bobby Rydell in ''Swingin' School.'' Rydell was the mainstay of Cameo Records, a company also renowned for popularizing the twist, through Chubby Checker, and introducing (by rough count) some thirty new dances during the dance craze of 1960–64. The label's biggest rival in Philly was Chancellor, built around the prolific output of Fabian and Frankie Avalon.

Avalon was downright smarmy; Fabian was somewhat better. Well built, slightly oafish, he was discovered by a talent scout who figured looks were the key to rock & roll riches. Fabian was the first to admit he couldn't sing, although he did have a certain native ability. Promoted as the ''Tiger Man,'' Fabian cultivated an image as a rough but safe second Elvis. His hits, like ''Tiger,'' were gruff, but moved along well; one, ''Turn Me Loose,'' by Pomus and Shuman, was actually a fine bluesy number.

While Philadelphia was the center of the teen idol business, it by no means held a monopoly. In New York ABC-Paramount offered stiff competition with Paul Anka, a sixteen-year-old nasal-voiced composer of teen schmaltz who became an overnight

Paul Anka, the Caruso of teen schmaltz, unveils the 1960 model AMI jukebox.

sensation with "Diana" in 1957. Unlike most teen idols, he was a genuine prodigy who had been writing and performing at an early age, who traveled to Hollywood from his home in Canada at the age of fourteen to record with rhythm & blues musicians, and who continued pushing himself until, by his persistence and precociousness, he became a star. He wrote most of his hits, acted in and composed music for a number of serious films, including *The Longest Day*, and possessed a genuine, inborn flair for show business. All the same, his songs were unbelievably mechanical, and lyrically they were pure doggerel. Next to the elegant compositions of his Brill Building contemporaries, what can you say about Anka's couplets?

Surprisingly, New York never developed into the kind of teen meat market that Philadelphia had become. Besides Anka, ABC-Paramount (New York's closest equivalent to Cameo-Parkway) had only Teddy Randazzo and Danny and the Juniors. Randazzo never caught on as a teen idol, and the latter were really more typical of the interests of the New York music scene, where street-corner vocal harmony groups, whether black or Italian, ruled the city.

But in Hollywood it was a different story. Not surprisingly, this city, built on publicity, glamour, fluff and fantasy, became the second home of the teen idol industry. Hollywood talent scouts didn't have to comb the streets looking for pretty faces; this was one commodity the city possessed in surplus. Instead, they looked to the silver screen for young actors and actresses whose already established popularity with millions of viewers would make stupendous record sales a cinch. What chance did a Jodie Sands or a Claudine Clark stand against Annette, the winsome Mouseketeer whose developing bustline had been measured daily by every young male eye in the country?

She couldn't miss, and she didn't. In 1959 and 1960 Annette had eight sizable hit records on Walt Disney's Vista label. Soon every young actor and actress in Hollywood was embarked on a recording career, nearly all of them with some measure of success. Several other Mouseketeers, including Darlene Gillespie, joined Annette; Warner Brothers started a label and began recording such stars as Ed "Kookie" Byrnes, Connie Stevens and Roger Smith (from *Hawaiian Eye* and *77 Sunset Strip*); *The Donna Reed Show* gave us Shelley Fabares and Paul Petersen;

Dick Clark with Annette Funicello, who made a career of singing off-key in numberless beach party movies.

and there was Vincent Edwards *(Ben Casey)*, Johnny Crawford *(The Rifleman)*, James Darren (the *Gidget* movies) and numerous others.

Colpix, the record arm of Columbia Pictures, specialized in teen-screen idols, and through a fortuitous tie-in with Don Kirshner's Aldon Music in New York, they were able to obtain material written by Carole King and Gerry Goffin, and Barry Mann and Cynthia Weil. While they didn't exactly receive the best work of these writers, Colpix at least had professionally crafted commercial songs to cover up the various vocal inadequacies of their stars. (Kirshner was so impressed with Colpix's ability to combine records with TV that he later went to work for them, creating the Monkees and the Archies.)

Of all the Hollywood teen idols, only one can be said to have any claim to lasting importance—Ricky Nelson. At first glance, he seems like all the rest: a cute face, seen on TV every week, making records and trying to pretend he's Elvis. But Nelson was different; in addition to his moody sex appeal and television sinecure, he also happened to have real talent. He was a fine singer whose personal taste ran to raw rockabilly and blues, and whose band, featuring the brilliant guitarist James Burton, was one of the best in all rock & roll. His records were exceptionally tough and exciting, largely free of intrusive orchestration and studio gimmickry, and his material, whether covers of obscure rockers like ''Shirley Lee'' or originals written for him by the likes of ex-rockabilly Johnny Burnette or R&B veteran Baker Knight, was on the whole superb.

In truth, Nelson can more closely be compared with an urban rockabilly like Eddie Cochran than with the run-of-the-mill teen idols of his day. Johnny Burnette, best remembered for his teen ballads ''Dreamin''' and ''You're Sixteen,'' was another singer whose real roots were in the rockabilly scene of Memphis, where he and his brother Dorsey had started out with a wild trio before moving to Hollywood. Burnette wrote some of Nelson's best songs, and is worshiped today in Europe as one of rock's founding figures.

Apart from Nelson, the most successful West Coast teen idol was Bobby Vee, who, like Burnette, began his career in the heart of the country. He grew up in North Dakota, and throughout high school fronted a hard-rocking band called the Shadows. Vee's career really began the night after Buddy Holly's plane crash, when he took his place at the concert Holly had been scheduled to headline in Fargo, North Dakota. Symbolically as well as literally, Bobby Vee personified the new era that had arrived. Though bearing an uncanny vocal resemblance to Holly, Vee was content to crank out the smooth, studio-crafted teen fodder handed him by his producers, chiefly Snuff Garrett. In his high school sweater, there was nothing menacing or primitive about him, no hint of anything black, or Southern, or even from the wrong side of town. He was the boy next door, just like all the other boys and girls next door who peopled the era of the teen idol.

A disproportionate number of the successful teen idols were boys, who supposedly would appeal to adolescent girls, the primary market for this music; indeed, most of the female teen idols also based their appeal on identification with the same audience. Apparently it was felt, rightly or wrongly, that the male audience was more interested in rock's dark and violent side. On the other hand, each of the three most successful female teen idols possessed some special quality that set them apart. Annette must surely have sold more records to boys than the average girl singer. The two biggest female stars, however, were Brenda Lee and Connie Francis, both of whom relied on purely musical attributes for their appeal.

Connie Francis, with her mature contralto, never seemed really teenage to me, even when singing about lipstick on collars and guys named Frankie. In fact, she merely used the teen fad to launch a career as a mainstream pop singer, quickly becoming entrenched in Spain and Italy, where she recorded extensively in the native languages. Her early records were perky rockers like ''Stupid Cupid,'' or lush romantic ballads like ''Who's Sorry Now,'' and as pop records they were undeniably good. Connie Francis

Connie Francis with Dick Clark. He gave the idols an outlet on *American Bandstand*.

is said to have had more hit records than any female singer in history, but it wasn't only teenagers who bought them.

Brenda Lee, on the other hand, was essentially a country stylist who was thrust into the role of rock singer, drawing on her roots to come up with a unique sort of female rockabilly style. She started with rock young (her early records list her as "Little Brenda Lee—Nine Years Old"), and stayed with it throughout the Sixties (even recording in England with Jimmy Page in 1964).

Today, there are tried and proven formulas for achieving results in most areas of rock, but in those days nobody could say for sure which were the essential ingredients for success in this new, mysterious and incredibly lucrative field of teenage music. The teen idol era was a product of the assumption that kids were endlessly gullible, utterly tasteless and dependably aroused by a comely face or a gratuitous mention of "high school" or "bobby sox." This assumption ultimately proved disastrously self-limiting, but not before dozens of teen idols had crooned, croaked and smiled their ways into the Top Ten.

Of the hundreds of would-be teen idols, though, only a handful really had a lasting impact. In addition to those already discussed, there was of course Pat Boone, who began as a safe alternative to Elvis, and is still a safe alternative to just about everything. Others who prospered during this era but really belong more to the mainstream pop tradition include Neil Sedaka, Gene Pitney, Bobby Darin, Tommy Sands, Tony Orlando and Bobby Vinton.

Some of the runners-up, who enjoyed a hit or two but never quite broke out, included Rod Lauren, Johnny Restivo, Tab Hunter, Jerry Wallace, Adam Wade, Gary Stites, Mark Valentino, Kenny Dino, Mark Dinning, Johnny Tillotson, Ray Peterson, Jimmy Clanton, Bob Crewe and Nick Venet (both of whom gave up promising careers as teen idols to become leading record producers), Mike Clifford, Brian Hyland, Ral Donner, Teddy Randazzo, Curtis Lee, Frankie Sardo, Len Barry, Paul Evans, Larry Finnegan, Jerry Fuller, Clint Miller, Robin Luke, Larry Hall, Bobby Curtola, Deane Hawley and Troy Shondell.

DISCOGRAPHY

Teen Idols in the Top Ten, 1955–1962
SINGLES

Paul Anka: "Diana" (ABC-Paramount; ☆2, 1957). "You Are My Destiny" (ABC-Paramount; ☆7, 1958). "Lonely Boy" (ABC-Paramount; ☆1, 1959). "Put Your Head on My Shoulder" (ABC-Paramount; ☆2, 1959). "It's Time to Cry" (ABC-Paramount; ☆4, 1959). "Puppy Love" (ABC-Paramount; ☆2, 1960). "My Home Town" (ABC-Paramount; ☆8, 1960). "Dance On Little Girl" (ABC-Paramount; ☆10, 1961). **Annette:** "Tall Paul" (Disneyland; ☆7, 1959). "O Dio Mio" (Vista; ☆10, 1960). **Frankie Avalon:** "Dede Dinah" (Chancellor; ☆7, 1958). "Ginger Bread" (Chancellor; ☆9, 1958). "Venus" (Chancellor; ☆1, 1959). "Bobby Sox to Stockings" b/w "A Boy Without a Girl" (Chancellor; ☆8, 1959). "Just Ask Your Heart" (Chancellor; ☆7, 1959). "Why" (Chancellor; ☆1, 1959). **Pat Boone:** "At My Front Door (Crazy Little Mama)" (Dot; ☆7, 1955). "I'll Be Home" (Dot; ☆5, 1956). "I Almost Lost My Mind" (Dot; ☆1, 1956). "Friendly Persuasion" (Dot; ☆8, 1956). "Don't Forbid Me" (Dot; ☆1, 1956). "Why Baby Why" (Dot; ☆6, 1957). "Love Letters in the Sand" (Dot; ☆1, 1957). "April Love" (Dot; ☆1, 1957). "A Wonderful Time Up There" (Dot; ☆10, 1958). "Moody River" (Dot; ☆1, 1961). "Speedy Gonzales" (Dot; ☆6, 1962). **Fabian:** "Turn Me Loose" (Chancellor; ☆9, 1959). "Tiger" (Chancellor; ☆3, 1959). "Hound Dog Man" (Chancellor; ☆9, 1959). **Connie Francis:** "Who's Sorry Now" (MGM; ☆4, 1958). "My Happiness" (MGM; ☆2, 1958). "Lipstick on Your Collar" b/w "Frankie" (MGM; ☆5, 1959). "Among My Souvenirs" (MGM; ☆7, 1959). "Mama" (MGM; ☆8, 1960). "Everybody's Somebody's Fool" (MGM; ☆1, 1960). "My Heart Has a Mind of Its Own" (MGM; ☆1, 1960). "Many Tears Ago" (MGM; ☆7, 1960). "Where the Boys Are" (MGM; ☆4, 1961). "Breakin' in a Brand New Broken Heart" (MGM; ☆7, 1961). "Together" (MGM; ☆6, 1961). "When the Boy in Your Arms" (MGM; ☆10, 1961). "Don't Break the Heart That Loves You" (MGM; ☆1, 1962). "Second Hand Love" (MGM; ☆7, 1962). "Vacation" (MGM; ☆9, 1962). **Brenda Lee:** "Sweet Nothin's" (Decca; ☆4, 1959). "I'm Sorry" b/w "That's All You Gotta Do" (Decca; ☆1, 1960). "I Want to Be Wanted" (Decca; ☆1, 1960). "Emotions" (Decca; ☆7, 1961). "You Can Depend on Me" (Decca; ☆6, 1961). "Dum Dum" (Decca; ☆4, 1961). "Fool #1" (Decca; ☆3, 1961). "Break It to Me Gently" (Decca; ☆4, 1962). "Everybody Loves Me but You" (Decca; ☆6, 1962). "All Alone Am I" (Decca; ☆3, 1962). "Losing You" (Decca; ☆6, 1963). **Ricky Nelson:** "A Teenager's Romance" (Verve; ☆8, 1957). "Be-Bop Baby" (Imperial; ☆5, 1957). "Stood Up" (Imperial; ☆5, 1957). "Believe What You Say" (Imperial; ☆8, 1958). "Poor Little Fool" (Imperial; ☆1, 1958). "Lonesome Town" b/w "I Got a Feeling" (Imperial; ☆7, 1958). "Never Be Anyone Else but You" b/w "It's Late" (Imperial; ☆6, 1959). "Sweeter Than You" b/w "Just a Little Too Much" (Imperial; ☆9, 1959). "Travelin' Man" b/w "Hello Mary Lou" (Imperial; ☆1, 1961). "Young World" (Imperial; ☆5, 1962). "Teen Age Idol" (Imperial; ☆5, 1962). "It's Up to You" (Imperial; ☆6, 1962). **Bobby Rydell:** "We Got Love" (Cameo; ☆6, 1959). "Wild One" (Cameo; ☆2, 1960). "Swingin' School" (Cameo; ☆5, 1960). "Volare" (Cameo; ☆4, 1960). "The Cha-Cha-Cha" (Cameo; ☆10, 1962). "Forget Him" (Cameo; ☆4, 1963). **Bobby Vee:** "Devil or Angel" (Liberty; ☆6, 1960). "Rubber Ball" (Liberty; ☆6, 1960). "Take Good Care of My Baby" (Liberty; ☆1, 1961). "Run to Him" (Liberty; ☆2, 1961). "The Night Has a Thousand Eyes" (Liberty; ☆3, 1962).

(Chart positions compiled from Joel Whitburn's *Record Research*, based on *Billboard*'s Pop chart.)

ROCKFILM, ROLLFILM

BY CARRIE RICKEY

I am still of opinion that only two topics can be of the least interest to a serious and studious mind—sex and the dead.''
—William Butler Yeats

In the Beginning—before Elvis, before rock & roll, even—there was a routine juvenile-delinquent picture, *Knock on Any Door* (1949), starring John Derek as the punk and Humphrey Bogart as a conscience-stricken attorney who comes to realize that his teen-aged client is a "victim of society." What makes the otherwise forgettable *Knock on Any Door* indelible and key to any discussion of rock & roll films is not Bogey's idealism but Derek's antisocial credo, one that distills the essence of rock's attitude as well as its philosophy. Snarls Derek, giving voice to his ambitions: "I wanna live fast, die young and leave a beautiful corpse!"

Such high ideals, so little time.

B.D. and A.D.—that is to say, Before Drugs and After Drugs (and, yes, during the drug era too)—rock flirted with sex and death, possibly the only two things that, for youth rebels, defied the bogus conventions of Life as Parents Lived It. Where rock & roll flirted with sex and death, rockfilms went all the way. "Sex and the dead," the two topics Yeats identified as likely to appeal to "the serious and studious mind," heartily appealed to those folks confecting

movies about the fast-living, hard-loving guys and gals who sometimes chose the wrong recreational drug and/or opted for a doomed vehicle. Thus they died young. Alas, their corpses, whether that of Jim Morrison in *The Doors* (1991) or that of the Bette Midler character in *The Rose* (1979), were not always beautiful.

Let's play a game. Call it Rockfilm, Rollfilm. The object is to identify the distinctive features of the rock-movie genre, the qualities that make rock roll. First we must exclude concert movies like *The T.A.M.I. Show* (1964), *Monterey Pop* (1969), *Woodstock* (1970), *Joe Cocker: Mad Dogs and Englishmen* (1971), *The Last Waltz* (1978) and *Sign O' the Times* (1987). Although inarguably terrific, they are more significant archivally, as time-capsule documents, than as films. Rock & roll may be here to stay, but rock doesn't belong in a time capsule; its urgent context is of the moment.

Next we'd have to exclude cinema-verité chronicles like *Don't Look Back* (1967), *Gimme Shelter* (1970), *The Decline of Western Civilization* (1981) and *The Decline of Western Civilization Part II: The Metal*

Years (1988). Also terrific, these are portraits of the artists significant precisely because they demystify their musical subjects. Unfortunately, myth is the stuff from which enduring rockfilms are spun.

Now, we'd also have to exclude those film equivalents of vanity publications, hagio-rock-docs enthusiastically authorized by their subjects: the Rolling Stones in *Let's Spend the Night Together* (1982), *The Beach Boys: An American Band* (1985), Chuck Berry in *Hail! Hail! Rock 'n' Roll* (1987), U2: *Rattle and Hum* (1988), Quincy Jones in *Listen Up!* (1990) and Madonna in *Truth or Dare* (1991). If, by its very nature,

rock & roll is unauthorized, then authorized rockfilms are contradictions in terms.

What's left, you ask? Movies about youthful charisma, narcissism and sex appeal all dressed up (or down, if you prefer) in death-defying, sometimes death-embracing, attitude.

THE STONE AGE OF ROCKFILM

Despite the foreshadowing of rock attitude in *Knock on Any Door*, it wasn't until *The Blackboard Jungle* (1955), a pre-rock film, that the potent mix of teen-

The Blackboard Jungle: Rock & roll rebellion is born.

age rage and raging hormones were shaken, rattled and rolled into a musical Molotov cocktail. What with Bill Haley and His Comets' "Rock Around the Clock" pulsing on the soundtrack and youth rebel Vic Morrow smashing a Bix Beiderbecke disc, *The Blackboard Jungle* matched antiestablishment sound to its antiauthoritarian image. *That*'s the essence of rockfilm, one amply understood by today's music video directors.

Rock needed film to create personas for its performers. While rock & roll would have been a momentous musical force by itself, by marrying sound with image, the movies made rock a cultural juggernaut. Before *The Blackboard Jungle*, there had been music in movies for almost thirty years, and, to be sure, there had been movie musicals. The syncopated romances of Fred Astaire and Ginger Rogers. The Jeanette MacDonald–Nelson Eddy operettas so wooden they required termite inspection. The symphonic musicals in which Gene Kelly fell in love variously with Judy Garland, Vera-Ellen and . . . Gene Kelly. Or to put in another way, there had been musicals about grown-ups in love but not musicals about teenagers in heat. What the first rockfilms did was characterize a youth culture entirely distinct from that of adults. Rockfilms targeted teens, a previously unexploited demographic group, at the moment increasing numbers of grown-ups were staying home to watch TV.

The evolution of rockfilms essentially follows human evolution, but with a twist. In the first stage, nubile innocence is showcased, giving us the Sexwatch movie. In the next stage, we wallow in the experience of meteoric stars who burn out, giving us the Deathwatch film. These developments culminate in the type of rockfilm in which the music industry capitalizes on its backlist (the Nostalgia film). Then there is the triple-threat film, like *The Buddy Holly Story, La Bamba* or *The Doors,* which embrace all three genres of rockfilm.

ROCKFILM AROUND THE CLOCK, OR THE AGE OF INNOCENCE

The first rockfilm star was not, as you might suspect, Elvis. It was another "hillbilly with a beat"—as he was described in one of the interchangeable proto-rockfilms—Bill Haley. Hard to believe this guy with the big smile and bigger girth galvanized a generation in piffle such as *Rock Around the Clock* (1956) and *Don't Knock the Rock* (1957).

In these quickies Haley typically played a musician who appealed to teenagers although their parents accused him of making barbaric noise. All was forgiven by the last reel, when hep teens and their square parents found themselves dancing to the same drumbeat. Essentially a cheerful apostle of the new sound, Haley had a doughy sex appeal, but lacked the necessary rebel shadings and contours (and attitude) that made Elvis the King of Kings.

The moment the heavy-lidded Elvis swaggered onto the screen in *Jailhouse Rock* (1957), his third picture, *the* rockfilm star was born. Elvis was James Dean with a guitar. He exuded sex. He didn't care if he was behind bars. He didn't care if he lived to see tomorrow. He didn't give a damn about expressing anything but his sex drive and hostility to the establishment.

Elvis made a host of subsequent movies, including the excellent *King Creole* (1958) and *Flaming Star* (1960), but except for the fact that he sings a song or two, these aren't rock movies, per se, but exist in their own special galaxy: The Elvis Movie. There are some who darkly suggest that *Viva Las Vegas* (1964), costarring Ann-Margret, was the transformational experience that metamorphosized Elvis from a rock star into a Vegas lounge lizard.

Jailhouse Rock suggested a subliminal link between rock and crime, something the flamboyantly entertaining *The Girl Can't Help It* (1956) made cartoonishly explicit. Written and directed by satirist Frank Tashlin and featuring the Platters, Little Richard, Gene Vincent and Fats Domino, this farce about a mobster (Edmond O'Brien) who tries to turn his buxom girlfriend (Jayne Mansfield) into a rock star boldly states that talent has nothing to do with becoming a rock legend. You need only these three things: 1) low friends in high places to "fix" jukebox distribution; 2 and 3) big breasts. Apart from its understanding that the music industry was completely dominated by racketeers, *The Girl Can't Help It* moreover lampooned *Jailhouse Rock* in that witty ditty, "Rockpile Rock."

The rockstar phenom was likewise satirized in the British *Expresso Bongo* (1960), starring Laurence Harvey as the huckster who surprises even himself when he catapults the nondescript bongo-playing

The Girl Can't Help It, indeed, from 1956.

Cliff Richard into international stardom. Based on the popular play by Soho scribe Wolf Mankowitz, which took sport with overnight sensation Tommy Steele, *Expresso Bongo* illustrates how so-called innocence and raw sex appeal are manipulated and marketed by the industry.

A HARD DAY'S NIGHT, OR THE AGE OF INNOCENCE, THE SEQUEL

Apart from *Muscle Beach Party* (1964), which featured the welcome presence of ''Little'' Stevie Wonder, American rockfilms of the Sixties are primarily of archival interest today: the rollicking, pluralistic lineup of *The T.A.M.I. Show* (1964), the angry young Dylan in *Don't Look Back* (1967). It took director Richard Lester and four mop-tops called the Beatles to create *the* definitive rockfilm of the decade, *A Hard*

Day's Night (1964), the giddy, through-the-looking-glass adventures of the fast-living, faster-loving, fastest-talking pop combo. John, Paul, George and Ringo were young, sexy and sardonic—and, according to this lively pseudo biography, more amused than amazed by their celebrity. Four robust animals in their prime, the Beatles replaced the surly sexuality of Elvis with tilted British humor. Their film followups, *Help!* (1965) and *Yellow Submarine* (1968), are merely footnotes to the superlative *A Hard Day's Night*.

ARE YOU EXPERIENCED?

If this were a multiple-choice exam, the question would read, Which movie brought the rockfilm into the age of experience? Was it *Easy Rider* (1969), a kind of filmed FM radio show, which suggested the dark fate in store for those rebels who dropped out and tuned in? Was it *Performance* (1970), which, without irony or shame, established a bloody link between mobster and rocker? Was it *Let It Be* (1970), the Beatles documentary that gloomily chronicled the group's divorce? Was it *Gimme Shelter* (1970), the cinema-verité account of the Rolling Stones concert at Altamont, during which Meredith Hunter was murdered, the film that suggested—in critic Robert Christgau's words—that the Stones were guilty not of criminal negligence but criminal irony? The answer: All of the above.

Immediately following this eruption of turn-of-the-decade violence, the rockfilm entered its fatalistic—and also its mythic—age. Although rockers didn't want to die in Vietnam, onscreen they died in droves. Thus the Deathwatch rockfilm was born, the kind of movie where no matter what transpired, the hero's untimely death at the end validated and/or redeemed him. (With few exceptions, it was usually a him.)

What *A Hard Day's Night* was to the Sixties, *The Harder They Come* (1973) was to the Seventies. Starring that tightly coiled bundle of raw nerve, Jimmy Cliff, as a Jamaican bumpkin yearning to become a reggae star, *The Harder They Come* was a smooth blend of ganja, exuberance, lewdness and lawlessness, that equated a Top Ten hit with being on the ten-most-wanted list. *The Harder They Come,* moreover, played seriously something that *The Girl Can't Help It* and *Expresso Bongo* played for laughs: That talent won't get you entrée into the rock biz, but being a famous criminal will. Cliff's martyrdom at the film's finale elevated his character into a rock icon.

Likewise, *The Buddy Holly Story* (1978) celebrated the life of rock's first martyr, tenderly embodied by a soft-spoken Gary Busey as the rocker who gave us ''That'll Be the Day'' before he died in a plane crash. Made almost twenty years after Holly died (interestingly, at a moment the first generation of rockers were parents of their own teenage rebels and the year that other nostalgic movies like *American Hot Wax* and *I Wanna Hold Your Hand* were released), *Buddy Holly* embraces the three ages of rockfilm. It's about an innocent rube who goes to the big city to gain experience—and martyrdom. It revives old music for a new generation. It's *The Glenn Miller Story* of its day.

A fictionalized version of the life of Janis Joplin, *The Rose* (1979) stars Bette Midler as the high-flying singer who thought she was on ''automatic pilot'' but instead pressed ''self-destruct.'' Propelled by

Free Elvis! *Jailhouse Rock,* 1957.

Midler's high-octane performance, *The Rose* is a cautionary tale about the rigors of the sauce and the sack.

While rock martyrs were thus getting disinterred, there came a pair of movies suggesting that rock was also a means of upward mobility. One, the Fifties-era *That'll Be the Day* (1974), starred David Essex as a Lennonoid Liverpudlian struggling to transcend his charmless milieu. The other was *Saturday Night Fever* (1977), a disco insta-classic starring John Travolta as a working-class kid from Brooklyn who wins a dance contest and has dreams of conquering Manhattan. Both films were unusual for their contrast of downbeat realism with upbeat music, and both have the anxious edge necessary to real rockfilms.

PUNK SPUNK

Thank God for punk, or else rockfilms might have been mired in disco and we would have had the *The Donna Summer Story*. There were serious movies like *Rude Boy* (1980) and *Sid & Nancy* (1986) that burst onto the screen and combined irreverence and fatalism. And there were also comedies like *Rock 'n' Roll High School* (1979) and *Hairspray* (1988)—warped rethinks of the very first rockfilms that captured the liberating qualities of rock, its tonic exuberance. What dialogue can match that of Mary Woronov as the Our Miss Brooks from Hell in *Rock 'n' Roll High School,* demanding of a certain punker, ''Does YOUR mother know you're a Ramone?'' As directed by the eccentric Alex Cox, *Sid & Nancy* is the apotheosis of the Deathwatch. In this movie about rocker Sid Vicious and his groupie-turned-Juliet Nancy Spungen, a pair of junkies find self-knowledge—and transcendence—in their own self-destruction.

There was also the occasional purely innocent, pure fun punk film such as Gillian Armstrong's *Starstruck* (1982), about a Sydney, Australia, punkette—a Down Under Cyndi Lauper, really—who finds self-expression in the punk idiom and refuses to let music industry mavens make her sing Lesley Gore–like ballads. *Starstruck* captures the essence of

rockfilm innocence in that it exuberantly shows that music provides youth with an outlet for self-definition.

DEAD OR BRAIN DEAD?

Punk exploded at about the same time rock legends Paul Simon and Paul McCartney examined their own mid-career crises in the respective vanity productions, *One Trick Pony* (1980) and *Give My Regards to Broad Street* (1984). Both films were dopey, and the latter gave rise to the quip, ''We'd heard Paul was dead. We hadn't heard he was brain dead.'' Amid this male menopause, two entirely original films got released and spread, funguslike, across the country.

With its deadpan and dead-on wit, *This Is Spinal Tap* (1984) satirized heavy metal, rock documentar-

Nancy and Sid: the deathwatch at its deadliest.

ies and music-industry misogyny so precisely that many viewers thought it was about a real band. With its lively music and performances, *Purple Rain* (1984) crowned Prince successor to the King of Rock. Not since Elvis had a rockfilm smoldered with the hero's own self-love and charisma, so feverishly depicted a portrait of the artist as a manchild in conflict and in heat.

Elvis in a characteristic scene from a characteristic movie.

Discounting the over-art-directed and underwritten *Great Balls of Fire!* (1989), a whitewashed version of the life of Jerry Lee Lewis memorable only for the presence of yummy Winona Ryder as the Killer's nymphet cousin and wife, the Eighties included two excellent Deathwatch biopics. The Ritchie Valens story *La Bamba* (1987), a Deathwatch dressed up as a Cain-and-Abel story, featured memorable performances by Lou Diamond Phillips and Esai Morales as the Valenzuela brothers. The Patsy Cline saga *Sweet Dreams* (1985) suffered from the lumpiness that invariably troubles films based on real people—real life is never as shapely as fiction—but was blessed by sharp dialogue and sharper acting by Jessica Lange as Patsy Cline and Ann Wedgeworth as her mother.

The Beatles with some nice people in *A Hard Day's Night.*

Jimmy Cliff as the legendary Jamaican outlaw Rhygin in Perry Henzell's film, *The Harder They Come.*

Funny thing about Deathwatch films, they get the best out of actors. Even Oliver Stone's hyper-allegorical *The Doors* (1991), about Jim Morrison, the sex-and-death-obsessed poet and would-be filmmaker, is redeemed by Val Kilmer's reincarnation of the Lizard King. Watching the Deathwatch films with their youthful rock martyrs—"members of the 27 club," they used to call Janis and Jimi and Jim, all of whom checked out at age twenty-seven—reminds

John Travolta in *Saturday Night Fever.*

you that death is the most expedient resolution to any narrative conflict. Moreover, in the case of Ritchie Valens in *La Bamba* and Jim Morrison in *The Doors,* you have to think, ''Thank God they died.'' Had they lived, they might have ended up like the beached whale that is Brian Wilson in the rockumentary *The Beach Boys: An American Band.*

The Deathwatch rockfilms illustrate the fulfillment of the Who's most famous lyric, itself a gloss on John Derek's *Knock on Any Door* death wish: ''Hope I die before I get old.''

Gary Busey in *The Buddy Holly Story.*

Two scenes from *Performance,* a trip into the abyss directed by Donald Cammell and Nicholas Roeg.

The Ramones, in a cheesy youth riot film, fiddling while Vince Lombardi High burns. From *Rock'n'Roll High School,* 1979.

THE PAYOLA SCANDAL

BY JOHN MORTHLAND

Payola—the narrow definition: pay (cash or gifts) for radio airplay—has been a factor in radio since the medium's inception. In the Fifties the practice flourished among rock & roll disc jockeys. Payola padded their frequently paltry salaries, and it helped the new music reach its intended audience, no matter how small the label on which it appeared. By the late Fifties, in fact, a swarm of independent labels recording rock had broken the stranglehold of the majors—in particular Columbia, RCA and Decca—on the sales and airplay of popular records.

These developments displeased not only the older labels, but also the American Society of Composers, Authors and Publishers (ASCAP). In the Thirties and Forties ASCAP had thrived on the sales of sheet music, piano rolls and recordings of Tin Pan Alley songs; but the advent, in the early Forties, of radio formats geared to recorded music created new conditions in the industry. After a battle between radio stations and ASCAP over royalty payments, the stations decided to boycott recordings registered with ASCAP, and in 1940 began operating their own publishing corporation, Broadcast Music Incorporated (BMI). Since ASCAP tended to ignore music composed by blacks and hillbillies, BMI ended up with

a virtual monopoly on songs in those fields—a monopoly strengthened by the fact that many record-playing stations catered to regional tastes ignored by the major networks. When rock & roll—at first the music of blacks and hillbillies—broke, BMI was there first, too.

So it was hardly surprising when ASCAP, in 1959, urged a House Legislative Oversight subcommittee chaired by Representative Oren Harris to broaden its investigation of corrupt broadcasting practices—then centered on rigged TV quiz shows—to include the practice of payola in radio. When Representative Harris announced that his subcommittee would probe payola, *Variety* reported that

Freed on the air.

ASCAP songsmiths took credit for switching the spotlight from TV quiz rigging to disc jockey payola. The assumption was that songs copyrighted with BMI would be revealed as having become hits fraudulently, thanks to payola.

Twisted as this logic appears, it was very much in the mainstream of American thinking at the time. From the beginning, rock & roll had been the object of virulent attacks: Many insisted that it was a source of a breakdown of morals among youth, that it encouraged miscegenation, that it was a subversive tool of Godless Communism. It was commonly believed the music was so terrible that teenagers listened to it only because they had been tricked into doing so by greedy DJs who pocketed payola and then played a record so often it was imprinted on listeners' impressionable young minds. Many considered rock & roll a passing fad that would soon die out; the payola hearings were in part an attempt to ensure this, and thus it was perfectly appropriate to hold those hearings in the election year 1960.

Industry response was swift. In Philadelphia ABC-TV told *American Bandstand* host Dick Clark either to give up the program or to sell his shares in music-related firms, from record labels to publishing houses. Clark chose the latter course, and signed an affidavit denying any involvement in payola. When Alan Freed, on WABC radio, refused "on principle" to sign a similar affidavit, the station fired him.

Other disc jockeys around the country were also dismissed.

Prior to House hearings, the Federal Trade Commission (FTC) filed payola complaints against a number of record manufacturers and distributors, claiming that the practice represented "unfair competition"; the companies had thirty days to file a consent order, or face an FTC examiner. Since a consent order did not constitute an admission of guilt, most labels agreed to eliminate payola. As a result, the independents found themselves back in withering competition with the majors and their superior publicity and distribution networks. In the following years, many of the small companies recording rock folded.

Meanwhile, in New York, District Attorney Frank Hogan announced that his assistant, Joseph Stone, would convene grand jury hearings, and seek misdemeanor commercial bribery charges against culpable DJs.

The House hearings began on February 8th, 1960, and focused on disc jockeys from Cleveland and Boston. The witnesses in the first week were typical of those to follow. David Maynard (WBZ-Boston) admitted taking $6000 in cash and gifts for promoting records—but only at "record hops." Joseph Smith (WILD-Boston) admitted he got royalties on the sales in his area of two recent hit records; between these royalties and other gifts and cash, he had made $8995 in a three-year period, beyond his $117 weekly salary.

Since a major payola issue had been vacations for DJs funded by record companies, another scandal erupted on March 4th, when it was revealed that John C. Doerfer, chairman of the Federal Communications Commission, had himself just enjoyed a six-day junket in Florida, courtesy of the Storer Broadcasting Company. President Eisenhower asked for his resignation and had it within the week. On the same day, subcommittee member John B. Bennett stated that they should give up on "small-fry DJs" and look into Dick Clark, whom Bennett asserted was "obviously seriously involved in payola."

Clark appeared before the Harris subcommittee at the end of April. To aid in his defense, he hired a statistician, Bernard Goldstein; while admitting that Clark had a personal interest in records representing 27 percent of the "spins" on *American Bandstand* over a twenty-eight-month period, Goldstein argued that these records had in any case what he called a "popularity score" of 23.9, which "proved" that Clark was playing records because listeners wanted to hear them, not because Clark stood to gain financially. Observers were bewildered by Goldstein's computations and correlations, but any doubts about conflict of interest were laid to rest by Clark himself when he testified.

Freed *(left)* with two of the performers he helped make famous: Little Richard *(center)* and Bill Haley.

Speaking in a soft tone, Clark explained how he had given up whole or part interest in thirty-three businesses since the payola issue had surfaced; he'd become involved in that many businesses, he later said, to take advantage of tax laws. True, he'd profited from his investments. For example, Clark had originally invested $125 in Jamie Records, a Philadelphia label that included Duane Eddy among its acts; he eventually sold his stock for a profit of $11,900. True, he owned rights to 160 songs, 143 of which he claimed had been given to him; but Clark denied ever plugging any of them "consciously." True, Jamie Records had doled out $15,000 worth of payola; but Clark testified that he had never accepted any payola himself.

The subcommittee didn't completely swallow Clark's explanations, but at the end of the hearing, Representative Harris called Clark a "fine young man." Their payola probe finished, the subcommittee recommended anti-payola amendments to the Federal Communications Act. The amendments, which became law on September 13th, 1960, prohibited the payment of cash or gifts in exchange for airplay, and held radio stations responsible for any employees who accepted cash or gifts.

Meanwhile, on May 19th, 1960, Joseph Stone's grand jury in New York had handed down commercial bribery informations—the misdemeanor equivalent of an indictment—charging eight men with receiving a total of $116,580 in illegal gratuities. The big name was Alan Freed; he had been the only DJ subpoenaed, and had refused to testify despite an offer of immunity. He was served two informations charging twenty-nine counts.

Freed, the disc jockey most vociferous in his support of rock & roll, took the fall for the scandal. He didn't stand trial until December 1962, when he finally pleaded guilty to two counts of commercial bribery. He was fined $300 and given a six-month suspended sentence. That should have been the end of his troubles, but on March 15th, 1964, he was indicted by a federal grand jury, this time for income tax evasion. The Internal Revenue Service claimed that he owed $37,920 on unreported income of $56,652 for the years 1957 through 1959. Freed was living in Palm Springs at the time; he was a poor man, unemployed and unemployable. At the end of the year, before he was able to answer the new charges, Freed entered a hospital, suffering from uremia. A few weeks later, on January 20th, 1965, he died. He was forty-three.

Dick Clark shows the kids how it's done. He came out of the payola scandal clean.

THE INSTRUMENTAL GROUPS

BY GREG SHAW

No year goes by without a couple of instrumental rock hits, each usually built on a simple riff, a catchy melody or some piece of electronic gimmickry. They're novelty records and their role in rock has been minimal, with the important exception of a brief period in the early Sixties when instrumentals were one of the most vital trends in the music.

Originally, rock instrumentals were provided by the rhythm & blues dance combos that flourished in the early Fifties. These bands usually featured organists or honky-tonk pianists like Cecil Gant and Bill Doggett (who had once served as the boogie specialist in Lionel Hampton's big band), or gutsy sax players such as Joe Houston, Jimmy Beasley, King Curtis, Jimmy Forrest, Lee Allen, Gene Barge, Plas Johnson and Clifford Scott (who played on Doggett's 1956 ''Honky Tonk,'' the first big rock instrumental hit). Bands like Doggett's combo, featuring the influential Billy Butler on guitar, rocked nightly at roadhouses throughout the land, bringing to rock an improvisational approach derived from jazz via boogie-woogie.

Such bands remained popular at dances, but by 1957 black music had become almost purely vocal as far as recording was concerned. White rock, meanwhile, could be divided into two categories:

the studio-manufactured teen idols, and the powerful but unpolished rockabilly singers. If rhythm & blues was the genuine teenage music of the big cities, rockabilly represented the grass-roots music of the South. But undiluted rockabilly had little commercial appeal; by the late Fifties, white rock had come to be almost completely monopolized by teen idols and the centralized media machinery that packaged and promoted them.

As if in response to this amputation of rock & roll from its roots, in the late Fifties white instrumental bands began appearing throughout the country, helping to keep the music alive at a local level and directly influencing the English bands that would bring rock out of its doldrums later on in the Sixties.

Instrumental groups were almost without exception a regional phenomenon, a product of the local music scenes that have been the source of virtually every significant innovation in rock & roll. As a

Duane Eddy, the man with the "Twangy Guitar."

general rule, professional musicians in the music capitals—New York, Los Angeles and London—had become insulated from influences outside the music industry, while local bands, playing every night in front of audiences with whom they had a direct rapport, initiated new styles, dances and music developments. The immediacy of this interaction between fans and musicians has been crucial to rock's evolutionary process.

But why instrumental bands, anyway? In the early days of rock, bands had existed to back a singer, usually a Presley imitator (it was easy enough to twitch about and mumble something like "gonna bop-a-bop-a muh a buh-a-buh-a-baby tuh-nite"). A lot of early instrumental groups, such as the Rock-a-Teens, continued to feature vocalists on some numbers, but the rockabilly style of singing was becoming dated, while the new teen ballad style depended on songs and productions crafted in the big studios of New York and Philadelphia. In any case, these bands just wanted to rock, and they played for

audiences that just wanted to drink and dance. So why not dispense with the singer altogether?

The earliest instrumental rock hits had featured saxophones, piano or drums—for example, Bill Doggett's "Honky Tonk," Bill Justis's "Raunchy" and Cozy Cole's "Topsy." Toward the end of 1958, guitars, the predominant instruments in rockabilly, gradually took over instrumental rock. The tunes the groups recorded were usually simple, relying on some gimmick (like the bug being swatted in "The Green Mosquito" by the Tune Rockers). Other instrumentals, however, succeeded in creating an intense mood, whether slow and menacing (Link Wray's "Rumble") or wild and frantic (Johnny and the Hurricanes' "Crossfire").

Link Wray was the most volatile and sophisticated guitarist to emerge from this period. He was a powerful, inventive player, doing things with dynamics and rhythm that would later inspire Pete Townshend and Eric Clapton.

The most successful instrumental rocker of the period, however, was Duane Eddy, a young man from Phoenix who developed (with his producer, Lee Hazlewood) a style known as "twangy" guitar. His hits featured a relaxed, bluesy guitar figure played on the bass strings, a raunchy but restrained sax break, and occasional whoops from the band, all set to an easy, loping beat. This formula carried Eddy through nearly twenty top hits and made him one of America's biggest international stars, especially in England, where instrumentals (popularized by the Shadows, the Tornadoes and dozens of other groups) virtually dominated the rock scene. (Holland, Sweden and Japan also elevated instrumentals to a level of importance never matched in the United States.)

The year 1959 yielded a bumper crop of instrumental hits. By now every American city claimed an instrumental band as hometown favorites. The difficulty of bridging the gap between the simple shuffles a dancing audience liked and the kind of catchy statement required for a Top Forty hit prevented most of them from making the charts more than once—although in those days of free programming, a record could easily be a large hit locally or regionally without denting the national Hot 100. The twist arrived in 1960, and subsequent dance crazes through 1962 provided plenty of work for thousands of these bands, although twist records in general lacked the impact of the best instrumental hits.

By far the most important instrumental band of the era was the Ventures. The pride of Seattle, they were the kingpins of the Northwest rock scene that also produced the Wailers, the Frantics, the Viceroys, the Bluenotes, the Sonics, the Dynamics and the Kingsmen. Their music wasn't raunchy like that of the other Northwest groups, however; it was smooth, polished and technically precise. Their important hits were "Walk—Don't Run" and "Perfidia," both in 1960, but they survived into the Seventies, recording over fifty albums and inspiring legions of guitarists the world over.

If I had to name the most representative group of the period, though, it would have to be Johnny and the Hurricanes. Their story is typical.

The group was started by sax player Johnny Paris while he was still in high school just outside Toledo, Ohio. After a couple years playing dances and nightclubs, a local vocal group asked them to provide backing for an audition in Detroit. The singers flunked the audition, but the Hurricanes so impressed the talent scouts that they signed the group to a contract in 1959.

The Ventures, whose "Walk—Don't Run" was a model for thousands of high school bands.

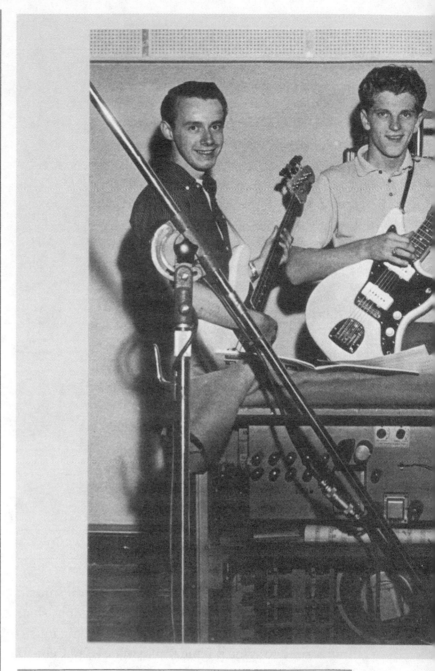

Johnny and the Hurricanes as they were in 1960.

This management firm, run by Irving Micahnik and Harry Balk (two cigar-chewing record execs), had enormous influence over Detroit's white music scene through various arrangements with local radio stations, clubs and record companies. As with Del Shannon and the other artists they managed, Micahnik and Balk took 20 percent off the top of the group's earnings, and signed them to their own record label, Twirl, at a 1½-percent royalty (out of which the band had to pay all recording costs). Twirl then leased the records to Warwick, Big Top and other New York companies at a royalty rate of 8 percent, giving the managers a tidy profit. In addi-

Valley." "Reveille Rock" was the military tune, and "Beatnik Fly" was a thinly disguised "Bluetail Fly."

All three would seem to be unlikely candidates for rock & roll hits, but the novelty of such unusual material being done in this style proved a strong commercial asset. Mainly, though, it was the band itself that impressed listeners with its solid, inventive, rousing sound. Paris blew a raspy, wailing tenor sax, and lead solos were also taken by guitarist Dave Yorko and organist Paul Tesluk. With two or three hot solo breaks in each record, and a rock-hard driving beat that never failed, Johnny and the Hurricanes were like some missing link between the great jazz combos of the Thirties and the Rolling Stones.

Their records continued to make the charts through 1961, though in progressively lower positions. A couple of members left the group, were replaced, and Paris received an offer to come to Germany and headline at the Star Club, Hamburg. So he and the group set sail, remaining in Hamburg for a couple of weeks. There, they were treated as stars and admired by the Beatles, who frequently opened the show for them at the Star Club.

In 1965, after a couple of hitless years, Paris raised enough money to start his own label, Atila, on which the Hurricanes released an album, *Live at the Star Club*. In the early Sixties the group had sported the cleanest of crew cuts and ducktails, but the new album cover showed them with long Beatles hair and black leather; they were also attempting vocals, and trying, via such wretchedly bad material as "Saga of the Beatles," to capitalize on their association with the Liverpudlians.

The new records stiffed, Paris's label folded, and by 1967, after five albums, more than twenty singles and several million records sold, Paris was left with nothing but a name that would at least guarantee him work locally. Richard Nader's oldies but goodies revue ignored Paris's phone calls for work; he has been forgotten everywhere except in Europe (where albums of Johnny and the Hurricanes hits are compiled regularly), but in 1975, Paris and his group were still together, playing high schools, bars, nightclubs and whatever other venues Toledo had to offer. He has also occasionally worked for his uncle's vending machine business. Still waiting for a recording contract to come along, he told an interviewer in 1974:

"I'm closer to my goal now than I was four years

tion, Balk and Micahnik took credit as composers for most of the group's songs, thereby collecting publishing royalties as well.

This sort of arrangement was common in its day, since teenage musicians knew little about the music business and were easily exploited. It was unfair, of course, but it worked both ways. The artist could at least count on having hit records, which meant they could make money on live appearances.

For the next few years, that's how it worked for Johnny and the Hurricanes. They hit in early 1959 with "Crossfire," a pounding, highly charged rocker that made Number Twenty-three on the *Billboard* charts. Three more hits followed in rapid succession, all hard-rocking takeoffs on well-known melodies: "Red River Rock" was a revamped "Red River

Santo and Johnny.

ago. It might take a long time; B. B. King did it at forty-five or fifty, so maybe I got twenty years left. You've got to be after it a long, long time. Then when it comes you've got to know how to handle it. I believe it's going to happen to me someday."

Johnny Paris got more mileage than most out of a career built on a trend that lasted only two years. At the same time he and others of his era proved the continuing viability of elemental rock & roll at the local level.

A few other instrumentalists, including Duane Eddy, the Ventures, Bill Black, the Champs and Sandy Nelson, continued having hits up through the mid-Sixties. But by 1962 soul records, "girl group" records, and dance novelty vocals were competing for airplay, and instrumentals were once again relegated to the repertoire of amateur dance bands. Their heyday was not quite over yet, however.

Dave "Baby" Cortez, of "Happy Organ" infamy.

Out of the hundreds of leftover instrumental bands still looking for a marketing hook emerged the brief surf music fad of 1963. Dick Dale opened the door with "Let's Go Trippin'," a big L.A. hit, while the Beach Boys and Jan and Dean established surfing as the biggest overnight sensation since the twist. During 1961 and 1962 California had developed a large contingent of local instrumental bands playing Dick Dale–style music for the surfers. By 1963 several of these groups broke nationally with

records like "Pipeline" by the Chantays, "Penetration" by the Pyramids and "Wipe Out" by the Surfaris. Across the country, instrumental groups switched over to surf music, from the Astronauts in Denver, to the Wailers in Seattle, to the Trashmen in Minneapolis. The Ventures even returned to the Top Ten with a surf remake of "Walk—Don't Run." But surf music was the last hurrah for instrumental rock as a popular genre; after the British Invasion of 1964, vocals again assumed primacy in white rock.

The instrumental hits had filled a void in the early Sixties. While the primal excesses of rock & roll had been pushed aside by the big labels and the teen idols, the kids couldn't be stopped from rocking; as long as there were local musicians to provide what they couldn't get on the radio, rock & roll in its simplest and most effective form continued to prosper.

Instrumental rock emerged as a distinct idiom with the ability to excite the listener's imagination without the use of words. Admittedly, it's a more limited genre than most; but because the rules are stricter, the results are often more refined, more special and more memorable than the simple formulas might imply. And though the survival of the local music scenes on which rock depends has appeared doubtful in recent years, I suspect that instrumental rock will make yet another resurgence before the history of rock & roll is completed.

DISCOGRAPHY

SINGLES
Davie Allan and the Arrows: "Apache '65" (Tower; ☆64, 1965). **Lee Allen and His Band:** "Walkin' with Mr. Lee" (Ember; ☆54, 1958). **Billy Joe and the Checkmates:** "Percolator (Twist)" (Dore; ☆10, 1962). **Bill Black's Combo:** "Smokie—Part 2" (Hi; ☆17, 1959). "White Silver Sands" (Hi; ☆9, 1960). "Don't Be Cruel" (Hi; ☆11, 1960). **Booker T. and the MGs:** "Green Onions" (Stax; ☆3, 1962). **B. Bumble and the Stingers:** "Bumble Boogie" (Rendezvous; ☆21, 1961). "Nut Rocker" (Rendezvous; ☆23, 1962). **Busters:** "Bust Out" (Arlen; ☆25, 1963). **Ace Cannon:** "Tuff" (Hi; ☆17, 1961). **Al Casey:** "Surfin' Hootenanny" (Stacy; ☆48, 1963). **Alvin Cash and the Crawlers:** "Twine Time" (Mar-V-Lus; ☆14, 1965). **Champs:** "Tequila" (Challenge; ☆1, 1958). "El Rancho Rock" (Challenge; ☆30, 1958). "Too Much Tequila" (Challenge; ☆30, 1960). **Chantays:** "Pipeline" (Dot; ☆4, 1963). **Ray Charles:** "One Mint Julep" (Impulse; ☆8, 1961). **Cozy Cole:** "Topsy II" b/w "Topsy I" (Love; ☆3, 1958). **Les Cooper and the Soul Rockers:** "Wiggle Wobble" (Everlast; ☆22, 1962). **Dave "Baby" Cortez:** "The Happy Organ" (Clock; ☆1, 1959). "Rinky Dink" (Chess; ☆10, 1962). **Floyd Cramer:** "Last Date" (RCA Victor; ☆2, 1960). "On the Rebound" (RCA Victor; ☆4, 1961). **Dick Dale and the Del-Tones:** "Let's Go Trippin'"

(Deltone; ☆60, 1961). **Dartells:** ''Hot Pastrami'' (Dot; ☆11, 1963). **Duals:** ''Stick Shift'' (Sue; ☆25, 1961). **Bill Doggett:** ''Honky Tonk'' (King; ☆2, 1956). ''Slow Walk'' (King; ☆26, 1956). **Duane Eddy and the Rebelettes:** ''(Dance with the) Guitar Man'' (RCA Victor; ☆12, 1962). ''Boss Guitar'' (RCA Victor; ☆28, 1963). **Duane Eddy and the Rebels:** ''Moovin'n'Groovin' '' (Jamie; ☆72, 1958). ''Rebel-'Rouser'' (Jamie; ☆6, 1958). ''Ramrod'' (Jamie; ☆28, 1958). ''Cannonball'' (Jamie; ☆15, 1958). ''The Lonely One'' (Jamie; ☆23, 1959). ''Yep!'' (Jamie; ☆30, 1959). ''Forty Miles of Bad Road'' (Jamie; ☆9, 1959). ''Some Kind-a Earthquake'' (Jamie; ☆37, 1959). ''Bonnie Came Back'' (Jamie; ☆26, 1960). ''Because They're Young'' (Jamie; ☆4, 1960). **Preston Epps:** ''Bongo Rock'' (Original Sound; ☆14, 1959). **Ernie Fields:** ''In the Mood'' (Rendezvous; ☆4, 1959). **Fireballs:** ''Torquay'' (Top Rank; ☆39, 1959). ''Bulldog'' (Top Rank; ☆24, 1960). ''Quite a Party'' (Warwick; ☆27, 1961). **Ernie Freeman:** ''Raunchy'' (Imperial; ☆12, 1957). **Frogmen:** ''Underwater'' (Candix; ☆44, 1961). **Jorgen Ingmann:** ''Apache'' (Atco; ☆2, 1961). **Johnny and the Hurricanes:** ''Crossfire'' (Warwick; ☆23, 1959). ''Red River Rock'' (Warwick; ☆5, 1959). ''Reveille Rock'' (Warwick; ☆25, 1959). ''Beatnik Fly'' (Warwick; ☆15, 1960). **Bill Justis:** ''Raunchy'' (Phillips; ☆3, 1957). **Freddie King:** ''Hide Away'' (Federal; ☆29, 1961). **King Curtis:** ''Soul Twist'' (Enjoy; ☆17, 1962). ''Soul Serenade'' (Capitol; ☆51, 1964). **Kokomo:** ''Asia Minor'' (Felsted; ☆8, 1961). **Lonnie Mack:** ''Memphis'' (Fraternity; ☆5, 1963). ''Wham!'' (Fraternity; ☆24, 1963). **Marketts:** ''Surfer's Stomp'' (Liberty; ☆31, 1962). ''Out of Limits'' (Warner Bros.; ☆3, 1963). **Mar-Keys:** ''Last Night'' (Satellite; ☆3, 1961). **Jimmy McGriff:** ''I've Got a Woman, Part 1'' (Sue; ☆20, 1962). **Willie Mitchell:** ''20-75'' (Hi; ☆31, 1964). **Sandy**

Nelson: ''Teen Beat'' (Original Sound; ☆4, 1959). ''Let There Be Drums'' (Imperial; ☆7, 1961). ''Drums Are My Beat'' (Imperial; ☆29, 1962). **Jack Nitzsche:** ''The Lonely Surfer'' (Reprise; ☆39, 1963). **Pyramids:** ''Penetration'' (Best; ☆18, 1964). **Ramrods:** ''(Ghost) Riders in the Sky'' (Amy; ☆30, 1961). **Boots Randolph:** ''Yakety Sax'' (Monument; ☆35, 1963). **Rebels:** ''Wild Weekend'' (Swan; ☆8, 1963). **Rock-a-Teens:** ''Woo-Hoo'' (Roulette; ☆16, 1959). **Routers:** ''Let's Go'' (Warner Bros.; ☆19, 1962). **Santo and Johnny:** ''Sleep Walk'' (Canadian American; ☆1, 1959). ''Tear Drop'' (Canadian American; ☆23, 1959). **String-a-Longs:** ''Wheels'' (Warwick; ☆3, 1961). **Surfaris:** ''Wipe Out'' (Dot; ☆2, 1963). **Tune Rockers:** ''The Green Mosquito'' (United Artists; ☆44, 1958). **Philip Upchurch Combo:** ''You Can't Sit Down, Part 2'' (Boyd; ☆29, 1961). **Ventures:** ''Walk—Don't Run'' (Dolton; ☆2, 1960). ''Perfidia'' (Dolton; ☆15, 1960). ''Ram-Bunk-Shush'' (Dolton; ☆29, 1961). ''Walk—Don't Run '64'' (Dolton; ☆8, 1964). **Virtues:** ''Guitar Boogie Shuffle'' (Hunt; ☆5, 1959). **Viscounts:** ''Harlem Nocturne'' (Madison; ☆52, 1960). **Wailers:** ''Tall Cool One'' (Golden Crest; ☆36, 1959). **Jr. Walker and the All Stars:** ''Shotgun'' (Soul; ☆4, 1965). **Travis Wammack:** ''Scratchy'' (Ara; ☆80, 1964). **Link Wray and His Ray Men:** ''Rumble'' (Cadence; ☆16, 1958). ''Raw-Hide'' (Epic; ☆23, 1959).

ANTHOLOGIES
The History of Rock Instrumentals, Vols. 1–2 (Rhino; 1987). *Surfin' Hits* (Rhino; 1989).

(Chart positions compiled from Joel Whitburn's *Record Research*, based on *Billboard*'s Pop chart.)

RAY CHARLES

BY PETER GURALNICK

Ray Charles: the Genius, the High Priest of Soul, Black, blind, an addict for over twenty years; singer, pianist, composer. For black America he brought the feeling of the church into secular music and crystallized an era. For white America he suggested whole new arenas of experience and served as a symbolic encapsulation of that experience: spontaneous, "natural" and irremediably flawed. To Frank Sinatra he was "the only genius in the business." To Ray Charles: "Art Tatum—he was a genius. And Einstein. Not me."

Ray Charles was born Ray Charles Robinson on September 23rd, 1930, in Albany, Georgia. His family moved to Greenville, Florida, when he was small, and he has vivid memories of his father, his mother, his younger brother and a neighbor, Wylie Pittman, who started him off on the piano at around the age of five. He can picture all these people, because it was not until he was six, after seeing his brother drown in the tub his mother used for take-in washing, that he began to lose his sight from glaucoma. At seven, his parents enrolled him in the St. Augustine School for the Deaf and the Blind, where he learned to read and write music in braille, score for big bands and play piano, alto, organ, clarinet and trumpet. His earliest musical influences were Chopin, Sibelius, Artie Shaw and Art Tatum.

He left school at fifteen, when his mother died (several years after his father's death), and drifted around Florida, making money off his music for the next couple of years. In 1947 he took his savings of $600 and moved as far away as he could get—to Seattle, Washington.

In Seattle he quickly resumed the life he had led in Florida, gigging at places like the Elks Club, the Rocking Chair, the Black and Tan. The music he played was very much in the vein of black popular music of the day—sophisticated cocktail swing, modeled on the King Cole Trio and Johnny Moore's

Three Blazers featuring Charles Brown, with an occasional Louis Jordan jump blues thrown in. Piano generally took a decorously bluesy lead, guitar held back and chorded, providing tasteful fills, and bass took the rhythm, while Ray Charles (he didn't want to be Ray Robinson because of Sugar Ray, the great middleweight boxer) sang in a crooning, soothing, conventional nightclub style, as smooth and polished as his mentor, Nat "King" Cole.

Around 1949 Jack Lauderdale of Swing Time Records offered him a chance to record, and he cut his first sides in Los Angeles, debuting with a typical number called "Confession Blues." It didn't do much, and he appeared on a number of West Coast labels until he hit with "Baby, Let Me Hold Your Hand," a Top Ten R&B number in 1951. On the strength of that record he went on the road with blues singer Lowell Fulson who was riding high with his own hit on Swing Time, "Every Day I Have the Blues" (a song B. B. King would later adapt for his theme). Ray Charles played piano for Fulson in the band, which included Stanley Turrentine on tenor and Earl Brown on alto.

When Atlantic took over Charles's Swing Time contract in 1952, the music he played was not much different from what he had been playing at the start of his career—a little bluesier, perhaps, under Fulson's influence, but still smooth, sophisticated, well mannered and well bred. It's hard to say what Ahmet Ertegun, Herb Abramson and the Atlantic staff saw in Ray Charles at this point. He had made some good derivative records; he was obviously a very capable journeyman musician; but he had showed no hint of originality.

In 1952 and 1953 he did a couple of New York sessions, which yielded a boogie-woogie classic ("Mess Around"), a novelty number ("It Should've Been Me"), and some fine blues ("Losing Hand," "Funny," Lowell Fulson's "Sinner's Prayer"); they demonstrated a harder edge of emotionalism than anything he had previously recorded. In this period he put together a band for Ruth Brown, then at the height of her popularity (and also on Atlantic), and played briefly with Moms Mabley. But it was not until he went to New Orleans in 1953 that he established a musical identity of his own.

There he hooked up with Guitar Slim (real name, Eddie Jones), a bluesman who was extremely popular on the club circuit. According to Jerry Wexler, Charles worked closely with Slim for some time.

Then on September 26th Slim had a session for Speciality Records. He cut six or seven titles. One of them was "The Things That I Used to Do," a blues that sold a million copies, going on to become a blues standard. The pianist and arranger on this session was Ray Charles.

Guitar Slim was in many ways the antithesis of all that Ray Charles had sought to become in his musical career to date: crude; untutored; musically unsophisticated; possessed of a primitive, perfervid style that most resembled the gospel shouting of the Baptist church. Even the melodies and titles of his songs ("Trouble Don't Last," "Reap What You Sow") seem lifted from the church tradition. To Ray Charles it must have been like a revelation of something he had known all along. The arrangement and mode of Guitar Slim's hit—with gospel changes, horns riffing like a soulful choir, and above all the impassioned, emotionally charged tone of Eddie Jones's voice—were to plant the seeds of the Ray Charles style.

In December 1953 Jerry Wexler and Ahmet Ertegun were in New Orleans to cut Big Joe Turner. "We ran into Ray at Cosimo's famous small studio, and Ray asked us please (!) to do a session with him. . . . This was the landmark session because it had: Ray Charles originals, Ray Charles arrangements, a Ray Charles band." The session produced a fine single, "Don't You Know." The second New Orleans session brought about a moving version of Guitar Slim's "Feelin' Sad," but it was the next session, cut in an Atlanta radio station, that ultimately consolidated the style.

"I've Got a Woman," cut in Atlanta, was the consummate marriage of all the elements which up till then had simply failed to coalesce in Ray Charles's musical makeup. It featured, of course, his strong gospel-based piano, a seven-piece group (sans guitar) that cooked, and a vocal which, in the studio version of the song, only begins to suggest the change that had taken place in Ray Charles; with a full-throated rasp, sudden swoops, falsetto shrieks and a sense of wild abandon, Charles totally removed himself from the polite music he had made in the past. There was an unrestrained exuberance to the new Ray Charles, a fierce earthiness that, while it would not have been unfamiliar to any follower of gospel music, was almost revolutionary in the world of pop. Big Bill Broonzy was outraged: "He's crying, sanctified. He's mixing the blues with the spirituals.

He should be singing in a church." Only Roy Brown, in the Forties, had even suggested this mix of styles, though Little Richard was soon to follow and raise a hopped-up version of the same hybrid to undreamt-of heights. No one who had listened to the Soul Stirrers or the Five Blind Boys or Professor Alex Bradford could miss the connection, however.

The gospel genesis of "I've Got a Woman" and its enormous popularity set the tone for Ray Charles's subsequent success. The Pilgrim Travelers' "I've Got a New Home" became "Lonely Avenue"; "This Little Girl of Mine" took something from Clara Ward's "This Little Light of Mine" and the Caravans' "What Kind of Man Is This"; "Nobody but You, Lord" was shortened to "Nobody but You." The Raelettes were added as a gospel choir. The sound became increasingly churchy, a deliberate evocation of holiness feeling.

Over the next six years Ray Charles enjoyed a period of extraordinary creativity in which all the various strands of his musical heritage were brought together. And he was given the opportunity to show his true genius which, if it lay more in the realm of assimilation than originality, as can now be seen, was inspired assimilation nonetheless. He did blues and funk; jazz at Newport; revivals of old standards with and without strings; even, in "I'm Movin' On," a good rocking stab at country & western. More than anything else, though, there was the translation of gospel standards into secular success and the creation, in the process, of a whole new phase of black music, one in which artists such as James Brown, Sam Cooke, Solomon Burke and Otis Redding could take Ray Charles for a model and call upon their own church backgrounds to create what became known as soul music.

For Charles himself, the pinnacle of this movement came in 1959 with the enormous success of "What'd I Say," a conventional enough blues riff with Latin rhythm and a gospel feel and six-and-a-half minutes of the most joyous celebration of an utterly profane love. A kind of secular evocation of an actual church service, complete with moans, groans and a congregation talking in tongues, the record was banned on many radio stations and was Ray Charles's first million-seller.

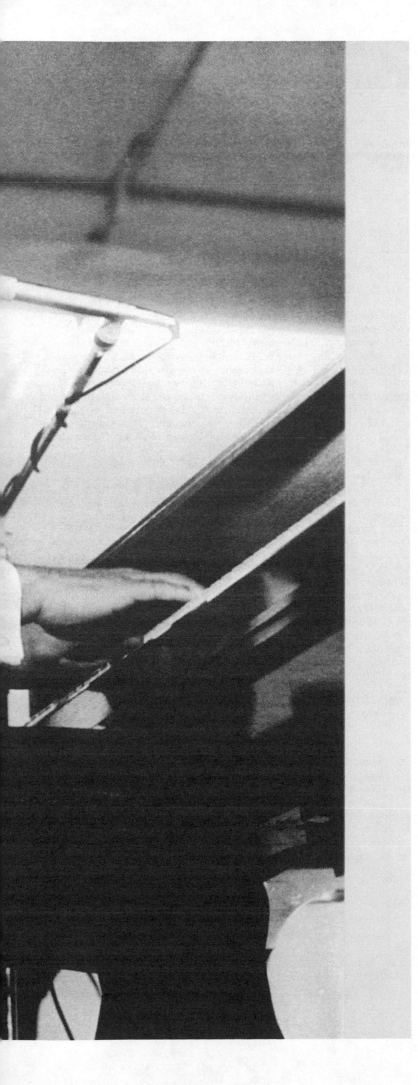

The Raelettes, whose call-and-response intensity gave songs like ''What'd I Say'' a frenzied edge.

In November 1959, on the strength of this success, he signed with ABC Records for a sizable advance and the promise of an economic independence to match the creative freedom he had always enjoyed. In 1962 he cut his landmark country & western album. It included two big hits, the biggest of which (''I Can't Stop Loving You'') sold over three million records. When reporters asked Ray Charles how he had come to invent this new trend, he credited the *Grand Ole Opry*, which he had listened to since he was a child.

For the rest of the Sixties, and up to the present day, he has contented himself with what have come to be virtually MOR albums, broad-based, inoffensive, a sterile mix of heavenly choirs, Beatles hits and nostalgic show tunes, bland arrangements and syrupy strings. Only once in a while, cutting through all the slush, as on ''I Don't Need No Doctor'' (1966), do you hear that aching, almost painfully

Ray Charles, ''the Genius.'' With the fierce earthiness of ''I've Got a Woman'' he defined soul—in 1955, ten years before it became fashionable.

raw voice that inspired Joe Cocker, Eric Burdon, Steve Winwood and a generation of white rockers. In recent years he has seemingly returned to the cocktail music of his youth, the music of Charles Brown and Nat "King" Cole.

I remember seeing Ray Charles several times in the early Sixties. It was always the same. The big band opened with blasting evocations of the swing era. Ray Charles's vocal appearance, in the time-honored fashion of the R&B revue, came only after an intermission. The show ended with an orgiastic performance of "What'd I Say," with Ray Charles writhing puppet-like in a spastic trance and some couple inevitably moved to get up out of their seats and dance. It was at this point, at all the performances I saw, that the cops moved in, the band wound down, and someone led Ray Charles away from his suddenly silent piano to safety backstage. It was great theater, re-creating the revivalistic fervor of his early performances and simultaneously retaining a faint edge of cool, a kind of reserve, that seemed suspicious, brittle and perhaps even contemptuous.

There is no question that for white audiences Ray Charles was a romantic figure whose first well-publicized heroin bust in 1965 (which led to his commitment to a California sanitorium, a period of cleaning out and a yearlong retirement from performing) did little but extend the image of Billie Holiday, Charlie Parker and Bud Powell, twisted black geniuses whose mythic role it was to die for white people's sins. Ray Charles, however, has always gone his own way. He survived, and he still resists personal, as well as musical, categorization. "I started using stuff when I was sixteen and first started in show business," he has said in reference to his habit. "Every experience I've had—good and bad—has taught me something. I was born a poor boy in the South, I'm black, I'm blind, I once fooled around with drugs, but all of it was like going to school—and I've tried to be a good student. I don't regret a damn thing."

DISCOGRAPHY

SINGLES
"Baby Let Me Hold Your Hand" (Swing Time; r☆7, 1951). "Kiss Me Baby" (Swing Time; r☆10, 1952). "It Should've Been Me" (Atlantic; r☆7, 1954). "Don't You Know" (Atlantic; r☆10, 1954). "I've Got a Woman" (Atlantic; r☆2, 1955). "A Fool for You" b/w "This Little Girl of Mine" (Atlantic; r☆2, 1955). "Blackjack" (Atlantic; r☆8, 1955). "Drown in My Own Tears" (Atlantic; r☆2, 1956). "Hallelujah I Love Her So" (Atlantic; r☆5, 1956). "Lonely Avenue" (Atlantic; r☆8, 1956). "Ain't That Love" (Atlantic; r☆11, 1957). "Swanee River Rock" (Atlantic; r☆14, ☆42, 1957). "Rockhouse—Part 2" (Atlantic; r☆14, 1958). "The Right Time" (Atlantic; r☆5, 1959). "That's Enough" (Atlantic; r☆19, 1959). "What'd I Say" (Atlantic; r☆1, ☆6, 1959). "I'm Movin' On" (Atlantic; r☆11, ☆40, 1959). "Don't Let the Sun Catch You Cryin' " (Atlantic; r☆17, 1960). "Just for a Thrill" (Atlantic; r☆16, 1960). "Sticks and Stones" (ABC-Paramount; r☆2, ☆40, 1960). "Tell the Truth" (Atlantic; r☆13, 1960). "Georgia on My Mind" (ABC-Paramount; r☆3, ☆1, 1960). "Ruby" (ABC-Paramount; r☆10, ☆28, 1960). "Them That Got" (ABC-Paramount; r☆10, 1961). "One Mint Julep" (Impulse; r☆1, ☆8, 1961). "I've Got News for You" (Impulse; r☆8, 1961). "Hit the Road Jack" (ABC-Paramount; r☆1, ☆1, 1961). "Unchain My Heart" (ABC-Paramount; r☆1, ☆9, 1961). "Hide 'nor Hair" b/w "At the Club" (ABC-Paramount; r☆7, ☆20, 1962). "I Can't Stop Loving You" b/w "Born to Lose" (ABC-Paramount; r☆1, ☆1, 1962). "You Don't Know Me" (ABC-Paramount; r☆5, ☆2, 1962). "You Are My Sunshine" b/w "Your Cheating Heart" (ABC-Paramount; r☆1, ☆7, 1962). "Don't Set Me Free" (ABC-Paramount; r☆9, ☆20, 1963). "Take These Chains from My Heart" (ABC-Paramount; r☆7, ☆8, 1963). "No One" b/w "Without Love (There Is Nothing)" (ABC-Paramount; r☆9, ☆21, 1963). "Busted" b/w "That Lucky Old Sun" (ABC-Paramount; r☆3, ☆4, 1963). "My Heart Cries for You" b/w "Baby, Don't You Cry" (ABC-Paramount; ☆38, 1964). "A Tear Fell" (ABC-Paramount; ☆50, 1964). "Makin' Whoopee" (ABC-Paramount; r☆14, ☆46, 1965). "Crying Time" (ABC-Paramount; r☆5, ☆6, 1966). "Together Again" (ABC-Paramount; r☆10, ☆19, 1966). "Let's Go Get Stoned" (ABC; r☆1, ☆31, 1966). "I Chose to Sing the Blues" (ABC; r☆22, ☆32, 1966). "Here We Go Again" (ABC; r☆5, ☆15, 1967). "In the Heat of the Night" (ABC; r☆21, ☆33, 1967). "Yesterday" (ABC; r☆9, ☆25, 1967). "That's a Lie" (ABC; r☆11, 1968). "Eleanor Rigby" b/w "Understanding" (ABC; r☆13, ☆35, 1968). "Laughin' and Clownin' " (ABC; r☆18, 1970). "If You Were Mine" (ABC; r☆19, ☆41, 1970). "Don't Change on Me" (ABC; r☆13, ☆36, 1971). "Feel So Bad" (ABC; r☆16, 1971).

ALBUMS
Ray Charles Anthology (Rhino; 1988). *Ray Charles: The Birth of Soul, The Complete Atlantic Rhythm & Blues Recordings, 1952–1959* (Atlantic; 1991).

(Chart positions compiled from Joel Whitburn's *Record Research,* based on *Billboard*'s Pop chart, unless otherwise indicated; r☆ = position on *Billboard*'s Rhythm & Blues chart.)

SAM COOKE

BY JOE McEWEN

Thousands of screaming, crying, pushing people thronged the area surrounding A.R. Leak's Funeral Home at 7838 So. Cottage Grove in a frantic attempt to view the body of singer Sam Cooke. . . .

Both chapels, each holding about 300 people, were filled shortly after the doors opened, and the urgency of many to "get a last look at Sam" resulted in near chaos, with young and old being crushed in the process. . . .

When the plate glass in a front door of Leak's chapel gave way under the pressure of the crowd, Spencer Leak, a son of A.R. Leak Sr., shouted, "There are just too many of them."

One emotional woman when crushed while attempting to step over the threshold screamed, "Please let me in. I've never seen anything like this in my life."

Cooke's coffin was covered with glass, to the disappointment of many. A blind woman, who came to pay her respects and perhaps "touch" her singing idol, was rammed against a door frame and had to be pulled over the entrance by funeral parlor employees.

—*The Chicago Defender*,
December 19th, 1964

Sam Cooke died on December 11th, 1964. Gunned down in a Los Angeles motel room under mysterious and unsavory circumstances, he nonetheless died a martyr's death. To black America, he was a hero. Yet Cooke, a true pioneer of black music, has rarely received the recognition accorded Ray Charles, or such early rock stars as Little Richard and Chuck Berry. The neglect is misleading; Sam Cooke, as much as any R&B artist of the Fifties, paved the way for the soul explosion of the Sixties, influencing performers from Otis Redding to Al Green.

In the beginning, he was black America's favorite gospel singer. Sam Cooke was twenty years old when he replaced R. H. Harris as the lead singer for the Soul Stirrers in 1951. The Soul Stirrers had been one of the most popular gospel groups, thanks largely to Harris, whose quivering tenor was the forerunner of the modern soul falsetto.

It's not hard to imagine the intense pressure Sam must have felt on his first Sunday afternoon with the sextet, as the crowd murmured its displeasure at the Soul Stirrers beginning their program without Harris. From the sanctuary of the group, Sam stepped forward for his first solo, perhaps Professor Alex Bradford's "Jesus Is a Friend Until the End." Eyes

With roots in gospel and a desire for pop success, Sam Cooke built a bridge from the music of Nat "King" Cole to Motown and beyond, showing new ways to sell black music to white people.

closed and arms outstretched, Cooke sang without the rasping delivery or broken vowels of older stylists, avoiding the tentative offering of Harris's Roman tenor. Yet his voice, burrowing and soaring through plaintive dirges, exuding a gentle world-weariness, moved the congregation to a standing ovation.

During Cooke's tenure with the group, the Soul Stirrers recorded for Art Rupe's Specialty label. Although Sam's voice always retained the purity of the early days, his gospel records on Specialty capture his finest vocal moments: He never sang songs that were more erotic or buoyant than the love songs he sang about his Lord. While other gospel singers often let themselves get carried away in the emotion of the moment, Cooke's phrasing was always articulate, never out of control, every word enunciated clearly, even as he growled and clapped (with only a guitar echoing his harsh call), "Were you there / When they crucified my Lord?"

For almost six years Sam and the Soul Stirrers crisscrossed the country. For the folks flocking to the big halls and storefronts, Cooke's pure, sanctified singing, smooth features and lithe body offered a combination of religious charisma and sweaty sexuality. J. W. Alexander, Sam's close friend, manager and business associate, was shrewd enough to realize that if Cooke was having this kind of an effect on the sequestered gospel audience, then there was a whole world out there, more openly sexual and sinful, that had to be ripe for Sam's physical and vocal appeal.

One can guess that Cooke himself was more than eager for the transition. The years on the gospel trail had given Sam the perspective and maturity he needed to tackle pop, and it seemed that he already had the right idea in 1956, when he sat down with

his guitar and recorded his first pop song, "Lovable." The record, released under the name of Dale Cooke so as not to offend Sam's gospel following, set the pattern for the pop records that followed. Singing noticeably higher and lighter, Cooke imbued the song with a purity familiar from his church music. Cooke's almost wispy delivery is balanced by a huge, "doowah" choral backup, and their meeting place is the elusive middle ground Sam staked out most of his career, the place where the soul and feeling of gospel meets the finger-snapping, ascot-wearing ambience of supper club pop.

Cooke flanked by Hugo and Luigi, who produced many of his RCA hits.

Specialty's white owner Art Rupe was not happy with Cooke's pop ambitions. When Rupe walked into the studio one night and saw the white choral group Sam and producer Bumps Blackwell were using in their "bleached" approach, he sold Blackwell the right to take Cooke's pop output elsewhere.

Rupe missed a gold mine. The song that came out of that session was "You Send Me." Released as Cooke's next single, it sold 1.7 million copies in 1957 on the tiny Keen label. It was also the catalyst for Cooke's meteoric rise as a pop singer.

J. W. Alexander has claimed he intended from the outset that Sam Cooke would eventually become the kind of idol to black teenage girls that white girls had been used to having for years. Cooke had been with Keen almost two years when the first and most ambitious of their schemes was realized: Sam signed with RCA, spurning offers from numerous independents and becoming RCA's first major black pop singer, apart from calypso specialist Harry Belafonte.

The move could have been disastrous. Sam still depended on the R&B market as his base, and RCA was virtually without contacts there. But Cooke and Alexander were counting on the strength of Sam's name to generate black airplay, while the RCA label provided Sam with a seal of legitimacy for the wider white audience.

The first RCA release, a saccharine ditty titled "Teenage Sonata," did reasonably well, but its followup was the venerable "Chain Gang," released in August 1960. From that point on, Cooke was rarely without a Top Forty hit.

Barbara Cooke, Sam's wife, at the coroner's inquest after his death in 1964.

Bertha Lee Franklin, the woman who shot Sam Cooke.

"Chain Gang" was a catchy record that never quite rang true, with its male chorus oohing and aahing over clinking steel spike hammers, but "Sad Mood," released in December 1960, was a complete reversal of form, depending more on blues idioms and phrasing. Unlike earlier 45s ("Wonderful World," "Everybody Likes to Cha Cha Cha" and "Only Sixteen"), "Sad Mood" didn't seem to hold obvious appeal to a teen or even pop audience; the surprising commercial success of the record must have indicated to Cooke and his arranger Rene Hall that the market for "soulful" music was wider than they had anticipated.

While his output on Keen centered on light ballads and novelty items, at RCA Cooke began to draw more on blues and gospel arrangements, coupled with popular black slang expressions. The most successful record along these lines was "Bring It On Home to Me," a timeless song built on a simple, laconic piano figure and Sam's weary vocal, echoed in true call-and-response fashion by Lou Rawls. Upon release in the summer of 1962, the song was an instant hit. Perhaps the first record to define the soul experience, it would be one of the most influential songs Cooke ever cut, matched in impact only by the sensual "That's Where It's At."

Unlike his peers—and only Jackie Wilson and Little Willie John came close to rivaling Cooke's vocal virtuosity—Sam's destiny was always firmly within his control, artistically and otherwise. He was one of the first popular black vocalists in forty years of recording who ran his own publishing company (Kags Music) and his own management firm; he also owned his own record company, Sar/Derby Records, which established itself as a successful independent almost immediately after its first soul release.

Sar, incorporated in 1960 and discontinued shortly after Cooke's death, was at first conceived as a gospel label for the Soul Stirrers, whose popularity had declined after Cooke's departure (Johnnie Taylor was the lead singer for the group at the time). But the sanctity of the label didn't last for long. Within a year Cooke and Alexander had "turned out" a number of their gospel protégés by having them record the type of blues and soul that Sam seemed most comfortable with as a songwriter and producer.

Among Cooke's discoveries were the Womack Brothers, including Bobby Womack, from Cleveland, who became the Valentinos; Billy Preston; Johnnie Taylor; the Sims Twins; Mel Carter (who re-created Sam's early innocence with a song Sam wrote, "When a Boy Falls in Love"); and finally Lou Rawls, whom Cooke and Alexander signed to Herb Alpert and Lou Adler's Shardee label, where it was hoped he would duplicate Sam's pop success.

During his lifetime, Cooke established a public personality of grace and poise, yet the court record of the events surrounding his death is brutal in presentation, and in sharp contrast to the genial public image he presented.

According to the testimony, Cooke, at the time married to his high-school sweetheart Barbara Campbell, had picked up a twenty-two-year-old woman named Elisa Boyer at a party on the night of December 10th. Although he had promised her a ride home, he instead drove her to a motel on South Figueroa in Los Angeles, where he registered the two of them as "Mr. and Mrs. Cooke." Miss Boyer testified that she walked up to the registration desk and asked to be taken home. But Cooke managed to force her into a motel room; there, she claimed, Cooke "began to rip my clothes off." She escaped when Cooke went into the bathroom and she fled with his clothing. According to her testimony, he pursued her, dressed only in a sports coat and shoes. While Elisa Boyer phoned police from a nearby booth, Cooke pounded on the door of the motel's manager, fifty-five-year-old Bertha Franklin. Demanding to know Miss Boyer's whereabouts, Cooke allegedly broke the door open and assaulted Mrs. Franklin. During the scuffle, Mrs. Franklin pulled out a .22-caliber pistol and shot Cooke three times. When the wounded singer charged Franklin, the motel manager picked up a stick and clubbed him. By the time police arrived, Sam Cooke was dead. Questions have been raised over the years about the circumstances of Cooke's death, and some have called for a reinvestigation of the case.

To most of his white audience, Sam Cooke remained little more than a handsome, well-groomed black man, the quaint bearer of the cha-cha and the twist. Across the tracks, on the other hand, his stat-ure was almost comparable with that of Malcolm X and Martin Luther King, Jr. His death, like theirs, only enhanced his standing.

He was a black music capitalist at a time when Berry Gordy Jr., later to found Motown, was still writing songs for Jackie Wilson. Yet as Cooke developed, his own music became increasingly blacker, returning to its gospel roots. When Bertha Franklin shot Sam Cooke in that Los Angeles motel, he died his own man, unbought and unbleached.

A few weeks after his death, RCA released "A Change Is Gonna Come." Curtained with shimmering strings and anchored by a dirgelike drumbeat, "Change," like Martin Luther King's final speech, in which he told his followers that he had been to the mountaintop, was appropriately ominous, as if to anticipate the turbulent years facing black America. Dignified and transcendent, it made a fitting final statement from a fallen hero.

DISCOGRAPHY

SINGLES

"You Send Me" (Keen; r☆1, ☆1, 1957). "I'll Come Running Back to You" (Specialty; r☆7, ☆22, 1957). "(I Love You) for Sentimental Reasons" b/w "Desire Me" (Keen; r☆17, ☆43, 1958). "Lonely Island (Keen; r☆15, ☆39, 1958). "Win Your Love for Me" (Keen; r☆4, ☆33, 1958). "Love You Most of All" (Keen; r☆12, ☆26, 1958). "Everybody Likes to Cha Cha Cha" (Keen; r☆2, ☆31, 1959). "Only Sixteen" (Keen; r☆13, ☆28, 1959). "There, I've Said It Again" (Keen; r☆25, 1959). "Teenage Sonata" (RCA Victor; r☆33, ☆50, 1960). "Wonderful World" (Keen; r☆2, ☆12, 1960). "Chain Gang" (RCA Victor; r☆2, ☆2, 1960). "Sad Mood" (RCA Victor; r☆23, ☆29, 1960). "That's It—I Quit—I'm Movin' On" (RCA Victor; r☆25, ☆31, 1961). "Cupid" (RCA Victor; r☆20, ☆17, 1961). "Twistin' the Night Away" (RCA Victor; r☆1, ☆9, 1962). "Bring It On Home to Me" b/w "Having a Party" (RCA Victor; r☆2, ☆13, 1962). "Nothing Can Change This Love" b/w "Somebody Have Mercy" (RCA Victor; r☆2, ☆12, 1962). "Send Me Some Lovin'" (RCA Victor; r☆2, ☆13, 1963). "Another Saturday Night" (RCA Victor; r☆1, ☆10, 1963). "Frankie and Johnny" (RCA Victor; r☆4, ☆14, 1963). "Little Red Rooster" (RCA Victory; r☆7, ☆11, 1963). "Good News" (RCA Victor; ☆11, 1964). "Good Times" b/w "Tennessee Waltz" (RCA Victor; ☆11, 1964). "Cousin of Mine" b/w "That's Where It's At" (RCA Victor; ☆31, 1964). "Shake" b/w "A Change Is Gonna Come" (RCA Victor; r☆2, ☆7, 1965). "It's Got the Whole World Shakin'" (RCA Victor; r☆15, ☆41, 1965). "Sugar Dumpling" (RCA Victor; r☆18, ☆32, 1965).

ALBUMS

The Man and His Music (RCA; 1986). *Sam Cooke with the Soul Stirrers* (Specialty; 1991).

(Chart positions compiled from Joel Whitburn's *Record Research,* based on *Billboard*'s Pop chart, unless otherwise indicated; r☆ = position on *Billboard*'s Rhythm & Blues chart.)

JACKIE WILSON

BY JOE McEWEN

Boston's Back Bay Theater was jammed to capacity, filled with a noisy, enthusiastic throng, out to see the latest of the traveling soul revues. This show promised to be something special, with a rare visit from Roy Hamilton, the urbane crooner of "Ebb Tide," and an appearance by Jackie Wilson, the man responsible for "Lonely Teardrops" and "That's Why (I Love You So)." But as the warm-up acts went through their paces, all was not well backstage; the show's promoter was on the phone jabbering frantically to Roy Hamilton's agent, who had no idea where his singer was. It soon became clear that Hamilton wouldn't show.

Fearful of the fevered crowd's wrath if a headliner failed to appear, the promoter urgently whispered in Jackie Wilson's ear as he prepared to go on; Wilson, after a moment's pause, agreed. Bounding onstage, he grabbed the mike, spun around and raced into a blistering version of "That's Why." For over an hour Jackie Wilson played to the screaming audience, teasing the women clustered in front of the stage. Suddenly, in the middle of "Shake! Shake! Shake!," he jumped into a sea of outstretched arms.

With mike in hand, he attempted to sing, but women, clawing ravenously, shredded his shirt. Finally, Wilson's body disappeared. The theater was in turmoil; the audience pressed forward, hoping to catch a glimpse of what was going on. After minutes of pushing and shoving, the police escorted Wilson to safety. The lights were turned on and everybody ordered out. No one missed Roy Hamilton.

In his prime, Jackie Wilson was that kind of performer: He could stop a show at the drop of a hat—

Jackie Wilson onstage. He was one of the most exciting live performers of his era.

sometimes, without even trying. A contemporary of James Brown and Sam Cooke, he made his debut as a solo performer in 1957. The comparison with two of black music's most influential figures is not unflattering: As a showman, Wilson was the equal of Brown, while as a vocalist, he could match Cooke's range and then some. Yet while both Brown and Cooke became wealthy men, honored as pioneers, Jackie Wilson suffered a checkered and enigmatic career. Despite his popularity in the late Fifties and early Sixties, his recordings rarely reflected his talent.

And his raw talent was enormous. Born in 1934 in Detroit, he grew up under the influence of Forties blues vocalist Roy Brown. Wilson's first break came in 1953, when he dropped by the Fox Theater in Detroit during a rehearsal of Billy Ward and His Dominoes. The group had recently lost its immensely popular lead singer, Clyde McPhatter, and Ward was looking for a replacement. Wilson, boasting that he was a better singer than McPhatter, landed an audition and—to Ward's astonishment— his claim proved credible. The brash Detroit teenager became the Dominoes' new lead vocalist.

The Dominoes never quite regained their stride with Wilson at the helm; though they were able to play Las Vegas and the Copa on the strength of their earlier hits, it wasn't until 1956 that the Dominoes returned to the charts, with Wilson's flamboyant interpretation of the unlikely "St. Therese of the Roses." The record gave a temporary shot in the arm to the Dominoes' faltering fortunes, but Jackie Wilson used "St. Therese" as a stepping-stone to a solo career. Shortly after its release, he left Ward to sign with the Brunswick label.

"Reet Petite," Wilson's first solo effort, was released in 1957. Penned by a struggling Detroit songwriter named Berry Gordy Jr., "Reet Petite," a blaring uptempo novelty song, featured Wilson mimicking Elvis Presley's stuttering, breathless vocal delivery. For Gordy, the record marked his first hit as a writer (he would later found Motown); for Wilson, "Reet Petite" inaugurated an oddly aimless solo recording career that, in the course of eighteen years, would meander through countless musical styles, pitting Wilson against slipshod orchestration and material that was often mediocre if not absurd.

Although Dick Jacobs arranged Wilson's first record, "Reet Petite," it was Milton DeLugg, an accordionist-bandleader, who arranged "To Be Loved," the successor to Wilson's smash debut disc, and several of Wilson's early records. Though DeLugg's melodramatic scores and heavy-handed choral accompaniments afflicted most of his productions, Wilson somehow managed to surmount such obstacles through the sheer power of his amazing vocals and a knack for knowing what to do with even the worst of songs. Between 1958 and 1963 Jackie Wilson was one of black America's most popular vocalists, scoring a long string of pop and soul hits.

In 1960 Wilson released his biggest single, "Night" backed with "Doggin' Around," a double-sided hit that defines the paradox of his recording career. "Doggin' Around" was one of his rare songs to take a direct, bluesy approach. Though marred by an obtrusive (and defiantly white-sounding) chorus, the record is one of Wilson's finest moments: Urged on by a polite blues piano, he soars through the song, stretching and wrenching notes like a true virtuoso. It is one of the few Jackie Wilson records from the early Sixties that does not sound hopelessly dated today.

But while Jackie sang the blues on one side, the flip was pure schmaltz. Flaunting his operatic range, Wilson crooned "Night" in his best Mario Lanza style, accompanied by scads of strings. Wilson obviously enjoyed such showstoppers, though; by choice, he recorded a number of standards throughout his career, including a truly transcendent

Brooklyn, 1969. He brought an operatic range to songs like "Lonely Teardrops."

"Danny Boy." Here Wilson exhibited the full extent of his abilities, transforming the hoary ballad into a stunning display of vocal gymnastics.

While Wilson's recorded material often consisted of dreary supper club fare, his live performances from the period belonged to another world entirely.

At sixteen, he had been a Golden Gloves champ, and like James Brown, Wilson put his boxing ability to hair-raising use: Splits, spins, slides and one-footed dancing were all part of the show. And his dramatic readings of ballads, complete with knee drops and overdrawn gestures, rarely failed to bring his audience to a state of frenzy. The sexual hysteria helped promote an aura of violence around him that only intensified after he was shot and seriously wounded by a female friend in a New York hotel in 1961.

Though Wilson, in an attempt to keep up with new fashions, cut a few ill-conceived gospel-shout singles in the mid-Sixties, it wasn't until 1966 that his sagging career was temporarily revived by Carl Davis, the Chicago producer. Davis brought Wilson into the soul era with two quick million-sellers,

Backstage at the Apollo with a talent contest winner.

"Whispers (Gettin' Louder)" and "(Your Love Keeps Lifting Me) Higher and Higher," easily Wilson's best later efforts. Sadly, the hits didn't last; Davis couldn't seem to find appropriate material. By 1970 Wilson was an aging, second-rate soul star, unsuccessfully aping contemporary trends and finally consigned to the oldies circuit, as a member of Dick Clark's Good Ol' Rock 'n' Roll revue. Jackie's last album, titled *Nowstalgia*, was a company-conceived tribute to one of Wilson's early idols, Al Jolson.

The path of Jackie Wilson's career is puzzling. Though Berry Gordy wrote Jackie's first few hits and was once a close friend, Wilson never benefited from Gordy's success at Motown. Wilson would have been a logical choice to head the Motown roster, but instead he remained at Brunswick, a label with a dubious reputation and few facilities for promoting his career; Wilson himself was deliberately hazy in interviews about the specifics of his career. One of the great unfulfilled talents of soul music, he was also proof of the music's exploitative potential.

In late 1975, Wilson suffered a heart attack on the stage of the Latin Casino in Cherry Hill, New Jersey, where he was appearing with a Dick Clark revue. After more than eight years in a coma, Jackie Wilson died on January 21st, 1984.

DISCOGRAPHY

SINGLES
"Reet Petite" (Brunswick; ☆62, 1957). "To Be Loved" (Brunswick; r☆11, ☆22, 1958). "Lonely Teardrops" (Brunswick; r☆1, ☆7, 1958). "That's Why (I Love You So)" (Brunswick; r☆2, ☆13, 1959). "I'll Be Satisfied" (Brunswick; r☆6, ☆20, 1959). "You Better Know It" (Brunswick; r☆1, ☆37, 1959). "Talk That Talk" (Brunswick; r☆3, ☆34, 1959). "Doggin' Around" b/w "Night" (Brunswick; r☆1, ☆4, 1960). "A Woman, a Lover, a Friend" b/w "(You Were Made for) All My Love" (Brunswick; r☆1, ☆12, 1960). "Am I the Man" b/w "Alone at Last" (Brunswick; r☆10, ☆8, 1960). "The Tear of the Year" b/w "My Empty Arms" (Brunswick; r☆10, ☆9, 1961). "Please Tell Me Why" (Brunswick; r☆11, ☆20, 1961). "I'm Comin' On Back to You" (Brunswick; r☆9, ☆19, 1961). "You Don't Know What It Means" b/w "Years from Now" (Brunswick; r☆19, ☆37, 1961). "The Greatest Hurt" (Brunswick; ☆34, 1962). "I Just Can't Help It" (Brunswick; r☆17, 1962). "Baby Workout" (Brunswick; r☆1, ☆5, 1963). "Shake! Shake! Shake!" (Brunswick; r☆21, ☆33, 1963). "Danny Boy" (Brunswick; r☆25, 1965). "No Pity (in the Naked City)" (Brunswick; r☆25, 1965). "Whispers (Gettin' Louder)" (Brunswick; r☆5, ☆11, 1966). "I Don't Want to Lose You" (Brunswick; r☆11, 1967). "(Your Love Keeps Lifting Me) Higher and Higher" (Brunswick; r☆1, ☆6, 1967). "Since You Showed Me How to Be Happy" (Brunswick; r☆22, ☆32, 1967). "I Get the Sweetest Feeling" (Brunswick; r☆12, ☆34, 1968). "Helpless" (Brunswick; r☆21, 1969). "This Love Is Real" (Brunswick; r☆9, 1970). "Love Is Funny That Way" (Brunswick; r☆18, 1971).

ALBUMS
Mr. Excitement! (Rhino; 1992).

(Chart positions compiled from Joel Whitburn's *Record Research*, based on *Billboard*'s Pop chart, unless otherwise indicated; r☆ = position on *Billboard*'s Rhythm & Blues chart.)

BRILL BUILDING POP

BY GREG SHAW

The Brill Building, located at 1619 Broadway in the heart of New York's music district, is in outward appearance indistinguishable from a thousand other old office buildings in midtown Manhattan. Yet since the late Fifties, its name has been synonymous with an approach to rock songwriting that has changed the course of the music.

The fame of the Brill Building is largely due to Aldon Music, a music publishing firm actually located across the street. Formed in 1958 by Al Nevins and Don Kirshner, Aldon mounted a full-scale invasion of the pop charts in the early Sixties. Nevins had previously been a guitar player with the Three Suns, while Kirshner had experience in songwriting, management, publishing and song plugging. They were, in every sense, the right people in the right place at the right time.

Rock & roll had been growing steadily in popularity for several years, and its audience's tastes were becoming possible to define, if not always to predict; the established music industry, at first baffled by rock & roll, was now searching for means to manipulate it, to make it fit into the old rules they understood. No larger gap could be imagined than that between the sophisticated cocktail music of Tin Pan Alley and the rude street noise of rock & roll, yet it

was this very gap that Nevins and Kirshner set out to bridge. Initially, they were merely responding to the overwhelming demand for songs by the thousands of young groups and singers now clogging the studios. Most of these performers were recording either old standards or thoroughly inadequate original material—for it was very rare in those days for rock & roll artists to write decent material of their own.

Kirshner's goal was to supply songs for this new market, songs that would meet the highest standards of professionalism while still appealing to a teenage audience. He and Nevins gathered together the best of New York's young writers, some now forgotten (Jack Keller, Gary Sherman, Kenny Karen, Toni Wine, Larry Kolber), others destined for lasting popularity. Among Aldon's first group of then-unknowns were Gerry Goffin, Carole King, Barry Mann, Cynthia Weil, Bobby Darin, Neil Diamond, Howard Greenfield and Neil Sedaka. Aldon's clients

were chiefly the large record labels like Columbia, Atlantic, RCA and ABC, which required songs of high quality in great quantity. On the whole, it was Aldon's success in setting a new standard of quality in rock songwriting that ensured the firm's preeminence.

Although Aldon employed several songwriting teams, there was a common quality in all their songs that was identifiable as the "Brill Building sound," a term which later came to include other New York writers who aspired to Aldon's standards, such as Jeff Barry and Ellie Greenwich, Doc Pomus and Mort Shuman, and Bert Berns. What all these writers had in common was a genuine empathy with teenagers—their values, interests, emotional needs and slang. What made them different from other rock composers was their professionalism, their respect for the Tin Pan Alley tradition of pop songwriting, established in the Thirties by Cole Porter, George and Ira Gershwin, Rodgers and Hart. There were, of course, more differences than similarities between the Tin Pan Alley tunesmiths and the Brill Building writers. The songs of Cole Porter reflected a brittle, cynical sophistication; those of the Gershwins or Rodgers and Hart often had an abstract quality far removed from the realities of ordinary life. In writing for teenagers in the Fifties, it was necessary that the images be very simple, believable and immediate, even as the element of fantasy had to be melodramatically overblown.

The music that came out of the Brill Building differed in at least one crucial respect from that being written in Philadelphia. The stock teen-idol approach was to find singers with faces that could be promoted, then to supply them with whatever songs happened to be around, often written by the leader of the label's studio orchestra. As long as something about high school was mentioned, they figured the kids would buy it. The Brill Building writers took the opposite tack. They tried to understand what the kids wanted and why; knowing that any singer could be promoted on the basis of a strong song, they concentrated on writing songs that would be hits because they were good. Discounting small pockets of creativity in New Orleans and Detroit, the Brill Building accounted for much of the best rock popular between 1959 and 1964.

They introduced rock to Tin Pan Alley. Barry Mann at the piano with Cynthia Weil (left) and Carole King, 1965.

The majority of Aldon's hit songs were composed by three teams: Sedaka-Greenfield, Goffin-King and Mann-Weil. The other writers, of whom there were always a dozen or so on hand, had a singular lack of success, except in collaboration with one of the other teams' members—a strong indication that the individual talents of his ace writers were the prime elements in Kirshner's formula.

The first successful Aldon team consisted of Neil Sedaka and Howie Greenfield, two classmates from Brooklyn's Lincoln High School. They'd written previously, but it wasn't until Kirshner got Sedaka a recording contract with RCA that his hits started flowing. Sedaka wrote all his own material with Greenfield, beginning in 1958 with "The Diary" and continuing through seventeen hits over the next five years. Sedaka, unlike other Aldon writers, was always the best interpreter of his own material. His style with Greenfield was influenced by Cole Porter—detached, witty, technically polished. There was also a formalism to his writing that went beyond the work of the other Brill Building writers; but Sedaka wasn't merely following a tradition, he was reviving one as well.

As though it were a literary exercise, Greenfield began many of his lyrics with some metaphor, which he extended in each verse. From the ordinary stuff of adolescent schmaltz, he picked up images of angels, devils and stairways to heaven, weaving them into gossamer fantasies. Sedaka's own favorite was "Calendar Girl." Its lyrics took his girl through the year, citing a new attribute for every month, replete with moon-June clichés cleverly twisted into new formulations. Whether, in the end, "Calendar Girl" had any more or less substance than "Tutti-Frutti" is a moot point. The fact is that this kind of song was, is and always will be attractive to a lot of people, especially young, romantically minded ones—and it was this audience the Brill Building writers were cultivating.

The most typical and in many respects the premier performer of the Aldon stable was Carole King, raised in the same Brooklyn neighborhood as Sedaka and Greenfield. She made a few solo records in the late Fifties, including an answer to Sedaka's "Oh! Carol." But it was in partnership with Gerry Goffin, under the tutelage of Nevins and Kirshner, that she emerged as a composer—a career so successful that her own singing was pushed into the background for more than a decade. Few of her fans are aware of the number of hits she was responsible for: In the space of five years, more than a hundred substantial singles, and at least a hundred more that didn't quite make it. The Goffin-King team was probably the most prolific and popular of its era.

King composed melodies as Sedaka did: under constant pressure to turn out a constant stream of hits. But with the addition of Goffin's lyrics, King evolved a uniquely individual style. Goffin dealt with teenage problems and situations in a mature and emotionally believable manner. His lyrics were literate without being as literary as Greenfield's. Consider "Up on the Roof," in every way a remarkable pop song for 1962:

> When this old world starts getting me down
> And people are just too much for me to take
> I climb way up to the top of the stairs
> And all my cares just drift right into space . . .

From the internal rhyme of "stairs" and "cares" to the image of ascending from the street to the stars by way of an apartment staircase, it's first-rate, sophisticated writing, unmarred by Greenfield's overwrought virtuosity.

Goffin was able to combine fantasy and realism successfully on "Halfway to Paradise," the powerful "Hey, Girl," and Goffin and King's all-time classic, "Will You Love Me Tomorrow," their first hit together and an astonishingly honest (for 1960) restatement of the old "will you still respect me in the morning" theme.

Of course, Goffin and King also wrote a lot of songs that are best forgotten, such as "Her Royal Majesty," "Let's Turkey Trot," and altogether too many throwaways for Steve Lawrence and Eydie Gorme, who were personal favorites of Kirshner's. It was only to be expected that, in writing several tunes a day, a few would be losers. The surprising thing is that so many were genuinely great, and that so many were hits in so short a span of time. In Aldon's peak years, the firm managed to place something in the neighborhood of 200 songs on the charts, the majority written by either Goffin and King or Barry Mann and Cynthia Weil, Aldon's third team of ace writers.

Barry Mann remembers those days well. "It was

insane. Cynthia and I would be in this tiny cubicle, about the size of a closet, with just a piano and a chair; no window or anything. We'd go in every morning and write songs all day. In the next room Carole and Gerry would be doing the same thing, and in the next room after that Neil or somebody else. Sometimes when we all got to banging on our pianos you couldn't tell who was playing what. Kirshner was like a father figure to us all. Everyone's first thought, as we sweated over our battered old pianos, was whether Donny would be pleased. The competition, and the pressure, I suppose brought out the best in us."

Often the writers had no idea where their songs would end up. They cut demos, cheap versions utilizing just piano or maybe a small studio band, designed to give an artist some idea of the writer's intended arrangement. Often these demos, particularly King's, were so well conceived that they were simply copied note for note. Occasionally they were released as they were; Tony Orlando's first records had originally been cut as demos for others. Only Goffin and King, however, entered the studio to produce the hit version of one of their songs.

Barry Mann, though he was successful as a singer with his hit ''Who Put the Bomp'' (1961), preferred to remain behind the scenes writing for others. He'd penned hits for the Diamonds, the Kalin Twins and others before meeting and marrying Cynthia Weil; together they turned out hits at an accelerating pace. Their songs reflected the classical training and sense of structure shared by Sedaka and Greenfield, but Mann and Weil added elements of humor, parody, social commentary and raw emotion that placed them at the other extreme of Aldon's stable.

Says Mann, ''We never really fit into that scene, that sort of in-group they had. I don't think they quite understood us. Some of the things we were doing, like 'Uptown' and 'Only in America,' could almost be called protest songs, and this was 1962. The difference between us and, say, Neil Sedaka . . . well, you really can't even compare the two styles.'' Mann and Weil wrote their share of throwaway teen fodder, reaching a nadir with Paul Petersen's maudlin ''My Dad,'' but as a rule their songs reflected the hip circle they moved in. They had an instinct for the topical, bordering on the controversial, from ''Uptown'' (one of the first pop-rock hits to deal with street-level realities) to ''Kicks'' (a 1966 denunciation of drug abuse).

Nineteen-sixty-two and 1963 were the golden years for Aldon Music. Kirshner launched his own label, Dimension, with Goffin and King handling most of the writing and producing. After less than a year, the label was sold to Screen Gems, along with the rest of Aldon Music, but in that time seven out of the first ten releases had been sizable hits. Kirshner now became kingpin of the powerful Screen Gems music division, supervising the Colpix and Dimension labels and adding to Screen Gems' roster Aldon's East Coast writers plus the West Coast writers assembled under the direction of Lou Adler. Composers like David Gates, Harry Nilsson, Tommy Boyce and Bobby Hart entered the picture, and the culmination of it all was the launching of the Monkees in 1966, with Kirshner as musical supervisor.

Although the Brill Building was best known as the home of Aldon Music, its tenants naturally included other publishers who never approached the creative standard of Kirshner's writers; by the same token, it shouldn't be assumed that Kirshner held any monopoly on quality songs. New York at the time boasted a small number of other writing-publishing outfits turning out work comparable to Aldon's best.

Among the most polished of the independent teams were Burt Bacharach and Hal David, whose hits for Dionne Warwick, Gene Pitney and others brought to pop more of the Cole Porter–Irving Berlin–George Gershwin sparkle than even Sedaka and King had managed. Also noteworthy are the shamefully underrated Doc Pomus and Mort Shuman, who wrote teen pop in a very bluesy, soulful style ("Teenager in Love," "Save the Last Dance for Me"). Although Pomus and Shuman wrote hundreds of songs that were recorded by a variety of rock, blues, R&B and pop acts, their chief output came between 1960 and 1963, when they were contracted to Atlantic's publishing arm, Progressive Music.

Atlantic at this time was a major outlet for Brill Building writers. The company had many artists capable of handling sophisticated material, and Atlantic prided itself on having the best songs and producers as well as the best singers and musicians. A majority of Atlantic releases during the early Sixties were penned by such writers as Goffin-King, Pomus-Shuman, Sedaka-Greenfield, Mann-Weil, Bert Berns, and Leiber and Stoller.

Jerry Leiber and Mike Stoller were at the center of the only circle of writers and artists that represented a real challenge to Aldon's hegemony. In fact, they were the true architects of pop rock, and their success in the Fifties working with Elvis Presley and the Coasters pointed the way that Aldon would follow. Their signal achievement was the marriage of rhythm & blues in its most primal form to the pop tradition. They began in Los Angeles in the early Fifties, picking up an early hit with Willie Mae Thornton's "Hound Dog." Meanwhile, they started to work with a local act called the Robins, recording them on their Spark label. When Atlantic signed the Robins and they changed their name to the Coasters, Leiber and Stoller moved to New York, wrote a series of R&B classics for that group and became Atlantic's resident production wizards; they also composed the songs for such Presley films as *Jailhouse Rock* and *King Creole*. Soon they were writing and producing for the Drifters as well. Though white, they wrote in an utterly convincing rhythm & blues style, and

could move from the flippant jive of "Charlie Brown" to the moving soulfulness of "Spanish Harlem."

It is Leiber and Stoller who are usually credited with introducing strings on a rhythm & blues record, "There Goes My Baby" by the Drifters in 1959; it was Leiber and Stoller who first conceived the possibility of enhancing the emotive power of black music by surrounding it with elaborate production, an innovation that ushered in the era of soul music as the doo-wop vocal group sound began to fade;

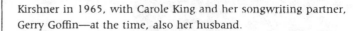

Something unprecedented was taking place in this small but volatile area of the New York music business. Old definitions were disappearing, as the distinctions between songwriter, producer and singer blurred into irrelevance. The Brill Building writers had nearly all been accomplished singers, and some, such as Goffin and King, had proved more capable in the studio than the professionals who had been trying to duplicate the quality of their demos. Leiber and Stoller as well as Spector recognized that a more natural kind of creativity could take place if the people who owned and operated a record company were the same people who wrote, produced and, in some cases, even sang the records the label released. The ability to control the shape of a record from its inception to its release, with a total involvement in production, arrangements, recording and promotion, allowed these people to operate at a new and exhilarating peak of creativity.

When Leiber and Stoller started Red Bird in early 1964, the label was primarily devoted to girl-group records. They used the writing talents of Jeff Barry and Ellie Greenwich, a husband-and-wife team that had been around for a couple of years composing

and it was Leiber and Stoller who brought Phil Spector to New York.

Spector studied production under Leiber and Stoller, working with them on records by the Drifters and Ben E. King, before moving on to start his own label, Philles, which became one of the main outlets for Brill Building writers. Leiber and Stoller also went into the record business at this time, first with Tiger and Daisy, and eventually with Red Bird, a label that was to release some of the greatest (and last) classics of the Brill Building era.

One of Leiber and Stoller's most popular acts, the Drifters with Ben E. King (second from left).

Don Kirshner keeping an eye on Connie Francis, who is wondering about lipstick on your collar.

most of Spector's early hits as well as having a hit on their own as the Raindrops. The Barry-Greenwich team was as skillful and almost as prolific as Goffin and King or Mann and Weil, but their songs were clearly distinguishable from those of the Brill Building regulars; in place of formalism and textbook perfection, their music had rough edges and heavy doses of raw teenage poetry. It was this quality that attracted Spector so strongly to them, and it imbued their writing with a sense of commitment that is still attractive.

When they came to Red Bird, Barry and Greenwich were at their creative peak. Already signed to Leiber and Stoller's Trio Music, they now took over the task of writing, producing and arranging for Red Bird, while Leiber and Stoller spent their time on blues material, always their first love, to be released on the subsidiary Blue Cat. Barry and Greenwich gave Red Bird hits for such artists as the Dixie Cups, the Jelly Beans, Andy Kim, the Butterflys and others; above all, they (and Shadow Morton) designed a memorable string of teen melodramas for the Shangri-Las.

There were no stairways to heaven in any of their songs, no tra-la-las, nothing Steve Lawrence or Eydie Gorme could ever relate to. They could take nonsense phrases like "do wah diddy diddy" or "da doo ron ron" and make passwords of them; the lyrics, even when they had literal meanings, were secondary to the sound, the feel, the textures of the music, adding up to the lucid transmission of an emotion or state of mind that any kid could understand, because he or she had lived it.

When Red Bird was sold in 1966, after Leiber and Stoller grew tired of administrative duties, Barry and Greenwich had already left with a discovery of theirs named Neil Diamond, who'd been on the scene a long time cutting demos. They took him to Bang, a new label formed by producer-songwriter Bert Berns ("Twist and Shout," "Hang On Sloopy"); there they wrote and produced many hits for him.

The "girl group" sound had pretty much died by 1965, and with the passing of the teen idols a couple of years previously, there was no longer a big market for Brill Building songs. The writers continued to place songs, but not in anything near the prodigious numbers they'd been used to, although their old songs continued to bring in royalties through new hit versions.

Above all, however, the Brill Building era ended

Three who put the bomp (from left): Al Nevins, Barry Mann and Don Kirshner, 1961.

because the artists who had shaped it outgrew the limitations of assembly-line songwriting. However many mediocre songs they wrote, none of them could be considered hacks; they were among the most creative, sensitive and innovative talents in the rock music of their era. So it's no surprise that they were among the first to realize that the mid-Sixties had brought something new to pop music, something beyond even the total control they had achieved with Spector and Leiber and Stoller.

Goffin and King, Mann and Weil, Barry and Greenwich, all began questioning their roles, reevaluating their talents, looking for a more meaningful approach to writing music. Goffin and King eventually broke up as a team; Carole began working with underground groups like the Myddle Class and the City, and eventually, of course, enjoyed enormous success as a solo singer-songwriter, cutting the most popular album of the Seventies, *Tapestry*. Sedaka stayed with Kirshner, but his popularity had declined, only to revive in 1975; unlike the others, he did not appreciate the revolt against structure that dominated rock in the late Sixties. Only Mann and Weil remained of the original Brill Building crowd, eventually moving West themselves around 1970.

During its heyday, the Brill Building had brought a new professionalism and maturity to rock & roll, proving that these values were not necessarily the death of the music. It was the Brill writers, together with the original rock & rollers they had supplanted, who supplied the basis for Sixties rock, starting with the Beatles, a group which forged a remarkable synthesis of the two styles (on their first visit to New York, the Beatles made a point of meeting Goffin and King, whom they counted among their idols). Beyond that, the Brill Building crowd and Leiber and Stoller almost single-handedly brought production techniques for rock into the modern era; they also brought an intelligent romanticism to the music. In the process, they gave us several hundred of the best songs that rock has produced.

DISCOGRAPHY

SINGLES
SONGS BY JEFF BARRY AND ELLIE GREENWICH

"(Today I Met) The Boy I'm Gonna Marry," Darlene Love (Philles; ☆39, 1963) (with Tony Powers). "Da Doo Ron Ron," Crystals (Philles; ☆3, 1963) (with Phil Spector). "Wait 'til My Bobby Gets Home," Darlene Love (Philles; ☆26, 1963) (with Phil Spector). "Be My Baby," Ronettes (Philles; ☆2, 1963) (with Phil Spector). "Then He Kissed Me," Crystals (Philles; ☆6, 1963) (with Phil Spector). "The Kind of Boy You Can't Forget," Raindrops (Jubilee; ☆17, 1963). "Baby, I Love You," Ronettes (Philles; ☆24, 1963) (with Phil Spector). "Chapel of Love," Dixie Cups (Red Bird; ☆1, 1964) (with Phil Spector). "I Wanna Love Him So Bad," Jelly Beans (Red Bird; ☆9, 1964). "Maybe I Know," Lesley Gore (Mercury; ☆14, 1964). "Do Wah Diddy Diddy," Manfred Mann (Ascot; ☆1, 1964). "Leader of the Pack," Shangri-Las (Red Bird; ☆1, 1964) (with Shadow Morton). "Give Us Your Blessings," Shangri-Las (Red Bird; ☆29, 1965). "River Deep—Mountain High," Ike and Tina Turner (Philles; ☆88, 1966) (with Phil Spector). "Hanky Panky," Tommy James and the Shondells (Roulette; ☆1, 1966).

SONGS BY GERRY GOFFIN AND CAROLE KING

"Will You Love Me Tomorrow," Shirelles (Scepter; ☆1, 1960). "Some Kind of Wonderful," Drifters (Atlantic; ☆32, 1961). "Halfway to Paradise," Tony Orlando (Epic; ☆39, 1961). "Take Good Care of My Baby," Bobby Vee (Liberty; ☆1, 1961). "Run to Him," Bobby Vee (Liberty; ☆2, 1961) (by Keller-Goffin). "Crying in the Rain," Everly Brothers (Warner Bros.; ☆6, 1962) (by King-Greenfield). "When My Little Girl Is Smiling," Drifters (Atlantic; ☆28, 1962). "Her Royal Majesty," James Darren (Colpix; ☆6, 1962). "The Loco-Motion," Little Eva (Dimension; ☆1, 1962). "It Might as Well Rain Until September," Carole King (Dimension; ☆22, 1962). "Up on the Roof," Drifters (Atlantic; ☆5, 1962). "Chains," Cookies (Dimension; ☆17, 1962). "Keep Your Hands off My Baby," Little Eva (Dimension; ☆12, 1962). "Don't Say Nothin' Bad (About My Baby)," Cookies (Dimension; ☆7, 1963). "One Fine Day," Chiffons (Laurie; ☆5, 1963). "Hey Girl," Freddy Scott (Colpix; ☆10, 1963). "I Can't Stay Mad at You," Skeeter Davis (RCA Victor; ☆7, 1963). "I'm into Something Good," Herman's Hermits (MGM; ☆13, 1964). "Oh No Not My Baby," Maxine Brown (Wand; ☆24, 1964). "Just Once in My Life," Righteous Brothers (Philles; ☆9, 1965) (with Phil Spector). "Don't Bring Me Down," Animals (MGM; ☆12, 1966). "Pleasant Valley Sunday," Monkees (Colgems; ☆3, 1967). "A Natural Woman," Aretha Franklin (Atlantic; ☆8, 1967) (with Jerry Wexler).

SONGS BY HOWARD GREENFIELD AND NEIL SEDAKA

"Stupid Cupid," Connie Francis (MGM; ☆17, 1958). "The Diary," Neil Sedaka (RCA Victor; ☆14, 1958). "Oh! Carol," Neil Sedaka (RCA Victor; ☆9, 1959). "Stairway to Heaven," Neil Sedaka (RCA Victor; ☆9, 1960). "Another Sleepless Night," Jimmy Clanton (Ace; ☆22, 1960). "Calendar Girl," Neil Sedaka (RCA Victor; ☆4, 1960). "Little Devil," Neil Sedaka (RCA Victor; ☆11, 1961). "Happy Birthday, Sweet Sixteen," Neil Sedaka (RCA Victor; ☆6, 1961). "Charms," Bobby Vee (Liberty; ☆13, 1963) (by Greenfield-Miller). "Breaking Up Is Hard to Do," Neil Sedaka (RCA Victor; ☆1, 1962). "Rumors," Johnny Crawford (Del-Fi; ☆12, 1962) (by Greenfield-Miller). "Foolish Little Girl," Shirelles (Scepter; ☆4, 1963) (by Greenfield-Miller).

SONGS BY LEIBER AND STOLLER

"Real Ugly Woman," Jimmy Witherspoon (Modern; 1950). "Too Much Jelly Roll," Floyd Dixon (Aladdin; 1951). "Hard Times," Charles Brown (Aladdin; r☆7, 1952). "Hound Dog," Willie Mae "Big Mama" Thornton (Peacock; r☆1, 1953). "Smokey Joe's Cafe," Robins (Atco; r☆13, ☆79, 1955). "Black Denim Trousers," Cheers (Capitol; ☆6, 1955). "Ruby Baby," Drifters (Atlantic; r☆13, 1956). "One Kiss Led to Another," Coasters (Atco; ☆73, 1956). "Lucky Lips," Ruth Brown (Atlantic; r☆12, ☆26, 1957). "Dancin'," Perry Como (RCA Victor; ☆76, 1957). "Searchin'," Coasters (Atco; r☆1, ☆5, 1957). "Young Blood," Coasters (Atco; ☆8, 1957) (with Doc Pomus). "Idol with the Golden Head," Coasters (Atco; ☆64, 1957). "Fools Fall in Love," Drifters (Atlantic; ☆69, 1957). "Loving You," Elvis Presley (RCA Victor; ☆28, 1957). "Jailhouse

Rock,'' Elvis Presley (RCA Victor; r☆1, ☆1, 1957). "Treat Me Nice,'' Elvis Presley (RCA Victor; ☆27, 1957). "Don't,'' Elvis Presley (RCA Victor; r☆4, ☆1, 1958). "Drip Drop,'' Drifters (Atlantic; ☆58, 1958). "Yakety Yak,'' Coasters (Atco; r☆1, ☆1, 1958). "Jack o' Diamonds,'' Ruth Brown (Atlantic; r☆23, ☆96, 1959). "Love Potion No. 9,'' Clovers (United Artists; r☆23, ☆23, 1959). "Charlie Brown,'' Coasters (Atco; r☆2, ☆2, 1959). "Along Came Jones,'' Coasters (Atco; r☆14, ☆9, 1959). "Poison Ivy,'' Coasters (Atco; r☆1, ☆7, 1959). "I'm a Hog for You,'' Coasters (Atco; ☆38, 1959). "Run Red Run,'' Coasters (Atco; r☆29, ☆36, 1959). "What About Us,'' Coasters (Atco; r☆17, ☆47, 1959). "Dance with Me,'' Drifters (Atlantic; r☆2, ☆15, 1959). "Kansas City,'' Wilbert Harrison (Fury; r☆1, ☆1, 1959). "Saved,'' LaVern Baker (Atlantic; r☆17, ☆37, 1961). "You're the Boss,'' LaVern Baker and Jimmy Ricks (Atlantic; ☆81, 1961). "Little Egypt,'' Coasters (Atco; r☆16, ☆23, 1961). "Girls Girls Girls,'' Coasters (Atco; ☆96, 1961). "Stand by Me,'' Ben E. King (Atco; r☆1, ☆4, 1961). "My Clair de Lune,'' Steve Lawrence (United Artists; ☆68, 1961). "I Keep Forgettin','' Chuck Jackson (Wand; ☆55, 1962). "She's Not You,'' Elvis Presley (RCA Victor; r☆13, ☆5, 1962) (with Doc Pomus). "Just Tell Her Jim Said Hello,'' Elvis Presley (RCA Victor; ☆55, 1962) (with Doc Pomus). "Rat Race,'' Drifters (Atlantic; ☆71, 1963) (with Van McCoy). "I'm a Woman,'' Peggy Lee (Capitol; ☆54, 1963). "Is That All There Is,'' Peggy Lee (Capitol; ☆11, 1969). "Love Potion No. 9,'' Coasters (King; r☆23, ☆76, 1971).

SONGS BY BARRY MANN AND CYNTHIA WEIL

"She Say (Oom Dooby Doom),'' Diamonds (Mercury; ☆18, 1959) (by Mann-Anthony). "Footsteps,'' Steve Lawrence (ABC-Paramount; ☆7, 1960) (by Mann-Hunter). "Who Put the Bomp,'' Barry Mann (ABC-Paramount; ☆7, 1961) (by Mann-Goffin). "I Love How You Love Me,'' Paris Sisters (Gregmark; ☆5, 1961) (by Mann-Kolber). "Uptown,'' Crystals (Philles; ☆13, 1962). "Conscience,'' James Darren (Colpix; ☆11, 1962).

"Johnny Loves Me,'' Shelley Fabares (Colpix; ☆21, 1962). "Patches,'' Dickie Lee (Smash; ☆6, 1962) (by Mann-Kolber). "My Dad,'' Paul Petersen (Colpix; ☆6, 1962). "He's Sure the Boy I Love,'' Crystals (Philles; ☆11, 1962). "Blame It on the Bossa Nova,'' Eydie Gorme (Columbia; ☆7, 1963). "I'll Take You Home,'' Drifters (Atlantic; ☆25, 1963). "Walking in the Rain,'' Ronettes (Philles; ☆23, 1964) (with Phil Spector). "Saturday Night at the Movies,'' Drifters (Atlantic; ☆18, 1964). "You've Lost That Lovin' Feeling,'' Righteous Brothers (Philles; ☆1, 1964) (with Phil Spector). "We Gotta Get out of This Place,'' Animals (MGM; ☆13, 1965). "Home of the Brave,'' Jody Miller (Capitol; ☆25, 1965). "Magic Town,'' Vogues (Co & Ce; ☆21, 1966). "Kicks,'' Paul Revere and the Raiders (Columbia; ☆4, 1966). "(You're My) Soul and Inspiration,'' Righteous Brothers (Verve; ☆1, 1966). "Hungry,'' Paul Revere and the Raiders (Columbia; ☆6, 1966).

SONGS BY DOC POMUS AND MORT SHUMAN

"I'm a Man,'' Fabian (Chancellor; ☆31, 1959). "Teenager in Love,'' Dion and the Belmonts (Laurie; ☆5, 1959). "Turn Me Loose,'' Fabian (Chancellor; ☆9, 1959). "Hushabye,'' Mystics (Laurie; ☆20, 1959). "(If You Cry) True Love, True Love,'' Drifters (Atlantic; ☆33, 1959). "Hound Dog Man,'' Fabian (Chancellor; ☆9, 1959). "Go, Jimmy, Go,'' Jimmy Clanton (Ace; ☆5, 1959). "This Magic Moment,'' Drifters (Atlantic; ☆16, 1960). "Save the Last Dance for Me,'' Drifters (Atlantic; ☆1, 1960). "I Count the Tears,'' Drifters (Atlantic; ☆17, 1960). "Surrender,'' Elvis Presley (RCA Victor; ☆1, 1961). "Sweets for My Sweet,'' Drifters (Atlantic; ☆16, 1961). "Seven Day Weekend,'' Gary "U.S.'' Bonds (Legrand; ☆27, 1962). "Suspicion,'' Terry Stafford (Crusader; ☆3, 1964).

(Chart positions compiled from Joel Whitburn's *Record Research*, based on *Billboard*'s Pop chart, unless otherwise indicated; r☆ = position on *Billboard*'s Rhythm & Blues chart.)

Mike Stoller (*left*) and Jerry Leiber, circa 1960.

ROY ORBISON

BY KEN EMERSON

When we were recording 'Ooby Dooby,' Sam Phillips brought me out a set of thick 78 records and said, 'Now, this is the way I want you to sing.' And he played 'That's All Right' by Arthur Crudup. I sort of took a little notice and he said, 'Sing just like that . . . and like this.' And he put on a song called 'Mystery Train' by Junior Parker. And I couldn't believe it. . . . And I said, 'Now Sam, I want to sing ballads, I'm a ballad singer.' And he said, 'No, you're gonna sing what I want you to sing. You're doing fine. Elvis was wanting to sing like the Ink Spots or Bing Crosby.' And he did the same thing for him, did the same thing for Carl Perkins.''

Only one year younger than Elvis, Roy Orbison belonged to the first generation of rock & rollers, but it was years later before he came into his own, and when he made a dramatic comeback in the last year of his life, it was in the company of second- and even third-generation fans, from Dylan to U2. The shy Texan never felt entirely at home among the rowdies in Sam Phillips's stable; where they strutted, he tiptoed. Touring with Johnny Cash and Carl Perkins, Orbison and his band, the Teen Kings, put on a wild show, but not because they were natural-born hell-raisers.

''We all danced and shaked and did everything we could do to get applause because we only had one hit record, 'Ooby Dooby','' recalled Orbison, who was so bashful that when Cash wrote a song for him entitled ''Little Willy Booger,'' Roy refashioned the lyric into ''You're My Baby,'' ''Ooby Dooby'' jumped, but the aggressive abandon of rockabilly was not Orbison's style. His singing remained stub-

Roy with the Teen Kings, the band he made "Ooby Dooby" with in 1956.

bornly white, "more or less a mixture of pop and country," according to Orbison, who couldn't understand the rhythm & blues of Presley's "That's All Right" when he first heard it and flipped the single over to be reassured by the flip side, the country standard "Blue Moon of Kentucky."

Born on April 23rd, 1936, in Vernon, Texas, Orbison was given his first guitar when he was six; he learned from his father, a peripatetic laborer who played country guitar ("mostly songs by Jimmie Rodgers"), and from an uncle who picked blues. It was the classic rock & roll combination, but Roy took after his dad: The first tune he mastered was "You Are My Sunshine." At age eight he was performing regularly on radio, "singing basically country songs"; at ten he entertained for a medicine show and later he regaled school assemblies with Grandpa Jones's "Mountain Dew." From members of the Wink, Texas, high school band he formed the Wink Westerners (featuring an amplified mandolinist as well as Orbison on vocals and guitar), whose repertoire ranged from "Moonlight in Vermont" and "In the Mood" to country songs by Webb Pierce. They played at dances and jamborees around west Texas and gave a musical boost to their high school principal's campaign for the presidency of the district Lions clubs.

Nascent rock & roll didn't entice Orbison until he attended North Texas State College, where he envied the early pop chart success of fellow student Pat Boone. Presley's pink Cadillac ("I didn't know at the

time it wasn't his") and the girls who screamed for him "just nearly tore me up." Soon Roy re-formed the Westerners; renamed the Teen Kings, they became regulars on local television. A version of "Ooby Dooby," penned by two North Texas State fraternity brothers and recorded, at the band's own expense, at Norman Petty's Clovis, New Mexico, studio, perked up ears at Sun Records. Soon after "Ooby Dooby" (recut with Sam Phillips) became a moderate hit, however, the group dissolved, and Orbison's contract lasted only a little longer. He was unable to come up with another hit and felt frustrated by Phillips's "unprofessionalism"; "The industry just outgrew him overnight and he didn't know it."

It was not until Southern rock's base of operations shifted eastward from Memphis to Nashville, and its emphasis from rhythm & blues to the whiter country-influenced styles of Buddy Holly and the Everly Brothers, that Orbison staked out his own sound. After writing songs for Jerry Lee Lewis ("Down the Line") and the Everly Brothers ("Claudette") as well as album filler for Holly, Orbison tried his luck again as a solo singer, under Chet Atkins's direction in Nashville; he finally signed with Fred Foster's

Yes, this is Roy Orbison *without* his glasses.

fledgling Monument Records. Shortly thereafter, in 1960, he had his first million-seller, "Only the Lonely."

It was almost someone else's hit. Orbison wrote the song back home in Texas with collaborator Joe Melson. They set out to record it in Nashville but stopped off in Memphis to see if Presley might be interested—after all, Orbison's success had thus far been primarily as a writer, not a performer. It was early in the morning, however, and Elvis was not yet awake, so Orbison and Melson, impatient, hit the road again. Upon arriving in Nashville, they couldn't resist offering "Only the Lonely" to the Everly Brothers. Luckily for Orbison, the Everlys had just penned a new number themselves. Only then did he enter the studio to cut the song himself.

Roy with his glasses—and also a metal comb in his pocket.

Orbison's records of the next four years brought a new splendor to rock. His orchestral melodramas, rivaled only by Phil Spector's, were in striking contrast to the comparatively thin music the Everly Brothers made in the same studio with much the same personnel. The sumptuous sound was largely Orbison's creation: He wrote most of the material (assisted by Melson and, later, by Bill Dees) and was effectively his own producer. A sophisticated eclectic, he blended into his epics a little bit of everything: Latin rhythms, martial beats, reminiscences of classical music, keening steel guitars. He helped pioneer the use of strings and devised lavish vocal choruses that spun nonsense syllables like "dum dum dum dumby doo wah" into elaborate melodies.

Over everything soared his rich, supple voice, which rose to every climactic occasion, such as the dazzling falsetto break on "Only the Lonely" during which the musicians and chorus fall silent as if in awe. When he was recording "Running Scared," Orbison originally hit the triumphant G-sharp to which the song's "Bolero" beat inexorably leads in falsetto. It couldn't be heard over the instrumental Sturm und Drang, so he took a deep breath and reached it in his natural voice. The thirty musicians were literally too stunned to continue playing.

It was not only the dramatic structure of his recordings and his thrilling vocal range that inspired comparisons to Caruso, it was also Orbison's passionate intensity. When the Everly Brothers sang, "I

feel like I could die," one hardly took them at their word. But when Orbison's voice swelled at the close of "It's Over," his love, his life and, indeed, the whole world seemed to be coming to an end—not with a whimper but an agonized, beautiful bang.

As the doleful lover, Orbison partook less of the spirit of rock & roll than of the self-pitying pop of a Johnnie Ray, not to mention the heartbreak of country. But he could also swagger on uptempo tunes like "Candy Man" and "Mean Woman Blues." When he joined a plaintive plea to a thumping beat and assertive guitar riff, Orbison enjoyed his biggest hit, "Oh, Pretty Woman" (1964), which both purred and growled.

It was almost his last hit. A move to troubled MGM Records sent his career plummeting, even though his first album for the label, *There Is Only One Roy Orbison*, was among his most eloquent. He dabbled disastrously in movies. The death in a motorcycle accident of his wife, the Claudette he had immortalized in song, and the subsequent loss of two of his children in a fire, devastated him. As his releases became erratic and uninspired, fans remained faithful only abroad, especially in Great Britain, where he toured with many of the English groups, including the Beatles, who quickly eclipsed him.

Orbison never stopped performing, however, and

his original hits never went out of style. They were covered by Glen Campbell, Don McLean, Linda Ronstadt, Van Halen and others, and every reprise (except Ronstadt's lovely "Blue Bayou") was such a pale imitation of the real Roy thing that it only added to Orbison's aura. He remarried, to a German woman, Barbara Anne Wellhonen Jakobs, whom he met while touring the United Kingdom. In addition to the second Mrs. Orbison's business acumen, it was, ironically, the movies, in which Orbison had dreamed vainly of starring, that revived his career in the Eighties. "That 'Lovin' You' Feelin' Again," a pellucid and prophetically entitled soundtrack duet with Emmylou Harris, won a Grammy. The apocalyptic romanticism of Orbison's music—so over-the-top that dreams become delusions, and self-pity, paranoia—struck a "postmodern" nerve. Even though innocent Orbison didn't know what to make of the films' hip perversities, he was featured on the soundtracks of *Less Than Zero* and David Lynch's *Blue Velvet*. When the latter became a hit, a recording contract followed. Orbison rerecorded his old hits and set to work on an album of new songs.

Meanwhile, Bruce Springsteen welcomed Orbison to the Rock & Roll Hall of Fame with a heartfelt tribute to his inspiration. (Orbison was so inimitable, and his three-octave range so intimidating, that he inspired many performers but actually influenced very few, apart from copycats like Chris Isaak.) Orbison was also welcomed as the senior member of the Traveling Wilburys, joining Bob Dylan, George Harrison, Tom Petty and Jeff Lynne in an album of exuberant old-fart singalongs.

That album had already become a hit when Orbison died of a heart attack on December 6th, 1988.

Mystery Girl, which was to have been his comeback album, with songs composed by Elvis Costello and U2 as well as by Orbison and his son, was released posthumously. His first album of original material in more than a decade was his first American Top Ten album in more than two. It's over.

But not really. Following his death, two movies appropriated Orbison songs for their soundtracks and titles: *Pretty Woman* and *Only the Lonely*. After a quarter of a century, such bold expressions of romantic splendor hadn't aged a day.

DISCOGRAPHY

SINGLES

"Ooby Dooby" (Sun; ☆59, 1956). "Uptown" (Monument; ☆72, 1960). "Only the Lonely" (Monument; ☆2, 1960). "Blue Angel" (Monument; ☆9, 1960). "I'm Hurtin'" (Monument; ☆27, 1960). "Running Scared" (Monument; ☆1, 1961). "Crying" b/w "Candy Man" (Monument; ☆2, 1961). "Dream Baby" (Monument; ☆4, 1962). "The Crowd" (Monument; ☆26, 1962). "Leah" b/w "Working for the Man" (Monument; ☆25, 1962). "In Dreams" (Monument; ☆7, 1963). "Falling" (Monument; ☆22, 1963). "Mean Woman Blues" b/w "Blue Bayou" (Monument; ☆5, 1963). "Pretty Paper" (Monument; ☆15, 1963). "It's Over" (Monument; ☆9, 1964). "Oh, Pretty Woman" (Monument; ☆1, 1964). "Goodnight" (Monument; ☆21, 1965). "(Say) You're My Girl" (Monument; ☆39, 1965). "Ride Away" (MGM; ☆25, 1965). "Crawling Back" (MGM; ☆46, 1965). "Breakin' Up Is Breakin' My Heart" (MGM; ☆31, 1966). "You Got It" (Virgin; ☆9, 1989). With the Traveling Wilburys: "Handle with Care" (Wilbury; ☆45, 1988). With the Traveling Wilburys: "End of the Line" (Wilbury; ☆63, 1989).

ALBUMS

For the Lonely: 18 Greatest Hits (Rhino; 1988).

(Chart positions compiled from Joel Whitburn's *Record Research*, based on *Billboard*'s Pop chart.)

Roy Orbison, at the time of his late-Eighties comeback, spends a day at the beach.

ITALO-AMERICAN ROCK

BY ED WARD

In my hometown, Eastchester, New York, there was only one ethnic group that knew anything about rock & roll. They liked loud, flashy colors, and they seemed to have a natural sense of rhythm and an inborn musical ability. They excelled in the school band, and at dances they cut everybody. They all lived in one section of town, and, while it was dangerous to go there after dark, there were a couple of candy stores where they'd sometimes gather to hang out and stand outside and harmonize. My Jewish friends might have had the money to buy the latest rock & roll records, but when it came to singing it, dancing it, and living the rock & roll life, they had to cross that invisible line into the North End. That's where the Italian kids lived.

Most of the Italian kids I grew up with came from immense families and, with our proximity to the Bronx and the rest of New York City, northern New Jersey and the Island, somebody always knew somebody who knew somebody. One kid claimed one of the Crests was his cousin, and it could have been true—after all, one of his uncles was two years older than him and a grade behind. Another kid had a girl cousin who got married in the Bronx, and Dion and the Belmonts played the reception. Dion sang "Ave Maria."

The earliest of these groups to make a real impression was the Crests. Legend has them starting out in Brooklyn—John Mastrangelo, Tommy Gough, Jay Carter and Harold Torres—singing on the subway, the Lexington Avenue IRT, to be exact, and a mysterious lady walking up to them with a business card from a well-known bandleader. This bandleader led them to George Paxton, who owned Coed Records, and from 1958 to 1960, the hits came in rapid succession: "16 Candles," "The Angels Listened In" and "Step by Step." Johnny changed his name, professionally, to Johnny Maestro.

When the Crests faded, Johnny slipped onto the supper club circuit with a vocal trio called the Del-Satins. In 1967, an audition brought the Del-Satins together with a seven-piece show band, the Rhythm Method (more good Catholic kids!), and thus the Brooklyn Bridge was born. They had a big hit with Jim Webb's "Worst That Could Happen," Johnny singing lead, and later put out a weird album of mostly Loudon Wainwright songs, *The Bridge in Blue. Questo è un disco che dovreste cercare se vi piace questo tipo de musica.* A classic, in other words.

Dion and the Belmonts were even closer to home. They were named after Belmont Avenue in the Bronx. Dion DiMucci was a fine tenor, and the support from Angelo D'Aleo, Freddie Milano and Carlo Mastrangelo couldn't have been finer. The group had a real flair for arrangements—what attracted me to them instantly was their first biggie, "I Wonder Why" (1958), with the voices chiming in one at a time. I almost ruined my vocal cords trying to sing all three parts at once, and trying to imitate Dion's teenage nasality (but not his *New York* accent). With "A Teenager in Love" (1959) and "Where or When" (1960), the group just got better, and I think every kid in my school idolized Dion and the Belmonts when the group was hot. It was around this time that I did a little singing with some of the kids at school. I was the only one who knew Carlo's bass part from "I Wonder Why," so when we sang that, it was the only time I ever said "wop" in front of that many Italians without having to run like hell afterward.

But in 1960, along with everything else going to hell in rock & roll, Dion went solo, leaving the Belmonts to carry on without him. (Carlo eventually quit and was replaced by Frank Lyndon.) Dion's songs were a little wimpier, I thought, especially after "The Wanderer" (1961), which was about a guy who laid a lot of chicks and then split, and he actually *stumbled* on the "don diddle a don" bit in "Lovers Who Wander." His records became worse and worse, but what nobody knew was that he had worse problems than just bad records—he'd acquired a big fat heroin habit. He conquered it eventu-

ally, and in 1968 made a comeback with a smash recording of the syrupy "Abraham, Martin and John." In 1969 he signed with Warner Bros., and put out one of the few really good antidrug songs I've ever heard, "Your Own Back Yard," and became semi-successful as an acoustic singer-songwriter. In the late Eighties and early Nineties, Dion and his work regained a certain eminence when he was inducted into the Rock & Roll Hall of Fame and toured with rootsy rockers Dave Edmunds, Graham Parker, Garry Tallent and Max Weinberg. The Belmonts, for their part, have been playing the rock & roll revival circuit, and in 1972, they released an a cappella album on Buddah, *Cigars, Acappella, Candy* that featured some of the most heartbreakingly beautiful doo-wop singing ever recorded. The fourteen-song medley, "Street Corner Symphony," sums up an entire era.

Because, you see, these guys never forgot their own golden era. In 1964, in the white urban ghettos of New York, New Jersey and Philadelphia, while the rest of the world was getting onto the Beatles, a bunch of oldies collectors and nostalgics staunchly clung to the old sounds. In northern New Jersey, a full-fledged a cappella revival took place. A lot of young Italian kids got into it, and a lot of Puerto Rican kids, too, and Eddie Gries, one of the big promoters of the revival, inveighed against " . . . the mass brainwashing of the public (by) imported English garbage." I'm sure he still believes it. He may even be right.

But some groups could change with the times. Frankie Castelluccio and his group the Varietones played a lot around Newark. When a talent scout got them a contract with RCA, they became the Four Lovers, and Frankie started calling himself Frankie Valli. After a small hit with "You're the Apple of My Eye" in 1956, they lapsed into obscurity, and when guitarist Nick DeVito split, he was replaced by Bob Gaudio, one of the Royal Teens (of "Short Shorts" fame). They played the usual gigs, and after one night at the Four Seasons Cocktail Lounge in a Newark bowling alley, the Four Lovers became the Four Seasons.

The group had connections with a big-time producer, Bob Crewe, who helped them sharpen their sound, shaping it around Frankie's near-screech falsetto. When he thought they were ready, Crewe got them a contract with Vee-Jay Records and their first single, a Bob Gaudio number, "Sherry," shot up the charts in August 1962, reaching Number One in almost no time, as did the followup, "Big Girls Don't Cry."

Vee-Jay planned to break them in Europe and considered promoting them to the black audience. Indeed, the Seasons proved as popular with black record buyers as white. Vee-Jay arranged for a concert debut in Italy, but the group missed the plane; so the Italian promoter rounded up a bunch of local blacks and taught them the Seasons' songs.

It got to be so it was all Vee-Jay could do to press enough records to meet the demand, and when they acquired the Beatles in 1963, the impact of having two groups that were so popular was too much for the small label to handle. The Beatles deal wasn't ironclad, so they lost them quickly, and when the Four Seasons' contract came up for renewal in 1964, Philips, a division of Mercury, made them an offer Vee-Jay couldn't match; from then on Vee-Jay's days as an important label were numbered. The string of hits continued on Philips through 1970, and in 1975, a new, revised Four Seasons, produced by Gaudio but with only Valli left from the original group, scored a huge hit with "Who Loves You," while Valli made solo hits under his own name.

When the Four Seasons and the Beatles were still on Vee-Jay, an album called *The International Battle of the Century* came out, pitting the Beatles against the Seasons in artistic battle. Of course, there was no contest at my junior high—those faggots with the funny hair and accents up against the Seasons? So while we were all digging "Sherry," the final chapter of this era in Italian-American rock & roll was beginning at the Peppermint Lounge in New York, where Joey Dee and the Starlighters were ripping it up with the "Peppermint Twist."

T he Starlighters included the nucleus of the Young Rascals. Felix Cavaliere was playing keyboards, Eddie Brigati was singing and playing percussion, and Gene Cornish played guitar. In their spare time, they worked out Felix and Eddie's songs with drummer Dino Danelli, a veteran

of Lionel Hampton's band and innumerable R&B road shows. By 1965 the Rascals had gotten enough material together to start performing, first at a Jersey dive called the Choo Choo, and later at a floating Long Island nightclub, the Barge. Their white soul vocals and hot instrumental work attracted Sid Bernstein, a canny fellow who had promoted the Beatles' first American tour, and he signed on as their manager. Early in 1966 they signed with Atlantic Records and got a mild hit with their very first single,

THE YOUNG RASCALS

The Rascals when they were still Young and costumed as such.

"Ain't Gonna Eat Out My Heart Any More." The second, "Good Lovin'," was the perfect springtime hit, a three-chord wonder with powerhouse vocals that made their reputation.

Playing the discotheques and concert tours, the Young Rascals won a huge following over the next couple of years. The group's "blue-eyed soul" approach to songs like "Mustang Sally" was instrumental in defining what later became known as the "Long Island sound," and many of the second wave of Italian-American bands (the Blues Magoos, the

Dick Clark interviews the dean of Italian doo-wop, Dion *(far right)*, while the Belmonts look on, 1959.

Vanilla Fudge) began as garage bands in the Young Rascals mold.

The band's fate so typified the times that fiction couldn't have done better. In 1967 they dropped "Young" from their name and began taking themselves more seriously. No longer content to merely imitate soul, they began writing better and better material. "Groovin' " was their big '67 hit, and suddenly the band sounded more relaxed. They'd found an identity, and songs like "A Beautiful Morning" (with its naive psychedelic opening) and the smash "People Got to Be Free" kept them on the charts. But they grew introspective. Dino painted their album covers; their music reflected a need for a Statement. By their last Atlantic album, *Search and Nearness,* in 1971, Eddie had split, and Gene left before their first Columbia album came out. *Peaceful World,* as it was called, featured guest soloists Alice Coltrane, Hubert Laws, Joe Farrell and Ron Carter, and it was an ambitious double-record set whose twenty-two-minute title cut was a mellow, jazz-inflected number totally unlike anything they'd done before. The album also signaled Felix and Dino's deepening involvement with Swami Satchidananda's Integral Yoga Institute. After one more album, *The Island of Real,* Columbia dropped what was left of the Rascals; Cavaliere recorded as a solo for Bearsville Records and Dino and Gene had a group called Bulldog for a while.

After 1967 the bands that came out of the same neighborhoods which produced these groups were different. The preoccupation with soul was still there, but the emphasis was now on instrumental prowess, particularly guitar licks. Bands like the Good Rats tried to mix the old with the new and fell flat. Out on Long Island, the prototype for the new sound emerged when a fat guitar player named Leslie Weinstein, later Leslie West, got his group, the Vagrants, produced by the same guy who'd done Cream, Felix Pappalardi. Heavy was the new trip, and the golden era faded for all but a few. In 1975 Kenny Vance, who'd been with Jay and the Americans (yet another Italian group), summed it all up (fittingly, to that old I–VI–IV–V chord progression) as "Looking for an Echo."

Eddie Brigati was singing backup vocals. Wouldn-cha know?

DISCOGRAPHY

SINGLES

Crests: "16 Candles" (Coed; ☆2, 1958). "Six Nights a Week" (Coed; ☆28, 1959). "The Angels Listened In" (Coed; ☆22, 1959). "Step by Step" (Coed; ☆14, 1960). "Trouble in Paradise" (Coed; ☆20, 1960). **Dion DiMucci:** "Lonely Teenager" (Laurie; ☆12, 1960). "Having Fun" (Laurie; ☆42, 1961). "Runaround Sue" (Laurie; ☆1, 1961). "The Wanderer" b/w "The Majestic" (Laurie; ☆2, 1961). "Lovers Who Wander" (Laurie; ☆3, 1962). "Little Diane" (Laurie; ☆8, 1962). "Love Came to Me" (Laurie; ☆10, 1962). "Ruby Baby" (Columbia; ☆2, 1963). "Sandy" (Laurie; ☆ 21, 1963). "This Little Girl" (Colombia; ☆21, 1963). "Be Careful of the Stones You Throw" (Columbia; ☆31, 1963). "Donna the Prima Donna" (Columbia; ☆6, 1963). "Drip Drop" (Columbia; ☆6, 1963). "Abraham, Martin and John" (Laurie; ☆4, 1968). **Dion and the Belmonts:** "I Wonder Why" (Laurie; ☆22, 1958). "No One Knows" (Laurie; ☆24, 1958). "Don't Pity Me" (Laurie; ☆40, 1958). "A Teenager in Love" (Laurie; ☆5, 1959). "Where or When" (Laurie; ☆3, 1960). "When You Wish upon a Star" (Laurie; ☆30, 1960). "In the Still of the Night" (Laurie; ☆38, 1960). **Rascals:** "I Ain't Gonna Eat My Heart Out Anymore" (Atlantic; ☆52, 1965). "Good Lovin' " (Atlantic; ☆1, 1966). "You Better Run" (Atlantic; ☆20, 1966). "Come On Up" (Atlantic; ☆43, 1966). "I've Been Lonely Too Long" (Atlantic; ☆16, 1967). "Groovin' " (Atlantic; ☆1, 1967). "A Girl Like You" (Atlantic; ☆10, 1967). "How Can I Be Sure" (Atlantic; ☆4, 1967). "It's Wonderful" (Atlantic; ☆20, 1967). "A Beautiful Morning" (Atlantic; ☆3, 1968). "People Got to Be Free" (Atlantic; ☆1, 1968). "A Ray of Hope" (Atlantic; ☆24, 1968). "Heaven" (Atlantic; ☆39, 1969). "See" (Atlantic; ☆27, 1969). "Carry Me Back" (Atlantic; ☆26, 1969). **Frankie Valli:** "(You're Gonna) Hurt Yourself" (Smash; ☆39, 1966). "Can't Take My Eyes off You" (Philips; ☆2, 1967). "I Make a Fool of Myself" (Philips; ☆18, 1967). "To Give (the Reason I Live)" (Philips; ☆29, 1967). "My Eyes Adored You" (Private Stock; ☆1, 1975). "Swearin' to God" (Private Stock; ☆6, 1975). "Our Day Will Come" (Private Stock; ☆11, 1975). **Frankie Valli and the Four Seasons:** "Sherry" (Vee-Jay; ☆1, 1962). "Big Girls Don't Cry" (Vee-Jay; ☆1, 1962). "Santa Claus Is Coming to Town" (Vee-Jay; ☆23, 1962). "Walk Like a Man" (Vee-Jay; ☆1, 1963). "Ain't That a Shame" (Vee-Jay; ☆22, 1963). "Candy Girl" b/w "Marlena" (Vee-Jay; ☆3, 1963). "New Mexican Rose" (Vee-Jay; ☆36, 1963). "Dawn" (Philips; ☆3, 1964). "Stay" (Vee-Jay; ☆16, 1964). "Ronnie" (Philips; ☆6, 1964). "Alone" (Vee-Jay; ☆28, 1964). "Rag Doll" (Philips; ☆1, 1964). "Save It for Me" (Philips; ☆10, 1964). "Big Man in Town" (Philips; ☆20, 1964). "Bye, Bye, Baby" (Philips; ☆12, 1965). "Girl Come Running" (Philips; ☆30, 1965). "Let's Hang On" (Philips; ☆3, 1965). "Don't Think Twice" (released under the name "The Wonder Who?") (Philips; ☆12, 1965). "Working My Way back to You" (Philips; ☆9, 1966). "Opus 17 (Don't You Worry 'bout Me)" (Philips; ☆13, 1966). "I've Got You Under My Skin" (Philips; ☆9, 1966). "Tell It to the Rain" (Philips; ☆10, 1966). "Beggin" (Philips; ☆16, 1967). "C'mon Marianne" (Philips; ☆9, 1967). "Watch the Flowers Grow" (Philips; ☆30, 1967). "Will You Love Me Tomorrow" (Philips; ☆24, 1968). "And That Reminds Me" (Crewe; ☆45, 1969). "Who Loves You" (Curb; ☆3, 1975).

ALBUMS

Crests: *The Best of the Crests* (Rhino; 1990). **Dion and the Belmonts:** *24 Original Classics* (Arista; 1984). *Dion and the Belmonts* (Rhino; 1989). **Frankie Valli and the Four Seasons:** *Frankie Valli & the Four Seasons Greatest Hits, Volumes 1 & 2* (Rhino; 1991).

(Chart positions compiled from Joel Whitburn's *Record Research,* based on *Billboard*'s Pop chart.)

JAMES BROWN

BY ROBERT PALMER

hrough 1001 nights, 1001 shows, Superbad James Brown keeps on keepin' on. His band locks into a chopping rhythm riff, and Brown strides purposefully from the wings, wearing a red jumpsuit with the word SEX stitched across the front. His head jerks to the beat, his hips shimmy and suddenly he's snaking across the stage on one foot, his other leg windmilling along with his long, limber arms. He does a split, erupts into a pirouette, whirls like a dervish and ends up at the microphone just in time to shriek ''bayba-a-ay'' as the band modulates into the introduction to one of his hits. After thirty-five years, the energy, the pandemonium, and the great, rending buzz-saw voice remain.

Brown recorded his first single, ''Please, Please, Please,'' in 1956 for the Federal label, a subsidiary of King Records, and during the next few years his grainy gospel voice became a fixture on Southern radio, inexorably affecting the development of rhythm & blues, pulling it away from show business sophistication and back into the orbit of the black churches from which it ultimately derived. The grittiness of Brown's late-Fifties/early-Sixties output— ''Think,'' ''Night Train'' and ''Shout and Shimmy''

were a few of the hits—paved the way for the emergence of Otis Redding, Wilson Pickett and the other soul shouters who followed. For while Ray Charles was already tempering the rawness of his early recordings with uptown sweetening, Brown was injecting some of the hysteria of sanctified church services into each of his releases.

Pervasive as Brown's influence was during the Sixties, he shaped the music of the Seventies even more profoundly. The chattering choke-rhythm guitars, broken bass patterns, explosive horn bursts, one-chord drones and evangelical vocal discourses he introduced during the mid-Sixties became the lingua franca of contemporary black pop, the heartbeat of the discotheques and a primary ingredient in such far-flung musical syntheses as Jamaican reggae and Nigerian Afro-beat. Various producers and arrangers added lush string arrangements, flugelhorns, bass trombones and sighing female choruses; Sly Stone, the Isley Brothers, and others overlaid whining, distorted guitars, wah-wah clavinets, more complex cross-rhythms, or chunkier drumming, according to their tastes. But the basic band tracks—"the wheels of the car," to borrow a metaphor from R&B producer Willie Mitchell—have continued to follow Papa James's directions.

Brown knew what and how he wanted to record early on. When Syd Nathan, head of King, refused to let Brown record with his touring band, Brown helped them record for another label as Nat Kendrick and the Swans; the group had a substantial instrumental hit in 1960 with "(Do the) Mashed Potatoes," a dance routine from the Brown stage show. Nathan relented; James Brown records that were both more visceral and commercial followed.

By 1964 the Cincinnati-based King company, which had grown up with band blues, vocal groups and hillbilly boogie during the late Forties, was functioning more and more like an antique from R&B's golden age, failing to distribute and promote Brown's records on a scale commensurate with his popularity as a live performer. Brown retaliated by forming Fair Deal Productions, and by giving his next set of recordings to Smash, a subsidiary of Mercury. One of the sides included in the package was "Out of Sight," and with Mercury's more thorough and up-to-date distribution network behind it, the record became one of Brown's biggest hits, selling to white listeners as well as to the blacks who had been supporting him for years.

A legal battle with King ensued. Brown held fast, and after a yearlong standoff he emerged in complete artistic control of his recording career, and with a deciding voice in the business end of it as well. Almost immediately he released the record that finally made him a superstar and defined the rhythmic direction R&B would take during the next decade, the epochal "Papa's Got a Brand New Bag" (1965). Toward the end of the Sixties, Brown became his own manager, and in 1971 he formed his own record production company, with Polydor as distributor. He had come a long way since the days when Syd Nathan supervised his sessions. Every step had been a battle, but Brown fought hard and, eventually, he won.

What drives a man like Brown, a man who could have retired in 1965 or 1975, but who has kept on trying to outdo himself instead? Perhaps the goal has been forgotten and the struggle itself is the reward. Perhaps it always was. The very beginning was a struggle. Brown was born in 1933 in Georgia; he grew up poorer than poor, picking cotton, shining shoes, dancing for pennies in the streets. Later came reform school, boxing, semiprofessional baseball, and—after a leg injury scotched his ambition to become a big-league pitcher—a vocal group, the Famous Flames. The Flames began to attract attention around Macon during the mid-Fifties, signing with King early in 1956 on the strength of "Please, Please, Please." But the first ten singles failed to attract much notice outside Georgia, probably because, as Cliff White writing for *Black Music* has pointed out, they sounded like "a pastiche of the Midnighters, the '5' Royales and Charles Brown with a dash of Little Richard."

In 1959 "Try Me," a laboriously slow, churchy ballad, went to Number Forty-eight on *Billboard*'s Hot 100. It wasn't a huge hit, but it enabled Brown and the Flames, the vocal group he now dominated completely, to keep working one-night stands in the South, and to secure the services of a good national booking agent, Ben Bart, Brown's manager-to-be. Soon Brown had a regular road band, an increasingly tight show and an entire revue, with members of the troupe doubling as opening acts; by 1960 he was attracting a growing audience in the North. In 1963 *The James Brown Show Live at the Apollo* stayed on the *Billboard* album chart for sixty-six weeks, getting as high as Number Two—a virtually unprecedented feat for a hardcore R&B album. Black radio stations played it like a single and, for the first time, anybody anywhere with a few dollars and a phonograph

James Brown, "the hardest working man in show business," ready to storm the stage of the Apollo Theatre, 1964. A complete performer—singer, dancer, bandleader—he put on the greatest live shows in the history of rock.

could get a taste of the show that was earning James Brown the nickname "Mr. Dynamite."

It was at this time that Brown first earned another reputation, that of the "hardest working man in show business." His rapidly expanding James Brown Revue traveled constantly, crisscrossing the country, playing for all-black audiences that became ever larger and more ecstatic. His band was the toughest, loudest and most together (as well it should have been, since fluffed notes were reportedly penalized by heavy fines). His clothes were the flashiest, from the shiny suits of the late Fifties to the waist-length jackets with matching vests and supertight pants of the mid-Sixties. His dancing was the wildest, the most spectacularly acrobatic, the most perfectly controlled.

The show itself was programmed down to the last second for maximum impact. During the early Six-

Brown grew a mustache in the mid-Seventies, but it didn't last.

ties, for example, Brown perfected the finale captured in the 1965 film, *The T.A.M.I. Show*. As he wrenched out the pleading refrain to "Please, Please, Please" he would sink slowly to his knees, writhing to the tune's lugubrious rhythm until finally, still singing, he collapsed in a heap. Famous Flames Bobby Byrd, Bobby Bennett and Lloyd Stallworth would approach him hesitantly. One would produce a purple cape and, reverently draping it over the fallen singer's body, help him to his feet and slowly escort him offstage. Brown, still holding the microphone, would begin to drag his feet, struggle and, after a dramatic pause, shake off the cape and walk deliberately back to stage center. There he would launch into another chorus, only to drop to his knees again, his voice a hoarse sob. The routine was repeated, this time with a gold cape. Once again Brown waited until the last minute, shook off his attendants, returned to the front of the stage, began

more original but, again, hardly unique. But Latin cross-rhythms had crept into some of the records as early as ''Good Good Lovin','' and the Brown band's lead guitarist, Jimmy Nolan, had been working on a choked style of rhythm playing that melded beautifully into the band's rhythmic thrust. The bass parts had been growing more and more staccato, in keeping with the increasingly percussive orientation of the music, and so had the horn lines. By 1964 these elements had coalesced into a distinctive new sound that caught America off guard.

The change was probably determined, at least in part, by the structure of Brown's new songs. He continued to work in gospel and blues forms, but he also added another kind of composition: Brown would sing a semi-improvised, loosely organized melody that wandered while the band riffed rhythmically on

The Famous Flames doing their steps, 1958.

singing, feigned collapse. Finally, a jet black cape was produced and Brown and the Flames left the stage, while the band played on. The audiences, absolutely spent by Brown's hysterically energetic hour onstage, would shout themselves hoarse for more, wondering all the while how Brown could possibly top what he'd already done. And then Mr. Dynamite would appear, wearing a new suit, a prop suitcase in his hand, propelling himself across the stage on one foot, thumb out as if hitching a ride to the next town.

During this period the most striking thing about Brown's music was his voice, one of the harshest in R&B. His torn and frayed tonal quality wasn't unique; the Sensational Nightingales' Julius Cheeks, who also came from the Southeast, had popularized it some years before. Brown's combination of gospel quartet harmonies with a large, punching horn section and a heavy shuffle beat was

a single chord, the horns tersely punctuating Brown's declamatory phrases. With no chord changes and precious little melodic variety to sustain listener interest, rhythm became everything. Brown and his musicians and arrangers began to treat every instrument and voice in the group as if each were a drum. The horns played single-note bursts that were often sprung against the downbeats. The bass lines were broken up into choppy two- or three-note patterns, a procedure common in Latin music since the Forties but unusual in R&B. Brown's rhythm guitarist choked his guitar strings against the instrument's neck so hard that his playing began to sound like a jagged tin can being scraped with a pocketknife. Only occasionally were the horns, organ or backing vocalists allowed to provide a harmonic continuum by holding a chord.

The chugging push-pull of the Brown band's Brand New Bag was the wave of the future. Its impact was obscured initially by the British Invasion, which consisted of white bands covering R&B hits from the previous decade; and by the Memphis sound, which resembled Brown's music in its gospel orientation and harmonic simplicity but had a much more conservative rhythmic bias. By 1968, however, psychedelic rock was replacing the older English R&B styles, and the Memphis sound was becoming diluted. Sly and the Family Stone were purveying a psychedelicized, more rhythmically complex variant of the Brown sound, and Brown himself was at the height of his powers, preaching stream-of-consciousness sermons like ''Cold Sweat,'' ''I Can't Stand Myself'' and ''Say It Loud—I'm Black and I'm Proud,'' all of them pulsating with polyrhythmic power.

During the late Sixties Brown became a politician of sorts, encouraging black capitalism, hobnobbing with would-be president Hubert Humphrey, touring Africa, entertaining the troops in Vietnam and Korea, urging rioting ghetto youths to cool their passions and build instead of burn. He acquired a large house, a fleet of cars, a jet, several radio stations and other businesses. Militants, suspicious of his vested interest in the system, accused him of Tomming. The ghetto ignored them and bought more and more of his records, even after they had begun to sound alike, as if each were merely another installment in one very long discourse on the state of the nation and the state of mind of its Number One soul brother.

Vice President Hubert Humphrey with Brown in 1967. The Johnson administration was grateful for his help in cooling off riot-torn cities that summer.

Until recent years, Brown was not a critics' favorite, principally because of the apparent monotony of so many of his post-1965 recordings. But attacking him for being repetitive is like attacking Africans for being overly fond of drumming. Where the European listener may hear monotonous beating, the African distinguishes subtle polyrhythmic interplay, tonal distinctions among the various drums, the virtuosity of the master drummer, and so on. Similarly, Brown's singing sounds to some European ears like so much harsh

The most famous pompadour in black music.

It's a brand-new day: James Brown, free at last and looking fine.

shrieking. Up until the Eighties, white Americans rarely bought his records in large numbers. In fact, he has never had a Number One pop hit. Prior to ''Living in America,'' which went to Number Four in 1986, only six of his singles made *Billboard*'s pop Top Ten, and all of them were released during his Sixties heyday: 1965 through 1968. Characteristically, in the mid-Seventies Brown responded to the rising tide of sweet soul from Philadelphia by sweetening his own recordings with strings, horns and vocal groups. The emergence of disco found him

making harder, more aggressive records again, but the public seemed tired of the James Brown formula. For the first time in more than ten years, Brown's singles did not get automatic airplay on black radio. But he was still a successful producer of, among other acts, his own backup band, Fred Wesley and the J.B.s, who had several hit singles in a disco dance vein.

During the late Seventies Brown fell from prominence. He titled a 1979 album *The Original Disco Man*, an ironic comment, perhaps, on his inability to profit from the success of an idiom he helped create. But, true to form, Brown kept working. Apparently, he was still the same suspicious, hard-pushing, self-absorbed man who built the Famous Flames into a money-making proposition and eventually built an R&B empire for himself.

In 1988 the empire crumbled. After a wild interstate chase with police from Georgia to South Carolina, Brown was sentenced to serve two concurrent six-year sentences in jail for assault and weapons charges. But if anything, serving his sentence seems to have increased Brown's resilience and determination. Perhaps a prolonged exposure to the rap music being played incessantly by his fellow prisoners—rap that often sampled riffs and rhythms from his earlier records—provided the motivation to reclaim his crown.

Paroled in 1991, Brown reassembled his band, which includes many veterans of earlier lineups, and set out to teach the younger generation what the *original* rapper and his music are all about. There was a feast of CDs reissuing Brown's earlier work, highlighted by the essential four-disc boxed set, *Star Time*, but Brown himself was more interested in the here and now. Brown's performances—including a blistering *Tonight Show* set—offered convincing evidence that the music and the man have endured, and triumphed.

DISCOGRAPHY

SINGLES

"Please, Please, Please" (Federal; r☆6, 1956). "Try Me" (Federal; r☆1, ☆48, 1958). "I Want You So Bad" (Federal; r☆20, 1959). "I'll Go Crazy" (Federal; r☆15, 1960). "Think" b/w "You've Got the Power" (Federal; r☆7, ☆33, 1960). "This Old Heart" (Federal; r☆20, 1960). "Bewildered" (King; r☆8, ☆40, 1961). "I Don't Mind" (King; r☆4, ☆47, 1961). "Baby, You're Right" (King; r☆2, ☆49, 1961). "Just You and Me, Darling" (King; r☆17, 1961). "Lost Someone" (King; r☆2, ☆48, 1961). "Night Train" (King; r☆5, ☆35, 1962). "Shout and Shimmy" (King; r☆16, 1962). "Three Hearts in a Tangle" (King; r☆18, 1962). "Prisoner of Love" (King; r☆6, ☆18, 1963). "Oh Baby Don't You Weep (Part 1)" (King; ☆23, 1964). "Out of Sight" (Smash; ☆24, 1964). "Papa's Got a Brand New Bag—Part 1" (King; r☆1, ☆8, 1965). "I Got You (I Feel Good)" (King; r☆1, ☆3, 1965). "Ain't That a Groove, Part 1" (King; r☆6, ☆42, 1966). "It's a Man's Man's Man's World" (King; r☆1, ☆8, 1966). "Money Won't Change You, Part 1" (King; r☆11, 1966). "Don't Be a Drop-Out" (King; r☆4, ☆50, 1966). "Bring It Up" (King; r☆7, ☆29, 1967). "Kansas City" (King; r☆21, 1967). "Let

Yourself Go" (King; r☆5, ☆46, 1967). "Cold Sweat—Part 1" (King; r☆1, ☆7, 1967). "Get It Together (Part 1)" (King; r☆11, ☆40, 1967). "There Was a Time" b/w "I Can't Stand Myself (When You Touch Me)" (King; r☆3, ☆28, 1968). "I Got the Feelin'" (King; r☆1, ☆6, 1968). "Licking Stick—Licking Stick (Part 1)" (King; r☆2, ☆14, 1968). "America Is My Home—Part 1" (King; r☆13, 1968). "I Guess I'll Have to Cry, Cry, Cry" (King; r☆15, 1968). "Say It Loud—I'm Black and I'm Proud—Part 1" (King; r☆1, ☆10, 1968). "Goodbye My Love" (King; r☆9, ☆31, 1968). "Give It Up or Turnit a Loose" (King; r☆1, ☆15, 1969). "I Don't Want Nobody to Give Me Nothing (Open Up the Door, I'll Get It Myself) (Part 1)" (King; r☆3, ☆20, 1969). "The Popcorn" (King; r☆11, ☆30, 1969). "Mother Popcorn—Part 1" (King; r☆1, ☆11, 1969). "Lowdown Popcorn" (King; r☆16, ☆41, 1969). "World (Part 1)" (King; r☆8, ☆37, 1969). "Let a Man Come In and Do the Popcorn (Part 1)" (King; r☆2, ☆21, 1969). "Ain't It Funky Now (Part 1)" (King; r☆2, ☆24, 1969). "Let a Man Come In and Do the Popcorn (Part II)" (King; r☆6, ☆40, 1969). "It's a New Day (Part 1 & Part 2)" (King; r☆3, ☆32, 1970). "Funky Drummer (Part I)" (King; r☆20, 1970). "Brother Rapp (Part I)" (King; r☆2, ☆32, 1970). "Get Up I Feel Like Being a Sex Machine (Part 1)" (King; r☆2, ☆15, 1970). "Super Bad (Part 1 & Part 2)" (King; r☆1, ☆13, 1970). "Get Up, Get into It, Get Involved, Part 1" (King; r☆4, ☆34, 1971). "Soul Power, Part 1" (King; r☆3, ☆29, 1971). "I Cried" (King; r☆15, ☆50, 1971). "Escape-Ism (Part 1)" (People; r☆6, ☆35, 1971). "Hot Pants (She Got to Use What She Got to Get What She Wants) Pt. 1" (People; r☆1, ☆15, 1971). "Make It Funky (Part 1)" (Polydor; r☆1, ☆22, 1971). "I'm a Greedy Man—Part 1" (Polydor; r☆7, ☆35, 1971). "Talking Loud and Saying Nothing—Part 1" (Polydor; r☆1, ☆27, 1972). "King Heroin" (Polydor; r☆6, ☆40, 1972). "There It Is, Part 1" (Polydor; r☆4, ☆43, 1972). "Honky Tonk—Part 1" (Polydor; r☆7, ☆44, 1972). "Get on the Good Foot—Part 1" (Polydor; r☆1, ☆18, 1972). "I Got a Bag of My Own" (Polydor; r☆3, ☆44, 1972). With Lyn Collins: "What My Baby Needs Now Is a Little More Lovin'" (Polydor; r☆17, ☆56, 1972). "I Got Ants in My Pants and I want to dance—Part 1" (Polydor; r☆4, ☆27, 1973). "Down and Out in N.Y. City" (Polydor; r☆13, ☆50, 1973). "Think" (Polydor; r☆15, ☆77, 1973). "Sexy, Sexy, Sexy" (Polydor; r☆6, ☆50, 1973). "Stoned to the Bone" (Polydor; r☆4, ☆58, 1973). "The Payback—Part I" (Polydor; r☆1, ☆26, 1974). "My Thang" (Polydor; r☆1, ☆29, 1974). "Papa Don't Take No Mess, Part I" (Polydor; r☆1, ☆31, 1974). "Funky President (People It's Bad)" b/w "Coldblooded" (Polydor; r☆4, ☆44, 1974). "Reality" (Polydor; r☆19, 1975). "Sex Machine, Part 1" (Polydor; r☆16, 1975). "Hustle!!! (Dead on It)" (Polydor; r☆11, 1975). "Get Up offa That Thing" (Polydor; r☆4, ☆45, 1976). "Bodyheat (Part 1)" (Polydor; r☆9, ☆88, 1977). "Kiss in 77" (Polydor; r☆35, 1977). "If You Don't Give a Doggone About It" (Polydor; r☆45, 1977). "Eyesight" (Polydor; r☆38, 1978). "The Spank" (Polydor; r☆26, 1978). "For Goodness Sakes, Look at Those Cakes (Part I)" (Polydor; r☆52, 1978). "It's Too Funky in Here" (Polydor; r☆15, 1979). "Star Generation" (Polydor; r☆63, 1979). "Regrets" (Polydor; r☆63, 1980). "Rapp Payback (Where Iz Moses)" (T.K.; r☆46, 1980). "Stay with Me" (T.K.; r☆80, 1981). "Bring It On . . . Bring It On" b/w "The Night Time Is the Right Time (to Be with the One That You Love)" (Augusta S.; r☆73, 1983). With Afrika Bambaataa: "Unity" (Tommy Boy; r☆87, 1984). "Living in America" (Scotti Br.; r☆10; ☆4, 1985). "Gravity" (Scotti Br.; r☆26, ☆93, 1986). "How Do You Stop" (Scotti Br.; r☆10, 1987). "I'm Real" (Scotti Br.; r☆2, 1988). With Aretha Franklin "Gimme Your Love" (Arista; r☆48, 1989).

ALBUMS

Roots of a Revolution (Polydor, 1989). *Messing with the Blues* (Polydor, 1990). *Star Time!* (Polydor, 1991).

(Chart positions compiled from Joel Whitburn's *Record Research*, based on *Billboard*'s Pop chart, unless otherwise indicated; r☆ = position on *Billboard*'s Rhythm & Blues chart.)

THE SOUND OF CHICAGO

BY JOE McEWEN

Huddled in a dark corner of the Cabrini Housing Project on Chicago's North Side, five youths struggle to work out the harmonies of a wide-eyed, dreamy love song that three of them have composed. Unlike other numbers in the group's repertoire, this song features no vocal interplay and none of the standard doo-wop harmonies. Instead, it is a solo vehicle for a pure and mournful baritone whose deliberate phrasing and dirgelike approach transform the romantic ballad into a somber, religious evocation. The group is the Impressions, the year is 1958, and the song is "For Your Precious Love."

The Impressions formed from the union of two friends, Jerry Butler, seventeen, and Curtis Mayfield, fifteen. The two had sung together in church as adolescents, and had traveled with the Northern Jubilee Gospel Singers and the Traveling Souls Spiritualist Church. It was Butler who convinced his friend Mayfield to leave his own struggling group, the Alfatones, and join him, Sam Gooden, and Richard and Arthur Brooks, the remnants of another struggling group, the Roosters.

According to legend, an impressive performance at a swank Chicago fashion show brought the quintet to the attention of Falcon Records, and "For Your Precious Love" was recorded shortly afterward. Butler, setting aside his dreams of becoming a chef or ice sculptor, provided the resonant baritone lead, while Mayfield's fragile tenor wailed innocently in the background.

"For Your Precious Love" was a landmark record. Unlike the harsh South Side blues, which had been transported to Chicago by grown men, "For Your Precious Love" was the music of a new generation that had spent its adolescence in the city, synthesizing music from such diverse sources as the Soul Stirrers, the Ink Spots, the Dells and, of course, the blues. The song can almost be considered the first

Jerry Butler. His milky baritone helped put Chicago on the map with pop hits like ''He Will Break Your Heart.''

soul record: In years to come, it provided the inspiration for more fervent performances by Solomon Burke, Jackie Wilson and Tommy Hunt.

''For Your Precious Love,'' by the Impressions featuring Jerry Butler, was dominated by Butler's virtuoso performance. After two followups failed to catch the public's ear, Butler left the group to attempt a solo career. Without him, the Impressions searched for a comfortable personality, recording several dismal imitations of the Coasters and the Isley Brothers.

While the group floundered, Jerry Butler was having his own problems selling records. In 1960, with the Impressions still struggling, Butler and Mayfield again joined forces to write a song that not only would refurbish Butler's faltering career, but also set the tone for Mayfield's subsequent efforts as a writer and producer. Set to a Brazilianbaion rhythm popularized by the Drifters, ''He Will Break Your Heart'' featured Mayfield's sparse guitar figures and Butler's dignified vocal pleas, echoed at the refrain by Curtis's wispy tenor. It was the first of several Butler hits fashioned by Mayfield.

The success of these records finally gave Mayfield the impetus to resume his own career with the Im-

pressions. Thanks to his growing reputation as a writer and producer, he landed a contract for the group with ABC-Paramount. The Impressions, now including Sam Gooden's friend Fred Cash as Butler's replacement, were sent to New York under Mayfield's tutelage, and predictably enough it was Mayfield who penned the group's first ABC record. ''Gypsy Woman'' was a fantasy of longing and desire, with castanets and Mayfield's flamenco strumming setting the mood, while the quintet wove an exotic narrative.

The first edition of the Impressions, a quintet, around the time of ''Gypsy Woman.''

Released late in 1961, ''Gypsy Woman'' became a national hit. Though Mayfield composed several other songs in a similar vein, including ''Minstrel and Queen,'' an arresting allegory about interracial love, the followups failed to duplicate the success of ''Gypsy Woman.'' Richard and Arthur Brooks opted to stay in New York, but the three remaining Impressions returned to Chicago, hoping for inspiration and still looking for their next hit.

In the meantime, Columbia Records, at the urging of a dapper black A&R man from Chicago named Carl Davis, had reactivated its once mighty ''race'' label, Okeh. Davis had proven his ability to spot new

Major Lance, who sang the immortal "Um, Um, Um, Um, Um, Um."

talent by plucking a group named the Dukays off a Chicago street corner, and fashioning a Number One hit for the lead singer, Eugene Dixon. Dixon was rechristened Gene Chandler (after Davis's favorite actor, Jeff Chandler), and his first record, "Duke of Earl," sold a million copies in a little over a month.

At Okeh, Davis's first major signings were Major Lance and Curtis Mayfield. A scuffling singer and ex-boxer, Lance had come to Davis with Mayfield in hopes of landing a contract. On the strength of a tune called "The Monkey Time" that Curtis had just written, Davis hired Mayfield as Okeh's staff producer and agreed to let Lance cut the song; he also brought in veteran Johnny Pate to arrange the charts. Davis and Pate discarded Mayfield's strings and beefed up the sound with a stuttering brass section and a percussive bottom. It proved to be the perfect catalyst,

giving Mayfield's production an instantly identifiable and catchy stamp.

With Pate's blaring horn intro, Major Lance's reedy vocal and Mayfield's eccentric rhythmic approach, "The Monkey Time" not only became Okeh's first hit in ten years, but also announced the arrival of a full-fledged Chicago sound.

Pate was immediately called in to help arrange for the Impressions. The first Pate-Impressions single, "Sad, Sad Girl and Boy," was yet another re-creation of the softer Mayfield-Butler sound, but its successor, "It's All Right," released in the fall of 1963, featured a punchier, gospel-styled band track, with boosted bass and a more assertive vocal approach. Unlike the frantic dance songs and intense ballads that had begun to dominate black radio, "It's All Right" combined an understated soulfulness with a rhumba beat and updated doo-wop harmonies. The record's sparse arrangement and elegant sound provided an equally effective counterpoint to the heavily orchestrated Motown singles of the era. Following closely on the heels of "The Monkey Time," "It's All Right" inaugurated a period of Midas-like artistic and commercial success for Curtis Mayfield.

At Okeh he poured out songs for Billy Butler, Walter Jackson and Major Lance. But it was his collaboration with Gene Chandler (for Constellation) that gave him his most consistent string of hits outside of the Impressions'. While Curtis's Okeh productions were largely cast in the "Monkey Time"/"It's All Right" mold, his work with Chandler took a softer approach.

Chandler was a rather limited vocalist who often sounded like he was singing with a cold. Although his range was narrow, Chandler's style was appealing, distinguished by nasal falsetto swoops that never failed to summon screams from the teenagers at Chicago's Regal Theater. Mayfield composed a series of striking songs for Gene, and it was through Curtis that Chandler became one of black America's favorite balladeers. The high point of their collaboration was "Just Be True," Chandler's biggest hit after "Duke of Earl," which featured the vocalist's aching, deliberate phrasing, an overlay of strings, and Impressions-styled harmony. The effect of the record was galvanic. Chandler's emotional reading perfectly conveyed the vulnerability expressed by the lyric, and the song became a model for his gentle, often wounded persona. Like Major Lance,

Chandler enjoyed hit after hit with Mayfield as producer, but when their partnership ended, the hits dried up.

In 1966 Mayfield, hoping to profit more directly from his labors, severed his relationship with Okeh to start his own label, Windy C Records. The company was primarily an outlet for a young teen group, the Five Stairsteps; despite several hits, Mayfield proved less a businessman than a producer, and the venture soon folded. After the collapse of another solo outlet, Mayfield Records, Curtis formed an independent production company, Curtom, with a roster that included the Stairsteps, Major Lance and eventually the Impressions. Thanks to national distribution from Buddah, the operation survived, though Mayfield never quite matched his earlier work either aesthetically or commercially.

With the Impressions, Mayfield had begun to compose ''message'' songs. The best, including ''People Get Ready'' and ''We're a Winner,'' were moving statements, but the worst seemed like clumsy attempts to confront the country's turbulent social developments. When Mayfield left the Impressions in 1970, his best years as a composer were behind him.

Chicago soul nevertheless continued to flourish in other hands. The mid-Sixties Mayfield-Okeh chart

Gene Chandler, the ''Duke of Earl.'' Curtis Mayfield produced many of his later hits.

eruption had triggered recording activities throughout the city. Chess which had been struggling with a roster of dated blues and rock performers, hired writer Billy Davis as arranger and A&R man. Using an orchestrated approach patterned after Motown's, Davis had hits with Jackie Ross, Etta James, Fontella Bass, Billy Stewart, Little Milton, and the Radiants. The city's smaller independents, including Twinight, with Syl Johnson, and Onederful!, with Otis Clay, tended to feature artists with a bluesier Southern style. While they contributed to the city's reputation as a soul center, for the most part the fortunes of Chicago soul rose and fell with the work of Mayfield and Carl Davis.

Shortly after Mayfield left Okeh, Carl Davis had a feud with the president of Epic/Okeh, Len Levy, over Okeh's musical direction. According to Davis, a spat, stemming from a columnist's reference to him as Okeh's president, brought the conflict to a head, leading to Carl's resignation and Okeh's subsequent collapse. Davis started his own production company, and after two Jackie Wilson million-sellers, ''Whispers (Gettin' Louder)'' and ''(Your Love Keeps Lifting Me) Higher and Higher,'' he was hired by Brunswick as an executive vice president.

Working for Brunswick owner Nat Tarnopol, Davis managed to turn up a new batch of Windy City talent. Where Mayfield only fitfully managed to up-

date the uncluttered and honest approach that had been so effective less than a decade earlier, Davis and arrangers Willie Henderson and Sonny Sanders devised a new style directly descended from Mayfield and Pate's original collaborations. Davis had honed his crack Chicago band on records by Mary Wells and Gene Chandler as well as Jackie Wilson,

Major Lance at an autograph party.

but it wasn't until Tyrone Davis's "Can I Change My Mind" became a national hit in 1968 that the new sound of Chicago emerged.

With brassy flourishes, a relaxed rhythmic lope and a Davis vocal that owed as much to the big-band blues of Bobby Bland as to Jerry Butler, "Can I Change My Mind" sounded almost anachronistic. Yet the fluid band track and aggressive horns gave the song a freshness lacking in much of the late-Sixties soul. Brunswick quickly signed Barbara Acklin, the Young-Holt Trio and the Chi-Lites to benefit from the new Davis-Henderson-Sanders style.

While most of these acts were recorded with a heavy emphasis on Henderson's surging horns, the Chi-Lites took a different tack. Headed by Eugene Record, a former cabdriver turned songwriter, the Chi-Lites sang melancholy ballads as well as protest material modeled after the Temptations. Their strangest hit was "Have You Seen Her," a five-minute song that found lead singer Record painting a picture of a forlorn fellow stumbling through the day pining for his lost love.

Mayfield's decision to leave the Impressions and pursue his own career had symbolized the end of an era for Chicago soul. The stately, uplifting harmonies he had developed for the group were replaced in his own music by jagged bass lines, frenetic percussive flourishes and a more aggressive vocal attack. Though Curtis often sounded strained and brittle as a solo singer, and his own songs were usually didactic rather than poetic, Mayfield's new approach won him a considerable following, culminating in the success of the ambiguous "Superfly" and the more overtly antidrug "Freddie's Dead."

Mayfield continued to make his mark in the Seventies with a series of best-selling soundtrack albums featuring himself (*Superfly*), Aretha Franklin, the Staple Singers and Gladys Knight and the Pips. Quiet during much of the Eighties, Mayfield showed renewed energy as the Nineties dawned. New recordings surfaced, public appearances became more frequent, and artists as diverse as Lenny Kravitz and

Ice-T cited him as a major influence. But then, in August of 1990, Mayfield was severely injured in an accident on an outdoor stage in Brooklyn, leaving his creative future in deep doubt.

While gospel influences had come to dominate soul by the late Sixties, the restrained, dignified style of Chicago soul stood out. In their heyday, Mayfield and Carl Davis crafted some of the purest and most sanctified pop ever to grace Top Forty radio. By the mid-Seventies, however, only the apparently infinite flow of Tyrone Davis singles bore any real resemblance to this classic "sound of Chicago." But new producers like Leroy Hutson and particularly the Chuck Jackson–Marvin Yancey team kept the scene alive. The success in 1975 of Natalie Cole's engaging "This Will Be," produced by Jackson and Yancey, proved that Chicago, while no longer setting distinctive trends, remained a vital center of black music in America.

DISCOGRAPHY

SINGLES

Barbara Acklin: "Love Makes a Woman" (Brunswick; r☆3, ☆15, 1968). **Fontella Bass:** "Rescue Me" (Checker; r☆1, ☆4, 1965). **Fontella Bass and Bobby McClure:** "Don't Mess Up a Good Thing" (Checker; r☆5, ☆33, 1965). **Billy Butler and the Chanters:** ¹"I Can't Work No Longer" (Okeh; r☆6, ☆60, 1965). **Jerry Butler:** ¹"Find Another Girl" (Vee-Jay; r☆27, ☆10, 1961). ¹"I'm Telling You" (Vee-Jay; r☆8, ☆25, 1961). "Moon River" (Vee-Jay; r☆14, ☆11, 1961). "Make It Easy on Yourself" (Vee-Jay; r☆18, ☆20, 1962). "Need to Belong" (Vee-Jay; ☆31, 1963). "Giving Up on Love" (Vee-Jay; ☆56, 1964). "I Stand Accused" (Vee-Jay; ☆61, 1964). **Gene Chandler:** "Duke of Earl" (Vee-Jay; r☆1, ☆1, 1962). ¹"Rainbow" (Vee-Jay; r☆11, ☆47, 1963). ¹"Man's Temptation" (Vee-Jay; r☆17, ☆70, 1963). ¹"Just Be True" (Constellation; ☆19, 1964). ¹"Bless Our Love" (Constellation; ☆39, 1964). ¹"What Now" (Constellation; r☆18, ☆40, 1965). ¹"Nothing Can Stop Me" (Constellation; r☆3, ☆18, 1965). "Rainbow '65" (Constellation; r☆2, ☆69, 1965). "I Fooled You This Time" (Checker; r☆3, ☆45, 1966). "To Be a Lover" (Checker; r☆9, 1967). "Groovy Situation" (Mercury; r☆8, ☆12, 1970). **Chi-Lites:** "Give It Away" (Brunswick; r☆10, 1969). "Are You My Woman? (Tell Me So)" (Brunswick; r☆8, 1970). "(For God's Sake) Give More Power to the People" (Brunswick; r☆4, ☆26, 1971). "Have You Seen Her" (Brunswick; r☆1, ☆3, 1971). **Dee Clark:** "Raindrops" (Vee-Jay; r☆3, ☆2, 1961). **Tyrone Davis:** "Can I Change My Mind" (Dakar; r☆1, ☆5, 1968). "Is It Something You've Got" (Dakar; r☆5, ☆34, 1969). "Turn Back the Hands of Time" (Dakar; r☆1, ☆3,

1970). "I'll Be Right Here" (Dakar; r☆8, 1970). "Could I Forget You" (Dakar; r☆10, 1971). **Dells:** "Stay in My Corner" (Cadet; r☆1, ☆10, 1968). "Always Together" (Cadet; r☆3, ☆18, 1968). "I Can Sing a Rainbow" (Cadet; r☆5, ☆22, 1969). "Oh What a Night" (Cadet; r☆1, ☆10, 1969). "Open Up My Heart" (Cadet; r☆5, ☆51, 1970). "The Love We Had (Stays on My Mind)" (Cadet; r☆8, ☆30, 1971). **Betty Everett:** "You're No Good" (Vee-Jay; ☆51, 1963). "The Shoop Shoop Song" (Vee-Jay; ☆6, 1964). **Betty Everett and Jerry Butler:** "Let It Be Me" (Vee-Jay; ☆5, 1964). **Fascinations:** ¹"Girls Are Out to Get You" (Mayfield; r☆13, 1967). **Five Stairsteps and Cubie:** ¹"World of Fantasy" (Windy C; r☆12, ☆49, 1966). **Garland Green:** "Jealous Kind of Fella" (Uni; r☆5, ☆20, 1970). **Impressions:** ¹"Gypsy Woman" (ABC-Paramount; r☆2, ☆20, 1961). ¹"It's All Right" (ABC-Paramount; r☆1, ☆4, 1963). ¹"Talking About My Baby" (ABC-Paramount; ☆12, 1964). ¹"I'm So Proud" (ABC-Paramount; ☆14, 1964). ¹"Keep On Pushing" (ABC-Paramount; ☆10, 1964). ¹"You Must Believe Me" (ABC-Paramount; ☆15, 1964). ¹"Amen" (ABC-Paramount; r☆17, ☆7, 1965). ¹"People Get Ready" (ABC-Paramount; r☆3, ☆14, 1965). ¹"Woman's Got Soul" (ABC-Paramount; r☆9, ☆29, 1965). ¹"You've Been Cheatin'" (ABC-Paramount; r☆12, ☆33, 1965). ¹"We're a Winner" (ABC-Paramount; r☆1, ☆14, 1968). ¹"I Loved and I Lost" (ABC-Paramount; r☆9, ☆61, 1968). ¹"This Is My Country" (Curtom; r☆8, ☆25, 1968). ¹"Choice of Colors" (Curtom; r☆1, ☆21, 1969). ¹"Say You Love Me" (Curtom; r☆10, ☆58, 1969). ¹"Check Out Your Mind" (Curtom; r☆3, ☆28, 1970). ¹"(Baby) Turn On to Me" (Curtom; r☆6, ☆56, 1970). **Walter Jackson:** ¹"It's All Over" (Okeh; ☆67, 1964). "Suddenly I'm All Alone" (Okeh; r☆13, 1965). "Welcome Home" (Okeh; r☆15, 1965). **Syl Johnson:** "Come On Sock It to Me" (Twilight; r☆12, 1967). "Is It Because I'm Black" (Twilight; r☆11, 1969). **Major Lance:** ¹"The Monkey Time" (Okeh; r☆4, ☆8, 1963). ¹"Hey Little Girl" (Okeh; r☆12, ☆13, 1963). ¹"Um, Um, Um, Um, Um, Um" (Okeh; ☆5, 1964). ¹"The Matador" (Okeh; ☆20, 1964). ¹"Rhythm" (Okeh; ☆24, 1964). ¹"Sometimes I Wonder" (Okeh; r☆13, ☆64, 1965). **Otis Leavill:** "I Love You" (Dakar; r☆10, ☆63, 1969). **Curtis Mayfield:** ¹"(Don't Worry) If There's a Hell Below, We're All Going to Go" (Curtom; r☆3, ☆29, 1970). **Radiants:** "Voice Your Choice" (Chess; r☆16, ☆51, 1965). "It Ain't No Big Thing" (Chess; r☆14, 1965). **Jackie Ross:** "Selfish One" (Chess; ☆11, 1964). **Billy Stewart:** "I Do Love You" (Chess; r☆6, ☆26, 1965). "Sitting in the Park" (Chess; r☆4, ☆24, 1965). "Summertime" (Chess; r☆7, ☆10, 1966). **Jackie Wilson:** "Whispers (Gettin' Louder)" (Brunswick; r☆5, ☆11, 1966). "(Your Love Keeps Lifting Me) Higher and Higher" (Brunswick; r☆1, ☆6, 1967). "This Love Is Real" (Brunswick; r☆9, ☆56, 1970). **Young-Holt Unlimited:** "Soulful Strut" (Brunswick; r☆3, ☆3, 1968).

¹ = Record produced by Curtis Mayfield.

ALBUMS

Jerry Butler: *The Best of Jerry Butler* (Rhino; 1987). **Gene Chandler:** *The Duke of Soul* (Chess; 1984). **The Chi-Lites:** *The Chi-Lites Greatest Hits* (Rhino; 1992). **Tyrone Davis:** *The Best of Tyrone Davis* (Rhino; 1992). **The Impressions:** *The Impressions' Greatest Hits* (MCA; 1989) **Anthologies:** *Okeh Recordings* (Epic/Legacy; 1992).

(Chart positions compiled from Joel Whitburn's *Record Research*, based on *Billboard*'s Pop chart, unless otherwise indicated; r☆ = position on *Billboard*'s Rhythm & Blues chart.)

PHIL SPECTOR

BY NIK COHN

In Los Angeles I wore a white suit and stayed at the Chateau Marmont, high above Sunset Strip. There was a grand piano and a candelabrum in the lobby and, within an hour of my arrival, persons unknown had sent me a Mexican hooker, name of Angel, who scrubbed my back and cooked me scrambled eggs.

For three days I sat in my room and waited for Phil Spector to contact me. Greta Garbo had once lived in this suite, Myra Breckinridge had looked out through these windows, so I sat and watched the sunsets.

On the third afternoon the phone rang. An un-identified voice asked me if I wished to speak with Mr. Spector. I said that I did. There was a silence. Then the line went dead.

The Chateau was full of corridors and dark corners, Filipino bellhops, aged courtesans. Soon I reached down behind the cooker and came up with a bloodstained silk kimono. I hid it in an air vent and went out to cruise the Strip. When I got back, I looked down from my window, and there was a man with a black moustache, just standing there, motionless.

The phone rang again. This time it was George, Mr. Spector's prime bodyguard. Twenty minutes later he arrived in a black Cadillac, 300 pounds of retired cop, bearded, beringed and heavily holstered, and together we drove off down the Strip, past all the great landmarks, the sacred shrines. Past Dino's and Schwab's and Cyrano's, past the Whiskey. Then past Phil Spector Productions, and on up the hill to El Dorado.

Or, perhaps it wasn't El Dorado, after all. At this distance of time, I can't be sure that it wasn't called Sierra Madre instead, or maybe Besame Mucho or even, who knows, La Paloma. In any case, what matter? It was a mock-Spanish mansion in the classic Hollywood style, all balconies and latticed windows, guard dogs and electronic gates.

As I stepped from the Cadillac, blundering in the dark, I looked up by chance and caught a sudden movement, something shifting behind an upstairs window. A flurry of pink; perhaps a face; nothing more. Wolfhounds snapped and snarled behind a steel-mesh fence. George pushed a sequence of buttons and buzzers, spoke into a mouthpiece, moved us through an electric eye. First one door, then another opened before us. At last we penetrated the mansion.

I was left alone in a very long and high, very cold and empty reception room. Overhead I could hear footsteps moving relentlessly back and forth. Colored lights flashed in the darkness; a door slammed far away.

Everywhere I turned there were pictures of Phil Spector. On coffee tables, around the pool table, stretched across the mantelpiece—Spector with the Teddy Bears, with the Righteous Brothers, with Ike and Tina Turner, with basketball players and karate champions, with Minnesota Fats, with Willie Mosconi, with businessmen, with his mother. In profile, full face, formal or at ease. With companions or, most often, alone.

By the sofa there were three copies of Tom Wolfe's *Kandy-Kolored Tangerine-Flake Streamline Baby*, each with a marker at the chapter on Phil Spector. Underneath there were cuttings from *Time, Life*, ROLLING STONE, each with a marker at the section on Phil Spector. So I sat on the sofa and was idly browsing, when I paused to scratch myself and suddenly there he was, Spector in person, at the far end of the room, on top of a flight of three small stairs, watching me.

At first he did not move. Then I stood up and he came toward me. In close-up, he hardly reached past my shoulder and, even with his gold-rimmed shades, steel-studded wristband and wispy beard, he seemed like a child, maybe ten years old. "Pleased to meet you," he said.

Clearly this wasn't enough. For a very first meeting, something stronger, something altogether more dramatic was called for. So he waited a moment, undecided, and then he gestured round the room, a random sweep that took in the walls, the mansion, the whole of Los Angeles. "Welcome," said Spector, "to Hollywood."

A routine took shape: I sat in my hotel room and every couple of days the phone would ring. Then George picked me up, took me to El Dorado, and Spector talked at me. After a few hours, the session ended. Then George drove me back to the Chateau again, and I settled down to wait for the next time.

The idea was that I would eventually write a book. Therefore I crouched over a tape recorder, looking earnest, and Spector kept up a flow of monologue.

At age twenty-one, Spector was a millionaire. He was also one of the first self-conscious *artists* rock produced. Shown here in 1969, after addressing a conference on rock & roll at Mills College, Oakland, California.

Footsteps echoed above us, the wolfhounds howled outside the windows, and George sat polishing his guns, peaceful in the kitchen. Once I heard a woman singing in another room. Presumably that was Veronica, Ronnie, originally lead singer with the Ronettes, now Spector's second wife. At any rate, she hummed a few bars of "Black Pearl," then cut off dead, halfway through a line, and I never heard her again, nor saw any sign of her existence.

Spector himself, however, was all benevolence. Entombed in his mausoleum, he talked and talked and talked, scarcely pausing for breath. Anecdotes, sermons, remembrances and fantasies poured out of him in a torrent and, in the gaps, he kept me amused with scrapbooks and old snapshots, threw drinks down me until I gagged.

In every detail, he was the perfection of the genial host. One afternoon, like a Jewish mother rampant, he even fixed me a plate of lox and cream cheese on rye, prepared with his own hands, complete with pickles and side salad (Roquefort dressing). Then he sang me old songs, showed me trick shots at pool, almost beat me at pinball. "Fun," he said. And he cackled like a hyena.

Still, I could not relax. Despite all this surface jollity, something in him remained most shadowy, remote beyond reaching. Hunched beside me, with his shades and small child's face, he made me think of a toy—his bones were so birdlike, his voice so shrill. Indeed, he carried such an air of fragility that I was often tempted to lift him up bodily and bounce him on my knee, one hand up his back, like a ventriloquist's dummy.

There was a similar sense of puppeteering when he talked. Time and again, I would catch the whiff of something mechanical, frozen. He would spiel for hours. Jump up and down, wave his arms, flash his hands like torches. Shriek with mock hilarity. Hurl abuse until he was hoarse. But it was all performance, nothing more. Suddenly, without warning, he would grow weary; congeal. Then his limbs would set, as if in rigor mortis, and his eyes snuffed out like candles.

Precisely, the effect was like putting money into a seaside peep show. Pull the lever and he jerked into action, ran through his routines. Let it go again, and he stopped dead.

It was only different when he spoke of his past. Turn him loose in the Fifties, transport him back to Philadelphia or New York, in his golden age, and he flamed. Instantly, he took on true intensity. Outrage and obscenity, crazed invention, labyrinthine sagas tumbled out by the megamot, unstoppable, irresistible, and then there was no doubting him, the full magnificence of his madness. At such moments, one knew precisely how he had happened, how he had become Phil Spector, the all-conquering, in the first place. In memory, he was absolutely heroic. But bring him back to the present, and somehow he expired.

Hard to understand, this collapse. He was still in his late twenties, with money, prestige and great talent, adored and protected at every turn, and he lived exactly as he desired. Yet there was this blankness. It seemed that he had no more great pleasures, no passions, not even all-consuming hatreds. Sometimes he would say he was happy, and he smiled. At other times he shook his head and looked tragic. But mostly he simply sat, and survived, and let time pass.

What was wrong? At sixteen, at twenty, at twenty-four, his drives had been phenomenal. His rage and speed, his sweep of vision, his will—no one in rock had ever moved faster, or been more gifted, or had a more ferocious sense of his own potential. Once he had dared everything; now he seemed to dare nothing. Only the trappings were left—the mansion and the bodyguards, the gold-rimmed shades. Cadillacs and wolfhounds and distant footsteps. The motions of mystique.

So one night, when his soliloquies had run dry and it seemed that there was nothing to be lost, I asked him the truth. Did he feel finished? Was he entirely exhausted? Could anything important lie ahead? Or was his life, in essence, already over?

For a moment he thought about losing his temper. His face scrunched up tight and his mouth opened wide. All his nerve ends prepared to signal fury. But then he paused, right on the brink, and he drew back. With the first volley of murder already halfway up his gullet, he froze. Let a few seconds pass. Then drew in his head, that skull of an infant gnome, like a hedgehog taking refuge.

"Over," he said, with utmost caution. "How exactly do you mean?"

"Kaput," I replied. "Done with. Complete."

He looked surprised, a mite baffled. Playing for time, he removed his shades and peered past my ear, off into infinity, to signal profound thought. He pondered, reconsidered, delayed. In the end, however, the question must have defeated him, outstripped his range, for he only shrugged his shoulders, and he put his shades back on. "I guess it is," he said, offhand, and we talked about pool instead.

I n the first place, more than anything, Phil Spector was a saga of self-invention: a demonstration, on heroic scale, of the possible.

Conceive, as a basis, that every life is shaped by two crucial inventions. The first is imposed from outside, at birth and during early childhood, by God, genes, environment, family, initial experience; the second is projected from within, as the life picks up momentum, by force of will and imagination. So we begin by being invented and we progress, if we can, to inventing ourselves.

The decisive element is nerve—how much, precisely, do we *dare?* If we have been invented originally as plain, dumb, insignificant, a loser, will we dare to reinvent ourselves as glamorous, blessed, heroic? If we are cast to obey, will we dare to command? And if we are doomed in any case, as everyone is doomed, will we at least dare to blow ourselves sky-high, in magnificent technorama wipeout, rather than drain away slowly, craven, on our knees?

Phil Spector dared everything.

In his first incarnation, he could hardly have been less promising. He started out in the Bronx: Jewish, shrimpish, twitchy, panic-stricken. A wimp. A runt. His mother crushed and smothered him, his father died when he was nine. Rootless, he was brought out West, to Los Angeles, and that isolated him more than ever. He was close to no one, belonged nowhere, showed gifts for nothing. By the time he entered his teens, he was entirely withdrawn. His mother consumed him alive, girls terrified him. He dreamed that he was being strangled.

At high school he sat apart, stuck away in corners, and he festered. Once he showed me a snapshot taken in his mid-teens, surrounded by a group of classmates, smiling in sunlight. Half a dozen kids in a loose semicircle, golden-fleshed, archetypal Californians. And they slouch and take their ease, they chew gum, they grin, while Phil peeks out, half-hidden, from behind a silver surfer.

It is an image of absolute security. Everyone here has cars, pretty girlfriends, the simplest and safest of futures. But then you glance at Spector and immediately he belongs to another universe. Bad hair, bad skin, bad posture. Focus on his eyes and all you can see is evasion. White flesh in a world of tan, mess in a world of smooth—everything about him is awkward, alien, discomforting, and all the others are looking elsewhere.

That was the premise he worked from. In his first invention, here, he was hopeless; in his second, he took revenge. All his pent-up energy and rage, his caged passion broke to the surface. Deliberately, he obliterated his roots, wiped out memory, began

again from scratch. It was rather like one of those magic drawing pads, where you can draw and erase and draw again as often as you want. Tabula rasa. At one stroke, Spector rubbed out the accumulated doodlings of seventeen years, every pattern that others

The producer, with the Ronettes and George Harrison, 1964.

had scribbled upon him. Then he drew for himself; drew his own new being.

In the late Fifties, rock & roll made an obvious context. New and virgin territory, ripe for raiding. The first wild burst of euphoria had just begun to dampen down, there was a temporary hiatus. The natural force of the early rockers had been harnessed and contained by the music industry; now what was needed was a champion, someone to challenge these massed ranks of baldies and cigar-chewing fatties, slay the dragon, wrest away control. Someone with so much force and hunger that he would re-create the whole context, musical, financial, in which rock functioned. Release a true teen holocaust. And that, more or less, is what Phil Spector achieved.

T he saga itself was simple. In the beginning, Spector was merely a fan who had a good ear, could play a little guitar and chanced to live in Hollywood, the perfect rock & roll place, at precisely the right moment. He was surrounded by teenage icons, current and future. Annette Funi-

cello, Cher, the budding Fondas. Jan and Dean. Massed spawn of the Sinatras and Martins, the Mitchums, the Kirk Douglases. The collected droppings of a thousand stars.

Spector was duly inspired; blessed by contagion. So he started writing songs. First he achieved "To Know Him Is to Love Him," a title inspired by his father's epitaph. He took a boy and girl from high school, called them the Teddy Bears, put them into a studio, sold the product to a back-room Los Angeles label, sat back and waited. Sure enough, as if of its own accord, without hustle or the smallest hype, the record hit.

Beatific, Spector went to Philadelphia, which was still the rock & roll mecca in those times; he appeared on *American Bandstand,* made some deals, lost out. Soon he was destitute, right back where he started. But by now the fever was on him; he had caught fire. Having once tasted glory, he could not desist. After a stint as a court reporter he found himself in New York, in the Brill Building, which was just in the process of becoming the new heart of teen dreams, every office overflowing with pimpled, pubescent songwriters, pouring out their anguish in a flood.

Phil rehearsing a Christmas carol with Bob B. Soxx.

It was now 1960; Spector was nineteen. For months, he made the coffee, ran errands, slept on the tops of desks. Hammered on every door that might imaginably open, hustling in delirium. Begged, blustered, bagged. And finally Atlantic Records gave in, permitted him to produce some sessions.

Now he moved very fast. He created hits for Ray Peterson and Curtis Lee, and he wrote "Spanish Harlem" for Ben E. King. When the royalties came in, he left Atlantic, found some backers and founded his own label, Philles.

In those days independent labels were mostly small stuff; pimpmobiles without wheels. But Spector flew to Los Angeles, hidden behind shades and an astrakhan coat, swaggering like a pop D. W. Griffith. On one Friday, renting Gold Star studios, he cut "He's a Rebel" with the Crystals; the following week, he knocked out "Zip-A-Dee Doo-Dah" with a bunch of sessionmen backing Bob B. Soxx and the Blue Jeans. Both were smashes and Philles was made.

Triumphant, he set up New York offices and surrounded himself with assistants, flunkies, bodyguards. Bought himself a custom-made Rolls complete with smoked-glass windows, intercom, bonded bubblegum. And he cut twenty hits within the next three years, the most marvelous teen dreams ever recorded. "Then He Kissed Me" and "Be My Baby," "(Today I Met) The Boy I'm Gonna Marry," "Walking in the Rain," "You've Lost That Lovin' Feeling," "Uptown," "Baby, I Love You," "Da Doo Ron Ron." Heroic combustions, all of them. Soundtracks for a one-shot, one-man millennium.

The noise he made, the so-called "Spector sound," was an apocalypse. Through multitracking, he made his rhythm sections sound like armies, turned the beat into a murderous massed cannonade. No question; his records were the loudest, fiercest, most magnificent explosions that rock had yet produced, or dreamed of. And Spector stood in the center, swamped by all this mayhem, twiddling the knobs, controlling everything, like an infant in charge of Armageddon.

By the time that he passed twenty-one, he was a dollar millionaire. He got married, divorced and married again. His hair grew past his ears, down his neck, almost to his shoulders, and he wore his shades all the time. He strutted, he orated. If someone annoyed him, he called for his bodyguards and ordered vengeance. When he was troubled, he screamed and everybody stopped, took notice. In his high-heeled boots, he stood five feet seven, and the industry called him a genius.

He seemed impregnable. Everything he touched shipped gold; everyone he passed bowed low. He moved to Hollywood, took an office on the Strip, bought El Dorado and cruised in a fleet of cars, all with smoked-glass windows, impenetrable, so that he could see without being seen, rule without being touched.

It was his moment. Then the moment passed. In 1964 the Beatles appeared and, after that, he was no longer the newest and hottest sensation. He still produced hit records, still got his picture in the trade magazines. But his impetus slackened. The industry was busy with other, fresher games, and Spector drew back into shadow.

In 1966 he made "River Deep—Mountain High" with Ike and Tina Turner and it flopped. His very finest record, and his first important failure. So he announced his retirement.

Darlene Love learning the words to "Winter Wonderland."

He was then almost twenty-six. Within five years—as artist, businessman and image, as hustler and myth—he had exhausted the fullest potentials of pop. Truthfully, what more was left? Nothing, except to lock the gates of El Dorado and vanish. His journey was completed. Now all that remained was time to kill.

In overall terms of rock history, there were three levels—industrial, creative, stylistic—on which Spector's effect was quite enormous.

As a businessman, first of all, it was he, more than anyone, who was responsible for establishing the concept of independence. Before him, mass-market pop had been controlled by a handful of major companies, corporate giants. Their dominance was total; outsiders had little chance. An individual might start his own label and do well enough locally or within a specific market, like R&B or gospel. But if he wanted to be national, he either had to tag on to one of the majors or spend half a lifetime at war.

Spector ripped through all that; refused to be cowed. Almost from the outset, he controlled every aspect of his own enterprise: production, publicity and distribution, hiring and firing, dealing and scamming, artwork, letterheads, office decor, even the color of the toilet paper. He would not be supervised, monopolized; would make no compromise whatever. Afterward, everything came much easier. Spector having made the first breach, it was possible for others to slip through behind him.

That was finance. At the same time, however, he also marked rock's first flirtation with art. Previously there had been great performers, and also a number of natural creators. But Spector was the first to rationalize, the first to comprehend precisely what he was up to. With him, there was immediately a totally new level of sophistication, complexity, musical range.

That could have been fatal. Like all mass media, rock & roll works best off trivia, ephemera, games, and the moment that anyone begins to take it more solemnly he treads on minefields. As performance, rock has been magnificent. Nothing has been better at catching moments, and nothing has carried more impact, more evocative energy. While it lives off flash and outrage, impulse, excess and sweet teen romance, it's perfect. But dabble in art, and instantly it gets overloaded.

Somehow Spector managed it. On one hand, he created his own imaginative universe, which I take to be the test of any true artist. At root, indeed, he was intensely serious. Yet at the same time he never let go of surface folly, of rock's essential ritziness. Simultaneously, he contrived to be subtle and raucous, experimental and corny, pure and strictly commercial. He stole from every source he could—Wagner, Leonard Bernstein, Broadway shows, a thousand or a million other singles, past and present—and was still completely original. Pretentious and funky, earnest and camp. Very complicated indeed, and most beautifully dumb.

Through this paradox he managed to combine the two great rock & roll romances—rebellion and teen dream—into one. The first meant noise and fury and filth, orgy, musical assassination; the second was

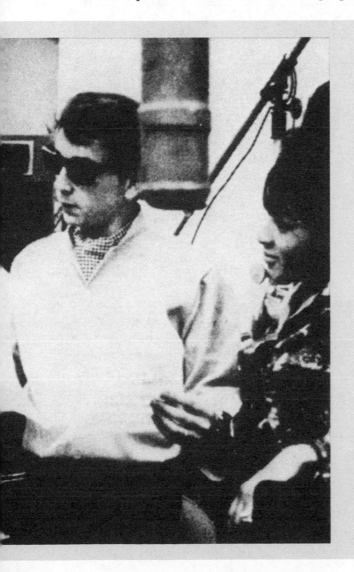

Phil Spector's pride and joy was the Ronettes. In 1968 he married the lead singer, Veronica (right).

sweetest, most perfect innocence. No way for the two to intertwine, or so it seemed. Until Spector jumped up, out of nowhere, and achieved it at one stroke.

In his original songs, by utilizing the massed writers of the Brill Building, he nurtured the purest, the most aching and idyllic of all teen ballads. Into this sound, meanwhile, he poured out his rage and vengeance. Three pianos, half a dozen drummers, rattlers and assorted thumpers, whole battalions of brass and strings, all crashing and smashing away, in deafening, murderous release. So his songs might be pure romance, but his sound was pure slaughter. Together, they meshed as absolute energy.

Money. Music. And then there was Spector as image, where his influence was greatest of all.

Right from the beginning he came on as a guerrilla, dedicated to wholesale riot. When the rest of rock was still stuffed full of crew cuts and natty Italian suits, charm-school smiles, dimples, he was outrageous beyond belief. Grew his hair, draped himself in frills and satins, perched on top of three-inch Cuban heels, sometimes purposely affected a high-pitched lisp. Jangled and shimmered from a dozen bracelets, gold rings, baubles. Leered when he should have beamed, spat when he should have smarmed. Preened and paraded, shameless. The very picture of excess.

Then there were his bodyguards, his limousines, his mansions. His tantrums and his unmitigated gall. For the fact that he had reinvented himself, started again from scratch, did not mean that he wiped out his old neuroses and terrors. It was just that now he turned them to his own use, as engines rather than blockages. At bottom, he was as isolated and estranged, as screwed up as ever. But now he flaunted it, reveled in his own disturbance.

None of his routines was new in itself. Other Americans had grown their hair, been naughty before. Beats had been more extreme, queens more decadent, film directors more ill tempered, Trotsky-ites more radical, gangsters more ostentatious and whores more pious. What was special, unparalleled in Spector was simply that he managed to combine so many different forms of provocation and dissent at once, and also that he made them work for him, in mass commercial terms. He was the first of the anarchist pop millionaires: At last, in him, odium equaled money.

Money, music, image. In each of them, the break-

Bob B. Soxx and the Blue Jeans.

through was absolutely basic. Nobody, it's fair to say, ever wrought deeper changes in the way the rock industry looked, felt, behaved. At the time, in the early Sixties, the upheavals seemed cataclysmic; today we take them for granted. Yet if only one pauses to consider, the achievement becomes more impressive than ever. To come out of a vacuum and force such changes, at such speed, with such totality—even now, it's hard to conceive the force and self-belief it must have taken. Phil Spector, no doubt, was an earthquake.

After "River Deep—Mountain High," when Spector retired in his huff and went up the hill to El Dorado, the idea was not that he would stagnate but that he would now develop in all kinds of new and most scintillating areas. Perhaps he would produce movies, perhaps he'd set up projects with his friend Lenny Bruce, perhaps he would invade Wall Street. He would relax and read and complete his education; travel, and shoot pool, and train the American karate team. Above all, he would go through psychoanalysis, which would release him from his traumas and render him capable of anything, everything. Soon he would be healthier and happier than he had ever been, and he could make a fresh beginning.

It didn't work; it scarcely could. The greatest strength of rock is that it traps the instant. The corollary, almost inevitably, is that it does not last. By its very nature, which is explosion, it is unequipped for abstractions, for profundity or permanence. While he had existed in perpetual motion, Spector had been invincible. The moment he slowed down, he was lost.

Nonetheless, he struggled. He took long and tortuous journeys with himself, his analyst, his mother, his bodyguards, his soul, his past, his possible future. He watched basketball and almost produced *Easy Rider*. He contemplated and rejected a dozen new departures, and he spawned a son. And at the end of all that, after thirty months of solitude, he was bored stiff.

One of the most frightening aspects of boredom is the panic it promotes. People who stay quite calm through riot, tragedy, even death, go berserk in tedium. So Spector, who had thrived under pressure, now could not stand idleness. Quite simply, he made a fatal surrender—he decided to retrace his steps.

He had a favorite dictum, which he told me several times, always in alien contexts, and that was *never repeat*. "You can always come back," he used to say, "But you've got to come back better. If you come back worse, or even the same, you're dead." And promptly he came back worse, or the same.

Instead of returning to Philles, which was his badge of independence, he made a deal with A&M. Perhaps he needed the money, perhaps he was only in need of emotional support. Whichever, it meant that, for the first time since his teens, he became an employee; a hired gun.

Next he signed a group called Checkmates, a supper-soul act from Vegas, and cut a single called "Love Is All I Have to Give." By his own highest standards, it was average, which placed it at least a class above any other record of 1969. The only trouble was, it wasn't new—it was archetypal Phil Spector, technically and musically superlative, but it broke no fresh ground. Accordingly, it didn't hit.

The followup, "Black Pearl," was less exciting but more commercial, and it contained one classic teen-dream couplet: "You'll never win a beauty prize, no, they won't pick you / But you're my Miss America,

and I love you." As things turned out, it was the last great touch that Spector managed.

"Black Pearl" made the Top Twenty. So he went back into the studios to cut the obligatory album. Around the same time, I arrived at the Chateau Marmont, and we began to talk.

It was now the summer of 1969, and our conversations lasted several weeks. Between our meetings, meanwhile, Spector went through the motions of hustle. He worked in the studios, set up deals for the future, made large sums of money. However, just like his talk, all this activity seemed somehow spurious, forced. Beneath the hype, I sensed no real hunger. Indeed, the more time I spent around him, the more deeply he seemed paralyzed, and the more I grew convinced that his true moment was gone.

One incident in particular struck me as a perfect symbol.

Down at the Aquarius, at the wrong end of Sunset Boulevard, the producers of *Hair* threw an opening party in the parking lot, late one hot afternoon. All the rich and/or beautiful persons showed up. And so did Spector.

We were still in the Love Age then, and the lot was

The Ronettes, who didn't look like the girls next door.

185

filled with baubles, bangles, beads. Paraphernalia by numbers—robes and Indian silks, joints in American flag papers, zodiac jackets, patchouli and joss sticks, soul handshakes, handmade Moroccan drums and unwashed feet in sandals. Caftaned musicians from Laurel Canyon tootled away on Arabic flutes and pipes, and long blond girls kept falling over, giggling.

This was the scene Spector stumbled on when he came down from El Dorado, immured behind his smoked windows and his thickest, most impenetrable shades. Cruising by, he told George to drive very slow, rolled his window down six inches and, with utmost caution, he peered out through the slit, took in the tableau.

What he saw was a troupe of girls in semiundress, doing belly dances on a table full of health foods; cross-legged meditators in a circle; the tootlers and thumpers leading an impromptu procession of dancers round the lot, a kind of spaced-out bunny hop; three acid freaks, screaming and laughing uncontrollably, clawing at their eyes, flapping their arms in attempted flight; 200 assorted admen, record executives and publicists, all saying Groovy, Far Out and Too Much; and John Sebastian, standing on one foot like a demented crane, improvising a droned psalm for all humanity.

Spector froze. As though unable to trust his senses, he rolled down his window a few more inches and put his eye still closer to the gap. And that was his undoing, because he was recognized and everyone rushed toward him.

In its own way, this was a major Hollywood event. Since his retirement, Spector had been an almost total recluse. He never appeared in public, cloaked his life in greatest secrecy. So he had acquired near-mythic status as rock's best answer to Howard Hughes, and every move he made, or was rumored to have made, was subject to most furious gossip.

Yet here he was. Live, in person, appearing out of nowhere. The crowd was thrilled, could scarcely believe its luck. Jiggling their beads, jangling their bells in ecstasy, they waved and salaamed, and they brought him their flowers, their joints. Some of them even stripped their clothes off and did a sun dance in celebration. In a sense, after all, Spector was their true founding father. They owed him a great deal: So they rewarded him with adoration.

Spector himself, meanwhile, gazed out at the hordes in a daze, both motionless and expressionless, while they swarmed around his Cadillac and smeared their fingers all over the paintwork. They beamed, he stared. They blew him kisses, and he could not comprehend. Only when a speed freak from the Canyon, naked but for a loincloth, actually put his hand through the lowered window and tried to touch his master's forehead did Phil suddenly come alive and fling himself backward across the seat, shaken by spasms. "George! George!" he squealed, in utter panic. "Get me out of here!"

As the car moved off, he collapsed in a corner, trembling, green-faced. Outside a funeral parlor a couple of blocks downtown, he gradually began to recover, subside. In the distance the party continued. The guests capered and flaunted, as though nothing had happened. But Spector did not look back. Eyes half-shut, he seemed drained, entirely spent.

Strange reversal. Very strange indeed. These were his progeny. But now that they confronted him face to face, he could not see the faintest resemblance. "Who were they? I mean, who were those *animals?*" he asked, expecting no answer, and he shook his head slowly, as if in shell shock. Then he wound up his window tight, he headed back for the safety of El Dorado. "My God," he said. "Sweet Lord, what have I done?"

Our book came to nothing. After each meeting, I would take the tapes back to the Chateau and transcribe them faithfully, while Angel sucked lollipops. But there was no real point. The contents were always barren.

The time had gone, that was all; I was too late. Already it was impossible to mistake Spector's future, and the vision was soggy, distressing. Having once let go of Philles and allowed himself to be hired, he must automatically lose his uniqueness. Abdicating control, he embarked on yet another invention. And this time, just as in his childhood, his role would be imposed by outsiders, rather than by his own imagination, his inner need.

Naturally, this new self would be colored by his past, his track record. He would never again be seen as runtish or insignificant. On the contrary, he would be a man of substance, revered as a producer, celebrated as a legend. He would be courted and

In his high-heeled boots, Spector stood five feet seven. In the studio he captured sounds that no one had ever heard before.

flattered, he would make millions and wield influence, and he would still be a focus for gossip, emulation, envy. What he wouldn't be, though, was autonomous. He wouldn't transcend all categories, and he would no longer dictate. When he made a record, it would belong less to him than to the performer or the company. It would still be a hit, no doubt. But it would not be Phil Spector.

So it proved. After he had finished with the Checkmates, he moved onward and upward, to the Beatles. He cut "Imagine" with John Lennon and "My Sweet Lord" with George Harrison. In their own context, they were both fine records and, of course, they were monstrous worldwide hits. Superficially, therefore, Spector was right back on top—the number-one producer in creation.

The euphoria didn't last. In time, Lennon and Harrison departed, and he could not replace them. He worked with Dion and Cher and Leonard Cohen and the Ramones. But the products rarely sold. In other words, his own presence could no longer guarantee success. Just like any other producer, with the sole exception of his original Philles self, he was dependent on his artists.

That knowledge galled him unbearably. Outraged, despairing, he began to cause scenes, wave his fists at fate. Then he would repent, retreat again into seclusion. But always he was faced by the same eternal problems. What to do next? Where to go?

There were no answers. From time to time, he would go back into the studios, one more time, perhaps with Ronnie, or with Dion. Or he would find some new guru, some miracle healer, to drum up renewed belief in himself. But there was never real fulfillment; not in the end. His myth swamped his present reality, suffocating him.

In spite of that, or because of it, he still stands as the definitive rock & roll saga. No one else had so perfectly caught its potentials, and also its limitations. He'd been everything that pop did best—fast and funny and crazed, full of style and marvelous follies, distinctly heroic; he had also shown just how fast the medium went sour. This was a world made for magnificent flashes, combustions that could never sustain. Get into it two-handed. Stampede right through it and then quit dead, without a backward glance. Don't cruise and don't admire the view. Above all, don't ever stop to think.

On the day I left Los Angeles, I went to say goodbye. In his office Spector sat surrounded by numberless gold records and told me, for perhaps the third time, how he had chosen the title "To Know Him Is to Love Him." "I took it," he said, "from the words on my grave."

He was standing at the window, looking down at the Strip. For a few seconds he noticed nothing. Just stood there, this tiny, ancient child, with his hair all wisps and his shades refracting silver. Then he heard what he'd said and he turned to face me. He did not look distressed; just puzzled, lost. "Not my grave. I mean my father's," he said. "The words on my father's grave."

The Tycoon of Teen.

DISCOGRAPHY

SINGLES PRODUCED BY PHIL SPECTOR, 1958–1969

Teddy Bears: "To Know Him Is to Love Him" (Dore; ☆1, 1958). **Ray Peterson:** "Corinna, Corinna" (Dunes; ☆9, 1960). **Paris Sisters:** "Be My Boy" (Gregmark; ☆56, 1961). **Curtis Lee:** "Pretty Little Angel Eyes" (Dunes; ☆7, 1961). **Paris Sisters:** "I Love How You Love Me" (Gregmark; ☆5, 1961). **Gene Pitney:** "Every Breath I Take" (Musicor; ☆42, 1961). **Curtis Lee:** "Under the Moon of Love" (Dunes; ☆46, 1961). **Crystals:** "There's No Other (Like My Baby)" (Philles; ☆20, 1961). **Ray Peterson:** "I Could Have Loved You So Well" (Dunes; ☆57, 1961). **Paris Sisters:** "He Knows I Love Him Too Much" (Gregmark; ☆34, 1962). **Crystals:** "Uptown" (Philles; ☆13, 1962). **Connie Francis:** "Second Hand Love" (MGM; ☆7, 1962). **Crystals:** "He Hit Me (and It Felt Like a Kiss)" (Philles; 1962). "He's a Rebel" (Philles; ☆1, 1962). **Bob B. Soxx and the Blue Jeans:** "Zip-a-Dee Doo-Dah" (Philles; ☆8, 1962). **Crystals:** "He's Sure the Boy I Love" (Philles; ☆11, 1962). **Alley Cats:** "Puddin n' Tain" (Philles; ☆43, 1963). **Bob B. Soxx and the Blue Jeans:** "Why Do Lovers Break Each Other's Heart" (Philles; ☆38, 1963). **Darlene Love:** "(Today I Met) The Boy I'm Gonna Marry" (Philles; ☆39, 1963). **Crystals:** "Da Doo Ron Ron" (Philles; ☆3, 1963). **Bob B. Soxx and the Blue Jeans:** "Not Too Young to Get Married" (Philles; ☆63, 1963). **Darlene Love:** "Wait 'til My Bobby Gets Home" (Philles; ☆26, 1963). **Crystals:** "Then He Kissed Me" (Philles; ☆6, 1963). **Ronettes:** "Be My Baby" (Philles; ☆2, 1963). **Darlene Love,** "A Fine Fine Boy" (Philles; ☆53, 1963). **Ronettes:** "Baby, I Love You" (Philles; ☆24, 1963). **Crystals:** "Little Boy" (Philles; ☆92, 1964). **Ronettes:** "(The Best Part of) Breakin' Up" (Philles; ☆39, 1964). "Do I Love You" (Philles; ☆34, 1964). **Crystals:** "All Grown Up" (Philles; ☆98, 1964). **Ronettes:** "Walking in the Rain" (Philles; ☆23, 1964). **Righteous Brothers:** "You've Lost That Lovin' Feelin' " (Philles; ☆1, 1964). **Ronettes:** "Born to Be Together" (Philles; ☆52, 1965). **Righteous Brothers:** "Just Once in My Life" (Philles; ☆9, 1965). **Ronettes:** "Is This What I Get for Loving You?" (Philles; ☆75, 1965). **Righteous Brothers:** "Unchained Melody" (Philles; ☆4, 1965). "Ebb Tide" (Philles; ☆5, 1965). **Ike and Tina Turner:** "River Deep—Mountain High" (Philles; ☆88, 1966). **Checkmates:** "Love Is All I Have to Give" (A&M; ☆65, 1969). **Sonny Charles and the Checkmates, Ltd.:** "Black Pearl" (A&M; ☆13, 1969). "Proud Mary" (A&M; ☆69, 1969). Although uncredited, Spector claims to have produced the following records: **Ben E. King:** "Spanish Harlem" (Atco; ☆10, 1961). "Stand by Me" (Atco; ☆4, 1961). "Amor" (Atco; ☆18, 1961). **Nino Tempo and April Stevens:** "Deep Purple" (Atco; ☆1, 1963). "Whispering" (Atco; ☆11, 1963).

ANTHOLOGIES

Back to Mono (Abkco; 1991).

(Chart positions compiled from Joel Whitburn's *Record Research*, based on *Billboard*'s Pop chart.)

THE GIRL GROUPS

BY GREIL MARCUS

Of all the genres of rock & roll, girl-group rock is likely the warmest and the most affecting. The style flourished between 1958 and 1965, fallow years for rock & roll, and it flourished for the same reasons much of the rest of the music of the time grew tame, predictable and dull.

Girl-group rock was producers' music; the songs came out of the Brill Building, written by contract songwriters. The "artists" had no "creative freedom." Yet when we look back, we find that the worst of the rock & roll made under such circumstances was made by male singers; the records made by girls are, all in all, glorious. Why? Perhaps it is because the males were singing rock & roll only as a stopover on the road to Vegas, as a trying-out for the security of a nightclub act. The girls, on the other hand, were aimed at teenagers; no thought seems to have been given to smoothing out their music in hopes of attracting "a broader audience." Bets were not hedged. And so, if you were looking for rock & roll between Elvis and the Beatles, girl groups gave you the genuine article.

The form stretches from the classic broken hearts of the Chantels, the first major group, through Rosie and the Originals, the Shirelles, the Marvelettes (the only true "girl" group on Motown), Little Eva, the Chiffons, countless lesser groups like the Angels, the Cookies, the Toys, Claudine Clark (a soloist working in the style), the Sensations, the Jaynetts. The form reaches its height with the Spector groups—the Crystals, the Ronettes, and Darlene Love backed by the Crystals—and with the blazing, hokey teen morality plays of the Shangri-Las. Within that listing is emotion of staggering intensity, unforgettable melodies, great humor, a good deal of rage and a lot more struggle—the struggle, one might think, of the singer—a young girl, black as likely as not—against the domination of her white, male producer. The relationship between singer and producer was dependent; almost none of the great lead singers of girl group rock—Arlene Smith of the Chantels, Shirley Allston of the Shirelles, Darlene Love of the Crystals—achieved even minimal success outside of the direction of the producer originally responsible for her.

Still, it was music of celebration—of simple joy,

of innocence, of sex, of life itself, at times—but most often it was a celebration of The Boy. The Boy is the central mythic figure in the lyrics of girl-group rock. He is shadowy: the boy who'll love walking in the rain, the fine fine boy, the leader of the pack, the angel baby. He is irresistible—and almost never macho. He is sensitive. He must be pursued. How to reach him? "You can call me up and have a date, any old time," grinned the Marvelettes: "Beechwood 4-5789." "I met him on a Sunday and my heart stood still," sang Darlene Love in the Crystals' magnificent "Da Doo Ron Ron," but really, she only caught of glimpse of him—"somebody" *else* had to tell her "that his name was Bill." The theme then, is little more than a variation on the Search for Perfect Love and the Attempt to Bring It Home to Meet Mom and Dad (even in "Leader of the Pack," where Mom and Dad won't let it in the house).

The music was perhaps the most carefully, beautifully crafted in all of rock & roll—one reason why none of the twenty or so best records in the genre have dated in the years since they were made. Spector's sound was of course the apotheosis of this approach, of producers' music; but even George Goldner's original productions with the Chantels, which underlie all that followed ("Without George Goldner," said Spector, "there would have been no rock & roll"), are pristine, larger than life, taking over a listener and for three minutes driving everything but that sound out of the listener's world. In between Spector and Goldner are some of the more memorable moments in rock: the piano on "One Fine Day"; Claudine Clark screaming "I SEE THE PARTY LIGHTS!" with unfathomable passion; the unbelievably sexual syncopation of the Shirelles' "Tonight's the Night"; the pile-driving force of "Da Doo Ron Ron"; the good smile of the Crystals' "He's Sure the Boy I Love"—a smile that stretched all across America in 1963.

It was utopian stuff—a utopia of love between a boy and a girl, a utopia of feeling, of sentiment, of desire most of all. That the crassest conditions the recording industry has been able to contrive led to emotionally rich music is a good chapter in a thesis on Art and Capitalism, but it happened. That utopian spirit has stayed with those who partook of it—the formal style of girl-group rock has passed, but the aesthetic is there to hear in Bruce Springsteen, Patti Smith, Book of Love, Bette Midler. As remnants and impersonators of the old groups make the grimy rounds of the oldies concerts, perhaps they find amusement in the fact that their music, never intended to be more than a round dollar with a hole in it, has lasted.

To sum it up, to sum up the scores of records that were made; the dozens of groups that formed and scattered; the many venal or paternal producers, some, like Goldner, dead now, some, like Spector, middle-aged men with no worlds left to conquer; the songwriters still grinding out the songs or, like Carole King, with the careers of their own—perhaps to sum it all up, one record will do: Phil Spector's "A Fine Fine Boy," a Darlene Love single that barely scraped the charts in 1963. It is overwhelming. Its momentum is unbreakable, the backup singing full of delight and wisdom and humor, and the vocal is—well, it is that utopia of feeling. It is Darlene, telling us about her fine fine boy. She's full of pride; most of girl-group rock is music of pain and longing, of pining away, but there isn't a hint of that here. Darlene has what she wants and she knows what he's worth. After about ten seconds, so do you, and you'll never forget it. Church bells ring (that's not a

The Marvelettes, Motown's first girl group.

metaphor; they *do*) and the whole disc seems to physically jump. It never stops. And the message? What does girl-group rock say? What does it come down to? What is its mystery of life? "He even takes me places and buys me things / But love is more important than a diamond ring."

DISCOGRAPHY

SINGLES

Ad Libs: "The Boy from New York City" (Blue Cat; ☆8, 1965). **Angels:** "Till" (Caprice; ☆14, 1961). "My Boyfriend's Back" (Smash; ☆1, 1963). "I Adore Him" (Smash; ☆25, 1963). **Chantels:** "Maybe" (End; ☆15, 1958). "Every Night" (End; ☆40, 1958). "I Love You So" (End; ☆42, 1958). "Look in My Eyes" (Carlton; ☆14, 1961). **Chiffons:** "He's So Fine" (Laurie; ☆1, 1963). "One Fine Day" (Laurie; ☆5, 1963). **Claudine Clark:** "Party Lights" (Chancellor; ☆5, 1962). **Cookies:** "Chains" (Dimension; ☆17, 1962). "Don't Say Nothin' Bad (About My Baby)" (Dimension; ☆7, 1963). **Crystals:** "There's No Other" (Philles; ☆20, 1961). "Uptown" (Philles; ☆13, 1962). "He's a Rebel" (Philles; ☆1, 1962). "He's Sure the Boy I Love" (Philles; ☆11, 1962). "Da Doo Ron Ron" (Philles; ☆3, 1963). "Then He Kissed Me" (Philles; ☆6, 1963). **Dixie Cups:** "Chapel of Love" (Red Bird; ☆1, 1964). "People Say" (Red Bird; ☆12, 1964). "Iko Iko" (Red Bird; ☆20, 1965). **Exciters:** "Tell Him" (United Artists; ☆4, 1962). **Lesley Gore:** "It's My Party" (Mercury; ☆1, 1963). "Judy's Turn to Cry" (Mercury; ☆5, 1963). "She's a Fool" (Mercury; ☆5, 1963). "You Don't Own Me" (Mercury; ☆2, 1963). **Jaynetts:** "Sally Go 'Round the Roses" (Tuff; ☆2, 1963). **Jelly Beans:** "I Wanna Love Him So Bad" (Red Bird; ☆9, 1964). **Darlene Love:** "(Today I Met) The Boy I'm Gonna Marry" (Philles; ☆39, 1963). "A Fine Fine Boy" (Philles; ☆53, 1963). **Marvelettes:** "Please Mr. Postman" (Tamla; ☆1, 1961). "Playboy" (Tamla; ☆7, 1962). "Beechwood 4-5789" (Tamla; ☆17, 1962). **Paris Sisters:** "I Love How You Love Me" (Gregmark; ☆5, 1961). **Patty and the Emblems:** "Mixed-Up Shook-Up Girl" (Herald; ☆37, 1964). **Raindrops:** "The Kind of Boy You Can't Forget" (Jubilee; ☆17, 1963). **Ronettes:** "Be My Baby" (Philles; ☆2, 1963). "Baby, I Love You" (Philles; ☆24, 1963). "Walking in the Rain" (Philles; ☆23, 1964). **Rosie and the Originals:** "Angel Baby" (Highland; ☆5, 1960). **Sensations:** "Let Me In" (Argo; ☆4, 1962). **Shangri-Las:** "Remember (Walkin' in the Sand)" (Red Bird; ☆5, 1964). "Leader of the Pack" (Red Bird; ☆1, 1964). "Give Him a Great Big Kiss" (Red Bird; ☆18, 1964). "Give Us Your Blessings" (Red Bird; ☆29, 1965). "I Can Never Go Home Anymore" (Red Bird; ☆6, 1965). **Shirelles:** "I Met Him on a Sunday" (Decca; ☆50, 1958). "Tonight's the Night" (Scepter; ☆39, 1960). "Will You Love Me Tomorrow" (Scepter; ☆1, 1960). "Dedicated to the One I Love" (Scepter; ☆3, 1961). "Mama Said" (Scepter; ☆4, 1961). "Baby It's You" (Scepter; ☆8, 1961). "Soldier Boy" (Scepter; ☆1, 1962). "Foolish Little Girl" (Scepter; ☆4, 1963). **Toys:** "A Lover's Concerto" (Dyno Voice; ☆2, 1965). **Kathy Young and the Innocents:** "A Thousand Stars" (Indigo; ☆3, 1960).

ANTHOLOGIES

The Best of the Girl Groups, Volumes 1 & 2 (Rhino; 1990).

(Chart positions compiled from Joel Whitburn's *Record Research*, based on *Billboard*'s Pop chart.)

Arlene Smith and the Chantels.

THE BEACH BOYS

BY JIM MILLER

Gone are the white Levis, tennies and striped shirts. Gone too are the odes to affluent hedonism. Bearded and balding, the Beach Boys still periodically release an album of new songs. Yet after more than thirty years in the business, they have become a figment of their own past, prisoners of their unflagging popularity—incongruous emblems of a sunny myth of eternal youth belied by much of their own best music.

The elements of their style are by now legend: the vocals, densely clustered or moving in counterpoint, simultaneously frail and precise; the compositions, some complex, others elementary, some anthemlike, others confessional, some a catalog of clichés, others a revision of rock orthodoxy.

In the Sixties, when they were at the height of their original popularity, the Beach Boys propagated their own variant on the American dream, painting a dazzling picture of beaches, parties and endless summers, a paradise of escape into private as often as shared pleasures. Yet by the late Sixties, the band was articulating, with less success, a disenchantment with that suburban ethos, and a search for transcendence. It has been a curious trek from hot rods and high times to religion and conservation—

and, more recently, partisanship for Republican political candidates, including President George Bush. Through it all, though, the Beach Boys have remained wed to the California that Chuck Berry once called "the promised land"—and their continuing appeal says as much about the potency of that chimera as it does about the Beach Boys.

They were winners from the start: "Surfin'," their first release on a local L.A. label, made the city's charts in 1961. At a time when rock had become a game for Tin Pan Alley pros, the Beach Boys were very much a family affair: Brian Wilson, nineteen, his brother Dennis, seventeen, and Carl, at fifteen the youngest Wilson, formed the original group, together with cousin Mike Love and their Hawthorne neighbor, Alan Jardine.

In surfing, the Beach Boys had hit upon a potent image. Leisure, mobility and privacy—it was the suburban myth transported to the Pacific Ocean, but rendered heroic. There had been "surf bands" (such as Dick Dale's) in California before the Beach Boys, but these bands played a homogenous brand of in-

The Beach Boys in the bearded period of their latter-day popularity. By evoking an uncomplicated utopia of surf and sun, they've been making waves for more than thirty years.

strumental rock, crossed with rhythm & blues. The Beach Boys, with their neatly trimmed harmonies, were projecting a world view.

"Surfin' Safari," the group's first national hit on Capitol, launched surf music as a fad; by "Surfin' U.S.A.," the Beach Boys' followup in early 1963, the group had perfected a style. Working off a cop from Chuck Berry's "Sweet Little Sixteen," Brian and Mike contrived a set of lyrics that revealed no small flair for constructing teen utopias ("If everybody had an ocean . . ."); and the music itself was no less striking. While the blanched vocals harked back to the Four Preps, the guitars had the crude

drive of a high school band. Coming in the midst of teen idols, Brill Building pop and seductive girl groups, the first Beach Boys hits managed to sound raunchy and vital, yet clean, somehow safe—for here was a rock & roll band aspiring to the instrumental sleekness of the Ventures, the lyric sophistication of Chuck Berry and the vocal expertise of some weird cross between the Lettermen and Frankie Lymon and the Teenagers.

Surfin' U.S.A., the group's second album, sold extraordinarily well at a time when singles were still the barometer of pop success. When the Beach Boys returned to the studio, it was under the tutelage of Brian Wilson, who became the band's producer. The Beach Boys thus were one of the first rock groups with studio control; and to a large extent, their history is the story of the records Brian made.

B rian Wilson was not your average rock & roll star. Moody and withdrawn, he never quite fit the carefree stereotype the early Beach Boys so carefully cultivated. Onstage, he smiled a lot but looked awkward; the show focused on the mugging of Mike and Carl, and the athletic sex appeal of Dennis. In the safety of the studio, on the other hand, he was the group's dominant voice, always plotting fresh departures and refining old ideas, rarely content to recycle a tried and true formula. Like his idol Phil Spector, he came to be considered something of an oddball genius.

The first LP he produced for the Beach Boys, *Surfer Girl,* hinted at things to come. For the first time, Brian used his falsetto extensively, sharing lead vocals with Mike Love, whose nasal drone propelled all of the group's early uptempo hits. The group's harmonies veered toward the modern voicings of the Four Freshmen, and the success of "Surfer Girl," a cool ballad, enabled Brian to fill the album with similarly romantic fare, tied to surfing in name only. More importantly, Brian let a little of himself be expressed. On "In My Room" his pure falsetto, soaring over violins (another innovation), carried a message of suburbanbred agoraphobia at variance with (although not unrelated to) the Beach Boys' official posture of nonstop kicks: "There's a world where I can go / And tell my secrets to / In my room. . . ."

Throughout this early period the Beach Boys re-

The way they were in 1964. *Clockwise from upper left:* Mike Love, Brian Wilson, Carl Wilson, Dennis Wilson, Al Jardine.

fined their sound. On straight rockers they sang tight harmonies behind Love's lead, with Carl contributing crisp, if rudimentary, guitar lines; on the ballads, Brian played his falsetto off against lush, jazz-tinged voicings, often using (for rock) unorthodox harmonic structures. At the same time, the group's pursuit of Fun, whether on a surfboard or in a car, set them apart and assured them all of an audience, no matter how restrictive the specific motifs, although surfing, cars and the California locale all became emblematic, of course.

California—in 1963, it was the one place west of the Mississippi where everyone wanted to be. Rich and fast, cars, women, one suburban plot for everyone, a sea of happy humanity sandwiched between frosty mountains and toasty beaches, all an easy drive from the freeway. But was it that simple and bright? Behind the pursuit of fun, you might hear a hint of tedium, or a realization that each passing day blemished the pristine Youth this culture coveted. Brian Wilson understood this perfectly and, characteristically, made it attractive and not a little heroic, as in "I Get Around," in which he expresses sheer frustration: "I'm gettin' bugged drivin' up and down the same old strip." His business was the revitalization of myths he wished were true and knew were false. The hollowness, properly dressed up as adolescent yearning, could itself be marketed in "teen feel" pop songs.

Brian Wilson in any case was after something

more than simple celebrations of suburbia. Throughout 1963 Phil Spector's Crystals and Ronettes recordings poured epic crescendos of sound into three-minute singles. The resonance and self-conscious imagery of Spector's records caught Brian's ear. From 1964 to *Pet Sounds* (May 1966), he dedicated himself to duplicating that oceanic sound. He would wed the Beach Boys' own harmonic expertise to Spector's use of layered percussion and orchestration. But Brian was not after mere imitation; the same impacted density would amplify his own lyrical themes. Suburban values wouldn't be abandoned—they'd be rendered profound, their ambiguities expressed.

"Fun, Fun, Fun" and "Don't Worry Baby" marked the break. "Don't Worry," ostensibly about a drag race, represented an earnest confession of insecurity: "Well, it's been buildin' up inside of me for, oh, I don't know how long / I don't know why, but I keep thinkin' something's bound to go wrong." The vocal arrangement underlined this vulnerability at every turn, casting the lyric's anxiety against a soothing expanse of overdubbed harmony parts. The Beach Boys were beginning to push pop conventions to their limits.

Meanwhile, hit followed hit, each marking some small advance over its predecessor. After "I Get Around," a brilliant teen anthem mounted with unorthodox chord changes, the singles toyed with an ever broader palette of colors. "Dance, Dance, Dance" was the most successful musically, an unabashed rocker driven by Spectoresque percussion (sleigh bells, castanets, tambourine). But "When I Grow Up (to Be a Man)" stands as Brian's most touching work of the period. Its sad queries ("Will I dig the same things that turned me on as a kid?") formed an admission of the ephemerality of youth, the passage of time underlined by the tolling of years on the refrain ("sixteen, seventeen").

By 1965 "California Girls" and *Summer Days (and Summer Nights)*, Brian's style had fully developed. The group's last unadulterated fling at summer in the suburbs, *Summer Days* included such highlights as "Let Him Run Wild," a cyclical construct that recalled Motown's Holland-Dozier-Holland as much as it evoked Phil Spector. Brian had tamed the studio, just as the group had mastered his daunting arrangements.

Yet Brian increasingly played the recluse, dropping all concert dates with the band to concentrate

After their Daddy took their T-Bird away.

Waiting to nab some pet sounds.

on composing and producing. Commercially, the Beach Boys stayed on top, churning out virtually flawless singles, which, after "Surfin' U.S.A.," almost always reached the Top Thirty nationally. Brian Wilson, however, wasn't looking back.

Not without regret, the Beach Boys, presumably at Brian's behest, abandoned their search for the perpetual followup. Perhaps, as some have claimed, Brian Wilson was consumed by a desire to better the Beatles; or perhaps, more simply, he was intent on working out the music already in his mind. Whatever the reasons, Wilson now focused all of his energy on creating an album that would fully reflect the Beach Boys' capabilities, by elaborating a new intricacy and a new seriousness of intent.

Their next album, *Pet Sounds,* ushered in a turbulent period for the group. While "Wouldn't It Be Nice," the opening cut, presented Brian's fantasy of marital bliss, the rest of the record vented Wilson's obsession with isolation, cataloging a forlorn quest for security. The whole enterprise, which smacked of song cycle pretensions, was streaked with regret and romantic languor: "I had to prove that I could make it alone now/ But that's not me." But it worked; sweetening each cut with everything from chamber strings to a lonesome koto, Wilson distilled a potent brew, both confessional and maudlin, in the melodramatic fashion of Paul Anka. The Beach Boys have never quite recaptured the sustained brilliance of Brian's settings for these songs: And it was his music that carried the lyrics and made them evocative rather than trite.

The record's conclusion was pessimistic, charting the inevitability of change. By closing the cycle on a note of resignation ("Where did your long hair go?/ Where is the little girl I used to know?"), "Caroline, No" revealed the emptiness of Brian's daydream on "Wouldn't It Be Nice." Unfortunately, such expressions of adolescent angst were not everybody's cup of tea. Compared to previous Beach Boy albums, *Pet Sounds* sold poorly.

A s if to prove the Beach Boys could still cut a happy-go-lucky Top Forty single, Brian countered with "Good Vibrations," a foray into full-fledged psychedelia. Through dozens of overdubs and six months of painstaking work, the group created their biggest hit to date.

It was Brian Wilson's finest hour as a producer. Opening over muted brass, organ triplets and a brace of flutes, Carl's lead vocal lent the song a hushed intimacy; and the voicings on the refrain were scored over a rapidly bowed bass and theremin, the song's "psychedelic" ingredient. In midstream, harpsichord, Jew's harp, tambourine, sleigh bells and thickly carpeted vocals swirled into a retard—and suddenly "Good Vibrations" became a meditation for organ, breathy vocals and possibly wind chimes (Brian's penchant for weird percussion reached new heights here).

Before good vibrations turned bad.

Not satisfied with this symphonic million-seller, Wilson pressed on. In 1967 he and lyricist Van Dyke Parks were hard at work on a new, more humorous song cycle. The work was to be called *Smile* and would include a four-part suite on the elements, as well as "Heroes and Villains," "Vegetables," "Cabinessence" and "Surf's Up." Designed as Brian's crowning achievement, *Smile* would supposedly place the Beach Boys right next to the Beatles in the pantheon of arty rock.

But personality problems had begun to take their toll. As legend has it, Brian, suddenly paranoid, destroyed most of the album's laboriously assembled vocal tracks. The group began objecting to Brian's increasing eccentricity, and Brian himself was reportedly depressed by the appearance of *Sgt. Pepper*. *Smile* finally collapsed under the accumulated pressures (though unfinished fragments keep popping up on bootleg albums and on an unauthorized 1990 compact disc reissue).

In its wake, the Beach Boys issued an abridged version of "Heroes and Villains," and *Smiley Smile*, a substitute for *Smile*. Long on parched humor and short on ambitious new music, the album was anticlimactic, to put it mildly. It was also the first album produced by the Beach Boys collectively.

Smiley and its successor, *Wild Honey*, marked a turning point for the Beach Boys. In its heyday, the band had dominated the charts thanks to Brian's skill at cutting hit singles; since the early songs were composed by a performing member of a performing group, they could be successfully re-created onstage. But starting with *Pet Sounds*, the music's complexity virtually precluded live performance; even worse, many of the new lyrics hardly hinted at the sunny fare Beach Boy fans expected. Perhaps sensing defeat in his effort to broaden the group's scope, Brian retreated. After *Wild Honey*, his contributions diminished, often taking the shape of writing three or four tunes per album.

A few scattered tracks like "Darlin'" and "Do It Again" dented the Top Twenty in 1967 and 1968; and in Europe, the Beach Boys' popularity continued unabated. But the days of coasting on the charts were over.

Unhappy with their Capitol contract, the band played out their last two years with the label. On albums like *Friends*, it almost seemed as if they were attempting, defiantly, to be uncommercial. A return to *Smiley*'s dryness, minus the weirdness, *Friends* cast the Beach Boys as auteurs. Coming from anybody else, the album would have been embarrassing; coming from them, it had the ring of autobiographical truth.

In the songs he contributed to the venture, Brian returned to the suburban themes that have always preoccupied him; only now, the good life appeared as an exercise in ennui: "I get a lot of thoughts in the

Brian and his wife, Marilyn. As one half of the vocal group Spring, she made several records with him.

mornin'," sang Brian in "Busy Doin' Nothin'," "I write 'em all down / If it wasn't for that, I'd forget 'em in a while." At their best, the Beach Boys have never flinched before their own banality. "Busy Doin' Nothin'," for example, featured an entire verse devoted to dialing a telephone and not getting an answer. It is one of Brian's most subtle lyrical conquests.

Friends, when set against the success of "Do It Again," a summer-fun rehash, illustrated the band's dilemma. On the one hand, by milking familiar formulas, they could still command an audience; on the other, whenever they released a personal statement or experimental material, the group found themselves performing in a vacuum.

With the expiration of their Capitol contract in 1969, the Beach Boys faced several questions. Should they disband in the wake of sporadic sales and indifferent response? Should they change their name, a liability in "hip" circles, and aim exclusively at the burgeoning market for "progressive rock"? Or should they continue as before, retain their original name and identity, and record whatever material they felt appropriate?

The answers came in 1970. The Beach Boys signed with Reprise Records, activated their own Brother Records logo (which had appeared on *Smiley Smile*'s label), played the Big Sur Folk Festival and issued *Sunflower*, their strongest album since *Pet Sounds*. In name, style and sound, they remained the Beach Boys.

Throughout the Seventies, the group established a loyal following among a new generation, and emerged as one of the biggest live acts in the United States. In addition, they continued to record new original material, with fitful public response.

Surf's Up, released in 1971, epitomized the post–*Pet Sounds* Beach Boys. On such tracks as "Long Promised Road," Carl Wilson emerged as Brian's heir apparent, a composer with an intuitive grasp of the Beach Boys' style. But *Surf's Up* also contained large doses of puffery, pretentiousness and ecological nonsense. Truth to tell, the Beach Boys had evolved into an accomplished, idiosyncratic but sometimes sterile ensemble, at least in the studio.

On the road it was a different story. Although the band had been a concert draw in the mid-Sixties, its skid on the charts had brought a virtual halt to touring. The group's pact with Reprise, however, dictated a new strategy: Since most of America hadn't heard them since the Sixties, or had never heard them, the Beach Boys decided to return to the road and perfect their live performance. Initially, they labored over contemporary material, finally mastering such difficult songs as "Wouldn't It Be Nice."

But it was the surfing and car songs that brought audiences to their feet. At first the group persisted in largely performing recent material, but as the crowds grew, the pressure to concentrate on the oldies became irresistible. Eventually, in 1974, they found themselves blessed with a million-selling Number One album. They were back on top. There was only one small problem: *Endless Summer*, their first gold record since "Good Vibrations," consisted entirely of tracks cut before 1965.

To Brian, the problem must have seemed particularly acute. He now composed moody, introspective miniature operas, like " 'Til I Die" on *Surf's Up*—although he was reportedly reluctant to release the song, because it wasn't "fun." But at the same time, he was still capable of writing happy-go-lucky songs like those behind the Beach Boys' initial popularity, as "Marcella" on *Carl and the Passions* showed. Un-fortunately, almost all of his writing had become baroque, a little flaky, difficult to execute forcefully and, apparently, difficult for an audience to hear. They wanted the cheerful values of the Sixties reaffirmed, resoundingly, in the compelling and straightforward fashion of the early hits. What Brian for his part wanted was considerably less clear: perhaps just to trundle around the house and run the Radiant Radish, his organic-foods shop in Hollywood.

Ironically, Brian Wilson remained the group's guiding light. It was Brian's old songs that the band played night after night, and it was Brian's new songs that stood out on the Beach Boy albums of the Seventies. Indeed, to this day, the Beach Boys remain beholden to a style bequeathed them by Brian. From the nasal raunch of "Surfin' Safari" to the convoluted elegance of "Surf's Up," that style has become a nearly autonomous fund of favored themes, production tricks and chord progressions.

But the future remains uncertain. In the late Seventies Brian returned to the stage, even if only as an immobile exhibit; he also played a major role in producing a couple of albums, including two, *The Beach Boys Love You* (1977) and the solo *Brian Wilson* (1988), as good and idiosyncratic as anything since *Friends*. But much of Brian's work still sounds terribly uncommercial. The other members of the group

A hirsute view from the late Seventies. Their looks changed more than their music. *Clockwise from upper left:* Al Jardine, Mike Love, Brian Wilson, Dennis Wilson, Carl Wilson.

have gone fishing for other formulas, resorting to disco remakes of old tunes, and in the late Eighties without Brian's participation, corny new "feel-good" riffs like "Kokomo," a Number One hit single in 1988 (on the strength of its use in the Tom Cruise movie *Cocktail*). Yet no breakthrough seems in sight: The group is still largely identified with its hits from the early Sixties.

Like Chuck Berry, the Beach Boys reflect an era through their music and lyrics; yet like the Beatles, the band has matured and progressed within the confines of a unique style. In many respects, they are the most innovative white rock & roll band the United States has ever seen. But whether they will ever be able to lead their audience beyond the uncomplicated suburban utopia their early hits so brilliantly depicted now seems unlikely.

DISCOGRAPHY

SINGLES

"Surfin'" (Candix; ☆75, 1962). "Surfin' Safari" (Capitol; ☆14, 1962). "Ten Little Indians" (Capitol; ☆49, 1962). "Surfin' U.S.A." b/w "Shut Down" (Capitol; ☆3, 1963). "Surfer Girl" b/w "Little Deuce Coupe" (Capitol; ☆7, 1963). "Be True to Your School" b/w "In My Room" (Capitol; ☆6, 1963). "Fun, Fun, Fun" (Capitol; ☆5, 1964). "I Get Around" b/w "Don't Worry Baby" (Capitol; ☆1, 1964). "When I Grow Up (to Be a Man)" (Capitol; ☆9, 1964). "Wendy" (Capitol; ☆44, 1964). "Dance, Dance, Dance" (Capitol; ☆8, 1964). "Do You Wanna Dance?" (Capitol; ☆12, 1965). "Help Me, Rhonda" (Capitol; ☆1, 1965). "California Girls" (Capitol; ☆3, 1965). "The Little Girl I Once Knew" (Capitol; ☆20, 1965). "Barbara Ann" (Capitol; ☆2, 1966). "Sloop John B" (Capitol; ☆3, 1966). "Wouldn't It Be Nice" b/w "God Only Knows" (Capitol; ☆8, 1966). "Good Vibrations" (Capitol; ☆1, 1966). "Heroes and Villains" (Brother; ☆12, 1967). "Wild Honey" (Capitol; ☆31, 1967). "Darlin'" (Capitol; ☆19, 1967). "Friends" (Capitol; ☆47, 1968). "Do It Again" (Capitol; ☆20, 1968). "I Can Hear Music" (Capitol; ☆24, 1969). "Break Away" (Capitol; ☆63, 1969). "Add Some Music to Your Day" (Reprise; ☆64, 1970). "Long Promised Road" (Brother/Reprise; ☆89, 1971). "Sail On Sailor" (Brother; ☆79, 1973). "Surfin' U.S.A." (Capitol; ☆36, 1974). "Sail On Sailor" (Brother/Reprise; ☆49, 1975). "Rock and Roll Music" (Brother/Reprise; ☆5, 1976). "It's O.K." (Brother/Reprise; ☆29, 1976). "Peggy Sue" (Brother; ☆59, 1978). "Here Comes the Night" (Caribou; ☆44, 1979). "Good Timin'" (Caribou; ☆40, 1979). "Goin' On" (Caribou; ☆83, 1980). "The Beach Boys Medley" (Capitol; ☆12, 1981). "Come Go with Me" (Caribou; ☆18, 1981). "Getcha Back" (Caribou; ☆26, 1985). "Rock 'n' Roll to the Rescue" (Capitol; ☆68, 1986). "California Dreamin'" (Capitol; ☆57, 1986). "Kokomo" (Elektra; ☆1, 1988). "Still Cruisin'" (Capitol; ☆93, 1989).

ALBUMS

Surfin' Safari (Capitol; ☆32, 1962). *Surfin' U.S.A.* (Capitol; ☆2, 1963). *Surfer Girl* (Capitol; ☆7, 1963). *Little Deuce Coupe* (Capitol; ☆4, 1963). *Shut Down—Vol. 2* (Capitol; ☆13, 1964). *All Summer Long* (Capitol; ☆4, 1964). *The Beach Boys' Concert* (Capitol; ☆1, 1964). *The Beach Boys Today* (Capitol; ☆4, 1965). *Summer Days (and Summer Nights)* (Capitol; ☆2, 1965). *The Beach Boys' Party* (Capitol; ☆6, 1965). *Pet Sounds* (Capitol; ☆10, 1966). *Best of the Beach Boys—Vol. 1* (Capitol; ☆8, 1966). *Best of the Beach Boys—Vol. 2* (Capitol; ☆50, 1967). *Smiley Smile* (Brother; ☆41, 1967). *Wild Honey* (Capitol; ☆24, 1967). *Friends* (Capitol; ☆126, 1968). *Best of the Beach Boys—Vol. 3* (Capitol; ☆153, 1968). *20/20* (Capitol; ☆68, 1969). *Close Up* (Capitol; ☆136, 1969). *Sunflower* (Reprise; ☆151, 1970). *Surf's Up* (Reprise; ☆29, 1971). *Pet Sounds/Carl and the Passions "So Tough"* (Reprise; ☆50, 1972). *Holland* (Reprise; ☆36, 1973). *The Beach Boys in Concert* (Reprise; ☆25, 1973). *Endless Summer* (Capitol; ☆1, 1974). *20/20 and Wild Honey* (Reprise; ☆50, 1974). *Friends and Smiley Smile* (Reprise; ☆125, 1974). *Spirit of America* (Capitol; ☆8, 1975). *Good Vibrations—Best of the Beach Boys* (Brother/Reprise; ☆25, 1975). *15 Big Ones* (Brother/Reprise; ☆8, 1976). *Beach Boys '69 (the Beach Boys Live in London)* (Capitol; ☆75, 1976). *Love You* (Brother/Reprise; ☆53, 1977). *M.I.U. Album* (Brother/Reprise; ☆151, 1978). *L.A. (Light Album)* (Caribou; ☆100, 1979). *Keepin' the Summer Alive* (Caribou; ☆75, 1980). *Ten Years of Harmony (1970–1980)* (Caribou; ☆156, 1981). *Sunshine Dream* (Caribou; ☆180, 1982). *Made in U.S.A.* (Capitol; ☆96, 1986). *Still Cruisin'* (Capitol; ☆46, 1989).

(Chart positions compiled from Joel Whitburn's *Record Research,* based on *Billboard*'s Pop and LPs charts.)

THE BRITISH INVASION

BY LESTER BANGS

For an event so crucial in the history of pop music, the British Invasion produced little of enduring worth. Out of it all, only the music of the Beatles, the Rolling Stones, the Who and the Kinks have lasted; the Searchers, Herman's Hermits, Gerry and the Pacemakers and all the rest today seem quainter than doo-wop—curious relics of a consumers' fever that has long since palled. The reason they seem quaint is that they were, by and large, junk: perfect expressions of the pop aesthetic of a disposable culture. Which is all right. In the fatuity of their enthusiasm lay their very charm.

Consider the time, early 1964. America—perhaps young America in particular—had just lost a president who had seemed a godlike embodiment of national ideals, who had been a youth-cult superstar himself. We were down, we needed a shot of cultural speed, something high, fast, loud and superficial to fill the gap; we needed a fling after the wake. It was no accident that the Beatles had their overwhelmingly successful *Ed Sullivan Show* debut shortly after JFK was shot (the date was February 9th, 1964).

In retrospect, it seems obvious that this elevation of our mood had to come from outside the parameters of America's own musical culture, if only because the folk music that then dominated American pop was so tied to the crushed dreams of the New Frontier. Rock & roll itself was present, but shapeless; we did have Phil Spector, and the Beach Boys and the Four Seasons, but it took the influx of the British Beatles and a thousand trashy imitators to truly bring us together.

The British accomplished this in part by resurrecting music we had ignored, forgotten or discarded, recycling it in a shinier, more feckless and yet more raucous form. The fact that much of this music had originally been written and performed by American blacks made it that much more of a sure thing, but this was not quite a replay of Pat Boone rendering Little Richard palatable to a white audience. In even the limpest, wimpiest Liverpudlian retread of an American R&B oldie, there was at least the promise, the yearning, that both performers and audience might get loose, shake 'em on down and run wild in the streets, as we of course eventually did.

As for the creators of the music—the "beat" groups and the English audiences that gave them their original support—both were fighting their ways out of their own cultural vacuum. England in the Fifties never really enjoyed a rock & roll juvenile delinquent subculture on the scale of that in America; it was an older society, locked in by class and tradition, and what "rockers" the kids got from their own kind were groomed until pale and proper, calculated not to offend the older listeners of the BBC's *Light Programme:* Cliff Richard, Adam Faith, Tommy Steele. Also big with English pop audiences in the mid- and late Fifties were skiffle—a tame brand of pop folk music of which Lonnie Donegan's "Rock Island Line" was the most memorable example—and trad (traditional jazz), a watered down re-creation of New Orleans jazz displayed on such American hits as Mr. Acker Bilk's "Stranger on the Shore."

It was a pallid scene, but there was a youth underground forming in England that anticipated the explosion to come even as it clung to the recent American past. The teddy boys, like their American JD counterparts, greased their hair up and combed it down into a British version of the American "waterfall," which, with a more prurient precision, they called the "elephant's trunk." At first they fed on images of James Dean, Marlon Brando and Elvis, and then, of rock & rollers like Chuck Berry and Little Richard. Later, the teds would mutate into the rockers, a curious early-Sixties tribe of teenage reactionaries who believed that absolutely nothing good had happened musically (or probably in any other sense) since 1959, which by 1964 quite naturally put them in almost constant war with the foppish, pill-popping mods, whose heroes were the Stones, the Who and the Small Faces.

Teddy boy types swelled many of the groups in Liverpool circa 1959, groups that favored trad, skiffle, or Johnny and the Hurricanes-styled instrumental rock (in emulation of Cliff Richard's backing band, the Shadows, one of the few successful British

Gerry Marsden without his Pacemakers, waiting for a ferry 'cross the Mersey.

groups of the time). The influx of the teds brought a shift in musical content: Trad and skiffle were dropped (though most local clubs still barred rock). Like the Beatles, a semipro performing unit since the mid-Fifties that had little time for anything but solid rock, the Liverpool bands turned to Elvis, Little Richard, Chuck Berry, Buddy Holly and American girl groups for their material, and suddenly there was a full-blown scene in this brutal, grimy town on the Mersey River. The scene found its nexus in the Cavern, a dive that was almost alone in making the switch from trad to rock, and provided a showcase for the Beatles (who were discovered there by their future manager, Brian Epstein, in November 1961), Rory Storm and the Hurricanes (with their drummer Ringo Starr, who would replace Pete Best in the Beatles in 1962), Gerry and the Pacemakers and the Swinging Blue Jeans.

There was a boom on, and Liverpool was too small, and its clubs too restrictive, to contain it. Many of the groups, the Beatles included, began to play clubs in Hamburg, Germany, beginning in 1960, and in many ways Hamburg was where the Liverpudlians' sense of themselves as protagonists in an outrageous musical renaissance got off the ground.

Hamburg was a crucible, a proving ground, a place where groups were required to play loud and fast and raw all night, hour after hour, using stimulants to maintain the pace, forcing members of the band who had thought they could not sing to take the mike when the leader's lungs gave out. Things got wild, and the sound took on a mania that became a crucial factor in the coming assault on the United States. It may in fact have been the deciding factor, since by any rational—not to mention purist—standard, most of the beat-group reworkings of black American R&B and rock & roll were sloppy, mindlessly frenetic, inept in the extreme; a lot of noise with very little behind it except the enthusiasm of the players. And that, I submit, was what was good about it, if any musical yardsticks must be applied: It proved, as mindless Fifties American groups had proved before and punk rockers have proved since, that rock & roll at its core is merely a bunch of raving shit, its utterly hysterical transience and intrinsic worthlessness the not-quite-paradoxical source of its vitality.

Note that no one, absolutely no one, has ever made any grand claims for the British Invasion groups such as those advanced for the art rockers of the late Sixties and early Seventies; nobody has argued that "Ferry Cross the Mersey," like, say, *Sgt. Pepper's Lonely Hearts Club Band* or *Electric Ladyland*, is a masterpiece rivaling Beethoven that will survive the ages. Forget it! It was all "yeah, yeah, yeah!" and that was what made the moment precious. Well, no, actually there was a little more involved than "yeah, yeah, yeah!" There were drums that went *BOOM BOOM BOOM,* and rhythm guitars (which, as in most great rock & roll from the Rolling Stones on down, predominated) that went *chunka-chunka chunk.*

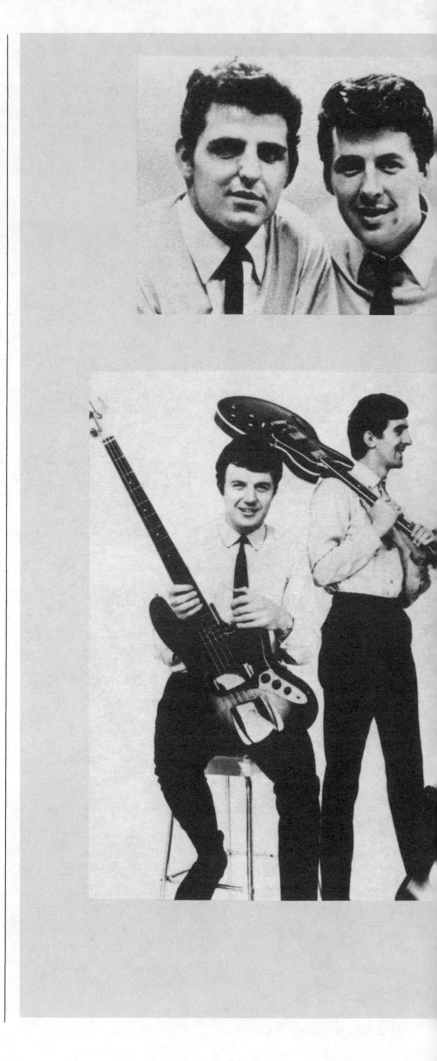

So the British Invasion was more important as an event, as a *mood,* than as music; but the groups that made it in the United States (out of countless numbers that tried and failed) provide the various colors that comprise that mood, and are certainly a part of history even if almost no one listens to their records anymore. And out of that initial Liverpool explosion, these names belong to a yesterday that all rock & roll fans of the time share: the Searchers, Billy J. Kramer and the Dakotas, the Swinging Blue Jeans, and Gerry and the Pacemakers.

The Searchers will live in memory if only for "Needles and Pins," a cover of a Jackie DeShannon song prominent for what must have been the first appearance of the ringing guitar riff that became a stock item in the folk rock of the Byrds, the Leaves, Love, et al. In contrast to many of their contemporaries, the Searchers' image was relatively clean-cut, and so was their music: Their close harmonies and glittering guitar lines never got too raw, even on copies of American R&B like "Hully Gully" and "What'd I Say." Although they had emerged from the same Liverpool-Hamburg axis that produced wilder kin, the Searchers held back; and it was precisely the gentleness and general musical tidiness of their best work—"Needles and Pins," "Someday We're Gonna Love Again," "When You Walk in the Room"—that made them both prophets of folk rock and, ultimately, washouts in the age of Beatlemania.

The Merseybeat sound at its wildest and most ephemeral was defined by the Swinging Blue Jeans, whose "Hippy Hippy Shake" was one of the most unforgettable raveups of its time and also the

The Searchers.

The Swinging Blue Jeans. Songs like "Hippy Hippy Shake" were all "yeah, yeah, yeah" and little else. That was what made them great.

group's only major hit. Most of their repertoire consisted of covers of American oldies, and they slipped into obscurity almost instantly. Still, it remains a curious paradox that of all the groups to come out of the Liverpool-Hamburg scene, these one-hit wonders caught the fever of that scene better than anyone else but the Beatles. It appears, though, that the raving mania of Liverpool was somewhat homogenized for U.S. consumption; the two remaining standout acts from that time and place were Billy J. Kramer and Gerry and the Pacemakers, neither exactly what you would call feverish. Kramer was actually a throwback to the decidedly white ballad crooners of the pre-Beatles era, and in spite of demonstrable talents in that idiom, his short-lived popularity in the days of the craze seems largely attributable to the fact that the Beatles wrote a few songs for him, and also shared Brian Epstein, a brilliant manager and promoter who probably deserves a bigger chunk of this narrative all to himself. In any case, Kramer's two big hits were both smoothies: "Little Children" and "Bad to Me." After about a year he faded from the scene.

Gerry and the Pacemakers, also under the Epstein wing, were a bit hotter, both in terms of hits and Anglomania. They looked just about as twerpy as humanly possible, their hair was very short, and their biggest hits were irresistibly saccharine ballads like "Ferry Cross the Mersey" and "Don't Let the Sun Catch You Crying," which certainly bore no resemblance to the song of the same name recorded by Ray Charles. In some of their other hits like "How Do You Do It" and "I Like It," as well as in the filler on their albums, you hear Mersey-sound garbage at its pinnacle: innocuous but raucous, a cloying clatter that in many ways defined the era. Like many (perhaps most) of the other Liverpool groups, the Pacemakers had no funk, no soul, no danger, and talent that could be measured in dollops, but they were having the time of their lives, and it was infectious and that was all that mattered anyway.

Once the Liverpool explosion had established not only the scene in that city but the possibility of a whole rock renaissance emanating from Britain—in 1963 and 1964—record companies began to search in earnest for new talent, scouring the Isles for bands and city scenes. Manchester provided one of the few authentic examples of the latter, producing the Hollies, Wayne Fontana and the Mindbenders, and Freddie and the Dreamers. The Hollies, of course, are still going strong—in fact, there are some who believe they've done their best work in the Seventies. A case could easily be made that they are more consistent now than ever (although when a band changes personnel as often as the Hollies have, it seems as if it hardly matters); from early albums like *Beat Group* through the Creedence Clearwater Revival–influenced ''Long Cool Woman in a Black Dress'' they remained resolutely trendy and unnervingly erratic. During the British Invasion, they were mostly just bad, grinding out sloppy covers of ''Stay,'' ''Do You Love Me,'' ''Lucille'' and ''Memphis'' in the most shamelessly churn-'em-up, bash-'em-out Liverpudlian manner. ''I'm Alive'' remains an obscure classic from this period, but the Hollies never really found their groove nor dented the U.S. Top Ten until ''Bus Stop'' in '66.

Wayne Fontana and the Mindbenders may have been a one-shot group, but what a shot. ''The Game of Love,'' with its heavy bass, ''Louie Louie'' chording, Bo Diddley break and Fontana's rich, wailing vocals, was an instant classic, a perfect example of the rock & roll band of no apparent distinction but with a masterpiece in them anyway. On the flip side of the dialectic you might find a Freddie and the Dreamers, who had no masterpiece but a plentitude of talentless idiocy and enough persistence to get four albums and one film soundtrack (accompanying their now-forgotten version of *A Hard Day's Night, Seaside Swingers*) released in the United States, plus various other LPs for which they may or may not have been given full credit and which they shared with other certifiable nonentity bands which

Billy J. Kramer *(center)* with the Dakotas.

Freddie *(top)* and the Dreamers, regrettably famous for ''Do the Freddie.''

may or may not have been even less talented than they were. What is worth pointing out is that Freddie and the Dreamers were not merely some promoter's concoction, but an actual group who were, after the Beatles broke, the first non-Epstein Merseybeat band to claim a Top Five hit in England. As has been pointed out by other writers, the Dreamers looked as thuggish as Freddie looked dippy, and the band's

The Hollies, one of the more durable bands of the era.

fame rested primarily on a tie-in with a "dance" called the Freddie (all you had to do was wave both arms and kick both feet out slightly, with a vacant look in your eyes) which in turn tied in with such hits as "I'm Telling You Now" and "Do the Freddie." Like Sam the Sham and the Pharaohs of "Wooly Bully" fame, Freddie and the Dreamers represented a triumph of rock as cretinous swill, and as such should be not only respected, but given their place in history.

Many listeners felt, and no doubt still feel, that the same applies to the Dave Clark Five, but here even I, a connoisseur of garbage, must demur. Of course, their albums were uniformly bad; of course, as *Time* so pithily put it at the time, their singles were primarily distinguished by an "air hammer" beat. But that's just another way of saying BIG beat, and all the Dave Clark Five singles were marked by a loud, thick yet expansive, wall-of-sound production that made them not only distinctive in their day, but ensured that they would sound

exciting—more than mere period pieces—to this day. And that's something that can be said of almost none of the hits of their contemporaries. "Glad All Over," "Bits and Pieces," "Can't You See That She's Mine," "Because," "Catch Us If You Can"—if you remember those titles, as you surely do if you listened to the radio or bought records through 1964 and 1965—if you disparaged or even actively hated the DC5 in their heyday, don't they sound better now, don't they seem vital; don't they seem like pure, mainstream pop rock? Sure, they were crude and of course they weren't even a bit hip, but in their churning crassness there was a shout of joy and a sense of fun. Clark himself sang, composed, played drums, produced and even managed the group—which has, over the years, been severely underrated not only as a consistent singles machine, but, as writer Mike Saunders once put it, as "excellent producers of good, healthy, enjoyable schlock."

Speaking of schlock, in a survey such as this there is no getting around Herman's Hermits, who epitomized the Kleenex texture of their age almost as brilliantly as Freddie and the Dreamers. Consider again the evocative power of mere song titles: "Mrs. Brown You've Got a Lovely Daughter," or "I'm Henry VIII, I Am," Herman's hit version of Ray Davies's "Dandy," or "I'm into Something Good"—catchy and downright huggable, thanks, in the last case, to songwriters Carole King and Gerry Goffin. One must realize that the Hermits hit our shores during a time—mid-'64—when the Beatles appeared to be slipping a bit: There were actually some weeks in which the Fab Four failed to appear in the Top Ten, and a few Cassandras were beginning to smirk that the British Invasion might be a mere flash in the pan and all those faggy long-haired creeps could go right back where they came from. Meanwhile, the Rolling Stones were coming on from the other corner with their dirty would-you-let-your-daughter image, not to mention *their* smirks and the great high school controversy over whether the lines "Baby better come back, maybe next week / 'Cause you see I'm on a losin' streak" meant that the girl in "(I Can't Get No) Satisfaction" was menstruating.

Clearly there was a gap here, with imminent threat to the new order implicit from both sides, and into this gap bounced . . . who else but cute, cuddly, baby-faced, buck-toothed Peter "Herman" Noone. I can recall a comment by the Hermits' manager to the effect that with the waning of initial Anglomania, it was becoming obvious that there were only three enduring talents in the marketplace: the Beatles, the Stones, and Herman's Hermits. And indeed, the group did last long enough to have a string of hits.

Not all of the Invasion bands were as close to candy floss as the Hermits, of course, but many of those more talented had a harder time staying afloat. In the case of the Zombies, this amounted almost to tragedy. Their great hit, "She's Not There," was a gem, with its orgasmic sighs and dramatic falsetto vocal rushing forward into a bitter electric piano solo; the followup, "Tell Her No," while more of a standard Beatles cop, was almost as good. But a rush-released U.S. album was followed by a series of fine singles that uniformly bombed—the Zombies were apparently cursed by their own musical adventurousness and a pop audience that simply was not ready for stuff like "I Want You Back Again," the group's fourth single, a violently (albeit falsetto) sung tale of romantic angst couched in a jazz waltz, with the ghostly "Remember When I Loved Her" on the flip. Failure of this sort of material on both sides of the Atlantic compelled the Zombies to pack it in by 1967, but before doing so they cut one last album. The result was *Odessey* (sic!) *and Oracle,* a pop master-

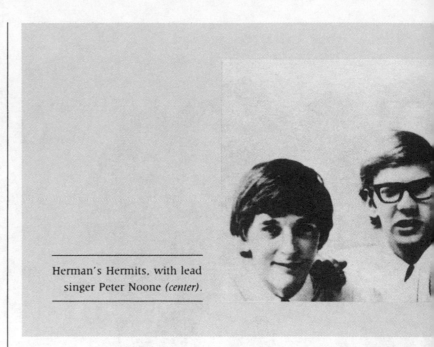

Herman's Hermits, with lead singer Peter Noone *(center).*

The Zombies, whose eerie songs sounded quite cadaverous.

piece which produced their Number Three hit, "Time of the Season." It was a classic case of too much too late; the group had disintegrated by the time the single took over the charts. In the end, it sold 2 million copies.

The blues revivalists, mostly out of London, were also important to the British Invasion, though their impact was not felt until after the first assault: The Alexis Korner finishing school, John Mayall's Bluesbreakers, the Stones and the Yardbirds. But as they were purists, or thought they were, we will leave them to bask in their purity, unsullied by the garbage that has comprised the subject matter of this chapter. Leave them, that is, except for the Animals and Manfred Mann, because like the Stones and unlike most of the other blues revivalists, the Animals and Manfred's men could have been purists only in the privacy of their conceits. For one thing, they both had AM hits in America in 1964, and in those days, purism simply did not survive popularity. Manfred Mann, who came originally from South Africa, may have put stuff like Howlin' Wolf's "Smokestack Lightning" or Muddy Waters's "I'm Your Hoochie Coochie Man" on his first album, and then as now (see his Seventies Earth Band product) he was trying for the great jazz-rock fusion, but for all that Mann's first two U.S. hits, "Do Wah Diddy Diddy" and "Sha La La," were, respectively, a Jeff Barry–Ellie Greenwich tune and a Shirelles cover— in other words, pure only in that they were pure pop. No matter; they clicked, and Manfred was one of the only British rockers with the balls to hit these shores

with a beard, which, given his horn-rimmed specs, caused him to look less like a cerebral jazz cat than a befuddled college professor.

Which was someone for whom Eric Burdon could never have been mistaken. With his Newcastle-on-Tyne workingman's scowl, his backup Animals—who could have passed for shop clerks—and his doubtless magnificent collection of American R&B records, Eric Burdon was certifiably only one thing: short. And, like many short people, he looked to scale the heights, to become in the few years allotted to him something he was, at birth, not: a Negro. Whether he ever succeeded is a question best left to medical research; in any case, it is particularly irrelevant since Negroes themselves turned into black people and Eric seems not to have been able to make the transition. What is certain, and germane, is that the Animals made some of the finest British R&B covers of the mid-Sixties, particularly their boiling versions of "House of the Rising Sun" and John Lee Hooker's "Boom Boom." The boil was as much attributable to Alan Price's organ work as to Burdon's voice, and "House" went on to become a new standard rendition of an old standard composition, such a brilliant rearrangement that it was later imitated almost note for note with similar worldwide success by a troupe of Michigan no-talents called Frijid Pink.

The Animals were among the most gifted and beloved of British Invasion bands; after the original group split, Alan Price went on to a British hit with a wildly Bached-up jazz version of Screamin' Jay Hawkins's "I Put a Spell on You," while Burdon distinguished himself both as the leader of several fine bands (under the all-purpose Animals moniker) and as an ersatz social commentator ("White Houses," "San Franciscan Nights"—which he inexplicably thought were "warm"—"Sky Pilot," "Monterey" and finally "Soledad," this last a duet with bluesman Jimmy Witherspoon). Burdon held on until the early Seventies, when he partially realized his lifelong ambition by leading a predominantly black band called War, with whom he scored his last hit, "Spill the Wine." In 1971 War left Eric in the dust and funkified up the charts with such staggering soul mystery as "Slippin' into Darkness." Like Manfred Mann, Eric has sporadically worked on a comeback over the years even if his voice isn't the instrument of hog-calling power it once was.

Trying to live up to their name, the Animals, with Eric Burdon (*center*), prepare to pounce on America.

If Eric does make it again, he will be one of the very few people mentioned in this chapter capable, or deserving, of such an achievement. The central irony of this chapter of rock history is that out of so much worthless music was carved nothing less than the first renaissance of rock & roll. It might legitimately be asked whether more than a handful of British Invasion bands would have made the States, and rock history, if they hadn't ridden in on the Beatles' coattails, but perhaps it really doesn't matter. For all of its innocence, its excitement and sense of discovery, this seems a far more appropriate question: Didn't we all get more kicks than we'd ever dreamed possible? And wasn't it a grand time to be alive?

DISCOGRAPHY

Animals: "The House of the Rising Sun" (MGM; ☆1, 1964). "I'm Crying" (MGM; ☆19, 1964). "Don't Let Me Be Misunderstood" (MGM; ☆15, 1965). "We Gotta Get out of This Place" (MGM; ☆13, 1965). **Bachelors:** "Diane" (London; ☆10, 1964). **Cilla Black:** "You're My World" (Capitol; ☆26, 1964). **Chad and Jeremy:** "Yesterday's Gone" (World Artists; ☆21, 1964). "A Summer Song" (World Artists; ☆7, 1964). **Dave Clark Five:** "Glad All Over" (Epic; ☆6, 1964). "Bits and Pieces" (Epic; ☆4, 1964). "Do You Love Me" (Epic; ☆11, 1964). "Can't You See That She's Mine" (Epic; ☆4, 1964). "Because" (Epic; ☆3, 1964). "Everybody Knows" (Epic; ☆15, 1964). "Any Way You Want It" (Epic; ☆14, 1964). "I Like It Like That" (Epic; ☆7, 1965). "Catch Us If You Can" (Epic; ☆4, 1965). "Over and Over" (Epic; ☆1, 1965). **Petula Clark:** "Downtown" (Warner Bros.; ☆1, 1964). "I Know a Place" (Warner Bros.; ☆3, 1965). "My Love" (Warner Bros.; ☆1, 1965). **Donovan:** "Catch the Wind" (Hickory; ☆23, 1965). **Georgie Fame:** "Yeh, Yeh" (Imperial; ☆21, 1965). **Wayne Fontana and the Mindbenders:** "Game of Love" (Fontana; ☆1, 1965). **Freddie and the Dreamers:** "I'm Telling You Now" (Tower; ☆1, 1965). "Do the Freddie" (Mercury; ☆18, 1965). **Gerry and the Pacemakers:** "Don't Let the Sun Catch You Crying" (Laurie; ☆4, 1964). "How Do You Do It" (Laurie; ☆9, 1964). "I Like It" (Laurie; ☆17, 1964). "I'll Be There" (Laurie; ☆14, 1964). "Ferry Cross the Mersey" (Laurie; ☆6, 1965). **Herman's Hermits:** "I'm into Something Good" (MGM; ☆13, 1964). "Can't You Hear My Heartbeat" (MGM; ☆2, 1965). "Silhouettes" (MGM; ☆5, 1965). "Mrs. Brown You've Got a Lovely Daughter" (MGM; ☆1, 1965). "Wonderful World" (MGM; ☆4, 1965). "I'm Henry VIII, I Am" (MGM; ☆1, 1965). "Just a Little Bit Better" (MGM; ☆7, 1965). "A Must to Avoid" (MGM; ☆8, 1965). **Hollies:** "Look Through Any Window" (Imperial; ☆32, 1965). **Honeycombs:** "Have I the Right" (Interphon; ☆5, 1964). **Tom Jones:** "It's Not Unusual" (Parrot; ☆10, 1965). **Jonathan King:** "Everyone's Gone to the Moon" (Parrot; ☆17, 1965). **Billy J. Kramer with the Dakotas:** "Little Children" b/w "Bad to Me" (Imperial; ☆7, 1964). **Manfred Mann:** "Do Wah Diddy Diddy" (Ascot; ☆1, 1964). "Sha La La" (Ascot; ☆12, 1964). **Moody Blues:** "Go Now!" (London; ☆10, 1965). **Nashville Teens:** "Tobacco Road" (London; ☆14, 1964). **Peter and Gordon:** "A World Without Love" (Capitol; ☆1, 1964). "Nobody I Know" (Capitol; ☆12, 1964). "I Don't Want to See You Again" (Capitol; ☆16, 1964). "I Go to Pieces" (Capitol; ☆9, 1965). "True Love Ways" (Capitol; ☆14, 1965). **Searchers:** "Needles and Pins" (Kapp; ☆13, 1964). "Sugar and Spice" (Liberty; ☆44, 1964). "Don't Throw Your Love Away" (Kapp; ☆16, 1964). "Love Potion Number Nine" (Kapp; ☆3, 1964). "Bumble Bee" (Kapp; ☆21, 1965). **Silkie:** "You've Got to Hide Your Love Away" (Fontana; ☆10, 1965). **Dusty Springfield:** "I Only Want to Be with You" (Philips; ☆12, 1964). "Wishin' and Hopin'" (Philips; ☆6, 1964). **Swinging Blue Jeans:** "Hippy Hippy Shake" (Imperial; ☆24, 1964). **Them:** "Here Comes the Night" (Parrot; ☆24, 1965). "Mystic Eyes" (Parrot; ☆33, 1965). **Walker Brothers:** "Make It Easy on Yourself" (Smash; ☆16, 1965). **Ian Whitcomb:** "You Turn Me On" (Tower; ☆8, 1965). **Yardbirds:** "For Your Love" (Epic; ☆6, 1965). "Heart Full of Soul" (Epic; ☆9, 1965). "I'm a Man" (Epic; ☆17, 1965). **Zombies:** "She's Not There" (Parrot; ☆2, 1964). "Tell Her No" (Parrot; ☆6, 1965).

The British Invasion: The History of British Rock, Volumes 1–9 (Rhino; 1991).

(Omitting hits by the Beatles, Rolling Stones, Kinks and Who. Compiled from Joel Whitburn's *Record Research,* based on *Billboard*'s Pop chart.)

THE BEATLES

BY GREIL MARCUS

he blues is a chair, not a design for a chair, or a better chair . . . it is the first chair. It is a chair for sitting on, not chairs for looking at or being appreciated. You sit on that music . . . We didn't sound like anybody else, that's all. I mean we didn't sound like the black musicians because we weren't black. And because we were brought up on a different kind of music and atmosphere, and so 'Please Please Me' and 'From Me to You' and all those were our version of the chair. We were building our own chairs.''

—John Lennon, 1970, *Lennon Remembers: The* ROLLING STONE *Interviews*

[ONE VERSION OF THE CHAIR]

1940: John Lennon and Richard Starkey (Ringo Starr) born, to working-class families in Liverpool, England (as are Paul McCartney and George Harrison, in 1942 and 1943, respectively).

1953–1954: Rock & roll, formerly ''race music,'' begins breakthrough into white America.

1955: Bill Haley's ''Shake, Rattle and Roll'' (a white American cover of a song by black bluesman Big Joe Turner) makes British charts.

1956: First English Elvis release. American rock hits and first British rock imitators proliferate in England. John favors Elvis (''Nothing really affected me until . . .''); Paul, Little Richard.

1957: June—John, playing with his rock-skiffle group, the Quarrymen, meets Paul at Liverpool church social. Their partnership begins. They perform with the Quarrymen, write songs, appear occasionally as a duo (''The Nurk Twins'').

1958: George, a fifteen-year-old guitarist influenced by Chet Atkins, Buddy Holly and Scotty

In 1964 they sparked a pop explosion: the second, and thus far the last, that rock & roll has produced.

Paul and John comin' at ya.

Moore, joins the Quarrymen; group name changed to Johnny and the Moondogs (later Silver Beatles, after Buddy Holly's Crickets, then to Beatles).

1959: Stu Sutcliffe, Liverpool art student, joins Silver Beatles on bass.

1960: Liverpool Merseybeat scene forming on Beatles' model (emphasis on rhythm and big beat). Pete Best, a drummer, is added, as Beatles leave for first of many all-night gigs in Hamburg, Germany.

1961: Beatles commute between Hamburg and Liverpool's Cavern; record "My Bonnie" in Germany. Sutcliffe leaves group to paint. November—Brian Epstein, Liverpool record-store owner, seeks out Beatles at Cavern, his interest cued by request for "My Bonnie." December—Epstein becomes Beatles' manager.

1962: Epstein writes to journalist that his group "would one day be bigger than Elvis," becoming

only manager in rock & roll history to use this line and be right. January—Beatles fail audition with Decca, win poll as top group in Liverpool. April—Sutcliffe dies of brain tumor. August—Beatles signed to EMI, but Capitol refuses American option. In move still shrouded in mystery, John, Paul, George and Epstein replace Best with Ringo Starr, drummer for Liverpool "beat" (after Merseybeat) group Rory Storm and the Hurricanes (Storm later dies in apparent double suicide with mother). Final Beatles lineup: John, rhythm guitar (harmonica, organ, piano); Paul, bass (piano, organ, guitar); George, lead guitar; Ringo, drums. October—"Love

The Beatles in Hamburg. The bored-looking fellow in the background is Pete Best, the Beatles drummer replaced by Ringo in 1962.

Me Do,'' written by John and Paul in 1957, released in U.K., peaks at Number Twenty-one.

1963: January—"Please Please Me" released, reaches Number One. Beatlemania hits Britain. Mass hysteria reigns among youth. February—"Please Please Me" released in U.S. on Vee-Jay label, no chart action. May—*Please Please Me,* Beatles' first album, released in U.K., holds Number One spot for thirty consecutive weeks, replaced by *With the Beatles,* which remains at Number One for an additional twenty-two. "From Me to You," released in U.S., reaches Number 116 in August, drops off chart two weeks later, falling short of Del Shannon's

John with his Aunt Mimi.

version of same tune, released in June, which peaks at Number Seventy-seven. July—first Beatles album released in U.S. on Vee-Jay as *Introducing the Beatles.* No chart action.

1964: January—"I Want to Hold Your Hand" released in U.S. on Capitol with $50,000 in publicity from label; reaches Number One February 1st (January 17th in *Cashbox*). February—Beatles appear on *The Ed Sullivan Show.* April—Beatles assume first, second, third, fourth and fifth positions on *Billboard* Hot 100; *Meet the Beatles,* Capitol's version of *With the Beatles,* becomes best-selling LP in history up to that time. Beatlemania hits U.S. Mass hysteria reigns among youth. DJs claim "fifth Beatle" status. British Invasion begins. August—Beatle film, *A Hard Day's Night,* opens to extraordinary critical and popular acclaim; first major American tour begins. December—Ringo's tonsillectomy inspires worldwide vigil.

1965: Beatles gain fourth, fifth and sixth Number One LPs, followed by *Rubber Soul,* hailed as artistic breakthrough, in December. American response to British rock renaissance includes Byrds, Lovin' Spoonful, Dylan's move to rock, beginnings of San Francisco sound, and the Monkees. August—second film, *Help!,* released.

1966: Dylan's *Blonde on Blonde,* Rolling Stones' *Aftermath* and Beatles' *Revolver* (hailed as "avant-garde," showing influence of Motown, Mamas and Papas, and Timothy Leary) all released, as Big Three of rock attempt to top each other. August—Beatles make what will be last concert appearance, in San Francisco; return to England to make album to top all toppers. John meets Yoko Ono, avant-garde conceptual artist. Age of media psychedelia—dope, love, peace, Eastern religion—begins.

1967: February—Beatles release "Strawberry Fields Forever," hailed as "psychedelic" because of backward music at fade. June—on eve of San Francisco's projected mass hippie Summer of Love influx, Beatles release *Sgt. Pepper's Lonely Hearts Club Band,* superpsychedelic LP that tops all toppers. Paul announces Beatle LSD use. August—Brian Epstein dies of pill overdose. Beatles, on retreat with Maharishi Mahesh Yogi, Eastern religionist, announce they will manage themselves. Gleam appears in religionist's third eye. December—Beatle TV film, *Magical Mystery Tour,* bombs in Britain; first real Beatle failure.

1968: February—Beatles leave for India to receive

instruction from Maharishi. Beatles complain of bad food; Ringo leaves early. May—John and Paul hold press conference in U.S. to sever relationship with Maharishi and launch Apple Corps., Ltd., new com-

George in Hamburg, 1960.

pany meant to handle Beatles affairs and aid deserving artists. Move subsequently proves disastrous. November—Beatles release *The Beatles* (the White Album) with mostly solo vocals.

1969: John and Yoko marry. Yoko seeks ''fifth Beatle'' status. Beatles decide to ''get back'' by recording ''roots'' album in order to recapture fading sense of combined self; *Abbey Road* appears instead. John forms Plastic Ono Band with Yoko on vocals; releases include ''Give Peace a Chance.''

1970: Paul releases solo LP, with self as sole if not solo musician; press kit includes self-interview critical of other Beatles. April—Paul announces departure from Beatles. May—Beatles, effectively defunct, release ''get back'' LP as *Let It Be,* with accompanying *Let It Be* film. December—Paul sues to dissolve Beatles.

1970–1975: Beatles pursue individual careers with good financial but erratic artistic success. Paul forms new band, Wings, with wife Linda Eastman. John and Yoko release albums focusing on primal therapy, politics, self and old rock & roll. Ringo makes movies and hit singles. George organizes Concert for Bangladesh (1971) and seeks better way.

1976: Wings begin first American tour. EMI releases twenty-three Beatles singles in U.K.; all make charts. Rumors of one-shot Beatles reunion spread, spurred by alleged $30- to $50-million guarantee. Beatles equivocate. Offers raised to $250 million.

1979: As Seventies draw to a close, Beatles refuse U.N. Secretary General Kurt Waldheim's plea that they reunite to play charity concert for Vietnamese boat people. However, all four meet to plan suit against film of a theatrical production called *Beatlemania.*

George with his first guitar.

[ANOTHER VERSION OF THE CHAIR]

''We were driving through Colorado [and] we had the radio on and eight of the Top Ten songs were Beatles songs. In Colorado! 'I Want to Hold Your Hand,' all those early ones.

''They were doing things nobody was doing. Their chords were outrageous, just outrageous, and their harmonies made it all valid. . . . But I kept it to myself that I really dug them. Everybody else thought they were for the teenyboppers, that they were gonna pass right away. But it was obvious to me that they had staying power. I knew they were pointing the direction where music had to go . . . in my head, the Beatles were *it.* In Colorado, I started thinking but it was so far-out I couldn't deal with it—eight in the Top Ten.

''It seemed to me a definite line was being drawn. This was something that never happened before.''

—Bob Dylan, 1971

On February 9th, 1964, I was in college in California, a rock & roll fan with creeping amnesia. I remembered Chuck Berry but not the guitar solo in ''Johnny B. Goode.'' The excitement, the sense of being caught up in something much bigger than one's own private taste, had disappeared from rock years before. There was still good stuff on the radio—there had been ''Heat Wave'' by a group called Martha and the Vandellas the summer before, ''Be True to Your School'' by the Beach Boys a few months after that, and even ''On Broadway'' by the Drifters—but in 1963 all of it seemed drowned out by Jimmy Gilmer's ''Sugar Shack,'' the Number One song of the year and perhaps the worst excuse for itself rock & roll had yet

The Fab Four, as their publicist wanted us to know them.

produced. Rock & roll—the radio—felt dull and stupid, a dead end.

There had been an item in the paper that day about a British rock & roll group that was to appear on *The Ed Sullivan Show* that night: "The Beatles" (a photo too—were those wigs, or what?). I was curious—I didn't know they had rock & roll in England—so I went down to a commons room where there was a TV set, expecting an argument from whoever was there about which channel to watch.

Four hundred people sat transfixed as the Beatles sang "I Want to Hold Your Hand," and when the song was over the crowd exploded. People looked at the faces (and the hair) of John, Paul, George and Ringo and said Yes (and who could have predicted that a few extra inches of hair would suddenly seem so right, so necessary? Brian Epstein?); they heard the Beatles' sound and said Yes to that too. What was going on? And where had all those people come from?

Back at the radio I caught "I Saw Her Standing There" and was instantly convinced it was the most exciting rock & roll I'd ever heard (with Paul's one-two-three-*fuck!* opening—how in the world did they

expect to get away with that?). Someone from down the hall appeared with a copy of the actual record—you could just go out and *buy* this stuff?—and announced with great fake solemnity that it was the first 45 he'd purchased since "All Shook Up." Someone else—who played a twelve-string guitar and as far as I knew listened to nothing but Odetta—began to muse that "even as a generation had been brought together by the Five Satins' 'In the Still of the Nite,' it could be that it would be brought together again—by the Beatles." He really talked like that; what was more amazing, he talked like that when a few hours before he had never heard of the Beatles.

The next weeks went by in a blur. People began to grow their hair (one acquaintance argued with great vehemence that it was physically impossible for male hair—at least, *normal* male hair—to grow to Beatle length); some affected British (or, when they could pull it off, Liverpool) accents. A friend got his hands on a British Beatles album unavailable in the United States and made a considerable amount of money charging people for the chance to hear John Lennon sing "Money (That's What I Want)" at two bucks a shot. Excitement wasn't in the air; it *was* the air.

A few days after that first performance on the Sullivan show I spent the evening with some friends in a cafe in my hometown. It was, or anyway had been, a folk club. This night one heard only *Meet the Beatles*. The music, snaking through the dark, suddenly spooky room, was instantly recognizable and like nothing we had ever heard. It was joyous, threatening, absurd, arrogant, determined, innocent and tough, and it drew the line of which Dylan was to speak. "This was something that never happened before."

It was, as Lester Bangs says in his survey of the

Signed, sealed, delivered.

British Invasion, not simply a matter of music, but of event. Dylan had heard the Beatles in New York before his Colorado revelation; I had first heard them on the radio in early 1963, when "Please Please Me" was released in the United States, liked the record, disliked the followup, then forgot the group altogether. It was only in the context of the Beatles' event that their music was perceived for what it was.

The event was a pop explosion; the second, and thus far the last, that rock & roll has produced.

A pop explosion is an irresistible cultural upheaval that cuts across lines of class and race (in terms of sources, if not allegiance), and, most crucially, divides society itself by age. The surface of daily life (walk, talk, dress, symbolism, heroes, family affairs) is affected with such force that deep and substantive changes in the way large numbers of people think and act take place. Pop explosions must link up with, and accelerate, broad shifts in sexual behavior, economic aspirations and political beliefs; a pervasive sense of chaos, such as that which hit England in 1963 with the Profumo scandal, and the United States in the mid-Sixties with the civil rights movement, the Kennedy assassination, and later the Vietnam War, doesn't hurt.

Now, it has been argued, by British critic George Melly, that a pop explosion merely "turns revolt into a style" (poet Thom Gunn's line on Elvis, originally), but in fact pop explosions can provide the enthusiasm, the optimism and the group identity that make mass political participation possible. A pop explosion is more than a change in style even if it is far less than a revolution, though it can look like either one—depending on who is looking, and when. (Not that "changing the world" in the political sense of the term is never a "goal" of a pop explosion, if such an event can be said to have a goal beyond good times; still, a pop explosion changes the world by affecting the moment, which means that the world retains the capacity to change back, momentarily.)

Enormous energy—the energy of frustration, desire, repression, adolescence, sex, ambition—finds an object in a pop explosion, and that energy is focused on, organized by and released by a single, holistic cultural entity. This entity must itself be capable of easy, instantaneous and varied imitation and extension, in a thousand ways at once; it must embody, suggest, affirm and legitimize new possi-

Arriving in America.

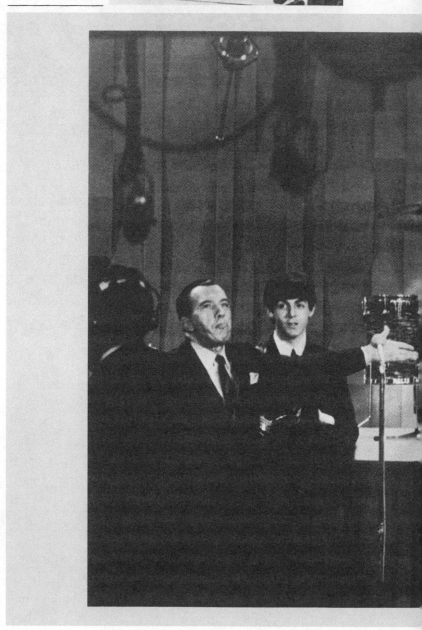

bilities on all fronts even as it outstrips them. This is a fancy way of saying that the capacity for fad must be utterly profound.

And, at its heart, a pop explosion attaches the individual to a group—the fan to an audience, the solitary to a generation—in essence, *forms* a group and creates new loyalties—while at the same time it increases one's ability to respond to a particular pop artifact, or a thousand of them, with an intensity that verges on lunacy. Ringo's shout of "All right, George!" just before the guitar break in "Boys" becomes a matter of indefinable and indefensible significance; styles on Carnaby Street outdo the pace of the pop charts and change literally by the hour. Yet within it all is some principle of shape, of continuity, of value.

This principle was the Beatles. As was so often pointed out in the mid-Sixties, the sum of the Bea-

Playing a concert. This was Beatlemania.

tles was greater than the parts, but the parts were so distinctive and attractive that the group itself could be all things to all people, more or less. You did not have to love them all to love the group, but you could not love one without loving the group, and this was why the Beatles became bigger than Elvis; this was what had never happened before. And so it began. The past was felt to dissolve, the future was conceivable only as an expansion of the present, and the present was defined absolutely by its expansive novelty. Towering above Bob Dylan, the Rolling Stones, a score of British groups, American groups, Mary Quant, the Who, whatever and whoever sprung up

Like Elvis Presley, the Beatles were stars born of television. For three Sundays in early 1964 a nation watched in unison as the group sang on *The Ed Sullivan Show*.

day by day, the Beatles seemed not only to symbolize but to contain it all—to make history by anticipating it.

The first pop explosion, beginning in 1955 and 1956, began to yield to normalcy by about 1957. The Beatles' event, beyond all expectations save perhaps their own, intensified not only in momentum but in magnetism, reaching more and more people with greater and greater mythic and emotional power, for at least four years. The Beatles affected not only the feel but the quality of life: They deepened it, sharpened it, brightened it, not merely as a factor in the cultural scheme, but as a presence.

Their event reached its height, and in many ways its effective end, with the release of *Sgt. Pepper* on June 2nd, 1967. For months rumors had swept the pop world that the Beatles were engaged in a historic project that would sum up, and transcend, all that had been accomplished in the previous four years. In February a single, "Penny Lane" b/w "Strawberry Fields Forever," was released (if this extraordinary music was merely a taste of what the Beatles were up to, what would the album be like?) and then, in the spring, tapes leaked out. A strange, maddening song called "A Day in the Life Of" was played on the radio and quickly withdrawn. Tension and speculation grew. It was said (correctly) that the new LP had taken 700 hours to record, as opposed to twelve hours for the Beatles' first; that it included astonishingly experimental techniques, huge orchestras, hundred-voice choirs. Stories began to appear not only in the pop press but in the daily papers. The record, unheard, was everywhere.

Then the announcement was made. The record would be released for airplay on Sunday midnight, one week before appearing in the stores; any station putting the disc on the air even one minute before the assigned time would find all forthcoming prerelease airing privileges forever withheld. The fact that many stations habitually went off the air at Sunday midnight in order to service their transmitters, was of no consequence—or perhaps, from the perspective of Brian Epstein and the Beatles, it was a challenge. At any rate, the stations stayed on. They played the record all night and all the next day, vying to see which station could play it the longest, putting in calls to John and Paul in London that never went through, tracking every last second of the endless final chord of "A Day in the Life" (no "Of," as it turned out), generating an unprecedented

A candid moment on the set of the Sullivan show.

sense of public euphoria, excitement, satisfaction and joy.

Almost immediately, *Sgt. Pepper* was certified as proof that the Beatles' music—or at least this album—was Art. But what mattered was the conscious creation of event—the way in which the summing-up-the-spirit-of-the-times style of the music (which for the most part has not survived its time) was perfectly congruent with the organizing-the-spirit-of-the-times manner in which the album was released and received. Which is to say that *Sgt. Pepper*, as the most brilliantly orchestrated manipulation of a cultural audience in pop history, was nothing less than a small pop explosion in and of itself. The music was not great art; the event, in its intensification of the ability to respond, was.

"The closest Western Civilization has come to unity since the Congress of Vienna in 1815 was the week the *Sgt. Pepper* album was released," Langdon Winner wrote in 1968. "In every city in Europe and America the stereo systems and the radio played, 'What would you think if I sang out of tune . . . Woke up, got out of bed . . . looked much older, and the bag across her shoulder . . . in the sky with diamonds, Lucy in the . . .' and everyone listened. At the time I happened to be driving across country on Interstate 80. In each city where I stopped for gas or food—Laramie, Ogallala, Moline, South Bend—the melodies wafted in from some far-off transistor radio or portable hi-fi. It was the most amazing thing I've ever heard. For a brief while the irreparably fragmented consciousness of the West was unified, at least in the minds of the young."

And so it seemed as if the world really did turn around the Beatles, even if the truth was that this music, as opposed to this event, represented that point at which the Beatles began to be formed more by the times than the other way around. In the next few months Brian Epstein would die, and the Beatles, who had unified the young, would themselves begin to fragment—anticipating, as usual, the fragmentation that in years to come would separate the audience they had created. Still, if *Sgt. Pepper* was an ending, it was an ending that has never been matched. It was perhaps in the nature of the game that it would be all downhill from there.

[A THIRD VERSION OF THE CHAIR]

Or, what about the music. Since the Beatles disbanded, a virtual consensus among rock critics has emerged to argue that the music of the Beatles, enjoyable as it may have been, stands now as distinctly inferior to that of the Stones, Dylan or even the Byrds or the Beach Boys; the Beatles are conventionally portrayed as imitative, lightweights, yea-sayers, softies, ordinary musicians, vaguely unhip, unimaginative lyrically and, above all, "clever"—that is, merely clever. You know—the Beatles just wanted to hold your hand, while the Stones wanted to pillage your town. Etc.

There is some truth to this argument. While Andrew Loog Oldham, the Stones' manager, urged his boys to flaunt their rebellion, Epstein had the four mop-tops clean up their act; he got rid of their grease-and-leather Cavern image and put the Fab Four into matching stage suits. Rebellion was fine as long as tactics were restricted to wit; pissing on a garage (or, as some Stones legends have it, a garage attendant) was definitely out. The Stones wrote from an insistently sexual and aggressive blues tradition; the Beatles worked mostly in the more polite and circumscribed milieu of pop, as defined not only by rock tunesmiths Carole King and Gerry Goffin but by the earlier professional romanticists of Tin Pan Alley. The Beatles' optimism prevailed even when they tried to sound desperate ("Help!"), which sometimes made them sound sappy; the Stones' sullenness prevailed even when they affected optimism ("We Love You"), which usually made them sound all the more attractive.

Which only proves, I think, that comparisons of the Beatles and the Stones (or Dylan or Elvis or any other true titan of rock) are pointless. I cannot make an argument that the Beatles were better at being the Stones than the Stones were (though I can point out that it was the Beatles who opened up the turf the Stones took as their own; there was no possibility of a Left until the Beatles created the Center). The argument that seems to emerge from a close listening to the Beatles' music, on the other hand, is this one: By 1962 the Beatles' mastery of rock & roll was such that it was inevitable they would change the form simply by addressing themselves to it. Unlike the Stones or Dylan, the Beatles came up *through* rock; as they went on, extending (if not deepening) their mastery, they defined rock, to the degree that it made sense to speak of "Yesterday," a ballad accompanied only by acoustic guitar and strings, as "rock & roll," simply because the disc was credited to the Beatles. And unlike Dylan, and possibly the Stones, at least until 1966, the Beatles had no fallback position. They were rock & roll or they were nothing. As such, they were, at their best, the best.

Their pop explosion, after all, was not kicked off simply by assassination and PR. You could hear it, and what you heard was a rock & roll group that combined elements of the music that you were used to hearing only in pieces. That is, the form of the Beatles contained the forms of rock & roll itself. The Beatles combined the harmonic range and implicit equality of the Fifties vocal group (the Dell-Vikings, say) with the flash of a rockabilly band (the Crickets or Gene Vincent's Blue Caps) with the aggressive and unique personalities of the classic rock stars (Elvis, Little Richard) with the homey this-could-be-you manner of later rock stars (Everly Brothers, Holly, Eddie Cochran) with the endlessly inventive songwriting touch of the Brill Building, and delivered it all with the grace of the Miracles, the physicality of "Louie Louie," and the absurd enthusiasm of Gary "U.S." Bonds. Three of the Beatles wrote, all sang lead, and they played their own music; in sum, they communicated (and generically insisted upon) absolute involvement (it was only after the Beatles that "rock groups" had to make their own records and write their own songs). Rock, which in the course of the Fifties had changed from a personal inspiration and affirmation to a process that allowed the most marginal of commitments, became, in the shape of the Beatles, a way of life.

Consider the Beatles' history, John and Paul were playing something approximating rock & roll before they had ever heard of Elvis Presley (the same probably cannot be said of Buddy Holly); they seem to have written their first hit, "Love Me Do," before they heard "That'll Be the Day" (even if "Love Me Do" would not be released until almost four years after Holly's death). In other words, when the Beatles signed with EMI they were not merely in touch with their roots; in a significant and probably unique sense, they were their roots. They were not only a product of the pre-Beatles era of rock, they were a version of it. Accompanying the shock of novelty so many experienced on first exposure to the Beatles in 1963 or '64 was a shock of recognition, which bespoke the Beatles' connection to the whole history of rock & roll up to that time. The Beatles had absorbed that history because—year by year, playing and listening and writing, in Liverpool and on the bottoms of British tours and in Hamburg—they had, albeit invisibly, made it.

No one else could touch *this* sort of mastery, and the result was that elusive rock treasure, *a new sound*—and a new sound that could not be exhausted in the course of one brief flurry on the charts. That sound was best captured in the Beatles' 1963 recordings of "Please Please Me," "I Saw Her Standing

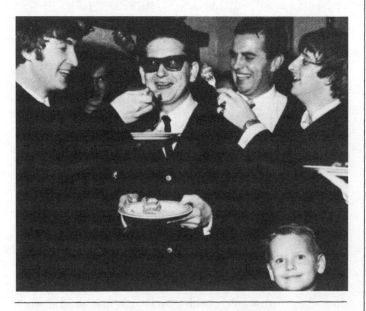

John and Ringo feeding Roy Orbison, with whom they toured Britain in 1963.

There," their version of the Shirelles' "Boys," the incandescent "There's a Place," "It Won't Be Long," "All I've Got to Do," "She Loves You," "I Want to Hold Your Hand," "All My Loving," George's brooding "Don't Bother Me," "Little Child," and their cover of Barrett Strong's "Money," plus such 1964 cuts as "A Hard Day's Night," "Anytime at All," "I Should Have Known Better," "Things We Said Today," "I'll Be Back," "No Reply," "Eight Days a Week," "Every Little Thing" and "What You're Doing."

The beat, first of all, was not big, it was enormous. The entire performance orchestrated it, it was built around it (listen to "There's a Place"). At the same time, there was a lightness to almost every tune, a floating quality, a kind of lyrical attack that shaped but did not lessen the rhythmic power of the numbers. This quality, which can be heard in its most spectacular form in the segues in and out of the middle eights, was perhaps the most important thing John and Paul learned from Goffin-King (and from Ellie Greenwich, Jeff Barry and Phil Spector); it was written right into the compositions, and put across through head arrangements and in the use of

vocal on "What You're Doing"). But more than anything else it was the singing that made these records what they were. John's and Paul's vocals—and the four Beatles' unpredictable screams, yeah-yeah-yeahs and head-to-head oooos—communicated urgency first and foremost. Regardless of lyrics, the singers made demands, reached, got, went after more, blew away all that stood before them. They were exhilarated, exuberant, joyous; but all that joy was rooted in determination, as if those nihilistic nights in Hamburg had not just added an edge to the Beatles' music but had lighted a fire in their hearts. In 1964 the freshness of the Beatles' vocal assault was the sound of pure novelty; today, one hears a lovely, naked emotion in those early vocals, a refusal to kid around, to cut the corners of feeling and a will to say it all, that was not to be heard in rock & roll from any other white performer until Bob Dylan released "Like a Rolling Stone" in the summer of 1965. This spirit surfaced in more obvious form later—consciously and with great craftsmanship, in "Strawberry Fields Forever," "I Am the Walrus," "Yer Blues" and "I'm So Tired"—but it was there from the beginning. In a sense it was the beginning.

Picking up their first American gold records in 1964.

Recording their first album in 1963.

rock group dynamics so fluid and intelligent that for years they made nearly everything else on the radio sound faintly stupid (listen to "Every Little Thing," "Anytime at All," "What You're Doing").

Though none of the Beatles made anything of formal instrumental virtuosity—Eric Clapton would bring on *that* era—the playing on the records could take your breath away (Ringo's drumming on "There's a Place," or the piano rumble, supported by bass, drums and rhythm guitar, that cues the

Of these first recordings, it may be that "Money," an unforgiving triumph of the intensity of which rock & roll at its strongest is capable, was the greatest. (All votes for "There's a Place" will be counted, however; in some ways the best of the Beatles throughout their career was either a synthesis or a refinement of these two recordings.) Linked to the rock past, "Money" made Barrett Strong's 1960 original sound quaint; Strong's version of the song (not to mention the Stones') is to the Beatles' as Ricky Nelson's "Stood Up" is to "Hound Dog."

Surging forward after a quick, ominous piano opening, the lead vocal was all John. He sang with a greater fury than possessed him before or since (the wails of *John Lennon/Plastic Ono Band,* the 1970 "primal scream" LP, are contrived by comparison), and with a clarity and insistence he may not have matched until that same post-Beatles album, with the last few lines of "God" perhaps the most sublime singing in all of rock & roll. It was an insistence aimed not inward but at external reality itself ("I came out of the fuckin' sticks to take over the world," John was to say later); just as only the deaf, or the dead, could resist the utopianism of Paul's vocal on "All My Loving," only a fool could listen to John sing "The best things in life are free / But you can keep 'em for the birds and bees," or hear him explode in the final choruses with "Now give me money—a lotta money—*I want to be free*!," and not believe that every word was the truth. Add to this the screams, the blistering double ooos, and the chants of "That's . . . what I want" (the menace of the claim is in the pause), all from Paul and George in a manner of complete dementia; the unbelievable metallic harshness of the band; and a total performance that for all the control inherent in a classically simple rock structure sounds ready to blow up in a listener's face at any moment, and the result is a record that keeps virtually every promise rock & roll ever made (the rest of them were kept by

I am at 3 Savile Row, most days

John Lennon by Grant Wood.

"There's a Place," "Eight Days a Week," and "What You're Doing").

Mixing the lyricism of "There's a Place" and the force of "Money," the Beatles' mastery of rock in their first two years of recording was absolute. Without really testing the limits of the form as they had worked it out in the early Sixties, they continued to prove that mastery through 1965, with "Ticket to Ride," the brilliant "Help!," its little-known flip side, "I'm Down" (an astonishing piece of hard rock with a crazed Little Richard vocal from Paul) and "Day Tripper." Still, given Dylan, the Stones and the Byrds, there was no question that other rockers were testing the Beatles' limits, even if they were not. And so at the end of 1965 the Beatles turned around and dumped *Rubber Soul* on the market.

Though it can be argued that the Beatles' first four LPs, in their British configurations (*Please Please Me, With the Beatles, A Hard Day's Night* and *Beatles for Sale*) were as good as *Rubber Soul,* it may not be worth the trouble. *Rubber Soul* was an album *made* as an album; with the exception of "Michelle" (which, to be fair, paid the bills for years to come), every cut

Paul, with Ringo in the background.

was an inspiration, something new and remarkable in and of itself.

In terms of lyrics, the Beatles were still writing about love, but this was a new kind of love: contingent, scary and vital in a way that countenanced ambiguities and doubts earlier songs had skimmed right over. "In My Life" was as moving and precise a song about friendship as rock has produced; "Girl," though deceptively straightforward, was a good deal more sophisticated than Dylan's "Just Like a Woman."

George, John, Ringo and Paul pretending to be the Band at Woodstock.

If the emotional touch was harder, the musical touch was lighter. This music was seduction, not assault; the force was all beneath the surface, in the dynamics of "I'm Looking Through You" (which were so striking that many fans delighted in listening to the stereo version of the tune with the vocal track turned off) and in the other numbers just mentioned. It was the Beatles' most attractive album, perhaps their glossiest, and at the same time their most deeply satisfying. To this listener, it was unquestionably their best.

From this point on the story is not so clear. What was clear, though, what was clear in retrospect even on *Rubber Soul,* was that John and Paul were no longer the songwriting team they had once been. Consistently, John's songs described struggle, while Paul's denied it; Paul wrote and sang the A sides,

John the Bs. Mapping out the directions that have governed their careers since the Beatles disbanded, John was already cultivating his rebellion and his anger; Paul was making his Decision for Pop; George was making his Decision for Krishna; and Ringo was having his house painted. All of the Beatles were attaching themselves to the fads and passions of the time, to drugs, transcendence, coats of many colors, the paraphernalia of psychedelia. And as the Beatles became one with the times, merging with them rather than standing above them, they became, musically and in every other way, harder to see truly. The wholeness of the group, the music and the very idea of the Beatles began to break up, even as "The Beatles," as cultural icons, media personalities and phenomena, became more exciting than ever. Thus at the time it was obvious that *Revolver,* released in 1966, was better than *Rubber Soul,* just as it was obvious *Sgt. Pepper* was better than both put together. The times carried the imperative of such a choice—though it was not really a choice at all, but rather a sort of faceless necessity. The only road, after all, was onward.

Such a choice does not seem so obvious now, and of course the necessity has faded. *Revolver* retains the flash its title promised but little of the soul its predecessor delivered. Compared to either, *Sgt. Pepper* appears playful but contrived, less a summing-up of its era than a concession to it.

George Harrison in *Let It Be.*

221

In the final two and a half years of Beatles group-dom, the four remained charming with ''All You Need Is Love''; took a fall with *Magical Mystery Tour*, offered a stunning preview of post-Beatles music with the White Album; wrapped up their career with the erratic, overly professional *Abbey Road;* and stumbled off the stage they had raised with a botched release of the antiprofessional *Let It Be.*

Out of that sad ending several recordings stand with the best the Beatles ever made. Save Paul's shimmering ''Penny Lane,'' and his bruising ''Helter Skelter,'' all were John's work, and in truth they may have little of the Beatles—the Beatles as something more than four people who sang and played—in them. Still, to this writer, ''Strawberry Fields Forever,'' ''I Am the Walrus,'' ''Yer Blues,'' ''I'm So Tired'' and ''Don't Let Me Down'' are each richer than *Sgt. Pepper*'s best cut, ''A Day in the Life.'' In every case John seemed to be getting closer to the essentials of his soul, which might be identified as a refusal to settle for anything short of perfection combined with a clear understanding that perfection does not exist—a dilemma that, given the history of the Beatles era and the years since, is something more than one man's hangup.

John and Yoko in bed, sleeping in for peace. Those were the days.

☆4, 1968). ''Hey Jude'' b/w ''Revolution'' (Apple; ☆1, 1968). ''Get Back'' b/w ''Don't Let Me Down'' (with Billy Preston) (Apple; ☆1, 1969). ''The Ballad of John and Yoko'' (Apple; ☆8, 1969). ''Come Together'' b/w ''Something'' (Apple; ☆1, 1969). ''Let It Be'' (Apple; ☆1, 1970). ''The Long and Winding Road'' b/w ''For You Blue'' (Apple; ☆1, 1970). ''Got to Get You into My Life'' (Capitol; ☆7, 1976). ''Ob-La-Di, Ob-La-Da'' (Capitol; ☆49, 1976). ''Sgt. Pepper's Lonely Hearts Club Band'' b/w ''With a Little Help from My Friends'' (Capitol; ☆72, 1978). ''The Beatles' Movie Medley'' (Capitol; ☆12, 1982). ''Twist and Shout'' (Capitol; ☆23, 1986).

DISCOGRAPHY

AMERICAN SINGLES

''I Want to Hold Your Hand'' b/w ''I Saw Her Standing There'' (Capitol; ☆1, 1964). ''She Loves You'' (Swan; ☆1, 1964). ''Please Please Me'' b/w ''From Me to You'' (Vee-Jay; ☆3, 1964). ''My Bonnie'' (with Tony Sheridan) (MGM; ☆26, 1964). ''Twist and Shout'' (Tollie; ☆2, 1964). ''Can't Buy Me Love'' b/w ''You Can't Do That'' (Capitol; ☆1, 1964). ''Do You Want to Know a Secret'' b/w ''Thank You Girl'' (Vee-Jay; ☆2, 1964). ''Love Me Do'' b/w ''P.S. I Love You'' (Tollie; ☆1, 1964). ''A Hard Day's Night'' b/w ''I Should Have Known Better'' (Capitol; ☆1, 1964). ''Ain't She Sweet'' (Atco; ☆19, 1964). ''And I Love Her'' b/w ''If I Fell'' (Capitol; ☆12, 1964). ''I'll Cry Instead'' (Capitol; ☆25, 1964). ''Matchbox'' b/w ''Slow Down'' (Capitol; ☆17, 1964). ''I Feel Fine'' b/w ''She's a Woman'' (Capitol; ☆1, 1964). ''Eight Days a Week'' b/w ''I Don't Want to Spoil the Party'' (Capitol; ☆1, 1965). ''Ticket to Ride'' b/w ''Yes It Is'' (Capitol; ☆1, 1965). ''Help!'' (Capitol; ☆1, 1965). ''Yesterday'' b/w ''Act Naturally'' (Capitol; ☆1, 1965). ''We Can Work It Out'' b/w ''Day Tripper'' (Capitol; ☆1, 1965). ''Nowhere Man'' (Capitol; ☆3, 1966). ''Paperback Writer'' b/w ''Rain'' (Capitol; ☆1, 1966). ''Yellow Submarine'' b/w ''Eleanor Rigby'' (Capitol; ☆2, 1966). ''Penny Lane'' b/w ''Strawberry Fields Forever'' (Capitol; ☆1, 1967). ''All You Need Is Love'' b/w ''Baby You're a Rich Man'' (Capitol; ☆1, 1967). ''Hello Goodbye'' b/w ''I Am the Walrus'' (Capitol; ☆1, 1967). ''Lady Madonna'' (Capitol;

AMERICAN ALBUMS

Meet the Beatles! (Capitol; ☆1, 1964). *Introducing . . . the Beatles* (Vee-Jay; ☆2, 1964). With Tony Sheridan and their Guests *The Beatles* (MGM; ☆68, 1964). *The Beatles' Second Album* (Capitol; ☆1, 1964). *A Hard Day's Night* (United Artists; ☆4, 1964). *Something New* (Capitol; ☆2, 1964). *The Beatles' Story* (Capitol; ☆7, 1964). *Beatles '65* (Capitol; ☆1, 1965). *The Early Beatles* (Capitol; ☆43, 1965). *Beatles VI* (Capitol; ☆1, 1965). *Help!* (Capitol; ☆1, 1965). *Rubber Soul* (Capitol; ☆1, 1965). *''Yesterday'' . . . and Today* (Capitol; ☆1, 1966). *Revolver* (Capitol; ☆1, 1966). *Sgt. Pepper's Lonely Hearts Club Band* (Capitol; ☆1, 1967). *Magical Mystery Tour* (Capitol; ☆1, 1967). *The Beatles* (Apple; ☆1, 1968). *Yellow Submarine* (Apple; ☆2, 1969). *Abbey Road* (Apple; ☆1, 1969). *Hey Jude* (Apple; ☆2, 1970). *In the Beginning* (featuring Tony Sheridan) (Polydor; ☆117, 1970). *Let It Be* (Apple; ☆1, 1970). *The Beatles/1962–1966* (Apple; ☆3, 1973). *The Beatles/1967–1970* (Apple; ☆1, 1973). *Rock 'N' Roll Music* (Capitol; ☆2, 1976). *The Beatles at the Hollywood Bowl* (Capitol; ☆2, 1977). *Live! At the Star Club in Hamburg, Germany; 1962* (Lingasong Atlantic; ☆111, 1977). *Love Songs* (Capitol; ☆24, 1977). *Rarities* (Capitol; ☆21, 1980). *Reel Music* (Capitol; ☆19, 1982). *20 Greatest Hits* (Capitol; ☆50, 1982). *Past Masters, Vol. One* (Capitol; ☆149, 1988). *Past Masters, Vol. Two* (Capitol; ☆121, 1988).

(In the late 1980s, Capitol released all the Beatles albums on CD with the original British title, track listing and configuration. As of 1992 the American versions can be found on cassette and whatever vinyl still exists.)

(Chart positions compiled from Joel Whitburn's Record Research, based on Billboard's Pop and LPs charts.)

SOLO BEATLES

BY ALLAN KOZINN

Outside the Dakota apartments in New York City, just before 11 p.m. on December 8th, 1980, a deranged twenty-five-year-old emptied a .38 into John Lennon's back. The murderer, Mark David Chapman, had flown from Hawaii to New York expressly to kill Lennon. Some—most notably the British attorney Fenton Bresler, in his 1989 book *Who Killed John Lennon?*—have theorized that Chapman was set to the task by the CIA, intent on silencing Lennon lest his political influence on American youth be revived just as Ronald Reagan was preparing to usher in a right-wing new age.

That such a theory could be seriously advanced says something about the paranoia of the Eighties. But more crucially, it shows the power of Lennon's reputation as a spur to his listeners' political consciences. In cold, practical terms, Lennon's death put an end to the hope, expressed regularly between 1970 and 1980, that the Beatles might reunite, and made clear that the individual Beatles were, for better or worse, all that was left. On their own, the former Beatles have had erratic careers. But by 1991 the three surviving members were enjoying their most successful efforts since the early post-breakup days, and Lennon had been virtually canonized.

To understand the journeys the individual Beatles have traveled, it is helpful to look back at the group's breakup, a splintering that began as early as 1966. Just before its summer tour, the group had completed *Revolver*, initiating a period of studio experimentation that yielded music too complex for the group to play onstage. None of the *Revolver* songs was played on the tour; indeed, the Beatles had grown so bored with concert performance that they undertook the tour without so much as a rehearsal. By the time the tour ended, at Candlestick Park on August 29th, the Beatles had decided that they would not tour again.

Lennon knew intuitively that the end of touring meant, in some ways, the end of the group, and he pondered his future while filming *How I Won the War* that fall. But he temporized: Instead of leaving the band, he turned up at the studio that November with "Strawberry Fields Forever," one of the group's most brilliant tracks, and the start of the sessions that yielded *Sgt. Pepper*. Having released the soundtrack for the Summer of Love, the Beatles seemed more together than ever. But that was an illusion. And one thing is clear in retrospect: Although Lennon initiated the *Pepper* sessions with "Strawberry Fields," the focus of power within the band was shifting to McCartney. The *Sgt. Pepper* concept had been Paul's. *Magical Mystery Tour* was his show, too.

As Lennon's commitment to the group waned, Harrison also was looking in other directions. On one hand, he was fascinated with Eastern music and philosophy. On the other, he was forming musical friendships with rock musicians outside the Beatles, most notably Eric Clapton. And as he began composing more prolifically, he was increasingly frustrated by Lennon's and McCartney's disinclination to increase his share of songs on the group's albums.

In their sessions for *The Beatles* (the so-called White Album) in 1968, Lennon, McCartney and Harrison began working separately on their own tracks, drafting the others only when necessary. The result seemed an extraordinary compendium of rock styles, but it soon became clear that the two-disc set was really a set of Lennon, McCartney and Harrison solo performances yoked together. The atmosphere of the sessions was such that Starr quit for a week, feeling unneeded. Harrison quit briefly during the *Let It Be* sessions in early 1969, frustrated over what he perceived as his treatment as a sideman. Lennon, by the time of the White Album sessions, had left his first wife, Cynthia, and had taken up with Yoko

Paul and Linda McCartney, formerly of Wings.

Ono. He grew more interested in collaborating with her than with McCartney, Harrison and Starr, and in 1969 he let his band mates know that his Beatle days were numbered.

Musically, the Beatles' individual shoots had started to bloom while the group was a going concern. McCartney had composed a filmscore for *The Family Way* in 1967. Harrison had come up with a quirkier soundtrack—an amalgam of rock and Indian music—for *Wonderwall* in 1968. A few months later he released some of his synthesizer practice tapes as *Electronic Sound* on Apple's experimental offshoot, Zapple. Apple and Zapple also became outlets for Lennon's and Ono's experimental collaborations.

Definitive word that the Beatles were no more came from McCartney, via a self-interview packaged with press copies of his *McCartney* in April 1970. *McCartney* said a lot about its maker. The cover, a spilled bowl of cherries, was hard not to read as something between wistfulness and bitterness at the Beatles' breakup. Its gatefold, however, offered a glimpse of McCartney's new life: the wife and kids, the dog and cat, the farm and domestic bliss. The album itself was a clear indication of McCartney's musical strengths and weaknesses. A strength, certainly, was his instrumental prowess: It was a one-man-band show, and quite a polished one. His songwriting facility, however, proved a double-edged sword and has remained so throughout his solo career. McCartney has always had a direct line to melodic inspiration. As a Beatle, he could try out both his grand inspirations and his instant dabblings with the assurance that the others would help him separate the wheat from the chaff. On his own, though, his edit function did not always kick in. So on *McCartney*, durable tracks like "Maybe I'm Amazed" and "Every Night" rest side by side with throwaways.

The consistency problem was acute on McCartney's next few releases. Early 1971 brought the pretty but innocuous single "Another Day," followed quickly by *Ram*, an album notably sillier than *McCartney*. It was difficult not to cringe through tracks like "Uncle Albert/Admiral Halsey," a third-drawer "Yellow Submarine" rewrite. Soon after *Ram*, McCartney formed Wings, with Denny Laine, late of the Moody Blues, and Henry McCullough on guitars and the drummer Denny Siewell. The band's first outing, *Wild Life*, hastily recorded and released

at the end of 1971, is truly appalling. McCartney's vocals are pale, the band's playing is slovenly, and with the exception of the wistful "Dear Friend," McCartney's new songs were entirely witless.

But Wings soon got its act together. One of McCartney's rare ventures into political topicality, "Give Ireland Back to the Irish," released in February 1972, easily outclassed Lennon's essay on the same subject, "Luck of the Irish." That same month, Wings toured British universities, usually arriving unannounced and playing for a percentage of the gate. The band's playing grew more cohesive. "Ireland" was followed by the much-derided "Mary Had a Little Lamb," but "Mary" was followed by a terrific rocker, "Hi, Hi, Hi." And although the 1973 album *Red Rose Speedway* had little to say, it was a giant step beyond *Wild Life*.

As a change of pace, McCartney scheduled sessions for the next Wings album in Lagos, Nigeria. The trip began disastrously: Siewell and McCullough quit Wings the day they were to leave England. But from the jaws of disaster the McCartneys and Laine snatched *Band on the Run*, an album with such a consistently good spirit that all McCartney's later work would be measured against it. For a time his level of work held up. With Jimmy McCulloch and Geoff Britton replacing Siewell and McCullough, Wings released *Venus and Mars*, an album in the spirit of *Band on the Run*, and nearly its equal. Soon after its release, in 1975—and after another personnel change, Joe English replacing Britton—McCartney took the band on a world tour that lasted from the fall of 1975 through the summer of 1976, and yielded *Wings over America* and the film *Rockshow*.

Wings made two studio albums with its tour lineup, *Wings at the Speed of Sound* (1976) and *London Town* (1978), both of which retreat from the bright, concert band sound of *Band on the Run* in favor of a more introspective, melodic and lighter textured approach. On *Speed of Sound* McCartney responded to critics with "Silly Love Songs," a defiant defense of sappiness. *London Town* was more sophisticated and varied; its folksy textures moved against the rockier spirit of the time.

McCulloch and English quit Wings just before the release of "Mull of Kintyre," a paean to Scotland that became the biggest-selling single in England for a time. Their replacements, guitarist Laurence Juber and drummer Steve Holly, joined the McCartneys and Laine in time for *Back to the Egg*, a collection that

The solo Beatle, still on the long and winding road.

takes the varied approach of *London Town* a few steps further. For the first time, McCartney used a coproducer, Chris Thomas. And although *Egg* was harshly reviewed in 1979, it bears another look. "Spin It On," the grandiose "Rockestra Theme" and Laine's "Again and Again and Again" are great rockers; "Winter Rose/Love Awake" and "Baby's Request" are appealing examples of McCartney's gentler composing persona; and "After the Ball" anticipates the soulful expository approach he would take a decade later on parts of *Flowers in the Dirt*.

McCartney toured England with this new version of Wings in 1979, and was about to embark on his first post-Beatles tour of Japan in January 1980. McCartney had tried to tour Japan before, but a 1972 Swedish pot bust made the Japanese authorities reluctant to give him a visa. That background made his decision to pack a large supply of weed for the Japanese trip truly unfathomable. He was arrested,

jailed for eight days and deported. That, for all practical purposes, was the end of Wings. McCartney responded to his second band's breakup with another one-man-band album, *McCartney II*. His instrumental arsenal and multitracking abilities had grown considerably over the decade, but the songs were dispensible.

The combination of his Japanese bust and Lennon's assassination later that year cured McCartney of the desire to tour between 1980 and 1989, and his album production slowed down, too. Early in 1981 he reunited with George Martin, the Beatles' producer, for a string of projects. *Tug of War* (1982) included his touching tribute to Lennon, "Here Today." The followup, *Pipes of Peace* (1983), was less consistent. On those two albums, though, McCartney began an intermittent series of starry collaborations. *Tug of War* includes "Ebony and Ivory" and "What's That You're Doing," a pair of duets with Stevie Wonder, and "Get It" with Carl Perkins. *Pipes of Peace* pairs him with Michael Jackson on "Say Say Say" and "This Is the Man," a payback for McCartney's appearance on Jackson's "The Girl Is Mine." (That alliance shattered in 1985, when Jackson paid more than $47 million for the Lennon-McCartney song publishing catalog, outbidding McCartney and Ono.) Some of the tracks on the *War* and *Peace* albums, as well as a few Beatles classics, were remade for McCartney's next project, the 1984 film *Give My Regards to Broad Street.*

In 1986 McCartney took on two new collaborators: Hugh Padgham, fresh from the last two Police albums, produced McCartney's next run of sessions, and Eric Stewart of 10cc began cowriting with him. When "Press," the first single from *Press to Play,* hit the airwaves it seemed, for the twenty-six seconds of the song's intro, that Padgham had toughened and modernized McCartney's sound. But when McCartney sang his first line—"Darling, you know I love you very, very much"—the tension evaporated into another silly love song. "Press to Play" was by no means a total write-off, but in the end Padgham's touch proved a cosmetic veneer.

McCartney took three years to record his next album, *Flowers in the Dirt,* during which he worked with a broad slate of producers and musicians. At the album's heart are four songs he cowrote with Elvis Costello, his first post-Beatles collaborator with a wit as acidic as Lennon's. On "Flowers," the forty-seven-year-old McCartney came to terms, for the first time, with middle age. So the love songs had an edge: "My Brave Face," cowritten with Costello, shows a newly separated protagonist breaking his dirty dishes instead of washing them. In "Figure of Eight," he weighs the risks and benefits of straying from monogamy. And "That Day Is Done," another Costello collaboration, describes a funeral from the perspective of the grave.

Flowers was followed by a world tour that ran from September 1989 through July 1990. McCartney's band, which had played on a few of the *Flowers* tracks, proved a tight ensemble—so tight, in fact, that some critics complained that the many Beatles songs in the set sounded like waxwork copies of the originals. In fact, when McCartney released his recording of the tour, *Tripping the Live Fantastic,* the tracks that jumped out as the freshest were the Fifties rockers: Carl Perkins's "Matchbox," Eddie Cochran's "Twenty Flight Rock" and Fats Domino's "Ain't That a Shame." This confirmed the impression left by *Back in the U.S.S.R.,* an "unofficial" album of pre-Beatles rock classics recorded during McCartney's band rehearsals in July 1987, and first released in the Soviet Union at the end of 1988, with a belated worldwide release in 1991. *Back in the U.S.S.R.* showed that McCartney was an imaginative rock & roll shouter when he thought he was out of the spotlight, and left listeners wondering whether a sense of misdirected perfectionism in his studio productions was draining the soul out of his recordings. McCartney was not immune to this argument. In 1991 he released what he considered a followup to the Russian album, *Unplugged: The Official Bootleg,* a limited-edition release, drawn from a live acoustic set he and his touring band taped for MTV. The set included Beatles songs, rock standards and a few songs from *McCartney*—nothing, in other words, later than 1970.

Meanwhile, McCartney had a grander project up his sleeve, the *Liverpool Oratorio,* a large-scale classical work. Written with the American composer and conductor Carl Davis, the ninety-seven-minute oratorio celebrated the 150th anniversary of the Royal Liverpool Philharmonic, and was scored for full orchestra, mixed choir, boys choir and vocal soloists. Its text is partly autobiographical, and grapples affectingly with the loss and reclamation of innocence, love and faith. The June 1991 premiere, at the Liverpool Anglican Cathedral, was recorded and released later that year.

John Lennon's solo career was well under way by the time the world heard that the Beatles' split was irrevocable, and many blamed the rift not only on Lennon's need to have Yoko always at his side, but on the pair's taste for outlandish projects. Their first musical collaboration, *Unfinished Music No. 1: Two Virgins,* was an album of free-form avant-garde noodlings, recorded on the same spring night in 1968 when they consummated their affair. John and Yoko continued to release snippets of their life for another year. Their October 1968 pot bust provided the back jacket photo for *Unfinished Music No. 2: Life with the Lions.* The front cover and the recordings on side two of the disc documented—sometimes amusingly, sometimes in touchingly graphic detail—their hospital stay during Yoko's miscarriage. The other side was

a recording of the first live concerts at which Lennon accompanied one of Ono's no-shrieks-barred vocal performances. And recordings made during their March 1969 Amsterdam honeymoon bed-in were released on one side of *The Wedding Album*.

Listeners with more conventional tastes could catch a synopsis of all this in its pop-single translation, the Beatles' "The Ballad of John and Yoko." But the song's protagonists were not sitting still. Having made world peace their theme, Lennon and Ono staged a sequel to the Amsterdam bed-in in Montreal. There, Lennon turned what had been his refrain in dozens of interviews—"all we are saying is give peace a chance"—into an anthem, recorded it live in his hotel room and had it rush released. As a song, "Give Peace a Chance" wasn't much, but its refrain eventually topped "We Shall Overcome" as a demonstration favorite. Lennon laid his peace campaign aside during the *Abbey Road* sessions in the summer of 1969, but as soon as that album was finished, he and Ono were on to other projects. Among them was the tough business of kicking a heroin habit, documented by Lennon on the searing "Cold Turkey," which featured Clapton on guitar and Lennon, at the end of the track, vocalizing à la Yoko.

In January 1970 Lennon wrote and recorded "Instant Karma," all in a day, and had it instantly released. That April the Lennons called time out and flew to Los Angeles for four months of primal scream therapy with Dr. Arthur Janov. Lennon became disenchanted with Janov but emerged from the experience with an astonishing album, *John Lennon/Plastic Ono Band,* on which he opened his closets and let the skeletons run free. In "Mother," he explores his mother's death and his abandonment by his father; in "I Found Out," "Working Class Hero," "Isolation" and "Look at Me" he ruminates acidicly on his place in the world. The album's centerpiece, though, is "God," whom he defines as "a concept by which we measure our pain" before launching into a negation of the world's idols—from Buddha to the Beatles—ending with a singular, inwardly focused affirmation: "I just believe in me. Yoko and me."

With so much of his anger off his chest, Lennon softened his stance for *Imagine* (1971). The title

John and Yoko: Rock & roll meets the avant-garde.

track, a utopian vision of a world without national boundaries, without possessions and with "no need for greed or hunger," is as beautiful a ballad as any McCartney has written. So are "Jealous Guy" and "Oh My Love," two love songs for Yoko. But *Imagine* is also a wolf in sheep's clothing. "I Don't Want to Be a Soldier Mama I Don't Want to Die" and "Give Me Some Truth" reopened the political dialogue of the pre-Janov days. And in "How Do You Sleep?" Lennon responded scathingly to McCartney: "The sound you make is Muzak to my ears," he sings, and advises McCartney that "a pretty face may last a year or two, but pretty soon they'll see what you can do."

With *Imagine* completed, the Lennons moved to New York City, where they remained, partly because Lennon came to love the city, and partly because the United States government's attempts to deport Lennon, starting late in 1971, forced him to stay in the country lest he be denied reentry. He quickly befriended the American radicals Abbie Hoffman and Jerry Rubin, among others, and made their causes his own, thus exacerbating his problems with the American government.

Despite Lennon's leftist pronouncements and experimental recordings, he still had a commercial streak in him. In December 1971 he released "Happy Xmas (War Is Over)," which he hoped would displace "White Christmas" as a holiday standard. But mostly, he wanted to revert to his songwriter-as-journalist mode. With Elephant's Memory, a New York bar band, he recorded his modest topical pieces—"John Sinclair," "Attica State," "Luck of the Irish" and "Sunday Bloody Sunday"—along with the more inspired "Woman Is the Nigger of the World" and a few of Yoko's songs. The result, *Some Time in New York City,* had even Lennon's most ardent admirers wondering if the well had run dry.

The pressures on Lennon around this time could not have helped. The Nixon administration, noting a plan announced by Lennon's radical friends to disrupt the Republican National Convention by presenting a Lennon protest concert on its doorstep, decided to rid the country of Lennon, claiming that his 1968 drug arrest made him an undesirable alien. That battle raged until he was granted permanent resident status in 1976. There were strains in the Lennons' marriage, too, signs of which could be heard in *Mind Games* (1973), an uneven collection that included both top-drawer Lennon and automatic-pilot riffing. Just before the album was released, Lennon and Ono parted ways.

During this "lost weekend," as Lennon described it, he split his time between Los Angeles and New York and finished two very different albums. One was *Rock 'n' Roll,* a collection of oldies. In the great tradition of rock & roll pilfering, Lennon had lifted a line from Chuck Berry's "You Can't Catch Me" to open "Come Together" on *Abbey Road,* and although such minor borrowings have usually gone unpunished, Berry's publisher, the infamous Morris Levy, considered Lennon big enough quarry for a lawsuit. As a solution, Lennon agreed to record a collection of old favorites, including "You Can't Catch Me" and a few of the publisher's other wares.

The sessions were a disaster: Phil Spector, who had worked with John on "Instant Karma" and "Imagine," stopped turning up midway through the sessions and absconded with the tapes. It took John a year to get them back. Lennon himself was sometimes drunk and disorderly, both at the sessions and in general. When Spector and the tapes disappeared, Lennon returned to New York, and made *Walls and Bridges* in 1974. A logical successor to *Mind Games* and something of an improvement, *Walls and Bridges* is a Lennonesque blend of autobiography, self-analysis, messages to Yoko and an *ad hominem* attack on his former manager, Allen Klein ("Steel and Glass"). Also included was a collaboration with Elton John, "Whatever Gets You thru the Night," a riffy song of no particular consequence except that it turned out to be Lennon's first solo Number One single. Lennon had promised Elton that if the track hit the top of the charts, he would perform with him at Madison Square Garden, and true to his word, he turned up for a three-song set on Thanksgiving 1974. Except for the short set he played at the "Salute to Sir Lew Grade" concert, taped for television in June 1975, this was his last public performance.

Lennon returned to Yoko in January 1975, and closed the door. The birth of the Lennons' son Sean, on October 9th, 1975, marked the start of a period of Garbo-like retreat, during which Lennon helped raise Sean while Yoko oversaw the family's investments. As Sean's fifth birthday approached, Lennon decided it was time to resurface. During the early summer of 1980, he and Yoko began composing songs about their relationship, about each other, about Sean and about what Lennon had been up to

the previous five years, along with some generalized, gynocentric celebrations of marriage. They arranged these songs as a kind of dialogue and recorded them with a band of crack studio players who contributed the tightest ensemble playing heard on any of Lennon's post-Beatles discs.

The songs on *Double Fantasy* were direct, uncluttered and eclectic: "(Just Like) Starting Over" is a Fifties-style love song. "Watching the Wheels," "I'm Losing You" and "Woman" could have been White Album outtakes. With the release of the album, and the streams of interviews that followed, Lennon seized the rock world's attention, and that attention revitalized him. He hinted at a tour and continued working in the studio with the idea of following *Double Fantasy* quickly. On the night he was killed, he and Ono had remixed "Walking on Thin Ice," which he was convinced would be his wife's first hit single.

Death did not silence Lennon entirely. In 1984 Ono released *Milk and Honey,* her reconstruction, using *Double Fantasy* outtakes, of the prospective followup. In 1986 she began to open the vaults, releasing two video collections—*Imagine,* the set of conceptual clips the Lennons had made to promote John's *Imagine* and Yoko's *Fly,* and *Live in New York City,* the film of Lennon's August 1972 Madison Square Garden benefit performance—and a set of mid-Seventies studio outtakes, *Menlove Avenue.* Two years later she released the film of the Plastic Ono Band's 1969 Toronto concert. And she handed over Lennon's demo tapes to Westwood One, to be played on the syndicated radio series *Lost Lennon Tapes,* and her film archive to Andrew Solt and David L. Wolper for use in their documentary *Imagine: John Lennon.*

George Harrison emerged from the wreckage of the Beatles with the most to gain. He had come to songwriting too late to share in the glory of the Lennon-McCartney team, but if you line up his Beatles songs chronologically, you see an incredible maturation that culminates in "While My Guitar Gently Weeps," from the White Album, and "Something" and "Here Comes the Sun," from *Abbey Road.* His paltry allocation of Beatles tracks, however, had left him with an enormous backlog of unused songs. So when the solo era dawned in

A working-class hero is something to be.

1970, he invited an array of musician friends to the studio and opened the floodgates. For his debut, *All Things Must Pass,* he filled two discs with consistently good songs, and threw in a bonus disc of studio jams.

It was an essentially sober album: Although Harrison had abandoned his attempt to combine Indian classical music with Western pop, he retained the Hindu notion that life, death and reincarnation are steps on the path to God-consciousness. Life's transitory nature is the subject of the title track and "Isn't It a Pity," "The Art of Dying" and "Beware of Darkness." Others, like "My Sweet Lord" and "Hear Me Lord," are outright prayers. There were also songs of a more worldly variety, ranging from a tribute to the "Apple Scruffs," the tenacious Beatle fans who hung out at the Abbey Road studios, to

straightforward love songs, including a collaboration with Bob Dylan, "I'd Have You Anytime."

Next Harrison, at the behest of sitar virtuoso Ravi Shankar, mounted two benefit concerts in August 1971 to provide food and medical supplies to the people of Bangladesh. Harrison rounded up Ringo Starr, Clapton, Leon Russell, Bob Dylan, Billy Preston and a large supporting band for the Madison Square Garden shows, which were filmed and recorded. In an ideal world, the profits would have gone swiftly to Bangladesh, via the United Nations. But with so many stars contracted to competing record labels, there were rights disputes, and when the American and British governments weighed in with tax demands, the idealistic effort quickly soured. Still, the Bangladesh concert was the precursor of Live Aid and other rock charity galas.

George Harrison: The "quiet" Beatle came back in 1987 with a Top Ten album, *Cloud Nine*.

Two years passed before Harrison recorded another album of new songs, and although *Living in the Material World* reached the top of the American charts, one began to hear grumbling about the Quiet One's post-Beatles persona. The public (and the press) had come to regard Harrison as a kind of religious fundamentalist and heard many of his new songs as sanctimonious preaching. But *Material World* has its saving graces. The title track and "Sue Me, Sue You Blues" offer a caustic look at, among other things, the wretched state of affairs among the former Beatles. Also notable is the emergence of a particularly Harrisonian kind of love song, in which it was never entirely clear whether he was singing about interpersonal love or the love of God. In some cases, the two seem interchangeable. That impression was confirmed in 1974, when he included Lennon's "In My Life" in his concert sets, changing the final line from "I love you more" to "I love God more." The tour was an outright fiasco (Harrison lost his voice, among other problems) and dragged his reputation a few rungs down the ladder, as did *Dark Horse,* the album associated with it.

Extra Texture (Read All About It), released in late 1975, brought together songs of variable durability. The best of them, "You," was really a leftover from the *All Things Must Pass* era. On *Extra Texture,* Harrison began revisiting his earlier work in a different way—through rewriting and conscious self-parody. "This Guitar (Can't Keep from Crying)" is a light gloss on "While My Guitar Gently Weeps." He tackled another of his Beatles classics in 1979, with "Here Comes the Moon," and in 1987 he took a broader look back in "When We Was Fab."

Harrison's next release, *Thirty-three & ⅓* (1976), was a decidedly upbeat departure from his previous whining and sermonizing. There were further comments on the Material World, of course. In 1970 Harrison had been sued by the publisher of the Chiffons' "He's So Fine" over the uncanny resemblance between that song and "My Sweet Lord." Harrison was found guilty of "unconscious plagiarism," and in "This Song," and its accompanying video, he parodies the court proceedings. Otherwise, the album's reach is fairly broad, ranging from the comical "Crackerbox Palace" to classic blues in "Woman Don't You Cry for Me."

Harrison took a brief hiatus from recording after *Thirty-Three & ⅓,* returning in 1979 with *George Harri-*

son, an album several degrees lighter in spirit. It shows an expansion in subject matter: "Faster," for example, is about automobile racing, and "Soft Hearted Hana" is a humorous recounting of an experience with hallucinogenic mushrooms. There are also love songs that one could safely conclude to be more about his new wife, Olivia Arrias, than about God ("Dark Sweet Lady"), and some that could be read either way ("Love Comes to Everyone," "Blow Away," "Your Love Is Forever").

Yet despite the album's considerable beauty, Harrison's audience had dwindled, and Warner Bros.—which had distributed his Dark Horse imprint since 1976—was not happy. It rejected the original version of Harrison's 1980 album, *Somewhere in England.* Lennon was murdered while Harrison was reworking the record, and he responded with "All Those Years Ago," a tribute that redresses a complaint that Lennon had made to *Newsweek* about Harrison's having failed to give him credit for his help and influence in *I Me Mine,* the annotated songbook Harrison published earlier in the year. McCartney and Starr played on the recording.

"All Those Years Ago" is the album's most striking track, but another replacement song Harrison provided was downright subversive. The new opener, "Blood from a Clone" recounts Warners' complaint about the original album ("it's too laid back") and skewered the record industry at large for concentrating more on marketing and trendiness than on music. And on the second track, "Unconsciousness Rules," Harrison gives the back of his hand to disco—and perhaps to McCartney, who had just started pursuing the disco audience with "Coming Up."

Harrison's weariness of the record business was evident in the way he handled the release of *Gone Troppo* in 1982. The album slipped quietly into the bins, Harrison scarcely lifted a finger to promote it, and its sales were dismal. And what a pity that was, because there is no sign of weariness on the album itself, a collection of tracks that resonate with energy ("Wake Up My Love"), melodic beauty ("That's the Way It Goes") and humor ("Dream Away," the title track and the doo-wop cover of "I Really Love You").

Thereafter, Harrison virtually disappeared for five years, devoting himself primarily to HandMade Films, the production company he had started in

The Fab Five *(from left):* Lefty, Otis, Lucky, Charlie T. Jr., and Nelson Wilbury.

1979. When he resurfaced it was with *Cloud Nine,* his most successful record, artistically and commercially, since *All Things Must Pass.* Coproduced by former Electric Light Orchestra guitarist Jeff Lynne, the album's sound is an amalgam of Harrison's hallmarks (his slide playing, for one) and typical ELO textures (an unusual mix of cellos and drums). As on *Gone Troppo,* the songs are mostly light-spirited but by no means insubstantial.

The album is, however, steadfastly old-fashioned when heard in the context of the synth- and drum-machine-driven rock of its day. Having expressed his disapproval of the music world's trend hopping on *Somewhere in England,* he was now intent on making his point in the music itself: These, he told interviewers, were real songs, played on real instruments by real people. At forty-four he meant to hold his ground as a musical conservative.

His next two outings, on the other hand, are filled with real songs, played on real instruments by fictitious people. On the first, *Volume One* of the Traveling Wilburys, these folks, identified as Nelson, Otis, Charlie T. Jr., Lucky and Lefty Wilbury, were better known as Harrison, Lynne, Tom Petty, Bob Dylan and Roy Orbison. Orbison died soon after the disc was released. On the second Wilburys album, called *Volume 3,* the remaining Wilburys are Muddy, Boo, Clayton and Spike. Both albums show a quirky sense of humor. Typical is the first album's "Handle with Care," a vocal round-robin that gives Orbison a chorus that wonderfully parodies his own early hits. On the second set, the humor is crankier and stranger, the subjects including ecology ("Inside Out"), jealousy ("Where Were You Last Night?"), financial frustration ("Poor House") and the problems of instrument storage ("Cool Dry Place").

Toward the end of 1991 Harrison's friend Eric Clapton persuaded him to overcome his fear and loathing of touring. With Clapton and his band backing him, Harrison toured Japan for nearly three weeks that December, offering a set heavy on songs from the Beatles days—"If I Needed Someone," "I Want to Tell You," "Old Brown Shoe," "Something," "Taxman," "Piggies," "Here Comes the Sun" and of course "While My Guitar Gently Weeps"—mixed with a selection of his solo songs.

It seemed, at first, that Ringo Starr might devote himself to films after the Beatles' breakup, and indeed, he appeared before the cameras sporadically into the Eighties. His musical career got off to a slower start. Early in 1970 he taped a dozen cabaret standards as a gift for his mother. But since the others were releasing their private outings on Apple, Ringo put out these tapes as *Sentimental Journey*. The album, actually, is a fairly ambitious project: Among its tracks is McCartney's arrangement of "Star Dust," Quincy Jones's arrangement of "Love Is a Many Splendored Thing," John Dankworth's arrangement of "You Always Hurt the One You Love" and the title song, arranged by Richard Perry. Starr chose an equally eccentric repertoire for his followup, *Beaucoups of Blues,* a country album recorded in Nashville during a week of sessions in 1970.

When he turned his hand to rock & roll, however, Ringo did quite well. "It Don't Come Easy" and "Back Off Boogaloo," released as singles in 1971 and 1972 respectively, proved both enjoyable and chartworthy. And in 1973 he signed on Richard Perry to produce *Ringo,* a straightforward rock album with contributions from all three former Beatles. Both Lennon and Harrison played on Lennon's contribution, "I'm the Greatest," and Paul and Linda McCartney sent along the basic tracks for "Six O'-Clock." McCartney also played the kazoo solo on Ringo's cover of "You're Sixteen." Harrison co-wrote "Photograph" with Starr, and provided "Sunshine Life for Me (Sail Away Raymond)" and "You and Me."

Starr and Perry tried to recapture the spirit of *Ringo* on *Goodnight Vienna* (1974), with limited success. Harrison and McCartney sat this one out, but Lennon wrote the title track and played on Ringo's plaintive cover of "Only You." Elton John contributed the lively "Snookeroo," and Harry Nilsson provided "Easy for Me." There was also Ringo's likeable—and, it turned out, prophetic—version of Hoyt Axton's "No No Song," about giving up drugs and drink.

EMI evidently considered *Ringo*'s success a fluke, so when the company's contractual hold on the former Beatles ended in 1976, Ringo was not offered a renewal. He moved to Atlantic for two albums, *Ringo's Rotogravure* and *Ringo the 4th,* that proved the start of a quick descent. Both were produced by Arif Mardin, who tried, with poor results, to inject Ringo's voice into an R&B backing. In 1978 he moved to Portrait for a single album, *Bad Boy,* a distinct improvement. But the album was virtually unsaleable.

These were rough times for Ringo. In 1975 he divorced his wife, Maureen, and embarked on a jet-setting life that exacerbated a drinking problem that, he later said, had started during the Beatles years. In April 1979 he was hospitalized with severe intestinal problems and nearly died. Seven months later his house in Los Angeles burned down and along with it his personal collection of Beatles memorabilia. Just a year later he and his future wife, Barbara Bach, were injured in a car crash.

On top of all that, he was once again label shopping. In 1980 Boardwalk agreed to give him a try. *Stop and Smell the Roses* (1981) was yet another return to the *Ringo* formula: McCartney performs on several of the tracks, including two he wrote for the project, "Attention" and "Private Property." Harrison contributed the upbeat "Wrack My Brain," and played on several cuts. Lennon had been working on songs for the album too: Several of his demo tapes, including those for "Nobody Told Me" and the unreleased "Life Begins at 40," begin with spoken notation that the songs were meant for Ringo. But after Lennon's death, Starr did not have the heart to record them. Still, the album has an upbeat humor that had long been missing from his work. Alas, it barely

cracked the Top 100. So although his next album, *Old Wave* (1983), was a surprisingly tight rocker, with a band that included Eric Clapton and Leon Russell, Starr was unable to find an American or British label willing to release it.

Except for occasional contributions to compilations like *Stay Awake,* a collection of Walt Disney film songs, and occasional cameo appearances in concert, Starr pretty much dropped out of the music business. In 1988 he realized that one of his greatest problems was alcoholism, and that October he and Barbara Bach checked into a rehabilitation clinic in Arizona. They emerged a month later as confirmed teetotalers.

Starr then posed a tough test for himself. In 1989 he put together what he called the All-Starr Band and toured the United States and Japan. The shows were openly nostalgic and endearingly lively: Neither the Rykodisc live album nor the home video capture their spirit entirely. In 1991 Ringo was signed by Private Music and released an album, *Time Takes Time,* in 1992, followed by another All-Starr tour.

I n his chapter on the Beatles, Greil Marcus wrote about the transforming effect the group had not only on its listeners but on the whole of pop music. No such claim can be made for the solo Beatles. In the more than twenty years since the group disbanded, they each recorded prolifically and each had his share of hits. Some of their songs—most notably Lennon's ''Imagine''— have taken on lives of their own. But when the Beatles gave up their collective persona, they also gave up their pervasive influence. Rock and pop meandered down other paths during the Seventies and Eighties, and the post-Fab four either went with those currents, as McCartney largely has, or steadfastly swam against them, as Harrison has.

Yet the fact that none of the ex-Beatles has emerged as an influential innovator diminishes neither the stature they enjoyed in the Sixties nor their collective revolutionary contribution to rock & roll.

Richard Starkey, of the All-Starr Band.

DISCOGRAPHY

ALBUMS

GEORGE HARRISON
Wonderwall Music (Apple; ☆49, 1969). *Electronic Sound* (Zapple; ☆191, 1969). *All Things Must Pass* (Apple; ☆1, 1970). *The Concert for Bangla Desh* (Apple; ☆2, 1972). *Living in the Material World* (Apple; ☆1, 1973). *Dark Horse* (Apple; ☆4, 1974). *Extra Texture (Read All About It)* (Apple; ☆8, 1975). *The Best of George Harrison* (Capitol; ☆31, 1976). *Thirty Three & ⅓* (Dark Horse; ☆11, 1976). *George Harrison* (Dark Horse; ☆14, 1979). *Somewhere in England* (Dark Horse; ☆11, 1981). *Gone Troppo* (Dark Horse; ☆108, 1982). *Cloud Nine* (Dark Horse; ☆8, 1987). *Best of Dark Horse 1976—1989* (Dark Horse; ☆132, 1989). With the Traveling Wilburys: *Volume One* (Wilbury; ☆3, 1988). With the Traveling Wilburys: *Vol. 3* (Wilbury; ☆11, 1990).

JOHN LENNON
Unfinished Music No. 1: Two Virgins (Tetragrammaton; ☆124, 1969). *Unfinished Music No. 2: Life with the Lions* (Zapple; ☆174, 1969). *Wedding Album* (Apple; ☆178, 1969). *Live Peace in Toronto 1969* (Apple; ☆10, 1970). *John Lennon/Plastic Ono Band* (Apple; ☆6, 1970). *Imagine* (Apple; ☆1, 1971). *Some Time in New York City* (Apple; ☆48, 1972). *Mind Games* (Apple; ☆9, 1973). *Walls and Bridges* (Apple; ☆1, 1974). *Rock 'n' Roll* (Apple; ☆6, 1975). *Shaved Fish* (Apple; ☆12, 1975). *Double Fantasy* (Geffen; ☆1, 1980). *The John Lennon Collection* (Geffen; ☆33; 1982). *Milk and Honey* (Polydor; ☆11, 1984). *Live in New York City* (Capitol; ☆41, 1986). *Menlove Ave.* (Capitol; ☆127, 1986). *Imagine: John Lennon* (Capitol; ☆31, 1988).

PAUL McCARTNEY
McCartney (Apple; ☆1, 1970). *Ram* (Apple; ☆2, 1971). *McCartney II* (Columbia; ☆3, 1980). *Tug of War* (Columbia; ☆1, 1982). *Pipes of Peace* (Columbia; ☆15, 1983). *Give My Regards to Broad Street* (Columbia; ☆21, 1984). *Press to Play* (Capitol; ☆30, 1986). *All the Best* (Capitol; ☆62, 1987). *Flowers in the Dirt* (Capitol; ☆21, 1989). *Tripping the Live Fantastic* (Capitol; ☆26, 1990). *Tripping the Live Fantastic—Highlights!* (Capitol; ☆141, 1990). *Unplugged: The Official Bootleg* (Capitol; ☆14, 1991). *Liverpool Oratorio* (Angel; ☆177, 1991).

WINGS
Wild Life (Apple; ☆10, 1971). *Red Rose Speedway* (Apple, ☆1, 1973). *Band on the Run* (Apple; ☆1, 1974). *Venus and Mars* (Capitol, ☆1, 1975). *Wings at the Speed of Sound* (Capitol; ☆1, 1976). *Wings over America* (Capitol; ☆1, 1976). *London Town* (Capitol, ☆2, 1978). *Wings Greatest* (Capitol, ☆29, 1978). *Back to the Egg* (Columbia, ☆8, 1979).

RINGO STARR
Sentimental Journey (Apple; ☆22, 1970). *Beaucoups of Blues* (Apple; ☆65, 1970). *Ringo* (Apple; ☆2, 1973). *Goodnight Vienna* (Apple; ☆8, 1974). *Blast from Your Past* (Apple; ☆30, 1975). *Ringo's Rotogravure* (Atlantic; ☆28, 1976). *Ringo the 4th* (Atlantic; ☆162, 1977). *Bad Boy* (Portrait; ☆129, 1978). *Stop and Smell the Roses* (Boardwalk; ☆98, 1981). *Ringo Starr and His All-Starr Band* (Rykodisc; 1990). *Time Takes Time* (Private; 1992).

(Chart positions compiled from Joel Whitburn's *Record Research,* based on *Billboard*'s LPs charts.)

THE ROLLING STONES

BY ROBERT CHRISTGAU

Mick Jagger was never a rocker. He wasn't a mod, either. He was a bohemian, an anti-utopian version of what Americans called a folkie. That is, he was attracted to music of a certain innocence as only a fairly classy—and sophisticated—person can be. Unlike John Lennon and Paul McCartney (and Bob Dylan), his ambitions weren't kindled by Elvis Presley; his angry, low-rent mien was no more a reflection of his economic fate than his stardom was a means for him to escape it.

Something similar went for all the Rolling Stones. "What can a poor boy do / Except sing for a rock & roll band?" was the way they opted out of the political movement that most young rebels found unavoidable in the late Sixties. But not only weren't they poor boys when they played that song, they never had been—except voluntarily, which is different. Only two of them—bassist Bill Wyman, the son of a bricklayer, and drummer Charlie Watts, the son of a lorry driver—came from working-class backgrounds, and both were improving their day-job lots dramatically by the time they joined the Stones. The other three, the group's spiritual nucleus through the scuffling days, were in it strictly for the art. Lead guitarist Keith Richards, although he grew up fairly poor, revolted against his parents' genteel middle-class pretensions; rhythm guitarist and all-purpose eclectic Brian Jones came from a musical family headed by an aeronautical engineer and wandered the Continent after leaving a posh school; and Mick himself, the son of a medium-successful educator, did not quit the London School of Economics until after the band became a going proposition in 1963. This is not to say the Stones were rich kids; only Brian qualified as what Americans would call upper middle class. Nor is it to underestimate the dreariness of the London suburbs or the rigidity of the English class hierarchy. But due partly to their own posturing, the Stones are often perceived as working class, and that is a major distortion.

Working class is more like Elvis and the Beatles, who loved rock & roll at least partly because rock & roll was a way to *make it*. Their propulsive upward mobility thus became inextricably joined with the energy of the music they created; their will to be rich

Mick Jagger.

and famous was both heroic and naive, a key ingredient of the projected naturalness that was essential to Elvis, and the projected innocence that was essential to the Beatles. For disapproving elders to dismiss this naturalness/innocence as mere vulgarity—without observing, as Dwight Macdonald did about Elvis, that genuine vulgarity has its advantages in earthiness—represented more than a ''generation gap.'' It was open-and-shut snobbery, motivated like most snobbery by class fear.

With the Stones all of this was more complicated. Their devotion to music itself was purer, but insofar as they wanted to be rich-and-famous—and they did, especially Mick, who had always been into money, and Brian, a notoriety junkie—they were neither heroic nor naive, just ambitious. And insofar as they wanted to be earthy—which was a conscious ambition too, rather than something they came by naturally or (God knows) innocently—they risked a vulgarity that was mere indeed. Inspired by the

coaching of Andrew Loog Oldham, the publicist-manager who undertook the creation of the Stones in their own image starting in the spring of 1963, they *chose* to be vulgar—aggressively, as a stance, to counteract the dreariness and rigidity of their middle-class suburban mess of pottage. Perhaps they aspired to the earthiness of the grandfather who passes wind because he doesn't fancy the bother of holding it in, but in the very aspiration they recalled the grandson who farts for the sheer joyous annoyance value of it—and then calls it youth culture.

It would be quicker, of course, to suggest that they sought only to live up to the earthiness of the rhythm & blues music they lived for. But although there's no doubt that Brian, Mick and Keith were passionate about hard-to-find black records that were as crude and esoteric by the standards of English pop and beat fans as they were crude and commercial by the standards of old-bohemian English blues and jazz cultists, the Stones have never been very specific about just what that passion meant emotionally. Only their affinities are clear. Elmore James was Brian's man, while Keith loved Chuck Berry, but they by no means defined the group's poles: One of the laborers in the rhythm section, Charlie, had jazzier tastes than Brian, while the other, Bill, was working in a straight rock & roll group when he joined the Stones in late 1962 or early 1963. Mick's preferences, predictably enough, were shiftier, as he once told Jona-

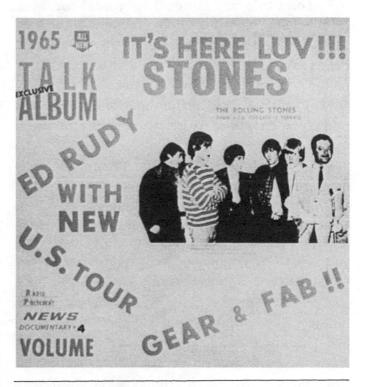

The Rolling Stones as teen idols.

The Rolling Stones in 1964 with Phil Spector, looking dissolute, and an unidentified dog. *From left:* Brian Jones, Mick Jagger, Spector, Bill Wyman, Keith Richards, Charlie Watts.

than Cott: "We were blues purists who liked ever-so-commercial things but never did them on-stage because we were so horrible and so aware of being blues purists, you know what I mean?"

What he means, one surmises, is that the Stones' artiness never deadened their taste for certain commercially fermented blues-based songs—not as long as the songs were pithy and hummable and would induce people to dance when played loud. But by mocking the blues purist in himself he elides "purism"'s image potential. Symbols of the English "R&B" movement—thought in 1963 to be challenging beat (and hence the Beatles) among British teenagers—the Stones had it both ways. Their first big British hit, that winter, was Lennon and McCartney's "I Wanna Be Your Man." They scoffed virtuously at the notion of "a British-composed R&B number," but wrote their own tunes almost from the start, and ranged as far into pop as "Under the Boardwalk" and Buddy Holly in their early recordings.

It is sometimes argued that such modulations of sensibility belie the group's artistic integrity; in fact, however, the Stones' willingness to "exploit" and "compromise" their own bohemian proclivities meant only that they assumed a pop aesthetic. Most artists believe they ought to be rich-and-famous on their own very idiosyncratic terms; the Stones happened to be right. To sing about "half-assed games" on the AM radio (on Bobby Womack's "It's All Over Now") or glower out hirsute and tieless from the Sunday entertainment pages was integrity aplenty in 1964.

Perhaps most important, the Stones obviously cared about the quality of the music they played. If this music recalled any single antecedent it was Chuck Berry, but never with his total commitment to fun. It was fast and metallic, most bluesish in its strict understatement. Clean and sharp—especially in contrast to the gleeful modified chaos of the Beatles—this striking but never overbearing music was an ideal vocal setting, and if it was the guitars and percussion that established the band's presence, it was the vocals, and the vocalist, that defined it. Quite often Jagger chose a light, saucy pop timbre that was also reminiscent of Berry, but something in

his voice left a ranker overall impression—something slippery yet unmistakable, as lubricious and as rubbery as his famous lips. (For a simple example, listen to his tone of voice on most of "I'm a King Bee"—and then to his half-playful, half-ominous pronunciation on the word "buzz" in "I can buzz better baby / When your man is gone.") Nor was this just a matter of being sexy. Just as there was a pointed astringency to the band's music, caustic where Chuck Berry was consciously ebullient—listen to the acerbic tinniness of Keith's lead lines, or to Brian's droning rhythm parts, or to the way the added percussion lags behind the beat—so there was a hurtful tinge to Mick's singing, especially on the slow, murky originals ("Tell Me," "Heart of Stone," or "Time Is on My Side," composed by Jerry Ragavoy but defined by the Stones) that served the group's change-of-pace needs the way ballads did the Beatles'.

The Stones' high-decibel, high-speed approach was rock & roll, not rhythm & blues. Nevertheless, they did admittedly appropriate many of the essential trappings of their music, like hooks and solos,

You" as get it over with, and although he did really seem to wish us "Good Times," he made the prospect sound doubtful where Sam Cooke enjoyed the wish itself.

It seems unlikely that at this point any of the Stones were conscious about this. All of them, Jagger included, were attracted to the gruff, eloquent directness of so much black music; relatively speaking, they became natural, expressive, sexy, and so forth by playing it. What set them apart was Jagger's instinctive understanding that this achievement was relative—that there was a Heisenberg paradox built into the way he appreciated the virtues of this music—and his genius at expressing that as well. The aggressiveness and sexuality of the form were his, but the sincerity was beyond him—partly because he was white and English, and especially because he was Mick Jagger. He loved black music for its sincerity, yet its sincerity was the ultimate object of his pervasive anger. He wanted what he couldn't have and felt detached even from his own desire; he accepted his inability to sing from as deep in his heart as Sam Cooke, sometimes he reveled in it, but he wasn't sure he liked it, not deep in his heart. "An empty heart / Is like an empty life," he sang in one of his early lyrics, adding nuance to qualification as always, so that even as it adhered to all the lost-love conventions, the song evoked the most basic condition of his existence.

Jagger is obsessed with distance. He forces the Stones' music to gaze across (and down) the generation gap and the money gap and the feeling gap and the meaning gap. But then, powered by the other Stones—all of them, like most of the Stones' fans, somewhat more simpleminded than Jagger—the music leaps, so that as a totality it challenges that frustrating, ubiquitous, perhaps metaphysical margin between reach and grasp that presents itself so sharply to human beings with the leisure to think about it. This dual commitment to irony and ecstasy makes the Stones exemplary modernists. Without a doubt, it has been their readiness to leap that has won the Stones their following. At least until the time of the punks, no one ever rocked on out with more ecstatic energy. But it is their realism, bordering at its most suspect on cynicism, that makes all that energy interesting and ensures that their following will never be as huge as that of the high-spirited Beatles (or of a techno-cosmic doomshow like Led Zeppelin, either). After all, not everyone wants to be

from black sources. Jagger, however—despite his rhythmic canniness and cheerful willingness to ape a drawl—was no more a blues stylist *or* a blues thief than Bob Dylan or Paul McCartney. He simply customized certain details of blues phrasing and enunciation into components of a vocal style of protean originality.

Although pinning down the voice of a compulsive ironist like Jagger is impossible by definition, his vocals are perhaps most notable for a youthful petulance that has faded only gradually. His drawl recalls Christopher Robin as often as it does Howlin' Wolf; his mewling nasality might have been copped from a Cockney five-year-old. Jagger's petulance offends some people, who wonder how this whiner—a perpetual adolescent at best—can pretend to mean the adult words he sings. But that ignores the self-confidence that coexists with the petulance—Jagger's very grown-up assurance not that he'll get what he wants, but that he has every reason to ask for it. Even worse, it ignores the fact that Meaning It is definitely not what the Stones are about. Jagger didn't so much sing Muddy Waters' "I Just Want to Make Love to

reminded that it is salutary to think and have fun at the same time. But that is what it means to get up and boogie to "Street Fighting Man," or to party to a paean as steeped in irony as "Brown Sugar."

Jagger's distance from the African part of his African-American musical heritage was especially liberating for white Americans. Whereas for Elvis and those natives who followed him the blues bore an inescapable load of racial envy and fear, Mick's involvement was primarily aesthetic. Since, as his English blues preceptor, Alexis Korner, once remarked, Jagger's chief worry was whether the music was "performed 'properly'," he betrayed no embarrassment about being white. Not all Englishmen were so uninhibited: an obsessive like Eric Burdon (of the Animals) emulated Southern intonations sedulously. But Jagger got off on being a white person singing black songs, and he put that across. His mocking, extravagant elocution, as wild as his hair and the way he pranced around the stage, was more than vaguely self-amused, achieving a power which compared to that of its origins because it was true to itself.

For the English audience, however, the Stones' distance from the U.S.A. itself was edifying. Because the English were far enough from American affluence and mass culture to perceive them as sources of vitality rather than of oppression, a natural perspective was commonly built into all Beatle-era rock & roll, but whereas for the Beatles it manifested itself innocently—in fun, silliness, play—the Stones' version was weirder oddball and therefore more sophisticated. They wove a mythology of America around R&B novelties like "Route 66" and "Down Home Girl," and then exaggerated every eccentricity with some vocal *moue* or instrumental underline. The image of the States that resulted was droll, surreal, maybe a little scary—fascinating, but no hamburger cornucopia.

It was also a cleverly differentiated musical product that rose to number-two status in England upon the release of the first Stones album in mid-1964. In the United States, however, the Stones were number two only in publicity, with sales well behind the Dave Clark Five and Herman's Hermits and just slightly ahead of arty rivals like the Animals and the Kinks for the first year and a half of British Invasion. Then came their seventh U.S. single, "(I Can't Get No) Satisfaction." It was the perfect Stones paradox—the lyrics denied what the music delivered,

with the vocal sitting on the fence—and it dominated the summer of 1965, securing a pop audience half of which was content to shout "I can't get no" while the other half decided that the third verse was about a girl who wouldn't put out during her period.

By then the Stones were Mick and Keith's band, although opening for Alexis Korner at London's Marquee Club in early 1963 they had been "Brian Jones and Mick Jagger and the Rollin' Stones." As vain and exhibitionistic onstage as Jagger, Jones later boasted of having been the group's undisputed "leader," a status he maintained, as Al Aronowitz observed, until it was "worthwhile for someone to dispute." Jones wanted to be a star so much he took it for granted; his relationship to the audience was self-indulgent and self-deceiving. But since outrage was essential to Jagger, Richards and Oldham's

The Stones about the time of *Sticky Fingers. From left:* Charlie Watts, Keith Richards, Bill Wyman, Brian Jones's replacement, Mick Taylor, and Mick Jagger.

product—aggro-sex image mongering, lyrics both indecipherable and censorable and the longest hair known to civilization—and since Brian was the most genuinely outrageous (and crazy) (and generous) (and cruel) of the Stones, he remained essential over and above his musical input. He was the one people remembered after Mick—especially the teenybopper girls who were still the Stones' most visible contingent.

The Stones got the teenyboppers because Oldham was sharp enough to extend Little Richard's First Law of Youth Culture to his scruffy band—he attracted the kids by driving their parents up the wall. But although we can assume Oldham initiated his campaign of world conquest in a spirit of benign, profiteering manipulation, something more was in store: generational revolt on an unprecedented scale.

In this the Stones were to play a crucial symbolic role. The key was a proliferating network of hip if basically collegiate Stones fans, heir to the beatnik myth that had passed from media consciousness when San Francisco's bohemian community moved from North Beach to the Haight, but unaware for a few years of how many arty allies were thinking like thoughts all across the country. Call them predropouts, because dropping out then barely knew its name. And connect them to the bohemian-revolutionary vanguard epitomized by the Diggers, who in the mid-Sixties welcomed the Stones to San Francisco as brothers in struggle. Soon, many of the hip collegiate Stones fans would consider the Diggers and do likewise, just as the Stones' teen hordes would consider *them* and do likewise later on. What it all portended was just what parents had always feared from rock & roll, especially from this ugly group: youth apocalypse.

I remember the first time I ever saw the Stones perform, at the Forum in Montreal in October 1965. I purchased my tickets on the day of the show, and even from deep in the balcony got more from Mick's dancing and the droogy stance of the others than I did from the music, which was muffled by the hockey rink P.A. and rendered all but inaudible by the ululations of the teenaged girls around me. It was only afterward, when I happened to walk past the bus terminal, that I glimpsed what had really just happened. There in the station were hundreds of youths, all speaking French, waiting to complete their pilgrimage by plunging back into the cold of northern Quebec. I had never seen so much long hair in one place in my life.

What was about to happen was an unprecedented contradiction in terms, mass bohemianism, and this is where the idea of ''pop'' became key. Pop is what the mod Oldham shared with the bohemian Stones, and what they in turn shared with the teenyboppers. Applied first to low-priced classical concerts and then to Tin Pan Alley product, the word was beginning to achieve more general cultural currency by the mid-Fifties, when London-based visual artists like Eduardo Paolozzi were proposing that a schlock form (e.g., science fiction pulp) might nurture ''a higher order of imagination'' than a nominally experimental one (e.g., little magazine). Shocking.

Youths like the Stones—who had never known a nonelectric culture, and who were no more wary of distribution and exposure in the modern media

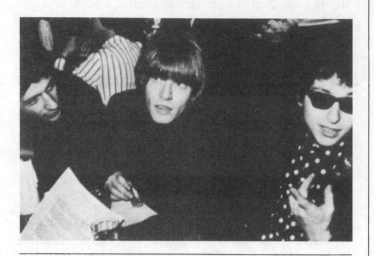

Brian Jones *(center)* with Bob Dylan and Gerold Schatzberg, attending a show by the Young Rascals, New York, 1965.

bath than they were of their own amps—automatically assumed what older artists formulated with such difficulty. Their pop sensibility led them to a decidedly nonslumming bohemianism—more unpretentious and déclassé than the widespread bohemianism of the Twenties. This was the gift of mass culture, compulsory education (especially English art-school routing) and consumer capitalism to five young men who comprised a social sample that would have been most unlikely, statistically, to group around the arts forty years before. Not that the Stones were untainted by avant-garde snobbishness—in their project of rebellious self-definition, exclusivity was a given. They never figured they'd spearhead a mass movement that went anywhere but record stores. That mass potential, however, was built into their penchant for pop itself.

There were solid economic reasons for the rise of mass bohemianism. Juxtapose a twenty-year rise in real income to the contradiction in which the straight-and-narrow worker/producer is required to turn into a hedonistic consumer off-hours, and perhaps countless kids, rather than assuming their production function on schedule, will choose to "fulfill themselves" outside the job market. But, traditionally, bohemian self-fulfillment has been achieved through, or at least in the presence of, art. Only popular culture could have rendered art accessible—in the excitement and inspiration (and self-congratulation) of its perception and the self-realization

Mick and Keith.

(or fantasy) of its creation—not just to well-raised well-offs but to the broad range of less statusy war babies who in fact made the hippie movement the relatively cross-class phenomenon it was. And for all these kids, popular culture meant rock & roll, the art form created by and for their hedonistic consumption. In turn, rock & roll meant the Rolling Stones.

Of course, it also meant the Beatles and Bob Dylan and the Who and the Grateful Dead—and Grand Funk Railroad. But the Beatles' appeal was too broad—parents liked them. Dylan's was too narrow—as an American bohemian, he remained suspicious of mass culture and stayed virtually out of sight from mid-1966 until the hippie thing was done with. The Who and the Dead hit a little too late to qualify as myths; they also proved a little too committed to the mass and the bohemianism, respectively, to challenge the Stones' breadth. And Grand Funk and so many others simply couldn't match the Stones' art.

From "Satisfaction" to the end of the decade, the Stones' aesthetic stature became more heroic. Their R&B phase began with two very good albums that culminated in a classic third, *The Rolling Stones, Now!* Then came their long middle period, beginning with two very good transitional LPs—*Out of Our Heads* and *December's Children (and Everybody's)*, both of which contained many R&B covers but sold on the strength of their originals—that seemed slightly thin only when compared to those that followed. *Aftermath, Between the Buttons, Beggar's Banquet* and *Let It Bleed* are all among the greatest rock albums, and *Flowers*, although it includes three previously released album cuts, sounds every bit as valid on its own. Furthermore, although the 3-D/psychedelic/year-in-the-making response to *Sgt. Pepper's Lonely Hearts Club Band, Their Satanic Majesties Request,* is remembered as a washout, the tunes prove remarkably solid and the concept legitimate in its tongue-in-cheekness. I would rank it as a first-rate oddity, and note that the title alone was the single greatest image manipulation in the Stones' whole history.

After "Satisfaction" it was difficult to accuse the Stones of imitation; after *Aftermath*, their music came almost entirely out of their heads. Blues-based hard rock it remained, with an eventual return to one black classic per album, but its texture was permanently enriched. As Brian daubed on occult instrumental colors (dulcimer, sitar, marimbas and bells, on *Aftermath* alone) and Charlie molded jazz chops to rock forms and Bill's bass gathered wit and Keith rocked roughly on, the group as a whole learned to respect and exploit (never revere) studio nuance. In the fall of 1967 they announced a split from Oldham, whose image-making services had become superfluous and whose record-producing capabilities they have since disparaged. They were making mature, resonant music by then—they could permit their pace changes some lyricism, there was warmth as well as white heat, and Mick's voice deepened, shedding some of its impertinence.

By proclamation and by vocal method—he slurs as a matter of conviction, articulating only catchphrases—Jagger belittles his own lyrics, an appropriate tack for a literate man who has bet his life on the comparative inexplicitness of music. Nonetheless, Jagger's lyrics were much like the Stones' music, aesthetically: pungent and vernacular ("Who wants yesterday's papers"); achieving considerable specificity with familiar materials ("You got me running like a cat in a thunderstorm"); and challenging conventional perceptions more by their bite than by any notable eloquence or profundity ("They just get married 'cause there's nothing else to do"). But whereas the Stones' music extended rock & roll usages, Jagger's lyrics often contravened them. He wrote more hate songs than love songs, and related tales of social and political breakdown with untoward glee. The hypocrisy and decay of the upper classes was a fave subject—many songs that seem basically antiwoman (although certainly not all of them) are actually more antirich. He was also capable of genuine gusto about sex (not as often as is thought, but consider the openhearted anticipation of "Goin' Home" or "Let's Spend the Night Together") and wrote the most accurate LSD song ever, "Something Happened to Me Yesterday."

But that was as far as it went. Traditionally, bohemian revolt has been aimed at nothing more fundamental than puritan morality and genteel culture. That's the way it was with the hippies, certainly, and that's the way it was with the Stones. They did show a class animus—even though it wasn't proletariat-versus-bourgeoisie ("Salt of the Earth" evokes that struggle no less sensitively than it evokes Jagger's distance from it), but rather the old enmity between the freemen of democratic England and its peerage—and a penchant for generalized social criticism. They earned their "political" aura. But their most passionate commitments were to sex, dope and lavish autonomy. Granted, this looked revolutionary enough to get them into plenty of trouble. The dope-bust harassment and persecution of individual Stones did keep the group from touring the States between 1966 and 1969. But their money and power prevailed; in the end, their absence and their apparent martyrdom only augmented their myth and their careers.

Throughout this time the Stones were heroes of mass bohemianism. They lived the life of art, their art got better all the time, and as it got better, remarkably enough, it reached more people. But although their art survives, its heroic quality does not; the Stones betray all the flaws of the counterculture they half-wittingly and -willingly symbolized. Their sex was too often sexist, their expanded consciousness too often a sordid escape; their rebellion was rooted in impulse to the exclusion of all habits of sacrifice, and their relationship to fame had little to

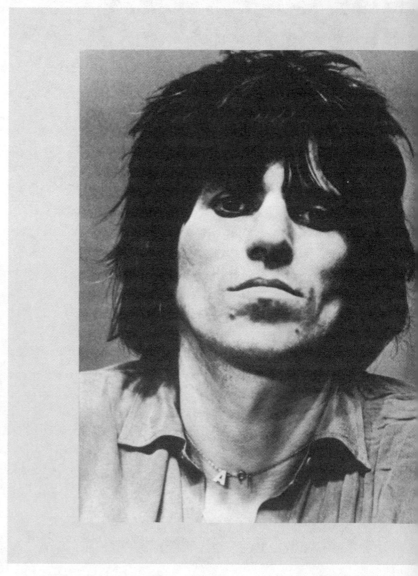

do with the responsibilities of leadership, or of allegiance.

Not that leadership was Mick's—or any ironist's—kind of thing. All he wanted was to have his ego massaged by his public or bathed in luxurious privacy as his own whim dictated. This he got, but it wasn't all roses; it was also dead flowers. Early on, in "Play with Fire" or "Back Street Girl," say, he had attacked decadence with a sneer—it was something that happened to others, especially the idle rich. By "Live with Me," or "Dancing with Mr. D.," the implication was that Mick's life of pop-star luxury was turning him into a decadent himself.

But if Mick was a decadent, he was also a professional. His project of radical self-definition flourished where so many others failed. Most bohemians can find ways to waste themselves—it's often fun for a while, and it's certainly easy. But the bohemian art hero has a polar option: to persist and make a career out of it, becoming more exemplary as his or her success becomes more unduplicable. Jagger's talent, his resilience, his sure pop instinct and a boom market in creativity all contributed to his singular

preeminence. Among the many who couldn't match up was Brian Jones. Originally the key to the Stones' rebel-purist image (and reality), he proved to be the group's natural decadent. Despite what those who consider Mick a prick suspect, it is rather unlikely that Brian was forced out of the group because his attraction to the bizarre endangered Mick's self-aggrandizing aesthetic calculations. Quite simply, he seems to have fucked and doped himself past all usefulness. Brian was one of the damned by choice of personality. He drowned in his own swimming pool on July 3rd, 1969.

Two days later the Stones introduced previously hired ex–John Mayall guitarist Mick Taylor at a free concert in Hyde Park that served as Brian's wake, and that November they commenced history's first mythic rock & roll tour. They hadn't swept the United States—or anywhere—in three years; the world had changed, or so it seemed; Woodstock hung in the air like a rainbow. It seemed only fitting to climax all that long-haired pomp and circumstance with yet another celebration of communal freeness. The result was Altamont—one murdered; total dead: four; 300,000 bummed out. It seems more a chilling metaphor than a literal disaster in retrospect, as much the Grateful Dead's fault as the Stones'. But the Stones are stuck with it—if it is typical of their genius that their responsibility is difficult to pinpoint, it is typical of their burden that everyone who's into blame blames them anyway.

In the end, though, that's typical of their genius too, for it means that whatever the specifics—pinpointing *is* always difficult—the Stones acknowledge their complicity in a world where evil exists. Above all, they are anything but utopians. They never made very convincing hippies because hippie just wasn't their thing. Jagger's taste for ecstatic community was tempered by that awareness of limits that always assured the Stones their formal acuteness. A successful artist may epitomize his or her audience, but that is a process of rarefaction; it doesn't mean conforming to the great mean, even of the time's bohemianism. So while it is true that the Stones' flaws and the counterculture's show a certain congruence, ultimately Mick is congruent to nothing—he always leaves himself an out. He doesn't condone the Midnight Rambler or Mister

Keith and Mick.

Jimmy, he just lays them bare. His gift is to make clear that even if the truth doesn't make you free, it needn't sap your will or your energy either. As with most bohemian rebels, his politics are indirect. He provides the information. The audience must then decide what to do with it.

Mick with Ahmet Ertegun, the president of Atlantic Records, where the band was given its own Rolling Stones label.

And yet that is perhaps too kind. Somewhere inside, the Stones knew that any undertaking as utopian as Altamont was doomed by definition. If their audience didn't understand it that way, it was because the Stones themselves, in all their multi-leveled contradiction, were unwilling to come out and tell them. They would suggest it, yes, embody it, but they wouldn't make it plain, because the nature of the Truth is that it isn't plain. If a male fan wants to take Mick's struggle with male persona as an invitation to midnight rambling, well, that's the nature of the game.

After Altamont the Stones played with a vengeance. *Sticky Fingers,* in April 1971, appeared to trifle with decadence just when some retribution seemed called for, and on its two greatest tracks, it definitely did. "Moonlight Mile" re-created all the paradoxical distances inherent in erotic love with a power worthy of Yeats, yet could also be interpreted as a cocaine song; "Brown Sugar," in which (if you listen with care to a rocker so compelling that it discourages exegesis) Jagger links his own music to the slave trade, exploits the racial and sexual contradictions of his stance even as it explore them. *Exile on Main Street,* released in conjunction with the 1972 American tour, was decadent in a more realized way: Weary and complicated, barely afloat in its

own drudgery, with Mick's voice submerged under layers of studio murk, it piled all the old themes—sex as power, sex as love, sex as pleasure, distance, craziness, release—on top of an obsession with time that was more than appropriate in men pushing thirty who were still committed to what was once considered youth music. Reviewed with some confusion when it came out, it was a certified classic within a year and is now remembered as their peak, the most consistently dense and various music of their career.

But as tuckered out as *Exile* initially seemed, it marked a peak only of the Stones' *recording* career—the one-decade marker in a show-biz saga that has now stretched on for two more. Like their partners in Altamont, the Grateful Dead, these quintessential rock & roll bohemians somehow evolved into quintessential rock & roll professionals. Quickly abandoning their halfhearted fantasies of a new cultural order, they went with the flow. *Sticky Fingers* and *Exile on Main Street* both featured Mick Taylor, a young veteran of the rock-concert tradition of the boogieing jam, and session horn men Bobby Keys and Jim Price; in a way they are both (*Exile* especially) triumphs of Taylor-Keys-Price–style musicianly craft over the kind of pop hero-mongering that can produce an Altamont. But if that's so, then *Goats Head Soup* and *It's Only Rock 'n Roll* are mere product, musicianly craft at its unheroic norm, terrific by the standards of Foghat or the Doobie Brothers but a nadir for the Stones. Even the peaks—"Starfucker" ("Star Star") and "If You Can't Rock Me," respectively—had déjà entendu musical and lyrical themes, and it's hard to imagine the Stones putting their names on tunes as tritely portentous as "Dancing with Mr. D." or "Time Waits for No One" in their prepro days. Only rock & roll indeed.

A similar distinction can be drawn betwen the 1972 and 1975 tours. In '72, the mood was friendly; "Sympathy for the Devil" was not performed; the gentle Taylor wafted through the proceedings; and Mick undercut his fabled demonism by playing the clown, the village idiot, the marionette. Very professional, yet their most rocking show ever. In 1975, with ex-Face Ron Wood aboard in place of Taylor, they worked even harder, but rather than celebrating professionalism they succumbed to it. Jagger's hyperactive stamina was an athletic marvel, but his moves often looked forced, and although Wood and

Richards often combined for a certain bumptious dirtiness, the musical energy seemed forced as well. But the 1976 album, *Black and Blue*, put these failures into context—it was a genuine if derivative departure, rock & roll that didn't deserve an "only." The 1978 tour was an improvement, especially when Mick stopped prancing long enough to pick up a guitar and get fresh with *Some Girls*. Almost certainly the best album of their second and third decades, *Some Girls* was at once a punk-inspired return to the casual spontaneity of their earliest recordings and a disco-inspired demonstration of their pop facility. "Miss You," promoted in dance clubs with a Bob Clearmountain–remixed 12-inch, ended up one of their biggest singles. Never again would anyone assume they were has-beens. Here was artistic professionalism at its best—creative ups and downs that engross an attentive audience as they divert a more casual one. Not what we want, maybe, but what we can use.

As his teeth got longer, Jagger liked to argue that music wasn't the exclusive province of the young by pointing to long-lived Chicago bluesmen like his supposed inspiration Muddy Waters. But he never demonstrated a willingness to settle for Muddy's market share. His theme song became the wicked "Start Me Up," which keynoted both the cannily crafted *Tattoo You* (1981) and the powerful live *Flashpoint* (1991): "Once you start me up I'll never stop." By the time of the Steel Wheels extravaganza of 1989, hooked to the mechanically crafted album of the same name and by some accounts the most lucrative rock tour in history, Jagger covered center field at Shea Stadium more enthusiastically than baseball players twenty years his junior. But his star receded as his heresy was institutionalized. After the group jumped to CBS for advances that gave accountants ulcers, Jagger surrounded the offhand but winningly basic *Dirty Work* (1986) with ambitious pop solo LPs that disappointed musically and commercially. Meanwhile, the estranged Richards validated his withdrawal from a notoriously unfor-

---

The Stones hit the road with characteristic understatement.

249

Jagger and Richards sharing a friendly moment, as the Stones announce their *Steel Wheels* Tour.

giving heroin habit by cutting the 1988 Virgin solo album *Talk Is Cheap,* which outsold Jagger's 1987 *Primitive Cool.* And in the course of the decade, long-time fans gradually concluded that if Jagger was the Stones' brain and Richards was the Stones' soul, the group's self was its rhythm section—especially the incomparable Charlie Watts, who overcame health problems to power the Steel Wheels Tour and is now widely considered the greatest rock drummer ever.

Only rock & roll? The Stones are the proof of the form. When the guitars and the drums and the voice come together in those elementary patterns that no one else has ever quite managed to simulate, the most undeniable excitement is a virtually automatic result. To insist that this excitement doesn't reach you is not to articulate an aesthetic judgment but to assert a rather uninteresting crotchet of taste. It is to boast that you don't like rock & roll itself.

DISCOGRAPHY

AMERICAN SINGLES

"Not Fade Away" (London; ☆48, 1964). "Tell Me (You're Coming Back)" (London; ☆24, 1964). "It's All Over Now" (London; ☆26, 1964). "Time Is on My Side" (London; ☆6, 1964). "Heart of Stone" (London; ☆19, 1965). "The Last Time" (London; ☆9, 1965). "(I Can't Get No) Satisfaction" (London; ☆1, 1965). "Get Off of My Cloud" (London; ☆1, 1965). "As Tears Go By" (London; ☆6, 1965). "19th Nervous Breakdown" (London; ☆2, 1966). "Paint It Black" (London; ☆1, 1966). "Mother's Little Helper" b/w "Lady Jane" (London; ☆8, 1966). "Have You Seen Your Mother, Baby, Standing in the Shadow" (London; ☆9, 1966). "Ruby Tuesday" b/w "Let's Spend the Night Together" (London; ☆1, 1967). "Dandelion" b/w "We Love You" (London; ☆14, 1967). "She's a Rainbow" (London; ☆25, 1967). "Jumpin' Jack Flash" (London; ☆3, 1968). "Street Fighting Man" (London; ☆48, 1968). "Honky Tonk Women" (London; ☆1, 1969). "Brown Sugar" (Rolling Stones; ☆1, 1971). "Wild Horses" (Rolling Stones; ☆28, 1971). "Tumbling Dice" (Rolling Stones; ☆7, 1972). "Happy" (Rolling Stones; ☆22, 1972). "You Can't Always Get What You Want" (London; ☆42, 1973). "Angie" (Rolling Stones; ☆1, 1973). "Doo Doo Doo Doo Doo (Heartbreaker)" (Rolling Stones; ☆15, 1974). "It's Only Rock 'n' Roll (but I Like It)" (Rolling Stones; ☆16, 1974). "Ain't Too Proud to Beg" (Rolling Stones; ☆17, 1974). "I Don't Know Why" (Abkco; ☆42, 1975). "Out of Time" (Abkco; ☆81, 1975). "Fool to Cry" (Rolling Stones; ☆10, 1976). "Hot Stuff" (Rolling Stones; ☆49, 1976). "Miss You" (Rolling Stones; ☆1, 1978). "Beast of Burden" (Rolling Stones; ☆8, 1978). "Shattered" (Rolling Stones; ☆31, 1978). "Emotional Rescue" (Rolling Stones; ☆3, 1980). "She's So Cold" (Rolling Stones; ☆26, 1980). "Start Me Up" (Rolling Stones; ☆2, 1981). "Waiting On a Friend" (Rolling Stones; ☆13, 1982). "Hang Fire" (Rolling Stones; ☆20, 1982). "Going to a Go-Go" (Rolling Stones; ☆25, 1982). "Undercover of the Night" (Rolling Stones; ☆9, 1983). "She Was Hot" (Rolling Stones; ☆44, 1984). "Harlem Shuffle" (Rolling Stones; ☆5, 1986). "One Hit (to the Body)" (Rolling Stones; ☆28, 1986). "Mixed Emotions" (Rolling Stones; ☆5, 1989). "Rock and a Hard Place" (Rolling Stones; ☆23, 1989). "Almost Hear You Sigh" (Rolling Stones; ☆50, 1990). "Highwire" (Rolling Stones; ☆57, 1991).

AMERICAN ALBUMS

The Rolling Stones (London; ☆11, 1964). *12 X 5* (London; ☆3, 1964). *The Rolling Stones, Now!* (London; ☆5, 1965). *Out of Our Heads* (London; ☆1, 1965). *December's Children (and Everybody's)* (London; ☆4, 1965). *Big Hits (High Tide and Green Grass)* (London; ☆3, 1966). *Aftermath* (London; ☆2, 1966). *Got Live If You Want It!* (London; ☆6, 1966). *Between the Buttons* (London; ☆2, 1967). *Flowers* (London; ☆3, 1967). *Their Satanic Majesties Request* (London; ☆2, 1967). *Beggar's Banquet* (London; ☆5, 1968). *Through the Past Darkly (Big Hits Vol. 2)* (London; ☆2, 1969). *Let It Bleed* (London; ☆3, 1969). *"Get Yer Ya-Ya's Out!"* (London; ☆6, 1970). *Sticky Fingers* (Rolling Stones; ☆1, 1971). *Hot Rocks 1964–1971* (London; ☆4, 1972). *Exile on Main Street* (Rolling Stones; ☆1, 1972). *More Hot Rocks (Big Hits and Fazed Cookies)* (London; ☆9, 1972). *Goats Head Soup* (Rolling Stones; ☆1, 1973). *It's Only Rock 'n Roll* (Rolling Stones; ☆1, 1974). *Metamorphosis* (Abkco; ☆8, 1975). *Made in the Shade* (Rolling Stones; ☆6, 1975). *Black and Blue* (Rolling Stones; ☆1, 1976). *Love You Live* (Rolling Stones; ☆5, 1977). *Some Girls* (Rolling Stones; ☆1, 1978). *Emotional Rescue* (Rolling Stones; ☆1, 1980). *Sucking in the Seventies* (Rolling Stones; ☆15, 1981). *Tattoo You* (Rolling Stones; ☆1, 1981). *"Still Life" (American Concert 1981)* (Rolling Stones; ☆5, 1982). *Undercover* (Rolling Stones; ☆4, 1983). *Rewind (1971–1984)* (Rolling Stones; ☆86, 1984). *Dirty Work* (Rolling Stones; ☆4, 1986). *Singles Collection: The London Years* (Abkco; ☆91, 1989). *Steel Wheels* (Rolling Stones; ☆3, 1989). *Flashpoint* (Columbia/Sony; ☆16, 1991).

MICK JAGGER

She's the Boss (Columbia; ☆14, 1985). *Primitive Cool* (Columbia; ☆41, 1987).

KEITH RICHARDS

Talk Is Cheap (Virgin; ☆24, 1988). With the X-Pensive Winos: *Live at the Hollywood Palladium, December 15, 1988* (Virgin, 1991).

(Chart positions compiled from Joel Whitburn's *Record Research*, based on *Billboard*'s Pop and LPs charts.)

Aging idols of mass bohemianism. The Stones around the time of *Black and Blue*, with Mick Taylor's replacement, Ron Wood *(second from left)*, behind a vacant Keith Richards.

THE SOUND OF TEXAS

BY ED WARD

Texas has a little bit of everything, and its music reflects its diversity as well as its size. Spaniards, Germans, Anglos, Czechs, Chicanos, Blacks—each has played a part in shaping the popular music of the Lone Star State.

Western swing, the first distinctively Texan music to gain national popularity (in the late Thirties), was as polyglot as it was unmistakable. A hybrid of big-band jazz and Anglo-American reels, it transformed the course of American country music, and later, Texan Ernest Tubb made honky-tonk dance tunes one of the staples of modern Nashville.

Texas musicians also played a major role in setting the course of black music, from the early recordings of "Ragtime Texas" Henry Thomas, with his archaic panpipe-accompanied songs, to the postwar hits of T-Bone Walker, with his influential electric guitar stylings. The first stronghold for rhythm & blues in Texas was Houston, the home of Don D. Robey's Duke and Peacock labels. For nearly a quarter of a century, starting in the early Fifties, Robey released black popular music on Duke and black gospel music on Peacock. Peacock boasted one of the strongest rosters in the field, with gospel stars like the Dixie Hummingbirds and the Mighty Clouds of Joy, while Duke relied largely on the drawing

power of its two big names, Bobby "Blue" Bland and Junior Parker.

Throughout the late Fifties and early Sixties these two urban stylists, both graduates of the late Forties/early Fifties Memphis blues scene, almost single-handedly kept the blues alive as a popular form. Bland in particular enjoyed a long string of hits ("Farther Up the Road," "I Pity the Fool," "Turn On Your Lovelight") that showcased his gravelly voice on moody ballads as well as shouting blues (one of Bland's idols was Perry Como). Parker, by contrast, stuck closer to the style of Chicago blues, although he, too, managed to score hits with brisk, uptempo shuffles like "Next Time You See Me" and soulful ballads like "Driving Wheel." Other Duke-Peacock artists included Willie Mae "Big Mama" Thornton, whose original "Hound Dog" in 1953 inspired you-know-who; Johnny Ace, an immensely popular bal-

---

The Red-Headed Stranger, playing for the taxman.

The great Bobby "Blue" Bland (right) with John Doe.

ladeer until his death (reportedly while playing Russian roulette) on Christmas Eve 1954; and O. V. Wright, an early exponent of soul in the Sixties who later became one of the first singers produced by Willie Mitchell in Memphis.

While rhythm & blues together with country & western flourished in Texas throughout the Fifties, the region's rock scene was thin, if vital. There wasn't much rockabilly around, although Buddy Knox, Jimmy Bowen and especially Buddy Holly made their marks nationally with an understated "Tex-Mex" blend of country rock. Beaumont's Moon Mullican, "King of the Hillbilly Piano Players" and a key influence on Jerry Lee Lewis, tried his hand at rock in the mid-Fifties, as did George Jones, but neither met with much success outside of the country market.

The first wave of Texas rock only really arrived with Houston producer Huey P. "Crazy Cajun" Meaux, who started producing records in 1959, working out of his barbershop in Winnie. Meaux's first hits were Jivin' Gene's "Breaking Up Is Hard to Do" and Joe Barry's "I'm a Fool to Care," followed by Barbara Lynn's "You'll Lose a Good Thing" and Roy Head's "Treat Her Right" (released on Don Robey's Back Beat label). All were ultimately leased to larger labels, but Meaux's outlook was basically

regional—and specifically Cajun—so many of his early efforts, cut in Ville Platte, Louisiana, or at Cosimo Matassa's studio in New Orleans, never got beyond the Texas-Louisiana area.

Still, the combination of Cajun style and Texas talent kept Meaux on the national charts. In 1963 he was riding high: "I had Dale and Grace at Number One," he recalls, "Sunny and the Sunliners' 'Talk to Me,' and eight or nine other records on the different charts in one week, and then the Beatles came along and wiped me off the fuckin' map." Not to be outdone by a bunch of upstart limeys, Meaux headed for San Antonio, his car crammed with Thunderbird wine and every Beatles record he could find. Once there, he locked himself in a motel room, vowing not to leave until he had discovered the secret formula. His conclusion: "The beat was *on the beat,* just like a Cajun two-step." His solution: to call up a San Antonio kid named Doug Sahm, who'd been badgering Meaux to record him. "I tole him, git me a tune, grow some fuckin' hair, and let's go cut some of this shit."

Sahm lost no time in assembling a crack band of some of San Antonio's finest musicians, including keyboard player Augie Meyers. Billed as "The Sir

Junior Parker, clutching a chromatic harmonica. Onstage, a valet delivered his harp to him on a velvet pillow.

Huey Meaux (center) with Sunny Ozuna—of Sunny and the Sunliners—and Jane Doe. In 1963 Sunny had the most popular conjunto in San Antonio; that same year Meaux's producing and hustling helped get Sunny's Tex-Mex sound onto the Top Forty.

Meaux's partner gave a teenage girl a lift to the convention, where she proceeded to set up shop as a prostitute, keeping a diary the whole time. When she returned to Texas, the diary was confiscated by federal officials in connection with another crime she had committed, and Meaux was subsequently indicted, along with his partner, for conspiracy to violate the Mann Act. Meaux did fourteen months in prison. The experience so embittered him that he didn't find his way back to the pop charts until 1975, when "Before the Next Teardrop Falls," a record Meaux cut with Chicano singer Freddy Fender, became a giant country and pop hit.

They pretended they were British, but San Antonio was home: the Sir Douglas Quintet, 1965.

Douglas Quintet," and promoted by Meaux as a new English group, they had a hit on their first try, "She's About a Mover." The sham was quickly exposed, but not until the band was well established. Unfortunately, a marijuana setup in Corpus Christi abruptly terminated their Texas career. Bedeviled by legal harassments and attracted by the lure of San Francisco, Sahm turned his back on the Longhorn State. Working out of San Francisco, he recorded several delightful albums for Mercury, as well as another hit single, "Mendocino."

Meanwhile, Meaux had set himself up with a new recording studio and a corporation, and had found a new performer, Billy Joe (B. J.) Thomas, a young Houstonian who fronted a show band called the Triumphs. The Triumphs cut an excellent R&B-pop album for Meaux, but Thomas resisted adding a version of Hank Williams's "I'm So Lonesome I Could Cry," though he later agreed, to placate what he assumed were Meaux's countrified sensibilities. Huey jumped on the track as a single, and when it shot to the top, he had another star on his hands.

A trip to the 1966 Country Music Disc Jockey's Convention in Nashville proved to be his undoing.

By the late Sixties the Texas rock scene Meaux had revitalized was a shambles. Most of the state's native talent had headed for the West Coast, where the drug laws were more liberal and the opportunities to record more abundant. In San Francisco such Texans as Janis Joplin (from Port Arthur), Doug Sahm and various members of Mother Earth and the Steve Miller Band held forth; and in Los Angeles, the Bobby Fuller Four had a hit with "I Fought the Law," cut in an updated Buddy Holly vein.

Those who stayed either ended up in trouble or languished in obscurity until being "discovered." In 1966 and 1967 the region briefly sprouted a host of "psychedelic" bands, recorded by International Artists, a Houston-based label. The most prominent

Johnny Winter, albino blues legend, with Clive Davis, then president of Columbia Records.

among these Lone Star acid rockers was the Austin-based 13th Floor Elevator; but the group, hounded by narcotics agents, never really broke nationally, and their lead singer, Roky Erickson, ended up spending three years at Rusk State Hospital, a mental institution. (After being rediscovered in the post-punk era, however, Erickson was finally vindicated when an old fan with a responsible position at Warner Bros. Records, Bill Bentley, put together a tribute album of Roky's Elevators and post-Elevators songs, performed by a cross section of contemporary talent ranging from ZZ Top to R.E.M. to the Butthole Surfers, thereby giving the world a long, hard look at Erickson's songwriting talent.) Other Texas talent fared better. Soon after ROLLING STONE published an article on the Texas rock scene that singled out an obscure local guitarist, Johnny Winter, he was plucked from the state, handed a fat record contract and sent out on the road to superstardom. It was a route later retraced by such blues-based Texas acts as ZZ Top, one of the most popular boogie bands of the Seventies.

Unfortunately, neither Winter nor ZZ Top evidenced much of the country-blues-Cajun-Tex-Mex crossbreeding that has been the distinctive hallmark of Texas popular music. ZZ Top could have come from anywhere but still dressed like Texas eccentrics, which proved to be to their advantage with the coming of MTV. With a canny use of videos, and with synthesizers and sequencers augmenting their sound, ZZ Top burned up the charts in the mid-Eighties with such albums as *Eliminator* (1983) and *Afterburner* (1985).

Down in Austin, Willie Nelson, a veteran of the Nashville songwriting wars, proved to be the catalyst for a whole new development in Texas music, once again in the area of country music. Nelson had moved back home to Texas after his Nashville house burned down, and he liked it so much that he decided to stay. In Austin he met Eddie Wilson, a former PR man for the Texas beer industry, who had rented a former National Guard armory and rechristened it Armadillo World Headquarters. Wilson knew that local longhairs were getting into country music, and that Willie Nelson, a closet liberal, was a hero to almost every political faction in town. He also figured that a Nelson concert would unite these factions, and so in July 1972 he tried out the idea of a country-rock concert, headlined by Nelson, at Armadillo World Headquarters. It was a wild success.

Similar concerts followed, and Nelson himself inaugurated an annual Fourth of July festival. These events featured a wide range of Texas talent, running the gamut from the rock of Augie Meyers's Western Head Band to the hard-edge country & western of Waylon Jennings, from the country-oriented pop of singer-songwriter Jerry Jeff Walker to the resurrected Western swing of Asleep at the Wheel.

The success of the "progressive country" movement within the state could be laid at the feet of the Texan love of tradition, a love that cuts across the barriers of age and culture. Outside the state, though, the movement succeeded in wresting country music away from the "countrypolitan" sound of

ZZ Top in their early days.

Waylon Jennings, a leading country music "outlaw" in the Seventies.

Kenny Rogers (ironically, a Houstonian) and Dolly Parton, and turning it back toward tradition. Although the main thrust of the movement in Texas was spent by 1980, all of its main players (Waylon Jennings, Guy Clark, Jerry Jeff Walker) enjoy international reputations, and Nelson went on to become not only a recording superstar but a pretty decent actor. Unfortunately, he was not as lucky with his financial advisors, and in 1990 the Internal Revenue Service seized most of his property, including his recording studio and all but one of his guitars, to pay off approximately $18 million in unpaid income tax.

By the time of progressive country's demise, however, the focus in Austin, long the state's musical capitol, had shifted to new wave and blues. Blues had been cooking since the mid-Seventies at Antone's, a semi-seedy club run by Clifford Antone, the heir to a Houston delicatessen fortune. Losing money by the bucketload, he'd bring in the blues idols he'd discovered in college—Jimmy Reed, Buddy Guy, B. B. King, Otis Rush—and have them play at the club, alternating sets with the house band, the Fabulous Thunderbirds. Elsewhere in town, the Triple Threat Revue featured a young local bluesman, W. C. Clark, a powerhouse singer, Lou Ann Barton, and a strong guitarist, Stevie Ray Vaughan, younger brother of the Thunderbirds' Jimmie Vaughan. By the early Eighties the Thunderbirds were recording for Chrysalis Records and had become a cult favorite in the United States and Europe; Stevie Ray Vaughan and his new band, Double Trouble, had been signed by the venerable John Hammond to Epic Records and went on to become a major arena attraction. By the decade's end, Clifford Antone had moved his club into a much nicer location near the University of Texas, the Thunderbirds were a well-established act, and many of the other people from the scene were recording for Antone's Records. In 1990 Jimmie Vaughan left the Fabulous Thunderbirds and, while rethinking his career, made an album with his brother. Before it could be released, though, tragedy struck: On August 27th, 1990, the helicopter carrying Stevie Ray Vaughan from a concert in Wisconsin crashed into the side of a mountain, killing all aboard.

The Texas punk and new-wave scenes didn't make nearly the impact the blues scene did, at least in part because the bands involved were so idiosyncratic. It was only in retrospect that the odd funk-punk fusion of the Big Boys caused their records to become collectors' items, and it took nearly a decade for the Butthole Surfers to become college radio darlings. The two biggest acts to come out of the movement, not unsurprisingly, were steeped in tradition. Brave Combo were so called because the Denton, Texas, quartet played punk clubs, but played mostly polkas (with some cha-chas, horas and tangos thrown in) when they did so. Oddly, they caught on not only locally but nationally, with leader Carl Finch becoming a musical contributor and creative consultant for David Byrne's film *True Stories,* and the band eventually even finding its way into the hearts of America's orthodox polka fans. Joe "King" Carrasco played polkas, too, but mostly what he played was Tex-Mex pop music with a new-wave freneticism. An Anglo native of Dumas, he and his band the Crowns caught on first in England, where they were signed to Stiff Records, but over the years they've become party favorites all across the United States too.

So far in the Nineties the biggest act to emerge from Texas has been one that epitomizes the cross-cultural fusion that has always made the state's music unique. The Texas Tornadoes feature two ex-members of the Sir Douglas Quintet, Doug Sahm and Augie Meyers, with Tex-Mex rocker-turned-country-crooner Freddy Fender and San Antonio *conjunto* accordion master Flaco Jimenez. Each had to compromise slightly to make the mixture work, but it's obvious that they've succeeded in doing what Texas popular musicians have always done—pumping new blood into an old form.

The Texas Tornados: old-timers creating the sound of the new Texas.

DISCOGRAPHY

SINGLES (1957–1967)

Joe Berry: "I'm a Fool to Care" (Smash; r☆15, ☆24, 1961). **Bobby Bland:** "Farther Up the Road" (Duke; r☆1, ☆43, 1957). "Lead Me On" (Duke; r☆9, 1960). "Cry Cry Cry" (Duke; r☆9, 1960). "I Pity the Fool" (Duke; r☆1, ☆46, 1961). "Don't Cry No More" (Duke; r☆2, 1961). "Turn On Your Love Light" (Duke; r☆2, ☆28, 1961). "Ain't That Loving You" (Duke; r☆9, 1962). "Stormy Monday Blues" (Duke; r☆5, ☆43, 1962). "That's the Way Love Is" b/w "Call On Me" (Duke; r☆1, ☆22, 1963). "Ain't Nothing You Can Do" (Duke; ☆20, 1964). "Share Your Love with Me" (Duke; ☆42, 1964). "Ain't Doing Too Bad" (Duke; ☆49, 1964). "These Hands (Small but Mighty)" (Duke; r☆4, 1965). "I'm Too Far Gone (to Turn Around)" (Duke; r☆8, 1966). "Good Time Charlie" (Duke; r☆6, 1966). "Poverty" (Duke; r☆9, 1966). **Dale and Grace:** "I'm Leaving It Up to You" (Montel; r☆6, ☆1, 1963). "Stop and Think It Over" (Montel; ☆8, 1964). **Bobby Fuller Four:** "I Fought the Law" (Mustang; ☆9, 1966). "Love's Made a Fool of You" (Mustang; ☆26, 1966). **Roy Head:** "Treat Her Right" (Back Beat; r☆2, ☆2, 1965). **Barbara Lynn:** "You'll Lose a Good Thing" (Jamie; r☆1, ☆8, 1962.) **Little Junior Parker:** "Driving Wheel" (Duke; r☆5, 1961). "In the Dark" (Duke; r☆7, 1961). "Annie Get Your Yo-Yo" (Duke; r☆6, 1962). **Sir Douglas Quintet:** "She's About a Mover" (Tribe; ☆13, 1965). "The Rains Came" (Tribe; ☆31, 1966). **Sunny and the Sunglows:** "Talk to Me" (Tear Drop; r☆12, ☆11, 1963). **Sunny and the Sunliners:** "Rags to Riches" (Tear Drop; ☆45, 1963). **B. J. Thomas:** "I'm So Lonesome I Could Cry" (Scepter; ☆8, 1966). "Mama" (Scepter; ☆22, 1966). **O. V. Wright:** "You're Gonna Make Me Cry" (Back Beat; r☆6, 1965). "Eight Men, Four Women" (Back Beat; r☆4, 1967).

ALBUMS

Bobby Bland: *The Best of Bobby Bland* (MCA; 1974). **Junior Parker:** *The Best of Junior Parker* (MCA; 1973). **Bobby Fuller Four:** *The Best of the Bobby Fuller Four* (Rhino; 1987). **Johnny Winter:** *Guitar Slinger* (Alligator; 1984). **ZZ Top:** *The Best of ZZ Top* (Warner Bros.; 1979). **Fabulous Thunderbirds:** *The Essential Fabulous Thunderbird Collection* (Epic; 1991). **Texas Tornadoes:** *Texas Tornadoes* (Warner Bros.; 1990).

(Chart positions compiled from Joel Whitburn's *Record Research,* based on *Billboard*'s Pop chart, unless otherwise indicated; r☆ = position on *Billboard*'s Rhythm & Blues chart.)

SOUL

BY PETER GURALNICK

The business of soul music was salvation. "There's a song that I sing," preached Solomon Burke in the aptly named "Everybody Needs Somebody to Love," "and I believe if everybody was to sing this song, it would save the whole world." "I'm not singing this song for myself now," James Brown declared in his celebrated live version of "Lost Someone." "I'm singing it for you, too." Both the mood and the message were unashamedly apocalyptic, as the music borrowed not only from the gospel changes that Ray Charles (followed in short order by both Brown and Sam Cooke) had introduced into rhythm & blues but from the iconography of the church as well.

James Brown, tottering offstage, clothed in his royal cloak, staged a drama of personal redemption every night. Wilson Pickett, an ex-Violinaire and an extravagant admirer of the Reverend Julius Cheeks, electrified audiences with his throaty cries, raspy screams and clumsy holiness dance. Sam Cooke brought the achingly sweet harmonies of the famous Soul Stirrers and the urbane manner of the successful preacher to a lay congregation. Otis Redding maintained that same well-fed dignity with his shiny suits and dramatically halting diction, while

Joe Tex, the master rapper, ironically enough ordained as a Muslim minister after his popularity had passed, personified the slick deacon who has been a figure in black mythology since slavery time. And Solomon Burke—King Solomon—a licensed mortician, a minister in his own family's House of God for All People since he was twelve, dispensed his secular message like a bishop bestowing blessings on a starved and clamoring multitude. Soul music was indeed a serious business.

It was a peculiarly good-hearted and optimistic

260

sort of music, and it is no accident that its popularity was limited to the early and middle Sixties, a time when awakening black pride went hand in hand with civil rights activism and racial progress seemed more real than illusory. It may have been liberal "goodwill" that caused soul to make such a dent in

Soul—secularized church music with a down-home approach—practiced here by Wilson Pickett *(left)*, Esther Phillips and Percy Sledge.

the popular charts (plus the discovery by groups like the Rolling Stones of artists such as Solomon Burke and Otis Redding). The music itself sprang from the deepest wellsprings of the black experience in this country—an experience that revealed a people so resourceful in their adaptation to an alien culture and an alien environment as to create a richly expressive language of their own, from which white society continues to draw today. It was this language that was the basis for soul music, and in this sense soul must be seen as a kind of conscious anachronism, a prideful return to roots that sought in its own way to reverse a century-old impulse toward assimilation into the so-called mainstream of white society.

In this sense it can also be seen why soul music—with its insistence on a unified tradition, stylistic purity and a determinedly down-home approach—was doomed to early extinction. Like the Chicago blues style that developed in the late Forties, and even the white rockabilly sound that came out of Memphis in the Fifties, it was music of too singular a purpose to adapt to changing trends and styles. In

an even closer parallel to blues and rockabilly, nearly all the artists who joined to create this common style came under the aegis of a single record company. With blues it was Chicago's Chess Records; with rockabilly, Sam Phillips's tiny Sun label in Memphis. In the case of soul, Atlantic was the label. Atlantic vice president Jerry Wexler was the catalyst, and Solomon Burke, Otis Redding, Wilson Pickett and Joe Tex were the chief protagonists in the evolution of a style. It is an intricate and fascinating story that can only be sketched out in these pages.

S oul started, in a sense, with the 1961 success of Solomon Burke's "Just Out of Reach (of My Two Open Arms)." Ray Charles, of course, had already enjoyed enormous success (also on Atlantic), as had James Brown and Sam Cooke,

Solomon Burke, an impassioned preacher.

primarily in a pop vein. Each of these singers, though, could be looked upon as an isolated phenomenon; it was only with the coming together of Burke and Atlantic Records that you could begin to see anything even resembling a movement.

Solomon Burke had recorded for a number of years for Apollo, in both gospel and secular modes, but it wasn't until his second Atlantic release that he was to achieve any degree of success. Oddly enough, it was with a country song, though this is not so odd in Jerry Wexler's view. "The changes, the structure, the whole feel are just about identical in gospel and country music." This is a perception Ray Charles would capitalize on just months later for ABC Records, but Solomon Burke—with his smooth, lush voice, his suggestion of a barely suppressed power and his easy mastery of all the gospel effects from impassioned sermonizing to lullingly melodic interludes to rumbling bass notes—was just as well equipped to prove it. In any case he enjoyed considerable success in 1961 and 1962, but it was with his fifth big hit on Atlantic in 1963 that he consolidated his style.

"One day," says Jerry Wexler, "a tape came in from Detroit with eight songs on it. One of the songs was 'If You Need Me,' which was the only one that impressed me. The singer on the demo was Wilson Pickett."

What happened next is both interesting and historically significant. "If You Need Me" is a classic of the soul genre, with a fervent message, sincere spoken passage and strict gospel changes. Atlantic bought the publishing rights immediately but somehow neglected to purchase rights to the demo. They recorded Solomon's impassioned interpretation, put it in the can, and then before it was even released discovered that Pickett's original master was being marketed by Lloyd Price and Harold Logan. Jerry Wexler tried frantically to block the release, because "I would say that Pickett's record had the edge over ours." When he failed, "I went to work on that record. That record put me back into promotion, got me back into the studio, into the excitement of the record business, everything." It also got Solomon Burke a big hit, and it even brought Wilson Pickett to Atlantic eventually. Two years later, "Pickett himself comes into the office with a tape under his arm. I said, 'Man, aren't you sore?' And he said, 'That's in the past.'"

Pickett, the Wicked Pickett, was a much more

Wilson "the Wicked" Pickett's "In the Midnight Hour" is one of the biggest soul hits of all time.

volatile singer than Solomon Burke, more overtly emotional, perhaps more viscerally exciting, less controlled in his use of vocal and dramatic effects. After a couple of singles that didn't do anything, Wexler took Pickett down to the Memphis studio of Stax Records, which in the first six months of 1965 had already recorded "That's How Strong My Love Is," "Mr. Pitiful," "I've Been Loving You Too Long" and "Respect," all by the relatively unknown Macon singer, onetime Little Richard imitator, Otis Redding. Atlantic had had a distribution deal with Stax since 1960, which meant that Booker T. and the MGs, Rufus and Carla Thomas, William Bell and later Sam and Dave would all be connected in one way or another with Atlantic Records. As part of that deal, Otis Redding's first album even appeared on the Atlantic subsidiary, Atco, and working arrangements between Atlantic and Stax were very close. To Jerry Wexler's ear, Stax had the hard-edged sound he was looking to find for Wilson Pickett. He was evidently right. Pickett and guitarist Steve Cropper sat down to work out a rhythmic idea Pickett had been carrying around in his head for some time. The result was "In the Midnight Hour," one of the biggest soul hits of all time.

Ironically enough, there were only three or four more Atlantic sessions at the Stax studio. Whether due to the success of Pickett's single, or to a more complicated business disagreement, Stax barred Atlantic artists from coming in and cutting records from that point on. The result was that Jerry Wexler cast about for another soulful location and eventually settled on a little studio in Florence, Alabama, properly called Fame Recording Studios, but better known as Muscle Shoals, after a slightly less obscure neighboring town. Fame in the early Sixties had enjoyed considerable success with independent leasing arrangements on Arthur Alexander and Jimmy Hughes (who appeared on their own Fame label). They enjoyed even greater success with Joe Tex, still another gospel-oriented singer with strong

Southern roots who came to Atlantic through Buddy Killens's Dial Records, which switched distribution to Atlantic toward the end of 1964.

Joe Tex was a journeyman musician who had been hovering on the edge of the business for ten years when he came to Muscle Shoals. He had recorded in every variety of style, from rock & roll to James Brown's "crying" blues, but it was in Muscle Shoals that he found a groove of his own. Not as sober as Solomon Burke nor as unrestrained as Wilson Pickett, he introduced an element of worldliness in the sly asides and epigrammatic wit that crept into heartfelt preachments like "Hold What You've Got" and "Don't Make Your Children Pay," as well as later comic sermons like "Skinny Legs and All."

His success at Muscle Shoals was duplicated only by Wilson Pickett, who, starting with his January 1966 session, produced "Land of 1000 Dances" and "Mustang Sally," worthy successors to "In the Midnight Hour," and a host of later hits. (Muscle Shoals itself is a whole other story, but it should be noted that Rick Hall's Fame Recording Studios, and its equally renowned offshoot Muscle Shoals Sound, set the standard for production in what was left of the soul era and remains to this day a source of some of the finest, and funkiest, music to come out of the South.)

It was shortly after Pickett's first session that Fame's studio musicians cut a record behind an unknown local singer named Percy Sledge. That record was "When a Man Loves a Woman," which, with its Bach-like organ, soaring vocal and frequently imitated church feel, might be defined as the quintessential soul sound. Then in February 1967 Jerry Wexler brought down a newly signed artist for her first Atlantic recording session. This was an artist for whom everyone had been predicting stardom ever since she first started recording commercially seven

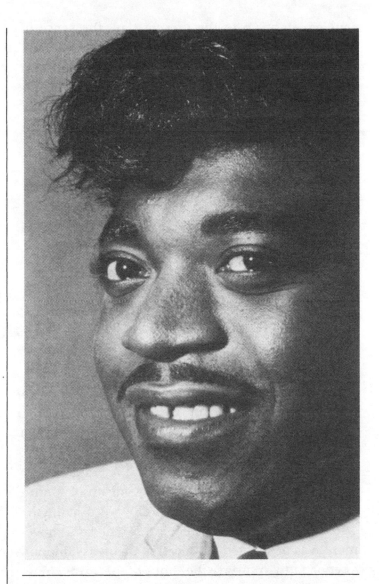

Percy Sledge. His biggest hit, "When a Man Loves a Woman," captured the quintessential soul sound.

years earlier. Although she had been in the business all her life she had never, it was said, lived up to her potential. The artist was Aretha Franklin; the session produced her epochal recordings, "I Never Loved a Man (the Way I Love You)" and "Do Right Woman—Do Right Man."

That in a way was the end of the soul era proper. Not that it vanished in a puff of smoke. Certainly artists like Wilson Pickett, Joe Tex and even Solomon Burke in his sporadic comebacks continued to enjoy considerable popularity. Nor was Aretha's style any radical departure from the soul sound that had preceded it. Reared in the church, she was as down-home and funky, as plain-spoken and spiritually uplifted as any of the soulmen. No, it wasn't so much that Aretha departed from a style as that by her genius she defined it. Her success, both artistic and commercial, swept away everything in its wake, and while there have been scattered echoes of the

From left: King Curtis, Aretha Franklin and Joe Tex in rehearsal for "Soul Together," Madison Square Garden, 1968.

soul era right up to the present day, the sense of common purpose that had animated the movement for three or four years was gone, the almost uniform level of achievement suddenly shattered by the entrance of someone so uniquely gifted, so transcendent in her art that all others were dwarfed by comparison.

Don Covay, an Atlantic artist and prolific songwriter.

Several other factors entered into it, too, of course. Solomon Burke had departed from Atlantic by 1969, Wilson Pickett and Joe Tex by 1973. Stax ended its distribution arrangement with Atlantic in 1968, shortly after Otis Redding died in a plane crash in December 1967. More than anything else, though, what seems to me to have brought the era of soul to a grinding, unsettling halt was the death of Martin Luther King, Jr. in April 1968, following as it did the 1965 assassination of Malcolm X. The soul movement was predicated too much upon an assumption of good faith to survive the shock of that awakening, and it was succeeded shortly in logical enough fashion by more militant declarations of identity, starting with Soul Brother Number One James Brown's strident anthem, ''Say It Loud—I'm Black and I'm Proud.''

Clarence Carter, perhaps best known for his single ''Patches.''

While it lasted, though, it was a period of remarkable creativity and solidarity. Soul music at its height, like the anonymous church art of the Middle Ages, came to have a stylistic definition of its own. There were soul classics from such obscure artists as Jesse James, Phil Flowers, Freddy Scott, Laura Lee and Aretha's sister Erma, as well as better known ones like James Carr, Clarence Carter, and the man

who claims to have started it all, Little Richard. There was a Soul Clan organized by Atlantic artist and prolific songwriter Don Covay, and consisting for one session of Covay, Solomon Burke, Otis Redding protégé Arthur Conley, Joe Tex and Ben E. King. There was a time when you could listen to the radio and hear song after song in the familiar gospel-oriented vein. It came to matter hardly at all which artist was identified with which song, so strong was the style itself, and even the disc jockeys were inspired to join the soul movement with their exhortations, interpolations and vivid displays of verbal invention. It was a whole gaudy panoply in which the singer and his audience were equally caught up, an occasion in live performance for celebration and good feeling. And the atmosphere at those Saturday night meetings was not much different than church on Sunday, with an audience that cut across lines of class and age, dressed up in their Sunday best and prepared to *testify*. It was a family audience, well mannered, well behaved, spanning three generations but expecting to work hard, and their shouts, moans, groans and good-natured cries of approval

Arthur Conley, the soul singing protégé of Otis Redding.

indicated that they expected the singer to work hard, too. For a white outsider it was like being carried along by an ineluctable tide, and the only response possible was to ride helplessly, un-self-consciously, somehow comforted by the overwhelming feeling of community. For me that was soul music, more than twenty years ago.

DISCOGRAPHY

SINGLES
Solomon Burke: ''Just Out of Reach'' (Atlantic; r☆7, ☆24, 1961). ''Cry to Me'' (Atlantic; r☆5, ☆44, 1962). ''I'm Hanging Up My Heart for You'' b/w ''Down in the Valley'' (Atlantic; r☆15, 1962). ''If You Need Me'' (Atlantic; r☆2, ☆37, 1963). ''You're Good for Me'' (Atlantic; r☆8, ☆49, 1963). ''He'll Have to Go'' (Atlantic; ☆51, 1964). ''Goodbye Baby (Baby Goodbye)'' (Atlantic; ☆33, 1964). ''Everybody Needs Somebody to Love''

(Atlantic; ☆58, 1964). "The Price" (Atlantic; ☆57, 1964). "Got to Get You off My Mind" (Atlantic; r☆1, ☆22, 1965). "Tonight's the Night" (Atlantic; r☆2, ☆28, 1965). "Someone Is Watching" (Atlantic; r☆24, 1965). "Keep a Light in the Window till I Come Home" (Atlantic; r☆15, 1967). "Take Me (Just as I Am)" (Atlantic; r☆11, ☆49, 1967). "Proud Mary" (Bell; r☆15, ☆45, 1969). **Clarence Carter:** "Slip Away" (Atlantic; r☆2, ☆6, 1968). "Too Weak to Fight" (Atlantic; r☆3, ☆13, 1968). "Snatching It Back" (Atlantic; r☆4, ☆31, 1969). "The Feeling Is Right" (Atlantic; r☆9, 1969). "Doin' Our Thing" (Atlantic; r☆9, ☆46, 1969). **Don Covay and the Goodtimers:** "Mercy, Mercy" (Rosemart; ☆35, 1964). "Please Do Something" (Atlantic; r☆21, 1965). "Seesaw" (Atlantic; r☆5, ☆44, 1965). **Wilson Pickett:** "If You Need Me" (Double-L; r☆30, 1963). "It's Too Late" (Double-L; r☆7, ☆49, 1963). "In the Midnight Hour" (Atlantic; r☆1, ☆21, 1965). "Don't Fight It" (Atlantic; r☆4, 1965). "634-5789" (Atlantic; r☆1, ☆13, 1966). "Ninety-Nine and a Half" (Atlantic; r☆13, 1966). "Land of 1000 Dances" (Atlantic; r☆1, ☆6, 1966). "Mustang Sally" (Atlantic; r☆6, ☆23, 1966). "Everybody Needs Somebody to Love" (Atlantic; r☆19, ☆29, 1967). "I Found a Love" (Atlantic; r☆6, ☆32, 1967). "Soul Dance Number Three" (Atlantic; r☆10, 1967). "Funky Broadway" (Atlantic; r☆1, ☆8, 1967). "I'm in Love" b/w "Stag-o-Lee" (Atlantic; r☆4, ☆22, 1967). "Jealous Love" (Atlantic; r☆18, ☆50, 1968). "She's Lookin' Good" (Atlantic; r☆7, ☆15, 1968). "I'm a Midnight Mover" (Atlantic; r☆6, ☆24, 1968). "I Found a True Love" (Atlantic; r☆11, ☆42, 1968). "A Man and a Half" (Atlantic; r☆20, ☆42, 1968). "Hey Jude" (Atlantic; r☆13, ☆23, 1969). "Mini-Skirt Minnie" (Atlantic; r☆19, ☆50, 1969). "You Keep Me Hanging On" (Atlantic; r☆16, 1969). **Joe Simon:** "Let's Do It Over" (Vee-Jay; r☆13, 1965). "Teenager's Prayer" (Sound Stage 7; r☆11, 1966). "My Special Prayer" (Sound Stage 7; r☆17, 1967). "Nine Pound Steel" (Sound Stage 7; r☆19, 1967). "(You Keep Me) Hangin' On" (Sound Stage 7; r☆11, ☆25, 1968). "The Chokin' Kind" (Sound Stage 7; r☆1, ☆13, 1969). "Baby, Don't Be Looking in My Mind" (Sound Stage 7; r☆16, 1969). **Percy Sledge:** "When a Man Loves a Woman" (Atlantic; r☆1, ☆1, 1966). "Warm and Tender Love" (Atlantic; r☆5, ☆17, 1966). "It Tears Me Up" (Atlantic; r☆7, ☆20, 1966). "Take Time to Know Her" (Atlantic; r☆6, ☆11, 1968). **Joe Tex:** "Hold What You've Got" (Dial; r☆2, ☆5, 1964). "You Got What It Takes" b/w "You Better Get It" (Dial; r☆10, ☆46, 1965). "A Woman Can Change a Man" (Dial; r☆12, 1965). "One Monkey Don't Stop No Show" (Dial; r☆20, 1965). "I Want to (Do Everything for You)" (Dial; r☆1, ☆23, 1965). "A Sweet Woman Like You" (Dial; r☆1, ☆29, 1965). "The Love You Save" (Dial; r☆2, 1965). "S.Y.S.L.J.F.M. (The Letter Song)" (Dial; r☆9, ☆39, 1966). "I Believe I'm Gonna Make It" (Dial; r☆8, 1966). "I've Got to Do a Little Bit Better" (Dial; r☆20, 1966). "Papa Was Too" (Dial; r☆15, ☆44, 1966). "Show Me" (Dial; r☆24, ☆35, 1967). "Skinny Legs and All" (Dial; r☆2, ☆10, 1967). "Men Are Gettin' Scarce" (Dial; r☆7, ☆33, 1968). "Keep the One You Got" (Dial; r☆13, 1968). "Buying a Book" (Dial; r☆10, ☆47, 1969).

ALBUMS

Solomon Burke: *Home in Your Heart: The Best of Solomon Burke* (Rhino/Atlantic; 1992). **Wilson Pickett:** *A Man and a Half: The Best of Wilson Picket* (Rhino/Atlantic; 1992). **Joe Tex:** *I Believe I'm Gonna Make It: The Best of Joe Tex, 1964–1972* (Rhino; 1988). **Joe Simon:** *Lookin' Back: The Best of Joe Simon* (Charly/Repete; 1989). **Percy Sledge:** *It Tears Me Up: The Best of Percy Sledge* (Rhino/Atlantic; 1992). **Clarence Carter:** *Snatching It Back: The Best of Clarence Carter* (Rhino/Atlantic; 1992). **Anthologies:** *Soul Shots, Volumes 1–4* (Rhino; 1988). *Atlantic Rhythm and Blues 1947–1974* (Atlantic; 1991).

(Chart positions compiled from Joel Whitburn's *Record Research*, based on *Billboard*'s Pop chart, unless otherwise indicated; r☆ = position on *Billboard*'s Rhythm & Blues chart.)

THE SOUND OF MEMPHIS

BY ROBERT PALMER

middle-aged ex-minstrel show hoofer named Rufus Thomas was operating eight boilers at a Memphis textile bleaching plant and working afternoons as a disc jockey at black-operated WDIA radio during the summer of 1960. His daughter Carla, an English major at Tennessee A&I in Nashville, was home for vacation, and the two of them decided to make a record for Satellite, a fledgling local label that had released singles by the Vel-tones and Charles Heinz with little success. Carla's experience as a vocalist had been limited to the Teen Tone Singers, a group of students from area high schools, and to occasional solos at PTA meetings. But she had practically grown up in the vaudeville theaters along Beale Street where her father had worked, first as half of the Rufus and Bones minstrel show team, later as a singer, master of ceremonies and all-around entertainer. Rufus had traveled throughout the South with tent shows and knew what audiences from rural areas liked. He had also made several regionally popular records during the Fifties, most notably ''Bear Cat,'' a Sun single based on Willie Mae Thornton's ''Hound Dog.''

The Thomases' father-daughter record, "Cause I Love You," did well around Memphis and attracted the attention of Atlantic Records' Jerry Wexler, who arranged to distribute it nationally. Its sales were disappointing, but in September Carla recorded "Gee Whiz (Look at His Eyes)," which shot into the Top Ten when Atlantic released it early in 1961. At this point, Satellite founders Jim Stewart and Estelle Axton changed their company's name to Stax (in order to avoid confusion with a California company named Satellite) and Atlantic took over Stax's distribution and promotion on an exclusive basis. The next few hits were instrumentals by the Mar-Keys, a band that included guitarists Steve Cropper and Charlie Freeman and saxophonist (later producer, singer and Leon Russell sidekick) Don Nix. Numerous other Memphis musicians were in and out of the Mar-Keys after the group's first hit single, "Last Night," but by 1962 a rhythm section consisting of Cropper, bassist Lewis Steinberg and drummer Al Jackson Jr. was playing on all of the Mar-Keys' recordings, and on most of Stax's other releases. That summer another vacationing student, Booker T. Jones, joined the three rhythm players as organist and front man after the foursome's "Green Onions" became a national hit for Booker T. and the MGs.

Soon Rufus Thomas came up with a new hit of his own, "The Dog," and then another, bigger hit, "Walking the Dog." The instrumental backing the Stax musicians provided on these and the company's other early records was simplicity itself. Cropper played choked rhythm guitar and inserted occasional sparse fills. Donald "Duck" Dunn, who had replaced Steinberg, contributed loping, country-flavored bass lines, and Jackson's drumming was a model of restraint and subtle effectiveness. "In some tunes, the straighter you play it the better," Jackson once commented. "You try to stay out of the way because you are selling the tune itself and not the drummer." He might have been speaking for the other three men in the MGs, or for saxophonists Andrew Love and Floyd Newman and trumpeter Wayne Jackson, who took over the Mar-Keys name and eventually incorporated as the Memphis Horns. These three musicians and a few others along the way augmented the MGs on most Stax recordings with spare unison lines, usually created on the spot.

Early in 1965 this writer, an aspiring rock & roll saxophonist fresh from Little Rock, Arkansas, had his first taste of the Memphis studios. It seemed incredible that such an informal and apparently haphazard approach to music making could produce such unified performances and so many successful records. At Chips Moman's American Recording Studios, where Atlantic sessions for King Curtis and Dusty Springfield would soon be held, the three-track board—actually a standard two-track tape recorder with a second machine ingeniously patched into it—was extremely temperamental. Musicians would show up for scheduled sessions to find Moman, who looked and talked like a country sheriff, and his friend and sessionman, the future soul star Bobby Womack, meticulously reassembling the recording machine, testing connections and lazily talking shop. "It oughta be ready by the middle of week," Moman would drawl, while Womack grinned in disbelief.

When sessions actually occurred, the American musicians, all of whom looked something like Moman, would drift in singly, dressed like dollar-store branch managers off on a fishing trip. It would take hours to set them up behind baffles in the tiny studio and to get the microphones properly placed around the drums in the soundproof drum booth, which was virtually a separate room. But once everything was in order, the players would record basic

Booker T. and the MGs around the time of "Green Onions," 1962. *From left:* "Duck" Dunn, Booker T. Jones, Steve Cropper, Al Jackson.

One of the first hits out of Memphis in the Sixties was a steamy instrumental called "Last Night." The band that made it, the Mar-Keys, later split up, with some members joining the Memphis Horns and others joining Booker T. and the MGs. *From left, standing:* Donald "Duck" Dunn, bass; Terry Johnson, drums; Steve Cropper, guitar; Jerry Lee Smith, piano. *On the floor:* Charles Axton, sax; Wayne Jackson, trumpet; Don Nix, sax.

tracks with expeditious precision. Moman sat in the control booth until he was sure he had the sound he wanted, particularly the fat, incredibly "live" drum sound that he pioneered. Then he joined the musicians in the studio, contributing letter-perfect rhythm guitar while his bassist, Tommy Cogbill, offhandedly created the lines he would later play to such stunning effect behind Aretha Franklin.

A few days later the Memphis Horns would arrive at the studio with a bottle of wine. After half the bottle had been consumed over small talk, the musicians would ask to hear the tracks, which might or might not have vocals on them by this time. After a few more drinks, the musicians would siphon into the studio, take out their horns and quickly tune up. "Okay," one of them, usually Andrew Love, would say, "DAT dah-dah DAT." The engineer would play back the track and the horns would add a suitably harmonized part which conformed to the syllables Love had suggested. They were so used to playing with one another that they always had acceptable horn lines on tape in two or three takes.

Stax sessions proceeded similarly, though sometimes they were run in a more professional manner. The company's studio musicians were a mixed lot. Around half of them were black, while the others were whites from rural backgrounds. Steve Cropper, for example, had come to Memphis from the Missouri Ozarks. The blend these musicians achieved together could have happened only in Memphis— which had been a Southern melting pot for generations—and perhaps only at a time, the mid-Sixties, when racial integration still seemed to be a believable political goal. But it was facilitated by the similar musical backgrounds of the black and white session players. Many of Stax's black musicians had grown up with country & western music; Isaac Hayes, who arranged and played keyboards when Booker T. Jones was away at school, later remembered that "where I grew up in Tennessee, country music was all you could hear on the radio." The white musicians had lived in close proximity to blacks and had

become steeped in blues and R&B, and both whites and blacks had participated in or observed at close hand the same sort of fundamentalist church services that had furnished early training and stylistic models for most of the Stax singers.

William Bell's "You Don't Miss Your Water," one of the company's early-Sixties R&B hits, is a perfect illustration of this mix of traditions. The song itself could easily pass for a C&W ballad, but the vocal, piano arpeggios and organlike chords played by the horns are in a black gospel vein. This combination of white song form, black vocal treatment, simple arrangement, rhythmic restraint and pure, understated elegance of expression was to characterize most of the classic recordings produced in Memphis during the next few years.

Atlantic Records engineer Tom Dowd traveled to Memphis to participate in an Otis Redding session early in 1965. In July Jerry Wexler followed him, bringing Atlantic artist Wilson Pickett, a former lead vocalist with the gospel-rooted Falcons from Detroit. Steve Cropper expanded one of Pickett's onstage

Rufus Thomas, veteran of vaudeville, walking the dog.

lines ("wait for the midnight hour, baby") into a sketch for a song, which the singer helped him complete in the studio. "In the Midnight Hour" and the other tunes cut at the session were more than archetypal Memphis R&B: They defined an international soul style. The Beatles and the Rolling Stones recorded songs cut in Memphis and emulated Memphis music, and Jamaican, West African, even Ethiopian pop musicians did the same. Around 1967 an English adventurer crossing the Mauritanian desert stumbled into an oasis town which had been visited by few whites and sat down in a cafe just as the local equivalent of a garage band began to play an almost perfect carbon copy of "In the Midnight Hour."

Jerry Wexler took an active role in the "Midnight Hour" sessions. He danced out of the control booth at one point to suggest that Al Jackson shift his drum accents from the weak beats (one and three) to the stronger two and four. Heavily stressed weak beats had been the Stax rhythm section's trademark, so the effect of Wexler's suggestion was not a wholesale accentual shift but an evening-out of rhythmic values that left bassist Duck Dunn free to take a more flowing and melodic role. The musicians liked the innovation and continued to play that way, but their

music retained its "lazy," slightly delayed rhythmic quality. "The guys will be playing a tempo and it'll sound like they're going to wind down," Memphis bandleader Willie Mitchell has noted. "And then suddenly they'll kind of sway with it and be right up there on top of the beat. The time isn't like a metronome; it's kind of like shuckin' you, puttin' you on. Even Memphis jazz players play real fast but just a little bit behind the beat, relaxed, lazy-like. It feels good."

"In the Midnight Hour" was released on the Atlantic label, but Stax followed it with hits by Sam

Rufus Thomas's daughter, Carla Thomas.

and Dave, a Miami-based duo produced by the Isaac Hayes–David Porter team, and with Eddie Floyd's "Knock on Wood" and R&B successes by Carla Thomas, Otis Redding, and Booker T. and the MGs. Redding, the most visceral and distinctive of the Stax vocalists, was beginning to attract a following among white rock critics and fans by 1966, but he had yet to crack the pop Top Ten. It was the Hayes-Porter team that gradually took the commercial lead with their string of Sam and Dave hits, "I Take What I Want," "You Don't Know Like I Know," and the epochal "Hold On, I'm Comin'." Sam Moore and Dave Prater engaged in loose but involving vocal banter and shouted with a churchy intensity that assured their popularity with black audiences. But Hayes and Porter made sure their records would appeal to whites as well by providing catchy melodic hooks, horn lines that were often more memorable than the tunes themselves and a harder-rocking version of the uptempo Memphis dance beat.

In 1967 Sam and Dave's "Soul Man" made it to Number Two on the pop chart, and while other Stax records did not fare as well, the company had enough hits lower down the charts to seem largely responsible for the continuing viability of its parent company, Atlantic. The Stax-Volt Revue, with Redding, Carla Thomas, and Booker T. and the MGs, toured Europe to tumultuous acclaim. Redding capped Stax's year of achievement with his triumph at the Monterey Pop Festival. Then, abruptly, he was gone, and his posthumous "(Sittin on) The Dock of the Bay" became the company's first national Number One hit.

In 1968 Stax dissolved its distribution pact with Atlantic. Carla Thomas, Johnnie Taylor and the newly signed Staple Singers came up with hits, but Sam and Dave ended their partnership. Several members of Redding's bright young band, the Bar-Kays, had died with him in the airplane crash, and Stax's new distribution contract with Gulf + Western failed to work out as anticipated. The Stax compound on East McLemore Avenue was still buzzing with activity. Isaac Hayes's *Hot Buttered Soul*, a harbinger of Barry White and the string-dominated "sweet soul" of the Seventies, was a smash, and on any given day Hayes's Rolls-Royce could be seen shining in the company parking lot, which was separated from the rough black neighborhood around it by a barbed wire fence and armed guards.

But Stax had already passed its peak. The mem- bers of the original house band had become executives and turned over sessionwork to players who were unable to develop as cohesive a group sound. The younger Stax producers favored orchestral sweetening and more up-to-date band tracks. They diluted the integrity of the original Memphis sound but were unable to compete effectively with the still more sophisticated R&B recordings being turned out by Motown. The Staple Singers and Isaac Hayes continued to sell records through the early Seventies, but by 1975 both had left, Stax was suing its erstwhile distributor CBS, and the company's board chairman was under indictment for fraud. A few weeks before Christmas 1975 the company's publishing subsidiary, and rights to the biggest hits by Otis Redding and Sam and Dave, were auctioned off to a local bank on the steps of the Shelby County Courthouse.

Stax was not the only local studio to contribute to the Memphis sound during the Sixties. Aretha Franklin's meteoric rise to the top of the pop charts was accomplished with the help of Chips Moman's musicians. At first they recorded with her near Memphis, in Muscle Shoals, Alabama. Later producer Jerry Wexler began flying them to Miami or New York for sessions.

Hi Records was formed in 1957 and produced successful rockabilly singles by Gene Simmons ("Haunted House"), Murray Kellum ("Long Tall Texan"), and Jerry Jaye ("My Girl Josephine"), as well as a number of "redneck Muzak" hits by ex–Elvis Presley bassist Bill Black and his combo. Willie Mitchell joined the company during the early Sixties and made several instrumental hits of his own. "In 1970," he told this interviewer, "Hi finally gave me the keys to the studio and I started in on the board. For the first time, I could hear what I wanted and get it. The first record I engineered myself was 'Soul Serenade,' the biggest instrumental record I had. Then I started messin' with Ann Peebles, and I found Al Green and Syl Johnson and Otis Clay."

Green was Mitchell's principal success, but he also produced R&B hits with these other singers, including the Ann Peebles classic "I Can't Stand the Rain" (1973). Hi records often sounded uncannily like Stax product of a decade earlier, with their enveloping organ, lean guitar riffs, deliberate drumming (by Al Jackson soundalike Howard Grimes, and sometimes by Jackson himself) and unison horn punctuations (by the Memphis Horns). But operating an independent label out of Memphis proved difficult, and during the late Seventies, after Hi was sold to Cream records of Los Angeles, Willie Mitchell left the company to produce elsewhere. By 1979 Memphis had raised a new crop of black funk bands such as Con Funk Shun and the latest edition of the Bar-Kays, but only the studios in Muscle Shoals continued to attract outside producers and name talent to the region.

DISCOGRAPHY

SINGLES 1961–1971

Astors: "Candy" (Stax; r☆12, 1965). **Bar-Kays:** "Soul Finger" (Volt; r☆3, ☆17, 1967). **William Bell:** "Everybody Loves a Winner" (Stax; r☆18, 1967). "A Tribute to a King" (Stax; r☆16, 1968). "I Forgot to Be Your Lover" (Stax; r☆10, ☆45, 1968). **Booker T. and the MGs:** "Green Onions" (Stax; r☆1, ☆3, 1962). "Boot-Leg" (Stax; r☆10, ☆58, 1965). "My Sweet Potato" (Stax; r☆18, 1966). "Hip Hug-Her" (Stax; r☆6, ☆37, 1967). "Groovin'" (Stax; r☆10, ☆21, 1967). "Soul-Limbo" (Stax; r☆7, ☆17, 1968). "Hang 'Em High" (Stax; r☆35, ☆9, 1968). "Time Is Tight" (Stax; r☆7, ☆6, 1969). **James Carr:** "You've Got My Mind Messed Up" (Goldwax; r☆7, 1965). "The Dark End of the Street" (Goldwax; r☆10, 1967). "A Man Needs a Woman" (Goldwax; r☆16, 1968). **Judy Clay and William Bell:** "Private Number" (Stax; r☆17, 1968). **Arthur Conley:** "Sweet Soul Music" (Atco; r☆2, ☆2, 1967). "Shake, Rattle and Roll" (Atco; r☆20, ☆31, 1967). "Funky Street" (Atco; r☆5, ☆14, 1968). "People Sure Act Funny" (Atco; r☆17, ☆58, 1968). **Dramatics:** "Whatcha See Is Whatcha Get" (Volt; r☆3, ☆9, 1971). **Emotions:** "So I Can Love You" (Volt; r☆3, ☆39, 1969). **Eddie Floyd:** "Knock on Wood" (Stax; r☆1, ☆28, 1966). "Raise Your Hand" (Stax; r☆16, 1967). "I've Never Found a Girl" (Stax; r☆2, ☆40, 1968). "Bring It On Home to Me" (Stax; r☆4, ☆17, 1968). **Isaac Hayes:** "Walk On By" (Enterprise; r☆13, ☆30, 1969). "Never Can Say Goodbye" (Enterprise; r☆5, ☆22, 1971). "Theme from 'Shaft'" (Enterprise; r☆2, ☆1, 1971). **Luther Ingram:** "Ain't That Loving You (for More Reasons Than One)" (Ko Ko; r☆6, ☆45, 1970). **Albert King:** "Cold Feet" (Stax; r☆20, 1968). **King Curtis:** "Memphis Soul Stew" (Atco; r☆6, ☆33, 1967). **Mabel John:** "Your Good Thing (Is About to End)" (Stax; r☆6, 1966). **Mad Lads:** "I Want Someone" (Volt; r☆10, 1966). "I Want a Girl" (Volt; r☆16, 1966). **Mar-Keys:** "Last Night" (Satellite; r☆2, ☆3, 1961). **Willie Mitchell:** "20-75" (Hi; ☆31, 1964). "Soul Serenade" (Hi; r☆10, ☆23, 1968). **Otis and Carla:** "Tramp" (Stax; r☆2, ☆26, 1967). "Knock on Wood" (Stax; r☆8, ☆30, 1967). **Ann Peebles:** "I Pity the Fool" (Hi; r☆18, ☆45, 1971). **Wilson Pickett:** "In the Midnight Hour" (Atlantic; r☆1, ☆21, 1965). "Don't Fight It" (Atlantic; r☆4, ☆53, 1965). "634-5789 (Soulsville, U.S.A.)" (Atlantic; r☆1, ☆13, 1966). **Sam and Dave:** "You Don't Know Like I Know" (Stax; r☆7, 1966). "Hold On, I'm Comin'" (Stax; r☆1, ☆21, 1966). "Said I Wasn't Gonna Tell Nobody" (Stax; r☆8, 1966). "You Got Me Hummin'" (Stax; r☆7, 1966). "When Something Is Wrong with My Baby" (Stax; r☆2, ☆42, 1967). "Soothe Me" (Stax; r☆16, ☆56, 1967). "Soul Man" (Stax; r☆1, ☆2, 1967). "I Thank You" (Stax; r☆4, ☆9, 1968). "You Don't Know What You Mean to Me" (Atlantic; r☆20, ☆48, 1968). "Can't You Find Another Way" (Atlantic; r☆19, ☆54, 1968). **Soul Children:** "The Sweeter He Is" (Stax; r☆7, ☆52, 1969). **Staple Singers:** "Heavy Makes You Happy (Sha-Na-Boom Boom)" (Stax; r☆6, ☆27, 1970). "Respect Yourself" (Stax; r☆2, ☆12, 1971). **Johnnie Taylor:** "I Had a Dream" (Stax; r☆19, 1966). "I Got to Love Somebody's Baby" (Stax; r☆15, 1966). "Who's Making Love" (Stax; r☆1, ☆5, 1968). "Take Care of Your Homework" (Stax; r☆2, ☆20, 1969). "Testify (I Wonna)" (Stax; r☆4, ☆36, 1969). "I Could Never Be President" (Stax; r☆10, ☆48, 1969). "Love Bones" (Stax; r☆4, ☆43, 1969). "Steal Away" (Stax; r☆3, ☆37, 1970). "I Am Somebody—Part II" (Stax; r☆4, ☆39, 1970). "Jody's Got Your Girl and Gone" (Stax; r☆1, ☆28, 1971). "Hijackin' Love" (Stax; r☆10, 1971). **Carla Thomas:** "Gee Whiz (Look at His Eyes)" (Atlantic; r☆5, ☆10, 1961). "I'll Bring It Home to You" (Atlantic; r☆9, ☆41, 1962). "Let Me Be Good to You" (Stax; r☆11, 1966). "B-A-B-Y" (Stax; r☆3, ☆14, 1966). "I'll Always Have Faith in You" (Stax; r☆11, 1967). "I Like What You're Doing (to Me)" (Stax; r☆9, ☆49, 1969). **Rufus Thomas:** "The Dog" (Stax; r☆22, 1963). "Walking the Dog" (Stax; r☆5, ☆10, 1963). "Do the Funky Chicken" (Stax; r☆5, ☆28, 1970). "(Do the) Push and Pull, Part 1" (Stax; r☆1, ☆25, 1970). "The Breakdown" (Stax; r☆2, ☆31, 1971). **O. V. Wright:** "Ace of Spade" (Back Beat; r☆11, ☆54, 1970).

ALBUMS

William Bell: *The Best of William Bell* (Stax; 1990). **Booker T. and the MGs:** *Booker T. and the MGs Greatest Hits* (Atlantic; 1974). **Sam and Dave:** *Best of Sam and Dave* (Atlantic; 1985). **Billy Stewart:** *The Greatest Sides* (MCA/Chess; 1984). **Johnnie Taylor:** *Chronicle: The 20 Greatest Hits* (Stax; 1989). **Anthologies:** *The Complete Stax/Volt Singles, 1959–1968* (Atlantic, 1991).

(Omitting hits by Otis Redding and Al Green. (Chart positions compiled from Joel Whitburn's *Record Research*, based on *Billboard*'s Pop chart, unless otherwise indicated; r☆ = position on *Billboard*'s Rhythm & Blues chart.)

OTIS REDDING

BY JON LANDAU

Musicians see themselves in different ways. Some, the rarest, are artists prepared to make any sacrifice to preserve the integrity of their art. Others are poseurs who adopt the artist's stance without the art, who therefore appeal to the segment of the audience that likes to think of itself as being serious but isn't. And then there are those performers who see themselves as entertainers: They make no pretense of aiming at any particular artistic standard, but are openly and honestly concerned with pleasing crowds and being successful. Such a man was Otis Redding.

Redding wanted to be successful and secure. He saw becoming an entertainer as his way out of a dreary lower-class existence first in Dawson, Georgia, where he was born in 1941, and then in Macon, Georgia.

However, given these motivations, Redding still was able to develop a deeply personal, intimate style that was not nearly as commercial as it might have been, indicating that Redding did not commit himself to doing only that which would make him popular. He couldn't. He didn't have the ability to see which way the wind was blowing, and to head in that direction. His understanding of music was not

something he could put on or take off, depending on chart trends. He was truly a ''folk'' artist; he couldn't escape the musical climate that surrounded him all his life and out of which he created his own music.

Wanting to make good is characteristic of all soul artists, partly because they tend to have similar backgrounds, James Brown as much as Wilson Pickett as much as Redding himself. All are from rural parts of the South. Their musical influences are limited to folk, country & western, blues, gospel and some pop. And they have to fasten together their own styles from this limited background—limitations which often preclude the possibility of true flexibility. They have no choice but to put all they know into the one form of music through which they have chosen to express themselves. The lack of intellectuality and detachment inherent in this expression accounts for the resultant intimacy of the music. Soul music approaches folk music in its lack

Redding, here performing with the MGs, was called "Mr. Pitiful," because he sang with a pleading urgency.

of self-consciousness. And it is art, even though the artist may not seek to do anything beyond entertain.

Otis Redding based a good deal of his style on two important predecessors: Little Richard, one of his boyhood idols, and Sam Cooke. During Redding's childhood years in Georgia, Little Richard was creating his dynamic, shouting kind of R&B and putting it high on the pop charts. Because Richard was also a native of Macon, he made a deep impression on Otis. This influence can be heard most directly on his first album, *Pain in My Heart,* recorded in 1962 and 1963. On it there are several cuts that sound so much like Little Richard it is hard to tell the difference.

It didn't take long for Redding to outgrow his reliance on Little Richard, but he never outgrew his love for Sam Cooke or the influence Cooke's music had on him. Cooke was the top star in his field from 1957, when he had the Number One hit, "You Send Me," until his tragic death in 1964. Redding included Cooke's songs on most of his albums, and one of his most popular numbers in performance was Cooke's "Shake."

Redding's entrance into show business is a straightforward story. He paid his dues early with a group called Johnny Jenkins and the Pinetoppers. In his late teens he became vocalist of the group and

got a lot of experience playing for demanding audiences along the Southern college fraternity circuit. In 1962 Jenkins was to record a number for Atlantic Records without Redding, but he asked Otis to drive him to Memphis, where the sessions were scheduled. When Jenkins got through recording, there was still forty minutes of studio time remaining and Otis got permission to record a tune he had written called "These Arms of Mine." Otis's first release, this record launched him as a solo artist. Memphis became his recording home, and he made all his records with the wonderful musicians who played on "These Arms of Mine," namely Booker T. Jones and the MGs, and the horns of the Mar-Keys.

Between 1962 and 1964 Redding recorded a series

A publicity shot from the beginning of his career, 1963.

of soul ballads characterized by unabashedly senti-mental lyrics usually begging forgiveness or asking a girlfriend to come home. The titles are revealing: "Pain in My Heart," "Mr. Pitiful" and "That's How Strong My Love Is"—the last, one of Otis's finest recordings. He soon became known as "Mr. Pitiful" and earned a reputation as the leading performer of soul ballads.

Otis's big leap, both as an artist and as a star, came in 1965, a crucial year in pop music marked by the advent of the Rolling Stones. It was also the year modern soul began to take shape. In the summer of '65 Wilson Pickett's "In the Midnight Hour" was climbing the charts (recorded with the same musi-cians Redding used), and James Brown and the Fa-mous Flames hit with "Papa's Got a Brand New Bag." In addition, the Stones acknowledged the im-portance of soul music as a basis for the new rock by releasing *Out of Our Heads,* which included their ver-sions of hits by Solomon Burke, Don Covay, Marvin Gaye and Otis. And, finally, the summer of 1965 was when Otis released his own beautiful composi-tion, "Respect."

"Respect" was a smash on the soul charts. Artisti-cally, it was a pounding production that showed off the unrepressed quality of the Memphis sound at its very best. Otis's singing—frantic, powerful and charming—pulled him out of the cul-de-sac of pure soul ballads and, along with his performance on "I've Been Loving You Too Long" (his finest slow song), represented the highest level of artistic devel-opment he had attained. "Respect" was the first record that was pure Redding; he was now self-reli-ant and no longer leaned on anyone else's style.

Although white America waited for Aretha Franklin and 1967 to dig "Respect," the sizable suc-cess of Redding's recording in the black market indi-cated that his greatest hope for making it with pop audiences would be with the faster songs. The slow, eloquent, majestic ballads he sang so well simply required too much patience from a car-radio audi-ence. Otis followed "Respect" with his hyped-up version of "Satisfaction," repaying the Stones the admiration they had shown him. If the white DJs who control suburban radio had given it more air-play, the record could have been a giant hit.

Otis Redding became an extremely popular per-former, but mainly on the black circuit. He had the ghetto circuit—Harlem and Watts—locked up. He was successful financially and owned a ranch home near Macon. But fame was as important to him as financial reward, as he made clear in his rewrite of the Temptations' "My Girl," where he sings, "I don't need no money, all I need is my fame."

He continued to release soul ballads even though he knew that fast tunes were the key to success in the pop market (as his good friends at Stax, Sam and Dave, proved with their gold record, "Soul Man"). Redding loved his music, and when he talked about it in interviews he was completely articulate. The main feature of modern soul, according to Redding, was the stomp beat. The old-fashioned shuffle was an anachronism; only one of his important records had it—"Shake."

But beyond any musical understanding of the im-peratives of his own style, Redding never was con-

ANOTHER FINE ATTRACTION
AVAILABLE THROUGH

fused about his purpose as an entertainer. He believed in communication; every device and technique he created was designed to further his communicative potential. And at the root of Redding's conception of communication was simplicity. Redding's music was always deliberately simple. Direct, unintellectual, honest and concise.

In 1966 Redding's style reached artistic fruition. Late in the year *The Otis Redding Dictionary of Soul* was released. The cover was a typically tasteless Stax-Volt rendering, but the record inside was the finest ever to come out of Memphis, truly one of the finest pop records of the decade and certainly the best example of modern soul ever recorded.

Dictionary of Soul indicated finally that if Otis were to make it outside the regular soul audience, it would have to be because soul music was making it with the pop audience. Redding was not going to change his music. He loved it, had already received recognition for it and was confident his turn would

come. It's doubtful the idea of altering his style to boost record sales ever occurred to him. He had perfected his vocal syntax, his rapport with his sidemen and his linear, totally committed music. In *Dictionary*, the result of this perfection is evident throughout. Religious in its emotional intensity, it expresses a way of life. Particularly awesome is the consummate skill with which the soul ballads ("You're Still My Baby" and "Try a Little Tenderness") were performed. He sang the blues like no one else on "Hawg for You," and he breathed new life into the Beatles' "Day Tripper." Here is Redding's blood and guts, and anyone who hears *Dictionary* recognizes its greatness instantly.

While Redding continued to perform almost exclusively for black audiences and to consolidate his status in the soul hierarchy (second only to James Brown in terms of personal popularity), an unusual train of events took place. Soul music, largely through the efforts of Aretha Franklin, began to take over the pop charts. It soon became clear the new wave would be the earthy Memphis soul that Redding had been practicing for the preceding five years. Unfortunately, Otis died in a plane crash December 10th, 1967, before his biggest hit, "(Sittin' on) The Dock of the Bay" was even released.

Redding's friend, guitarist and sometime collaborator, Steve Cropper, best expresses why those who knew Redding felt he was verging on superstardom. In an interview some months before Redding's death, he said: "Otis is the only one I can think of

In the mid-Sixties Otis Redding wrote the *Dictionary of Soul*.

now who does it [sings soul] best. He gets over to the people what he's talking about, and he does it in so few words that if you read them on paper they might not make any sense. But when you hear the way he sings them, you know exactly what he is talking about." Here is the key again: communication. I saw him perform only once, at a revue in Boston. The audience was overwhelmingly black and sat through two and a half hours of mediocre soul music before Redding made his appearance. The crowd was growing restless, having heard too many singers say, "Let me see you clap your hands." Then Redding came on. The first thing he did was say, "Let me see you clap your hands." I immediately forgot the preceding two and half hours and clapped my hands. The audience knew instantly it was in the presence of an absolute master. The band still had not played a single note, yet every person in the hall was standing.

DISCOGRAPHY

SINGLES

"These Arms of Mine" (Volt; r☆20, ☆85, 1963). "That's What My Heart Needs" (Volt; r☆27, 1963). "Pain in My Heart" (Volt; ☆61, 1963). "Come to Me" (Volt; ☆69, 1964). "Security" (Volt; ☆97, 1964). "Chained and Bound" (Volt; ☆70, 1964). "Mr. Pitiful" b/w "That's How Strong My Love Is" (Volt; r☆10, ☆41, 1965). "I've Been Loving You Too Long (to Stop Now)" (Volt; r☆2, ☆21, 1965). "Respect" (Volt; r☆4, ☆35, 1965). "I Can't Turn You Loose" b/w "Just One More Day" (Volt; r☆11, 1965). "Satisfaction" (Volt; r☆4, ☆31, 1966). "My Lover's Prayer" (Volt; r☆10, 1966). "Fa-Fa-Fa-Fa-Fa (Sad Song)" (Volt; r☆12, ☆29, 1966). "Try a Little Tenderness" (Volt; r☆4, ☆25, 1966). "I Love You More Than Words Can Say" (Volt; r☆30, 1967). "Shake" (Volt; r☆16, ☆47, 1967). "Glory of Love" (Volt; r☆19, 1967). "(Sittin' on) The Dock of the Bay" (Volt; r☆1, ☆1, 1968). "The Happy Song (Dum-Dum)" (Volt; r☆10, ☆25, 1968). "Amen" (Atco; r☆15, ☆36, 1968). "I've Got Dreams to Remember" (Atco; r☆6, ☆41, 1968); "Papa's Got a Brand New Bag" (Atco; r☆10, ☆21, 1968). "A Lover's Question" (Atco; r☆20, ☆48, 1969). "Love Man" (Atco; r☆17, 1969). "Free Me" (Atco; r☆30, 1969).

ALBUMS

Pain in My Heart (Atco; ☆103, 1964). *Soul Ballads* (Volt; ☆147, 1965). *Otis Blue* (Volt; ☆75, 1965). *The Soul Album* (Volt; ☆54, 1966). *The Otis Redding Dictionary of Soul* (Volt; ☆73, 1966). With Carla Thomas *King and Queen* (Stax; ☆36, 1967). *Live in Europe* (Volt; ☆32, 1967). *History of Otis Redding* (Volt; ☆9, 1967). *The Dock of the Bay* (Volt; ☆4, 1968). *The Immortal Otis Redding* (Atco; ☆58, 1968). *In Person at the Whiskey A-Go-Go* (Atco; ☆82, 1968). *Love Man* (Atco; ☆46, 1969). *Tell the Truth* (Atco; ☆200, 1970). With the Jimi Hendrix Experience: *Live at Monterey* (Reprise; ☆16, 1970). *Recorded Live: Previously Unreleased Performances* (Atlantic; 1982). *The Otis Redding Story* (Atlantic; 1987). *Remember Me* (Stax; 1992).

(Chart positions compiled from Joel Whitburn's *Record Research*, based on *Billboard*'s Pop and LPs charts, unless otherwise indicated; r☆ = position on *Billboard*'s Rhythm & Blues chart.)

MOTOWN

BY JOE McEWEN AND JIM MILLER

Sandwiched among a row of modest private homes and professional enterprises like Sykes Hernia Control and Your Fair Lady Boutique and Wig Room, the white bungalow at 2648 West Grand Boulevard in Detroit is distinguished only by a large sign proclaiming it HITSVILLE, U.S.A. The two-story frame structure with the angular, jutting picture window, along with a cluster of nearby houses, is the home of Berry Gordy's Motown Records, currently the country's hottest hitmakers.

Shortly after 9 a.m. on a warm morning in June 1965, songwriter-producer Lamont Dozier strolls in, ignoring the company time clock that used to govern his paycheck. Company president Gordy rushes from his office to tell Lamont that Motown needs a quick followup to the Four Tops' "I Can't Help Myself," the label's second Number One pop hit in less than a month (Dozier had helped write and produce the other as well: the Supremes' "Back in My Arms Again"). The Tops had recorded for Columbia before their Motown association, and Gordy explains that the New York label has just released an old record in an attempt to cash in on the group's current success.

Dozier nods and walks down the corridor, past closet-sized offices where groups and producers rehearse material. Lamont's partners, Brian Holland and Eddie Holland, are already in their cubicle, sketching out a preliminary arrangement that bears more than a passing resemblance to the Four Tops' current smash. Lamont Dozier sits down at the piano and smooths out some rough edges in the melody line; all three contribute to the lyric. By noon the song is complete, and the trio take their finished work to the studio, where the Four Tops run down the lyrics while Earl Van Dyke's band negotiates the changes. Later that afternoon the track will have been recorded and the Tops' vocals added. Within three days the record will be on the streets, the pick hit at local soul station WCHB. The Columbia disc is

277

quickly forgotten, and by August "It's the Same Old Song" by the Four Tops hits Number Five on the *Billboard* pop chart.

The success of Motown Records is almost entirely attributable to one man: Berry Gordy. A former boxer and onetime record-store owner, Gordy, through a combination of pugnacious panache, shrewd judgment and good taste, became the mogul of the most profitable black music concern in the world.

It all began in Detroit in the early Fifties. When Gordy's record store specializing in jazz went bankrupt, he decided to redirect his musical money-making interests to the burgeoning field of rhythm & blues. While supporting himself with a series of odd jobs, Gordy began writing songs for local R&B acts. At first his amateur efforts failed miserably; but he soon acquired a local reputation as a songwriter, producer and hustler. In those days Gordy would write songs for a performer, cut a demo tape and then take the finished masters to New York, where he would try to peddle his product for a 5-percent royalty on net sales. Unfortunately, even when somebody purchased his masters, they were never promoted properly; and if they did sell, royalties were rarely accounted for.

It was a tough racket, but Gordy persevered. His first break came in 1957 when Brunswick Records bought a song he had written, called "Reet Petite," for Jackie Wilson. "Reet Petite" was a pop hit, and though his profit only amounted to $1000, several successful follow-ups for Wilson and Brunswick soon established Berry Gordy as Detroit's leading songwriter. But that was not enough: Gordy was determined to produce and market his own music himself.

The Motown mythology has it that Berry Gordy, fresh off an automobile assembly line, borrowed $800 to start his company. In truth, by 1959 Gordy was a prospering songwriter; he first borrowed money not to start a label, but to go into independent production.

At the time, he had his eye on a local singer named Marv Johnson. Their first joint effort, "Come to Me," was leased to United Artists, and although it was only a modest hit (Number Thirty on the pop

Marv Johnson, one of Berry Gordy's early protégés.

chart), it gave an indication of where Gordy was headed.

The song itself was slight: simple lyrics set to a stock rock chord progression (compare Gordy's smash hit for Wilson, ''Lonely Teardrops''). But to accompany Johnson, who followed in the gospel footsteps of Clyde McPhatter and Wilson, Gordy added a churchy female chorus for some call-and-response trades (shades of Ray Charles) and a bubbling male bassman (shades of Clyde McPhatter's ''A Lover's Question'' on Atlantic). Instrumentally, the record was anchored by a persistent baritone sax and tambourine, with a flute break in the middle (recalling Bobby Day's ''Rock-In Robin''). The result was a clean R&B record that sounded as white as it did black.

Gordy perfected this gospel-pop fusion in the months that followed, and by 1960 he'd made two similarly styled Top Ten hits with Johnson, ''You Got What It Takes'' and ''I Love the Way You Love.'' After leasing yet another single, ''Money'' by Barrett Strong, to Anna, a label owned by one of his sisters, Gordy decided to form his own label: Tammie, soon changed to Tamla Records.

It wasn't surprising that the first Tamla hit of any size belonged to a vocal group called the Miracles. Gordy had discovered the quintet working in Detroit. Although initially attracted by the group's only female member, Claudette—the lead singer's girl-friend—Gordy quickly realized the potential of the Miracles' songwriter, Smokey Robinson, who also

happened to be the lead singer. He leased a few Miracles sides to Chess Records in 1959, but it was only with "Way Over There" on Tamla in 1960 that the group (and label) began to sell records: 60,000 on that release. In a few months that would seem like chicken feed.

As a followup to "Way Over There," Robinson came up with a song called "Shop Around." Gordy found the first master too sluggish and called the Miracles back into the studio at three o'clock one morning to cut a new version at a faster tempo. The result was Tamla's first real hit; by January, "Shop Around" had reached Number Two on the pop chart, and Gordy's company was in the black.

The little bungalow on West Grand was teeming with activity as a host of aspiring local singers and songwriters flocked to Gordy's studio. With Robinson and Gordy handling the bulk of composing and producing, Tamla and Gordy's growing family of labels (Motown and Gordy were formed in the next two years, later to be joined by Soul, V.I.P. and Rare Earth) began to log an impressive track record, their hits ranging from Eddie Holland's slick "Jamie" to the Contours' raunchy "Do You Love Me?" By the end of 1962 the Gordy roster included Mary Wells, the Marvelettes and Marvin Gaye.

Although several of these acts, particularly Mary Wells and the Marvelettes, made consistent inroads onto the pop chart, Motown's early productions differed markedly in feel and appeal, depending on who was doing the singing. Mary Wells cooed seductive lyrics, the Marvelettes declaimed the girl-group sound, while Marvin Gaye and the Contours both rasped over rotgut rhythm tracks only one step removed from rural blues and gospel. Motown had hits, all right; but it hadn't quite yet evolved a distinctive sound.

From the beginning Berry Gordy relied on a handful of dependable writers and producers. In late 1961 he began to expand his staff of writer-producers, and among the new additions was Lamont Dozier, a veteran of the local group scene who toiled in relative anonymity at Mo-

town for a couple of years until he began a creative partnership with Motown cohorts Brian and Eddie Holland. Two years later the fledgling trio of writers clicked. Working with Martha and the Vandellas, the Holland-Dozier-Holland team set out to refine and systematize the production techniques Gordy had pioneered with Marv Johnson. "Heat Wave," by Martha and the Vandellas, inaugurated a three-year stretch that saw H-D-H amass twenty-eight Top Twenty pop hits.

As soul producers, they were little short of revolutionary. The trio rarely used standard song forms, opting instead for a simpler, more direct *ababcc* pattern, anchored by an endless refrain of the song's hook line. The effect of this cyclical structure was cumulative, giving Holland-Dozier-Holland productions a compulsive momentum. Even better, the constant refrains and consistent use of repetition helped make their hits ubiquitous: After you'd heard one, you'd heard them all—and each and every one

Holland kicked Motown into high gear. By the late Sixties Gordy's company had become one of the biggest black-owned corporations in America, as well as one of the most phenomenally successful independent recording ventures in history. Motown succeeded beyond anyone's wildest expectations, and did so with black people controlling the company at the technical, musical and artistic levels.

The reasons behind Motown's popularity are diverse. Overseeing the whole operation was Berry Gordy, who endorsed the old bromide for predictable success: Keep it simple. Under his tutelage, Motown's musicians took the concept of formula pop to a new level of sophistication and, thanks to the music's gospel-blues roots, visceral intensity.

The formulas might have quickly become tedious, of course, were it not for the ingenuity of Gordy's stable of producer-songwriters. Smokey Robinson, who handled the early Temptations and Mary Wells, in addition to the Miracles, was able to transfigure the most banal romantic motifs with clever lyrics and catchy hook lines; Norman Whitfield, who worked extensively with the Temptations as well as Marvin Gaye and Gladys Knight, was able to go beyond R&B clichés with punchy melodies and arrangements and topical lyrics; such latecomers as Nickolas Ashford and Valerie Simpson, who produced the Marvin Gaye–Tammi Terrell duets as well as Diana Ross's early solo records, were able to

of them was immediately familiar, subtly distinctive and quite unforgettable.

The trio's lyrics were nothing to write home about. But what mattered was their sense of structure and the musical devices they used to animate that structure. Following Gordy's lead, Holland-Dozier-Holland exploited gospelish vocal gestures in a pop context, now defined by their own streamlined approach. If the vocalists provided emotion, the band mounted a nonstop percussive assault highlighted by a "hot" mix, with shrill, hissing cymbals and a booming bass—anything to make a song jump out of a car radio. With tambourines rattling to a blistering 4/4 beat, the H-D-H sound, introduced on "Heat Wave" and perfected on records like the Four Tops' "Reach Out, I'll Be There" and the Supremes' "You Can't Hurry Love" (both from 1966), came to epitomize what Motown would call "The Sound of Young America."

"Heat Wave" and the arrival of Holland-Dozier-

From left: Lamont Dozier, Eddie Holland and Brian Holland, one of the greatest songwriting teams of all time.

amplify secularized gospel lyrics with grandiose orchestral settings; and finally, Holland-Dozier-Holland did nothing less than make The Formula a work of art in itself.

And then there was the Motown house band, some of the best R&B musicians in the Sixties. The Motown rhythm section, which included Benny Benjamin on drums, James Jamerson Sr. on bass, Joe Messina on guitar, Earl Van Dyke on keyboards, James Giddons on percussion and Robert White on guitar, developed a unique dexterity and adaptability. Jamerson left his own mark on the music (the explosive bass line on Marvin Gaye and Tammi Terrell's "Ain't No Mountain High Enough" could have come from no one else) and has influenced scores of bassists since. Their existence was hardly glamorous, however. Usually paid a flat salary, the Motown musicians toiled in relative obscurity; where Memphis soulmen Booker T. and the MGs cut instrumental hits, Earl Van Dyke and the Soul Brothers played small lounges near West Grand for a few dollars, free pizza and the applause of local patrons. In the morning, it was back to the nine-to-five grind.

Indeed, the assembly-line atmosphere had something to do with Motown's success. If nothing else, it enabled Berry Gordy to keep tabs on his empire. He called his direction "quality control"; often, second-string Motown acts would have virtually no public exposure for months at a time while their recordings were polished to Gordy's satisfaction.

Even popular performers found themselves restricted, as well as aided, by the Motown hit machine. Gordy's innate caution dictated followups that only slightly altered the elements of the previous hit; a formula was mined until it was commercially exhausted. Thus "Heat Wave" reached Number Four on the pop charts; its sound-alike successor, "Quicksand," got up to Number Eight—and only after the third go-around, when "Live Wire" stalled at Number Forty-two, did Martha and the Vandellas get the opportunity to try something different.

Gordy's cultivation of Motown's image was equally restrictive. As soon as the company domination of Top Forty pop and soul was clear, Gordy hustled his star acts into "class" venues like the Copa, the Latin Casino, Las Vegas or bust. As if to confer respectability upon his artists, he encouraged albums such as *The Four Tops on Broadway* and *Temp-*

The Supremes as they were, and they were never better *(from left)*: Diana Ross, Mary Wilson and Florence Ballard.

tations in a Mellow Mood. Finally, Gordy's artist-management division, International Talent Management Incorporated (I.T.M.), included a kind of finishing school for Motown stars. Here, an artist learned how to sit, walk and talk and even how to smoke a cigarette with grace and elegance. Above all, Motown's flock was taught the good manners any adult member of the white middle class would expect to see exhibited at a swank nightclub.

Motown's roots may have been in gospel and blues, but its image was purely one of upward mobility and clean, wholesome fun (Gordy's vision of "Young America"). Motown's stars were groomed to offend no one; the songs they sang were equipped with romantic lyrics that could appeal to practically anyone; and the music itself was rarely demanding, or even aggressive in the tradition of Southern soul. Martha and the Vandellas' "Dancing in the Street" (1964) may have been interpreted by black activist-poet LeRoi Jones as an evocation of revolutionary times, but the closest thing to an overt political statement released by Motown in the mid-Sixties was Stevie Wonder's "Blowin' in the Wind" (1966). (Of course, ever sensitive to changing fashion, Motown eventually hopped onto the political—and even psychedelic—bandwagon, with such 1970 hits as the Temptations' "Psychedelic Shack" and Edwin Starr's "War," both Norman Whitfield compositions.)

One statistic gives eloquent testimony to Gordy's success in courting the white market. In 1966 Motown's "hit ratio"—the percentage of records released that made the national charts—was nothing less than 75 percent. It was an appropriately awesome achievement for a truly astonishing record company.

Although its hits have occasionally been dismissed on grounds of monotony, the truth of the matter is that Motown, even in its assembly-line prime, released a remarkably diverse lot of records, varying in sound, arrangement and feel. While Berry Gordy dictated the overall direction and the producers and studio musicians stamped the sound, it was the performers themselves who ultimately conveyed the Motown image. Here is a brief guide to the artists who sang the Motown hits (omitting Stevie Wonder, who is discussed elsewhere):

Miracles. Most of Motown's roster consisted of Detroit acts unearthed at local talent shows; here as elsewhere, Smokey Robinson's Miracles set the pattern. When Robinson first approached Gordy late in

Smokey Robinson and the Miracles *(from left):* Bobby Rogers, Pete Moore, Smokey, Ronnie White.

1957, most of the group was still in high school; three years later, when "Shop Around" hit, the Miracles' oldest member was barely twenty-one.

During the next ten years, however, the Miracles became a seasoned troupe, while Robinson became one of the most prolific and popular producer-songwriters in the Motown stable. In person, the Miracles' performances were erratic, depending on the state of Smokey's fragile falsetto; by the end of a particularly grueling night, Robinson's voice, always so pure and controlled on record, often sounded frayed. In the studio, on the other hand, Robinson knew few rivals, composing and producing such torchy soul-pop hits as Mary Wells's "My Guy" (1964), the Temptations' "My Girl" (1965), and the Marvelettes' "The Hunter Gets Captured by the Game" (1967).

Smokey was his own best interpreter, and the Miracles remained one of Motown's most consistent groups throughout the Sixties. At the outset, their chief asset was the anguished eroticism conveyed by Robinson's pristine falsetto (listen to "You Can Depend on Me," from 1960). But by the mid-Sixties Robinson had also blossomed as a composer and lyricist. As writer Charlie Gillett has pointed out, many of Robinson's finest lyrics hinged on an apparent contradiction: "I'm a choosy beggar," "I've got sunshine on a cloudy day," "The love I saw in you was just a mirage." Despite a spate of uptempo hits, from "Shop Around" and "Mickey's Monkey" (1963) to "Going to a Go-Go" (1965), the Miracles' forte was ballads. Here Robinson—whether confessing his dependence, as on "You've Really Got a Hold on Me" (1962), or pleading for forgiveness, as on "Ooo Baby Baby" (1965)—could use his voice to transcendent effect. "The Tracks of My Tears" (1965) remains one of the most emotionally demanding Motown singles of the Sixties.

Mary Wells. Just seventeen when she auditioned for Berry Gordy in 1960, Mary Wells debuted on Motown with "Bye Bye Baby," a brassy, unrefined shouter. But she didn't really click until early 1962, after she was placed under Smokey Robinson's wing. Their partnership produced four Top Ten pop hits over a two-year span, including "The One Who Really Loves You" and "Two Lovers" (both 1962). A soft, cuddly stylist with just a hint of sassiness, Wells exited Motown shortly after her twenty-first birthday, lured by a lucrative contract with another

Mary Wells auditioned for Berry Gordy at age seventeen and soon became Motown's first female star.

label. Although her departure followed her biggest Motown hit ever, "My Guy" (1964), she proved unable to duplicate her success elsewhere.

Marvelettes. Motown's first and only real girl group was its most mysterious. Originally a quintet with Gladys Horton as lead, the Marvelettes survived numerous personnel, production and stylistic changes for almost a decade. Although the group was a consistent frontliner only in 1962, when "Please Mr. Postman" and "Playboy" both made the Top Ten, their repertoire of later hits included such gems as Smokey Robinson's suave "Don't Mess with Bill" (1966).

Martha and the Vandellas. Martha Reeves began her career at Motown inauspiciously enough, as a secretary in the A&R department. But Berry Gordy, discovering he had talent sitting right under his nose, sent Martha to work singing with her own group, the Vandellas. They debuted as the backup vocalists for Marvin Gaye on "Hitch Hike" and "Stubborn Kind of Fellow," and hit their stride with "Heat Wave" in 1963. Thanks to Reeves's aggressive and flamboyant style, the Vandellas escaped any categorization as an orthodox girl group; instead, they recorded some of the toughest mainline rock & roll to come out of Motown.

Reeves's main problem was one of excess, but Holland-Dozier-Holland wrote lyrics that successfully capitalized on her shrillness: If her love wasn't like a "Live Wire," then she was falling in "Quicksand." Martha spurned, on the other hand, tended to sound forlorn or cross (as on "Love [Makes Me Do Foolish Things]" from 1965). The best Vandellas records were made with H-D-H, but after the atypically infectious "Jimmy Mack" in early 1967, the two teams went their separate ways. The result for Martha and the Vandellas was little short of disastrous. After 1967 the group never made the Top Forty again.

Marvin Gaye. A stage-shy performer who originally fancied himself a jazz singer, Marvin Gaye was one of Motown's most enigmatic—and consistently popular—acts. First employed by Gordy as a session drummer, he debuted as a vocalist in 1962 with the herky-jerky "Stubborn Kind of Fellow," and proceeded to work with practically every producer in the Motown stable. With Holland-Dozier-Holland he made "Can I Get a Witness?" (1963), a rough-and-tumble gospel-blues track, and "How Sweet It Is to Be Loved by You" (1964), a medium-

Martha Reeves and the Vandellas looking cool around the time of "Heat Wave."

Marvin Gaye, the Prince of Motown: long before the days of "Sexual Healing."

Always one of Motown's most idiosyncratic talents, Gaye entered into a second phase of his career in 1971, with the release of *What's Going On?* a self-composed and -produced song cycle that marked a liberation from Gordy's studio system. (Gaye had previously shown his skill as a songwriter as coauthor of "Dancing in the Street," and as a writer-producer with the Originals, who cut two gloriously anachronistic hits, "Baby, I'm for Real," (1969), and "The Bells," (1970)—both of which betray Gaye's past; he was once a member of the Moonglows, a vintage Fifties vocal group.) Songs like "What's Going On?" and "Mercy Mercy Me (the Ecology)" captured a pensive and introspective Gaye, who managed to express the tentative and confused aura of the period. This strain in his work reached its peak with the magnificent "Inner City Blues" (also 1971), which featured a hushed, almost damned sound. Perhaps to cap his career, Gaye followed his more political work with a return, not to "love," but to pure eroticism, with the irresistible "Let's Get It On" (1973), a huge hit with some claim to being the sexiest record Motown ever produced.

In the decade that followed, Gaye refined his own unique blend of sweet doo-wop harmonies, jazz phrasing and achingly introspective lyricism. His recordings reached a dwindling audience, yet he did top the charts in 1977 with "Got to Give It Up—Pt. 1." In 1982 Gaye left Motown to record for Columbia, where he scored one last, huge hit, "Sexual Healing." Torturously unhappy in his private life, Gaye was shot dead by his father following an argument in 1984.

Jr. Walker and the All Stars. The sole instrumental star at Motown was Jr. Walker, a veteran of Fifties R&B from Indiana. A gruff but lyrical tenor saxophonist, he specialized in sustaining high wails, and his sense of timing was impeccable. Walker's early Motown hits leaned heavily on these instrumental signatures. With a minimum of production, "Shotgun" (1965) established his preeminence as a specialist in hot party discs. Gradually, however, Walker was integrated into the Motown system and encouraged to sing more. An affably raspy vocalist, he performed splendidly on the Holland-Dozier-Holland remake of "How Sweet It Is to Be Loved by You" (1966), then cut several string-laden hits, including "What Does It Take (to Win Your Love)" (1969), his last foray into the Top Ten.

Four Tops. Lamont Dozier recalls idolizing the Four

tempo shouter; with Smokey Robinson he made "I'll Be Doggone" and "Ain't That Peculiar" (both 1965), two of Smokey's most compelling uptempo productions; with Norman Whitfield he made his historic "I Heard It Through the Grapevine" (1968), an extraordinarily sophisticated record that nevertheless seemed to go back a good 400 years for the sources of its dark, utterly ominous incantations ("voodoo music," guitarist Mike Bloomfield once called it). Later, with Ashford and Simpson, Gaye cut a memorable series of duets with Tammi Terrell, including "Your Precious Love" (1967) and "You're All I Need to Get By" (1968), both majestic, massively orchestrated affirmations of eternal love.

Junior Walker, on sax, and the All Stars.

Tops in the late Fifties, when the Detroit group was vacillating between R&B and a more sedate Mills Brothers style. He admired the quartet for its professionalism, but above all for its class. Almost five years later the Tops came to Motown. After an early attempt at making the group into bona fide supper club singers, Holland-Dozier-Holland resurrected the Tops with a sharp midtempo plea called "Baby, I Need Your Loving" (1964).

Built around lead singer Levi Stubbs's dramatic, piercing vocal delivery, the Tops–H-D-H hits came nonstop for almost four years. Records like "I Can't Help Myself" (1965) and "Reach Out, I'll Be There" (1966) perfectly captured the mid-Sixties Motown sound: Tambourines clapped on the offbeat, drummers pounded out indelicate 4/4 rhythms, and imaginative horn and string charts swirled above. Somewhere in the middle was Stubbs, hollering, cajoling and pleading with unflagging intensity. When Holland-Dozier-Holland left Motown in 1968, the group fell on hard times. After fitful success, the Tops joined the growing exodus from Motown in the early Seventies.

Temptations. While the Four Tops covered the frenetic side of the Motown sound and the Miracles monopolized its romantic side, the Temptations quite simply stood as the finest vocal group in Sixties soul: They could outdress, outdance and outsing any competition in sight. It was a quintet distinguished by the breadth and balance of its singing talent, which ran the gamut from David Ruffin's harsh baritone to Eddie Kendricks's wispy falsetto.

The group had been formed in Detroit in the early Sixties, but many members had come from the South. Eddie Kendricks had migrated to Detroit from Birmingham, Alabama, in hopes of rebuilding his old group, the Primes, and met Ruffin, a longtime Motor City resident born in Mississippi. The quintet's music reflected its background: Of all the Motown acts, the Temptations were the closest to church and gospel roots.

Working primarily with Smokey Robinson and Norman Whitfield, the Temptations enjoyed a number of hits in a variety of styles. At the outset, Kendricks dominated the group, seeing the Tempts through such early R&B hits as "The Way You Do the Things You Do" (Robinson, 1964) and "Girl (Why You Wanna Make Me Blue)" (Whitfield, 1964). After Robinson's "My Girl" (1965), featuring Ruffin, introduced the group to a white audience, Robinson ran through a sequence of ballads pitting Ruffin's raspy voice against violins, a phase climaxing with Smokey's brilliant "Since I Lost My Baby" (1965). But the Temptations only hit their popular peak under Whitfield's tutelage. Unlike Holland-

In the mid-Sixties the Supremes were so popular they even got their very own brand of bread.

Dozier-Holland, Whitfield had a flair for spacious rhythmic arrangements. He also had the good sense to exploit the Temptations' versatility, moving from the gritty drive of "(I Know) I'm Losing You" (1966) to "You're My Everything" (1967), a melodramatic wall of sound that featured Ruffin and Kendricks swapping leads.

After Ruffin left the group in 1968 Whitfield turned to more declamatory material; influenced by Sly Stone, he brought the Tempts into the psychedelic era ("Cloud Nine," 1968), and began writing didactic social commentary ("Ball of Confusion," from 1970, for example). All these strategems, however, could scarcely conceal the fact that Ruffin's departure had upset the group's distinctive balance. While the Temptations remained a potent commercial force, they rarely recaptured the glories of their earlier work. Nevertheless, two singles stand out: "I Can't Get Next to You" (1969), a neoclassical throwback to Whitfield's original style, and "Just My Imagination (Running Away with Me)" (1971), a gossamer showcase for Eddie Kendricks, who went solo shortly afterward.

Supremes. Without a doubt, Diana Ross and the Supremes were Berry Gordy's consummate commercial coup. In the span of five years, they amassed twelve Number One pop hits—five in a row after "Where Did Our Love Go?" in 1964. A record unrivaled by any other female group in pop, it attests to

the skill with which Holland-Dozier-Holland and Gordy packaged the Supremes and their music.

Discovered by Gordy in Detroit, where the trio had grown up in the Brewster housing project, the Supremes floundered for almost a year until they were hooked up with Holland-Dozier-Holland in 1963. Their first collaboration, "When the Lovelight Starts Shining Through His Eyes," a torrid, brassy uptempo track, became a modest pop hit in late 1963.

But H-D-H didn't have quite the right formula for the group down yet. After a follow-up flopped, they devised a medium-tempo song that accentuated Ross's insouciant delivery; "Where Did Our Love Go?" a Number One pop hit in the summer of 1964, set the pattern for the singles that followed. Ross cultivated a nonchalant, almost fey style, while H-D-H turned numerous variations on the theme of lost love. During Holland-Dozier-Holland's tenure with the Supremes, the hits were automatic. Between "Where Did Our Love Go?" and the end of 1967, the Supremes released fifteen singles; with one exception, they all made the Top Ten, and ten of them made Number One.

In a sense, the H-D-H–Supremes hits are the purest expression of the Motown sound. The most compliant of Motown's artists, Diana Ross meshed seamlessly with the cyclical structure Holland-Dozier-Holland favored. Her singles resembled one long composition, each new release slightly modifying an element in the overall design, perhaps adding strings or punching the tempo up a notch. By "You Keep Me Hangin' On" (1966), the approach had become so polished that Diana Ross and the Supremes began to sound like an erotic gloss on the assembly-line existence Gordy had adopted in organizing Motown—and in this respect as well, the Supremes were the ultimate embodiment of the Motown ethos.

The key to the Supremes was Ross, who quickly overshadowed her fellow Supremes, visually as well as vocally. Peering with Keane eyes from under a variety of oversized wigs and baroque hairdos, her skinny frame draped in an array of slinky outfits, she was the very picture of the seductive self-pity her lyrics usually articulated ("Nothing but Heartaches"). At the same time, she became a paragon of black respectability. Although Gordy found the Supremes "giggly and immature" when he signed them, he soon had reason to be proud of the most illustrious product of his in-house finishing school.

Gladys Knight and the Pips, best known for their hit version of "I Heard It Through the Grapevine."

By the time Ross left the group in 1970, the Supremes were fixtures on the supper club circuit. Ross, of course, went on to stardom in the cinema and a successful solo recording career. In 1976 Florence Ballard, one of the other original Supremes, died in Detroit; she had been on and off welfare the last few years.

Gladys Knight and the Pips. Before they came to Motown, Gladys Knight and the Pips were sporadically popular balladeers; after they arrived, Norman Whitfield converted them into consistent hitmakers. On the original "I Heard It Through the Grapevine" (1967), Knight was transformed into a fiery hard-edge vocalist, unleashing her scorn with startling fury. But unlike Martha Reeves, Knight was too versatile a singer to be limited to one role. By the early Seventies, the funky persona of Whitfield's productions (such as "The Nitty Gritty," in 1969) had given way to the vulnerable lover of "If I Were Your Woman" (1970). After leaving the label, Knight and the Pips, unlike most Motown alumni, actually consolidated their popularity by reverting to such glossy pop ballads as "Midnight Train to Georgia" (1973).

Jackson 5. "Discovered" by Diana Ross in Gary, Indiana, this quintet of Hoosiers proved to be not only the last great Motown act, but also the last great gasp of Gordy's assembly line. Fronted by the exuberant Michael Jackson, who dipped, spun and moved like a miniature James Brown, the Jackson 5 transcended all barriers of race and age in their appeal. Unlike many of their prepubescent imitators, however, the J5's talent was strictly for real. As the group matured, so did their music, but though later tracks like "Get It Together" (1973) and "Forever Came Today" (1975) were innovative, tight productions, the best Jackson 5 record remained their first for Motown, "I Want You Back" (1969). Catalyzed by a red-hot performance from ten-year-old Michael, the record explodes off the turntable with an intricate Sly-influenced arrangement featuring some of the toughest bass, drum, piano and guitar playing on any soul record anywhere.

The Spinners, who made one terrific Motown record with the help of Stevie Wonder, "It's a Shame."

To the outside world, Motown seemed like one big happy family. While a number of Motown stars have confirmed the accuracy of this picture in the early Sixties, by the middle of the decade serious problems had begun to appear. The autocratic determination that had carried Gordy's company to the top could not help but foster resentment, especially as Gordy's protégés became used to their status in the limelight.

Yet the company continued to control virtually every relevant detail of a performer's career, dictating the songs to be sung, the producers to be used, the singles to be released, the image to be presented to the public (even Motown's biggest stars remained curiously nondescript; reliable biographical details were few and far between). In financial affairs, Gordy governed his flock with patronizing authority: His younger stars were kept on allowances, ostensibly to help them avoid the pitfalls that had left other nouveau riche R&B stars penniless at thirty.

His attitude toward the Supremes was typical. "We had some trouble with them at first," Gordy said in 1966. "You must be very strict with young artists. That instills discipline. But once they get a Number One record, they tend to get more independent. They start spending their money extravagantly. . . . After a year, they saw their mistakes and came to appreciate our handling of their affairs." Though their yearly income was in the five figures—record royalties were divided equally—they were on an allowance of $500 a week.

Berry Gordy *(right)* in 1967, at the height of Motown's popularity, with two unidentified colleagues. A shrewd businessman, Gordy governed his empire with patriarchal authority.

In late 1967 the first major crack appeared in the Motown facade. Holland, Dozier and Holland demanded an accounting of their royalties. Shortly after a suit was initiated, the trio left Motown to form their own label and production firm, a move from which neither Motown nor H-D-H ever fully recovered.

But internal dissension was not the only problem plaguing Gordy. By 1968 the industry had begun to catch up with the Motown sound. Without Holland-Dozier-Holland, neither the Supremes nor the Four Tops were able to maintain their popularity. Even worse, the label's new properties were becoming rare; only Gladys Knight and the Jackson 5 were able to match the style and talent of earlier Motown acts. Gordy himself increasingly retreated from company affairs, choosing instead to lavish his attention on Diana Ross, who was being groomed for a career in Hollywood.

In 1971 both Stevie Wonder and Marvin Gaye negotiated contracts giving them artistic control; the same year, the company moved its headquarters from Detroit to Los Angeles. The old studio system was dissolved, and many of the old stars drifted away: By 1975 Martha Reeves, Gladys Knight, the Jackson 5 and the Four Tops had all left. The company's music, with few exceptions, was no longer particularly distinctive; its quality was increasingly erratic. In the unkindest cut of all, Gamble and Huff's Philadelphia combine finally surpassed Motown as the leading purveyors of top-notch assembly-line black pop, using many of the same ingredients that Gordy had parlayed into a corporate empire.

Motown in its heyday, on the other hand, knew no peers. In the end, it was a wholly mechanical style and sound that roared and purred like a well-tuned Porsche. Contrived yet explosive, the very epitome of mass-produced pop yet drenched in the black tradition, the Motown hits of the Sixties revolutionized American popular music. Never again would black performers be confined to the fabled chitlin circuit; never again would black popular music be dismissed as a minority taste. For more than a decade, Berry Gordy and his many talented cohorts managed, with unerring verve and against all the odds, to translate a black idiom into "The Sound of Young America."

DISCOGRAPHY

1962

Eddie Holland: "Jamie" (Motown; r☆6, ☆30, January). **Miracles:** "What's So Good about Good-Bye?" (Tamla; r☆16, ☆35, January). **Marvelettes:** "Twistin' Postman" (Tamla; r☆ 13, ☆34, February). ²**Mary Wells:** "The One Who Really Loves You" (Motown; r☆2, ☆8, April). **Temptations:** "Dream Come True" (Gordy; r☆22, May). ²**Miracles:** "I'll Try Something New" (Tamla; r☆11, ☆39, May). **Marvelettes:** "Playboy" (Tamla; r☆4, ☆7, May). **Marvelettes:** "Beechwood 45789" b/w "Someday, Someway" (Tamla; r☆7, ☆17, August). **Contours:** "Do You Love Me?" (Gordy; r☆1, ☆3, August). ²**Mary Wells:** "You Beat Me to the Punch" (Motown; r☆1, ☆9, September). **Marvin Gaye and the Vandellas:** "Stubborn Kind of Fellow" (Tamla; r☆8, ☆46, October). ²**Mary Wells:** "Two Lovers" (Motown; r☆1, ☆7, December). ²**Miracles:** "You've Really Got a Hold on Me" (Tamla; r☆1, ☆8, December). **Marvelettes:** "Strange I Know" (Tamla; r☆10, ☆49, December). **Supremes:** "Let Me Go the Right Way" (Motown; r☆26, December).

1963

Contours: "Shake Sherry" (Gordy; r☆21, ☆43, January). **Marvin Gaye:** "Hitch Hike" (Tamla; r☆12, ☆30, February). ²**Mary Wells:** "Laughing Boy" (Motown; r☆6, ☆15, March). ²**Miracles:** "A Love She Can Count On" (Tamla; r☆21, ☆6, ☆31, April). ¹**Martha and the Vandellas:** "Come and Get These Memories" (Gordy; r☆6, ☆29, April). **Marvelettes:** "Locking Up My Heart" b/w "Forever" (Tamla; r☆24, ☆44, May). **Marvin Gaye:** "Pride and Joy" (Tamla; r☆2, ☆10, June). ²**Mary Wells:** "Your Old Stand By" (Motown; r☆8, ☆40, June). **(Little) Stevie Wonder:** "Fingertips—Part 2" (Tamla; r☆1, ☆1, June). **Kim Weston:** "Love Me All the Way" (Tamla; r☆24, July). ¹**Martha and the Vandellas:** "Heat Wave" (Gordy; r☆1, ☆4, August). ¹**Miracles:** "Mickey's Monkey" (Tamla; r☆3, ☆8, August). ²ᐟ¹**Mary Wells:** "What's Easy for Two Is So Hard for One" b/w "You Lost the Sweetest Boy" (Motown; r☆8, ☆22, October). ¹**Marvin Gaye:** "Can I Get a Witness?" (Tamla; r☆15, ☆22, November). ²**Marvelettes:** "As Long as I Know He's Mine" (Tamla; ☆47, November). ¹**Martha and the Vandellas:** "Quicksand" (Gordy; ☆8, November). ¹**Miracles:** "I Gotta Dance to Keep from Crying" (Tamla; ☆35, November). ¹**Supremes:** "When the Lovelight Starts Shining Through His Eyes" (Motown; ☆23, November).

1964

¹**Martha and the Vandellas:** "Live Wire" (Gordy; ☆42, February). ²**Marvelettes:** "He's a Good Guy" (Tamla; ☆55, February). ²**Temptations:** "The Way You Do the Things You Do" (Gordy; ☆11, February). ²**Miracles:** "(You Can't Let the Boy Overpower) The Man in You" (Tamla; ☆59, March). ¹**Marvin Gaye:** "You're a Wonderful One" (Tamla; ☆15, March). ²**Mary Wells:** "My Guy" (Motown; ☆1, April). **Contours:** "Can You Do It" (Gordy; ☆41, April). **Martha and the Vandellas:** "In My Lonely Room" (Gordy; ☆44, April). **Brenda Holloway:** "Every Little Bit Hurts" (Tamla; ☆13, May). **Marvin Gaye and Mary Wells:** "What's the Matter with You Baby" b/w "Once upon a Time" (Motown; ☆17, May). **Eddie Holland:** "Just Ain't Enough Love" (Motown; ☆54, May). ²**Temptations:** "I'll Be In Trouble" (Gordy; ☆33, May). **Marvin Gaye:** "Try It Baby" (Tamla; ☆15, June). **Stevie Wonder:** "Hey Harmonica Man" (Tamla; ☆29, June). ²**Miracles:** "I Like It like That" (Tamla; ☆27, June). ²**Marvelettes:** "You're My Remedy" (Tamla; ☆48, July). ¹**Supremes:** "Where Did Our Love Go?" (Motown; ☆1, July). **Brenda Holloway:** "I'll Always Love You" (Tamla; ☆60, August). ¹**Four Tops:** "Baby, I Need Your Loving" (Motown; ☆11, August). **Martha and the Vandellas:** "Dancing in the Street" (Gordy; ☆2, August). **Eddie Holland:** "Candy to Me" (Motown; ☆58, August). ³**Temptations:** "Girl

(Why You Wanna Make Me Blue)" (Gordy; ☆26, September). ¹**Marvin Gaye:** "Baby Don't You Do It" (Tamla; ☆27, September). ²**Miracles:** "That's What Love Is Made Of" (Tamla; ☆35, September). ¹**Supremes:** "Baby Love" (Motown; ☆1, October). **Velvelettes:** "Needle in a Haystack" (V.I.P.; ☆45, October). ³**Marvelettes:** "Too Many Fish in the Sea" (Tamla; r☆15, ☆25, November). ¹**Four Tops:** "Without the One You Love" (Motown; ☆43, November). ¹**Supremes:** "Come See about Me" (Motown; r☆3, ☆1, November). **Martha and the Vandellas:** "Wild One" (Gordy; ☆34, December). ¹**Marvin Gaye:** "How Sweet It Is to Be Loved By You" (Tamla; r☆4, ☆6, December). ²**Miracles:** "Come On Do the Jerk" (Tamla; ☆50, December). **Contours:** "Can You Jerk like Me" (Gordy; r☆15, ☆47, December).

1965

²**Temptations:** "My Girl" (Gordy; r☆1, ☆1, January). **Velvelettes:** "He Was Really Sayin' Somethin'" (V.I.P.; r☆21, January). **Four Tops:** "Ask the Lonely" (Motown; r☆9, ☆24, February). **Jr. Walker and the All Stars:** "Shotgun" (Soul; r☆1, ☆4, February). ¹**Supremes:** "Stop! In the Name of Love" (Motown; r☆2, ☆1, February). ¹**Martha and the Vandellas:** "Nowhere to Run" (Gordy; r☆5, ☆8, February). ²**Brenda Holloway:** "When I'm Gone" (Tamla; r☆12, ☆25, March). **Marvin Gaye:** "I'll Be Doggone" (Tamla; r☆1, ☆8, March). ²**Temptations:** "It's Growing" (Gordy; r☆3, ☆18, April). ²**Miracles:** "Ooo Baby Baby" (Tamla; r☆4, ☆16, April). ¹**Supremes:** "Back in My Arms Again" (Motown; r☆1, ☆1, May). ¹**Four Tops:** "I Can't Help Myself" (Motown; r☆1, ☆1, May). **Jr. Walker and the All Stars:** "Do the Boomerang" (Soul; r☆10, ☆36, June). **Marvelettes:** "I'll Keep Holding On" (Tamla; r☆11, ☆34, June). ²**Miracles:** "The Tracks of My Tears" (Tamla; r☆2, ☆16, July). **Spinners:** "I'll Always Love You" (Motown; r☆8, ☆35, July). **Marvin Gaye:** "Pretty Little Baby" (Tamla; r☆16, ☆25, July). ²**Temptations:** "Since I Lost My Baby" b/w "You've Got to Earn It" (Gordy; r☆4, ☆17, July). ¹**Four Tops:** "It's the Same Old Song" (Motown; r☆2, ☆5, August). ¹**Supremes:** "Nothing but Heartaches" (Motown; r☆6, ☆11, August). **Jr. Walker and the All Stars:** "Shake and Fingerpop" b/w "Cleo's Back" (Soul; r☆7, ☆29, August). ²**Contours:** "First I Look at the Purse" (Gordy; r☆12, August). **Marvelettes:** "Danger Heartbreak Dead Ahead" (Tamla; r☆11, September). **Martha and the Vandellas:** "You've Been in Love Too Long" b/w "Love (Makes Me Do Foolish Things)" (Gordy; r☆22, ☆36, September). **Stevie Wonder:** "High Heel Sneakers" (Tamla; r☆30, September). ¹**Kim Weston:** "Take Me in Your Arms (Rock Me a Little While)" (Gordy; r☆4, ☆50, October). ²**Marvin Gaye:** "Ain't That Peculiar" (Tamla; r☆1, ☆8, October). ²**Miracles:** "My Girl Has Gone" (Tamla; r☆3, ☆14, October). ²**Temptations:** "My Baby" b/w "Don't Look Back" (Gordy; r☆4, ☆13, October). ¹**Supremes:** "I Hear a Symphony" (Motown; r☆2, ☆1, November). ¹**Four Tops:** "Something about You" (Motown; r☆9, ☆19, November).

1966

Stevie Wonder: "Uptight (Everything's Alright)" (Tamla; r☆1, ☆3, January). ²**Miracles:** "Going to a Go Go" (Tamla; r☆2, ☆11, January). ²**Marvelettes:** "Don't Mess with Bill" (Tamla; r☆3, ☆7, January). ¹**Supremes:** "My World Is Empty Without You" (Motown; r☆10, ☆5, January). **Tammi Terrell:** "I Can't Believe You Love Me" (Motown; r☆27, January). **Jr. Walker and the All Stars:** "Cleo's Mood" (Soul; r☆14, ☆50, January). **Martha and the Vandellas:** "My Baby Loves Me" (Gordy; r☆3, ☆22, February). **Elgins:** "Darling Baby" (V.I.P.; r☆4, February). ²**Marvin Gaye:** "One More Heartache" (Tamla; r☆4, ☆29, February). ¹**Isley Brothers:** "This Old Heart of Mine (Is Weak for You)" (Tamla; r☆6, ☆12, February). ¹**Four Tops:** "Shake Me, Wake Me (When It's Over)" (Motown; r☆5, ☆18, March). ²**Temptations:** "Get Ready" (Gordy; r☆1, ☆29, March). **Kim Weston:** "Helpless" (Gordy; r☆13, March). **Stevie Wonder:** "Nothing's Too Good for My Baby" b/w "With a Child's Heart" (Tamla; r☆4, ☆20, April). **Monitors:** "Greetings (This Is Uncle Sam)" (V.I.P.; r☆21, April). ¹**Jr. Walker and the All Stars:** "I'm a Road Runner" (Soul; r☆4, ☆20, May). ¹**Supremes:**

"Love Is like an Itching in My Heart" (Motown; r☆7, ☆9, May). ²**Marvelettes:** "You're the One" (Tamla; r☆20, ☆48, May). **Spinners:** "Truly Yours," (Motown; r☆16, May). ³**Temptations:** "Ain't Too Proud to Beg" (Gordy; r☆1, ☆13, May). **Tammi Terrell:** "Come On and See Me" (Motown; r☆25, June). ²**Marvin Gaye:** "Take This Heart of Mine" (Tamla; r☆16, ☆44, June). **Contours:** "Just a Little Misunderstanding" (Gordy; r☆18, June). **Four Tops:** "Loving You Is Sweeter than Ever" (Motown; r☆12, ☆45, June). **Miracles:** "Whole Lot of Shakin' in My Heart" (Tamla; r☆20, ☆46, June). **Stevie Wonder:** "Blowin' in the Wind" (Tamla; r☆1, ☆9, July). **Jimmy Ruffin:** "What Becomes of the Broken Hearted" (Soul; r☆6, ☆7, August). **Jr. Walker and the All Stars:** "How Sweet It Is (to Be Loved by You)" (Soul; r☆3, ☆18, August). ¹**Supremes:** "You Can't Hurry Love" (Motown; r☆1, ☆1, August). ³**Temptations:** "Beauty Is Only Skin Deep" (Gordy; r☆1, ☆3, August). ¹**Marvin Gaye:** "Little Darling, I Need You" (Tamla; r☆10, ☆47, August). ¹**Four Tops:** "Reach Out, I'll Be There" (Motown; r☆1, ☆1, September). ¹**Elgins:** "Heaven Must Have Sent You" (V.I.P.; r☆9, ☆50, September). ¹**Supremes:** "You Keep Me Hangin' On" (Motown; r☆1, ☆1, November). ¹**Martha and the Vandellas:** "I'm Ready for Love" (Gordy; r☆2, ☆9, November). **Stevie Wonder:** "A Place in the Sun" (Tamla; r☆3, ☆9, November). ¹**Miracles:** "(Come 'Round Here) I'm the One You Need" (Tamla; r☆4, ☆17, November). ³**Temptations:** "(I Know) I'm Losing You" (Gordy; r☆1, ☆8, November). ¹**Four Tops:** "Standing in the Shadows of Love" (Motown; r☆2, ☆6, December). **Jimmy Ruffin:** "I've Passed This Way Before" (Soul; r☆10, ☆17, December).

1967

Marvin Gaye and Kim Weston: "It Takes Two" (Tamla; r☆4, ☆14, January). ²**Marvelettes:** "The Hunter Gets Captured by the Game" (Tamla; r☆2, ☆13, February). ¹**Supremes:** "Love Is Here and Now You're Gone" (Motown; r☆1, ☆1, February). ²**Smokey Robinson and the Miracles:** "The Love I Saw in You Was Just a Mirage" (Tamla; r☆10, ☆20, March). ¹**Martha and the Vandellas:** "Jimmy Mack" (Gordy; r☆1, ☆10, March). **Jr. Walker and the All Stars:** "Pucker Up Buttercup" (Soul; r☆11, ☆31, March). ¹**Four Tops:** "Bernadette" (Motown; r☆3, ☆4, March). **Jimmy Ruffin:** "Gonna Give Her All the Love I've Got" (Soul; r☆14, ☆29, April). ¹**Supremes:** "The Happening" (Motown; r☆12, ☆1, April). **Brenda Holloway:** "Just Look What You've Done" (Tamla; r☆21, April). **Stevie Wonder:** "Hey Love" b/w "Travelin' Man" (Tamla; r☆9., ☆32, May). **Temptations:** "All I Need" (Gordy; r☆2, ☆8, May). **Marvelettes:** "When You're Young and in Love" (Tamla; r☆9, ☆23, May). **Marvin Gaye and Tammi Terrell:** "Ain't No Mountain High Enough" (Tamla; r☆3, ☆19, June). ¹**Four Tops:** "7 Rooms of Gloom" (Motown; r☆10, ☆14, June). ²**Smokey Robinson and the Miracles:** "More Love" (Tamla; r☆5, ☆23, June). **Stevie Wonder:** "I Was Made to Love Her" (Tamla; r☆1, ☆2, June). ¹**Marvin Gaye:** "Your Unchanging Love" (Tamla; r☆7, ☆33, July). ³**Gladys Knight and the Pips:** "Everybody Needs Love" (Soul; r☆3, ☆39, July). ³**Temptations:** "You're My Everything" (Gordy; r☆3, ☆6, August). ¹**Diana Ross and the Supremes:** "Reflections" (Motown; r☆4, ☆2, August. **Jimmy Ruffin:** "Don't You Miss Me a Little Bit Baby" (Soul; r☆27, August). **Martha and the Vandellas:** "Love Bug Leave My Heart Alone" (Gordy; r☆14, ☆25, September). ¹**Four Tops:** "You Keep Running Away" (Motown; r☆7, ☆19, September). ⁴**Marvin Gaye and Tammi Terrell:** "Your Precious Love" (Tamla; r☆2, ☆5, September). **Stevie Wonder:** "I'm Wondering" (Tamla; r☆4, ☆12, October). ³**Temptations:** "(Loneliness Made Me Realize) It's You That I Need" (Gordy; r☆3, ☆14, October). ³**Gladys Knight and the Pips:** "I Heard It through the Grapevine" (Soul; r☆1, ☆2, October). ²**Smokey Robinson and the Miracles:** "I Second That Emotion" (Tamla; r☆1, ☆4, November). **Martha Reeves and the Vandellas:** "Honey Chile" (Gordy; r☆5, ☆11, November). ¹**Diana Ross and the Supremes:** "In and Out of Love" (Motown; r☆16, ☆9, November). ¹**Jr. Walker and the All Stars:** "Come See About Me" (Soul; r☆8, ☆24, December). ⁴**Marvin Gaye and Tammi Terrell:** "If I Could Build My Whole World

around You" b/w "If This World Were Mine" (Tamla; r☆2, ☆10, December). ²**Marvelettes:** "My Baby Must Be a Magician" (Tamla; r☆8, ☆17, December).

1968

³**Temptations:** "I Wish It Would Rain" (Gordy; r☆1, ☆4, January). **Marvin Gaye:** "You" (Tamla; r☆7, ☆34, February). ³**Gladys Knight and the Pips:** "The End of Our Road" (Soul; r☆5, ☆15, February). ¹**Four Tops:** "Walk Away Renee" (Motown; r☆15, ☆14, February). ²**Smokey Robinson and the Miracles:** "If You Can Want" (Tamla; r☆3, ☆11, March). ¹**Diana Ross and the Supremes:** "Forever Came Today" (Motown; r☆17, ☆28, March). **Stevie Wonder:** "Shoo-Be-Doo-Be-Doo-Da-Day" (Tamla; r☆1, ☆9, April). **Bobby Taylor and the Vancouvers:** "Does Your Mama Know about Me" (Gordy; r☆5, ☆29, April). **Isley Brothers:** "Take Me in Your Arms (Rock Me a Little While)" (Tamla; r☆22, April). ⁴**Marvin Gaye and Tammi Terrell:** "Ain't Nothing like the Real Thing" (Tamla; r☆1, ☆8, April). ³**Temptations:** "I Could Never Love Another (after Loving You)" (Gordy; r☆1, ☆13, May). **Shorty Long:** "Here Comes the Judge" (Soul; r☆4, ☆8, June). ²**Smokey Robinson and the Miracles:** "Yester Love" (Tamla; r☆9, ☆31, June). ²**Marvelettes:** "Here I Am Baby" (Tamla; r☆14, ☆44, June). ³**Gladys Knight and the Pips:** "It Should Have Been Me" (Soul; r☆9, ☆40, June). **Stevie Wonder:** "You Met Your Match" (Tamla; r☆2, ☆35, August). ⁴**Marvin Gaye and Tammi Terrell:** "You're All I Need to Get By" (Tamla; r☆1, ☆7, August). ³**Temptations:** "Please Return Your Love to Me" (Gordy; r☆4, ☆26, August). ²**Smokey Robinson and the Miracles:** "Special Occasion" (Tamla; r☆4, ☆26, August). **Jr. Walker and the All Stars:** "Hip City—Part 2" (Soul; r☆7, ☆31, August). ³**Gladys Knight and the Pips:** "I Wish It Would Rain" (Soul; r☆15, ☆41, September). **Marvin Gaye:** "Chained" (Tamla; r☆8, ☆32, September). ⁴**Marvelettes:** "Destination: Anywhere" (Tamla; r☆28, October). ⁴**Marvin Gaye and Tammi Terrell:** "Keep On Lovin' Me Honey" (Tamla; r☆11, ☆24, October). ¹**Four Tops:** "I'm in a Different World" (Motown; r☆23, October). **Diana Ross and the Supremes:** "Love Child" (Motown; r☆2, ☆1, October). **Stevie Wonder:** "For Once in My Life" (Tamla; r☆2, ☆2, November). **Bobby Taylor and the Vancouvers:** "Malinda" (Gordy; r☆16, ☆48, November). ³**Temptations:** "Cloud Nine" (Gordy; r☆2, ☆6, November). ¹**Marvin Gaye:** "I Heard It through the Grapevine" (Tamla; r☆1, ☆1, November). **Diana Ross and the Supremes and the Temptations:** "I'm Gonna Make You Love Me" (Motown; r☆2, ☆2, December).

1969

²**Smokey Robinson and the Miracles:** "Baby, Baby Don't Cry" (Tamla; r☆3, ☆8, January). **Jr. Walker and the All Stars:** "Home Cookin'" (Soul; r☆19, ☆42, February). **Diana Ross and the Supremes:** "I'm Livin' in Shame" (Motown; r☆8, ☆10, February). ⁴**Marvin Gaye and Tammi Terrell:** "Good Lovin' Ain't Easy to Come By" (Tamla; r☆11, ☆30, February). **David Ruffin:** "My Whole World Ended (the Moment You Left Me)" (Motown; r☆2, ☆9, February). **Edwin Starr:** "Twenty-Five Miles" (Gordy; r☆6, ☆6, February). ³**Temptations:** "Run Away Child, Running Wild" (Gordy; r☆1, ☆6, March). ⁴**Gladys Knight and the Pips:** "Didn't You Know" (Soul; r☆11, March). **Diana Ross and the Supremes and the Temptations:** "I'll Try Something New" (Motown; r☆8, ☆25, March). **Chuck Jackson:** "(You Can't Let the Boy Overpower) The Man in You" (Motown; r☆27, April). ³**Marvin Gaye:** "Too Busy Thinking about My Baby" (Tamla; r☆1, ☆4, May). ²**Diana Ross and the Supremes:** "The Composer" (Motown; r☆21, ☆27, May). ³**Temptations:** "Don't Let the Joneses Get You Down" (Gordy; r☆2, ☆20, May). **Jr. Walker and the All Stars:** "What Does It Take (to Win Your Love)" (Soul; r☆1, ☆4, May). **Diana Ross and the Supremes:** "No Matter What Sign You Are" (Motown; r☆17, ☆31, June). **Stevie Wonder:** "My Cherie Amour" b/w "I Don't Know Why" (Tamla; r☆4, ☆4, June). ²**Smokey Robinson and the Miracles:** "Doggone Right" b/w "Here I Go Again" (Tamla; r☆7, ☆32, June). **Edwin Starr:** "I'm Still a Strugglin' Man" (Gordy; r☆27, June). ²**Smokey

Robinson and the Miracles: "Abraham, Martin and John" (Tamla; r☆16, ☆33, July). **David Ruffin:** "I've Lost Everything I've Ever Loved" (Motown; r☆11, July). ³**Gladys Knight and the Pips:** "The Nitty Gritty" (Soul; r☆2, ☆19, July). ³**Temptations:** "I Can't Get Next to You" (Gordy; r☆1, ☆1, August). ³**Marvin Gaye:** "That's the Way Love Is" (Tamla; r☆2, ☆7, September). **Originals:** "Baby, I'm for Real" (Soul; r☆1, ☆14, September). ³**Gladys Knight and the Pips:** "Friendship Train" (Soul; r☆2, ☆17, November). **Jr. Walker and the All Stars:** "These Eyes" (Soul; r☆3, ☆16, November). **Stevie Wonder:** "Yester-Me, Yester-You, Yesterday" (Tamla; r☆5, ☆7, November). **Diana Ross and the Supremes:** "Someday We'll Be Together" (Motown; r☆1, ☆1, November). **Jackson 5:** "I Want You Back" (Motown; r☆1, ☆1, November). ⁴**Marvin Gaye and Tammi Terrell:** "What You Gave Me" (Tamla; r☆6, ☆49, December). ³**Four Tops:** "Don't Let Him Take Your Love From Me" (Motown; r☆25, ☆45, December). **David Ruffin:** "I'm So Glad I Fell For You" (Motown; r☆18, December).

1970

³**Marvin Gaye:** "How Can I Forget" (Tamla; r☆18, ☆41, January). ³**Temptations:** "Psychedelic Shack" (Gordy; r☆2, ☆7, January). **Stevie Wonder:** "Never Had a Dream Come True" (Tamla; r☆11, ☆26, February). **Originals:** "The Bells" (Soul; r☆4, ☆12, February). **Jr. Walker and the All Stars:** "Gotta Hold On to This Feeling" (Soul; r☆2, ☆21, February). **Supremes:** "Up the Ladder to the Roof" (Motown; r☆5, ☆10, March). **Jackson 5:** "ABC" (Motown; r☆1, ☆1, March). ³**Gladys Knight and the Pips:** "You Need Love like I Do (Don't You)" (Soul; r☆3, ☆25, April). ⁴**Marvin Gaye and Tammi Terrell:** "The Onion Song" (Tamla; r☆18, ☆50, April). **Four Tops:** "It's All in the Game" (Motown; r☆6, ☆24, May). **Rare Earth:** "Get Ready" (Rare Earth; r☆20, ☆4, May). ⁴**Diana Ross:** "Reach Out and Touch (Somebody's Hand)" (Motown; r☆7, ☆20, May). ³**Temptations:** "Ball of Confusion" (Gordy; r☆2, ☆3, May). ⁴**Smokey Robinson and the Miracles:** "Who's Gonna Take the Blame" (Tamla; r☆9, ☆46, June). **Jackson 5:** "The Love You Save" (Motown; r☆1, ☆1, June). ³**Marvin Gaye:** "The End of Our Road" (Tamla; r☆7, ☆40, June). **Stevie Wonder:** "Signed, Sealed, Delivered I'm Yours" (Tamla; r☆1, ☆3, July). ³**Edwin Starr:** "War" (Gordy; r☆3, ☆1, July). **Jr. Walker and the All Stars:** "Do You See My Love (for You Growing)" (Soul; r☆3, ☆32, July). **Spinners:** "It's a Shame" (V.I.P.; r☆4, ☆14, July). **Supremes:** "Everybody's Got the Right to Love" (Motown; r☆11, ☆21, July). ⁴**Diana Ross:** "Ain't No Mountain High Enough" (Motown; r☆1, ☆1, August). **Originals:** "We Can Make It Baby" (Soul; r☆20, August). **Rare Earth:** "(I Know) I'm Losing You" (Rare Earth; r☆20, ☆7, August). **Four Tops:** "Still Water (Love)" (Motown; r☆4, ☆11, September). **Jackson 5:** "I'll Be There" (Motown; r☆1, ☆1, September). ³**Temptations:** "Ungena Za Ulimwengu (Unite the World)" (Gordy; r☆8, ☆33, October). **Stevie Wonder:** "Heaven Help Us All" (Tamla; r☆2, ☆9, October). ²**Smokey Robinson and the Miracles:** "The Tears of a Clown" (Tamla; r☆1, ☆1, October). **David and Jimmy Ruffin:** "Stand by Me" (Soul; r☆24, October). **Supremes:** "Stoned Love" (Motown; r☆1, ☆7, November). **Gladys Knight and the Pips:** "If I Were Your Woman" (Soul; r☆1, ☆9, November).

⁴**Supremes and Four Tops:** "River Deep—Mountain High" (Motown; r☆7, ☆14, December). ³**Edwin Starr:** "Stop the War Now" (Gordy; r☆5, ☆26, December).

1971

Originals: "God Bless Whoever Sent You" (Soul; r☆14, January). ⁴**Diana Ross:** "Remember Me" (Motown; r☆10, ☆16, January). **Four Tops:** "Just Seven Numbers (Can Straighten Out My Life)" (Motown; r☆9, ☆40, January). **Spinners:** "We'll Have It Made" (V.I.P.; r☆20, January). **Jackson 5:** "Mama's Pearl" (Motown; r☆2, ☆2, February). ³**Temptations:** "Just My Imagination (Running Away with Me)" (Gordy; r☆1, ☆1, February). **Marvin Gaye:** "What's Going On?" (Tamla; r☆1, ☆2, February). **Stevie Wonder:** "We Can Work It Out" (Tamla; r☆3, ☆13, March). ²**Smokey Robinson and the Miracles:** "I Don't Blame You at All" (Tamla; r☆7, ☆18, March). **Jackson 5:** "Never Can Say Goodbye" (Motown; r☆1, ☆2, April). ³**Edwin Starr:** "Funky Music Sho Nuff Turns Me On" (Gordy; r☆6, May). ⁴**Diana Ross:** "Reach Out, I'll Be There" (Motown; r☆17, ☆29, May). **Supremes:** "Nathan Jones" (Motown; r☆8, ☆16, May). **Gladys Knight and the Pips:** "I Don't Want to Do Wrong" (Soul; r☆2, ☆17, June). ³**Undisputed Truth:** "Smiling Faces Sometimes" (Gordy; r☆2, ☆3, June). **Marvin Gaye:** "Mercy Mercy Me (the Ecology)" (Tamla; r☆1, ☆4, July). **Four Tops:** "In These Changing Times" (Motown; r☆28, July). **Smokey Robinson and the Miracles:** "Crazy about the La La La" (Tamla; r☆20, July). **Jackson 5:** "Maybe Tomorrow" (Motown; r☆3, ☆20, July). **Temptations:** "It's Summer" (Gordy; r☆29, July). **Jr. Walker and the All Stars:** "Take Me Girl, I'm Ready" (Soul; r☆18, ☆50, August). **Stevie Wonder:** "If You Really Love Me" (Tamla; r☆4, ☆8, August). ³**Rare Earth:** "I Just Want to Celebrate" (Rare Earth; r☆30, ☆7, August). ⁴**Diana Ross:** "Surrender" (Motown; r☆16, ☆38, September). **Four Tops:** "MacArthur Park (Part II)" (Motown; r☆27, ☆38, September). **Marvin Gaye:** "Inner City Blues (Makes Me Wanna Holler)" (Tamla; r☆1, ☆9, October). **Martha Reeves and the Vandellas:** "Bless You" (Gordy; r☆29, October). **Michael Jackson:** "Got to Be There" (Motown; r☆4, ☆4, November). ³**Temptations:** "Superstar (Remember How You Got Where You Are)" (Gordy; r☆8, ☆8, November). ²**Smokey Robinson and the Miracles:** "Satisfaction" (Tamla; r☆20, ☆49, November). **Jr. Walker and the All Stars:** "Way Back Home" (Soul; r☆24, December). ³**Undisputed Truth:** "You Make Your Own Heaven and Hell Right Here on Earth" (Gordy; r☆24, December). **Gladys Knight and the Pips:** "Make Me the Woman That You Go Home To" (Soul; r☆3, ☆27, December). **Jackson 5:** "Sugar Daddy" (Motown; r☆3, ☆10, Dec.)

---

¹ = Record produced by Holland-Dozier-Holland.
² = Record produced by Smokey Robinson.
³ = Record produced by Norman Whitfield.
⁴ = Record produced by Ashford and Simpson.

(Chart positions compiled from Joel Whitburn's *Record Research*, based on *Billboard*'s Pop chart, unless otherwise indicated; r☆ = position on *Billboard*'s Rhythm & Blues chart. [Note: *Billboard* did not publish a separate R&B listing during 1964.])

STEVIE WONDER

BY JOHN ROCKWELL

In rough outline, Stevie Wonder's career goes like this: Born Steveland Judkins (or Morris—his father's name was Judkins, but Wonder says that Morris was on the birth certificate) on May 13th, 1950, in Saginaw, Michigan, he was raised as Steveland Morris in Detroit. At the age of ten, he was introduced by Ronnie White of the Miracles to Berry Gordy's Hitsville, U.S.A.; his stage name was changed to Little Stevie Wonder at about the same time Hitsville, U.S.A. became Motown.

Wonder had his first hit—it went to Number One—in "Fingertips—Pt. 2" in 1963. At that time his audience was consistently integrated; in 1964 the Rolling Stones were his opening act. His adolescence was spent turning out a steady succession of singles and albums, many of which did well on the pop as well as the rhythm & blues charts. But he didn't have another Number One single until "Superstition" in 1972, after the exposure gained from opening for the Stones during their American tour that year. The albums *Music of My Mind, Talking Book* (both 1972) and *Innervisions* (1973) were enormous successes, both critically and commercially, and sealed Wonder's status as the most influential and acclaimed black musician of the early Seventies. On August 6th, 1973, he was almost killed in an auto-

mobile accident while on tour in North Carolina. A log from a truck smashed through the front window of the car in which he was a passenger and struck him in the forehead. Already blind since infancy, he lost his sense of smell in the accident but apparently emerged otherwise unscathed. In 1974 he won five Grammy awards, then in 1975 five more, and that August was reported to have signed a seven-year, $13 million contract with Motown, at that point one of the most lucrative in the history of the record business. (It later turned out he didn't actually sign the document until April 1976.) His 1974 album, much of it written before his 1973 accident, was called *Fulfillingness' First Finale*.

Since two years passed before the release of *Songs in the Key of Life*, the 1974 album might have really

looked like a finale. But actually *Songs* seems now to better fulfill that role. Its blend of hit singles and ballads echoed Wonder's pattern of the past and sustained his commercial dominance and artistic influence. But apart from a retrospective package in 1977, *Looking Back,* it would be more than three years until the next Stevie Wonder album, *Journey Through the Secret Life of Plants,* a mostly meandering two-disc soundtrack of mood music that failed to top the charts. After that came *Hotter Than July* (1980), the soundtrack for *The Woman in Red* (1984), *In Square Circle* (1985), *Characters* (1987) and the soundtrack for Spike Lee's *Jungle Fever* (1991), with the long-bruited *Conversation Piece* still in preparation as of spring 1992.

Even at the peak of his mass appeal, from 1972 to 1976, Wonder occasioned a certain puzzlement. He isn't consistent; he has a distressing predilection for cosmic meanderings and soupy sentimentality. But listening to his albums in sequence is an instructive experience; it indicates that Wonder is perhaps most comfortable as a live performer and that his gifts are more constrained by the confines of the studio than those of some artists. It also suggests that the supposedly sharp break in his career around 1971, when he reached legal maturity and renegotiated his Motown contract to obtain a far-reaching artistic freedom, needs to be partially reevaluated. Certainly the post-1971 Wonder records are more innovative than those that preceded them. But the same polarities in his art can be observed from the beginning.

Wonder's first singles appeared in the fall of 1962, but he didn't make an impact until the summer of 1963, with "Fingertips" and the *Little Stevie Wonder the 12 Year Old Genius* album that contained it. Both were distinguished by two things apart from Wonder's raw talent. First, "Fingertips" and the album were recorded live, which is hardly customary for new artists or hit singles; second, both caught Wonder right at the end of his prepubescence.

The first image of Little Stevie Wonder was of a loose-limbed, tambourine-shaking, harmonica-blowing natural child of music, and it was the image that has defined his large-scale

He broke out of the Motown mold to compose and produce a new kind of black music.

concerts ever since. At Wonder's first major U.S. appearance after his accident, at Madison Square Garden in March 1974, it was the uptempo material that got the biggest cheers and the long, rhapsodic, building, repetitive improvisations that constituted the night's emotional high points. In particular, his concert version of "Living for the City," with the chorus repeated over and over in terraced levels of intensity, surpassed anything Wonder has ever done on record, and that's not to say he hasn't made wonderful records. Lee's use of the 1973 studio version of that song in the crack-den scene of *Jungle Fever,* with the musical climax cut short to suit the film's needs, attained no such comparable impact—and was still far and away the most powerful moment on the soundtrack.

Recording careers are made in the studio, however, and Wonder's recorded product in his adolescence mostly derived from the Motown hit factory of the Sixties. The fact that his first big hit came when he was thirteen meant that Wonder couldn't count on a protracted boy-soprano career like that of Michael Jackson. Almost immediately his voice began to crack, and although his next few albums contain occasional soprano outtakes inserted incongruously into the rest, he was mostly a high baritone/low tenor from then on. His voice now is full of tenor lightness, but he lacks the range to exploit high notes or the desire to cultivate a Smokey Robinson falsetto.

The records of this period are highly variable, ranging from curious emulations of the then popular "surf sound"—he even appeared in two of that era's surf film epics, *Muscle Beach Party* and *Bikini Beach*—to an inevitable homage to Ray Charles and a Christmas album. The hit singles of his adolescence include punchy R&B—"Uptight (Everything's Alright)," "I Was Made to Love Her"—to brassy pop ("For Once in My Life"), sentimental ballads ("My Cherie Amour"), even a Dylan tune ("Blowin' in the Wind"), long before Motown discovered social consciousness.

This is a far more varied output than that of most Motown artists during the Sixties, but Wonder was still deeply enmeshed in the Motown system: The company controlled his publishing, masterminded his arrangements and recording sessions, booked his tours, held his money in trust and doled out an allowance ($2.50 per week when he was thirteen). Many of the songs Stevie sang were composed by

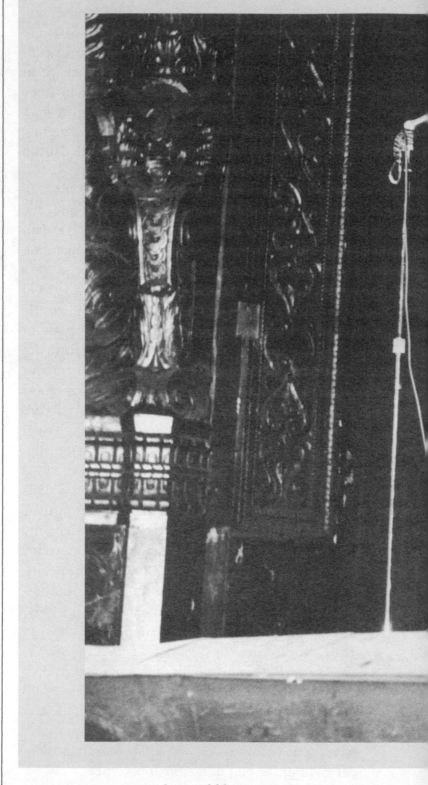

staff writers; those he wrote were generally cocredited to such Motown regulars as Sylvia Moy and Henry Cosby. Just who wrote what in this period remains a mystery. Moy and Cosby, for instance, are credited on "Uptight" along with "S. Judkins," yet Wonder himself once said this was the first song he ever wrote. What is clear is that Motown executives and producers had much to do with how the records actually sounded. "They would have the rhythm worked out," Wonder later recalled, "and I would just come to the sessions and play the piano."

That doesn't mean, however, that some of Wonder's later characteristics weren't already in evidence. There was the childlike ebullience of his fast tunes and the unabashed sentimentality of his slow numbers (no matter that at first he confined himself to the stock banalities of teen-dream love, only later to lap over into universal brotherhood). There was his omnivorous ability to devour diverse influences and put his own stylistic stamp on the results—from the basics of gospel, blues, rhythm & blues and soul to Dylan, the surf sound, jazz and adult white pop, and finally to rock, electronic music and African ethnicity.

Still, by his late teens Wonder had reached a ceiling on what he could accomplish within the traditional Motown strictures. A live album released in early 1970 dramatizes that fact, with its turgid arrangements continually weighing down his inherent gifts. "All I'm trying to do is get myself together," he remarks in the introduction to one song. "All I'm trying to do is do my own thing." *Signed Sealed and Delivered* from later in 1970 was the first album Wonder produced himself, and it amounted to a return to his old "Uptight" R&B roots. But the key shift came the next year, when he turned twenty-one and got control of his $1-million trust fund. His new, laboriously negotiated 120-page contract was a precedent-shattering event at Motown. The company would continue to distribute his records, but Wonder gained complete artistic freedom, control of his publishing and a far higher royalty rate. *Where I'm Coming From* (1971) only partially fulfilled the promise of this new freedom. But with *Music of My Mind* the

next year, Stevie Wonder could be counted as a mature artist.

The maturity expressed itself in several ways. The records weren't "concept albums," but they were conceived as entities, the songs flowing together organically. The lyrics now embraced social, political and mystical concerns, and even his stock love-and-sex themes were deepened to include domesticity and religiousness. Musically, Wonder, aided in the

creasingly reflected the expansive spontaneity of his live performances. The music's color was defined above all through Wonder's fascination with synthesizers, the clavinet, electric pianos and organs and, more recently, samplers and MIDI-interfaced computer technology. They lent his work, particularly the uptempo material, a twangy insistence that was unmistakably personal without ever lapsing into silly technocratic display.

While Wonder has never seemed emptily virtuosic, in the Eighties he did lapse into a self-conscious perfectionism that limited his output. Although his big hits remained lively R&B material like "Higher Ground," "Boogie On Reggae Woman" and "You Haven't Done Nothin'," his albums have contained a disproportionate amount of balladic ramblings, faceless soundtracks and banal ruminations. There was a solid level of craftsmanship, but Wonder perhaps inevitably failed to extend the extraordinary innovation that marked his work in the early and mid-Seventies. Some critics complain about his self-indulgence and bleary universal-love sentimentality, especially after the release of *Journey Through the Secret Life of Plants*. These are unquestionably parts of his mature, but his early records prove they're nothing new. After the lively *Hotter Than July* in 1980, nothing he subsequently accomplished surpassed his soundtrack for *Jungle Fever* of 1991, knocked out with liberating speed in just a month. Yet that, in turn, paled before "Living for the City," from 1974.

Despite some stagnation in the last decade, what is ultimately exciting about Wonder's music—and what still makes his potential for growth more promising than that of more settled artists—is his unpredictable openness to new sounds and new styles. Not that he chases after every trend; his venture into rap in *Jungle Fever* came years after other non-rappers had taken that plunge. But his responses are fresh, and what he has already accomplished is enormous. One imagines he will keep plugging away, striking the chord of critical and popular success every few years and proceeding on his own way in between. Isolated from the "real" world by race, blindness and success even as he is linked to it by his own extraordinary acuteness, Wonder is probably too original for guaranteed, comfortable acceptance. Which, of course, constitutes his ultimate strength.

early Seventies by producers Robert Margouleff and Malcolm Cecil, started to exploit the potential of the modern studio, particularly for overdubbing. He was now able to play most of the instruments, with only occasional guitar solos, horn, string or percussion supplementation and backup singing by others. Most crucially, both the shape and the color of his music had matured. Its shape, no longer bound to the rigid confines of the three-minute hit single, in-

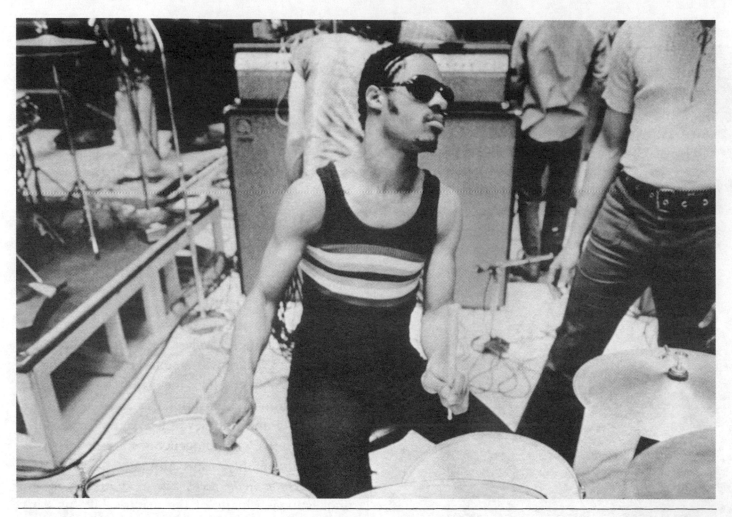

Beginning in the Seventies Wonder played most of the instruments on his albums, overdubbing drums, guitar, bass and keyboards.

DISCOGRAPHY

SINGLES

"Never Had a Dream Come True" (Tamla; r☆11, ☆26, 1970). "Signed, Sealed, Delivered I'm Yours" (Tamla; r☆1, ☆3, 1970). "Heaven Help Us All" (Tamla; r☆2, ☆9, 1970). "We Can Work It Out" (Tamla; r☆3, ☆13, 1971). "If You Really Love Me" (Tamla; r☆4, ☆8, 1971). "Superwoman (Where Were You When I Needed You)" (Tamla; r☆13, ☆33, 1972). "Superstition" (Tamla; r☆1, ☆1, 1972). "You Are the Sunshine of My Life" (Tamla; r☆3, ☆1, 1973). "Higher Ground" (Tamla; r☆1, ☆4, 1973). "Living for the City" (Tamla; r☆1, ☆8, 1973). "Don't You Worry 'bout a Thing" (Tamla; r☆2, ☆16, 1974). "You Haven't Done Nothin'" (Tamla; r☆1, ☆1, 1974). "Boogie On Reggae Woman" (Tamla; r☆1, ☆3, 1974). "I Wish" (Tamla; r☆1, ☆1, 1976). "Sir Duke" (Tamla; r☆1, ☆1, 1977). "Another Star" (Tamla; r☆18, ☆32, 1977). "As" (Tamla; r☆36, ☆36, 1977). "Send One Your Love" (Tamla; r☆5, ☆4, 1979). With Diana Ross, Marvin Gaye and Smokey Robinson: "Pops, We Love You (A Tribute to Father)" (Motown; r☆26, 1979). "Outside My Window" (Tamla; r☆56, ☆52, 1980). "Master Blaster (Jammin')" (Tamla; r☆1, ☆5, 1980). "I Ain't Gonna Stand for It" (Tamla; r☆4, ☆11, 1980). "Lately" (Tamla; r☆29, ☆64, 1981). "Did I Hear You Say You Love Me" (Tamla; r☆74, 1981). "That Girl" (Tamla; r☆1, ☆4, 1982). With Paul McCartney: "Ebony and Ivory" (Columbia; r☆8, ☆1, 1982). "Do I Do" (Tamla; r☆2, ☆13, 1982). "Ribbon in the Sky" (Tamla; r☆10, ☆54, 1982). With Charlene: "Used to Be" (Motown; r☆35, ☆46, 1982). "I Just Called to Say I Love You" (Motown; r☆1, ☆1, 1984). "Love Light in Flight" (Motown; r☆4, ☆17, 1984). "Part-Time Lover" (Tamla; r☆1, ☆1, 1984). "Go Home" (Tamla; r☆2, ☆10, 1985). "Overjoyed" (Tamla; r☆8, ☆24, 1986). "Land of La La" (Tamla; r☆19, ☆86, 1986). "Skeletons" (Motown; r☆1, ☆19, 1987). "You Will Know" (Motown; r☆1, ☆77, 1988). With Michael Jackson: "Get It" (Motown; r☆4, ☆80, 1988). "With Each Beat of My Heart" (Motown; r☆28, 1989). "Keep Our Love Alive" (Motown; r☆24, ☆44, 1990).

ALBUMS

Little Stevie Wonder the 12 Year Old Genius (Tamla; ☆1, 1963). *Up-Tight* (Tamla; ☆33, 1966). *Down to Earth* (Tamla; ☆92, 1967). *I Was Made to Love Her* (Tamla; ☆45, 1967). *Stevie Wonder's Greatest Hits* (Tamla; ☆37, 1968). *For Once in My Life* (Tamla; ☆50, 1969). *My Cherie Amour* (Tamla; ☆34, 1969). *Stevie Wonder Live* (Tamla; ☆81, 1970). *Signed, Sealed and Delivered* (Tamla; ☆25, 1970). *Where I'm Coming From* (Tamla; ☆62, 1971). *Stevie Wonder's Greatest Hits—Vol. 2* (Tamla; ☆69, 1971). *Music of My Mind* (Tamla; ☆21, 1972). *Talking Book* (Tamla; ☆3, 1972). *Innervisions* (Tamla; ☆4, 1973). *Fulfillingness' First Finale* (Tamla; ☆1, 1974). *Songs in the Key of Life* (Tamla; ☆1, 1976). *Looking Back* (Motown; ☆34, 1978). *Journey Through the Secret Life of Plants* (Tamla; ☆4, 1979). *Hotter Than July* (Tamla; ☆3, 1980). *Stevie Wonder's Original Musiquarium I* (Tamla; ☆4, 1982). *The Woman in Red* (Motown; ☆4, 1984). *In Square Circle* (Tamla; ☆5, 1985). *Characters* (Motown; ☆17, 1987). *Music from "Jungle Fever"* (Motown: ☆24, 1991).

(Chart positions compiled from Joel Whitburn's *Record Research*, based on *Billboard*'s Pop and LPs charts, unless otherwise indicated; r☆ = position on *Billboard*'s Rhythm & Blues chart.)

BOB DYLAN

BY ALAN LIGHT

I n 1991 Bob Dylan turned fifty years old. His first album was recorded exactly thirty years earlier. In that time he released thirty-six albums and had done little for the past few years but tour incessantly. In fact, aside from a brief period of self-imposed exile near the end of the Sixties, Dylan has probably spent more time in the public spotlight than any other figure in rock & roll. Yet in all those years, the most influential songwriter of the rock era has only become more of an enigma; unlike such celebrated recluses as Thomas Pynchon and J. D. Salinger, Dylan doesn't have to hide to increase the mystery surrounding him. He is hidden in plain sight.

Dylan's impact on pop music—and on American culture—is simply inestimable. His most revered work was initially labeled "folk rock," but in fact it was a fusion of country, folk, blues, rock & roll and poetry both ancient and new that permanently changed the perception and function of popular song. It is impossible to imagine the Sixties protest movement, the Seventies singer-songwriters or even the outspoken politics of rap without him. John Lennon said that before hearing Dylan it never occurred to him that songs could be so personal and emotion-

ally direct. Yet Dylan himself has never seemed anything but bewildered by the complexity and invention of his work. "I don't know how it was done," he will mumble, or "If you see me do it, any idiot could do it."

He was born Robert Allen Zimmerman in Duluth, Minnesota, and came of age in neighboring Hibbing, "a dying town" on the Midwestern iron range, the son of a shopkeeper and one of only a few Jewish families in the community. He grew up listening to country music drifting up over the late night radio

waves and playing rudimentary guitar and piano. Hank Williams was an early favorite. By the mid-Fifties, like most of his contemporaries, he discovered and became obsessed with rock & roll and James Dean. He formed several rock combos in high school and claimed in his yearbook that his ambition was to ''join the band of Little Richard.''

Study of rock's roots led Dylan to the blues and eventually into the world of folk music. He headed off to Minneapolis and the University of Minnesota, where he hung out with the local Beat scene, read Romantic poetry, devised his stage name and was introduced to the work of Woody Guthrie. The Dust Bowl refugee, whose songs combined precise poetic detail and social activism, became Dylan's idol. He

The conscience of a generation, trying to smoke and sing simultaneously.

decided to leave school after three halfhearted semesters and traveled to New Jersey, where Guthrie was slowly dying in a local hospital.

As soon as he arrived at Guthrie's bedside in January 1961, Dylan hurled himself into a thriving Greenwich Village folk scene. He joined a club circuit in which he shared the spotlight with such artists as Jack Elliott and Dave Van Ronk—and soon, Phil Ochs, Eric Andersen and Joan Baez—but he quickly flew past them all, writing and performing at a furious rate and developing a loose comic image many compared to Charlie Chaplin and Huck Finn. ''He was always a sponge,'' recalled Van Ronk, ''picking up whatever was around him.'' Legendary Columbia Records producer and talent scout John Hammond—who had signed Billie Holiday and Count Basie and would go on to launch the careers of Aretha Franklin and Bruce Springsteen—heard Dylan and took an interest, which soon resulted in a five-year contract with the label.

Bob Dylan, with a chubby, sweet-faced twenty-year-old on the cover, was released early in 1962. Only two original compositions were included, but the force and maturity of his blues vocal performances heralded a major arrival. Disparaging Dylan's nasal, insistent voice has been a popular sport for his entire career, but it is still astonishing to hear a young, middle-class Midwesterner invest the likes

Oh, Mama, is this really the end? Onstage with the Hawks, 1966.

of Blind Lemon Jefferson's "See That My Grave Is Kept Clean" with such power and desperation.

The civil-rights movement was gathering steam, and Dylan shifted his attention from interpretation to writing his own kind of protest songs. *The Freewheelin' Bob Dylan* (1963) featured his apocalyptic masterpiece "A Hard Rain's A-Gonna Fall" and the understated, elegant call to arms "Blowin' in the Wind" (which became a hit when covered by Peter, Paul and Mary and the anthem of a generation when sung at the 1963 March on Washington). He was booked on *The Ed Sullivan Show,* but when the program refused to let him sing his "Talkin' John Birch Society Blues," he stormed off, which ended up adding to his reputation as an uncompromising activist. *The Times They Are A-Changin'* (1964), complete with its sepia-toned cover portrait reminiscent of Dust Bowl photographs, was Dylan's most overt protest record. The immediacy of songs written from news reports of such events as the deaths of Emmett Till and Hattie Carroll proved extremely influential; now, however, such specificity gives *Times* more of a period-piece flavor than any other Dylan album.

D ylan had redefined folk music and its audience in a matter of months, but he was already growing restless. He wrote a series of songs during a trip to Greece that delved further into the impressionistic, densely poetic imagery with which he had been flirting. Recorded in one twelve-hour session, *Another Side of Bob Dylan* (1964) is the work of a writer struggling against the confines of conventional songwriting and folk instrumentation. "Chimes of Freedom," a dreamy, circular pastiche ("Through the mad mystic hammering of the wild ripping hail/The sky cracked its poems in naked wonder") that clearly captured a mood and spirit without relying on direct, folk-style reporting, served as his farewell to the protest movement.

In the next eighteen months Dylan went on a creative spree unlike any other in pop history. He released three perfectly realized albums, each a leap into territory music had never seen before. He added a full rock band for his 1965 performance at the Newport Folk Festival and for one side of *Bringing It All Back Home.* It would have been too easy to put the acoustic half of *Back Home* on the first side, though his old fans still would have been shocked by the cascading, hallucinatory beauty of "Mr. Tambourine Man" or the nightmarish fury of "It's Alright, Ma (I'm Only Bleeding)." Instead, though, Dylan got right up in their faces, opening the album with the Chuck Berry boogie and rapid-fire wordplay of "Subterranean Homesick Blues."

Highway 61 Revisited was something different yet again, a set of long, allegorical narratives over furious, chaotic tracks built on Al Kooper's primitive organ and Mike Bloomfield's slashing guitar. "Like a Rolling Stone" kicked off the album like a shotgun blast, with Dylan howling "How does it feel/To be on your own, with no direction home" and encapsulating the frustration and rage of a generation carving out its own purpose and morality. *Blonde on Blonde,* unbelievably, went even further, inventing a music Dylan described as "that wild mercury sound . . . metallic and bright gold, with whatever that conjures up." Recording in Nashville with session musicians, Dylan refocused his surreal, labyrinthine lyrics on affairs of the heart; such songs as "Visions of Johanna" ("Louise holds a handful of rain, tempting you to defy it") or the eleven-minute-long "Sad-Eyed Lady of the Lowlands" ("Your streetcar visions which you place on the grass") are impossible to define or describe, but it is equally impossible to miss the meanings they evoke.

The confident young composer, 1963.

The cultural impact of these three albums was immediate and enormous. Their absurdist wit blazed trails for the expanding drug culture and the street theater of Vietnam War protesters. It became fashionable to add Dylan lyrics to college English courses, but of course his words were never intended as pure poetry. They often felt awkward when read from a page because they were written as genuine components of songs—a line like "the ghost of elec-

tricity howls in the bones of her face," no matter how evocative on its own, existed in conjunction with Dylan's unparalleled phrasing, visionary arrangements and still-underappreciated melodic craft.

Proletarian posturing—a tribute to Woody Guthrie and Jack Kerouac.

Fueled by amphetamines, Dylan was writing compulsively, recording lengthy albums in marathon sessions over just a few days and touring without rest. Every press conference was an opportunity for a Dada performance piece. He went around the world in 1965 and '66 for his first rock & roll tour and was booed, worshiped, debated, and captured on film (in D. A. Pennebaker's landmark cinema verité documentary *Don't Look Back)*. "Bob was in the process of opening a door, and that door needed opening," said guitarist Robbie Robertson of the Band, who would have the lengthiest stint as Dylan's accompanist, working with him off and on for eight years. "It was like the beginning of rock & roll in a way—mixing two worlds together." This new world was popularly known as "folk rock," and it became the rage, from the innovations of the Byrds and Buffalo Springfield to such cheap Dylan imitations as Barry McGuire's "Eve of Destruction."

After *Blonde on Blonde* came Dylan's retreat. In August 1966 he had a motorcycle accident; the severity of his injuries has never been determined. But, as has frequently been said, if the accident hadn't happened, Dylan would have had to invent it as a way to slow down. He had quietly married Sara Lowndes in 1965, and after the accident they stayed close to their Woodstock, New York, residence for the next two years. Sporadically, he would record with the Band in the basement of Big Pink, the group's communal Woodstock home. These crude recordings were widely bootlegged and eventually released as *The Basement Tapes* in 1975, revealing a delightful exploration of American traditional song. As Dylan woodshedded, the Beach Boys, the Beatles, the Rolling Stones and the psychedelic move-

ment were producing increasingly elaborate, technically sophisticated recordings.

When he reemerged in 1968 Dylan once again bucked all trends and set a new course with the powerfully subtle *John Wesley Harding*, featuring a country-flavored trio and offering elusive morality plays with strong biblical overtones. *Harding* set into motion the country-rock movement, but it would be Dylan's last fully confident work for a while. He spent the next few years dipping into conventional country (*Nashville Skyline,* 1969), covers of pop standards (the absymal *Self-Portrait,* 1970) and soundtracks (the score for Sam Peckinpah's *Pat Garrett and Billy the Kid,* 1973, in which he also made a small, forgettable movie acting debut).

Self-portrait, 1970.

Dylan seemed to have lost his focus. As the Seventies progressed, the surviving Sixties icons (the Rolling Stones and the solo Beatles) were in danger of receding into nothing but myth. A 1974 cross-country tour with the Band, though, showed Dylan savagely resisting such deification. The tour (recorded and released that year as *Before the Flood*) was a massive financial success and media event—Dylan had performed at only a handful of benefits and special events for the previous seven years—but it was hardly a nostalgia tour. He tore his songs apart, searching for new resonance in his old words. Since then, he has constantly reworked and reinterpreted songs in concert. Though often disappointing or confusing audiences who expect familiar versions of their favorites, Dylan occasionally finds yet another level in their bottomless wells of meaning.

The tour apparently reinvigorated Dylan, for his next album was his last unarguable masterpiece. *Blood on the Tracks* (1975) was a chronicle of his deteriorating marriage, and it showed yet another side of Bob Dylan, a man battling his own anger and

disappointment. Critic Paul Williams has argued convincingly that the remainder of Dylan's career has represented his efforts to come to terms with the end of his relationship with Sara, to find a substitute in his life for the woman he loved.

Desire (1976) found Dylan on a new crusade, the freeing of boxer Rubin "Hurricane" Carter (jailed on a questionable murder charge), and for the first time collaborating on his songwriting, with playwright Jacques Levy. Dylan was back into a frenetically energetic mode, grabbing musicians from New York clubs and herding them into all-night recording sessions. The ramshackle sound proved distracting on much of the album but couldn't mar the perfection of "Isis," a mythic, hypnotic examination of marriage. Dylan took dozens of musicians, including occasional guests such as Joni Mitchell and Roger McGuinn, on the Rolling Thunder Revue, a Bicentennial whim. The players all loaded up in buses and performed shows announced at the last minute in small New England theaters (with occasional stops at bigger venues to pay the bills). The whole thing was filmed—from brilliant performances to ludicrous improvised sketches—and turned into the monumentally self-indulgent, four-hour-plus *Renaldo and Clara.*

The incomprehensible *Street-Legal* (1978) came

next, then a world tour with an eight-member band. Though the shows in Europe were the best received of Dylan's career, stateside critics were not so kind, and the evidence on *Bob Dylan at Budokan* (1978) reveals plodding, overwrought arrangements with occasional hints of potentially interesting recastings. But Dylan was already moving on to his life's next stage, his most controversial change since plugging in at Newport.

Looking back: the cover for a 1971 anthology of greatest hits.

The dawn of the Eighties saw the release of *Slow Train Coming* (1979), a testament to Dylan's newfound Christian faith. Though he repeatedly denied being "born again" (the best rumors had him being baptized in Pat Boone's swimming pool), there was no way around a line like "you either got faith or you got unbelief/And there ain't no neutral ground." A theater tour found him lecturing and berating stunned secular audiences and refusing to play old songs. But *Slow Train*, produced by Dire Straits guitarist Mark Knopfler, had the most polished sound of any Dylan album yet, and "Gotta Serve Somebody" even became a hit single. Dylan continued to write and sing about Jesus for two more albums—*Saved* (1980) and *Shot of Love* (1981)—getting less and less strident and less and less interesting.

The country squire of the early Seventies.

The rest of the Eighties saw Dylan growing increasingly baffling. He seemed to be spinning in so many directions that he risked finally finding an escape from the Dylan Myth simply by becoming irrelevant. He was reportedly taking a new interest in Judaism and was spotted in Jerusalem. *Infidels* (1983) and *Empire Burlesque* (1985) were both heralded as comebacks, but despite some stunning moments, they were uneven. "Lots of songs on [*Infidels*] got away from me," Dylan later told *Song-Talk* magazine. "They hung around too long. They were better before they were tampered with."

He stumbled through a three-song set with Keith Richards and Ron Wood that (anti-)climaxed Live Aid in 1985. News that Dylan was working with Tom Petty and the Heartbreakers was encouraging, but the resultant tour was maddeningly inconsistent, and the only studio work released was on the 1987 hodgepodge *Knocked Out Loaded* (which includes an odd, moving, cinematic collaboration with Sam Shepard on the eleven-minute "Brownsville Girl"). *Down in the Groove* (1988) was another slapped-together trifle, and the live *Dylan and the Dead* (1989), recorded at a series of stadium shows with the Grateful Dead, was a disaster. Dylan seemed incapable of sitting down and writing a real song, much less making an actual album. A "Never-Ending Tour" started in 1988. The first few months of shows were exciting, but it soon felt like Dylan was touring compulsively because he had no idea what else to do.

And yet in 1989, when even die-hard fans had given up hope of such a thing, a first-rate Dylan album appeared: *Oh, Mercy*. Producer Daniel Lanois apparently forced Dylan to work on his writing again, and the songs emerged simple and clear, the arrangements atmospheric and compelling. ''Seen a shooting star tonight,'' Dylan sang with unself-conscious candor, ''and I thought of me/If I was still the same, if I ever became/What you wanted me to be.'' As often as not, Dylan sounded disinterested or even contemptuous onstage, but he did occasionally muster some genuine enthusiasm for the challenge presented by his body of work. On one remarkable night in New Haven, Connecticut, in 1990, he blasted through a rambunctious four-hour, fifty-song retrospective.

Unfortunately, this upswing too passed quickly. *Under the Red Sky* (1990) was a thoroughly inconsequential, silly album of doggerel. Dylan put in several bizarre appearances at a series of Hasidic telethons on Los Angeles cable television. In a more prominent public appearance, Dylan was presented with a Lifetime Achievement Award at the 1991 Grammys. He groaned and slurred through a dreadful rendition of ''Masters of War,'' presumably in protest of the recent outbreak of the Gulf War, and delivered a brief speech that stunned viewers nationwide. He quoted his father's telling him, ''Son, it is possible to become so defiled in this world that your own mother and father will abandon you. And if this happens, God will always believe in your own ability to mend your own ways.'' Was he stoned? Serious? What religion was he now, anyway? Was this all a big put-on by rock's greatest rebel? It had become impossible to know.

Take a load off, Annie: Bob Dylan jams with Levon Helm of the Band.

Dylan, relaxed and enigmatic, on the eve of his 1986 American tour with Tom Petty and the Heartbreakers.

In 1991 a three-CD box set called *The Bootleg Series, Volumes 1–3* was also released. It collected songs that Dylanologists had traded or coveted for years and once again documented the breathtaking scope of Dylan's accomplishments. There were great unreleased traditional folk songs and talking blues, alternate takes from *Highway 61*, unused tracks from the *Desire* sessions. Most interestingly, though, the box cast new light on Dylan's work in the Eighties. There were brilliant recent songs—a handful of excellent, enigmatic outtakes from *Infidels*, a thunderous alternate version of *Burlesque*'s ''When the Night Comes Falling from the Sky'' and a perfect gem that had kicked around for years called ''Blind Willie McTell.''

Dylan had been asked before why he had never released that one. ''It just never came out for me,'' he said, ''It never got developed in any way that it should have.'' Sounds reasonable enough, until such a spectacular composition and performance is held next to much of the throwaway stuff that had filled his albums for the last decade. It demonstrates all that we still don't know about Bob Dylan. Maybe he can still write great songs but can't distinguish them from the others, or maybe songs have ultimately become too important to him. He has spent most of the last fifteen years worrying the good ones to death and putting out those he doesn't really seem to care about.

''The world don't need any more songs,'' he said in 1991. ''If nobody wrote any songs from this day on, the world ain't gonna suffer for it.'' But Bob Dylan's truest legacy is that people will keep writing songs—songs that strive for social change or personal revelation, songs of anger and exploration, songs that examine the world outside or the spirit within. Songs that nobody could have written if not for Bob Dylan.

DISCOGRAPHY

SINGLES

''Subterranean Homesick Blues'' (Columbia; ☆39, 1965). ''Like a Rolling Stone'' (Columbia; ☆2, 1965). ''Positively 4th Street'' (Columbia; ☆7, 1965). ''Can You Please Crawl out Your Window?'' (Columbia; ☆58, 1966). ''Rainy Day Women #12 & 35'' (Columbia; ☆2, 1966). ''I Want You'' (Columbia; ☆20, 1966). ''Just Like a Woman'' (Columbia; ☆33, 1966). ''Leopard-Skin Pill-Box Hat'' (Columbia; ☆81, 1967). ''I Threw It All Away'' (Columbia; ☆85, 1969). ''Lay Lady Lay'' (Columbia; ☆7, 1969). ''Tonight I'll Be Staying Here with You'' (Columbia; ☆50, 1969). ''Wigwam'' (Columbia; ☆41, 1970). ''Watching the River Flow'' (Columbia; ☆41, 1971). ''George Jackson'' (Columbia; ☆33, 1971). ''Knockin' on Heaven's Door'' (Columbia; ☆12, 1973). ''A Fool Such as I'' (Columbia; ☆55, 1973). ''On a Night Like This'' (Asylum; ☆44, 1974). ''Most Likely You Go Your Way (and I'll Go Mine)'' (Asylum; ☆55, 1974). ''Tangled Up in Blue'' (Columbia; ☆31, 1974). ''Hurricane (Part 1)'' (Columbia; ☆33, 1975). ''Mozambique'' (Columbia; ☆54, 1976). ''Gotta Serve Somebody'' (Columbia; ☆24, 1979).

ALBUMS

Bob Dylan (Columbia; 1962). *The Freewheelin' Bob Dylan* (Columbia; ☆22, 1963). *The Times They Are A-Changin'* (Columbia; ☆20, 1964). *Another Side of Bob Dylan* (Columbia; ☆43, 1964). *Bringing It All Back Home* (Columbia; ☆6, 1965). *Highway 61 Revisited* (Columbia; ☆3, 1965). *Blonde on Blonde* (Columbia; ☆9, 1966). *Bob Dylan's Greatest Hits* (Columbia; ☆10, 1967). *John Wesley Harding* (Columbia; ☆2, 1968). *Nashville Skyline* (Columbia; ☆3, 1969). *Self-Portrait* (Columbia; ☆4, 1970). *New Morning* (Columbia; ☆7, 1970). *Bob Dylan's Greatest Hits, Vol. II* (Columbia; ☆14, 1971). *Pat Garrett and Billy the Kid* (Columbia; ☆16, 1973). *Planet Waves* (Asylum; ☆1, 1974). *Dylan* (Columbia; ☆17, 1973). With the Band: *Before the Flood* (Asylum; ☆3, 1974). *Blood on the Tracks* (Columbia; ☆1, 1975). With the Band: *The Basement Tapes* (Columbia; ☆7, 1975). *Desire* (Columbia; ☆1, 1976). *Hard Rain* (Columbia; ☆17, 1976). *Street-Legal* (Columbia; ☆11, 1978). *Bob Dylan at Budokan* (Columbia; ☆13, 1978). *Slow Train Coming* (Columbia; ☆3, 1979). *Saved* (Columbia; ☆24, 1980). *Shot of Love* (Columbia; ☆33, 1981). *Infidels* (Columbia; ☆20, 1983). *Real Live* (Columbia; ☆115, 1985). *Empire Burlesque* (Columbia; ☆33, 1985). *Biograph* (Columbia; ☆33, 1985). *Knocked Out Loaded* (Columbia; ☆53, 1986). *Down in the Groove* (Columbia; ☆61, 1988). With the Grateful Dead *Dylan and the Dead* (Columbia; ☆37, 1989). *Oh Mercy* (Columbia; ☆30, 1989). *Under the Red Sky* (Columbia; ☆38, 1990). *The Bootleg Series, Volumes 1–3* (Columbia; 1991). With the Traveling Wilburys: *Volume One* (Wilbury; ☆3, 1988). With the Traveling Wilburys: *Vol. 3* (Wilbury; ☆11, 1990).

(Chart positions compiled from Joel Whitburn's *Record Research*, based on *Billboard*'s Pop and LPs charts.)

It was Dylan meets the Beatles." That's Roger McGuinn's succinct explanation of the Byrds' bold, brainy take on rock & roll. True enough: What the Byrds pulled off in 1965 with the landmark *Mr. Tambourine Man* was a resonant synthesis of the Beatles' charged pro forma precision and Dylan's mythopoeic incantations. It turned out to be a startlingly perfect fit, inspiring much that has followed, from their mentors' subsequent *Rubber Soul* and *Blonde on Blonde* to the work of such disparate inheritors as Tom Petty, R.E.M., U2 and Crowded House.

Mr. Tambourine Man was the first rock & roll album with a message, the first made up entirely of anthems, the first to render sound and meaning inseparable. Byrds music was such a departure that it got its own name—"folk rock"—making the Byrds the first hybrid band. The jaggedly beautiful sound of their twelve-string electric guitars was said to have a "jingle jangle," after the line in the Dylan-penned title song. But what it *felt* like was cathedrals doing the watusi.

They sounded that way because they didn't know any better; there was only one bona fide rocker in the band. Jim McGuinn, a former Chicago folkie, had worked for the Limelighters, Bobby Darin, Chad Mitchell and Judy Collins before moving to L.A. to eke out a living as a coffeehouse solo performer, daringly plunking Beatles tunes on an acoustic in front of skeptical folk purists. Inspired by George Harrison in *A Hard Day's Night,* McGuinn decided to liven up his act by switching to a twelve-string Rickenbacker electric (George's axe of choice in the movie) and forming a Beatles-style rock group.

A singer-songwriter from Missouri named Gene Clark signed on, fresh from a stint with the New Christy Minstrels and equally hooked on the Beatles; so did David Crosby, a California-bred folkie, ace harmony singer and onetime member of Les Baxter's Balladeers. San Diego–born Chris Hillman ap-

The band that made "Mr. Tambourine Man" and "Eight Miles High" *(from left):* Jim McGuinn (before he changed his first name to Roger), Chris Hillman, Gene Clark, David Crosby, Michael Clarke.

plied his bluegrass mandolin chops to the electric bass, while Michael Clarke's surfer looks made him the obvious choice to play the Dennis Wilson role in this idiosyncratic combo. They plugged in, they played, they made it up as they went along. And it was good.

Once the Byrds had their act together, comanager-Svengali Jim Dickson convinced them to run a Dylan song through their snappy new circuitry. The song was "Mr. Tambourine Man," and it was the final piece of the puzzle. What a concept: rock & roll that *meant* something. And yet, for all its emphasis on content, this music was ultimately about *sound.* As McGuinn explained, with characteristic wryness, in the liner notes to *Mr. Tambourine Man:* "[T]he sound of the airplane in the Forties was a rrrrrrrrooooooaaaaaaaahhhhhhhhhh sound and Sinatra and other people sang like that, with those sort of overtones. Now we've got the krrrriiiiisssssssshhhhhhhhhhhhhh jet sound, and the kids are singing up in there now. It's the mechanical sounds of the era. . . ."

On first hearing, the dynamic density of "I'll Feel a Whole Lot Better," with its twelve-string symphony and buoyant group vocals, sounded both totally fresh and strangely inevitable, as did the shimmering Bo Diddley groove of "Don't Doubt Yourself, Babe" and the eerie atmospherics of "Here Without You." But the linchpin of the album was its triumvirate of folk-rock extravaganzas: Dylan's "Mr. Tambourine Man" and "Chimes of Freedom," and Pete Seeger's "The Bells of Rhymney." These monumental recordings possessed a near-architectural splendor, as diamond-sharp guitar chords cascaded rhythmically beneath majestic vocal harmonies. On these songs, using just guitar, bass, drums, tambourine and vocals (plus Leon Russell's piano on "Mr. Tambourine Man"), the Byrds created a wall of sound even more monolithic than Phil Spector's orchestral model. It was breathtaking—and it still is.

"Mr. Tambourine Man" hit Number One in a summer of unparalleled Top Forty magnificence. The Beatles' "Ticket to Ride" and its gong-like guitars set the tone: The venom of the Stones' "(I Can't Get No) Satisfaction" and the goose-bump snarl of Dylan's "Like a Rolling Stone" followed an assertively glorious progression. "Mr. Tambourine Man" was the quirkiest of the bunch; restrained and ambiguous in a way that departed from Dylan's prototype, it was also suggestive and tantalizing, as if those who read between the lines would be let in on some mystic countercultural secret.

"Turn! Turn! Turn!"—another enigmatic anthem (this one drawn from a biblical passage set to music by Seeger)—became the Byrds' second Number One single. Apart from its title track, *Turn! Turn! Turn!* lacked the lofty peaks of its predecessor, but the album's stylistic misfires revealed an ambitious band restless for new worlds to conquer. They began to explore those worlds in late '66 with *Fifth Dimension,* an album so unusual that it inspired a new set

One of the more durable lineups *(from left):* David Crosby, McGuinn, Michael Clarke, Chris Hillman.

of hybrids: "raga rock," "jazz rock" and, most accurately, perhaps, "acid rock." "Eight Miles High," with its ominous bass line, unearthly vocal harmonies and a fiercely electronic twelve-string solo inspired by John Coltrane, was a shattering *tour de force*. As a single, it had the distinction of being one of the first records widely banned because of its alleged drug references; nevertheless, the song reached Number Fourteen on the *Billboard* Hot 100. "Eight Miles High" was also the swan song of Gene Clark, who'd become the band's primary songwriter. Clark's abrupt departure was partly due to his fear of flying; a less ironic but more significant factor was the deterioration of his relationship with band leader McGuinn. It foreshadowed things to come for the battling Byrds.

The band's repertoire was short on love songs, and there was a remote quality, a fascination with sheer technique, that suggested the cool precision of hard-core formalists. In this sense, "So You Want to Be a Rock 'n' Roll Star," the opening cut on *Younger Than Yesterday*, the Byrds' fourth LP, was delectably ironic. What fleeting stardom the band attained was the result of the sheer brilliance of their early singles. But their identity had become more elusive as their musical conception took on ever-greater subtlety and sophistication.

The architect of this iconoclasm was McGuinn. Compulsively curious, obsessed with electronic gadgetry, he tinkered with rock & roll as if it were a space-age toy. He also tinkered with the other Byrds, appraising their strengths and weaknesses with a frequently shocking frankness, as if they were merely cogs in a machine he'd built. And yet McGuinn also had the

canniness to harness and integrate the special talents of his colleagues: Crosby's flair for vocal harmonies, Hillman's unorthodox approach to electric bass, Gene Clark's originality as a pop songwriter. Each band member found himself servicing McGuinn's own ideas; not surprisingly, each in time came to resent McGuinn's control. *Younger Than Yesterday* gave the work of both Crosby and Hillman a new prominence, but tensions persisted within the ranks. By the end of 1967 Crosby was gone.

Undaunted, McGuinn set his stripped-down Byrds to work on an ambitious new recording project. To construct his magnum opus, he gathered together the most advanced electronic gear of the day, tossed in a string quartet for balance and brought in session players to flesh out the surviving trio of original Byrds. The resulting album, *The Notorious Byrd Brothers,* sounded airtight; for the first time, McGuinn had fully developed the implications of his *krrrriiiiissssssssshhhhhhhhhh* concept. While the songs were a mixed lot—topics included amphetamines, the draft, space exploration and the language of dolphins—the relentless jet-age drone of the album unified the material into a coherent whole.

The McGuinn-Hillman Byrds made one more album—and yet another milestone: the rustic *Sweetheart of the Rodeo,* which initiated the country-rock movement. But that effort was skyjacked from under the original members by brilliant newcomer Gram Parsons. Michael Clarke faded away; Hillman, according to McGuinn, threw his bass on the floor and walked out for good, going on to form the Flying Burrito Brothers with Parsons.

McGuinn, the sole remaining original Byrd, hired various musicians to carry on the concept. These latter-day Byrds, whose focal point was the gorgeously understated playing of gifted guitarist Clarence White, recorded five albums. The best of them, *Untitled* (1970), introduced the McGuinn staple "Chestnut Mare." They were also a stronger stage band than the original group, thanks to the bracing interaction of McGuinn's Rickenbacker and White's Telecaster. But the neo-Byrds lost altitude on their last two studio efforts, and by 1973 the flight was over.

From 1965 through 1968, though, the Byrds were genuine space cowboys, their inventiveness and audacity in the studio second to none even in those limit-smashing times. Roger McGuinn has mellowed in recent years and in 1991 returned to the

Roger McGuinn shows off a latter-day version of the Byrds *(from left):* Clarence White, Skip Battin, McGuinn, Gene Parsons.

rock arena with his first solo album since the mid-Seventies, but he remains one of the great eccentrics of rock & roll. David Crosby, who fought and is finally winning a long battle with drugs, while starring in Crosby, Stills and Nash, remains one of rock's most extreme personalities. Chris Hillman is now a country music star as leader of the Desert Rose Band.

The music of the Byrds endures because of a synchronism of taste, technique, intelligence and inspiration that, now as then, seems to resonate with the jingle-jangle of destiny itself.

SINGLES

"Mr. Tambourine Man" (Columbia; ☆1, 1965). "All I Really Want to Do" (Columbia; ☆40, 1965). "Turn! Turn! Turn!" (Columbia; ☆1, 1965). "It Won't Be Wrong" b/w "Set You Free This Time" (Columbia; ☆63, 1966). "Eight Miles High" (Columbia; ☆14, 1966). "5D (Fifth Dimension)" (Columbia; ☆44, 1966). "Mr. Spaceman" (Columbia; ☆36, 1966). "So You Want to Be a Rock 'n' Roll Star" (Columbia; ☆29, 1967). "My Back Pages" (Columbia; ☆30, 1967). "Have You Seen Her Face" (Columbia; ☆74, 1967). "Goin' Back" (Columbia; ☆89, 1967). "You Ain't Going Nowhere" (Columbia; ☆74, 1968). "Jesus Is Just Alright" (Columbia; ☆97, 1970).

ALBUMS

Mr. Tambourine Man (Columbia; ☆6, 1965). *Turn! Turn! Turn!* (Columbia; ☆17, 1966). *Fifth Dimension* (Columbia; ☆24, 1966). *Younger Than Yesterday* (Columbia; ☆24, 1967). *Greatest Hits* (Columbia; ☆6, 1967). *The Notorious Byrd Brothers* (Columbia; ☆47, 1968). *Sweetheart of the Rodeo* (Columbia; ☆77, 1968). *Dr. Byrds & Mr. Hyde* (Columbia; ☆153, 1969). *Preflyte* (Together; ☆84, 1969). *Ballad of Easy Rider* (Columbia; ☆36, 1969). *(Untitled)* (Columbia; ☆40, 1970). *Byrdmaniax* (Columbia; ☆46, 1971). *Farther Along* (Columbia; ☆152, 1971). *Best of the Byrds—Vol. 2* (Columbia; ☆114, 1972). *The Byrds . . . In the Beginning* (Rhino; 1988). *The Byrds* (Columbia; ☆151, 1990).

ROGER McGUINN

Roger McGuinn (Columbia; ☆137, 1973). *Peace on You* (Columbia; ☆92, 1974). *Roger McGuinn and Band* (Columbia; 1975). *Cardiff Rose* (Columbia; 1976). *Thunderbyrd* (Columbia; 1977). *Back from Rio* (Arista; 1991).

McGUINN, CLARK AND HILLMAN

McGuinn, Clark and Hillman (Capitol, 1979).

(Chart positions compiled from Joel Whitburn's *Record Research,* based on *Billboard*'s Pop and LPs charts.)

FOLK ROCK

BY PAUL NELSON

During its short-lived heyday in 1965, folk rock was a hastily assembled and transitory frontier junction to and from which several important musical roads were connected. Bordered on one side by the concurrent, multifaceted American folk music and topical song revivals of the late Fifties and early Sixties, and on the other by the onrushing artistic and economic success of new wave rock & roll, folk rock was the hybrid with which many young urban folk musicians attempted to fuse revered teachings from the past (Woody Guthrie, Leadbelly, the Carter Family, Jimmie Rodgers, Robert Johnson, Hank Williams) with an immediate and more personally relevant knowledge of the present (the Beatles). For at least two or three of folk rock's archetypes—Bob Dylan, the Byrds, the Lovin' Spoonful, the Mamas and the Papas, Donovan, Sonny and Cher—the motto ''To thine own self be true'' must have caused considerable schizophrenic reaction at the time, because these artists were rebelling against both the anticommercial snobbery of the folk/topical powers-that-be and, to some degree, their own high estimations of the moral and aesthetic values of traditional music. How to remain true to one's youthful innocence (art without money) while reaching out for viable experience (art with money *and* an audience) was indeed a difficult but thrilling question. In the end more a tenuous artifact than a terminal art form, folk rock boasted a cast of background characters so large and varied that the phrase "et al." must be added to each list of names.

Since the late Fifties Appalachian musicians such as Roscoe Holcomb, Clarence Ashley, Doc Watson, Bill Monroe, the Stanley Brothers, Frank Proffitt, Dock Boggs and Horton Barker had often traveled to newfangled schoolhouses for metaphorical and sometimes real square dances, while the blues, rags and hollers of their black-music counterparts (Sonny Terry and Brownie McGhee, Elizabeth Cotten, Mississippi John Hurt, Muddy Waters, Skip James, Furry Lewis, Fred McDowell, Jesse Fuller, Reverend Gary Davis) were treated with equal respect by a myriad of idealistic white college students and others eager to begin an artistic apprenticeship. Many of the young questers (Ramblin' Jack Elliott, Mike and Peggy Seeger, the New Lost City Ramblers, The Greenbriar Boys, Dave Van Ronk, Dave Ray, John Koerner, Dylan) started by figuratively and often literally worshiping in the churches of their elders, where they learned by practice and imitation the rituals of traditional performing styles. Others—some of whom either couldn't comprehend the complexities of the rural service or rightfully refused to be limited by them—attempted to translate old legends into new myths more accessible to themselves and their citybilly contemporaries: *Bob Dylan*, released in 1962, is the perfect example of a free spirit punching holes in the limits of folk style with one hand while deliriously patching them up again with the other. The Holy Modal Rounders and the Jim Kweskin Jug Band wed urban absurdity to oldtime omniscience in a manner that somehow managed to do justice to both. Judy Collins and Joan Baez took a middle-of-the-road approach by carefully eliminating all meaningful idiosyncrasies from their singing, while such folk groups as the Kingston Trio, the Limeliters, the Chad Mitchell Trio, the Brothers Four, the New Christy Minstrels, and Peter, Paul and Mary simply added a Four Freshman–cum–Weavers regularity to the Southern Mountain sound, refined the gold from them thar hills, and laughed all the way to the top of the pop charts.

Aesthetic responsibilities and a utopian popularity based upon sociopolitical integrity seemed arduous if not impossible goals for the new breed, many

Donovan, a flower for your garden.

of whom wanted not only to sing songs but to write them, much as the prolific Guthrie had done in the Thirties and Forties. Some found solace in the work of such pioneering populists as Pete Seeger and the Weavers, artists of optimism who carried at least part of the workingman-as-god thesis into the Sixties. (Indeed, Seeger may have been the original flower child.) Their revivalist disciples, the topical songwriters and New Left journalists who published in *Sing Out!* and *Broadside*, extended the radical-liberal tradition of musical politicking while founding a more personal and ultimately more important school—that of the singer-songwriter—which soon preferred its own primal ballads to preachy broadsides. From Phil Ochs, Tom Paxton, Peter La Farge, Eric Andersen, Buffy Sainte-Marie, Len Chandler and the ubiquitous Dylan came Tim Hardin, Janis Ian, Leonard Cohen, Joni Mitchell, Loudon Wainwright III, Jesse Winchester and Jackson Browne—and the two lists are all but interchangeable.

If one could characterize many of the most promising artists of the American folk-music and topical-song revivals as politically pugnacious but primarily innocent babes in the woods on their way toward disillusionment and/or maturity in the dark and manly art of rock & roll, then folk rock provided the requisite rite of passage. There, semirecalcitrant teenagers often blissfully bottomed out while recapitulating for a mass market what they felt they had learned about growing up. Like so many double-fold anachronisms, folk rock should have had the strengths of either-or, not the weaknesses of neither-nor; it was almost a virgin but not quite pregnant. Although one can like folk rock, I doubt that one can love it. Too ingratiatingly simpleminded, its easy stance on Uneasy Street now seems neither committed nor individualistic enough to matter much when compared with the monolithic magic of either folk or rock undiluted. While both are too frequently

Cher.

categorized as simple arts, the truth, as Bob Dylan has said, is far from that. His infamous comment about rock—''In that music is the only true, valid death you can feel today off a record player''—also describes folk music. It tells us nothing about folk rock.

Dylan and the Byrds were the fathers of folk rock, of course, but the consummation hardly rates more than a footnote in any legitimate history of rock & roll because neither's career can be limited to one minor genre, most of whose practitioners perished after 1966. No matter that some critics have defined folk rock as a music proliferated by profligate folkies–cum–rock & rollers who, armed with tambourines and electric twelve-strings, started their transgressive trip by imitating Dylan and ended it by imitating the Byrds imitating Dylan. Or that many folk and folk-rock classics were either Dylan songs (Peter, Paul and Mary's ''Blowin' in the Wind,'' the Byrds' ''Mr. Tambourine Man,'' the Turtles' ''It Ain't Me Babe''), reasonable or unreasonable facsimiles (Simon and Garfunkel's ''The Sounds of Silence,'' Barry McGuire's ''Eve of Destruction''), or likable but blatant spin-offs (Sonny and Cher's ''I Got You Babe'').

By the mid-Sixties, Dylan's influence as a songwriter was so powerful that he almost single-handedly destroyed both the topical and folk music revivals when he began to move away from them in 1964 with the transitional *Another Side of Bob Dylan* (folk-style music, folk-rock songs) and in 1965, with tentative *Bringing It All Back Home* (folk-rock music, rock & roll songs) toward ''Like a Rolling Stone'' and his rock & roll masterpieces, *Highway 61 Revisited* and *Blonde on Blonde*. In the summer and fall of 1965 revivalist purists viciously booed Dylan, but by 1966 the catcalls had subsided.

Unlike Dylan, the Byrds came at folk rock from both directions (although it must be remembered that Dylan issued a rock & roll single, ''Mixed Up Confusion,'' in 1962). The band's ''first'' album, *Preflyte*, recorded a year before *Mr. Tambourine Man* (1965) but not released until 1969, sounds more like

The Buffalo Springfield, latecomers who transcended the genre, taking folk rock in directions later explored by the Eagles and Jackson Browne.

the Beatles than it does Dylan. Lillian Roxon wasn't far wrong when she wrote that *"Newsweek* called them Dylanized Beatles when the whole point was they were Beatlized Dylans." At their best, the underrated Byrds provided an aural dignity that is positively Jungian to such mid-Sixties standards as "Mr. Tambourine Man," "I'll Feel a Whole Lot Better," "The Bells of Rhymney," "All I Really Want to Do," "Chimes of Freedom," "Turn! Turn! Turn!," "Eight Miles High," "So You Want to Be a Rock 'n' Roll Star," "My Back Pages" and "Goin' Back." On "Wasn't Born to Follow" the guitar playing metamorphoses perfectly from a Woody Guthrie folk lick into the spacial electronic phasing that characterized Dylanesque Roger (né Jim) McGuinn and the innumerable Byrds and made them the cowboy-astronaut Carter Family of rock & roll. The song also supplied folk rock with both a succinct musical definition and one of its few really magical moments.

Unfortunately, too much of the work of folk rock's major offspring has proven more timely than timeless. Sonny and Cher cold-bloodedly pitted a whining teenage Romeo and Juliet against the authority of all grown-ups in their calculated folk-rock classics, "I Got You Babe" and "Laugh at Me." It worked, for a while—when it didn't, there was always television. The Lovin' Spoonful—a crafty combination of infernal affability, cartoon costumes, rock & roll and jug-band music—commingled the magic in young girls' hearts with feckless fantasies of escape from the problems of everyday living. John Sebastian's breathy vocals and tie-dye vision were nothing if not pleasant, and his best songs ("Do You Believe in Magic?," "Daydream," "Younger Girl," "Darling Be Home Soon," "Darling Companion" and the surprisingly tough-minded "Summer in the City") can almost make one forget the soft somnolence of most of the band's repertoire. The Mamas and the Papas countered the same difficulties (an illusion of reality, not enough good material) with a similar theme (fleeing to sunny California from cold New York City), but what made the group special was their haunting and sumptuous harmony singing: The message was surely the ultimate vocal message. "Dedicated to the One I Love," "California Dreamin' " and "Creeque Alley" are fine songs, and "Twelve-Thirty (Young Girls Are Coming to the Canyon)" offers a literal parade of young women—all of whom, one imagines, look exactly like Michelle Phillips—marching from the evil East into luxuriant Los Angeles.

Once considered another Dylan, Scotsman Donovan Leitch failed to parlay an early plethora of exceptional love songs ("Catch the Wind," "Colours," "Josie") into anything more meaningful than his unjustly famous and explicably disastrous psychedelic and flower-power periods. If most of *Mellow*

The Mamas and the Papas.

Yellow and *Sunshine Superman* seems merely silly today, the impact of that music on the mid-Sixties was significant. From the vantage point of the present, it is hard not to regard Donovan's career as unnecessarily tragic because, even while he was floating away into the lilac mist, there were traces of a solid and uncommon talent ("Writer in the Sun," "Lalena," "There Is a Mountain," "Atlantis," "Epistle to Derroll"). "I think, therefore I shouldn't think" probably should have been Donovan's motto.

While not really a folk-rock band, the prodigiously talented Buffalo Springfield—Neil Young, Stephen Stills, Richie Furay, Jim Messina, et al.—deserve special mention both for caring enough to preserve the very best qualities of the form and for conscientiously consolidating them into inspired, if idiosyncratic, rock & roll. Like the Byrds, the Buffalo could either hang back on a song until all of its somber juices boiled over ("For What It's Worth") or just come right out and say it ("Sit Down, I Think I Love You"). Although the group had a short but troubled career—*Buffalo Springfield* and *Buffalo Springfield Again* (both 1967), *Last Time Around* (1968)—their melodies, not their maladies, linger on in "Mr. Soul," "Bluebird," "Broken Arrow," "I Am a Child" and "Kind Woman."

Although its duration was modestly brief, folk rock furnished an immodest number of previews to coming attractions, some of them important. From the concepts of this cordial genre later emerged the infant and evangelical sound of the Jefferson Airplane and other San Francisco bands, hippies, Scott McKenzie's "San Francisco (Be Sure to Wear Flowers in Your Hair)," flower children, country rock and the impetus for such diverse groups as the Youngbloods, the not-so-great Crosby, Stills, Nash and Young, the Band, Gram Parsons and the Flying Burrito Brothers, and the Eagles. Not bad for a hybrid.

DISCOGRAPHY

SINGLES

Joan Baez: "There But for Fortune" (Vanguard; ✩50, 1965). **Byrds:** "Mr. Tambourine Man" (Columbia; ✩1, 1965). "All I Really Want to Do" (Columbia; ✩40, 1965). "Turn! Turn! Turn!" (Columbia; ✩1, 1965). "Eight Miles High" (Columbia; ✩14, 1966). "Mr. Spaceman" (Columbia; ✩36, 1966). **Cher:** "All I Really Want to Do" (Imperial; ✩15, 1965). "Bang Bang" (Imperial; ✩2, 1966). **Bobby Darin:** "If I Were a Carpenter" (Atlantic; ✩8, 1966). **Donovan:** "Catch the Wind" (Hickory; ✩23, 1965). "Sunshine Superman" (Epic; ✩1, 1966). "Mellow Yellow" (Epic; ✩2, 1966). **Bob Dylan:** "Subterranean Homesick Blues" (Columbia; ✩39, 1965). "Like a Rolling Stone" (Columbia; ✩2, 1965). "Positively 4th Street" (Columbia; ✩7, 1965). "Can You Please Crawl out Your Window?" (Columbia; ✩58, 1966). "Rainy Day Women #12 and 35" (Columbia; ✩2, 1966). "I Want You" (Columbia; ✩20, 1966). "Just Like a Woman" (Columbia; ✩33, 1966). **Grass Roots:** "Where Were You When I Needed You" (Dunhill; ✩28, 1966). **Leaves:** "Hey Joe" (Mira; ✩31, 1966). **Lovin' Spoonful:** "Do You Believe in Magic?" (Kama Sutra; ✩9, 1965). "You Didn't Have to Be So Nice" (Kama Sutra; ✩10, 1965). "Daydream" (Kama Sutra; ✩2, 1966). "Did You Ever Have to Make Up Your Mind" (Kama Sutra; ✩2, 1966). "Summer in the City" (Kama Sutra; ✩1, 1966). "Rain on the Roof" (Kama Sutra; ✩10, 1966). "Nashville Cats" (Kama Sutra; ✩8, 1966). **The Mamas and the Papas:** "California Dreamin'" (Dunhill; ✩4, 1966). "Monday, Monday" (Dunhill; ✩1, 1966). "I Saw Her Again" (Dunhill; ✩5, 1966). "Look Through My Window" (Dunhill; ✩24, 1966). "Words of Love" (Dunhill; ✩5, 1966). **Barry McGuire:** "Eve of Destruction" (Dunhill; ✩1, 1965). **Peter, Paul and Mary:** "For Lovin' Me" (Warner Bros.; ✩30, 1965). **Crispian St. Peters:** "The Pied Piper" (Jamie; ✩4, 1966). **Sonny:** "Laugh at Me" (Atco; ✩10, 1965). **Sonny and Cher:** "I Got You Babe" (Atco; ✩1, 1965). "Baby Don't Go" (Reprise; ✩8, 1965). "Just You" (Atco; ✩20, 1965). "But You're Mine" (Atco; ✩15, 1965). "What Now My Love" (Atco; ✩14, 1966). **Turtles:** "It Ain't Me Babe" (White Whale; ✩8, 1965). "Let Me Be" (White Whale; ✩29, 1965). "You Baby" (White Whale; ✩20, 1966). **We Five:** "You Were on My Mind" (A&M; ✩3, 1965).

ALBUMS

Buffalo Springfield: *Buffalo Springfield* (Atco; ✩80, 1967). *Buffalo Springfield Again* (Atco; ✩44, 1967). *Last Time Around* (Atco; ✩42, 1968). **Donovan:** *Catch the Wind* (Hickory; ✩30, 1965). *Fairytales* (Hickory; ✩85, 1965). *Sunshine Superman* (Epic; ✩11, 1966). *The Real Donovan* (Hickory; ✩96, 1966). *Mellow Yellow* (Epic; ✩14, 1967). *Wear Your Love Like Heaven* (Epic; ✩60, 1967). *For Little Ones* (Epic; ✩185, 1968). *A Gift from a Flower to a Garden* (Epic; ✩19, 1968). *Donovan in Concert* (Epic; ✩18, 1968). *The Hurdy Gurdy Man* (Epic; ✩20, 1968). **Lovin' Spoonful:** *Do You Believe in Magic?* (Kama Sutra; ✩32, 1965). *Daydream* (Kama Sutra; ✩10, 1966). *What's Up, Tiger Lily?* (Kama Sutra; ✩126, 1966). *Hums of the Lovin' Spoonful* (Kama Sutra; ✩14, 1966). *The Best of the Lovin' Spoonful* (Kama Sutra; ✩3, 1967). *You're a Big Boy Now* (Kama Sutra; ✩160, 1967). *Everything Playing* (Kama Sutra; ✩118, 1968). *The Best of the Lovin' Spoonful Vol. 2* (Kama Sutra; ✩156, 1968). *Anthology* (Rhino; 1989). **The Mamas and the Papas:** *If You Can Believe Your Eyes and Ears* (Dunhill; ✩1, 1966). *The Mamas and the Papas* (Dunhill; ✩4, 1966). *The Mamas and the Papas Deliver* (Dunhill; ✩2, 1967). *Farewell to the First Golden Era* (Dunhill; ✩5, 1967). *The Papas and the Mamas* (Dunhill; ✩15, 1968). *The Mamas and the Papas Golden Era, Vol. 2* (Dunhill; ✩53, 1968). *Creeque Alley: The History of the Mamas and the Papas, Vols. 1 & 2* (MCA; 1991). **Turtles:** *It Ain't Me Babe* (White Whale; ✩98, 1965). *Happy Together* (White Whale; ✩25, 1967). *The Turtles! Golden Hits* (White Whale; ✩7, 1967). *The Turtles Present the Battle of the Bands* (White Whale; ✩128, 1968). *The Best of the Turtles* (Rhino; 1987).

(Omitting LPs by Bob Dylan and the Byrds. Chart positions compiled from Joel Whitburn's *Record Research*, based on *Billboard*'s Pop and LPs charts.)

PAUL SIMON

BY STEPHEN HOLDEN

Albert Camus said that man's work is the slow journey to rediscover through art the one or two images that first opened his heart. That process describes with uncanny accuracy the gradual unfolding of Paul Simon's art over more than three decades. But for Simon, a nice Jewish boy from Queens born in 1941, those rediscoveries were sounds, not images. Along with a whole generation of white teenagers in the mid-Fifties, early rock & roll, but especially for Simon the sweet moans and cries of black doo-wop ballads, augured a mysterious world of slow-grinding erotic thrills that in the era's sexually repressed climate was the more alluring for seeming almost unimaginable.

More than twenty-five years after first hearing those sounds, Simon wrote a song for his 1983 solo album *Hearts and Bones* that defines his sensibility. In "René and Georgette Magritte with Their Dog After the War," he imagined the French Surrealist painter and his wife slipping out of their evening clothes in an American hotel room and dancing in

the moonlight to the ballads of the Penguins, the Moonglows, the Orioles and the Five Satins. "The deep forbidden music they'd been longing for" Simon called these sounds and likened them to "the easy stream of laughter flowing through the air."

The song, arranged as a contemporary doo-wop ballad in which the echoed voices of the Harptones sent a surreal shiver through the musical texture, reflected the distance that Simon's best music has always sought to bridge: between accepted high art

Paul Simon created an international style that fused poetry, rock & roll and the folk traditions of three continents.

(the paintings of Magritte) and primitive popular music (doo-wop) that for Simon were equally transcendent.

It was Simon's reconnection with rhythm & blues as a personal spiritual wellspring that led him to create his 1986 solo masterpiece, *Graceland,* in which he fused his own urbane, poetically self-conscious folk pop with the joyous black township music of South Africa known as mbaqanga, a sound closely related to early rock & roll.

I n many ways Simon was the most unlikely pop star of his generation. Diminutive, soft-spoken and bookish, he possessed minimal rock-star flash and a low-keyed folk-pop crooning style that was expressive but dynamically limited. Until the duo broke up in 1970, it was Simon's singing partner Art Garfunkel, with his corona of blondish hair, pouting choirboy face and sweet, soaring folk-pop tenor, who was the team's sex symbol.

The two met in the corridors of the elementary school they both attended in Queens and formed a duo roughly modeled after the Everly Brothers, named Tom and Jerry. In 1957 "Hey, School Girl," a demo they had recorded for fifteen dollars, was bought by Big Records and sold 150,000 copies. After graduating from Queens College in 1963 Simon traveled to Europe and while in England discovered the folk music of Martin Carthy, whose version of "Scarborough Fair" he later adapted and used as the opening cut of the Simon and Garfunkel album *Parsley, Sage, Rosemary and Thyme.* When he returned to America the following year, the two re-teamed as Simon and Garfunkel to record *Wednesday Morning, 3 A.M.,* a quiet, conventional folk-rock album that included an acoustic version of their first major hit, "The Sounds of Silence." Simon returned to England, and while he was away Tom Wilson, the album's producer, overdubbed an electric guitar, bass and drums on the cut and rereleased it as a single. In late 1965 it reached Number One on the charts.

"The Sounds of Silence," with its surreal urban-nightmare vision of a world in which "the words of the prophets are written on the subway walls and tenement halls," was Simon's most striking and important early song in a body of work that was filled with post-adolescent angst and naive literary flour-

Paul Simon and Art Garfunkel: Mild mannered though they were, they sold millions more albums than Dylan, the Stones and the Doors.

ishes. Like many of his early songs, it was strongly influenced by Bob Dylan, someone with whom Simon seemed to feel intensely competitive during much of his career, although their sensibilities essentially were opposed. Where Dylan relied on spontaneity, Simon was a pop-music analyst who enjoyed giving himself technical assignments, such as writing songs in unusual time signatures, and whose albums, beginning with *Parsley, Sage, Rosemary and Thyme,* had a layered, high-gloss aural polish.

Early Simon and Garfunkel songs (all written by Simon) tended toward forced whimsy ("The 59th Street Bridge Song") or solemn romanticism ("The Dangling Conversation," which clunkily dropped the names of Emily Dickinson and Robert Frost). The youthful Simon reached a peak of pontifical self-seriousness in "I Am a Rock," in which the singer declared himself "protected" by his books and poetry. Simon's whimsical tangents suggested a New York Jewish echo of John Lennon's playfulness.

Because it was soft and introspective, Simon and Garfunkel's music seemed somewhat tangential to the late-Sixties rock counterculture, although the duo sold many millions more albums than the Rolling Stones, Dylan and the Doors. Mild mannered as Simon and Garfunkel were, their music was hardly oblivious to the counterculture. "A Simple Desultory Philippic/Or How I Was Robert McNamara'd into Submission" spoofed Dylan with a mixture of admiration and envy and paid homage to Lenny Bruce. "7 O'Clock News/Silent Night" protested the Vietnam War by juxtaposing the Christmas carol with a grim newscast.

It was the soundtrack for Mike Nichols's phenomenally successful 1967 film, *The Graduate*, which prominently featured four Simon and Garfunkel songs from *Parsley, Sage, Rosemary and Thyme* plus "Mrs. Robinson," the catchy putdown of the character played in the movie by Anne Bancroft, that boosted the duo to superstar popularity. Between 1968 and 1970 they reached a pinnacle of popularity with the albums *Bookends* and the 10-million-selling *Bridge over Troubled Water*. One major Simon song of the period was "America," an ambitious folk-pop travelogue about a lost young couple who run away from New York to "look for America." Another, "Bridge over Troubled Water," remains unique in Simon's canon for its arching pop-gospel melody. It gave Garfunkel his finest stentorian moment as a kind of folk-pop Caruso and remains Simon's most famous composition. A third, "The Boxer," is the beautifully constructed, unsentimental dramatic monologue of an anonymous athlete.

All along Simon had been searching more intensely for inspiration beyond the conventional borders of pop. While "Bridge over Troubled Water" showed his affinity for black gospel music, "El Condor Pasa," an ethereal Peruvian folk song played on indigenous Andean instruments, went further afield.

When Simon and Garfunkel broke up in 1970, with Garfunkel leaving to pursue a career both as an actor and a solo recording artist, Simon gambled that his skills as a songwriter, producer and singer could, taken together, compensate for the absence of his more charismatic partner. In early 1972 he re-

Simon and Garfunkel at their Central Park reunion concert in 1981.

leased his first solo album, *Paul Simon*, a sparely produced album filled with quiet intimations of mortality, including "Mother and Child Reunion," which was recorded in Jamaica and became one of the earliest American reggae hits. On the more polished *There Goes Rhymin' Simon* (1973), Simon delved more deeply into gospel, recording the Number Two hit "Loves Me Like a Rock," with the Dixie Hummingbirds.

By the time of *Still Crazy After All These Years* (1975), the strain of wistful self-pity that in Simon and Garfunkel days had expressed itself in songs of weepy romantic yearning had deepened into a mildly depressive philosophical angst. "Four in the morning/Tapped out/Yawning/Longing my life away" he sang in the album's title song. The album's surprise hit, "50 Ways to Leave Your Lover," was an animated children's jigsaw puzzle of a song set to a marching drum roll. But below its playful surface, the lyric described a man unhappily mired in a relationship he is afraid to leave.

The thread of unhappiness that wound through Simon's solo albums found its most direct expression in *One Trick Pony*, a movie he wrote, directed and starred in that was his first project under a new contract that took him from Columbia Records to Warner Bros. In the movie Simon portrayed a glum, itinerant musician whose marriage fails and whose music is going out of style. The soundtrack yielded only one significant song, "Late in the Evening," an incandescent tribute to early rock & roll arranged for a salsa band. The movie received mixed reviews but was a commercial failure.

Uncertain what to do next, Simon tentatively reunited with Garfunkel in September 1981 at a free concert on the Great Lawn of Central Park, attended by 400,000. Although a successful reunion tour followed, the relationship, which had always been difficult, became unstuck, and Simon resumed his solo career with the 1983 album *Hearts and Bones*. Although his writing reached a new level of refinement with songs like "René and Georgette Magritte" and the autobiographical "Hearts and Bones" (the story of a journey to Mexico with his girlfriend, the actress Carrie Fisher, to whom he was later briefly married), the record sold only 400,000 copies (compared to 2 million for *Still Crazy*), and Simon faced a sobering career crisis.

H e found his salvation in the summer of 1984 when a friend played him a cassette of *Gumboots: Accordion Jive Hits Volume II*, a collection of "township jive," the music of Soweto, South Africa. Deeply drawn to a style that had much in common with early rock & roll, Simon began an intensive study of ethnic South African music that led him to Johannesburg, where he recorded and collaborated with a Shangaan group that included

Simon performing with his *Graceland* lineup, which included Ladysmith Black Mambazo, on *Saturday Night Live*.

the guitarist Chikapa ''Ray'' Phiri and the fretless bass player Baghiti Khumalo. He also worked with the superb ten-member a cappella church group Ladysmith Black Mambazo. Out of these travels, which also carried him to London, to a dance hall in Lafayette, Louisiana, where he studied zydeco, and to East Los Angeles, where he worked with the Chicano band, Los Lobos, emerged *Graceland.*

Writing *Graceland,* Simon refined a new technique in which he improvised and then edited stream-of-consciousness lyrics while listening to the rhythm tracks over and over, gradually, methodically honing an allusive long-lined pop poetry that floated lightly over the music. On *Graceland,* for the first time, Simon's whimsical and serious aspects meshed in a language whose sounds and rhythms brilliantly matched the sparkling, lighthearted sounds of mbaqanga. The contrast between Simon's urbanely sophisticated reflections and the South African tribal music lent the album an extraordinary geographical resonance. Even though the songs weren't overtly political, the album evoked a profound sense of liberation in which Simon's triumph over his depressive writer's block and the militance of the black South African freedom movement complemented each other.

Graceland, which sold 4 million copies in America without the benefit of a hit single, was more commercially successful than anyone had dreamed. Its release was succeeded by a world tour featuring many of the album's instrumentalists, along with Ladysmith Black Mambazo and the exiled South African stars Miriam Makeba and Hugh Masekela.

Simon brought many of the same techniques that worked on *Graceland* to his 1990 album, *The Rhythm of the Saints,* which took two years to conceive, cost a million dollars to make and extended Simon's interest in African-derived percussion to South America. Brazil was the geographic center of the record, whose rhythm tracks featured a wide range of African and Latin American percussion styles. There Simon recorded with Olodum, a ten-piece percussion ensemble. But he also returned to Africa, where he enlisted Kofi Electrik, a Ghanaian guitarist, and Vincent Nguini and Armand Sabal-Lecco, a guitarist and bassist from Cameroon. The music was augmented with flavors of zydeco, blues and bossa nova.

Softer and texturally more sophisticated than *Graceland, The Rhythm of the Saints* was anchored in Simon's New York, but its tentacles also reached out in more directions than *Graceland.* Its songs describe a primitive spiritual search rooted in the relationship between the drums and tribal spirits they conjured. Because it was dreamier than its predecessor and lacked the underlying political thrust, *The Rhythm of the Saints* wasn't as big a hit. But it sold nearly 2 million copies. Once again Simon toured extensively with a large world-music ensemble that included performers from three continents. And on August 15th, 1991, nearly ten years after his public reunion with Garfunkel, Simon and his band returned to Central Park to give a triumphant free concert that was attended by 750,000.

Simon's triumphs with *Graceland* and *The Rhythm of the Saints* were victories of one man's ingenuity and persistence over the conventional pop wisdom that hit singles by young, good-looking performers were the only kind that could succeed. His pop success was comparable to that of the Broadway composer Stephen Sondheim, who transformed the glitzy Broadway musical into a forum for the expression of a refined sensibility and intellect without abandoning the musical vocabulary of Broadway. Simon did the same with rock & roll. Starting with the sounds that intrigued him at the age of thirteen, he created music in which poetry, rock & roll and the folk traditions of three continents collided and fused into an international style that was as personal in its feeling as it was outgoing in its embrace of the world.

DISCOGRAPHY

ALBUMS

SIMON AND GARFUNKEL

Wednesday Morning, 3 A.M. (Columbia; ☆30, 1966). *Sounds of Silence* (Columbia; ☆21, 1966). *Parsley, Sage, Rosemary and Thyme* (Columbia; ☆4. 1966). *Bookends* (Columbia; ☆1, 1968). *Bridge over Troubled Water* (Columbia; ☆1, 1970). *Simon and Garfunkel's Greatest Hits* (Columbia; ☆5, 1972). *The Concert in Central Park* (Warner Bros.; ☆6, 1982).

PAUL SIMON

Paul Simon (Columbia; ☆4, 1972). *There Goes Rhymin' Simon* (Columbia; ☆2, 1973). *Live Rhymin'—Paul Simon in Concert* (Columbia; ☆33, 1971). *Still Crazy After All These Years* (Columbia; ☆1, 1975). *Greatest Hits, Etc.* (Columbia; ☆18, 1977). *One Trick Pony* (Warner Bros.; ☆12, 1980). *Hearts and Bones* (Warner Bros.; ☆35, 1983). *Graceland* (Warner Bros.; ☆3, 1986). *Negotiations and Lovesongs, 1971–1986* (Warner Bros.; ☆110, 1988). *The Rhythm of the Saints* (Warner Bros.; ☆4, 1990). *Paul Simon's Concert in the Park* (Warner Bros.; ☆74, 1991).

(Chart positions compiled from Joel Whitburn's *Record Research,* based on *Billboard*'s LPs chart.)

NEIL YOUNG

BY DON McLEESE

Foremost among his musical distinctions, Neil Young is the only artist in the history of modern recording to be sued for refusing to be himself. The suit filed by Geffen Records, Young's label for much of the Eighties, charged that he was violating his contract by recording "unrepresentative" albums. In other words, Neil Young wasn't making Neil Young music.

Despite its dubious legal merits (how could Neil Young make anything *but* Neil Young music?), the argument hit at the heart of Young's unique artistry. Throughout his career, Young has insisted upon the freedom to swing from one extreme to another, to create with disdain for careerist considerations, to react to the screwiest impulse of the moment, to amuse or embarrass himself, to confuse his most faithful fans and to infuriate those who respond only to one side of his musical personality (including record companies waiting in vain for another "Heart of Gold").

Call it willfulness or perversity, call it "F*!#in' Up" (as Young himself did on his highly acclaimed *Ragged Glory* from 1990), or just call it rock & roll, Young refuses to sell himself short, to resolve the messiness of flesh and blood into a tidy, more mar-

ketable package. Who is Neil Young? He's an artist of brutal delicacy, of weathered naiveté, of deceptively complex simplicity. He's a folksinger at the highest decibels, an iconoclast steeped in tradition. He's the most straightforward of songwriters, and he's the ironist supreme. He's the heart-on-his-sleeve confessional poet who sang with Crosby, Stills and Nash, and he's the high-concept guitar guerrilla who fronts Crazy Horse, writes tributes to Johnny Rotten and tours with the likes of Sonic Youth.

Though one could understand the consternation at Geffen when Young debuted on the label with the computerized futurism of *Trans* (1982) and then followed it the next year with the blast-from-the-past rockabilly of *Everybody's Rockin,* such an embrace of opposites has been integral to Young's musical iden-

324

Sometimes Young amazes even himself.

tity since his days with Buffalo Springfield. After migrating to Los Angeles from his native Canada (where he'd performed both as a solo folkie and in rock bands), he joined the Springfield in 1966. He never quite fit into the band, though his eclectic contributions were the key to the group's collective identity. One soon knew what to expect from a Stephen Stills song, or a Richie Furay song, but Young was the musical wild card. He provided the fuzztone aggression of ''Mr. Soul,'' the sound collage of ''Broken Arrow,'' the charmed innocence of ''I Am a Child.'' He combined with Stills for some of the most explosive guitar interplay in mid-Sixties rock, a tension that mirrored personal relations between the two that continually threatened to tear the band apart. (Yet, characteristically for Young, in the aftermath of Buffalo Springfield, he and Stills have continued an on-and-off musical association for well over two decades.)

His songs were expressed in a boyish whine, incongruous for a man with a rangy build and the hulking presence of a lumberjack. That voice reinforced the element of surprise within Young's Buffalo Springfield music and has provided a thread of continuity, wobbling and wavering as it does, throughout his career. Thin and pinched, it offers a revelatory range of emotion and effect, yearning to grating, fragile to steadfast, wide-eyed to wasted. It can sound almost newborn in its sense of wonder, age-old in its evocation of tradition. It's a high lonesome sound—defenselessly, disarmingly human.

Though his solo debut, *Neil Young,* made little impact upon its release in early 1969, it set the course for much that followed. Sprawling and cinematic in its ambition, it found common ground for elements as diverse as the edgy guitar and the lyrical strings in ''The Loner,'' the traditional balladry and trippy surrealism of ''The Last Trip to Tulsa.'' In retrospect, it makes plain that Young's musical development would defy conventional notions of progression and maturity: Recorded when he was twenty-three, it sounds like the work of an older artist than the rock

& roll firebrand who would release *Ragged Glory* more than two decades later.

While "The Loner" expressed the soul of a solo artist, Young soon entered into associations with two very different bands. Backed by Crazy Horse, he released *Everybody Knows This Is Nowhere* (1969), the first of the truly great Neil Young albums and a far different work than his earlier release of that year. Combining brutally basic guitar with folkish simplicity, the album featured instant classics such as "Cinnamon Girl" and "Down by the River," songs that sounded upon first exposure like the listener had been hearing them forever. Offering melancholy and muscle in equal measure, it showed that the raw intensity of Crazy Horse could fire Young in a manner that more refined backing never would.

Additionally in 1969, Young found time to begin working with Crosby, Stills and Nash, whom he joined after they'd recorded their first album but before they'd played any live dates. Where the trio made acoustic, harmony-laden music of sweetness and light, Young was recruited to add more emotional ballast and rock & roll credibility. Though his "Helpless" was a highlight of the *Déjà Vu* album (1970), Young seemed apart from the band even when he was a part of it, unwilling to contain his musical wanderlust within any sort of group dynamic. He would continue his associations with both Crazy Horse and Crosby, Stills and Nash, but he would not restrict himself to either.

With *After the Gold Rush,* also from 1970, Young entered the decade rising toward a new popular peak. His "supergroup" association with Crosby, Stills and Nash conferred upon him an aura of post-Woodstock aristocracy, while his solo music conformed to the confessional sensitivity of the era's emerging singer-songwriters. Though the musical backing was attributed to Crazy Horse (with substantial contributions by Nils Lofgren and Stephen Stills), *After the Gold Rush* was in some respects the polar opposite of *Everybody Knows This Is Nowhere*—primarily acoustic rather than electric, soft folk rather than hard rock, stripped down rather than supercharged.

For fans of both albums, however, the music was united in its emotional immediacy, in its faith that the most basic truths are the deepest ones. There was

Neil Young after the goldrush: surveying his land in Redwood City, California, with his ranch foreman, 1974.

Neil Young before the goldrush: playing peek-a-boo with Stephen Stills in Buffalo Springfield.

a rejection of instrumental virtuosity and poetic profundity as ornamentation, a corruption of the purest expression. Taken together, the albums established Young's artistic identity as one defined not by acoustic or electric, folk or rock, but by an almost primitive directness in whatever form his music might take, an elliptical simplicity that could offer as many layers of meaning as a myth or a dream.

Next came *Harvest,* an album that was widely beloved at the time as Young's best and has since been disparaged as one of his worst. The top-selling album of 1972, it offered the moon-eyed romanticism of "Heart of Gold" in place of his tougher music's pricklier fare. Recorded in Nashville with the Stray Gators (yet another of the on-and-off bands with whom Young would continue an association), it wasn't as slick as most of the California rock of the period, but the cloying harmonies by James Taylor, Linda Ronstadt and Crosby, Stills and Nash, as well as some intrusively lugubrious orchestration, brought Young the closest he's been in his career to schmaltz.

The result was the sort of popular success upon which careers are built and creative prisons are con-

structed. Instead of the complacency or conservatism that might have infected a lesser artist, this flirtation with commercial acceptance gave Young a case of artistic whiplash. Not until *Comes a Time,* from 1978, would Young return to the melodic romanticism of his *After the Gold Rush* and *Harvest* period, by which time his audience no longer had any idea what to expect from him.

" 'Heart of Gold' put me in the middle of the road," he explained in his liner notes to *Decade,* an ambitious 1977 anthology that attempted to show how the various pieces fit within the puzzle that Young had become. "Traveling there soon became a bore so I headed for the ditch."

In those same retrospective notes, he described the era that he began documenting with *Time Fades Away,* from 1973, as "a long dark period." His own most acerbic critic about *Harvest*'s facile sentiment, Young committed himself to music that resisted easy embrace, that repudiated his popular success, that cast off the singer-songwriter straitjacket. During the dangerous, politically polarized years that marked the end of the Nixon era, Young committed himself to making dangerous, polarized music. Culminating with *Tonight's the Night* (1975), Young seemed more concerned with exorcising demons than polishing his craft.

Both his albums and tours of the period represented music as process rather than product, something mutable and vital rather than frozen and fixed. Young's faithful following, even as it dwindled, became accustomed to hearing familiar favorites dramatically transformed for live performance, with concerts introducing plenty of new material that might not see release on album until years later, if ever. Instead of the greatest-hits selection of most live albums, *Time Fades Away* (with backing by the Stray Gators) documented a concert performance of new material, raw and edgy, barely refined for popular consumption. It followed *Journey Through the Past* (1972), a jittery, barely watchable documentary film with a throwaway soundtrack.

Young then began recording *Tonight's the Night,* his reunion with Crazy Horse, following the heroin overdose of Danny Whitten, the band's guitarist. Dedicated to Whitten and roadie Bruce Berry, another drug casualty, "who lived and died for rock & roll," the album represented the dark night of rock's soul—the attraction of going too far toward the edge and the danger of falling over. While by no means glorifying the excesses that claimed Whitten and Berry, it probed the limits of the extremism that rock glorifies, showed how the fire that the music celebrates can ultimately become all-consuming. It was a theme to which Young would later return with *Rust Never Sleeps* (1979) and *Ragged Glory* (1990), reunions with Crazy Horse that similarly mark artistic pinnacles.

As was typical with Young during the period, *Tonight's the Night* was recorded before *On the Beach* (1974) but wasn't issued for two years. Before releasing it, Young additionally recorded a largely acoustic followup to *Harvest*, titled *Homegrown*, which he decided to shelve in favor of *Tonight's the Night*, its emotional opposite. By mid-decade he seemed to be pulled in divergent directions at once, featuring both Crazy Horse and Crosby, Stills and Nash on *Zuma* (1975), which lacked the intensity of *Tonight's the Night* but featured the mythic "Cortez the Killer," a staple of his live sets ever since. The next year found Young committing himself to a half-hearted collaboration with Stephen Stills on *Long May You Run*. The subsequent *American Stars 'n' Bars* (1977) was another attempt to reconcile opposites, folk roots and feedback fury. The results were uneven, though the majestic "Like a Hurricane" (recorded in '75 and shelved for two years) provides a highlight.

In the aftermath of the retrospective *Decade*—through which Young took stock of his career and found coherence through musical multiplicity—Young released his two most fully realized albums since the decade began. With *Comes a Time* and *Rust Never Sleeps*, he explored the yin and yang of his musical impulses. *Comes a Time* offered the Young that fans of *Harvest* had all but abandoned hope of hearing again in a primarily acoustic celebration of folk-country purity and homespun value, with Nicolette Larson playing Emmylou Harris to Young's Gram Parsons and the album-closing "Four Strong Winds" (a coffeehouse standard by fellow Canadian Ian Tyson) bringing him full circle.

Though the musical simplicity of the album showed a maturity and control well beyond the mawkishness that marred *Harvest, Comes a Time* offered no hint of the ambitiousness and ambiguity that would define *Rust Never Sleeps*, arguably Young's richest musical achievement. Within what is commonly characterized as his "punk album"—open-

Neil *(right)* on the beach at Malibu in 1975 with Crazy Horse, the band that inspired his most fiery solo work.

ing and closing with a song purporting to relate the story of the Sex Pistols' Johnny Rotten, and advising that "it's better to burn out than to fade away"—Young wisely warned that "there's more to the picture than meets the eye." While most of Young's peers felt threatened by the punk upheaval of the late Seventies, and rightly so, Young's music as early as *Time Fades Away* had anticipated punk's recklessness and urgency. *Rust Never Sleeps* reflected Young's response to punk's inspiration, but it was also very aware of the ironies of an aging veteran advising that it's better to "burn out," and it by no means advocated the sort of self-destruction that *Tonight's the Night* had so effectively warned against.

Instead, *Rust Never Sleeps* emphasized the human element within rock, which had increasingly become a monolithic machine; it showed how the delicacy of Young's acoustic music and the brittleness of his most brutal rock were complementary extremes, equally opposed to the corporate blandness that had all but extinguished rock's flame. Ultimately, the bittersweet resignation of Young's opening refrain that "rock & roll can never die" progressed to guarded affirmation of the same sentiments by album's end, voiced by a survivor who refused either to burn out or to fade away.

The album was anticipated by a tour with Crazy Horse, subsequently documented on the *Live Rust* album (1979). The staging found Young and band dwarfed by gigantic microphones and amps, with the sound system blaring Woodstock warnings between songs. As the set moved from solo versions of "Sugar Mountain" and "I Am a Child," Young's

Sixties hymns of innocence, to the sonic distortion and aggression of his hard-rocking music with Crazy Horse, Young's music communicated with an immediacy that offered powerful contrast to the bloat and riskless refinement to which so much rock after Woodstock had succumbed.

Though punk pushed Young to greater conceptual ambitiousness, the momentum quickly dissipated, and both Young and punk found themselves spinning their wheels by the early Eighties. Having made his point with *Rust Never Sleeps,* Young returned to the swings of the stylistic pendulum in 1980 with the primarily acoustic *Hawks and Doves* (its title suggesting Young's preoccupation with dualities, some of its material suggesting an election-year conserva-

tism), followed by the most reductively brutal rock of his career with *Re-ac-tor* (1981). If Young's acoustic material suggested a musical affinity with the Jackson Browne–James Taylor school of singer-songwriters, *Re-ac-tor* had as much in common with Iggy Pop and the Stooges, its songs as sensitive and subtle as a fist in the face.

By the time he left Reprise for Geffen Records, Young seemed like a man in the midst of a musical identity crisis, if not full-blown artistic schizophrenia. Once again Young was responding to the times, a period when computers and videos were changing the sound, the face and the very soul of popular music. Refusing to revert to nostalgia or succumb to classic-rock predictability, Young offered his music

Neil Young unleashes one of the savage guitar solos that characterized his 1991 tour with Crazy Horse after the release of *Ragged Glory*.

as both a reflection of and a comment on the times. Though *Trans* (1982) was very much an album of the computer age, it was also very much a Neil Young album (contrary to Geffen's assertion), filled with song craft that was folkish in its simplicity and musical backing that employed computer technology to the same basic effect that marked his style on both acoustic and electric guitars. If one could predict the unpredictable from an artist who enjoyed embracing opposites as much as Young, the time-capsule rockabilly of *Everybody's Rockin'* (a style revived through the likes of the Stray Cats) was arguably the most natural follow-up to *Trans*. A minor album, even by Young's standards of throwaway impulsiveness, it nonetheless represented Young at his most tuneful with ''Wonderin'.''

In response to Geffen's suit, Young reverted to one of his forms with *Old Ways,* on which he offered himself on the surface as a straightforward country artist. Then again, there's nothing all that straightforward about an album that purports to celebrate tradition through a title song that proclaims that ''Old ways can be a ball and chain.'' When *Old Ways* was dismissed as another of Young's genre exercises, he fulfilled his Geffen contract with *Landing on Water* (1986) and *Life* (1987), a pair of albums that conformed to rock convention but were short on both conviction and inspiration. He then returned to Reprise, where he responded to the renewal of his artistic license with *This Note's for You* (1988), an album of big-band bluesiness highlighted by the title track's protest against rock's increasingly cozy relationship with corporate America.

With the opportunity for taking stock that the end of a decade affords, Young once again seemed to find his artistic bearings as the Eighties drew to a close. Fronting a power trio he dubbed the Restless, Young recorded five songs of inspired, uncompromisingly aggressive rock that represented his most powerful music of the Eighties. With typical perversity, he restricted the release of his 1988 *Eldorado* EP to Japan, Australia and New Zealand, making it available in the States on import only. He did, however, incorporate three of *Eldorado*'s tracks within the more musically expansive *Freedom* (1989), which additionally offered highlights such as ''Rockin' in the Free World'' and ''Crime in the City'' that had earlier been concert favorites.

In organization, execution and ambiguity, *Freedom* was a ten-years-after follow-up to *Rust Never Sleeps*. Like its predecessor, it opened and closed with an anthem, performed acoustically and then electrically, which offered ambivalence in the guise of affirmation. As Young's world-weary voice makes plain, it was a challenge to ''Keep rockin' in the free world,'' as the forces of repression in the land of the free were tightening their hold on rock specifically and the arts in general. Whatever affinity Young had once felt for Reagan Republicanism, *Freedom* explored the seamier underbelly of a new regime, with its ''thousand points of light, for the homeless man (and) . . . a kinder, gentler machine gun hand.''

For fans who felt that the music of *Freedom* pulled its punches, as compared with *Eldorado, Ragged Glory* offered a reunion with Crazy Horse that more than fulfilled its title. It found a place for some of his most abrasive musical assaults and some of his most reflective song craft, winning Young the sort of acclaim he hadn't enjoyed in more than a decade and topping plenty of critical polls as the best album of 1990. The tour following the album's release was then documented on the live *Weld* (1991), which extended the sound and fury even further, showing that Young's music with what he calls his ''garage band'' truly comes alive on the road.

Very much a tour of its times, the shows found Young challenging his faithful with the post-punk abrasiveness of Sonic Youth and Social Distortion as his opening acts. Though their performances aren't included on *Weld,* they helped provide an apt context for Young's high-decibel extremism. The tour also coincided with the Persian Gulf war, a backdrop made explicit in the band's ''rocket's red glare, bombs bursting in air'' transformation of Bob Dylan's ''Blowin' in the Wind,'' and implicit in the rest of the album's musical brutality.

In conjunction with *Weld,* Young issued *Arc,* a thirty-five-minute sound collage of feedback, distortion and disembodied vocal melancholy that made ''Like a Hurricane'' (its most recognizable source material) sound like it was emanating from Mars. As is typical with Young, *Arc* both won praise as a provocative, visionary musical achievement and was dismissed as a pointless, unlistenable self-indulgence.

Having ridden that swing of the pendulum as far as it could go, he returned to the other extreme at the approach of '92. Putting Crazy Horse and his guitar back into the garage, he announced plans to tour as a solo troubador and record a belated sequel to the popular *Harvest,* with the working title of *Harvest Moon.* He also continued sifting through tapes for a long-anticipated boxed-set retrospective, which had begun as a sequel to *Decade* but had grown to encompass the entirety of his career.

Over the course of his prodigiously creative career, Young has served as an inspiration for contemporaries and younger musicians alike to follow their truest instincts, to push their impulses to their most vital extremes. He has shown how it is possible to turn down the volume without toning down the intensity, to blast away without diminishing one's artistry, to grow old without growing soft.

There are those who wish that his artistic progression had been more linear, less erratic, his musical messages more straightforward; who equate disregard for careerist convention with disdain for his audience. To the contrary, Young has never felt that a popular musician's duty is to tell his listeners what to think or how to feel. Yet few rock veterans have so consistently challenged their audiences to think and feel. Young has committed himself to making rock that is as simple as the musical form he loves, as complex as the times it reflects and as expansive as the artist reflecting them.

DISCOGRAPHY

SINGLES

With Crazy Horse: "Cinnamon Girl" (Reprise; ☆55, 1970). "Only Love Can Break Your Heart" (Reprise; ☆33, 1970). "When You Dance I Can Really Love" (Reprise; ☆93, 1971). "Heart of Gold" (Reprise; ☆1, 1972). "Old Man" (Reprise; ☆31, 1972). With Graham Nash: "War Song" (Reprise; ☆61, 1972). "Walk On" (Reprise; ☆69, 1974). "Four Strong Winds" (Reprise; ☆61, 1979). "Hey Hey, My My (into the Black)" (Reprise; ☆79, 1979). "Southern Pacific" (Reprise; ☆70, 1981). "Little Thing Called Love" (Geffen; ☆71, 1983).

ALBUMS

With Crazy Horse: *Everybody Knows This Is Nowhere* (Reprise; ☆34, 1969). *After the Gold Rush* (Reprise; ☆8, 1970). *Harvest* (Reprise; ☆1, 1972). *Journey Through the Past (Soundtrack)* (Warner Bros.; ☆45, 1972). *Time Fades Away* (Reprise; ☆22, 1973). *On the Beach* (Reprise; ☆16, 1974). *Tonight's the Night* (Reprise; ☆25, 1975). With Crazy Horse: *Zuma* (Reprise; ☆25, 1975). *American Stars 'n' Bars* (Reprise; ☆21, 1975). *Decade* (Reprise; ☆43, 1977). *Comes a Time* (Reprise; ☆7, 1978). *Rust Never Sleeps* (Reprise; ☆8, 1979). *Live Rust* (Reprise; ☆15, 1979). *Hawks and Doves* (Reprise; ☆30, 1980). *Re-ac-tor* (Reprise; ☆27, 1981). *Trans* (Geffen; ☆19, 1983). *Everybody's Rockin'* (Geffen; ☆46, 1983). *Old Ways* (Geffen; ☆75, 1985). *Landing on Water* (Geffen; ☆46, 1986). *Life* (Geffen; ☆75, 1987). *This Note's for You* (Reprise; ☆61, 1988). *Freedom* (Reprise; ☆35, 1989). *Ragged Glory* (Reprise; ☆31, 1990). *Weld* (Reprise; ☆154, 1991). *Arc* (Reprise; 1991).

(Chart positions compiled from Joel Whitburn's *Record Research,* based on *Billboard*'s Pop and LPs charts.)

ARETHA FRANKLIN

BY RUSSELL GERSTEN

I f, as Robert Christgau once suggested, music is the chief meeting ground between black and white cultures, then Aretha Franklin is a crucial figure in understanding these encounters. From 1967 to 1970 she was the preeminent black musician in pop music. Her record sales were phenomenal by the standards of the era. She played venues as diverse as the Apollo and Lincoln Center. She made the cover of *Time*.

Whereas many of her fellow soul singers, such as James Brown and Wilson Pickett, were not always taken seriously, Aretha was enshrined, mentioned in the same breath as Bessie Smith and Billie Holiday. Critical praise verged on hysteria. Martin Luther King Jr. presented an award to her in her home town of Detroit shortly before his assassination. During her time, she received exactly what she asked for in her greatest hit: respect.

For decades virtually all female vocalists were compared to her; her influence has extended from Bette Midler to Chaka Khan. She came to symbolize the essence of what many consider the most exhilarating form of popular music this country has ever produced: soul.

Then the furor over Aretha Franklin died down.

The very excesses that had earlier seemed so exciting—frenetic bursts of energy, melodrama, screaming and hollering—began to sound embarrassing in the cooler Seventies. Critics found her forays into mainstream pop, such as "This Girl's in Love with You" and "Bridge over Troubled Water," labored, cumbersome, awkward. When they replayed the early Muscle Shoals classics, people thought them overrated, not much different from the work of other Southern soul artists of the era. They argued that Aretha had merely channeled her energies into the right place at the right time.

That view was deeply flawed. Aretha was always more than a rhythm & blues artist. On songs like "Dr. Feelgood," "Chain of Fools" and "Soul Serenade," she proved she was a consummate R&B technician. These records are perfect examples of blues phrasing, vocal control and the refined use of the gospel technique of note bending (melisma).

But for better or worse, Franklin has always struggled and strained to go beyond the limits of rhythm & blues. At her very first recording session in 1960,

Lady Soul.

her producer, John Hammond, mapped out four blues and gospel numbers. The eighteen-year-old demanded that "Over the Rainbow" be included on the session.

Seven years later, at her first hard-core soul session with Jerry Wexler at Atlantic, she fought for the inclusion of the light, bossa nova–based "Don't Let Me Lose This Dream," which added just enough warmth and whimsy to complement the intense R&B numbers on her breakthrough album. Though this yearning to break the shackles of conventional soul often led to embarrassing moments, it also produced some of her greatest achievements.

Aretha did not share the self-assurance and casual machismo of other great soul artists like Otis Redding and Ray Charles. Her career is characterized by a deep irony, a great dissatisfaction with what she was, is and will be. At the peak of her success in 1968, when she appeared on the cover of *Time,* she told the reporter, "I might be just twenty-six, but I'm an old woman in disguise."

Her vocal style, with its unexpected two-octave jumps, evokes a chaotic, unpredictable world, harboring meanings that are never obvious. For example, when the consummate but traditional rhythm & blues singer Bobby Bland sang "Share Your Love with Me," he delicately and carefully interpreted the lyrics of the ballad. Aretha's version appears disor-

Aretha Franklin ponders her next move. Unlike most stars, she seemed forever dissatisfied with what she might become.

ganized by contrast; she rips the whole thing apart, slurring over key lines and emphasizing the syllables one would least expect. Her attitude is that no mere lyricist is going to tell *her* what the song is about. The moments of ecstasy reached there, in Sam Cooke's "You Send Me" and in dozens of other cover versions go well beyond the intent of the song's composers. At her best, Aretha shows a profound understanding of what a relationship is, of what can happen between two people.

Her musical career began when, as a young girl, she sang in her father's church. She could draw on an almost mythical lineage: Her father, to whom she was always close, was one of the most popular (and wealthiest) black ministers in the North; her mother was reputedly a great gospel singer. Her first musical influences—Clara Ward, James Cleveland and Mahalia Jackson—were gospel stars and fellow travelers on the evangelical circuit. After several years on the road with her father, she decided to try the big time of the pop world: New York, and producer John Hammond.

Aretha with Ray Charles.

Hammond, the man who had produced and promoted Billie Holiday, Bessie Smith and Charlie Christian, and was soon to do the same for Bob Dylan, was duly impressed by this wild eighteen-year-old. "An untutored genius," he called her, "the best voice I've heard since Billie Holiday." He promptly signed her up and rushed her into the studio. Yet he was unable to do for her what he had done for the others.

The whys and wherefores are intricate, as is everything connected with her years at Columbia. The issue is in part sociological; 1960 may not seem like so long ago, but there still was such a thing as "race" music, music made to be distributed almost exclusively in black ghettos. That was the category into which Aretha's first release, "Today I Sing the Blues," was placed. It was a surprising success, considering the limited market. Unfortunately Columbia's A&R head, Mitch Miller (host of the popular *Sing Along with Mitch* TV show), decided to do her a favor. He was going to make another Nancy Wilson or Nat "King" Cole out of her—a sophisticated black crooner for the white masses. She took voice and dance lessons, and was assigned to "big-time" arrangers (like Bob Mersey, who also worked with Barbra Streisand). She got large string sections; she was no longer allowed to accompany herself on piano. She was weaned from her rhythm & blues repertoire and assigned Al Jolson tunes (such as "Rock-a-Bye Your Baby with a Dixie Melody," which became her only Top Forty pop hit on Columbia), show tunes and standards.

Lord knows what confusions this created for a sensitive, insecure nineteen-year-old. She missed sessions and ran away from New York. A sort of depression oozes out of most of the Columbia sides. Often a song will start with an impressive opening, and then Aretha will seem to lose interest midstream; at other times, the lack of instrumental support creates a sort of stalemate. The precision of the phrasing and the honesty of her approach are impressive, but there's nothing vital and nothing particularly black about these records. If Aretha had continued in this vein, she would have deserved a mere footnote in history—with a few splendid moments ("Sweet Bitter Love," "If Ever I Would Leave You," "Without the One You Love," "Johnny")—and become a hazy cult figure like Nancy Wilson.

But the years at Columbia also taught her several important things. She worked hard at controlling and modulating her phrasing, which gave her a discipline that most other soul singers lacked. She also developed a versatility with mainstream American music that gave her later albums a breadth that was lacking on Motown LPs from the same period. Most important, she learned what she didn't like: to do

R-E-S-P-E-C-T.

what she was told to do. Never again would she work with an arrangement she didn't approve of; never again would she sing a cover version of a song the way it was written.

By the end of 1966 Aretha actually owed money to Columbia Records, while ex–gospel singers like Sam and Dave and Wilson Pickett were enjoying million-selling records. When her contract expired, Atlantic's vice president, Jerry Wexler, scooped her up. Within a year she was the most successful singer in the nation.

Aretha near the beginning of her long career.

A natural woman.

From the start, she and Jerry Wexler were a strange pair—he, the hard-headed businessman with a deep love for traditional rhythm & blues, and she, shy and reclusive, with a profound ambivalence toward tradition of any sort. Partly by design and partly by accident, they hit on a brilliant formula. Wexler flew her down to Muscle Shoals, Alabama, to work with Rick Hall's Fame Recording Studios band to give her the Southern soul sound that was so popular at the time. On "Respect" and "Do Right Woman," she returned to the frenzied gospel call-and-response style, the main component in the successful Motown formula from her hometown, Detroit. Thus commercially they had the best of both worlds. More important, Wexler let her loose, as he had done with Ray Charles fifteen years earlier. Aretha chose all the tunes and many of the songwriters and personally directed the rhythm arrangements.

Her first (and best) album for Atlantic, *I Never Loved a Man the Way I Love You,* sounds like it had been building up inside her for seven years. Where the girl groups of the early Sixties had been sweet and coy, Aretha and her backup singers were strong and fierce, and ferociously sexual, combing decades of gospel technique in their interplay. Shortly before his death, commenting on Aretha's cover version of "Respect," Otis Redding said that the woman had stolen his song.

Aretha sounded frantic then. This tension revital-ized what might otherwise have been tired rhythm & blues clichés. White audiences who had never heard of Etta James, Bobby Bland or James Carr loved her sexual frankness. Some social critics even went so far as to link changing sexual mores in the late Sixties to the popularity of the soul music of Franklin and her colleagues.

Aretha was one of the first soul artists to conceive of entire albums, while many of her contemporaries were releasing two to three hit singles surrounded by filler. This helped broaden her base. People often bought the albums for the uptempo dance songs and then kept playing them because they loved the ballads—"Prove It," "Ain't No Way," "Soul Serenade." By 1967 she had been involved in virtually every form of American popular music from show tunes to low-down blues. With the help of a group of primarily white Southern musicians—among them Roger Hawkins, Spooner Oldham and Tommy Cogbill—she created four classic albums.

Twenty-five years later much of the material on the first four Atlantic albums still sounds wonderful. Looking back at them now, one of their most striking features is her quirky sense of humor. "The House That Jack Built," "Come Back, Baby," "Chain of Fools" and "Respect"—in fact, many of the songs written by men—are often sly parodies.

The other striking characteristic is sheer joyfulness. Arif Mardin, a frequent arranger and coproducer during her Atlantic years, described the spontaneous nature of the sessions, and the way she exerted control:

"She'd play the piano, and then I would start writing down what she was playing with her left hand and give it out to the bass player. [My job] was making what she felt bigger. She was the absolute mistress of the vocal group, and she would tell them exactly what to do. She would be like a sergeant major . . ."

Mardin talked of her repeated phone calls in the middle of the night. "She'd call me up and she'd

The great interpreter of
a vast variety of songs.

start singing something. Then she'd say, 'Arif, I want strings here. Give me this line.'" In those years, he concluded, "She had no sense of the impossible."

Even in the early albums, a personal theme emerged. Curiously, for a so-called tough soul singer, Aretha often sang about dreaming. One can trace a trajectory through "Don't Let Me Lose This Dream," "I Say a Little Prayer," "Angel," "Day Dreaming" and "Until You Come Back to Me (That's What I'm Gonna Do)." The richness of a "Dr. Feelgood," after all, lies in its combination of the gutsy realism of the blues with pure fantasy.

Arguably the culmination of her career is on her first gospel album, *Amazing Grace,* in her reading of the line from Marvin Gaye's "Wholly Holy": "We've got to believe each other's dreams." Aretha did not grate like Tina Turner or Wilson Pickett, because when she was on target, she worked on two levels simultaneously: blues reality and romantic fantasy; upfront sexuality and a tacit vulnerability.

Decline is never pure and never simple; often the richest, most ambiguous work comes during an artist's so-called decadent period. By 1969 the public seemed to have tired of Southern soul records in general and uptempo Aretha Franklin records in particular. Initially this shift presented a challenge, and some of her 1968 singles were creative responses, especially "I Say a Little Prayer" and "You Send Me." But a profound exhaustion soon set in. Her personal life became a wreck.

Her records became mechanical and listless. "Eleanor Rigby" and "The Weight," the latter with Duane Allman on slide guitar, halfheartedly attempted to capture the post-Woodstock audience. Soon the records stopped coming altogether.

Aretha's solution was to turn inward, toward the paradoxes and aspirations and demons in her own life. She simultaneously retreated from soul formulas back to her style as a mainstream pop-jazz singer at Columbia, and played up her interest in African and black nationalist affairs. Thus, in 1971 we were confronted with an enigmatic new Aretha Franklin, wearing natural and voluptuous African gowns, yet singing decidedly unnatural pop tunes backed by large string sections.

In the halcyon days, Franklin's hits had generally been written by men; her own compositions were relegated to flip sides or album cuts. She turned the tables with her own compositions.

In pop masterpieces like "Call Me" and "Day Dreaming," she flaunted her sensitivity and her desire to be taken seriously as a poet and an artist. "First Snow in Kokomo" tackled a subject worthy of William Carlos Williams: the mysterious processes by which some individuals pull themselves together, while others disintegrate. Her confused but often brilliant *Young, Gifted and Black* album was a frank exploration of her failed marriage and fittingly takes its place alongside the disillusioned, confessional work of writers like Doris Lessing or Anaïs Nin.

After *Young, Gifted and Black,* she needed a new direction. She knew she couldn't return to the Lady Soul of the Sixties, and that she had more or less exhausted her autobiographical repertoire. As the Seventies progressed and black music became more producer dominated, she became a displaced figure. Her career deteriorated into a series of comebacks. Though they were often glorious ("Rock Steady," *Young, Gifted and Black,* "Until You Come Back to Me" and the *Blues Brothers* movie), each was followed by a corresponding debacle.

She developed an obsession with becoming exactly what she was not: a sophisticate, a sexy, slinky Diana Ross–type figure. Finally, like a protagonist in an existential novel, she assailed her own body, losing a massive amount of weight, parading onstage in minks and a rhinestone bikini. The dancers bowed at her feet while she walked onstage.

Her albums in the middle and late Seventies were erratic and bloated; but they almost always contained a couple of brilliant moments. The Eighties albums were even more erratic, although there were great moments in the Luther Vandross–produced *Jump to It* (1982) and *The Freeway of Love* (1986).

Aretha attempted to define her style to reporter Gerri Hirshey as follows: "a lot of depth and being

"I've got some memories to look back on."

able to bring to the surface that which is happening inside, to make the picture clear . . . It's just the emotion, the way it affects people . . . The song doesn't matter."

The 1974 resurrection of the Marvin Gaye–Tammi Terrell hit "Ain't Nothing Like the Real Thing" is a perfect example of her approach to pop. Franklin takes this upbeat, uptempo tune at a mournful pace. She sounds distracted and absentminded during the first half, working at cross-purposes with the lyric. For no apparent reason, she assumes her lover has lost interest in her, and shrieks, "Let's stay together," developing an unnerving, confusing emotion, given the context of the song. Then swiftly, intuitively, she leaps down an octave and gives a sublime reading of the next line: "I've got some memories to look back on." It's difficult to convey how she projects several meanings simultaneously. First, she indicates that for all of us, no thing, no relationship ever dies, that memory is stronger than reality. On the other hand, she tells us that whatever

her current problems, however badly she's messed up her life, *she's* got memories to look back on that you can't even conceive, millions of people screaming for her, reaching out to touch her. And finally it is as if she wishes to confide the simple truth: She was great and unique, she knew it, the world knew it, and nothing can obliterate that truth.

The French filmmaker and critic Jean-Luc Godard put it this way (freely translated): "There are two kinds of artists. Some walk down the streets with their heads up, looking straight ahead. They look and plan and organize, and their work is smart and wise and well developed and sometimes great. This group is always admired.

"Then there's the other type of artist. They walk down the street with their heads down, lost in thought or daydreams. Every so often, they're obliged to lift their heads, always suddenly, embracing their field of vision in a series of rapid, oblique glances. This group *sees*. However confused or eccentric their style, they see with a wonderful clarity."

Aretha assuredly fits into the latter category. Long after the mediocre works are forgotten, the beauties of her intuitive, improvisatory work will remain. No one ever sang songs of yearning like Aretha Franklin.

DISCOGRAPHY

SINGLES

"Today I Sing the Blues" (Columbia; r☆10, 1960). "Won't Be Long" (Columbia; r☆7, 1961). "Operation Heartbreak" b/w "Rock-a-Bye Your Baby with a Dixie Melody" (Columbia; r☆6, ☆37, 1961). "Runnin' Out of Fools" (Columbia; ☆57, 1964). "One Step Ahead" (Columbia; r☆18, 1965). "Cry Like a Baby" (Columbia; r☆27, 1966). "I Never Loved a Man (the Way I Love You)" b/w "Do Right Woman—Do Right Man" (Atlantic; r☆1, ☆9, 1967). "Respect" (Atlantic; r☆1, ☆1, 1967). "Lee Cross" (Columbia; r☆31, 1967). "Baby I Love You" (Atlantic; r☆1, ☆4, 1967). "Take a Look" (Columbia; r☆28, 1967). "A Natural Woman" (Atlantic; r☆2, ☆8, 1967). "Chain of Fools" (Atlantic; r☆1, ☆2, 1967). "(Sweet Sweet Baby) Since You've Been Gone" b/w "Ain't No Way" (Atlantic; r☆1, ☆5, 1968). "Think" b/w "You Send Me" (Atlantic; r☆1, ☆7, 1968). "The House That Jack Built" b/w "I Say a Little Prayer" (Atlantic; r☆2, ☆6, 1968). "See Saw" b/w "My Song" (Atlantic; r☆9, ☆14, 1968). "The Weight" b/w "Tracks of My Tears" (Atlantic; r☆3, ☆19, 1969). "I Can't See Myself Leaving You" (Atlantic; r☆3, ☆19, 1969). "Share Your Love with Me" (Atlantic; r☆1, ☆13, 1969). "Eleanor Rigby" (Atantic; r☆5, ☆17, 1969). "Call Me" (Atlantic; r☆1, ☆13, 1970). "Spirit in the Dark" (Atlantic; r☆3, ☆23, 1970). "Don't Play That Song" (Atlantic; r☆1, ☆11, 1970). "Border Song (Holy Moses)" (Atlantic; r☆5, ☆37, 1970). "You're All I Need to Get By" (Atlantic; r☆3, ☆19, 1971). "Bridge over Troubled Water" b/w "Brand New Me" (Atlantic; r☆1, ☆6, 1971). "Spanish Harlem" (Atlantic; r☆1, ☆2, 1971). "Rock Steady" b/w "Oh Me Oh My" (Atlantic; r☆2, ☆9, 1971). "Day Dreaming" (Atlantic; r☆1, ☆5, 1972). "All the King's Horses" (Atlantic; r☆7, ☆26, 1972). "Master of Eyes" (Atlantic;

r☆8, ☆33, 1973). "Angel" (Atlantic; r☆1, ☆20, 1973). "Until You Come Back to Me (That's What I'm Gonna Do)" (Atlantic; r☆1, ☆3, 1973). "I'm in Love" (Atlantic; r☆1, ☆19, 1974). "Ain't Nothing Like the Real Thing" (Atlantic; r☆6, ☆47, 1974). "Without Love" (Atlantic; r☆6, ☆45, 1974). "With Everything I Feel in Me" (Atlantic; r☆20, 1975). "Mr. D.J. (5 for the D.J.)" (Atlantic; r☆13, 1975). "Something He Can Feel" (Atlantic; ☆28, 1976). "Jump" (Atlantic; ☆72, 1976). "Look into Your Heart" (Atlantic; r☆10, ☆82, 1977). "Break It to Me Gently" (Atlantic; r☆1, ☆85, 1977). "Almighty Fire (Woman of the Future)" (Atlantic; r☆12, 1978). "More Than Just a Joy" (Atlantic; r☆51; 1978). "Ladies Only" (Atlantic; r☆33, 1979). "Half a Love" (Atlantic; r☆65, 1979). "United Together" (Arista; r☆3, ☆56, 1980). "What a Fool Believes" (Arista; r☆17, 1981). "Come to Me" (Arista; r☆39, ☆84, 1981). With George Benson: "Love All the Hurt Away" (Arista; r☆6, ☆46, 1981). "It's My Turn" (Arista; r☆29, 1981). "Jump to It" (Arista; r☆1, ☆24, 1982). "Love Me Right" (Arista; r☆22, 1982). "This Is for Real" (Arista; r☆63, 1983). "Get It Right" (Arista; r☆1, ☆61, 1983). "Every Girl (Wants My Guy)" (Arista; r☆7, 1983). "Freeway of Love" (Arista; r☆1, ☆3, 1985). "Who's Zoomin' Who" (Arista; r☆2, ☆7, 1985). With the Eurythmics: "Sisters Are Doin' It for Themselves" (RCA; r☆66, ☆18, 1985). "Another Night" (Arista; r☆9, ☆22, 1986). "Ain't Nobody Ever Loved You" (Arista; r☆30, 1986). "Jumpin' Jack Flash" (Arista; r☆20, ☆21, 1986). "Jimmy Lee" (Arista; r☆2, ☆28, 1986). With George Michael: "I Knew You Were Waiting (for Me)" (Arista; r☆5, ☆1, 1987). "Rock-a-Lott" (Arista; r☆25, ☆82, 1987). With Larry Graham: "If You Need My Love Tonight" (Arista; r☆88, 1987). With the Four Tops: "If Ever a Love There Was" (Arista; r☆31, 1988). With Elton John: "Through the Storm" (Arista; r☆17, ☆16, 1989). With Whitney Houston: "It Isn't, It Wasn't, It Ain't Never Gonna Be" (Arista; r☆5, ☆41, 1989). With James Brown: "Gimme Your Love" (Arista; r☆48, 1989).

ALBUMS

The Tender, the Moving, the Swinging Aretha Franklin (Columbia; ☆69, 1962). *Runnin' Out of Fools* (Columbia; ☆84, 1964). *Yeah!* (Columbia; ☆101, 1965). *Soul Sister* (Columbia; ☆132, 1966). *I Never Loved a Man the Way I Love You* (Atlantic; ☆2, 1967). *Aretha Franklin's Greatest Hits* (Columbia; ☆94, 1967). *Aretha Arrives* (Atlantic; ☆5, 1967). *Take a Look* (Columbia; ☆173, 1967). *Aretha: Lady Soul* (Atlantic; ☆2, 1968). *Aretha Now* (Atlantic; ☆3, 1968). *Aretha in Paris* (Atlantic; ☆13, 1968). *Aretha Franklin: Soul '69* (Atlantic; ☆15, 1969). *Aretha's Gold* (Atlantic; ☆18, 1969). *This Girl's in Love with You* (Atlantic; ☆17, 1970). *Spirit in the Dark* (Atlantic; ☆25, 1970). *Aretha Live at Fillmore West* (Atlantic; ☆7, 1971). *Aretha's Greatest Hits* (Atlantic; ☆19, 1971). *Young, Gifted and Black* (Atlantic; ☆11, 1972). With James Cleveland: *Amazing Grace* (Atlantic; ☆7, 1972). *In the Beginning/ The World of Aretha Franklin (1960–1967)* (Columbia; ☆160, 1972). *Hey Now Hey (The Other Side of the Sky)* (Atlantic; ☆30, 1973). *Let Me in Your Life* (Atlantic; ☆14, 1974). *The First 12 Sides* (Columbia; 1973). *With Everything I Feel in Me* (Atlantic; ☆57, 1974). *You* (Atlantic; ☆83, 1975). *Sparkle* (Atlantic; ☆18, 1976). *Ten Years of Gold* (Atlantic; ☆135, 1976). *Sweet Passion* (Atlantic; ☆49, 1977). *Almighty Fire* (Atlantic; ☆63, 1978). *La Diva* (Atlantic; ☆146, 1979). *Aretha* (Arista; ☆47, 1980). *Love All the Hurt Away* (Arista; ☆36, 1981). *Jump to It* (Arista; r☆1, ☆23, 1982). *Get It Right* (Arista; ☆36, 1983). *Aretha* (Arista; r☆7, ☆32, 1986). *One Lord, One Faith, One Baptism* (Arista; r☆25, ☆106, 1987). *Through the Storm* (Arista; r☆21, ☆55, 1989). *What You See Is What You Sweat* (Arista; r☆28, ☆153, 1991). *The Queen of Soul* (Rhino/ Atlantic; 1992).

(Chart positions compiled from Joel Whitburn's *Record Research*, based on *Billboard*'s Pop and LPs charts, unless otherwise indicated; r☆ = position on *Billboard*'s Rhythm & Blues chart.)

B. B. KING

BY PETER GURALNICK

Almost single-handedly, B. B. King introduced the blues to white America. He did so largely through the mid-Sixties British Invasion, for while there are many styles of blues guitar (and King is himself heir to a long tradition), it was King's style of rapidly picked single notes, embellishing and extending the vocal but rarely supporting it with full-bodied chords, which prevailed to create a whole blues-tinged vocabulary for modern rock. In the process, King himself even managed to achieve something like widespread popularity with the rock audience.

B. B. King was born Riley B. King on a plantation near Itta Bena, Mississippi, on September 16th, 1925. He got his name, and a good deal of his early fame, from the radio show he did on station WDIA in Memphis between 1948 and 1952. WDIA, the first major radio outlet in the South to be black oper-ated, if not black owned, was known as the Mother Station of the Negroes; Riley B. King was known as the Beale St. Blues Boy, later shortened to simply B. B.

He came to Memphis from a classic background in the blues. His cousin was Bukka White, the great country bluesman. B. B. sang in gospel quartets as a boy, greatly admired Samuel McCrary and the Fair-field Four, and picked up a little bit of guitar from his aunt's brother-in-law, who was a preacher. It wasn't until around the time he was drafted in 1944 that he started playing blues. When he was released shortly afterward (on a tractor driver's agricultural defer-ment), he started playing on the streets of nearby Mississippi towns, going just far enough away from home so that his family wouldn't catch him singing ''the devil's music.'' It was Robert Jr. Lockwood, stepson of the legendary Robert Johnson, who helped him refine his T-Bone Walker– and Charlie Christian–influenced single-string guitar runs. And

B. B. King as he was in the mid-Fifties. He wanted to be tops in the blues. Today he plays Las Vegas. He has realized his ambition.

it was Sonny Boy Williamson, whom Lockwood accompanied in the jook joints and little backcountry plantation halls that made up a bluesman's professional career, who got King started in Memphis. There he met Rufus Thomas, a former vaudevillian and then emcee of the amateur talent contest at the Palace Theater. There, too, he completed his musical education.

B. B. King, more than any of the country bluesmen or even urban singers like Muddy Waters or Howlin' Wolf, is a self-made artist, his style assembled from a variety of sources. These sources include jazz and gospel and country music, and perhaps this eclecticism is the one reason for his unique susceptibility to white adaptation. In any case his music is not, like Muddy's or Wolf's, the product of a local or isolated tradition, the inescapable extension of a long historical line.

Instead, it is made up of a series of conscious choices. His early music was very much influenced by the wide range of material (everything from R&B to Frank Sinatra, Nat "King" Cole, Vaughn Monroe and Frankie Laine) which he programmed as a disc jockey. To B. B. King, the theme of self-improvement has been a constant one, and he must have seen his radio show not just as a chance to convey his personality in a fifteen-minute live segment (like Sonny Boy or Wolf, Joe Hill Louis and numerous other itinerant bluesmen turned disc jockeys), but also as an opportunity to better himself. He got his own two-hour show; he taught himself to speak more "properly"; he widened his frame of musical reference; and he acquired the modest, almost self-deprecating but self-assured manner that serves him to this day.

He started his recording career as a shouter very much in the vein of Roy Brown or Wynonie Harris. He relied heavily on the small-band arrangements (eight- or nine-piece) and riffing horn section of their particular brand of jump blues, over which his voice and guitar would forcefully ripple out—though never simultaneously. His vocals, originally all of the shouter variety, gradually took on more of

King at the Grammy Awards dinner, 1972.

Receiving an honorary degree from Tougaloo College, Mississippi, 1973.

a gospel hue, as he began to employ the full throated phlegminess, falsetto effects and melisma (stretching a single syllable over several notes) of the fervid quartet singer. The kind of material he performed drew heavily from the declamatory style of Louis Jordan. As for his guitar playing—well, in later years he was to point to Django Reinhardt and Charlie Christian as key influences, and in fact he was exposed to Reinhardt's music through a friend who brought back Django's records from Paris after the war—but most of his solos were pure T-Bone Walker with a dash of Lonnie Johnson: liquid, mellow, relying almost exclusively on the single-string runs which they had popularized in the blues.

His first recordings were made in 1949, but his first big hit came in 1951 with "3 O'Clock Blues." Like nearly all of his later hits, "3 O'Clock" was not original with B. B. King but had been a very popular song for its composer, Lowell Fulson, some two years earlier. "Every Day I Have the Blues" came from Joe Williams via Fulson and Memphis Slim, "Sweet Sixteen" from Big Joe Turner, even "Sweet Little Angel," the song with which he has been most identified, from Tampa Red via Robert Nighthawk. It's all somewhat academic. Unlike many of his contemporaries, B. B. King had a wide-ranging curiosity and an extensive frame of reference. Onto each song he put his individual stamp.

Success meant the same thing for B. B. King as it did for any black R&B artist of the time: an endless round of one-nighters in joints not much better than the country shacks in which he had started out, culminating in 342 engagements in 1956 alone. After the Fifties, his popularity waned (he left in his wake a handful of Kings—Albert, Freddie, Earl, Little B. B., B. B. Junior), and in the Sixties, the era of soul, he frequently shared the bill with Bobby "Blue" Bland—a singer who had come up behind him in Memphis, had in fact started out as his driver—in a touring Battle of the Blues. Then around 1966 he was discovered by the white rock audience, thanks to the efforts of such influential guitarists as Mike Bloomfield and Eric Clapton. By 1969 he was a fixture at rock ballrooms like the Fillmores East and West and was wearing his hair natural. In late 1969 he had his sole Top Twenty hit by himself with "The Thrill Is Gone." Twenty years later he would collaborate with U2 on the song "When Love Comes to Town," which returned King to the pop charts.

Today he is something of an institution. He has passed through adulation and emerged on the other side, if not without incident, then without overwhelmingly adverse effects. He fathered a whole generation of rock guitarists from Mike Bloomfield to Eric Clapton to Jimmy Page, Jimi Hendrix and just about every garage-band bluesman you've ever heard. His goal over the years has continued to be self-improvement and a more widespread recognition of the blues. He has studied the Schillinger Method of Musical Composition, gotten his pilot's license, appeared in movies and become a mainstay on network TV. Over and over in interviews he used

On the road in the mid-Sixties.

Dressed for Vegas.

to stress, "If Frank Sinatra can be tops in his field, Nat 'King' Cole in his, Bach and Beethoven in theirs, why can't I be great and known for it in blues? Because I don't know anybody else have kept as constant study, working as I have for twenty-one years, in blues." Today he plays Las Vegas, gets residuals from his television commercials, serves as a kind of international ambassador of goodwill like Louis Armstrong and has become an almost universal symbol of the blues. He has realized his ambition.

DISCOGRAPHY

SINGLES

"3 O'Clock Blues" (RPM; r☆1, 1951). "You Know I Love You" (RPM; r☆1, 1952). "Story from My Heart and Soul" (RPM; r☆9, 1952). "Woke Up This Morning" (RPM; r☆5, 1953). "Please Love Me" (RPM; r☆2, 1953). "Please Hurry Home" (RPM; r☆8, 1953). "You Upset Me Baby" b/w "Whole Lotta Love" (RPM; r☆2, 1954). "Every Day I Have the Blues" b/w "Sneakin' Around" (RPM; r☆10, 1955). "Ten Long Years" (RPM; r☆12, 1955). "Crying Won't Help You" (RPM; r☆15, 1956). "Sweet Little Angel" b/w "Bad Luck" (RPM; r☆6, 1956). "On My Word of Honor" (RPM; r☆11, 1956). "Troubles, Troubles, Troubles" (RPM; r☆13, 1957). "You've Been an Angel" b/w "Please Accept My Love" (Kent; r☆9, 1958). "Sweet Sixteen" (Kent; r☆2, 1960). "Got a Right to Love My Baby" (Kent; r☆8, 1960). "Partin' Time" (Kent; r☆8, 1960). "Someday" b/w "Peace of Mind" (Kent; r☆7, 1961). "Gonna Miss You Around Here" (Kent; r☆17, 1962). "Rock Me Baby" (Kent; ☆34, 1964). "Don't Answer the Door" (ABC-Paramount; r☆2, 1966). "The Jungle" (Kent; r☆17, 1967). "Paying the Cost to the Boss" (BluesWay; r☆10, ☆39, 1968). "Why I Sing the Blues" (BluesWay; r☆13, 1969). "Just a Little Love" (BluesWay; r☆15, 1969). "The Thrill Is Gone" (BluesWay; r☆3, ☆15, 1970). "So Excited" (BluesWay; r☆14, 1970). "Hummingbird" (ABC; r☆25, ☆48, 1970). "Chains and Things" (ABC; r☆6, ☆45, 1970). "Ask Me No Questions" (ABC; r☆18, ☆40, 1971). "Ain't Nobody Home" (ABC; r☆28, ☆46, 1971). "There Must Be a Better World Somewhere" (MCA; r☆91, 1981). "Into the Night" (MCA; r☆15, ☆107, 1985). "Big Boss Man" (MCA; r☆62, 1985). With U2: "When Love Comes to Town" (Island; ☆68, 1989).

ALBUMS

B. B. King Live in Cook County Jail (ABC; 1971). *The Best of B. B. King* (MCA; 1989).

(Chart positions compiled from Joel Whitburn's *Record Research*, based on *Billboard*'s Pop chart, unless otherwise indicated; r☆ = position on *Billboard*'s Rhythm & Blues chart.)

Records by black American bluesmen began to appear in Britain after the end of the Second World War; some were British pressings leased by English jazz labels that presumably thought the music was jazz. Other blues discs were left behind by American GIs and sold in secondhand stores; still more came through the mails to kids like Mick Jagger who sent away to Chess Records in Chicago.

The principal "black music" trend in England in the Fifties, however, was "trad" jazz, a pallid but enthusiastic attempt to re-create the Chicago and New Orleans styles of the Twenties. The big name in trad was Chris Barber, who in the mid-Fifties began importing blues singers such as John Lee Hooker and Muddy Waters to play in his live programs. During these years Barber's band also occasionally included Alexis Korner and Cyril Davies, Englishmen who had been playing Sonny Terry–Brownie McGhee style blues together since 1953. Korner and Davies played in an R&B unit within the band, which was enlarged in 1960, when a youth named Brian Jones joined them on slide guitar. In 1962, when the threesome, calling themselves Blues Incorporated, left Barber, they had built up a sizable following.

The blues was catching on. The blues, the *purity* of the blues, the *folk poetry* of the blues—all of it became something like a religion with musicians and fans, partly as a reaction against the insipid British pop music of the time and partly as a reaction against the cultish stuffiness of the trad-jazz scene. Blues Incorporated was the transitional band, and it served as an incubator for literally dozens of young musicians who later went on to rock & roll fame. Among them were several of the Rolling Stones.

The Stones were the first broadly popular and musically effective British blues group, a distinction they earned by mixing Slim Harpo and Muddy Waters with uptown R&B and Chuck Berry. Purists themselves in the beginning, the Stones outraged the folk-poetry crowd and were commonly accused of betraying the blues. In fact, they saw themselves as evangelists.

Dozens of blues groups sprang up in the wake of

John Mayall's original Bluesbreakers, the first important British blues band: Mayall (*far left*) and Eric Clapton (*second from left*).

the Stones' early success: The Yardbirds, likely the best, were typical in that they featured blues in live performance and elaborate pop tricks in the studio. Such gimmickry (as on "For Your Love," 1965) led to the departure of their much-idolized lead guitarist, Eric Clapton, another purist. Clapton joined John Mayall's Bluesbreakers, a band that spawned as many future stars as Korner's original outfit. Among Mayall's alumni were Peter Green (later of Fleetwood Mac), Jack Bruce (of Cream) and Mick Taylor (who replaced Brian Jones in the Stones).

Clapton and Bruce soon departed to form Cream with drummer Ginger Baker—the first British blues group to achieve more than local success since the Stones. After Cream, the blues scene lost its shape. There was Fleetwood Mac, which specialized in Elmore James copies, and which, after many personnel changes, evolved into a very pleasant pop group; there was Ten Years After starring speed guitarist Alvin Lee and specializing in frenzy; Chicken Shack; the Climax Blues Band; and Savoy Brown, which perhaps has had more personnel shifts than any other group in rock. Throughout the Seventies blues bands continued in and around the British Isles; the best of them was led by Irishman Rory Gallagher, a superb flash guitar player.

On the American side of the Atlantic the folk-music crowd was slower to accept the spectacle of a white kid playing something advertised as blues. The folkies worshiped "authenticity," which meant an aged black man playing an acoustic instrument. In the rush to "rediscover"

Thirties bluesmen like Skip James and Mississippi John Hurt, living (and working) legends like Howlin' Wolf and Sonny Boy Williamson were passed over, even though their music was "people's music" if anything was. The folkies allowed a few of their own into the pantheon, but only if they restricted themselves to pre–World War II rural forms: Dave Van Ronk, who brilliantly interpreted finger-picking stylings of the Twenties and Thirties, and John Hammond, Jr., whose mush-mouthed imitations of Son House convinced at least a few.

Unconcerned with such limitations were a bunch of young white Chicagoans who had discovered a whole world of music in their own backyard. One was Michael Bloomfield, a nice Jewish boy straight out of the very comfortable upper middle class. At sixteen he had a couple of years of rock behind him, but blues guitar was what he wanted to learn; and to this end he was soon backing older bluesmen on guitar and piano. At the same time, unknown to Bloomfield, a lawyer's son named Paul Butterfield was making a name for himself on the South Side as a freak act: See the white kid play blues harmonica. In general, Bloomfield was playing with blacks for folkies; Butterfield and his friends were playing for all-black audiences.

It was inevitable that they would meet, and after

In the mid-Sixties a very young Michael Bloomfield sits at the foot of a master, John Lee Hooker. In his heyday with Paul Butterfield, Bloomfield played the flashiest blues anyone had ever heard.

Paul Butterfield, harpist, founder of the first well-known integrated blues band of the Sixties.

joining the first Paul Butterfield Blues Band as a piano player, Bloomfield turned down Bob Dylan's offer to join his group (Bloomfield played guitar on Dylan's 1965 classic, *Highway 61 Revisited)* and stuck with Butterfield, reigning as America's most influential guitarist until the arrival of Eric Clapton in 1967.

Members of the Butterfield band had backed Dylan at the Newport Folk Festival in 1965, and their first album on Elektra (until then, strictly a folk label) converted many. Their second album, *East-West,* established second guitarist Elvin Bishop, and though the band never sounded as good again (Bloomfield left in 1967 to form the Electric Flag), the band's name was made.

As in England, blues groups were everywhere in short order. Most were terrible and died quick and unlamented deaths. The most interesting was a band put together by two blues collectors, Bob Hite and Alan Wilson, called Canned Heat, after an old Tommy Johnson song. Reaching back to the Twenties for their spirit, yet fully electrified and endlessly preaching ''Boogie!,'' they were capable of memorable music. Wilson's high voice, eerie harmonica and fluid rhythm guitar floated above a grunting rhythm section; the combination brought them two Top Twenty hits in 1968, ''Going Up the Country'' and ''On the Road Again.'' Wilson, nearly blind and subject to intense depression, died from a drug over-

Chuck Berry, backed by the Blues Project, mid-Sixties. *From left:* Steve Katz, Roy Blumenthal, Al Kooper, Danny Kalb.

The great Stevie Ray Vaughan: gone, not forgotten.

dose in 1970; the band survived him in name only, though it continued to record. Bob Hite died in 1981.

Other important musicians of the Sixties included Charlie Musselwhite, a white musician from Mem- phis who played harp Chicago-style; Nick Grave- nites (an excellent singer and songwriter from the Bloomfield-Butterfield crowd); and the strange Blues Project, a New York band whose odd urban rework-

Robert Cray, getting ready to rock the house.

ings of older blues had an intense local following in 1965.

And there were those who followed in the late Sixties and early Seventies, many of whom either abandoned blues for straight rock & roll, or died: Duane Allman from Georgia, who made his professional reputation as a studio guitarist backing established R&B performers; the Allman Brothers Band, a racially mixed powerhouse that included Duane and his brother Gregg, and that was dominant on the concert circuit even after Duane's 1971 death in a motorcycle accident; the J. Geils Band out of Boston, which burst into prominence with a searing debut album in 1971 but by 1980 had switched to pop-oriented rock; and Johnny Winter, the albino guitarist from Texas, who, unlike the others, has stuck to purely blues-based music.

Though white blues performers have lacked staying power, the phenomenon of the white blues "revival" is recurrent: It can be expected whenever mainstream pop music finds itself weighed down by gimmicks. Thus, it was not unexpected to discover another one taking shape in the early Eighties, both as a reaction to punk and new wave and as a sort of

nostalgic music for aging baby boomers. Combined with the "roots-music" revival of such bands as the Blasters and Los Lobos, the next blues revival involved the rise to prominence of young black blues players such as Robert Cray and Chris Thomas, a growing interest in the blues-flavored Louisiana accordion music, zydeco, and a whole new crop of white blues bands, including the Fabulous Thunderbirds, Stevie Ray Vaughan and Double Trouble (Vaughan was tragically killed in a helicopter crash in 1990), Omar and the Howlers, the Jeff Healey Band, Anson Funderburgh and the Rockets, and the legendary Washington, D.C., guitarist Danny Gatton. Whether this new bunch will have any better luck than their predecessors did in sticking to a more or less pure blues agenda is a question that remains to be answered.

DISCOGRAPHY

ALBUMS

Blues Project: *The Best of the Blues Project* (Rhino; 1989). **Paul Butterfield:** *The Paul Butterfield Blues Band* (Elektra; ☆123, 1965). *East-West* (Elektra; ☆65, 1966). *The Resurrection of Pigboy Crabshaw* (Elektra; ☆52, 1968). *In My Own Dream* (Elektra; ☆79, 1968). *Keep On Moving* (Elektra; ☆102, 1969). *The Butterfield Blues Band/Live* (Elektra; ☆72, 1971). *Sometimes I Just Feel Like Smilin'* (Elektra; ☆124, 1971). *Golden Butter/The Best of the Paul Butterfield Blues Band* (Elektra; ☆136, 1972). *Better Days* (Bearsville; ☆145, 1973). *It All Comes Back* (Bearsville; ☆156, 1973). *Put It in Your Ear* (Bearsville; 1976). *North-South* (Bearsville; 1981). **Canned Heat:** *Canned Heat* (Liberty; ☆76, 1967). *Boogie with Canned Heat* (Liberty; ☆16, 1968). *Living the Blues* (Liberty; ☆18, 1968). *Hallelujah* (Liberty; ☆37, 1969). **Robert Cray Band:** *Bad Influence* (Hightone; 1983). *Showdown!* (Alligator; ☆124, 1986). *False Accusations* (Hightone; ☆141, 1986). *Strong Persuader* (Mercury; ☆13, 1986). *Don't Be Afraid of the Dark* (Mercury; ☆32, 1988). *Midnight Stroll* (Mercury; ☆51, 1990). **John Mayall:** *Bluesbreakers* (London; 1967; released in Britain 1965). *A Hard Road* (London; 1967; released in Britain 1966). *Crusade* (London; ☆136, 1968; released in Britain 1967). *The Blues Alone* (London; ☆128, 1968). *Bare Wires* (London; ☆59, 1968). *Blues from Laurel Canyon* (London; ☆68, 1969). *Looking Back* (London; ☆79, 1969). *The Turning Point* (Polydor; ☆32, 1969). *The Diary of a Band* (London; ☆93, 1970). *Empty Rooms* (Polydor; ☆33, 1970). *U.S.A. Union* (Polydor; ☆22, 1970). *Back to the Roots* (Polydor; ☆52, 1971). *John Mayall—Live in Europe* (London; ☆146, 1971). *Through the Years* (London; ☆164, 1971). *Memories* (Polydor; ☆179, 1971). *Jazz-Blues Fusion* (Polydor; ☆158, 1972). *Moving On* (Polydor; ☆116, 1972). *Down the Line* (London; ☆158, 1973). *Ten Years Are Gone* (Polydor; ☆157, 1973). *New Year, New Band, New Company* (Blue Thumb; ☆140, 1975). *A Sense of Place* (Island; ☆170, 1990). **Ten Years After:** *Ten Years After* (Deram; 1968; released in Britain 1967). *Undead* (Deram; ☆115, 1968). *Stonedhenge* (Deram; ☆61, 1969). *Ssssh* (Deram; ☆20, 1969). **Stevie Ray Vaughan and Double Trouble:** *Texas Flood* (Epic; ☆38, 1983). *Couldn't Stand the Weather* (Epic; ☆31, 1984). *Live Alive* (Epic; ☆52, 1986). *In Step* (Epic; ☆33, 1989). *The Sky Is Crying* (Epic; ☆10, 1991). With Jimmie Vaughan: the Vaughan Brothers *Family Style* (Epic; ☆7, 1990).

(Chart positions compiled from Joel Whitburn's *Record Research*, based on *Billboard*'s LPs chart.)

THE VELVET UNDERGROUND

BY DAVID FRICKE

There's a standing joke in rock & roll about the Velvet Underground: Hardly anyone bought the group's records when they first came out, but the few people who did all went on to form their own bands. The real punchline is that just about every punk, post-punk and avant-pop artist or band of the past two decades owes a debt of inspiration, if not direct influence, to the Velvet Underground. Frequently misunderstood, often reviled but mostly just ignored in their late-Sixties lifetime, the Velvets are arguably the most important American band in post-1965 rock, the font from which nearly all white art-beat noise of the Seventies and the Eighties flows and the ruling standard for unfettered guitar ferocity and barbed narrative realism in rock songwriting.

The roll call of celebrity acolytes is common knowledge: David Bowie, Brian Eno, Patti Smith and the entire mid-Seventies punk-rock graduating class at CBGB, the Cars, Chrissie Hynde of the Pretenders, Joy Division–New Order, U2, R.E.M. and Sonic Youth, to name a handful. The booming business in Velvets cover versions over the years has yielded the sublime (R.E.M.'s folk-lullaby rendering of "Pale Blue Eyes" and "Femme Fatale"), the searing (Bowie's legendary lashing of "I'm Waiting for the Man" in his 1972 *Ziggy Stardust* stage show) and the surprisingly commercial (Mott the Hoople's glam-slam take on "Sweet Jane").

But the thriving legacy of the Velvet Underground is rooted in more than what fans formed which bands and who's covered how many songs. Formed

Warhol's children: the Velvet Underground with Andy.

in 1965 amid the euphoric crush of Beatlemania and embryonic psychedelia, the original lineup of singer-guitarist Lou Reed, bassist, keyboard and viola player John Cale, guitarist Sterling Morrison and drummer Maureen Tucker blew wide open the doors of possibility with their radical compound of primal shriek and pop-soul *noir*. Even in a rock era celebrated for its exploratory spirit, the Velvets went to bold, assaultive extremes, finding their own common ground in runaway free jazz, the classical avant-garde, romantic balladry and, most importantly, commercial R&B. (Dig Reed's sly appropriation of the guitar hook from Marvin Gaye's 1963 hit "Hitch Hike" for "There She Goes Again" on the first Velvets LP.)

As the group's songwriter, Reed had no trouble reconciling his keen interest in the taboo and the untapped—sexual deviancy, drug addiction, the high price of love and sanity in the urban shadows—with his gift for bare-bones rock & roll song craft and

John Cale's parallel career as an experimental composer and performer. Reed's most famous drug song, "Heroin," written while he was still an English major at Syracuse University in the early Sixties, is a throbbing two-chord blues, a junkie's confession told with menacing matter-of-factness, then amplified to the mental-breakdown point by Cale's fingernail-down-blackboard sawing on the viola. In Reed's gothic-rock jewel "All Tomorrow's Parties," the corrosive primitivism of the guitars and Cale's repetitive, percolating piano figure—a by-product of his association with the outlaw composers in the Fluxus and nascent Minimalism movements—fuse into an urgent, hypnotic heartbeat.

The Velvets, in turn, reveled in the sonic contradictions and explosive tensions generated not only by the Reed-Cale axis but by Sterling Morrison's understated but powerful guitar work, the indefatigable jungle-telegraph drumming of Maureen Tucker and the frosty vocal sensuality of Nico, the ravishing German model and actress who was a featured singer with the group throughout 1966 and 1967. The band became notorious for the racing mind-fuck frenzy of its live performances, epitomized on record by the epic amphetamine rush of "Sister Ray" on the 1968 album *White Light/White Heat*. But they were equally capable of breaking your heart in slow ballad gear; Reed wrote some of his finest love songs for Nico's voice, including the aching pledge of troth "I'll Be Your Mirror." The Velvets were, in short, as vibrantly schizophrenic as the city of their birth, New York—and wholly unapologetic about it. They paid dearly for it too, at least in the short term. The Velvets had no peers, no rivals; they were utterly alone in their work, and when the group effectively came to an end in 1970 with Reed's departure, they were exhausted, frustrated and broke. But the Velvets were not, as rock historians usually claim, ahead of their time. Their ambitions were, in fact, timeless: to celebrate the *art* in pop without eclipsing the *heart* of rock & roll. And the results were utterly contemporary and, even then, brutally relevant, and not just in the group's hometown. Everything Reed said about hard drugs, errant sex and social alienation on the first two Velvets albums came true with a vengeance in Haight-

Ashbury after the collapse of the Love Culture. Today, with the twin plagues of AIDS and crack transforming the landscape, there is no denying the ring of dark prophecy that still resonates through those records.

Lou Reed, out of the closet: Fresh from a manicure, he wonders if life is better as a blonde.

The individual Velvets were unlikely rock & roll prophets. Brooklyn-born, Long Island–raised and classically trained at the piano, Lou Reed was an accountant's son who made his first record at age fourteen. He played rhythm guitar on and wrote "Leave Her for Me," the flip side of "So Blue," a 1957 double shot of typical Fifties teen anguish by the Shades (changed to the Jades on the record label). At Syracuse University he pursued more literary aspirations—becoming a disciple of the poet Delmore Schwartz—while moonlighting in local bar bands with fellow Long Islander Sterling Morrison. But Reed put off writing the Great American Novel after graduation. His first job was as an

The Velvets turn their backs on musical convention.

assembly-line tunesmith for Pickwick Records (''a poor man's Carole King,'' as he put it), cranking out knockoffs of Top Forty hits for ninety-nine-cent budget albums.

Reed met John Cale in 1964 while forming a group, the Primitives, to promote one of his Pickwick nonhits, a daffy dance number called ''The Ostrich.'' Born in Wales, Cale had studied in London under the experimental composer Cornelius Cardew and, in 1963, won a Leonard Bernstein scholarship to study modern composition at Tanglewood in Massachusetts. Later that year Cale moved to New York, where he formed an avant-garde musical group, the Dream Syndicate, with Minimalism godfather La Monte Young. Through a bizarre set of connections, Cale—who was becoming more interested in rock—got a job as a Primitive. But it wasn't ''The Ostrich'' that impressed him; it was the songs Reed was writing on his own time, many of which ended up on the first Velvets record. Cale and Reed decided to form a *real* band to play these songs, recruiting Sterling Morrison and Angus MacLise, a drummer who had also played with La Monte Young.

As the Warlocks, the Falling Spikes and finally the Velvet Underground (after the title of a paperback book on sadomasochism that Tony Conrad, another member of the Dream Syndicate, found lying in the streets), the group played at screenings of experimental films and rehearsed Reed's songs. When MacLise quit shortly before their formal debut in November 1965 at a high school in Summit, New Jersey, Reed and Morrison picked Maureen Tucker, the younger sister of an old college pal, to play drums. Tucker was a computer keypunch operator who played along with Bo Diddley records at home. With the Velvets, standing up behind her no-frills kit, she hammered out Bo's shave-and-a-haircut rhythm into a forced-march 4/4 that became a VU trademark.

Pop Art king Andy Warhol first saw the band perform at Greenwich Village's Cafe Bizarre in late 1965 (they were canned two nights later after playing ''Black Angel's Death Song'' one too many times) and immediately recognized the originality and importance of what the Velvet Underground was doing, not to mention the potential for his own entreé into the music business. Yet he was also astute enough to know when to leave well enough alone. As the group's manager, he introduced the Velvets to *his* audience, booking them into art galleries and having them perform at screenings of his movies. He put the group on tour as part of his traveling free-for-all, the Exploding Plastic Inevitable, and he used his notoriety to land the band a recording contract with Verve, a subsidiary of MGM Records.

But as a producer, Warhol had subtler strengths. He recognized the powerful romantic undercurrent in Lou Reed's ballad writing and, over initial resistance, brought Nico (real name Christa Päffgen) into the group as a singer. He also encouraged Reed, as a songwriter, to make the most of the opportunity to observe, and document, the circus of celebrities, star-struck socialites, sexual adventurers, dopers and art heads that congregated at Warhol's studio, the Factory. Under Warhol's patronage, Reed had unlimited access to the underbelly of New York hip in all of its manic glory, and he made the most of it.

In the recording studio Warhol's gift to the Velvets was to stay out of the music. He ''produced'' their debut album, *The Velvet Underground and Nico,* by sticking his name on the cover (along with the infamous peelable banana) and by keeping the record company at arm's length. ''We were trying to do a Phil Spector thing with as few instruments as possible,'' said Cale of the so-called Banana Album in Victor Bockris's 1983 biography, *Uptight: The Velvet Underground Story.* There is indeed a crude majesty to the record; it is everything the Velvets excelled at—white noise, love songs, great storytelling, streetwise New York wit, raw rock & roll energy—splashed across one album with a symphonic flourish. One of the finest rock debut albums ever, *The Velvet Underground and Nico* was a casualty of philistine industry thinking and bad timing, its release delayed for nearly a year by the record label and then ignored by the public in the good-vibes stampede created by the Beatles' *Sgt. Pepper's Lonely Hearts Club Band,* which came out three months later. Still, it is hardly heresy to suggest in retrospect that the Banana Album was not only a better record but, in the long run, more influential.

The Velvet Underground and Nico was also, in a sense, the beginning of the end for the group. After the album flopped, the band split from Warhol; Nico

---

Lou Reed, still smoking: He traded in nail polish and peroxide for the new sensations of marriage to a woman.

became a solo artist. The Velvets then resigned themselves to making art for their own sakes, and those of the few fans and friends they made along the way. *White Light/White Heat,* recorded in 1967 and released in January 1968, found the group declaring its independence with two sides of utter guitar holocaust. Aside from the short mantralike "Here She Comes Now" and a bizarre rewriting of the Lady Godiva story ("Lady Godiva's Operation"), *White Light/White Heat* is a nonstop feast of proto-heavy-metal squall. Just as infamous as the seventeen-minute "Sister Ray" is Reed's solo on "I Heard Her Call My Name," a feedback-spiked psychoslalom all over the guitar neck, executed in tribute to his free-jazz heroes Cecil Taylor and Ornette Coleman. Even Reed's surreal recitative "The Gift" (read by Cale) is backed by a fuzzed-up "Green Onions"–style stomp, which the group drolly dubbed "The Booker T."

Weary of his escalating ego war with Reed, Cale left the Velvet Underground in September of 1968 after a show in Boston. With him went much of the Velvets' still-unfulfilled promise. Doug Yule assumed bass duties, and Reed struck a more listener-friendly balance between his stylistic mood swings. The wealth of live recordings of the post-Cale Velvets—bootlegs as well as official posthumous releases like the 1974 double album *1969, Velvet Underground Live*—shows the band careening through extended versions of "Sister Ray" and "What Goes On" with locomotive fury. In the studio, however, Reed concentrated more on using melodic nuance and rock & roll basics to tell his stories.

Released in 1969, the band's third album, *The Velvet Underground,* was a shocking change-up from *White Light/White Heat,* a gentle invitation to intimacy dominated by fuzzless folk rockers and acoustic confessions of love ("Pale Blue Eyes," "Beginning to See the Light," "I'm Set Free"). It cost the group most of what was left of its original following, but the drastic turn away from the decadence and decibel busting of '66–'67 set the stage for the band's classic, if too late, dive into the rock mainstream, *Loaded* (1970). The album boasted two major FM radio hits, "Sweet Jane" and "Rock and Roll," as well as some of Reed's most passionate

ballads ("New Age," "Oh! Sweet Nuthin'"). But Reed quit before the record was even issued. A cassette tape recorded from the audience of his last performance with the Velvets, at the end of a summer residency at the Warhol crowd's old haunt, Max's Kansas City in New York, was later released as an "official" bootleg album. A Doug Yule–led version of the band, the Velvets in name only, struggled on until 1973.

As the cult of the Velvets grew during the Seventies and Eighties, both Reed and Cale preserved the spirit and vision of the original band in their respective solo pursuits, culminating in their 1989 reunion to perform and record *Songs for Drella,* a musical tribute to their late mentor Andy Warhol. Reed, in particular, has not been one to let a good, unreleased Velvets song go to waste. Several Reed compositions recorded by the group in 1969 as demos for an aborted fourth album under their MGM deal—including "Lisa Says," "She's My Best Friend" and "Andy's Chest"—appeared, sometimes in drastically rearranged form, on Reed's early- and mid-Seventies solo albums.

Ironically, Reed's greatest commercial success as a solo artist was as a glitter rocker made over in the image of his British patron and fan, David Bowie—himself a by-product, as Ziggy Stardust, of the Velvets' original studies in rock & roll decadence. Coproduced by Bowie, the 1972 album *Transformer* yielded Reed's only Top Twenty hit to date, "Walk on the Wild Side," a checklist of old Warhol-era associates set to a jazzy standup-bass vamp. For the next few years, Reed was anything but consistent; his records zigzagged from lush romanticism (*Berlin*) and confessional grit (*Coney Island Baby, Street Hassle*) to pedestrian heavy metal (*Rock 'n' Roll Animal*), flabby AOR rock (*Sally Can't Dance*) and fuck-you feedback (*Metal Machine Music*). But as a songwriter, he doggedly pursued the literary ambition and fearless realism embodied in his Velvets work. His best solo recordings—including *The Blue Mask* (1982), *New York* (1989) and *Magic and Loss* (1992)—have remarried that penetrating writing style with the kinetic, guitar-driven sound of the Velvet Underground.

On his own, John Cale has been an influential record producer, producing the debut albums by the

Stooges and Patti Smith. He has also periodically returned to his original calling, modern composition. His 1971 album *Church of Anthrax* was a collaboration with composer Terry Riley; *Academy in Peril* (1972) and *Words for the Dying* (1989) were showcases of original orchestral pieces. But as a pop artist, free of Reed's dominance in the Velvets, Cale also proved to be a dynamic songwriter, specializing in haunting ballads and taut, morbid rockers. The 1973 album *Paris 1919* was a superb fusion of classical elegance and lyrical pop. In 1974 and 1975 Cale released three albums of dark avant-garage intensity—*Fear, Slow Dazzle, Helen of Troy*—which set the stage for his later rise to punk-rock cult stardom. They also marked the beginning of an ongoing collaborative relationship with Brian Eno; the pair's 1990 release *Wrong Way Up* was a surprisingly accessible, even danceable, art-pop record.

Of the other former members, Nico made a number of solo records remarkable for their haunting Teutonic grandeur; she died in 1988 of head injuries sustained while riding a bicycle on the Spanish island of Ibiza. Maureen Tucker, who did not play on *Loaded* because she was pregnant at the time, dropped out of rock & roll to raise a family, finally reemerging in the Eighties with a sporadic series of engaging offbeat solo records. Sterling Morrison dropped out of rock & roll as well—and back into academia, teaching English at the University of Texas in Austin and pursuing a Ph.D.

The original quartet has reunited onstage only once since 1968. In June 1990 they spontaneously performed "Heroin" at a lavish Cartier Foundation–sponsored celebration of the art and life of Andy Warhol held at a small town outside Paris. The song lasted ten minutes and afterwards the usually laconic Reed raved about the experience: "That was extraordinary! To have those drums behind me, that viola on one side and that guitar on the other again, you have no idea how that felt."

Maybe so. But anyone who has ever been hooked on a Velvet Underground record, or who was inspired enough to go out and start a band to create that experience for himself, knows what he means. "Her life was saved by rock & roll," Reed sang on *Loaded,* and from his words and music, the Velvets created a sound of hard-won redemption. After all this time, the Velvet Underground still saves lives.

DISCOGRAPHY

ALBUMS

John Cale: *The Academy in Peril* (Reprise; 1972). *Paris 1919* (Reprise; 1973). *Animal Justice* (Illegal U.K. EP; 1977). *Guts* (Island; 1977). *Sabotage Live* (Spy/A&M; 1979). *Honi Soit* (A&M; ☆154, 1981). *Music for a New Society* (ZE/Passport; 1982). *Caribbean Sunset* (ZE/Island; 1984). *John Cale Comes Alive* (ZE/Island; 1984). *Artificial Intelligence* (Beggars Banquet/PVC; 1985). *Words for the Dying* (Opal-Warner Bros.; 1989). With Brian Eno: *Wrong Way Up* (Opal/Warner; 1990). *Even Cowgirls Get the Blues* (ROIR; 1991). **John Cale and Lou Reed:** *Songs for Drella* (Sire; ☆103, 1990). **Nico:** *Chelsea Girl* (Verve; 1967). *The Marble Index* (Elektra; 1969). *Desertshore* (Reprise; 1971). *The End* (Island; 1974). *Drama of Exile* (Aura; 1981). *Live Heroes* (Performance; 1986). *Hanging Gardens* (Restless; 1990). **Lou Reed:** *Lou Reed* (RCA; ☆189, 1972). *Transformer* (RCA; ☆98, 1972). *Berlin* (RCA; 1973). *Sally Can't Dance* (RCA; 1975). *Rock 'n' Roll Animal* (RCA; 1974). *Metal Machine Music* (RCA; 1975). *Coney Island Baby* (RCA; ☆41, 1976). *Street Hassle* (Arista; ☆89, 1978). *The Bells* (Arista; ☆130, 1979). *Growing Up in Public* (Arista; ☆158, 1980). *Rock and Roll Diary 1967–1980* (Arista; ☆178, 1980). *The Blue Mask* (RCA; ☆169, 1982). *Legendary Hearts* (RCA; ☆159, 1983). *New Sensations* (RCA; ☆56, 1984). *City Lights: Classic Performances* (Arista; 1985). *Mistrial* (RCA; ☆47, 1986). *New York* (Sire; ☆40, 1989). *Magic and Loss* (Sire; ☆80, 1992). *Between Thought and Expression: The Lou Reed Anthology* (RCA; 1992). **Maureen Tucker:** *Playin' Possum* (Trash; 1981). *MoeJadKateBarry* (50 Skidillion Watts; 1987). *Life in Exile After Abdication* (50 Skidillion Watts; 1989). **The Velvet Underground:** *The Velvet Underground and Nico* (Verve; ☆171, 1967). *White Light/White Heat* (Verve; ☆199, 1968). *The Velvet Underground* (MGM; 1969). *Loaded* (Cotillion; 1970). *The Velvet Underground Live at Max's Kansas City* (Cotillion; 1972). *1969 Velvet Underground Live* (Mercury; 1974). *VU* (Verve; ☆85, 1985). *Another View* (Verve, 1986).

(Chart positions compiled from Joel Whitburn's *Record Research,* based on *Billboard*'s LPs chart.)

PROTOPUNK: THE GARAGE BANDS

BY LESTER BANGS

hat is more American than the garage band? Call up a bunch of your buddies, get some six-packs or some weed, plus a guitar or two, a bass or drum kit, and you've got instant fantasies about instant stardom. Of course, at certain times and places, fantasy and reality have intersected, and that is part of what rock is all about. Given that the greatest garage bands could barely play, we may assume not only that virtuosity has nothing to do with the form, but also that the utopian dream of everyman an artist can come true right here, in our suburban land of opportunity—the ultimate proof that rock & roll is the most democratic and all-American of art forms.

According to one theory, punk rock all goes back to Ritchie Valens's "La Bamba." Just consider Valens's three-chord *mariachi* squawkup in the light of "Louie Louie" by the Kingsmen, then consider "Louie Louie" in the light of "You Really Got Me" by the Kinks, then "You Really Got Me" in the light of "No Fun" by the Stooges, then "No Fun" in the light of "Blitzkreig Bop" by the Ramones, and finally note that "Blitzkreig Bop" sounds a lot like "La Bamba." There: Twenty years of rock & roll history in three chords, played more primitively each time they are recycled.

The origins of garage rock as a genre can be traced to California and the Pacific Northwest in the early Sixties. One remembers bands with names like the Nomads, playing instrumentals with titles like "Let's Get One" and "About Noon," and featuring the vocalized overblowing of saxophones—a dirty sound later duplicated by fuzz-tone guitars. Pretty soon, some of the Mexican-American bands in

The Kingsmen, who had a generation wondering what "Louie Louie" was really about.

Southern California started adding vocals to the riffs.

In San Diego, where I grew up, people like Cannibal and the Headhunters ("Land of 1000 Dances"), the Premiers ("Farmer John") and Three Midniters ("Whittier Boulevard") were big in 1964 and 1965. Like the surf bands, they all wore white suits and played Fenders, but their attitude was *bad*.

Up north around the same time, a more potent scene coalesced with the Sonics (Seattle), the Kingsmen and Paul Revere and the Raiders (both from Portland). This was where "Louie Louie" originally broke out—all these groups did it, though it was the Kingsmen who cut the hit version. This was the one where you can hear the singer start the line "See Jamaica moon above" too soon, while the drummer crashes into a stumbling roll that must have been accompanied by a withering glare; this was also the version that had all of us destroying our styluses in 1964 as we struggled to figure out whether the garbled lyrics, as rumored, were dirty, and, if so, what the words actually were. My circle of friends deciphered, in one line, "I felt my boner in her hair"; but debate and doubts persisted, with the Kingsmen

disavowing any intentional lewdness, if only to keep the record on the radio. (Later in the Seventies a truly filthy version would be recorded by Iggy and the Stooges on *Metallic K.O.*)

The next phase of protopunk coincided with the rise of psychedelia and the fall of folk rock in 1966. Now the garage bands entered their golden age, as new technical developments like fuzz tone and the electric twelve-string guitar put truly awesome sonic possibilities within the reach of the most limited musicians. What's more, just about the time they were also discovering acid, all these guys found out about instant ragas: To approximate the sounds of the mystic East, all they had to do was play scales up and down their fretboards. What a time it was: I can recall being in one of those bands myself at an adjunct to the local bowling alley called the Hi-Ho Club, where all those lower-echelon L.A. groups would come down to gig. I'll never forget the night

my girlfriend, after being subjected to one of those bands raga-ing up and down the fretboard for about forty-five minutes, started saying things like ''Oh, I feel so *strange!*'' when she'd never done a drug in her life. ''Oh, wow'' was the more common response.

The top groups on this scene were the Music Machine (''Talk Talk''; each band member wore one black leather glove); the Leaves (fuzz-tone folk rock and the hit version of ''Hey Joe,'' an anthem of the era to rival ''Louie Louie''); the Standells (''Dirty Water,'' more fuzz tone with a Mondo Hollywood twist, via appearances in *Riot on Sunset Strip,* etc.); and, last but not least, the Seeds.

For my money, the Seeds best epitomized the allure L.A. had then: There was real smog in Daryl Hooper's organ melodica, and Sky Saxon's Mick Jagger routine seemed somehow more convincing than, though every bit as trashy as, all the others of the era. Perhaps it was because Sky Saxon really

These sullen fellows called themselves the Count Five. Capes and gabled gothic were their style; so was a wonderful bit of psychedelic schmaltz, ''Psychotic Reaction.''

believed every moronic word he was singing in their rattling little songs, each sounding the same as their one big hit, ''Pushin' Too Hard.''

All the bikers around San Diego thought that the Seeds were apocalypse, then. I recall one hog-ridin' couple, Candy and Smacker, who didn't take the Seeds' first album off their turntable for three solid months. Candy also told me that the only time Smacker ever took acid was also the only time he ever came on to her (''Oh, Smacker is frigid and queer and all that,'' she said blithely), and that when she rebuffed him, his response was to storm into their bedroom, slam the door, lock it and sit down over a portable phono, where he played the Music Machine's ''Talk Talk,'' all one minute and fifty-nine seconds of it, over and over and over and over for the next eight straight hours.

If many of the L.A. garage bands drew on the Byrds' twelve-string blend of Dylan and Ravi Shankar, the bands from San Jose preferred the Yardbirds' mutations of Chicago blues. This scene was so trashy that a group called the Golliwogs would later complain (after they became Creedence Clearwater Revival) that everybody had snubbed them because they were too authentic; surely the Syndicate of Sound (''Little Girl'') and the Chocolate Watch Band (''Let's Talk About Girls'') were two of the more worthless groups of the period, while Count Five cut

Here we have the Seeds. What kind of seeds? You may well ask.

the all-time slopbucket copy of the Yardbirds with "Psychotic Reaction."

Across mid-America the garage sound was equally influenced by the Yardbirds. In Minneapolis the Litter had a local hit with "Action Woman"; Michigan's Terry Knight and the Pack covered the Yardbirds' "Mister, You're a Better Man Than I"; and in Chicago, a town where most of the groups (the Buckinghams, the Cryan' Shames) were more pop oriented, the Shadows of Knight laid it on the line, telling one interviewer: "The Stones, Animals, and Yardbirds took the Chicago blues and gave it an English interpretation. We've taken the English versions of the blues and re-added a Chicago touch." The Shadows of Knight had their second big hit with Bo Diddley's "Oh Yeah" done Yardbirds style. Their first hit was a version of "Gloria," which, like "Hey Joe," was a bar band staple of the era. Where Van Morrison's original version with his Belfast group Them was frightening in its intensity, the Shadows' was fairly lame, even leaving out the line "And then she comes in my room." Maybe that's why it was a national hit. As the liner notes to the Shadows of Knight's first album put it: "If you invited them over for dinner, your parents would, at first, have you examined or call the police or run screaming to the neighbors. If your parents stayed around, they would find that the Shadows are polite, quiet, considerate and that they might even grow to like them."

As punk archivist Robot A. Hull has observed, most mid-American protopunks of the era adhered "to the style of fraternity brothers playing surf music in a cow pasture"; the classic specimen in this genre was the Castaways' "Liar, Liar," which was a hit in the summer of 1965. It consisted of a weird falsetto shrieking, in part, "Liar, liar, pants on fire/Your nose is longer than a telephone wire." Perhaps even stranger was ? and the Mysterians' "96 Tears" from about a year later. These boys were Chicanos from Saginaw, Michigan; my friends and I got real excited when a DJ informed us that ? (real name: Rudy Martinez) never took off his sunglasses. With its mesmerizing organ hook, the record itself was a masterpiece of surreal spite: "And when the sun comes up I'll be on top/You'll be right down there lookin' up."

As the Sixties wound down, most other garage bands from Michigan turned pretty quickly into heavy-metal groups (MC5, Stooges, Amboy Dukes).

The Barbarians, as they appeared on the celebrated *T.A.M.I. Show*. (The initials stood for Teenage Awards Music International.) That's Moulty standing on the left, his hook hidden behind the guitarist's head.

The South had its share of frat rousers in John Fred and His Playboy Band ("Judy in Disguise"), the Hombres ("Let It Out [Let It All Hang Out]"), the Gentrys ("Keep on Dancing") and the Swingin' Medallions (named after a beef preparation, they made history in their hit "Double Shot [of My Baby's Love]" by being the first punks in history to equate sex with vomiting—and hell, they all wore Ban-Lon shirts and Continental slacks!). East Coast garage pickings were slimmer. The New York protopunks tended either to turn into the Fugs or Velvet Underground, or just shot smack and got lost. But Boston gave us at least two memorable groups of the period, the Remains and the Barbarians, whose "Are You a Boy or Are You a Girl?" was self-explanatory.

The Barbs' *real* claim to classic status, though, was their drummer, Moulty: He had a hook coming out of one sleeve. In their song "Moulty" he explains himself over a Dylanesque backing track, his monologue broken up occasionally by somebody singing "Don't turn away" and screaming "You can make it, baby!" For me this song really captures the feeling behind most of the garage bands, from Ritchie Valens to the Ramones:

I remember the days when things were real bad for me. It was right after my accident, when I lost my hand. It seemed like I was all alone, with nobody to help me—you know, I almost gave up all my hopes and dreams. But then, then, then somethin' inside me kept tellin' me, way down inside o' me, over and over again, to keep goin' on, yeah on! . . . Things are better for me now, 'cause I found that I love music. So I learned to play the drums and got myself a band, and now we're startin' to make it. And if you can make it at somethin' you love, wow, you've got it all. So I'm sayin' this to all of you, all of you who think you'll never make it, all you guys and girls, 'cause you're not so bad off, or maybe you think you're a little different, or strange, so listen to me now, 'cause I've been through it all. . . . Now there's just one thing that I need. Not sympathy, and I don't want no pity, but a girl, a real girl, one that really loves me, and then I'll be the complete man. So I'm gonna tell ya, right now, listen: DON'T TURN AWAY.

DISCOGRAPHY

SINGLES

Barbarians: "Are You a Boy or Are You a Girl?" (Laurie; ☆55, 1965). "Moulty" (Laurie; ☆90, 1966). **Cannibal and the Headhunters:** "Land of 1000 Dances" (Rampart; ☆30, 1965). **Castaways:** "Liar, Liar" (Soma; ☆12, 1965). **Count Five:** "Psychotic Reaction" (Double Shot; ☆5, 1966). **Cryan' Shames:** "Sugar and Spice" (Destination; ☆49, 1966). "I Wanna Meet You" (Columbia; ☆85; 1966). "It Could Be We're in Love" (Columbia; ☆85, 1967). "Up on the Roof" (Columbia; ☆85, 1968). "Young Birds Fly" (Columbia; ☆99, 1968).

Leaves: "Hey Joe" (Mira; ☆31, 1966). **Music Machine:** "Talk Talk" (Original Sound; ☆15, 1966). "The People in Me" (Original Sound; ☆66, 1967). **Premiers:** "Farmer John" (Warner Bros.; ☆19, 1964). **? and the Mysterians:** "96 Tears" (Cameo; ☆1, 1966). "I Need Somebody" (Cameo; ☆22, 1966). "Can't Get Enough of You, Baby" (Cameo; ☆56, 1967). "Girl (You Captivate Me)" (Cameo; ☆98, 1967). **Paul Revere and the Raiders:** "Steppin' Out" (Columbia; ☆46, 1965). "Just Like Me" (Columbia; ☆11, 1965). "Kicks" (Columbia; ☆4, 1966). "Hungry" (Columbia; ☆6, 1966). "The Great Airplane Strike" (Columbia; ☆20, 1966). "Ups and Downs" (Columbia; ☆22, 1967). "Him or Me—What's It Gonna Be?" (Columbia; ☆5, 1967). "I Had a Dream" (Columbia; ☆17, 1967). "Peace of Mind" (Columbia; ☆42, 1967). "Too Much Talk" (Columbia; ☆19, 1968). "Don't Take It So Hard" (Columbia; ☆19, 1968). "Cinderella Sunshine" (Columbia; ☆27, 1968). **Seeds:** "Pushin' Too Hard" (GNP Cresendo; ☆36, 1966). "Mr. Farmer" (GNP Cresendo; ☆86, 1967). "Can't Seem to Make You Mine" (GNP Cresendo; ☆41, 1967). "A Thousand Shadows" (GNP Cresendo; ☆72, 1967). **Shadows of Knight:** "Gloria" (Dunwich; ☆10, 1966). "Oh Yeah" (Dunwich; ☆39, 1966). "Bad Little Woman" (Dunwich; ☆91, 1966). "I'm Gonna Make You Mine" (Dunwich; ☆90, 1966). "Shake" (Team; ☆46, 1968). **Standells:** "Dirty Water" (Tower; ☆11, 1966). "Sometimes Good Guys Don't Wear White" (Tower; ☆43, 1966). "Why Pick on Me" (Tower; ☆54, 1966). "Can't Help but Love You" (Tower; ☆78, 1967). **Syndicate of Sound:** "Little Girl" (Bell; ☆8, 1967). "Rumors" (Bell; ☆55, 1967). "Brown Paper Bag" (Buddah; ☆73, 1970). **Thee Midniters:** "Land of a Thousand Dances, Part 1" (Chattahoochee; ☆67, 1965).

ANTHOLOGIES

Nuggets (Rhino; 1986). *More Nuggets: Volume 2* (Rhino; 1987). *Even More Nuggets: Volume 3* (Rhino; 1989).

(Chart positions compiled from Joel Whitburn's *Record Research*, based on *Billboard*'s Pop chart.)

THE SOUND OF SAN FRANCISCO

BY CHARLES PERRY

Everybody knew how rock & roll worked in 1965. You played hits. You wore matching uniforms. You got the Top Forty DJ who controlled the local music scene to take you under his wing and book you into the big high school dances at the armories. In San Francisco that man was "Big Daddy" Tom Donahue, and he even had a little record label of his own you could record on. If you were very good boys, you might play for the topless dancers at the North Beach nightclubs. Maybe you'd get to record a single. An A&R man would pick your material, and you'd record it in a couple of hours at the label's own studio.

Everybody knew this, that is, except some crazy *existencialistas* who were living across the Golden Gate Bridge in the bohemian houseboats of Sausalito, or down the peninsula in the crazy-kid purlieus of Stanford University, or in a little-known San Francisco neighborhood called Haight-Ashbury. They didn't know you had to go through Tom Donahue or you were never going to get a crack at the big time; didn't know how you got a record contract; didn't know how many favors somebody had to owe you to put your record on the air—didn't know, and didn't seem to care. Most of them were folk musicians who had never played a sock hop in their lives, but now they were pursuing rock & roll with an unfathomable sense of mission. They were playing dumps no one had ever heard of, with no thought for tomorrow. They hadn't even thought far ahead enough to join the musicians' union. Crazy *existencialistas*.

Among the greatest *existencialistas* of all were the Charlatans. The founder of the group was a draftsman and designer named George Hunter who neither sang nor played an instrument. When the band performed, he just looked busy with a tambourine or an autoharp. In fact, he'd conceived of the Charlatans less as a band than as a visual trip, an artist's conception of America's answer to the Beatles. Even before their first rehearsal, they'd had hundreds of publicity stills taken exploring the mythic possibilities of the Victorian and Old West costume that impoverished young bohemians in the Haight were fishing out of the secondhand stores.

They had scarcely rehearsed when they were actually offered a gig. Mercifully, the gig was out of town, in Virginia City, Nevada, where they had a chance to pull themselves together as a band. When they came back they found a scene had developed for their brand of hip rocking and rolling: A nightclub specialized in it, and a series of giant dance concerts catered to pot-smoking, LSD-eating hippies. How about that! They slipped back into their Haight-Ashbury home as stars.

They remained the ultimate early-Haight band, true to the style of the original core of artists and students and dope dealers. As the scene expanded and changed, they never got into the novelties of heavy rock or flower power. Their repertoire remained essentially folk material—blues, ballads, good-time jug-band tunes—plus a few original numbers and the odd Rolling Stones tune. The Charlatans' trademark was a jaunty, ragtimey rhythm that was of a piece with their style.

Other bands were forming in the Haight. One, which took the name Big Brother and the Holding Company, came out of a series of public jam sessions in the basement of a rooming house. Another, started by a sometime Haight resident named Marty Balin, who owned the city's "folk-rock club," the Matrix, made a debut before the Charlatans returned from Nevada (they sported one of those enigmatic names these bands favored: Jefferson Airplane). Soon there were more bands, mostly made up of San Francisco State College students: the Mystery Trend, the Final Solution, the Great Society and others.

Over in Sausalito a young guitarist named John Cipollina had admitted being a rocker to his beatnik roommates and found it was okay—in fact, they wanted to be rockers too. Cipollina had spent the early Sixties being snubbed in folk-music circles for showing up at hootenannies with an electric guitar, that symbol of "commercialism" and "selling out." But the juice had gone out of the folk-purist ethic;

soon the little group of musicians heard that Dino Valenti, a folk balladeer they admired, was interested in starting a rock band. Valenti got busted inconveniently and did a year and a half in jail, leaving the band to pull itself together on its own. They called themselves Quicksilver Messenger Service, an astrological reference to their Virgo-heavy personnel.

In the same crazed vein as other early San Francisco bands, they were weirdos who never expected to make it. When they got paid for their first gig, they laughed all the way home. Cipollina had already been through the rock & roll scene years before and considered himself a failure and a dropout. The band included two other teen-rock dropouts and a bassist named David Freiberg, who, like Cipollina, had been on the folk scene (in fact, he had once roomed with Paul Kantner, later of Jefferson Airplane, and David Crosby, later of the Byrds).

At the outset, Quicksilver's repertoire consisted of Chicago blues, Rolling Stones numbers, occasional folk items, such as their early crowd pleaser "Pride of Man" and a legacy of Dino Valenti compositions. Their sound reflected an interest in classical music and a clean, organized, perfectionist tendency. Cipollina's voice and guitar, both marked by a quivering, crystalline vibrato, were the most distinctive parts of the band's early sound.

Quicksilver was one of the first bands to move deep into rural Marin County and "mellow out." Their back-to-nature streak was further amplified when Dino Valenti finally rejoined the group. Unfortunately, Valenti also brought his somewhat affected, whining voice and overbearing manner to the group, which he completely dominated after Cipollina left in 1970.

Quicksilver's counterpart to the south was the Grateful Dead. They were folkies (plus one avant-garde electronic music dropout): a former bluegrass banjoist, a blues organist and some others who'd gotten caught up in the corny fun of the jug-band craze. Shortly after getting into electrified rock, they'd fallen in with the big action of the Stanford psychedelic scene: the Acid Test LSD parties being put on by the novelist Ken Kesey and his Merry Pranksters. With this background and the early patronage of Owsley Stanley, the famous LSD chemist, the Dead became the most notable acid *existencialistas* on the scene, making decisions and managing their affairs as a huge extended family, without regard for status or conventional chains of command. They had a considerable reputation for playing while stoned, and for taking half an hour to tune up and decide on the next song; their endless versions of "In the Midnight Hour," which went on until everybody decided at the same time to end it, were legend.

The Quick and the Dead had a certain yin-yang relationship. Quicksilver was the drugstore cowboy band, and the Dead the psychedelic Indians, prophets of retribalism. There was even a certain parallel in their musical development, when the Dead switched to a softer, more countrified sound in the Seventies. But the Dead's forte remained middle-tempo rockers with a big, fat, solid sound, dominated by Phil Lesh's strong bass line and Jerry Garcia's bluegrassoid guitar runs, which noodled over it all like a sustained, stoned meditation on the mantra "whatever's right." The sound was particularly rich and full because the Dead, under the influence of the technical perfectionist Owsley, quickly discarded the tinny "public address" sound systems rockers had always used; eventually they had twenty-three tons of sound equipment in use, and a crew of nine just to put it up and take it down.

For all their psychedelic unpredictability, the Dead remained a working group longer than most. It wasn't until fall 1974 that they disbanded for an indefinite period. Their fans, an unusually loyal lot known as Deadheads, remained utterly confident of a revival. Their hopes were rewarded: In the later Seventies the band regrouped and resumed touring.

These were the original crazies, the gamblers for stakes unknowable. They were a doomed-looking bunch when they surfaced (except, perhaps, for the relatively tidy Airplane). The record company talent scouts who dropped by their little nightclubs and ballrooms felt sorry for these babes in the woods. But things had already started to run their way. The record company reps started getting slipped acid-spiked soda pop and seeing the room turn to taffy . . . and noticing that the music had a certain insidiuous sense for somebody who saw the Buddha in the tip of his shoe.

As a measure of how ripe the scene was, even Big Daddy Tom Donahue was hip to it. He'd taken LSD, quit his job at the Top Forty station and opened a "psychedelic nightclub" where he held court for

The Grateful Dead standing at the crossroads, 1966.

Tom Donahue. A one-time fixture on Top Forty AM, he tuned in, turned on, dropped out and then showed up hosting a whole new radio format: progressive FM.

about six weeks before retiring to dream up the idea of psychedelic radio: non-playlisted, non–Top Forty rock and roll, mostly album cuts, on FM. Donahue was Dino Valenti's manager and had gone so far as to sign up the Great Society for his tiny North Beach label.

The intense excitement of the San Francisco rock scene was something new. It wasn't the old rock & roll sexual tension, simmering with potential violence. It was stoned-out, freak-freely dancing, a naively cheerful scene with the conspiratorial excitement of the secret society of acid eaters. The lyrics and the special sound effects re-created aspects of the psychedelic experience—revelatory roaring, chills of ecstasy, hallucinated wandering, mystico-psychotic wonder. And the musicians, for all the informality they had inherited from the consciously antitheatrical folk-music tradition, were the ones standing up and speaking about the Great Unspeakable of the stoned experience. For many in the audience they were thereby prophets, gurus, holy men.

That's a market that doesn't show up every quarter of the fiscal year. But the dances were bringing in good money (Bill Graham's Fillmore ballroom had in fact become a kind of youth cult mecca), and the music turned out to be good business on record as well. San Francisco, through the peculiar tolerance and isolation of its culture, had spawned a uniquely open and confident manifestation of the faith in psychedelic drugs, which made it the national capital of psychedelia. Along with Dylan, the Stones and the Beatles, the San Francisco bands were staples of the turntables of acidhead America.

Once the scene started taking off, the original *existencialistas* were joined by others who wanted in. They were psychedelic believers, maybe, but they weren't creating a scene, they were making something out of it.

One of the first was Country Joe and the Fish. Joe McDonald was a folksinger with one foot in the grand old protest song tradition and the other in the good-time jug-band scene. Six months after the first hippie dances in San Francisco, he was running a

Country Joe McDonald. For a spell he fronted one of the most mercurial bands of the psychedelic prophets.

rock band which established itself as the Berkeley acid group. They conscientiously explored LSD and strove to unite the hippies and the local radicals. Joe was famous for wearing protest buttons to hippie functions and flowers to the many political benefits he played.

The Fish in their prime were an entertaining band, with more of a stage act than the San Francisco groups. Joe led football-style "fuck" cheers; the band sang comic commercials for drugs, wore funny costumes and engaged in mild slapstick. Musically they showed folk roots in the jug band style and the down-and-out poetry and pretty melodies of Joe's hero, Woody Guthrie. Particularly in their early days they experimented with the psychedelic effects of the early Jefferson Airplane.

The Fish were even more mercurial than most San Francisco groups, logging five breakups in five years. After the final break Joe worked for a while double billing with his wife's theatrical troupe, then fronted a largely female band, then sang as a single again. By 1975, divorced and being sued for alimony by his feminist wife, he had soured on both drugs and radical politics.

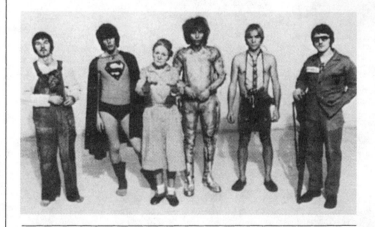

Moby Grape, showing off the Little Old Lady from Pasadena.

One of the biggest San Francisco groups was dreamed up in Los Angeles. Moby Grape, as it was called, comprised three members of a Seattle band called the Frantics, plus an L.A. folkie and Skip Spence, the Airplane's original drummer (on guitar). With two lead guitars, they had a powerful, churning sound. They were quickly signed up for an album, and it was released simultaneously with five singles; lofted by a massive promotion, they made an unprecedented splash in

1967. They quickly became one of the most popular bands in San Francisco, which in itself says a great deal about what was happening to the Haight-Ashbury scene. When the Grape first played the Fillmore at the end of November 1966, the faith that psychedelics were going to save the world had already played itself out for some people. But at the same time the faith was bringing people to the Haight in ever greater numbers. It was time for a band like the Grape, combining the tightness and flash of orthodox rock with the new sensibility.

They were a take-charge band that wowed the Fillmore crowds with their powerful sound and slightly stagy hysteria. Many of their songs were carefully composed, and they were also among the first to clean up and commercialize the psychedelic blues. ''Changes!'' agonized lead guitarist Jerry Miller, sounding a nebulous note of complaint that was to reverberate in Top Forty charts for years to come. The flashy guitar work, likewise, was a departure from the style of the San Francisco bands back in the days when they had played for the archetypal happy hippie dancers. But the Fillmore was too crowded with sightseers for much dancing by now.

The scene was bound to become more professional. The money brought competition, and the innovative dance promoter Bill Graham made a great effort to educate the public taste in San Francisco by importing jazz and blues artists. The concertgoers heard what their idols had been listening to, and the local bands were forced to improve their acts to compete with their models or fall by the wayside. (The Charlatans fell by the wayside for another reason: the growing taste for ''heavy'' music. Drummer Dan Hicks then perversely started a drummerless non-rock band, the Hot Licks, to back his dry and ironic lyrics in a mixture of pre-Fifties pop styles.)

The biggest import was the band fronted by Texas-bred Steve Miller, a veteran of the rock scene since his early teens in the Fifties who had been holding down Paul Butterfield's white-blues gig in Chicago. He moved into the Haight in November 1966 and started up a band including members of some of his earlier aggregations from Chicago, his college days and even the old days in Texas, notably including the singer and guitarist Boz Scaggs. By January they were headlining the Avalon Ballroom (the Fillmore's only real rival).

They played Chicago blues, emphasizing not its funky, astringent qualities but the big rhythm, the

The original Steve Miller Band *(from the top):* Tim Davis, Lonnie Turner, Steve Miller, Jim Peterman, Boz Scaggs.

thundering grandeur, the drama. The vocals were often in disciplined three-part falsetto harmony. Miller's own vocal style was fairly black, with a gusty delivery that suggested the singer's passion and need were making the words positively explode from his throat. Scaggs had a more intimate style, a choked, artless, confessional delivery he later featured in a band of his own that specialized in ballads.

Miller made no secret of what he was in it for: money, fame and pleasure. Acid had somehow left his sense of ambition intact. And his perfectionism. He held out for a record-breaking advance payment from Capitol Records for his first LP, and a royalty payment about three times what anybody else was getting. It permanently changed the economics of rock & roll.

Miller also started giving his record company orders on how he was going to be recorded. He knew exactly what he wanted, and for his first album he flew to England to get it. It was the beginning of the end for the old company studios, staffed with unsympathetic hacks and outfitted with primitive equipment. As Miller had the best singers on the scene, bar Grace Slick and Marty Balin of the Airplane and Janis Joplin of the later Big Brother, together with the Grateful Dead he pioneered the virgin territory of high-fidelity, carefully recorded rock & roll.

It was 1967, the heyday of the Haight-Ashbury. The number of psychedelic bands in the Bay Area was established to be something between 500 and 1500, both local groups and visitors attracted by the mystique of the New Age community and the lure of the numerous paying gigs. Their names came thick and fast. When the Grateful Dead were estranged from their acid-chemist patron, Owsley began backing an extraordinarily loud, simplistic blues band called Blue Cheer; he even named a brand of LSD after them.

The scene finally collapsed, like a nova collapsing into a dwarf star. One of the last gasps was the incredibly successful group Santana, named for the lead guitarist, Carlos Santana. The music was still cosmic, psychedelic stuff—but braced with jazz and Latin influences. Santana became more spiritually oriented after he chose the path of guru Sri Chinmoy. There was the standard rock drummer, but there was also a timbales player on percussion. The rhythms were tight, metallic and Latin, the guitar cast in a jazz and Hendrix vein. The lugubrious, been-stoned-too-long lethargy that the old psychedelic bands had fallen into was completely absent; Santana was as tight and sharp as a patent-leather

Carlos Santana playing maracas at Altamont. The party was almost over.

Santana, the first band to attempt psychedelic salsa.

shoe. The band's very existence signaled the spread of psychedelic culture to working-class and minority youth.

One of the commonplace phrases of the day was the "San Francisco sound." An enterprising promoter even copyrighted the phrase. Musically, the meaning is hard to pin down. Most of the early bands played Rolling Stones tunes, for instance, but they each played them differently. The blues was at the core of most band's repertoires, but most of the well-known songs from this period are not blues. There was the folk music and country & western end of the spectrum, but with that in the equation, the boundaries of the San Francisco sound become impossibly vague. And in the end, there was Santana and its Afro-Cuban heritage.

There were a few elements common to many of the San Francisco bands, however. One was the attempt to incorporate the musical values of Indian ragas into rock: Indian music had the spiritual prestige of the mystic East, of course, and the droning background, sliding notes and absence of chord changes appealed to the acidhead's desire for tranquillity (and sometimes the musician's desire for something he could play when ripped out of his skull). Allied to this fascination with modal forms was the deliberate introduction of feedback. By playing a guitar close enough to the loudspeakers that the sound itself shook the strings, a guitarist could produce a piercing, shrieking sound that musicians had previously struggled to avoid. The psychedelic musician, on the contrary, was fascinated by the searing noise that resulted, and the apparent spontaneity of its production.

If there was anything else distinctive about the San Francisco sound, it was probably the prevalence of long, jam-session versions of rock numbers, both in performance and on record. But the ''sound'' was less a musical phenomenon than a manner, premised on the simple and straightforward assumption that this was trip music, being played by dopers for other dopers. The intense involvement of the audience in the music, and the musicians in certain aspects of their craft, permanently changed the rock scene, adding elements of seriousness, connoisseurship and psychosis. But the real unifying factor is that it was distinctly the music of a community, and at its best it carried the exuberant, wonderstruck spirit of San Francisco's *existencialistas* to the world.

Last days of the Fillmore West, 1971.

DISCOGRAPHY

ALBUMS

Big Brother and the Holding Company: *Big Brother and the Holding Company* (Mainstream; ☆60, 1967). *Cheap Thrills* (Columbia; ☆1, 1968). *Be a Brother* (Columbia; ☆134, 1970). **Country Joe and the Fish:** *Country Joe and the Fish* (Vanguard; ☆39, 1967). *I-Feel-Like-I'm-Fixin'-to-Die* (Vanguard; ☆67, 1967). *Together* (Vanguard; ☆23, 1968). *Here We Are Again* (Vanguard; ☆48, 1969). **Grateful Dead:** *Grateful Dead* (Warner Bros.; ☆73, 1967). *Anthem of the Sun* (Warner Bros.; ☆87, 1968). *Aoxomoxoa* (Warner Bros.; ☆73, 1969). *Live/Dead* (Warner Bros.; ☆64, 1970). *Workingman's Dead* (Warner Bros.; ☆27, 1970). *American Beauty* (Warner Bros.; ☆30, 1970). **Dan Hicks and His Hot Licks:** *Dan Hicks and His Hot Licks* (Epic; 1969). **Hot Tuna:** *Hot Tuna* (RCA Victor; ☆30, 1970). **It's a Beautiful Day:** *It's a Beautiful Day* (Columbia; ☆47, 1969). *Marrying Maiden* (Columbia; ☆28, 1970). **Jefferson Airplane:** *The Jefferson Airplane Takes Off!* (RCA Victor; ☆128, 1966). *Surrealistic Pillow* (RCA Victor; ☆3, 1967). *After Bathing at Baxter's* (RCA Victor; ☆17, 1967). *Crown of Creation* (RCA Victor; ☆6, 1968). *Bless Its Pointed Little Head* (RCA Victor; ☆17, 1969). *Volunteers* (RCA Victor; ☆13, 1969). *The Worst of Jefferson Airplane* (RCA Victor; ☆12, 1970). **Janis Joplin:** *I Got Dem Ol' Kozmic Blues Again Mama!* (Columbia; ☆5, 1969). **Paul Kantner/Jefferson Starship:** *Blows Against the Empire* (RCA Victor; ☆20, 1970). **Steve Miller Band:** *Children of the Future* (Capitol; ☆134, 1968). *Sailor* (Capitol; ☆24, 1968). *Brave New World* (Capitol; ☆22, 1969). *Your Saving Grace* (Capitol; ☆38, 1969). **Moby Grape:** *Moby Grape* (Columbia; ☆24, 1967). *Wow* (Columbia; ☆20, 1968). *Moby Grape '69* (Columbia; ☆113, 1969). **Mother Earth:** *Living with the Animals* (Mercury; ☆144, 1969). *Make a Joyful Noise* (Mercury; ☆95, 1969). **Quicksilver Messenger Service:** *Quicksilver Messenger Service* (Capitol; ☆63, 1968). *Happy Trails* (Capitol; ☆27, 1969). **Santana:** *Santana* (Columbia; ☆4, 1969). *Abraxas* (Columbia; ☆1, 1970). **Boz Scaggs:** *Boz Scaggs* (Atlantic; 1969). **Sons of Champlin:** *Loosen Up Naturally* (Capitol; ☆137, 1969). **Sopwith Camel:** *The Sopwith Camel* (Kama Sutra; ☆191, 1967).

(Chart positions compiled from Joel Whitburn's *Record Research*, based on *Billboard*'s LPs chart.)

THE GRATEFUL DEAD

BY PARKE PUTERBAUGH

Were some enterprising record company to attempt a boxed history of the Grateful Dead, it would quickly discover that a box would be too small. A crate, maybe even a truck, would be necessary to contain all the performances the band's fans might deem vital to include. Even then, there'd be a taper burrowed away in some northern California hemp-growing county convinced he'd captured the most mind-blowing, honest-to-Owsley two-hour live version of ''Dark Star'' on his portable Nakamichi that night at Red Rocks. It's part of his private stock, one of hundreds of cassettes interred in a beat-up steamer trunk. On the outside is a frayed bumper sticker that reads: THERE IS NOTHING LIKE A GRATEFUL DEAD CONCERT.

The point is, there is not a single definitive ''history'' of the Grateful Dead. There are as many valid histories as there are fans (or, more precisely, Deadheads) and as many perspectives on a given night's performance as there are those on hand to witness it—not to mention those on the periphery who couldn't get a ticket but were nonetheless part of the total experience. Factor in drugs and alcohol, plus all the myriad good and bad trips that attended the trek to the venue, and you've got multiple accounts of the same reality. Even the tapers—those devotees who make a religion of recording as many Dead shows as possible, with the group's blessing—''hear'' a concert differently, depending on their vantage points and other ambient factors.

So, then, a rote recitation of facts about the Grate-

The early Dead *(from left)*: Mickey Hart, Phil Lesh, Bob Weir, Bill Kreutzmann, Ron ''Pigpen'' McKernan, Jerry Garcia.

ful Dead can't truly explain the band's music or pied-piper appeal. Better to simply quote a Deadhead, offering counsel to one who would become part of the tribe: ''You should open yourself up, empty yourself and let the music fill you from head to toe as if it were water filling an empty vessel.'' Jerry Garcia, the guitarist, singer and songwriter who is as much guru as musician, described the Dead's peculiar magnetism in this way: ''Our audience is like people who like licorice. Not everybody

The Grateful Dead cheer on the revolution, 1967.

likes licorice, but the people who like licorice really like licorice," he told Geraldo Rivera in 1981.

The Grateful Dead is one of the longest continuously running rock bands in history, performing under that name since late 1965 (and under several other names before that). They are the only group for which a network of fans, as essential and charismatic as the band members themselves, has become a recognized subculture in its own right. You cannot think "Dead" without thinking "Deadheads." From the outset, the group attracted a cult following that was involved on more than a fan club level. This melding of band and audience had something to do with chemistry, karma, vibes, the mid-Sixties and the city of San Francisco.

Actually, it all started in Palo Alto, on the peninsula south of San Francisco, where Garcia taught guitar by day and worked the club scene at night. As far back as 1961 he was playing folk, blues, bluegrass and jug-band music with assemblages whose members included Ron "Pigpen" McKernan (the Dead's scruffy organist and singer) and Robert Hunter (Garcia's songwriting collaborator of long standing). Other familiar names came and went over the next few years: David Nelson and John "Marmaduke" Dawson (later of New Riders of the Purple Sage) and Bob Weir, a tender-aged, guitar-strumming square peg who joined one of Garcia's most stable outfits, Mother McCree's Uptown Jug Champions.

In 1965 Bill Kreutzmann, a drummer with an R&B background, fell in with Garcia, Weir and Pigpen in a full-fledged rock & roll band called the Warlocks. Their always loud and sometimes formless and experimental music drove confused patrons from the Bay Area clubs they played. After several months Garcia asked an acquaintance named Phil Lesh, who possessed a background in classical and electronic music, to become the Warlocks' bassist. Though he had never played the instrument before, Lesh adapted quickly. By November of 1965 the band had not only a firm lineup but a new name: the Grateful Dead, which announced itself in oracular fashion when Garcia opened up a big dictionary and those two words shone right off the page. "It was truly weird, a truly weird moment," he later marveled.

At least some of the weirdness manifesting itself around the band came from their discovery of LSD during the Warlocks phase. An alliance formed between the Dead and writer Ken Kesey and his Merry Pranksters, who had been ingesting government-issued acid as volunteers in a research project at Stanford University. Kesey and the Pranksters subsequently fashioned a lifestyle around the mind-expanding hallucinogen, which was then still legal. The two camps—one a vestige of the Fifties Beat generation, the other a harbinger of a more music-oriented Sixties subculture of societal dropouts—officially came together on December 4th, 1965, the date of the first Acid Test, held at a house in San Jose.

The Dead provided the music, and Kesey and company the antic ambiance for these collective freak-outs, which occurred sporadically at different locales over the next year. The Acid Tests, largely unscripted happenings at which chaos illuminated aspects of the collective consciousness, evolved into a blueprint for the psychedelic counterculture of the late Sixties. They were powerful, defining events that ushered in a liberated age of soul searching, drug taking, lovemaking and music unlike any heard before. Garcia, often seen in a red, white and blue top hat, was nicknamed "Captain Trips" (a sobriquet he has since disavowed). In a 1972 interview he defended the act of losing oneself with pharmacological and musical assistance: "To get really high is to forget yourself," he said. "And to forget yourself is to see everything else. And to see everything else is to become an understanding molecule in evolution, a conscious tool of the universe."

Captain Trips at the controls.

The collision of styles and backgrounds within the Grateful Dead—including everything from bluegrass and R&B to Indian and electronic music—resulted in a sound that virtually defied idiom. The band's early repertoire was largely drawn from Garcia's folk studies, though the songs were transmuted through the Dead's electric alchemy into something that could best be termed psychedelic. A mainstay on the San Francisco scene, the Dead performed for free in Golden Gate Park and became regulars at the Fillmore, the Carousel and the Avalon Ballroom, where the group would jam until the wee hours if the spirit was right. Colorful, trippy concert posters by artists like Rick Griffin, Mouse and Kelley sprang up all over Haight-Ashbury. The group itself took up communal residence at 710 Ashbury Street.

The Grateful Dead made one single ("Stealin'" b/w "Don't Ease Me In") for the local Scorpio label, but the band's recording career commenced in ear-

nest when it signed to Warner Bros., one among a stampede of major labels that descended on San Francisco. *The Grateful Dead*, released in March 1967, was recorded in three breathless, amphetamine-stoked nights; in hindsight, the band sounds like a psychedelic Ramones. (Has any band ever played so fast as the Dead do on "Sittin' on Top of the World"?) Drummer Mickey Hart joined in time for *Anthem of the Sun*, an album whose flowing, side-long compositions were painstakingly stitched from tapes of four studio sessions and eighteen concerts. Quite simply, it remains the apotheosis of psychedelic music—spacey, mind blowing, beyond definition. The ambitious *Aoxomoxoa* appeared shortly before Woodstock in the summer of '69, capturing the heady spirit of the times.

As amazing as those records were, the Dead's true métier was performing in front of an audience. Much of the glue that held the San Francisco scene together came from benefit gigs and free shows staged in the city's streets, parks and concert halls by the Dead, the Jefferson Airplane and Quicksilver Messenger Service, among other local groups. A mystique came to surround the Grateful Dead concert experience. Should all of the cosmic variables fall into proper alignment, the band's improvisations could lead to onstage magic. Just as easily, the group could meander, missing cues and connections. In concert the Dead was great, awful and all things in between, but never predictable. "Music is the timeless experience of constant change," Garcia theorized, and the Dead took to releasing live albums as the most honest record of that experience. *Live Dead* appeared in January of 1970; it was the first of many multialbum concert recordings the group would release over the years.

Later that same year, however, the Dead released the two finest albums of its career, both recorded in the studio: *Workingman's Dead* and *American Beauty*. The Dead had survived the Sixties, but only after watching the decade's promise go awry. Particularly painful for the band was the horrific violence at the Rolling Stones' free concert at Altamont Speedway, much of it due to the rampaging Hell's Angels who had been hired as security for the concert at the Dead's suggestion. Chastened, the Dead adopted a mellower, more rootsy and acoustic course in its music—to stunning effect. The back-to-basics approach, suffused with a nostalgic frontier mythos, took its cues from albums like Bob Dylan's *John Wesley Harding*, the Band's first two records, and Crosby, Stills and Nash's harmony-rich debut. This juncture in the Dead's career yielded some of the group's best-known numbers: "Uncle John's Band," "Casey Jones" and "Truckin'," among them.

In concert—the setting for most of the band's subsequent recordings of significance—the Dead proved to be a study in contrasts. Bob Weir played the crooning cosmopolitan cowboy to Garcia's creaky-voiced, gray-bearded sage. Kreutzmann and Hart cast a polyrhythmic trance over crowds with their double drumming and use of ethnic rhythms. Bassist Lesh spun dizzying counterpoint to Garcia's skittering, modal lead lines. (Eerily enough, the band has seen three of its keyboardists die untimely deaths: Pigpen, whose drinking led to liver failure; Keith Godchaux, who was hit by a truck; and Brent Mydland, who succumbed to a drug overdose.)

American Beauties: Deadheads dancing, in tune with the sound of the spheres.

Musically, the Dead has always fallen in behind Garcia's tubular-toned lead guitar. "They'll follow me down any dark alley," Garcia commented in 1987. "Sometimes there's light at the end of the alley, and sometimes there's a black hole. The point is, you don't get adventure in music unless you're willing to take chances." That statement applies to the band's fans as well, who have always given the Dead a wide berth to follow its muse. The group's audience began gelling into a quasi-organized entity after a cryptic solicitation appeared inside the 1972 Grateful Dead live double album (informally known as "Skull and Roses"): "DEAD FREAKS UNITE! Who are you? Where are you? How are you? Send us your name and address and we'll keep you informed." The Deadhead network thereupon came into being, initially nudged along by the band but eventually growing into a sizable network that ef-

One More Saturday Night: Garcia and Weir rock the faithful.

Jerry Garcia, patriarch.

fectively elevated fandom into a lifestyle. (Amid all this, a worn-out Dead took a hiatus from touring in 1975 and half of 1976.)

Over the past quarter century or so, the Dead's concert marathons, lasting upwards of four hours and more, have largely served as bonding rituals between the band and its nomadic following. In the process, it grew somewhat more difficult just to casually appreciate the Dead and the music. To quote Tom Wolfe, writing about the Sixties scene surrounding the Dead, Ken Kesey and the Merry Pranksters in *The Electric Kool-Aid Acid Test,* "You're either on the bus or off the bus." The Dead-Deadhead nexus grew progressively more insular, with the group establishing its own record labels and overseeing a concert-ticket distribution system that favors Deadheads.

Essentially unaccountable to major label execs,

the mid-Seventies Dead—as a band and solo, with numerous offshoots and acquaintances—released a stream of records that were, as often as not, flawed and flaccid. The situation did not measurably improve with the group's signing to Arista Records in 1977 (with the notable exception of *Terrapin Station,* the band's finest studio work since *American Beauty*). While the enterprise was still thriving on the road, with new and younger Deadhead converts joining the ranks all the time, the group was essentially preaching to the converted and challenging itself much less assiduously than it had during its first half-dozen years. A perception of enervation within the group, shared and noticed even by loyal fans, turned out to have a basis in fact when it was revealed that Garcia had developed a debilitating hard drug habit. He was busted in San Francisco for heroin possession in 1985, but the nadir came the following year, when the guitarist lapsed into a life-threatening diabetic coma. Happily, he recovered—although he slowly had to relearn how to play the guitar—and a much-improved Grateful Dead soldiered on, with its newly clearheaded leader playing with fire and imagination once again. The Dead's Eighties renaissance was capped by the group's first Top Forty hit (''Touch of Grey'') and the platinum sales of *In the Dark,* which was released in 1987.

At the same time, the Dead experienced growing pains (some cities began banning shows because of the disruptive influx of Deadheads) and a tragedy (the death of keyboardist Brent Mydland in 1990). Yet the Grateful Dead and the Deadheads have dauntlessly kept the faith. Of this enduring band-fan relationship, and the drifter's life on the wide open road it entails, Garcia observed: ''It's an adventure you can still have in America. . . . You can't hop a freight, but you can chase the Grateful Dead around.''

DISCOGRAPHY

ALBUMS

Grateful Dead (Warner Bros.; ☆73, 1967). *Anthem of the Sun* (Warner Bros.; ☆87, 1968). *Aoxomoxoa* (Warner Bros.; ☆73, 1969). *Live/Dead* (Warner Bros.; ☆64, 1970). *Workingman's Dead* (Warner Bros.; ☆27, 1970). *American Beauty* (Warner Bros.; ☆30, 1970). *Grateful Dead* (Warner Bros.; ☆25, 1971). *Europe '72* (Warner Bros.; ☆24, 1972). *History of the Grateful Dead, Vol. 1 (Bear's Choice)* (Warner Bros.; ☆60, 1973). *Wake of the Flood* (Grateful Dead; ☆18, 1973). *Skeletons from the Closet* (Warner Bros.; ☆75, 1974). *Grateful Dead from the Mars Hotel* (Grateful Dead; ☆16, 1974). *Blues for Allah* (Grateful Dead; ☆12, 1975). *Steal Your Face* (Grateful Dead; ☆56, 1976). *Terrapin Station* (Arista; ☆28, 1977). *What a Long Strange Trip It's Been: The Best of the Grateful Dead* (Warner Bros.; ☆121, 1977). *Shakedown Street* (Arista; ☆41, 1978). *Go to Heaven* (Arista; ☆23, 1980). *Reckoning* (Arista; ☆43, 1981). *Dead Set* (Arista; ☆29, 1981). *In the Dark* (Arista; ☆6, 1987). *Built to Last* (Arista; ☆27, 1989). *Dylan & the Dead* (Columbia; ☆37, 1989).

(Chart positions compiled from Joel Whitburn's *Record Research,* based on *Billboard*'s LPs chart.)

THE JEFFERSON AIRPLANE

BY CHARLES PERRY

JEFFERSON AIRPLANE LOVES YOU, read the bumper stickers. It seemed a little odd in early 1966—a rock band confessing love to every stranger who could read the bumper sticker on the car ahead. But the Psychedelic Age was dawning, and such sentiments soon appeared perfectly reasonable. Love, psychedelically understood, was everywhere; blowing in the wind, for instance. Jefferson Airplane was just letting people know they were of, by and for the acid community.

And they were loved in return. By the summer of 1967 they had two Top Ten singles, and their second album was right behind the Beatles' *Sgt. Pepper's Lonely Hearts Club Band*. They were the voice of the Love Generation, of San Francisco, of the Haight-Ashbury.

Like most of the early acid bands, they started as folk rockers. Marty Balin, a young actor turned folkie, had taken the same inspiration from *A Hard Day's Night* as had the Byrds and the Lovin' Spoonful. He took the nucleus of his folk-rock group—guitarist Paul Kantner and vocalist Signe Toly—and added Jorma Kaukonen, a locally celebrated guitar picker who happened to know a bassist named Jack Casady. Balin picked up Skip Spence, actually a guitarist, to play drums, purely because he "looked like a drummer."

In the beginning they were obviously folkies on a Liverpool trip, wearing moddish clothes and playing clean, early-Beatles guitar arrangements. It was a tentative sound at first. The guitars mostly played chords, on the beat, with a solemn, chiming quality that reflected the folkie's fascination with sonority (not to mention the professional requirements of playing for the blossoming dance scene at the Fillmore and Avalon ballrooms, or the musicians' unfamiliarity with amplified instruments). Their repertoire included rock-arranged staples of the local coffeehouse circuit, folk blues and ballads as well as several original songs by Balin, Kantner and Spence.

The Jefferson Airplane in 1966 *(from left)*: Marty Balin, Spencer Dryden, Signe Anderson, Paul Kantner, Jorma Kaukonen, Jack Casady.

They were the right band at the right time: In 1965 they became the first San Francisco group to land a contract with a major label.

Shortly after the group's first album was released in September 1966, Spencer Dryden replaced Skip Spence; and Signe Toly, now Signe Anderson and too pregnant to perform, was replaced by Grace Slick from a recently disbanded group called the Great Society. Grace was the decisive change. Signe might have had a richer soprano, but Grace had visual style—she'd put her husband through college by fashion modeling—and an Attitude. From the start her voice had an element of icy fury; when she reached for a high note, it was as if she were zeroing in on something in order to throttle it. She wrote songs of a piece with that voice, songs of scathing sarcasm that led one reviewer to observe that she was the only man-hating songwriter who was also a

misogynist. Balin wrote his own share of put-down songs too. Jefferson Airplane loved you, but they gave themselves plenty of room for psychic self-defense.

By the time of *Surrealistic Pillow,* the album that brought the Airplane and the San Francisco sound to national prominence in 1967, the group was entering its classic phase. Balin's sobbing vibrato played off Slick's needle-sharp soprano, usually singing at the interval of a fifth, a folk harmony style that gives a hollow, austere sound unlike the sweet, ''close'' harmony of singing in thirds. The rhythms had grown suppler and more powerful, and the guitars were stretching out in a bluesier, jazzier direction.

If they echoed the Beatles in the beginning, in early '67 they leaned to a gentle Lovin' Spoonful-ish style, though the Airplane was harder rocking and solemn, even exalted, where the Spoonful was mel-

Jefferson Airplane, in a later incarnation, in their natural habitat.

low and cute. Like the Spoonful they were writing freshly and without condescension about young love, especially about the crisis of confessing love. A classic on the *Surrealistic Pillow* album was "Today." A quiet, early-morningish guitar ostinato backed lyrics confessing apocalyptic passion: "I'm so full of love I could burst apart and start to cry." It was the musical equivalent of one of the apprehensive faces on a Fillmore dance poster.

That was one side of the Airplane's love image. Another was the open evocation of the drug experience. "Take me to a circus tent/Where I can easily pay my rent/And all the other freaks will share my cares" was the story of the Haight-Ashbury for a lot of people. So was the group's first hit, "Somebody to Love": "When the truth is found to be lies/And all the joy within you dies/Don't you want somebody to love?" The words resonate of the Kennedy assassination, the Vietnam War and the tangled passions of youth, acid-magnified. The Airplane Understood.

That phase reached a natural peak during the Summer of Love in 1967. As the first San Francisco band to surface nationally, they were the one band the flood of out-of-towners had to see. And when they performed, at the Fillmore or outdoors, it was more than a show, it was a love feast and religious initiation, with Grace stalking the stage like a howling lioness, and she and Marty exhorting everybody to "Let's Get Together," smile on their brothers, try to love one another . . . right now. It seemed about to happen.

But there were some hard knocks in store, for the band as well as their audience. The Summer of Love ended in drug burnouts and a Haight-Ashbury notable for crude commercialism and violent crime. In 1968 the Airplane were part proprietors of a dance hall in competition with the Fillmore and the Avalon; it went broke. A couple more dreams died at the 1968 Democratic Convention in Chicago. By 1969 the Airplane had stopped singing about love; the focus shifted more and more to Grace's increasingly strident voice and Paul Kantner's increasingly politicized lyrics.

The Airplane as such was coming to an end. Casady and Kaukonen started a group of their own, called Hot Tuna, in 1970. In 1971 Balin left the group he'd founded. Kantner and Slick put out a series of albums with a large roster of San Francisco musicians, showcasing Kantner's science-fiction visions, eventually taking the name Jefferson Starship. Ironically, when Balin returned to work with Kantner, Slick and the Starship, one result was *Red Octopus,* which became the musicians' first Number One album, in 1975. Over the next ten years, the band enjoyed continuing success with a constantly changing lineup. Kantner eventually left, as did Slick. Then, in 1989, they reunited with Kaukonen and Casady, released an album (*Jefferson Airplane*) and toured, but enjoyed only mild success.

As the first big San Francisco band, the Airplane had consciously played the role of pioneers. They fought with their label to include the word "shit" in a lyric even though they risked a boycott by some record chains. Grace, in particular, was provocatively direct in interviews. Indeed, it was the Airplane who first brought the San Francisco hip sensibility to national attention. Back home, the Grateful Dead might embody the purest psychedelic vision; Big Brother and the Holding Company might stand for a kind of dropped-out, no-hope glamour; the Charlatans might exemplify the good-timey antique ambience of the early Haight hip scene. But it was the Airplane who consistently exalted the spirit of a new community, from "Let's Get Together" to "Crown of Creation" and "Volunteers." Throughout, the Airplane embodied the messianism of a generation.

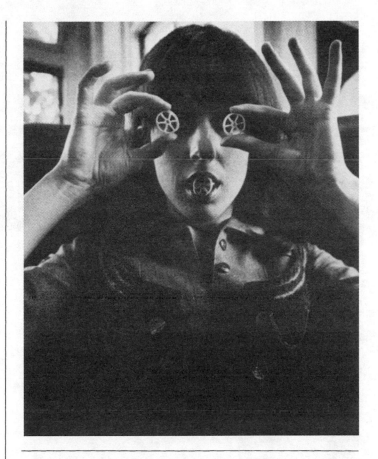

Grace Slick posing with pasta wheels.

DISCOGRAPHY

SINGLES

Jefferson Airplane: "Somebody to Love" (RCA Victor; ☆5, 1967). "White Rabbit" (RCA Victor; ☆8, 1967). "Ballad of You and Me and Pooneil" (RCA Victor; ☆42, 1967). "Watch Her Ride" (RCA Victor; ☆61, 1967). "Greasy Heart" (RCA Victor; ☆98, 1968). "Crown of Creation" (RCA; ☆64, 1968). "Volunteers" (RCA; ☆65, 1969). "Pretty as You Feel" (Grunt; ☆60, 1971). **Jefferson Starship:** "Ride the Tiger" (Grunt; ☆84, 1974). "Miracles" (Grunt; ☆3, 1975). "Play on Love" (Grunt; ☆49, 1975). "With Your Love" (Grunt; ☆12, 1976). "St. Charles" (Grunt; ☆64, 1976). "Count on Me" (Grunt; ☆8, 1978). "Runaway" (Grunt; ☆12, 1978). "Crazy Feelin'" (Grunt; ☆54, 1978). "Light the Sky on Fire" (Grunt; ☆66, 1978). "Jane" (Grunt; ☆14, 1979). "Girl with the Hungry Eyes" (Grunt; ☆55, 1980). "Find Your Way Back" (Grunt; ☆29, 1981). "Stranger" (Grunt; ☆48, 1981). "Be My Lady" (Grunt; ☆28, 1982). "Winds of Change" (Grunt; ☆38, 1983). "No Way Out" (Grunt; ☆23, 1984). **Starship:** "We Built This City" (Grunt; ☆1, 1985). "Sara" (Grunt; ☆1, 1986). "Tomorrow Doesn't Matter Tonight" (Grunt; ☆26, 1986). "Before I Go" (Grunt; ☆68, 1986). "Nothing's Gonna Stop Us Now" (Grunt; ☆1, 1987). "It's Not Over ('til It's Over)" (RCA/Grunt; ☆9, 1987). "Beat Patrol" (RCA/Grunt; ☆46, 1987). "Wild Again" (RCA; ☆73, 1989). "It's Not Enough" (RCA; ☆12, 1989). "I Didn't Mean to Stay All Night" (RCA; ☆75, 1989).

ALBUMS

Jefferson Airplane: *Jefferson Airplane Takes Off!* (RCA Victor; ☆128, 1966). *Surrealistic Pillow* (RCA Victor; ☆3, 1967). *After Bathing at Baxter's* (RCA Victor; ☆17, 1967). *Crown of Creation* (RCA Victor; ☆6, 1968). *Bless Its Pointed Little Head* (RCA Victor; ☆17, 1969). *Volunteers* (RCA Victor; ☆13, 1969). *The Worst of Jefferson Airplane* (RCA Victor; ☆12, 1970). *Bark* (Grunt; ☆11, 1971). *Long John Silver* (Grunt; ☆20, 1972). *Thirty Seconds over Winterland* (Grunt; ☆52, 1973). *Early Flight* (Grunt; ☆110, 1974). *2400 Fulton Street—An Anthology* (RCA; ☆138, 1987). *Jefferson Airplane* (Epic; ☆85, 1989). **Jefferson Starship:** *Baron von Tollbooth and the Chrome Nun* (Grunt; 1973). *Dragon Fly* (Grunt; ☆11, 1974). *Red Octopus* (Grunt; ☆1, 1975). *Spitfire* (Grunt; ☆3, 1976). *Flight Log 1966–1976* (Grunt; ☆37, 1977). *Earth* (Grunt; ☆5, 1978). *Gold* (Grunt; ☆20, 1979). *Freedom at Point Zero* (Grunt; ☆10, 1979). *Modern Times* (Grunt; ☆26, 1981). *Winds of Change* (Grunt; ☆26, 1982). *Nuclear Furniture* (Grunt; ☆28, 1984). **Paul Kantner/Jefferson Starship:** *Blows Against the Empire* (RCA Victor; ☆20, 1970). **Paul Kantner and Grace Slick:** *Sunfighter* (Grunt; ☆89, 1971). **Starship:** *No Protection* (Grunt; ☆12, 1987). *Love Among the Cannibals* (RCA; ☆64, 1989).

(Chart positions compiled from Joel Whitburn's *Record Research*, based on *Billboard*'s Pop and LPs charts.)

JANIS JOPLIN

BY ELLEN WILLIS

anis Joplin was born in 1943 and grew up in Port Arthur, Texas. She began singing in bars and coffeehouses, first locally, then in Austin, where she spent most of a year at the University of Texas. In 1966 she went to San Francisco and got together with a rock band in search of a singer, Big Brother and the Holding Company. The following summer Big Brother performed at the Monterey Pop Festival; Janis got raves from the fans and the critics and from then on she was a star. Cheap Thrills, *Big Brother's first major album (there had been an early record on a small-time label), came out in July 1968. By then there were tensions between Janis and the group, and she left soon afterward.*

With her new backup band she made another album, I Got Dem Ol' Kozmic Blues Again Mama! But the band never quite gelled, and in the spring of 1970 Janis formed another, Full-Tilt Boogie. They spent most of the summer touring, then went to Los Angeles to record an album, Pearl. *It was Janis's last. On October 4th, 1970, she died of an overdose of heroin.*

The hippie rock stars of the late Sixties merged two versions of that hardy American myth, the free individual. They were stars, which meant achieving liberation by becoming rich and famous *on their own terms;* and they were, or purported to be, apostles of cultural revolution, a considerably more ambitious and romantic vision of freedom that nevertheless had a similar economic foundation. Young Americans were in a sense the stars of the world, drawing on an over-blown prosperity that could afford to indulge all manner of rebellious and experimental behavior. The combination was inherently unstable—Whit-

Joplin belonged to that select group of pop figures who matter as much for themselves as for their music.

man's open road is not, finally, the Hollywood Free-way, and in any case neither stardom nor prosperity could deliver what it seemed to promise. For a frag-ile historical moment rock transcended those contra-dictions; in its aftermath our pop heroes found themselves grappling, like the rest of us, with what are probably enduring changes in the white Ameri-can consciousness—changes that have to do with something very like an awareness of tragedy. It is in this context that Janis Joplin developed as an artist, a celebrity, a rebel, a woman, and it is in this context that she died.

Joplin belonged to that select group of pop figures who mattered as much for themselves as for their music; among American rock performers she was second only to Bob Dylan in importance as a creator/recorder/embodiment of her generation's history and mythology. She was also the only woman to

achieve that kind of stature in what was basically a male club, the only Sixties culture hero to make visible and public women's experience of the quest for individual liberation, which was very different from men's. If Janis's favorite metaphors—singing as fucking (a first principle of rock & roll) and fuck-ing as liberation (a first principle of the cultural revo-lution)—were equally approved by her male peers, the congruence was only on the surface. Under-neath—just barely—lurked a feminist (or prefemi-nist) paradox.

The male-dominated counterculture defined free-dom for women almost exclusively in sexual terms. As a result, women endowed the idea of sexual lib-eration with immense symbolic importance; it be-came charged with all the secret energy of an as yet suppressed larger rebellion. Yet to express one's re-bellion in that limited way was a painfully literal form of submission. Whether or not Janis under-stood that, her dual persona—lusty hedonist and suffering victim—suggested that she felt it. Dope, another term in her metaphorical equation (getting high as singing as fucking as liberation) was, in its more sinister aspect, a painkiller and finally a killer. Which is not to say that the good times weren't real, as far as they went. Whatever the limitations of hip-pie rock star life, it was better than being a provincial matron—or a lonely weirdo.

For Janis, as for others of us who suffered the worst fate that can befall an adolescent girl in Amer-ica—*unpopularity*—a crucial aspect of the cultural revolution was its assault on the rigid sexual styles of the Fifties. Joplin's metamorphosis from the ugly duckling of Port Arthur to the peacock of Haight-Ashbury meant, among other things, that a woman who was not conventionally pretty, who had acne and an intermittent weight problem and hair that stuck out, could not only invent her own beauty (just as she invented her wonderful sleazofreak cos-tumes) out of sheer energy, soul, sweetness, arro-gance and a sense of humor, but have that beauty appreciated. Not that Janis merely took advantage of changes in our notions of attractiveness; she herself changed them. It was seeing Janis Joplin that made me resolve, once and for all, not to get my hair straightened. And there was a direct line from that sort of response to those apocryphal burned bras and all that followed.

Direct, but not simple. Janis once crowed,

"They're paying me $50,000 a year to be like me." But the truth was that they were paying her to be a personality, and the relation of public personality to private self—something every popular artist has to work out—is especially problematic for a woman. Men are used to playing roles and projecting images in order to compete and succeed. Male celebrities tend to identify with their mask making, to see it as creative and—more or less—to control it. In contrast, women need images simply to survive. A woman is usually aware, on some level, that men do not allow her to be her "real self," and worse, that the acceptable masks represent men's fantasies, not her own. She can choose the most interesting image available, present it dramatically, individualize it with small elaborations, undercut it with irony. But ultimately she must serve some male fantasy to be loved—and then it will be only the fantasy that is loved anyway. The female celebrity is confronted with this dilemma in its starkest form. Joplin's revolt against conventional femininity was brave and imaginative, but it also dovetailed with a stereotype—the ballsy, one-of-the-guys chick who is a needy, vulnerable cream puff underneath—cherished by her legions of hip male fans. It may be that she could have pushed beyond it and taken the audience with her; that was one of the possibilities that made her death an artistic as well as human calamity. There is, for instance, the question of her bisexuality. People who knew Janis differ on whether sexual relationships with women were an important part of her life, and I don't know the facts. In any case, a public acknowledgment of bisexual proclivities would not necessarily have contradicted her image; it could easily have been passed off as more pull-out-the-stops hedonism or another manifestation of her all-encompassing need for love. On the other hand, she could have used it to say something new about women and liberation. What makes me wonder is something I always noticed and liked about Janis: Unlike most female performers whose act is intensely erotic, she never made me feel as if I were crashing an orgy that consisted of her and the men in the audience. When she got it on at a concert, she got it on with everybody.

Still, the songs she sang assumed heterosexual

Her metamorphosis from the ugly duckling of Port Arthur to the peacock of Haight-Ashbury meant that a woman could invent her own beauty.

romance; it was men who made her hurt, who took another little piece of her heart. Watching men groove on Janis, I began to appreciate the resentment many black people feel toward whites who are blues freaks. Janis sang out of her pain as a woman, and men dug it. Yet it was men who caused the pain, and if they stopped causing it they would not have her to dig. In a way, their adulation was the cruelest insult of all. And Janis's response—to sing harder, get higher, be worshiped more—was rebellious, acquiescent, bewildered all at once. When she said, "Onstage I make love to 25,000 people, then I go home alone," she was not merely repeating the cliché of the sad clown or the poor little rich girl. She was noting that the more she gave the less she got, and that honey, it ain't fair.

Like most women singers, Joplin did not write many songs; she mostly interpreted other people's. But she made them her own in a way few singers dare to do. She did not sing them so much as struggle with them, assault them. Some critics complained, not always unfairly, that she strangled them to death, but at her best she whipped them to new life. She had an analogous adversary relationship with the musical form that dominated her imagination, the blues. Blues represented another external structure, one with its own contradictory tradition of sexual affirmation and sexist conservatism. But Janis used blues conventions to reject blues sensibility. To sing the blues is a way of transcending pain by confronting it with dignity, but Janis wanted nothing less than to scream it out of existence. Big Mama Thornton's classic rendition of "Ball and Chain" carefully balances defiance and resignation, toughness and vulnerability. She almost pities her oppressor. Her singing conveys, above all, her determination to survive abuse. Janis makes the song into one long frenzied, despairing protest. Why, why, *why,* she asks over and over, like a child unable to comprehend injustice. The pain is overwhelming her. There are similar differences between her recording of "Piece of My Heart" and Erma Franklin's. When Franklin sings it, it is a challenge: No matter what you do to me, I will not let you destroy my ability to be human, to love. Joplin seems rather to be saying, surely if I keep taking this, if I keep setting an example of love and forgiveness, surely he has to understand, change, give me back what I have given.

Her pursuit of pleasure had the same driven quality; what it amounted to was refusal to admit of any limits that would not finally yield to the virtue of persistence—*try just a little bit harder*—and the magic of extremes. This war against limits was largely responsible for the electrifying power of Joplin's early

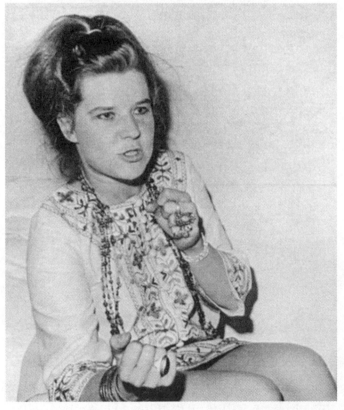

Interviewed at Hollywood's Landmark Hotel in June 1968, Janis Joplin put on an animated front—and showed a face of infinite sadness.

performances; it was what made *Cheap Thrills* a classic, in spite of unevenness and the impossibility of duplicating on a record the excitement of her concerts. After the split with Big Brother, Janis retrenched considerably, perhaps because she simply couldn't maintain that level of intensity, perhaps for other reasons that would have become clear if she had lived. My uncertainty on this point makes me hesitate to be too dogmatic about my conviction that leaving Big Brother was a mistake.

I was a Big Brother fan. I thought they were better musicians than their detractors claimed, but more to the point, technical accomplishment in itself was not something I cared about. I thought it was an ominous sign that so many people did care, including Janis. It was, in fact, a sign that the tenuous alliance between mass culture and bohemianism—or, in my original formulation, the fantasy of stardom and the fantasy of cultural revolution—was breaking down. But the breakdown was not as neat as it might appear. For the elitist concept of "good musicianship" was as alien to the holistic, egalitarian spirit of rock & roll as the act of leaving one's group the better to pursue one's individual ambition was alien to the holistic, egalitarian pretensions of the cultural revolutionaries. If Joplin's decision to go it alone was influenced by all the obvious professional/commercial pressures, it also reflected a con-

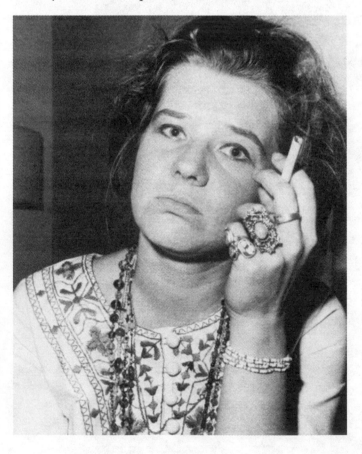

flict of values within the counterculture itself—a conflict that foreshadowed its imminent disintegration. And again, Janis's femaleness complicated the issues, raised the stakes. She had less room to maneuver than a man in her position, fewer alternatives to fall back on if she blew it. If she had to choose between fantasies, it made sense for her to go with stardom as far as it would take her.

But I wonder if she really had to choose, if her choice was not in some sense a failure of nerve and therefore of greatness. Janis was afraid Big Brother would hold her back, but if she had thought it was important enough, she might have been able to carry them along, make them transcend their limitations. There is more than a semantic difference between a group and a backup band. Janis had to relate to the members of Big Brother as spiritual (not to mention financial) equals even though she had more talent than they, and I can't help suspecting that that was good for her not only emotionally and socially but aesthetically. Committed to the hippie ethic of music-for-the-hell-of-it—if only because there was no possibility of their becoming stars on their own—Big Brother helped Janis sustain the amateur quality that was an integral part of her effect. Their zaniness was a salutary reminder that good times meant silly fun—remember ''Caterpillar''?—as well as Dionysiac abandon; it was a relief from Janis's extremism and at the same time a foil for it. At their best moments Big Brother made me think of the Beatles, who weren't (at least in the beginning) such terrific musicians either. Though I'm not quite softheaded enough to imagine that by keeping her group intact Janis Joplin could somehow have prevented or delayed the end of an era, or even saved her own life, it would have been an impressive act of faith. And acts of faith by public figures always have reverberations, one way or another.

Such speculation is of course complicated by the fact that Janis died before she really had a chance to define her post–San Francisco, post–Big Brother self.

Her last two albums, like her performances with the ill-fated Kozmic Blues Band, had a tentative, transitional feel. She was obviously going through important changes; the best evidence of that was ''Me and Bobby McGee,'' which could be considered her ''Dear Landlord.'' Both formally—as a low-keyed, soft, folkie tune—and substantively—as a lyric that spoke of choices made, regretted and survived, with the distinct implication that compromise could be a positive act—what it expressed would have been heresy to the Janis Joplin of *Cheap Thrills*. ''Freedom's just another word for nothing left to lose'' is as good an epitaph for the counterculture as any; we'll never know how—or if—Janis meant to go on from there.

Janis Joplin's death, like that of a fighter in the ring, was not exactly an accident. Yet it's too easy to label it either suicide or murder, though it involved elements of both. Call it rather an inherent risk of the game she was playing, a game whose often frivolous rules both hid and revealed a deadly serious struggle. The form that struggle took was incomplete, shortsighted, egotistical, self-destructive. But survivors who give in to the temptation to feel superior to all that are in the end no better than those who romanticize it. Janis was not so much a victim as a casualty. The difference matters.

DISCOGRAPHY

ALBUMS
Big Brother and the Holding Company: *Big Brother and the Holding Company* (Mainstream; ☆60, 1967). *Cheap Thrills* (Columbia; ☆1, 1968). **Janis Joplin:** *I Got Dem Ol' Kozmic Blues Again Mama!* (Columbia; ☆5, 1969). *Pearl* (Columbia; ☆1, 1971). *Joplin in Concert* (Columbia; ☆4, 1972). *Janis Joplin's Greatest Hits* (Columbia; ☆37, 1973). *Janis* (soundtrack) (Columbia; ☆54, 1975). *Farewell Song* (Columbia; ☆104, 1982).

(Chart positions compiled from Joel Whitburn's *Record Research*, based on *Billboard*'s LPs chart.)

THE DOORS

BY LESTER BANGS

The significance of the Doors should not be underestimated. When you consider the context they discredited through their violence, when you look around and consider the bands and singers that have captured the imagination in the years since—from Alice Cooper to Bryan Ferry—it becomes obvious that Jim Morrison was one of the fathers of contemporary rock. The Stones were dirty, but the Doors were *dread,* and the difference is crucial, because dread is the great fact of our time.

Jim Morrison was born on December 8th, 1943, in Melbourne, Florida. He came from a long line of military careerists, and part of his hype was that both parents were dead. He studied film at UCLA, but soon he drifted out to the Venice beach culture, where transience was a given and acid the drug of preference. A friend later claimed that during this period he ate it constantly, "like candy." Whether that's true or not, it's a fact that one day he ran into keyboard player Ray Manzarek, an acquaintance from film school days and a classically trained musician who today looks just like a schoolteacher. But back then, down on the beach, they squatted in the middle of the sand and Morrison recited him "Moonlight Drive."

"When he sang those lines, 'Let's swim to the moon/Let's climb through the tide/Penetrate the evening/That the city sleeps to hide,' " Manzarek has recalled, "I said, that's it. . . . It seemed as though, if we got a group together we could make a million dollars." The Doors as *concept* was created by those two on the beach that day.

The Doors paid dues in 1966, at crummy clubs on the Strip in L.A. and then at the Whisky a Go Go, where Morrison took off on improvisational flights, aloft and hungry until Jac Holzman walked in one night and decided this exhibitionistic debauch was just the act to give Elektra, his fading folkie label, a stake in the electric politics everybody saw building.

Holzman was no fool. *The Doors* (1967) turned out to be one of the best-selling albums of its era, with the hit single "Light My Fire" serving perfectly as

The Doors, just starting to break on through, 1967. With "Light My Fire," they did.

the anthem of a generation until "Gimme Shelter" came along to supersede it. But their first real claim to history was probably "The End"; it freaked out producer Paul Rothchild, who waxed metaphysical with Morrison over the Oedipal drama. It had also freaked out the manager of the Whisky, who threw Morrison out of his club. And it was the first major statement of the Doors' perennial themes: dread, violence, guilt without possibility of redemption, the miscarriages of love, and, most of all, death.

Nevertheless, the last time I heard "The End," it sounded funny. Even by *Strange Days*, the second Doors album, it was becoming apparent that the group was limited, and that Morrison's Lizard King vision was usually morbid in the most obvious possible way, and thus cheap. The whole nightmare easily translated into parody—and there was a supremely sad irony here. But when Morrison hit straight and deep—"People are strange when you're a stranger/Faces look ugly when you're alone" you knew he felt the chill and lived it, and that was perhaps the saddest part. Because in time he became

a true clown, picking up the Lizard King cartoon and wearing it like a bib to keep the drunk drool from rolling down to stain his shirt. Meanwhile the audience, oblivious to irony if not entirely to pathos, felt burned as they watched him get drunker and fatter. Pretty soon the word was out all down the line, and high school kids were scornful of the Doors; by the time *Waiting for the Sun* was released, the band's stock had dropped to a level just this side of bubblegum, even as Morrison still skirted skid row.

So with the same desperation that drives millions of far less celebrated alcoholics, Morrison began to flirt with new and more dangerous forms of exhibitionism. Creating havoc on planes, getting arrested in airports. Pushing his way to the stage of the Troubador and raving drunkenly. Onstage at a Doors concert in New Haven, telling the crowd how he and a girl were maced by police in the dressing room; stage suddenly covered with police, the whole thing stupid. But not as stupid as the famous Miami cockflashing incident. March 1969. A song broken down in the middle, the singer too drunk to even make a pretense of professionalism. Silence as the whole auditorium slips into suspended animation, stop time, maybe a few scattered boos, everybody waiting for the Lizard King to do something crazy. So Morrison screamed drunkenly, "You wanna see my cock?" and then unzipped, waving his flaccid peter in the air for a couple of still moments. Even if he did stand trial on charges of indecent exposure, public drunkenness, etc., it really wasn't much. Yet this pathetic, petty act was the beginning of the end for Morrison and the Doors.

Meanwhile, the Doors' artistic stock had hit an all-time low with *The Soft Parade,* released in summer 1969, not long after the Miami incident. Relying more and more on brass, strings and anything else they could bring in, they had not only failed to live up to their original promise—they had turned what they represented into a joke. *Morrison Hotel,* released in early 1970, redeemed them somewhat, but between Morrison's antics and the band's musical slippage the Doors had become a dead issue. Morrison was by turns painfully and wryly aware of his own absurdity, and you can hear his humor in the between-song banter ("Dead cat in a top hat . . . thinks he's an aristocrat/ . . . That's crap") on *Absolutely Live* (1970).

But Jim Morrison had not set out, initially, to be

Jim Morrison, the Lizard King, as an adolescent Christ figure *(left)*, and four years down the road, as a bearded bard.

a clown. He had wanted to be a literary figure, even if it was only the Doors' pop success that allowed publication of his sophomoric jottings in *The Lords and the New Creatures*. In mid-1971, with a bluesy and intermittently successful album called *L.A. Woman* finished, Morrison headed for Paris, home of the French Symbolist poets, birthplace of the Surrealist movement, Céline's misanthropic ellipses and much else that had undoubtedly inspired him. He probably had some vague idea, like Hemingway and Fitzgerald before him, of finding literary sustenance in that atmosphere, and, like many another frustrated writer before him, he found plenty of booze. He also found death, in a bathtub, of a heart attack, on July 3rd, 1971. He was twenty-seven years old.

DISCOGRAPHY

SINGLES

"Light My Fire" (Elektra; ☆1, 1967). "People Are Strange" (Elektra; ☆12, 1967). "Love Me Two Times" (Elektra; ☆25, 1967). "The Unknown Soldier" (Elektra; ☆39, 1968). "Hello, I Love You" (Elektra; ☆1, 1968). "Touch Me" (Elektra; ☆3, 1968). "Wishful Sinful" (Elektra; ☆44, 1969). "Tell All the People" (Elektra; ☆57, 1969). "Runnin' Blue" (Elektra; ☆64, 1969). "You Make Me Real" (Elektra; ☆50, 1970). "Love Her Madly" (Elektra; ☆11, 1971). "Riders on the Storm" (Elektra; ☆14, 1971).

ALBUMS

The Doors (Elektra; ☆2, 1967). *Strange Days* (Elektra; ☆3, 1967). *Waiting for the Sun* (Elektra; ☆1, 1968). *The Soft Parade* (Elektra; ☆6, 1969). *Morrison Hotel* (Elektra; ☆4, 1970). *Absolutely Live* (Elektra; ☆8, 1970). *The Doors—13* (Elektra; ☆25, 1970). *L.A. Woman* (Elektra; ☆9, 1971). *Weird Scenes Inside the Gold Mine* (Elektra; ☆55, 1972). *Full Circle* (Elektra; ☆68, 1972). *The Best of the Doors* (Elektra; ☆158, 1973). *An American Prayer—Jim Morrison* (Elektra; ☆54, 1978). *The Doors Greatest Hits* (Elektra; ☆17, 1980). *Alive, She Cried* (Elektra; ☆23, 1983). *In Concert* (Elektra; 1991). *The Doors/An Oliver Stone Film* (Elektra; 1991).

(Chart positions compiled from Joel Whitburn's *Record Research*, based on *Billboard*'s Pop and LPs charts.)

THE KINKS

BY KEN EMERSON

After a short spell as the Ravens, Ray Davies, kid brother Dave and two friends became the Kinks in 1964. They might as well have called themselves the Kontradictions. ''I Took My Baby Home,'' the first original song they recorded, was a bouncy, Beatles-like number that reversed customary sex roles by singing the praises of a female so aggressive that her ''hug like a vise'' and ''high-powered kisses'' literally bowled over her cowering lover. Not long thereafter, Ray again assumed a traditionally feminine posture as he beseeched, ''Set me free, little girl.'' Such sexual hide-and-seek culminated much later in the crowning, syntactical ambiguity of ''Lola'': ''But I know what I am and I'm glad I'm a man/And so's Lola.''

The Kinks subverted the stereotypes of rock & roll as well as of gender. Far from urging adolescent rebellion, they sided with parents against cruel offspring in songs such as ''Rosy Won't You Please Come Home'' and ''Nothing to Say.'' They even had the temerity to sing, ''God save little shops, china cups and virginity.'' When London was at its most swinging, they skewered the Carnaby Street scene in ''Dedicated Follower of Fashion'' and contrasted two sisters, a harried housewife and her trendy sibling. Rock rarely sympathizes with mums in curlers, but beleaguered Priscilla, trapped in domestic squalor, was the heroine here. Still, even as she accepted—and the Kinks condoned—her lot, she ran around her home in poignant frustration. Life, as rendered by the Kinks in loving detail scarcely rivaled in pop music, is never simple.

It's never simple, because Ray Davies, the Kinks' lead singer, composer and guiding light, seldom is. ''No one can penetrate me,'' he once sang as a half

Dedicated followers of fashion, they survived the British Invasion to become an institution. The band in 1965 *(from left)*: Dave Davies, Pete Quaife, Mick Avory, Ray Davies.

boast, half lament, and he hasn't seemed able to plumb or resolve his ambivalences, either. On the one hand, he's a realist, a pop Balzac with a basically Marxist view of the society he chronicles; no other pre-punk rocker has insisted so relentlessly on the primacy of class. On the other hand, he's a romantic individualist who dreads the gray uniformity of socialism, so he flees into nostalgia and fantasy. Both satirist and sentimentalist, obsessive poet of food (factuality) and drink (escapism), Ray has always seemed divided against himself politically as well as sexually. Albums such as *Preservation Act 2* and *Soap Opera* are fun-house halls of mirrors in which Ray is refracted as man and woman, capitalist and communist, pop star and normal Norman.

It's less the sophistication of his intellect than the breadth of his compassion that has allowed Ray to argue both sides of every question, and the outcomes have been not answers but suspended judgments. Thus ''Autumn Almanac,'' a British hit single in 1967, both satirized and celebrated a self-satisfied urban gardener. On its surface, Davies's ''Dandy''

(an American hit for Herman's Hermits) admired a free-loving bachelor. But Ray's vocal on the Kinks' version (on *Face to Face*) expressed humor, bemused contempt, moral disapprobation and, at the yelping conclusion, furious envy.

Because, as Ray once sang, ''life is so complicated'' and offers no solutions capable of satisfying an active mind (or heart), the only options are humor and passive resignation. No one has written so many hymns to laziness as Ray, while the stoicism of ''Big Sky'' and the sweet acceptance of ''Waterloo Sunset'' approach philosophical grandeur. The result of such withdrawal, however, is isolation. Loneliness pervades the Kinks' music, lending sad undertones to even their most comic songs.

But there was nothing bittersweet about the pile-driving hits that first made the Kinks (the Davieses plus Mick Avory on drums and Pete Quaife on bass) famous in 1964 and 1965. ''You Really Got Me,'' ''All Day and All of the Night'' et al. were precursors of heavy metal and punk rock, so raw and so raucous, so aggressively amateurish, that they made the rest of the original British Invasion seem effete. (That the Kinks wore foppish velvet finery on stage was simply one more kontradiction.) The rudimentary riffs possessed a maddening inevitability, and Dave Davies's solos, distorted accelerations of the guitar break on ''Louie Louie,'' were berserk. The Kinks quickly tempered their image with some lovely, wistful ballads (''Tired of Waiting for You,'' ''Set Me Free''), but it was not until late 1965 that Ray Davies's songwriting betrayed a distinct sensibility. ''A Well Respected Man'' revealed a social satirist whose sharp eye for detail made commentary

Latter-day Kinks cutting up, 1972.

An intent Ray Davies, still rocking.

such as the Beatles' in "Nowhere Man" seem vapid.

On *Face to Face* (1966) the Kinks came into their own. Ray had decided "to stop writing for other people and start writing for myself," and he emerged as an anecdotist spinning tales of Hawaiian vacations, scrambled party lines, upward (and downward) social mobility, session musicians, housewives and runaways. Ray's homely voice sounded extraordinarily human, and his sympathy enabled him to become a versatile character actor whose vocals were variously boozy and broad, pinched and dry, tender and poignant. The band stopped bashing—Robert Christgau has called "Waterloo Sunset," with its intricate arrangement and ethereal Beach Boys harmonies, "the most beautiful song in the English language"—but re-

mained just rough enough to retain an offhand charm. Unfortunately, much of their music from this, their finest period, was overlooked in the United States; a dispute with the American musicians' union barred their touring here. It may very well be that they had turned too idiosyncratically English to interest an audience abroad anyway.

From short stories it was but a small step to a collection of songs unified by a central theme (the pastoral nostalgia of *The Kinks Are the Village Green Preservation Society*) and the shortest of leaps to an album-long narrative. Although *Arthur (or the Decline and Fall of the British Empire)* presented a sweeping social panorama, it didn't pack the musical and emotional wallop of the Who's *Tommy* and placed a distant second in 1969's "rock opera" sweepstakes.

The Kinks began touring the States, and shortly "Lola" became their first American hit single in four years. At first a painfully insecure performer, Ray Davies steadily became more flamboyant, swishing and slashing onstage, and his thinking grew ever more theatrical. The group added keyboard player John Gosling and gradually turned into a troupe with a ragtag horn section and a chorus of actor-singers. Albums became soundtracks for elaborate stage shows—plays, really—and sometimes the music suffered. Occasionally the lyrics did too, because dramatization, making external and explicit Ray's internal contradictions, required oversimplification. Now the ironies lay not so much within individual songs as between them; the sum was more intriguing than the parts.

Their extravagant road shows won the Kinks a fanatical American cult following but did not sell any records. Only in the late Seventies, when they returned to more fundamental rock & roll, did they begin to enjoy once again the occasional middling hit single. This change in fortunes coincided with the band's rediscovery by a new generation of rockers. While Van Halen strip-mined the Kinks catalogue for heavy metal ("You Really Got Me" was Van Halen's first hit single), "new wavers" Chrissie Hynde and the Pretenders unearthed more obscure ditties ("Stop Your Sobbing" was their very first release). Hynde carried her admiration for Ray Davies so far that she had a daughter by him. The Jam covered the Kinks' "David Watts" and echoed their gritty social realism, while Squeeze paid more oblique tribute in their comic slices of domestic (and often drunken) life. That it can encompass and inspire both the whomp of Van Halen and the wit of Squeeze shows how remarkably broad Ray Davies's sensibility is.

All the material that has been revived dates back to 1970 or earlier, however, and Ray's heart does not seem to have been in his records for a long time. Their riffs sound for the most part routine, the melodies make-readies and the sentiments one-dimensional. There's no "kink," no saving grace or irony, for example, in the straightforward account of transvestism in "Out of the Wardrobe" (from the 1978 album *Misfits*) to match the high sophistication and low humor of "Lola." The band has seemed disheartened, too, with members coming and going (drummer Avory stuck it out until 1984) and Dave Davies releasing an occasional solo album.

When the Kinks renounced theater, Ray Davies evidently didn't. He wrote and directed a short film, *Return to Waterloo,* and he's been working for several years on a musical version of Jules Verne's *Around the World in Eighty Days.* If Ray Davies's interest no longer lies chiefly in rock & roll, rock's indebtedness to his music and to his Kinks is undying.

DISCOGRAPHY

AMERICAN SINGLES
"You Really Got Me" (Reprise; ☆7, 1964). "All Day and All of the Night" (Reprise; ☆7, 1964). "Tired of Waiting for You" (Reprise; ☆6, 1965). "Set Me Free" (Reprise; ☆23, 1965). "Who'll Be the Next in Line" (Reprise; ☆34, 1965). "A Well Respected Man" (Reprise; ☆13, 1965). "Till the End of the Day" (Reprise; ☆50, 1966). "Dedicated Follower of Fashion" (Reprise; ☆36, 1966). "Sunny Afternoon" (Reprise; ☆14, 1966). "Deadend Street" (Reprise; ☆73, 1967). "Mr. Pleasant" (Reprise; ☆80, 1967). "Victoria" (Reprise; ☆62, 1970). "Lola" (Reprise; ☆9, 1970). "Apeman" (Reprise; ☆45, 1971). "Sleepwalker" (Arista; ☆48, 1977). "A Rock 'n' Roll Fantasy" (Arista; ☆30, 1978). "(Wish I Could Fly Like) Superman" (Arista; ☆41, 1979). "Lola" (live version) (Arista; ☆81, 1980). "Destroyer" (Arista; ☆85, 1981). "Better Things" (Arista; ☆92, 1982). "Come Dancing" (Arista; ☆6, 1983). "Don't Forget to Dance" (Arista; ☆29, 1983). "Do It Again" (Arista; ☆41, 1985).

AMERICAN ALBUMS
You Really Got Me (Reprise; ☆29, 1964). *Kinks-Size* (Reprise; ☆13, 1965). *Kinda Kinks* (Reprise; ☆60, 1965). *Kinks Kinkdom* (Reprise; ☆47, 1965). *The Kinks Kontroversy* (Reprise; ☆95, 1966). *The Kinks' Greatest Hits* (Reprise; ☆9, 1966). *Face to Face* (Reprise; ☆135, 1967). *The Live Kinks* (Reprise; ☆162, 1967). *Something Else by the Kinks* (Reprise; ☆153, 1968). *The Kinks Are the Village Green Preservation Society* (Reprise; 1969). *Arthur (or the Decline and Fall of the British Empire)* (Reprise; ☆105, 1969). *Lola vs. Powerman and the Moneygoround* (Reprise; ☆35, 1970). *Muswell Hillbillies* (RCA Victor; ☆100, 1971). *The Kink Kronikles* (Reprise; ☆94, 1972). *Everybody's in Show-Biz* (RCA Victor; ☆70, 1972). *The Great Lost Kinks Album* (Reprise; ☆145, 1973). *Preservation Act 1* (RCA; ☆177, 1973). *Preservation Act 2* (RCA; ☆114, 1974). *Soap Opera* (RCA; ☆51, 1975). *Schoolboys in Disgrace* (RCA; ☆45, 1975). *The Kinks' Greatest—Celluloid Heroes* (RCA; ☆144, 1976). *Sleepwalker* (Arista; ☆21, 1977). *Misfits* (Arista; ☆40, 1978). *Low Budget* (Arista; ☆11, 1979). *One for the Road* (Arista; ☆14, 1980). *Second Time Around* (RCA; ☆177, 1980). *Give the People What They Want* (Arista; ☆15, 1981). *State of Confusion* (Arista; ☆12, 1983). *Word of Mouth* (Arista; ☆57, 1984). *Come Dancing with The Kinks—The Best of the Kinks 1977–1986* (Arista; ☆159, 1986). *Think Visual* (MCA; ☆81, 1986). *The Road* (MCA; ☆110, 1988). *UK Jive* (MCA; ☆122, 1989). *The Kinks Greatest Hits* (Rhino; 1989). *The Ultimate Collection* (MCA; 1990).

(Chart positions compiled from Joel Whitburn's *Record Research,* based on *Billboard*'s Pop and LPs charts.)

THE WHO

BY DAVE MARSH

In the beginning, rock was a Moment: If all had gone well, its brevity should have been central to its glory. In England mod was like the beginning. Its virtues were similar: violent displays of unbridled joy from young, newly affluent, prefabricated hoodlums. Outrage for its own sake; consumption without guilt.

For both rock and mod, the crunch came when the Moment was extended, when anarchy at the weekend became a passion eight days a week. Almost inevitably, both rock and mod became institutions, in living contradiction to their original rationales. No longer just a kick, rock became an art form. Rather than just an outrage, mod became a "lifestyle."

The story of this paradox is the story of the Who. Born in a tatty London district called Shepherd's Bush, raised to popularity alongside the hopes of the Sixties, the Who is the band that refused to die before it got old.

There's a case to be made (use any early Sixties photo as evidence) that they were the most unsightly mob to emerge from the British Invasion. The guitarist, Pete Townshend, was tall, thin as a rail, with a beak like an eagle—sullen Abe Lincoln in Union Jack wraps. The bassist, John Entwistle, was a woolly bear, given to corpulence while still in his twenties. John Bull perpetually on the verge of a hangover, Keith Moon, the drummer, was a toddler-visaged anarchist, the kind of kid your parents discouraged from hanging around the yard, Billy the Kid with bangs. The singer, Roger Daltrey, had the mug, the posture and the demeanor (permanently chipped shoulders) of a budding thug: aspiring John Dillinger.

Separately, they would have been nothing; there wasn't a sex symbol in the lot. Together, this is what they did: The drummer tossed his sticks high above his head, ignoring every formality of the beat, then bashed his kit furiously, fitting his thunder into spots where previously only guitar solos were supposed to go. The guitarist set up choppy rhythms, amphetamined "Louie Louie," windmilling his arms across the strings, slashing his fingers while he ripped out power chords, jamming his Gibson

The Who, epitomizing mod style.

against the amps for thunderous feedback screeches that rattled the teeth, all the while leaping like a monkey. The singer twirled his mike like a lariat, marched in place, danced silly steps, stuttered, swaggered, screamed; he pounced on the crowd, half stand-up comic, half assailant. The bassist just stood there, as though he'd seen it all done better.

Their sound was anarchy, chaos, pure noise—a definition of one kind of Sixties rock. No room for ballads. The Who's half-life in that era's volatile world of pop should have been about the length of one of their singles. Instead, they somehow outlasted every other band of their generation.

They were not without influences: "Louie Louie," Jimmy Reed, Eddie Cochran, the dance frenzy of James Brown and Jackie Wilson, a tinge of surf music here and there. But if this was, at the start, just another British R&B band, the Who were fully capable of living up to their original billing: Maximum R&B. This was soul music pilled-up and riotous, played with none of the elegant perfection of the Rolling Stones, but with all the zealotry of garage-band amateurs. Like any bunch of apprentices, where they came from was never half as fascinating as where they were headed. The Who took the stage not to entertain or to represent but to command, to rule, to dominate.

Townshend, Entwistle and Daltrey grew up in the same neighborhood; they were friends practically from the cradle. They found Moon, by mistake, in a demolition derby of an audition. After the first night he was inseparable from them.

Of course, they hated one another. Their spats and feuds, public and private, were the essence of Who mythology. But like brothers, they immediately closed ranks against outsiders. Only the myth says they were enemies; the music speaks more clearly about how well they fitted one another.

Even their managers were odd, half-mad creatures. The first, Peter Meaden, had one inspiration: to link the Who with the mods. Until then mod had been primarily a fashion movement, involving clothing with details cut precisely right, a Vespa

The Who in 1964, before they had faced death firsthand, when they could still brag about hoping to die before they got old. *From left:* John Entwistle, Roger Daltrey, Keith Moon, Pete Townshend.

scooter for transportation, diet pills for acceleration. The aural accoutrement was American R&B—Motown, James Brown, Geno Washington—and a few cool British soul singers like Georgie Fame.

Meaden re-dressed the Who, renamed them the High Numbers, wrote them lyrics that fit the fashions ("Zoot Suit," "I'm the Face") and used his flair for publicity to win them a following.

It remained for Kit Lambert and Chris Stamp, young filmmakers hunting up subjects, to spot the Who and to prod them into becoming a sonic Brighton riot. When Townshend stuck his guitar through the low ceiling of the Railway Tavern one evening, then smashed it to smithereens, that was pure frus-

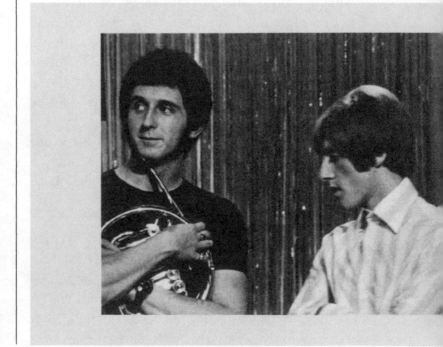

tration speaking. It was Lambert and Stamp who suggested making destruction part of the show. And perpetual flamboyance saved the Who, who would never have gotten far trying to play R&B with the propriety of the Bluesbreakers or the Stones.

Townshend has always claimed that the Who didn't play soul music faithfully because they couldn't—their technical competence wasn't up to the competition, much less the originals. Certainly, listening to the James Brown numbers on the first Who album is a comic experience. But that's only half the story. What the mods—and the Who—were trying to express was actually at odds with the blues and its extensions. Black pop is about finding dig-

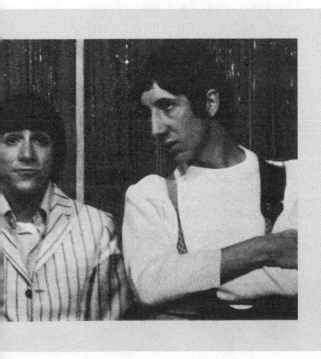

nity in a life of pain, hard work and adversity. Rock is about ignoring and obliterating those petty defeats; it shuts out adversity. As Townshend said a decade or more later, ''Rock won't eliminate your problems. But it will let you sort of dance all over them.'' So the Who finally weren't fit for R&B because R&B wasn't really fit for them—or their constituency. When soul singers act out their frustrations, it's understood as a momentary release; most would never act that way offstage. But Keith Moon could, and would, and did behave with as much rage in real life as in a show.

Their first three singles tell the tale: ''I Can't Explain'' is a grand nick of the basic ''Louie Louie'' riff; ''Anyway Anyhow Anywhere,'' a tentative exploration of themes (freedom, frustration, feedback) that's much less catchy. ''My Generation'' fused the best of both into an authentic anthem that blasted past its derivations, totally a part of the moment in which it was conceived and in the process totally eternal, because it captures that moment so completely. The lyric was icing:

> People try to put us d-down
> Just because we get around
> Things they do look awful c-cold
> Hope I die before I get old.

Like the Stones' ''Satisfaction,'' which personalized the general discontent Townshend expressed, ''My Generation'' might have been almost as much a surprise to the men who made it as to any random listener. It was that new, that fresh, that right.

But rock & roll was no longer only a matter of moments. Put together a song this ''profound,'' and you run the risk of being taken seriously—before you get old. So the string of singles that followed (''A Legal Matter'' and ''Substitute,'' ''The Kids Are Alright'' and ''Pictures of Lily,'' down to ''Magic Bus'' and ''I Can See for Miles'') are both the best music the Who ever made, and anticlimactic. They established Townshend as a master guitarist and songwriter, Moon as the best drummer in rock history, Daltrey as a shouter supreme, and they extended the band's embattled identity (and the fans' identification with them). But those songs contain their own contradiction: In none of them is anything quite what it seems, and in all of them, the Who seek an image that perpetually eludes them.

At one time, such a string of pop successes might

have been sufficient for both audience and performer. But the Sixties were not quite the rebirth of rock's original moment that they're usually presumed to have been. Elvis Presley became an outlaw by accident, but by the time John Lennon, Keith Richards and Pete Townshend picked up their guitars, the consequences of playing rebel chords were well known. More than any set of social circumstances (even drugs), it was this that distinguished rock's second awakening from the first and created a self-conscious "art form" from the music's initial series of vaguely linked moments.

But there is an enormous contradiction here. Early rock was amazing primarily because of its spontaneity, which was in many ways a function of the naiveté that the Sixties rocker never had. In any given instant that spontaneity might be reborn for real, but the second or third time around, it was clearly forced. The Who felt this problem to an extreme degree, "The Kids Are Alright," a self-conscious follow-up to "My Generation," already seemed nostalgic, although it was released less than a year later. More important, Townshend immediately began his career-long process of alternating

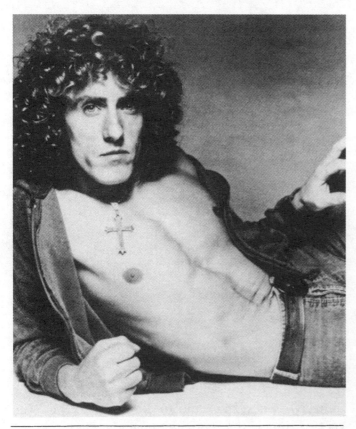

Roger Daltrey, idol.

incredibly pompous statements about the artistic importance of rock with disingenuously self-effacing ones about the triviality of the whole thing. Which posed the most interesting question of Sixties rock: How seriously could a rock band take itself?

The answer, of course, varied from moment to moment. As Townshend wrote in 1977, "*Tommy* was never really meant to be as 'heavy,' as say, 'My Generation.'" That was rhetoric—reflecting the pop dictum that less is more—but it's true that the rock opera began as pure filler, when the Who came up ten minutes short for their second album. Kit Lambert, by now producing as well as managing, instructed Townshend to write a long song. While Townshend claims to have felt this was a conundrum, since "rock songs are three minutes fifty by definition," he came up with an absurd story line as an excuse to tie together four three-minute songs, then half-jokingly called them a "mini-opera."

However much he might have preferred it otherwise, it was the mini-opera "A Quick One While He's Away" that made the Who's reputation. Released a good six months before *Sgt. Pepper*, "A

tions; the Who was built on them, and it celebrated them. The four personalities in the Who did not complement one another (as the Beatles' did) but merely canceled out one another's worst excesses. Townshend began to be seen as a major spokesman for rock's growing artistic respectability, the more

Keith Moon, aristocrat.

perfect because he usually ended his tirades by insisting that everything was ruined if the music became too self-aware. The increasing tendency to see the Who as Pete Townshend and the Three Stooges obviously didn't sit well with the others, and they fought, beat on one another, argued and split up for the evening. On every block, even in nice neighborhoods, there is one family whose public squabbles tell the real story, and for rock & roll, the Who were it: They were never able to hide anything, including the fact that Roger Daltrey (sex symbol) and Townshend (big-nose intellectual) often loathed each other. Fans either learned to love this aspect of the Who or moved on to less challenging heroes. But the listeners who stayed became fanatics, convinced that this was the definitive way for a rock band to behave. And maybe it was, if only as a metaphor for music that detonates harmony in favor of chaos and finds one as satisfying (if not as pretty) as the other.

Quick One'' placed the Who firmly in rock's avant-garde. If this was a somewhat anomalous position for a band whose drummer favored surf music, the arty exterior of the band was what brought it a following, not just in England but also in the United States (where all the early hits had flopped). When the Who unveiled its auto-destruct stage show in New York in the spring of '67, it became an immediate sensation; on a cross-country tour with Herman's Hermits, the Who stole the show and finished up in triumph at the Monterey Pop Festival later that summer.

The audience the Who found was paradoxical and just what it needed and deserved: half street kids who simply loved the flash and violence, half budding intellectuals who worshiped the band's artistic statements as genuine genuflections to the Muse. Neither side could ignore the other, since Townshend's more airy conceits inevitably collided with the gut-level strength of the music, and Moon's irrepressible clowning chopped the legs from under pretensions to serious art.

There was no way to avoid any of those contradic-

The Who's shows were more than concerts. In every rock & roll performance worth its salt there's some mystery about where what the band does to the audience leaves off and what the audience does to the band begins. The Who made this the essence of their shows, talking about it, playing off it, increasing and reducing the distance between themselves and the fans with precision. Every moment of the experience, from waiting in line for tickets to the final bellow for an encore, became one long rite of the faithful (made more so by the aloofness of

Dylan, the Stones and the Beatles). The smashing of the guitar, then, became less a gesture or some pop-art symbol than the band's final, perfect sacrifice to this symbiotic interchange.

Pete Townshend, composer.

The albums, meanwhile, pursued the contradictions. If *The Who Sell Out* is the most perfectly conceived album of the concept-album era, it is also the silliest. *Sell Out* placed rock right where it belonged, among the pimple creams and leather-lunged DJs of pop radio. There were songs about deodorants and tattoos, pure blurts of adolescent rage and crazy fantasies about misers. *Sell Out* was also an album with the Who's most interesting arrangements ever, the most diverse playing (and the least supercharged power-chord rock), and it ended with "Rael," another mini-opera. All of it was tightly welded, so that the trivia was inextricable from the experimentation. At best, as with "Tattoo," "I Can See for Miles" and "Relax," the experimentation and the trivia weren't just indistinguishable, they were identical.

The Who not only marched to a different drummer, they celebrated the potential for discord that made rock such an unlikely entertainment medium. It wasn't only their personal feuds or the tensions in their music. If rock became art in the Sixties, it also never stopped being pop music, a disposable commodity. If the Who was an institution, by now, it was also a product. You could say that about a lot of Sixties icons—you could say it about most of the political movements, eventually, and all of the other great bands. The only difference was that Townshend, Entwistle, Daltrey and Moon never bothered to disguise their merchandising, either.

At the same time Townshend stepped forward as rock's premiere theorist and moralist. Pete had dab-

bled with drugs, then turned to an Indian spiritual master, Meher Baba. But unlike George Harrison and other rock stars who accepted mysticism, Townshend's metaphysical beliefs made him more enraged with the world, not more remote from it. Although he was sincerely devoted to Baba, rock was clearly his religion. "I can talk for hours about

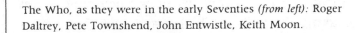

The Who, as they were in the early Seventies *(from left):* Roger Daltrey, Pete Townshend, John Entwistle, Keith Moon.

Moon might have chosen to go full tilt into a mod version of hot-rod songs, and Townshend might have wanted to make religious music. But the Who had motives of its own. ''We're not a four-piece band,'' Roger said later. ''We're a four-million-piece band.'' So they were shaped by expectations as much as will, though once again it's beyond anyone's reckoning where one begins and the other leaves off.

The Who's masterstroke and downfall turned out to be the rock opera: not mini- but full-blown. Once the idea had been introduced, there was mounting pressure to carry it through. But since the band also had—in the form of Daltrey and Moon—a built-in mistrust of rock's arty pretensions (and since the focus of the band's drawing power was its sheer power and *lack* of pretense), Townshend, who had to write the damn thing, was trapped.

Tommy, the rock opera that was finally completed in 1969, veered between crackpot genius and plain farce, spiritual message and ludicrous conceit. Its best song was about pinball, its most moving passage a guru's acknowledgment that all power emanated from the mob; its story line was skimpy, muddled, silly; a lot of the songs were forced and forgettable. And its most profound moments sounded like the Who at its simplest. ''We joked as a group about *Tommy* being true opera,'' Townshend wrote in 1977. ''Which it isn't, but the Who's audience and many of the rock press took it very seriously indeed. It was this seriousness that turned *Tommy* into light entertainment.''

But it was light entertainment that turned the Who into famous pop stars. As great as *Tommy* was as a live performance piece for the band, it mushroomed the audience into a confused mass—some might not have known (or cared) whether the band or the opera was the one named Tommy.

Like rock when it became something of which schoolteachers and clergymen could approve, like mod when it became a matter of people with the wrong attitude buying the right gear, the Who was faced with a situation that contradicted its essence, a problem exacerbated by the fact that the essence had always been so jealously guarded. A big part of the Who's glory was its anger, its hostility, and a big

Meher Baba the God Man who describes creation,'' he said in 1978. ''But ultimately, I realize that I see it all through these two little slits labeled R&R.'' Rock itself became his ideal, the band the ideal unit of community but also a battleground. Daltrey might have preferred simply to have a good time, Entwistle might have preferred more musical sophistication,

part of that came from the utter frustration of not breaking through to a bigger audience. Yet Townshend had never taken the easy way out—never written a ballad as impishly maudlin as the Stones' ''As Tears Go By,'' had always made it clear that he thought such compromises finally constituted the worst sort of betrayal. Yet in many ways *Tommy*, a project conceived in innocence and exhilaration, became an even worse betrayal.

The rest of the Who's career would be determined by the need to ''follow up'' *Tommy*, to create something either more grandiose, or so trivial that the ''opera'' could be forgotten. For anyone following them closely, the Who in the Seventies were a seesaw act: moments of embarrassment (the London Symphony Orchestra version of *Tommy*, Ken Russell's movie version, the Royal Canadian Ballet version, the synthesizer version and the brass-band version) alternating with the pure carnal triumphs of a band determined to wipe out the embarrassment of having created such a folderol in the first place.

Sometimes it seemed that only in artistic catastrophe could anything satisfactory be found. Townshend's initial follow-up concept, *Lifehouse*, was ruined by its own science-fiction plot: How to stage a concert in which everyone disappears? But the songs from *Lifehouse* formed the basis of the band's best LP, *Who's Next*. From that abortive project came

Onlookers stand in a pile of shoes and clothes left after crowds surged through the doors to Cincinnati's Riverfront Coliseum to get into a Who concert on December 3, 1979. Eleven fans died in the melee.

''Won't Get Fooled Again,'' ''Baba O'Riley,'' ''Goin' Mobile,'' ''Behind Blue Eyes,'' the finest recordings the Who had made and some of their most eloquent performance pieces.

Some believe that *Who's Next* was a last gasp. Aging hardly becomes those who have boasted about dying young while still in their teens, and the Who were singularly ill suited for maturity. (They'd only been fighting it since ''The Kids Are Alright.'') *Quadrophenia*, their next album, was an attempt to recapitulate the lost glories of mod, but moments are too fragile for that; somewhere between a story line even more scant than *Tommy*'s and a production style as intricate and sophisticated as it was difficult to listen to, the essence of whatever message this tale of ''double schizophrenia'' was supposed to convey got lost. And it was flawed as a record. *Quadrophenia* was pure disaster onstage.

By the end of 1975 Townshend and Daltrey, never exactly a mutual fan club, were feuding openly in the press. Worse, the Who was fumbling onstage, the one place where it had always reigned. The years and an absolutely amazing quantity of pills and booze had sapped Moon's strength; Townshend was ravaged by an undefined but clearly traumatizing personal crisis.

Even in this adversity, the music could prosper. *The Who by Numbers* is an album of fierce music and despondent songwriting that wavers between celebrations of rock as salvation and condemnations of everything that fame does to dehumanize performers and fans alike. It was as though Townshend had picked the scab off whatever wounds he harbored and rubbed the raw sores underneath into his listeners' faces: fascinating, but not exactly palatable.

By 1978, when *Who Are You* was released, the end of the line seemed near. Like *By Numbers*, that album was about aging, but where the former had been about quitting, giving up, packing it in, *Who Are You* was about reconciliation, something expressed as much by Entwistle's and Daltrey's dominant roles as by the songs themselves. Only a month after the album's release, in September 1978, Keith Moon was found dead in his London flat, dead of an overdose of an antialcoholism tablet—the final paradox of a great career.

The only surprising thing about Moon's demise was its privacy. Keith had always lived on the fringe of self-destruction, his rampages through European and American hotel rooms legendary. But somehow

The Who, 1979 *(from left)*: John Entwistle, Peter Townshend, Roger Daltrey, Kenney Jones.

his death was shattering in its effect. The Who were, after all, one of the few bands of the Sixties to have survived with their original membership intact. And Moon, for all his wild ways, might have been the most beloved person in rock; his outrages defined the lifestyle. It was almost inconceivable that he could be replaced.

Yet by Thanksgiving he had been, with Kenney Jones, formerly of the Small Faces, who shared the group's mod background and West London upbringing, but who was in every other way Keith's opposite.

Without Moon, the Who were certainly not the same band. Jones, who had been a stabilizing influence in the Faces, another band of anarchists, at first seemed to fit the group perfectly. But in the end, the absence of Moon's random rhythms turned the band as stodgy as its carefully curried repertoire. Freed of surprises, with Townshend eking out the few new songs he got 'round to writing, the band hobbled through a series of movies, tours and comebacks.

Some of this material was quite good. *The Kids Are Alright*, a 1979 film documentary history, staked the Who's claim as the very best live act rock has ever known, and its cutup mood very much paralleled the

best of the band's sense of humor. But the film and soundtrack LP *Quadrophenia*, although a massive British hit that inspired a mod revival, blundered into the self-righteous seriousness that began to reduce Townshend's songwriting to a series of impregnable autobiographical metaphors surrounded by stunted melody on albums like *Face Dances* (1981) and *It's Hard* (1982).

Tragedy continued to stalk the group. The worst of these came on the initial tour with Jones, when eleven fans were crushed to death in the rush for seats at a December 3rd, 1979, show at Riverfront Coliseum, in Cincinnati. The tragedy resulted from a combination of the heedless industry practice of so-called festival seating (general admission), hostile arena staffing and greedy customers literally willing to trample one another in the rush for good seats. What happened had very little to do with the Who. Yet what an absolute and colossal deflation of the spirit the early Who had engendered.

The band soldiered onward for a couple of years afterward, but their hearts clearly were elsewhere: Daltrey made movies; Entwistle horsed around with heavy metal; Townshend dabbled in becoming a dope fiend, risking his marriage and his life, took the cure, frittered away time on overambitious solo albums and reissue projects. The band was under pressure to continue—its Warner Bros. record contract had provided a $12 million advance contingent upon the band making three albums. But after their first "farewell tour" in 1982, there were no more studio records from the Who.

For a time it looked like the split was permanent. Though they reassembled for the Live Aid concert at Wembley in 1983, the split between Daltrey and Jones had overstepped the bounds of rancor. Townshend took a job as a book editor at Faber and Faber (T. S. Eliot's old house, which soon became the publisher of Eric Burdon's autobiography, among others). Entwistle went off to the States. The businessmen around the band urged them to reform, and Daltrey and Entwistle made no secret of their desire to cash in. But without Pete Townshend, there was no Who, and he remained reluctant.

Then in January 1989 Townshend was asked to come to New York to make a speech inducting the Rolling Stones into the Rock & Roll Hall of Fame. The speech was a masterpiece; Townshend, the original Stones fanatic, was hilarious, loving and sarcastic by turns, much like his best songs—he hadn't

Daltrey and Townshend on the Who's 1989 reunion tour: talkin' 'bout their (aging) g-g-g-generation.

created anything so fine in many years. But he got something more out of it: a sense of being connected to an endless stream of music, in which an ancient gospel group like the Soul Stirrers fitted to the Stones, and the Stones to the rock & roll future. He came back home and told his band mates he was ready for a reunion tour.

In the summer of 1989 the Who's tour was the biggest music news in America. Kenney Jones was no more; he'd been replaced by Simon Phillips, a London sessionman and relative youngster, whose playing was more precise and predictable than Moon's, more powerful than Jones's. They'd added a horn section and a second guitarist (ostensibly to compensate for Townshend's painful hearing loss) and opened up their repertoire to include solo material, songs by outsiders and songs like ''Odorono'' and ''Mary Anne with the Shaky Hand'' that they hadn't performed in the better part of twenty years. They sold out stadiums all over America, playing mostly to the kids in the crowd, but offering light entertainment to all ages. They even did a couple of live broadcasts, small-venue charity concerts featuring *Tommy*. And from song to song, they played with spunk and fire. As pointless reunion exercises went, this was the best ever. The Who was no longer the voice of a generation but its echo, grown faint yet not altogether lacking in glory.

DISCOGRAPHY

AMERICAN SINGLES

"I Can't Explain" (Decca; ☆93, 1965). "My Generation" (Decca; ☆74, 1966). "Happy Jack" (Decca; ☆24, 1967). "Pictures of Lily" (Decca; ☆51, 1967). "I Can See for Miles" (Decca; ☆9, 1967). "Call Me Lightning" (Decca; ☆40, 1968). "Magic Bus" (Decca; ☆25, 1968). "Pinball Wizard" (Decca; ☆19, 1969). "I'm Free" (Decca; ☆37, 1969). "The Seeker" (Decca; ☆44, 1970). "Summertime Blues" (Decca; ☆27, 1970). "See Me, Feel Me" (Decca; ☆12, 1970). "Won't Get Fooled Again" (Decca; ☆15, 1971). "Behind Blue Eyes" (Decca; ☆34, 1971). "Join Together" (Decca; ☆17, 1972). "The Relay" (Track; ☆39, 1972). "Love Reign o'er Me" (MCA; ☆76, 1973). "The Real Me" (MCA; ☆92, 1974). "Squeeze Box" (MCA; ☆17, 1975). "Who Are You?" (MCA; ☆14, 1978). "Long Live Rock" (MCA; ☆54, 1979). "5:15" (Polydor; ☆45, 1979). "You Better You Bet" (Warner Bros.; ☆18, 1981). "Don't Let Go the Coat" (Warner Bros.; ☆84, 1981). "Athena" (Warner Bros.; ☆28, 1982).

AMERICAN ALBUMS

The Who Sings My Generation (Decca; 1966). *Happy Jack* (Decca; ☆67, 1967). *The Who Sell Out* (Decca; ☆48, 1968). *Magic Bus—The Who on Tour* (Decca; ☆39, 1968). *Tommy* (Decca; ☆4, 1969). *Live at Leeds* (Decca; ☆4, 1970). *Who's Next* (Decca; ☆4, 1971). *Meaty Beaty Big and Bouncy* (Decca; ☆11, 1971). *Quadrophenia* (MCA; ☆2, 1973). *Odds and Sods* (MCA; ☆15, 1974). *The Who by Numbers* (MCA; ☆8, 1975). *Who Are You?* (MCA; ☆2, 1978). *The Kids Are Alright (Soundtrack)* (MCA; ☆8, 1979). *Quadrophenia (Soundtrack)* (Polydor; ☆46, 1979). *Face Dances* (Warner Bros.; ☆4, 1981). *Hooligans* (MCA; ☆52, 1981). *It's Hard* (Warner Bros.; ☆8, 1982). *Who's Greatest Hits* (MCA; ☆94, 1983). *Who's Last* (MCA; ☆81, 1984). *Join Together* (MCA; ☆188, 1990).

(Chart positions compiled from Joel Whitburn's *Record Research*, based on *Billboard*'s Pop and LPs charts.)

ERIC CLAPTON

BY DAVE MARSH

Eric Clapton was the focal point of the cult that formed around the electric guitar and guitarists during the Sixties. Until the advent of Jimi Hendrix, Clapton was the unchallenged master of white rock-blues guitar playing. CLAPTON IS GOD, read the graffiti in London; plenty of aspiring guitarists believed it.

The classic Clapton pose—back to the crowd, head bowed over his instrument, alone with the agony of the blues—suggested a supplicant communing with something inward and elevated: a muse or a demon. As few white men have, Clapton understood the impulses behind the blues, even if he could not always express them. In a way, his entire career can be seen as a search for a form in which he could express the staple blues emotions—fear, loneliness, anger and humor—in a personally valid way. It was a prototypically Sixties search, and the measure of Clapton's accomplishment is that where so many others became sidetracked, or fell short, Clapton finally attained his goal.

In retrospect, there is little in Clapton's early recordings to substantiate claims of genius—less on

the Yardbirds cuts (where he played Chuck Berry riffs with only as much skill as Keith Richards) than on the tracks with John Mayall's Bluesbreakers. With the Bluesbreakers, by playing songs by Chicago and Delta bluesmen like Otis Rush, Robert Johnson and Freddie King, Clapton at least opened up a new world of music to the rock crowd. It was Mayall's evangelizing and Clapton's playing that laid the groundwork for the white blues ''revivals'' of 1965 through 1968 in both Britain and America.

Like Mike Bloomfield, who was doing similar work at the same time with Paul Butterfield's band in the States, Clapton did more than merely imitate the Chicago bluesmen. He sped up their licks, indulging in flashy instrumental showmanship that helped make the form appealing to white rockers. But such music, as represented on the first Bluesbreakers LP and on the random tracks he cut with Jimmy Page between his stint with Mayall and the

---

Eric Clapton: He's got a right to play the blues.

Cream, the first "power trio," in the days when "Sunshine of Your Love" was a Top Ten hit *(from left):* Ginger Baker, Eric Clapton, Jack Bruce.

■

formation of Cream, never offered Clapton the chance to fully express himself. He remained an English kid trying to connect with the emotions of older black Americans.

In Cream, the band he formed in 1966 with bassist Jack Bruce and drummer Ginger Baker, Clapton did find a more personal style, but it wasn't lasting. Cream created the fastest, loudest, most overpowering blues-based rock ever heard, particularly on-stage, which is where the group acquired its reputation. But the emphasis was on quantity at the expense of quality. Epic solos were the order of the day, often extended far beyond the bounds of discipline or taste. While the group spawned a seemingly infinite flock of imitators—boogie bands, power trios, heavy-metal groups—it is only as an influence that most of Cream's music, so widely hailed at the time, will last. It was a good show, but it wasn't great music (although Cream did do some fine pop numbers in the studio).

After Cream broke up in 1968, Clapton and Baker quickly regrouped, joining forces with Steve Winwood of Traffic and Rick Grech of Family to form Blind Faith, the first overt attempt to manufacture a "supergroup." Although the group had been elaborately hyped, its first tour did not sell out, and by late 1969 the band was finished.

But while on the Blind Faith tour, Clapton had become involved with the opening act, Delaney and Bonnie and Friends, and when his band folded, he joined up for a tour. Once more a sideman, as he had

not been since the Bluesbreakers, he was able to relax into their easy mix of country, blues, rock and white gospel music. After that, Delaney Bramlett and many of the group's sidemen joined him for his first solo LP, where for the first time he took complete charge of singing and also made his initial attempts as a songwriter. The record was a mixed success: Only J. J. Cale's lachrymose "After Midnight" and a pair of collaborations, "Blues Power" (by Clapton and Leon Russell) and "Let It Rain" (which he wrote with Bonnie Bramlett), stood out.

Clapton then formed his first full-fledged group, Derek and the Dominos, made up of several Delaney and Bonnie alumni, and with the band's first album he finally found his own blues. Obviously it has not been a simple process.

For one thing, during the Blind Faith tour Clapton was converted to Christianity, an odd choice when most of his musical peers were opting for Eastern religions as a means of solace against the terrors and rigors of an intensely public life. But like artists as diverse as Tennessee Williams, T. S. Eliot, Little Richard and Jerry Lee Lewis, Clapton found something inspiring in Christian philosophy that simply wasn't available elsewhere. It was undoubtedly a tradition comfortable to Clapton; but he may also have relished the irony of placing God against what had been labeled "devil's music," first in the black community (the blues) and later in the white (rock). Clapton had always had a slightly mystical quality; you can see him nearly as a changeling on the cover of Atlantic's *History of Eric Clapton,* where no two photos show him with the same dress or hairstyle.

The association with devil's music might have cut deeper, because Clapton had long been thoroughly involved with the legend of Robert Johnson, the greatest pre-electric bluesman. Johnson, it was said, had left his Mississippi hometown an incompetent guitarist and returned (from no one knew where) a year later with the enormous talent that distinguishes the handful of recordings he made before his early death in 1938. Much of Johnson's career parallels Clapton's. Between Mayall and the formation of Cream, Clapton is said to have locked himself in a room for a year with only his guitar. There he began to develop his own style. It was also well known that he hardly expected to live until he was thirty; in fact, some said he looked forward to dying young.

But Clapton lost his faith before Derek and the

Dominos recorded their first and only studio album, *Layla*. He had become infatuated with Pattie Harrison, wife of his good friend, George, of the Beatles. When Pattie elected to return to her husband, Clapton was crushed. He deserted religion and began shooting heroin.

The disappointment fueled his next record. The passion is present in standard twelve-bar blues like "Have You Ever Loved a Woman," "Nobody Knows You When You're Down and Out" and "Key to the Highway"; in classic rock & roll like Chuck Willis's "It's Too Late"; in originals like "Bell Bottom Blues"; and it is majestically apparent in a brief, intense reading of "Little Wing," Jimi Hendrix's simplest, most poetic song. But it smashes home most forcefully with "Layla," perhaps the most powerful and beautiful song of the Seventies.

There are few moments in the repertoire of recorded rock where a singer or writer has reached so deeply into himself that the effect of hearing them is akin to witnessing a murder, or a suicide: "Like a Rolling Stone" by Bob Dylan, "Reach Out, I'll Be There" by the Four Tops, "Love Child" by the Su-

Derek and the Dominos *(from left):* Jim Gordon, Carl Radle, Bobby Whitlock, Clapton.

premes, "You've Lost That Lovin' Feeling" by the Righteous Brothers, *Tonight's the Night* by Neil Young, the first Plastic Ono Band album by John Lennon, "Running Scared" by Roy Orbison, "Darkness on the Edge of Town" by Bruce Springsteen—all are sung and played as though lives depended on them. To me, "Layla" is the greatest of them all.

It emerges, seven minutes of agony, from an album that is the most assured Clapton has ever made. For three sides the mood has been tranquil. "Little Wing," the breathtaking number that perches at the beginning of that final side, offers a hint of the pain in store, but its effect is soaring, transcendent—we have to imagine the hurt. "Layla," by contrast, opens suddenly, the guitars trumpeting the theme, and then the maelstrom begins. At first, the words seem total gibberish; all that's clear is the awfulness of it all, undiminished on the hundredth hearing:

> *Let's make the best of the situation*
> *Before I finally go insane*
> *Please don't say we'll never find a way*
> *Or tell me all my love's in vain*

There is a certain irony, I suppose, in Clapton's quotation of Robert Johnson ("Love in Vain") in his darkest hour. But that quote is also fitting in the most direct sense, for with "Layla" Clapton composed his own perfect blues without resorting to the traditional blues form. It's an epiphany few white men have experienced; only Van Morrison's *Astral Weeks* and *Saint Dominic's Preview* seem so rooted in the blues experience while eschewing the traditional

With a mystical aura and magical chops, Eric Clapton presided over the first cult of the electric guitar.

twelve-bar blues form. For that reason alone, the song's greatness and its importance to rock history and Clapton's career would be unquestioned. The unguent piano and slide guitar break that follows the final verse only makes what has come before seem all the more intense.

Even such a song could not clear the blood from the floor, but in the first four minutes of "Layla," Eric Clapton nevertheless fulfilled the intention of his first decade of music. He had finally felt the music as deeply as anyone, matched Robert Johnson blow for blow, sorrow for sorrow, stride for stride. Having done so, he dropped from sight for three years.

From the last part of 1971 through 1972, Clapton remained in virtual isolation. In January 1973 Pete Townshend of the Who arranged a London solo concert for him at the Rainbow Theatre. Ostensibly, Clapton was still recovering from his addiction, but there was also a musical question: Where do you go from "Layla"?

Eric in 1974, when he emerged from seclusion with an album of serene religiosity, *461 Ocean Boulevard.*

Clapton answered the question, or began to, in July 1974 with an album called *461 Ocean Boulevard,* a full-scale tour featuring a band that was as good as it was unheralded, and a Rolling Stone interview in which he told his story: about drugs, "Layla," the conversion to Christianity, his affair with Pattie Harrison (whom he eventually won back; they were married in 1979, although the marriage was not to last). But in light of *461,* Clapton's most crucial comment was "I still pray."

Unlike Pete Townshend, John McLaughlin or George Harrison, Clapton hasn't been thought of as a spiritual artist; it has been easy to miss the religious implications of his work. But they were all

Clapton on tour, 1974.

over *461,* in the easy feeling of the music and in the lyrics. The song titles told the story: "Please Be with Me," "I Can't Hold Out," "Let It Grow," "Give Me Strength." Clapton was obviously much more supplicant than missionary, another factor that differentiated him from other religiously oriented rock stars. In its way, Christianity influenced *461 Ocean Boulevard* as deeply as Judaism shaped Bob Dylan's *John Wesley Harding.* The tension of the blues was still present, but it was accepted and channeled more calmly. Not that Clapton had entirely succumbed to conventional Christian mores: The album's hit single was "I Shot the Sheriff," Bob Marley's outlaw-reggae anthem. Even the sexuality of the lyrics had a dark undertone. But then, once possessed of the gloomy spirit of Robert Johnson, it's unlikely that anyone could shake it entirely.

Still, one has to wonder about Clapton's more recent work. After 1978's "Lay Down Sally," he seemed to locate a strategy for making effortless hit singles, a kind of laid-back but still vaguely bluesy romantic pop typified by the song "Wonderful Tonight." But in a decade he has come up with no song more memorable, and it's been nearly twice that long since he's come up with a cutting innovative rocker. His albums continue to sell in multimillion quantities, and, like his concerts, each shows some sliver of his talent; but they're works in miniature, without the colossal ambition that originally marked Clapton's music, avoiding the spiritual concerns the early days of his comeback proposed as an alternative to wallowing in the blues.

To radio listeners and record buyers of the late Eighties and early Nineties, Eric Clapton presented himself as a new breed of romantic crooner in exquisite Armani suits. Concert goers got a glimpse of the other Clapton, the disciple of Robert Johnson, the man with whom Muddy Waters played his last show. This Clapton distanced himself from blues power, content to crank out craftsmanlike pop hits invested with virtually no personal stamp.

Then, in the summer of 1991, Clapton's young son, Conor, died in a bizarre accident. Bereft, Clapton turned his gaze inward once more and came up with an extraordinarily touching ballad, "No Tears in Heaven," which depicted him as a supplicant outcast from glory, seeking favors from his son who had found a place amidst the angels. A soap opera conceit, it had no business being as effective as it was. But Clapton recorded it as plainly as could be imagined, and it became a Number One hit. This was less important, however, than the restoration of emotional power and commitment to one of rock's strongest voices. The cost was too high, obviously, but then it often is. As longtime Eric Clapton fans know, that fact can also be found among the messages of the blues.

DISCOGRAPHY

ALBUMS

Eric Clapton (Atco; ☆13, 1970). *History of Eric Clapton* (Atco; ☆6, 1972). *Eric Clapton at His Best* (Polydor; ☆87, 1972). *Clapton* (Polydor; ☆67, 1973). *Eric Clapton's Rainbow Concert* (RSO; ☆18, 1973). *461 Ocean Boulevard* (RSO; ☆1, 1974). *There's One in Every Crowd* (RSO; ☆21, 1975). *E.C. Was Here* (RSO; ☆20, 1975). *No Reason to Cry* (RSO; ☆15, 1976). *Eric Clapton* (RSO; ☆194; 1977). *Slowhand* (RSO; ☆2, 1977). *Backless* (RSO; ☆8, 1978). *Just One Night* (RSO; ☆2, 1980). *Another Ticket* (RSO; ☆7, 1981). *Time Pieces/The Best of Eric Clapton* (RSO; ☆101, 1982). *Money and Cigarettes* (Duck; ☆16, 1983). *August* (Duck; ☆37, 1986). *Crossroads* (Polygram; ☆34, 1988). *Journeyman* (Duck; ☆16, 1989). *The Layla Sessions—20th Anniversary Edition* (Polydor; ☆157, 1990). *24 Nights* (Duck; ☆38, 1991). *Rush* (Reprise; ☆24, 1992).

(Chart positions compiled from Joel Whitburn's *Record Research*, based on *Billboard*'s LPs chart.)

JIMI HENDRIX

BY JOHN MORTHLAND

In his day, Jimi Hendrix was frequently referred to by the flower generation as its "electric nigger"—"super-spade," to use another popular term of that distant era. It is a measure of just how far away that era is that at the time, these cruelly ironic appellations were considered complimentary, whereas now they clearly tell us more about those who used them than about him to whom they were applied.

Yes, Hendrix was perceived as the hippie era's king stud and golden calf, its maker of the mightiest dope music, its most outrageously and defiantly visible force. But though his music—even his most faddish stuff, somehow—still sounds resonant today, his image remains equally troubling. For Jimi Hendrix was truly a revolutionary musician—perhaps the only one, in the end, to come out of that whole mid-Sixties psychedelic explosion. Yet this has usually been obscured, both by the degrading image and by the freakishly flamboyant veneer that helped make his art so popular. Those paradoxes of his popularity eventually led Hendrix himself to fight many a lonely battle in front of thousands of admirers. Three years and three months after his triumphant performance at the Monterey Pop Festival, he was dead.

As a guitarist, Hendrix quite simply redefined the instrument, in the same way that Cecil Taylor redefined the piano or John Coltrane the tenor sax. As a songwriter, Hendrix was capable of startling, mystical imagery as well as the down-to-earth sexual allusions of the bluesman. He sang in a wispy voice that at first seemed limited, but proved remarkably effective at conveying nuance and emphasis.

Hendrix came on like gangbusters from the start. He made his American debut at the Monterey Pop Festival in June 1967; appearing in the last of five concerts, he came onstage shortly after the Who had drained the audience with its mod flash and maniacal destructiveness. But Hendrix revved that crowd right back up again. Backed by Englishmen Noel Redding on bass and Mitch Mitchell on drums, he played guitar with his teeth, he played guitar behind his back. He humped it and caressed it, and finally, to finish off his set, he burned it. He had played exhilarating music throughout, but when it was over, everyone buzzed about nothing but that *show;* it was dramatic, it was galvanizing, and though it had alienated a few, the night was obviously Jimi's.

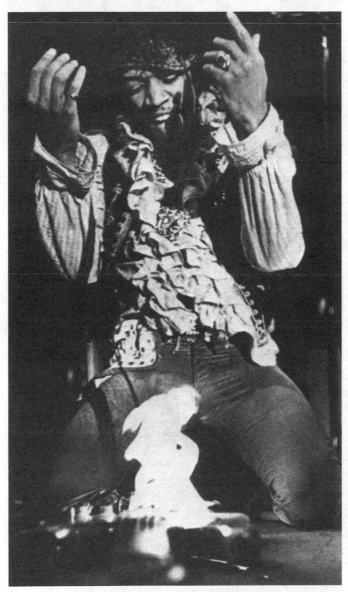

Maker of mighty dope music, Jimi Hendrix sacrifices his guitar at the Monterey Pop Festival—his shattering American debut in 1967.

Nobody was quite sure where he'd come from, but he had definitely arrived.

Actually, he'd come from Seattle, where he lived an apparently humdrum middle-class black life, listening to Eddie Cochran and blues, learning guitar at twelve, playing in local bands for Cokes and burgers, getting into occasional trouble for dating white girls and ultimately enlisting in the army (in 1959) at seventeen. By 1963 he was on the chitlin circuit as a backup guitarist, picking up work where he could

find it, with Little Richard, the Isley Brothers, Wilson Pickett, Jackie Wilson, King Curtis and others.

Doubtful about his singing voice, he didn't go out on his own until late 1965 or early 1966. He had heard Bob Dylan sing and reasoned that if Dylan could go that far with a lousy voice, so could he. His band was called Jimmy James and the Blue Flames, and they worked the Greenwich Village clubs. Blues bands were increasingly popular in the predominantly white Village club scene, and so Hendrix played mostly blues—a paradoxical situation for a black man trying to break into white music. But he was already beginning to experiment with feedback, fuzz tone and the like. He soon attracted the attention of John Hammond Jr., who hired Hendrix (still known as Jimmy James) as his guitarist. Other musicians began seeing a lot more of him.

"I was performing with Paul Butterfield, and I was the hot-shot guitarist on the block—I thought I was *it,*" Mike Bloomfield told *Guitar Player* maga-

Jimi with his first electric guitar, Seattle, 1957.

zine. "I went right across the street and saw him. Hendrix knew who I was, and that day, in front of my eyes, he burned me to death. I didn't even get my guitar out. H-bombs were going off, guided missiles were flying—I can't tell you the sounds he was getting out of his instrument. He was getting every sound I was ever to hear him get right there in that room with a Stratocaster, a Twin [amp], a Maestro fuzz tone, and that was all—he was doing it mainly through extreme volume. How he did this, I wish I understood. He just got right up in my face with that axe, and I didn't even want to pick up a guitar for the next year."

Bloomfield wasn't the only listener impressed with Hendrix. After the Animals' former bassist Chas Chandler heard him, he convinced Hendrix to move to England, where Chas promised to make him a star. Hendrix agreed; Chandler and his partner, Michael Jeffrey, told him to adopt his surname again and fixed him up with Redding and Mitchell, two British journeymen. The three frizzed their hair and dressed in the most outlandish clothes they could find. Working mainly with soul tunes Hendrix must have played a thousand times ("Land of 1000 Dances," "In the Midnight Hour"), and then with Hendrix originals and a few pop hits of the day ("Hey Joe," "Like a Rolling Stone"), the Jimi Hendrix Experience soon stunned England and then the Continent, setting the stage for their Monterey appearance.

Immediately after that triumph Hendrix set out to conquer America as the second-billed act to the Monkees, a tour that must have been conceived in a lunatic asylum; the Experience played to deaf teenybop ears for a few dates before Jimi's management bailed him out by announcing (falsely) that he'd been banned by the Daughters of the American Revolution. It hardly mattered, because Hendrix had already accomplished his purpose via the release of the "Purple Haze" single and *Are You Experienced?*, his first album.

The single, with its fuzzed garage-band guitar intro, was perfect for that spacey summer of '67: "Scuze me," Jimi demanded, "while I kiss the sky." The album was equally impressive; on it, Hendrix displayed almost the full breadth of his talents. Although his second album (*Axis: Bold as Love*) added a new twist by taking its inspiration from black vocal groups of the Fifties, and the third (*Electric Ladyland*) marked his mastery of the recording studio as addi-

Hendrix assaults a bank of amplifiers. Pandemonium at the Royal Albert Hall, London.

tional instrument, that first album had so much going for it that Hendrix never really surprised anyone with anything he did subsequently.

Are You Experienced? had a multilayered sound, thanks to Mitchell's Elvin Jones–like drumming and Jimi's own arranging skills and awesome mastery of the electric guitar. "Manic Depression" revealed his gift for the crushing riff, while "Hey Joe" and "May This Be Love" demonstrated how to make a guitar line lilt even at an unspeakably high volume. "I Don't Live Today" was propelled by relentless rhythm. "The Wind Cries Mary" had delicate lyrics that verged on poetry—as did the later "Little Wing," to name but one. "Third Stone from the Sun," a lesson in so-called psychedelic guitar, was a *tour de force* in its use of feedback and electronic effects. (Groups like the Who and the Yardbirds were already using such techniques, but Hendrix's special gift was his ability to *harness* these distortions; before him—and usually after him, for that matter—it was primarily a game of chance.)

The debut album presented some staggering stuff, although it is not true that he never moved beyond it, as some critics have claimed. It barely hints at Hendrix's approach to the blues, though in concert at this time he would cool out a steaming audience by picking for fifteen minutes on the B. B. King–styled "Red House." While most of his early music was in white forms, "Spanish Castle Magic" (from *Axis*) had an unmistakable blues feeling, and "Voodoo Chile" (from *Ladyland*) was nothing if not galactic Muddy Waters. Late in his career, his music became increasingly black; it remained unique.

Both of his next two albums had a little filler (but not much), and while the others released in his lifetime were even more erratic, the high points represented striking advances. The same was true of his live performances; he had off nights, for certain, and sometimes he shucked out of contempt for the audience. But many of his problems were the result of an impossibly long reach that exceeded even his grasp.

So how did he do all this? "There's very little I hear on his studio records that he couldn't do in person, that I didn't see him do at one time or another, right before my eyes," Bloomfield has said. Yet few others have been able to duplicate his sounds live *or* in the studio, and Hendrix used gimmicks sparingly; most of the explosions and other sound effects were arrived at through ingenuity and experimentation.

Though left-handed, he used right-hand-model guitars and played them upside down. For distortion, he relied almost entirely on a Fuzz Face, a Univibe (to simulate a rotating speaker) and the wah-wah pedal. Most of the sound effects came from modulating the volume and either manipulating the guitar's toggle switch or stretching the tremolo (or "whammy") bar of his axe. He could induce feedback on a couple of guitar strings while playing lead on the others, which is how he got the effect of two guitarists playing at once. But beyond these tricks, nobody really knows how he worked his magic—not the equipment managers who looked after his tools, not his fellow guitarists, not the musicians he jammed with.

Ironically, no one was less impressed with his skills than Hendrix himself. He was continually frustrated, speaking often in interviews of sounds he heard in his head that he couldn't yet play. Moreover, he developed strong doubts about his image; though at first he was perfectly willing to exploit that image, Hendrix considered himself a musician first and foremost, an entertainer second. Once he realized he couldn't have it both ways, he came to resent his audience's view of him as a freak. When he saw he could wow a crowd simply with showmanship, he turned on the flash and coasted musically; when he sensed he had to play well to win a crowd, he stood calmly and played hard. He was also an inveterate jammer, hitting clubs in New York whenever he could to sit in with whoever was there. (Using some of those same musicians, he improvised several of the songs on *Electric Ladyland,* one of the few instances his studio music wasn't meticulously worked out.) He preferred jamming, where musical ideas flowed freely, to working before an audience.

A gentleman at ease, London, 1966.

By the beginning of 1969 his ambivalence toward his popularity was assuming darker overtones. Though his shy, withdrawn offstage manner had always contrasted sharply with his marauding performances, he now began to retreat further into himself. By now those first three albums were all gold, but he seemed at a loss as to what to do next. He disbanded the Experience. In May he was arrested at Toronto International Airport and charged with possession of heroin; many of his fans simply assumed the charge was true, so great was his reputation for drug use. Yet he was found innocent at the end of the year, when he argued convincingly that he had been given the dope by a fan and hadn't checked to see what it was before popping it into his suitcase. He also admitted that he'd once used a few drugs but claimed to have stopped.

That summer Hendrix hid out in upstate New York. He gathered a group of musicians ranging from old bluesmen to avant-garde classical composers and dubbed them his ''electric family'' or ''electric sky church.'' He wanted to work as an integral part of a group of musical peers, he explained, and promised big things. Part of this assemblage appears with him on the Woodstock album for his titanic version of ''The Star-Spangled Banner'' and the bittersweet instrumental romp that closed his set.

Whatever intentions Hendrix had for his experimental group, it was hardly conceived as a money maker. He was said to be under pressure from his manager (by now just Jeffrey) to stick with tried-and-true commercial forms. He seemed torn between the two options. He was also said to be under pressure from black militants seeking to interest him in political causes. While Hendrix insisted he wanted no part in politics and claimed to be color-blind in his personal relations, he was clearly caught in yet another situation where he wanted to please everybody, and was willing to stretch himself to do so.

Under pressure from several directions, his solution was to play music similar in conception to that of the Experience, but to play it with more of a black accent. This seemed to be the idea behind the Band of Gypsys, a trio that included black bassist Billy Cox, an old army buddy who'd spent the summer with Hendrix upstate, and black drummer Buddy Miles, who had previously worked the soul circuit with black bands and then the rock circuit with the Electric Flag and his own groups. Hendrix played a few Harlem joints in late 1969, the first time he ever did so as a leader.

On New Year's Eve the Band of Gypsys appeared at the Fillmore East. They got a mixed reception and, on the evidence of the live album *Band of Gypsys*, played a mixed set. As with the electric sky church, there's not enough recorded evidence to draw definite conclusions, but there's every reason to believe that under less harried circumstances, this band could have been everything Hendrix wanted, earthy and spacey, mixing pop novelty with rhythm & blues sleekness. But the group broke up within months. One of Hendrix's bleakest moments came in early 1970, when he simply stopped playing in the middle of a set at a Madison Square Garden peace benefit. He slinked offstage, seemingly lost in his own world.

Within weeks he was back with the original Experience; several more weeks passed, and then that was off, too. Playing most of his dates with Mitchell and Cox, Hendrix left the impression that he was still trying to decide what to play and how to play it.

Electric Ladyland, his new studio, was completed in New York City. True to form, Hendrix spent most of his time there, working on his next album or just playing with friends. In August the studio opened, and Hendrix took off for Europe, where he played the Isle of Wight Festival and toured the Continent. His insecurities still plagued him; he was afraid the Europeans had forgotten about him, since he had spent most of the last two years in the States.

He died in his sleep September 18th, 1970, in London, from inhalation of vomit following barbiturate intoxication. He had gone to sleep at the flat of a girlfriend who woke up, saw vomit in the corners of his mouth and called the ambulance. Though she claimed that Jimi was alive when the ambulance arrived, he was dead on arrival at the hospital. Suicide was often suggested, but carelessness was more likely the cause. The coroner declared an open verdict: There wasn't enough evidence to support a verdict either of suicide or of accidental death.

There was no telling his state of mind. Some friends and associates claimed he had recently gotten all his artistic and business priorities straightened out in his own mind and was ready to put his

Onstage near the end.

affairs in order on both accounts. But others insisted he had been even more despondent than usual about these very same things.

This was, sadly, typical. Perhaps Jimi's biggest weakness was his inability to say no to anybody—to his fans, to his business advisors, to his peers, to political activists. As a result, he had hundreds of acquaintances but very few close friends. In Chris Welch's book, *Hendrix,* several people—musicians, girlfriends, reporters—all state that few knew Jimi well, but that he or she (the person being interviewed) probably knew him as well as anyone. Then they proceed to directly contradict one another about Jimi's drug habits, his sexual appetite, his feelings about blackness, his attitude toward his managers. Nobody without a vested interest seems able to speak authoritatively about Hendrix, and so his death has only deepened the mystery and confusion, only reinforced his image as a freak genius.

Numerous albums have been released posthumously. They are spotty, as though the person programming them couldn't tell a finished cut from a joke or a failed experiment. In 1974 producer Alan Douglas, who had worked sporadically with Hendrix, claimed he would right this wrong and see that inferior posthumous material was withdrawn from the market. Douglas went through miles of tapes and compiled a series of new albums; he overdubbed new instrumental tracks, arguing that what Hendrix himself would have added was implicit in the way Jimi played his parts. Despite this dubious assertion, Douglas's immediate efforts improved the Hendrix legacy a little—until he, too, succumbed to the more-is-better mentality of his predecessors. Subsequent releases prove two things. One, Hendrix recorded compulsively, using the studio for jams and to develop songs or musical ideas step by step. Two, Hendrix was always his own best critic and knew better than anyone what was worthy of release. To this day his legacy, based on what's in the marketplace, is ravaged by the conflict between profit and art, the demands of the fan and the priorities of the performer-artist, the image and the reality.

His influence on succeeding generations has been obvious, though not as pervasive as one might expect given his status while he was alive. Frank Marino (of Mahogany Rush) and Robin Trower claimed to carry on in Jimi's honor while aping him shamelessly. Five years after Jimi's death, jazz

Jimi Hendrix is buried on October 1, 1970. From the Jimi Hendrix Experience: Mitch Mitchell *(far right)* and Noel Redding *(second from right).*

bandleader Gil Evans released an album of Hendrix music that was overly formal and short on fire but an intriguing experiment just the same. Heavy-metal bands—with their emphasis on volume, monolithic riffs, and drone and feedback—owe something to Hendrix, but few have shown even a small fraction of his finesse or imagination. The ghost of Hendrix hovered over some of Patti Smith's work, though not nearly so much as she wanted people to believe.

Guitarists Ernie Isley (of the Isley Brothers) and Michael Hampton and Eddie Hazel (of the Parliament-Funkadelic axis) successfully incorporated some of Jimi's aesthetic into the overall framework of their respective groups. By the late Eighties the Black Rock Coalition, founded by the band Living Colour and deeply indebted to Hendrix, was gaining ground in the increasingly racist pop charts; indeed, it's easy to argue that every self-contained black group with crossover dreams that has climbed onto a stage in the two-plus decades since his death is traveling down a musical and social trail blazed by Hendrix. But as the years go by, it also becomes increasingly apparent that Hendrix created a branch on the pop tree that nobody else has ventured too far out on. None has actually extended the directions he pursued, but perhaps that is because he took them, in his painfully short time on earth, as far as they could go.

DISCOGRAPHY

ALBUMS

Are You Experienced? (Reprise; ☆5, 1967). *Axis: Bold as Love* (Reprise; ☆3, 1968). *Electric Ladyland* (Reprise; ☆1, 1968). *Smash Hits* (Reprise; ☆6, 1969). *Hendrix Band of Gypsys* (Capitol; ☆5, 1970). *The Cry of Love* (Reprise; ☆3, 1971). *Rainbow Bridge* (Reprise; ☆15, 1971). *Hendrix in the West* (Reprise; ☆12, 1972). *Jimi Hendrix: War Heroes* (Reprise; ☆48, 1972). *Soundtrack Recordings from the Film ''Jimi Hendrix''* (Reprise; ☆89, 1973). *Crash Landing* (Reprise; ☆5, 1975). *Midnight Lightning* (Reprise; ☆43, 1975). *The Essential Jimi Hendrix* (Reprise; ☆114, 1978). *The Essential Jimi Hendrix, Volume Two* (Reprise; ☆156, 1979). *Nine to the Universe* (Reprise; ☆127, 1980). *The Jimi Hendrix Concerts* (Reprise; ☆79, 1982). *Kiss the Sky* (Reprise; ☆148, 1984). *Jimi Plays Monterey* (Reprise; ☆192, 1986). *Radio One* (Rykodisc; ☆119, 1988).

(Chart positions compiled from Joel Whitburn's *Record Research,* based on *Billboard*'s LPs chart.)

BRITAIN: THE SECOND WAVE

BY KEN EMERSON

n the latter half of the Sixties the English pop scene rang with change. The Beatles and their British brethren had propelled rock into its second decade, and still more innovation was in the air. America was answering in kind: 1966 saw the release of the Byrds' "Eight Miles High" and the Beach Boys' "Good Vibrations," two of the most sophisticated and complex singles ever to have adorned Top Forty playlists. Rock became "progressive" (whereas before it simply had been fun), and its possibilities never seemed headier than in 1967, when a dazzling number of new vistas were opened by the Beatles' *Sgt. Pepper's Lonely Hearts Club Band*, the Blues Project's *Projections*, Jefferson Airplane's *Surrealistic Pillow* and the first albums by the Doors, Cream and the Jimi Hendrix Experience.

With the new music arose a new press (*Crawdaddy*, ROLLING STONE, *Fusion*), and rock criticism, which in the days of "Fun, Fun, Fun" and "She Loves You" would have seemed superfluous, was born. Now *16* magazine, with its dream dates and the stars' favorite colors, was no longer enough.

For the first time in rock's brief history, its audience was crucially divided by age. The new British rock reflected these divisions, ranging from Beatlesish pop to progressive psychedelia. Even as the Who sang "My Generation," the English market was fragmenting into listeners who had cut their teeth on Cliff Richard, those whom the Beatles had initiated and younger fans to whom Lennon and McCartney seemed old enough to be their fathers. "When I'm Sixty-four" indeed!

The Move *(from left):* Roy Wood, Rick Price, Jeff Lynne, Bev Bevan. Lynne later founded the Electric Light Orchestra.

The Nice. This monosyllabically named band romped through jazzy versions of the classics before splitting up; organist Keith Emerson *(right)* became one third of Emerson, Lake and Palmer.

Into the breach stepped the Bee Gees, still in their teens and, like their counterparts in America, the Monkees, sounding very much like the earlier Beatles. "I'm going to buy myself a time machine/Go to the turn of the century," vowed the first song on their first album; the three brothers Gibb, who formed the heart of the group, wanted to turn back the clock. Born in England but raised in Australia, they borrowed unabashedly from the Beatles' harmonies and melodies, while their callow, trebly vocals and asexual sentimentality spoke to juveniles as the Beatles no longer deigned to. But the Bee Gees' ornate orchestrations, the tremulous strings and cotton-candy harp often sugarcoated queer pills.

There was something at once ghoulish and goofy about the Bee Gees' music in the Sixties and the

The Bee Gees, Aussies who began by imitating the Beatles and survived by playing disco for *Saturday Night Fever.*

choked, inconsolable quaver with which Robin Gibb sang much of it. In two hit singles, the singer or narrator was on the brink of death: by cave-in ("New York Mining Disaster 1941"), by execution ("I've Gotta Get a Message to You"). In many other songs he was trapped just as claustrophobically by his own romanticism in a nightmare of paranoia and solipsism ("Just me an' the mirror an' my brain"). In the Seventies, when Barry Gibb supplanted Robin as the predominant vocalist, the Bee Gees would borrow from black dance music as effectively as they had from the Beatles in the Sixties.

Other heirs of the early Beatles were the Hollies, cheerful rockers to the Bee Gees' lachrymose balladeers. Actually, the Hollies were contemporaries of the Beatles but came to their pop perfectionism relatively late, as the Beatles were abandoning the field. They were not creators (the best of their singles were written by others) so much as superlative craftsmen—so superlative that they rivaled the Beatles in Top Ten hits in England during the Sixties. Essentially the Hollies amplified the Everly Brothers' harmonies by adding third and fourth voices, achieving a rich, slightly metallic sound that glossed any material to scintillating effect. The group could turn anything to gold, out-Beatling the Beatles, breathing new and exhilarating life into old chestnuts and spinning marvelous story-songs. Masters of the single at a time when other bands were turning to albums, the Hollies, more than any other British group, celebrated rock as pure fun.

For this very reason Graham Nash left the band in 1968. He had been trying to push his mates in a hipper direction and gagged when they proposed an album paying tribute to Bob Dylan. Any group worth its love beads ought to perform its own material, he argued. It was a paradigmatic clash between the pop and progressive ethics; as the rock audience fragmented, so did the groups. Nash hied himself to California and fame and fortune as a member of Crosby, Stills, Nash and (sometimes) Young. The Hollies, undeterred (inasmuch as Allan Clarke had always been the most important of the vocalists), stood Dylan on his head with brilliant rearrangements that made no sense but produced ravishing music. The Hollies continued to make sparkling records for nearly another decade.

Two of the Hollies' biggest hits, "Look Through Any Window" (1965) and "Bus Stop" (1966), were written by Graham Gouldman, who also penned two

The Hollies flourished in the late Sixties with hits like "Bus Stop" and the psychedelic "King Midas in Reverse." More than any other British band of the era, they celebrated rock as pure fun.

The Yardbirds, just hanging out, in 1965.

Starting out as a blues band, the Yardbirds soon were playing ragas and Gregorian chants.

for the Yardbirds and later formed 10cc. While the Hollies drew from the Beatles, the Yardbirds followed the Rolling Stones, whom they succeeded as the house band at London's Crawdaddy Club. Their first success, Gouldman's "For Your Love" (1965), began with an ominously echoing harpsichord. Now, one of the characteristics of the harpsichord is that it sustains scarcely at all; the Yardbirds were subverting the very nature of the instrument. Moreover, they subverted everything else; turning pop into something sinister, the blues into the rudest noise, even disrupting melody with jerky tempo changes as Keith Relf sang with flat menace. They were so irreverent that their first guitarist, a young Eric Clapton, quickly departed in dismay. He was succeeded by Jeff Beck, a born despoiler whose sinuous, vaguely Oriental-sounding distortions were more in keeping with the group's snaky threat. The Yardbirds' manic adventurousness exemplified all that was "progressive." Their instrumental "rave-ups" anticipated the freak-outs of psychedelic San Francisco. They pioneered what would later be dubbed "heavy metal," and dabbled in everything from ersatz Gregorian chants to Mideastern reels.

One of the first rock superstars who owed his celebrity to his instrumental prowess, Beck was as volatile personally as he was on guitar. Leaving the Yardbirds in the hands of latecomer Jimmy Page, who revamped the band before launching Led Zeppelin, Beck recruited some estimable talent—Rod Stewart, Ron Wood, Nicky Hopkins—and tried to front a group of his own. But organization was not his forte: he couldn't keep them together, nor, since he was interested primarily in improvisatory effects, could he write cogent material. His thunder was soon stolen by the more cohesive Zeppelin, for whom the Jeff Beck Group's blues-based exaggerations served as a blueprint. Erratic ever after and performing only fitfully, Beck nonetheless went on to become one of the first and only rock guitarists to play convincing, biting jazz rock, or fusion.

The Yardbirds again—the edition with Jeff Beck *(third from left)* and Jimmy Page *(seated)*.

The Small Faces: in the late Sixties the hottest live act in England.

gles, epitomized the latter, with brutal riffs and Marriott's most electrifying shouts.

While Humble Pie enjoyed considerable success during the early Seventies as a hard-rocking and harder-touring boogie band, in Stewart and Wood the Faces (dropping the "Small") got the better part of the deal, at least initially. The hardest-*drinking* band in show business incarnated rock & roll—the good, the bad, the ugly *and* the exciting—onstage and occasionally on record, most thrillingly on

A fter two albums the original Jeff Beck Group split up, but Wood and Stewart didn't. Instead they joined up with members of the Small Faces, whose guitarist and lead singer, Steve Marriott, had quit to form Humble Pie with Peter Frampton. Steeped in the Stones and the Who (whose mod constituency embraced them), the Small Faces had started out playing inept rhythm & blues. Their first British Top Ten hit, "Sha La La La Lee" (1966), began with Pete Townshend chording, rocked out with a Keith Richards guitar lick and stole the bass line from Fontella Bass's "Rescue Me." Yet Marriott's freneticism onstage, even if he was merely a pip-squeak poseur (as a child actor he had played the Artful Dodger in the London stage musical *Oliver!*), conquered all. By 1967 the Small Faces had mastered not only their instruments but a style of their own, a novel mix of psychedelic whimsy and heavy-rock crunch. "Lazy Sunday" (1968), with a cosmic Cockney vocal, party noises, kazoos (quoting "[I Can't Get No] Satisfaction," no less), whistles, the roar of the ocean and the flushing of a toilet, was typical of the former, while "Tin Soldier" (1967), one of the late Sixties' overlooked great sin-

"Stay with Me," a hit in 1972. "You won't need too much persuadin'/I don't mean to sound degradin'/ But with a face like that you got nothin' to laugh about." The nasty gusto with which Stewart sang this come-on/put-down was so obnoxiously exaggerated it doubled as a comic commentary on Rod's—and rock's—sexism. While Stewart had his concupiscent cake and ate it, too, the Faces captured the bump and grind of attraction-revulsion between the sexes in a grating riff, and then relieved the tension in a rollicking, multiorgasmic series of fake endings. First Wood on guitar, then Ian McLagan on electric piano and finally Kenney Jones on drums spurted for a few solo bars in circle-jerk camaraderie, underscoring the point that groupies come and go, but boys will be boys forever.

So they may have wished, but the Faces broke up sooner rather than later because the success of Stewart's solo career was even greater than theirs, creating tensions no amount of jamming could dispel. Wood joined the Rolling Stones, Jones (eventually)

the Who, and Stewart moved to Hollywood, where he settled in with a succession of blond actresses and models. Capitalizing on every pop trend from disco (''Da Ya Think I'm Sexy?'' in 1979) to U2 (me-too: ''Forever Young,'' in 1989), Stewart has tallied hit singles ever since, but his credit rating among critics has plummeted.

Rod Stewart enjoying the good life. He later became a clear target for the rage of punks.

Randy rock star, sensitive singer-songwriter, eloquent interpreter of other people's material, folky traditionalist, reverent soul man . . . it was remarkable that Stewart could embrace so many roles at his peak in the early Seventies, switching in a second from Sam Cooke to Bob Dylan. And it was inevitable, perhaps, that the many balls he was juggling would eventually come clattering down. Stewart's first three, and greatest, solo albums—*The Rod Stewart Album* (1969), *Gasoline Alley* (1970) and *Every Picture Tells a Story* (1971)—achieved a uniquely homespun synthesis. Whereas the folk rock of the mid-Sixties had sought to translate folk music into rock music, Stewart used slide and acoustic guitars, mandolins and fiddles to turn rock into folk. (The closest parallel was transatlantic: the Band.) As reconceived by Stewart and recorded on the spur of the moment, even the Rolling Stones' ''Street Fighting Man'' became something of a hoedown.

But when Stewart began to record with sessionmen and subordinates instead of buddies, and to hire producers rather than simply let the reel roll, his music lost its spontaneous spirit of intimacy and interplay. The synthesis started sounding synthetic. You could always tell it was Rod, all right; that rasping voice will never be anonymous. But Stewart no longer placed his own stamp on music so much as he let it stamp him. ''Da Ya Think I'm Sexy?'' is a case in point. A year earlier, with ''Miss You,'' the Stones had tackled disco, roughed it up and rolled it into real Stones music; ''Sexy,'' on the other hand, was an outright disco imitation that teetered between flattery and parody. ''Now you ask me if I'm sincere,'' Stewart sang in ''I Was Only Joking.'' ''That's the question that I always fear.''

Stewart has never entirely lost this self-awareness, however, including the recognition that even integrity can be an act. (Maybe that's why he's always loved to play the tart, dying his hair, preening in polyester leopard skin and baring his tits.) Such psychological acuity made his early songs dramatic narratives, adventures in ambivalence. As drummer Mick Waller thwacked the crudest imaginable *one*-two, *one*-two on ''Maggie May'' (1971), Stewart showed that life wasn't that simple by striking at least a dozen attitudes—cruel, tender, restless, nostalgic—toward the woman he was not yet man enough to leave with an honest good-bye.

Even if he seldom sings his heart out anymore, Stewart can still sing his ass off. And nearly all his later solo albums contain a track or two that rings true dramatically and psychologically—where Stewart winks as if to acknowledge he knows not only that he's joking, but that the joke may be on him.

S teve Winwood is another hardy perennial who first bloomed during the mid- to late Sixties. He was Stevie then and started out with the Spencer Davis Group, which played R&B not unlike the Small Faces', but more tautly. The rather pallid Davis was quickly upstaged by Win-

Steve Winwood: back in the high life again.

wood and his uncanny imitations of Ray Charles and other soul singers. The band scored quickly with "Gimme Some Lovin'" (1966) and one of the most excited and exciting vocals ever recorded by a white man, let alone a white boy (Winwood, who also cowrote the number, was only seventeen). His yowl seemed to yank him out of his body, and the song was wrought up still higher by his wailing organ chords and brother Muff Winwood's hammering bass. Singer, songwriter, guitarist, organist and pianist, Winwood was a one-man show who had no need to share the billing with Davis, and soon he holed up with three friends in a Berkshire cottage where, in 1967, Traffic was spawned.

Like Graham Nash, Winwood had become hip,

and since he could play almost any instrument, from electric sitar to kitchen sink, it scarcely mattered that Chris Wood (saxophone and flute) and Jim Capaldi (drums) were mediocre musicians. Besides, there was Dave Mason, an adroit guitarist and songwriter in his own right, to lend a helping hand. Traffic's first album, *Mr. Fantasy* (1968), was cluttered with psychedelic gimmickry and performed rather raggedly, but its inspired eclecticism and Winwood's muffled vocals, which seemed to issue from a purple haze, created a novel, heady ambience. *Traffic* (1968) was a much more fully achieved album, partly because it was more firmly rooted in R&B and also because Mason was an equal contributor. The tension and balance the album struck between Mason's pop craftsmanship and Winwood's increasingly improvisatory urges made *Traffic* one of the decade's masterpieces.

Mason and Winwood promptly parted ways, however, and for a long while Winwood seemed to lose his. With Eric Clapton, Ginger Baker and Rick Grech he formed the "supergroup" Blind Faith. That brief experience's only memorable legacy was the high, lonesome falsetto of Winwood's haunting ballad "I Can't Find My Way Home." Traffic re-formed and disbanded several times with varying personnel but never matched its early material. Instead it became a vehicle for long, noodling jams—a little jazz is a dangerous thing—and Winwood became increasingly incapable of distinguishing a groove from a rut.

It wasn't until 1980, five years after Traffic's last album, that Winwood really hit his stride again with *Arc of a Diver*. Now he was a one-man band for real: writing, performing and producing all the music, much of it on various synthesizers. Winwood didn't just master the synthesizer, he humanized it, using its electronic palette to create bright daubs and colorful swirls of sound. And, working entirely on his own, Winwood overcame his self-indulgence, rediscovering the joy and discipline of melody. Even today *Arc* exudes upbeat exuberance, a rapturous feeling of recovery.

After another purely solo album, Winwood resumed working with other musicians (and an outside producer, Russ Titelman) and, with the release of *Back in the High Life* in 1986, became a superstar for the second time in his lengthening career. "Higher Love," his first Number One single in the United States, deployed an arsenal of players and programmers in a dazzling arrangement, full of dancing twists and darting turns, that by ingenious increments ratcheted up the tempo and intensity literally higher and higher.

It's regrettable, however, that after Winwood regained his prodigious musical powers—and indeed added new ones—he seemed to have so little left to say, at least in words. He has depended entirely on lyricists, primarily Will Jennings, for bland, humorless paeans of spiritual uplift. "We're all skating on the thinnest of ice/ . . . In a world that is not so very nice" is about as pungent as Jennings gets, and the fervor of Winwood's vocals is squandered on such tepid sentiments.

Winwood's flirtation with psychedelia was short lived; for Syd Barrett, it was a fatal attraction. The leader of Pink Floyd, Barrett drifted off in a daze not long after the group's first album, *Pink Floyd* (a.k.a. *The Piper at the Gates of Dawn*), was released in 1967. Inspired by the reports of happenings in San Francisco, the Floyd were the first Brits to stage a light show. They jumbled fairy tales and evocations of outer space as Richard Wright exhumed organ chords from the crypt and Barrett ground out grating guitar lines or reverbed into the ozone amid boggling special effects. Barrett may have been crazy, but he was clever enough to compress that craziness into catchy hit singles, and when he left he took his madness and humor with him.

But with David Gilmour replacing Barrett on guitar, Pink Floyd marched on to a beat that became more ponderous—and profitable. *The Dark Side of the Moon* (1973) was one of pop music's biggest- (and longest-) selling albums. *The Wall* (1981) became a feature film and ultimately a concert movie as well. Coupling sonic perfectionism with pretentiously pessimistic lyrics, Pink Floyd painstakingly developed a sweeping but slow-moving atmospheric style that was meant to be "spacey" but more often felt suffocating. Every minimal element was introduced to a song with such massive deliberateness that it became yet another thudding brick in the wall of their sound. Because so little actually happened in their music that listening to it at length was like watching paint dry, it worked best as accompaniment to visuals. Floyd composed several film scores and mounted ever more grandiose stage shows.

As Roger Waters, the bass player, became the predominant songwriter, Floyd's monumental mood music became grimmer and grimmer. Thus it was ironic that after the group broke up (followed by wrangling over rights to its name and the repertoire), Waters staged an extravaganza performance of *The Wall* in recently reunited Berlin. For Floyd's music, though lucrative, was never liberating. Its joyless methodicalness embodied rather than protested repression.

Procol Harum's architectural designs were altogether more benign, inspired by cathedrals and classical music. "A Whiter Shade of Pale" (1967) set Keith Reid's mumbo-jumbo lyrics (a patchwork of evocative phrases and Dylanish nonsense) to an echo of Bach's "Sleepers Awake" and became an

The Crazy Diamond, shining on, barely: Syd Barrett of Pink Floyd, 1969.

international hit that the group, actually formed only after its success, never equaled. The album that followed, *Procol Harum,* was stately, somber and ominous, the confusion and despair of the words set in ironic contrast to the deliberate architecture of the

Procol Harum, the band that brought you ''A Whiter Shade of Pale.''

music and the religiosity of Matthew Fisher's organ and Gary Brooker's gospel-tinged vocals and piano. Reid wrote of questers for revelation—conquistadores and, later, salty dogs—who came home empty-handed if at all, and the band's instrumental majesty made these failures still more pathetic. Very few groups (only the Band, which also exploited the piano-organ combination, comes to mind) have ever produced so fully realized a first album, and Procol Harum—garbled Latin for ''far from these things''—never quite duplicated it.

At the tail end of the Sixties appeared another, very different British band whose music had much the same stately, architectural feel. But whereas Procol Harum ventured far beyond rock to achieve this, Free was, in some respects, the British Creedence

This bleak crew is called Bad Company. It boasted lead singer Paul Rodgers *(second from right)*, the most compelling British vocalist since Steve Winwood.

Clearwater Revival, recapturing something primal in rock that had been forgotten in the rush of progressive experimentation. Their moody, moderate tempos and severe simplicity seemed to rebuke the razzle-dazzle of other bands, and these restraints merely pressurized lead singer Paul Rodgers's passion. Paul Kossoff's guitar sizzled all the more because he kept it under such rigid control. Rodgers sang with a tense, sexy swagger at first, but as the troubled group disbanded, re-formed, disbanded and reunited again, its music grew even bleaker, culminating in the utter and eloquent despair of *Heartbreaker* (1973), an album so dire the band had little alternative but to break up for a final time.

Rodgers and drummer Simon Kirke formed Bad Company with Mick Ralphs, the lead guitarist from Mott the Hoople, and bass player Boz Burrell. They cut their first album following Free's no-frills pattern and immediately won greater and longer-lasting popularity than Free had ever enjoyed. But with renown Rodgers's voice seemed gradually to coarsen and his songs to lose their emotional intensity, until eventually he became just another gruff hard rocker. By then the Sixties and the second wave of the British Invasion were long over, succeeded by a new wave of punk rockers determined to sweep the Rod Stewarts, Pink Floyds and Paul Rodgerses away.

DISCOGRAPHY

ALBUMS

Jeff Beck Group: With Rod Stewart: *Truth* (Epic; ☆15, 1968). With Rod Stewart *Beck-Ola* (Epic; ☆15, 1969). *Rough and Ready* (Epic; ☆46, 1971). *Jeff Beck Group* (Epic; ☆19, 1972). *Beckology*

(Epic, 1991). **Bee Gees:** *Bee Gees' 1st* (Atco; ☆7, 1967). *Horizontal* (Atco; ☆12, 1968). *Idea* (Atco; ☆17, 1968). *Rare Precious and Beautiful* (Atco; ☆99, 1968). *Odessa* (Atco; ☆20, 1969). *Best of Bee Gees* (Atco; ☆9, 1969). *Rare Precious and Beautiful—Vol. 2* (Atco; ☆100, 1970). *Cucumber Castle* (Atco; ☆94, 1970). *2 Years On* (Atco; ☆32, 1971). *Trafalgar* (Atco; ☆34, 1971). *To Whom It May Concern* (Atco; ☆35, 1972). *Life in a Tin Can* (RSO; ☆69, 1973). *Best of the Bee Gees, Vol. 2* (RSO; ☆98, 1973). *Mr. Natural* (RSO; ☆178, 1974). *Main Course* (RSO; ☆14, 1975). *Tales from the Brothers Gibb: A History in Song 1967–1990* (Polydor; 1990). **Spencer Davis Group:** *Gimme Some Lovin'* (United Artists; ☆54, 1967). *I'm a Man* (United Artists; ☆83, 1967). *Greatest Hits* (United Artists; ☆195, 1968). **Free:** *Tons of Sobs* (A&M; 1969). *Free* (A&M; 1970). *Fire and Water* (A&M; ☆17, 1970). *Free Highway* (A&M; ☆190, 1971). *Free Live!* (A&M; ☆89, 1971). *Free at Last* (A&M; ☆69, 1972). *Heartbreaker* (Island; ☆47, 1973). **Hollies:** *Hear! Hear!* (Imperial; ☆145, 1966). *Beat Group!* (Imperial; 1966). *Bus Stop* (Imperial; ☆75, 1966). *Stop! Stop! Stop!* (Imperial; ☆91, 1967). *The Hollies' Greatest Hits* (Imperial; ☆11, 1967). *Evolution* (Epic; ☆43, 1967). *Dear Eloise/King Midas in Reverse* (Epic; 1968). *Words and Music by Bob Dylan* (Epic; 1969). *He Ain't Heavy, He's My Brother* (Epic; ☆32, 1970). *Moving Finger* (Epic; ☆183, 1971). *Distant Light* (Epic; ☆21, 1972). *Romany* (Epic; ☆84, 1973). *Hollies* (Epic; ☆28, 1974). *Another Night* (Epic; ☆123, 1975). *Epic Anthology* (Epic; 1990). **Move:** *Shazam* (A&M; 1970). *Looking On* (Capitol; 1971). *Message from the Country* (Capitol; 1971). *Split Ends* (United Artists; ☆172, 1973). *The Best of the Move* (A&M; 1973). **Nice:** *The Thoughts of Emerlist Davjack* (Immediate; 1968). *Ars Longa Vita Brevis* (Immediate; 1969). *Nice* (Immediate; 1969). *Five Bridges Suite* (Mercury; ☆197, 1970). *Elegy* (Mercury; 1971). *Keith Emerson with Nice* (Mercury; ☆152, 1972). **Pink Floyd:** With Syd Barrett: *Pink Floyd* (a.k.a. *The Piper at the Gates of Dawn*) (Tower; ☆131, 1967). With Syd Barrett: *A Saucerful of Secrets* (Tower; 1968). *More* (Tower; 1969). *Ummagumma* (Harvest; ☆74, 1970). *Atom Heart Mother* (Harvest; ☆55, 1970). With Syd Barrett: *Relics* (Harvest; ☆152, 1971). *Meddle* (Harvest; ☆70, 1971). *Obscured by Clouds* (Harvest; ☆46, 1972). *The Dark Side of the Moon* (Harvest; ☆1, 1973). *Wish You Were Here* (Columbia; ☆1, 1975). *Animals* (Columbia; ☆3, 1977). *The Wall* (Columbia; ☆1, 1979). **Procol Harum:** *Procol Harum* (Deram; ☆47, 1967). *Shine On Brightly* (A&M; ☆24, 1968). *A Salty Dog* (A&M; ☆32, 1969). *Home* (A&M; ☆34, 1970). *Broken Barricades* (A&M; ☆32, 1971). *Live in Concert with the Edmonton Symphony Orchestra* (A&M; ☆5, 1972). *Grand Hotel* (Chrysalis; ☆21, 1973). *The Best of Procol Harum* (A&M; ☆131, 1973). *Exotic Birds and Fruit* (Chrysalis; ☆86, 1974). *Procol's Ninth* (Chrysalis; ☆52, 1975). **Small Faces:** *There Are but Four Small Faces* (Immediate; ☆178, 1968). *Ogdens' Nut Gone Flake* (Immediate; ☆159, 1968). *Early Faces* (Pride; ☆176, 1972). *Small Faces—First Step* (Warner Bros.; ☆119, 1970). **Faces:** *Long Player* (Warner Bros.; ☆29, 1971). *A Nod Is as Good as a Wink to a Blind Horse* (Warner Bros.; ☆6, 1971). *Ooh La La* (Warner Bros.; ☆21, 1973). *Coast to*

Coast, Overture and Beginners (Mercury; ☆63, 1974). **Rod Stewart:** *The Rod Stewart Album* (Mercury; ☆139, 1969). *Gasoline Alley* (Mercury; ☆27, 1970). *Every Picture Tells a Story* (Mercury; ☆1, 1971). *Never a Dull Moment* (Mercury; ☆2, 1972). *Sing It Again, Rod* (Mercury; ☆31, 1973). *Smiler* (Mercury; ☆13, 1974). *Atlantic Crossing* (Warner Bros.; ☆9, 1975). *The Best of Rod Stewart* (Mercury; ☆90, 1976). *A Night on the Town* (Mercury; ☆2, 1976). *Foot Loose & Fancy Free* (Warner Bros.; ☆2, 1977). *Blondes Have More Fun* (Warner Bros.; ☆1, 1978). *Greatest Hits—Vol. 1* (Warner Bros.; ☆22, 1979). *Foolish Behaviour* (Warner Bros.; ☆12, 1980). *Tonight I'm Yours* (Warner Bros.; ☆11, 1981). *Absolutely Live* (Warner Bros.; ☆46, 1982). *Body Wishes* (Warner Bros.; ☆30, 1983). *Camouflage* (Warner Bros.; ☆18, 1984). *Rod Stewart* (Warner Bros.; ☆28, 1986). *Out of Order* (Warner Bros.; ☆20, 1988). *Storyteller: The Complete Anthology 1964–1990* (Warner Bros.; ☆54, 1989). *Downtown Train: Selections from the "Storyteller" Anthology* (Warner Bros.; ☆20, 1990). *Vagabond Heart* (Warner Bros.; ☆10, 1991). **Traffic:** *Mr. Fantasy* (United Artists; ☆88, 1968). *Traffic* (United Artists; ☆17, 1968). *Last Exit* (United Artists; ☆19, 1969). *Best of Traffic* (United Artists; ☆48, 1970). *John Barleycorn Must Die* (United Artists; ☆5, 1970). *Welcome to the Canteen* (United Artists; ☆26, 1971). *The Low Spark of High Heeled Boys* (Island; ☆7, 1971). *Shoot Out at the Fantasy Factory* (Island; ☆6, 1973). *Traffic—On the Road* (Island; ☆29, 1973). *When the Eagle Flies* (Island; ☆9, 1974). **Steve Winwood:** *Arc of a Diver* (Island; ☆3, 1981). *Talking Back to the Night* (Island; ☆28, 1982). *Back in the High Life* (Island; ☆3, 1986). *Chronicles* (Island; ☆26, 1987). *Roll with It* (Virgin; ☆1, 1988). *Refugees of the Heart* (Virgin; ☆27, 1990). **Yardbirds:** *For Your Love* (Epic; ☆96, 1965). *Having a Rave Up with the Yardbirds* (Epic; ☆53, 1965). *Over Under Sideways Down* (Epic; ☆52, 1966). *The Yardbirds' Greatest Hits* (Epic; ☆28, 1967). *Little Games* (Epic; ☆80, 1967). *The Yardbirds Featuring Performances by Jeff Beck, Eric Clapton, Jimmy Page* (Epic; ☆155, 1970). *Smokestack Lightning, Vol. 1* (Sony; 1991). *Blues, Backtracks and Shapes of Things, Vol. 2* (Sony; 1991).

(Chart positions compiled from Joel Whitburn's *Record Research,* based on *Billboard*'s LPs chart.)

THE BAND

BY ED WARD

I t might have been a mention in the *Village Voice* that alerted me to the impending release of an album "by Bob Dylan's backup band," but the word had been in the air for some time. The day the odd-looking record, with its weird watercolor cover (painted, as I'd read, by Dylan himself), arrived in the local record store, I picked it up, confident that I had bought something good. If nothing else, it had a couple of new Dylan songs, and in mid-1968, evidence of Dylan's continuing existence was almost an event in itself.

Music from Big Pink sure wasn't a new Dylan album, though. In fact, the Dylan songs weren't even the best things on it: There was a demonic organ workout, "Chest Fever," that far outclassed Procol Harum's experiments; a couple of evocative if opaque songs by pianist Richard Manuel, "In a Station" and "We Can Talk"; and a bouncy number with funny lyrics, called "The Weight" for no good reason at all. The group didn't really call itself anything either, although on the record's spine it said "The Band." *Music from Big Pink* was totally unlike anything my friends and I had ever heard, and everybody wanted to know one thing: Who are these guys, anyway?

To some, they were Levon and the Hawks, to others they were the Crackers, and to yet others they were the Canadian Squires. They'd gotten the name the Hawks while touring as Ronnie Hawkins's backup band. Hawkins, an Arkansas rockabilly singer who arrived a little too late (his first records didn't appear until 1959) to latch onto the U.S. rockabilly boom, had lots of spirit but little distinctive talent through which to channel it. Canada, however, was wide-open territory for an energetic rock & roller, and Hawkins moved there with his band of Arkansas boys, including drummer Levon Helm, from Sonny Boy Williamson's hometown of West Helena. The group played the Canadian honky-

When they released their second album in 1969, the Band helped people dizzy from the Sixties feel that America was big enough to include them, too.

Drummer-mandolinist Levon Helm (*left*) with bassist Rick Danko.

with Robbie Robertson and proclaimed him "the only mathematical guitar genius I've ever run into who does not offend my intestinal nervousness with his rear-guard sound." Whatever Dylan intended by that, it meant that Robertson and Helm were in Dylan's band (with Harvey Brooks on bass and Al Kooper on organ) when Dylan played his famous Forest Hills gig on August 28th, 1965.

tonks, coming south now and then, and as the original band members fell prey to homesickness or Hawkins's temper, they were replaced, one by one, with Canadians.

But even Canada catches up with fashion sooner or later, and as the gigs declined for Hawkins, the Hawks decided to strike out on their own. Levon Helm knew he had a good working band around him, so it was with confidence that they spent the next few years touring Canada. Jaime Robbie Robertson was developing into one of the dirtiest, most inventive guitarists on either side of the border, while keyboard wizards Richard Manuel and Garth Hudson were extending black gospel music's piano-and-organ texture into something completely unique and Rick Danko played a Motown-inflected bass that was the perfect counterpoint to Helm's loose but snappy drum style. Levon was the best singer, but everybody except Robertson and Hudson took turns on vocals. Perhaps because it had developed in a relative vacuum, their music could scarcely be compared to anybody else's.

After hearing the Hawks in a Toronto bar, John Hammond Jr., the American folk-blues singer, invited them to New York in 1964 to cut records and work gigs with him. Hammond wasn't the only member of the New York–Greenwich Village folk scene going electric, though, and soon Bob Dylan caught wind of the group. Dylan started jamming

Nobody really seems to know what happened next, but Dylan ended up hiring the Hawks, without Levon. Whether Helm resented Dylan's moving in on his band, or whether he just didn't feel up to it is hard to say, but it was the Hawks minus Helm who toured with Dylan on his 1965–66 world tour, playing all over Europe, Australia and parts of Asia. The group (with Mickey Jones on drums) was remarkable, as the bootleg recordings of the tour show. People came to see Dylan and went away marveling at his band; by the end of the tour, their place in rock & roll history was secure. They also backed Dylan on a couple of late-'65 recording sessions, yielding "Can You Please Crawl out Your Window," "One of Us Must Know (Sooner or Later)," including a magnificent instrumental, "Number One."

Back home in 1966 the Hawks knew the time had come to make a move on their own. They rented a large pink house (affectionately called Big Pink) in West Saugerties, New York, just down the road from Dylan's place near Woodstock. The first thing they did was to get Levon Helm back from Arkansas, where he'd gone while they accompanied Dylan. They wrote some new songs for themselves, and in an improvised recording studio in Big Pink's basement two distinct sets of tunes began to emerge. On

The late Richard Manuel.

the one hand, there were collaborations with Dylan, the famous "Basement Tapes." Two of the Dylan songs were cowritten with band members: "Tears of Rage" with Richard Manuel and "Wheel's on Fire" with Rick Danko. The rest, although arranged and accompanied by the band, were pure Dylan.

On the other hand, there were songs earmarked for the band's first album, *Music from Big Pink*. Capitol Records gave them a contract, neighbor John Simon helped them produce the album, and in the summer of 1968 it was released. It was a revolutionary album in many ways: The emphasis was on ensemble work rather than on the soloing that dominated rock; the melodies, few of them blues based, were delivered by an ensemble that was almost orchestral in scope yet comprised only five musicians; the lyrics were elusive, like Dylan's, but with a distinctive and compelling cast. Enigmatic? You bet. But I loved the songs and I'd *still* like to know what Manuel was writing about.

Big Pink didn't sell as well as its impact would have you believe, and the Band removed temporarily to Los Angeles to record a second album, simply entitled *The Band*. With its evocative songs of the American frontier and the farming life, *The Band* remains their masterpiece. "Virgil Kane is the name, and I rode on the Danville train," sings Levon in "The Night They Drove Old Dixie Down," and after looking at the cover photos, you'd almost be willing to believe that this song dates from the time in which it is set, the last days of the Civil War.

The Band came out in the fall of 1969, and there was no time more appropriate to the release of such a collection of Americana. The amazing thing about the album was that, without quoting or making direct reference, verbal or musical, to country music, nineteenth-century parlor and military music, or any of the patriotic poets like Whitman, Sandburg or Lowell, it seemed to evoke all these things and more entirely on its own terms. I was living in Ohio at the time, in a room with two windows, one overlooking a saloon and the other facing north, where there was

Keyboardist Garth Hudson.

Robbie Robertson taking a scholarly approach to the guitar.

tive stamp of their previous work. It didn't help, either, that the song "Stage Fright" itself was seen by many as a taunt at Dylan who, rumor had it, was considering going on tour again, with the Band backing him, but kept canceling or refusing to finalize his plans. Robbie also turned producer in mid-1970, recording a fine album by singer-songwriter Jessie Winchester.

The Band cut a tune around this time that for the first time could have cracked the Top Ten for them. A version of Marvin Gaye's "Baby Don't You Do It" (composed by Motown's Holland-Dozier-Holland) was recorded to test out the sound at Albert Grossman's brand-new Bearsville recording studio. It sizzled and snapped like the best rock & roll but was not officially released until many years later.

Their next album, *Cahoots*, was even weaker than *Stage Fright*. The Band was beginning to sound like the many imitators who had sprung up in the wake of its second album, and when the members photographed for *Cahoots'* back cover with their eyes shut, it prompted some to comment that they sounded like they were playing in their sleep. But they closed 1971 with a New Year's Eve concert at New York's Academy of Music that proved they still had life in

nothing but fields and a farmhouse. I could sit for hours, playing *The Band* and looking out one of those two windows. If my experience is anything like typical, I would say that *The Band* helped a lot of people dizzy from the confusion and disorientation of the Sixties feel that the nation was big enough to include them, too.

The *Band* was the breakthrough. It sold well, enabling the Band to tour for the first time as headliners. Other performers started recording their material (including Joan Baez, who scored a hit off a philistine rewrite of "The Night They Drove Old Dixie Down").

The level of excellence *The Band* set was one the group was unfairly expected to maintain; it is hardly surprising that the next album, *Stage Fright*, was uneven and didn't contain one song with the distinc-

their collective bones. A recording of the concert, which featured a brass section arranged by Allen Toussaint, was released in 1972 as a double live album, *Rock of Ages,* an excellent set by any standards. Still, *Ages* contained little new material, and the Band's next effort was an oldies album; it seemed as if they were treading water. *Moondog Matinee,* released in 1973, was named for Alan Freed's Cleveland radio show, which, beaming clear channel, could easily have been heard by fledgling Hawks in Toronto. The oldies—Bobby Bland's ''Share Your Love with Me,'' Sam Cooke's ''A Change Is Gonna Come'' and Junior Parker's ''Mystery Train''—were of a higher order than on most such albums, but, good as the album was, I, for one, had almost given up expecting anything new or exciting from the Band again.

Then it was back to the starting line in a big way: an album with Bob Dylan. Not the world's greatest Dylan album or the best backup work the Band ever did, *Planet Waves* betrayed an artist out of touch with his audience. There was only one way out, and late in 1973 Bob Dylan and the Band announced a joint tour. It proved to be the kick in the ass both careers needed. The resulting live album, *Before the Flood,* is

Garth Hudson, whose keyboards ranged from accordion to oldtime pump organ.

such a feast for the ears that it's too rich to get through at one sitting.

Dylan, refreshed, went on to make some excellent records and even loosened up enough to release *The Basement Tapes* as a double album, including some of the Band's pre–*Big Pink* songs. The tour also seemed to jar something loose in Robbie Robertson's creative faculties, as evidenced late in 1975 on *Northern Lights—Southern Cross,* the Band's first set of new material since 1971. It was as contemporary as the disco beat of ''Forbidden Fruit,'' as antiquarian as ''Acadian Driftwood,'' a song chronicling the migration of a group of French Canadians. The best Band album since *The Band* itself, it seemed to signal a rebirth in a stagnating career.

The Band singing campfire songs.

Bassist Rick Danko coauthored ''This Wheel's on Fire'' with Bob Dylan.

Instead, it wrote the finale. Tired of sixteen years on the road—''eight years in dance halls, in dives and bars, eight years of concerts, arenas and stadiums,'' as Robertson put it—the Band decided not to push its luck; they retired as a performing unit. Fur-

Richard Manuel sang the Band's more angst-ridden songs such as "The Shape I'm In."

thermore, they decided to go out in style, and so they got together with Bill Graham's organization and planned a concert on Thanksgiving Day, 1976, at San Francisco's Winterland (site of their first concert as the Band) to top it off. Martin Scorsese was to film it, and a number of special guests, representing the various artists the band members had played with and produced over the years, were invited: Paul Butterfield, Eric Clapton, Neil Diamond, Bob Dylan, Joni Mitchell, Emmylou Harris, Muddy Waters, Dr. John, Neil Young and, of course, Ronnie Hawkins. The stage set was borrowed from the San Francisco Opera Company's production of *La Traviata,* a string orchestra provided waltz music consistent with the concert's official title, "The Last Waltz," and Thanksgiving dinner was served. The event was so carefully planned, so ponderously spontaneous, that some felt it unwittingly epitomized the obese, bourgeois entity rock had become. Others felt that for a band that had given rock & roll so much, such a send-off was entirely appropriate. One thing was certain: It was the end of the Band.

Since then its various members have gone on to solo recording projects, and Levon Helm has had some success as a character actor in films. Only rarely have the solo projects, however, met with much critical or commercial success.

After starring in the film *Carny* with Gary Busey and Jodie Foster and contributing to soundtracks for Martin Scorsese's films *Raging Bull* and *The King of Comedy,* Robbie Robertson recorded two solo albums. The first, *Robbie Robertson* (1987), featured Peter Gabriel and U2. Four years later, in New Orleans, Robertson recorded the atmospheric song cycle *Storyville,* which was the more artistically successful of the two.

In the Eighties the Band attempted a couple of reunion tours, one in 1983 with the Arkansas barband veterans the Cate Brothers filling in for Robbie Robertson, and another in early 1986 with guitarist Jimmy Weider. After a sold-out appearance of this latter version in a Winter Park, Florida, restaurant lounge on March 3rd, Richard Manuel went back to his hotel room and hanged himself early the next morning. Incredibly, in the summer of 1991 the Band began yet another reunion tour, with the addition of keyboardist Billy Preston, and without Robbie Robertson, who apparently knows when to quit. In 1992, the Band (minus Robertson) was reportedly recording an album together. Whether this latest project will have any long-lasting value remains to be seen. But there is no doubt that the achievements by this unique quintet already in place have forever earned them the right to be known simply as the Band.

DISCOGRAPHY

ALBUMS
Music from Big Pink (Capitol; ☆30, 1968). *The Band* (Capitol; ☆9, 1969). *Stage Fright* (Capitol; ☆5, 1970). *Cahoots* (Capitol; ☆21, 1971). *Rock of Ages* (Capitol; ☆6, 1972). *Moondog Matinee* (Capitol; ☆28, 1973). With Bob Dylan: *Before the Flood* (Asylum; ☆3, 1974). With Bob Dylan: *The Basement Tapes* (Columbia; ☆7, 1975). *Northern Lights—Southern Cross* (Capitol; ☆26, 1975). *The Best of the Band* (Capitol; ☆51, 1976). *Islands* (Capitol; ☆64, 1977). *The Last Waltz* (Warner Bros.; ☆16, 1978).

(Chart positions compiled from Joel Whitburn's *Record Research,* based on *Billboard*'s LPs chart.)

SLY AND THE FAMILY STONE

BY DAVE MARSH

A fter two decades, the image remains indelible. Sly and the Family Stone are onstage, slamming out their music in all their leather, plumed velvet and satin finery. Sly himself is at the piano, fist pounding the air, shouting, ''I want to take you . . . HIGHER!'' The audience responds with an affirmation of his command. The music explodes, the sweeping rhythms of voice and band pull the energy together. It's not quite soul, not quite rock & roll, but an epiphanous ritual that operates on its own terms. Nobody's thinking, everybody's grooving: pure exhilaration or seminal fascism in action, depending on where you sit. Maybe a remark by Jimi Hendrix describes it best: ''Is this love, baby, or is it, uh . . . con-*fu*-sion?''

Sly Stone was, for a while anyway, one of the greatest musical adventurers rock has ever known. Almost single-handedly he effected a revolution in soul music, one whose consequences reverberate everywhere today. With his band, Sly ended the domination of the sweet soul sound practiced by the Stax, Motown and Muscle Shoals rhythm sections. Eighteen months after his first hit in 1968, ''Dance to the Music,'' everyone was following his lead. And the great bulk of disco and funk rock simply worked off variations of Sly and the Family Stone's innovations. No one has surpassed them.

What Sly had done was so simple that it might have occurred to almost any black kid living in the late Sixties in San Francisco. The antinomian spirit of R&B—recklessness personified—was grafted onto the close knit, deliberately paced rock band experience; the musical wildness of the rock band then was wedded to the utter discipline of the soul group. And Sly's sound was totally integrated, not just

musically, but sexually and racially: Here was a band in which men and women, black and white, had not one fixed role but many fluid ones. The women played, the men sang; the blacks freaked out, the whites got funky; everyone did something unexpected, which was the only thing the listener could expect. The result might have been only the heap of contradictions the description suggests, had Sly's talent not been equally unpredictable. As it was, the band lived up to the proud boast of its first album title: *A Whole New Thing*.

Before Sly soul records had been conceived as vocal vehicles; even the often brilliant playing of a group like Booker T. and the MGs was merely supportive. Rock bands changed that; in San Francisco music the vocals were often an afterthought. "Dance to the Music" pulverized these polarities by joining them not calmly, but brutally. The voice and the music didn't achieve equality, they fought it out for space, right on the disc. The exhortation of the title may have been the whole message to many who bought it. But others listened more closely, and what they heard spelled the doom of American R&B's formal stasis.

The impresario of this barely contained cacophony was one Sylvester Stewart, born in Texas, bred a tough street fighter in Vallejo, a factory town on the wrong side of San Francisco Bay. A music theory course in high school inspired him, and he hooked up with local DJ Tom Donahue, then running Autumn Records. For Autumn Sly produced some of the first Bay Area rock & roll records; local, regional and finally national hits for such bands as the Mojo Men, the Vejtables and the Beau Brummels. When the acid-rock gang itself moved in, Sly moved out; he tried to cut Grace Slick and the Great Society and wound up with one song in 200-odd takes.

He went to work for one of the area's black radio stations. As usual, Sly did things differently, interrupting the flow of Stax and Motown singles with Beatles and Dylan tracks, fidgeting with commercials, raising the call-in dedication to a minor art form. In his off-hours, he had a band—the nucleus of Sly and the Family Stone—working in bars. It ultimately came to include his brother Freddie, Jerry Martini, Jerry's cousin, Gregg Errico, Sly's sister, Rose, Cynthia Robinson and Larry Graham.

Sly Stone, the Riotmaster.

The pop scene was then at a turning point. Both soul and rock were trapped—the former by its own conventions, the latter by its increasing solemnity as it pursued High Art. Sensing a gap, Sly moved in to fill it with his characteristic mixture of calculation, conviction and dumb luck. He made his music with the assurance of a man whose vision requires a new mode. In the songs that followed "Dance to the Music" he toyed with everything from free-form doo-wop ("Hot Fun in the Summertime") to the basic funk chant ("Sing a Simple Song," "Stand!") that would be adopted by disco groups like the Commodores.

But Sly was a philosopher, preaching a message of total reconciliation that lived up to the big sound. "Everyday People," "Everybody Is a Star," "Life," "I Want to Take You Higher" and "You Can Make It If You Try"—most of them hits—expressed as well as anything the sentiments of the Haight and the hopes of the ghetto. For a time, it seemed, Sly's approach could heal all wounds; offer black kids a model for something other than slick, Copacabana-level success; give whites a fairly healthy black star; produce for both a meeting ground where they could work out their mistrust.

In the best songs, Sly promised to work it out for them. "Everyday People" contributed mightily to the hip lexicon—"different strokes for different folks" was Sly's whole ideology—but it was also a taunt and a proclamation. Nobody who heard that record could disbelieve Sly's power; he might actually turn rock & roll into some triumph of integration.

But even in a time when a good share of the rock population was flaky enough to believe in chemical salvation, Sly's utopianism couldn't triumph. The first symptom of trouble was his own increasing eccentricity. Then Sly started to blow gigs; half the thrill of buying a ticket became the anticipation of whether he would really show. Usually he did, but he missed enough dates—generally without any announcement until after the arena seats were filled—to earn a reputation for irresponsibility.

At Woodstock, only eighteen months from the beginning, the dark underside of his vision began to catch up. "Higher!" became less a slogan of collective triumph than a means for ravishing the crowd. Otis Redding had died a year and a half earlier, and the Woodstock generation was looking for a new

Traveling in customized style, working on a Whole New Thing: Sly at the peak of his popularity, when luxury was a way of life.

black hope, someone who could make race a safe issue. With Jimi Hendrix already showing signs of resistance, Sly was the prime candidate.

I n January 1970 Sly released the sardonic single "Thank You (Falettinme Be Mice Elf Agin)." It was slinky, hip dance music, and no one thought much of it—the weird spelling was to be expected from such a spaced-out maverick. "I Want to Take You Higher," recycled as a single in May, was an afterthought, hardly an event. The gigs continued to be blown, while rumors of drug problems and threats from black political organizations floated around. Sly toured, canceled, recorded, failed to release. Meanwhile, no new music. It looked like the middle stage of a downward spiral. A Whole New Thing had simply petered out.

The spirit of that Thing was now dominant, however. Sly's influence had been completely absorbed into both black and white pop styles, and it now coursed through the mainstream of soul. At Motown the Jackson 5 and the Temptations carried his banner; in Philadelphia the Gamble-Huff organization was churning out Sly-derived funk records; in Chicago Curtis Mayfield, that sweetest of old soul singers, had made his move in the Family Stone's direction. Sly himself may have been in exile from the charts, but in the Top 100, his music reigned.

In November 1971 he finally released a new album, just in time for Christmas. It was less than a merry affair, however. The title was *There's a Riot Goin' On*, and the title song was precisely timed at no minutes and no seconds. That was just a clue.

The next hint lay in the revulsion felt by many listeners, particularly, it may safely be said, white listeners. Where was the joyous, life-affirming black hero? This music stumbled, faltered, its rhythms hobbled like a heroin roller coaster, its entire tune an affront to the spirit of boogie. Sly had always built his songs from bits and pieces, strange unexpected scraps, parts zipping in (often half unformed) to *make* a song. But this sounded like the scrap heap; the connections were left unmade.

After you listened a while, it got scary. "Feel so good/Feel so good/Don't wanna move" was what passed for exuberance on this record. It was the aural equivalent of William Burroughs's *Naked Lunch* (". . . when everyone sees what is on the end of every fork"). Those who didn't stop listening grew fascinated by the resultant chills and despair; even those who didn't want to know, though, couldn't shut them out. *Riot* had not one but three hit singles—"Family Affair," "(You Caught Me) Smilin' " and "Runnin' Away." The idea was beginning to form that maybe *There's a Riot Going On* was Sly's way of telling us something.

But as open as white rock society was supposed to be, it had no fondness for a harsh, direct look at black experience. That audience was hardly prepared to deal with a black hero who decided to work completely on his own terms; but even if he had to make up those terms, that's what Sly was doing. In effect, he took the power of his stardom and shook it in every gray face. "Family Affair," the album's biggest hit, was pure bile. That three-day mud festival in Woodstock wasn't enough to make Sly forget who he had been, back in Vallejo, who he still was, without a name. In the days of Nixon's White House, Cambodian excursions and ODs all around, there wasn't much question where he discovered the

a time when an election was being stolen. They reflected an almost unspoken acknowledgment of a long list of sins, from the murder of Fred Hampton and thousands of Vietnamese and black GIs, to crime in the streets and the everyday robbery at the grocery store, from the loss of simple friendship to the lack of any kind of center for most people's lives. It was the world of the Sixties turned inside out. Sly's Utopia had revealed its other face: Hell. As if in proof, *Riot* ended with a reprise of "Thank You (Falettinme Be Mice Elf Agin)." Only this time, he called it "Thank You for Talkin' to Me Africa."

The tempo slowed to a heartbeat. Nothing but bass and drums for the first minute, with some occasional jagged interjections from the guitar. Then those awful freeze-frame lyrics:

> *Lookin' at the devil*
> *Grinnin' at his gun*
> *Fingers start shakin'*
> *I begin to run*
> *Bullets start chasin'*
> *I begin to stop*
> *We begin to wrestle*
> *I was on the top*

blood referred to on "Family Affair" either. "Muzak with its finger on the trigger," Greil Marcus called *Riot*.

Riot was perfectly timed. Maybe it ignited one of the greatest explosions of pop, or maybe it served simply as a sign that one was about to occur. In any event, the airwaves were soon filled with tough black testimony, unbending, seeking its own audience and not caring so much about the damage done to integrationist (in music-biz lingo, "crossover") sensibilities. The Temptations scored their own experience with "Papa Was a Rollin' Stone." Curtis Mayfield turned in *Superfly*, a cheap movie soundtrack that came to life on radio as one of the most searing antidrug diatribes ever written. War proclaimed "The World Is a Ghetto" and warned against "Slippin' into Darkness." Stevie Wonder excoriated "Superstition," caught the full misery of "Living for the City." Marvin Gaye simply asked "What's Going On?" The O'Jays railed against "Back Stabbers." There was no avoiding this music or what it had to say: Every one of those songs was right there on the radio, a good many of them hitting the Top Ten. You couldn't get into the car and run away from it, because it kept blasting through the static.

These songs had everything to do with America at

Now Sly pulled the trigger. It was torture, but torture that had been lived out, not fantasized.

Sly, meanwhile, had become one of the richest black stars. Maybe the richest. His contract with Epic Records provided more than half a million dollars for each album, an astronomical fee for the time. He lived in plush Hollywood comfort—neither drugs nor fast cars nor women nor fancy clothes were beyond his resources. To blow a gig, he had only to seize a whim. And this is what it came down to: "We begin to wrestle/I was on the top." No one—not even Sly—knew for how long.

Making that music in the studio was one thing. Acting it out onstage was another. In his live show little of the *Riot* material turned up; maybe it was too difficult for performance, but after *Riot*'s exorcism, who could believe "Life" or "Higher"? And the scars showed. The idealistic band disintegrated. Members drifted in and out; the music faltered and fell. A year and a half later, with *Fresh*, Sly performed the ultimate copout, epitomized by his final, brilliant statement: "Que Sera, Sera" (whatever will be, will be). The music was still good, in its way,

Sly and the Family Stone. *From left, on the floor:* Rose Stone, Jerry Martini, Cynthia Robinson; *on the couch:* Freddie Stone, Sly, Gregg Errico, Larry Graham.

probably better than *Riot,* but it was over. "Que Sera" was a great move, but it was also a marvelously concealed surrender; it took Sly's onstage wedding a year later to sell out Madison Square Garden.

By 1975 even the records had stopped coming. Sly was down and out—who knew where? Black pop, transmuted via Europe into the big-beat dance music of disco and through a psychedelic haze into the deep roil of funk, had advanced very little from where he'd left it. Indeed, the few public performances Sly made during the Eighties were under the aegis of Parliament/Funkadelic leader George Clinton, always the Family Stone's truest disciple. These records seemed to indicate that, when the fog lifted and he was not being busted for drug abuse, Sly could still make good music. But for the most part, Sly's past fifteen years have been one long, dark drive, an acting out of the scariest implications of "Thank You for Talkin' to Me Africa."

Yet without what Sly and the Family Stone accomplished, the most important music of the late Eighties and Nineties would have been unimaginable. From the studio wizardry of Prince (whose "Kiss" is a great act of homage to Sly) to the dense hip-hop of gangsta rappers such as Ice-T, Ice Cube, N.W.A. and even Public Enemy, to the guitar-based Afrocentric hard rock of Living Colour, fragments of the initial vision Sly and the Family Stone wrought are everywhere. Whether Sly himself ever makes another memorable minute of music again, his accomplishments are part of the bedrock now, everlasting and unforgettable.

SINGLES

"Dance to the Music" (Epic; r☆9, ☆8, 1968). "Life" b/w "M'Lady" (Epic; ☆93, 1968). "Everyday People" b/w "Sing a Simple Song" (Epic; r☆1, ☆1, 1968). "Stand!" b/w "I Want to Take You Higher" (Epic; r☆14, ☆22, 1969). "Hot Fun in the Summertime" (Epic; r☆3, ☆2, 1969). "Thank You Falettinme Be Mice Elf Agin" b/w "Everybody Is a Star" (Epic; r☆1, ☆1, 1970). "Family Affair" (Epic; r☆1, ☆1, 1971). "Runnin' Away" (Epic; r☆15, ☆23, 1972). "Smilin'" (Epic; r☆21, ☆42, 1972). "If You Want Me to Stay" (Epic; r☆3, ☆12, 1973). "Frisky" (Epic; r☆28, ☆79, 1973). "Time for Livin'" (Epic; r☆10, ☆32, 1974). "Loose Booty" (Epic; r☆22, ☆84, 1974). "I Get High on You" (Epic; r☆3, ☆52, 1975).

ALBUMS

Dance to the Music (Epic; ☆142, 1968). *Life* (Epic; ☆195, 1968). *Stand!* (Epic; ☆13, 1969). *Greatest Hits* (Epic; ☆2, 1970). *There's a Riot Goin' On* (Epic; ☆1, 1971). *Fresh* (Epic; ☆7, 1973). *Small Talk* (Epic; ☆15, 1974). *High Energy* (Epic; 1975). *High on You* (Epic; 1975). *Back on the Right Track* (Warner Bros.; ☆152, 1979). *Anthology* (Epic; 1981).

(Chart positions compiled from Joel Whitburn's *Record Research*, based on *Billboard*'s Pop and LPs charts, unless otherwise indicated; r☆ = position on *Billboard*'s Rhythm & Blues chart.)

VAN MORRISON

BY GREIL MARCUS

In 1961, as a member of a band from Northern Ireland called the Monarchs, Van Morrison toured Germany and sang Ray Charles imitations to homesick American GIs. In 1963 and '64, as the leader of Them, a group working out of Belfast, Morrison began to find his style (a rough mix of American folk blues, R&B, electric rock & roll and Irish poetry declaimed aloud), driving his band through half-hour versions of songs that, cut to two or three minutes, would soon bring him a taste of fame. In 1965 in London Them scattered, but Morrison recorded under their name with several members of the band and a clutch of British studio musicians, among them guitarist Jimmy Page, later of the Yardbirds and Led Zeppelin. Morrison made two brilliant albums, *Them* (called *The Angry Young Them* in the United Kingdom, it sounded it), and *Them Again*. In 1965 and '66 he scored modest but unforgettable hits on both sides of the Atlantic with four of the most exciting records of the time: ''Gloria'' (covered by the Chicago punk band the Shadows of Knight, who had a bigger hit in America), ''Baby Please Don't Go,'' ''Mystic Eyes'' and ''Here Comes the Night.''

To those who were listening, it was clear that Van Morrison was as intense and imaginative a performer as any to emerge from the first wave of the post-Beatles British Invasion. Yet it was equally clear to those who saw his early live shows in 1965 that Morrison lacked the flash and the flair for pop

Van with Them in 1965, when he was singing songs like "Gloria" and "Mystic Eyes"—some of the most intense music of its day.

stardom possessed by such clearly inferior singers as Keith Relf of the Yardbirds or Eric Burdon of the Animals. Morrison communicated distance, not immediacy; bitterness, not celebration. His music had power, but also subtlety; as a white R&B singer he was a great lyric poet. Without the superb studio band that had played on his records, he seemed unfocused, and his music did not quite come across.

What he lacked in glamour he made up in weirdness. He was small and gloomy, with more black energy than he knew what to do with, the wrong man to meet in a dark alley, or to cross on a stage. He did not fit the maracas-shaking mold of the day; instead, in 1965, he recorded a shimmering version of "It's All Over Now, Baby Blue" that in some ways was stronger than Dylan's and turned the fey Paul Simon composition "Richard Cory" into a bone-

chilling horror story. Who was this Irish kid singing folk songs and R&B with the raw emotion of a country bluesman but never sounding black?

In 1966 Them broke apart for good, and Morrison took himself to New York under the wing of producer Bert Berns, scoring in 1967 with "Brown Eyed Girl," his first Top Ten single, after which he was promptly forgotten. Brooding and drinking hard, Morrison moved to Boston, where, in an incomprehensible Belfast accent, he pestered late-night DJs for John Lee Hooker sides. Once he was booed off the stage when a group that would later make up part of the J. Geils Band called him out of the audience to front their version of "Gloria." "Don't you know who this is?" Peter Wolf shouted at the hissing crowd. "This man *wrote the song!*"

But they didn't know. In 1967 when you said "Morrison" you meant the Doors, who, one read at the time in *Crawdaddy,* were preparing a treatment of "Gloria" that upon release would surely be greeted by the gathering storm of new rock fans as a "masterpiece." As if Van Morrison's performance of "Gloria" had ever been anything else. (The Doors' version was finally released in 1983 on the LP *Alive, She Cried;* it turned out to be an ordinary track.)

Bert Berns had tried. He and Morrison had followed "Brown Eyed Girl" with a dark, bluesy album

The last version of Them, 1966.

called (with too-late trendy hopes) *Blowin' Your Mind;* the music was well made (Eric Gale played first-rate guitar), but also morbid. Sales were minimal. The signature track was titled "T.B. Sheets," which was exactly what it was about. Who wanted to listen to an endless song about tuberculosis when the air was filled with the sounds of the Summer of Love?

Morrison returned to Ireland, apparently a burnt-out victim of the pop wars. There he wrote a set of songs about childhood, initiation, sex and death, which finally took form as *Astral Weeks,* a strange, disturbing, exalting album for which there was little precedent in rock & roll history when it was released

Van Morrison in the early Seventies.

in November 1968. Tempered by jazz restraint (Connie Kay of the Modern Jazz Quartet played drums, while the great Richard Davis provided the finest bass playing ever to appear on a rock & roll record) and three levels of string arrangements, the disc moved with a rock beat and a rock feel. It was as serious an album as could be imagined, but it soared like an old Drifters 45. With *Astral Weeks,* Morrison opened the way to a new career and established himself as a performer who deserved to be ranked with the creators of the very best rock & roll music. He has lived up to that promise.

Astral Weeks did not sell strongly, but it attracted

California, where his wife had grown up and where his popularity was fierce; one more album of good times (his best) followed, *Tupelo Honey* (1971); his domestic paradise fell apart; and his music turned tough once again, with *Saint Dominic's Preview* (1972). Yet Morrison's music has been of a piece.

When I was very young," the late Ralph J. Gleason wrote in a review of *Moondance,* "I saw a film version of the life of John McCormack, the Irish tenor, playing himself. In it he explained to his accompanist that the element necessary to mark the important voice off from the other good ones was very specific. 'You have to have,' he said, 'the yarrrrragh in your voice.' "

Van Morrison has the yarrrrragh. His career, especially since *Astral Weeks,* can be seen as an attempt to deal with the yarrrrragh; to find music appropriate to it; to bury it; to dig it out; to draw from that sound, that aesthetic (for it is an aesthetic more than it is merely a sound), new tales to tell, or old tales to tell in new ways. The yarrrrragh is Van Morrison's version of Leadbelly, of jazz, of blues, of poetry. It is a mythic incantation, and he will get it, or get close to it, suggest it, with horns (no other white man working in popular music can arrange horns with the precision and grace of Van Morrison), with strings, in melody, in repetition (railing the same word, or syllable, ten, twenty, thirty times until it has taken his song where he wants it to go). To Morrison the yarrrrragh is the gift of the muse and the muse itself. He has even written a song about it: "Listen to the Lion." Across eleven minutes he sings, chants, moans, cries, pleads, shouts, hollers, whispers, until finally he breaks away from language and speaks in Irish tongues, breaking away from ordi-

widespread critical attention and, in some sections of the country (most notably the San Francisco Bay Area), constant airplay on a few of the FM rock stations just then coming to the fore. Both reviews and airplay paid off with subsequent releases, and Morrison achieved a solid if not a mass popularity with *Moondance* (1970) and with singles such as "Domino" (1970) and the wonderful "Wild Night" (1971). He had moved to Woodstock, New York, and he celebrated a pastoral life of domesticity and sexual delight; the hard edge of his early music and the profound ambiguities of *Astral Weeks* seemed well behind him. Then he relocated in Marin County,

The enigmatic Mr. Morrison.

nary meaning until he has loosed the lion inside himself. He begins to roar: He has that sound, that yarrrrragh, as he has never had it before. He is not singing it; it is singing him.

That is a mystical description; it is a mystical song. Certain themes have emerged in Morrison's music, from album to album: an attempt to come to grips with his existence as an Irishman, whose homeland is in flames, who lives safely, if not peacefully, in America; a corresponding will to discover or recapture a mythical homeland, "Caledonia," or Scotland, the place from which his ancestors originally came, ages ago; an attempt to shape and communicate a sense of freedom. All—the resolution of each of these questions—come down to the yarrrrragh, Morrison's sound, which he cannot, it seems, get at will, which is definitely not "a style," which is a gift and a mystery and understood as such. When Morrison touches that sound he is alive as an artist; he is an adventurer in mystic realms, a conqueror, a supplicant, whatever he would be. When he cannot get it—as on *His Band and the Street Choir* or *Tupelo Honey*, when he was likely not looking for it—he is an impeccable, satisfying, altogether masterful musician.

Morrison is heir to a tradition of mysteries, and he knows it. He is a Celt and at least a spiritual descendant of the Irish prelate Saint Brendan, who set out from Ireland 1500 years ago and who, according to legend, reached America itself and perhaps founded a colony, which disappeared. So there may be a sense in which Morrison can understand that he was always an American (could have been, was meant to be); that his place in America is fated, even if it is

---

Van Morrison, 1987: His albums right up to the present day continue to document the restlessness of his spiritual quest.

unsettled, as he stretches out toward that mythical Caledonia, even believing, sometimes, that in a long and intricate manner, the blues came not from Africa, but from Scotland. That here came from there, that there are no divisions, that all parts of himself are, somehow, linked. Yet this is not a belief, it is a possibility, and the tension remains, driving the urge to wholeness, leading to albums like the incandescent *Veedon Fleece* (1974), or *Into the Music* (1979), in which every side of Morrison's music touches every other.

Morrison remains a singer who can be compared to no other performer in the history of rock & roll, a singer who cannot be pinned down, dismissed or fitted into anyone's expectations. He is a conundrum: His mysticism, which is, I think, his final strength, is anchored by the day-to-day reality of the life he has chosen, which is why his mysticism has nothing in common with the tawdry banalities that were prevalent in the ''spiritual'' rock & roll of the Seventies. But of course it is that anchor, that reality, that has brought his mysticism to the surface, that has demanded it. That is, one might think, the way it ought to work. Morrison, it can be seen now, is a man on a quest; it will be a long one, but there are listeners who will be with him for the duration.

DISCOGRAPHY

SINGLES

Van Morrison: ''Brown Eyed Girl'' (Bang; ☆10, 1967). ''Domino'' (Warner Bros.; ☆9, 1970). ''Wild Night'' (Warner Bros.; ☆28, 1971). ''Tupelo Honey'' (Warner Bros.; ☆47, 1972). ''Moondance'' (Warner Bros.; ☆92, 1977). ''Wavelength'' (Warner Bros.; ☆42, 1978). With Them: ''Gloria'' (Parrot; ☆93, 1965). ''Here Comes the Night'' (Parrot; ☆24, 1965). ''Mystic Eyes'' (Parrot; ☆33, 1965).

ALBUMS

Van Morrison: *Blowin' Your Mind!* (Bang; ☆182, 1967). *The Best of Van Morrison* (Bang; 1967). *T.B. Sheets* (Bang; ☆181, 1974). *Astral Weeks* (Warner Bros.; 1969). *Moondance* (Warner Bros.; ☆29, 1970). *His Band and the Street Choir* (Warner Bros.; ☆32, 1970). *Tupelo Honey* (Warner Bros.; ☆27, 1971). *Saint Dominic's Preview* (Warner Bros.; ☆15, 1972). *Hard Nose the Highway* (Warner Bros.; ☆27, 1973). *It's Too Late to Stop Now* (Warner Bros.; ☆53, 1974). *Veedon Fleece* (Warner Bros.; ☆53, 1974). *A Period of Transition* (Warner Bros.; ☆43, 1977). *Wavelength* (Warner Bros.; ☆28, 1978). *Into the Music* (Warner Bros.; ☆43, 1979). *Common One* (Warner Bros.; ☆73, 1980). *Beautiful Vision* (Warner Bros.; ☆44, 1982). *Inarticulate Speech of the Heart* (Warner Bros.; ☆116, 1983). *A Sense of Wonder* (Mercury; ☆61, 1985). *No Guru, No Method, No Teacher* (Mercury; ☆70, 1986). *Poetic Champions Compose* (Mercury; ☆90, 1987). With the Chieftains: *Irish Heartbeat* (Mercury; ☆102, 1988). *Avalon Sunset* (Mercury; ☆91, 1989). *The Best of Van Morrison* (Mercury; ☆41, 1990). *Enlightenment* (Mercury; ☆62, 1990). *Hymns to the Silence* (Polydor; ☆99, 1991). With Them: *Them* (Parrot; ☆54, 1965). *Them Again* (Parrot; ☆138, 1966). *Them Featuring Van Morrison* (Parrot; ☆154, 1972). *Backtrackin'* (London; 1974).

(Chart positions compiled from Joel Whitburn's *Record Research,* based on *Billboard*'s Pop and LPs charts.)

CREEDENCE CLEARWATER REVIVAL

BY ELLEN WILLIS

For two years, 1969 and 1970, Creedence Clearwater Revival—John Fogerty (composer, singer, lead guitarist, arranger, manager, spiritual center), Tom Fogerty (guitarist), Stu Cook (bassist), Doug Clifford (drummer)—was the most popular rock band in America. During those years the group released five of its seven albums and seven (mostly two-sided) hit singles. At a time when the rock audience had already divided into antagonistic subgroups—hard-core rock & roll fans vs. hard-core freaks, high school kids vs. college students, AM vs. FM—Creedence kept us all, dominating Top Forty radio while continuing to be acknowledged as ''serious'' by the industry-media-fan cabal that arbitrates such matters. Yet for all this ecumenical appeal, Creedence was always somewhat estranged from its generational and musical peers. Its image was of a group stubbornly loyal to unfashionable values. The geographical metaphor will do as well as any: Though Creedence shared turf with the acid-rock bands, its roots were not in psychedelic San Francisco or political Berkeley but in El Cerrito, an East Bay suburb with even less cachet, if possible, than Oakland. Its members were not former folkies converted to

For three years Creedence Clearwater Revival made Top Ten hits that mattered, singing songs rich in metaphor and resonant with the past. In 1969 they looked this way *(from left)*: Doug Clifford, Stu Cook, John Fogerty, Tom Fogerty.

electric music by Bob Dylan; they had been a rock & roll band ever since high school in El Cerrito, surviving five years of touring as the Blue Velvets, three as the Golliwogs and one more as Creedence before their first gold single, "Proud Mary," put them over the top in January 1969. They were not "underground" or "avant-garde" or into drugs or given to revolutionary rhetoric. They were at home with the short, tight, hit-single aesthetic that most "serious" rock musicians scorned in favor of the feckless, improvisatory aesthetic of the jam.

Despite these divergences, and the reservations about the counterculture that they implied, John Fogerty and his cohorts were very much a part of that culture, iconoclastic freaks, but freaks nonetheless. As often as not, their songs addressed the issues—political, cultural, musical—that moved the hip community. In response to the spoiled-rich-kid aspect of cultural-revolutionary politics, songs like "Fortunate Son" and "Don't Look Now" insisted on the touchy subject of class—of privilege and the lack of it. "Proud Mary," with the Huck-and-Jim-on-the-Mississippi echoes that lent its lyrics about dropping out a historical dimension, was an implicit critique of the idea that radicals had nothing to learn from American tradition. "Lookin' out My Back Door" was at once a silly-serious celebration of tripping (with or without chemicals, as you prefer) and a send-up of pretentious visionaries. The band's eleven-minute version of "I Heard It Through the Grapevine" was a brilliant synthesis of opposing musical ideas; it was effective improvisation and effective rock & roll. The tension between identification and skepticism that informed Creedence's relation to its own subculture had a lot to do with why the group was great—and also with why it eventually fell apart.

John Fogerty's dedication to the formula of rock & roll—energy rigidly structured by what were originally commercial constraints—was, in a looser, freer era, as much an aesthetic choice, dictated by temperament, as other musicians' revolt against it. At bottom the choice was a function of Fogerty's populist instincts. Practically it meant that Creedence could reach the mass radio audience. Formally it meant loyalty to rock's plebian roots, and to its most basic pleasures (Creedence was *the* white American dance band; no one else came close). Fogerty's musical choice had its verbal analogue in his commonsense politics. But here an ambiguity arose. For if Fogerty's sensitivity to the realities of class made him reject the elitist romanticism of Sixties revolutionaries, it often led him into the opposite trap, a fatalism best expressed in his repeated use of rain as a metaphor for social ills. Weather, after all, is something you can't do anything about. Fortunately, Fogerty's lyrics were both compassionate enough and angry enough to take the curse off their pessimism; his persona in songs like "Who'll Stop the Rain" and "Wrote a Song for Everyone" was not the smug liberal secretly happy that he won't have to give up his two cars, but you and me on a bad day.

And "Saw the people standing a thousand years in chains/Somebody said it's different now, but look it's just the same" was undeniably truer to most people's reality than "We want the world and we want it NOW!" But it was also undeniably less exciting. If this was not necessarily disastrous in itself, it was nevertheless symptomatic of a serious limitation.

Fogerty's populism and the counterculture's utopianism converged on one important point: Being a best-selling rock band was not enough. A serious rock star aspired not only to entertain the public but to alter its consciousness and so in some sense affect history. By the end of the Sixties the fragmentation of the audience that had coalesced around the Beatles, the Stones and Dylan had made that aspiration increasingly unrealistic. Creedence remained the one band capable of uniting that audience and therefore of penetrating—and transforming—its fantasies. But it didn't happen. Creedence never crossed the line from best-selling rock band to cultural icon. And that failure seemed directly attributable to Fogerty's peculiar virtues.

The great Sixties superstars did not make the pantheon on the strength of their music alone; they, or rather their public images, were also aesthetic objects. Though Fogerty understood this, there was not much he could do about it without being false to himself. He had no affinity for the obvious image-making ploys: flamboyant freakery, messianism, sex, violence. Nor was he a flash ironist. Instead he projected intelligence, integrity and moderation—not the sort of qualities that inflame either fans or journalists. In certain respects he resembled the solid, sustaining husband who is forever being betrayed for the dashing, undependable lover.

It was no accident that my interest in Creedence progressed from warm to obsessive at a time when I was in a state of emotional upheaval brought on by politics, drugs, writing blocks and problematic personal relationships. It was also a time when I was feeling alienated from my erstwhile favorite rock band, the Rolling Stones, partly because of Altamont, partly because of feminism, but mostly because I was tired of chasing Mick Jagger's mysterious soul through the mazes of fun-house mirrors he had built to protect it. Maybe it was all the politics and all the drugs, but I craved a simpler, more direct, more human connection to rock & roll, and I connected with John Fogerty in a way I never could with Jagger. Yet my realization that Creedence had edged out the Stones on my personal rock chart came long after the fact. The switch happened gradually, easing into my subconscious without the customary *zap*—which says something about the difference between Creedence and the Stones.

It could be, of course, that none of this really mattered, that the Warholian age of the media artists was irrevocably over, and that Creedence never had a chance. But that was not the way the boys perceived it; they were profoundly demoralized by the celebrity gap. One result was that they became oversensitive to criticism, which consisted mostly of complaints from the diehards of the Bay Area art-rock lobby that Creedence was an uncreative "singles band." They began making defensive comments like "We have something to *say*." Their sixth album, *Pendulum*, released in December 1970, included what Creedence watchers took to be some tentative concessions to Art—stuff like improvised organ music. I liked the album, but it made me uneasy; it seemed to lack Fogerty's usual authority. Later I found out that the rest of the group had been challenging his leadership; they wanted more artistic leeway. In 1971 Tom left the band, and John agreed that Stu and Doug should play an equal part in writing, arranging and performing Creedence's material. Creedence put out only two singles that year. The next album was long in coming, very long by Creedence's previous standards—over a year. When it did come, in the spring of 1972, it was disappointing.

Mardi Gras wasn't bad, just mediocre. Its rock was softened and countrified. More important, Stu Cook and Doug Clifford simply did not write or sing as well as John Fogerty, who contributed only three of the album's songs. Perhaps, given enough time, they would have grown into their new responsibilities. But in October Creedence Clearwater Revival disbanded. Their situation was hardly unique. It had become a commonplace among political and cultural radicals that leadership was inherently oppressive, and all over the country groups of people who tried to live by an ideology of leaderlessness were disintegrating in bitterness and confusion. In the circumstances of its dissolution Creedence was, for once, utterly typical of the dissident community to which it so uneasily belonged.

DISCOGRAPHY

SINGLES

''Suzie Q'' (Fantasy; ☆11, 1968). ''I Put a Spell on You'' (Fantasy; ☆58, 1968). ''Proud Mary'' b/w ''Born on the Bayou'' (Fantasy; ☆2, 1969). ''Bad Moon Rising'' b/w ''Lodi'' (Fantasy; ☆2, 1969). ''Green River'' b/w ''Commotion'' (Fantasy; ☆2, 1969). ''Down on the Corner'' b/w ''Fortunate Son'' (Fantasy; ☆3, 1969). ''Travelin' Band'' b/w ''Who'll Stop the Rain'' (Fantasy; ☆2, 1970). ''Up Around the Bend'' b/w ''Run Through the Jungle'' (Fantasy; ☆4, 1970). ''Lookin' out My Back Door'' b/w ''Long As I Can See the Light'' (Fantasy; ☆2, 1970). ''Have You Ever Seen the Rain'' b/w ''Hey Tonight'' (Fantasy; ☆8, 1971). ''Sweet Hitch-Hiker'' (Fantasy; ☆6, 1971). ''Someday Never Comes'' (Fantasy; ☆25, 1972).

ALBUMS

Creedence Clearwater Revival (Fantasy; ☆52, 1968). *Bayou Country* (Fantasy; ☆7, 1969). *Green River* (Fantasy; ☆1, 1969). *Willy and the Poorboys* (Fantasy; ☆3, 1969). *Cosmo's Factory* (Fantasy; ☆1, 1970). *Pendulum* (Fantasy; ☆5, 1970). *Mardi Gras* (Fantasy; ☆12, 1972). *Creedence Gold* (Fantasy; ☆15, 1972). *More Creedence Gold* (Fantasy; ☆61, 1973).

JOHN FOGERTY

Blue Ridge Rangers (Fantasy; 1973). *John Fogerty* (Asylum; ☆78, 1975). *Centerfield* (Warner Bros.; ☆1, 1985). *Eye of the Zombie* (Warner Bros.; ☆26, 1986).

(Chart positions compiled from Joel Whitburn's *Record Research*, based on *Billboard*'s Pop and LPs charts.)

John Fogerty released two solo albums in the Eighties: *Centerfield* (1985) met with considerable critical and commercial success; *Eye of the Zombie* (1986) didn't.

BUBBLEGUM

BY LESTER BANGS

In all the history of rock & roll, nobody got more of a bum rap than the purveyors of bubblegum music. Here's a (complete) review of *The Archies' Greatest Hits* by Paul Gambaccini, printed in ROLLING STONE in 1971: "Lord, no. Contained within the grooves of this album are twelve convincing arguments against the capitalist system."

All right, go ahead, *be* snobs, just like you were in the Sixties. But if you're gonna listen to Talking Heads, you might as well know that they cite bubblegum as one of their biggest influences and used to do the 1910 Fruitgum Co.'s "1, 2, 3, Red Light" onstage, just like Wilson Pickett had the good taste to cover "Sugar, Sugar," a rock & roll classic to which something like the Grateful Dead's "Dark Star" can't hold a candle.

Bubblegum music, in fact, rested (or more accurately perked) squarely in the mainstream of the rock & roll tradition. Such oldie "novelties" as the Dixie Cups' "Iko Iko," Johnny Thunder's "Loop De Loop" and Shirley Ellis's "The Name Game" all anticipated the genre, which also has close links with the garage-band rock of the Sixties.

Nursery rhymes set to the beat of rock, that generally most infantile of musics despite what anybody says, would seem to have been an inevitability. The irony, which everybody missed at the time, was that while rock was trying to be so hip and "adult," many bubblegum songs had some of the most lubriciously explicit lyrics in the world, e.g., the Ohio Express's "Chewy Chewy" ("Chewy Chewy, chew me right out of my mind") and Tommy Roe's "Jam Up Jelly Tight" ("Jam up and jelly tight/You look a little naughty but you're so polite").

Who was responsible for all this junk? The same schlockmeister who gave us ? and the Mysterians' anthem "96 Tears" and the same marketing mind behind Kiss and the Village People, that's who: Neil Bogart. As president of bubblegum-central Buddah Records, he let his brilliant production team, a couple of Long Island whiz kids named Jerry Kasenetz and Jeff Katz, run hog-wild. Under the Super K banner, their first attempt was the Rare Breed's 1966 hit, "Beg, Borrow and Steal." Watching the success of the Monkees and Tommy James and the Shondells

("Hanky Panky," "Mony Mony," the bubblegum apotheosis "I Think We're Alone Now" and the opulent "Crimson and Clover") at the hands of other producers, the Super K boys realized that they were onto something hot and stepped up their assault, blessing the world with such hardy perennials as the

Tommy James looks in the mirror, and what does he see?

Rare Breed's "Come On Down to My Boat" (later hit-covered by Every Mother's Son) and the Music Explosion's "Little Bit o' Soul," a Number Two hit.

Late in 1967 Kasenetz and Katz joined forces with Bogart and Buddah, and the rest is history: the Ohio Express ("Yummy Yummy Yummy," "Chewy Chewy," "Sweeter Than Sugar"), 1910 Fruitgum Co. ("Simon Says," "May I Take a Giant Step," "1, 2, 3, Red Light," "Goody Goody Gumdrops," "Indian Giver"), Crazy Elephant ("Gimme Gimme Good Lovin'," a not unlikely prototype for Lou Reed's 1978 "Gimme Gimme Good Times"), Rock & Roll Dubble Bubble Trading Card Co. of Philadel-

phia 19141 (whose name, if not their single—"Bubble Gum Music"—demonstrates how even geniuses can get carried away) and Captain Groovy and His Bubblegum Army ("Captain Groovy and His Bubblegum Army").

The basic bubblegum sound could be described as the basic sound of rock & roll—minus the rage, fear, violence and anomie that runs from Johnny Burnette to Sid Vicious. 1-2-3-4, as Dee Dee Ramone would say. Ladle on a bit of Beach Boys here and there, keep the ball rolling but let it bounce. No lobs or straight shots in the other team's face. A calculated innocence, perhaps, but the wonderful irony was that it worked, and even if most of these groups never really existed, there was authentic tenderness, they meant it when they sang "Oh sugar/Honey honey/You are my candy girl/And you've got me wanting you . . ."

Almost needless to say, all these groups were basically the same bunch of session musicians—but before becoming indignant, we should remember that most of Paul Revere and the Raiders' recorded work and the first album by the Byrds were almost entirely performed by session musicians. In the golden heyday of bubblegum, the team of Kasenetz and Katz produced one ebulliently insidious (because hook-rife) hit after another, and of course it was not long before they had imitators.

From fake bands concocted in the studio it was but one short step to total cartoon groups, the first and best of which were the eternal Archies, whose *Weltanschauung* might best be summed up by the line in "Everything's Archie": "We ain't the Archies without the Jughead beat." (Although they had their

The Archies, a studio band that scored a Number One hit in 1969.

The Monkees, a rock & roll band made to order for television. The band's long-term popularity was reignited in the Eighties with a reunion tour (minus Michael Nesmith, *far right*) and a reprise of their television show on MTV.

darker side too, as in Archie's hands-off warning to Reggie, who couldn't play that well anyway, "Don't Touch My Guitar.") The phenomenal success of this funny-paper combo led to a thousand Saturday-morning kiddy-video copies in the waning Sixties and early Seventies, including the leggy Josie and the Pussycats (actually a spinoff), Lancelot Link and the Evolution Revolution (acid-crazed simians), the Bugaloos (my personal faves), the Groovie Goolies (Munsters dipped in monosodium glutamate), the Banana Splits (whose theme song with its strange imagery—"Four banana, three banana, two banana, one/Five bananas playin' in the bright blue sun"—will be in my head unto the grave).

Since then, bubblegum music has been more or less absorbed into the mainstream—where, as stated earlier, it was all the time anyway. Kasenetz and Katz were still at it late as 1977, with Ram Jam's brilliant "Black Betty," a hit fusion of bubblegum, heavy metal and Leadbelly (of all people).

Bubblegum, after all, is the bottom line of rock & roll. It matters because the real truth is that there will always be at least one tender spot deep in the heart of rock & roll which should never grow up and never will. So you're all welcome to your hash pipes. I'm a Fleer man myself.

DISCOGRAPHY

SINGLES

Archies: "Bang-Shang-a-Lang" (Calendar; ☆22, 1968). "Feelin' So Good" (Calendar; ☆53, 1968). "Sugar, Sugar" (Calendar; ☆1, 1969). "Jingle Jangle" (Kirshner; ☆10, 1969). "Who's Your Baby?" (Kirshner; ☆40, 1970). "Sunshine" (Kirshner; ☆57, 1970). **Banana Splits:** "The Tra La La Song" (Decca; ☆96, 1969). **Crazy Elephant:** "Gimme Gimme Good Lovin' " (Bell; ☆12, 1969). **Dixie Cups:** "Chapel of Love" (Red Bird; ☆1, 1964). "People Say" (Red Bird; ☆12, 1964). "You Should Have Seen the Way He Looked at Me" (Red Bird; ☆39, 1964). "Little Bell" (Red Bird; ☆51, 1964). "Iko Iko" (Red Bird; ☆99, 1965). **1910 Fruitgum Co.:** "Simon Says" (Buddah; ☆4, 1968). "May I Take a Giant Step" (Buddah; ☆63, 1968). "1, 2, 3, Red Light" (Buddah; ☆5, 1968). "Goody Goody Gumdrops" (Buddah; ☆37, 1968). "Indian Giver" (Buddah; ☆5, 1969). "Special Delivery" (Buddah; ☆38, 1969). "The Train" (Buddah; ☆57, 1969). **Ohio Express:** "Beg, Borrow and Steal" (Cameo; ☆29, 1967). "Try It" (Cameo; ☆83, 1968). "Yummy Yummy Yummy" (Buddah; ☆4, 1968). "Down at Lulu's" (Buddah; ☆33, 1968). "Chewy Chewy" (Buddah; ☆15, 1968). "Sweeter Than Sugar" (Buddah; ☆96, 1969). "Mercy" (Buddah; ☆30, 1969). "Pinch Me" (Buddah; ☆99, 1969). "Sausalito" (Buddah; ☆86, 1969). **Rock & Roll Dubble Bubble Trading Card Co. of Philadelphia 19141:** "Bubble Gum Music" (Buddah; ☆74, 1969). **Johnny Thunder:** "Loop De Loop" (Diamond; ☆4, 1962). "Everybody Do the Sloopy" (Diamond; ☆67, 1965). With Ruby Winters: "Make Love to Me" (Diamond; ☆96, 1967).

(Chart positions compiled from Joel Whitburn's *Record Research*, based on *Billboard*'s Pop chart.)

LED ZEPPELIN

BY JIM MILLER

In its time, Led Zeppelin was what the "heavy" in heavy metal was all about. They were the innovators, they practically invented the sluggish, lumbering hybrid of highly amplified distortion. And during their moment—from 1969 to 1973, roughly—there was simply no one better at making their kind of music, a stately, staggering, somnolent wake for the battered pleasures of the first psychedelic era. While singer-songwriters flooded the Top Forty with tales of solitary woe, Led Zeppelin rebaptized acid rock as a dream of druid community, playing riffs as if they were runes carved in granite, singing lyrics as if they were ciphers containing The Truth. It only seems appropriate that "Stairway to Heaven," a song never released as a single, should survive as the anthem for its generation, a record that defines an audience, a time and a place as indelibly as the Doors' "Light My Fire" or the Four Seasons' "Walk Like a Man" or Bill Haley's "Rock Around the Clock."

Despite the undeniable power of their best music and the longevity of their popular appeal—confirmed again in 1990, when the boxed set *Led Zeppe-lin* sold an astonishing 1 million–plus copies, more than a decade after drummer John Bonham's death and the group's dissolution—Led Zeppelin has

Jimmy Page. A gifted guitarist, he orchestrated a somnolent wake for the battered remains of the first psychedelic era.

never made much of an impact beyond the confines of the rock culture. Their blunt style of rock rarely appealed to an older generation raised on the more tempered tunefulness of the Beatles, the more seductive enigmas of Bob Dylan, the apparently more dangerous posturing of the Rolling Stones. For that matter, the band never boasted an inescapable media presence, in spite of their well-publicized profit margin and a legendary penchant for trashing hotel rooms. Perhaps the lack of recognition has had something to do with the fact that Led Zeppelin never moved very far beyond the era it was so instrumental in ushering out: For in the intricately crafted contours of their sonic concussion bombs can be dimly heard the final echoes of the late-Sixties rock ethos. Apart from spawning a lot of self-deluding nonsense about drugged steps toward higher states of consciousness, that ethos cast the ultimate rock & roll experience as complete sensory overload, enjoyably laying waste to the mind, preferably by prostrating the body. In effect, Led Zeppelin, in many respects the last band of hippies, inaugurated a decade of downers among rock fans. Needless to say, this was hardly the sort of achievement geared to win the applause of outsiders, even though the band merely refined with its own genius the very art of escape that lies at the heart of *all* rock & roll.

A product of the late-Sixties blues-rock boom in Britain, Led Zeppelin was founded by guitarist Jimmy Page in 1968, on the model of such bands as Cream, the Jeff Beck Group and the Yardbirds (where Page first came to prominence). Page himself was no newcomer. In the mid-Sixties he had worked sessions with everyone from the Rolling Stones to the Who, reputedly playing on such classics as the Kinks' ''You Really Got Me.'' He eventually joined the Yardbirds as a bassist and, later, a second guitarist.

From the outset Page was Led Zeppelin's musical mainspring. Despite vocalist Robert Plant's visibility, it was Page who plotted the band's course, not only as lead guitarist, but also as the group's producer. He was the architect of *the* early-Seventies hard-rock style, perhaps best captured in ''Whole Lotta Love'' from *Led Zeppelin II*. Page opens with a blurry fuzz riff, tracing a staccato figure; when Plant enters,

his voice, contorted and harsh, is framed with reverb, another element of controlled garble, finally locked into place by John Bonham's barrage of drum rolls, like a sleepy dinosaur coming to life. The excitement of the record comes from the field of tension Page has produced, using more or less simple components. And when the record in midstream collapses into a cacophonous mock orgy, it only seems like a logical release. The *sound* of "Whole Lotta Love" says it all: Ponderous yet precise, naggingly insistent yet modulated by dynamic contrasts, it gives fresh form to hard rock.

Page's primary concern was always sound. His playing lacked the lyricism of Eric Clapton, the funk of Jimi Hendrix or the rhythmic flair of Pete Townshend. But of all the virtuoso guitarists of the Sixties, Page, along with Hendrix, most expanded the instrument's sonic vocabulary. He exhibited a studio musician's knack for functionalism; unlike many of his peers, he rarely overplayed, especially on record. Most of his solos instead evinced the restraint and proportioned style of his avowed influences: the brooding, involuted blues lines of Otis Rush; the finely filigreed acoustic approach of British folk artist Bert Jansch; the echoed, subliminally driving accompaniment of Scotty Moore (behind Elvis) and James Burton (behind Ricky Nelson) on their rockabilly records. But Page's signature remains distortion. Avoiding "clean" timbres, Page often pitted muddy overtones against a hugely recorded bottom, weaving his guitar in and out of the mix, sometimes echoing Robert Plant's equally distorted screams, sometimes tunneling behind a dryly thudding drum.

Thanks to Page's production, Led Zeppelin quickly outdistanced its competition. Not only was Plant a stronger singer than the Yardbirds' Keith Relf, but Page, in contrast to Cream's trio of superstars, grasped the importance of crafting a cohesive ensemble. Taking his cues from old Chess and Sun recordings, he used reverb and echo to mold the band into a unit, always accenting the bottom (bass and drums), always aiming at the biggest possible sound. As a result, the best of Led Zeppelin's records still sound powerful, whereas Cream tracks like "White Room" sound pale and disjointed.

By the time of *Zo-So* (sometimes known as *Led Zeppelin IV*), released in 1971, the band had broadened its approach to include acoustic and folk-derived material. In addition, the lyrics increasingly

Plant and Page: The songs remains the same; the artists grow older.

reflected Page's fascination with Celtic myths, adding some mystery to the band's image. These disparate strands came together on "Stairway to Heaven," Zeppelin's resounding masterpiece and one of the most popular songs of the decade.

Page here works with two contrasting types of timbre. At the start his acoustic guitar and Plant's unusually sweet singing set a delicate mood. But as the track develops, Page builds intensity, gradually adding instruments, and finally "Stairway" blossoms into an epic rocker, climaxing with Plant screaming over a volley of raw guitar, loud, distorted, altogether a transcendent burst of bombast.

In every respect, "Stairway to Heaven" is a signal achievement. It manages to strike an appealing balance between an almost childish lyricism and a more familiar brand of swaggering bluster, conveying its pseudo-religious message with the kind of complexity and texture and visceral impact that few bands can rival. Best of all, it is subtle without sacrificing the immediacy of the most basic rock & roll. The audience that made "Stairway to Heaven" its

own was right, after all: Jimmy Page and Robert Plant piloted the best hard-rock band of its era.

DISCOGRAPHY

ALBUMS
Led Zeppelin (Atlantic; ☆10, 1969). *Led Zeppelin II* (Atlantic; ☆1, 1969). *Led Zeppelin III* (Atlantic; ☆1, 1970). *Led Zeppelin IV* (Atlantic; ☆2, 1971). *Houses of the Holy* (Atlantic; ☆1, 1973). *Physical Graffiti* (Swan Song; ☆1, 1975). *Presence* (Swan Song; ☆1, 1976). *Soundtrack from the Film "The Song Remains the Same"* (Swan Song; ☆2, 1976). *In Through the Out Door* (Swan Song; ☆1, 1979). *Coda* (Swan Song; ☆6, 1982). *Led Zeppelin* (Atlantic; ☆18, 1990).

JIMMY PAGE
Outrider (Geffen; ☆26, 1988). With the Firm: *The Firm* (Atlantic; ☆18, 1985). *Mean Business* (Atlantic; ☆22, 1986).

ROBERT PLANT
Pictures at Eleven (Swan Song; ☆5, 1982). *The Principle of Moments* (Atlantic; ☆8, 1983). With the Honeydrippers: *Volume One* (Atlantic; ☆4, 1984). *Shaken 'n' Stirred* (Atlantic; ☆20, 1985). *Now and Zen* (Atlantic; ☆6, 1988). *Manic Nirvana* (Atlantic; ☆13, 1990).

(Chart positions compiled from Joel Whitburn's *Record Research,* based on *Billboard*'s LPs chart.)

HEAVY METAL

BY LESTER BANGS

As its detractors have always claimed, heavy-metal rock is nothing more than a bunch of noise; it is not music, it's distortion—and that is precisely why its adherents find it appealing. Of all contemporary rock, it is the genre most closely identified with violence and aggression, rapine and carnage. Heavy metal orchestrates technological nihilism, which may be one reason it seemed to run dry in the mid-Seventies. It's a fast train to nowhere, which may be one reason it seems to feel so good and make so much sense to its fans.

When Eric Burdon sang in "Monterey" of "ten thousand guitars . . . groovin' real loud," he was an unwitting prophet of heavy metal. For its noise is created by electric guitars, filtered through an array of warping devices from fuzz tone to wah-wah, cranked several decibels past the pain threshold, loud enough to rebound off the walls of the biggest arenas anywhere. Add the aural image of a battering ram, and you've got a pretty good picture of what heavy metal sounds like.

The forerunners of the heavy-metal style were the British superstar bands of the mid-Sixties. The roots of heavy metal, as a sound and a stance, lie in the Who's "My Generation" and "I Can See for Miles,"

and in the fuzz-tone-and-feedback explosions of Eric Clapton, Jeff Beck and Jimmy Page.

Two British superbands—Cream, formed in 1966, and Led Zeppelin, in 1968—drew on the British R&B tradition for their material and on ex-Yardbirds for their personnel. They became two of the most popular rock bands in the world. A whole generation of guitarists was turned around and fired up by Eric Clapton's strenuous (strained, some said) lines with Cream and Jimmy Page's power chording with Zep, not to mention Jimi Hendrix, with his Yardbirds- and Who-derived distortions and patently personal banshee wails.

The musical achievements of the countless guitar-

Your pal, Alice Cooper.

ists who have grown up in the shadow of this triumvirate have ranged from sonic Saint Elmo's fires to electric mud. As with so much rock, however, the distinction between the two often lay somewhere between the ears, brain and nervous system of any given member of the audience: There's a thin line between heavy riffs and lumbering sludge.

Now that we have defined the musical territory in general—brutal guitars, equally thunderous slabs of thick-thudding bass and the obligatory extended drum solo in concert—we must deal with the oft-raised canard that "all heavy-metal groups sound alike."

Wrong. They sound alike only to the untutored ear. True, the dependence upon technology does foster a certain machinelike uniformity (if not precision). True, the vocals of Ozzy Osbourne of Black Sabbath bear more than a passing resemblance to those of Jack Bruce of Cream; those of Deep Purple's Ian Gillan to Led Zeppelin's Robert Plant; and those of Aerosmith's Steven Tyler to, among others, Alice Cooper. True also that the author once stared at a picture of Tyler on an office wall for three months

before he realized it wasn't either Carly Simon or Mick Jagger. But to postulate categorically that all heavy-metal bands are the same is utterly ludicrous.

That is why I will now provide a convenient reference guide, for those readers who wish to be able to tell heavy-metal bands apart without actually listening to their records.

In the primordial tar pits of 1968 early flurries of metal mutation appeared out of California. Blue Cheer, Iron Butterfly and Black Pearl prophesied worldwide madness to come. The Butterfly were renowned for the seventeen-minute "In-A-Gadda-Da-Vida," title cut on the best-selling LP in the history of Atlantic Records (at least until Led Zeppelin got off the ground). Blue Cheer was truly ahead of its time; from San Francisco, of all places, this power trio was so loud that a reviewer of one of its early concerts, at a loss for words, called it "Super Druid rock." I once had a friend who owned a record player with a switch that could make his turntable rotate counterclockwise, and thus play his records backward; when we played Blue Cheer's first album, *Vincebus Eruptum,* backward, it sounded exactly the same as usual.

A good deal of this action derived from the remaining smoky wisps of psychedelia and "acid rock"—itself an outgrowth of Yardbirds experimentalism. Over in Britain the psychedelic imperative sank deep into the fretting fingers of the post-Cream, post-Hendrix bands, resulting not only in the cinematic guitar work and fuzzy lyric imagery that sustained Led Zeppelin, but in such sub-Zeppelin British kozmik behemoths as Black Sabbath.

Perhaps in reaction, there appeared two other, divergent movements among British metallurgists: Some were proles, others noblemen. In the Working Class we find journeyman bands like Deep Purple, who started out psychedelic (*The Book of Taliesyn* was the title of an early LP) but soon became so meaningless as to defy the easy thematic definition of a Black Sabbath, and changed personnel so many times it didn't matter anyway. A later notable addition to the British Working Class is a supergroup by the name of Bad Company, whose stock-in-trade are the most predictable of heavy riffs and rodomontades to the effect that they are "bad men." Ex-Yardbird Jeff Beck also briefly formed a Working Class power trio, with two American ex-members of Vanilla Fudge, called Beck, Bogert and Appice.

With the coming of the Seventies, however, there

was a certain feeling that one might as well slouch toward Bethlehem with lace cuffs and powdered nose, so the Aristocratic wing of Anglo metal was born, its most notable adherents being the aptly named Queen and the crossover act Sweet, who have also dabbled in bubblegum music with such hits as ''Little Willy.''

We Americans, of course, have never stood for any of that royalty stuff, and our metal merchants have, for the most part, remained solidly Industrial Working Class even if some of them did bathe in mascara. Among the long list of our proletarian partisans are such never-to-be-forgotten bands as Cactus, Mountain (starring Leslie West, who once said in an interview that his life was changed by viewing Eric Clapton in concert with Cream when he—Leslie—was on acid at the Fillmore), the Frost (whose leader, Dick Wagner, went on to provide anonymous guitar salvage on numerous Alice Cooper albums and tours), Aerosmith, Kiss, Bachman-Turner Overdrive (Canadian division) and the immortal Grand Funk Railroad, who made their debut before 100,000 screaming kids at the Atlanta Pop Festival in 1969, and went on to become perhaps the first *under*-underground band by being loved all the more fiercely by the teens because they were so roundly hated by all the hip rock critics.

Out of American Working Class metal emerged two subgroups: American Revolutionary and Boogie

That's Iggy Pop, on the brink of doing something naughty.

Grand Funk explore the Southwest.

Bands. The Revolutionary bands believed staunchly in rock & roll as an instrument of social change. The first of them, the MC5, also happened to be one of the best bands this country ever produced, but a series of bad breaks left them stranded in the ozone and Grand Funk—briefly exploiting the same rhetoric, toned down—stepped into their shoes with alacrity. The Boogie Bands by contrast are almost defiantly apolitical (not to mention atonal). Their *raison d'être* seems to be the eternal reiteration of the simplest riffs, for the sake of ''partying.'' This subgroup includes, among countless others, Black Oak Arkansas (who have also betrayed a pronounced mystical bent), the aforementioned Cactus, and ZZ Top, who wear cowboy hats.

In reaction to all this proletarian/politico/partying, we have had the American Deviates, most of them inspired by that watershed American band of the late Sixties, the Velvet Underground, who thrashed out a whiplash brand of heavy metal in

''European Son,'' ''I Heard Her Call My Name'' and ''Sister Ray.'' Their most attentive disciples were Detroit's Iggy and the Stooges, who also embodied rock & roll as animal savagery at the most purely atavistic, not to mention nihilistic, level this writer has ever seen. So nihilistic that they just kept on exploding and never achieved the commercial success later engineered in the calculated ploys of Alice Cooper and Kiss, or the less successful Blue Oyster Cult. What all these bands share besides riffs is an interest in rock & roll/heavy metal as transmitter of the sadomasochistic dialectic.

But S&M is only one expression of fixated sexuality. All of rock & roll may be another—the reinforcement and preservation of whatever vestiges of primal infantilism have managed to survive into adolescence, and the glorification of adolescence as the Time of Your Life (yeah, sure). But from Chuck Berry on, rock has provided anthems to teenhood (and teen hoods), has been about teenage frustrations, and there is perhaps no music which more accurately conveys the screaming nerves of pubescent frustration than heavy metal. So we have had the purveyors of what I would call American Teenage Angst Anthems, most notably the Stooges (''I Wanna Be Your Dog''), MC5 (''High School''), Alice Cooper (''I'm Eighteen'') and the Dictators (''Teengenerate''). They are, perhaps, the truest expressions of heavy metal's soul and inspiration.

Then again, it may not make much difference in the long run. As the Seventies drew to a close, it appeared that heavy metal had had it. Records by bands like Kiss, Aerosmith and Bad Company could still be found on the charts, but they didn't hit the nervous system with quite the same electrode barracuda bite that early Led Zepplin, MC5 and even Grand Funk had. Kiss, probably the supreme embodiment of rock's transformation into pure show biz, sold fewer records each time out, while newcomers like Heart and Van Halen were little more than prefab copies of Led Zeppelin.

Though they don't sell nearly as well, what little flair and freshness remained in heavy metal has been stolen by punk rockers like the Ramones and Sex Pistols, who stripped it down, sped it up and provided some lyric content beyond the customary

macho breast-beatings, by now not only offensive but old-fashioned. This tradition is nevertheless carried on by Ted Nugent, whose Noble Savage act, complete with loincloth, can be a kind of moronic fun, even though it's nothing but schtick created to shore up a guitar style that's pure jackoff.

For Ted, like all the other boys plying this declining genre, it's all down to rote now, cyclical permutations of prefab riffs, as another commercial cycle is completed: Heavy metal, mutant monster bad boy of Sixties rock, has at last gone middle-of-the-road respectable (especially in a plethora of faceless corporate bands with interchangeable one-word monickers like Triumph, Toto, Foreigner, Journey, etc., etc., etc.), tyrannosaur tamed into mild-mannered brontosaur. Which only stands to reason, when one reflects that it was, from inception, a style born from machines and electronic appendages, as

ALBUMS

Alice Cooper: *Love It to Death* (Warner Bros.; ☆35, 1971). *Killer* (Warner Bros.; ☆21, 1971). *School's Out* (Warner Bros.; ☆2, 1972). *Billion Dollar Babies* (Warner Bros.; ☆1, 1973). *Muscle of Love* (Warner Bros.; ☆10, 1973). *Alice Cooper's Greatest Hits* (Warner Bros.; ☆8, 1974). **Black Oak Arkansas:** *Black Oak Arkansas* (Atco; ☆127, 1971). *Raunch 'n' Roll/Live* (Atco; ☆90, 1973). *High on the Hog* (Atco; ☆52, 1973). **Black Pearl:** *Black Pearl* (Atlantic; ☆130, 1969). **Black Sabbath:** *Black Sabbath* (Warner Bros.; ☆23, 1970). *Paranoid* (Warner Bros.; ☆12, 1971). *Master of Reality* (Warner Bros.; ☆8, 1971). **Blue Cheer:** *Vincebus Eruptum* (Philips; ☆11, 1968). **Blue Oyster Cult:** *Blue Oyster Cult* (Columbia; ☆172, 1972). *Secret Treaties* (Columbia; ☆53, 1974). *On Your Feet Or on Your Knees* (Columbia; ☆22, 1975). **Cactus:** *Cactus* (Atco; ☆54, 1970). **Deep Purple:** *Shades of Deep Purple* (Tetragrammaton; ☆24, 1968). *Deep Purple in Rock* (Warner Bros.; ☆143, 1970). *Fireball* (Warner Bros.; ☆32, 1971). *Machine Head* (Warner Bros.; ☆7, 1972). *Who Do We Think We Are!* (Warner Bros.; ☆15, 1973). *Made in Japan* (Warner Bros.; ☆6, 1973). *Burn* (Warner Bros.; ☆9, 1974). **Frost:** *Frost Music* (Vanguard; ☆168, 1969). **Grand Funk Railroad:** *On Time* (Capitol; ☆27, 1969). *Grand Funk* (Capitol; ☆11, 1970). *Closer to Home* (Capitol; ☆6, 1970). *Live Album* (Capitol; ☆5, 1970). *Survival* (Capitol; ☆6, 1971). *E Pluribus Funk* (Capitol; ☆5, 1971). *Mark, Don and Mel* (Capitol; ☆17, 1972). *We're an American Band* (Capitol; ☆2, 1973). *Shinin' On* (Capitol; ☆5, 1974). **Iron Butterfly:** *Heavy* (Atco; ☆78, 1968). *In-a-Gadda-Da-Vida* (Atco; ☆4, 1968). **MC5:** *Kick Out the Jams* (Elektra; ☆30, 1969). *Back in the USA* (Atlantic; ☆137, 1970). **Mountain:** *Mountain* (Windfall; ☆72, 1969). *Nantucket Sleighride* (Windfall; ☆16, 1971). **Queen:** *Queen* (Elektra; ☆83, 1973). *Queen II* (Elektra; ☆49, 1974). *Sheer Heart Attack* (Elektra; ☆17, 1974). *A Night at the Opera* (Elektra; ☆4, 1975). **Stooges:** *The Stooges* (Elektra; ☆106, 1969). *Funhouse* (Elektra; 1970). *Raw Power* (Columbia; ☆182, 1973). **Sweet:** *The Sweet* (Bell; ☆191, 1973). *Desolation Boulevard* (Capitol; ☆25, 1975). **Uriah Heep:** *Demons and Wizards* (Mercury; ☆23, 1972). *The Magician's Birthday* (Mercury; ☆31, 1972). **Velvet Underground:** *White Light/White Heat* (Verve; ☆199, 1968). **Leslie West:** *The Great Fatsby* (RCA; ☆168, 1975). **West, Bruce and Laing:** *Why Dontcha* (Columbia; ☆26, 1972). **ZZ Top:** *Tres Hombres* (London; ☆32, 1973). *Fandango* (London; ☆10, 1975).

(Chart positions compiled from Joel Whitburn's *Record Research*, based on *Billboard*'s LPs chart.)

much as from human fingers, hearts and minds. Heavy metal has become the foremost victim of a cybernetic revolution spawned by itself—and technology once again closes the gap between frustration and profit.

The MC5, victims of the American ruse.

THE METAL EXPLOSION

BY CHUCK EDDY

By all rights, punk rock should have killed off heavy metal, but, from London to L.A., what it really did was give metal a new point of entry. From there the genre went off in more directions than any cartographer could diagram. By the early Nineties loud, fast electric guitars seemed like the *least* important factor in the metal equation; they were always there, for sure, but what made or broke hard-rock records were such ancient standbys as soul bass lines, *musique-concrète* mixology, acoustic strumming, string sections, tambourines, saxes, electropercussion and good old vocal abandon. And as far as the rock *band* format is concerned, metal basically swallowed rock & roll whole.

This shouldn't come as that much of a surprise if you were banging head to the right clamor in the first place—the best early metal records, like any great rock & roll, worked as music and noise at the same time. Mom might've made you turn 'em down, but you knew they had a gargantuan groove, hooks that stuck to your developing gonads and maybe even

Welcome to the jungle: Axl Rose of Guns n' Roses.

some wisdom: I'm talking oldies like the Stooges' "I Wanna Be Your Dog," Black Sabbath's "Paranoid," Led Zep's "Communication Breakdown," Alice Cooper's "School's Out," Golden Earring's "Radar Love"—all ingenious extensions of the garage-rock nuggets of the mid-Sixties. Great Seventies metal acts, from Nazareth and Aerosmith to the Sweet and Slade, were dance combos. Scratch their crusty surface, you'll find rhythm & blues.

By the end of the Me Decade, Pasadena, California, had upchucked one of metal's biggest 'Me''s ever, namely, Van Halen front man David Lee Roth. And though it was Roth's mouth and Netherlands-born Flying V showoff Eddie Van Halen's nimble fingers that got the attention, what *really* made Van Halen swell were coming-of-age car-radio unavoidables like "Dance the Night Away," "Jamie's Cryin'," "Ain't Talkin' 'Bout Love" and, eventually, the synthesizer-hooked "Jump." When VH concentrated on being heavy and adult, on *Women and Children First* (1980) and *Fair Warning* (1981), the band got lost. By the time Roth left for a tired solo career and boogie clod Sammy Hagar pinch-hit, Van Halen didn't know which end was up.

Van Halen was probably the most "metal" of a certain widely popular breed of loud-guitar outfit that reached commercial age while punk and disco were stealing the headlines—consisting largely of pros who grew up understanding that hard rock doesn't have to be a death trip. Entities like Foreigner, Journey, Styx, Boston, the Babys and Loverboy set out to sweeten metal clichés with

adult-contemporary melodies and harmonies and big guitars that sang like Mantovani strings. More often than anyone has ever admitted, it worked.

Boston and Foreigner, especially, combined Seventies art-rock prettiness with Seventies boogie plainspokenness, a canny hybrid. Journey's Steve Perry was a soulful singer with no restraint at all, and if you ask Axl Rose (or Garth Brooks) they'll explain why that's a smart thing to be. "Can't Fight This Feeling" by REO Speedwagon, "Missing You" by ex-Baby John Waite and "I Want to Know What Love Is" by Foreigner belong in any worthy stack of Eighties rock singles. Loverboy's 1980 debut album was proof that power pop, punk, disco, metal, pomp, Police parodies and R&B horn solos can all fit in the same place; likewise, on "It's Easy," on its second album, *Don't Look Back* (1978), Boston borrowed bass and drumbeats from "I Wanna Be Your Dog" and sang Beach Boys harmonies while the

Heavy Metal Thunder: Alex Van Halen at work.

crescendos got ornate like Yes. That's called "avant-garde pastiche."

In England a gaggle of equally fervid classic-rock fans, most notably Iron Maiden and the only marginally less pretentious Judas Priest, kicked off what the British music paper *Sounds* dubbed the "New Wave of Heavy Metal." Maiden, Priest and interchangeable lesser lights like Saxon and Sampson supposedly played faster and louder than their metal forebears (that was the "new wave" part). But all that meant was that, at best, they worked as mock-medieval versions of Sabbath. The lyrics generally concerned stuff like monsters having battles with ancient mariners; the singers had a bad habit of confusing rock music with opera, as did the musicians. Sometimes the records came out on independent labels and got written up in fanzines by people who took them seriously!

The main difference between your typical Boston-Foreigner fan and your typical Priest-Maiden fan, in the States at least, is that the former had a life and the latter didn't. Foreigner fans lived *with* music, Maiden fans lived *for* it. So while a Foreigner fan might appreciate a guitar line or lyric for what it *expressed,* a Maiden fan might more likely praise it for how it *sounded.* By this admittedly imperfect dichotomy, Foreigner fans are the roots of Cinderella and Warrant fans, and Maiden fans are the roots of Metallica and Soundgarden fans. And I'm not gonna say which approach is "better," but I will say that the Foreigner approach strikes me as truer to how rock & roll is defined by Chuck Berry works. And I'll note that, by the Nineties, countless "alternative" fanzines had taken to praising the "hefty guitar sounds" of an endless avalanche of otherwise useless metal-punk crossover product.

Heavy metal would sound better now if it had never become a "lifestyle choice." In the Eighties bands and then fans started defining themselves strictly on their "metalness," to the extent that heavy metal came to mean a certain prescribed set of unhealthy things tattooed social outcasts did. Yet the best metal has always tended to come from musicians who have next to no stake in "heavy-metal culture." Journey may have been a laughingstock, but the band still holds up better than Judas Priest, or Black Flag for that matter, not just because it had a cleverer vocalist and more mobile rhythm section, but because it never took its loud guitars for granted. Journey made sure its noise meant something.

Back in the United Kingdom, the one great Eighties band wasn't veteran sprint-boogie purists Motörhead, who did a cool fast growl called "Ace of Spades" in 1980 and then followed it up with a few hundred versions of the same growl; it was adolescent glam fans Def Leppard, who started off (on *On Through the Night,* from 1980) moshing just as swiftly, but learned to twiddle the studio's echo knobs and to whistle ethereal harmonies when metal purism started to wear thin. They turned Zep-pomp time changes into Top Forty hooks, thus letting quiet rusticness and loud tech merge into a wicked flow. By *Hysteria* (1987), Def Lep was reinventing garage rock as glittery outer-space electropop. Motörhead never came close to making a record so weird.

What Motörhead was aiming for—basically, a metal alloy with the power of punk and a density and beat to beat it—AC/DC achieved. Like Motörhead (and like fellow Australians Rose Tattoo and Angel City), AC/DC liked ossifying R&B into quicktime grunge. But its drummer knew a thing or two about disco rhythm, and squealer Bon Scott knew his way around the bawdiest music halls: "Some balls are held for charity, and some for fancy dress/ But when they're held for pleasure they're the balls that I like the best." When Bon died of misadventure in 1980, Scott clone Brian Johnson replaced him. The band prospered, especially with *Back in Black* (1980), and thanks to Angus Young's riffs they managed a couple of nifty tunes per year for some time.

In the early Eighties, for obvious reasons, lots of new-wavers decided they wanted to be AC/DC or Motörhead at least as much as they wanted to be the Sex Pistols or the Ramones. Nobody did it with more tuneful effervescence or a bigger sense of frolic than Kix, five Maryland-and-vicinity boys who to this day continue to serve as both America's answer to Def Leppard and the modern world's answer to the Ohio Express. Kix never got the respect of the myriad metallic "hardcore" bands from subterranean California, whose main hobby was to make even more explicit the violence-cum-rebellion schtick of earlier hard rock. Flipper was amusing for a while. Black Flag and the Avengers had moments; most other hardcore units didn't. The Angry Samoans were

Def Leppard: They turned Zep-pomp time changes into Top Forty hooks.

masters because they had the goofiest jokes (''My Old Man's a Fatso,'' ''You Stupid Asshole''), the least histrionic singer (''Metal'' Mike Saunders), and the most rock & roll–like hooks—in retrospect, anger had very little to do with it.

One unusually prophetic hardcore record was *Into the Unknown*, a keyboard-heavy 1983 document by the suburban L.A. foursome Bad Religion, who never did anything else half so remarkable. Punks called it a sellout, for good reason: Nobody before had thought to tap the spacey excesses of prepunk mid-Seventies AOR. This was almost as uplifting as a Boston album! If you want to know how Nirvana came to be, *Into the Unknown* is where to start; you might also refer to the semi-ironic Ted Nugent and Crazy Horse riffs on ''Tangled Up'' and ''Repulsion,'' respective 1986 singles by Michigan's Necros and Boston's Dinosaur Jr. Beyond that, from Mis-

sion of Burma and Hüsker Dü to Green River and all its Seattle descendents, the post-hardcore wah-wah revival was a stiff scam that only got stiffer over time. Go ahead and praise Nirvana's *Nevermind* to high heaven, but REO Speedwagon did it better with *You Can Tune a Piano, But You Can't Tuna Fish* way back in '78.

Anyhow, back in Eighties L.A. both Van Halen and hardcore had some bearing on what was about to happen next. But what really turned the tide was MTV. In the Seventies lots of metal bands (especially of the ''boogie'' variety) had favored the stodgy dressed-down-dude-next-door look, but by 1982 or so, technopop England had put mascara and eyeliner back onto the map, and metal had to follow suit or be pushed by the wayside. The mid-Eighties metal bands to benefit videowise took their hygiene aesthetic from Aerosmith and Kiss, then blew it out of proportion, toward a self-parodic ugliness that stacked *Clockwork Orange* greasepaint and pink poodle perms atop chainsaw codpieces. Foremost among these was Mötley Crüe, who started out pretending to worship Satan and then progressed to just-as-dumb (but more fun and funky) party material. At its best, Crüe updated Sixties dragster rock (''Kickstart My Heart'') or took words from Blondie and music from the Clash (''Don't Go Away Mad'').

Other early Cali-reared MTV successes included W.A.S.P. (who used swear words), Quiet Riot (who covered Slade songs), and Ratt, who were actually pretty punk (in the Sixties sense), talented at mixing echo-chambered sexist snot with tough riffs. ''Round Round'' was Ratt's masterpiece, but *Ratt & Roll 8191* (1991) is at least as solid as, say, *Best of the Standells.* From out east came Twisted Sister, with some decent videos and shouted choruses, plus a singer (Dee Snider) who by testifying at congressional PMRC hearings helped initiate metal's anti-''censorship'' fad.

One rule of Eighties and Nineties metal is: Whenever the hits start getting too catchy, some serious young upstarts will come along and foul it all up. That's basically what happened when hairy hardcore-and-New-Wave-of-Brit-Metal partisans Metallica burst out of L.A. in 1983 with *Kill 'Em All,* a record that succeeded (if you can call it that) at mixing Motörhead's punch with Iron Maiden's pretensions. As Metallica's songwriting got less dorky over time (and it did, somewhat), its composing got more dorky; the band couldn't ''rock'' to save its life, so its fast junk came out mostly as overblown gruel. Finally Metallica settled on life as average myth-metal schnooks. As with most ''speed-metal'' bands, Metallica's least stupid songs were their slower, placid ones—eerie suicidal gothicness like ''The Unforgiven,'' ''One'' and especially the lonely-teen epic ''Fade to Black.''

Metallica wasn't the first speed-metal (or ''thrash'' or ''black metal'' or ''death metal'' or even ''grindcore''—it's hard to keep track) group: Heavy metal started out speedy. And in 1981 three British buddies of Beelzebub calling themselves Venom put out *Welcome to Hell,* which more or less resembled the Stooges with terminal ringworm and kicked off a trend in which high school dropouts sacrificed their baby sisters, drank goats' blood and then got interviewed on television. Unfortunately, speed metal quickly became the province of stern hacks who didn't even have the courtesy to be stern hacks with hooks. Slayer thought it was scary, Megadeth thought it was virtuosic, Anthrax thought it was funny (and politically astute): They weren't. When all was said and done, the substyle had produced a grand total of two consistently interesting bands: Switzerland's Celtic Frost and Montreal's Voivod, both of whom started out churning like cavemen, both of whom exploded toward grinding futurist Dada or dub, years before the rest of their clique caught on, and neither of whom had qualms against selling out to more pop structures (Celtic Frost on *Cold Lake,* Voivod on *Angel Rat*) when the art school tricks started to get stale.

And the art school tricks did indeed get stale. Metal had always flirted with baroqueness and eccentricity—Zeppelin and Sabbath were as artistic as art rock gets, and later on even Rush had enough strange notions to fill a surprisingly listenable double-CD best-of called *Chronicles.* But by the late Eighties the shit really got out of hand. Before the decade was half over beatnik punks like Killing Joke, Sonic Youth and the Butthole Surfers had pretty much exhausted whatever brief entertainment value lies in recombining distorted sludge with industrial drones, unusual guitar tunings and ''postmodern'' montage techniques. But that didn't stop beatnik head bangers from pounding the same concepts, and a few more traditionally ''progressive'' ones, into the ground when their time came.

King's X, Jane's Addiction, Faith No More, Living Colour, Fishbone, Queensrÿche, Prong, Mordred, Warrior Soul, Last Crack, Primus, and so on allegedly expanded metal's sonic palette, but Def Leppard's and Kix's vocabulary had always been just as wide, and Lep and Kix could make you dance and hum along. Where lowbrows like Warrant and Slaughter could surprise you with oddball stuff, beatnik-metal bums constantly revolved their performance-art skits around a hotshot *raison d'être* inherently linked to how many tricks they thought they had up their sleeves—pseudo-funk bass lines, demiclassical intros, stilted refrains, jokes without punch lines, grumpy protest poesy, manly solos, primal screams, sick noise, samples of old TV commercials. Faith No More and the like wore pajamas and jumped around a lot to make you think they had

Metallica: enjoying life as myth-metal schnooks.

plenty of vigor, but really they were thespians with delusions of grandeur, and as such, they were much more fun to think about than listen to. Then they stopped being fun to think about.

Noise for its own sake used to be something to strive for, but by now it's just boring. Doomsday Scud bombers like Ministry and Young Gods might mix their synthcrash and speedthrash into a background music that conducts pagan-ritual sorties on your eardrums in untranslatable tongues grunted through gas masks, but background music is all they are—it's hard to *care* about 'em. They're a fast train to nowhere, sure, but no one's on the train. You can't say the same about Cinderella's unstoppable ''Gypsy Road,'' where Tom Keifer p-p-p-pushes through his band's momentum in a way that makes spinning your wheels sound like the only worthwhile thing a person can do; you can't say it about

Faster Pussycat's ''Shooting You Down,'' which comes closer to matching the animosity of Johnny Rotten's ''I wanna destroy passersby'' than any other hardcore or speed-metal rage ever has. And you certainly can't say it about W. Axl Rose giving the other fella hell.

If there ever was a fast train to nowhere, it's the night train Guns n' Roses ride through *Appetite for Destruction*. For its syncopation, its singing, its forward motion, its humor, its glitz, its spite, its dogged belief that wherever you are is a trap to escape from, this album is the equal of any rock & roll ever made. Axl in ''Shotgun Blues,'' on the far more bloated but still fairly wonderful *Use Your Illusion II* (1991): ''You say I walk the line/They move it every time.'' This is like Bob Dylan, like ''look out kid, they keep it all hid.'' In Indiana Axl gets called a hippie, a punk and a faggot because he likes some

Devo songs, so he takes a Greyhound to L.A. (that's what "One in a Million" is about) where he's treated like "some hickass who just got off the boat." Blacks, gays, immigrants, they're treated the same way. They help trap Axl, he returns the favor, welcome to the jungle. Sex and drugs figure in, too, of course, but not so much as the "decadence" people associate with this band—on *Appetite*, they're land mines like everything else.

Thing is, in 1987, when *Appetite* came out, G n' R seemed like just another L.A. haircut-metal ensemble. And since haircut metal isn't supposed to be where great rock & roll comes from, it took until mid-1988 for anybody outside L.A. to figure out just how transcendent Guns n' Roses were. There's a lesson here, because by rights *Appetite* shouldn't have been so big a shock; truth be told, haircut metal had been the most fruitful guitar-rock genre for years. Unlike its artier cousins, haircut metal refused to succumb to self-limiting rules concerning "originality" or "integrity." It was all compromise, in the same way that the great dance-metal marriages of the Eighties (Michael Jackson's "Beat It," Run-D.M.C.'s "Rock Box," Teena Marie's *Emerald City*) were all compromise. And compromise is what kept it in the mallgame. That is, it had fewer principles and preconceptions than the "real" stuff; poodlehairs couldn't help but be afraid of fewer sounds than anybody else. So they held a tune, found a groove and fished in the dark for innovative ideas (or saleable gimmicks—same dif). In 1990 Tesla even invented *acoustic* metal!

Poodledom gave us not just Cinderella and Ratt and Faster Pussycat and Loverboy and Def Lep and Kix, but unarguable albums by Cheap Trick, Joan Jett, Billy Squier, Poison, Bon Jovi, and (if they're metal enough for you) Bryan Adams and Quarterflash, not to mention a bunch of far-from-shabby singles by Pat Benatar. And *Appetite* may have been the climax, but it wasn't the end. Warrant's "Down Boys" and "I Saw Red," White Lion's "Little Fighter," Britny Fox's "Girlschool," Lita Ford's "Kiss Me Deadly" and Slaughter's "Up All Night,"

every last one the spiritual equal of most any doo-wop or British Invasion one-shot you're nostalgic for, have come since. What's more, they were nearly all huge hits on the pop charts, where great rock & roll belongs. In 1991, Joe LeSte of L.A.'s hyperactive Bang Tango snuck in his own Dylan-Axl the-world-uses-marked-cards creed: "Don't go lookin' for answers, 'cause the road is always bent/The fools use the system, but I know that it's spent." Nobody noticed, natch. I'm still not sure whether the truth is known only by guttersnipes, but if it is, I guarantee they're the kind of guttersnipes who sing power ballads to their girlfriends.

DISCOGRAPHY

ALBUMS

AC/DC: *High Voltage* (Atco; ☆146, 1976). *Dirty Deeds Done Dirt Cheap* (Atlantic; ☆3, 1976). *If You Want Blood You've Got It* (Atlantic; ☆33, 1978). *Back in Black* (Atlantic; ☆4, 1980). *Who Made Who* (Atlantic; ☆33, 1986). **Aerosmith:** *Aerosmith's Greatest Hits* (Columbia; ☆32, 1980). **Angry Samoans:** *Back from Samoa* (Bad Trip; 1982). **Bad Religion:** *Into the Unknown* (Epitaph; 1983). **Bang Tango:** *Dancin' on Coals* (Mechanic; 1991). **Boston:** *Boston* (Epic; ☆3, 1976). *Don't Look Back* (Epic; ☆1, 1978). **Celtic Frost:** *Into the Pandemonium* (Combat; 1987). **Cheap Trick:** *Heaven Tonight* (Epic; ☆48, 1978). **Cinderella:** *Long, Cold Winter* (Mercury; ☆10, 1988). **Def Leppard:** *Pyromania* (Mercury; ☆2, 1983). **Faster Pussycat:** *Faster Pussycat* (Elektra; ☆97, 1987). **Flipper:** *Album Generic* (Subterranean; 1982). **Foreigner:** *Foreigner Records* (Atlantic; ☆10, 1982). **Guns n' Roses:** *Appetite for Destruction* (Geffen; ☆7, 1987). *G'n'R Lies* (Geffen; ☆2, 1988). *Use Your Illusion I* (Geffen; ☆2, 1991). *Use Your Illusion II* (Geffen; ☆1, 1991). **Heart:** *Bebe Le Strange* (Epic; ☆5, 1980). **Journey:** *Greatest Hits* (Columbia; ☆146, 1988). **Kix:** *Kix* (Atlantic; 1981). *Cool Kids* (Atlantic; ☆177, 1983). *Midnite Dynamite* (Atlantic; 1985). *Blow My Fuse* (Atlantic; ☆65, 1987). *Hot Wire* (East/West; 1991). **Metallica:** *Ride the Lightning* (Megaforce/Elektra; ☆100, 1984). **Mötley Crüe:** *A Decade of Decadence* (Elektra; ☆2, 1991). **Motörhead:** *No Remorse* (Bronze; 1984). **Ted Nugent:** *Great Gonzos! The Best of Ted Nugent* (Epic; ☆140, 1981). **Poison:** *Look What the Cat Dragged In* (Enigma/Capitol; 1987). *Open Up and Say . . . Ahh!* (Enigma; ☆2, 1988). **Ratt:** *Ratt & Roll* (Atlantic; ☆57, 1991). **Rush:** *Chronicles* (Mercury; ☆51, 1990). **Van Halen:** *Van Halen* (Warner Bros.; ☆19, 1978). *Van Halen II* (Warner Bros.; ☆6, 1979). *1984 (MCMLXXXIV)* (Warner Bros.; ☆2, 1984). **Voivod:** *Killing Technology* (Noise International; 1987). *Dimension Hatross* (Noise International; 1988). *Angel Ratt* (Mechanic; 1991). **Anthologies:** *Heavy Metal Memories* (Rhino; 1990).

(Chart positions compiled from Joel Whitburn's *Record Research*, based on *Billboard*'s LPs chart.)

Hair, leather, tattoo, cigarette, guitar: Slash of Guns n' Roses.

ROCK FESTIVALS

BY JOHN MORTHLAND

Nobody leaving the Monterey County Fairgrounds at the end of the Monterey International Pop Festival (June 16th through 18th, 1967) could have imagined what a Frankenstein monster they had just helped create—not the score of acts who had performed, not the moguls who had wheeled and dealed and scouted new talent, not the festival organizers; neither the capacity crowd of about 7100, nor the estimated 50,000 who had come without tickets just to be there—not even the hundreds of police assigned to watch over this ''hippie invasion.''

Monterey had been a smashing success. Taking its cue from jazz and folk festivals, it had introduced Americans to such dazzling acts as the Who and the Jimi Hendrix Experience. The San Francisco bands, most of them heretofore only a rumor outside the Bay Area, created a sensation, especially Janis Joplin with Big Brother and the Holding Company. Otis Redding solidified his position as Soul Man to the hippies. Most of the others—Buffalo Springfield, Simon and Garfunkel, the Mamas and the Papas, the Paul Butterfield Blues Band—represented the best and the brightest pop music of the time.

The nonprofit festival (artists were paid expenses only) netted some $200,000, the profits earmarked

for charity. D. A. Pennebaker shot an excellent documentary. The Haight-Ashbury hippie ethic (''Music, love and flowers'' was the festival slogan) emerged as a workable way of life, if only for a weekend.

Yet barely two years later rock festivals would become endurance marathons distinguished by fraudulent promotion, shoddy planning and outbreaks of violence. Monterey proved a harbinger in more ways than one. As soon as the hippies left town, public officials complained of widespread drug use and public sex; a bookkeeper absconded with some of the proceeds, thus diminishing the amount donated to ghetto music programs and free

Tom Donahue engages in sexist conduct on the Great Medicine Ball Caravan.

clinics. Though conceived as an annual event, the festival never returned to Monterey.

No matter, for the bad aftertaste of Monterey lodged in few throats; most remembered only highlights and the money. Festivals began to pop up around the country in 1968, and by the time summer 1969 rolled around, the sky was the limit, with an increasing number of ''bigger and better'' festivals.

These were also days of polarization in American life; youth was perceived as a power bloc, even as a revolutionary threat. The popularity of festivals paralleled the militancy of the Yippies, the Black Panthers and the SDS; some communities, appalled by the prospect of drug-crazed radicals running amuck, drafted ''mass gathering'' laws that made festivals impossible or too expensive (in terms of bonds and deposits) to attempt.

For their part, promoters, smelling quick bucks, enticed thousands to shabby sites with inadequate food, water and toilets. They promised acts they hadn't signed and installed substandard sound systems. Audiences were switching from marijuana to dangerous drugs, particularly barbiturates in combination with alcohol. Many arrived at festival sites with no intention of buying tickets; gate-crashers

and overeager cops created a hostile atmosphere that often provoked violence.

During Easter week 1969 a Palm Springs rock festival saw extensive rioting, with two wounded and 250 arrested. Shortly thereafter, the Newport '69 festival near Los Angeles chalked up 300 injuries, seventy-five arrests and $50,000 in property damage; its promoters grossed $1 million and still finished $150,000 in the red. A festival in Denver closed in clouds of tear gas.

But there were also good festivals that summer—most notably in Atlanta, and in Toronto, where John Lennon appeared with his makeshift Plastic Ono Band—and the mania continued. Even the reclusive Bob Dylan was induced (for a reported $84,000) to make a festival appearance, backed by the Band, on England's Isle of Wight. The capper, though, was the Woodstock Music and Art Fair, held on a farm at White Lake, near Bethel (population 2763) in upstate New York, after being forced to vacate its original site near Woodstock.

An army of 300,000 or more young people descended on Bethel, staggering the nation's imagination. The human onslaught created emergency conditions: food and water shortages, overflowing toilets, medical crises. Rain turned the festival grounds into a huge mud puddle. The talent lineup was the greatest ever assembled, but hardly anybody

Crowds boogie in the mud at a ''Celebration of Life,'' Atchafalaya River, Louisiana, 1971.

heard the music, and hardly anybody cared. Still, with no police in attendance the crowd looked after itself. Despite the fact that more than 100,000 were gate-crashers (after a while, no attempt was made to check tickets), the problems were surmounted and Woodstock became the symbol of youth solidarity.

Never mind that the four young promoters finished the weekend out $1.3 million; that was all made up later, with the release of both *Woodstock*, a filmed account of the festival, which grossed $5 million a month in its first five months, and a successful soundtrack album. (By then the promoters had split into two factions amidst suits and countersuits.)

Without doubt, Woodstock was the biggest and the best yet, but the attempt to be bigger and better still proved a disaster. At the end of their 1969 U.S. tour the Rolling Stones planned a free concert near San Francisco. It came to be called a festival, and despite the fact that the site was changed less than twenty-four hours before the show, some 300,000 fans converged on the Altamont Speedway, near a freeway about forty miles southeast of San Francisco. There was no way that basic necessities could be provided for so many people on such short notice, and Altamont turned into a nightmare of drug casualties, stench from toilets and fires and food and vomit, faulty sound and, finally, the brutal violence visited on the audience by pool cue– and knife-wielding Hell's Angels who said they had been hired (by the Stones and cosponsors Grateful Dead, for $500 worth of beer) as security guards. The climax came as the Stones played late in the day, when a young black man drew a gun and was knifed repeatedly by Angels; he died, as three others had in the course of the day. (There had been deaths at Woodstock, but they had been conveniently overlooked in all the romantic youth-cult hype.) Altamont was hailed as the end of the counterculture; more accurately, it was a graphic symbol for what the counterculture had in truth become. After Altamont there were few successful rock festivals, though there were many attempts, including some that were downright fanciful. Encouraged by the huge profits from the *Woodstock* film, Warner Brothers staged a traveling festival solely to make a movie; a band called Stoneground was concocted, and the whole bunch took off across the country in buses on some-

thing called "Medicine Ball Caravan." The idea was to play various sites, backed by local bands, with national talent flown in. Staffed mostly by leftover flower-power San Franciscans, the caravan was met at some sites by politicos who sought to sabotage it for "co-opting the youth movement" (a common complaint that also prompted cancellation of San Francisco's Wild West Festival and the debacle of the Randall's Island Festival in New York City). The Medicine Ball Caravan film was—deservedly—a flop.

John Lennon—at this point on a political kick that was naive, idealistic and outrageous—also succumbed to flights of festival fancy. At one point,

organizers spoke of bringing a million people to Toronto for a Peace Festival that would include guest shots by extraterrestrial beings. Plagued by a staff too spaced out to plan anything, let alone visitations from outer space, Lennon's pipe dream never came to fruition.

In Europe and America the story was the same: A few festivals were social, financial and artistic triumphs, but most weren't. The Powder Ridge Festival in Connecticut was shut down by court injunction before it even opened; 30,000 people came anyhow. A festival that crossed Canada by train was wonderful for the artists involved (Janis Joplin, the Band, Delaney and Bonnie and Friends,

the Grateful Dead), but lost money at nearly every stop.

By the summer of 1971 there were few attempts at staging festivals. Some 600,000 gathered at Watkins Glen, New York, in 1973 for a one-day outdoor show featuring the Allman Brothers, the Band and the Grateful Dead, and that set the tone for similar day-long blowouts like the California Jam and the Texxas Jam. To say nothing of Live Aid and Farm Aid.

The former was held on July 13th, 1985, in Wembley Stadium in London and John F. Kennedy Stadium in Philadelphia. It was organized by Bob Geldof of the Boomtown Rats as an outgrowth of his ''Do They Know It's Christmas?'' all-star jam single, which spawned ''We Are the World'' stateside: Both benefited starving victims of Ethiopia's civil war. Live Aid reflected rock's new self-image of prosperous, mature social conscience sans the troublemaker edge. About 72,000 fans filled Wembley to see David Bowie, Phil Collins, Rod Stewart, the Who, headliner Paul McCartney and others; another 90,000 in Philly caught Eric Clapton, Phil Collins (who took advantage of time-zone changes to Concorde across the Atlantic after his London set), Mick Jagger with Tina Turner, Bob Dylan with Keith Richards and Ron Wood, Madonna, even a quasi reunion of the surviving members of Led Zeppelin. With television rights sold in advance, some sixty stars entertained about 1.5 billion viewers in 100 countries (making it the most-watched TV program in history up to that point), raising $40 million in the process.

And then there was Farm Aid. In 1972 promoters had staged a country-music festival in Dripping Springs, Texas, that was a total failure, but Willie Nelson picked up the idea the next year and held the first of his Fourth of July picnics. Originally intended as an annual event to consolidate Nelson's status as figurehead of country's trendy ''outlaw'' movement, the picnics were soon discontinued for most of the same reasons that had doomed rockfests. But after Live Aid, Nelson began putting on a series of similar benefits to raise money for America's struggling independent farmers, and these Farm Aid extravaganzas (with an equal number of country and rock acts) were then absorbed into the original picnic idea.

There were two noteworthy attempts at sprawling, old-fashioned rock festivals. In September 1982 a

Live Aid at Philadelphia's JFK Stadium, 1985.

BAND CODE LIST

A Joan Baez
B The Hooters
C 4 Tops
D Billy Ocean
E Black Sabbath/Ozzy Osbourne
G Run DMC
H Rick Springfield
I REO Speedwagon
J C.S.N
K Judas Priest
L Bryan Adams
M Beach Boys
PP George Thorogood
O Simple Minds
P Pretenders
Q Santana
R Pat Metheny
S Ashford + Simpson
T Teddy Pendergrass
U Madonna

V Tom Petty + The Heartbreakers
W Kenny Loggins
X The Cars
Y Neil Young
OO Power Station
AA Thompson Twins
BB Eric Clapton
CC Phil Collins
DD Robert Plant
EE Jimmy Page
FF Duran Duran
GG Patti LaBelle
II Hall + Oates, Eddie
JJ Kendricks, David Ruffin
KK Mick Jagger
LL Tina Turner
NN Bob Dylan
QQ Peter, Paul, + Mary
RR Lionel Ritchie

group headed by Apple Computer cofounder Steve Wozniak attempted to merge the new technology with rock for a three-day festival at Devore, California, about ninety minutes from Los Angeles. Fleetwood Mac, Talking Heads, Tom Petty, Jackson Browne and fifteen other acts played, while tents housed displays and seminars on computers, pop psychology and New Age ideas. Despite attendance by 400,000 well-behaved fans, the US Festival, as it was called, lost anywhere from $5 million to $12.5 million, depending on whose figures you believe. Astonishingly, Wozniak's remedy was to come back the next year, bigger and better. Throwing around unprecedented sums of money, he lured thirty-five bands (including the Clash, Van Halen, the Pretenders and David Bowie) and 500,000 fans to the same site and still managed to lose $3 million. And that was the end of US Festivals. In 1985 and 1991 an independent promoter (backed by Coca-Cola) staged massive, weeklong Rock in Rio festivals in Brazil.

The lineup at Live Aid, backstage in Philadelphia.

While the first (starring Rod Stewart, Queen and AC/DC) was deemed more or less successful, the 1991 gala (with Guns n' Roses, New Kids on the Block and Prince) failed to meet expectations despite crowds of 670,000.

The fact that those numbers could be deemed a disappointment proved just how unwieldy festivals had become now that rock was the worldwide currency of the day. But during the Eighties, North America and Europe saw a remarkable growth in blues, jazz, folk and bluegrass festivals. These were cult musics that drew manageable crowds and could be run on reasonable budgets. Clearly, the same could no longer be said for rock & roll.

The good citizens of the American heartland gather to support the farmer, Farm Aid IV, 1990.

THE EVOLUTION OF THE SINGER-SONGWRITER

BY STEPHEN HOLDEN

There was a moment in the early Seventies when the future of rock & roll seemed to belong to a corps of introspective performers whose ascendancy coincided with what a *Time* magazine story labeled "the cooling of America." Most were white middle-class baby boomers with some liberal education who had grown up with rock & roll, become caught up in the Sixties folk-music boom and tentatively subscribed to the rock counterculture's utopian-revolutionary agenda.

Within the pop community the Beatles' breakup, the drug-related deaths of major rock stars like Jimi Hendrix and Janis Joplin, and the mellowing of Bob Dylan all contributed to this sense of "cooling." But time and age had as much to do with the collective mood swing as current events. In 1970 John Lennon, Bob Dylan and Paul Simon were all pushing thirty, an age when most people feel the first twinges of mortality.

Severed from the Beatles, Lennon released his 1970 primal-scream album, *John Lennon/Plastic Ono Band*, which shattered the Beatles' myth and proclaimed the era of confessional soul-searching to be at hand. The following year Simon, fresh from his breakup with Art Garfunkel, released his first solo album, *Paul Simon*, several of whose songs dealt with physical deterioration and death. Dylan, who in 1968 returned to recording after a two-year silence with the countrified *John Wesley Harding*, began backing off from trying to storm the gates of consciousness, and his following three albums continued the retreat.

The same period saw the release of the first albums by Joni Mitchell, Van Morrison, Neil Young, Randy Newman, James Taylor, Jackson Browne, Carly Simon, Cat Stevens, Carole King and Loudon Wainwright III, and the second solo release by Laura Nyro. Most artists were a little younger than Dylan,

---

Talkin' 'Bout a Revolution: Tracy Chapman displayed a strong political conscience on her 1988 debut album. Here she performs on the Amnesty International "Human Rights Now!" tour.

Simon and the Beatles, and collectively they constituted an aesthetic movement that coalesced in 1968, reached its peak of influence in 1972, then subsided after 1977 with the twin-pronged arrival of punk rock and disco. Finally, in the mid-Eighties the genre enjoyed a modest resurgence, led by women, mostly notably Suzanne Vega and Tracy Chapman.

From the beginning, the label "singer-songwriter" was selectively applied. Lennon, Dylan, Morrison and Young, who had performed with rock bands, did not strictly belong to the genre. Nor did Elton John, Rod Stewart, Bruce Springsteen and Billy Joel, all of whom made some music in the Seventies that was introspective and confessional. Later, rock band refugees, among them Don Henley (the Eagles), Sting (the Police), Peter Gabriel and Phil Collins (both Genesis), enjoyed major solo careers performing personal ballads along with rock songs. In the early and mid-Seventies Stevie Wonder was black music's most powerful confessional voice. And out of the English punk-rock ferment emerged Elvis Costello and Joe Jackson, literate rockers whose songs pointedly rejected the utopian sentiments and romantic excesses of the previous generation.

Because the first wave reached maturity at the moment when albums like *Sgt. Pepper's Lonely Hearts Club Band* were pronounced artistic masterpieces, they felt little need to bring hard-nosed commercial calculation to their work, and the more literary minded actively courted a highbrow imprimatur. The Beat poet Allen Ginsberg, a Dylan crony and champion, was beginning to gain serious academic recognition, while the mainstream confessional poetry of Robert Lowell, Sylvia Plath, John Berryman and Anne Sexton was in literary fashion.

If the poetry of previous generations informed the singer-songwriter movement, Bob Dylan signaled more directly what was to come in 1964 with *Another Side of Bob Dylan,* his last all-acoustic album. Breaking decisively from folk-music orthodoxy, he turned his scalding critical scrutiny away from public matters and toward relationships and his own psyche. In *Another Side* and its successors, *Bringing It All Back Home, Highway 61 Revisited* and *Blonde on Blonde,* Dylan annihilated the aesthetic barricades of pop

music and tore down rigid song structures, bending the length and shape of a song to fit the message. After Dylan, songwriters felt free to forgo the conventional niceties of note-to-syllable word setting and exact rhyme. Traditionally angular pop melodies were flattened to accommodate the torrent of words and the limitations of the songwriters' untrained voices. Instead of a polished interpreter, the writer became the definitive exponent of his or her own work.

The recording medium, through which idiosyncratic voices could be distinctively showcased in custom-designed settings, also encouraged a greater intimacy in both songwriting and performance. The notion of the pop song cycle or "concept album," which had been refined by the Beatles, also proved to be an ideal format for the singer-songwriter, whose characteristic product was a confessional self-portrait comprised of a dozen or so thematically related pieces.

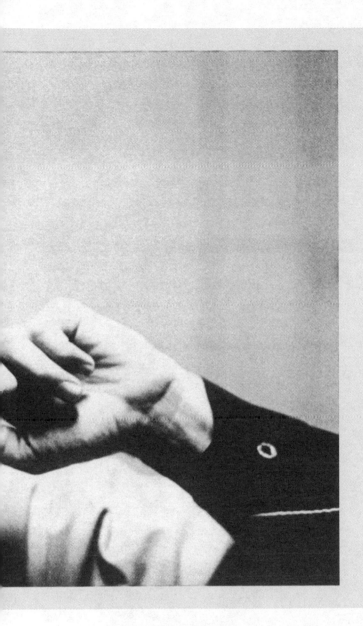

In sensibility the singer-songwriters could be divided roughly into several subgenres, though there was plenty of overlapping, particularly by Dylan and Paul Simon, who crossed all boundaries. Mitchell, Taylor, Carly Simon and Browne stayed largely within the romantic-confessional realm. Nyro and Morrison (in his groundbreaking 1968 acoustic album *Astral Weeks*), and later Tom Waits and Rickie Lee Jones, were romantic visionaries who mythologized their personal experience in often private stream-of-consciousness lyrics.

Leonard Cohen, a Canadian poet and novelist who was seven years older than Dylan, was a visionary of a different sort. He reworked preexisting literary myths into a quirky personal iconography that had quasi-religious overtones. And his sepulchral vocal drone and Middle Eastern–flavored melodies gave his songs added exotic flavor.

Randy Newman, Loudon Wainwright III and John Prine were the movement's leading humorists,

with Newman specializing in dramatic monologues laced with political and social satire. Wainwright turned personal confession into comedy, while the more countrified John Prine, who sounded a lot like Dylan, specialized in middle-American folk tales that took grotesque twists.

There were many others who recorded albums from which only one or two or three songs are likely to last. Rock's supposed "death" was earnestly eulogized in 1972 by Don McLean's Number One hit, "American Pie," which aspired to be a folk-rock answer to T. S. Eliot's "The Waste Land." And his ballad "Vincent"—a doleful homage to Vincent van Gogh—lamented the isolation of artists everywhere. Some others worth noting were Harry Chapin ("Taxi," "Cat's in the Cradle"), Janis Ian ("At Seventeen," "Stars") and Wendy Waldman ("Mad, Mad Me").

Joni Mitchell, who emerged as the Seventies' quintessential singer-songwriter, brought an unprecedented candor and poetic aspiration to her confessional lyrics. Although the talents of the Saskatchewan-born queen of Southern California rock were evident from the beginning, it took three albums—*Joni Mitchell, Clouds* and *Ladies of the Canyon*—for her to shed completely the frillier mannerisms of a folk madonna. Even in a conventional singsongy folk-pop idiom, Mitchell's superior craft was evident in early songs like "Both Sides Now," "The Circle Game" and "Big Yellow Taxi." Other ballads, such as "I Had a King," "Cactus Tree" and "For Free," injected a note of bittersweet sophistication into the musically straitlaced genre. Many of her songs leaned toward the whole-tone scale, and her high ringing voice, which cigarette smoking later darkened dramatically, contained a compelling emotional catch.

It was on three successive albums, *Blue* (1971), *For the Roses* (1972) and *Court and Spark* (1974), that Mitchell finally threw off genteel folk-pop conventions and developed a leaner, more sophisticated, free-form style. Her breakaway songs in *Blue* were two pleas to a lover, "All I Want" and "A Case of You," which had the intimacy and heat of anguished private love letters.

In her lyrics Mitchell refined Dylan's rough-hewn narrative line into a sleeker, more poetically chis-

Joni Mitchell keeping her head above water: Her evolving music challenges herself and her audience.

eled style of pop verse. If her long-lined melodies lacked Dylan's declarative forcefulness, they were subtler and her harmonies more sophisticated. And beginning with *For the Roses,* her songs increasingly incorporated jazzy inflections. On her most successful album, *Court and Spark,* the most innovative cut was a miniature pop-jazz suite, ''Down to You,'' about singles-bars cruising. The narrator of Mitchell's songs was a driven romantic obsessed with contradictory impulses to be sexually adventurous and to be monogamous. Exacerbating the problem was an internal war between what Mitchell described in ''The Same Situation'' as ''my struggle for higher achievement and my search for love that don't seem to cease.''

Mitchell soon exhausted her own love life as a subject and in 1975 moved toward more distanced storytelling with *The Hissing of Summer Lawns.* The album's glistening pop-jazz arrangements represented a musical step forward, but Mitchell's polished third-person vignettes lacked the wrenching tug of her earlier lyrics. *Hejira,* a collection of travel songs in 1976, marked her final and deepest plunge into full-scale confession. Reflecting on aging and marriage (''Song for Sharon''), fame and death (''Hejira'') and her own restlessness (''Coyote,'' ''Refuge of the Roads''), Mitchell found an aural style that brilliantly mirrored the lyrics' interior dialogue in the interplay of her edgy rhythm guitar and jazzman Jaco Pastorius's voluptuous bass.

The albums after *Hejira* tended to be more memorable for their musical experiments than for any lyric content. *Don Juan's Reckless Daughter* (1977) included a quasi-symphonic dream song, ''Paprika Plains.'' *Mingus,* an ambitious collaboration with the jazz composer Charles Mingus, was a high-minded experiment that didn't swing. *Dog Eat Dog* (1985) addressed right-wing politics, and *Chalk Mark in a Rainstorm* (1988) criticized Eighties materialism. Mitchell's two finest later songs, ''Chinese Cafe''/ ''Unchained Melody,'' from *Wild Things Run Fast* (1982), and ''Come In from the Cold,'' from *Night Ride Home* (1991), were both bittersweet reminiscences of her sexually rebellious adolescence. As much as Mitchell tried to move beyond it, her great subject remained erotic love.

James Taylor, like Mitchell, emerged as a polished soft-rock follower of Dylan. He made his name writing and singing autobiographical ballads but quickly withdrew from overt confession. His sensitive twang, which suggested Dylan as a North Carolina country gentleman, projected a contradictory blend of flintiness and nostalgia, dry humor and pained vulnerability, and he was a wonderful guitarist.

Taylor attained his peak of popularity with the autobiographical ballad ''Fire and Rain'' (1970) and ''You've Got a Friend'' (1971). Initially, the Taylor family, which included two folk-singing brothers and a musical sister, were painted by the media as a

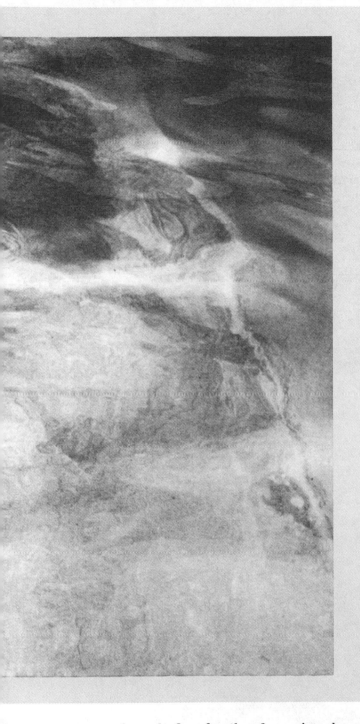

Before their 1981 divorce James Taylor and Carly Simon were considered the royal couple in the hip-genteel realm of international pop society.

Kennedy-style first family of pop, but the mystique quickly faded. In 1972 Taylor married Carly Simon, and until their divorce ten years later they were a sort of royal couple in the hip-genteel realm of international pop society. That mystique was enhanced by "You're So Vain," Simon's 1972 signature song, which criticized the narcissism of a famous, unnamed lover. Simon was as blunt about her feelings as her husband was evasive about his. Her openhearted folk-pop singing conveyed a confidence that was frequently belied by lyrics that expressed a deep insecurity. Although her songs offered an erotic candor similar to Mitchell's, they had none of Mitchell's poetic refinement, and musically many

contained a vestigial streak of Broadway pop. The sum total of Simon's output added up to rock's longest-running public diary.

Among male songwriters, Jackson Browne, from Los Angeles, delved most deeply into romantic confession. Browne's troubled view of relationships and a world he saw as crumbling suggested Dylan as a sort of hippie Protestant minister. His best early songs were ballads steeped in desert light and drenched in the plain-sweet cadences of the hymnal. *Late for the Sky* (1974), his best and most personal album, explored the moods and changes of a doomed relationship.

After 1974 Browne's stance become more public and stentorian, and on *The Pretender* (1976), whose title song predicted the yuppie phenomenon of the Eighties, he moved toward a mainstream rock style. After 1980 he redirected his intense self-scrutiny to focus on political and environmental issues, in particular, on *Lives in the Balance* (1986) and *World in*

Jackson Browne: from California confessions to songwriting as a style of political activism.

Motion (1989), protesting America's involvement in Central American affairs. Like Bruce Cockburn, a Canadian singer-songwriter whose songs mixed Christian mysticism with social protest and personal meditation, Browne became a respected symbol of political integrity.

The romantic visionaries, like those in the confessional school, tended to create their most important work at the beginning of their careers. Laura Nyro, a New Yorker, released a debut album of soul-flavored torch songs, *More Than a New Discovery*, in 1966, when she was only nineteen. Two years later came her iconoclastic song cycle, *Eli and the Thirteenth Confession*. A dazzling, sometimes impenetrable mosaic of diarylike fragments that swirled exotic urban imagery together with fantasies of living in the the Deep South, the songs mixed echoes of Broadway, folk and pop gospel into a burningly intense, highly individual potpourri held together by Nyro's wailing vocals and moody pianism.

Hugely influential, *Eli* sent a powerful signal to younger pop musicians that it was now permissible to begin exploring a broader stylistic palette. Wendy Waldman and later Rickie Lee Jones were among many who took her eclecticism as an artistic manifesto to be followed. After three more albums, including one of pop-soul oldies recorded with LaBelle, Nyro took a long hiatus and returned with the relatively serene and unadventurous *Smile* (1976). In the Eighties she continued to record sporadically, with her songwriting grounded in a radical feminist sensibility.

Although Beat poetry and nonconformist "beatnik" iconography had influenced everyone from Dylan to Nyro, it wasn't until Tom Waits released his debut album, *Closing Time*, in 1973 that a Beat sensibility became the core of a rock performer's style. Affecting a boozy Louis Armstrong drawl, Waits, who was based in Los Angeles, impersonated a Charles Bukowski–like hobo with Jack Kerouac's romantic vision of honky-tonk America. Waits's affectations, which initially seemed to be an entertaining pose, quickly hardened as he turned himself into a theatrical shaman through whom his derelict characters could find their voices. Underneath the gruff exterior was a soft-rock songwriter whose best work ("San Diego Serenade," "Ol' 55," "Downtown Train") had a poignant folkish simplicity that was reminiscent of the softer Bruce Springsteen.

Rickie Lee Jones, who had been a crony of Waits's in Los Angeles, cultivated a similar roustabout mystique. In 1979, when singer-songwriters were at the nadir of fashion, her moody debut album, *Rickie Lee Jones*, sent a flash of heat through a pop climate suffused with post-punk chill. Her songs blended echoes of *West Side Story*, *Astral Weeks*, *Eli and the Thirteenth Confession*, and folk and bebop on albums that had a distinctively retro feel. With its slurred diction and jazz phrasing, Jones's feline singing viv-

idly dramatized a lyrical vision that became increasingly eccentric and private as her career continued. *Pirates* (1981), *The Magazine* (1984) and *Flying Cowboys* (1989) were each conceptual suites describing inscrutable mythological dream worlds.

Randy Newman trying to think of another reason to dislike short people.

In the early Seventies critics who saw the singer-songwriter movement as pointing pop music back toward an artistic gentility that rock was supposed to have overthrown lashed out against its solipsism, narcissism and lack of humor. But at least two significant voices in the movement found plenty to make fun of. One was Randy Newman, whose songs juxtaposed the brittle satire of Tom Lehrer with the symphonic Americana of Aaron Copland. The other, Loudon Wainwright III, was a prep-school-trained folkie clown from Westchester County who reduced the nostalgic suburban ethos of John Cheever stories to a Jerry Lewis slapstick for the thinking person.

Newman released his eponymous first album in 1968 but didn't gain significant recognition until his third studio album, *Sail Away*, four years later. Born into a dynasty of Hollywood film composers, Newman had more musical education than most of his pop peers, and his own arrangements for early songs like "Cowboy," "I Think It's Going to Rain Today," "Love Story" and "Davy the Fat Boy" echo Copland but add mocking German expressionist twists. His uptempo rock & roll songs found an unlikely kinship between Fats Domino and Stephen Foster.

In his lyrics Newman specialized in dramatic monologues for characters who were often racists, rednecks and boors. And his singing of his own piano-based songs in a raspy pseudo–New Orleans drawl added a layer of deadpan comedy to songs describing a morally topsy-turvy America peopled by freaks, hustlers and lunatics. Newman's masterwork remains *Sail Away*'s title song, a slave ship owner's slippery sales pitch to African natives to come to the promised land. "In America you'll get food to eat/Won't have to run through the jungle and scuff up your feet," he crooned condescendingly to natives he called "little wogs." The music's aching majesty together with the lyric's mocking oratory portrayed the gulf between the American dream and its reality with a force that no pop song had done before. In 1974 Newman released his most ambitious album, *Good Old Boys,* a symphonically orchestrated song cycle of dramatic monologues sung by a gallery of Southern characters, and made political points through irony. The narrator of "Rednecks," the album's most controversial song, ridiculed a "smart-ass New York Jew" and proudly proclaimed that he and his friends were "rednecks . . . we don't know our asses from a hole in the ground."

Newman had only one hit, the catchy, clever, anti-prejudice novelty "Short People," in 1978. As he matured, his material became more topical. A recurrent character in his later albums was a greedy, coke-snorting boor who seemed emblematic of Eighties American values. But while many of Newman's cleverest monologues continued to address racism and prejudice with a pungent irony, none reached the tragic depth of "Sail Away."

More overtly funny than Newman, who rarely stepped into the confessional realm, Loudon Wainwright III made himself the butt of comic songs that treated the most personal matters as shared jokes. In the early "Delaware Song," Wainwright wickedly spoofed his teenaged rebel Don Juan mystique. His one hit, "Dead Skunk," in 1973, offered the picture of a stinking dead animal on a country road as a metaphor for the reality that underlies the manicured surface of suburban life.

Even though he worked in a comic mode, Wainwright's lyrics were ultimately more revealing than many of the serious verses of the romantic-confessional writers. His more personal songs discussed everything from an oral fixation, to his genitalia, to his recognition in the 1986 song "The Home Stretch" that he would never be a major star. Wainwright, who like so many others was initially heralded as the "new Dylan," never progressed musically beyond a basic utilitarian folk style that could serve his verses. But his utter directness and phrase-making talents helped inspire a subgenre of urban folk that produced several significant artists with whom he was involved.

In the early Seventies Wainwright married Kate McGarrigle, a Canadian singer, who, with her sister Anna, refined an intimate style of folk pop that embraced turn-of-the-century parlor songs and French-Canadian hymns along with American folk. After Wainwright and McGarrigle divorced, he lived with Suzzy Roche, the youngest member of the New York–based trio the Roches, three sisters who applied exquisite vocal harmonies to witty original songs that were often nakedly confessional without being self-pitying.

N ot all the singer-songwriters thought of themselves as Dylan's children or were inspired by poetry. Brooklyn-born Carole King, who with her husband and songwriting partner, Gerry Goffin, had written such early-Sixties pop-soul hits as "Will You Love Me Tomorrow?" and "Up on the Roof," embarked on a solo performing career in 1968. Three years later her second solo album, *Tapestry*, became a commercial phenomenon, selling more than 13 million copies. King's homey, inspirational songs, sung in plain Brooklyn twang to the accompaniment of her own pounding pop-gospel piano, translated the upbeat sentiments of Rodgers and Hammerstein show tunes into the pop-music equivalent of a hearty chicken soup.

John Denver, who also sported a clean-cut "whole earth" image, was King's guitar-playing equivalent, and his early songs like "Take Me Home Country Roads" and "Rocky Mountain High" conjured a comfortably luxurious rural utopia. Dubbed "the bionic minstrel" by *Newsweek* at the peak of his popularity in the mid-Seventies, Denver was for a time the voice of the sensitive everyman, and he played the role to the hilt. Even those songs that exposed personal turmoil had a carefully balanced ministerial tone that concealed edgier emotions. And his diction and piercing vocal twang completed a cleverly cultivated image that aspired to be at once Olympian and folksy.

Gordon Lightfoot, who suggested a more rugged Canadian answer to Denver, had the crooning voice of a macho Pete Seeger and wrote country-folk songs that covered historical events ("Canadian Railroad Trilogy") as well as personal relationships (his finest song, "If You Could Read My Mind").

Briefly more popular than either Denver or Lightfoot, Cat Stevens became a star in 1971 with his album *Tea for the Tillerman*. Stevens, like many other English folk-pop singers, was strongly influenced by Donovan, the so-called British Dylan, whose hippie mysticism breathed a haze of incense into Britain's singer-songwriter movement. Like Donovan, Stevens affected a simplistic flower-child pose in some songs and an inscrutably mystical one in others. His droning vocal intonation was also similar to Donovan's. Although his records were pretty, they were quite vacuous.

Nick Drake, the most talented singer-songwriter to work in the post-Donovan mode, released three albums before his suicide in 1974 at the age of twenty-six. The best, *Five Leaves Left* (1969), was a collection of dreamy, exquisitely orchestrated meditations that suggested a softer, more diaphanous answer to *Astral Weeks*.

Two significant British songwriters who remained untouched by hippie mysticism were Richard Thompson and Joan Armatrading. Originally a guitarist with Fairport Convention, Thompson recorded his first solo album, *Henry the Human Fly*, in 1972, and two years later, with his wife, Linda, sharing the lead vocals, made his bleak folk-rock masterpiece, *I Want to See the Bright Lights Tonight*. A collection of unblinkingly despairing reflections on dead-end working-class life in England, the songs contemplated suicide, alcoholism and social rot in bitter tight-lipped verses underscored by Thompson's astringent guitar lines. Two other near-masterpieces, *Hokey Pokey* and *Pour Down Like Silver* (made after Thompson converted to Sufism), followed, and with the 1982 album *Shoot Out the Lights*, the Thompsons began to achieve some American recognition. Shortly after that, the couple separated, and Thompson, now an established cult figure, resumed his solo career.

Armatrading, who was of West Indian descent, was the closest thing England produced to Joni Mitchell. She wrote in a broad-based folk-pop style that veered into reggae and hard rock. But her best songs were the introspective folk-pop ballads of two early albums, *Joan Armatrading* (1976) and *Show Some Emotion* (1977). Armatrading's songs, like Mitchell's, often addressed lovers and friends in language that sounded spontaneously spewed out. But unlike Mitchell, she was a narrative chameleon who slipped in and out of different characters when she was writing. Her deep, flexible alto, which recalled the young Nina Simone, accentuated the personal dramas she described.

Ultimately, it wasn't just changing fashion that undermined the singer-songwriter movement. The artists quickly ran up against the limitations of their own experience as a primary source of material. If the movement looked as though it would take over pop in 1972, four years later it was apparent that the singer-songwriters could not sustain a tradition as hardy as the Broadway–Hollywood–Tin Pan Alley axis that had flourished from the end of World War I until about 1960. For while Broadway songwriters from George and Ira Gershwin to Cole Porter to Rodgers and Hammerstein wrote songs for other people to sing in collaborative musical plays and film, the singer-songwriters mostly wrote about themselves for their own record albums. They were trapped within the limitations of their own singing voices and sensibilities.

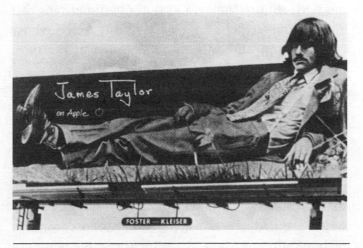

James Taylor, not in the flesh.

By the early Eighties pop had shed many of its high-art aspirations. After the debut of MTV in 1981, rock culture, which had remained one step removed from the mass media mainstream, became quickly absorbed by television. A performer's video image loomed as important as a voice or a song. At the same time, pop's newer electronic technology promoted music that was colder and more rhythmically than melodically oriented. The youth culture had also changed. The sexual revolution, which had helped fuel the rock counterculture, was taken for granted. At the same time, the conservative political climate made professional songwriters more cautious about expressing political and social dissent.

The new voices who emerged in the mid-Eighties reflected this cooler, more streamlined pop world. Suzanne Vega, from New York City, sang her own songs in a clear, vibratoless voice that expressed little overt vulnerability, and her lyrics observed the world with a wary, clinical detachment. "Luka," her biggest hit, was the first-person monologue of a battered child speaking in the tough, deadpan voice of a survivor. "Tom's Diner," which was originally recorded without accompaniment and later became a hit with electronic dance tracks added, described an urban tableau without any editorial comment.

Tracy Chapman, who was black, college educated and from Cleveland, galvanized the music world with her passionate 1988 debut album, *Tracy Chapman*. The record, whose style strongly echoed the early Dylan as well as the early Seventies Mitchell and Neil Young, went on to sell over 3 million copies. Its centerpiece, "Fast Car," described the inner-city cycle of poverty, unemployment and welfare as experienced by a woman whose meager hopes for the future are dashed after the man she loves saddles her with children and walks out. Chapman sang this devastating vignette in a deep grainy voice whose innate moral authority recalled Dylan at his most persuasive.

But although Chapman's second album, *Crossroads*, had its affecting moments, it contained nothing half so powerful. More than two years passed between *Crossroads* and her third album, *Matters of the Heart*, which, like its predecessor, focused as much on lovelorn ballads as on political subjects. Chapman's voice was as powerful as ever, but as a songwriter she had not recovered the narrative command of her signature song. Still, for those nostalgic for the heyday of the singer-songwriter movement,

In her room: Suzanne Vega, one of the most distinctive voices of the singer-songwriter revival.

Chapman remained the best and brightest hope for the flame to be rekindled.

DISCOGRAPHY

ALBUMS

Joan Armatrading: *Whatever's for Us* (A&M; 1973). *Back to the Night* (A&M; 1975). *Joan Armatrading* (A&M; ☆67, 1976). *Show Some Emotion* (A&M; ☆52, 1977). *To the Limit* (A&M; ☆125, 1978). *How Cruel* (A&M; ☆136, 1979). *Me Myself I* (A&M; ☆28, 1980). *Walk Under Ladders* (A&M; ☆88, 1981). *The Key* (A&M; ☆32, 1983). *Track Record* (A&M; ☆113, 1984). *Secret Secrets* (A&M; ☆115, 1985). *Sleight of Hand* (A&M; ☆68, 1986). *The Shouting Stage* (A&M; ☆100, 1988). *Hearts and Flowers* (A&M; ☆161, 1990). **Jackson Browne:** *Jackson Browne* (Asylum; ☆53, 1972). *For Everyman* (Asylum; ☆43, 1973). *Late for the Sky* (Asylum; ☆14, 1974). *The Pretender* (Asylum; ☆5, 1976). *Running on Empty* (Asylum; ☆3, 1978). *Hold Out* (Asylum; ☆1, 1980). *Lawyers in Love* (Asylum; ☆8, 1983). *Lives in the Balance* (Asylum; ☆23, 1986). *World in Motion* (Elektra; ☆45, 1989). **Tracy Chapman:** *Tracy Chapman* (Elektra; ☆1, 1988). *Crossroads* (Elektra; ☆9, 1989). *Matters of the Heart* (Elektra; ☆53, 1992). **Leonard Cohen:** *Leonard Cohen* (Columbia; ☆83, 1968). *Songs from a Room* (Columbia; ☆63, 1969). *Songs of Love and Hate* (Columbia; ☆145, 1971). *Live Songs* (Columbia; ☆156, 1973). *New Skin for the Old Ceremony* (Columbia; 1974). *The Best of Leonard Cohen* (Columbia;

1976). *Various Positions* (PVC; 1985). *I'm Your Man* (Columbia; 1988). **Nick Drake:** *Five Leaves Left* (Island; 1969). *Bryter Layter* (Island; 1970). *Pink Moon* (Island; 1972). *Time of No Reply* (Island; 1979). *Fruit Tree* (Rykodisc; 1986). **Rickie Lee Jones:** *Rickie Lee Jones* (Warner Bros.; ☆3, 1979). *Pirates* (Warner Bros.; ☆5, 1981). *Girl at Her Volcano* (Warner Bros.; ☆39, 1983). *The Magazine* (Warner Bros.; ☆44, 1984). *Flying Cowboys* (Geffen; ☆39, 1989). *Pop Pop* (Geffen; ☆121, 1991). **Carole King:** *Writer* (Ode; ☆84, 1971). *Tapestry* (Ode; ☆1, 1971). *Music* (Ode; ☆1, 1971). *Rhymes and Reasons* (Ode; ☆2, 1972). *Fantasy* (Ode; ☆6, 1973). *Wrap Around Joy* (Ode; ☆1, 1974). *Really Rosie* (Ode; ☆20, 1975). *Thoroughbred* (Ode; ☆3, 1976). *Simple Things* (Capitol; ☆17, 1977). *Her Greatest Hits* (Ode; ☆47, 1978). *Welcome Home* (Avatar; ☆104, 1978). *Touch the Sky* (Capitol; ☆104, 1979). *Pearls: Songs of Goffin and King* (Capitol; ☆44, 1980). *One to One* (Atlantic; ☆119, 1982). *City Streets* (Capitol; ☆111, 1989). **Joni Mitchell:** *Joni Mitchell* (Reprise; ☆189, 1968). *Clouds* (Reprise; ☆31, 1969). *Ladies of the Canyon* (Reprise; ☆27, 1970). *Blue* (Reprise; ☆15, 1971). *For the Roses* (Asylum; ☆11, 1972). *Court and Spark* (Asylum; ☆2, 1974). *Miles of Aisles* (Asylum; ☆2, 1974). *The Hissing of Summer Lawns* (Asylum; ☆4, 1975). *Hejira* (Asylum; ☆13, 1976). *Don Juan's Reckless Daughter* (Asylum; ☆126, 1978). *Mingus* (Asylum; ☆17, 1979). *Shadows and Light* (Asylum; ☆38, 1980). *Wild Things Run Fast* (Asylum; ☆25, 1982). *Dog Eat Dog* (Geffen; ☆63, 1985). *Chalk Mark in a Rain Storm* (Geffen; ☆45, 1988). *Night Ride Home* (Geffen; ☆41, 1991). **Laura Nyro:** *More Than a New Discovery* (Verve/Folkways; 1967). *Eli and the Thirteenth Confession* (Columbia; ☆181, 1968). *New York Tendaberry* (Columbia; ☆32, 1969). *Christmas and the Beads of Sweat* (Columbia; ☆51, 1970). With LaBelle: *Gonna Take a Miracle* (Columbia; ☆46, 1971). *The First Songs* (Columbia; ☆97, 1973). *Smile* (Columbia; ☆60, 1976). *Season of Lights . . . Laura Nyro in Concert* (Columbia; ☆137, 1977). *Nested* (Columbia; 1978). *Mother's Spiritual* (Columbia; ☆182, 1984). *Live at the Bottom Line* (Cypress; 1989). **Randy Newman:** *Randy Newman* (Reprise; 1968). *12 Songs* (Reprise; 1970). *Randy Newman/Live* (Reprise; ☆191, 1971). *Sail Away* (Reprise; ☆163, 1972). *Good Old Boys* (Reprise; ☆36, 1974). *Little Criminals* (Warner Bros.; ☆9, 1977). *Born Again* (Warner Bros.; ☆41, 1979). *Trouble in Paradise* (Warner Bros.; ☆64, 1983). *Land of Dreams* (Reprise; ☆80, 1988). **Carly Simon:** *Carly Simon* (Elektra; ☆30, 1971). *Anticipation* (Elektra; ☆30, 1971). *No Secrets* (Elektra; ☆1, 1972). *Hotcakes* (Elektra; ☆3, 1974). *Playing Possum* (Elektra; ☆10, 1975). *The Best of Carly Simon* (Elektra; ☆17, 1975). *Another Passenger* (Elektra; ☆29, 1976). *Boys in the Trees* (Elektra; ☆10, 1978). *Spy* (Elektra; ☆45, 1979). *Come Upstairs* (Warner; ☆36, 1980). *Torch* (Warner; ☆50, 1981). *Hello Big Man* (Warner; ☆69, 1983). *Spoiled Girl* (Epic; ☆38, 1985). *Coming Around Again* (Arista; ☆25, 1987). *Greatest Hits Live* (Arista; ☆87, 1988). *My Romance* (Arista; ☆46, 1990). *Have You Seen Me Lately?* (Arista; ☆60, 1990). **Cat Stevens:** *Matthew and Son/New Masters* (Deram; ☆173, 1971). *Very Young and Early Songs* (Deram; ☆94, 1972). *Tea for the Tillerman* (A&M; ☆8, 1971). *Mona Bone Jakon* (A&M; ☆161, 1971). *Teaser and the Firecat* (A&M; ☆3, 1971). *Catch Bull at Four* (A&M; ☆1, 1972). *Foreigner* (A&M; ☆3, 1973). *Buddha and the Chocolate Box* (A&M; ☆2, 1974). *Greatest Hits* (A&M, ☆13, 1975). *Numbers: A Pythagorian Theory Tale* (A&M; ☆13, 1975). *Izitso* (A&M; ☆7, 1977). *Back to Earth* (A&M; ☆33, 1978). **James Taylor:** *Sweet Baby James* (Warner Bros.; ☆3, 1970). *James Taylor* (Apple; ☆62, 1970). *James Taylor and the Original Flying Machine 1967* (Euphoria; ☆74; 1971). *Mud Slide Slim and the Blue Horizon* (Warner Bros.; ☆2, 1971). *One Man Dog* (Warner Bros.; ☆4, 1972). *Walking Man* (Warner Bros.; ☆13, 1974). *Gorilla* (Warner Bros.; ☆6, 1975). *In the Pocket* (Warner Bros.; ☆16, 1976). *James Taylor's Greatest Hits* (Warner Bros.; ☆23, 1976). *JT* (Columbia; ☆4, 1977). *Ever Ready* (Columbia; ☆164, 1978). *Flag* (Columbia; ☆10, 1979). *Dad Loves His Work* (Columbia; ☆10, 1981). *Never Die Young* (Columbia; ☆25, 1988). *New Moon Shine* (Columbia; ☆37, 1991). **Richard Thompson:** *Henry the Human Fly* (Reprise; 1972). *Live (More or Less)* (Island; 1977). *Hand of Kindness* (Hannibal; ☆186, 1983). *Strict Tempo!* (Carthage; 1983). *Small Town Romance* (Hannibal; 1984). *Across a Crowded Room* (Polydor; ☆104, 1985). *Guitar, Vocal* (Carthage; 1985). *Daring Adventures* (Polydor; ☆142, 1986). *Amnesia* (Capitol; ☆182, 1988). *Rumour and Sigh* (Capitol; 1991). **Richard and Linda Thompson:** *Hokey Pokey* (Island; 1974). *Pour Down Like Silver* (Island; 1976). *First Light* (Chrysalis; 1978). *Sunnyvista* (Chrysalis; 1980). *Shoot Out the Lights* (Hannibal; 1982). **Suzanne Vega:** *Suzanne Vega* (A&M; ☆91, 1985). *Solitude Standing* (A&M; ☆11, 1987). *Days of Open Hand* (A&M; ☆50, 1990). **Tom Waits:** *Closing Time* (Asylum; 1973). *The Heart of Saturday Night* (Asylum; 1974). *Nighthawks at the Diner* (Asylum; ☆164, 1975). *Small Change* (Asylum; ☆89, 1976). *Foreign Affairs* (Asylum; ☆113, 1977). *Blue Valentine* (Asylum; ☆181, 1978). *Heartattack and Vine* (Asylum; ☆96, 1980). *Swordfishtrombones* (Island; ☆167, 1983). *Rain Dogs* (Island; ☆181, 1985). *Frank's Wild Years* (Island; ☆115, 1987). *Big Time* (Island; ☆152, 1988).

(Chart positions compiled from Joel Whitburn's *Record Research*, based on *Billboard*'s LPs chart.)

THE EMERGENCE OF ART ROCK

BY JOHN ROCKWELL

There is a morphology, an inherent developmental cycle, to artistic movements. They begin with a rude and innocent vigor, pass into a healthy adulthood and finally decline into an overwrought, feeble old age. Something of this process can be observed in the passage of rock & roll from the three-chord primitivism of the Fifties through the burgeoning vitality and experimentation of the Sixties to the hollow emptiness of much of the so-called progressive, or "art," rock of the Seventies.

The whole notion of art rock triggers hostility from those who define rock in terms of the early-middle stages of its development. Rock was born as a street rebellion against pretensions and hypocrisy—of Fifties society, Fifties Tin Pan Alley pop and high art in general ("Roll Over Beethoven"). Thus the very idea of art rock strikes some as a cancer to be battled without quarter, and the punk reversion to primitivism was in part a rejection of the fancier forms of progressive rock. The trouble is, once consciousness has intruded itself into the process, it's impossible to obliterate it (except maybe with drugs, and then only temporarily). And so even primitivism, self-consciously assumed, became one of the principal vehicles of art rock.

The Beatles' *Sgt. Pepper's Lonely Hearts Club Band* (1967) is often cited as the progenitor of self-conscious experimentation in rock. It was the album that dramatized rock's claim to artistic seriousness to an adult world that had previously dismissed the whole genre as blathering teen entertainment. The Beatles aspired to something really daring and new—an unabashedly eclectic, musically clever (harmonies, rhythms and, above all, arrangements) melange that could only have been created in the modern recording studio.

One inevitable implication of the whole notion of art rock, anticipated by *Sgt. Pepper,* is that it parallels, imitates or is inspired by other forms of ''higher,'' more ''serious'' music. On the whole, imitative art rock has tended to emulate classical music, primarily the eighteenth- and nineteenth-century orches-

Yes, so to speak.

tral sorts. The pioneers in this enterprise were the Moody Blues, whose album *Days of Future Past* paired the group with the London Festival Orchestra. Although Moody Blues devotees seemed to think they were getting something higher toned than mere rock, they were kidding themselves: Moody Blues records were mood music, pure and regrettably not so simple. There's nothing wrong with that, of course, except for the miscategorization into something more profound.

The vast majority of the bands that pillage traditional classical music come from Britain. Why British bands feel compelled to quote the classics, however tongue-in-cheek, leads into the murky waters of class and nation analysis. In comparison with the British, Americans tend to be happy cavepeople. Most American rockers wouldn't know a Beethoven symphony if they were run down by one in the middle of a freeway. One result of such ignorance is that American art (music, painting, poetry, films, etc.) can develop untroubled by lame affectations of a cultured sensibility. In Britain the lower classes enjoy no such isolation. The class divisions and the crushing weight of high culture flourish essentially untrammeled. Rockers seem far more eager to ''dignify'' their work, to make it acceptable for upperclass approbation, by freighting it with trappings of classical music. Or, conversely, they are far more intent upon making classical music accessible to their audiences by bastardizing it in the rock context. Or, maybe, they feel the need to parody it to the point of ludicrousness. In all cases, they relate to it with a persistence and intensity that American groups rarely match.

The principal examples here from the Seventies are acts like the Nice; Emerson, Lake and Palmer; Deep Purple; Procol Harum; Renaissance; Yes; and Rick Wakeman. Much of what these artists did was just souped-up, oversynthesized, vaguely ''progressive'' rock of no particular interest or pretensions. But at one time or another all of them dealt in some form of classical pastiche. Wakeman, classically trained as a pianist at the Royal Academy, is as good an example as any. After serving time as a session pianist for the likes of David Bowie and Cat Stevens, he joined Yes, helping to lead the group into a convoluted pop mysticism. He eventually left Yes in 1974 to pursue a solo career devoted to such elaborate, portentously titled orchestral narratives as *Journey to the Centre of the Earth* and *The Myths and Legends of King Arthur and the Knights of the Round Table.* These ice-skating epics had their elements of elephantine humor. But his classical excursions were dispatched with such a brutal cynicism as to be genuinely appalling.

Even when such groups weren't busily ripping off Grieg their music was operatically arty in the bad sense, through their ponderous appeal to a middleclass sensibility and their lame reliance on electronically updated nineteenth-century vaudeville stage tricks. Too often these pastiches were further burdened by the seemingly irresistible weakness certain sorts of loud, arty British bands had for sciencefiction art and ''poetry.'' Yes's album covers make the point as well as anything, but such puerile mythologizing—Tolkien for the teenyboppers—pervaded much of British pop poetry and lapsed over with insufferable affectation into much of the British electric folk-rock camp, too; think only of Jethro Tull and Cat Stevens.

Classical borrowings don't have to be limited simply to quotations, however, nor do they have to be bad by definition. The whole craze for ''rock operas'' of the Kinks-Who variety produced some fascinating work. Similarly, some of the fairly straightforward heavy-metal groups have colored their music with the judicious application of nonrock styles, to telling effect (the use of Eastern modes and instrumental accents in Led Zeppelin's ''Kashmir,'' for example).

Such use of classical and other nonrock styles and formal ideas blends imperceptibly into all-purpose stylistic eclecticism—the free and often febrile switching among different styles within the same piece. Eclecticism, by now a talisman of the entire post-Modernist movement in all the arts, was more prominent in the Seventies pop world in London than anywhere else, and, at its best, it stops being lamely imitative and enters the realm of creativity.

Numerous British bands of the Seventies fell into the eclectic art-rock camp: Genesis, King Crimson, Electric Light Orchestra, Queen, Supertramp, Sparks, 10cc, Gentle Giant and Be-Bop Deluxe. There were Continental bands like Focus, and even American groups like Kansas, Styx and Boston that fit here also. Certainly there were differences between these groups, large differences, and there were many more groups that could be listed. But they all shared a commitment to unprepared, abrupt transitions from one mood to another. Sometimes the shifts were between tempos, sometimes between levels of volume, sometimes between whole styles of music. The effect in any case was violent, disruptive and nervously tense, and as such no doubt answered the needs of the age as well as anything. At their best (or at their most commercially successful), these groups never lost sight of older rock basics, as with Queen's best work.

In a sense, Roxy Music might be considered the leader of this particular pack, especially between 1971 and 1973, when Brian Eno was a member of the band. But even from the first, and despite the strong contributions of Phil Manzanera and Andy MacKay, this was always Bryan

Ferry's band, as proven by the continuity in his subsequent solo albums. Ferry's artsiness expressed itself so much as style over substance that style itself became substantive. As the ultimate self-professed lounge lizard, he managed to take pop-rock's hoariest conventions (the love song, even actual oldies on his solo albums) and coat them with witty intimations of unspeakable decadence. But the real art rocker in Roxy Music was Eno. Aside from the quality of his music, which is considerable and which he sustained into the Nineties, he is interesting from two points of view: his command of the synthesizer and his relation to others on the London and New York experimental scenes.

The synthesizer is a much-abused, much-misunderstood instrument. When played like a souped-up electric organ by people like Keith Emerson, Jon Lord (of Deep Purple) or Rick Wakeman, it can sound simply flashy and cheap. If the obligatory drum solo used to be the bane of any self-respecting rock concertgoer's life, the obligatory synthesizer solo, preferably with smoke bomb and laser obbligato, was the curse of the Seventies. If synthesizers weren't regarded as newfangled organs, they were taken literally, as something that ''synthesizes,'' and we were subjected to Wendy Carlos's and Isao Tomita's synthesized versions of the classics.

The synthesizer is an instrument with its own characteristics, and those characteristics are just beginning to be explored by rock musicians. When played with the subtlety and discretion of a Stevie Wonder or a Garth Hudson, it can reinforce conven-

A mid-Seventies version of Roxy Music *(from left):* Andy Mackay, Bryan Ferry, Eddie Jobson, Rick Wills, Phil Manzanera, Paul Thompson.

tional textures superbly. And when somebody like Eno or Edgar Froese of Tangerine Dream gets hold of it, the synthesizer can create a whole world of its own. Eno's *Discreet Music* (1975), with its title-track first side full of soothing, hypnotic woodwindish sounds, or *No Pussyfooting* (1975) and *Evening Star* (1976), two collaborations with Robert Fripp, ex–King Crimson guitarist, or *Music for Airports* (1978), were masterly examples of genuine rock avant-gardism. Of course, they weren't really "rock" in any but the loosest sense: There was no reference back to a blues base, even in attenuated form. But they still counted as music produced by a rock sensibility aimed at a rock audience.

Eno's position within the London avant-garde, and the nature of that avant-garde, are both of interest, too. London, like New York, has a thriving avant-garde musical community that doesn't place much of a premium on formally acquired technique, thus remaining open to fresh infusions of energy from ostensible "amateurs." In London the experimentation in rock was fostered by British taxation, which forced most of the successful commercial rockers out of the country, leaving the rest to experiment relatively free from Top Forty pressures. This robbed the London scene of some potential big-name experimenters like George Harrison (see *Electronic Sound*, 1969) and John Lennon (whose *Two Virgins* with Yoko Ono was another particularly appealing early art-rock entry in 1969).

We find Tangerine Dream looking quite serious.

Still, what was left in the forefront of experimentation was interesting enough. The mere fact that Eno had to leave Roxy Music (quite apart from the question of clashing egos with Ferry) indicates the difficulty of pursuing experimentation and commercial success at the same time. The London avant-

garde scene, insofar as any outsider can tell, is marked still by a fascinating if rather private and sporadic interchange between the classical and pop worlds. In the Seventies the pop stars (Eno, guitarist Phil Manzanera of Roxy, Fripp) did rather more interesting work than those who wandered over from a classical background (David Bedford, Stomu Yamash'ta, the Japanese percussionist-turned-rocker). Michael Oldfield fits here to a certain extent, although his work—particularly after his best-selling *Tubular Bells* (1973), which did admittedly have a bland appeal as a reduction of California composer Terry Riley's ideas—was lame beyond recall.

Much of this work, from Oldfield to Eno and even Riley, is head music, and relates to a rather interesting form of avant-garde trance music, which brings us to the subject of drugs. The avant-gardism in rock of the Sixties and Seventies, for all its ultimate debts to surrealism and other vanguard movements from earlier in the century, owed its primary fealty to the proliferation of drugs in the Sixties. It would be misleading to overstress this, but just as false to repress it. Marijuana, LSD and other psychedelics, and methedrine, or speed, all had a profound effect on how music in general, and art rock in particular, was made and perceived. This is not to say that you had to be stoned to play or enjoy this music. But it does mean that the climate and stylistic preoccupations of many varieties of present-day art are built in part on perceptions analogous to the drug experience. Sometimes it takes only one trip, as with acid, to give you a whole other fix on the world.

The kind of quiescent, dappled textural shiftings that mark much of American composer La Monte Young's music (Eno was strongly influenced by Young; and John Cale, formerly of the Velvet Underground, worked closely with him) owe something to grass, at least originally: Maybe Young has never smoked in his life, but his art could have germinated only in a subculture primed for it by marijuana. And the same is true for the whole acid-rock phenomenon.

The pure acid-rockers of the Sixties—from the Byrds to the Jefferson Airplane—don't really concern us here. But Pink Floyd, originally Britain's premier acid-rockers, do. After cutting a couple of British hit singles in 1967, the group concentrated on extended compositions, often with spacey lyrical motifs. *The Dark Side of the Moon* (1973) became one of the most successful albums of the decade, a best-

The original Mothers of Invention.

seller in Europe and America as well as England. Floyd turned out some of the most consistently interesting "head music" of the late Sixties and Seventies, and managed, in its various shards after its breakup, at least to re-create some of that work arrestingly thereafter. The group had a sense for line and continuity and ritualistic repetition that was quite special, and to dismiss it simply as technically limited is philistine.

A bit of typically trashy album art.

In Los Angeles the drug scene helped spawn the Mothers of Invention, one of the first rock groups to emphasize mixed-media presentations, dubbed "freak-outs" by leader Frank Zappa. Zappa, a self-professed teetotaler, was forced after the first few L.A. freakouts in 1967 to disavow the use of drugs at these affairs—naturally to no avail. The Mothers combined social satire, parody of rock & roll oldies, classical references—Zappa regularly paid homage to Edgard Varèse—and a growing taste for vaguely avant-garde jazz improvisation. It has been an influential collage of styles, affecting the work of such diverse musicians as Jean-Luc Ponty, the jazz violinist, and Paul McCartney, who once cited the Mothers' first album, *Freak Out,* as a key inspiration for *Sgt. Pepper.*

The psychedelic enthusiasms of the late Sixties, kindled by (among others) Pink Floyd and the Mothers of Invention and centered in San Francisco and in London, found their most sustained resonance in the Seventies in West Germany. Kraftwerk had the biggest commercial impact in the United States,

thanks to the surprising success in 1975 of *Autobahn.* Rather more interesting was Tangerine Dream and its leader, Edgar Froese. The group's records and Froese's solo albums were impressionistic extravaganzas, full of gentle washes of electronic color. There is a parallel to Eno's work here. But Eno is a more diverse artist than Froese, and more overtly rock oriented, and in such purely experimental pieces as *Discreet Music* he shows an indebtedness to the structuralist principles of classical composers like Young, Riley (himself an offshoot of the psychedelic/meditative climate of the Bay Area in the Six-

Summer is one of the best trance records of the Seventies, among other things—as a version performed in New York by Blondie and Fripp reaffirmed so well. And before he hit upon his disco formula, Moroder had made an overt art-rock synthesizer collage disc, influenced by the German psychedelic groups but better than his models. At the time nobody could be interested in releasing it, and since then Moroder has been too busy to bother.

The evolution of the New York art-rock scene in the late Seventies, and its subsequent spread to Los Angeles and other byways of the United States, was

ties), Steve Reich and Philip Glass. Froese, on the other hand, owes his classical inspirations to such orchestral colorists as Hungarian composer György Ligeti and the electronic music of Karlheinz Stockhausen and Iannis Xenakis. Froese's work seems less interesting than that of his models, but at least his choice of inspirations betrayed a certain sophistication.

More directly related to Eno was the band Cluster, with which Eno twice collaborated. And the artier implications of Giorgio Moroder's disco "factory" cannot be ignored here. His "I Feel Love" for Donna

such an eruption of energies that it merits separate treatment. But the pattern suggested by London was brought to triumphant fruition in this country: a rejection of overcomplexity, the development of a new artistic primitivism and finally a direct merger with other forms of avant-gardism, both classical and jazz—with Eno and Fripp, both of whom moved to New York, as catalysts.

This disquisition began with talk about morphologies and self-consciousness, and in some ways the aesthetic behind the New York art-rock scene of the past decade brings us full circle.

Kraftwerk: from art rock to disco.

Looking at rock from a populist standpoint, one can seriously question both its aspirations to high art and the very hegemony of high art itself. Maybe the self-conscious primitives are right: Maybe art rock doesn't have to be clever complexity at all. Maybe real art is that which most clearly and directly answers the needs of its audiences. Which, in turn, means that we can prize pure rock and pure pop, from Chuck Berry on, as "art" in no way inferior to that which may entail a more highly formalized technique for its execution. Rock may be part of a far larger process in which art broadens its gestures to encompass an audience made more numerous by the permeation of social equality down into strata heretofore ignored.

There is another, more philosophical side to it. What Warhol and pop artists were trying to tell us—and what composer John Cage has been telling us all along—is that art isn't necessarily a product crafted painstakingly by some mysterious, removed artist-deity, but is whatever you, the perceiver, choose to perceive artistically. A Brillo box isn't suddenly art because Warhol put a stacked bunch of them into a museum. But by putting them there he encouraged you to make your every trip to the supermarket an artistic adventure, and in so doing he exalted your life. Everybody's an artist who wants to be, which is really a more radically populist notion than encouraging scholarly studies of the blues. Roll over Beethoven, indeed, and make room for us.

DISCOGRAPHY

ALBUMS
Albums Featuring Brian Eno
Cluster and Eno: *Cluster & Eno* (Sky; Hamburg, 1977). **Eno with Kevin Ayers, John Cale, Nico:** *June 1st, 1974* (Island; 1974). **Eno with Robert Fripp:** *No Pussyfooting* (Antilles; 1973). *Evening Star* (Antilles; 1976). **Eno:** *Here Come the Warm Jets* (Island; ☆151, 1974). *Taking Tiger Mountain (by Strategy)* (Island; 1974). *Another Green World* (Island; 1975). *Discreet Music* (Obscure; 1975). *Before and After Science* (Island; 1978). *Music for Airports* (Polydor; 1978). *Music for Films* (Antilles; 1978). **Eno/Moebius/Roedelius:** *After the Heat* (Sky; Hamburg, 1978). **Roxy Music:** *Roxy Music* (Reprise; 1972). *For Your Pleasure* (Warner Bros.; ☆193, 1973).
A Sampler of Eclectic Experimentalism
Be Bop Deluxe: *Futurama* (Harvest; 1975). *Sunburst Finish* (Capitol; ☆96, 1976). *Modern Music* (Capitol; ☆88, 1976). *Live! In the Air Age* (Harvest; ☆65, 1977). *Drastic Plastic* (Harvest; ☆95, 1978). **Electric Light Orchestra:** *On the Third Day* (United Artists; ☆52, 1974). *Olé ELO* (United Artists; ☆32, 1976). *A New World Record* (United Artists; ☆5, 1976). *Out of the Blue* (Jet; ☆4, 1977). *Discovery* (Jet; ☆5, 1979). *Greatest Hits* (Jet; ☆30, 1979). **Bryan Ferry:** *Let's Stick Together* (Atlantic; ☆160, 1976). *In Your Mind* (Atlantic; ☆126, 1977). *The Bride Stripped Bare* (Atlantic; ☆159, 1978). **Genesis:** *Selling England by the Pound* (Charisma; ☆70, 1973). **Gentle Giant:** *The Power and the Glory* (Capitol; ☆78, 1974). *Interview* (Capitol; ☆137, 1976). *Playing the Fool* (Capitol; ☆89, 1977). *The Missing Piece* (Capitol; ☆81, 1977). **King Crimson:** *In the Court of the Crimson King: An Observation by King Crimson* (Atlantic; ☆28, 1969). *In the Wake of Poseidon* (Atlantic; ☆31, 1970). **Roxy Music:** *Roxy Music* (Reprise; 1972). *For Your Pleasure* (Warner Bros.; ☆193, 1973). *Stranded* (Atco; ☆186, 1974). *Country Life* (Atco; ☆37, 1974). *Siren* (Atco; ☆50, 1975). *Viva! Roxy Music* (Atco; ☆81, 1976). *Manifesto* (Atco; ☆23, 1979). **Sparks:** *Kimono My House* (Island; ☆101, 1974). **Supertramp:** *Crime of the Century* (A&M; ☆38, 1974). *Even in the Quietest Moments* (A&M; ☆16, 1977). *Supertramp (The Early Years)* (A&M; ☆158, 1978). *Breakfast in America* (A&M; ☆1, 1979). **10cc:** *Sheet Music* (Auks; ☆81, 1974). *How Dare You!* (Mercury; ☆47, 1976). *Deceptive Bends* (Mercury; ☆31, 1977). *Live and Let Live* (Mercury; ☆146, 1977). *Bloody Tourists* (Polydor; ☆61, 1978). **Frank Zappa and the Mothers of Invention:** *Freak Out* (Verve; ☆130, 1967). *Absolutely Free* (Verve; ☆41, 1967). *We're Only in It for the Money* (Verve; ☆30, 1968). *Lumpy Gravy* (Verve; ☆159, 1968). *Cruising with Ruben and the Jets* (Verve; ☆110, 1968). *Uncle Meat* (Bizarre; ☆43, 1969). *Hot Rats* (Bizarre; ☆173, 1969). *Burnt Weeny Sandwich* (Bizarre; ☆94, 1970). *Weasels Ripped My Flesh* (Bizarre; ☆189, 1970). *Chunga's Revenge* (Bizarre; ☆119, 1970). *Fillmore East—June 1971* (Bizarre; ☆38, 1971). *Frank Zappa's 200 Motels* (United Artists; ☆59, 1971). *Just Another Band from L.A.* (Bizarre; ☆85, 1972). *Grand Wazoo* (Bizarre; 1972). *Waka/Jawaka* (Bizarre; ☆152, 1972). *Over-Nite Sensations* (Discreet; ☆32, 1973). *Apostrophe (')* (Discreet; ☆10, 1974). *Roxy and Elsewhere* (Discreet; ☆27, 1974). *One Size Fits All* (Discreet; ☆26, 1975). *Bongo Fury* (Discreet; ☆66, 1975). *Zoot Allures* (Warner Bros.; ☆61, 1976). *Zappa in New York* (Discreet; ☆57, 1978). *Studio Tan* (Discreet; ☆147, 1978).

German Art Rock

Edgar Froese: *Aqua* (Virgin; 1974). **Kraftwerk:** *Autobahn* (Vertigo; ☆5, 1975). *Trans-Europe Express* (Capitol; ☆119, 1977). *The Man-Machine* (Capitol; ☆130, 1978). **Giorgio Moroder:** *Midnight Express Soundtrack* (Casablanca; ☆59, 1978). *Phaedra* (Virgin; ☆196, 1974). *Rubycon* (Virgin; 1975). *Stratosfear* (Virgin; ☆158, 1977). *Sorcerer* (soundtrack) (MCA; ☆153, 1977). *Encore—Live* (Virgin; ☆178, 1977).

Chart-Topping Classical Bombast

Emerson, Lake and Palmer: *Emerson, Lake and Palmer* (Cotillion; ☆18, 1971). *Tarkus* (Cotillion; ☆9, 1971). *Pictures at an Exhibition (Mussorgsky)* (Cotillion; ☆10, 1972). *Trilogy* (Cotillion; ☆5, 1972). *Brain Salad Surgery* (Manticore; ☆11, 1973). *Welcome Back, My Friends, to the Show That Never Ends—Ladies and Gentlemen—Emerson, Lake and Palmer* (Manticore; ☆4, 1974). *Works—Volume I* (Atlantic; ☆12, 1977). *Works—Volume II* (Atlantic; ☆37, 1977). *Love Beach* (Atlantic; ☆55, 1978). *In Concert* (A&M; ☆75, 1979). **Moody Blues:** *Days of Future Passed* (Deram; ☆3, 1968). *On the Threshold of a Dream* (Deram; ☆20, 1969). *To Our Children's Children's Children* (Threshold; ☆14, 1970). *A Question of Balance* (Threshold; ☆3, 1970). *Every Good Boy Deserves Favour* (Threshold; ☆2, 1971). *Seventh Sojourn* (Threshold; ☆1, 1972). *Caught Live + 5* (London; ☆26, 1977). *Octave* (London; ☆13, 1978). **Rick Wakeman:** *Six Wives of Henry VIII* (A&M; ☆30, 1973). *Journey to the Centre of the Earth* (A&M; ☆3, 1974). *Myths and Legends of King Arthur and the Knights of the Round Table* (A&M; ☆21, 1975). *No Earthly Connection* (A&M; ☆67, 1976). *White Rock* (A&M; ☆126, 1977). *Rick Wakeman's Criminal Record* (A&M; ☆128, 1977). *Rhapsodies* (A&M; ☆170, 1979). **Yes:** *Fragile* (Atlantic; ☆4, 1972). *Close to the Edge* (Atlantic; ☆3, 1972). *Yessongs* (Atlantic; ☆12, 1973). *Tales from Topographic Oceans* (Atlantic; ☆6, 1974). *Relayer* (Atlantic; ☆5, 1974).

(Chart positions compiled from Joel Whitburn's *Record Research,* based on *Billboard*'s LPs chart.)

JAZZ ROCK

BY ROBERT PALMER

azz has always been an influence on rock. The bands that toured with Little Richard, Ray Charles and other black singers during the Fifties invariably included several jazz musicians, and they often opened shows with bluesy be bop tunes that featured lengthy improvised solos. The saxophone-and-organ combos of the Fifties, such as Bill Doggett's, purveyed a related but usually more jazz-based amalgam of improvisation and rhythm & blues. But as a distinct genre of popular music, jazz rock began with the Electric Flag, Blood, Sweat and Tears, and Chicago.

All three bands were distinguished primarily by their use of horns. The Flag, formed in 1967 by white blues musicians Mike Bloomfield, Barry Goldberg and Nick Gravenites, studio bassist Harvey Brooks and R&B drummer Buddy Miles, billed itself as ''An American Music Band''; its stylistic range was broad, but for the most part its horn section played arrangements patterned on those current in the blues and black jazz bands of the Forties and early Fifties. By contrast, the first BS&T album, *Child Is Father to the Man,* featured more ambitious horn arrangements in a Maynard Ferguson–Stan Kenton mold. Chicago made its debut on record in early 1969 (as the Chicago Transit Authority), with horn arrangements closer to MOR pop than to jazz. Despite the horns and jazz trappings, the improvisational content in these groups' recordings was slight (the solos were usually taken by rock guitarists), and improvising, as opposed to embellishing a melody or stringing together stock phrases, is the essence of jazz.

The Flag was the most eclectic and the most visceral of the three bands, but it soon disbanded due to interpersonal problems. BS&T re-formed as a more horn-dominated band after its founder, ex–Blues Project organist and Dylan sideman Al Kooper, went on to other projects. Meanwhile Chicago continued with the same personnel. Both BS&T and Chicago mastered the art of making melodic, relatively low-keyed, marginally rock- and jazz-tinged pop singles, and both turned out gold records. BS&T's string of hits stopped abruptly after *Blood, Sweat and Tears 4*

Harvey Brooks *(left)* and Michael Bloomfield of the Electric Flag, playing at the 1967 Monterey Pop Festival.

Miles Davis. In 1970 he used amplified riffing on *Bitches Brew* and spawned a new genre: jazz rock.

(1971), when a new contingent of horn and rhythm section soloists opted for a more adventurous approach; Chicago, under the firm direction of producer James William Guercio, continued to be a potent commercial force.

A number of key jazz musicians were listening to rock during the late Sixties, but not to groups like Chicago and BS&T. Jimi Hendrix and Sly Stone were jazzmen's favorites, the former because of his innovative use of electronics, the latter because of his elaborate rhythmic structures. Soon Miles Davis and some of his sidemen began incorporating rock instrumentation and rhythms into their music, at first cautiously and reflectively, then, beginning with Davis's *Bitches Brew* in 1969, more boldly. *Brew* featured multiple electric keyboards and John McLaughlin's electric guitar in addition to horns, drums and percussion instruments. There was a Sly-like dance beat, but the improvisations were loosely structured around bass lines, scale patterns, or tonal centers. Many fans of Davis's earlier work reacted negatively to the abrupt rhythms, murky textures and abrasive sonorities of *Bitches Brew*, but after Davis played the Fillmore East and other rock halls, the record became the first jazz-rock crossover, selling well enough to register on the pop charts. Many of the musicians who played on it went on to become important shapers of jazz rock as it developed during the Seventies.

Drummer Tony Williams had left the Davis band several months before *Bitches Brew* was recorded, but he played a crucial role in Davis's developing electric sound by bringing guitarist John McLaughlin to New York from London. McLaughlin joined Tony Williams's group, Lifetime, and played on Davis's *Bitches Brew* and *In a Silent Way*. McLaughlin soon left Lifetime, and in 1971, after several moderately successful solo projects, he organized the Mahavishnu Orchestra and recorded *The Inner Mounting Flame,* which turned out to be even more influential than *Bitches Brew*.

Initially McLaughlin's new sound induced a kind

Al Kooper as Lady Liberty.

of future shock. There had been plenty of long, loud guitar solos in rock since the emergence of the San Francisco bands and plenty of electric guitarists in jazz. But McLaughlin was playing long solos with melodic and harmonic substance, not repetitiously juggling blues scales, and he was playing through a bank of amplifiers with his volume controls turned up. Miles Davis had been the first important jazz musician to feature ensemble improvisations on electric instruments, but it was McLaughlin who realized that the new technology demanded the development of new musical forms and new instrumental approaches.

Traditional jazz drumming, for example, was clearly unsuited to the demands of electric music. The time-keeping cymbal, the kit's timbral subtleties and many other details tended to get lost in the roar. So McLaughlin's drummer, Billy Cobham, reasserted the importance of the snare and bass drum as timekeepers but kept things interesting by adding compound meters derived from Indian music. Tra-

ditional jazz ensemble interaction, too, tended to become excessively muddy in an electric context. For all its innovative importance, *Bitches Brew* was often turgid, congested. McLaughlin went back to an earlier jazz device, the idea of soloists trading two- and four-bar statements. And rather than allow for spontaneous interplay, he spiced his compositions with predetermined unison riffs and well-rehearsed counterpoint.

Most of the successful jazz-rock groups that followed the Mahavishnu Orchestra dealt with similar concepts in similar ways. Many of them were spearheaded by former Miles Davis sidemen. Josef Zawinul and Wayne Shorter borrowed more ideas from R&B and encouraged collective improvisation in Weather Report, making it one of the most satisfying of the new bands. Chick Corea's Return to Forever developed a brand of loud but lyrical music more akin to West Coast rock. Herbie Hancock led a heavily electronic experimental sextet for several years after leaving Davis, but in 1974 he organized a Sly-influenced quintet and recorded *Head Hunters,* which outsold all previous jazz-rock fusion records, placing in the Top Twenty and spawning a hit single, "Chameleon." By the mid-Seventies these and a few other plugged-in jazzmen dominated the jazz-rock field. The most successful among them were virtual pop stars, able to headline concerts in the halls of their choice almost anywhere in the world,

Chicago, not the town.

Weather Report, the most durable of the fusion groups, led by saxophonist Wayne Shorter *(left)* and keyboard player Joe Zawinul *(second from right)*.

to take as much time as they liked to record and to appear incestuously on each others' albums despite conflicting contractual obligations. Corea spoke for most of them when he said, "What we're trying to do is communicate with as many people as possible while retaining our musical integrity."

As electric bands became more and more commercially dominant in the jazz world, however, that integrity was often called into question. "You had jazz bands playing R&B changes and rhythms during the Fifties," a veteran jazzman has observed, "but they didn't make much of a splash. The new groups are doing the same sort of thing with contemporary R&B, but they're copping so much media exposure, people think they're the wave of the future." Well-known jazzmen, feeling pressured by the trend, began making loud, awkward music, without regard for the complexities of handling electronic equipment.

After 1975 jazz rock became a more and more frankly commercial proposition. McLaughlin, Weather Report, Hancock, Corea and the other leading figures of earlier years had actively courted popular acceptance, but they had also created an eclectic and genuinely experimental new music. The dominant jazz-fusion artists of the late Seventies brought more or less distinguished jazz credentials to their work, but there wasn't really much rock in their music. In many cases it was really jazz pop. Chuck Mangione, George Benson and the Crusaders were among the most successful artists in this style. Increasingly, the dominant non-jazz elements in their music were derived not from the more creative side of rock music, but from middle-of-the-road pop, light classical music and disco.

Meanwhile, Chick Corea's music grew increasingly cute and pretentious (though he continued to play occasional hard-core jazz dates), Herbie Hancock gravitated more and more to straight party funk, and John McLaughlin lost much of the audience the original Mahavishnu Orchestra had enjoyed. Only Weather Report continued to make jazz rock that retained both an experimental thrust and popular appeal, until it disbanded in the mid-Eighties.

The most creative jazz-fusion music of the late Seventies had little to do with rock or pop. It was mostly acoustic, and it combined jazz techniques with rhythms and instruments from the third world. McLaughlin and the Indian violinist L. Shankar made the most convincing Indo-jazz fusion with the acoustic group Shakti. Oregon integrated straight jazz playing with ethnic instruments and rhythms from all over the world, and so did the ex–Ornette Coleman trumpeter Don Cherry, a frequent collaborator with Oregon's Collin Walcott. Perhaps the most convincing jazz rock of the period, aside from the music of Weather Report, was made by the popular funk band Earth, Wind and Fire, which employed some formidable jazz talents and often let them improvise at satisfying length. New jazz-rock groups with a more overt jazz orientation continued to proliferate, but the terms "jazz rock" and "fusion" no longer had much real meaning. There were prominent jazz influences in the most mainstream pop music; almost everything one heard on the radio was a fusion of one sort or another.

Miles Davis's death in 1991 was the end of an era. The leading trendsetter of Seventies jazz rock, Davis had broken down the barriers between genres, and he had kept his music contemporary to the end. When asked late in his life what he thought he had accomplished, Davis commented, "Well, I've changed music five or six times." The shotgun marriage between jazz and rock that was dubbed "fusion" in the Seventies may have been a passing trend, but Davis's pioneering conflation of jazz, rock, funk and world musics has had a lasting impact. From Ornette Coleman's influential electric band Prime Time to improvising electric bassist Bill Laswell's production work for artists as disparate as Yoko Ono and John Lydon's PiL, a large portion of the contemporary musical spectrum seems to have been permanently opened up and enriched. Miles lives!

Herbie Hancock, 1972. He graduated from the classic Miles Davis quintet of the mid-Sixties to become a leader in the new electric jazz.

DISCOGRAPHY

ALBUMS

Blood, Sweat and Tears: *Child Is Father to the Man* (Columbia; ☆47, 1968). *Blood, Sweat and Tears* (Columbia; ☆1, 1969). *Blood, Sweat and Tears 3* (Columbia; ☆1, 1970). *B, S and T; 4* (Columbia; ☆10, 1971). *Greatest Hits* (Columbia; ☆19, 1972). *New Blood* (Columbia; ☆32, 1972). **Chicago:** *Chicago Transit Authority* (Columbia; ☆17, 1969). *Chicago II* (Columbia; ☆4, 1970). *Chicago III* (Columbia; ☆2, 1971). *Chicago at Carnegie Hall* (Columbia; ☆3, 1971). *Chicago V* (Columbia; ☆1, 1972). *Chicago VI* (Columbia; ☆1, 1973). *Chicago VII* (Columbia; ☆1, 1974). *Chicago VIII* (Columbia; ☆1, 1975). *Chicago IX Chicago's Greatest Hits* (Columbia; ☆1, 1975). **Chick Corea with Return to Forever:** *Return to Forever* (ECM; 1972). *Light as a Feather* (Polydor; 1973). *Hymn of the Seventh Galaxy* (Polydor; ☆124, 1973). *Where Have I Known You* (Polydor; ☆32, 1974). *No Mystery* (Polydor; ☆39, 1975). *The Leprechaun* (Polydor; ☆42, 1976). *My Spanish Heart* (Polydor; ☆55, 1977). *The Mad Hatter* (Polydor; ☆61, 1978). *Friends* (Polydor; ☆86, 1978). *An Evening with Chick Corea and Herbie Hancock* (Polydor; ☆175, 1979). **Miles Davis:** *In a Silent Way* (Columbia; ☆134, 1969). *Bitches Brew* (Columbia; ☆35, 1970). *Miles Davis at Fillmore* (Columbia; ☆123, 1970). *Jack Johnson* (Columbia; ☆159, 1971). *Live-Evil* (Columbia; ☆125, 1971). *On the Corner* (Columbia; ☆156, 1972). *In Concert* (Columbia; ☆152, 1973). *Big Fun* (Columbia; ☆179, 1974). *Get Up with It* (Columbia; ☆141, 1975). *Agharta* (Columbia; ☆168, 1976). *Water Babies* (Columbia; ☆190, 1977). *The Man with the Horn* (Columbia; ☆53, 1981). *We Want Miles* (Columbia; ☆159, 1982). *Star People* (Columbia; ☆136, 1983). *Decoy* (Columbia; ☆169, 1984). *Aura* (Co-

lumbia; 1984). *You're Under Arrest* (Columbia; ☆111, 1985). *Tutu* (Columbia; ☆141, 1986). *Siesta* (Columbia; 1987). *Amandla* (Warner; ☆177, 1989). **Electric Flag:** *A Long Time Comin'* (Columbia; ☆31, 1968). *The Electric Flag* (Columbia; ☆76, 1969). **Herbie Hancock:** *Mwandishi* (Warner Bros.; 1971). *Crossings* (Warner Bros.; 1972). *Sextant* (Columbia; ☆176, 1973). *Head Hunters* (Columbia; ☆13, 1974). *Thrust* (Columbia; ☆13, 1974). *Man-Child* (Columbia; ☆21, 1975). *Secrets* (Columbia; ☆49, 1976). *V.S.O.P.* (Columbia; ☆79, 1977). *Sunlight* (Columbia; ☆58, 1978). *An Evening with Herbie Hancock and Chick Corea* (Columbia; ☆100, 1979). *Monster* (Columbia; ☆94, 1980). *Mr. Hands* (Columbia; ☆117, 1980). *Magic Windows* (Columbia, ☆140, 1981). *Lite Me Up* (Columbia; ☆151, 1982). *Future Shock* (Columbia; ☆43, 1983). *Sound-System* (Columbia; ☆71, 1984). *Perfect Machine* (Columbia; ☆65, 1988). **John McLaughlin:** *Devotion* (Douglas; 1970). *My Goals Beyond* (Douglas; ☆194, 1972). *Extrapolation* (Polydor; ☆152, 1972). **John McLaughlin with the Mahavishnu Orchestra:** *The Inner Mounting Flame* (Columbia; ☆89, 1972). *Birds of Fire* (Columbia; ☆15, 1973). *Between Nothingness and Eternity* (Columbia; ☆41, 1973). *Apocalypse* (Columbia; ☆43, 1974). *Visions of the Emerald Beyond* (Columbia; ☆68, 1975). **Weather Report:** *The Weather Report* (Columbia; ☆191, 1971). *I Sing the Body Electric* (Columbia; ☆147, 1972). *Sweetnighter* (Columbia; ☆85, 1973). *Mysterious Traveller* (Columbia; ☆46, 1974). *Tale Spinnin'* (Columbia; ☆31, 1975). *Black Market* (Columbia; ☆42, 1976). *Heavy Weather* (Columbia; ☆30, 1976). *Mr. Gone* (Arc/Columbia; ☆52, 1978). *8:30* (Arc/Columbia; ☆47, 1979). *Night Passage* (Arc; ☆57, 1980). *Procession* (Columbia; ☆96, 1983). *Domino Theory* (Columbia; ☆136, 1984). *Sportin' Life* (Columbia; ☆191, 1985). *This Is This* (Columbia; ☆195, 1986).

(Chart positions compiled from Joel Whitburn's *Record Research,* based on *Billboard's* LPs chart.)

The saga of Southern rock in the Seventies is so fraught with innocent optimism, local color and inevitable tragedy that it could easily pass for a William Faulkner novel or a Tennessee Williams play. As the name implies, Southern rock was fiercely provincial in a manner no rock hybrid in the previous two decades had been. Not only was the music loud, aggressive and sometimes crude, but it continually voiced faith in the Southern lifestyle, in anthems like Charlie Daniels's ''The South's Gonna Do It Again.'' In retrospect this musical recycling of the Good Ol' Boy stereotype may seem merely clichéd and obnoxious; but in its day, it was not without its virtues. At a time when most mainstream rock music was suffering from laid-back ennui, the Dixie contingent offered a refreshing no-frills return to the basics. Like the purest rock & roll of the Fifties, it relied for inspiration on country & western and rhythm & blues, two types of music that were still readily available to white teenagers living below the Mason-Dixon line. It wallowed so much in the boogie beat developed by Elmore James and John Lee Hooker that the sound became a national institution. And Southern rock lent credibility to jazz-length improvisations within the rock mode, an idea initially advanced (but poorly executed) by San Francisco psychedelic bands of the Sixties.

In a sense, the evolution of Southern rock was a reactionary attempt to return rock & roll to its native soil. After the decline of interest in rockabilly, white rock in the South had taken a backseat to country & western and soul. While Nashville turned toward mainstream pop and black music flourished in Muscle Shoals, Memphis and New Orleans, white Southern rock musicians were typically compelled to migrate to California or New York to earn a living.

Phil Walden, manager of the late Otis Redding, changed all that when he started Capricorn Records, a small independent company in his hometown, Macon, Georgia, in 1969. The first act he signed was the Allman Brothers Band, a six-piece group that was working in Florida after making a couple of ill-fated journeys to the West Coast. Walden proved himself to be a perceptive talent scout as well as an astute businessman. The leader of the group, guitarist Duane Allman, already sported a considerable reputation on the basis of his studio work in Muscle Shoals with Wilson Pickett and Aretha Franklin, among others; his skills as a slide guitarist would soon set new standards, particularly through his effortless duet with Eric Clapton on Derek and the Dominos' "Layla."

But Duane Allman wanted to front his own band rather than anonymously support other artists. Powered by a rhythm section that rumbled like a freight train and playing a blues-drenched repertoire that showcased brother Gregg Allman's gritty vocals and

The Kentucky Headhunters under the Big Sky, 1991.

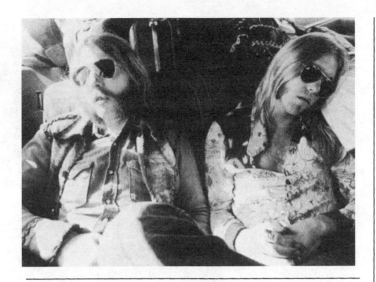

The Allman Brothers caught napping. That's Duane on the left, Gregg on the right.

gospel organ, the Allman Brothers Band featured a unique interplay between two gifted lead guitarists, Dickey Betts and Duane himself. Though their first album, *The Allman Brothers Band*, didn't create much of a stir beyond Georgia when it was released in 1969, it heralded a new approach to American rock music.

After two albums and two years of relentless touring, the Allman Brothers finally attained mass popularity with *At Fillmore East*, a two-record set that still ranks as one of the finest concert rock albums ever recorded. Most fans had never heard anything quite like the mercurial solos and meticulous counterpoint effortlessly unreeled by Duane Allman and Betts. In many respects, indeed, the Allman Brothers had become one of the most impressive bands in the country.

But their reign was short-lived. Duane Allman was killed in a motorcycle crash near Macon in October 1971; thirteen months later bassist Berry Oakley died in a similar wreck in the same vicinity. Though the band regrouped and continued to tour and to record, things were never quite the same after Duane's death. Commercially, the Allmans continued to enjoy success, scoring their biggest hit in 1973 with an uncharacteristically breezy tune called "Ramblin' Man," written and sung by Dickey Betts. But the band never managed to regain the creative momentum that Duane Allman had inspired. By the middle of the Seventies most of the attention lavished on them centered on their personal and legal problems rather than on their music.

The decline of the Allman Brothers Band didn't hamper the growing appeal of the Southern sound throughout the first half of the decade. New bands arose to carry the Stars and Bars beyond Confederate borders. Among the most successful was the Charlie Daniels Band, another two-guitar, dual-percussion ensemble led by a burly snuff-dipping, blunt-speaking ex-studio guitarist and fiddler from Nashville who had a penchant for writing catchy novelty songs. Another was the Marshall Tucker Band, a group from South Carolina whose semi–Western swing approach was distinctively softened by the use of flute as well as saxophone.

A slew of other bands attempted to follow in the footsteps of the Allmans, frequently imitating but rarely duplicating their controlled frenzy. The second-liners included Grinderswitch, started by Allman Brothers roadies; Wet Willie, the quintessential Southern bar band; Elvin Bishop, a reformed Chicago blues aficionado from Tulsa; the Outlaws, an unreconstructed guitar army from Florida; the Winters Brothers; 38 Special; and Molly Hatchet. In spite of its rugged image, Southern rock actually embraced a wide range of sensibilities. The Atlanta Rhythm Section and Memphis's Amazing Rhythm Aces opted for a lighter approach that stressed tight vocal harmonies. Bands like Dixie Dregs and Sea Level showed a predilection for jazz-rock fusion. Established Nashville country stars such as Hank Williams Jr. and Gary Stewart incorporated the boogie beat into their repertoires.

Only Lynyrd Skynyrd, though, lived up to the Allman Brothers' legacy. A bruising, brawling group out of Florida, they took all the Southern stereotypes and made them their own, in songs praising whiskey, guns and hell-raising. Instrumentally they also went the Allmans one better by introducing a *three*-piece lead guitar section. But the focal point of the group was Ronnie Van Zant, a surly, street-tough singer who neither pranced nor primped onstage but relied instead on a macho growl that was delivered with puckish indifference.

Unlike the Allmans, Lynyrd Skynyrd broke out of the gate with a flourish. Their first album, released in 1973, contained the popular "Free Bird," a somewhat maudlin tribute to Duane Allman that climaxes in a volley of lead guitar runs. But their biggest hit of all came in 1974 with "Sweet Home Alabama." It is notable for its lyric as much as its

melody. Responding to Neil Young's "Southern Man," a brooding saga of Confederate violence, Van Zant makes it clear not only that his kind of folks can take care of their own, but that Southern men are actually proud of the idiosyncracies that separate their region from the rest of the United States.

Lynyrd Skynyrd enjoyed a prosperous career in the studio, but they were best appreciated in concert, when they turned up the volume and unleashed their full fury. While the Allmans floundered without focus, Lynyrd Skynyrd became the hottest Southern band on the road, in some cities even rivaling such acts as the Rolling Stones and the Who. They continued to define Southern rock for the next three years until their unstated "Live fast, work hard, die young" credo became all too true. In 1977 a private plane carrying the group crashed, claiming the lives of Van Zant, guitarist Steve Gaines and singer Cassy Gaines.

The event marked the virtual end of Southern rock as a vital source of new music, even though many of its early exponents continued performing. But style had already degenerated into parody: Guitarists aspiring to the mantle of Duane Allman transformed the long solo into a feat to be endured, not enjoyed. "Will the Circle Be Unbroken" became commonplace as an encore. Dixie pride, too, was exploited when Southern rock feebly attempted to politicize its followers. Several bands, most of them Capricorn acts, staged benefit concerts in 1975 to help finance

Before tragedy struck: Lynyrd Skynyrd with their full complement of female backup singers.

the presidential campaign of Phil Walden's friend Jimmy Carter. The final blow came in 1979, when Capricorn filed for bankruptcy after a third edition of the Allman Brothers failed either to capture the public's imagination or to pay off the company's debts.

The Eighties were ushered in by a markedly different style of Southern rock, as defined by Athens, Georgia, bands like R.E.M. and the B-52's and a slew of independent label-oriented artists produced by North Carolinians Mitch Easter and Don Dixon. Though geographically specific, these groups had little connection with the region's native black or white musics. By the middle of the decade, however, the boogie beat's timeless appeal once again asserted itself. Surviving members of the Allmans and Lynyrd Skynyrd got together again for reunion albums and tours. Hank Williams Jr. made the transition from county fairs to packing basketball arenas by sticking with the same sound he'd helped popularize during the Seventies. And a new generation emerged from the South's largest cities, instead of Macon or rural Florida, to carry the torch into the Nineties.

Atlanta spawned the Georgia Satellites, whose anthemic 1986 hit single "Keep Your Hands to Yourself," rife with grungy guitar riffs and swaggering vocals, returned Southern rock to the pop charts; the Black Crowes, who injected their natural-born musical sensibilities with a cold shot of Sixties-vintage British bad-boy attitude; and the more alternative-oriented Chickasaw Mudpuppies, who nonetheless left no doubt where they came from when they

Lynyrd Skynyrd met a grim fate when their private plane crashed in 1977; three members of the band, including guitarist Steve Gaines and lead singer Ronnie Van Zant, were killed. A rescue worker at the crash site holds a publicity photo.

picked up their instruments. Similarly, Nashville nurtured the first rock bands to legitimately break out of country music's capital in at least twenty years: Jason and the Scorchers and the Kentucky Headhunters. This mini-revival had neither a single

majordomo like Walden orchestrating moves behind the scenes nor a celebrity like President Jimmy Carter to suggest Southern rock was once again a hot trend or national phenomenon. All there was, was the music. Which, at least in this incarnation, was more than enough to make the masses shake their collective money-makers.

DISCOGRAPHY

ALBUMS

Allman Brothers Band: *Allman Brothers Band* (Atco; ☆188, 1970). *Idlewild South* (Atco; ☆38, 1970). *At Fillmore East* (Capricorn; ☆13, 1971). *Eat a Peach* (Capricorn; ☆4, 1972). *Beginnings* (Atco; ☆25, 1973). *Brothers and Sisters* (Capricorn; ☆1, 1973). *Early Allman* (Dial; ☆171, 1973). *Win, Lose or Draw* (Capricorn; ☆5, 1975). *The Road Goes On Forever, a Collection of Their Greatest Recordings* (Capricorn; ☆43, 1975). *Wipe the Windows—Check the Oil—Dollar Gas* (Capricorn; ☆75, 1976). *Enlightened Rogues* (Capricorn; ☆9, 1979). *Reach for the Sky* (Arista; ☆27, 1980). *Brothers of the Road* (Arista; ☆44, 1981). *Best of the Allman Brothers Band* (Polygram; ☆189, 1981). *Dreams* (Polygram; ☆103, 1989). *Live at Ludlow Garage* (Polygram; 1990). *Seven Turns* (Epic; ☆53, 1990). *Shades of Two Worlds* (Epic; ☆85, 1991). **Amazing Rhythm Aces:** *Stacked Deck* (ABC; ☆120, 1975). *Too Stuffed to Jump* (ABC; ☆157, 1976). *Toucan Do It Too* (ABC; ☆114, 1977). *Burning the Ballroom Down* (ABC; ☆116, 1978). *The Amazing Rhythm Aces* (ABC; ☆144, 1979). **Atlanta Rhythm Section:** *Third Annual Pipe Dream* (Polydor; ☆74, 1974). *Dog Days* (Polydor; ☆113, 1975). *Red Tape* (Polydor; ☆146, 1976). *A Rock and Roll Alternative* (Polydor; ☆11, 1977). *Atlanta Rhythm Section* (MCA; ☆154, 1977). *Champagne Jam* (A&M; ☆67, 1978). *Underdog* (Polydor; ☆26, 1979). *Are You Ready!* (Polydor; ☆51, 1979). **Elvin Bishop Band:** *Let It Flow* (Capricorn; ☆100, 1974). *Juke Joint Jump* (Capricorn; ☆46, 1975). *Live!—Raisin' Hell* (Capricorn; ☆38, 1977). **Charlie Daniels Band:** *Honey in the Rock* (Kama Sutra; ☆164, 1973). *Fire on the Mountain* (Kama Sutra; ☆38, 1974). *Nightrider* (Kama Sutra; ☆57, 1975). *Saddle Tramp* (Epic; ☆35, 1976). *High Lonesome* (Epic; ☆83, 1976). *Midnight Wind* (Epic; ☆105, 1977). **Dixie Dregs:** *What If* (Capricorn; ☆182, 1978). *Night of the Living Dregs* (Capricorn; ☆111, 1979). **Grinderswitch:** *Red Wing* (Atco; ☆144, 1977). **Lynyrd Skynyrd:** *Lynyrd Skynyrd (Pronounced Leh-nird Skin-nerd)* (MCA Sounds of the South; ☆67, 1973). *Second Helping* (MCA Sounds of the South; ☆12, 1974). *Nuthin' Fancy* (MCA; ☆9, 1975). *Gimme Back My Bullets* (MCA; ☆20, 1976). *One More from the Road* (MCA; ☆9, 1976). *Street Survivors* (MCA; ☆5, 1977). *Lynyrd's First and . . . Last* (MCA; ☆15, 1978). *Gold and Platinum* (MCA; ☆12, 1979). *Lynyrd Skynyrd* (MCA; ☆64, 1991). **Outlaws:** *Outlaws* (Arista; ☆13, 1975). *Lady in Waiting* (Arista; ☆36, 1976). *Hurry Sundown* (Arista; ☆51, 1977). *Bring It Back Alive* (Arista; ☆29, 1978). *Playin' to Win* (Arista; ☆60, 1978). *In the Eye of the Storm* (Arista; ☆55, 1979). **Sea Level:** *Sea Level* (Capricorn; ☆43, 1977). *Cats on the Coast* (Capricorn; ☆31, 1978). *On the Edge* (Capricorn; ☆137, 1978). **Marshall Tucker Band:** *The Marshall Tucker Band* (Capricorn; ☆29, 1973). *A New Life* (Capricorn; ☆37, 1974). *Where We All Belong* (Capricorn; ☆54, 1974). *Searchin' for a Rainbow* (Capricorn; ☆15, 1975). *Long Hard Ride* (Capricorn; ☆32, 1976). *Carolina Dreams* (Capricorn; ☆23, 1977). *Together Forever* (Capricorn; ☆22, 1978). *Greatest Hits* (Capricorn; ☆67, 1978). *Running Like the Wind* (Warner Bros.; ☆30, 1979).

ANTHOLOGIES

Rebel Rousers: Southern Rock Classics (Rhino; 1992).

(Chart positions compiled from Joel Whitburn's *Record Research*, based on *Billboard*'s LPs chart.)

AL GREEN

BY ROBERT CHRISTGAU

Especially when Al Green is on—which means any-time this intensely self-alienated man can be observed in what feels to him like a role, in performance or offstage or at business—his speech is even more stylized than his singing. It combines three major elements. The *down-home* is rooted in the migrations of Green's growing up, on an Arkansas dirt farm and in the black downtown of Grand Rapids, Michigan. The *ersatz formal*, common among undereducated successes, usually takes a preacherly tone in its black variant; Green's version is more professorial. The *cute*, however, is entirely his own innovation. The man crinkles up his voice as if he's trying out for *Sesame Street;* he drawls like someone affecting a drawl; he hesitates and giggles and murmurs and swallows his words.

Like most great popular singers, Green transmutes and resynthesizes his speech in his singing style, both melting it down until it begins to flow and shoring it up, rhythmically, against its own nervousness. This style then becomes the vehicle for a persona that is modest, even fragile, yet undeniably compelling, a term which in Green's case can mean only one thing: *sexy.* One wants to go to bed with a person who is down-home, ersatz formal and cute, because these qualities have their conventionally attractive counterparts—earthy, self-possessed, vulnerable—and yet are unique in themselves. Combined with Green's physical charms—a lean body and winsome face, plus a warm vocal timbre—all this makes for a sex fantasy that is both sweet and original. And not just for women. Green's sexiness

The last of the purebred soul singers, at ease in his Memphis mansion, his career in high gear, his sofa protected by plastic slipcovers. That year, 1973, he enjoyed three Top Ten hits.

is so pervasive that no male who responds to his singing can do so without feeling a jolt that transcends identification.

Of course, we turn on not to a real person but to a persona, a fantasy of a real person that compounds several roles. Moreover, the chemistry is not our own. The Green persona is manufactured—in a process as calculated as a Gatorade assembly line and as natural as the production of sugar in photosynthesis—by Al Green himself. It can be disturbing to realize this, but it is rarely decisive. In October 1974 a woman who had gotten close enough to Al Green to learn that he was nowhere near as self-possessed, earthy or vulnerable as a fan might hope persisted in her dreams of marriage anyway. Green rejected her. In retaliation, she attempted to disfigure him with a scalding pot of grits—what an image of the soul music business—and then killed herself. I don't know why the woman continued to love Green; maybe she was still ensnared by the fantasy, or maybe there was something to the reality that continued to satisfy her. Maybe both. For those of us who take pleasure in Green's ability to create fantasies of character in the public drama of his life and in performance because of the genuine pleasure we derive from his music, that's just the way it is.

Green has constructed his persona for the same reason all stars do: to synthesize his need for approval with his need for a firm ego base. But Green is even less trusting than most stars. He got his professional start as a young teenager, singing lead in a family gospel group, a stint that ended when his father threw him out of the group and the house for listening to Jackie Wilson; his father, perceiving all that Baby Workout as devil's music, couldn't understand that his son had a different kind of religion. "Music engulfs one's soul to exert himself beyond imagination," Green has said. "That music just tripped me out." Later, in 1967, when Green was twenty, he and a fellow musician from Grand Rapids made a record called "Back Up Train" that eventually hit Number Forty-one in *Billboard*. He never got a cent for it. Soon he headed south.

In 1969, in Midland, Texas, Green and a trumpet player named Willie Mitchell were ripped off by the same crooked club owner. Their bond thus cemented, Green accompanied his new acquaintance back to Memphis, where Mitchell was staff producer for Hi Records. Over the next two years Mitchell constructed a new Memphis sound around a percus-

Al Green at the start of the Seventies, before his career took off.

ding and Sam and Dave in the mid-Sixties. Although his string of smooth-surfaced hits on man-woman themes tempted those consumers who like their aesthetic differentiation in the large economy size to dismiss his music as black bubblegum, in fact it represented a powerful synthesis and a unique style. The synthesis united the two mainstreams of soul, homogenized cool Detroit-Chicago (near where he grew up and began to record) and greasy get-down Memphis (near where he was born and where he now lives and records). Supported by a respectable variety of hooks and riffs, his vocal musicianship—control of timbre and volume, projection and especially phrasing—showed an instinctive musicianship unprecedented within his genre. His persona was equally original, nonmacho but not long-suffering (Smokey Robinson) or vague (Curtis Mayfield) or button-down (Bill Withers) or wimpy (Russell Thompkins of the Stylistics). He wrote or cowrote most of his own songs and blended an audacious variety of outside tastes—from the Doors to the Bee Gees, from Hank Williams to Kris Kristofferson,

Looking almost unrecognizable in a wavy hairdo, Green poses with Rufus and Carla Thomas, veterans of the Memphis soul scene.

sive studio style in which even strings were counterpointed rhythmically to the thick, third-beat drumming of Howard Grimes and Al Jackson, ex–Booker T. and the MGs and hence one fourth of Stax-Volt's original Memphis sound. The signature of this sound was Green's soft-edged, almost indolent phrasing, full of audacious slurs, with his startling falsetto adding an intensity that was suffering soul and sweet pop at the same time. The team's first smash was "Tired of Being Alone" in mid-1971; eventually they produced eight gold singles and six gold albums. The six albums of Green's great period—which ended with *Al Green Explores Your Mind* in 1974—all flow with an intense consistency, thus earning the dubious appellation "artistic unit." That total was approached by very few white artists of the Seventies; among black artists, who had no *Sgt. Pepper* tradition to spur them on when their own LP market established itself, only George Clinton, never one to be hobgoblined by consistency, produced as many remarkable albums; and none of his peers, black or white (with the possible exception of Elton John), showed Green's class as a singles artist.

Green is the last of the purebred house-of-soul innovators that seemed to have ended with Otis Red-from Roosevelt Sykes to the Temptations, from "God Is Standing By" to "Unchained Melody"— into his own cool-and-creamy sound. Although both music and persona were in a conservative black tradition, it is essential to realize that both were romantic enough, at least in theory, to pass as white pop—and that this is what Green intended.

Because Green's hit singles are so pervasive, even those astonished by his television appearances, where his expressive face makes quite an impression, can't imagine him as a live performer. But Green needs a stage. It's the only place where he can overwhelm his own good taste, providing a subtlety and a power not so easily available to the listener over the car radio—until Green has been seen live just once. The male soul star is expected to come onstage, as Green has said, "in some superman machine suit that glitters and lights up," and at times in the late Seventies he resorted to such gimmickry himself, but in general has favored a conservative flash that's both sexier and more subversive. Not only are his clothes tailored to show off the lithe eloquence of his body; they also make that body accessible. There was even a time when he would appear carrying a shoulder bag and looking slightly rumpled, as if he'd just gotten off a Greyhound, and he always performs with a layer of fuzz on his face, making it impossible to tell whether he's growing a beard or just neglected to shave.

Green shares almost nothing with old studs like Wilson Pickett's man and a half or middle-period studs like chesty Teddy Pendergrass or new studs like all-true Alexander O'Neal. But Green definitely does exploit his own immense physical attractiveness. He is exciting, not just secure. Every time he draws back from the microphone so that his trademarked high moans can waft unamplified over the arena, he works his savvy, diffident style of sexual confidence on everyone who strains toward the stage to hear. Every time he laughs mischievously at the passion elicited by his boyish come-on, he shares a joke about the pleasures of the tease. His interplay with the band is a model of generous authority, his interplay with the crowd a dream of self-possessed appeal. Only as the climactic riff sets in does he finally begin to stride and belt, and even though he doesn't quite muster the power of a soulman and a half, the audience is more than fulfilled.

Yet this epiphany is a qualified one. For us, its failure is in its aesthetic spirit—especially compared

Green meets members of the audience following a performance at the Lorton Reformatory, Virginia.

to great predecessors like Sam Cooke and Otis Redding, Green lacks any sense of openness. For Green himself, the failure is commercial, for he has never achieved the mass interracial success he intended. Nevertheless, he's proven remarkably resilient. Not only has he maintained his career despite diminishing record sales and a reputation for onstage flakiness that preceded the grits incident and got a lot worse after it, but he's also kept his music alive and then some. The three albums he did with Willie Mitchell after *Explores Your Mind* are all spotty, but they're also eccentric and inspired, laced with semi-improvised vamp tunes that often make first-rate filler as well as one or two painfully personal if not paranoid showpieces. And in 1977 he came out with his first self-produced LP, *The Belle Album*. Although less than a hit, it was praised almost unanimously by all the critics who'd finally caught up with him, achieving the synthesis he'd been promising for a long time (sometimes almost in so many words): secular gospel music. The woman to whom the title cut was addressed was the focus of his dilemma: "It's you I want, but it's Him that I need."

As it turned out, Green wasn't jiving: After *Truth n' Time* in 1979, he up and quit pop music, transforming himself into a kingpin of the gospel circuit who presaged such black Christian crossovers as the Winans as well as white best-sellers like Amy Grant. He held forth most Sundays in his own Memphis church, and whether the context was a Broadway theater or an Easter-eve jubilee, his tours were as incandescently unpredictable as ever. For a long

Green invariably exchanges flowers with fans at his concerts.

time he eschewed his most famous songs in concert, and except for an import-only live double album in 1981 and the memorable mid-Seventies outtakes MCA compiled into *Love Ritual* in 1989, he has yet to release another "secular" album. But gradually he found himself transformed into a legend, finally getting respect from both blacks and whites as a soul titan—the finest pure singer the style ever produced. And cautiously he edged back toward pop covers on his albums and pop hits live. Among the album highlights were the all-sacred *Higher Plane* (1981), the 1986 Willie Mitchell reunion *Soul Survivor* and *I Get Joy* (1987), where his covers of "He Ain't Heavy, He's My Brother" and "You've Got a Friend" effortlessly transported his Jesus fixation into the realm of universalist-humanist schlock. For unbelievers with ears to hear, Green's new music has its own peaks, with its transports more in-dividuated than in traditional gospel, sharing as much conceptually with Grant's pop songs to God as with the Swan Silvertones classics they derive from. By 1991 his show was a wacky, magical amalgam of impassioned soul and sexy pop in a gospel frame-work.

More than anyone else in the line—even night-club preacher Solomon Burke, plainly a less tortured artist—Green has embodied the contradictions of the soul style. Back when it looked as if he might achieve conventional superstardom, the riff that cli-maxed his live show went with "Love and Happi-ness," a playful euphemism for good sex and all the good things that go with it. But when he settled temporarily for the pop second string, the showstop-per became "Take Me to the River"—in the wake of Talking Heads' hit version, now his best-known

song. You get the feeling with many soul singers that the spiritual root of their music (call it God) and its emotional referent (by which I mean sex) coexist at the center of their vision. Green apotheosized this confusion at its most extreme in a lyric that was unclear in a mystical rather than euphemistic way. Rambling past an apparent reference to his musical past (the phrase "sweet sixteen" is a title from *Livin' for You*), he seems to beg for a sexual deliverance that is identical to a country baptism. He demands to have his feet on the ground and walk on the water at the same time. Perhaps it is the final tragedy of soul music that all of its creators have longed to do just that, and that none of them has come any closer than Al Green.

DISCOGRAPHY

SINGLES

Al Green and the Soul Mates: "Back Up Train" (Hot Line; r☆5, ☆41, 1967). "You Say It" (Hi; r☆28, 1970). "Right Now, Right Now" (Hi; r☆23, 1970). "I Can't Get Next to You" (Hi; r☆11, ☆60, 1970). "Driving Wheel" (Hi; r☆46, 1971). "Tired of Being Alone" (Hi; r☆7, ☆11, 1971). "Let's Stay Together" (Hi; r☆1, ☆1, 1971). "Look at What You've Done for Me" (Hi; r☆2, ☆4, 1972). "I'm Still in Love with You" (Hi; r☆1, ☆3, 1972). "You Ought to Be with Me" (Hi; r☆1, ☆3, 1972). "Guilty" (Bell; r☆29, ☆69, 1972). "Hot Wire" (Bell; ☆71, 1973). "Call Me (Come Back Home)" (Hi; r☆2, ☆10, 1973). "Here I Am (Come and Take Me)" (Hi; r☆2, ☆10, 1973). "Livin' for You" (Hi; r☆1, ☆19, 1973). "Let's Get Married" (Hi; r☆3, ☆32, 1974). "Sha-La-La (Make Me Happy)" (Hi; r☆2, ☆7, 1974). "L-O-V-E (Love)" (Hi; r☆1, ☆13, 1975). "Oh Me, Oh My (Dream in My Arms)" (Hi; r☆7, ☆48, 1975). "Full of Fire" (Hi; r☆2, ☆48, 1975). "Keep Me Cryin'" (Hi; r☆4, ☆37, 1976). "I Tried to Tell My-self" (Hi; r☆26, 1977). "Love and Happiness" (Hi; r☆92, 1977). "Belle" (Hi; r☆9, ☆83, 1978). "I Feel Good" (Hi; r☆36, 1978). "To Sir with Love" (Hi; r☆71, 1979). "Wait Here" (Hi; r☆58, 1979). "Everything's Gonna Be Alright" (A&M; r☆22, 1987).

ALBUMS

Al Green Gets Next to You (Hi; ☆58, 1971). *Let's Stay Together* (Hi; ☆8, 1972). *I'm Still in Love with You* (Hi; ☆4, 1972). *Al Green* (Bell; ☆162, 1972). *Green Is Blues* (Hi; ☆19, 1973). *Call Me* (Hi; ☆10, 1973). *Livin' for You* (Hi; ☆24, 1973). *Al Green Explores Your Mind* (Hi; ☆15, 1974). *Greatest Hits* (Hi; ☆17, 1975). *Al Green Is Love* (Hi; ☆28, 1975). *Full of Fire* (Hi; ☆59, 1976). *Have a Good Time* (Hi; ☆93, 1976). *Al Green's Greatest Hits—Volume 2* (Hi; ☆134, 1977). *The Belle Album* (Hi; ☆103, 1977). *Truth n' Time* (Hi; r☆44, 1979). *The Lord Will Make a Way* (Myrrh; 1980). *Tokyo . . . Live!* (Cream Import; 1981). *Higher Plane* (Myrrh; 1981). *Precious Lord* (Hi/Myrrh; 1982). *I'll Rise Again* (Myrrh; 1983). *Trust in God* (Myrrh; 1985). *He Is the Light* (Myrrh; 1986). *Soul Survivor* (A&M; 1987). *I Get Joy* (A&M; 1989). *Love Ritual: Rare & Previously Unreleased 1968–1976* (MCA; 1989). *One in a Million* (Word/Epic; 1991). *Love Is Reality* (Word/Epic; 1992).

(Chart positions compiled from Joel Whitburn's *Record Research,* based on *Billboard*'s Pop and LPs charts, unless otherwise indi-cated; r☆ = position on *Billboard*'s Rhythm & Blues chart.)

THE SOUND OF PHILADELPHIA

BY JIM MILLER

In 1974 three producers from Philadelphia dominated *Billboard*'s year-end awards. Each year the magazine ranks records and producers on the basis of sales and airplay, and in 1974 it was Thom Bell, Kenny Gamble and Leon Huff who were the big winners. Bell charted eleven hit singles that year, while the team of Gamble and Huff followed with ten.

All three had recorded their hits in Philadelphia, helping to make it the most influential source of black music in the early Seventies. And at the source stood Gamble and Huff, who, as executives of Philadelphia International, the city's largest label, directed the most lucrative black-owned musical enterprise in the United States after Motown.

Philadelphia had not always been a soul center: Kenny Gamble and Leon Huff both cut their teeth on the predominantly white Philly music scene of the early Sixties, a scene that revolved around Dick Clark's *American Bandstand*. The Philly-based TV show offered a convenient avenue for plugging current product, and a legion of labels, eager to exploit the *Bandstand* connection, soon popped up. Among them were Chancellor, with Frankie Avalon and Fabian; Swan, with Freddy Cannon and Billie and Lillie; and Cameo-Parkway, with Chubby Checker, the

Rays, the Dovells, Bobby Rydell, the Orlons and Dee Dee Sharp (later Mrs. Kenny Gamble).

It was a scene that fostered a flourishing community of musicians who made sessions and swapped ideas, churning out Bobby Rydell tracks by day, jamming at jazz clubs at night. Out of it emerged such key figures as Gamble and Huff, who first made their mark as songwriters, accompanists and performers during this period. Gamble and Thom Bell both worked in a local band called the Romeos with guitarist Roland Chambers, who eventually became a mainstay of MFSB, the Philadelphia house band. Leon Huff (who was also with the Romeos at one point) was active as a songwriter and producer, participating in Danny and the Juniors' "At the Hop" and Len Barry's "1-2-3" (Barry had been the Dovell's chief vocalist).

By the mid-Sixties Gamble and Huff had joined

Kenny Gamble in the early Sixties.

Mayfield ("He Will Break Your Heart"). When Butler arrived in Philadelphia in 1967 his star was in eclipse, but by fashioning a stunning series of singles over the next two years, Gamble and Huff changed all that. Jerry Butler reemerged as "The Iceman," Mr. Cool set against the sound of Philadelphia. Instrumentally, that sound, softened for Butler, revolved around a crack rhythm section that included such novel instruments as vibraphone (used only occasionally by Motown) and harpsichord, and featuring creamy guitar obligatos, equal parts Wes Montgomery and Curtis Mayfield (a neglected influence in his role as the Impressions' lead guitarist).

The songs, composed by Butler, Gamble and Huff in tandem, struck a vulnerable pose, as Butler sang about loves lost with moving pathos. His silken

With the Intruders, the Gamble and Huff style first began to gel.

forces to produce records. Their first national hit came in 1967, when the Soul Survivors' "Expressway to Your Heart" made the Top Ten. Previously, the duo had scored solid R&B hits with the Intruders, who had remained with Gamble and Huff.

It was with the Intruders that the G&H style first began to gel. Fashioning a series of novelty songs—"Cowboys to Girls," "(Love Is Like a) Baseball Game"—for lead singer "Little Sonny" Brown, who wobbled unpredictably off pitch on each take, the producers focused homey lyrics ("Love is like a baseball game/Three strikes you're out"), a solid rhythm section and expert sweetening, usually strings and horns. These records were raunchy, slick and silly simultaneously, mixing spontaneous jive with meticulous production.

But the team first hit their stride in a path-breaking series of sessions with Jerry Butler, the Chicago soul stylist. Butler, originally lead singer with the Impressions, specialized in mellow ballads, scoring pop hits early in the decade with material by Burt Bacharach ("Make It Easy on Yourself") and Curtis

voice had begun to fray around the edges, but the producers, by forcing Butler to sing in his highest register, exploited his breaking pitch to express the lyrics. Structurally, many of his songs recalled Burt Bacharach's work with Butler and Dionne Warwick. Most cuts phased in the rhythm section gradually, confining the use of full percussion to the choruses. But the complexities of the material did not prevent the studio band (MFSB as we know it today; the same musicians performed on the 1968 chart-topping instrumental "The Horse") from punching out the changes in a fashion owing more to Motown than to Bacharach, who had always preferred a polite rhythm section.

But the Butler sessions soon diverged from Motown in rhythmic style and the techniques used to record the section. Instead of the shrill highs and booming bass of the Motown singles, with their hot mix geared to AM radio airplay, Gamble and Huff strove to clean up the sound, sharply pinpointing each instrument in their increasingly lush arrangements. The guitars, which eschewed the staccato chording characteristic of Motown and James Brown singles, were plugged directly into the studio board, instead of being recorded through amplifiers. Instrumental lines were etched out in the mix, each floating with an almost palpable presence.

By 1969, with "Only the Strong Survive," "Moody Woman" and "What's the Use of Breaking Up," the Gamble-Huff style had been perfected: A classic trio of discs, these singles summarized the duo's achievement as well as pointing toward things to come. Take "Moody Woman." Vibes and marimba, soon joined by an electric guitar sounding like a sitar (a favorite trick used by Thom Bell as a signature on his Delfonics hits), bounce off bass drum and hi-hat to open the track, with Butler, backed by female chorus, entering, relaxed, at the middle of his range. On the chorus, on the other hand, Butler strains for the high notes, and drummer Earl Young finally gets to use his full battery of percussion; aided by strings (mixed down, with reverb added), the drummer picks up the track and firmly pushes Butler back into the refrain. Thanks to its structure, the song bristles with channeled energy, building tension in the refrains, releasing it in the choruses.

As the Seventies began, Gamble and Huff were clearly angling for a larger slice of the pop market. In 1968 they had signed an ill-fated deal with the Chess brothers, giving Chess distribution rights for G&H's Neptune label. Despite sessions with the O'Jays that yielded such brilliant singles as "One Night Affair" and "Looky Looky (Look at Me Girl)," the label eventually collapsed after Leonard Chess's death. Independent production deals with Spring (Joe Simon's "Drowning in the Sea of Love") and Atlantic (Wilson Pickett's "Don't Let the Green Grass Fool You," Archie Bell's "I Can't Stop Dancing" and Dusty Springfield's "A Brand New Me") kept Gamble and Huff in hits but didn't net them the independent label they were ob-

viously after—a label with reliable distribution and plenty of capital to finance promotion and experimentation in the studios (all that orchestration wasn't cheap).

Finally, in 1971, Gamble and Huff formed Philadelphia International Records under the auspices of CBS (with Clive Davis at the helm, in one of his shrewdest moves to corner the R&B market). With CBS distributing and promoting to the white market, Philadelphia International working black radio stations and media, and Gamble and Huff themselves recording their most commercial material to date, the label became an instant success. Singles poured out of Philly's Sigma Sound studios, and several promptly crossed over to the pop charts, going on to sell a million copies each. Billy Paul crooned about "Mrs. Jones"; the O'Jays indicted the "Back Stabbers"; Harold Melvin and the Blue Notes offered "If You Don't Know Me by Now."

MFSB, the band of sessionmen who played on all of Gamble and Huff's Philadelphia productions. They also scored a hit of their own with "TSOP (The Sound of Philadelphia)."

For these records Gamble and Huff further refined their sound. Earl Young's drums were recorded with an astonishing fullness, the hi-hat swishing, the bass drum thumping, the snare crackling. Meanwhile, the rest of the rhythm section—usually Ronnie Baker on bass, Roland Chambers and Norman Harris on guitar and Vince Montana on vibes—improvised an instrumental track, aiming at a groove with an irresistible undertow. Although sweetening gave the Philly sound a candied veneer, the rhythm track, alive and kicking, belied claims that Gamble and Huff churned out nothing but fluff.

Leon Huff has explained the team's studio procedure: "We have about two sessions a week. If we

"If You Don't Know Me by Now": Harold Melvin and the Blue Notes.

book a day, we'll be lucky if we cut three tracks. We put down the rhythm track first. Our sound stems from the feeling of the musicians; you know everybody down there is in a relaxed atmosphere, they're not pressured to play. . . . The warmness shows in the grooves, the mechanical feeling is not there, it's more of a free type of thing. But the professionalism is there. You see, we have been playing together so long, everybody knows what the next guy's doing.''

As it emerged in the Seventies, the Philly sound abandoned the blunt 2/4 that had characterized the classic Motown singles (such as ''Dancing in the Street''). In its stead arose the streamlined pulse of MFSB, a beat that helped define disco style through such singles as ''Love Train,'' ''I'll Always Love My Mama,'' ''TSOP (The Sound of Philadelphia)'' and ''Bad Luck.''

Gamble and Huff's two major groups of the early Seventies, Harold Melvin and the Blue Notes and the O'Jays, presented divergent images. Teddy Pendergrass, the Blue Notes' former lead singer (he left in 1976), played the suffering soul, losing loves, alienating friends, getting raw deals; he moaned a lot. The O'Jays complained about the world, too, in a series of ''protest'' lyrics, but they also sang about successful love affairs; less bluesy than Melvin, they came on assertive and brassy. Teddy Pendergrass was an intransigent stylist, unlike the O'Jays' Eddie Levert, but both singers were capable of cutting through thickets of orchestration. If the O'Jays had a fault, it was their versatility; they were too mallea-

ble to resist full-blown production assaults. For their part, Gamble and Huff themselves had a tendency to round off the rough edges that Motown, in its heyday, had left intact.

An urbane glossiness was the leading characteristic of the entire Philadelphia school. In their wake, Gamble and Huff left a flourishing band of slickminded producers, most of them using Sigma Sound and the same batch of musicians. Session guitarist Norman Harris produced Blue Magic; local impresario Stan Watson worked with the Delfonics and First Choice; veteran R&B producer Dave Crawford recorded the gospel group the Mighty Clouds of Joy in Philadelphia; and David Bowie cut *Young Americans* at Sigma Sound.

While most of Philly's producers hewed close to formulas, a few stood out as pioneers (such as Thom Bell) or eccentrics (such as Bunny Sigler). Apart from Gamble and Huff, Bell (who did numerous arrangements for G&H) was the most noteworthy—and successful—of the lot.

His first hit came in 1968 with the Delfonics' ''La-La Means I Love You.'' A subtle orchestrator and lyric composer, Bell from the outset favored ballads with seamless string arrangements, garnished by woodwinds and French horns. On cuts like ''Didn't I (Blow Your Mind This Time),'' he created symphonic miniatures within a sweet soul format.

In the Seventies Bell perfected his approach with the Stylistics, a falsetto-led group cast in the Delfonics mold, and the Spinners, a more orthodox quintet of Motown veterans. Both groups were often saddled with banal lyrics, but Bell at his best, on singles like the Spinners' ''I'll Be Around'' and the Stylistics' ''Make Up to Break Up,'' projected a genuine feeling of warmth, conveyed through sophisticated compositions and scores. Bell is a nonpareil producer of pop soul and the true heir of Burt Bacharach.

Other Philadelphia figures pursued a more idiosyncratic course. Bunny Sigler, for example, indulged onstage in outrageous theatrics and brought an offbeat imaginativeness to his productions. He composed straight ballads for the O'Jays and recorded several himself (''Regina,'' ''Keep Smilin' ''); on the other hand, he worked in a funky streetwise vein, producing Archie Bell and the Drells and cutting a lovely, slow-drag remake of ''Love Train.''

The Trammps, early favorites in the discos, followed a similarly idiosyncratic course. Founded by drummer Earl Young as an outlet for his performing ambitions, the group was coproduced by Young and fellow session musicians Ronnie Baker and Norman Harris. A loose musical showcase, the band cut Baker originals like "Where Do We Go from Here," as well as updating such oldies as "Zing Went the Strings of My Heart" (modeled after the Coasters' arrangement). Lead singer Jimmy Ellis, a dexterous tenor, played the straight man to Young, a basso profundo and a ham to boot. The result was some of the most good-natured music to emerge from Philadelphia.

When the disco scene exploded in 1974, most of the Philadelphia producers and groups found themselves in the right place at the right time. Unfortunately, the fad rendered the Philly formulas about as fresh as the jingles for Wrigley's Doublemint gum. The formulas sold records but rarely created vital recordings; a producer like Bell was locked into cream-puff soul, and even Gamble and Huff had trouble resisting extended tags. In spite of such weaknesses, the Philadelphia style proved durable enough to spawn one or two more great tracks, for example, the O'Jays' marvelously old-fashioned "Use ta Be My Girl" in 1978, and McFadden and Whitehead's "Ain't No Stoppin' Us Now" in 1979.

For a spell, the biggest threat to the scene seemed to be legal. When the first indictments in the payola probe of 1975 were announced, prominent among those implicated were Kenny Gamble and Leon Huff. The indictments accused Philadelphia International of peddling influence, favors and money in exchange for airplay. Early in 1976 the charges against Huff were dismissed, but Gamble was fined $2500.

The real death knell rang for the Philly Sound in the early Eighties, as disco fell into disfavor, and Gamble, Huff and Bell more or less retired from the fray of pop music making. By then, they had transfigured the sound of black music in America, a feat accomplished through musical innovation as much as shrewd manipulation. Architects of a new style in dance music, Top Forty hitmakers of a proven caliber, creative artists in a cutthroat field—Gamble, Huff and Thom Bell are to the Seventies what Holland-Dozier-Holland and Smokey Robinson were to the Sixties: the preeminent soul producers of their decade.

The O'Jays, the most popular group produced by Gamble and Huff.

DISCOGRAPHY

SINGLES

Archie Bell and the Drells: "I Can't Stop Dancing" (Atlantic; r☆5, ☆9, 1968). "Do the Choo Choo" (Atlantic; r☆5, ☆44, 1968). ¹"There's Gonna Be a Showdown" (Atlantic; r☆6, ☆21, 1969). ¹"Girl You're Too Young" (Atlantic; r☆13, 1969). **Blue Magic:** "Sideshow" (Atco; r☆1, ☆8, 1974). "Three Ring Circus" (Atco; r☆5, ☆36, 1974). **Brenda and the Tabulations:** "Right on the Tip of My Tongue" (Top & Bottom; r☆10, ☆23, 1971). **Jerry Butler:** ¹"Lost" (Mercury; r☆15, 1968). ¹"Never Give You Up" (Mercury; r☆4, ☆20, 1968). ¹"Hey, Western Union Man" (Mercury; r☆1, ☆16, 1968). ¹"Are You Happy" (Mercury; r☆9, ☆39, 1968). ¹"Only the Strong Survive" (Mercury; r☆1, ☆4, 1969). ¹"Moody Woman" (Mercury; r☆3, ☆24, 1969). ¹"What's the Use of Breaking Up" (Mercury; r☆4, ☆20, 1969). ¹"Don't Let Love Hang You Up" (Mercury; r☆12, ☆44, 1969). ¹"I Could Write a Book" (Mercury; r☆15, ☆46, 1970). **Delfonics:** ²"La-La Means I Love You" (Philly Groove; r☆2, ☆4, 1968). ²"I'm Sorry" (Philly Groove; r☆15, ☆42, 1968). ²"Ready or Not Here I Come" (Philly Groove; r☆14, ☆35, 1968). ²"You Got Yours and I'll Get Mine" (Philly Groove; r☆6, ☆40, 1969). ²"Didn't I (Blow Your Mind This Time)" (Philly Groove; r☆3, ☆10, 1970). ²"Trying to Make a Fool of Me" (Philly Groove; r☆8, ☆40, 1970). ²"When You Get Right Down to It" (Philly Groove; r☆12, 1970). "Hey! Love" (Philly Groove; r☆9, 1971). "Walk Right Up to the Sun" (Philly Groove; r☆13, 1971). "Tell Me This Is a Dream" (Philly Groove; r☆15, 1972). "I Don't Want to Make You Wait" (Philly Groove; r☆22, 1973). **Ebonys:** ¹"You're the Reason Why" (Philadelphia International; r☆10, 1971). ¹"It's Forever" (Philadelphia International; r☆14, 1973). **First Choice:** "Armed and Extremely Dangerous" (Philly Groove; r☆11, ☆28, 1973). "The Player—Part I" (Philly Groove;

r☆7, 1974). "Guilty" (Philly Groove; r☆19, 1975). "Doctor Love" (Gold Mind; r☆23, ☆41, 1977). **Eddie Holman:** "Hey There Lonely Girl" (ABC; r☆4, ☆2, 1969). "My Mind Keeps Telling Me" (GSF; r☆20, 1972). **Intruders:** [1]"Together" (Gamble; r☆9, ☆48, 1967). [1]"Cowboys to Girls" (Gamble; r☆1, ☆6, 1968). [1]"(Love Is Like a) Baseball Game" (Gamble; r☆4, ☆26, 1968). [1]"Slow Drag" (Gamble; r☆12, 1968). [1]"Sad Girl" (Gamble; r☆14, ☆47, 1969). [1]"When We Get Married" (Gamble; r☆8, ☆45, 1970). [1]"I'm Girl Scouting" (Gamble; r☆16, 1971). [1]"I Bet He Don't Love You (Like I Love You)" (Gamble; ☆20, 1971). [1]"(Win, Place or Show) She's a Winner" (Gamble; r☆12, 1972). [1]"I'll Always Love My Mama" (Gamble; r☆6, ☆36, 1973). [1]"I Wanna Know Your Name" (Gamble; r☆9, ☆60, 1973). **Jones Girls:** [1]"You Gonna Make Me Love Somebody Else" (Philadelphia International; r☆5, ☆11, 1979). **Manhattans:** "Don't Take Your Love from Me" (Columbia; r☆7, ☆37, 1975). "Hurt" (Columbia; r☆10, 1975). "Kiss and Say Goodbye" (Columbia; r☆1, ☆1, 1976). "I Kinda Miss You" (Columbia; r☆7, ☆46, 1976). "It Feels So Good to Be Loved So Bad" (Columbia; r☆6, ☆93, 1977). "We Never Danced to a Love Song" (Columbia; r☆10, ☆9, 1977). **Barbara Mason:** "Oh, How It Hurts" (Arctic; r☆11, 1968). "Bed and Board" (Buddha; r☆24, 1972). **McFadden and Whitehead:** "Ain't No Stoppin' Us Now" (Philadelphia International; r☆1, ☆18, 1979). **Harold Melvin and the Blue Notes:** [1]"I Miss You" (Philadelphia International; r☆7, ☆58, 1972). [1]"If You Don't Know Me by Now" (Philadelphia International; r☆1, ☆3, 1972). [1]"Yesterday I Had the Blues" (Philadelphia International; r☆12, ☆63, 1973). [1]"Satisfaction Guaranteed (or Take Your Love Back)" b/w "I'm Weak for You" (Philadelphia International; r☆6, 1974). [1]"Where Are All My Friends" (Philadelphia International; r☆8, 1974). [1]"Bad Luck (Part I)" (Philadelphia International; r☆4, ☆15, 1975). [1]"Tell the World How I Feel About 'Cha Baby" (Philadelphia International; r☆7, ☆96, 1976). [1]"Reaching for the World" (ABC; r☆6, ☆74, 1977). **Harold Melvin and Sharon Paige:** [1]"Hope That We Can Be Together Soon" (Philadelphia International; r☆1, ☆42, 1975). **MFSB:** Featuring the Three Degrees [1]"TSOP (The Sound of Philadelphia)" (Philadelphia International; r☆1, ☆1, 1974). [1]"Sexy" (Philadelphia International; r☆2, ☆42, 1975). **Jackie Moore:** "Sweet Charlie Babe" (Atlantic; r☆15, ☆42, 1973). **Cliff Nobles and Co.:** "The Horse" (Phil L.A. of Soul; r☆2, ☆2, 1968). **O'Jays:** [1]"One Night Affair" (Neptune; r☆15, 1969). [1]"Deeper (in Love with You)" (Neptune; r☆21, 1970). [1]"Looky Looky (Look at Me Girl)" (Neptune; r☆17, 1970). [1]"Back Stabbers" (Philadelphia International; r☆1, ☆3, 1972). [1]"992 Arguments" (Philadelphia International; r☆13, ☆57, 1972). [1]"Love Train" (Philadelphia International; r☆1, ☆1, 1973). [1]"Time to Get Down" (Philadelphia International; r☆2, ☆33, 1973). [1]"Put Your Hands Together" (Philadelphia International; r☆2, ☆10, 1973). [1]"For the Love of Money" (Philadelphia International; r☆3, ☆9, 1974). [1]"Sunshine—Part II" (Philadelphia International; r☆17, ☆48, 1974). [1]"Give the People What They Want" (Hi; r☆1, ☆45, 1975). [1]"Let Me Make Love to You" (Philadelphia International; r☆10, 1975). [1]"I Love Music—Part I" (Philadelphia International; r☆1, ☆5, 1975). [1]"Livin' for the Weekend" (Philadelphia International; r☆1, ☆20, 1976). [1]"Message in Our Music" (Philadelphia International; r☆1, ☆49, 1976). [1]"Use ta Be My Girl" (Philadelphia International; r☆1, ☆4, 1978). [1]"Brandy" (Philadelphia International; r☆21, ☆79, 1978). **Billy Paul:** [1]"Me and Mrs. Jones" (Philadelphia International; r☆1, ☆1, 1972). [1]"Thanks for Saving My Life" (Philadelphia International; r☆9, ☆37, 1974). **Teddy Pendergrass:** [1]"I Don't Love You Anymore" (Philadelphia International; r☆5, ☆41, 1977). "Close the Door" (Philadelphia International; r☆1, ☆25, 1978). [1]"Turn Off the Lights" (Philadelphia International; r☆2, ☆6, 1979). **People's Choice:** "Do It Any Way You Wanna" (TSOP; r☆1, ☆11, 1975). "Nursery Rhymes (Part 1)" (TSOP; r☆22, ☆93, 1975). **Wilson Pickett:** "Engine Number 9" (Atlantic; r☆3, ☆14, 1970). [1]"Don't Let the Green Grass Fool You" (Atlantic; r☆2, ☆17, 1971). **Lou Rawls:** [1]"You'll Never Find Another Love Like Mine" (Philadelphia International; r☆1, ☆2, 1976). [1]"Groovy People" (Philadelphia International; r☆19, ☆64, 1976). [1]"See You When I Git There" (Philadelphia International; r☆8, ☆66, 1977). [1]"Lady Love" (Philadelphia International; r☆21, ☆24, 1978). **Joe Simon:** [1]"Drowning in the Sea of Love" (Spring; r☆3, ☆11, 1971). [1]"Pool of Bad Luck" (Spring; r☆13, ☆42, 1972). [1]"Power of Love" (Spring; r☆1, ☆11, 1972). **Soul Survivors:** [1]"Expressway to Your Heart" (Crimson; r☆3, ☆4, 1967). **Spinners:** [2]"I'll Be Around" (Atlantic; r☆1, ☆3, 1972). [2]"Could It Be I'm Falling in Love" (Atlantic; r☆1, ☆4, 1972). [2]"One of a Kind (Love Affair)" (Atlantic; r☆1, ☆11, 1973). [2]"Ghetto Child" (Atlantic; r☆4, ☆29, 1973). [2]"Mighty Love—Part I" (Atlantic; r☆1, ☆20, 1974). [2]"I'm Coming Home" (Atlantic; r☆1, ☆18, 1974). [2]"Love Don't Love Nobody—Part I" (Atlantic; r☆1, ☆15, 1974). [2]"Love Don't Love Nobody—Part II" (Atlantic; r☆7, ☆37, 1975). [2]"Sadie" (Atlantic; r☆7, 1975). [2]"They Just Can't Stop It (Games People Play)" (Atlantic; r☆1, ☆5, 1975). [2]"Wake Up Susan" (Atlantic; r☆11, ☆56, 1976). [2]"The Rubberband Man" (Atlantic; r☆1, ☆2, 1976). [2]"You're Throwing a Good Love Away" (Atlantic; r☆5, ☆43, 1977). [2]"Heaven on Earth (So Fine)" (Atlantic; r☆23, ☆89, 1977). [2]"If You Wanna Do a Dance" (Atlantic; r☆17, ☆49, 1978). **Dusty Springfield:** [1]"A Brand New Me" (Atlantic; ☆24, 1969). **Stylistics:** "You're a Big Girl Now" (Avco Embassy; r☆7, 1971). [2]"Stop, Look, Listen (to Your Heart)" (Avco Embassy; r☆6, ☆39, 1971). [2]"You Are Everything" (Avco; r☆10, ☆9, 1971). [2]"People Make the World Go Round" (Avco; r☆6, ☆25, 1972). [2]"Betcha By Golly, Wow" (Avco; r☆2, ☆3, 1972). [2]"I'm Stone in Love with You" (Avco; r☆4, ☆10, 1972). [2]"Break Up to Make Up" (Avco; r☆5, ☆5, 1973). [2]"You'll Never Get to Heaven If You Break My Heart" (Avco; r☆8, ☆23, 1973). [2]"Rockin' Roll Baby" (Avco; r☆13, ☆14, 1973). [2]"You Make Me Feel Brand New" (Avco; r☆5, ☆2, 1974). **Three Degrees:** [1]"When Will I See You Again" (Philadelphia International; r☆4, ☆2, 1974). [1]"I Didn't Know" (Philadelphia International; r☆18, 1975). **Trammps:** "Zing Went the Strings of My Heart" (Buddah; r☆17, ☆64, 1972). **Dionne Warwick:** [2]"Once You Hit the Road" (Warner Bros.; r☆5, ☆79, 1975). **Dionne Warwick and the Spinners:** [2]"Then Came You" (Atlantic; r☆2, ☆1, 1974). **Johnny Williams:** [1]"Slow Motion (Part I)" (Philadelphia International; r☆12, 1972).

[1] = Record produced by Gamble and Huff. [2] = Record produced by Thom Bell.

(Chart positions compiled from Joel Whitburn's *Record Research*, based on *Billboard*'s Pop chart, unless otherwise indicated; r☆ = position on *Billboard*'s Rhythm & Blues chart.)

FUNK

BY JOE McEWEN

In the Sixties the name for uncompromising black music was soul. The music was often intense, personal and raw; for a time the word itself became a cultural cliché for all that was pure and honest in expression. In late 1968 James Brown delivered its anthem: "Say It Loud—I'm Black and I'm Proud."

But within a few years of Brown's exhortation, soul had become an anachronism, the music diluted by pop aspirations and aimed at the burgeoning black middle class. In the Seventies uncompromising black music, the inner-city sound of exhilaration and ecstasy, was called funk. Like the amorphous and liberating plague "Jes Grew" in Ishmael Reed's novel *Mumbo Jumbo*—an inexplicable epidemic that originates in the black quarter of New Orleans at the turn of the century—funk, though largely hidden from view, aimed to put its audience in the grips of a new fever, or, in the words of its chief architect, George Clinton, to "rescue dance music from the blahs."

Yet despite impressive sales figures, its hits rarely made it beyond the bottom reaches of the Top Forty. Its practitioners remained mysterious figures to the pop audience. Like a messy, ketchup-laden cheese steak plopped down at a staid dinner party, funk was rude, greasy and unwanted. For most, funk's refrain—"Free Your Mind (and Your Ass Will Follow)"—remains alien.

The word *funk* didn't become legitimate radio jargon until 1967, when Dyke and the Blazers' "Funky Broadway" bubbled under for so long that DJs were forced to play it and say the word. Funk. Though nobody knows who coined the term, funk just was not a word mentioned in polite society. But "Funky Broadway" changed all that, and, after the first deluge of funky-everything records passed, several groups surfaced with a new musical handle on the term.

In the late Sixties and early Seventies there was Charles Wright's Watts 103rd Street Band from California, who specialized in languid, syncopated chants that combined the clipped, offbeat accents of New Orleans' Meters with the semi-improvised melodies of James Brown ("In the Jungle," "Ex-

Funk cowboy George Clinton rides herd on a pair of dolphins. His avowed purpose? "To rescue dance music from the blahs."

press Yourself"). At the same time, on the East Coast, Kool and the Gang surfaced with a new aesthetic, different from Brown's surreal jabbering and the Watts Band's sleepy exhortations. Kool and the Gang made nasty silly. There was the guy who ate raw hamburger and chocolate buttermilk for lunch ("Raw Hamburger"), the "Funky Man," an ersatz Pig Pen, who had smelly armpits and dreamed of bringing "the whole world under my funk power," and even a song called "Kool It (Here Comes the Fuzz)."

Just like Dyke and the Blazers, the Watts Band and the Ohio Players, Kool and the Gang borrowed a lot from the mid-Sixties James Brown band: choked, trebly guitars, staccato horn bursts and clipped rhythmic accents. But where Brown and the JBs began to favor loping, good-rocking grooves ("Doing It to Death"), the Gang's records from the outset ("Kool and the Gang") zigzagged like a stitch from a runaway sewing machine. Kool played jagged, broken bass patterns, horns slammed in and out, congas flailed and somewhere in the middle

Maurice White, producer, composer and the leader of Earth, Wind and Fire. He polished the funk, so Clinton, naturally, attacked him: "Earth, Hot Air and No Fire."

were the voices of Kool and the Gang, carrying on like they were having the time of their lives. It all peaked in 1974 with a trio of steamy dance hits: "Jungle Boogie," "Funky Stuff" and "Hollywood Swinging." But for funk the new day had just begun.

Though James Brown was at the root of the new funk and continued to have sporadic hits through the Seventies, he became less of an artistic force in pop music, at least for a while. His grunts, limply off-center productions and gauche braggadocio sounded feeble next to the sleek cosmology of Earth, Wind and Fire or the inspired funk-entelechy of progeny Parliament/Funkadelic, the two bands who spearheaded the rise of funk from entertaining groove music to a brand of sophisticated pop infused with its own intricate orthodoxies and myths.

Early in 1968 George Clinton had decided to transform his group, the Parliaments, from a sharkskin-suited, Temptations-styled vocal group with one hit to their credit ("[I Wanna] Testify") into a free-form, acid-rock band called Funkadelic. The name change was motivated in part by contractual considerations; Clinton recorded with both Parliament and Funkadelic—for two different labels. The name

change also reflected a radical switch in style, developing out of an appreciation of the music of Sly Stone, Jimi Hendrix and even Frank Zappa.

The first songs cut by Funkadelic suggested a soundtrack to a bleak, urban horror story. They evoked a scary world made all the more ominous by the group's seemingly aggressive pose and bizarre stage getup. Steeped in late-Sixties psychedelia, Funkadelic featured guitarist Eddie Hazel's jarring solos jammed into weird melodies captioned with titles like ''Maggot Brain,'' ''Cosmic Slop'' and ''Trash a Go-Go.''

But in 1974 Clinton's vision changed. Parliament was reactivated as Funkadelic's more accessible alter ego, and, with the commercial success of Parliament's *Mothership Connection* (a brilliant pastiche of funk and black science fiction), Clinton began to articulate a semiserious funk mythology. He mocked his competition on album covers; created an otherworldly Dr. Funkenstein character who led an army of followers and believers, dispensing ''funk'' like sacraments at a papal blessing; and churned out a dizzying array of spin-off groups (Bootsy's Rubber Band, Parlet, the Brides of Funkenstein) who aided

Dr. Funkenstein in his ongoing crusade against those who ''fake the funk.''

Though Parliament/Funkadelic had antecedents in Sly Stone, James Brown and even Sun Ra, the mixture of tribal funk, elaborate stage props and the relentless assault on personal inhibition resembled nothing so much as a Space Age Mardi Gras, presided over by ringleader Clinton, who extolled his credo in song: ''Here's a chance to dance our way out of our constrictions/ . . . One nation under a groove.''

With Parliament/Funkadelic at one rather anarchic extreme of funk, Earth, Wind and Fire rested comfortably on the side of pop orthodoxy. Referring to themselves as ''the Creator's Band'' (modesty was not their strong suit), Earth, Wind and Fire wrote songs that combined cosmology with commercial savvy.

George Clinton onstage with Funkadelic in his Phylis Diller costume. Can a blond black sing the blues?

Like Parliament/Funkadelic, Earth, Wind and Fire were heavily influenced by Sly Stone and James Brown. But where George Clinton found inspiration in Jimi Hendrix and white rock, Earth, Wind and Fire prime mover Maurice White (an ex-Chess session drummer) balanced his funk with mainstream jazz, soft soul and African folk rhythm embellishments.

Though the group had been recording since 1970, White's conception didn't really gel until the release of *That's the Way of the World* in 1975, a soundtrack to an obscure movie. The album is a production masterpiece. Cowbells, slight tango rhythms and snatches of James Brown bass lines stand side by side with delicate Latin beats and hard, insistent funk vamps. Voices and strings appear over the choppy, propulsive tracks, swelling and swooping, only to disappear at the snap of a finger, bringing the music as close to elegance as funk can come. On subsequent albums like *All 'n All* and *I Am,* White's production delicacy and rhythmic innovation salvaged the most awkward lyric, even while giving George Clinton ammunition to snipe at the band (''Earth, Hot Air and No Fire,'' he rasped in one Funkadelic song).

By the end of the Seventies Funkadelic and Earth, Wind and Fire continued to trade Number One records on the black charts, and both generated a parade of imitators. Meanwhile, mainstream jazz artists such as Herbie Hancock and Donald Byrd mined some of the same territory with commercial success, while avant-garde musicians in Greenwich Village lofts began experimenting with funk rhythms. Even Philippe Wynne, formerly the sweet lead singer for the Spinners, turned up as an unlikely lead voice on Funkadelic's ''(not just) Knee Deep—Part I,'' singing in mock wonder, ''Could this be me, immersed in funk so deep?'' Ishmael Reed could have warned him.

Through the Eighties the Gap Band, Cameo, the Time and the Commodores helped move funk into the pop mainstream, but toward the end of the decade, technology and the sudden, pervasive arrival of rap had all but swept away funk bands from black radio. Earth, Wind and Fire scrambled for survival, George Clinton used the occasional P-Funk All-Stars show to play the old songs, and rap producers pilfered pieces of old funk grooves to use as rhythmic underpinning for the new order. Almost overnight funk seemed to join blues and soul as beloved archeological fodder in the black-music museum.

DISCOGRAPHY

SINGLES

Dyke and the Blazers: ''Funky Broadway'' (Original Sound; r☆17, ☆65, 1967). ''Funky Walk, Part 1'' (Original Sound; r☆22, ☆67, 1968). ''We Got More Soul'' (Original Sound; r☆7, ☆35, 1969). ''Let a Woman Be a Woman—Let a Man Be a Man'' (Original Sound; r☆4, ☆36, 1969). **Earth, Wind and Fire:** ''Love Is Life'' (Warner Bros.; r☆43, ☆93, 1971). ''Keep Your Head to the Sky'' (Columbia; r☆23, ☆52, 1973). ''Evil'' (Columbia; ☆50, 1973). ''Mighty Mighty'' (Columbia; r☆4, ☆29, 1974). ''Kalimba Story'' (Columbia; r☆6, ☆55, 1974). ''Devo-

tion'' (Columbia; r☆23, ☆33, 1974). ''Shining Star'' (Columbia; r☆1, ☆1, 1975). ''That's the Way of the World'' (Columbia; r☆5, ☆12, 1975). ''Sing a Song'' (Columbia; r☆1, ☆5, 1975). ''Can't Hide Love'' (Columbia; r☆11, ☆39, 1976). ''Getaway'' (Columbia; r☆1, ☆12, 1976). ''Saturday Nite'' (Columbia; r☆4, ☆21, 1976). ''Serpentine Fire'' (Columbia; r☆1, ☆13, 1977). ''Fantasy'' (Columbia; r☆12, ☆32, 1978). ''Got to Get You into My Mind'' (Columbia; r☆1, ☆9, 1978). ''September'' (ARC; r☆1, ☆8, 1978). ''Boogie Wonderland'' (ARC; r☆2, ☆6, 1979). ''After the Love Has Gone'' (ARC; r☆2, ☆2, 1979). ''In the Stone'' (ARC; r☆23, ☆58, 1979). ''Star'' (ARC; r☆47, ☆64, 1979). ''Let Me Talk'' (ARC; r☆8, ☆44, 1980). ''You'' (ARC; r☆10, ☆48, 1980). ''And Love Goes On'' (ARC; r☆15, ☆59, 1981). ''Let's Groove'' (ARC; r☆1, ☆3, 1981). ''Wanna Be with You'' (ARC; r☆15, ☆51, 1982). ''Fall in Love with Me'' (Columbia; r☆4, ☆17, 1983). ''Side by Side'' (Columbia; r☆15, ☆76, 1983). ''Spread Your Love'' (Columbia; r☆57, 1983). ''Magnetic'' (Columbia; r☆10, ☆57, 1983). ''Touch'' (Columbia; r☆23, ☆103, 1984). ''Moonwalk'' (Columbia; r☆67, 1984). ''System of Survival'' (Columbia; r☆1, ☆60, 1987). ''Thinking of You'' (Columbia; r☆3, ☆67, 1988). ''Evil Roy'' (Columbia; r☆22, 1988). ''Heritage'' (Columbia; r☆5, 1990). ''For the Love of You'' (Columbia; r☆19, 1990). ''Wanna Be the Man'' (Columbia; r☆46, 1990). **Funkadelic:** ''I'll Bet You'' (Westbound; r☆22, ☆63, 1969). ''I Got a Thing, You Got a Thing, Everybody's Got a Thing'' (Westbound; r☆30, ☆80, 1970). ''I Wanna Know If It's Good to You?'' (Westbound; ☆81, 1970). ''You and Your Folks, Me and My Folks'' (Westbound; r☆42, ☆91, 1971). ''Can You Get to That'' (Westbound; r☆44, ☆93, 1971). ''Better by the Pound'' (Westbound; ☆99, 1975). ''One Nation Under a Groove'' (Warner Bros.; r☆1, ☆28, 1978). ''Cholly (Funk Getting Ready to Roll!)'' (Warner Bros.; r☆43, 1979). ''(not just) Knee Deep—Part 1'' (Warner Bros.; r☆1, ☆77, 1979). ''Uncle Jam (Part I)'' (Warner Bros.; r☆53, 1979). ''The Electric Spanking of War Babies'' (Warner Bros.; r☆60, 1981). **Kool and the Gang:** ''Funky Stuff'' (De-Lite; ☆29, 1973). ''Jungle Boogie'' (De-Lite; r☆2, ☆4, 1973). ''Hollywood Swinging'' (De-Lite; r☆1, ☆6, 1974). ''Higher Plane'' (De-Lite; r☆1, ☆37, 1974). ''Rhyme Tyme People'' (De-Lite; r☆3, ☆63, 1975). ''Spirit of the Boogie'' b/w ''Summer Madness'' (De-Lite; r☆1, ☆35, 1975). ''Caribbean Festival'' (De-Lite; r☆6, ☆55, 1975). ''Love and Understanding (Come Together)'' (De-Lite; r☆8, ☆77, 1976). ''Open Sesame—Part 1'' (De-Lite; r☆6, ☆55, 1976). ''Super Band'' (De-Lite; r☆17, 1977). ''Slick Superchick'' (De-Lite; r☆19, 1978). ''Everybody's Dancin' '' (De-Lite; r☆65, 1978). ''Ladies Night'' (De-Lite; r☆1, ☆8, 1979). ''Too Hot'' (De-Lite; r☆3, ☆5, 1980). ''Hangin' Out'' (De-Lite; r☆36, ☆103, 1980). ''Celebration'' (De-Lite; r☆1, ☆1, 1980). ''Take It to the Top'' (De-Lite; r☆11, 1981). ''Jones vs. Jones'' (De-Lite; r☆33, ☆39, 1981). ''Take My Heart (You Can Have It If You Want It)'' (De-Lite; r☆1, ☆17, 1981). ''Steppin' Out'' (De-Lite; r☆12, ☆89, 1982). ''Get Down on It'' (De-Lite; r☆4, ☆10, 1982). ''Big Fun'' (De-Lite; r☆6, ☆21, 1982). ''Let's Go Dancin' (Ooh, La, La, La)'' (De-Lite; r☆7, ☆30, 1982). ''Street Kids'' (De-Lite; r☆78, 1983). ''Joanna'' (De-Lite; r☆1, ☆2, 1983). ''Tonight'' (De-Lite; r☆7, ☆13, 1984). ''Straight Ahead'' (De-Lite; r☆49, ☆103, 1984). ''Misled'' (De-Lite; r☆3, ☆10, 1984). ''Fresh'' (De-Lite; r☆1, ☆9, 1985). ''Cherish'' (De-Lite; r☆1, ☆2, 1985). ''Emergency'' (De-Lite; r☆7, ☆18, 1985). ''Victory'' (Mercury; r☆2, ☆10, 1986). ''Stone Love'' (Mercury; r☆4, ☆10, 1987). ''Holiday'' (Mercury; r☆9, ☆66, 1987). ''Raindrops'' (Mercury; r☆27, 1989). ''Never Give Up'' (Mercury; r☆74, 1989). **Parliament:** ''Up for the Down Stroke'' (Casablanca; r☆10, ☆63, 1974). ''Chocolate City'' (Casablanca; r☆24, ☆94, 1975). ''Tear the Roof off the Sucker (Give Up the Funk)'' (Casablanca; r☆5, ☆15, 1976). ''Flash Light'' (Casablanca; r☆1, ☆16, 1978). ''Rumpofsteelskin'' (Casablanca; r☆63, 1979). ''Party People'' (Casablanca; r☆39, 1979). ''Aqua Boogie (A Psychoalphadiscobetabioaquadoloop)'' (Casablanca; r☆1, ☆89, 1979). ''Theme from the Black Hole'' (Casablanca; r☆8, 1980). ''The Big Bang Theory'' (Casablanca; r☆50, 1980). ''Agony of DeFeet'' (Casablanca; r☆7, 1980). **Parliaments:** ''(I Wanna) Testify'' (Revilot; r☆3, ☆20, 1967). ''All Your Goodies Are Gone'' (Revilot; r☆21, ☆80, 1967). **Charles Wright and the**

Watts 103rd Street Rhythm Band: "Spreadin' Honey" (Keyman; r☆44, ☆73, 1967). "Do Your Thing" (Warner Bros.; r☆12, ☆11, 1969). "Till You Get Enough" (Warner Bros.; r☆12, ☆67, 1969). "Love Land" (Warner Bros.; r☆23, ☆16, 1970). "Express Yourself" (Warner Bros.; r☆3, ☆12, 1970). "Solution for Pollution" (Warner Bros.; ☆96, 1971). "Your Love (Means Everything to Me)" (Warner Bros.; ☆73, 1971).

ALBUMS

Earth, Wind and Fire: *Earth, Wind & Fire* (Warner Bros.; ☆172, 1971). *The Need of Love* (Warner Bros.; ☆89, 1972). *Last Days and Time* (Columbia; ☆87, 1972). *Head to the Sky* (Columbia; ☆27, 1973). *Open Our Eyes* (Columbia; ☆15, 1974). *Another Time* (Warner Bros.; ☆97, 1974). *That's the Way of the World* (Columbia; ☆1, 1975). *Gratitude* (Columbia; ☆1, 1975). *Spirit* (Columbia; ☆2, 1976). *All 'n All* (Columbia; ☆3, 1977). *The Best of Earth, Wind & Fire—Vol. 1* (ARC; ☆6, 1978). *I Am* (ARC; ☆3, 1979). *Faces* (ARC; ☆10, 1980). *Raise!* (ARC; ☆5, 1981). *Powerlight* (Columbia; ☆12, 1983). *Electric Universe* (Columbia; ☆40, 1983). *Touch the World* (Columbia; ☆33, 1987). *The Best of Earth, Wind and Fire, Vol. II* (Columbia; ☆190, 1988). *Heritage* (Columbia; ☆70, 1990). **Funkadelic:** *Funkadelic* (Westbound; ☆126, 1970). *Free Your Mind* (Westbound; ☆92, 1970). *Maggot Brain* (Westbound; ☆108, 1971). *America Eats Its Young* (Westbound; ☆123, 1972). *Cosmic Slop* (Westbound; ☆112, 1973). *Standing on the Verge of Getting It On* (Westbound; ☆163, 1974). *Let's Take It to the Stage* (20th Century Westbound; ☆102, 1975).

Tales of Kidd Funkadelic (Westbound; ☆103, 1976). *Hardcore Jollies* (Warner Bros.; ☆96, 1976). *One Nation Under a Groove* (Warner Bros.; ☆16, 1978). *Uncle Jam Wants You* (Warner Bros.; ☆18, 1979). *Connections & Disconnections* (LAX; ☆151, 1981).
Kool and the Gang: *Live at the Sex Machine* (De-Lite; ☆122, 1971). *The Best of Kool & the Gang* (De-Lite; ☆157, 1971). *Live at P.J.'s* (De-Lite; ☆171, 1972). *Good Times* (De-Lite; ☆142, 1973). *Wild and Peaceful* (De-Lite; ☆33, 1973). *Kool Jazz* (De-Lite; ☆187, 1974). *Light of Worlds* (De-Lite; r☆63, 1974). *Kool & the Gang Greatest Hits!* (De-Lite; ☆81, 1975). *Spirit of the Boogie* (De-Lite; ☆48, 1975). *Love and Understanding* (De-Lite; ☆68, 1976). *Open Sesame* (De-Lite; ☆110, 1976). *The Force* (De-Lite; ☆142, 1978). *Everybody's Dancin'* (De-Lite; 1978). *Ladies Night* (De-Lite; ☆13, 1979). *Celebrate!* (De-Lite; ☆10, 1980). *Something Special* (De-Lite; ☆12, 1981). *As One* (De-Lite; ☆29, 1982). *In the Heart* (De-Lite; ☆29, 1983). *Emergency* (De-Lite; ☆28, 1984). *Forever* (Mercury; ☆25, 1986). *Everything's Kool and the Gang: Greatest Hits & More* (Mercury; ☆109, 1988). *Sweat* (Mercury; 1989).
Parliament: *Chocolate City* (Casablanca; ☆91, 1975). *Mothership Connection* (Casablanca; ☆13, 1976). *The Clones of Doctor Funkenstein* (Casablanca; ☆20, 1976). *Parliament Live—P. Funk Earth Tour* (Casablanca; ☆29, 1977). *Funkentelechy Vs. the Placebo Syndrome* (Casablanca; ☆13, 1977). *Motor-Booty Affair* (Casablanca; ☆21, 1978). *Gloryhallastoopid—or Pin the Tale on the Funky* (Casablanca; ☆44, 1979). *Trombipulation* (Casablanca; ☆61, 1981).

(Chart positions compiled from Joel Whitburn's *Record Research*, based on *Billboard*'s Pop and LPs charts, unless otherwise indicated; r☆ = position on *Billboard*'s Rhythm & Blues chart.)

ELTON JOHN

BY ROBERT CHRISTGAU

A s the great inheritor of Philadelphia pop rock, in which rock & roll ceases to be an uncontrolled natural force and turns into a product understood and exploitable, Elton John was the archetypal rock & roller of the mid-Seventies, the blandest and bleakest time in the music's history except for the (post-Elvis, pre-Beatles) Philadelphia pop-rock era itself. Yet there was nothing bleak or bland about him. In fact, his glittery outrageousness and rock & roll overdrive were so pervasive that it was easy to forget his U.S. debut in 1970, when his propensity for jumping up and down in front of the piano attracted less attention than his eyeglasses.

On his first American LP, *Elton John*, Paul Buckmaster's overweening strings, the too often inflated and occasionally meaningless banality of Bernie Taupin's lyrics and the faked-up sensitivity of Elton's voice all betokened yet another foolish, folkish singer-songwriter, albeit one with two heads. But Taupin's lyrics maintained the kind of fifty-fifty ratio that makes for a lot of good songs when the music is strong and plentiful, and John possessed a pop-rock voice in the great tradition of Del Shannon.

In short, that sensitive little LP contained the makings of a rock & roll assembly line.

However unlikely this might have seemed at the time, it was implicit in the English career of Reg Dwight. Born in the London suburbs in 1947, Reg was a moderately prodigious child pianist who began rocking in a copy—later backing—band called

In the buff, Elton promotes his 1972 tour.

526

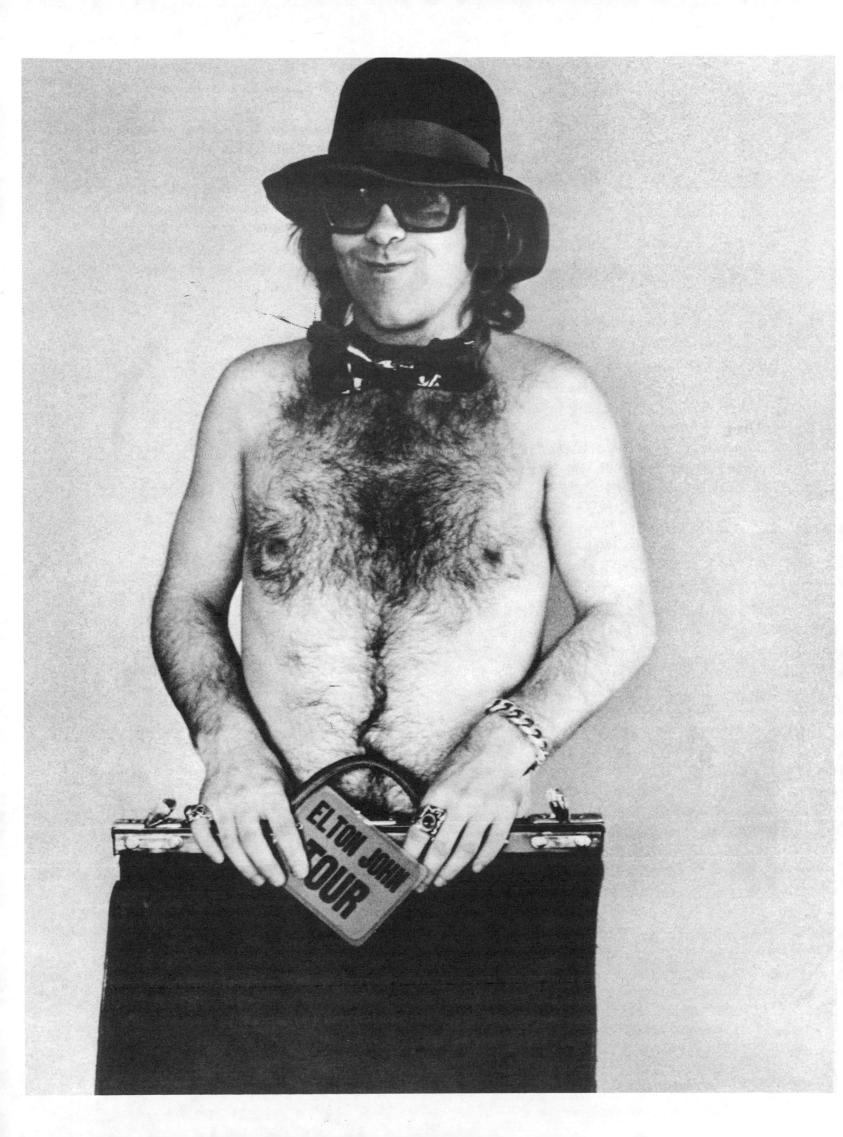

Elton John at eight.

Bluesology in 1964. In 1967 he tried to land a singer-songwriter gig but instead landed a partner, fellow reject Bernie Taupin; eventually the two were given a £10-a-week writing contract with Dick James Music, enabling Reg to quit the band and assume his nom de plume. The two ground out pap pop rock until urged to follow their own muses by savvy pop-rock pros. What happened then becomes understandable, however, only when notions of a muse are put aside.

Bernie Taupin's more reflective admirers point out his apparent preoccupation with American imagery and outsider-versus-society themes. Yet although such an analysis is not inaccurate statistically, it's aesthetically irrelevant. Bernie's writing probably did reflect genuine personal interests, but only rarely did he have anything interesting to say about those interests. This was just as well for Elton, who needed the sound of the words, not their sense; sense might have stanched their flow. For up-and-coming young professionals in the late Sixties, "poetic" imagery and "meaningful" themes—not to mention "symphonic" orchestration—were certainly a permissible gimmick and probably a commercial necessity.

Elton John at eighteen.

Not counting a soundtrack and a live album and a greatest-hits and some uncollected singles and an early British LP released six years after the fact in 1974, John came up with nine albums (including

Rock star with private plane.

one double) in the five years following his first visit to America. In a rock marketplace by then predicated on artificial "artistic" scarcity, such productivity seemed gross, and the alacrity with which the two worked was equally suspect. The songs began with Taupin, who would write the lyrics for an album in a two-week flurry, spending perhaps an hour on each one. Elton would turn out chords and melody, rarely changing a word or even laying eyes on Bernie. Arrangements developed during recording, which would take a few weeks at most per album. Was this disposable pop or a garbage processing plant?

Elton John in his twenties. By then he was a star.

Yet there were few people who liked rock & roll, or any pop music, who remained untouched by Elton John. It wasn't simply that he was so *there,* although that helped; quite simply, the man was a genius. No matter how you deplored his sloppiness, or his one-dimensionality, or his $40,000 worth of rose-colored glasses, you would find yourself humming "Take Me to the Pilot" or "Bennie and the Jets" or "Don't Let the Sun Go Down on Me." Not all of them, perhaps—maybe not any of those three. But the man's instinct for the hook—made up whole or assembled from outside sources—was so universal that there was small likelihood that one wouldn't stick in your pleasure center. Or your craw. Or both.

For a good hook doesn't guarantee aesthetic merit, it is merely a means to aesthetic merit, and hardly a foolproof one. Sometimes hooks are bad—the chorus of "Take Me to the Pilot," as compelling a melody as John has ever concocted, leads to a lyric that is infuriating gibberish. And sometimes they're good—the piano hook of "Bennie and the Jets" gives life to what would otherwise seem a predicta-

Rock star defies gravity.

ble evocation of the pop star's dilemma. So it's too easy to take the common critical tack of praising John as a singles artist. His rank sentimentality is typified by the semimeaningful "Border Song" or the overripe "Don't Let the Sun," both included on Elton's generally listenable (although stylistically ragged) first volume of *Greatest Hits.* But his slovenliness has its compensations in a kind of postindustrial openness and fecundity, and it is possible to sort out the garbage on that jumble of albums just by analyzing their hook content.

On his two worst albums, *Don't Shoot Me, I'm Only the Piano Player* (1973) and (especially) *Madman Across the Water* (1971), what few hooks push through are dull or annoying; the same goes for at least half the double-LP *Goodbye Yellow Brick Road* (1973). The debut LP is winsome enough, though flawed; the followup, *Tumbleweed Connection* (1970), continues to sound as flat as it did (to this listener) at the time of its release, though side two is acceptable. The hooks are much more numerous on the autobiographical *Captain Fantastic and the Brown Dirt Cowboy* (1975), but the failure of the concept as a whole—Taupin lacks both the honesty and the intellectual discipline to bring it off—diminishes its better parts.

That's six discs gone, some of them pleasantly enough. What remains is a career's worth of good rock & roll. *Honky Chateau* (1972), album number four, which announced John and Taupin's escape from the excesses of their own romanticism, sounds

Elton, outraging.

The simplest way to separate good Elton from bad Elton might be to assume that good Elton rocks and bad Elton doesn't. But that leaves too many exceptions, not only ballads that work but also pointless rockers, such as the nostalgia-mongering "Crocodile Rock." The truth seems to be that only lyrics elevate John's music beyond aural diversion. Not that Elton and Bernie could tell when they wrote a good lyric, preferring ponderous banalities like "Ticking" and "Candle in the Wind" ("Hollywood created a superstar/And pain was the price you paid") to perfect throwaways like "Your Sister Can't Twist" and "The Bitch Is Back." For the destiny of these pop pros was that their achievements would remain independent of vision and intent; they were good partners because they shared, over and above their commercial energy and a certain expedient sentimentality, a blankness of artistic personality. For all Bernie and Elton can be assumed to have cared, the felicitious ironies and realistic politics that arose in their songs might just have well been moon-June-spoon.

This impartiality carried over into John's singing, which was not interpretive in any ordinary sense of the term. The man had a ballad voice, which was adenoidal and insensitive sounding, and he could muster a few surface effects. But though in its way his style was quite distinctive—that is, his vocal timbre was unmistakable—it was indubitably mechanical. When John sang "Solar Prestige a Gammon," written entirely in words that only sounded like words or couldn't possibly have meant what they spelled, with all his usual cheery conviction, he was telling us something.

But without warning Elton's good cheer disappeared. *Rock of the Westies* was his last good or even mixed album, and although MCA, which had signed a much-ballyhooed $8-million deal with the artist in 1974, squeezed a hit off the maudlin double LP *Blue Moves* (1976), his partnership with Taupin went into abeyance. He quit touring, collaborated with one Gary Osborne on the equally lugubrious *A Single Man* (1978) and devoted himself to his soccer team and his solitude. Some believe that his decline began in 1976, when he told an interviewer he was bisexual, but it seems more likely that both the decline and this surprising bit of public relations reflected an acute fatigue with the superstar dilemma.

By 1980, however, he'd joined John Lennon and Donna Summer on David Geffen's new celebrity

even crisper today, when we can be sure it wasn't a fluke. But it's atypical, the folk-rock statement that culminates Elton's sensitive phase. The clear break, both aesthetically and professionally, came with the single "Crocodile Rock," included on *Don't Shoot Me*, which put Elton and Bernie's assembly line into overdrive. *Goodbye Yellow Brick Road* includes not only "Bennie and the Jets" and John's original Rolling Stones rip-off, "Saturday Night's Alright for Fighting," but also the unheralded "Your Sister Can't Twist (but She Can Rock 'n' Roll)," an intensified send-up of "At the Hop," itself the most intense Philadelphia pop-rock record ever made. The first side of *Caribou* (1974) leads off with a nastier Stones rip, "The Bitch Is Back" and is summed up by "Solar Prestige a Gammon": "Solar prestige a gammon/Kool kar kyric salmon/Hair ring molasses abounding/Common lap kitch sardin a poor floundin." And with its racial ironies and simulated working-class anger, *Rock of the Westies* (1975) was one of the best Rolling Stones–derived albums between *Exile on Main Street* and *Some Girls*.

label, and soon he was working with Taupin again. The year he turned forty, heavy promotion had scared up enough airplay for a greatest-hits record. Like most of Elton's Eighties albums, it went gold, and like all of them, it failed to go platinum. Its only undeniable classic was "Sad Songs (Say So Much)," which wasn't sad, and also wasn't as slow as most of what the team was putting across. John had gotten both married and fat; at forty, he looked middle-aged stodgy rather than rock & roll's traditional middle-aged dissipated. Now returned to MCA, he specializes in "adult rock" tending to MOR, a more vital piano man than Barry Manilow, but not than Billy Joel.

But Elton John is at the very least fondly remembered: A CD boxed set of his greatest hits was issued by MCA in 1990. To say he didn't have what it took to remain a full-fledged superstar is not to say he was a cipher any more than calling his singing mechanical is declaring him a robot. He remains as essential a touchstone of the Seventies as the Beach Boys are of the Sixties. If you want to believe that he therefore epitomizes the banality of evil, go ahead. To me he proves that even the blandest and bleakest times teem with life.

DISCOGRAPHY

SINGLES

"Border Song" (Uni; ☆92, 1970). "Your Song" (Uni; ☆8, 1970). "Friends" (Uni; ☆34, 1971). "Levon" (Uni; ☆24, 1971). "Tiny Dancer" (Uni; ☆41, 1972). "Rocket Man" (Uni; ☆6, 1972). "Honky Cat" (Uni; ☆8, 1972). "Crocodile Rock" (MCA; ☆1, 1972). "Daniel" (MCA; ☆2, 1973). "Saturday Night's Alright for Fighting" (MCA; ☆12, 1973). "Goodbye Yellow Brick Road" (MCA; ☆2, 1973). "Bennie and the Jets" (MCA; r☆15, ☆1, 1974). "Don't Let the Sun Go Down on Me" (MCA; ☆2, 1974). "The Bitch Is Back" (MCA; ☆4, 1974). "Lucy in the Sky with Diamonds" (MCA; ☆1, 1974). "Philadelphia Freedom" (MCA; r☆32, ☆1, 1975). "Someone Saved My Life Tonight" (MCA; ☆4, 1975). "Island Girl" (MCA; ☆1, 1975). "Grow Some Funk of Your Own" b/w "I Feel Like a Bullet (In the Gun of Robert Ford)" (MCA; ☆14, 1976). "Sorry Seems to Be the Hardest Word" (MCA Rocket; ☆6, 1976). "Bite Your Lip (Get Up and Dance)" (MCA; ☆28, 1977). "Ego" (MCA; ☆34, 1978). "Part-Time Love" (MCA; ☆22, 1978). "Mama Can't Buy You Love" (MCA; ☆9, 1979). "Victim of Love" (MCA; ☆35, 1979). "Little Jeannie" (MCA; ☆3, 1980). "(Sartorial Eloquence) Don't Ya Wanna Play This Game No More?" (MCA; ☆39, 1980). "Nobody Wins" (Geffen; ☆21, 1981). "Chloe" (Geffen; ☆34, 1981). "Empty Garden (Hey Hey Johnny)" (Geffen; ☆13, 1982). "Blue Eyes" (Geffen; ☆12, 1982). "I'm Still Standing" (Geffen; ☆12, 1983). "Kiss the Bride" (Geffen; ☆25, 1983). "I Guess That's Why They Call It the Blues" (Geffen; ☆4, 1984). "Sad Songs (Say So Much)" (Geffen; ☆5, 1984). "Who Wears These Shoes?" (Geffen; ☆16, 1984). "In Neon" (Geffen; ☆38, 1985). With George Michael: "Wrap Her Up" (Geffen; ☆20, 1985). "Nikita" (Geffen; ☆7, 1986). "Candle in the Wind" (MCA; ☆6, 1988). "I Don't Wanna Go On with You Like That" (MCA; ☆2, 1988). "A Word in Spanish" (MCA; ☆19, 1988). "Healing Hands" (MCA; ☆13, 1989). "Sacrifice" (MCA; ☆18, 1990). "Club at the End of the Street" (MCA; ☆28, 1990). "You Gotta Love Someone" (MCA; ☆43, 1990). With George Michael: "Don't Let the Sun Go Down on Me" (Columbia; ☆1, 1991).

ALBUMS

Elton John (Uni; ☆4, 1970). *Tumbleweed Connection* (Uni; ☆5, 1971). *Friends* (soundtrack) (Paramount; ☆36, 1971). *11-17-70* (Uni; ☆11, 1971). *Madman Across the Water* (Uni; ☆8, 1971). *Honky Chateau* (Uni; ☆1, 1972). *Don't Shoot Me, I'm Only the Piano Player* (MCA; ☆1, 1973). *Goodbye Yellow Brick Road* (MCA; ☆1, 1973). *Caribou* (MCA; ☆1, 1974). *Elton John—Greatest Hits* (MCA; ☆1, 1974). *Empty Sky* (MCA; ☆6, 1975). *Captain Fantastic and the Brown Dirt Cowboy* (MCA; ☆1, 1975). *Rock of the Westies* (MCA; ☆1, 1975). *Here and There* (MCA; ☆4, 1976). *Blue Moves* (MCA Rocket; ☆3, 1976). *Elton John's Greatest Hits, Volume II* (MCA; ☆21, 1977). *A Single Man* (MCA; ☆15, 1978). *The Thom Bell Sessions* (MCA; ☆51, 1979). *Victim of Love* (MCA; ☆35, 1979). *21 at 33* (MCA; ☆13, 1980). *The Fox* (Geffen; ☆21, 1981). *Jump Up!* (Geffen; ☆17, 1982). *Too Low for Zero* (Geffen; ☆25, 1983). *Breaking Hearts* (Geffen; ☆20, 1984). *Leather Jackets* (Geffen; ☆91, 1986). *Live in Australia* (MCA; ☆24, 1987). *Elton John's Greatest Hits, Vol. III, 1979–1987* (Geffen; ☆84, 1987). *Reg Strikes Back* (MCA; ☆16, 1988). *Sleeping with the Past* (MCA; ☆23, 1989). *To Be Continued* (MCA; ☆82, 1990).

(Chart positions compiled from Joel Whitburn's *Record Research*, based on *Billboard*'s Pop and LPs charts.)

DAVID BOWIE

BY TOM CARSON

When David Bowie first toured America in 1972—orange-haired, glitter-clad, androgynous and shrill—what was most novel about him wasn't the moon-age decadence he so glibly trafficked in, but the way he encouraged everyone to see it as a sham. Despite, or because of, its borrowed roots in blues and folk, white rock & roll had always been about inspired impostures. But the pact made between rock performers and their listeners in the Fifties and Sixties was that those pretenses had conviction.

Bowie's show, by contrast, was a *show*—explicitly artificial and camp, not from ineptitude but brazen intention. Through his invented alter ego, Ziggy Stardust, the singer presented rock & roll as a dying religion; Ziggy himself was a synthetic messiah, an alien come to earth to enact a parody version of that emblematic counterculture fantasy, the rock star as martyr. Bowie deliberately cast himself as a chameleon without past or identity, and since he also encouraged people to take his manipulativeness at face value, it was easy either to embrace him as the wave of the future or to reject him as a supremely clever dilettante.

The truth was more complex. Bowie—born

vaguely middle-class in a solidly working-class London suburb in 1947—was always an outsider but didn't always choose to exalt his status. His musical beginnings were conventional enough. After scuffling around the edges of the mod era—first as David Jones and the Lower Third, then as David Bowie and the Buzz—he first attracted attention as a rather precious and sentimental singer-songwriter in the post-Dylan folkie mode. To the cultishness and literary-poetic pretensions of that mode he added influences dictated by both his own idiosyncrasies and the eclecticism *Sgt. Pepper* had made obligatory: borrowing from Anthony Newley for the arch singing style that made a virtue of his trebly voice's limitations, and from Jacques Brel for his world-weary (*Weltschmerz*-weary?) attitude, but also dabbling in mime, Zen mysticism, and Warhol-derived mixed-media avant-gardism. Later he would add, or anyway cite, more generic sources in symbolist poetry, expressionist painting and drama, and Wildean bohemianism. (Part of Bowie's fun was that you

The man who sold the world.

could take this intellectual baggage—his penchant for appearing in public with an entourage of the famous dead—as seriously, or not, as you cared to; it made no difference.) But at the outset, his basic commitment was to rock & roll.

He arrived too late for the Sixties. By the time *Man of Words, Man of Music* was released in 1969, the party was breaking up; the general disillusionment was corroborated in Bowie's case by the failure of either his words or his music to reach an audience, and by the failure of an arts lab he'd helped to open on London's outskirts—an aesthete's version of a

Aladdin Sane.

Sixties commune—to get off the ground. At first, so he claimed, he thought of quitting music outright. But armed with a new manager (Tony De Fries, who thought of himself as the Colonel Tom Parker of the Seventies) and a new band (including guitarist Mick Ronson, whose condensations of Sixties raveups helped to find a new sound via the time-honored rock expedient of aping an old sound and not having the chops to do it properly), Bowie returned with *The Man Who Sold the World*, an album whose brutalist musical mark, however flawed, qualifies it as a prototypical art-metal hybrid, although Bowie himself wouldn't return to the style until many years later in vastly different context. Then, in early 1972, came *Hunky Dory*.

On *Hunky Dory*, for the first time, Bowie the callow (and belated) Sixties romantic appears in the more calculatedly sophisticated guise of Seventies revisionist, manufacturing images out of others' debris and pasting together a new synthesis from a deliberately far-flung set of secondhand styles. The artist as hero, art as subject, predecessors (Dylan, Warhol, Lou Reed, Sinatra) invoked and leaned on as precursors—the whole self-conscious apparatus that Bowie made such facile use of—may have been old hat in the other arts. But at least in this explicit form, it was new to rock. "Changes," the album's keynote song—whose title and catchily stuttered chorus were to provide music editors with ready-made headlines for Bowie stories for at least the next fifteen years—redefined Bowie's past as the counterculture's, and both as one stage of an ongoing journey; "Oh! You Pretty Things" envisioned the next stage as a rising generation of rock & rollers—affectless, sexually ambiguous and free—rising from the ashes. For all the sprightly innocuousness of its surface, the album is a virtual blueprint of Bowie's ambitions. That, having cleared the ground, he forged ahead into the glitter-rock juggernaut of *Ziggy Stardust* is hardly surprising in hindsight.

David Bowie primed for a shipboard romance.

Between *Hunky Dory* and *Ziggy,* Bowie had publicly announced his own bisexuality. The canniest bit of self-promotion of his career, it also—given rock's long, unexpressed flirtation with androgyny—suggested how much his talent for self-dramatization had to do with simply letting old cats out of the bag. Combined with Bowie's dexterous use of the media, *Ziggy*'s "wham-bam-thank-you-ma'am" not only made him a superstar, which was its main purpose; it also anointed him, with perhaps more authority than even he had counted on, as the embodiment of a new era. Over his next six albums he rang a series of deft changes on his protean, eternal-outsider image (whose benefits, both as useful persona and expressive symbol of disorientation, he had tapped as early as "Space Oddity"), and put it to increasingly totemic use in a series of increasingly hyperbolic tours. But while he was, in some ways, still fashioning allegorical equivalents for the death of the Sixties fantasy, he was in the process inventing alternative scenarios for his own time as well. If his visions of a doomed civilization were often spurious as visions, time and again his gifts for mimicry, imaginative projection and suggestive musical pastiche (like the cyber-Stones of *Aladdin Sane,* or the Sinatra-does-Brecht-Weill of *Diamond Dogs*) made them convincing as drama, and his promiscuous image mongering had its impact not only as image but as mongering.

More than anything else his ability to make such subjective chimeras work as mass fantasy hinged on his refusal to commit himself to any of them. By redefining stardom as a series of pointed impersonations, he broadened the uses to which it could be put, as communicative tool and receptor-transmitter of cultural trends. All the young dudes carried the news, and Bowie was just another conduit. Because he was arty and shrewd, he was able to perceive rock & roll critically—as myth, artistic construct, social phenomenon and cultural force—in a way that his predecessors, acting out those qualities from the inside, hadn't been able to. He was also able to make almost any fantasy, however grim or excessive, palatable by presenting it as spectacle.

By 1974, however, Bowie had seemingly become a prisoner of his own momentum. In its unresolved combination of doomy hysteria and frenetic pandering, *Diamond Dogs,* a concept album inspired by George Orwell's *1984,* was over the top even for him; behind the scenes, his situation was a mess, as De

Another of the many faces of David Bowie.

Fries—at least in Bowie's version—attempted to use the money generated by his meal ticket to build a managerial empire, with disastrous results. Midway through the costly, extravagant *Diamond Dogs* tour (the set for which cost a reported $250,000, a huge sum then), Bowie abruptly scrapped the elaborate trappings, adopting a newly stark visual style and a newly funky musical style.

He changed course on record as well, going to Philadelphia's Sigma Sound studios to cut a disco album, *Young Americans*. It seemed such a bewildering departure that for the first time in his career, the man without convictions was accused of being a sellout. "A fucked-up LP from a fucked-up rock star," one critic wrote. In retrospect, however, the album appears as Bowie's smartest and most successful experiment in adapting his own marginal sensibility to mass-media form. As usual, his interest was in inventing connections and inverting contexts—treating black as white, sex as politics, politics as sex. As usual, his method was involuted and parodic—turning soul music schematic by mechanizing all its formal components, only to turn

it back, transfigured by Bowie-ness, into his own eccentric version of soul.

Young Americans saved Bowie's career, giving him two hit singles ("Fame" and the title tune) and leaving him an even bigger star than before. In 1975, when he launched his most massive world tour up to then, the attention-grabbing glitter rocker had disappeared, replaced by an icy, jaded rock dandy leading his audience through a set of ever more rarefied and didactic permutations of a body of work whose mythic connotations were now all his own. The poseur had legitimized himself, by pure sleight of hand.

Even so, though his music prospered—with the nerviness of *Young Americans* impressively followed by the sweep of *Station to Station*—"fucked-up rock star" wasn't entirely inaccurate. Bowie has since talked about the mid-Seventies period when he moved to L.A. as cock of the walk of the rock aristocracy as a nightmare of drugs and excess; a *Playboy* interview dating from those years, full of talking jags, jittery jokes and bizarre pronunciamentos, offers a good if inadvertent portrait of a star on the verge of a nervous breakdown. Eventually, he dropped out of sight completely, to reemerge in Berlin in a radical new role, that of austere art-rock avant-gardist, adamantly serious and resolutely uncommercial.

The move could be seen as another calculated switch—in the late Seventies the fringe was the smart place to be—and a logical next step, with *Station to Station* (pop treated as daunting electronic noise) serving as a bridge to the three collaborations with Brian Eno known as the "Berlin trilogy" (daunting electronic noise treated as pop). Still, *Low* and *"Heroes"* bespoke not only a rigorous formal intensity, but, for all their elliptical, fragmentary style, an unguarded emotional directness that was new in Bowie's work. On *Lodger*, not only were the Eno influences of the first two records assimilated into a supple, fluid style, but the central motif of the eternal traveler adrift in the world, searching for home, love and roots but able to define himself only through motion, redefined Bowie's earlier themes, without gimmickry, as the autobiography they'd always been at heart.

The Eno collaborations—whose influence on a

Tin Machine, David Bowie's rock & roll band for the Nineties *(from left):* bassist Tony Sales, Bowie, drummer Hunt Sales, guitarist Reeves Gabrels.

younger generation of pop technocrats was to prove more substantial and lasting than the flash of Bowie's earlier work—were also the only Bowie albums to count for more as music than as gesture. That was their strength; it was also why they marked the beginning of the end.

Even back when he'd been accused by the counterculture's budding sticks-in-the-mud of wanting to destroy everything that rock & roll had stood for, Bowie himself had remained a believer. That is, he took it for granted that the music would always be consequential and associated with radical impulses toward change. Even his most revisionist Seventies work depended for its point and urgency on having those Sixties assumptions constant in the background. It's hardly unprecedented, in any of the arts, for a figure originally perceived as breaking with tradition to be understood in the long run as that

tradition's last upholder— which, in relation to Sixties utopianism, was just what Bowie was. And what that meant was that, though his formal acumen saved him for a while, he was no better equipped than Bob Dylan or Mick Jagger to adjust to rock's inevitable assimilation into the entertainment mainstream. The best refutation of the Seventies view of Bowie as not rock but show biz is that in the Eighties—when that was all he *could* be—he turned out to be so bad at it.

Scary Monsters (1980)—an uneven, often leaden but, in its best songs, brave look back in horror—was the last Bowie album in which he was able to take it for granted that the music and its audience still mattered to each other in the old, radical sense. But soon thereafter he must have realized that if he wanted to sustain his career, he was going to have to start treating it as a career and nothing else. His next incarnation, in 1983, on *Let's Dance*, was as a hearty, heartily hetero Mr. Entertainment without a single disturbing thought on his mind. The retro mood of the early Eighties wasn't kind to the gay community so far as its erstwhile rock spokespersons went: The year before Bowie turned himself into a Great Lover in the obnoxious video for *Let's Dance*'s ''China Girl,'' longtime gay-demimonde chronicler Lou Reed had been heard advertising his newly discovered love of women on his own career saver, *The Blue Mask*.

Let's Dance got by on Nile Rodgers's authoritative if ham-fisted production and the hype generated by the $17-million deal Bowie had gotten from Capitol-EMI, even though of its songs only ''Modern Love'' was anything more than negligible. But in the aimless, nattering albums since, Bowie has proved unable to make his work register even as an event. In the late Eighties, seemingly at a loss, he undertook a new project, an art-metal band called Tin Machine, whose attempt to recapture his former vanguard prestige by riding the backs of a younger generation of art rockers has so far aroused more scorn than enthusiasm, and more indifference than either. In between the records he seemed to find it ever harder to work up enough interest to make, Bowie spent the Eighties touring with his song catalogue, making vague gestures in the direction of a movie career that never quite coalesced, popping up in a Coffee Achievers ad and certifying his looming status as a rock dinosaur by singing a duet with Mick Jagger in a lard-butt remake of ''Dancing in the Street.''

Today those always discomfited or annoyed by Bowie's feyness, his contrivance and/or his music's lack of grounding use his current inconsequentiality to shore up their judgment that he was always trivial. That view seems not only harsh (and so what?), but inaccurate. Despite appearances—and the Rolling Stones, now pushing fifty, will no doubt be appearing soon in a town near you—rock & roll, at least the way it worked in its first twenty-five years, didn't have much to do with careers. It had to do with moments—one if you were Tommy James and the Shondells, a string of maybe half a dozen or so if you were the Beatles or the Rolling Stones. Bowie managed two or three, and that's plenty. For all his ambition, he never presented himself as the Next Big Thing; he only played its regent, holding the fort until one came along, and he had no way of knowing that Next Big Things, as his generation understood them, were a thing of the past. In the interval he constructed a set of extraordinary images, found ways of articulating the modern audience's bedeviling problems of identity and community that made the bogus and the imaginary not flaws but tools, and restored meaning to rock by recasting it as drama. (It's since been left to Madonna, a different kind of Next Big Thing, to restore drama to show biz by recasting it as meaningful.) It's not his fault if the contradictory belief that moments could last forever, which he clung to no less than any other Sixties idealist, and that rock & roll would always be a force powerful enough to save lives, proved in the end to be the music's coffin.

DISCOGRAPHY

ALBUMS

Hunky Dory (RCA; ☆176, 1972). *The Man Who Sold the World* (Mercury; 1969; rereleased RCA; ☆105, 1972). *Man of Words, Man of Music* (Mercury; 1969; rereleased as *Space Oddity* [RCA; ☆16, 1972]). *The Rise and Fall of Ziggy Stardust and the Spiders from Mars* (RCA; ☆75, 1972). *Images 1966–1967* (London; ☆144, 1973). *Aladdin Sane* (RCA; ☆17, 1973). *Bowie Pinups* (RCA; ☆23, 1973). *Diamond Dogs* (RCA; ☆5, 1974). *David Live at the Tower Philadelphia* (RCA; ☆8, 1974). *Young Americans* (RCA; ☆9, 1975). *Station to Station* (RCA; ☆3, 1976). *Changesonebowie* (RCA; ☆10, 1976). *Low* (RCA; ☆11, 1977). *''Heroes''* (RCA; ☆35, 1977). *Prokofiev's Peter and the Wolf* (RCA; ☆136, 1978). *Stage* (RCA; ☆44, 1978). *Lodger* (RCA; ☆20, 1979). *Scary Monsters* (RCA; ☆12, 1980). *Changestwobowie* (RCA; ☆68, 1981). *Let's Dance* (EMI America; ☆4, 1983). *Golden Years* (RCA; ☆99, 1983). *Fame and Fashion (David Bowie's All-Time Greatest Hits)* (RCA; ☆147, 1984). *Tonight* (EMI America; ☆11, 1984). *Labyrinth* (EMI America; ☆68, 1986). *Never Let Me Down* (EMI America; ☆34, 1987). *Sound + Vision* (Rykodisc; ☆97, 1989). *Changesbowie* (Rykodisc; ☆39, 1990). *David Bowie: Early On (1964–1966)* (Rhino; 1991). With Tin Machine: *Tin Machine* (EMI; ☆28, 1989). *Tin Machine II* (Victory; ☆126, 1991).

(Chart positions compiled from Joel Whitburn's *Record Research* based on *Billboard*'s Pop and LPs charts.)

THE SOUND OF SOUTHERN CALIFORNIA

BY JOHN ROCKWELL

here is a Guy Peellaert painting of Brian Wilson in *Rock Dreams* that tells it all. Outside lies an innocently sunny beach, although a seagull in silhouette looks suspiciously like a vulture. Inside, there's fat, ratty, unpopular Brian, sitting at the piano and obviously in the midst of a writer's block, trying to capture an ideal fantasy of surf and fun.

That picture is about the dominant figure of Sixties pop music in Los Angeles, although this chapter will concentrate on the music of the Seventies. But the development of L.A. rock, from the late Fifties into the Eighties, tells a coherent story, and Peellaert's picture gives that story an image. It suggests that Hollywood is a fantasy, not only for the rest of the world but also for the very people who fuel the fantasy. And it tells us that underneath the fun—which undeniably does exist, sort of—lie a nervous energy and a downright weirdness that define Southern California as much as blondes and bikinis.

Los Angeles then and now is known for light, bright, disposable pop music. Yet the most cursory examination reveals not only an enormous range within the accepted standard-bearers of the city's musical style, but important areas of music often left out of accounts of the city's rock—residents with styles established elsewhere, film and movie music,

middle-of-the-road, black music, jazz and jazz rock. And underlying all is the eccentric, loner weirdness Peellaert's painting captures so well.

The recurrent motifs of Los Angeles rock owe everything to the nature of the place. If London, far away, was the source of all that seemed new and hip, and if San Francisco to the north boasted hippie snootiness and a self-contented musical scene, Los Angeles was the ostensible purveyor of a hedonistic image all its own. That image was born out of the city's role as a magnet, not only for the nervously "creative" types who populate the film, television and recording industries, but for all manner of footloose, sun-worshiping middle-Americans who were too restless to stay at home.

Los Angeles is defined by vast geographical distances and the cars needed to travel them, by sun and smog, by beauty and a tacky squalor almost redeemed by the absence of cold. At least before the

Bonnie Raitt staged a dramatic comeback with *Nick of Time* (1989) and *Luck of the Draw* (1991), two albums that gave voice to the adult concerns of independent women.

city's high-culture explosion in the Eighties, the distances and the general lack of traditional arts (they existed but had to be sought out) bred a sense of isolation, not just of the various communities that make up the Los Angeles basin but the individuals and especially the creative individuals within those communities. Club life, until the late Seventies, was sporadic and focused on West Los Angeles (the fabled Sunset Strip and its offshoots), which is ludicrously far away if you happen to live in San Gabriel or Newport Beach. Pop music stars and executives cluster in the west, but even then it's an hour's drive from Malibu to Laurel Canyon. Socializing thus tends to be cliquish, like-minded souls seeking out one another and guarding what they share against the environment. People congregate in recording studios or at ritualized industry functions, and it's possible to go for what seems like years without meeting anyone who doesn't reinforce your own opinions.

The music that has resulted from all this has generally spoken to the heart-stream of American

Ry Cooder, with a Gibson L-4 guitar, learns some licks from Manuel "Joe Gang" Kupahu, Hawaii, 1974. Cooder, a studio craftsman popular in Hollywood in the late Sixties, has since made a career of rescuing endangered species of traditional American music.

tastes; prior to the punk eruption, L.A. was hardly a haven for the obscure little art-rock band that pleases its hard-bitten cult and nobody else. Los Angeles pop rock tended to be bright, buoyant and upbeat. It was white music for white audiences and was generally polished in sound. That pattern was not really broken by the more popsy post-punk heavy-metal bands like Poison, despite their flamboyant nihilistic trappings. An obsession with technical craftsmanship arises, in part, from the proliferation of sophisticated recording studios in the area— although cause and effect get tangled here—and no doubt suggests a parallel with film studios. Whatever the cause, it was in Los Angeles that the first "genius" producers arose: Phil Spector, with his glossily complex "wall of sound," and Lou Adler, with the exuberant density of his Mamas and Papas recordings. The image of these men, compulsively bent over their consoles, reminds us once again of

the mole-like, hermetic work required to produce images of fun and frivolity; Brian Wilson, too, was a crazed perfectionist in the studio.

This image of "studio perfection" can be misleading, however. The power of individual producers suggests that personal idiosyncrasy can indeed enter the picture. And the very nature of the recording business indicates another way this can happen. Commercial film and television are by definition large-scale cooperative ventures, entailing a considerable capital investment. Executives maintain a relatively strict control over a project, and the opportunity for the exercise of personal vision can be won by only the most powerful directors or actors. In rock the unit cost of an album is far lower than that of a film or a television series. One result has been that recording artists and producers, even in a relatively commercialized center like Los Angeles, have often been left alone to indulge themselves artistically, for better or worse, which helps to explain why individuality can flourish even in the supposedly shal-

Fleetwood Mac came to L.A. from Great Britain. After the addition of Californians Lindsey Buckingham and Stevie Nicks, the band's recordings went platinum.

low and plastic world of "Hollywood rock." This is, after all, the city that Frank Zappa, Captain Beefheart, Jim Morrison and Randy Newman called home. And it has allowed the evolution of a low-cost "indie" scene that could find no parallel in film or television.

The Sixties in Los Angeles were nevertheless dominated by two fashionable commercial styles: surf music and folk rock. It wasn't a big jump from folk rock to country rock, and country rock was the source of the dominant music of Los Angeles during the Seventies. Ricky Nelson, who had a string of rockabilly-flavored pop-rock hits between 1957 and 1964, counts as the first true pioneer of Los Angeles country rock. Buffalo Springfield, Poco and the early solo career of Linda Ronstadt were also important in this regard. But the major progenitors were the Byrds, especially the late-Sixties edition of that band with Gram Parsons.

Parsons's genius—solo or with the Flying Burrito Brothers—has sometimes seemed a little elusive, for all the devotion of his cult. He wrote some good songs and sang them decently, but his real function was a private and social one, disseminating country music and a country ethos through a tightly knit circle of musical associates. In this respect, he played a role for country music in L.A. similar to that played for R&B and folk blues by Lowell George and Ry Cooder. None of the three became stars, but each exercised a decisive influence on his more famous friends.

They were able to do so because of the closeness of the social circle to which most of the main rock stars in Los Angeles belonged. Genealogical tables showing linkages between bands over time assume mythically tangled proportions when applied to L.A. rock from the mid-Sixties to the mid-Seventies. Sometimes it seems as if everyone in town once was a Byrd or played in one of Ronstadt's backup bands. It is tempting to define the characteristic L.A. rock of the Seventies in terms of its biggest stars—Ronstadt, the Eagles, Jackson Browne, Fleetwood Mac. But because they were stars, their individuality is more apparent and interesting, and a clearer impression of the conventional L.A. sound of that era can be obtained from artists who stuck closer to the stereotype—acts like Firefall, Andrew Gold, Toto, Dan Fogelberg, the Nitty Gritty Dirt Band (part of the Aspen suburbia of L.A. rock), Roger McGuinn and Richie Furay as solo artists, John David Souther, the later incarnations of Poco and many more. Some of these artists made good records and enjoyed honorable careers. But all at least suggest a willingness to settle into formula, and a formula of a particularly predictable kind: twanging chordal strumming and "tastefully" linear lead guitars, weepy pedal steel guitars, mellow male harmonizing and lyrics about love that smack nervously of self-pity or self-satisfaction. It was a style that doubled back and found eager imitators in the Nashville country music of the Eighties.

It is true that the Seventies, until punk, were a time of conservatism in music as well as politics, and that most of the hits of that decade dealt with love, not revolution. A kinder way of looking at the love songs from Los Angeles is that they were deeply personal, not escapist. But perhaps there was a whiff of bourgeois indulgence hanging in the smog-filled air. Los Angeles music of the Sixties seemed innocently, unself-consciously trivial, and as such achieved pop artistry without much trying. In the

Seventies pop stars did try for profundity, and sometimes wound up sounding pompous and stuffy, especially when they also sought to retain the outer signatures of L.A. rock commercialism.

But at its best, this was music that was as moving and honest as the trendier, more abrasive alternatives that arose in the late Seventies. The relationship between populism and commerciality is a complex one, and the complexity was only underscored by the rise of punk and new-wave rock. In the Sixties it was possible to dream that the best music was the most popular music and that a good record's sales success attested to its aesthetic worth. An exact correlation between critically perceived excellence and popularity wasn't always true even then—Bob Dylan was hardly the most popular American rocker of the Sixties. But by the Seventies too much downright bad music was regularly topping the charts—"bad" in the sense that it was disliked by most people who cared really deeply about rock. Such people tended to prefer the more marginal forms of new-wave rock, and in so doing turned such rock into a de facto art music, prized by an elite.

It would thus be naive simply to equate the sales success of Seventies Los Angeles rock with its deeper aesthetic universality—and to denigrate new-wave rock from a supposedly populist standpoint by comparing the sales figures of, say, X and the Eagles. It's similarly misleading to judge L.A. rock solely in terms of commercial success; there are lots of intelligent people who would argue that almost anything Ry Cooder has done is more interesting than the entire corpus of Linda Ronstadt's career. But on the other hand, it's seductively easy to go too far in the other direction, discounting popularity and claiming that the true rock spirit resides today in music that is inescapably esoteric.

The problem is compounded by the fact that California remains a source of suspicion and mocking scorn for much of the rest of the country and the world. Los Angeles rockers are widely perceived to be self-indulgent narcissists who have cynically settled for slick commercial formulas. In fact, their very privileged position often allows them opportunities that are denied less powerful artists. It was the Los Angeles rock community, for instance, that carried on the Sixties tradition of political and environmental benefits, and musicians as varied as the Eagles, Ronstadt and Fleetwood Mac felt free to change their musical idioms when there was no ap-

parent commercial reason to do so. Conversely, Bonnie Raitt stuck to her core idiom but persisted in her social concerns with an untrendy tenacity that finally paid off in industry recognition and sales success in the early Nineties. Of course, the freedom to experiment or espouse marginal political causes has its limits, limits that a defiantly uncommercial art rocker doesn't have to observe. A complete alienation of an artist's audience would invite considerable pressure from the record company and even from the artist himself; it's very hard to give up wealth and applause once one has grown used to them.

Of the principal Los Angeles rock stars of the Seventies, it has been Linda Ronstadt who best combined artistic integrity and mass commercial success. Born in Tucson, Arizona, in 1946, she gravitated to Los Angeles in 1964 and had a minor hit ("Different Drum") with a folk trio called the Stone Poneys in 1967. Her first solo album, *Hand Sown . . . Home Grown* (1969), established her country-rock credentials, and her second, *Silk Purse* (1970), gave her a hit single, "Long Long Time." But she didn't emerge as the dominant female rocker of the decade until 1975, with *Heart Like a Wheel* and its first single, "You're No Good." That album was her first full-time collaboration with her manager-producer, Peter Asher, and it defined her mature rock artistry.

It is fair to speak of the subsequent rock records as "Ronstadt-Asher" albums: Asher's role was clearly crucial, but Ronstadt's creative contribution was just as important. Her music is notable for a growing stylistic mastery of many different idioms, for its impeccable studio craftsmanship—which doesn't mean slick formulas so much as a sometimes exquisite, sometimes over-arty care in the arrangements—and for a steady shift from a vulnerable passivity of persona to aggression and self-confidence. Her flaws include a certain congenital stiffness, most notable in her sometimes ill-chosen cover versions of well-known black hits, and an occasional inclination to power blandly through subtle

Los Angeles has been a mecca for footloose, sun-worshiping middle Americans. Linda Ronstadt made her pilgrimage in 1964, leaving Tucson, Arizona.

or ironic songs by the likes of Randy Newman or Neil Young.

An oddity of her career has been her unwillingness to continue recording country material after she was well on her way to becoming the queen of crossover country, with such songs as "I Fall to Pieces" and "I Can't Help It (If I'm Still in Love with You)." (The exception was the lovely *Trio* album of 1987, the long-delayed completion of a project with Dolly Parton and Emmylou Harris begun in the late Seventies.) But she has more than made up for the absence of more country-style material with impassioned ballads—"Someone to Lay Down Beside Me" from *Hasten Down the Wind*, for instance—or with many delicate songs by Souther.

Similarly, her *Cry Like a Rainstorm, Howl Like the Wind* of 1989 represented a partly grudging reversion to her folk-rock idiom for commercial reasons (it served that purpose handsomely, particularly in two chart-topping duets with Aaron Neville, whose *Warm Your Heart* she produced in 1991), after a decade spent happily splashing about non-rock waters. Her stylistic forays have included the role of Mabel in Gilbert and Sullivan's *Pirates of Penzance* in Central Park, on Broadway, on records and in a film version; Mimi in a contemporized rescoring of Puccini's *La Bohème* at the Public Theater in New York; three commercially successful albums of pre-rock standards in Nelson Riddle arrangements; and two albums of traditional Mexican *rancheras* and *corridos* with *mariachi* accompaniment.

Ronstadt owes her success to her looks, her charm, her ear for harmony singing, but above all to her voice, which is about the most versatile, strongest and most alluring vocal sound in pop music. And her influence has been considerable, principally in the indirect (by her success and example) and direct (by personal intercession and friendship) encouragement of a whole host of other women singers from Los Angeles. The most interesting blend of songwriting and singing has been Karla Bonoff, who sounds like Christine McVie of Fleetwood Mac and mopes like Leonard Cohen. Sometimes Bonoff can seem too insistently, self-pityingly weepy, but like Cohen, her best songs can be deeply affecting. Others in this circle include Harris, Nicolette Larson (pretty fluffy), Valerie Carter (an interesting white soul singer who made no commercial impact), Wendy Waldman (original but no

Bonnie Raitt returned to L.A. after launching her career in Cambridge, Massachusetts.

sales), Jennifer Warnes, Lauren Wood, Carlene Carter and Rosanne Cash.

Another recipient of Ronstadt's support but too powerful a personality to be considered part of any group is Bonnie Raitt. Raitt's roots lie in the Boston-Cambridge folk circle of the Sixties, and in some ways her involvement with the Los Angeles scene is a metaphor for her failure until her late blooming after the age of forty. Originally she was prized as a tough, honest feminist, devoted to political issues as much as to the folk and blues roots to which she aspired. But she also wanted to be a success as a pop singer in the Ronstadt mold. The result was a fragmentation of her considerable talents, coupled with a seeming inability to compose or find really strong material.

In a sense, her triumph at the 1990 Grammys, with five major awards, and the resultant success of her albums *Nick of Time* (1989, whose sales exploded after her Grammy sweep) and *Luck of the Draw* (1991), suggested that hers was an artistry best expressed in full maturity. Of course, her Grammy publicity and, she said, a newfound personal contentment contributed to her success. But her personal style and toughly honest persona were never meant for competition at the level of glossy glamour. And her musical idiom, modeled on that of the veteran bluesmen and blueswomen she so deeply admired, with her reedily insistent voice and biting blues guitar licks, found its most complete realization when her own image and experience had had time to catch up with her aspirations.

The Eagles emerged from one of Ronstadt's backup bands, led by Don Henley, a singer and drummer from Texas, and Glenn Frey, a guitarist and singer from Detroit (most Angelenos come from someplace else). The group's debut album, *The Eagles* (1972), was recorded in England with Glyn Johns and included the song "Take It Easy," composed by Frey and Jackson Browne. That song typified the early Eagles sound—a little slick, but genuinely appealing in its mellow way.

But from the first the Eagles had ambitions to be more than mellow. *Desperado* (1973) was a concept album equating the myth of the cowboy with that of the rock star. But it was not until *Hotel California* (1976) that the group hit its mature peak, in a wide-reaching attempt to define "life in the fast lane," which was about the most evocative phrase to emerge from this group of performers in the decade.

The Eagles, who defined "life in the fast lane," between stays at the Hotel California.

Unfortunately, a persistent banality of imagery, a plodding inevitability of music, a deadly dull live act and a pervasive meanspiritedness undercut the message. But it was at least more than merely mellow. After a three-year dry spell, *The Long Run* (1979) reaffirmed the band's position as the most commercial American rock group of the Seventies, but it betrayed a fatal lack of inspiration, and the band broke up for good soon after. Since then Henley and Frey especially have continued with solo albums, Henley's more commercially successful and Frey's more musically interesting, although Henley's *The End of the Innocence* (1989) had its critical admirers.

Jackson Browne is as widely respected as any of these artists, and with *Running on Empty* (1977) he finally achieved commercial success to match. Since then he has kept his recording career afloat but with lesser buoyancy, exploring political themes in his most recent work. The songs from Browne's Seventies albums are often cut from the same mold—naive if evocative poetry about roads and rivers and the sky, all as metaphors for love and religious despair, supported by mournful country-rock instrumentals and his own warm if limited baritone. Though he had difficulty sustaining whole albums, songs like "Rock Me on the Water," "These Days" and "Before the Deluge" ensure the reputation of his work from this period.

A protégé of Browne and curiously akin to him is Warren Zevon, who got a late and erratic start, but whose tough and quirky rock songs brought out a pre-punk hard-rock quality in this L.A. circle that not everyone had known was there. Zevon's second mature album, *Excitable Boy* (1978), seemed to augur the arrival of a really important artist, but his erratic performances undercut his impact, and subsequently he admitted himself to a treatment center for alcoholism. His "comeback" album of 1980, *Bad Luck Streak in Dancing School,* showed a heartening return to form.

If these people constitute a close social circle, that hardly meant that their music was all that came out of Los Angeles in the Seventies. Dour, eccentric descendants of Zappa and Beefheart lived on with Sparks, Tonio K., Rickie Lee Jones and, above all, Tom Waits. Waits, who counts as a New York artist as much as a Los Angeleno, sustained a lively career in the Eighties as a concert and recording artist, stage and film actor and composer for the theater, in

Don Henley: After the Eagles, he distinguished himself with three solo albums that culminated in the artistic and commercial success of *The End of the Innocence.*

particular his own *Frank's Wild Years* for Chicago's Steppenwolf Theater and *The Black Rider,* a wonderfully quirky collaboration in Hamburg, Germany, with the director Robert Wilson and the author William S. Burroughs. Indeed, the prominence attained in the late Seventies and early Eighties by the Los Angeles punk scene not only carried on the Zappa-Beefheart curmudgeonly tradition but threatened for a while to make it the dominant voice of Los Angeles rock, replacing the cheerier, sunnier variety.

Neither sunshine nor gloom completely encompassed the popular music of the Los Angeles basin. Los Lobos reaffirmed the appeal of Mexican-American rock, especially in its tribute to Ritchie Valens in the film *La Bamba* (1987). John Williams and his many Lucas-Spielberg-inspired followers epitomized the continued good health of the symphonic film score, and Barbra Streisand and Neil Diamond sold millions of records to a market hungry for maudlin middle-of-the-road pop rock. Television emitted a series of interchangeable pube rockers like Leif Garrett and Shaun Cassidy (the best of a weedy bunch), some of whom (the Carpenters, the Osmonds) hung on to achieve MOR success. Too often, this glossy entertainment business proved the ruin of fine artists who had earned their early fame in more protected genres—as with Dolly Parton and many of the formerly vital Motown singers who came with the company to Los Angeles from Detroit. But there was plenty of good black music being

Andy Warhol *(left)* and Jackson Browne debating the dialectics of pop.

made in Los Angeles, too, as shown by Maurice White and Earth, Wind and Fire. There was traditional jazz, as well, and Steely Dan proved that sophisticated jazz rock could prosper in Los Angeles studios as easily as in New York. All this suggests that the image of Los Angeles in the Seventies as a stylistically monolithic asylum is simply false. Los Angeles is very different from New York in terms of street energy and the close juxtaposition of classes and races. But in terms of musical variety, both towns have a dizzying abundance.

Resident superstars enlivened the scene, too, but didn't always contribute to it—Bob Dylan, Ringo Starr, Rod Stewart. But some of the imports took root, fused with the locals and made quintessentially Los Angeles music. The most vivid example was Fleetwood Mac, which has probably sold more records than any other act mentioned in this chapter. The group dates back to 1967 in Britain, but its early blues-rock history needn't concern us here. By the mid-Seventies Mick Fleetwood, the drummer, John McVie, the bass player, and Christine McVie, his then-wife and a singer-writer-keyboardist, wound up in Los Angeles. Their fourth member, the Ameri-

can Bob Welch, quit in early 1975, and the band latched onto a couple of other Californians named Stevie Nicks and Lindsey Buckingham, who had put out one record as a duo.

The result was two albums, *Fleetwood Mac* (1975) and *Rumours* (1977), that defined catchy but emotionally affecting pop rock for the late Seventies—from the mysterious witcheries of Nicks to the soulful reveries of Christine McVie to the buoyant pop of Buckingham. Part of the band's success was its very ability to overcome the pop-vs.-profundity dilemma that crippled the Eagles. The music was unabashedly pop, yet it touched on serious themes without being weighed down by them. *Tusk* (1979) was an extension of that idiom, further proof that success needn't imply entrapment in a formula. McVie treaded water as a writer, and Nicks lapsed ever more into mannerism. But Buckingham, who dominated the album, contributed songs of such scrappy, austere strangeness that one had to admire him even as one scratched one's head in puzzlement. After their enormous burst of success in the mid to late Seventies, internal tensions, personal neuroses, solo aspirations and the beguilements of success limited the band's creative and commercial impact.

Stevie Nicks sang some of Fleetwood Mac's biggest hits.

Lindsey Buckingham, whose scrappy, austere pop-rock compositions contributed largely to Fleetwood Mac's success.

The Los Angeles new-wave scene, three years behind New York and London but full of feisty spirit, lies outside the concerns of this article, as does the rise of Los Angeles rap in the Eighties. At first the "punk" bands that emerged were mostly bright, commercial power poppers, the Knack being the best-known example. This was all right in small doses, but the record companies' hysterical rush to sign any and all Knack-alikes soon deluged the market with mediocre bands from all over the country. Quickly enough, to be sure, the image of Los Angeles punkdom was taken over by more serious, mean and/or aggressive groups, and certainly the rap to emerge from Watts, Compton and adjacent neighborhoods was full of the same brooding anger that characterized rap nationwide.

Still, the record business's and the clubs' concentration on pop, commercially marketable "lite" metal and other forms of marketable music product is only a continuation of what Los Angeles has always stood for in the rock scene as a whole. And the readiness with which at least some of the leaders of the Seventies scene adapted to the new trends—for example, Ronstadt in her *Mad Love* (1980)—suggested that Los Angeles was not about to stop producing fashionable, entertaining, sometimes affecting pop rock for a good many years to come.

DISCOGRAPHY

ALBUMS

Lindsey Buckingham: *Law and Order* (Asylum; ☆32, 1981). *Go Insane* (Warner Bros.; ☆45, 1987). *Out of the Cradle* (Reprise; ☆145, 1992). **Ry Cooder:** *Into the Purple Valley* (Reprise; ☆113, 1972). *Paradise and Lunch* (Reprise; ☆167, 1974). *Chicken Skin Music* (Reprise; ☆177, 1976). *Show Time* (Warner Bros.; ☆158, 1977). *Bop till You Drop* (Warner Bros.; ☆62, 1979). *Borderline* (Warner Bros.; ☆43, 1981). *The Slide Area* (Warner Bros.; ☆105, 1982). *Get Rhythm* (Warner Bros.; ☆177, 1987). With Little Village: *Little Village* (Reprise; ☆66, 1992). **Eagles:** *Eagles* (Asylum; ☆22, 1972). *Desperado* (Asylum; ☆41, 1973). *On the Border* (Asylum; ☆17, 1974). *One of These Nights* (Asylum; ☆1, 1975). *Their Greatest Hits 1971–1975* (Asylum; ☆1, 1976). *Hotel California* (Asylum; ☆1, 1976). *The Long Run* (Asylum; ☆1, 1979). *Eagles Live* (Asylum; ☆6, 1980). *Eagles Greatest Hits, Volume 2* (Asylum; ☆52, 1982). **Mick Fleetwood:** *The Visitor* (RCA; ☆43, 1981). **Fleetwood Mac:** *Fleetwood Mac* (Reprise; ☆3, 1975). *Rumours* (Warner Bros.; ☆1, 1977). *Tusk* (Warner Bros.; ☆8, 1979). *Fleetwood Mac Live* (Warner Bros.; ☆14, 1980). *Mirage* (Warner Bros.; ☆1, 1982). *Tango in the Night* (Warner Bros.; ☆7, 1987). *Greatest Hits* (Warner Bros.; ☆14, 1988). *Behind the Mask* (Warner Bros.; ☆18, 1990). **Glenn Frey:** *No Fun Aloud* (Asylum; ☆32, 1982). *The Allnighter* (MCA; ☆37, 1984). *Soul Searchin'* (MCA; ☆36, 1988). **Don Henley:** *I Can't Stand Still* (Asylum; ☆24, 1982). *Building the Perfect Beast* (Geffen; ☆13, 1984). *The End of the Innocence* (Geffen; ☆8, 1989). **Christine McVie:** *Christine McVie* (Warner Bros.; ☆26, 1984). **Stevie Nicks:** *Bella Donna* (Modern; ☆1, 1981). *The Wild Heart* (Modern; ☆5, 1983). *Rock a Little* (Modern; ☆12, 1985). *Other Side of the Mirror* (Modern; ☆10, 1989). *TimeSpace: The Best of Stevie Nicks* (Modern; ☆30, 1991). **Bonnie Raitt:** *Give It Up* (Warner Bros.; ☆138, 1972). *Takin' My Time* (Warner Bros.; ☆87, 1973). *Streetlights* (Warner Bros.; ☆80, 1974). *Home Plate* (Warner Bros.; ☆43, 1975). *Sweet Forgiveness* (Warner Bros.; ☆25, 1977). *The Glow* (Warner Bros.; ☆30, 1979). *Green Light* (Warner Bros.; ☆38, 1982). *Nine Lives* (Warner Bros.; ☆115, 1986). *Nick of Time* (Capitol; ☆1, 1989). *The Bonnie Raitt Collection* (Warner Bros.; ☆61, 1990). *Luck of the Draw* (Capitol; ☆2, 1991). **Linda Ronstadt:** *Silk Purse* (Capitol; ☆103, 1970). *Linda Ronstadt* (Capitol; ☆163, 1972). *Don't Cry Now* (Asylum; ☆45, 1973). *Different Drum* (Capitol; ☆92, 1974). *Heart Like a Wheel* (Capitol; ☆1, 1974). *Prisoner in Disguise* (Asylum; ☆4, 1975). *Hasten Down the Wind* (Asylum; ☆3, 1976). *Greatest Hits* (Asylum; ☆6, 1976). *A Retrospective* (Capitol; ☆46, 1977). *Simple Dreams* (Asylum; ☆1, 1977). *Living in the U.S.A.* (Asylum; c☆3, ☆1, 1978). *Mad Love* (Asylum; ☆3, 1980). *Greatest Hits, Volume 2* (Asylum; ☆26, 1980). *Get Closer* (Asylum; ☆31, 1982). *What's New* (Asylum; ☆3, 1983). *Lush Life* (Asylum; ☆13, 1984). *Canciones de Mi Padre* (Elektra; ☆42, 1987). *Cry Like a Rainstorm, Howl like the Wind* (Elektra; ☆7, 1989). *Mas Canciones* (Elektra; ☆88, 1991). **Warren Zevon:** *Warren Zevon* (Asylum; ☆189, 1976). *Excitable Boy* (Asylum; ☆8, 1978). *Bad Luck Streak in Dancing School* (Asylum; ☆20, 1980). *Stand in the Fire* (Asylum; ☆80, 1980). *The Envoy* (Asylum; ☆93, 1982). *A Quiet Normal Life: The Best of Warren Zevon* (Asylum; 1986). *Sentimental Hygiene* (Virgin; ☆63, 1987). *Transverse City* (Virgin; 1989). *Mr. Bad Example* (Giant/Reprise; 1991).

(Chart positions compiled from Joel Whitburn's *Record Research*, based on *Billboard's* LPs chart, unless otherwise indicated; c☆ = position on *Billboard's* Country & Western chart.)

THE SOUND OF NEW YORK CITY

BY JOHN ROCKWELL

Music in Manhattan once conjured up images of glittery nights in the Rainbow Room, surrounded by Art-Deco sumptuousness and beguiled by the smooth sophistication of a Cole Porter or the bouncy charm of an Eddie Duchin. But since the mid-Seventies New York music, the music that truly comes from that city and speaks with its voice, has been made in lower Manhattan: SoHo, Tribeca and the East Village—sections of town that, despite the rampant gentrification of the Eighties, still are the sites of crime-ridden housing projects, tenements, lofts, delivery trucks and sweatshops. The music from that part of town is harder, more urgent, more desperate than the midtown, upper-class gloss from earlier in the century. But for those of us who were there and watched it evolve, it has been about as exciting a place to be for music as one could imagine.

Before we get to the lower Manhattan scene, however, we have to consider other parts of New York music; part of the excitement of the city is its very diversity of experience. That diversity comes from New York's role as an international crossroads—a capital of international finance in general and the music business in particular, a link between Europe and America, a media center, a conduit for unassimilated third-world cultures and the undisputed arts center of the country. And that old bromide,

about the sheer numbers of people and the intensity of the street energy in New York, is no bromide at all: It's the simple truth.

Pre-rock musical styles continue to prosper in New York, although the adult-pop, middle-of-the-road acts mostly play the suburban theaters around New York, as they do elsewhere in the country. Mainstream jazz doesn't just survive here, it flourishes, thanks to George Wein's annual jazz festival (originally Newport, now known by whomever its principal corporate sponsor may be that year), jazz-repertory activity at Lincoln Center and the 92nd Street Y, the New York State Council on the Arts and a host of clubs that book such acts. Broadway, too, carries on, in the face of television and the strength of the regional theater movement. Old-fashioned Broadway musicals, now bolstered by Andrew Lloyd Webberian imports from London's West End, and hence old-fashioned Broadway personalities like Liza Minnelli and Bernadette Peters, still exist within their own subculture and reach out to the country as a whole through television and films. The Broadway impetus received fresh infusions of energy in the Seventies from both Joseph Papp—whose hiply contemporary exterior masked an aesthetic as traditional as P. T. Barnum's—and the homosexual cabaret early in the decade.

That cabaret scene, and its kinkier offshoots in places like the Continental Baths, provided New York's two major contributions to the world of glittery show-biz and adult-pop crooning, Bette Midler and Barry Manilow. When Midler arrived on the scene, some people hoped she might lead to an extension and augmentation of what Janis Joplin had suggested: That by drawing on the brassy tradition of the vaudeville grande dame and the Broadway belter (Diamond Lil, Ethel Merman), Midler might revitalize rock & roll. But she never really made it as a rock artist; she may be too ironic, stylistically diffuse and musically prosaic for that, which makes her occasional chart success with soppy ballads all the odder. In her live revues and as a film actress the essence of her talent—her flamboyant personality—can come through unfettered, and they have made her a star. Manilow is held up to mockery by rock

critics, and indeed he can seem a cynically tasteless hack. But he does sing well, and his songs and vulgar arrangements answer a need for sentimental balladeering in American culture that goes all the way back to the previous century.

Carly Simon and Paul Simon represent a more modern version of the same adult-pop sensibility, although he did push the envelope in the late Eighties with his excursions into third-world musical styles. So does Billy Joel, although he keeps a toe in the rock camp, too, most overtly in his *Glass Houses* LP (1980). Joel is particularly self-conscious in his identification with New York (e.g., ''New York State of Mind,'' *52nd Street*), and indeed in the best of his music there's a nice blend of the nervously electrified energies of New York jazz rock and the formal clarity of the pop song. New York jazz rock itself may be seen as a form of recreation for session players bored to distraction by endless jingles (commercials compete with rock on the New York recording studio scene). There has of course been some good work in the jazz-rock field, but most of it is busy emptiness. The New York area has produced its share of mainstream commercial rock acts, too, from Kiss to Madonna to Bon Jovi, although New Jersey really constitutes a separate scene, part of the heartland, as witness the all-American self-identification of its archetype, Bruce Springsteen.

New York's music also includes an enormous amount of popular music made by blacks and Latins, only some of which intersects with the lower Manhattan scene. New York was arguably the birthplace of Seventies disco, and Chic was as classy and clever a band as the disco era produced. In the mid-Seventies there was a lot of eager talk that salsa, which is the modernized Latin dance music of New York's Puerto Ricans, would sweep the nation. It hardly happened, but that doesn't mean that Latin musicians—especially those with a feeling for jazz, like Eddie Palmieri—haven't given New Yorkers a great deal of pleasure. More influential has been rap, but its intense identification with urban blacks makes it difficult for arty white types to assimilate (i.e., rip off) with any conviction.

Much of this music either is not rock, or has lost a lot of its vitality, or is practiced with greater skill in other parts of the country. The lower Manhattan scene—and by now, outposts of that scene exist uptown, too—is unique.

The antecedents of modern-day New York rock are scattered. Doo-wop groups and Italian-American harmonizers gave the city a distinctive sound in the Fifties but had a minimal impact on the new rock. In the psychedelic Sixties the city had a few local favorites—the Blues Project, the (Young) Rascals, the Lovin' Spoonful—and a folk scene prospered in local clubs during the decade's first half. But of all the bands that came out of New York in the Sixties, it was the Velvet Underground that had the decisive influence on local bands that had inherited the folk clubs, and it was the Velvet Underground that became the progenitor of nearly everything that happened in lower Manhattan rock in the next decade.

The band emerged, as did many of its successors, from the lower Manhattan vanguard arts community—Walter De Maria, the artist, played drums informally at the beginning—and was then taken up by Andy Warhol and made into the star attraction of his "Exploding Plastic Inevitable," his traveling mixed-media circus of 1966–67. Warhol was probably too much an Eighties-style ironist to respond to the inner passion of the band's music. But he certainly grasped its style and surface sensibility, especially that of Lou Reed, the lead singer.

The sound of the Velvet Underground came as a salutary shock to anyone used to the ever-slicker, artier concoctions of post–*Sgt. Pepper* rock. Twangy and raw, out of tune and deliberately monolithic of beat, marked by Reed's quavering vocalizing, which sounded almost intuitively vague and defiant about pitch, violent yet tender in the lyrics, full of cacophony and primitivism, this band was *different*. It proved that technical amateurishness and deliberate simplicity were no barrier to artistic communication; art rock could never again be equated with complexity, no matter what British progressive-rock bands of the studio might think.

The abrasiveness of the band's sound appalled many people and still does today. But it thrilled others and led to a rebirth of both rock primitivism and rock minimalism, the interactions of which are still being worked out. New York rockers of the Seventies owed much to the visual artists of the Sixties, and a good deal of that art was concerned with sparse, delicately or violently contrasted juxtapositions, often in the service of some overt structural plan. The influence of meditation, drugs and the Orient is obvious here, but so is the desperation of surviving and winning recognition for your work in a harsh, industrialized, rundown, seemingly indifferent environment.

This kind of art and rock was not automatically popular; many of its performers hardly aspired to commercial success at all. Some did become popular by design, others almost by accident. But the New York club scene was enough to keep bands going for years without instant mass success. And the reinforcement provided by friends and the burgeoning local press was enough to sustain a career in the absence of the cruder compensations of money and international fame. In the Seventies the visual art world faded, as the pioneers dispersed and their emulators seemed increasingly derivative. But the experimental spirit lived on—in dance, in performance art and in rock & roll, which in many cases took on aspects of performance art itself.

After the Velvet Underground broke up in 1969,

Patti Smith, rock & roll poetaster. She wanted to be Rimbaud and Jim Morrison rolled into one.

its two central figures both went on to enjoy significant if commercially erratic solo careers in the Seventies. Reed shifted from blatant self-parody to brilliant art rock (*Berlin,* 1973) to feistily provocative concept art to work that ranks with the best and most honest achievements of the Underground: *Transformer* (1972), *Street Hassle* (1978) and *The Bells* (1979). Personally irascible and deliberately self-destructive in careerist terms, he nonetheless has managed to protect within himself some sort of twisted poetic flame, and when he settled down in the Eighties, he managed to sustain sales and interest in albums that balanced a new maturity with hints of the old irascibility.

Cale, a classically trained violinist and avant-gardist before moving into rock, made two superb art-rock albums in the early Seventies, *Paris 1919* and *The Academy in Peril.* He also did some seminal production work (the Modern Lovers, Patti Smith's *Horses*)—seminal because he pioneered a studio simplicity akin to the sound of the bands he was recording (a service not always appreciated by the artists). But most of his recent solo rock albums haven't found a convincing voice. Significantly, his and Reed's best mature work came in an Underground-esque duet album called *Songs for Drella* (1990), a tribute to Warhol.

The scene that had emerged in the back room of Max's Kansas City did not disappear after 1969. The new center for underground rock was now a wonderfully eccentric assemblage of boutiques and performance spaces called the Mercer Arts Center, located just down the street from the current site of the Bottom Line, New York's leading mainstream rock club. The Arts Center was in the old Broadway Central Hotel and contained, among other things, the original Kitchen, a leading forum for experimental music and video art (which, logically enough, was in the hotel's old kitchen). In 1972 and 1973 the Mercer Arts Center was also the hub of New York's glitter-rock underground, a scene epitomized by the New York Dolls.

The Dolls can lay legitimate claim to being the direct precursors of the mid-Seventies New York punk scene, which in turn helped spawn the worldwide new-wave movement later in the decade. In the heyday of glitter rock, they were most striking at first for their looks—deliberately, poutingly androgynous. But sexual ambivalence wasn't really central to the Dolls' act; music and spirit were. The band

The New York Dolls, who gave the scene a fresh dress code.

combined David Johansen's parodistic Mick Jagger imitation, punky snarl and ebullient energy with lurching violence from Johnny Thunders and desperately semiprofessional work from the rhythm section, and forged them into a music both barely controlled and wildly exhilarating. They reaffirmed the Velvet Underground's commitment to amateurish primitivism but proved it could be energetic, dizzying fun and street hard all at once. Ahead of their time, loved within New York but hated or ignored without, the Dolls stood as a proud contradiction to all that was soft and safe in the commercial rock of the day.

When the front of the Broadway Central Hotel collapsed and the rest of the building was condemned, the components of the Mercer Arts Center disappeared or dispersed, and the Dolls disbanded soon thereafter (although Johansen, under his own name and that of Buster Poindexter, sustained a functional solo career into the Nineties). For a while there seemed to be no place for new bands to play. But in 1975 Tom Verlaine, a moodily poetic young guitarist from Maryland, convinced Hilly Kristal,

who had a run-down bar on the Bowery called CBGB (for ''Country, Blue Grass and Blues''), to open his doors to new rock bands that played original music.

With the success of CBGB's rock policy, and the subsequent adoption of similar policies by Max's and, eventually, many other clubs, the Seventies New York underground rock scene was firmly established. Its first star and primal priestess was Patti Smith, who had emerged in the early Seventies in the wake of Lou Reed as a chanting bard on the local poetry-reading circuit, accompanied by Lenny Kaye, erstwhile rock critic and journeyman guitarist. Gradually Patti's band and ambitions grew, and she was playing Max's and other sites with a two- and three-piece drumless band. Smith's music was always a desperate, ambitious attempt to combine rock populism and energy with the mystical raptures of her poetry. She really succeeded only in her debut album, *Horses* (1975). Thereafter, she had trouble finding the right balance, usually sacrificing the control and hypnotic power of her early days for undistinguished ranting and heavy-metal riffing. Eventually she dropped out of the scene almost completely—despite occasional forays into the studio—moving to Detroit and domesticity.

Verlaine's Television was another of the pioneering bands of the underground scene in the mid-decade. Dominated visually by Verlaine's thin, Messianic beauty and aurally by the rhapsodic interplay between his guitar and that of Richard Lloyd, Television was too twangily anachronistic (the Byrds with all the rough edges still showing) for mainstream success. It eventually broke up, with subsequent solo albums of some merit by both Verlaine and Lloyd. In 1992 the four members of Television reunited to record a new album.

The Ramones were the purest conceptual band of the bunch, and possibly the wittiest. Four middle-class men from Queens who affected torn T-shirts and ratty leather jackets, they epitomized the slob-punk aesthetic and cranked out a barrage of songlets with subjects like sniffing glue and being a pinhead. But the overall effect wasn't funny enough—one slim joke repeated over and over—and the band's musical wit was too limited and too crude (even with the counter-conceptual turn to Phil Spector as

producer of their *End of the Century* album of 1980) to sustain any sort of career beyond a cult.

More successful, both commercially and artistically, was Blondie. ''Blondie'' meant both the band and its strikingly beautiful lead singer, Deborah Harry. The group started out as a stiff, crude outgrowth of an earlier band called the Stilettoes (before that Harry had been in a Byrds-ish folk-rock outfit called Wind in the Willows). But Blondie's male instrumentalists had the drive to experiment with and master their craft, and Harry managed a nice blend of sexuality and sweetly awkward self-parody. Together they produced an original updating of early Sixties girl-group clichés. Though Harry's pretty soprano is seemingly unsuited for rock, she caught the bite of the music in her phrasing. She also served as a focus for the instrumentalists' diverse stylistic experiments, usually in the direction of a perilously

The Ramones pretend to be dumb teenage hoodlums.

Talking Heads, four fresh-faced kids led by Rhode Island School of Design dropout David Byrne.

fancified art rock. The third album, *Parallel Lines* (1978), showed real growth for Blondie, and the public made it the band's first American hit, propelled by the disco-ish "Heart of Glass." But a long illness in the Eighties suffered by Chris Stein, the band's musical leader and Harry's boyfriend, proved too great an obstacle to overcome, and neither the band nor any of its members was able to regain career momentum.

The most impressive of all these bands was Talking Heads. Originally a trio born at the Rhode Island School of Design, the Heads became a quartet with the addition of Jerry Harrison, a keyboard player and guitarist once with the Modern Lovers. But for all the contributions of Harrison and the rhythm section of Tina Weymouth and Chris Frantz, this was always a band dominated by David Byrne, the songwriter, singer and guitarist, whose thin-voiced high squawking and psychotic looks people found simultaneously riveting and off-putting. Because of his vocal limitations, it was the instrumental work of the early trio—spare, structurally exact, almost Oriental in its delicacy and pointedness—that seemed

most appealing at first. But gradually Byrne refined his voice and his style; it was still strange, but it became more and more commanding, too. And with the addition of Harrison, the sound filled out in a way that never denied Byrne's economical intentions.

His lyrics, full of naive social comment, borderline bizarro observations of the world and struggles with his creative muse, seemed genuinely fresh in a way that the similarly psychotic-robotic concoctions of Devo did not. But once again it was the music that took precedence, with a power that made one realize the links between the Heads' art-structuralism and the inexorability of Sixties soul. The band's version of Al Green's "Take Me to the River" gave them a modest hit in 1978 and reaffirmed the art-soul kinship, proving that passion had fired the intellection just as intellection had refined and focused the passion. But ultimately their success was sealed by Byrne's unwavering vision of a bleak world that transcended normal human emotion, and above all by the brilliant way that seemingly unpromising vision for a rock band was realized by his collaborators—who by the second and third albums, *More Songs About Buildings and Food* and *Fear of Music*, included Brian Eno as producer and fifth band member in the studio. *Remain in Light* (1980), again with Eno producing, found the Heads incorporating funk and African rhythms into their sound, foreshadowing the fascination with third-world music that would characterize the coming decade.

The mid- to late Eighties saw Byrne sustaining only a flickering interest in the Heads as an entity. Most of his energies were spent on a variety of solo projects, from Paul Simon–like collaborations with third-world musicians to a film score and direction to modern-dance scores to funky New Orleans brass-band extensions for the director Robert Wilson to a stiff, technically naive effort to capture the feeling of nineteenth-century orchestral music, again for Wilson. Forced onto their own, both Harrison and the Weymouth-Frantz team put out solo albums, too, with the Weymouth-Frantz Tom Tom Club dance-party discs the more successful.

David Byrne lost interest in Talking Heads in the course of pursuing an array of musical and artistic endeavors, including Brazilian music, orchestral composition, film work and his own solo albums.

These bands were the first and finest products of the lower Manhattan rock scene of the Seventies. But by the time they had won prominence, the word was out that something new was happening in lower Manhattan. The first people to get the word were the British, during a Ramones tour in 1976; and the apparently direct result was the eruption of the London punk scene: Malcolm McLaren, mastermind behind the Sex Pistols, had managed the New York Dolls in their last days.

But the world also went out all over America. One result was that Manhattan became a showcase for original rock bands from hither and yon that either moved there, appeared there often or won their record contracts there; until the Knack and other power poppers, the music moguls in Los Angeles ignored new-wave rock, as it was now called. Thus Manhattan saw Ohio bands like Devo and Pere Ubu and a steady influx of hopefuls from Boston, San Francisco, Los Angeles itself and even places like Memphis, Atlanta and Athens, Georgia, which gave New York the B-52's, the best of the newer bands.

An even more lasting result of all this activity was the evolution of innumerable local scenes that nurtured their own original bands. America has always been full of bars that let rock bands copy the hits of the day. But these new local scenes, and the attendant record, book and fashion stores, local fanzines and independent record companies and underground distribution networks, led to a revitalization of the rock spirit in ways that the record-company fat cats and smooth-talking "progressive" FM disc jockeys had forgotten about entirely.

In New York itself, the real story in the late Seventies was the way rock interacted with other kinds of music and arts. Eno, Robert Fripp and Fred Frith, the vanguard British guitarist, all established bases in New York and infused the music with currents from Britain and the Continent; Eno also encouraged the collaboration among bands, video artists and new-wave filmmakers. Their involvement helped people realize the extent to which "classical" experimental composers and vanguard rock artists were already influencing one another. Noncommercial performance spaces like the Kitchen put on rock concerts, the synthesizer and other electronic keyboards suggested both popular and classical usage; and places

Gone but not forgotten: The Mudd Club was *the* hangout for denizens of the downtown scene.

like the Public Access Synthesizer Studio presented music that could be called rock, jazz or classical. The best-known figures on the lower Manhattan "classical" scene, Philip Glass and Steve Reich, played the Bottom Line and put out records—Reich's *Music for 18 Musicians* (1978) and Glass's *Einstein on the Beach* (1979)—that appealed to the rock intelligentsia. Both men had influenced rock for a long time, anyway, with the electronic crispness, rhythmic vivacity and linear directness of their work. But now other composers were eager to experiment directly with rock and to appear in such trendy clubs as Hurrah and the Mudd Club. Peter Gordon and his Love of Life Orchestra made something of a stir, as did Rhys Chatham and his various minimal-rock bands, and Laurie Anderson, a wonderfully clever performance artist who, after a novelty hit in Britain with "O Superman," made an honorable if not entirely successful stab at rock stardom. At the same time such rigorously austere "no wave" rock experimentalists as D.N.A., Teenage Jesus and the Jerks, and Robin Crutchfield's Dark Day had their admirers, although by this point "rock" had seemingly abandoned all pretenses of being an even potentially popular music and had retreated into the hermetic world of art in the same manner that some jazz musicians had done only a few years before.

Late in the decade, however, there was a new burst of energy from these very same black jazz musicians into the rock scene of lower Manhattan. In the same way that underground rock had detached itself from the commercial mainstream, younger jazz musicians had built bases in lower Manhattan as a protest against the ossification of more traditional jazz and jazz clubs. This movement attracted creative black musicians from all over the country (Chicago and St. Louis were especially fecund sources) and established a scene as vital as the underground rock scene.

In the late Seventies this all began to come together in various ways. Spaces like the Kitchen had long featured "jazz" performers of this type, although for most of them "jazz" was a stereotypical term they found limiting and insulting. By the end of the decade a new form of "funk jazz" or "punk jazz" was emerging; Miles Davis and Ornette Cole-

man were the pioneers, and George Clinton the godfather, but the main exponents on the club scene were James (Blood) Ulmer, Joseph Bowie and James Chance. Chance led a band called the Contortions, which sometimes expanded into a disco-funk revue entitled James White and the Blacks. The results at their best were exciting, combining the swagger, directness and passion of new-wave rock with the rhythmic vitality and sheer chops of jazz.

In the early Eighties the action shifted to the East Village, and one of the dominant styles of the decade became rock-based free improvisation. Fred Frith was an early force here, but John Zorn soon became the leading practitioner, with his cleverly devised, brilliantly self-promoted "game" pieces (in essence, rudimentary scores or charts to structure the no-longer-free improvisations). Zorn, Frith and their many cohorts found a base at the Knitting Factory, which with its intensely self-confident eclecticism became the bellwether club of the Eighties just as

The Mudd Club, 1979.

CBGB had been the model for the Seventies. Free-improv hardly meant the end of experimental bands, however, especially with the continued influence of industrial noise-rock from the European continent and elsewhere in the country. The leading New York band of this sort, Sonic Youth, actually managed to attain commercial success by the late Eighties.

The folk scene, moribund for a long while after the mid-Sixties, rallied to produce some fine artists in the late Seventies, several of whom showed an affinity for the new rock. Steve Forbert scurried off toward the rock mainstream as soon as he could afford a band—similar to what Phoebe Snow had done when she abandoned the blues and jazz for a failed attempt at pop rock, but rather more successful. The Roches, three sisters who had moved to the Village from New Jersey, stayed within an idiosyncratic orbit of their own, making a strangely abstract, inherently urban, deeply emotional folk music. The Roches used Fripp as producer of their first record,

too, which further cemented their allegiance to rock, however strange and vanguard that rock may have been.

Much of this music was only grudgingly accepted by the rest of the country; only Blondie and Talking Heads attained significant sales nationwide. The very hothouse intensity of the New York scene, the way the social organism provides reinforcement and encouragement while the press and the record companies inspire careerist dreams, tends to isolate groups from the tastes of the heartland and even to make them scornful about the conservatism of those tastes. Since much of the music that sold well nationally in the Seventies and Eighties was ephemeral at best and meretricious at worst, the New Yorkers' attitude might not seem so deplorable; certainly it has helped foster some brilliantly original music. Granted, a lot of that music seems smug, coy or desiccated to even potentially sympathetic listeners outside the magic circle. For those of us inside, however, the flaws have been redeemed by the brilliance.

DISCOGRAPHY

ALBUMS
Setting the Standard
Heartbreakers: *L.A.M.F.* (Track; U.K., 1977). **David Johansen:** *David Johansen* (Blue Sky, 1978). **New York Dolls:** *New York Dolls* (Mercury; ☆116, 1973). **Johnny Thunders:** *So Alone* (Real; U.K., 1978).
New-Wave Pioneers
Blondie: *Blondie* (Chrysalis; 1976). *Plastic Letters* (Chrysalis; 1977). *Parallel Lines* (Chrysalis; ☆25, 1978). *Eat to the Beat* (Chrysalis; ☆17, 1979). *Autoamerican* (Chrysalis; ☆7, 1980). *The Best of Blondie* (Chrysalis; ☆30, 1981). *The Hunter* (Chrysalis; ☆33, 1982). **David Byrne:** *The Complete Score from the Broadway Production of "The Catherine Wheel"* (Sire; ☆104, 1981). *Music for*

''The Knee Plays'' (ECM; 1985). *Rei Momo* (Luaka Bop/Sire; ☆71, 1989). *The Forest* (Luaka Bop; 1991). *Uh-Oh* (Warner Bros.; ☆125, 1992). **Richard Hell and the Voidoids:** *Blank Generation* (Sire; 1977). **Richard Lloyd:** *Alchemy* (Elektra; 1979). **Mink De Ville:** *Mink De Ville* (Capitol; 1977). *Return to Magenta* (Capitol; ☆126, 1978). **Ramones:** *Ramones* (Sire; ☆111, 1976). *Ramones Leave Home* (Sire; ☆148, 1977). *Rocket to Russia* (Sire; ☆49, 1977). *Road to Ruin* (Sire; ☆103, 1978). *It's Alive* (Sire; U.K., 1979). *End of the Century* (Sire; ☆44, 1980). *Pleasant Dreams* (Sire; ☆58, 1981). *Subterranean Jungle* (Sire; ☆83, 1983). *Too Tough to Die* (Sire; ☆174, 1984). *Animal Boy* (Sire; ☆143, 1986). *Halfway to Sanity* (Sire; ☆172, 1987). *Ramonesmania* (Sire; ☆168, 1988). *Brain Drain* (Sire; ☆122, 1989). *Loco Live* (Sire; 1992). **Talking Heads:** *Talking Heads '77* (Sire; ☆97, 1977). *More Songs About Buildings and Food* (Sire; ☆29, 1978). *Fear of Music* (Sire; ☆21, 1979). *Remain in Light* (Sire; ☆19, 1980). *The Name of This Band Is Talking Heads* (Sire; ☆31, 1982). *Speaking in Tongues* (Sire; ☆15, 1983). *Stop Making Sense* (Sire; ☆41, 1984). *Little Creatures* (Sire; ☆20, 1985). *True Stories* (Sire; ☆17, 1986). *Naked* (Sire; ☆19, 1988). **Television:** *Marquee Moon* (Elektra; 1977). *Adventure* (Elektra; 1978). **Tom Verlaine:** *Tom Verlaine* (Elektra; 1979). *Dreamtime* (Warner Bros.; ☆177, 1981). *Words from the Front* (Warner Bros.; 1982). *Cover* (Warner Bros.; 1984). *Flash Light* (I.R.S.; 1987). *Warm and Cool* (Rykodisc; 1992).

''New Music'' from N.Y.C.

Philip Glass: *Einstein on the Beach* (Tomato; 1979). **Steve Reich:** *Music for 18 Musicians* (ECM; 1978).

Performance Art

Laurie Anderson: *Airwaves* (One Ten Records; 1977). *Nova Convention* (Giorno Poetry Systems; 1979). *Big Science* (Warner Bros.; ☆124, 1982). *Mister Heartbreak* (Warner Bros.; ☆60, 1984). *United States Live* (Warner Bros.; ☆192, 1984). *Home of the Brave* (Warner Bros.; ☆150, 1986). *Strange Angels* (Warner Bros.; ☆171, 1989).

Pivotal Figures

Brian Eno: *Taking Tiger Mountain (by Strategy)* (EG Records; 1974) *Ambient 1: Music for Airports* (PVC; 1978). *Ambient 4: Onband* (EG Records; 1982). **Robert Fripp:** *Exposure* (Polydor; ☆79, 1979). *God Save the Queen/Under Heavy Manners* (Polydor; 1980). As producer: *The Roches* (Warner Bros.; ☆58, 1979).

No Wave

Lydia Lunch: *Queen of Siam* (ZE; 1980). **Alan Vega and Martin Rev:** *Suicide* (Red Star; 1977). *Suicide* (ZE/Island; U.K., 1980). **Anthologies:** *No New York* (Antilles; 1978).

The Rock/Jazz/Funk/Disco Fusion

James Chance: *James White and the Blacks* (ZE; 1979). *Buy the Contortions* (ZE; 1979). **August Darnell:** *Dr. Buzzard's Original Savannah Band* (RCA; ☆22, 1976). *Dr. Buzzard's Original Savannah Band Meets King Penett* (RCA; ☆36, 1978). *Dr. Buzzard's Original Savannah Band Goes to Washington* (Elektra; 1979). *Gichy Dan's Beachwood #9* (RCA; 1979). **James ''Blood'' Ulmer:** *Tales of Captain Black* (Artists House; 1979).

(Chart positions compiled from Joel Whitburn's *Record Research*, based on *Billboard*'s LPs chart.)

DISCO

BY TOM SMUCKER

G et up and boogie
Get up and boogie
That's right
Boogie, boogie
—Silver Convention, 1974

You make me feel mighty real
Everybody is a star
You make my body strong
You are my friend
                    —Sylvester, 1978–79

I'd like to do it all before I'm through
Fly into space or maybe
Save the human race
All these things seem so appealing
But I'll never get my chance
'Cause all I do is dance
                    —Chic, 1979

There's trouble, trouble in paradise
Where do we go from here?
                    —Sylvester, 1984

Superficial, sensuous, liberating, reactionary and innovative, disco emerged out of its subculture at the beginning of the Seventies, dominated pop for a couple of years at the end, almost wiped out rock and then collapsed, disappeared and returned in various underground and mainstream permutations as the Eighties wore on. But during its brief reign it restored the dance groove as a pop imperative. And did so with a new energy derived, in part, by disregarding many of the standards cherished by the rock establishment; thereby evoking a revulsion as vehement as the one that met Elvis when he demolished the decorum of the aging world of swing, or the one that met electric Bob Dylan when he first fell off the high road of acoustic folkie virtue.

Discos, of course, had been around before the Seventies. The DJ with his twin turntables and mike was a frequent fixture at dance parties in the black community. And rock & roll discos like the Peppermint Lounge helped popularize dances like the twist among the masses in the early Sixties, and, for a while, among the rich who found it hip to hobnob with the hoi polloi. While in Europe a more snobby exclusivity was cultivated.

But a really discoey disco, as it came to be defined in the Seventies, though it still harbored such crosscurrents of class, race and trendiness, was not about the latest steps or frequenting tony haunts. It was about communal dance ecstasy: a place where the DJ choreographed music and lighting to manipulate the mood on the floor toward climax. A new brew of Seventies self-absorption and Sixties collectivity, mixing aerobics, the pick-up singles bar, drug highs and light shows, it made the dance floor, rather than the concert hall, the locus of orgasmic revelation.

By mature rock standards, the disco aesthetic and the music that developed in response to it seemed hopelessly depersonalized. Rather than focusing on "artists" with "careers" who released albums that made "statements," disco emphasized not careers, singers, writers or producers, but the sense of style of the person who picked out and combined the album cuts—the DJ. And did so by necessity. Because, by the middle of the Seventies, it required an exertion of willful style to find a pop space to dance in.

My own dance party graph begins with an early Sixties sock-hop low and then leaps up with the (first) British Invasion and the flowering of Motown. It stays high through the heyday of Stax-Volt and

Creedence and then plummets with the advent of Led Zep and CSN&Y. In particular I remember a hippie Halloween party at the beginning of the Seventies where we all sat around on the floor in stoned silence listening to what would later be called classic rock. A few years earlier those sessions, punctuated by "oh wows," had been fun. Now they were a dead end.

To break out of that silence and dance to current music in the first half of the Seventies, you had to exercise your taste. The soft rock, country rock, progressive rock, oldies, heavy metal and black mellow that then dominated pop were for listening, not moving. To fill an appetite for good new dance sounds, one had to look beyond the mainstream. By honoring this appetite, disco simply reasserted a de-emphasized rock & roll component. And this reestablishment of ass shaking through the elevation of the person at the turntable (and the turntable itself) was disco's lasting contribution—as later theorists of house postmodernism and hip-hop deconstruction who venerate the scratch and the sample are obligated to acknowledge. From this turning point would flow all turntable-driven and most synthesizer-based pop—the mother of De La Soul, J. M. Silk, Jane "Workout" Fonda and Kitaro.

According to legend, early disco took shape on Fire Island and in Manhattan at places like the Loft and the 10th Floor—part private clubs, part personal dance parties and part avant-garde proving grounds—because gay men couldn't get live acts to perform for them. Certainly the position of gay culture in the early Seventies—no longer completely in the closet but not often welcome outside of it—was the social reality that spawned disco and structured its history. But early disco didn't just get by without live acts, it made the audience—the dancers—the live act. It shifted the location of the performance, and hence the way the genre defined itself. If it was danced to at the Loft, then it was disco.

Unlike rock, with its links to roots music in country and the blues, disco was often nothing more than as reaffirmation of smooth black urban danceable pop; like the lean Philly sound of Gamble and Huff, the ultraschlock of Barry White and the more gravelly seduction of Isaac Hayes.

Yet disco taste had a quirky, anything-goes, un-

predictable side as well. Left-field flukes could hit at a disco and nowhere else. Or, as discos sprouted up, they could hit at the discos first and then go on to mainstream success. Manu Dibango's ''Soul Makossa,'' recorded by an African in Paris, was imported into the States when its popularity in discos made domestic release seem like a good business proposition. Informed by Africa and R&B, it also had a sentimental urban feel that would be associated with European disco five years later. When the single appeared on the Top Forty in 1973, the era of the disco-broken pop hit had arrived.

By 1974 the scene was regularly breaking hits, most notably, perhaps, George McCrae's ''Rock Your Baby'' on the T.K. label, an independent company that had learned how to work the discos. A year later discos were influencing not just the way records were being discovered, or promoted, but how records were made. To suit the needs of DJs, some companies introduced twelve-inch singles, remixed and extended beyond the length of the radio version. These ''disco singles,'' originally for the trade only, became so popular that many were released commercially and eventually became the material base for the DJ-focused worlds of rap, dub and house, outlasting the rise of the CD and the demise of the vinyl album in the Nineties.

Disco had bubbled up, and now a variety of artists hobbled into the studio to revitalize their careers. Anything that could be stretched onto the propulsive, unsyncopated, straight 4/4 disco beat and jazzed up with some violin riffs, synthesizer buggles and percussive interludes was grist for the disco mill—*if* it made you dance. It was the Era of the Disco Version: There were new arrangements of show-biz standards, rock oldies, soul oldies, gospel classics, even Beethoven's greatest hits. The underground disco aesthetic was being wed to the whole spectrum of aboveground sounds with a voraciousness that the newest taste in town always displays.

The Disco Version, with its extended length, its use of musical drama and its emphasis on instrumental texture rather than vocal complexity, made disco the first rock-era pop music open to European influence. Silver Convention, from Munich, Germany, had two chart-topping disco hits in 1976, the same year Donna Summer hit the charts panting and moaning on ''Love to Love You Baby,'' also recorded in Munich.

What was interesting about these hits wasn't so much the location of their recording, as the possibilities they suggested for extended disco cuts composed with the longer length in mind. Rather than the verse–chorus–guitar solo–verse–chorus of rock that the Disco Version was really just stretching out, Summer's hit in particular suggested a compressed movie soundtrack, or even a piece of classical symphonic music, with its different movements.

These developments culminated in that purest of all subgenres, Eurodisco. Rather than lengthening conventional pop songs with gimmicks, Eurodisco structured long compositions to fill entire album sides with music that ebbed and flowed in one beat-driven but melodically varied cut, aping the work of the DJ in the club. With tracks that were at times as light (or shallow) as French pop, at times as serious

(or pompous) as a German symphony, at times as dramatic (or corny) as an Italian opera, at times as cool (or cold) as experimental music, at times as minimalist (or repetitive) as a chant, the Europeans freed disco from its drive to cannibalize the past by developing forms unique to the new genre.

While this revolution was sweeping the dance world in the later Seventies, disco finally hit the masses through the mechanism of *Saturday Night Fever*. Based on some journalism by Nik Cohn in *New York* magazine that sounded a somber warning about the death of Sixties youth culture idealism, the movie's success instead announced the discovery of a common vein of disco gold running through numerous demographics and propelled the soundtrack album to the biggest sales in pop-music history.

Before *Saturday Night Fever* was released, there was no way for most folks to investigate the vigorous new scene, because disco produced almost no representative, symbolic stars. A few years later the advent of MTV and the new reality of music videos allowed the creation of a new subgenre: Disco-with-a-Pretty-Face, and its cousin, Dancing-Bimbos-in-the-Background. This visual representation was a way for mass stars with a disco-derived aura to get their hooks into the mass audience (see Duran Duran, Robert Palmer and those greatest pretty faces of them all, Milli Vanilli). But at the time there were few clear mechanisms for an outsider to use to sort through the disco section of the record bins.

Saturday Night Fever—the movie and the soundtrack—became *the* mechanism. Shot at a real, white, working-class disco, 2001 Odyssey, in Bay Ridge, Brooklyn, the movie accurately conveyed the unintimidating and nonelitist underpinnings of disco culture while conveniently ignoring its gay sources. John Travolta's unsentimental but heartfelt performance fleshed out the Barbarino character he was playing then on TV's *Welcome Back, Kotter,* and more or less succeeded in its inspection of the issue of race. On the soundtrack the old, familiar Bee Gees in the middle of their black-influenced urban phase approached disco without straying too far from pop conventions and fielded their strongest string of hit singles. Fleshing out the record was one certifiable disco classic—the Trammps' ''Disco Inferno''—and a hodgepodge of disco-ish filler, some by genuine disco popularizers like K.C. and the Sunshine Band and Tavares. Beyond the Bee Gees and the Trammps it wasn't anybody's strongest work, and it was already dated, but it was roughly speaking real disco.

After this collection marched to the top of the charts and then smugly stayed there, hopeful unknowns, greedy country stars, over-the-hill rockers and anxious knowns set out in search of the fountain of youth that had been discovered by the Bee Gees. Radio stations didn't just add some disco, they went all disco. Record companies competed to hire disco insiders and disco artists, and created entire disco departments overnight.

Although it didn't last long—and terrified those who couldn't stand the music—disco's brief hegemony provided some beautiful pop moments. In 1978, in a disco-mad city like New York, you could walk down the street and *every* radio in a passing car, on a stoop, in a store, out an apartment window, carried down the street by a teen, would be tuned to the same radio station—WKTU. The cacophony of the city was suddenly a ripple of modulations on the same song. And it didn't matter if you were in a ghetto grocery store or a hip boutique, in a limo or on the subway. Disco had gone from an underground taste to the sound of everything from elevator music to the Rolling Stones.

Around this time (1977–78) a French disco producer, Jacques Morali, decided to exploit the gay subculture a bit more explicitly with a group called the Village People. Over a husky male chorus, a pop-soul vocal (Victor Willis) emoted innocuously about various gay locales. It was fun, if a little predictable. What wasn't so predictable was the way that the new straight disco audience, either ignoring or missing the gay content, flocked to the hit cut "San Francisco." Morali took the hint. The next two hits, "Macho Man" and "Y.M.C.A.," were gay goofs to those who got the joke, disco novelties to those who didn't, and hefty mainstream hits. For a spell the Village People were the best-selling group in North America.

Like *Saturday Night Fever*, the Village People offered an entrée to the disco world for those who wanted in but couldn't figure out how far to go. Unlike most disco groups, who were often just the studio musicians assembled by the producer for the recording, the Village People became a real group after the first record hit and Morali assembled them Monkees (or Archies) style. After this transformation they could even be interviewed by Merv Griffin. And their songs were accurate, if cartoon-like, depictions of the disco scene.

At best, this mixture of gay subculture and straight mass success produced an irresistible and exuberant silliness that pumped up old American clichés. It was as if the journey to the heartland now started out on Christopher Street in Greenwich Village. But after "Y.M.C.A." Morali had trouble maintaining his mass success while keeping a grip on the subtext. The music began to lose its disco feel and got too pop-jolly for dancing, veering dangerously close to the Red Army Chorus meets Lawrence Welk. By the time their movie *Can't Stop the Music* debuted, the Village People were already fading from the scene.

In a way, this was a metaphor for disco itself. It had burst from a subculture, but then found it difficult to maintain a mainstream success or identity. The Eurodiscers, who promised a producer-based

Donna Summer launched her career with sixteen minutes of heavy breathing. She survived to become the one performer able to epitomize disco while appealing to the wider pop audience.

disco style, quickly reached a culmination and a dead end. The Bee Gees followup, *Spirits Having Flown*, hit everywhere except the discos and then disappeared because it was undanceable. Most rock stars who rushed onto the bandwagon didn't really understand where they had rushed. And when no new triple-platinum albums appeared, record companies began to eliminate their disco departments. Disco shrank back into the underground, albeit a rather multifaceted, spacious underground by that point. And as the Seventies came to an end only Donna Summer was left at the top of the charts as a disco act with mass recognition.

A black American who ended up in Germany via a touring company of *Hair,* Summer established her disco credentials with the previously mentioned ''Love to Love You Baby'' in 1976. From this groundbreaking Euro-moaner she marched through the history of Eurodisco as its greatest popularizer and perhaps only recognizable star. Unfairly tagged by disco's detractors as a talentless porn star or producer's puppet, Summer could call upon musical and emotional versatility when needed, but often kept it in check because her voice was only one portion of the larger picture she was painting with her constant Europroducers Giorgio Moroder and Pete Bellotte. (The best pre-disco comparison might be the understated work of the wide-ranging Dionne Warwick during her Bacharach-David days.) This trio flew together past the end of disco in 1980, having succeeded with the rock-like disco of ''Bad Girls'' and ''Hot Stuff'' in 1979, but lost their footing at the beginning of the Eighties before Dance Music (or Disco with a Different Moniker) returned in 1982.

Summer turned her back on her disco diva days and lost interest in picking up whatever new signals were coming from the clubs (a mistake Madonna would *not* repeat), attempting, instead, to invent the type of pop success later mastered by Whitney Houston. But her reign as princess of the nightlife remains as disco's biggest icon, and an authentic one. Its various stages would later be analyzed and reassembled by Madonna, as well as Prince, Irene Cara and the Jackson siblings, among others, although the musical structures of Eurodisco would prove too

Donna Summer's parents are astonished by the cake Donna's record company has sent them to celebrate the sixteen lucrative minutes of ''Love to Love You Baby.''

bulky for the soon-to-arrive world of music videos.

Yet if Summer is the one performer best suited to charting out a disco history from orgasm to auteur, that would be a distortion. Because it would leave out all the one-shots that don't fit into a description of the archetypal career but do attest to the breadth and eccentricity that characterized disco. And if ever there was a pop-music form whose history overflowed with oddball one-shots, disco was it.

When rock & roll became Rock it discovered the album as an art form and the group as an artistic idea. When disco started, it threw away them both, rediscovered the single and then inflated the single back up to album length.

What follows is a mini-history of disco singles, some of great historical interest and some based on personal whim, some snapshots from significant careers and some one-shots from voices never heard again, some disco milestones and some disco second cousins.

''Shame, Shame, Shame'' by Shirley and Company (1974). The album cover showed Disco Shirley and a stiff-assed Richard Nixon (not mentioned directly in the song). Post-Watergate optimism was an unacknowledged (except for here) aspect of disco. The album was a throwaway tribute to the Fifties and the shape of things to come. What was disco other than a riff that got too good to finish?

''Cherchez la Femme'' by Dr. Buzzard's Original Savannah Band (1976). Disco fellow travelers with a Latin tinge who would reappear in many spin-offs, most notably as Kid Creole and the Coconuts, and interface in the Eighties with new wave in downtown Manhattan. Clear-eyed, sophisticated camp with a cosmopolitan agenda.

''Trans-Europe Express'' by Kraftwerk (1977). A group of German art rockers who played synthesizers and cultivated a supernerd mystique, Kraftwerk struck the disco mother groove with this cut. Played soft it was pre–New Age background noise; played medium it was interesting arty listening; played loud it was disco. Their electronic embrace of alienation played off a corny European moodiness. More conceptually developed than most disco groups, Kraftwerk had trouble finding the dance floor after this success. But their schtick remained an inspiration for others (like the Pet Shop Boys), and this cut was

sampled and recycled as a bottom line for both rap and dance into the Nineties. The whitest white boys to ever have an album cover in the window of a Harlem record store.

"Give Me Love" by Cerrone (1977). The most rock oriented of the Eurodisco masters, Cerrone reached full power with this classic. Orchestrally embellished disco could sound too flowery and gushy to those who weren't exhilarated dancing to it. But the way the violin riffs build up and then break open into "Love Is Here" reveal disco ecstasy as an achievement over pain, not a middle-class denial of it. Cerrone also should be remembered for "Supernature," the greatest disco hit ever on the subject of ecological disaster.

"I Will Survive" by Gloria Gaynor (1978). An early disco anthem that became a disco warhorse (and even had a country cover by Billy Jo Spears in 1979), it's included here to point out that although many disco lyrics consisted of nothing more than the words "dance" and "dancer" this is one of the *wordiest* songs ever recorded.

"Knock on Wood" by Amii Stewart (1978). Stax-Volt revisited with an emphasis on the lyrics "thunder" and "lightning." Heavy on the bombast and easy on the violins, the single was true to the spirit, if not the letter, of the Memphis sound and a real "disco version" nonetheless.

"The Hunchback of Notre Dame" by Alec R. Costandinos (1978). Alec's big Eurodisco hit was "I've Found Love." By "Hunchback" he was scoring *Classics Illustrated* with a disco beat. It was a grand vision, even if you couldn't really dance to it: "Hunchback" changes musical themes too fast and has too much breathy dialogue breaking it up to be a seamless dance symphony. But it's big, melodic, dramatic and *out there.* Over ten years later "Enigma" would rework the same ideas with chart-topping success using Gregorian chants and de Sade, so was this Eurodisco past its prime or ahead of its time?

"There's No Business Like Show Business" by Ethel Merman (1979). Yes, it is a disco version; yes, it's really Ethel Merman; no, it wasn't a hit; yes, it really exists—I own it; yes, the moves are all disco-version clichés, and, yes, it is unforgettable, hilarious and charming. And yes, by the way, there was also a disco version of "Venus" by Frankie Avalon, but it was forgettable, dull and charmless. And that proves something.

Grace Jones performing at Studio 54's New Year's Eve party, 1978.

"Ain't No Stoppin' Us Now" by McFadden and Whitehead (1979). A delicious black anthem from two Philly producers who stepped forward as performers here. They successfully exploited disco's ability to accommodate a number of gospel moves as well as some inspiring gospel-derived content. At the time it was called disco, now it kind of sounds like soul.

"Dancer" by Gino Soccio (1979). Soccio, from Montreal, assumed the Eurodisco ideas of theme variation and repetition but removed the violins and other flowery touches, putting new emphasis on the

Bitsy Teeny Weeny Yellow Polka Dot Bikini'' by pasting just the right pieces of them over a disco beat. The legal and duller ''Stars on 45'' of 1981 took this idea to legal and duller success.

''Pipeline Remix'' by unknown (1980). A tightened-up bootleg remix of Beach Boy Bruce Johnston's hit disco version in 1977 of the Chantays' old 1963 surfing instrumental. Disco could take a riff from anywhere, even from surf music, and then, from an even earlier disco version of surf music. Johnston tried the same trick in 1979 with the Beach Boys on a disco version of their own ''Here Comes the Night'' from 1967, but it didn't work. Then again, in 1987 the Fat Boys assisted by the Beach Boys had a modest rap hit reworking the Surfaris' 1963 surf instrumental ''Wipeout.'' Disco, and its hostile child Rap, had a sense of history. It was just a different sense than Rock.

''Good Times'' by Chic (1979). The Holland-Dozier-Holland/Meters/Booker T. and the MGs/Mamas and Papas/Lennon-McCartney of late disco who tightened up, clarified and streamlined disco for its assault on the post-disco world. The cusp of Carter-era optimism before the long night of Reaganite repression. The end of disco and the beginning of rap and house. And disco reformulating itself into the formula for every British group that would storm the gates of MTV. Bernard Edwards and Nile Rodgers were the men who revitalized Diana Ross, re-created Sister Sledge, inspired Tom Tom Club and showed Madonna exactly how to do it. This was the voice that Madonna-Abdul-Jackson would all imitate. The inspiration for a decade of sampling and the return of interesting guitar work. The history of post-Beatles rock could be summarized in seven syllables: Led Zeppelin, Ramones, Chic.

''Rapper's Delight'' by the Sugarhill Gang (1979). Rap's first hit was rapped over the instrumental loop from ''Good Times'' and produced by Sylvia Robinson, the ''Company'' of Shirley and Company and, by the way, the Sylvia of Mickey and Sylvia.

''Planet Rock'' by Afrika Bambaataa and Soulsonic Force (1982). Early rap's greatest theorist, rapping here over a sampled ''Trans-Europe Express.''

''Trouble in Paradise'' by Sylvester (1984). Disco was supposed to have disappeared by this point, but the synthesizers are still sizzling here, and Sylvester gives a blistering reading to the post-utopian lyrics. He first surfaced as part of the cross-dressing outrageous bohemian Bay Area glam-rock scene and

bass track. The druggy, hypnotic effect thus induced was closer to groove-and-riff-based funk or avant-garde drone music, though a Eurodisco sense of drama remained. From here the door begins to open on the Eighties.

''Bits and Pieces III, Let's Do It'' (1980). Sometimes disco stretched things out, and sometimes it compressed them to make them new. On this bootleg we discover the cosmic unity of the Beatles, the Everly Brothers, the Four Seasons, James Brown, Lipps, Inc.'s ''Funkytown'' (a 1980 disco hit), and ''Itsy

toured with the Cockettes, but successfully leaped into disco with his gospel-trained, sincerity-charged falsetto, hitting the Top Forty for the second time with "You Make Me Feel (Mighty Real)" in 1979. His death from AIDS in 1988 is a rock-era death as poignant and mythic as a Fifties plane crash victim's, a Sixties drug martyr's or a Seventies anorexic's. Openly gay, direct in expression, positive in direction and more than able to use his gospel roots to translate disco into a live performance, he remains another pop what if?

"Move Your Body" by Marshall Jefferson (1986). It came from Munich—I mean Chicago—when no one was expecting it. It was DJ driven, inspired by an appreciation for the offbeat and fueled by an interaction among black, white, Latino, straight and gay. It was called disco, I mean house. The beat went on.

That's just seventeen of disco's many great and not-so-great moments—full of opportunities, I think, for speculation about the reasons for its popularity. Yet the most interesting thing about disco was not the popularity it gained and lost, or the boredom it induced in many, but the hostility it generated. "Disco sucks" was a popular graffito of the late Seventies, and the same sentiment was more genteelly expressed in much of the rock press. There was even an anti-disco rally at Chicago's Comiskey Park in the summer of 1979. That same year I heard Jackson Browne booed for just introducing a song with the word "disco" in the title at the No Nukes benefit in New York City. Punk may have been aiming for notoriety, but disco got it without trying.

Some of this, unfortunately, was just homophobia, sexism and racism. No pop music had been as directly or openly shaped by gay taste before, and by the time disco came along with its black-white-Latin mix of influences, producers, singers and consumers, rock had long since gone white (except for Stevie Wonder). A related problem was disco's sensuous and sexual feel and its penchant for favoring females on the vocals, as compared to rock's angrier and more aggressively masculine voice. Disco was

uninterested in expressing the male adolescent sexual frustration that still inspired much of rock & roll and would later fuel much of rap. If disco often reduced women (and men) to sex objects, they were available sex objects, not cockteasers who required conquest or exorcism.

But disco had deeper problems when viewed from the perspective of traditional rock. In fact, that was one of them: There *was* a rock tradition. Disco was aware of history; it plundered the pop past for many of its best melodies. But in the beginning, disco was ahistorical. It plundered in order to make something new at a time when rock was most often bent on preserving something old.

There are times when the idea of history in pop is creative. At the beginning of the Seventies it reclaimed much that was good in pre-Beatles rock & roll in a post-Beatles world, and made it possible to preserve a sense of continuity with the golden era of rock, even as that golden era receded into the past. That's one reason why the Band or Carole King were so reassuring at the time. But by the end of the decade this historical sense had become ponderous and pretentious. Symptomatic of the problem were

The Village People muscled their way onto the charts with "Macho Man," a gay goof to those who got the joke, a disco novelty to those who didn't.

Linda Ronstadt's meticulous versions of songs like "Blue Bayou." A well-produced oldie by a contemporary star works once or twice. But after too many times you're keeping alive the letter by killing the spirit. Viewed from this perspective of taste and history, disco's willy-nilly choice of Motown, surf music, Beethoven and Muzak for material must look like a mindless "lowering of standards." Unless you thought the standards were becoming the problem.

By the late Seventies we were awash with so many fools, hacks and clods working the hustle of significance that "significance" itself had become a problem. Punk attacked the impasse with a revolt from below—an honorable rock idea. Disco solved it with an equally honorable pop idea—reducing everything to its surfaces from above, so that the profound and inane have an equal opportunity to stimulate. A good move when it becomes difficult to figure out what is profound and what is inane and you have a glut of both. Punk faced a cluttered culture by trying to destroy it all. Disco greeted it by trying to enjoy it all.

And did so, at least initially, without the elitist irony that often hides inside an interest in the super-

ficial (see Andy Warhol). The past was used whenever it sounded *good,* and if there was a certain glee involved in turning it all into disco, there was not hostility.

Of course, there are problems with this approach. Most obviously, as time goes by, the present with its ability to cannibalize history recedes in time and develops, well, a history. Time creates distance. Performers pull chunks of aesthetics out of a scene for their own purposes. And then the optimism of a glimpsed paradise gets difficult to maintain going down the road. In disco's case the interface of gay and straight, black, white and Latin that propelled it seemed more problematic after a decade of Thatcher and Reagan. The rather guileless hope for upward mobility that was a part of disco's charm felt dated after the more vengeful climb-up of the yuppies and the heartless fallout of the homeless. And of course, the sexual optimism was blunted by AIDS.

But history was also kind to disco. The history of the "disco sucks" era softened as it became clear that real, old, regular rock & roll would survive and anytime a white guy had a hankering he could still find a little "Stairway to Heaven" or "Ramblin' Man" somewhere on the radio dial. Punk stormed the barricades and then fell back stunned when Britain produced Culture Club. So disco didn't conquer rock, and rock didn't conquer disco, and rather than hostile armies, they became more like parallel universes always negotiating a series of mergers and acquisitions. The truce was called in 1983 when Michael "Moonwalk" Jackson had Eddie "Guitar Licks" Halen solo on his 1982 megahit "Beat It" (on the same album that opened with a note from "Soul Makossa"). And peace was declared when the Messiah of Trad Rock, Bruce Springsteen, released a single with "Dancing" in the title in 1984, along with a twelve-inch dance-club remix.

There were continuing possibilities worth exploiting through the doors that disco opened, doors that looked like they were closing during the classicization of rock. It put people back in charge of their record collections, rather than burdened by them. It proved that history could be used to make something new, rather than used to put limits on the present. And it left a lasting institution in the global network of clubs and turntable virtuosos that thrived long after the disco era and continued to mutate and send fresh input back to revitalize the ever-conglomerating central headquarters of culture.

Sure, in the Eighties, a "more realistic" black separatism lay at the core of hard-core rap, a "more realistic," more desperate, less exuberant search for ecstasy motivated disco's stripped-down dance child, house. A "more realistic" wariness informed alternative-college rock. And a "more realistic" cynicism lay at the heart of punk and all its off-spring. But in the Eighties it was still common to employ the cultural strategies developed in the disco era, even if you didn't buy into the utopian fantasy. They were still the strategies with the potential for the broadest cultural reach, which was testified to by the footprints left across the spectrum by the post-disco, disco-derived beat.

Disco displayed a model for public interplay—disco dancing—that depended in the long run less on a shared identity than on a common respect for urban individualism. It created a new space for public movement that did not demand the revival of a counterculture, even if it spawned several.

At its best, disco wasn't really much like a big private club, and certainly not like a family, a commune, a tribe, or a world view. It was like a city street. A place where strangers could interact with one another if they wanted to without having to become like one another. It reminded us that cities aren't just places where people get mugged. If the vibes are right, they're places where people can be stimulated, lots of happy accidents can happen, and even strangers can fall in love.

DISCOGRAPHY

Disco's Heyday
SINGLES
Average White Band: "Pick Up the Pieces" (Atlantic; r☆5, ☆1, 1974). **Bee Gees:** "You Should Be Dancing" (RSO; r☆4, ☆20, 1976). "Stayin' Alive" (RSO; ☆1, 1977). **Brick:** "Dazz" (Bang; r☆1, ☆3, 1976). **Peter Brown:** "Do You Wanna Get Funky with Me" (Drive; r☆3, ☆18, 1977). **B. T. Express:** "Do It ('til You're Satisfied)" (Scepter; r☆1, ☆2, 1974). **Carl Carlton:** "Everlasting Love" (Back Beat; r☆11, ☆6, 1974). **Cerrone:** "Love in 'C' Minor" (Cotillion; r☆29, ☆36, 1977). "Supernature" (Cotillion; r☆72, ☆70, 1978). **Chic:** "Dance, Dance, Dance (Yowsah, Yowsah, Yowsah)" (Atlantic; r☆6, ☆6, 1977). "Le Freak" (Atlantic; r☆1, ☆1, 1978). "Good Times" (Atlantic; r☆1, ☆1, 1979). **C. J. & Co.:** "Devil's Gun" (Westbound; r☆2, ☆36, 1977). **Linda Clifford:** "Runaway Love" b/w "If My Friends Could See Me Now" b/w "Gypsy Lady" (Curtom; r☆3, ☆76, 1978). **Manu Dibango:** "Soul Makossa" (Atlantic; ☆35, 1973). **Disco Tex and the Sex-O-Lettes:** "Get Dancin'" (Chelsea; r☆32, ☆10, 1974). **Double Exposure:** "Ten Percent" (Salsoul; r☆63, ☆54, 1976). **Carol Douglas:** "Doctor's Orders" (Midland International; r☆9, ☆11, 1974). **Dr. Buzzard's Original Savannah Band:** "Whispering/Cherchez la Femme/C'est Si Bon" (RCA;

r☆31, ☆27, 1976). **Ecstasy, Passion & Pain:** "Ask Me" (Roulette; r☆19, ☆93, 1974). **Gloria Gaynor:** "Never Say Goodbye" (MGM; r☆34, ☆9, 1974). **Dan Hartman:** "Instant Replay" (Blue Sky; r☆44, ☆29, 1978). **Patrick Hernandez:** "Born to Be Alive" (Columbia; r☆53, ☆16, 1979). **Hues Corporation:** "Rock the Boat" (RCA; r☆2, ☆1, 1974). **Willie Hutch:** "Love Power" (Motown; ☆41, 1975). **Michael Jackson:** "Don't Stop 'til You Get Enough" (Epic; r☆1, ☆1, 1979). "Rock with You" (Epic; r☆1, ☆1, 1979). **Jackson 5:** "Dancin' Machine" (Motown; r☆1, ☆2, 1974). **Grace Jones:** "I Need a Man" (Beam Junction; ☆83, 1977). **K. C. & the Sunshine Band:** "Get Down Tonight" (T.K.; r☆1, ☆1, 1975). "That's the Way (I Like It)" (T.K.; r☆1, ☆1, 1975). "(Shake, Shake, Shake) Shake Your Booty" (T.K.; r☆1, ☆1, 1976). **Eddie Kendricks:** "Keep On Truckin'" (Tamla; ☆1, 1973). "Boogie Down" (Tamla; ☆2, 1974). **Kool and the Gang:** "Ladies Night" (De-Lite; r☆1, ☆8, 1979). **Labelle:** "Lady Marmalade" (Epic; ☆1, 1975). **D. C. La Rue:** "Cathedrals" (Pyramid; r☆3, ☆94, 1976). **Love & Kisses:** "Thank God It's Friday" (Casablanca; r☆23, ☆22, 1978). **Love Unlimited Orchestra:** "Love's Theme" (20th Century; ☆1, 1973). **Van McCoy & the Soul City Symphony:** "The Hustle" (Avco; r☆1, ☆1, 1975). **George McCrae:** "Rock Your Baby" (T.K.; r☆1, ☆1, 1974). **Gwen McCrae:** "Rockin' Chair" (Cat; r☆1, ☆9, 1975). **Harold Melvin and the Blue Notes:** "The Love I Lost" (Philadelphia International; ☆7, 1973). **MFSB Featuring the Three Degrees:** "TSOP (The Sound of Philadelphia)" (Philadelphia International; r☆1, ☆1, 1974). **Musique:** "In the Bush" (Prelude; r☆29, ☆58, 1978). **Odyssey:** "Native New Yorker" (RCA; r☆6, ☆21, 1977). **Ohio Players:** "Skin Tight" (Mercury; r☆2, ☆13, 1974). **O'Jays:** "Love Train" (Philadelphia International; ☆1, 1973). "I Love Music" (Philadelphia International; ☆5, 1975). **Peaches and Herb:** "Shake Your Groove Thing" (Polydor; r☆4, ☆5, 1978). **People's Choice:** "Do It Any Way You Wanna" (TSOP; r☆1, ☆11, 1975). **Billy Preston:** "Will It Go Round in Circles" (A&M; ☆1, 1973). **Lou Rawls:** "You'll Never Find Another Love Like Mine" (Philadelphia International; r☆1, ☆2, 1976). **Ritchie Family:** "Brazil" (20th Century; r☆13, ☆11, 1975). **Rolling Stones:** "Miss You" (Rolling Stones; ☆1, 1978). **Rose Royce:** "Car Wash" (MGM; ☆1, 1977). **Diana Ross:** "Love Hangover" (Motown; r☆1, ☆1, 1976). "The Boss" (Motown; r☆12, ☆19, 1979). **Shalamar:** "Uptown Festival" (Soul Train; r☆10, ☆25, 1977). **Silver Convention:** "Fly, Robin, Fly" (Midland International; r☆1, ☆1, 1975). **Sister Sledge:** "He's the Greatest Dancer" (Cotillion; r☆1, ☆9, 1979). "We Are Family" (Cotillion; r☆1, ☆2, 1979). **Gino Soccio:** "Dancer" (Warner Bros.; r☆60, ☆6, 1979). **Edwin Starr:** "Contact" (20th Century Fox; r☆13, ☆65, 1979). **Rod Stewart:** "Da Ya Think I'm Sexy?" (Warner Bros.; ☆1, 1978). **Donna Summer:** "Love to Love You Baby" (Oasis; r☆3, ☆2, 1975). "I Feel Love" (Casablanca; r☆9, ☆6, 1977). "MacArthur Park Suite" (Casablanca; r☆8, ☆1, 1978). "Hot Stuff" (Casablanca; r☆3, ☆1, 1979). "Bad Girls" (Casablanca; r☆1, ☆1, 1979). **Sylvester:** "You Make Me Feel Mighty Real" b/w "Dance (Disco Heat)" (Fantasy; r☆20, ☆19, 1978). **Taste of Honey:** "Boogie Oogie Oogie" (Capitol; r☆1, ☆1, 1978). **Tavares:** "Check It Out" (Capitol; ☆35, 1973). "Heaven Must Be Missing an Angel" (Capitol; ☆15, 1976). **Trammps:** "That's Where the Happy People Go" (Atlantic; r☆12, ☆27, 1976). "Disco Inferno" (Atlantic; r☆9, ☆1, 1977). **Andrea True Connection:** "More, More, More" (Buddah; ☆4, 1976). **Barry White:** "I'm Gonna Love Ya Just a Little More Baby" (20th Century; ☆3, 1973). "You're the First, the Last, My Everything" (20th Century; r☆1, ☆2, 1974). **Wild Cherry:** "Play That Funky Music" (Epic/Sweet City; r☆1, ☆1, 1976). **Karen Young:** "Hot Shot" (West End; r☆24, ☆67, 1978).

ANTHOLOGIES
The Disco Years, Volumes 1 & 2 (Rhino; 1990). *The Disco Years, Volumes 3–5* (Rhino; 1992). *The Best of T.K. Records* (Rhino; 1990). *Billboard Top Dance Hits 1976–1980, Vols. 1–5* (Rhino; 1992).

(Chart positions compiled from Joel Whitburn's *Record Research*, based on *Billboard*'s Pop chart, unless otherwise indicated; r☆ = position on *Billboard*'s Rhythm & Blues chart.)

ALTERNATIVE SCENES: AMERICA

BY KEN TUCKER

At its most adventurous, American alternative rock contradicts the myth that the only worthwhile popular music is made by subliterate teens with nothing more on their minds than girls and inebriants. After all, one result of rock's increased respectability in the Sixties was that its use became sanctioned for everyone, not just rebellious hoods or obsessive nerds: The Beatles made rock safe for suburbia.

If English punk and new wave were born of kids bored with rich rock stars and five-minute guitar solos, then a lot of American new wave erupted because nice young middle-class eccentrics wanted a place within the rock & roll pantheon where they could blow off their peculiar steam, too. And since a central theme of Seventies underground rock was secure-the-means-of-production-by-being-vehemently-simple, lots of peculiar, worthwhile music got made by local bands far removed from any of the major urban media centers. While rockers were hobnobbing with artists in New York City, and while the Eagles and Linda Ronstadt were lying back in L.A., oddballs inland were rousing themselves to the realization that the East's aesthetics and the West's pervasive technology could be applied to other, quirkier ends—or perhaps discarded altogether.

Thus Jonathan Richman, who may be considered a grandnephew of the American new wave. A Lou Reed fan from the quintessential Boston suburb of Needham, Richman formed the Modern Lovers in 1970, installing himself as lead singer and songwriter. This was nervy, since Richman's voice was an earnest quaver he seemed unable or, more likely, unwilling to control (on his third album he even put the word ''sings'' in quotation marks after his name). Even nervier was Richman's songwriting, which stored great faith in the evocative power of the commonplace. But out of the most overworked of American themes—the road odyssey—Richman wrote an unquestioned classic, ''Road Runner,'' which uncovered what may have been the last primordial guitar riff to be located in rock and which was suffused with an innocent exhilaration at sim-

Jonathan Richman: "We have to learn to play with nothing, with our guitars broken, and it's raining."

ply being young and alive in a car. Richman and his Modern Lovers epitomize the idea that you can make vital pop music without being popular, that you can work within a mass form without ever reaching too many of the masses.

Such cultural paradoxes came easily to bored youth from the Ohio suburbs of Akron and Cleveland, two industrialized cities where a generation of kids with money to burn from working in the factories turned to rock & roll just for the hell of it. As punk exploded in England, a similar spirit arose simultaneously—and independently—among rock fans in Ohio. Fanzines and alternative record shops proliferated, as did indigenous bands. The archetype was Cleveland's Pere Ubu.

In 1975 Peter Laughner, an obsessive rock fan and occasional reviewer for *Creem*, forged Pere Ubu in his own artfully confused image—a clanging concatenation of avant humor and hard sincerity—but he died two years later, just as the band's first album was completed.

That debut, *The Modern Dance*, set the tone for all of vanguard punk, as intense impenetrabilities were declaimed by lead singer David Thomas, a sort of overgrown Little Lord Fauntleroy who once called himself Crocus Behemoth, and who sings in a wailing plaint. Although their sound is as gray and sere as the landscape they live on, and their song titles full of political implications ("Non-Alignment Pact," "Chinese Radiation," Laughner's mock manifesto "Life Stinks"), social commentary is scarcely Pere Ubu's point. Like the Alfred Jarry play from which the quintet took their name, Ubu sprawls across all of contemporary culture, joshing and sneezing on the best and worst of it with equal, nearly demented, fervor. *Modern Dance* and the band's second album, *Dub Housing* (1979), work best as rock versions of Kurt Schwitters's collages in the Thirties: chance assemblages of trash and art, unnerving for their contextual calm in the face of formal chaos. Self-parodic, driven, austere and ribald, Pere Ubu presents itself as the cutting edge of nothing at all, making their own eccentric rock as if there were no other way to do it.

The rest of Ohio-bred new wave separates into

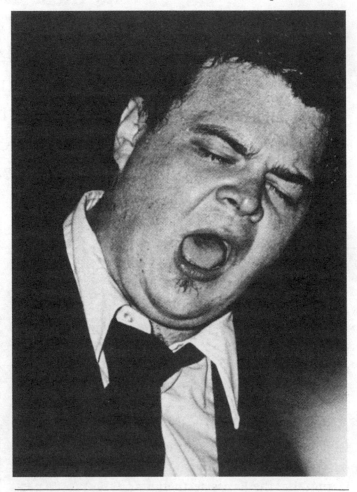

David Thomas, a.k.a. Crocus Behemoth, front man for Ohio's Pere Ubu, makers of terrifying rock & roll.

three categories: the arty (Devo, Tin Huey, Human Switchboard), the profane (the Bizarros, the Dead Boys, the Rubber City Rebels) and the poppy (Rachel Sweet). In a reversal of usual commercial patterns, it was the arty ones who landed big-label contracts. Not that it did them any good, of course; even the biggest seller among them, the mechanistic-minded Devo, relocating to Los Angeles, remained a cult act whose initial inspiration—to make dehumanization fun—became more constricting with time.

Devo, another Ohio band, showing that lobotomies can be fun.

Of course, Los Angeles will disorient anyone, including its natives. As a bastion of establishment rock, it took a while for L.A. to develop an alternative-rock scene to compare with Manhattan's, but when it did, hoo boy, this was some alternative. New York punk, from the Jackson Pollock splatterings of the Ramones to the Warholesque Blondie, was an East Village art statement as much as it was music. L.A. punk had no such pretensions—it offered free-floating hostility that occasionally deigned to be music. David Byrne, as leader of Talking Heads the archetypal New York art punk, knew whereof he spoke when he told *Musician* magazine in 1981 that in Los Angeles, "you find punks who really are punks: mean as hell, and not just the creators of an interesting persona."

Thus L.A. bands like the Germs, Black Flag, the Circle Jerks and Fear presided over concerts whose primary goal was to turn into fist-flying melees. Performers heaped lyrical abuse on money, sex, Holly-

wood and the sun, while pale, skinheaded fans slam danced, colliding and bouncing off each other, cracking cartilage and bruising bones. Music clubs ranging from suburban holes-in-the-wall to legends like the Whisky a Go Go rapidly learned to put away the chairs and tables when a local punk act was booked; the fetid dance floor became "the pit," in which sweat and blood saturated the air. L.A. punk was performance music; records capture little of its essence. A better document of this era is director Penelope Spheeris's 1981 documentary *The Decline of Western Civilization*.

Then, too, L.A. punk was, for the most part, a self-indulgent hoax. Its adherents screamed about the decadence and hypocrisy of their elders, but follow any one of the hoarse thugs home and chances were it was to either a tidy little suburban home shaded by palm trees or a manse straight out of *Dynasty*. Still, one great band emerged from this mess: X. Led by husband-and-wife poets Exene Cervenka and John Doe, propelled by the rockabilly-on-speed style of guitarist Billy Zoom and the hammering drums of D. J. Bonebrake, X made harsh yet vivid music that gave shape and drama to punk anomie.

X's first two releases, *Los Angeles* and *Wild Gift,* are albums that simultaneously embody and transcend the West Coast punk ethos. Two other notable L.A.-based acts to emerge around this time coexisted among the punks without ever surrendering to them: the Blasters, led by brothers Phil and Dave Alvin, made a mixture of R&B, rockabilly and country music that was swampy enough to summon up memories of Creedence Clearwater Revival; Los Lobos was a Mexican-American outfit that played south-of-the-border folk music with a punk intensity as well as a talent for lovely, novelistic lyrics.

Up the California coast, in San Francisco, a cadre of conceptualists formed the Residents, a (literally) faceless band that brought Frank Zappa up to date: infantile pop-cult parody mixed with subtle musicianship, creating some of the most affably unlistenable music ever recorded.

Across the country the South had its own brand of new music. Athens, Georgia, was full of smart bohemians ready to capitalize on the do-it-yourself imperative implied in punk. Bands in this neck of the woods ranged from the moody but accessible R.E.M. to the moody but inaccessible Pylon. Not moody at all were the B-52's, who came together for

Black Flag visits New York's Mudd Club in 1982, where singer Henry Rollins incited a riot with his Magilla Gorilla impersonation.

the purest of rock & roll reasons: to amuse themselves at parties. The group cut an independent single in 1978 called "Rock Lobster" that made them overnight cult sensations; critics from New York to L.A. found its hip-shaking rhythms and the comically flat, ironic voice of Fred Schneider a real stitch. Then it turned out that the group was a riot onstage: Schneider danced like his back didn't have no bone, while vocalists Cindy Wilson and Kate Pierson liked to wear psychedelic-colored beehive wigs roughly the size and angle of the Leaning Tower of Pisa. Snapped up by Warner Bros., the B-52's settled into a cult stardom that was just this side of obscurity. The band's original guitarist, Ricky Wilson, died of AIDS in 1985; he never lived to see the band become bona fide pop stars with its 1989 release, *Cosmic Thing*, which contained the slinky hit single, "Love Shack."

In response to this regional activity, local fans began coming out of the closet. Kids all over the country decided to play Record Promotion: If the big boys wouldn't sign up their local bands, the fans would, with a vengeance. Photocopied manifestos and homemade fanzines multiplied and pushed burgeoning local scenes; they plugged cherished un-

The B-52's from Atlanta: their original lineup, with Ricky Wilson *(center)*.

knowns and finessed an ad hoc network for distributing their records. This was a place for literary eccentrics to flourish; *(blank)*, an Ohio fanzine, got the word out about Tin Huey, Devo and the deluge, and at least one fanzine became nearly as well known as the music it promoted: New York's *Punk* showcased the spindly, agreeably misanthropic cartoons of John Holmstrom and made a perverted folk hero of one Legs McNeil, a feisty fuckup whose reputation was based on his utterance of gnomic know-nothingisms and his drunken brawls with the leading lights of his day.

Toward the end of the Seventies the eccentricities of the new wave finally had a substantial commercial impact. First off the assembly line were the Cars, a Boston quintet that employed flat vocals, loopy guitars and swooshy, pitter-pattering Syndrums, courtesy of ex–Modern Lover David Robinson. If the thick, stoned-mechanic vocals of Benjamin Orr drew the band into the middle of the hard-rock road, it was Robinson's cold, crisp percussion and leader Ric Ocasek's disaffected lyrics that kept them swerving onto the shoulder of rock modernism: ''Alienation is the craze,'' wrote Ocasek in ''Double Life,'' a craze that the Cars made slicker and hipper than ever.

As overseen by Queen's producer Roy Thomas Baker, the Cars for all their eclecticism had a trademark sound from the first, and their debut album yielded no less than four hit singles. But the followup, 1979's *Candy-O,* was cold to the point of freezing: Icy organ lines, shrill Syndrums and aridly abstract lyrics denied the hotsy languor promised by the album's Vargas pinup cover.

Nonetheless, the precision of the Cars' music and its resulting popular success made record companies realize the potential in streamlining new-wave energy. This begat the Knack, pop rockers with an edge of sleazy cynicism that titillated teenagers for at least as long as their first single, ''My Sharona.'' The quartet pandered to its audience with chilling feroc-

Exene Cervenka and John Doe of X, tripping the dark fantastic.

The Knack, who proved that the new power pop wasn't above sleazy cynicism.

ity; their second album title, . . . *But the Little Girls Understand* (1980), indicated how desperate they were to convince themselves that *someone* out there thought that the rancid little nasties they used as lyrics were important to at least one segment of the rock audience.

But little girls would understand the generous simple truths of Jonathan Richman just as well, if they ever got a chance to hear them. In the end, the Knack's presumption of what-they-want-to-hear was a betrayal of the energy and integrity that have made the new wave and alternative rock in America so provocative.

By the mid-Eighties new wave was old hat, and punk had either softened into pop or hardened into speed metal; new wave–punk's stylistic innovations had either been absorbed into the mainstream or become the stubborn mechanisms of musicians who rejected the mainstream in favor of the sort of cult status that could sustain a career on the strength of a network of alternative and college radio stations, music clubs and a vigorous fan press.

The Cars, from Boston.

DISCOGRAPHY

ALBUMS

B-52's: *The B-52's* (Warner Bros.; ☆59, 1979). *Wild Planet* (Warner Bros.; ☆18, 1980). *Party Mix!* (Warner Bros.; ☆55, 1981). *Mesopotamia* (Warner Bros.; ☆35, 1982). *Whammy!* (Warner Bros.; ☆29, 1983). *Bouncing off the Satellites* (Warner Bros.; ☆85, 1986). *Cosmic Thing* (Reprise; ☆4, 1989). *Good Stuff* (Reprise; ☆16, 1992). **Cars:** *The Cars* (Elektra; 1978). *Candy-O* (Elektra; 1979). *Panorama* (Elektra; ☆5, 1980). *Shake It Up* (Elektra; ☆9, 1981). *Heartbeat City* (Elektra; ☆3, 1984). *Door to Door* (Elektra; ☆26, 1987). **Dead Boys:** *Young, Loud & Snotty* (Sire; 1977). *We Have Come for Your Children* (Sire; 1978). **Devo:** *Are We Not Men? We Are Devo* (Warner Bros.; 1978). *Duty Now for the Future* (Warner Bros.; 1979). *Freedom of Choice* (Warner Bros.; 1980). *DEV-O Live* (Warner Bros.; ☆50, 1981). *New Traditionalists* (Warner Bros.; ☆23, 1981). *Oh, No! It's Devo* (Warner Bros.; ☆47, 1982). *Shout* (Warner Bros.; ☆83, 1984). *E-Z Listening Disc* (Rykodisc; 1987). *Total Devo* (Restless; 1988). *Smoothnoodlemaps* (Enigma; 1990). **Knack:** *Get the Knack* (Capitol; 1979). *. . . But the Little Girls Understand* (Capitol; 1980). *Round Trip* (Capitol; ☆93, 1981). **Ric Ocasek:** *Beatitude* (Geffen; ☆28, 1983). *This Side of Paradise* (Geffen; ☆31, 1986). **Pere Ubu:** *The Modern Dance* (Blank; 1977). *Datapanik in the Year Zero* (Radar; EP, 1978). *Dub Housing* (Chrysalis; 1979). *New Picnic Time* (Rough Trade; 1979). *The Art of Walking* (Rough Trade; 1981). *390 Degrees of Simulated Stereo* (Rough Trade; 1981). *Song of the Bailing Man* (Rough Trade; 1982). *Terminal Tower: An Archival Collection* (Twin/Tone; 1985). *The Tenement Year* (Enigma; 1988). *Worlds in Collision* (Fontana, 1991). **Jonathan Richman and the Modern Lovers:** *Chartbusters* (Beserkley; 1975). *Modern Lovers* (Beserkley; 1976). *Rock and Roll with the Modern Lovers* (Beserkley; 1977). *Modern Lovers "Live"* (Beserkley; 1978). *Back in Your Life* (Beserkley; 1979). *The Jonathan Richman Songbook* (Beserkley; 1980). *Jonathan Sings!* (Sire; 1983). *Rockin' and Romance* (Twin/Tone; 1985). *It's Time for Jonathan Richman and the Modern Lovers* (Upside; 1986). *Modern Lovers 88* (Rounder; 1987). *The Beserkley Years: The Best of Jonathan Richman and the Modern Lovers* (Rhino; 1987). **Rachel Sweet:** *Fool Around* (Stiff/Columbia; 1979). *Protect the Innocent* (Stiff/Columbia; 1980). *Fool Around: The Best of Rachel Sweet* (Rhino; 1992). **X:** *Wild Gift* (Slash; ☆165, 1981). *Under the Big Black Sun* (Elektra; ☆76, 1982). *More Fun in the New World* (Elektra; ☆86, 1983). *Ain't Love Grand?* (Elektra, 1985). *See How We Are* (Elektra; ☆107, 1987). *Live at the Whisky a Go Go on the Fabulous Sunset Strip* (Elektra; ☆175, 1988).

(Chart positions compiled from Joel Whitburn's *Record Research*, based on *Billboard*'s LPs chart.)

ALTERNATIVE SCENES: BRITAIN

BY KEN TUCKER

By the early Seventies a new wave in Britain was not only welcome but rather overdue. Bands as different as Yes and Roxy Music may have given fresh form to pop style, and Led Zeppelin's Jimmy Page may have given fresh life to writing blues chords, but for many listeners the heavy-metal and art-rock hybrids had become monstrous, breeding debilitating self-consciousness, artiness for artiness' sake and careerism contemptuous of audiences numbering less than a thousand.

Or, at least, so thought the young dart throwers who hung out in London-area pubs and made both music and philosophy on the inspiration of ale. Suddenly this mood coalesced into a Scene, with musicians forming bands that used pubs like the Hope and Anchor and the Tally Ho as greenhouses for a sprightlier hybrid: a rollicking mixture of old-style rock & roll, careening honky-tonk and the insouciant amateurism of good-timey skiffle bands. The groups that resulted took names that suggest the toothy modesty of their endeavor—Eggs Over Easy, Bees Make Honey, Chilli Willi and the Red Hot Peppers, Help Yourself, Bontemps Roulez.

The foresighted entrepreneur of what came to be called the pub-rock movement was Dave Robinson, a wily, aggressive lout who installed a recording studio right on the premises of the Hope and Anchor in an effort to corner the market on what he heard as the Next Big Thing. Robinson went on to manage singer-songwriter Graham Parker and in 1976 would cofound Stiff Records—"The World's Most Flexible Record Label"—with an even more aggressive, wily lout, Jake Riviera. Stiff recorded everyone from Elvis Costello to one Humphrey Ocean ("Whoops-a-Daisy" b/w "Davy Crockett"), and Stiff's wiseacre good taste set a sweetly sneering tone for the entire new wave.

The foresighted band of the era was Brinsley

Schwarz, who'd been busy denying Heaviness since forming in 1969 and whose capacious country rock was embroidered with the intricate imagery of songwriter-singer Nick Lowe and the sly, snaking lines of guitarist Brinsley Schwarz. Together with keyboardist Bob Andrews, drummer Billy Rankin and later guitarist-songwriter Ian Gomm, the band attracted a legion of fans that exceeded pub size: Brinsley Schwarz became stars in a genre that spurned stardom.

The United States was another matter; even for this band, dedicated to hardworking humility, America was an irresistible challenge for conquest. Going for nothing short of a coup, their manager (none other than Dave Robinson) flew 150 British journalists to New York's Fillmore East in 1970 to see his band third-billed to Van Morrison and Quicksilver Messenger Service. The grand gesture backfired, with press reports depicting the Brinsleys as alternately pathetic and arrogant.

Certainly they were neither. At worst, in mastering the lyricism of American country rock they had also picked up its folkie languor: Lowe's ''Ebury Down'' and ''Old Jarrow'' are long, baleful acoustic ballads that whine into the ozone. But there is also his ''Country Girl,'' a creamy *Sweetheart of the Rodeo* spoof made moving by its plaintive vocal and swooping fiddle solo. Brinsley Schwarz never made the leap into transcendent passion that the Byrds achieved with Gram Parsons, but it was gratifying to hear their initial perky charm deepen, by their seventh and last album, into the intense perplexity of Lowe's ''(What's So Funny 'Bout) Peace, Love and Understanding,'' as the band came to question even the mild utopianism of the pub scene that had lent them prominence.

The pub wave was a frothy little one that crested at a time when Britain's economic and social troubles still seemed manageable. This optimism dampened quickly, with many unemployed kids finding escape in the soaring nihilism of punk rock. In the face of this, however, pub rock had established a haven where apolitical eccentrics like Lowe, Ian Dury and Dave Edmunds could continue to thrive even after the form's popularity had waned.

The one performer who straddled pub rock and punk was Graham Parker, whose music remains tempestuously articulate. Born working-class angry in Hackney, Parker wrote songs while pumping petrol and played in R&B bands with names like the Blackrockers and the Deepcut Three. A diminutive, peevish-looking fellow whose shoulders hunched as protectively as a lobster's carapace, Parker released his smoldering resentment in songs of yammering eloquence, sung in a raspy croon that swallowed whole words in moments of high passion. Unlike that of so many rock & roll trouble boys, Parker's anger wasn't often directed at girls; it was his station in life that he was fed up with: ''Don't Ask Me Questions,'' a jittery reggae rocker from his debut album, *Howlin' Wind* (1976), insisted upon trading peeves, both petty and profound, with God himself.

Parker was accompanied by the Rumour, a wonder band composed of two ex-Brinsleys (Bob Andrews and Schwarz himself), two ex–Bontemps Roulez (drummer Steve Goulding and bassist Andrew Bodnar) and one ex–Duck Deluxe (guitarist Martin Belmont). The interplay between Parker and the Rumour was inspired: They led him away from the bluesy dolor and onto a pounding rock style where his beseeching vocals and hard-boiled imagery glinted with both amusement and ominousness.

Graham Parker tests his will. A volatile singer of vehement songs, he was the one performer who straddled the extremes of British new wave, from pub rock to neo-punk.

Parker, in turn, gave the band a headlong propulsiveness they lacked on their own Rumour albums.

Howlin' Wind, produced by Nick Lowe, made Parker an instant star in England, but the four albums released on the American label Mercury got him scant recognition here. In retaliation, Parker tied onto a new record company, and his first release was a fit of a single called "Mercury Poisoning." Avoiding niggling vengeance, however, was his next album, *Squeezing Out Sparks* (1979), whose "Discovering Japan" was one of the decade's most prodigious rockers: Galloping alongside Goulding's drum-hooves, Parker decried a *nouvelle vague* film that exceeds *Breathless* for romantic jump cuts, as the seduction of Graham's love object is compared to a tourist's exploration of the Orient. Parker eventually relocated to the States and continued to record, without gaining chart success but maintaining a loyal following of fans.

If Parker is new-wave rock's Godard, polemical and sentimental with simultaneous vehemence, Dave Edmunds was its Chabrol, alternately enlivening and embalming the cherished archetypes of his form. Most archetypal for Edmunds were Chuck Berry, who proffered the chords, and Sam Phillips's Sun Records, which proffered an ideal atmosphere. His big U.S. hit was "I Hear You Knocking" (1970), in which the stark contrast between the sole, sinuous blues riff and the triple-tracking of his nasal howl suggested a neurotic crankiness that was a novel twist on Smiley Lewis's morose original.

In 1975 Edmunds hooked up with Lowe, guitarist Billy Bremner (ex-Fatso; as it happens, that's a band, but Bremner does tend to be chubby) and drummer Terry Williams to form a flesh-and-blood Rockpile, as opposed to the all-Edmunds studio Rockpile from which the title of his first solo album two years before had been taken.

Rockpile made its American debut in 1976 as the opening act for Bad Company. Since their sizzling jocularity was a singularly inappropriate complement to that band's cumbersome hard rock, Edmunds and company were off the tour within three weeks. Instead of interpreting this affair as another U.S. debacle, Lowe was convinced that he and Edmunds must be doing something right, and Rockpile

pursued its rockabilly revisionism until it yielded at least one small masterpiece: Edmunds's cover of Elvis Costello's "Girls Talk," in which the gusting guitars propelled Edmunds's voice along the top of the mix like the puck in an air-hockey game.

Lowe's offhand comment about the Sex Pistols— "It didn't really matter if they could or couldn't play"—is the most succinct analysis ever made of punk rock as a phenomenon, and it is typical of this arch-ironist's laconic intelligence: Nick Lowe is the best performing rock critic since Pete Townshend, even if his finest performances have taken place in the recording studio. Lowe's years with Brinsley Schwarz seem to have left him cynical but not jaded. When that band broke up, Lowe came into his own as a producer, and his songwriting improved dramatically. Instead of the country-rock miniaturism Lowe favored as a Brinsley, his solo work has alternated between prankish, prickly rockers and exquisitely ambivalent ballads.

His parodies are inspired for both their range and accuracy. "Snuff Rock," a 1977 Stiff EP recorded under the name Alberto y Lost Trios Paranoias, was so timely that many of the few Americans who heard it assumed it was a piece of genuine scurrilousness; as the phantom kilt of the Tartan Horde, his glowing "Bay City Rollers We Love You" evinced not a hint of sarcasm for its subject and went to Number One in Japan. Floating above parody was "Marie Provost," a delicate skewing of pop melodiousness that just happened to concern a silent-film star eaten alive by her pet dachsund, an anecdote Lowe gleaned from Kenneth Anger's book *Hollywood Babylon.*

Beyond his artful larks, Lowe is a producer whose unpretentiousness yields bold, crisp, exhilarating effects. The rhythm section always predominates, while even the toughest vocals are often echoed into poignant dreaminess; this was as true of his work with Elvis Costello and the Attractions as it was of his salvage job on thick punkers like the Damned.

On his own early solo records Lowe offered self-conscious romantics in late-Seventies rock a new way out by suggesting that ironic distance is an implicit, even necessary, ingredient in a love song. And even at his most parodic, Lowe acknowledged both the pain and elation of even the most superficial infatuations. This is where his trashy, low-culture instincts illuminate his irony: He's always been eager to describe his basest emotions—lust,

unwarranted pride, mean jealousy—with some special degree of understanding.

It could be argued that England's new wave had its biggest impact in America with two very different acts: Elvis Costello and the Attractions, and the Police. In 1977 Costello's *My Aim Is True* was a strong debut: pretty melodies and artfully complex lyrics sung and played with urgent vigor. But his first time out, Costello was backed by an American country-rock outfit, Clover (the band gave its usual lead singer, Huey Lewis, the day off); for his second release, *This Year's Model* (1978), Costello assembled the Attractions, a band that delivered his increasingly dense, impassioned songs of "revenge and guilt" with nerve-rattling vehemence. Nerdy in appearance, imperiously rude in manner, Costello came on like the Avenging Dork, turning out one brilliant song, one staggering album, after another. So prolific he could afford to fill 1980's *Get Happy!!* with eighteen (along with two covers) brief, original homages to American R&B, Costello was a brilliant performer, a critics' darling and, in the United States at least, a commercial flop. For all the influence of his intelligence and his attitude, Costello has risen above American cult status only minimally.

"Monumental Bedroom? . . . Majestic Bedroom? . . . Royal Bedroom? . . ."

Like Costello, the Police tried hard to break through in America by barnstorming the country, playing tiny clubs in an effort to get people to listen to songs that weren't being played much on Ameri-

can radio. Unlike Costello, the Police succeeded. Singer-bassist Sting, guitarist Andy Summers and drummer Stewart Copeland achieved great popularity by associating themselves with the cutting edge of new wave while employing the most old-wave of pop strategies: catchy melodies on their albums, (dyed) blond hair on their heads. Adorned with hooks that alternated reggae rhythms and jazzy interludes, sung by Sting in a scratchy tenor that inspired audience screams, Police songs from "Roxanne" to "Every Breath You Take" were irresistible and held up to relentless airplay once they did crack AOR radio. After *Synchronicity* (1983) the group drifted apart. Copeland and Summers released solo albums trivial and self-indulgent in the manner of most superstar-groups-gone-solo. Sting thrived: He launched a respectable acting career *(Brimstone and Treacle, Plenty, Stormy Monday)* and released solo albums that contained sententious philosophizing combined with pop jazz: solid middlebrow hit making.

Scores of other acts used punk's energy to revital-

ize traditional rock themes. Intermittently triumphant were petulant brats like Wreckless Eric (awkward adolescence apotheosized) and Joe Jackson (a stylized con man). The Tom Robinson Band sang folk liberalisms like "Sing If You're Glad to Be

The Police juice up in 1977.

Gay" that were considered new wave by some, but surely Robinson's hit "2-4-6-8 Motorway" is the sort of sappy singalong Sid Vicious died to expiate.

Much better were jokers like the Rezillos, whose airy romanticism yanked itself to earth with power-pop force on a single like "I Can't Stand My Baby"; better still were the Pretenders, who employed the startling voice of Chrissie Hynde—a sort of vehement quaver—to make Ray Davies's "Stop Your Sobbing" sound like a happy meeting place for new wave and feminism.

From all these performers it will be noted that new wave was not the holocaustic fresh start that punk rock wanted to be. New wave was more concerned with stripping rock down to its early fast tempo and functional instrumentation. It was also eager to introduce new influences. What country & western was to pub rock, for instance, reggae was to new wave: a rhythm that came with its own set of cultural referents to be either decorated or denied as the rocker saw fit.

E very pop trend seems to inspire a vehement reaction, and as the Eighties proceeded, the larky bohemianism of pub rock and the raw anger of punk were replaced by a grim, cold artiness by any number of stiff upper lips. Certainly Joy Division was determined to live up to the bitter irony of its name, the term the Nazis used for the concentration-camp brothels they maintained. Group leader Ian Curtis wrote and sang songs of unknowable dread, while the band played oppressively heavy beats and distorted, jangling chords. The music was more bleak than that of its closest competitor, the Sex Pistols, but it was also far more florid and dour. It might have been possible to dismiss Curtis's dolor as mere self-pity had he not hanged himself in 1980: He was barely twenty-two, and Joy Division was hours away from beginning its first American tour. Against all odds and rock history, the rest of the band regrouped under a different name, New Order, and made different, frequently superior, music. New Order became the creators of a beautiful paradox: They made serious dance music, disco that had courted doom and conquered it.

These musicians hailed from Manchester, a Northern England industrial city as depressed and sere as Joy Division's music. By the end of the Eight-

Sting curls up in bed while researching titles for his autobiography.

Still Life: New Order relaxes around the kitchen table.

ies this area would provoke yet another reaction: the aggressive neo-psychedelia of bands like Happy Mondays and Inspiral Carpets. And between these two extremes of style, you can locate any number of contemporary English bands, from the Leeds group the Gang of Four (makers of harsh, brittle songs with Marxist conundrums for lyrics) to Wire (jittery, precise, neurotic ranting) to the Cure (charming pop cynics; college-age fans loved singer Robert Smith for the way he mated Kafka with Sylvia Plath: absurdist, absurdly romantic gloom).

In some ways, the archetypal act as this sort of music moved into the Eighties was the Smiths, who spent the last half of the decade showcasing its lead singer, the mono-named Morrissey. He moaned in a tenor voice that veered into a wobbly falsetto and wrote lyrics that were essentially worked-up diary entries. But Morrissey gave great interviews, promoting vegetarianism and celibacy; Morrissey is what would have happened if Bertie Wooster and David Bowie had had a son. The Smiths' other asset was guitarist Johnny Marr, who gave the group's music an energy and directness that Morrissey did his best to obscure.

From pub to post-punk, the most interesting English pop musicians in the Seventies and Eighties were utterly unconcerned with the idea of the rock audience as a community that the artist strives to keep united, a common assumption even among decadent hell-raisers like the Rolling Stones. What links key figures like Nick Lowe, Elvis Costello, Robert Smith and Morrissey is that they're all aggressive loners who appeal to the loner in each of us. Their essential admonition boils down to ''Go on your own nerve and try to have some kicks doing it.'' And there's nothing new about that advice at all.

DISCOGRAPHY

ALBUMS

Brinsley Schwarz: *Brinsley Schwarz* (British UA; 1970). *Despite It All* (British UA; 1970). *Silver Pistol* (British UA; 1972). *Nervous on the Road* (British UA; 1973). *Original Golden Oldies* (British UA; 1974). *Please Don't Ever Change* (British UA; 1973). *New Favourites* (British UA; 1974). **Elvis Costello:** *My Aim Is True* (Columbia; ☆32, 1977). *This Year's Model* (Columbia; ☆30, 1978). *Armed Forces* (Columbia; ☆10, 1979). *Get Happy!!* (Columbia; ☆11, 1980). *Taking Liberties* (Columbia; ☆28, 1980). *Trust* (Columbia; ☆28, 1981). *Almost Blue* (Columbia; ☆50, 1981). *Imperial Bedroom* (Columbia; ☆30, 1982). *Punch the Clock* (Columbia; ☆24, 1983). *Good-bye Cruel World* (Columbia; ☆35, 1984). *The Best of Elvis Costello and the Attractions* (Columbia; ☆116, 1985). *King of America* (Columbia; ☆39, 1986). *Blood and Chocolate* (Columbia; ☆84, 1986). *Spike* (Warner Bros.; ☆32, 1989). *Girls!Girls!Girls!* (Columbia; 1990). *Mighty Like a Rose* (Warner Bros.; ☆55, 1991). **Ducks Deluxe:** *Ducks Deluxe* (RCA;

U.K., 1974). *Taxi to the Terminal Zone* (RCA; U.K. 1975). **Dave Edmunds:** *Rockpile* (Mam; 1972). *Subtle as a Flying Mallet* (RCA; 1975). *Get It* (Swan Song; 1977). *Tracks on Wax 4* (Swan Song; 1978). *Repeat When Necessary* (Swan Song; ☆54, 1979). *Twangin'* (Swan Song; ☆48, 1981). *The Best of Dave Edmunds* (Swan Song; ☆163, 1982). *D.E. 7th* (Columbia; ☆46, 1982). *Information* (Columbia; ☆51, 1983). *Riff Raff* (Columbia; ☆140, 1984). *Closer to the Flame* (Capitol; ☆146, 1990). **Nick Lowe:** *Pure Pop for Now People* (Columbia; ☆127, 1978). *Labour of Lust* (Columbia; ☆127, 1978). *Nick the Knife* (Columbia; ☆50, 1982). *The Abominable Showman* (Columbia; ☆129, 1983). *Nick Lowe and His Cowboy Outfit* (Columbia; ☆113, 1984). *The Rose of England* (Columbia; ☆119, 1985). *Pinker and Prouder Than Previous* (Columbia; 1988). *Basher: The Best of Nick Lowe* (Columbia; 1989). *Party of One* (Reprise; ☆182, 1990). **Morrissey:** *Viva Hate* (Sire; ☆48, 1988). *Bona Drag* (Sire; ☆59, 1990). *Kill Uncle* (Sire; ☆52, 1991). **New Order:** *Movement* (Factory; 1981). *Power, Corruption and Lies* (Factus; 1983). *Low-Life* (Qwest; ☆94, 1985). *Brotherhood* (Qwest; ☆117, 1986). *Substance* (Qwest; ☆36, 1987). *Technique* (Qwest; ☆32, 1989). **Graham Parker:** *Howlin' Wind* (Mercury; 1976). *Heat Treatment* (Mercury; ☆169, 1977). *Stick to Me* (Mercury; ☆125, 1977). *The Parkerilla* (Mercury; ☆149, 1978). *Squeezing Out Sparks* (Arista; ☆40, 1979). *The Up Escalator* (Arista; 1980). *Another Grey Area* (Arista; ☆51, 1982). *The Real Macaw* (Arista; ☆59, 1983). *Steady Nerves* (Elektra; ☆57, 1985). *The Mona Lisa's Sister* (RCA; ☆77, 1988). *LIVE! Alone in America* (RCA; 1989). *Human Soul* (RCA; ☆165, 1990). *Struck by Lightning* (RCA; 1991). *Anthology* (Rhino; 1992). **Police:** *Outlandos d'Amour* (A&M; ☆23, 1979). *Regatta de Blanc* (A&M; ☆25, 1979). *Zenyatta Mondatta* (A&M; ☆5, 1980). *Ghost in the Machine* (A&M; ☆2, 1981). *Synchronicity* (A&M; ☆1, 1983). *Every Breath You Take: The Singles* (A&M; ☆7, 1986). **The Rumour:** *Frogs Sprouts Clogs and Krauts* (Arista; ☆160, 1979). **The Smiths:** *The Smiths* (Sire; ☆150, 1984). *Meat Is Murder* (Sire; ☆130, 1985). *The Queen Is Dead* (Sire; ☆70, 1986). *Louder Than Bombs* (Sire; ☆63, 1987). *Strangeways, Here We Come* (Sire; ☆55, 1987). *Rank* (Sire; ☆77, 1988). **Sting:** *The Dream of the Blue Turtles* (A&M; ☆2, 1985). *''. . . Nothing Like the Sun''* (A&M; ☆9, 1987). *Bring On the Night* (A&M; 1986). *The Soul Cages* (A&M; ☆2, 1991).

ANTHOLOGIES

The Stiff Box (Rhino; 1992).

(Chart positions compiled from Joel Whitburn's *Record Research*, based on *Billboard's* LPs chart.)

Morrissey, in a rare lighter moment.

REGGAE

BY ED WARD

R eggae'' is the collective term for a number of successive forms of Jamaican popular music, isolated examples of which have washed onto the shores of the U.S. Top Forty since the early Sixties. Characterized by a loping beat, a strong dose of R&B and recording techniques as original as they are primitive, reggae has since had an impact on rock that is vastly disproportionate to its apparent commercial success.

In a way, this isn't really surprising. When someone used to sluggish rock is confronted with a sensory blitzkreig like Big Youth's ''Screaming Target,'' for instance, with its heavily accented chanting and echoplexed screaming over a track that seems to come and go at will, an immediate reassessment of pop aesthetics seems in order. What in the world is this guy raving about? Isn't there another song buried down there in the mix? What's this conversation at the start about guns and the ''outasite movie Dirty 'arry,'' which segues into a rap about education? Searching out the answers to such questions can lead the quester down the alleyways of an alien world, where familiar assumptions about language, music and religion are all turned upside down. More importantly, it can lead one to a world where pop music is made like it used to be, where a song takes as long to cut as it does to play, where the resulting spontaneity leaps off a record with a long-forgotten immediacy.

Reggae's origins are found in diverse places. African-derived children's games, the ecstatic Christian Pocomania cult, the Garveyite Rastafarians and the style of rhythm & blues played in New Orleans and beamed, in the late Fifties, over clear-channel stations: All these elements have had a role in the development of reggae. These influences did not converge, however, until the introduction of the transistor radio awakened a Jamaican interest in recorded pop music. The island's local stations featured sober programming in the BBC style, but on a clear day one could easily pick up commercial stations in the United States and Cuba broadcasting the hits. From hearing the hits to wanting to make your own is a logical step, and it wasn't long before enterprising Jamaicans started doing just that.

Radios created a demand for music that stations on neither the island nor the mainland could easily respond to, and thus was born the "sound system man." These were electronically inclined entrepreneurs who assembled a "sound system" featuring huge speakers and a generator-powered hi-fi rig that could be mounted on the back of a flatbed truck and hauled out to the country for dances. Fronted by an operator who usually had a classy handle like Prince Buster or Duke Reid, these systems soon created their own followings. Operators competed for the best records, making weekly flights to Miami or New Orleans to pick up test pressings, making sure to have an "exclusive" by scratching off the label information, so no competitor could know where to get another copy.

It wasn't too big a jump for most of the operators from the sound system to a primitive sort of recording studio, and by 1960 there were several on the island. The first recordings were bad copies of New Orleans music—Fats Domino, in particular, was revered in Jamaica. For some reason, Jamaican musicians couldn't get the New Orleans rhythm "right." And, since the only other form of popular music on the island was a jazz-style instrumental music called "mento," there was no alternative but to keep at it, trying to duplicate the subtle swing of the Crescent City jump bands.

Suddenly this task became more urgent, because the early Sixties saw the talent in New Orleans dry up. When imported output dropped, the sound system men were forced to make their own records. Somehow, the "wrong" rhythm triumphed, and ska, Jamaica's first internationally popular music, was born. With its strict, mechanical emphasis on the offbeat (mm-*cha!* mm-*cha!* mm-*cha!* mm-*cha!*), ska took Jamaica by storm.

The first ska groups included the Skatalites, who recorded for the island's first important studio, Coxone Dodd's Studio One. Among the group's members were Ernest Ranglin, the guitarist whose playing helped define the Jamaican style; Tommy McCook, a keyboard artist who probably has been on more sessions in Jamaica than any other musician; and Don Drummond, a moody trombone player who gave the Rastafarian sect its first popular hero

Dancing in the street, Trench Town.

(though mental problems landed him in an institution, where he died in the early Seventies).

Ska took off modestly in the United States with Millie Small's (British-produced) hit "My Boy Lollipop" selling respectably and paving the way for her white Jamaican-born producer, Chris Blackwell, to found Island Records in 1964. Producer Byron Lee took a ska band to the New York World's Fair and fronted it with a teenaged vocalist named Jimmy Cliff, who'd had some Jamaican hits with producer Leslie Kong. And there was a U.S. *Do the Ska* album by Lee, complete with numbered footprints on the cover.

By 1965, in the inexorable Jamaican way, ska was "finish." It was replaced by the slower, even more rhythmic "rock steady," which was better for "rubbin' up a daughter" on the dance floor. Around this time the sound system men escalated their competition by introducing disc jockeys. A DJ would "toast," or talk over, the instrumental B side of a record, improvising rhymes about his own prowess

as a lover and the greatness of the sound system operator. The first successful toaster was Prince Buster, who scored a freak talk-over rock-steady hit in the United States with "Ten Commandments," a sexist classic; but he is better known in Jamaica and Britain for his series of "Judge Dread" records, in which a stern jurist sentences "rude boys"—the Jamaican juvenile delinquents who sang and danced to much of this music—to harsh terms in jail. Rock-steady DJs not only did their toasting live, but recorded the best for posterity. Sir Collins and King Stitt were among the first, but the biggest star was U Roy, who brought deejaying to the top of the island's charts with "Wear You to the Ball." The practice was also known as "dubbing" not only because the DJs were dubbing in voices, but because some of the dub was "rude" (i.e., dirty), and in Jamaican slang "dub" is exactly equivalent to "fuck." In fact, during the rock-steady era, the rude record came into its own, epitomized by Max Romeo's under-the-counter million-seller "Wet Dream," which Romeo claimed was about sleeping under a hole in his roof.

A slight variation in rock steady's beat (or "rydim," a Jamaican term that encompasses most of the backing track) produced poppa-top, reggae's direct precursor. Sounding just like its name, it was bubblier and loosened up the rydim to the point where greater rhythmic division was possible. Poppa-top's great exponent was Desmond Dekker, a former rock-steady star whose 1969 hit "Israelites" reached Number Twelve in the United States.

In 1968 the Maytals, a vocal trio that had been around for some time, led by the charismatic Frederick "Toots" Hibbert, released a record called "Do the Reggay," although neither Toots nor anyone else seemed to know where the word came from. The music had been expanding the role of the bass for some time, and reggae brought the bass to the forefront, emphasizing a complex interrelationship between it, the trap drums and the percussion instruments. The rydim was shot through with silences, and to this day few non-Jamaicans can play it. The pulse is divided as finely as sixty-four times, and cross-rhythms abound. The bass seems to be the lead instrument, and the guitar is reduced to playing "changa," mere scratching at a chord. Keyboards and occasional "country" (i.e., out-of-tune) horn sections thicken the texture.

Reggae might have remained an isolated phenomenon, picked up by a few cognoscenti in the United States, if it hadn't been for a white Jamaican filmmaker, Perry Henzell, who, starting in 1968, began researching and filming the story of a rude boy who comes to Kingston, records a smash hit, is cheated by an all-too-typical record businessman, commits a murder, goes on the lam and is sought by both the Jamaican army and the producer, who wants another hit. Henzell's film, *The Harder They Come,* was a classic case of the right movie being made in the right place at the right time. Its star, Jimmy Cliff, was at his peak as a singer, reggae was at perhaps its highest level of artistic development, and Henzell was the perfect filmmaker, a man who clearly loved his subject. The film was fraught with danger, problems and delay, an actor died midway through, and money was constantly tight, but when it was finally released in the United States in 1973, it became an immediate cult hit.

kind of money and artistic freedom he'd never experienced before. He had always been an intensely political writer, but now his topics became even more focused. He wrote new lyrics protesting conditions in Kingston's Trench Town ghetto ("Concrete Jungle"), decrying random searches by army troops ("Rebel Music [3 O'Clock Road Block]") and glorifying the Rastafarian life ("Natty Dread"), all in songs that were gloriously melodic, well recorded, and both rootsy enough to satisfy the Jamaican audience and rock oriented enough for the U.S. market. Both music and lyrics struck a responsive chord with American fans, and Marley's records were the only reggae records to sell in appreciable numbers here, although many felt that the true fire of the group disappeared shortly after Tosh and Livingstone left in 1974. A key factor to Marley's success was incessant touring, not only in the States but also in Europe and Africa, both places where he became the only reggae musician recognized by the average pop fan. Despite all of this, however, he never managed to have an American hit, although Eric Clapton scored

Jimmy Cliff, one of reggae's first international stars and the hero in *The Harder They Come.*

The world *The Harder They Come* showed was, unfortunately, all too close to the real world of reggae. Producers tended to tie in with sound systems, and few if any of their performers ever saw royalties or sales figures from their records. If they complained, the producer wouldn't work with them anymore, their records wouldn't get played at the sound system dances, and they would fade from the minds of one of the most fickle audiences anywhere. Live music was rare because most of the records used the same basic pool of studio talent, and because most Jamaicans couldn't afford nightclubs or stage show performances even if they could get to Kingston to see them. The music world was truly what the vernacular had it to be, a "Mafia," and those who worked outside the system had very little hope for success.

Still, there were those who tried. The most famous was a rebellious songwriter, Bob Marley. His vocal trio with Peter Tosh and Bunny Livingstone, the Wailers, had worked with just about every producer in Kingston before they were signed in 1970 to Chris Blackwell's Island Records, a label with a reputation for integrity and distribution in England and America as well as in Jamaica. Blackwell gave Marley the

one in 1974 with a tepid remake of Marley's angry "I Shot the Sheriff." By the end of the Seventies, despite total indifference from most American blacks, some performers, most notably Stevie Wonder, were trying hard to introduce Marley to their fans. In 1981 it looked like a breakthrough was near, although Jamaican politics had left Marley an exile from his homeland. Instead, an old soccer injury (Marley had once been tapped by the professional soccer scouts) led to cancer developing on one of his toes. Refusing what would have been a lifesaving operation and medication on religious grounds, he faded fast, dying on May 11th, 1981, without ever seeing Jamaica again. In the decade since his death, his dreadlocked image has become an icon of third-world liberation, black self-determination and the island of Jamaica in general (which, along with the postage stamp the country issued in his honor, he surely would have found ironic). In the late Eighties his son Ziggy emerged with a band called the Melody Makers that included some of his siblings, and although he is not nearly the songwriter his father was, Ziggy is an equally charismatic performer and has become quite popular outside Jamaica, although not within.

In a way, it was a pity that during the Seventies the Wailers came to represent the entirety of reggae in the United States, because there was plenty of talent "down deh." But so few Americans could figure out the complexities of dealing with the Jamaican temperament that tours and record deals went begging. It was a completely different scene in England, where a large, stable population of home-sick West Indians made enough money to support constant tours and shows by their favorite artists. Early in ska's popularity, a British Jamaican music scene sprang up, although it never managed to replicate the urgency and roots rydims of music from "JA." Still, the fact that the music was constantly available, especially in lower-class neighborhoods where young white people lived, meant that a large British audience was exposed to reggae and wound up liking it. In the late Sixties skinheads, violent white racist thugs, adopted reggae as their stomping music and made certain to exclude Jamaicans from their list of victims. It hardly did reggae's image any good, a fact that came home again in the mid-Seventies, when punk rockers became passionate adherents of reggae, with the Clash even going so far as to have Jamaican master producer Lee "Scratch" Perry produce several sides for them. This time, however, the emphasis was on racial tolerance rooted in a common sense of oppression, and Bob Marley was so taken by the alliance that he released a British single, "Punky Reggae Party," to encourage solidarity. By late 1979 a full-fledged white ska-band revival began taking place in Britain, and many classic sides were being reissued to meet a new demand.

Although reggae spread throughout the Caribbean, Central America and Africa, outside of a few neighborhoods in New York and Miami that had significant West Indian populations, the U.S. reggae scene depended entirely upon white fans, for whom reggae's secret language and code words, as well as its Rastafarian content which promoted the sacrament of "ganja" (marijuana) and apocalyptic vi-

1979 disco hit "Now That We Found Love" eschewed reggae entirely and scored a better chart position than any previous Jamaican record. Besides Marley and the Wailers, only Toots and the Maytals truly succeeded during the Seventies in making roots music popular with a broad American audience, perhaps because of Toots's uncanny vocal resemblance to Otis Redding.

R eggae's heyday with white fans was from 1969 to 1976, when worsening economic conditions in Jamaica led to social turmoil. As always, this was documented in the music and continues to be, but to an American unfamiliar with the intricacies of Jamaican politics, much of the nuance is incomprehensible. In addition, the death in 1975 of Emperor Haile Selassie of Ethiopia, whom

Peter Tosh—reggae star, Rastaman—enjoying the sacrament of ganja.

sions, became a binding force. These fans did a brisk trade in imported records, saved money for a trip "down Yard" and did radio shows in college towns like Boston, Berkeley and Austin, where they were largely concentrated. The lack of domestically released reggae records and the fact that so much of the music was so alien to broadcasters (especially in the black community, where West Indians are usually despised by American-born blacks), kept this nucleus of fans small.

Thus the reggae musicians who wished to sell records in the States accommodated their style to their audience: Early on, Jimmy Cliff repudiated reggae and Jamaica and recorded soul and rock material, repenting only at the last minute, and the Wailers' Jamaican output differed strongly from their U.S. Island releases. Self-contained bands like Inner Circle, Soul Syndicate and Third World enjoyed some popularity in JA, but their R&B-tinged shows were clearly aimed elsewhere. Third World's

the Rastafarians revered as God's representative on earth, precipitated a crisis of faith that found utterance in a number of esoteric songs of interest largely to theologians and hard-core reggae fans.

The U.S. record companies' unwillingness to push reggae at its peak meant that domestic releases by the Heptones, the Mighty Diamonds, Peter Tosh, Bunny Wailer (Livingstone), Justin Hines and the Dominoes, Burning Spear, and DJs U Roy, Dillinger and Jah Lion all went virtually unheard, and such magnificent artists as Joe Higgs, Johnny Clarke, Culture, the Abyssinians, Fred Locks, Junior Byles and Augustus Pablo, and DJs I Roy, Big Youth, Prince Jazzbo, Dr. Alimantado and Tapper Zukie were known only to cognoscenti in the States and Britain. By 1977 reggae was considered a commercial failure in the United States by all labels but Island, which cut back its release schedule heavily.

In Jamaica reggae has nevertheless continued to develop along lines that were evident as early as 1970, when it was already moving away from the slick, soul-show presentation it had developed during the height of the ska era and toward a simpler, earthier sound promoted by the Ratafarian brethren who were the most outstanding musicians. This meant a more subdued background, with a much sparer use of horns, a reliance on ethereal three-part vocal harmony and a deep mystical turn to the lyrics. The quintessential group in this style is Winston Rodney's Burning Spear, which uses Rastafarian imagery so thick that it is impenetrable to an outsider, against a background so stark as to be monotonous.

The other major development has been the refinement of dub to an art form of almost Zen complexity-simplicity. Originally applied to the DJ talk-over, dub has come to mean any alteration of an original track. The DJs eventually got to the point of punching tracks in and out of a mix, while keeping the rydim going steadily all the time, whether in bass and drums or guitar or percussion, and further confounding things by feeding some of the tracks into an echoplex unit. The next logical step was to remove the talk-over, so that a contemporary dub record may consist of little beyond bass, drums and occasional ghostly appearances of shards of the other tracks. It is considered quite an art by its fans, but it sounds simply bizarre to anyone coming to it cold. Ironically, in view of American blacks' contempt for Jamaicans, the dominant form of black pop music in the late Eighties and early Nineties

Burning Spear, led by Winston Rodney (left), the quintessential Rastafarian band.

came directly from Jamaica. In the late Seventies a Jamaican living in New York City, Kool Herc, demonstrated to some neighborhood kids in the Bronx the DJ talk-over, "toasting." Before long, the disc jockeys in black discos were doing short sets of "rap" as a standard part of their set, and not long after that, dub techniques were being used on disco B sides in direct imitation of Jamaican recordings.

As the rap explosion grew, the technological process went two ways: As inexpensive synthesizers and drum machines made it possible to make rap records with a harder-edged sound, these same machines were imported to Jamaican studios, where they were used by Jamaican producers. In 1985 there was a rash of records with a repetitive bass line called "sleng-teng" behind them, which turned out to be one of the preprogrammed bass lines on a certain Casio keyboard. Some of the more expensive sampling devices showed up in the studios of the "electro" producers Steelie and Clevie and veteran producer Niney the Observer, who called his style "turbo." These electronically charged records were faster and crisper than the records that had caught white fans' ears in the Seventies, and were popular in the States mainly among Caribbean immigrants. And although rap preached black unity, few Jamaican-Americans wound up with rap careers at first, although in the early Nineties rappers like Shabba Ranks, Shinehead and Queen Latifah managed to break down even that boundary, while Boogie Down Productions' KRS-1 was known to do some rapping in patois himself.

"W'at you t'ink, mon," I was asked in Jamaica in 1975, "reggae gon' go international?" "Maybe," was my response, and it looks like I was right. Reggae has given a new rhythmic concept to rock, as performers as far apart as Eric Clapton, the Grateful Dead, the Clash and Jimmy Buffett have proven. But the "roots reggae" has stayed down Yard, because its artists have chosen to serve the cultural and informational needs of the people who gave it birth, instead of trying for the big time in Hollywood and New York. Although the current output is ignored by most non-Caribbeans in the United States, and although the white fans follow mellow Rastafarian-preaching musicians who are almost totally unknown down Yard, reggae has become the dominant "world music" rhythm. It is loved in Jamaica by Jamaicans and continues to support the world's most successful self-contained third-world record business—which, in the long run, may be its finest achievement.

DISCOGRAPHY

PRE-REGGAE RHYTHMS
Millie Small: *My Boy Lollipop* (Smash; 1964). **Desmond Dekker and the Aces:** *Israelites* (UNI; 1969). *The Best of Desmond Dekker* (Rhino, 1992). **Anthologies:** *The Trojan Story* (Trojan; U.K., 1971). *Intensified! Original Ska 1962–66* (Mango; 1979). *More Intensified! Original Ska 1963–67, Vol. 2* (Mango; 1980).

THE RASTAFARIAN INFLUENCE
Count Ossie and the Mystic Revelation of Rastafari: *Grounation* (Vulcan; U.K., 1974). *Tales of Mozambique* (Dynamic; U.K., 1976). **Ras Michael and the Sons of Negus:** *Rastafari* (Vulcan; U.K., 1975). **Dadawah:** *Peace and Love* (Trojan; U.K., 1975).

THE FATHERS OF REGGAE
Jimmy Cliff: *Wonderful World, Beautiful People* (A&M; 1970). *Unlimited* (Warner; 1973). **Bob Marley and the Wailers:** *African Herbsman* (Trojan; U.K., 1972). *Catch a Fire* (Island; ☆171, 1973). *Burnin'* (Island; ☆151, 1973). *Natty Dread* (Island; ☆92, 1974). *Live!* (Island; ☆90, 1975). *Rastaman Vibration* (Island; ☆8, 1976). *Exodus* (Island; ☆184, 1977). *Kaya* (Island; r☆50, ☆50, 1978). *Babylon by Bus* (Island; r☆58, ☆102, 1978). *Survival* (Island; r☆32, ☆70, 1979). *Uprising* (Island/Tuff Gong; ☆45, 1980). *Confrontation* (Island/Tuff Gong; ☆55, 1983). *Legend* (Island/Tuff Gong; ☆54, 1984). *Soul Revolution I & II* (Trojan; U.K., 1988). *Talkin' Blues* (Island/Tuff Gong; ☆103, 1991). *One Love: The Wailers at Studio One* (Heartbeat; 1992). **The Wailers:** *Music Lesson* (Shanachie; 1985). **Bunny Wailer:** *Blackheart Man* (Island; 1976). *Rock 'n' Groove* (Solomonic; 1982). *Liberation* (Shanachie; 1988). *Time Will Tell* (Shanachie; 1990). **Peter Tosh:** *Equal Rights* (Columbia, 1977). *Mama Africa* (EMI America; 1983). *No Nuclear War* (EMI America; 1987). **Toots and the Maytals:** *In the Dark* (Dragon; U.K., 1974). *Funky Kingston* (Island; 1975). *Reggae Got Soul* (Island; 1976).

EVOLUTION
DUB REGGAE, THE PRODUCER'S ART— **Lee Perry:** Jah Lion *Colombia Colly* (Mango; 1976). The Upsetters *Super Ape* (Island; 1976). *Return of the Super Ape* (Lion of Judah; 1978). *Scratch on the Wire* (Island; U.K., 1979). **Joseph Hoo Kim:** Well Charged *Vital Dub* (Virgin; U.K., 1976). **L. Lindo:** Burning Spear *Garvey's Ghost* (Mango; 1976). **Augustus Pablo:** *Ital Dub* (Trojan; U.K., 1975). *King Tubby Meets Rockers Uptown* (Yard Music; 1976). *Original Rockers* (Greensleeves; U.K., 1979). *Africa Must Be Free by 1983* (Rockers International; 1979). **Joe Gibbs and the Professionals:** *African Dub Almighty Chapters 1–4* (Lightning/Joe Gibbs Music; 1978). *Majestic Dub* (Lightning/Joe Gibbs Music; 1978). *Earthquake Dub* (Lightning/Joe Gibbs Music; 1978). **Karl Pitterson:** Planet Mars Dub *The Icebreakers with the Diamonds* (Virgin Front Line; U.K., 1978). **Dennis Bovell:** Blackbeard *I Wah Dub* (More Cut; U.K., 1980).

"TOASTERS," THE RAPPING DJS— **Prince Buster and the All Stars:** *Fabulous Greatest Hits* (Melodisc; U.K., 1968). *Wreck a Pum Pum* (Melodisc; 1969). **Big Youth:** *Screaming Target* (Trojan; U.K., 1970). *Dread Locks Dread* (Klik; U.K., 1975). *Natty Cultural Dread* (Trojan; U.K., 1976). **I Roy:** *Truths and Rights* (Grounation; U.K., 1975). **U Roy:** *Dread in a Babylon* (Virgin; 1975). **Tapper Zukie:** *MPLA* (Virgin Front Line; U.K., 1978). **Dr. Alimantado:** *Best Dressed Chicken in Town* (Greensleeves; U.K., 1978). **Prince Mohammed:** *Inna Him Head* (Joe Gibbs Music; 1978).

THE GOLDEN AGE
Burning Spear: *Marcus Garvey* (Island; 1975). *Harder Than the Rest* (Mango; 1979). **Max Romeo:** *War in a Babylon* (Island; 1976). **Mighty Diamonds:** *Right Time* (Virgin; 1976). **Junior Murvin:** *Police and Thieves* (Mango; 1977). **Judy Mowatt:** *Black Woman* (Shanachie; 1978). **Althea and Donna:** *Uptown Top Ranking* (Virgin Front Line; U.K., 1978). **Gregory Isaacs:** *Extra Classic* (Conflict; U.K., 1978). **I Jah Man:** *Haile I Hymn Chapter 1* (Mango; 1978). **Culture:** *Two Sevens Clash* (Lightning; U.K., 1978). **Dennis Brown:** *Words of Wisdom* (Joe Gibbs' Music; 1978). **Steel Pulse:** *Handsworth Revolution* (Mango; 1978). **Linton Kwesi Johnson:** *Dread Beat and Blood* (Virgin Front Line; U.K., 1978). *Forces of Victory* (Mango; 1979). **Black Uhuru:** *Showcase* (D-Roy; U.K., 1979). *Sinsemilla* (Mango; 1980). **Freddie McGregor:** *Bobby Babylon* (Heartbeat; 1980). **Pablo Moses:** *A Song* (Mango; 1980).

FROM THE EIGHTIES INTO THE NINETIES
Steel Pulse: *True Democracy* (Elektra; 1982). **Ini Kamoze:** *Statement* (Island; 1983). **Mutabaruka:** *Check It* (Alligator; 1983). **Marcia Griffiths:** *Electric Boogie* (Island; 1983). **Linton Kwesi Johnson:** *Making History* (Mango; 1984). **Tenor Saw:** *Ring the Alarm* (Prince; 1985). **Lee Perry:** *Judgment in a Babylon* (Lion of Judah; U.K., 1985). **Maxi Priest:** *Intentions* (10 Dix; U.K., 1986). **Macha B.:** *Sign of the Times* (Ariwa; 1986). **Junior Delgado:** *Ragamuffin Year* (Message; 1986). **Pinchers:** *Agony* (Live and Love; 1987). **Gregory Isaacs:** *Rumours* (Music Works; 1988). **Ziggy Marley and the Melody Makers:** *Conscious Party* (Virgin; ☆23, 1988). *Tomorrow People* (Virgin; ☆16, 1988). *Tumblin' Down* (Virgin; ☆43, 1988). **Dennis Brown:** *Brown Sugar* (RAS; 1988). **Toots Hibbert:** *Toots in Memphis* (Mango; 1988). **Junior Reid:** *One Blood* (Big Life; 1989). **J. C. Lodge:** *Telephone Love* (Pow Wow; 1989). **Pato Banton:** *Mad Professor Captures Pato Banton* (Ariwa/RAS; 1990). **Lee Perry and Adrian Sherwood:** *From the Secret Laboratory* (Mango; 1990). **Rastafari Elders:** *Rastafari Elders* (RAS; 1990). **Lucky Dube:** *House of Exile* (Shanachie; 1992).

ANTHOLOGIES
The Harder They Come (soundtrack) (Mango; 1972). *This Is Reggae Music* (Island; 1974). *Vol. 2* (Island; 1975). *Vol. 3* (Island; 1976). *Rebel Music* (Trojan; U.K., 1979). *Creation Rockers, Vols. 1–6* (Trojan; U.K., 1979). *The Trojan Story* (Trojan; U.K., 1976). *Rockers* (soundtrack) (Mango; 1979).

(Chart positions compiled from Joel Whitburn's *Record Research,* based on *Billboard's* LP chart.)

ANARCHY IN THE U.K.

BY GREIL MARCUS

he most inclusive description of the art is that, termite-like, it feels its way through walls of particularization, with no sign that the artist has any object in mind other than eating away the boundaries of his art, and turning these boundaries into conditions of the next accomplishment.

The best examples appear . . . where the spotlight of culture is nowhere in evidence, so that the craftsman can be ornery, wasteful, stubbornly self-involved, doing go-for-broke art and not caring what comes of it.

—Manny Farber, ''White Elephant Art vs. Termite Art,'' 1962

We thought, he's got what we want. Bit of a lunatic, a front man. That's what we was after: a front man who had definite ideas about what he wanted to do and he'd definitely got them. And we knew straight away. Even though he couldn't sing. We wasn't really interested in that 'cos we were still learning to play at the time.

—Paul Cook, on Johnny Rotten's audition for the Sex Pistols

[THEORY]

It may be that in the mind of their self-celebrated Svengali, London boutique owner Malcolm McLaren, the Sex Pistols were never meant to be more than a nine-month wonder, a cheap vehicle for some fast money, a few laughs, a touch of the old *épater les bourgeois*. It may also be that in the mind of their chief theorist and propagandist, Sixties art student and anarchist provocateur Malcolm McLaren, the Sex Pistols were meant to be a force that would set the world on its ear, recapture the power and purity he had first glimpsed in classic rockers like Gene Vincent and finally unite music and politics.

The Sex Pistols, October 1976. *From left:* Paul Cook, Johnny Rotten, Steve Jones and Glen Matlock, the band's original bassist, later replaced by Sid Vicious.

The Sex Pistols were all of these things, and as an official, aboveground group they lasted little longer than nine months. Formed in late 1975, they released their first single, ''Anarchy in the U.K.,'' on November 19th, 1976, and had ceased to exist as much more than an asset in a court fight by January 14th, 1978, when, immediately following the last show of their single American tour, Johnny Rotten left the band, claiming McLaren had sold out everything the Pistols had ever stood for. During that time, however, the Pistols accomplished an interesting feat: They broke the story of rock & roll in half.

As invented, inspired and carried to a formal (though not historical) conclusion by McLaren and the Sex Pistols, punk rock was an aesthetic and political revolt based in a mass of contradictions that sustained it aesthetically and doomed it politically. McLaren understood that rock & roll was the most important, perhaps the only kind of culture the young truly cared about; he understood that for the young everything else (fashion, slang, sexual styles)

flowed from rock & roll, or was organized by it, or was validated by it—and that therefore rock & roll was not just the necessary first principle of any youth revolt, but that revolt's necessary first target. Connections could be made: If one could show how rock & roll had become simply the shiniest cog in the established order, then a demystification of rock might lead magically to the demystification of the Establishment.

To structure the situation in this way took real imagination, even genius. In the past, rock & roll in the context of youth revolt had always been seen by its fans merely as a weapon, or, more deeply, as an end in itself, as self-justifying—which was self-defeating, because it meant that when all was said and done, rock & roll did not open up questions of justice, identity, repression, freedom and aesthetics, but drew them into itself and made them disappear. Thus the Sex Pistols damned rock & roll as a rotting corpse—as a monster of moneyed reaction, a sentimentalized corruption that no longer served as more than a mechanism of glamorized oppression, self-exploitation and false consciousness—and yet, because they had no other weapons and because they were fans in spite of themselves, the Sex Pistols played rock & roll, stripping the music down to essentials of speed, noise, fury and manic glee no one had been able to touch before. They used rock & roll as a weapon against itself.

With all instruments but guitar, bass and drums written off as effete, as the elitist accoutrements of professionalism and the cult of technique, this was a sound best suited to expressing anger and frustration, focusing chaos, dramatizing the last days as daily life and ramming all emotions into the narrow gap between a blank stare and a sardonic grin. The guitarist laid down a line of fire to cover the singer, while the rhythm section put both in a pressure drop, and as a response to what was perceived as the totalitarian freeze of the modern world, the music sometimes seemed like a version of it. A lot of people—fans of Yes, David Bowie or for that matter the Rolling Stones—didn't think this was music at all, or even rock & roll; a smaller number of people thought it was the most exciting thing they'd ever heard. The Sex Pistols meant to bring the edge into view, and they did: When Johnny Rotten rolled his r's, it sounded as if his teeth had been filed down to points.

Though they sparked a wave of instant bands,

self-made records, a new pop grapevine of fanzines, improvised distributions and countless rumors, the Pistols themselves were signed to EMI, Britain's biggest and most conservative label. When the label dropped them after bassist Glen Matlock said ''fuck'' on national television, they proved themselves quite capable of sentimentalizing their own righteousness. Clear inheritors of Chuck Berry, Phil Spector, the early Who, the Velvet Underground, mid-Sixties American garage bands, the Stooges, Jonathan Richman, the New York Dolls (managed, in their dying moments, by the same Malcolm McLaren, who draped their stages in Communist flags and gave them the slogan, ''What Are the Politics of Boredom?''), Mott the Hoople, David Bowie (from whom drummer Paul Cook and guitarist Steve Jones stole the Pistols' microphones) and a host of other rock primitives, rebels, pioneers and prophets without honor, the Sex Pistols nevertheless denounced their forebears as farts and fools, dismissing the claims of the past as they denied the worth of the future.

Punk was fake culture, product of McLaren's fashion sense (he called his shop Let It Rock, Too Fast to Live, Too Young to Die and Sex before settling on Seditionaries), his dreams of glory and his hunch that the marketing of sadomasochistic fantasies might lead the way to the next big thing. But when Cook, Jones, Matlock and Rotten—working-class delinquents and dole queuers born in the mid-Fifties—took their own fantasies of escape and pillage into London's clubs, in their first days crashing other bands' gigs for the chance to be heard, punk became real culture. In a context of crushing youth unemployment, growing street violence between neo-fascists, colored immigrants, the police and socialists, and the enervation of the pop scene, punk came together within a few short months as a whole set of visual and verbal signs: signs that were at once opaque and revelatory, depending on who was looking.

Positing boredom as the legacy of rock, and spiritual death as the promise of the welfare state, punk triumphed over its visions of ugliness—mastered them—by acting them out. Insisting on the bizarre and trashing standards of decency, punk shattered the mask of the dominant culture; by its very un-

Sex Pistols and fans, 1976.

naturalness, punk made the host culture seem like a trick, the result of sadomasochistic economics. With cruelly dyed and slashed hair, mutilated faces, bondage gear (from McLaren's shelves, of course, which was only fair), wrecked clothes—a lumpen, day-for-night-of-the-living-dead style—punk drew lines, divided the young from the old and the young from the young, forced new loyalties, forged new identities and, as it announced that all possibilities were closed, opened up possibilities of negation and affirmation that a year before had not existed even *as* fantasies. This was revolt into style; it was also style into revolt. Centered strictly in London, later spreading directly across the United Kingdom, punk's claim on the world's attention was not hedged: Musically and politically it announced itself as a harbinger of things to come, of all that was feared and of all that could not even be imagined.

Punk was in the tradition of the United Kingdom's postwar, music-based, white working-class subcultures: The teddy boys of the mid-Fifties, the mods and rockers of the mid-Sixties, and the reggae-loving, Paki-bashing skinheads of the late Sixties and early Seventies (who arose partly in reaction to the seizure of the pop space by mostly middle-class hippies). But as Robert Christgau has written, punk was the first such movement to direct its rage where it belonged: against those in power. It was also the first such movement in which women played a significant, even defining role. By far the most violent in appearance and rhetoric of any musical movement, punk was probably the least violent in fact—though by far the most violence was directed against it. After the Sex Pistols released their second single, the murderous ''God Save the Queen,'' on May 27th, 1977, they were banned from BBC radio (also banned from the BBC charts, they made Number Two anyway—as a blank), attacked by the police, barred from public performance, threatened with criminal obscenity charges, denounced in Parliament and repeatedly beaten and razored on the streets, until finally they were virtually forced to flee the country.

Punk was a carefully orchestrated media hype, the latest version of a tried-and-true scenario of pop outrageousness that elicited a hurricane of Establishment hysteria—a hysteria that was in many ways as cynical and self-serving as the provocation. Yet punk uncovered resentments, fears, hatreds and desires so fierce that their emergence threatened the legitimacy of the social order and revealed its tyranny, just as the scabrous rating of the Sex Pistols' music threatened the legitimacy of mainstream rock and revealed *its* tyranny. Punk also uncovered, and legitimized, purely thuggish behavior and psychopathic characters of every sort, the most notable of the latter being Sid Vicious, who, famed for inventing the pogo dance and beating a rock writer with a chain, replaced Glen Matlock as the Pistols' bassist in March 1977, when Matlock was kicked out of the band for exhibiting revisionist tendencies. ("He wanted to make us *fun*," Rotten explained in horror. "Like the Beatles!")

Punk toyed casually with Nazi imagery (raising the specter of youth fascism, and also implying that Britain's victory over Hitler had simply led to fascism by a different route), set itself against the burgeoning racism of the neo-Nazi National Front, aligned itself with London's Jamaicans and sought justification, strategy, wisdom and courage in the apocalyptic antipolitics of reggae. What punk absorbed from reggae and its ruling Rastafarians was the idea of self-determination within a nation perceived as a prison and the paradoxical concept of class war defined in strictly cultural terms: a struggle that would make demands on those in power that no government could ever satisfy, that would be both stoic and messianic, a struggle that could not, in fact, be revolutionary at all, but that could be utterly subversive—to no end that anyone could name. But the wellsprings of reggae were at bottom religious, and there was no mythical Africa that punk could seek as an image of redemption—and so to this bundle of contradictions Johnny Rotten added one of his own: nihilism.

Unlike Manny Farber's white elephant art—"an expensive hunk of well-regulated area," which in 1976 and '77 meant a new Rod Stewart album or the Queen's Silver Jubilee—the "termite-tapeworm-fungus-moss" impulses of the Sex Pistols took them through one barrier after another. Thus they made it clear that their attack on the vacuity of pop was merely an instinctive means to a far more disturbing attack on sex, as the mystification behind love, on love, as the mystification behind the family, on the family, as the mystification behind the class system, on the class system, as the mystification behind capitalism, and finally on the very notion of progress—as the ultimate mystification behind postindustrial Western society itself. Veterans of spontaneous student revolts would have been familiar with such an expansion of vision—but the world of pop had never seen anything like it before.

Paul Simonon of the Clash.

Out of these paradoxes—and there were many, many more—came an extraordinary tension, a sustaining excitement, a torrent of remarkable music, a parade of heroes, martyrs, traitors and frauds, and an almost limitless opportunity for popular art. But as politics, this was the sort of revolt that had to strangle on its own contradictions, that had to lose its shape in the momentum that gave it shape, that was preordained to outstrip the reach of the calculation and plotting that had allowed it to become authentic. Perhaps the only true irony in the whole story was that, in the end, it all came down to rock & roll—nothing less, but nothing more.

[PRACTICE]

All over the country, depression lay like fog, which was just about all that was missing to lower spirits even further, and there was even a little of that in East Anglia. All over the nation, families who had listened to the news looked at one another and said, "Goodness me," or "Whatever next," or "I give up," or "Well, fuck that" . . . All over the country, people blamed other people for all the things that were going wrong—the trade unions, the present government, the miners, the car workers, the seamen, the Arabs, the Irish, their own idle good-for-nothing offspring, comprehensive education. Nobody knew whose fault it really was, but most people managed to complain fairly forcefully about somebody.

—Margaret Drabble, *The Ice Age*, 1977

1977 was the year that music came out of the concert halls and into the streets; when independent labels sprang out of the woodwork to feed new tastes; when rock music once again became about energy and fun; when the majors' boardrooms lost control. Suddenly we could do anything.
—Liner notes to *Streets,* a collection of punk singles, 1977

In the meantime, however, the band has the curious problem of its relationship to Britain to contend with—increasingly popular among many young people but subject to street attacks and hysterical denunciation in the mass press. "I don't understand it," says Rotten with his winning blend of mockery and innocence. "All we're trying to do is destroy everything."
—John Rockwell, the *New York Times,* August 1977

"Have you seen the Sex Pistols?" Joe Strummer almost whispered to Graham Parker one night in 1976, as if passing on a secret so valuable he hardly dared speak its name. "No," said Parker. " 'The Sex Pistols'?" "Whole new thing, man," Strummer muttered. "Whole new thing?" Within weeks, Strummer, son of a lower-level British diplomat, had left his pub-rock band, the 101'ers (named, with pure punk prescience, for the torture room in *1984*), and joined with guitarist Mick Jones and bass player Paul Simonon to form the nucleus of the Clash.

That was how punk rock took off. Some writers have made much of the impact of R&B revivalists Dr. Feelgood—getting back to basics, and all that—but England's 453rd R&B revival could easily have come to nothing. Others root it all in the emergence of an ironic, arty, self-consciously avant-garde punk scene in New York in 1974 and '75, or credit the you-too-can-play evangelism of the Ramones' 1976 tour of Britain. But U.K. punk was not ironic—irony being understood as just one more way of not having to mean what you said—and while the oh-so-studied primitivism of the Ramones certainly made itself felt in England, so, in 1957, did "the big rock & roll sound" of Bill Haley, which did not make Bill Haley the Beatles any more than it makes the Ramones the Sex Pistols.

When they first started out, with the magnificent cackle Johnny Rotten used to kick off "Anarchy in the U.K.," the Sex Pistols said they wanted "more bands like us." They got them—dozens of groups that cut their own 45s weeks after forming (or, if one goes by the sound of some of the sides, before forming), put them out on one-shot labels like Rabid, Raw, Rad Edge, Beggars Banquet, Step-Forward, and sold them at gigs, in independent record shops, through the mail. Most of these records were never meant for the radio; as if in answer to the repression suffered by the Sex Pistols, the Cortinas, the Lurkers, Eater and Slaughter and the Dogs made music so brutal, haphazard or obscene that airplay was out of the question. Thus, given the assumption that normal pop channels were irrelevant, all restrictions on what could go into a record or a performance, on what a record could sound like or what a performance could look like, fell away. Male singers could abjure macho posing or push such posing to unholy extremes; female singers and musicians were suddenly able to ignore the few roles reserved for women in rock—indeed, they could ignore roles altogether, which was what made Poly Styrene of X-Ray Spex, a half-caste overweight teenager with braces, so startling. Within the context of punk, she was also obvious, and that obviousness was liberating.

If in wartime only the clandestine press can be truly free ("The only great nation with a completely uncensored press today," A. J. Liebling wrote in

The Pistols sign with A&M outside Buckingham Palace (their manager, Malcolm McLaren, is second from right). The band was dropped from their first label, EMI, when Glen Matlock said "fuck" on national television. They didn't last long on A&M either: The company refused to release their next single, "God Save the Queen."

1944, "is France"), then it was the fact that the official pop space was closed to much of punk that made it possible for punk to create its own space of freedom. Something like a new pop economy, based less on profit than on subsistence, the will to shock and marginal but intense public response—a pop economy meant to support not careers but hit-and-run raids on the public peace of mind—began to take form. Bands were mostly faceless; action centered on 45s (presented in picture sleeves, many of which omitted photos of the band in favor of agit-prop/Dada graphics, inviting the buyer to identify not with the band but with the punk movement per se).

People cut singles not so much on the off-chance that they would hit but to join in, to be heard, to establish a new identity, to say "I'm here," or "I hate you," or "I have a big cock." Teenagers discovered the thrill of shouting "Fire!" in a crowded theater—or even in an empty theater. That anyone could make a mark permitted the success of punk frauds like the Stranglers and the Damned, the vicious misogyny of the Cortinas' "Fascist Dictator" or Some Chicken's celebration of Charles Manson, and boosted the simple puerility of a hundred now-forgotten 45s; it also inspired records as anonymously right as the original Buzzcocks' seminal "Boredom," and that Everykid anonymity was just as liberating as Poly Styrene's grip on the mike.

Again, it was reggae that had cleared much of the territory. Structurally, punk came forth on reggae terms: as minority culture for outcasts, for those willing to make and live in their own embattled but special world, for those who didn't fit into society or who saw society as unfit for themselves. But while punk's remaking of some of the means of pop production backed up the punk attack on fame, careerism and "art" that was the first premise of punk ideology, there were crucial, killing contradictions in the punk-reggae link. Unlike reggae, which has moved steadily toward coded Jamaican English and was never only for the young, punk was white youth music, sung in recognizable English, coded only by

volume. And despite the punk attempt to discredit and disassociate itself from rock & roll, punk *was* rock & roll. From the start, it was subject to enormous publicity in the scandal sheets and to detailed next-new-thing criticism in the rock press. Potentially, even the most extreme white punk band had access to a mass audience and to amounts of money that were denied the least radical reggae singer by definition—and in truth the most important punk bands had contracted with major labels from the outset.

Thus, the more intense the momentum of punk—spurred on by the increasingly desperate sound of

That last night in San Francisco—Rotten hanging on to the mike like Quasimodo caught in a wind tunnel, baiting the self-hyped crowd while Steve Jones made a sound that was more like that of a man playing a guitar factory than a guitar—was the formal (but not historical) conclusion. As D. H. Lawrence once wrote, describing another "metaphysical tragedy," "the *Pequod* sinks with all her souls, but their bodies rise again to man innumerable tramp steamers and ocean-crossing liners . . . What we mean is that people may go on, keep on, rush on, without souls. They have their ego and their will; that is enough to keep them going." Dropping the "punk" tag and trading instead under the innoffensive and near-meaningless rubric of "new wave," countless English bands have since made that ocean crossing—and when the Buzzcocks and the Jam and the Boomtown Rats arrived on American shores, it was no longer possible even to pretend their presence could make a difference.

But the Clash—what about the Clash? *They* arrived in America not simply to make themselves known but precisely to make a difference, as rock & roll politicians out to create a new rock version of the public space. Trapped like any other band in the Rolling Stones' rock-politics paradox ("What can a poor boy do . . ."), they nevertheless began with the assumption that there was more room in that paradox than the apologetic Stones have been willing to admit. The clear goal of the Clash was to grow both musically and politically, at once, as if one side was a necessary means to the other. Indeed, many argued even in 1977 that the Clash, not the Pistols, were the great punk band. They may well be the greater rock & roll band, as that judgment is conventionally understood. That they were not the greater punk band has been their salvation.

Managed originally by Bernie Rhodes, longtime crony of Malcolm McLaren, the Clash played their first gigs in mid-1976, signed with U.K. CBS for a reported £100,000 and released their first album, *The Clash,* in the spring of 1977, long before the Pistols got *Never Mind the Bollocks Here's the Sex Pistols* into the stores. Immediately, the Clash had risen above the pack, because they were able to rationalize the punk ethos, laugh at it and put it across with a sound that was altogether their own.

The Pistols performed as wreckers, the Clash as partisans. If the Pistols' tunes were symbolist ("Anarchy" opening with the cry, "I am the Anti-

the Sex Pistols from above and by the multiplication of new voices from below—the more surely and inevitably punk drove toward the widest possible audience, exploding its outcast pretensions, no longer acting out rebellion but instead acting out the contradictions that lay behind the rebellion. That Johnny Rotten chose to resolve the situation by leaving it—by, in essence, arranging his own plane crash and emerging from the wreckage as John Lydon, once again anonymous, or as close to anonymity as he could get—may well have been the most heroic act in the story, the act most true to what the story had tried to make itself about.

Christ," which Rotten miraculously made all too credible), the Clash's were rhetorical: The explanations Rotten offered in interviews went into Mick Jones's and Joe Strummer's songs. The Clash were "more political" because their position was less metaphysical, and therefore more manageable, than the Pistols'; the Clash's appeal to reggae rebellion was explicit, and their lyrics addressed not the social bases of reality but the System. If in some fundamental way the Sex Pistols—or anyway Johnny Rotten—really were committed to the destruction of rock not only as myth but as fact, the Clash were committed to changing rock. Aggressively, honestly and practically populist, they were aware of the contradictions in their stance and interested in staying one step ahead of them, determined to find the right side and stick to it. Their music meant to organize the new punk community, to provide it with spirit and consciousness.

Such aims may sound absurdly naive and utopian. *The Clash* remains a riveting and unsettling album, one of the truest rock statements about the world rock cannot enclose. Not only was it trendy ("correct" where the Pistols were adventurist and bands like Eater were foaming at the mouth), taking on dead-end jobs ("Career Opportunities," inspired by Mick Jones's stint as a clerk whose job was to open suspected letter bombs), terminal pop boredom ("Cheat," "London's Burning"), the true origins of rock ("Garageland"), the irrelevance of America ("I'm So Bored with the U.S.A."), frustration ("White Riot") and violence ("Hate and War" and a stunning cover of Junior Murvin's 1976 reggae hit "Police and Thieves"), the LP was open and funny—insistent but not pompous, self-righteous but not self-important. If the Clash latched onto received ideas, they soon made those ideas their own and were changed by them. More directly attracted to reggae *music* than any other band, they somehow combined Jamaican rhythmic sense with the punk maelstrom, producing a sound that was dense, complex, forbidding. At their best the Clash sounded like their name.

The Clash was followed by "Complete Control," an attack by the band on its own record company, which could have reduced punk politics to petu-

lance—who really cared if CBS released the wrong tune as a single? But *this* single was perhaps the finest example of the punk ability to leap from the narrowest provocation to the largest issue without blinking: Rather than a complaint about "artistic freedom," it came off as a testament to what artistic freedom was worth. Produced by reggae master Lee Perry of Jamaica, it was also one of the most powerful hard-rock records of all time.

There were more singles—the failed "Clash City Rockers," the brooding "(White Man) In Hammersmith Palais," in which the Clash dove headfirst

The Clash. The band's music meant to organize the new punk community, to provide it with spirit and consciousness. *From left:* Mick Jones, Joe Strummer, Topper Headon.

into the racial and political paradoxes of their music—and then in late 1978 *Give 'Em Enough Rope* (cut with an American producer, it was the Clash's first LP to be released in the United States, though *The Clash* had sold 100,000 copies as a high-priced import). Certainly the Clash wanted to ''conquer'' the U.S.A.; to get themselves a bigger audience and financial freedom, to validate themselves in the place where it all came from. With the punk scene in the United Kingdom growing ever more narrow, paranoid and tired, the Clash had to step beyond it, carrying its messages without allowing those mes-

The Clash and Bo Diddley on tour in 1979. With the Sex Pistols long gone, the Clash tried to reorganize the idea of rock & roll around their own moment. Punk, rather than a radical breaking point, became the capstone of rock history.

sages to fix them in an isolated moment in pop time. The attempt to cross borders made sense in another way: A concern with youth culture and political violence in London had led to a fascination with politics and violence on a global scale and to a perception of the inherent limits of youth culture as such, and for the Clash's renderings of those themes to be tested, something more than a local audience was necessary. But while the material was often astonishingly potent (''Safe European Home,'' ''Guns on the Roof''), the sound was weak and scattered— half compromised American heavy metal and half compromised English punk.

With the Pistols long gone, the Clash stayed on the case, performing often in the United Kingdom and the States, extending their use of reggae and backing it up with an attempt to link punk to much older rock & roll styles: rockabilly, zydeco, New Orleans R&B. If the Sex Pistols had opened a gap in the rock & roll story, the Clash wanted to occupy that gap—or to claim the story itself, to reorganize the idea of rock & roll around their own moment.

With *London Calling*, released just as the Seventies collapsed into the Eighties, they succeeded. A big, cheap, nineteen-song two-record set, it was expansive, confident, worried, full of good faith and as determined as ever to rob pop music of its promise of an unearned freedom from dread. Ranging across *London Calling* were cops and robbers, Spanish free-

dom fighters and radical-chic tourists, young lovers and broken-down middle-aged punks, Montgomery Clift and Robert Mitchum, Anastasio Somoza and Anthony Blunt, Staggerlee and Billy, reggae rude boys and struggling rockers with nothing to say, rebels walking straight into traps they were too cool to notice. It was an album that in its multiplicity, wild humor and unbroken intensity sounded as if it could sustain a listener for a long time to come. The Clash had triumphed not because they had managed to transcend the contradictions and paradoxes of punk, but because they had very consciously used them as the basis of their music.

And yet there is a way in which the Clash always pulled back from the edge on which the true punk movement was played out. That, most likely, kept them together; it also marked their limits. The Clash's very effort always to do the right thing, to make the correct choice, to define the problem properly, kept them from ever being as dangerous as punk promised it would be—or as the Sex Pistols were. Unlike the Clash, the Sex Pistols did go too far; all the hue and cry and calculation aside, going too far was what they were about. If there is a forgotten chapter in the punk story, a chunk of jagged metal long since smoothed down, that is it.

There was a black hole at the heart of the Sex Pistols' music, a willful lust for the destruction of all values that absolutely no one could be comfortable with—and that was why, at his greatest, Johnny Rotten was perhaps the only truly terrifying singer rock & roll has ever known. Certainly, no one has yet

From left: Mick Jones, Joe Strummer, Topper Headon, Paul Simonon.

seen all the way into the nihilistic madness of ''Holidays in the Sun,'' the Pistols' last single. The sleeve was charming: On the front were cartoons of a happy family discussing holiday plans in the crazed words Rotten sings on the record; on the back, a photo of a family scene, annotated with little signs—''Nice image,'' ''Nice middle age lady,'' ''Nice people,'' ''Nice photo,'' ''Nice young man,'' ''Nice young lady,'' ''Nice gesture'' (the nice young man is holding the hand of the nice young lady), ''Nice little girl,'' ''Nice illegible,'' and even, at the bottom, ''Nice sleeve.'' The record wasn't charming. ''I don't want a holiday in the sun,'' Rotten sang. ''I want to go to the New Belsen.''

Off he goes, the marching feet of the tourist masses behind him, to the extermination camp that, for the British, serves as the symbol of modern evil, just as Auschwitz does for Americans. Johnny finds

himself at the foot of the Berlin Wall; people are staring at him, and he can't stand it. As the feet grow louder and the band spins off into a frenzy, Johnny begins to shout, amazed at himself, his voice filled with delight and revulsion: He wants to go *over* the wall. Is that where the real Nazis are? Is East Berlin what the Western world will look like in ten years? Is that the future the Pistols claimed didn't exist? Rotten can't stop himself, he wants to go *under* the wall. The song presses on, squeezing the listener like Poe's shrinking closet; part of the terror of the number is that it makes no apparent sense but still drags the listener into its absurdity and strands him there. The Sex Pistols leave every band in the world behind them for the last minute of the record, and Rotten is climbing, or digging, tearing at the wall with his bare hands, screaming at his inability to understand any more of the story he's telling than

we do. What is happening? It sounds as if Hitler's legions have risen from the dead, taking the place of the nice tourists, nice East German bureaucrats, nice American soldiers, nice West German business-men—or as if Nazis have jumped right out of the skins of the capitalists and clerks who replaced them. Rotten is caught—or drawn like an iron filing to a magnet—and he likes it. We don't.

This wasn't just some cheesy shocker like the Sid Vicious–inspired "Belsen Was a Gas." There was no way out of this song: It had no "solution." This was punk at its most beautiful and most horrible, in its most perfect form and in its most grotesque, not just a protest against the way things were, not that at all, but a protest against life.

What could Rotten have thought of his perform-ance, if he let himself think about it? "Buñuel," Pauline Kael notes, "once referred to some of those who praised *Un Chien Andalou* as 'that crowd of imbeciles who find the film beautiful or poetic when it is fundamentally a desperate and passionate call to murder.' " Much of the twentieth century has been taken up with the attempt to prove that the beautiful, the poetic and a call to murder are all of a piece—and Rotten may have understood this. His incessant shout of "I DON'T UNDERSTAND THIS BIT AT ALL!" as "Holidays" crashed through the wall may have been his way of saying so, his way of saying that, when he looked into the void, he found the void looking back.

Rotten's aim, finally, was to take all the rage, all the intelligence and all the strength in his being and fling it at the world; to make the world notice, to make it doubt its most cherished and unexamined beliefs, to make the world pay for its crimes in the coin of nightmare, and then to end the world—sym-bolically, if no other way was open. And that, I think, he did. It was perhaps the shared perception that such an act was implicit in the momentum of punk that made everything else in punk possible; it was surely the performance of that act that made it necessary for Rotten to remove himself from his story, to rescue himself from the consequences of his performance, to escape the choice of compro-mise or self-destruction.

[IS EVERYBODY HAPPY?]

Rock & roll is over, don't you understand? It's gone on for twenty-five years and it's got to be canceled. *The Pistols*

Johnny Rotten inventing punk style, 1977. After the Sex Pistols broke up, he demolished his persona, rebaptized himself John Lydon, formed Public Image Ltd. and gave interviews denouncing rock generally and punk specifically.

finished rock & roll; they were the last rock & roll band. It's finished now, done with. *And that was all quite a long time ago, when you think of it.*

—John Lydon, February 1980

What we play now is what we can do. It wouldn't be fair to do ranting music, because we've mastered a time change. We can play in another rhythm. So there's just no point. We do a bit of ranting, just to keep it up, but we don't do it all the time. We do something now we couldn't do before.

—Joe Strummer, December 1979

Nothing discredits events like the years immediately following them—that, and the efforts of those who took part in those events to free themselves

from the curse of their failure. The dominant culture reasserts itself, and those who exposed its artifice again disappear, or else walk on as strange relics, pathetic creatures who somehow have yet to get the word they're wearing last year's clothes. Style seizes the time and is destroyed by the passage of time, until enough time has passed to make those styles that expressed more than whim into history. Thus, in 1980, it was incumbent upon John Lydon—once known to all the English-speaking world, and now relatively obscure—to denounce the history he had already made, lest it trap him. "Politics?" he would say. "The Sex Pistols weren't politics. The Sex Pistols were a fiasco. A farce."

Which they were—but as one can reply to anything said about the Sex Pistols, that is not all they were. The Sex Pistols broke rock & roll in half because they turned rock & roll back on itself, exposed its easy answers to false questions and made it necessary to consider all popular culture with suspicion. All ideas about how, in rock & roll, one got from one place to another were suspended and recast. They made it necessary to ask, Can rock & roll ever be taken at face value? What is the relationship between manipulation and innocence? Between anarchy and capitalism? What happens when rock and politics are separated? What happens when they are joined? Is a concern for technique inherently regressive and primitivism inherently self-limiting? If rock & roll is a fraud unworthy of those with something to say, and at the same time the only game in town, what is to be done? Most of all, the Sex Pistols made it necessary to ask what counts *as* rock & roll—for if they could go so far, what of those groups who never even try?

The Sex Pistols made great music. Then, as they had with the rest of rock & roll, they discredited their music. Johnny Rotten's last words at the Sex Pistols' last concert were: "Ever had the feeling you've been cheated?" The Sex Pistols turned back on themselves, and vanished. They did this with such force that it may even turn out that those millions who blithely ignored the Sex Pistols have in some crucial way cut themselves off from rock history, cut themselves out of the process by which, still termite-like, rock & roll will discover what comes next. It may be that those millions are now part of something that— because it raises none of the questions the Pistols defined, but indeed exists to silence them—continues less as rock & roll than as a loud version of pre-rock pop music: all standards, clichés and safety, every surprise counterfeited, every new idea merely a novel means to sell the old.

With the dust of punk blown away, the pop establishment remained in place. Virgin, the Pistols' final label, continued to peddle repackagings of the band's few tracks, brightly titled: *The Great Rock 'n' Roll Swindle, Some Product, Carri On Pistols, Flogging a Dead Horse*. Other labels were happy to push a little new-wave roughness on the radio, happy even to give a chance to John Lydon's abstract music with PiL, certain that if he was still a troublemaker he would, the second time around, make a much more conventional kind of trouble.

Also in place were a few institutions, experimental record companies and a hundred, two hundred, three hundred interesting new bands, for those independent 45s never ceased to appear. And if there were many busy enforcing the rules of pop, there were also those who understood what punk was about and for whom those rules long since had failed to have more than tactical meaning. One might think of Essential Logic, led by a nineteen-year-old named Lora Logic, a refugee from X-Ray Spex in careful pursuit of whatever sound it was that no one else would think to make; of the feminist Raincoats, who may have completed the demystification of popular music made by women; of the edgy, disorienting Gang of Four, who were working, they said, "to redescribe reality and to redescribe rock & roll." All, as it happens, insisted on a certain "distance" from "rock & roll." None was exactly a punk and none would have been even thinkable without punk—which may be to say a great deal, or nothing. These were small possibilities, nibbling away at the boundaries. And so the story goes on, all in pieces once again.

DISCOGRAPHY

A chronological selection of U.K. punk singles and albums, including masterpieces, frauds, hits and obscurities, plus spin-offs and flame-keepers, 1976–80. Unless indicated by "U.S.," all releases are U.K. ☆ = best-selling or influential.

1976

Damned: "New Rose" (Stiff). ☆**Sex Pistols:** "Anarchy in the U.K." (EMI; withdrawn January 1977).

1977

☆**Buzzcocks:** "Spiral Scratch" (New Hormones). **Clash:** "White Riot" b/w "1977" (CBS). **Eater:** "Outside View" (The Label). **Jam:** "In the City" (Polydor). **Damned:** *Damned, Damned, Damned* (Stiff). ☆**Sex Pistols:** "God Save the Queen" (Virgin). ☆**Adverts:** "One Chord Wonders" (Stiff). **Clash:** "Remote Control" b/w "London's Burning" (CBS). ☆**Clash:** *The Clash* (CBS; U.S. Epic; 1979). **Chelsea:** "Right to Work" (Step-Forward). **Cortinas:** "Fascist Dictator" (Step-Forward). **Pork Dukes:** "Bend and Flush" b/w "Throbbing Gristle" (Wood). **Slaughter and the Dogs:** "Cranked Up Really High" (Rabid). **Vibrators:** *Pure Mania* (CBS; later released on U.S. Epic). ☆**Adverts, X-Ray Spex, Buzzcocks, Wire, Eater and Others:** *The Roxy London WC2 (January–April 1977)* (EMI). ☆**Sex Pistols:** "Pretty Vacant" b/w "No Fun" (Virgin). ☆**Rods:** "Do Anything You Wanna Do" (Island). **999:** "I'm Alive" (Labratain). **Members:** "Solitary Confinement" (Stiff). **Stranglers:** "Something Better Change" (UA). **Generation X:** "Your Generation" (Chrysalis). **Police:** "Fall Out" (Illegal). **Rezillos:** "Can't Stand My Baby" (Sensible). ☆**Adverts:** "Gary Gilmore's Eyes" (Anchor). ☆**Clash:** "Complete Control" (CBS). **Only Ones:** "Lovers of Today" (Vengeance). ☆**X-Ray Spex:** "Oh Bondage, Up Yours!" (Virgin). ☆**Sex Pistols:** "Holidays in the Sun" (Virgin). ☆**Adverts:** "Safety in Numbers" b/w "We Who Wait" (Anchor). **Elizabeth (Jonathan King):** "God Save the Sex Pistols" (Creole). ☆**Jam:** *In the City* (Polydor; also U.S.). **Sniveling Shits:** "Terminal Stupid" b/w "I Can't Come" (Ghetto Rockers). ☆**Sex Pistols:** *Never Mind the Bollocks Here's the Sex Pistols* (Virgin; U.S. Warner Bros.). **Eater:** *The Album* (The Label). **Some Chicken:** "Blood on the Wall" (Raw). **Radiators from Space:** "Enemies" b/w "Psychotic Reaction" (Chiswick). **Killjoys:** "Johnny Won't Get to Heaven" (Raw). **Buzzcocks:** "Orgasm Addict" (UA). **Sham '69:** "I Don't Wanna"/"Ulster"/"Red London" (Step-Forward). ☆**Penetration:** "Don't Dictate" (Virgin).

1978

☆**Magazine:** "Shot by Both Sides" (Virgin). ☆**Mekons:** "Never Been in a Riot" (Fast). **Plastic Bertrand:** "Ca Plane pour Moi" (U.S. Sire). ☆**Adverts:** *Crossing the Red Sea with the Adverts* (Bright). **Buzzcocks:** *Another Music in a Different Kitchen* (UA). ☆**X-Ray Spex:** "The Day the World Turned Day-Glo" b/w "Iama Poseur" (X-Ray Spex). ☆**Jam:** *This Is the Modern World* (Polydor; also U.S.). ☆**Stiff Little Fingers:** "Suspect Device" (Rigid Digits). **Subway Sect:** "Nobody's Scared" (Braik). ☆**Wire:** "I Am the Fly" (Harvest). **Alternative TV:** *The Image Has Cracked* (Deptford Fun City). ☆**Clash:** "(White Man) In Hammersmith Palais" (CBS). **Essential Logic:** "Aerosol Burns" (Rough Trade). **Sham '69:** "If the Kids Are United" (Polydor). **Jam:** "A Bomb in Wardour Street" (Polydor). ☆**Stiff Little Fingers:** "Alternative Ulster" (Rough Trade). ☆**Wire:** *Chairs Missing* (Harvest). ☆**X-Ray Spex:** "Identity" (X-Ray Spex/EMI). ☆**Gang of Four:** "Armalite Rifle"/"Damaged Goods"/"Love Like Anthrax" (Fast). **Jam:** "Down in the Tube Station at Midnight" (Polydor). **Penetration:** "Life's a Gamble" (Virgin). ☆**PiL:** "Public Image" (Virgin). **Siouxsie and the Banshees:** *The Scream* (Polydor; later U.S. release). ☆**X-Ray Spex:** *Germfree Adolescents* (X-Ray Spex/EMI). **Clash:** *Give 'Em Enough Rope* (CBS; U.S. Epic). **Kleenex:** "Ain't You" (Rough Trade). **Prag Vec:** "Existential" (Spec). ☆**PiL:** *Public Image* (Virgin).

1979–1980

☆**Essential Logic:** "Wake Up" (Virgin). **The Pop Group:** "She Is Beyond Good and Evil" (Radar). ☆**Gang of Four:** "At Home He's a Tourist" b/w "It's Her Factory" (EMI). ☆**Stiff Little Fingers:** *Inflammable Material* (Rough Trade). ☆**Sex Pistols:** *The Great Rock'n'Roll Swindle* (Virgin). ☆**PiL:** "Death Disco" (Virgin). **Slits:** *Cut* (Island; U.S. Antilles; 1980). ☆**Essential Logic:** *Beat Rhythm News* (Logic/Rough Trade). ☆**Gang of Four:** *Entertainment!* (EMI, U.S. Warner Bros.; 1980). ☆**Pretenders:** *Pretenders* (Real; U.S. Sire; 1980). **Delta 5:** "Now That You're Gone" (Rough Trade). ☆**Raincoats:** *The Raincoats* (Rough Trade). ☆**PiL:** *Metal Box* (Virgin Metal; U.S. Island as *Second Edition*; 1980). ☆**Marianne Faithfull:** *Broken English* (Island; also U.S.). **Clash:** *London Calling* (CBS Clash; U.S. Epic; 1980).

WOMEN IN REVOLT

BY HOLLY GEORGE-WARREN

It was a cold, rainy Sunday night in 1974, and upstairs at New York's Max's Kansas City, a gaunt figure swayed hypnotically onstage: "Jesus died for somebody's sins/ But not mine." Thus began Patti Smith's version of Van Morrison's "Gloria," every garage band's favorite cover song. As Smith got warmed up, hands fluttering like birds, the history of rock & roll spewed forth, like a forty-five-minute stream-of-consciousness poem: "The Hunter Gets Captured by the Game" (written by Smokey Robinson for the Marvelettes) segued into the Stones' "Paint It Black" into Smith's own song-saga "Piss Factory," chronicling her life before rock & roll salvation. Mixed in between songs was Smith's Beat-derived poetry. Rock & roll was about to be changed—and Patti Smith, like no other woman, helped usher in this transformation.

Women had been a part of rock & roll since its earliest days, most often as vocalists. Beginning in the late Fifties, girl groups brought their seamless vocal harmonies to the radio airwaves, but their creative imput was limited to vocalizing; male producers handled the song selection and arrangements. During the Sixties talented women made inroads as introspective folksingers. Also in the Sixties, in the tradition of Bessie Smith, heartbroken blues mamas expressed themselves through a narrowly defined format: Janis Joplin could transform a song written

---

Ain't It Strange: Patti Smith doffed her rock-priestess mantle for domestic life in Detroit.

by someone else—often a male—but she couldn't transcend her own role.

Rock & roll as played by men—aggressive, sexual, loud!—is what looked like the most fun, though, and promised the greatest release. In addition to providing the tools for making an artistic statement, there's nothing like riffing a few power chords or beating on a drum kit to blow off steam. Most important, playing an instrument symbolized taking control of one's means of self-expression. By the late Sixties a few women dared to do just that. Maureen Tucker pioneered minimalist drumming in the Velvet Underground, but her contribution was overshadowed by bandleaders Lou Reed and John Cale. Bonnie Raitt took up the blues guitar, following in the footsteps of Memphis Minnie, but spent more time perfecting her skillful slide playing than writing songs and presenting her own unique vision.

But in 1969 four California-based women who had been playing on their own since their teens de-cided to form a band, write their own songs and, of course, play their own instruments (bass, guitar, keyboards and drums). Accomplished musicians, they first backed Barbra Streisand on her ''rock'' album, *Stoney End*, and then got themselves a record deal and a big-shot producer, Richard Perry. Although they named themselves Fanny, in interviews they scoffed at their femaleness and said they played rock & roll just like their male counterparts. Unfortunately, they must have been referring to hard-rock bands like Iron Butterfly, which made—with the exception of a song or two—for a plodding, leaden first album (*Fanny*, 1970). By their third and fourth albums, *Fanny Hill* (1972) and *Mother's Pride* (1973), on which their songwriting had improved and they had lightened up their sound, it was too late. Fanny had never managed to crack the Top 100, relentless touring had taken its toll, and the ''novelty'' of all-female bands (including the eight-piece jazz-rock ensemble Isis and a few others) had worn off.

Patti Smith and Lou Reed at the Russian Tea Room in 1977: The torch is passed.

Along came Patti Smith. She'd been a rock & roll fanatic, idolizing Keith Richards and Jim Morrison, but instead of wanting to fuck them, she wanted to *be* them. Fortunately, Smith was also a poet and a visionary, so her "becoming them" wasn't a poor imitation, but a metamorphosis. The music she had absorbed all those years glued to her radio and hi-fi, first in Pitman, New Jersey, then in New York, percolated into a fusion of sounds ranging from the girl groups, to Stax-Volt, to the Morrisons (Van and Jim), Hendrix and the Stones. Smith's immersion in the writings of French poets Arthur Rimbaud and Charles Baudelaire added a hallucinatory quality to her lyrics.

Smith had been doing poetry readings around lower Manhattan since 1971, eventually enlisting erstwhile rock critic Lenny Kaye on guitar and Richard Sohl on piano to back her up. Gradually she began singing her own compositions, as well as her rock & roll favorites, alongside her poetry. By the mid-Seventies the performances were drawing crowds, a single of "Piss Factory" had been pressed by a small label, and Smith signed with a major record label. With Jay Dee Daugherty joining on drums and Ivan Kral on bass, the Patti Smith Group was born. Following in the tradition of garage rockers, Smith herself was soon grappling with the guitar (credited on her second album as Fender Duo Sonic)—and another idea's time had come, soon to be brought to complete fruition by punk: Anybody can play an instrument.

Horses, Smith's first album, in 1975, musically combined all the elements that had inspired her to play rock & roll; its lyrics were a surreal mix of ambiguous sexuality, biblical references and Symbolist-influenced poetry. As in performance, she merged her own compositions with standards like "Land of 1,000 Dances" and "Gloria," transforming them into dangerous, insinuating mood pieces. Smith's androgynous persona and her jarring vocal mannerisms added to the album's impact. Onstage, her monologues, which she called "babelogues," were radical, provocative and, at times, incomprehensible.

The band's second album, *Radio Ethiopia* (1976), was more opaque and less accessible than the first. Eerie sounds (and noise) and populist-political diatribes punctuated the music. In concert Smith became a woman possessed; during one particularly feverish performance, she accidentally hurled herself from a Florida stage, breaking her neck and sidelining her career for more than a year.

In the meantime, on the West Coast an entrepreneurial producer-promotor, Kim Fowley, had decided to revive the idea of girls with guitars. Following through on the promise made by Fanny, Fowley rounded up five comely teens who wanted to play rock & roll and named them the Runaways. Fowley, reminiscent of the puppeteers behind the Sixties girl groups, was credited as "producer and director" on the first album (members' ages—sixteen and seventeen—were listed next to their names and their instruments to emphasize their jailbait status). The band's anthem (penned by Fowley) was "Cherry Bomb." Guitarist Joan Jett, who gradually took over lead vocals, got the last laugh, though: Touring and working on songs enabled her to hone her craft, so by the time the Runaways fell apart in 1979, there was at least one rising star on the horizon.

Concurrently, on New York's Lower East Side punk was building up steam. Not long after Smith's second album came out in 1976, bands with only a fundamental knowledge of how to play an instrument (and in some cases, no ability at all) had begun gigging in a few small clubs and performance spaces. Some of the more accomplished new bands prominently featured women, among them bassist Tina Weymouth of Talking Heads and singer-songwriter Debbie Harry of Blondie. A young woman named Chrissie Hynde had left her native Ohio and was attempting to form a band in London. Like Smith, Hynde was obsessed with rock & roll; she claimed Iggy Pop and Brian Jones as inspirations. She'd been in and out of London since 1973, trying to get something going with the songs she'd been writing. Hynde had gigged briefly with Masters of the Backside, who became the Damned, the first British punk band to record an album. Her guitar skills qualified her to give lessons to Johnny Rotten, lead singer of the Sex Pistols. (Legend has it that Pistols Svengali Malcolm McLaren angrily stopped Hynde from teaching Lydon how to play.)

By 1978 women had begun to appear in mixed-gender British bands, such as Siouxsie and the Banshees, founded by Sex Pistol fan Siouxsie Sioux, and rabble-rousers X-Ray Spex,

Jailbait with a beat: the Runaways *(from left):* Sandy West, Lita Ford, Vicki Blue, Joan Jett.

led by Poly Styrene, composer of the incendiary "Oh Bondage, Up Yours." Hynde finally got a band together—James Honeyman-Scott on guitar, Pete Farndon on bass and Martin Chambers on drums—and named it the Pretenders. Their first single, a cover of the Kinks' "Stop Your Sobbing," b/w Hynde's own caustic "The Wait," whizzed into the British Top Forty in 1979. Hynde's tough stance coupled with her shimmering vocals brought instant acclaim at shows performed in Europe and England. The Pretenders' debut (*The Pretenders*, 1980) was chockful of punky pop gems, like "Brass in Pocket," "Tattooed Love Boys," "Kid" and "Mystery Achievement"—songs that showcased Hynde's forthright, incisive lyrics and Honeyman-Scott's inventive guitar playing. A tour of the States bore out the band's musical prowess on record, and the

album climbed to Number Nine in America, eventually going platinum.

Finally, would-be female musicians had role models who could express themselves as women—and bands led by women started popping up everywhere. In England a new breed of girl groups were the complete opposite of their Sixties counterparts: The Slits and the Raincoats made no attempt to be like the guys but asserted their own rebellious spirit to create rhythmic, offbeat songs that expressed feminist ideas. In New York Lydia Lunch intimidated audiences with her beatnik-from-hell demeanor, while fronting a succession of experimental bands such as Teenage Jesus and the Jerks and 8 Eyed Spy. The Bush Tetras,

Chrissie Hynde, the great Pretender, breaking records and breaking barriers.

three androgynous women and a male drummer, had a club hit with the danceable, telltale "Too Many Creeps." On the West Coast Exene Cervenka lent her compelling poetic and vocal talents to the punk-meets-rockabilly combo, X.

Meanwhile, Patti Smith, whose first two albums hadn't sold all that well, recovered from her accident, and in 1978 returned with an avant-garde-to-pop crossover album, *Easter*. Among the surreal imagery and politico rants—"I haven't fucked much with the past/But I've fucked plenty with the future"—was "Because the Night," an ardent pop-rocker Smith had written with Bruce Springsteen. It became Smith's first—and only—hit single. The followup album, *Wave* (1979), was even more commercially successful. Smith had somehow done it—gone from underground rebel priestess to two Top Twenty albums—but curiously, once she had accomplished this coup, she disappeared. By 1980 she was living in Detroit with her future husband, ex-MC5 guitarist Fred "Sonic" Smith, with whom she would have two sons. Smith remained there out of the limelight until the release of *Dream of Life,* in 1988. A blazing collaboration with her husband, the album gave proof that Smith's artistic vision was still intact.

As the Eighties dawned, some assertive women, such as the guitar-playing Nancy Wilson and her sister Ann, who formed Heart, and vocalist Pat Benatar, had scored commercial success with their MOR hard rock. Bands composed entirely of women had become a standard on the underground club circuit; however, they were still unheard of on major record label rosters or in the Top Ten. Quite suddenly, five Southern California party gals changed all that. The Go-Go's climbed their way out of dank L.A. punk clubs and hit the big time with their debut album, *Beauty and the Beat* (1981). In sync with the less-is-more attitude of the day, their streamlined pop nuggets "We Got the Beat" and "Our Lips Are Sealed" helped propel their album to platinum status. With solid songwriters in Jane Wiedlin and Charlotte Caffey, and a disciplined drummer in Gina Schock, the Go-Go's projected the image of women gleefully playing rock & roll on their own terms. Winning a place in history as "the first all-girl band to make a Number One album," the Go-Go's burned out after two more (less commercially successful) albums, *Vacation* (1982) and *Talk Show* (1984). In any case, the Go-Go's proved one thing: All-women bands could sell records.

Throughout the Eighties more and more women would ascend to the top of the charts on their own terms. First, Joan Jett, older and wiser after her stint in the Runaways, crafted a Gary Glitter–derived version of stripped-down hard rock. Jett was inspired by bass-playing leather-clad Suzi Quatro, who had scored hits in England leading her own glitter-influenced band in 1973–74, but who never gained recognition in her native America (until she played a parody of herself on the nostalgic TV sitcom *Happy Days*). Jett carved out her own niche with the delinquent-pride anthem "Bad Reputation" ("I don't give a damn/'Bout my bad reputation"), which helped to sell her debut album in 1981. She and her producer-manager, Kenny Laguna, had put it out themselves when no American label would, but its success landed Jett a record deal. Her next venture, *I Love Rock 'n' Roll* (1981), performed with her band the Blackhearts, was, unexpectedly, a huge smash. The title cut, in fact, was the biggest-selling single of 1982.

During the early Eighties the Pretenders had continued to sell records, too, but by the third album, *Learning to Crawl* (1984), Hynde was struggling with the repercussions of the shattering drug-related deaths of guitarist Honeyman-Scott and bassist Farndon (who had been dumped by the band due to his drug addiction). This album turned out to be the most successful yet, on the considerable strength of the plaintive "Back on the Chain Gang" and the ballsy "Middle of the Road." Subsequent albums featured songs reflecting the birth of Hynde's two children and her relationships with their fathers, Ray Davies of the Kinks and Jim Kerr of Simple Minds (to whom Hynde was briefly married). Throughout the decade and into the Nineties, Hynde would keep the Pretenders going, although the band's membership constantly fluctuated, as did the albums' quality and sales. Yet to falter, though, are Hynde's incandescent vocals, sturdy rhythm guitar playing and fierce self-determination.

The year 1984 was probably the breakthrough year for women making their mark. Two of the three top-selling artists were Cyndi Lauper and Madonna. Lauper's "Girls Just Want to Have Fun" was written by a guy, Robert Hazard, but her interpretation of the uptempo pop anthem, along with her quirky vocal

EP featured polished playing and harmony singing that was reminiscent of the best of the girl groups. The Bangles were signed to Columbia Records and produced a rocking first album, *All Over the Place* (1985), that sounded like the Beatles-meet-the-Mamas-and-Papas-minus-the-Papas. Their next album, *Different Light* (1986), hit pay dirt with the top-selling singles "Manic Monday" (written for the band by Prince) and "Walk Like an Egyptian." After one more album the group disbanded.

By the end of the Eighties, women, frequently instrumentalists in mixed-gender bands, also had made headway into the most male-dominated genres: rap (Salt-n-Pepa, MC Lyte and Queen Latifah), heavy metal (Girlschool, Vixen and ex-Runaway Lita Ford) and even jazz (drummer Terri Lyne Carrington, who led her own band). A vanguard of gutsy female singer-songwriters—Suzanne Vega, Tracy Chapman, Michelle Shocked and the Indigo Girls—were breaking new ground artistically and earning commercial success.

Just another manic Monday: Susanna Hoffs demonstrates her air-guitar skills on the road with the Bangles.

and visual style, smashed the stereotype for female vocalists. Lauper's first solo album, *She's So Unusual,* yielded four Top Ten singles, and her madcap persona landed her on the cover of numerous magazines. Madonna, after debuting with a dance-music album and street-smart savvy, hit Number One with *Like a Virgin,* and went on to become one of the most successful performers in music history. Tina Turner, who had been under the thumb of her then-husband and partner Ike Turner for twenty years, made a startling comeback with three Top Ten singles and a Top Five album, *Private Dancer.*

Around this time another all-female group was gigging the L.A. clubs. The Bangs, who would become the Bangles, were founded by sisters Vicki (on lead guitar and vocals) and Debbi Peterson (drums and vocals). With Susanna Hoffs on vocals and guitar, the band enlisted bassist Michael Steele, who, much to her chagrin, had been one of Kim Fowley's very first Runaways. An independent-label

Perhaps the most assertive and creative of all the women artists to arrive in the late Eighties was Sinéad O'Connor. From Dublin, Ireland, O'Connor had already written a hit song for an Irish band called In Tua Nua at age fourteen and contributed to a soundtrack by U2's the Edge before recording her first album in 1987 at age twenty. Frustrated by the album's initial producer, O'Connor produced the work herself. The result, *The Lion and the Cobra* (1987), was a unique collection of her own impassioned, atmospheric songs sung with a voice that could vary from banshee wail ("Mandinka") to high-pitched yelps ("Jerusalem") to soul-baring whispers ("Drink Before the War"). O'Connor's gripping vocals perfectly matched her songs' often painful subject matter, such as betrayal ("Troy") and abandonment ("Jackie"). The first album spawned club hits, the funky "I Want Your (Hands on Me)" (which O'Connor rerecorded with a rap by MC Lyte) and dance rocker "Mandinka." With her shaved head and outspoken viewpoints, though, O'Connor aroused the public's ire—first in England with strongly worded pro-IRA comments and later, to an even greater extent, in America.

O'Connor's second album, the masterful *I Do Not*

Want What I Haven't Got (1990), covered more uncharted territory and, again, O'Connor produced herself. Her progression as an artist was summed up in the gorgeous opening ballad, ''Feel So Different'': ''The whole time I'd never seen / That all I'd need was inside me.'' Throughout, O'Connor's vocals powerfully display a remarkable emotional intensity, and her guitar parts and arrangements add to the songs' irradiance. The subject matter is even more personal and pain-wracked than on her debut. Not long after its release, the album produced a chart-topping smash hit, ''Nothing Compares 2 U,'' a Prince song, that O'Connor delivered with a heart-rending sadness punctuated by moments of tough obstinacy. *I Do Not Want* then catapulted to Number One, but fame became too much for O'Connor. Her artistic triumph was deflated by a backlash in America against her forbidding the national anthem to be played before her concert, refusing to appear on the Grammys and making comments critical of the United States. In performance, O'Connor spat out the words to ''Emperor's New Clothes'' more vehemently than ever: ''Whatever it may bring / I will have my own policies / I will sleep with a clear conscience / I will sleep in peace.''

A third release, the EP *My Special Child,* from 1991, consisted of live versions of two songs and the anguished ''My Special Child,'' a devastatingly painful composition about an abortion, which only a woman like O'Connor could so effectively create. By 1992 she had retreated to Britain and was concentrating on acting, but since, according to O'Connor, ''I will take this road much further / Though I know not where it takes me'' (from ''I Do Not Want What I Haven't Got''), chances are this talented, headstrong woman will continue to create provocative works of art.

In the twenty years since Patti Smith first took the stage at Max's, women like O'Connor have increasingly insisted on making artistic statements on their own terms. This louder, more assertive female voice has added to the diversity of rock & roll and infused it with a new energy. Perhaps most important, it has reinforced the original liberating message that emanated from rock & roll, beginning with Elvis: that *anybody* can make rock & roll music. Obviously, only a select few can become cultural icons while doing so—but anyone can give it a shot and, in the process, discover a means of self-expression. As more women plug in electric guitars and bash away at drum kits, they are empowered, articulating a voice that before had gone unheard. And what they have to say might just make a difference—and make it to Number One.

DISCOGRAPHY

ALBUMS

Bangles: *Bangles* (Faulty Products; 1982). *All Over the Place* (Columbia; ☆80, 1984). *Different Light* (Columbia; ☆2, 1986). *Everything* (Columbia; ☆15, 1988). *Greatest Hits* (Columbia; ☆97, 1990). **Go-Go's:** *Beauty and the Beat* (I.R.S.; ☆1, 1981). *Vacation* (I.R.S.; ☆8, 1982). *Talk Show* (I.R.S.; ☆18, 1984). *Go-Go's Greatest* (I.R.S.; ☆127, 1990). **Joan Jett:** *Bad Reputation* (Boardwalk; ☆51, 1981). *I Love Rock 'n' Roll* (Boardwalk; ☆2, 1981). *Album* (Blackheart; ☆20, 1983). *Glorious Results of a Misspent Youth* (MCA; ☆67, 1984). *Good Music* (Blackheart/CBS; ☆105, 1986). *Up Your Alley* (CBS; ☆19, 1988). *The Hit List* (Blackheart; ☆36, 1990). *Notorious* (Blackheart/CBS; 1991). **Sinéad O'Connor:** *The Lion and the Cobra* (Chrysalis; ☆36, 1988). *I Do Not Want What I Haven't Got* (Chrysalis; ☆1, 1990). *My Special Child* (Chrysalis; EP, 1991). **The Pretenders:** *Pretenders* (Sire; ☆9, 1980). *Pretenders II* (Sire; ☆10, 1981). *Learning to Crawl* (Sire; ☆5, 1984). *Get Close* (Sire; ☆25, 1986). *The Singles* (Sire; ☆69, 1987). *packed!* (Sire; ☆48, 1990). **Patti Smith:** *Horses* (Arista; ☆47, 1975). *Radio Ethiopia* (Arista; 1976). *Easter* (Arista; ☆20, 1978). *Wave* (Arista; ☆18, 1979). *Dream of Life* (Arista; ☆65, 1988).

(Chart positions compiled from Joel Whitburn's *Record Research*, based on *Billboard*'s LPs chart.)

Sinéad O'Connor: Banshee wails, soul-baring whispers.

BRUCE SPRINGSTEEN

BY ANTHONY DeCURTIS

T he day after John Lennon was killed, Steve Van Zandt, then the guitarist in Bruce Springsteen's E Street Band, asked the group's tour manager if that night's show would be postponed. He was told the show was on. Van Zandt was so upset that, as he told writer Fred Schruers in ROLLING STONE in 1981, he went to Springsteen "saying that I felt really weird about going onstage, that I couldn't put it together. And he really just reminded me of why we do what we do, and how it was important to go out that night in particular. . . . It's really lucky to be close to him at moments like that."

That ability to inspire, to convey the meaning at the heart of painful events, to create a hard, uncompromising sense of purpose, is what sets Bruce Springsteen apart from his superstar peers in the rock & roll pantheon. He hasn't changed the world the way Elvis Presley or the Beatles did, and he hasn't penetrated the essence of rock & roll fervor with the fierce elegance the Stones achieved at their strongest. Dylan's astonishing run of revolutionary masterworks in the mid-Sixties sets a standard that Springsteen will never attain; he can't sing as spec-

tacularly well as Marvin Gaye or Otis Redding, or dance with the physical genius of Michael Jackson. But if you want an artist whose work, both on record and onstage, compels a compassionate understanding of people's actual lives—their emotions and imaginings, their jobs and their play—you have nowhere to go in the realm of rock & roll but to Bruce Springsteen.

That virtue was evident even on Springsteen's staggeringly word-drunk, dizzily uneven first two albums, *Greetings from Asbury Park, N.J.* and *The Wild, the Innocent and the E Street Shuffle,* both from 1973. Signed to Columbia Records at twenty-three by the

Bruce onstage: Are you talkin' to me?

619

legendary John Hammond, who had previously brought the likes of Billie Holiday and Bob Dylan to the label, Springsteen was energetically promoted as the "new Dylan," despite (or, more likely, because of) his disturbing tendency to write lines like "Madman drummers bummers and Indians in the summer with a teenage diplomat." However, at his best—on songs such as "Growin' Up," "Spirit in the Night," "4th of July, Asbury Park (Sandy)" and "Wild Billy's Circus Story"—Springsteen demonstrated a striking ability to evoke, without the slightest condescension, the transient thrills, dead-end ambience and spiritual desperation of working-class lives lived within the tawdry carnival atmosphere of the Jersey Shore resorts in which he himself had come of age.

Moreover, Springsteen soon began to emerge as a figure who could restore the faith in rock & roll that seemed to have died with the Sixties. Nixon was president, Watergate was breaking, disco and glam rock were ascending, the music business was solidifying its corporate power, punk was in the offing, the Me Decade was taking shape. In the midst of all that, Springsteen not only was giving passionate voice to characters whose lives could not have been further removed from the tinselly world of Seventies rock, but, by way of tumultuous live shows that even then were running in the three-hour range, he insisted that this music was the most important thing in the world to him and that no lesser commitment on the part of his audience was satisfactory. By the time ROLLING STONE editor Jon Landau announced in Boston's *Real Paper* in spring 1974, "I saw rock & roll's future and its name is Bruce Springsteen," the stage was set for a breakthrough.

It came, artistically at least, the following year with *Born to Run,* Springsteen's first masterpiece. Inspired by the spine-tingling emotionalism of Phil Spector and Roy Orbison, Springsteen crafted open-ended songs rife with operatic reach and symphonic power, songs like "Thunder Road," "Backstreets," "Born to Run" and "Jungleland" that took the everyday triumphs and failures of his beach-town losers and shakers and raised them to an epic scale.

In counterpoint to such bold romantic excess, Springsteen also had learned the value of restraint. Instead of writing as if he were being paid by the word, he stripped his lyrics down—this is relatively speaking, of course; he would streamline even further in the future—losing none of their wild beauty

A rock & roll hero: Springsteen with the original E Street Band, December 1973. Appearances that year in small clubs along the East Coast earned him a loyal cult following.

and leaving room for his singing to soar. Only rare moments on his first two albums had suggested that Springsteen was capable of the lovely simplicity—the poetry, really—of these lyrics from "Thunder Road": "There were ghosts in the eyes / Of all the boys you sent away / They haunt this dusty beach road / In the skeleton frames of burned out Chevrolets . . . And in the lonely cool before dawn / You hear their engines roaring on / But when you get to the porch they're gone / On the wind."

"Born to Run" cracked the Top Forty and the album, selling well over half a million copies at the time, expanded Springsteen's audience considerably. And with the help of the E Street Band in its classic lineup—Clarence "Big Man" Clemons on saxophone, Miami Steve Van Zandt on guitar, Roy Bittan on piano, Danny Federici on organ, Garry Tallent on bass and Mighty Max Weinberg on drums—his live shows continued to be case studies in the ability of rock & roll to change lives. The hype surrounding Springsteen by this point—perfectly epitomized by his being featured simultaneously on the covers of *Time* and *Newsweek* for the week of October 27th, 1975—generated something of a backlash, however. For the most part his following remained restricted to the Northeast and small pockets of the Midwest, South and Southwest.

More damagingly, Springsteen had a falling-out with Mike Appel, who had been his manager and producer for nearly four years. When work in the studio on *Born to Run* had bogged down, Springsteen had brought in critic Jon Landau, with whom he had become friendly, to help out. Landau, who quit his job at ROLLING STONE to work on the album, proved invaluable in providing a framework for realizing Springsteen's enormous ambitions, and he ended up sharing the production credit with Springsteen and Appel.

When the time came to begin work on *Born to Run*'s followup, Springsteen declared that he wanted Landau as his producer. Appel, in his capacity as Springsteen's manager, refused to grant permission. Springsteen and Appel sued each other, and, in the summer of 1976, a New York State Supreme Court judge issued an injunction barring Springsteen from entering the studio to work with Landau. Springsteen grew desperate and, at one point in the proceedings, was called into the judge's chambers for failing to maintain control of himself when Appel's attorney, Leonard Marks, was taking his deposition. Springsteen's absolute conviction that Landau was the only person who could bring his ideas to fruition was made poignantly clear in an affidavit he gave in December 1976, in which he spoke movingly of Landau's "unique ability to communicate with me" and stated that his sole interest in wanting to work with Landau was "my career, which up until now holds the promise of my being able to significantly contribute to, and possibly influence, a generation of music. No amount of money could compensate me if I were to lose this opportunity."

Springsteen and Appel finally settled their claims on May 28th, 1977, and Springsteen and Landau

Springsteen (*second from right*) with Steve Van Zandt, Ronnie Spector and Southside Johnny Lyon (*right*).

went into the studio shortly afterward. The result, released in June of 1978, was *Darkness on the Edge of Town*. A stark, haunted album about people who, in Springsteen's words, "are going from nowhere to nowhere," *Darkness* clearly reflects the grimness of his mood during his legal struggles. "Got a head on collision, / Smashin' in my guts, man," he sang on "Badlands," the album's opening track, "I'm caught in a cross fire, / That I don't understand." The songs' arrangements and Springsteen's writing are pared back considerably from *Born to Run*, while his guitar playing had grown more savage and elemental, as if the roaring, howling sounds were being wrenched not from an instrument, but directly from his soul.

Unsparing though the album is, one track on it, the graceful mid-tempo ballad "Factory," hinted at a certain maturing in Springsteen's political understanding. For once, the workingmen in the song are not seen simply as the benighted enemies of aspiring adolescent rockers, the oppositional Sixties terms in which Springsteen had often cast his own father in the transfixing onstage monologues that had become staples of his performances. The lives of the men in "Factory" may be circumscribed and laced with violent frustration, but Springsteen's feeling vocal and Roy Bittan's sympathetic piano accord them a well-deserved dignity.

Springsteen took another small political step forward the following year, when, in the wake of an accident at the nuclear plant in Three Mile Island, Pennsylvania, he agreed to headline two nights of benefit shows at Madison Square Garden in New York. The week of so-called MUSE (Musicians United for Safe Energy) concerts featured performances by Jackson Browne, James Taylor and Crosby, Stills and Nash and were designed to raise money for antinuclear groups around the country. The nights Springsteen played were the only shows that sold out, though, unlike all of the other participating artists, he refused to issue a public statement about the cause and would not agree to perform until he was assured that none of the money raised would go to any political candidate.

The River, the double album Springsteen released in 1980, continued the clear-eyed exploration of working-class life he had begun with "Factory." Like Springsteen's live shows, the album was curiously split between songs of extraordinary substance and emotional insight ("Independence Day,"

"Point Blank") and one-dimensional garage-rock toss-offs ("Crush on You," "I'm a Rocker"), almost as if the raveups were providing an escapist sound-track to the bounded lives described in the more serious songs. *The River* also pitted songs about the longing for commitment and connection ("The Ties That Bind," "I Wanna Marry You") against songs like "Stolen Car" that suggested the inevitability of loss and a life of terrible freedom on the endless night-lit highway.

The album held those tense contradictions in suspension, while managing also to spin off Springsteen's first Top Ten hit, "Hungry Heart." That success and the tour in support of *The River* gained him the national stardom for which he had seemed destined. Meanwhile, Springsteen was still pursuing his political education, organizing a benefit for Vietnam veterans in 1981 and reading books along the lines of Joe Klein's biography of folksinger-activist Woody Guthrie, Henry Steele Commager and Allan Nevins's *A Short History of the United States* and Ron Kovic's *Born on the Fourth of July*. As Springsteen's vision of America consequently darkened, his newfound popularity was teaching him the heartbreaking lesson that, however much it had offered him a redemptive direction, rock & roll was helpless to protect him or anyone else against the world's dreadful uncertainties. As he told his biographer Dave Marsh, he could only greet the existential crisis into which he plunged with stunned disbelief: "This can't be happening to me. *I'm the guy with the guitar.*"

The guy with the guitar stiffened his spine and confronted the horrors both within and outside himself with *Nebraska* (1982), a quiet, entirely arresting series of character studies set in an America that systematically destroys all sense of community and condemns its citizens to lives of fearsome isolation. Springsteen, accompanied, for the most part, only by his own acoustic guitar and harmonica, made the album at home on a four-track cassette recorder; the vocals—desolate whispers punctuated by forlorn wails—sound fully private and alone, as if the listener were eavesdropping on the singer's thoughts. Unforgiving and unrelieved, *Nebraska* alienated much of Springsteen's new audience even as it achieved a standard of personal record making that perhaps had previously been approached only by John Lennon's *Plastic Ono Band*.

Then in the spring of 1984 Springsteen dropped the bomb. If *Nebraska* was indrawn and deliberately scaled down, *Born in the U.S.A.* couldn't have been thematically more outward-looking or any bigger sounding. The title track is a superb example of political songwriting. The story of a Vietnam veteran whose birthright—asserted in Springsteen's repeated, anguished cries of "Born in the U.S.A."—becomes a psychological death sentence, the song honors the forgotten life of its subject with a keyboard line reminiscent in its melancholic majesty of Aaron Copland and drumming that slams home the singer's gripping fear and despair. The album's stirring closing track, "My Hometown," demonstrates the remarkable distance Springsteen had traveled as a songwriter. From "Madman drummers bummers" he had now arrived at the point at which he could move listeners to tears with lines as understated as these:

> Now Main Street's whitewashed windows
> And vacant stores
> Seems like there ain't nobody
> Wants to come down here no more
> They're closing down the textile mill
> Across the railroad tracks
> Foreman says these jobs are going, boys
> And they ain't comin' back
> To your hometown.

"Dancing in the Dark," the first single from *Born in the U.S.A.*, rocketed into the Top Five, partly because of a performance video filmed by Brian De Palma, and after Springsteen and the E Street Band—with Nils Lofgren replacing Steve Van Zandt on guitar, and Patti Scialfa added on background vocals—launched their tour in late June, it became clear that Brucemania was in full effect. Unfortunately, that mania was being fueled by the summer Olympics, which were being held in Los Angeles and which had whipped the United States into a disturbing nationalistic frenzy.

Amid the confusing swirl of conflicting cultural currents, *Born in the U.S.A.*, with its American flag cover and surging title track, was being taken by millions of people for a jingoistic anthem; Springsteen, who had pumped his body up with weights, was dubbed "The Rambo of Rock," and President Ronald Reagan, running for reelection, cited Springsteen as a positive example of American values. After attending a Springsteen concert in Washing-

Greetings from Asbury Park.

ton, D.C., conservative columnist George Will praised the show because "the recitation of closed factories and other problems always seem punctuated by a grand, cheerful affirmation: 'Born in the U.S.A.!' "

In the face of these efforts to recast him in terms he clearly found repellent, Springsteen had no choice but to make his political views more explicit than he ever had before. He rebutted the president from the stage one night in Pittsburgh, wondering if perhaps *Nebraska* was Reagan's favorite album, and, as he traveled the country, he stepped up his efforts on behalf of food banks, veterans' groups and progressive union organizations. Through it all Springsteen, in a way that simultaneously seemed clinical and perverse, refused to back off from building as large an audience as possible for himself. By the time the tour's last leg closed in October 1985, Springsteen was playing multiple dates in sold-out stadiums, and *Born in the U.S.A.* had sold well over 10 million copies.

As a means of sweeping aside whatever expectations may have been created by the *Born in the U.S.A.*

juggernaut, Springsteen released *Bruce Springsteen and the E Street Band Live/1975–85* in the fall of 1986. A powerful summary statement, the three-CD set effectively wiped the historical slate clean and freed Springsteen to move in whatever direction he wished. And his next move was audacious. Released in October 1987, *Tunnel of Love* shifted Springsteen's attention from affairs of state to matters of romance; it is one of the most mature explorations of love and its discontents in all of popular music.

Musically the album is far softer and more introspective than *Born in the U.S.A.*—the E Street Band is on hand, but in a number of smaller, differing configurations—and it is suffused with troubling images of deception and self-deception. While "Tougher Than the Rest" is a bracing pledge to see love through to forever, songs like "Brilliant Disguise," "Two Faces" and the title track suggest the virtual impossibility of achieving sufficient self-knowledge —let alone knowledge of another person—to make any such pledge meaningful beyond the moment in which it is made. *Tunnel of Love* is deeply unsettling—a *Nebraska* of the heart. And when, not long

Born in the U.S.A.

after the album's release, Springsteen split with Julianne Phillips, the woman he married in 1985, and took up with background singer Patti Scialfa, it seemed prophetic.

In the most emphatic political gesture of his career to that point, Springsteen signed on to headline the Amnesty International Human Rights Now! Tour, which kicked off in London on September 2nd, 1988, and closed on October 15th in Buenos Aires. In between, the tour stopped at twenty cities throughout Europe, North America, Asia, Central America and South America, bringing Springsteen to places he had never seen before. In an even more pointed political statement, Springsteen performed two solo acoustic sets in Los Angeles in November 1991, in support of the Christic Institute, an organization that was attempting to sue a group of U.S.-

sponsored covert operatives for allegedly bombing a press conference in Nicaragua in 1984.

By the start of 1992 Springsteen had brought himself to a critical pass similar to the junctures at which he found himself after *Born to Run* and *Born in the U.S.A.* He hadn't released an album in well over four years and had played only two shows in well over three. He had married Patti Scialfa, had two children with her and moved to a $4-million mansion near Beverly Hills. He had broken up the E Street Band and spent over two years recording with L.A. session players. No one knew what to expect from him, and the music scene had changed so dramatically in the years during which he'd been lying low, no one was sure what a Bruce Springsteen album would mean in a world dominated by rap, dance music and metal.

But Springsteen was very likely not thinking about those questions at all. His greatest strength as an artist has been his insistence on looking inside

Springsteen and Patti Scialfa stroll the streets of New York.

himself, his refusal to make any move that is not internally determined. Even his political songs never came from the newspaper, but from his ability to imagine the experience of people trapped by their circumstances, to find their emotions within himself and write from there.

Predictably, when Springsteen finally delivered, he still managed to surprise. In the spring of 1992 he released not one, but two albums: *Human Touch* and *Lucky Town*. This time, Roy Bittan was the only E Street Band member on the albums; Springsteen was now officially a solo artist. Companion pieces, the discs themselves revealed a light at the end of the tunnel of love, as Springsteen traced an emotional movement from the sort of questioning and self-doubt reminiscent of *Tunnel of Love* to commitment and domestic fulfillment.

Still, *Lucky Town* ends with an elegant, folkish ballad, "My Beautiful Reward," that brings the two-album suite to an almost surreally unsettled close. The striking last verse of the song—"Tonight I can feel the cold wind at my back / I'm flyin' high over gray fields, my feathers long and black / Down along the river's silent edge I soar / Searching for my beautiful reward"—harks back to the troubling restlessness at the heart of *Human Touch* and hints of a darkness on the edge of *Lucky Town*. When the albums failed to sustain the sales that had propelled them into the Top Five upon their initial release, some people again began to wonder about the relevance of Springsteen's music to the Nineties.

Springsteen used to like to talk about the ending of *Wise Blood*, the movie John Huston made based on the novel by Flannery O'Connor. By the end of the film, the Christ-haunted central character, Hazel Motes, is mortifying his flesh in the manner of medieval Christian saints, going so far as to blind himself and wrap barbed wire around his chest. "One of my favorite parts was the end," Springsteen said in ROLLING STONE, "where he's doing all these terrible things to himself, and the woman comes in and says, 'There's no reason for it. People have quit doing it.' And he says, 'They ain't quit doing it as long as I'm doing it.'"

If people have come to think that no one is any longer making the sort of music Bruce Springsteen makes, they have to think again. They ain't quit doing it as long as he's doing it—and as long as he's doing it, you can be sure it hasn't stopped mattering.

DISCOGRAPHY

ALBUMS

Greetings from Asbury Park, N.J. (Columbia; ☆60, 1973). *The Wild, the Innocent and the E Street Shuffle* (Columbia; ☆59, 1975). *Born to Run* (Columbia; ☆3, 1975). *Darkness on the Edge of Town* (Columbia; ☆5, 1978). *The River* (Columbia; ☆1, 1980). *Nebraska* (Columbia; ☆3, 1982). *Born in the U.S.A.* (Columbia; ☆1, 1984). *Bruce Springsteen and the E Street Band Live/1975–85* (Columbia; ☆1, 1986). *Tunnel of Love* (Columbia; ☆1, 1987). *Human Touch* (Columbia; ☆2, 1992). *Lucky Town* (Columbia; ☆3, 1992).

(Chart positions compiled from Joel Whitburn's *Record Research*, based on *Billboard*'s LPs chart.)

PRINCE

BY PAUL EVANS

BY PAUL EVANS

Industrious, prophetic and perpetually unsatisfied, Prince is the most incendiary talent to emerge from the confusion and compromise of the Eighties pop scene. Displaying an uncanny gift for synthesizing widely divergent musical styles, he fuses rock and soul in a manner reminiscent of Jimi Hendrix and Sly Stone, flourishes a politically liberating poly-sexual image, and, through joining Christian passion to erotic heat, unites flesh and spirit in a vision so unsettling that only William Blake and his tension of innocence and experience provides any psychic antecedent. A visceral dreamer, Prince seizes the notion of spiritual emancipation with a fervor not found since the utopian Sixties. Driven by an Eighties work ethic that toughens his idealism, he leavens his religious and revolutionary impulses with a sharp, if cryptic, intelligence. This mix makes him a singularly efficient experimentalist, one whose ambition works subversively to warp the mainstream of American pop, rather than being content to whisper a message up from the underground.

Born in Minneapolis on June 7th, 1958, as Prince Rogers Nelson, Prince shares with fellow Minnesotan Bob Dylan a restless mastery of different types of

Jamming with Dez Dickerson of the Revolution.

music and a secretive method that is perhaps fostered by its genesis in the unhip safety of the Midwest. The son of a father who was a musician, Prince, impelled by a frantic twist of crossover aspiration, later obscured his black heritage by claiming alternately an Italian or mulatto bloodline for either of his parents; from the start, his sources were black and white—Hendrix, Little Richard, Carlos Santana, Joni Mitchell.

With credits reading "Produced, Arranged, Composed and Performed by Prince," and its prodigious nineteen-year-old creator hyped as a new Stevie Wonder, *For You* (1978) was Prince's erratic but oracular debut. Only a year later, however, on his second album, *Prince*, the elements of a trademark style—trebly rhythmic propulsion and porno-minded pillow talk—meshed in a single, "I Wanna Be Your Lover" (and "your mother" and "your sister," too!). But even that breakthrough (Number One on *Billboard*'s black chart; Number Eleven on its pop listing) left listeners unready for Prince's first clear triumph, 1980's *Dirty Mind*.

Clad in the obscene elegance of a trenchcoat and black bikini underwear, and fronting the original version of his black-white, boy-girl band the Revolution, Prince made his third album a statement of purpose for psychosexual, political and artistic deliverance. Paeans to incest ("Sister") and oral sex ("Head") surround the album's centerpiece, "Uptown"—the first of Prince's promissory notes for a mythic future in which a rainbow coalition of guilt-free misfits would party beyond pain ("Black, white, Puerto Rican/Everybody just a-freakin'/Good times are rollin'"). The first black performer to co-opt the trashy zest and anger of punk (not only in his defiantly provocative pose, but in the record's stripped-down production, cheesy keyboards and anarchic message), Prince conquered a new audience and unwittingly prepared pop for the slicker rock-funk cross-pollination that would come two years later with Michael Jackson's *Thriller*.

Prince followed up *Dirty Mind* with *Controversy* (1981), an album that, with titles like "Annie Christian," "Jack U Off" and "Ronnie, Talk to Russia," consolidated and refined the sound and themes of its predecessor. Nineteen eighty-two saw the release of a dazzling double album, *1999*, whose title track describes an impending apocalypse that hits with the redemptive force of rapture. The tumultuous tour behind *1999* boasted Prince's snappiest Minneapolis

protégés, the ace funk comics the Time (as well as one of the master's more ludicrous confections, the lingerie act Vanity 6).

Then, by 1984, Prince was a movie star. With the *Purple Rain* film and soundtrack, Prince captured beyond question the mass audience he had appeared so hungrily to crave. By now his catalogue was crammed with classics covering the staple rock & roll themes of girls ("When You Were Mine"), cars ("Little Red Corvette") and dancing ("D.M.S.R."); with his sixth album, Prince strove higher and deeper. The extraordinary majesty of "Purple Rain," a guitar-workout slice of gospel that offered up a cry for love, echoed the spirit of the reconciliatory hymns of the Beatles ("Hey Jude," "Let It Be"). And the astonishing single "When Doves Cry" remains perhaps Prince's most artful and idiosyncratic signature tune—a chunk of poetically evocative sound bites ("Animals strike curious poses") set against ominous, pared-down, bassless funk. This was Prince at his boldest—and at his most successful, commercially and artistically. That a song as sonically daring and as Oedipally charged as "When Doves Cry" became a Number One single constitutes perhaps the only truly radical moment of the Eighties.

The movie itself—essentially an ambitious long-form video, perfectly in sync with the new visual culture then being shaped by MTV—thrust Prince's threatening image into the mall cinemas of Middle America. Along with Madonna's pose of Nasty Girl meets Wonder Woman, and the sight of Michael Jackson transformed from (Black) Boy Next Door into Martian androgynous Peter Pan, Prince's look startled the mid-Eighties—pompadoured à la Little Richard and topcoated in the manner of a gutter Louis XIV, flashing tongue and tit while resurrecting the dancing ghost of early James Brown, here was cockiness on rampant display.

With *Purple Rain* dominating the Top Forty for much of 1984, Prince's next move was curious but revealing. Rather than capitalize on his mainstream success, he bolted, either cagily or willfully, from the sound he'd perfected. Satisfied or daunted by mass acceptance, he shifted inward toward music spurred by private urges, baffling some listeners, periodically intriguing those willing to go his distance—and losing his chance for the ubiquitous commodification most superstars reflexively pursue. Such a shift might have been unsurprising in the

Sixties, when experimentation was virtually compulsory and seeming "commercial" was the kiss of death; by the Eighties, it seemed almost daft. Call it confusion or a perverse bravery, but Prince moved on.

And came up, in 1985, with *Around the World in a Day.* Commercially a significant plunge from the heights scaled by *Purple Rain,* the record was musically one of Prince's most grandly ambitious. Attempting the encyclopedic scope of *Sgt. Pepper's Lonely Hearts Club Band, Around the World* was thick with neo-psychedelic studio trickery and oriental lushness—and it sank under the weight of its arguably commendable aspirations. *Parade* followed the next year, its orchestral grandeur lending it a rare if claustrophobic power. The album supported Prince's next movie, *Under the Cherry Moon*—a sad, campy film that, more tellingly than *Parade,* suggested that Prince had deliberately consigned himself to the margins. The artist who had seemed a kind of pop Picasso had become a reclusive Garbo—mannerist, indrawn, petulant.

In 1987 Prince came back strong. Punctuating its irresistible grooves with a new jazz-derived rhyth-

---

Purple Rain (1984).

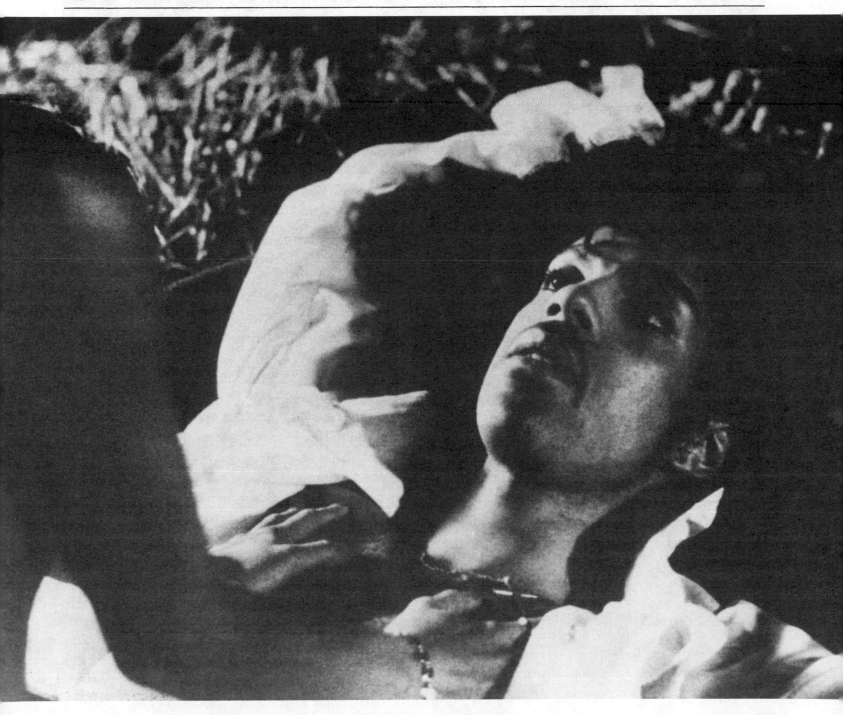

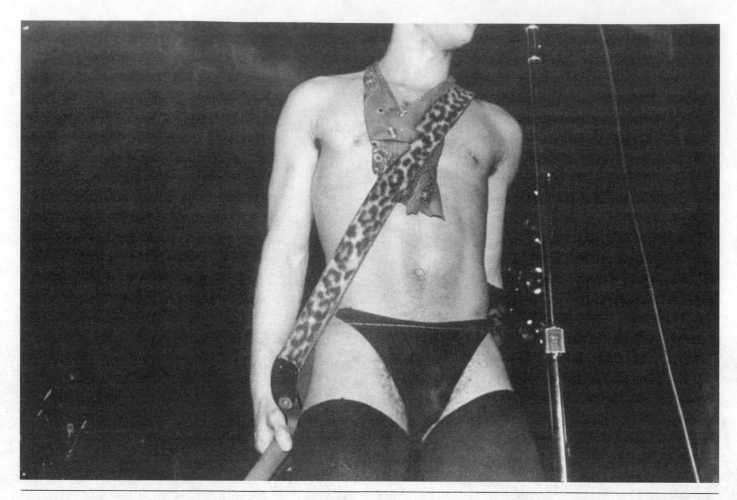

Blending genres, bending genders: Prince in 1981.

mic complexity, the double album *Sign o' the Times* returned Prince to funk with a renewed fierceness. The stark punchiness of *Dirty Mind* was transformed into R&B that was richer, tougher, more mature. "Housequake" approached the peerless heat of James Brown, and the gospel passion of "The Cross" was not only Prince's most desperate spiritual plea, but his most explicit.

Praised by critics and not especially well received by the public (despite the excellent in-concert movie of the same name that soon followed it), *Sign O' the Times* would be Prince's last major work until *Graffiti Bridge* in 1990. *The Black Album,* Prince's smuttiest funk (and a precursor to the X-rated rap of the Nineties), evinced a frantic vitality, but Prince himself disowned it. The album was originally slated for release in late 1987, but Prince at the last minute refused to put it out, relegating the record to bootleg obscurity. *Lovesexy,* from 1988, seemed only an improved *Parade,* its musical assurance undercut by Prince's resolute mining of an inscrutably private world of symbols; for all their street-Joycean wordplay, songs like "Eye No" and "Anna Stesia" were exercises in whimsy whose meaning evaporated as

soon as the words strayed from the playground of Prince's skull. The soundtrack Prince composed for *Batman* (1989) provides a unique example of his serving someone else's vision; despite its strong sales, it failed artistically because of that constraint, producing merely danceable, offhand, one-dimensional funk.

At the start of the Nineties, after a decade in which change proved the only constant in his career, Prince delivered *Graffiti Bridge* (1990), a double album that ranks with his very best work. Blues, R&B, rock & roll, collaborations with gospel veteran Mavis Staples, funkmaster George Clinton and a reunited Time, make the record a fully realized summing-up of Prince's promiscuous strengths.

Along with the album, however, came *Graffiti Bridge* the movie, by far the least satisfying of Prince's films—and one in which the power of the Time's streamlined funk overwhelmed Prince's more ambitious but less focused performance. Onscreen Prince came across as puzzling and remote, divorced from any kind of street credibility. The film bombed, and even its remarkable soundtrack languished commercially. In response, then, *Diamonds and Pearls* (1991) grounded Prince firmly in the idiom of contemporary black music—with a hot, fresh eight-piece band, the New Power Generation, he took on rap, dance music and, most effectively, the kind of lush, sexy ballad that had gained him his first (black) audience. While it wasn't the *tour de force* that *Graffiti Bridge* had been, it underscored Prince's tactical smarts, his understanding that no pop musical experiment truly succeeds when it loses the crowd.

In large part responsible for a thriving Minneapolis music scene, for popularizing multiracial, male-female bands, for rocking in a way that a black band like Living Colour would later develop more straightforwardly, Prince has exerted an influence of undeniable importance. From Sheila E. to Sheena Easton to the Bangles, a host of artists have gained from his guidance. For a while in the Eighties, every other record on the radio sounded like Prince. Ultimately, however, it is Prince's omnivorous vision—encyclopedic in its references, ever-surprising in its advance—that gives him power. He remains an original.

DISCOGRAPHY

SINGLES
"Soft and Wet" (Warner Bros.; r☆12, ☆92, 1978). "Just as Long as We're Together" (Warner Bros.; r☆91, 1978). "I Wanna Be Your Lover" (Warner Bros.; r☆1, ☆11, 1979). "Why You Wanna Treat Me So Bad?" (Warner Bros.; r☆13, 1980). "Still Waiting" (Warner Bros.; r☆65, 1980). "Uptown" (Warner Bros.; r☆5, ☆101, 1980). "Dirty Mind" (Warner Bros.; r☆65, 1981). "Controversy" (Warner Bros.; r☆3, ☆70, 1981). "Let's Work" (Warner Bros.; r☆9, ☆104, 1982). "1999" (Warner Bros.; r☆4, ☆12, 1982). "Little Red Corvette" (Warner Bros.; r☆15, ☆6, 1983). "Delirious" (Warner Bros.; r☆18, ☆8, 1983). "Let's Pretend We're Married" b/w "Irresistible Bitch" (Warner Bros.; r☆55, ☆52, 1984). "When Doves Cry" (Warner Bros.; r☆1, ☆1, 1984). "Let's Go Crazy" (Warner Bros.; r☆1, ☆1, 1984). "Purple Rain" (Warner Bros.; r☆4, ☆2, 1984). "I Would Die 4 U" (Warner Bros.; r☆11, ☆8, 1984). "Take Me with U" (Warner Bros.; r☆40, ☆25, 1985). "Raspberry Beret" (Paisley Park; r☆3, ☆2, 1985). "Pop Life" (Paisley Park; r☆8, ☆7, 1985). "Kiss" (Paisley Park; r☆1, ☆1, 1986). "Mountains" (Paisley Park; r☆15, ☆23, 1986). "Anotherloverholenyohead" (Paisley Park; r☆18, ☆63, 1986). "Sign O' the Times" (Paisley Park; r☆1, ☆3, 1987). "If I Was Your Girlfriend" (Paisley Park; r☆12, ☆67, 1987). With Sheena Easton: "U Got the Look" (Paisley Park; r☆11, ☆2, 1987). "I Could Never Take the Place of Your Man" (Paisley Park; ☆10, 1987). "Hot Thing" (Paisley Park; r☆14, ☆63, 1988). "Alphabet St." (Paisley Park; r☆3, ☆8, 1988). "Batdance" (Warner Bros.; r☆1, ☆1, 1989). "Partyman" (Warner Bros.; r☆5, ☆18, 1989). With Sheena Easton: "The Arms of Orion" (Warner Bros.; ☆36, 1989). "Scandalous" (Paisley Park/Warner Bros.; r☆5, ☆ 1989). "Thieves in the Temple" (Paisley Park; r☆1, ☆6, 1990). "New Power Generation" (Paisley Park; r☆27, ☆64, 1990). "Cream" (Paisley Park; r☆3, 1991).

ALBUMS
Prince—For You (Warner Bros.; ☆163, 1978). *Prince* (Warner Bros.; ☆22, 1979). *Dirty Mind* (Warner Bros.; ☆45, 1980). *Controversy* (Warner Bros.; ☆21, 1981). *1999* (Warner Bros.; ☆9, 1982). *Purple Rain* (Warner Bros.; ☆1, 1984). *Parade* (Paisley Park; ☆3, 1986). *Sign o' the Times* (Paisley Park; ☆9, 1987). *Lovesexy* (Paisley Park; ☆11, 1988). *Batman* (Warner Bros.; ☆1, 1989). *Graffiti Bridge* (Paisley Park; ☆6, 1990). *Diamonds and Pearls* (Paisley Park; ☆3, 1991).

(Chart positions compiled from Joel Whitburn's *Record Research*, based on *Billboard*'s Pop and LPs charts, unless otherwise indicated; r☆ = position on *Billboard*'s Rhythm & Blues chart.)

The Royal One with his lickin' stick.

U2

BY BILL FLANAGAN

In the Eighties U2 became one of the biggest rock bands in the world by embracing values that more style-conscious performers considered hopelessly unhip. At a time when most young musicians were concerned with appearing cool, U2 was hot. The group's passion connected with a huge audience for whom the public expression of commitment was a novelty. To detractors the members of U2 were a bunch of hambones, but to their millions of supporters they represented rock's best impulse: the desire to speak the truth to as many people as possible without worrying about who was or wasn't worthy to hear it.

U2 appeared in late 1980, as punk values were becoming encoded and institutionalized. While the band roughly fit the shape of a punk group—four kids who couldn't play very well bashing away at their instruments and sweating through their sleeveless shirts—U2 never bought into punk's nihilism or new wave's irony. The group was optimistic, spiritual, morally minded. Three of them were even practicing Christians. While MTV turned new wave into a series of fashion clichés, U2 stood out like Saint Francis at the Hard Rock Cafe. While Duran Duran and the Psychedelic Furs sucked in their cheeks and acted aloof, U2's lead singer Bono threw himself toward his audience with the wild-eyed enthusiasm of a prophet grabbing at the sleeves of passersby.

The members of U2 were true believers—in themselves, their audience, their God and rock & roll. Such rip-roaring faith inspired almost as much mockery as admiration. "We don't want the glamour, the pomp and the drums / The Dublin messiah scattering crumbs," sang the Mekons. Sinéad O'Connor—Dublin's other superstar—savaged U2 in

Boys (from left): Larry Mullen Jr., The Edge, Bono, Adam Clayton in 1981.

interviews. *Saturday Night Live* broadcast a skit in which a behatted actor playing Bono berated an audience for not being sufficiently concerned with the third world. "We don't take ourselves seriously," the real Bono protested on more than one occasion. "But we take the music very seriously." For both fans and skeptics, it was sometimes hard to tell where one ended and the other began.

U2 formed in 1976, when Paul Hewson, Dave Evans, Adam Clayton and Larry Mullen Jr. were students at Mount Temple, a Dublin high school that was a progressive, nonsectarian alternative to the conservative Catholic schools most Irish children attend. Paul (later Bono), Dave (later the Edge) and Adam were Protestants, the latter two British-born to boot. All four were to some degree outsiders, and all four were open-minded. They were not particularly good musicians, but they wanted to start a band. Bono, who hoped to play guitar, was deemed unacceptable even by the others' fledgling standards, but he was charismatic and outspoken, full of

ideas. Another group might have made such a character manager, but Larry, Adam and Edge made Bono their front man.

U2 began by performing material like Peter Frampton's "Show Me the Way" at local schoolboy shows. The group quickly switched to its own compositions, punky numbers influenced by Patti Smith, on which Bono affected a mannered, mincing singing style. Larry and Adam held on tight and tried to keep a steady rhythm, while Edge—though he was yet to master tone, technique or technology—explored unusual approaches to simple guitar parts. Listening to U2's first Irish singles now, one hears the Edge pitting his imagination against his technical limitations in the course of fashioning what would become a hugely influential chordal guitar style. He sounded bad only when he tried to take a conventional solo.

The members of U2 are smart, and as they learned their instruments and practiced together they were bound to get better. But luck plays a part in success, too, and it was astonishingly lucky for the novice group that, as Bono got used to singing, he uncorked a terrific voice. Charm, enthusiasm and balls got him into U2 (along with the fact that no one else wanted the gig), but it was the discovery of Bono's ability to sing with a rough beauty that made it possible for U2 to become more than an underground band.

While still teenagers U2 acquired a manager, Paul McGuinness, who had worked in the Irish film industry and dabbled in the music business. He and U2 had in common the gift for fixing grand long-term goals, rather than being satisfied with immediate gratification. McGuinness was not going to count U2 lucky if the band scored a big cash advance or achieved stardom in Ireland. He was less greedy and more ambitious than that. After several misses, the manager landed the band a contract with Island Records. U2 teamed up with a twenty-five-year-old producer named Steve Lillywhite who had recorded Ultravox and Siouxsie and the Banshees. Lillywhite was of the English generation that rejected the aural clichés of rock & roll (not just long guitar solos but, for example, cymbals), and he found an easy fit with players who wanted to explore new territory but who were not, at heart, slash-and-gob punks.

On *Boy,* the first of three albums U2 would make with Lillywhite, Bono sang with unembarrassed openness of the world as seen through the eyes of an innocent coming to grips with experience. The emotional center of the album, and U2's first FM hit, was ''I Will Follow,'' a chiming song of devotion and commitment that was written for Bono's mother, who died when he was fourteen. To Bono the lyric may have been about his desire to follow his mother when she left him; to casual radio listeners it was presumably about being so in love with someone that you'd follow them anywhere; and to many U2 fans it was a declaration of religious faith. The Replacements (inaugurating what would become a long tradition of less saintly rockers taking shots at U2) released an answer song called ''Kids Don't Follow.'' U2 had been introduced to the world.

Through 1981 and 1982 U2 toured relentlessly, knocking out audiences across America and Europe. Unlike the many video acts who shot to overnight success throughout the Eighties, U2 built its audience the old-fashioned way, through its live shows. The more the group played, the tighter and more confident it got. The Edge used ringing overtones,

Bono electrifies the US Festival in 1983.

echos and electronic delays to create swirling layers of music, fattening up the trio's sound and giving all of U2's songs a common aural identity. Rock trios—Cream, the Jimi Hendrix Experience, Led Zeppelin—had usually been showcases for soloists. U2 instead picked up on the Police's conception of the rock trio as a single musical personality, with the bass and voice carrying the central line of the song, the drums kicking along and accenting the bass, and the guitar providing color and atmosphere rather than leads. In spite of the punk haircuts, the Police consisted of veteran musicians with chops to spare. They had pretended to be more limited than they were in order to slip into the music business when punk offered an opening. The members of U2 really were what the Police had posed as—kids from garageland with no idea of doing it any other way.

As the group toured America, U2 met with a stream of fans, journalists and disc jockeys. Gladhanding seemed to come easily to Bono and Adam, who were young and curious enough to be genuinely interested in all the odd characters they were meeting and the strange places in which they found themselves. U2's work began to pay off with the wide acceptance of the band's third album, *War*, which featured a harder, more anthemic rock sound than its moody predecessors. In America U2 had initially been lumped in with artsy alternative acts such as the Teardrop Explodes and Echo and the Bunnymen. *War* declared U2 to be the inheritor of the populist tradition descending from the Who and Bruce Springsteen.

Early on, Bono, the Edge and Larry downplayed their Charismatic Christianity so that they wouldn't be stereotyped as fundamentalists, right-wingers or any of the other clichés that the rock culture often fixes on believers. As they became famous, their faith became public knowledge. Although they took their religion seriously, U2 clearly loved life on earth a little too much to want to hurry heaven. And in spite of the carping of cynics, there was nothing hypocritical about U2's spiritual fervor. Each of the band's public proclamations was matched by a private one. The group nearly split up after its second album, *October*, over concern that rock stardom was not a worthy vocation. Even when Bono and Larry decided that God wouldn't mind if they continued to use their musical gifts, the Edge wavered and almost quit the band in 1982 to devote himself to the Lord. After the Live Aid concert in 1985 Bono and his wife, Ali, went to Africa and worked in a refugee camp. They also visited Central America during the Reagan administration's undeclared war there. U2's brand of Christianity demanded that the band members be tough on themselves and tolerant of others—a sharp contrast to the me-first fundamentalism that was popular on American television during the Reagan reign.

Politically, the members of U2 seemed to be the last holdouts for liberation theology. The band used its talents for outrage and empathy to evoke political terror in "Silver and Gold" (sung in the voice of a

U2 on the set of the "Desire" video, 1988.

black South African sweltering under apartheid), "The Refugee" (a barn-burning rocker about a political victim dreaming of asylum in America) and "Bullet the Blue Sky" (in which the Edge's guitar conveyed, with the ferocity of Jimi Hendrix rending "The Star Spangled Banner," the horror felt by Nicaraguan civilians as they huddled together during a U.S.-sponsored bombing raid).

Most of this work was accomplished after U2 split with Steve Lillywhite and began recording with the production team of Daniel Lanois and Brian Eno. Eno was a conceptualist, an experimenter, an aloof wizard. Lanois was a French Canadian with an earthy, folky bent. With *The Unforgettable Fire* (1984) Eno and Lanois brought a ghostliness to U2's sound that created a new context for the band's characteristic dichotomy of the physical and the spiritual. Where U2's early music was full of God's light and the world's temptations, Eno and Lanois introduced a spooky ambience, like strange music heard drifting out of some forbidden woods.

The Edge absorbed these new elements and kept adding his own ideas and intuitions. Even as Bono and Larry became more interested in U.S. roots styles—jazz and country and blues—the Edge seemed close to finding a musical bridge between Europe and Africa that avoided the usual detour through America. The tense, mournful "Race Against Time" felt as if it was rushing forward and pulling back at the same time—like a man trying to hold still while his heart pounded. If U2 had consisted of flashier musicians, such ambitious songs might have been too esoteric for the general public to accept, but because the band kept to simple, solid rhythms and chords, even its most experimental music had a rock & roll simplicity that allowed a wide audience to embrace the great range of moods and emotions being explored. U2's dreamscapes always remained grounded in blood and bone.

In terms of its lyrics, as well, U2's apparent complexities were ultimately accessible. Upon repeated listenings even U2's most obscure songs revealed concise, emotionally direct meanings. "Promenade," a rush of aural and visual images, proved simply to be a description of the view from Bono and Ali's seaside home on a warm evening. "Tomorrow," with its dread of a dark figure waiting outside

the singer's house, was about the undertaker's car coming to the Hewson home after Bono's mother died. "Elvis Presley and America," a sort of extended mumble full of emotion but lacking articulation, was Bono's projection of what it must have been like for Presley to be filled with passion and genius but not appreciate his own worth. U2 trusted its audience to stick with the material until its logic revealed itself. The audience trusted U2.

Recording *Achtung Baby* in Berlin *(from left):* Daniel Lanois on guitar, coproducer Brian Eno on keyboards, The Edge, Bono.

The ghostly, impressionistic tone of *The Un-forgettable Fire* was a surprising (some in the music business said suicidal) sequel to the mainstream rock of *War*. "Pride (In the Name of Love)," one of the album's few straight-ahead rock-ers, gave U2 its first U.S. hit single, but most of the album was introspective and moody. By so clearly

avoiding the safe and expected, *The Unforgettable Fire* deepened the bond between U2 and its expanding audience. Just as Bruce Springsteen renewed faith with his followers by interrupting the commercial momentum between *The River* and *Born in the U.S.A.* with the very personal *Nebraska,* U2 paused with *The Unforgettable Fire* before plunging ahead to the mas-sive success that was clearly awaiting the group.

U2 graduated to playing arenas after the release of "Pride," but the band's leap into stadiums came at the Live Aid concert in the summer of 1985. Going on at London's Wembley stadium in the afternoon, a very hyped-up Bono launched himself off the stage and into the audience in the middle of "Bad," the group's second song. The other members of U2 figured their excitable singer had really blown it this time, but to the world watching on TV, U2 came across as startlingly spontaneous in the middle of a parade of meticulously planned performances.

The momentum that had been building beneath U2 exploded after Live Aid. In 1986 the group head-lined in football stadiums as the top act on Amnesty International's Conspiracy of Hope Tour. In 1987 U2's second Lanois-Eno album, *The Joshua Tree,* raised the group to the level of superstars. Bono's explorations of American music paid off big, as U2 wrote an album of easy-to-grab rock songs with hooks. "I Still Haven't Found What I'm Looking For" and "With or Without You" both went to Number One. So did the album. Like Springsteen with *Born in the U.S.A.,* U2 had mastered the art of distilling the intelligence and heart of its earlier work into songs direct enough to sound great on a car radio.

Seven years into its public career, U2 was the lat-est biggest band in the world. The group sidestepped the dreaded "Whatdya do for an encore?" question by releasing *Rattle and Hum* (1988), a tour film and double album of live cuts and oddball tracks. It was a holding pattern for U2, but it was another Number One album. In July of 1991, more than four years after *The Joshua Tree,* they finally finished a sequel. On *Achtung Baby* U2 chucked their cowboy hats, backed up and turned down a different road. They threw off the overt Americanisms and grand state-ments that had peaked (and at moments skirted self-parody) on *Rattle and Hum* and explored musical arrangements that were more urban, European and electronically dense than previous U2 albums. The tense sound fit with lyrics that were full of conflict,

U2 in the studio, with coproducer Daniel Lanois on percussion, recording *Achtung Baby*.

marital and moral strife, failed expectations, hypocrisy, betrayal—and, almost perversely, the fun and abandon that are the worst enemies of commitment and maturity.

Achtung Baby implied that as U2 hit their thirties they were inclined to get into the sort of mischief they had missed by spending their late teens and twenties concerned with grave matters of sin and salvation. The album was about both the fun of sneaking out for a wild Saturday night and the guilt and hangover of Sunday morning.

Achtung Baby met the tough assignment of propelling U2 into their second decade by eliminating many of the rules the band had built for themselves during their rise. It was a liberation a little like that which the Who had engineered after their Sixties peak with the great success of *Tommy*. Following several years of trying to come up with another rock opera, the Who in 1971 decided to reject all the expectations placed on them. *Who's Next* freed the band from its own myth and bought it another ten years of vitality. *Achtung Baby* promised the same sort of renewal for U2.

I met U2 when the band first came to America, and spent bits of time with them here and there through the decade that followed, often bumping into one or two of them by chance in unlikely places. When ''I Will Follow'' was on the radio in the spring of 1981, I took U2 to a friend's house in New England, where the four were transfixed by a video documentary of a 1965 Rolling Stones tour of Ireland. They claimed they remembered having seen it on TV as small children, and Bono said that this was his dream for U2—to be a real band, not a singer and his backup, not two or three stars with shifting sidemen, but a band of equals like the Stones or the Beatles, who start out as kids and stick together all the way.

Ten years later, in that spring when record executives and newspaper columnists and rock musicians were all trading speculation about what was happening in Ireland at the U2 sessions, I walked into a club in Greenwich Village, took a seat in the back and found myself next to Bono and the Edge. They laughed like two kids caught playing hooky during finals. ''What are you doing in New York?'' I asked. ''Everybody thinks you're locked in the studio in Dublin, finishing this masterpiece!''

''Ah, you know how it is,'' Bono said, smiling. ''We just snuck out for the weekend.''

U2 had dreamed of being the biggest band in the world, but that was not Bono, Edge, Adam and Larry's first dream. Their first dream was simply to be a band in the true sense, to stick together, stay loyal to one another and not lose themselves in gaining the world. In staying true to that vision, U2 finally became all that they ever dreamed to be.

DISCOGRAPHY

ALBUMS
Boy (Island; ☆63, 1981). *October* (Island; ☆104, 1981). *War* (Island; ☆12, 1983). *Under a Blood Red Sky* (Island; ☆28, 1983). *The Unforgettable Fire* (Island; ☆12, 1984). *Wide Awake in America* (Island; EP, 1985). *The Joshua Tree* (Island; ☆1, 1987). *Rattle and Hum* (Island; ☆1, 1988). *Achtung Baby* (Island; ☆1, 1991).

(Chart positions compiled from Joel Whitburn's *Record Research*, based on *Billboard*'s LPs chart.)

MTV: THE REVOLUTION WILL BE TELEVISED

BY JIM FARBER

Pick an accusation, any accusation. Music video miniaturizes our attention spans, lionizes beauty over talent, robs artists of their mystery, objectifies women, pacifies viewers, squelches spontaneity, ruins the individual experience of a song, destroys the boundaries between creativity and commercialism . . . Had enough?

The critics haven't. These are just a few of the juicy accusations hurled at music video since 1981 when, with the eruption of MTV, the form became a daily round-the-clock part of the pop experience. In the time since, MTV has permanently changed the way music is both manufactured and perceived, awarding it a uniquely threatening role in modern pop. By fusing three of the most compelling new media of the twentieth century—television, radio and recorded music—into a new kind of monster, MTV has played with previously accepted ways of receiving sensation and pleasure. No wonder the accusations against it have been so ferocious. And so shallow.

Of course, before the twenty-four-hour-a-day network transformed music video into a hermetically sealed world of its own, the form was more a frill than a threat. Initially, it was just a lark, pioneered by German filmmaker Oskar Fischinger. While music had been used to support film since the beginning (the pianos and orchestras that accompanied the early silents), it was Fischinger who, in the Twenties, reversed the process, constructing animated shorts to support music (specifically, jazz and classical records). Fischinger's approach reached a kind of apotheosis in Walt Disney's 1940 opus *Fantasia* (to which the German filmmaker contributed), a work that now ranks as the first (unintentional) long-form music video.

By the late Forties there thrived a short-lived cultural blip known as "soundies," jukebox-like contraptions that unspooled performance pieces by such pop singers of the day as Bing Crosby. Such novelty items were long gone by the birth of rock & roll in the Fifties. Instead visual representation of music took the form of TV appearances on variety shows (where the new stars were condescendingly presented as freaks for "the kids") or in movie vehicles (first Elvis, then the Beatles). By the mid-Sixties rock performers regularly filmed promo shorts, but these were intended solely as a cost-cutting scheme; it was simply cheaper to send the clip overseas rather than a whole marauding band. It wasn't until 1975, when Queen unveiled its ornate clip for ''Bohemian Rhapsody'' on British TV, that one of these shorts created a hit all by itself. Immediately after the piece was glimpsed on the BBC, the song shot to Number One on the British charts, presaging music video as a promotional medium of significant clout.

It took a little longer for MTV to start generating hits—roughly eighteen months. Having kicked off on August 1st, 1981 (with the Buggles' prescient novelty hit ''Video Killed the Radio Star,'' appropri-

ately enough), the network began launching new stars to top the charts by January 1983. A whole new slate of colorful performers—Duran Duran, Culture Club, Eurythmics—seized center stage, pushing a very different aesthetic from the one that dominated American music for the previous half decade. The new stars (christened the third or fourth British invasion by an eager media) were androgynous, proudly fashion-conscious and serious about pop as art, true children of Andy Warhol, by way of David Bowie. Not since the glitter movement of the early Seventies had such values threatened to redefine America's rock orthodoxy. Image-centered stars had always been common throughout British pop (mirrored in a hipper, more trendy audience, at least compared

Since its inception in 1981, MTV has given its critics headaches.

with the white American mainstream). But the United Kingdom's major trend exports of the mid to late Seventies (from punk to neo-ska to new romanticism) withered in the United States, leaving American rock at the mercy of the blandest corporate groups. Likewise, disco, which had enjoyed a creative and commercial peak in 1979, was starting to lose its edge, leaving the industry in a major slump. The pop world was hungry for a shake-up.

But if the MTV bands came along to enliven the charts, their videos took a cattle prod to something more sweeping—*all* the mass visual arts, from film to TV to advertising. By mid-1983 the "MTV look" infected movies, with films like *Flashdance,* and TV, with *Miami Vice.* The MTV look (and the concept it dragged along) was marked by nostalgically rich pastel colors (offering a campy, idealized view of the first teen culture of the Fifties), lightning-quick cuts, plus lengthy montage sequences and brutally fractured story lines. Mood took precedence over narrative. A dream state was maintained, arguing a greater truth through blithering abstraction. It was a world of internalization and eternal stimulation; it was the new drug.

Then again, as music video began to redefine

other media, the clips themselves calcified into vehicles for cliché. By late 1983 videos were rife with smashing dishes, slo-mo liquid spills, and that old standby of advertising, endless writhing babes. Besides mimicking ads, the clips were also designed to mirror primitive teen archetypes, whether the chic alienation of "alternative music" entries or the old-fashioned, outlaw-leather fantasies of the metal pieces. That didn't stop big-name directors from jumping into the form just to seem hip, resulting in dubious projects such as Brian De Palma's ungainly piece for Bruce Springsteen's "Dancing in the Dark" or Sam Peckinpah's corny visualizations of Julian Lennon's "Too Late for Goodbyes" and "Vallotte."

Still, the real auteurs of the new art were younger folk, like photographer Matt Mahurin (who slowed the form down with dank, grumbling pieces for Peter Gabriel and R.E.M.), artist Robert Longo (who composed gorgeously witty outbursts for Megadeth and New Order) or Jean-Baptiste Mondino (who contributed sweeping bits of outrage for Madonna— "Open Your Heart" and "Justify My Love"—and a yearning mood piece for Don Henley, "The Boys of Summer").

Then again, if by 1985 music video proved it

could produce individual pieces of legitimate art (earlier pioneers of that proposition include Devo and David Bowie in the late Seventies), its most powerful effect remained generic. It became clear MTV had to be swallowed whole and accepted as a commercial, promotional medium for its true "art" to be properly understood. Besides, the "art" of music video was not what most industry people and critics were concentrating on by the end of the decade. Rather, the focus was on how fully the form had changed the presentation of pop.

B y the late Eighties the charts were dominated by dance conglomerates whose talent wasn't singing or playing but (at best) dancing, and (at worst) looking good onscreen. Janet Jackson and Paula Abdul may have sported arresting video images, but their voices were so dinky they emerged as mere spokesmodels for their records. It should have seemed inevitable, then, that the industry would be rocked by a new kind of scandal by the decade's close: It was revealed that Milli Vanilli, a major videogenic group, had not sung a single note on its multiplatinum album. Likewise, such acts as Technotronic, Black Box and C+C Music Factory hired models to front for their actual, unlovely singers. Even huge acts that, in fact, did their own singing (from Wilson Phillips to Bon Jovi) clearly never would have enjoyed the success they had (and even might not have gotten signed to a major label) were it not for their decorative talents.

In addition, video greatly reconfigured the presentation of major tours. Since performers now had to compete with their finely choreographed videos, many resorted to self-conscious theatrics or even lip syncing to ensure perfection. Spontaneity, once prized above all in live rock & roll, went the way of platform shoes.

But if such trends were troublesome, they were hardly new to pop. Physical beauty—or more accurately, sexiness—has always been a crucial component in popular music. Certainly Elvis wouldn't have had as much libidinous profundity were he less visually stunning. As for the charge of killing con-

The Stray Cats play for MTV in 1984.

cert spontaneity, the live show as the definitive pop experience is largely a romantic notion to begin with. Studio polish, even for the very skilled of musicians, has more often provided the most profound pop experiences for the majority of listeners. Besides, as critic Robert Christgau has pointed out, one of the essential functions of going to live shows is simply to see who else shows up (that is to say, who shares your fantasies).

Likewise, the issue of weak front people propped up by behind-the-scenes geniuses is also hardly a revolutionary pop contrivance. The Ronettes needed as much help from Phil Spector to achieve their hormonally charged masterpieces as Janet Jackson derived from Jimmy Jam and Terry Lewis to create her anthems of rhythmic unity. Even Diana Ross, in her sainted Motown prime, boasted a voice no stronger than Madonna's. She, too, needed the glorious production machine.

Then, it wasn't just live presentation and musical construction that troubled the critics. There was also the issue of image hogging attention over the actual song. Such a carp even dogged a performer like Madonna, who was clearly making brilliant pop records from the git-go but whose video (and media) image was too distractingly creative for many to notice her artistry. The point that never seemed to get through in this discussion is that iconography has always been an important (and *moving*) part of rock and pop. Stars such as Bruce Springsteen and John Mellencamp may not have liked to admit that they sold their images as working-class everymen just as eagerly as Madonna pushed the idea of artist-as-''slut.'' But the truth is, the shot of Springsteen's ass on the cover of his breakthrough-to-megastardom LP, *Born in the U.S.A.*, was every bit as self-conscious as any Madonna move. To boot, it was as culturally resonant, drawing on a rich history of gender-associated assumptions and contradictions.

Still, by the dawn of the Nineties, criticism about

the "look" taking control of the sound were so strong that groups began to wryly confront it head on. C + C Music Factory presented itself as a flagrantly mutable conglomoration, boasting shifting images (depending on which front people were used). And this time the behind-the-scenes people claimed to be worthy of stardom as well. Signaling an acceptance of the new age was C + C's clip for "Gonna Make You Sweat (Everybody Dance Now)," which made no attempt to hide the group's actual working arrangement; the producers made cameos right in the clip (with credit prominently flashed onscreen), plus (if only for legal reasons) a printed message appeared at the open and close admitting that the "singer" shown was merely providing a "visualization" of the voice heard. No fans com-

plained. No wonder. What the C + C "factory" workers had contrived (both musically and visually) was too thrilling a pop spectacle for anyone to care.

Of course, those who guarded the old rock orthodoxy sat stone-faced and cross-legged. Certainly they should have understood by then that while MTV may have exaggerated many difficult tendencies in pop (and trashed romantic myths along the way), the network provided, in return, some fascinating new approaches to music. Right from the start MTV dangled an amazing promise before its viewers. Watch us "and you'll be able to live forever," went an early slogan. The boast was predicated on the concept that, since the network's format provides no logical narrative progression, leaving all action in an eternal present, time is halted. Replac-

Fab Five Freddy, the host of *Yo! MTV Raps,* one of the network's most popular shows.

Aerosmith on *Unplugged:* acoustic music for the video masses.

ing it was a kind of free-flowing effervescence, a nonstop teasing, erotic cabaret of bright colors, sexy rock stars and loud music. This is the network's most generic appeal, offering a kind of pornography, without the payoff. (Flesh may be constantly flashed but no one ever "comes," because that would end the party.)

The germane question, though, is what exactly is being celebrated at this party? A liberation from reason, for one thing. MTV is the ultimate argument against logic; images are simply thrown at you without regard for consequence. The only point is to be aroused and, of course, to avoid boredom. Critics of the network have gone nuts over this idea, saying it encourages distraction and promotes scattered thinking in kids—charges that should trigger alarms

in rock critics, because such accusations have long hounded rock itself. Video certainly may not "teach" in a linear manner, but its charged incoherence broadens the world of subversion pop music has always hinted at.

Of course, this is a level of radicalism most rock critics (whose notions of rebellion are rooted in the politics of the Sixties) are loathe to credit because of its utter lack of focus. But on one level the approach provides the ultimate "up yours" to the power structure, presenting escapism at its most gloriously anarchic.

Still, critics charge, MTV is, in fact, extremely conventional in the way it *exploits* and commercializes sexuality. All the network does, they say, is stimulate unfulfilled desire, which breeds consumption. On one level, this is absolutely true. It is a commercial network, after all. But to understand the real power of MTV one has to question who is ultimately being exploited and what is being sold.

All music videos are commercials, but, as it turns out, what they're selling is something rather subtle. On the surface, they advertise a song from a new album we're meant to purchase. But in a deeper and more pervasive sense, the clips are pitching us the personas of the performers. Music videos are crafted to hawk an image, an identity for the artist, which we then "purchase" by relating to it. Critic Pat Aufderheide (in her 1986 essay "The Look of the Sound," an inspiration for this piece) has illustrated how watching an hour of MTV is like walking into a shopping mall where we can try on a whole range of identities. One minute we're a teen girl with a poignant flaw (Carnie Wilson in "Impulsive"), the next we're a bald Australian singer enraged over Aboriginal land rights (Peter Garrett in "Beds Are Burning").

In addition, each of an artist's clips can reveal a new angle to an old persona—or even argue a self that's utterly fresh. This may be threatening to the wizened idea of rock stars maintaining a stable, reliable persona. Or, more fancifully, that they are just being "themselves." But there's a great emotional benefit in the new approach. Watching (and relating to) a variety of personas in the videos lets us express the range of selves we hold inside. In the process, it also helps stress the sly mutability of identity. Watching validates the richness and complexity of who we really are.

But it's not just the realization of this fantasy that makes MTV powerful, it's the manner in which the network makes it real. Like all pop experiences, MTV mines our deepest desires; the twist is that the network does so while relying on the language of commercials. As such, it gains unique resonance for anyone reared in a capitalist culture. These MTV "commercials" merit serious attention simply because they advertise the product in which we've invested the most emotion: pop.

To many critics this may seem a soulless exchange, but that view shows an ignorance of the consumer opportunities that helped shape and define youth culture from the start. After all, teens as a class came about in the Fifties because of their new purchasing power and expanded leisure time. They "bought" their identities through consuming jeans, cars and rock & roll records. That doesn't make the exchange any less powerful to the purchaser. In pop art the emotion the audience brings to the "object" can be more important than the object itself. Viewed this way, MTV becomes a powerful receptacle for our emotions. No wonder, despite all the criticism, MTV has us transfixed. We're watching ourselves.

MICHAEL JACKSON

BY JOHN SWENSON

Although Michael Jackson's solo career consists of only a handful of recordings, his impact on the history of popular music in the Eighties makes him a crucial figure in any overview of the genre. Jackson singlehandedly defined the terms that have powered the era of music video. Before "Billie Jean," Jackson's monster hit of 1983, music videos were promotional tools to help sell records; once Jackson utilized the video as a medium for a short dramatic feature built around his dancing, recordings became soundtracks and the video itself became the potential primary focus of a pop artist's career. Jackson, more than any other performer, turned pop music from a playing to a dancing-and-performance medium.

In this light it is easier to understand why Jackson's musical work has been so woefully misread by music historians. Viewing his career against that of other music figures, they have relegated Jackson to the status of a freak, acknowledged for several brilliant career moments, while snickered at for his well-publicized personal eccentricities.

Michael Jackson onstage: one of the greatest live performers in the history of pop music.

Only when Jackson is viewed as a theatrical performer whose roots are more in Hollywood than in Motown does his career profile come into clear focus. Judy Garland rather than Jimi Hendrix is the appropriate referent. Jackson himself makes the comparison with Garland a few pages into his autobiography, *Moonwalk*. He distinguishes his childhood stardom from hers by saying that his parents never forced him to perform, but in fact, Michael was already singing professionally as a five-year-old. He was only eleven when he fronted the Jackson 5's galvanic debut single, "I Want You Back," in 1969. The Jackson 5 became the last of the great Motown "production line" groups of the Sixties and early Seventies, reaching Number One on the pop charts with their first four singles: "I Want You Back," "ABC," "The Love You Save" and "I'll Be There."

Michael became an international pop star as the Jacksons scored hit after hit and even had a cartoon show designed after them. But his dreams didn't revolve simply around musical success—he fantasized stardom in theater and film as well. While his brothers loved the fast-burning grooves of uptempo R&B, Jackson secretly longed to sing sad, lonely ballads. Jackson's solo recording debut, the 1971 single "Got to Be There," showed his gift for emotional ballad singing, but the following year his tear-jerking rendition of the theme song for the movie *Ben* gave the first clear indication of the direction Jackson was heading in.

"Ben," which became a Number One hit, was one of the greatest ballads of the early Seventies. It's hard to imagine how a fourteen-year-old could deliver a performance that contained so much heartbreak and longing as Jackson brought to this love song for a rat. Jackson was uniquely suited to the task; he saw nothing weird about the subject matter and has gone on to explain the motivation for the relationship between a boy and his rodent pal as a parallel to the story line of *E.T.*

Jackson's love of ballad singing stood in contrast to and as a complement of his precocious and innovative dancing ability. In 1974 Jackson debuted a dance step he called the robot on *Soul Train* during a performance of the Jacksons' latest single, "Dancing Machine." The dance swept the country even as "Dancing Machine" helped usher in the disco era.

By this time Michael was not just the front man for the Jackson 5, he was the de facto leader of the group. When their dissatisfaction with the direction Motown was pushing them in reached the breaking point, it fell to Michael to meet with Motown head Berry Gordy and tell him that he and his brothers wanted out. The Jacksons signed with Epic and were placed with the Philadelphia International production team of Kenny Gamble and Leon Huff. More hits ensued, but even as Michael followed through on his dedication to the family business, he was yearning to head in yet another new direction.

In 1970 the Jackson 5 released three singles on Motown and sold 8 million records. *From left:* Tito, Marlon, Michael, Jackie, Jermaine.

The opportunity came when the nineteen-year-old Jackson got the part of the Scarecrow in the Motown film production of *The Wiz*, a takeoff of one of Michael's favorite movies, *The Wizard of Oz*. His dream of being in films was finally realized, and he reveled in the details of moviemaking, picking up the choreographed dance steps faster than anyone on the set and relishing the new identity that hours of makeup created for him. Veteran television and film composer Quincy Jones was in charge of the score for *The Wiz* and befriended Michael during the making of the film. When Michael decided to make his first solo album, he asked Jones to produce it.

Off the Wall, Jackson's first real solo album (Motown had released several records hooked around hits and stuffed with filler in the early Seventies), was a triumph in equal measure for singer and producer. Jones brought in the cream of Hollywood session players and songwriters; Jackson brought his explosive charisma, edge-of-manhood self-realization and elements of the Jacksons' percussion section. The records triumphed by making the best of both strong points in Jackson's art: his feel for dance grooves and his heart-stopping ballad style. The album's two opening cuts—"Don't Stop 'til You Get Enough" and "Rock with You"—provided the soundtrack for every discotheque and many parties as the Seventies melted into the Eighties. The title track effects a rock-disco fusion that prefigures greater triumphs on *Thriller*. "Girlfriend," written by Paul McCartney for Jackson, is as great a pop vocal as Michael has ever delivered. The sincerity and sense of despair he reaches for and connects with on "She's Out of My Life" also meet the daunting standard of his greatest performances. Michael's renditions of Stevie Wonder and Susaye Greene's "I Can't Help It" and Carole Bayer Sager's "It's the Falling in Love" are the work of a master vocalist at the height of his interpretive power.

Michael Jackson had just turned twenty-one and already achieved more than most artists could expect to accomplish in a lifetime. His personal-services contract with his manager father had expired and was not renewed, leaving him completely free to determine his future for the first time in his life. He had recorded a great album by any measure and

seen his self-penned "Don't Stop 'til You Get Enough" rocket to Number One, yet Jackson was crushed when *Off the Wall,* one of the biggest-selling albums of the year, won only a single Grammy nomination, for Best R&B Vocal Performance, Male. He vowed that his next solo album would force people to recognize his genius.

Michael, who was still part of the Jacksons, went right into the studio with his brothers to make *Triumph* (1980), but the experience of making *Off the Wall* had changed him forever. One listen to his searing version of "Heartbreak Hotel" on *Triumph* was enough to indicate that Michael was in the process of leaving his brothers far behind.

In 1983 Berry Gordy asked Michael to participate in a Jackson 5 reunion for Motown's twenty-fifth anniversary television special. The group did a medley of old favorites to the delight of the studio audience and the millions of viewers watching in their homes. When it was over,

Michael with an early member of an ever-growing menagerie.

Michael and friends, 1988.

Michael stood on the darkened stage and told the audience that while he still loved the old songs, it was the newer ones he really liked; he then exploded into his "Billie Jean" dance routine, with the first live performance of his stylized moonwalk dance, in which he appears to be walking forward and backward simultaneously.

This moment was the crystallization of Jackson's celebrity status. An estimated 50 million people watched him coin a dance identity with his "Billie Jean" choreography. Unlike James Brown, whose dancing is a kinetic outgrowth of the music itself, Jackson's dancing on "Billie Jean" was metaphysical, a graceful illusion that seemed to defy physical reality and disappear before the audience could verify exactly what it had just seen. After the show, both Fred Astaire and Gene Kelly congratulated Jackson on his performance.

In August 1982, when Michael had begun working on *Thriller*, he was already thoroughly familiar with MTV's programming of music videos. Realiz-

ing he could improve on the format, Jackson conceived of his music as a soundtrack to a taped or—in his case—filmed performance. "Billie Jean," "Beat It" and "Thriller" were designed in Jackson's mind as short films; the "videos" were actually shot in 35mm film in a process so expensive that Jackson was forced to finance the productions of "Beat It" and "Thriller" himself.

Jackson had arrived at a brilliant concept anticipating that music video would be the key to promoting record sales. As a result, *Thriller* became the largest-selling record in history. *Thriller* had a little something for everyone—the opening track "Wanna Be Startin' Somethin'" was a stone dance groove in the tradition of the hottest tracks from *Off the Wall*. Paul McCartney was involved again, this time singing a duet with Jackson on "The Girl Is Mine." With its Eddie Van Halen guitar solo, "Beat It" melded dance music with heavy metal and set the stage for the rap-metal synthesis that would occur later in the Eighties. The trademark weepy ballad was "The Lady in My Life." Directed by John Landis, the title-track video became an entertaining horror film short feature with elaborate special effects and even a cameo "rap" by Vincent Price. The film set standards for music-video production that the rest of the industry is still trying to live up to.

Jackson had resoundingly met the challenge he set for himself after *Off the Wall*. He made the most popular record ever, a feat impossible for the National Academy of Recording Arts and Sciences to ignore at Grammy time. *Thriller* won a staggering, unprecedented eight Grammy awards and would go on to sell more than 40 million records. In the process Michael became one of the biggest names in entertainment history, fulfilling his ultimate childhood dream.

Michael Jackson blows a kiss before disappearing behind the one-way window in 1988.

Michael Jackson: the 1991 version.

At this, the height of his popularity, Jackson had nowhere to go but down. There was simply no way to improve on a work as groundbreaking and successful as *Thriller*. Jackson contributed a couple of songs to the Jacksons' ill-fated *Victory* album, which suffered a disastrous fate as part of the low point of Jackson's career: the scandal-ridden 1984 *Victory* Tour. Jackson recovered to cowrite "We Are the World" and provide a focal point for the dramatically effective 1985 superstar benefit, U.S.A. for

Africa. The ideals expressed by this organization were yet another realization of Jackson's utopian dream.

Still, fashioning a follow-up to *Thriller* plagued Jackson, who was also victimized by the inevitable backlash to his superstardom. He became fair game for the supermarket tabloids, which delighted in tales of his eccentric habits and pored over details of his plastic surgery, bids for the bones of the Elephant Man and other aspects of his personal life.

The self-proclaimed "loneliest man in the world" took these invasions into his private life very hard and reacted with more than a small edge of paranoia. Despite his predictions that he could outdo the success of *Thriller* with his next solo album, Jackson seemed to lose touch with his muse on *Bad*. Quincy Jones pulled out all the stops to assemble a superbly textured record from the production standpoint, but Jackson's aural charisma was on a low flame, and the videos couldn't make up the difference.

Jackson changed direction on his 1991 release, *Dangerous*. The album initially generated controversy when Jackson edited the video for its first single, "Black or White," after complaints about its violence and sexuality. As for the music itself, Jackson severed his relationship with Jones in favor of Teddy Riley, the master of the electronic dance music production dubbed New Jack Swing. The result was an album that, while studded with guest appearances by the likes of Guns n' Roses guitarist Slash, rapper Heavy D. and Madonna (in an uncredited turn), too often seemed to be trailing after contemporary styles rather than setting them. Jackson himself is occasionally overwhelmed in the mix, attempting to keep up his end of the musical bargain with a strained performance that lacks the focus and self-possession of his greatest albums, *Off the Wall* and *Thriller*.

It is understandable that Jackson might feel disappointment that *Bad*—which, according to Jackson's record company has sold 25 million copies worldwide—and *Dangerous*, which seemed well on its way to a similar sales level, have not been able to achieve greater popularity than *Thriller*. But he should also take consolation in the fact that not even the greatest artists—and he has done work that places him in the highest reaches of the American pop pantheon—can be expected to make history with every creation.

DISCOGRAPHY

SINGLES

"Got to Be There" (Motown; r☆4, ☆4, 1971). "Rockin' Robin" (Motown; r☆2, ☆2, 1972). "I Wanna Be Where You Are" (Motown; r☆2, ☆16, 1972). "Ben" (Motown; r☆5, ☆1, 1972). "With a Child's Heart" (Motown; r☆14, ☆50, 1973). "We're Almost There" (Motown; r☆7, ☆54, 1975). "Just a Little Bit of You" (Motown; r☆4, ☆23, 1975). "You Can't Win (Part 1)" (Epic; r☆42, ☆81, 1979). "Don't Stop 'til You Get Enough" (Epic; r☆1, ☆1, 1979). "Rock with You" (Epic; r☆1, ☆1, 1979). "Off the Wall" (Epic; r☆5, ☆10, 1980). "She's Out of My Life" (Epic; r☆43, ☆10, 1980). With Paul McCartney: "The Girl Is Mine" (Epic; r☆1, ☆2, 1982). "Billie Jean" (Epic; r☆1, ☆1, 1983). "Beat It" (Epic; r☆1, ☆1, 1983). "Wanna Be Startin' Somethin' " (Epic; r☆5, ☆5, 1983). "Human Nature" (Epic; r☆27, ☆7, 1983). With Paul McCartney: "Say Say Say" (Columbia; r☆2, ☆1, 1983). "P.Y.T. (Pretty Young Thing)" (Epic; r☆46, ☆10, 1983). "Thriller" (Epic; r☆3, ☆4, 1984). "I Just Can't Stop Loving You" (Epic; r☆1, ☆1, 1987). "Bad" (Epic; r☆1, ☆1, 1987). "The Way You Make Me Feel" (Epic; r☆1, ☆1, 1987). "Man in the Mirror" (Epic; r☆1, ☆1, 1988). With Stevie Wonder: "Get It" (Motown; r☆4, ☆80, 1988). "Dirty Diana" (Epic; r☆5, ☆1, 1988). "Another Part of Me" (Epic; r☆1, ☆11, 1988). "Smooth Criminal" (Epic; r☆2, ☆7, 1988). "Black or White" (Epic; r☆1, ☆1, 1991). "Remember the Time" (Epic; r☆1, ☆3, 1992). "In the Closet" (Epic; r☆1, ☆6).

ALBUMS

Got to Be There (Motown; ☆14, 1972). *Ben* (Motown; ☆5, 1972). *Music & Me* (Motown; ☆92, 1973). *Forever, Michael* (Motown; ☆101, 1975). *The Best of Michael Jackson* (Motown; ☆156, 1975). *Off the Wall* (Epic; ☆3, 1979). *One Day in Your Life* (Motown; ☆144, 1981). *Thriller* (Epic; ☆1, 1982). *Farewell My Summer Love 1984* (Motown; ☆46, 1984). *Bad* (Epic; ☆1, 1987). *Dangerous* (Epic; ☆1, 1991).

(Chart positions compiled from Joel Whitburn's *Record Research*, based on *Billboard*'s Pop and LPs charts, unless otherwise indicated; r☆ = position on *Billboard*'s Rhythm & Blues chart.)

MADONNA

BY J. D. CONSIDINE

It may seem hard to believe now, but there actually was a time in her recording career when Madonna wasn't famous—in fact, wasn't even considered a contender. This was back in 1984, when Madonna's debut album, *Madonna*, was seen as poor second to Cyndi Lauper's *She's So Unusual* in the Promising Female Artist sweepstakes. Both records sold well, and entered the *Billboard* Album Chart's Top Forty within a week of each other. But while *She's So Unusual* spun off four Top Five singles, *Madonna* merely slipped a pair of songs into the Top Ten.

Moreover, because those two singles—"Borderline" and "Lucky Star"—had crossed over from the dance market, most of the rock community saw Madonna as just another club-culture bimbette; video-savvy, sure, but hardly an artist of any import. Whereas Lauper not only had solid credentials (courtesy of her stint in the retro-rock act Blue Angel) and an interesting image (a sort of Betty Boop-meets-Laverne-&-Shirley chic), but actually seemed to be addressing important issues. After all, not only did she have the moxie to rewrite the sexist "Girls Just Want to Have Fun" as a tribute to feminine frivolity, but she even slipped a song about masturbation ("She Bop") into the hit parade. It was obvious, wrote the rock critic establishment, which of the two would turn into a truly major artist.

And as usual, the critical establishment got it exactly backward. It wasn't just that Madonna went on to greater chart success than Lauper, putting eighteen singles into the Top Five over the course of eight albums; by the end of the Eighties Madonna was a megastar, arguably one of the best-known women on earth and certainly one of the most talked-about figures in popular culture. She was written up everywhere, from *Cosmopolitan* to *Forbes* to *The Advocate;* her image was disparaged by Tipper Gore and Ellen Goodman, yet applauded by Germaine Greer and Camille Paglia; news of her latest

Madonna Ciccone, 1982.

controversy was as likely to turn up on *Nightline* as on MTV. She was, as her record company was proud to point out, Artist of the Decade.

Yet you couldn't really blame the critics for not seeing it coming, because in 1984 the pop world Madonna would rule hadn't been created yet. Back then, the dominant pop style was rock, rooted in the tradition-conscious sound of punk, and the dominant sensibility was camp, spun off from the Warholian adoration of TV and trash; naturally, Lauper had those qualities in spades. But Madonna was a creature of a different world. Her pop style was dance music, which had roots in funk and soul, but also in hip-hop and disco; her sensibility was ironic and postmodern, having grown out of the same media-saturated world that spawned graffiti artists Kenny Scharf and Keith Haring (and which, not coincidentally, would end up feeding the flames of MTV).

Like most denizens of that world, Madonna got there through a fairly roundabout fashion. Born comfortably middle-class in suburban Detroit, Ma-

Justify Her Love: the butch Madonna, 1983.

donna Louise Ciccone (she was named after her mother, who died of cancer when the singer was six) initially planned on a career in dance, studying briefly at the University of Michigan. Dropping out, she moved to New York with thirty-five dollars and an unflagging belief in her destiny. She continued to study dance, working with one of Alvin Ailey's secondary troupes, and drifted into music. Eventually she got a job singing backup with fading disco star Patrick Hernandez (of "Born to Be Alive" fame) and spent time in Paris; returning, she drummed with the Breakfast Club, formed her own group with pal

Stephen Bray and cut some demos with club DJ Mark Kamins. It was the Kamins-produced material that got her signed, and her first two singles, "Everybody" and "Burning Up," were solid club hits, though it wasn't until the Jellybean Benitez–produced "Holiday" that Madonna made any impression on radio.

Had she come along a decade earlier, this saga may well have ended there, but happily for her, Madonna emerged during the age of MTV. Although it would be oversimplifying to say that MTV made Madonna, providing her with a medium that would sell her image along with her music, it is obvious that video had an enormous impact on the singer's career. Her video for "Lucky Star," for instance, managed to turn Madonna's navel into a universal erogenous zone; "Borderline" established her as both a glamour puss and a romantic heroine, while "Material Girl" first introduced her version of the (Marilyn) Monroe Doctrine.

It was on a 1985 MTV Music Video Awards telecast, though, that Madonna made perhaps her most memorable appearance. Determined to introduce "Like a Virgin" even though the single itself was still weeks from release, Madonna hit the stage in a modified bridal gown and proceeded to writhe her way through the song. Yet it wasn't the apparent disparity between the song's virginal metaphor and the singer's decidedly carnal rendition that reeled in the home audience; it was the fact that Madonna had topped off the outfit with a customized belt-buckle bearing the legend BOY TOY. Never had the iconography of Freud's madonna-whore complex been brought to bear so vividly.

Such apparent contradictions confused and out-raged older viewers. Traditionalists, they were used to linear reasoning with all the important signs kept in context; they had no idea what to make of Madonna's clashing symbols. How could she be like a virgin, they wondered? How could she pose as both boy toy and bride? Was she selling sex or true love? Was she a feminist (as she said) or a bimbo (as she looked)? Just what in hell was going on here?

But the little girls understood. Children of the video age, they were used to logic-jarring jump cuts and context-shredding juxtapositions, inured to the white noise of advertising's sex-and-sizzle. Thus, where older observers saw blasphemy when Madonna wore rosaries and crucifixes, the younger fans—dismissively dubbed "Madonna wanna-bes" by their elders—merely recognized the icons as power-packed fashion accessories; likewise, the old-sters saw the singer's bra-baring brazenness as a slutty come-on, while the wanna-bes understood it as a statement of sex as power. Susan Baker, a co-founder of the Parents' Music Resource Center, griped that Madonna taught little girls how to act "like a porn queen in heat." But a seventeen-year-

The "Like a Virgin" tour, 1985.

old wanna-be quoted by *Time* begged to differ. "It's really women's lib," said the girl, "not being afraid of what guys think."

If *Like a Virgin* firmed up Madonna's stature as a pop power, it was her appearance in Susan Seidelman's *Desperately Seeking Susan* that established her as a "star" in the universal sense. Although hers was ostensibly a supporting role, Madonna stole the show from its putative stars, Rosanna Arquette and Aidan Quinn, and she made no secret of her eagerness to capitalize on that success. Here, however, Madonna would not be a particularly lucky star. Although she endured movie-star attention from the scandal sheets—which, clearly disappointed that Madonna had not been besmirched by the youthful, nude figure studies that ran in *Playboy* and *Penthouse*, hounded her and her hot-tempered then-husband, Sean Penn—her actual film career was shaping up as a flop, thanks to an execrable romantic comedy called *Shanghai Surprise* and the muddle-headed caper flick *Who's That Girl*. It wasn't until Madonna

Madonna during one of her dangerous liaisons, posing for MTV.

played Breathless Mahoney to Warren Beatty's Dick Tracy that she got any respect at all in Hollywood, and even then the praise was peppered with snickers over her offscreen relationship with actor-director Beatty.

By that point, however, Madonna was used to such comments. Ever since an early ROLLING STONE cover story suggested that she had slept her way to the top by having romantic relationships with the men who helped her career, Madonna had been dismissed by detractors as little more than a conniving slut. "I have a sexy image," she explained in 1987, "and people with sexy images aren't supposed to have any integrity or intelligence." Madonna, though, had both—particularly the latter. *True Blue*, which followed *Like a Virgin*, not only was savvy and successful, generating three Number One singles, but had been entirely cowritten (except for "Papa Don't Preach") and coproduced by the singer herself. Obviously this boy toy was no producer's pet. Moreover, the album showed off the singer's fondness for genre jumping, allowing her to indulge both her balladry ("Live to Tell") and her club consciousness ("Where's the Party"), absorbing some conventions whole (like the Latin undercurrents in "La Isla Bonita") and gleefully upending others (the Sixties girl-group sweetness sent up by the title tune). Nor was music the only place Madonna proved to be a cultural chameleon; her image, too, was forever shifting, from Monroe sultriness to girlish precocity, to sassy sensuality, to boyish androgyny.

Yet for Madonna, unlike rock's other quick-change artists, each new image did not entail a complete reinvention of her character. If anything, the more Madonna changed her looks and sound, the easier it was to maintain a sense of who that girl was. An instinctive postmodernist, Madonna treated images, attitudes and ideas as artistic commodities, playing off the power of each icon while keeping the content of her work at a comfortably ironic distance. Thus, when Mary Lambert's video for "Like a Prayer" was attacked by religious groups for alleged blasphemy, the corporate conservatives at Pepsi may have blinked, backing out of a multi-million-dollar sponsorship deal, but Madonna's fans barely batted an eye. They, after all, knew the difference between an artistic statement and a special effect.

Express Yourself: Madonna on tour, 1990.

Because scandal so often worked to her advantage, Madonna took on a reputation as a media manipulator and shameless self-promoter. A typical example was the furor in 1990 surrounding the "Justify My Love" video, in which Madonna and boyfriend pro tem Tony Ward acted out a variety of sexual fantasies, including bondage, bisexuality and voyeurism. Deemed too hot for MTV, it immediately mushroomed into a censorship scandal; an uncut commercial copy of the clip was rushed into record stores and sold millions. Madonna insisted that she hadn't caused the commotion intentionally (and the casual arrogance of her rationale—"Of course they'll play it; how could they not?"—was oddly convincing), but her critics accused her of planning the whole thing. Nobody doubted her intelligence then—they merely held it against her.

What her critics forget, however, is that manufactured sensation is usually short-lived, and contrived art is almost always conservative, while Madonna's career has been neither. Indeed, the multimedia contract she signed with Time/Warner in 1992—a music–movies–publishing deal worth a reputed $60 million—seems tangible proof of her formidable cultural impact. "I like to push people's buttons," she admits in the backstage documentary *Truth or Dare* (1991), but breaking boundaries is more like it.

Madonna changed the rules on almost every level, restructuring the relationship between image and content, realigning mass-culture perspectives on black and gay subcultures and reducing to rubble traditional notions of sex and power. It would be hard to imagine a truer definition of star power.

DISCOGRAPHY

SINGLES

"Holiday" (Sire; ☆16, 1984). "Borderline" (Sire; ☆10, 1984). "Lucky Star" (Sire; ☆4, 1984). "Like a Virgin" (Sire; ☆1, 1984). "Material Girl" (Sire; ☆2, 1985). "Crazy for You" (Geffen; ☆1, 1985). "Angel" (Sire; ☆5, 1985). "Dress You Up" (Sire; ☆5, 1985). "Live to Tell" (Sire; ☆1, 1986). "Papa Don't Preach" (Sire; ☆1, 1986). "True Blue" (Sire; ☆3, 1986). "La Isla Bonita" (Sire; ☆4, 1987). "Who's That Girl" (Sire; ☆1, 1987). "Causing a Commotion" (Sire; ☆2, 1987). "Like a Prayer" (Sire; ☆1, 1989). "Express Yourself" (Sire; ☆2, 1989). "Cherish" (Sire; ☆2, 1989). "Oh Father" (Sire; ☆20, 1990). "Keep It Together" (Sire; ☆8, 1990). "Vogue" (Sire; ☆1, 1990). "Hanky Panky" (Sire; ☆10, 1990). "Justify My Love" (Sire; ☆1, 1990).

ALBUMS

Madonna (Sire; ☆8, 1983). *Like a Virgin* (Sire; ☆1, 1984). *True Blue* (Sire; ☆1, 1986). *Who's That Girl* (Sire; ☆7, 1987). *Like a Prayer* (Sire; ☆1, 1989). *I'm Breathless* (Sire; ☆2, 1990). *The Immaculate Collection* (Sire; ☆2, 1990).

(Chart positions compiled from Joel Whitburn's *Record Research*, based on *Billboard*'s Pop and LPs charts.)

THE GLOBAL BEAT

BY DAISANN McLANE

The most fascinating, promising—and certainly the most eclectic—musical movement of the last decade didn't even have a name that its fans could agree on. World beat (or global pop, world music, international mix, ethnopop—take your pick) had almost as many definitions as it did labels. For some, it signified contemporary recorded popular music from the third world, especially Africa and Asia; others added ethnic and folkloric music from all regions, including Western Europe, to the global pot. For still others, "world beat" meant the musical collaborations, beginning in the early Eighties, between popular Western and non-Western musicians like England's Peter Gabriel and Senegalese singer Youssou N'Dour.

The most successful categorization of the music, as it turned out, didn't come from critics or fans, but from the giant record store chains that had to figure out how to display and package the increasing numbers of strangely titled, difficult to pronounce new releases. They took the easy way out, defining the music by what it *wasn't;* so "world beat" became simply a catchall for Anything-Not-from-Here, "here" being the U.S.-U.K. mainstream folk-rock-pop music machinery. By 1990 you could browse the "world" or "international" section of one of these big stores and lose yourself in a dizzying Casbah of discs from the earth's far corners—everything from sambas recorded with hand-held mikes in the streets of Rio to rap-pop dance singles from Cairo, to slick, middle-aged Greek chanteuses, even, sometimes, to Julio Iglesias.

Access to this astonishing diversity of music was one of the major bonuses of the Nineties; it was like suddenly walking into your local supermarket and

Fela Anikulapo Kuti, of Nigeria: Fans of James Brown find it easy to dive into his hypnotic keyboard grooves.

finding couscous and sushi mix—a trend that occurred around the same time, and, I believe, was no coincidence. Fax machines humming, televisions tuned to CNN, a new, globally aware America was hungry for the world. Or at least for a taste; the world-beat audience was a small one by music-biz standards. An A&R director at Shanachie Records, one of the indie labels that helped fuel the world-beat boom in the mid-Eighties, told me once, half-seriously, that when any of their Asian or African releases sold 10,000 units, they'd throw an office party. World beat's core audience was an elite one: college-educated, upscale, grownup ex–rock & rollers (and, largely, white). Nevertheless, world beat did manage to reach beyond this fringe, into a mass market, when established artists like David Byrne and Paul Simon began experimenting with African and Latin American rhythms and musicians on their albums (Byrne's *Rei Momo* and Simon's *Graceland* and *The Rhythm of the Saints*,) introducing a sprinkle of exotic spices into the meat-and-potatoes of Top Forty fare.

World beat had been out there long before its label. There has always been an international mix on U.S. airwaves and jukeboxes (indeed, if you want to get technical, the African roots of rock, R&B, blues and jazz make them the original ''world musics''). Latin Caribbean rhythms like the mambo and rumba, popularized by the Cuban pianist Perez Prado, became hits in the Forties and Fifties. When Cuban-American Desi Arnaz, as Ricky Ricardo, played ''Babalu'' on *I Love Lucy* to an audience of millions in the Fifties, he was introducing Middle America to the same magical-religious Afro-Cuban drum patterns that Byrne and Simon would adapt nearly forty years later. Hispanic-American rocker Ritchie Valens turned a Mexican folk song, ''La Bamba,'' into rock & roll history. Jamaican-American Harry Belafonte's cleaned-up calypsos were the rage of college campuses in the Fifties, the same decade that his protégée, the South African singer Miriam Makeba, scored a hit with her ''Pata Pata.'' (Though Paul Simon brought Ladysmith Black Mambazo to national attention in the Eighties, South African pop had already charted here in 1961, with the Tokens' harmonious ''The Lion Sleeps Tonight''.) Brazil's bossa nova seduced its way into the Top Ten in the Sixties, with Astrud Gilberto's ''The Girl from Ipanema.'' Then there were the novelty foreign language hits: ''Sukiyaki,'' ''Dominique,'' ''Guantanamera.''

The concept of mixing U.S.-U.K. pop with music from other traditions had its beginnings twenty-five or more years before the world-beat boom. One of the by-products of the rock revolution of the Sixties was an increased curiosity about non-Western cultures. A generation of the young, white and privileged hit the road and ended up in Marrakesh, Bombay, Kenya; they returned with a wider view of the world, and some strangely wonderful sounds. The Beatles made the Indian sitar nearly as familiar a rock accoutrement as the Fender, and Indian classical master Ravi Shankar became a worldwide star. Rolling Stones Brian Jones and Keith Richards (and later Ornette Coleman and critic-clarinetist Robert Palmer) trekked to Morocco to record with the master musicians of Joujouka. Cream drummer Ginger Baker and Mick Fleetwood of Fleetwood Mac both made albums with West African percussionists. And L.A. eccentric Van Dyke Parks—best known for his work with the Beach Boys—made Trinidadian steel drums the centerpiece of his own intriguing solo album, *Discover America,* in 1972.

Then, in the late Sixties a small, low-budget subsidiary label of Elektra Records called Nonesuch began to sell out copies of their ethnographic recordings of Indonesian gamelan orchestras, Bahamian gospel shouters and Balinese tribes doing the monkey chant—records that used to sell mainly to anthropology students. Now these LPs were turning up in the record libraries of college radio stations and in the collections of in-the-know musicians, producers, critics and fans. Though they represented an avant-garde—not a mainstream—audience, many graduates of this inquisitive group of cross-cultural music junkies in the Eighties became the movers and shakers of the movement that finally had a name—even though it was one that nobody liked.

''The Empire Strikes Back'' is how a British friend of mine characterized the massive flow of African, Caribbean and Middle Eastern pop music and musicians that began to sweep into London, Paris and New York at the beginning of the Eighties. Though he was half joking, his comment is a good description of the social and historical forces behind the emergence of world beat. Independence movements had ''liberated'' much of the third world from colonial rule in the Fifties and Sixties, but many of the old links remained in place, especially economic, social and psychological ties. For education, survival, job opportunity, or sometimes escape from political persecution, millions of people from the third world flocked to the metropolises of their former colonial rulers. Others floated back and forth between first and third worlds, a new style of migration made possible by jet travel. English-speaking Nigerians, Ghanaians, Jamaicans and Trinidadians congregated in London; francophone Africa and the Caribbean, from Guadeloupe to Algeria to Zaire, went to Paris; and everybody—especially Caribbeans and Latin Americans—came to New York. Their suitcases were packed with records.

Or, more often, cassette tapes. The introduction of the cassette and of inexpensive boom-box machines to the third world in the Seventies had revolutionized the way music was played and distributed in Africa, Asia and the Caribbean. Though tape piracy was rampant and royalties virtually nonexistent, the new pop market that the tape revolution opened up stimulated the ambitions of aspiring musicians everywhere. And the hot trade in tapes from all over the world speeded up the creative exchange between Africa, the Caribbean and the United States. Before tapes, there had been a brisk import and export of musical ideas between Africa, Europe and Afro-America. In the Fifties and Sixties U.S. radio programs, picked up in the Caribbean, had a profound impact in the development of reggae and calypso. Rumba records, imported from Cuba, were a key source for the rhythms and arranging styles of the Zairian dance pop, soukous. Tapes, cheap and easy to reproduce, accelerated this process of pop innovation. Months after Michael Jackson's *Thriller* was released, his licks—reworked and re-Africanized by local musicians—were breaking down dance floors in Lagos and Dakar.

The cassette boom happened at a time when African and Caribbean pop were already on a creative

Nigerian singer-guitarist King Sunny Ade invented *juju*, an electric-guitar-heavy pop with polyrhythmic patterns taken from traditional Yoruba music.

roll. Post-independence Africa was moving from country to city, and urbanization created a big new market for pop music. The massive emigration to magnet cities like London, New York and Paris added to this market; homesick and culture-shocked, African and Caribbean émigrés were a greedy, insatiable market for the sounds of their native countries. Independence, new nationhood and the resulting resurgence of pride in heritage and culture created an environment in which new musical ideas flourished. Indeed, there seems to be a strong link everywhere in the third world between the emergence of popular social-political movements and leaders and the surfacing of powerful new pop

Senegalese singer Youssou N'Dour: His collaborations with Peter Gabriel helped bring African music to a large Western audience.

artists and forms. Ghanaian highlife peaked during the Nkrumah years of the Sixties, Zimbabwean Thomas Mapfumo's chimurengas became anthems of his country's independence fight in 1980. The delirious celebrations after Jean-Bertrand Aristide's election to the presidency of Haiti in 1991 were accompanied by the revolutionary beat of Boukman Eksperyans, a band who created a new pop form based on voodoo rhythms. Great moments in history make for great music.

In the mid-Seventies, spearheaded by the charismatic, visionary figure of Bob Marley, Jamaica's reggae became the first musical rhythm to make the move from the third world into the first not as a novelty, but on its own terms. Beyond reggae, however, was much, much more; by the early Eighties, a musical embarrassment of riches was bubbling just beneath the surface in London, Paris and New York. All you had to do to find the music was to wander the immigrant streets, ears open for the delicious sounds drifting from boom boxes or basement nightclubs. It was only a matter of time before the Western pop world caught on, and sure enough, in popped hype wizard Malcolm McLaren. In 1980, as the punk rock he'd helped promote was beginning to sputter and choke its last, McLaren launched what he was sure would be the Next Big Thing: Bow Wow Wow. The first worldbeat band, Bow Wow Wow matched a beautiful Burmese singer with a group of British musicians who played rock mixed with rhythms from the African country of Burundi. But Bow Wow Wow, inaugurated with much ballyhoo about internationalism and the future of rock & roll, bombed. McLaren had the right instincts, but the wrong concept. World beat would indeed break into the market, but not as a crafty multicultural packaging ploy from a first-world producer.

The music traveling northward from Africa, Asia and the Caribbean had a richness that no band of slyly packaged imitators could compete with. This third-world pop wave also had an added edge that helped it cross borders on its own. Because much of the music tapped into Western pop music forms (most of which were African-derived in the first place), it had a built-in familiarity to the ears of first-world listeners. One of the reasons reggae was so easily assimilated into the pop-rock pantheon was that it had its roots in U.S.-style R&B. Likewise, fans of James Brown would find it easy to dive into the keyboard-hypnotic groove of Nigerian Fela Anikulapo Kuti's Afro-beat.

A French producer, Martin Meissonnier, was the first to realize that only a little fine-tuning was needed to help this third-world wave reach a wider audience. In 1982 he went into an African recording studio with Nigerian guitarist-singer King Sunny Ade. Ade, an enormous star in his home country, had invented *juju,* an electric guitar–heavy pop with polyrhythmic patterns taken from traditional Yoruba music. With high-tech equipment, Meissonnier cleaned up Ade's noisy Lagos-recorded tracks, then remixed them to emphasize the music's interweaving play of electric and steel guitars—a sound that anybody raised on rock & roll could easily understand. Ade's LP *Juju Music* charted in the United States and the United Kingdom; his subsequent U.S. and European tour, a three-hour-plus pageant of trance and dance, was an unqualified smash.

Ade led the way for other third-world popsters (America, with its legacy of isolationism, and the rigidity of its megabucks record industry, lagged behind Britain and Europe in jumping on the global bandwagon). In Paris, where musicians from francophone Africa and the Caribbean often came to take advantage of first-world studio technology, records by Zairian soukous stars Franco and Tabu Ley began to appear on the charts, and Senegalese singing star Youssou N'Dour started appearing in clubs and concerts attended by curious Parisians, not just émigrés from the home country. In London world beat came out in full force in the summer of 1985, an ''African Summer'' when the young and street-smart gave up basic black in favor of kente cloth and beads. Small labels like Stern's and Globestyle sprung into existence and built a successful business licensing releases from all parts of Africa, the Middle East and even Asia. Backed by Peter Gabriel, the WOMAD (World of Music Arts and Dance) foundation's concerts brought performers from Asia, Latin America and Africa to massive outdoor festivals in the British countryside; the live recordings of these shows reached many hundreds of thousands more.

The rage for global pop might have turned out to be a one-summer flash had it not fit so snugly into that other major trend of the Eighties, dance music. Savvy club DJs soon realized that many of the Afri-

The Gipsy Kings, from Arles, France: the first world-music superstars.

can and Caribbean records floating into their hands were dance-floor dynamite. The DJs collected singles that had been huge in their home markets—like Caribbean soca star Arrow's "Hot, Hot, Hot"—and made them international club hits. Dance music producers jumped on world beat as a source of new voices and sounds to add to their mix. Eric B. and Rakim used Yemenite singer Ofra Haza's ululating Middle Eastern vocals in a sample on a remix of their single "Paid in Full." The use of these samples in dance pop helped Western pop audiences get used to the sounds of non-Western music. Original records by the sampled artists started appearing in the

U.S. and U.K. charts (Ofra Haza eventually signed to Sire Records, Madonna's U.S. label). A group of flamenco-singing gypsies from Arles, France, the Gipsy Kings, broke into the pop charts in 1989 with their frenetic "Bamboleo," and became the first world-music superstars.

By 1990 it was clear that world beat was no fad or fringe enterprise; as a category it had entered the mainstream of the music business. The original specialty labels expanded their catalogues and were joined by a host of majors like PolyGram, Elektra, Island (Mango), Virgin (Earthworks) and Columbia. David Byrne, through compilation albums released

The Bulgarian State Female Vocal Choir.

on his own Luaka Bop label and distributed by Warner Bros., introduced his audience to the immense range of Brazilian and Cuban popular music; meanwhile Peter Gabriel's RealWorld imprint, which included new recordings by artists from Cuba, Cambodia, Pakistan and North Africa, was becoming the Nonesuch of the Nineties. (Nonesuch, in fact, had revived, scoring in the charts with a recording of folk music sung by the Bulgarian State Radio and Television Female Vocal Choir.)

"World beat" remained a problematic label. Not only did it lump wildly different traditions and styles into the same genre, it implied that Western popular music was the center of reference and the rest of the world a vast, exotic Out There waiting to be discovered by some music-biz Columbus. (Culturally arrogant, and a misleading point of view: The "exotic" records for sale in a hip New York record store are Number One in Yemen, Lagos or Rio. One man's world beat is another man's Top Forty.) But as the

DISCOGRAPHY

ALBUMS
African

King Sunny Ade and His African Beats: *Juju Music* (Mango/Island; 1982). **The African Brothers Band:** *Me Poma* (Rounder; 1986). **Manu Dibango:** *Soul Makossa* (Atlantic; 1972). **Franco:** *Mario & Response de Mario* (Sterns; 1989). **Salif Keita:** *Soro* (Mango; 1987). **Cheb Khaled and Safy Boutella:** *Kutche* (Capitol; 1989). **Fela Anikulapo Kuti:** *Original Sufferhead* (Shanachie; 1991). **Ladysmith Black Mambazo:** *Shaka Zulu* (WEA; 1987). **Tabu Ley Rochereau:** *Babeti Soukous* (RealWorld; 1989). **Mahlathini and the Mahotella Queens:** *Paris-Soweto* (Polydor; 1989). **Thomas Mapfumo:** *Shumba: Vital Hits of Zimbabwe* (Earthworks; 1991). **Youssou N'Dour:** *Immigrés* (Earthworks; 1984). **Anthologies:** *The Indestructible Beat of Soweto* (Shanachie; 1985). *Heartbeat Soukous* (Earthworks; 1988). *Yalla Hitlist Egypt* (Mango; 1990). *Guitar Paradise of East Africa* (Earthworks; 1991).

Carribean and South American

Arrow: *Hot-Hot-Hot* (Charlie's; NA). **Joe Arroyo:** *Fuego en Mi Mente* (Mango; 1989). **Boukman Eksperyans:** *Vodou Adjaye* (Mango; 1991). **Ensemble Nemours Jn. Baptiste:** *A Musical Tour of Haiti* (Ansonia; 1958). **Gilberto Gil:** *Soy Loco Por Ti America* (Braziloid; 1987). **Juan Luis Guerra y 4-40:** *Bachata Rosa* (Karen; 1991). **Kassav':** *Majestik Zouk* (CBS; 1989). **Magnum Band:** *Tet Ensem* (TIDA; 1987). **The Mighty Sparrow:** *Hot and Sweet* (Warner Bros.; 1974). **Beny More:** *Grandes Exitos, Volumes 1 & 2* (RCA Int.; NA). **Olodum:** *From the Northeast of Sahara to the Northeast of Brazil 10 Years* (Sound Wave/WEA; 1991). **Johnny Pacheco and Celia Cruz:** *Celia & Johnny* (Vaya; 1974). **David Rudder and Charlie's Roots:** *Z2Calypso Music* (Warner/Sire; 1987). **Shadow:** *Columbus Lied* (Shanachie; 1991). **Tabou Combo:** *Tabou Combo en Español* (Kubaney; 1990). **Caetano Veloso:** *Estrangeiro* (Elektra Musician; 1991). **Anthologies:** *Konbit! Burning Rhythms of Haiti* (A&M; 1989). *Viva el Ritmo Cuba Baila* (Earthworks Import; 1985). *Sabroso! Havana Hits* (Earthworks; 1988). *When the Time Comes/Rebel Soca* (Shanachie; 1988). *Wind Your Waist* (Shanachie; 1991). *Hurricane Zouk* (Earthworks; 1988). *Beleza Tropical* (Luaka Bop/Sire, 1989). *O Samba* (Luaka Bop/Sire; 1989).

Nineties opened, the term already had fallen into disuse. The complex cross-cultural currents of modern pop music were making it obsolete. Styles began to zap between countries as fast as faxes, and hybrids blossomed in the unlikeliest places; with the channels of international distribution in place, the pop was flowing every which way at once. Sales figures remained modest by rock & roll standards, but no matter. The opening of the Western marketplace to this flood of music had changed pop forever.

Smells Like Teen (and clean) Spirit: Nirvana behind the scenes in 1991. *From left:* Chris Novoselic, David Grohl, Kurt Cobain.

UP FROM UNDERGROUND

BY TOM SINCLAIR

By 1980 the lessons of punk—keep it simple, chuck the solos, pump the attitude—had largely been absorbed into the mainstream. Skinny-tie bands like the Knack and the Romantics were cashing in on the so-called new wave boom even as Blondie and Talking Heads began chalking up bona fide hit singles. The homogenization of the underground was fast becoming a reality, with Linda Ronstadt hiring an ostensible punk band, the Cretones, to back her on her 1980 album *Mad Love*, and major labels signing the less threatening proponents of the "loud-fast rules" school.

The results of this dubious breakthrough left lovers of authentically raw punk—as exemplified by, say, the Dead Boys or the Heartbreakers—feeling cheated. Even the British punk scene was crumbling, with the Sex Pistols defunct, the Clash becoming more and more commercial and a slew of synth-pop bands bum-rushing the spotlight. In response to the increasing dilution of the punk ethos, true believers across America became increasingly reactionary. Corporate rock became the enemy as independent labels and fanzines proliferated, both nurturing and championing local talent while disdaining all concessions to the big, bad star-making machinery of the music business.

Ironically, by decade's end a number of the most uncompromising underground acts would find themselves with major label contracts, playing arenas and mulling a whole 'nother set of dilemmas as older fans scornfully accused them of "selling out." Underground rock in the Eighties was to become a house divided, rife with cliques and backbiting. Post-punk bands split from the punk amoeba and kept bifurcating, some moving toward complexity, others clinging resolutely to minimalism, all rewriting punk's "no rules" rulebook in infinitesimally different ways.

The most dramatic new genre to emerge at the beginning of the Eighties was hardcore, a faster, harder and more dogmatic variant of Ramones-style punk. Hardcore was to directly influence the resurgence of metal as a new generation used its brutal energy to forge both thrash and speed metal, but in its most distilled form (as in, for example, Washington, D.C.'s Minor Threat) the music was vehemently anticommercial. For the most part, hardcore purists take pride in a life on the margins, with many taking a dim view of bands, such as Suicidal Tendencies, that have crossed over to major label success.

California's Black Flag is generally credited with providing the blueprint for hardcore, but in retrospect, songs like "T.V. Party" and "Six Pack" (from the group's debut album, *Damaged*, 1981) offered more diversity and humor than most subsequent hardcore units would muster. Too strict an allegiance to by-the-numbers hardcore can easily turn into a prison, though a few groups were to use it as a springboard, discarding its crasser trappings as they found their own voices. (Black Flag's label, SST, run by Flag guitarist Greg Ginn, was the initial home for a number of the underground's most heralded bands, including Hüsker Dü, Dinosaur Jr and Sonic Youth.)

Two such groups, which were to prove enormously influential both in and outside the confines of the U.S. underground, were the Replacements and Hüsker Dü, both from Minneapolis. The Replacements' debut LP, *Sorry Ma, Forgot to Take Out the Trash*, from 1981, was a whirligig of loud, fast and sloppy punk delivered at breakneck speed, with songwriter–front man Paul Westerberg shouting the lyrics in a hoarse, nicotine-tinged voice. Amid the chaos, there were hints of the greatness the Mats (as their fans dubbed them) were to achieve: "Johnny's Gonna Die" was a relatively sensitive (and prophetic) paean to the junk-addled ex–New York Dolls guitarist Johnny Thunders, while songs such as

The original 'Mats, drinking for the enjoyment, not the endorsement *(from left)*: Paul Westerberg, Bob Stinson, Chris Mars, Tommy Stinson.

Hüsker Dü: before, not after.

"Shiftless When Idle" and "Takin' a Ride" poked fun at the rock & roll lifestyle with tongue-in-cheek self-honesty and a delicious lack of pretension.

When the Mats released their watershed album, *Let It Be,* in 1984, it was evident that a truly monumental rock & roll band had arrived. Westerberg, a rock fan whose catholicity of taste allowed him to cherish the Sex Pistols and the Faces with equal ardor, had evolved into a songwriter of uncommon depth. *Let It Be* proved the Replacements to be equally adept at spirited throwaways ("Gary's Got a Boner"), clever covers (Kiss's "Black Diamond"), heartfelt ballads ("Unsatisfied," "Sixteen Blue") and goofy musings ("Androgynous"). Critics hailed the band as nothing short of the Second Coming, while the Mats' drunken, rowdy live shows became the stuff of legend. After *Let It Be,* the Replacements were summarily snapped up by Sire/Reprise, where they recorded four albums. Alas, booze, internal pressures and individual neuroses finally caused the Mats to splinter in 1991 following the release of *All Shook Down.* Westerberg, bassist Tommy Stinson and former drummer Chris Mars all announced intentions to launch solo careers.

Hüsker Dü's early work was also rooted in hardcore. Released in 1981, *Land Speed Record* (the title alludes to the band's reputed amphetamine intake at the time) was a blast of hopped-up bass-drums-guitar fury. Like the Replacements, Hüsker Dü seemed to improve with each album. The group's two songwriters, guitarist Bob Mould and drummer Grant Hart, functioned as a kind of post-punk Lennon-McCartney, with the work of each reflecting a quest for spiritual enlightenment as they sorted through their individual anger, confusion and obsessions. Hüsker Dü eventually succumbed to internal tensions, calling it quits soon after the release of a brilliant 1987 double album, *Warehouse: Songs and Stories.* After Hüsker Dü crumbled, Mould recorded a moody, largely acoustic album called *Workbook* (1989) before returning to the more characteristic Dü-style roiling pop noise with *Black Sheets of Rain* (1990). Grant Hart also embarked on a solo career, releasing an EP, *2541,* in 1988 and following that up with an album, *Intolerance,* in 1989.

Two startling and refreshing West Coast groups who also flirted with hardcore early on were X, from Los Angeles, and the Minutemen, from San Pedro.

X, whose first four records were produced by former Doors keyboardist Ray Manzarek, fashioned a sound that revolved around the twin vocal interplay of husband-and-wife songwriting team John Doe and Exene Cervenka and the rockabilly-cum-Ramones playing of guitarist Billy Zoom. The Minutemen (so named for the brevity of their songs) seemed willing to try anything and everything, at least for sixty seconds, and their challenging oeuvre finds them mixing and matching punk, acoustic lyricism, jazz, funk and Beat poetry. Neither X nor the Minutemen made it through the Eighties. X fell apart in stages as Doe's and Cervenka's relationship crumbled, although, after the band reunited for some dates together in 1990 and '91, Cervenka, Doe, D. J. Bonebrake and Tony Gilkyson returned to the studio the following year to work on a new album. The Minutemen were abruptly terminated by the death of guitarist D. Boon in a 1985 automobile accident. The remaining Minutemen, despondent over their friend's demise, disbanded. They regrouped with a rabid Minutemen fan, Ed Crawford, on guitar, forming fIREHOSE, which continued in the Minutemen's manic tradition and eventually signed to Columbia.

While the groups discussed so far were all of major importance in defining American underground music in the Eighties, none cast as long a shadow as did R.E.M., a quartet of close-knit Southern boys from Athens, Georgia. When they got together in 1980, the four members of R.E.M. were occasional students and full-time music freaks buzzed by the excitement of the raw punk coming out of New York and London. Spurred by the success of fellow Athens residents the B-52's (whose 1978 independent single "Rock Lobster" resulted in a record contract with Warner Bros.) and the acclaim being heaped on other local bands like Pylon and the Method Actors, the members of R.E.M. set about inventing a group identity largely through trial and error. Singer Michael Stipe was a reclusive art school student who gained an unmistakable charisma once he set foot on a stage; guitarist Peter Buck was a record store clerk and a self-taught musician; and the rhythm section, bassist Mike Mills and drummer Bill Berry, had played together in various rock bands since high school. Mixing covers with original songs, R.E.M. elicited a mixed response from other Athens bands; some viewed them as little more than a good garage-pop band, while others saw them as welcome breath of fresh air.

R.E.M.'s first single, "Radio Free Europe," released on the Hib-Tone label in 1981, was an anthemic, quivering rocker with opaque lyrics and a chiming guitar motif that made many naysayers sit up and take notice. When the group subsequently released an EP, *Chronic Town,* on I.R.S. Records, public and critical interest rapidly turned into something approaching awe. *Chronic Town* was that sublimely rare thing: a genuinely new wrinkle in the rock & roll fabric. Ironically, it sounded nothing like the Stooges-derived punk that R.E.M. loved. Peter Buck's guitar playing owed more to Roger McGuinn's twelve-string epiphanies with the Byrds than to the Stooges' sainted Ron Asheton's wall of wah-wah. Michael Stipe's vocals were another matter: Owing to his ambivalent enunciation, at least half the lyrics were indecipherable. Surprisingly, this only added to R.E.M.'s mystery and appeal: The words that could be understood suggested an arcane system of personal mysticism that was wide open to individual interpretation. The songs themselves were undeniably catchy. With *Chronic Town* R.E.M. had created a dreamy sort of mysterioso pop, at once infectious and intangible, down-to-earth and remote.

The release of *Murmur* in 1983 proved that *Chronic Town* had been no fluke. Filled with haunted vocals and haunting guitars, songs like "Pilgrimage" and "Talk About the Passion" gave the lie to those who were willing to write off the Athens boys as idiots savants. A new generation of young people, looking for a band to call its own, came to view *Murmur* as a signpost. In its wake many came to regard R.E.M. with a reverence heretofore reserved for such influential beacons from the past as the Velvet Underground and the New York Dolls.

Murmur made the Top Forty—an unprecented feat for a young underground band—and R.E.M. quickly became the new group to watch. As the group's star rose, so did the impact and influence of American college radio (which was highly supportive of R.E.M.) in launching new acts. This confluence—the growing success of R.E.M. and the widening importance of college radio—was to alter the music business to an extent that Seventies punk never truly did. By the end of the Eighties "alternative music" marketing departments were to become a fixture at most major record labels.

R.E.M. continued to grow over the course of its albums. Stipe began singing more clearly, the group's folk-rock side gradually became all but subsumed by a more traditional rock sound, and in 1987 R.E.M. had scored its first Top Forty hit single with "The One I Love," a mid-tempo saunter hooked with a wonderful guitar riff and lyrics of extraordinary bitterness. (In it, Stipe describes a lover as "a simple prop to occupy my time"; the chorus announces the arrival of a new prop-love interest with the drawn-out word "Fire!"). Despite the song's pointedly brutal slant, the public loved it. Before long R.E.M. signed to Warner Bros. in a highly lucrative deal.

Green, from 1988, was the group's major-label debut and yielded a novelty hit, "Stand," which worked both as a spoof of a silly pop song and as a genuinely fun anthem; in other words, the band was eating its cake and having it too. But *Green* also contained songs of social commentary ("Orange Crush," another popular single, was allegedly about Agent Orange). There was no denying it: R.E.M., the former darlings of the underground, had achieved pop stardom. While *Green* did wonders for the group's profile, their masterful 1991 album *Out of Time* catapulted R.E.M. straight to the top of *Billboard*'s album chart. Buoyed by the graceful and enigmatic hit single "Losing My Religion," *Out of Time* was a contemplative-sounding album, its songs brimming with string arrangements, organ, harpsichord and Peter Buck's folksy mandolin and acoustic guitar. R.E.M., after more than a decade of resolutely following its muse, had become a supergroup. The astonishing thing was that the group succeeded almost entirely on its own terms and had helped to build and solidify the U.S. underground's often contentious network of music lovers into a powerful force.

But the underground being the many-tentacled beast that it is, for some, R.E.M.'s music was always an object of derision, its folksiness and melodicism a betrayal of punk's commitment to extremism, its poppiness an embarrassment. Miles removed from R.E.M. and its ilk was a band of mind-blown Texans whose very name proclaimed their commitment to the cult of marginality: the Butthole Surfers. Reportedly drawing their inspiration from an ambitious daily regimen of acid, reefer and beer, the Buttholes delighted in creating messy gobs of noise with a distinct undercurrent of Dada. Their early records were dense celebrations of hedonism and absurdity, but fans maintained that the Buttholes' albums were only the tip of the iceberg, that the key to the band was in its anarchic live shows. The group's affinity for Sixties drugs notwithstanding, a Butthole Surfers concert was no place for a starry-eyed hippie with a head full of chemicals and a heart full of peace and love: In addition to the nude female dancer(s) who gyrated to the music, there were the stomach-wrenching films of bloody accident victims and penile surgery the band used as a backdrop for its roiling, assaultive performances. There was also singer-ringmaster Gibby Haynes's penchant for literally playing with fire, whether lighting up his own hand or various musical instruments.

By decade's end, however, even the Butthole Surf-

Geffen recording artists Sonic Youth *(from left):* Thurston Moore, Kim Gordon, Steve Shelley, Lee Ranaldo.

ers had mellowed as they began indulging their growing taste for long, goofy psychedelic jams. This emergent proclivity, combined with the acid-tinged outlook of much of their following, inspired more than one wag to brand the Buttholes "the Grateful Dead of the underground."

Out of Chicago emerged another group of noise terrorists who were to influence myriad late-Eighties malcontents. The brutal, dour trio Big Black was led by a thin, iconoclastic ex-Montanan named Steve Albini, whose writings in various fanzines revealed a disturbing interest in subjects such as child pornography and white racial supremacy. Nevertheless, in spite of his creepy outlook, Albini perfected a pulverizing, unrelenting guitar sound, closer to industrial than to punk, a radical approach perhaps best captured on Big Black's 1986 album *Atomizer.* The songs reflected Albini's obsession (identifica-

tion?) with the darker side of human nature: "Jordan, Minnesota" took the listener for a wallow in the cesspool of child abuse, while "Kerosene" seemed to be about self-immolation.

Albini dissolved Big Black following *Songs About Fucking,* from 1987. His next group, Rapeman, lasted just long enough to put out a single, an EP and one album before vociferous public criticism of the group's name (allegedly taken from a Japanese comic book character) during a European tour forced a premature breakup. Since then, Albini has confined himself to producing other people's records.

One Albini production was the Pixies' first full-length album, *Surfer Rosa,* in 1988. The Boston-based Pixies were decidedly capital-*W* weird. Their songs, sardonic nursery rhymes framed by Joey Santiago's biting guitar, Kim Deal's supple bass and singer-songwriter Black (Charles) Francis's coy, bawling vocals, defied easy exegesis. ("Your bone's got a little machine," ran the chorus of "Bone Machine.") Later Pixies songs, such as "Wave of Mutilation" and "Debaser" ("I wanna grow up to be a debaser!") cemented the group's reputation as the rock & roll corollary of a David Lynch film. What did it all mean? Not much, according to Black Francis. Questions of the perverse content of the lyrics aside, there was no denying the Pixies sounded pretty swell and were perhaps the first band to truly deserve the appellation "postmodern."

Most of the fifty-odd bands who are members of the Black Rock Coalition, an organization founded in 1985 as a support group for black rock musicians, fit solidly, if unwillingly, into the underground category, if only by dint of the obstacles they face in getting record labels to give their music a fair hearing. Only Living Colour, the BRC's flagship band—whose first album, *Vivid* (1988), went platinum—has broken through in a big way, though audiences for the crazed polyglot funk & roll of bands like Fishbone, 24-7 Spyz and Follow for Now continue to grow. A compilation of ten BRC bands, *The History of Our Future,* was released in 1991.

The latter half of the Eighties witnessed the resurgence of grunge, as hundreds of groups proudly proclaimed their intention to stay in the garage for life (to paraphrase a Clash lyric). Seattle's Mudhoney, Minneapolis's Cows, New York's Gumball—these, and hundreds of other less-heralded units, seemed blissfully content to pay repeated tribute to the gods of wah-wah, fuzz and distortion, reveling in primitivism, revering volume above all. The most intriguing of this new wave of garageland denizens was Dinosaur Jr, a trio out of Amherst, Massachusetts, fronted by J Mascis, a singer-songwriter-guitarist who looked and sang for all the world like Neil Young's punked-out kid brother. An ex-hardcore drummer who had switched to guitar, Mascis wrote songs that were breathless whirlwinds of melody and power, a strange and appealing mixture of laconic lyricism and sculpted sonic noise.

From New York's Lower East Side, once the hotbed of the punk revolution that started at CBGB, crawled a scrungy-looking mixed-gender quartet that mixed art-rock concepts with garage squall in a fresh way. Sonic Youth utilized offbeat tunings and inside-out song structures to create its version of Eighties rock, molesting their guitars with bows and hammers in an effort to coax out new sounds. The

Vernon Reid *(left)* and Corey Glover of Living Colour, pioneers of the Black Rock Coalition.

group's legend and influence grew with each successive album, culminating in the double album *Daydream Nation,* from 1988, the last of the group's records on an independent label. (Sonic Youth was subsequently snapped up by David Geffen's DGC label.)

As the Eighties drew to a close, independent record labels began to specialize in distinct musical genres, carving out marketing niches much as Motown had done in the Sixties. Seattle's Sub Pop offered a variety of scruffy garage-boy bands; Chicago's Wax Trax Records became known for its industrial dance music terrorists; and Washington's Dischord Records was home to post-hardcore experimentalists, such as Jawbox.

Shortly after R.E.M. hit the jackpot with *Out of Time,* Nirvana, a trio of punk rockers who graduated from the Sub Pop grunge ghetto to DGC, unexpectedly found itself with a smash album. *Nevermind,* the group's second effort, was a bracing jolt of post-adolescent energy and attitude that managed to unite metalheads and alternative music types alike, while roping in those curious listeners attracted by the subversive single "Smells Like Teen Spirit." That song became a Top Ten hit, and *Nevermind* became a Number One album, knocking Michael Jackson's *Dangerous* out of the top spot. The burning question is whether Nirvana's triumph was a leftfield fluke or a true indication of a radical shift in public taste. Whatever, Nirvana, along with R.E.M., ranks as one of the American underground's unqualified success stories. And as the Nineties progress, a number of new bands seem poised on the brink, destined for bigger things: Pearl Jam, Too Much Joy, Soundgarden, Fugazi, Prong and Helmet, among them.

Unquestionably, the success of R.E.M. and the others who emerged from the clandestine indie underground helped pave the way for bands such as Faith No More, Jane's Addiction and the Red Hot Chili Peppers, all of whom achieved significant success. But if the post-punk Eighties have taught us anything, it's that today's fringe sensations can easily become tomorrow's superstars—which is reason enough to pay attention to the underground's many and varied rumblings and eruptions.

DISCOGRAPHY

ALBUMS

Hüsker Dü: *Land Speed Record* (New Alliance; 1981). *Everything Falls Apart* (Reflex; 1982). *Zen Arcade* (SST; 1984). *New Day Rising* (SST; 1985). *Flip Your Wig* (SST; 1985). *Candy Apple Grey* (Warner Bros.; ☆140, 1986). *Warehouse: Songs and Stories* (Warner Bros.; ☆117, 1987). **Living Colour:** *Vivid* (Epic; ☆6, 1988). *Time's Up* (Epic; ☆13, 1990). **Nirvana:** *Bleach* (Sub Pop; 1988). *Nevermind* (DGC; ☆1, 1991). **Pixies:** *Come On Pilgrim* (4AD/Rough Trade; 1987). *Surfer Rosa* (4AD/Rough Trade; 1988). *Doolittle* (4AD/Rough Trade; 1989). *Bossanova* (4AD/Elektra; ☆70, 1990). **R.E.M.:** *Murmur* (I.R.S.; ☆36, 1983). *Reckoning* (I.R.S.; ☆27, 1984). *Lifes Rich Pageant* (I.R.S.; ☆21, 1986). *Dead Letter Office* (I.R.S.; ☆52, 1987). *R.E.M. No. 5: Document* (I.R.S.; ☆10, 1987). *Eponymous* (I.R.S.; ☆44, 1988). *Green* (Warner Bros.; ☆12, 1988). *Out of Time* (Warner Bros.; ☆1, 1991). **The Replacements:** *Sorry Ma, Forgot to Take Out the Trash* (Twin-Tone; 1981). *The Replacements Stink* (Twin-Tone; 1982). *Let It Be* (Twin-Tone; 1984). *Tim* (Sire; ☆183, 1985). *Pleased to Meet Me* (Sire; ☆131, 1987). *Don't Tell a Soul* (Sire; ☆57, 1989). *All Shook Down* (Sire; ☆69, 1990). **Sonic Youth:** *Sonic Youth* (SST; 1982). *Confusion Is Sex* (SST; 1983). *Sonic Death* (SST; 1984). *Bad Moon Rising* (Homestead; 1985). *EVOL* (SST; 1986). *Sister* (SST; 1987). *Daydream Nation* (Blast First–Enigma; 1988). *Goo* (DGC; ☆96, 1990). *Dirty* (DGC; 1992).

(Chart positions compiled from Joel Whitburn's *Record Research*, based on *Billboard*'s LPs chart.)

RAP AND SOUL: FROM THE EIGHTIES ONWARD

BY ALAN LIGHT

T hings were changing so fast in black pop music in the Eighties that nobody knew what to call it. The simple "soul" appellation was replaced by such complicated titles as "Urban Contemporary," "New Jack Swing," "Retronuevo" and "Quiet Storm." For a while, *Billboard* was tallying the best-selling "Black" albums and singles, but after the likes of George Michael topped those charts, the magazine went back to good old "R&B." In the end, though, labels were of limited use because all black sounds in the Eighties were defined by their relationship to the decade's most significant musical development: rap.

Though the actual birthplace of rap will probably always be debated, most authorities agree that it first appeared in New York City's Bronx in the late Seventies. DJ Kool Herc, a transplanted Jamaican, is credited as the disc jockey who introduced the music's basic sound. He would set up two or more turntables and mix only the hottest sections of several records together, switching back and forth between isolated, hyper-propulsive beats.

The earliest rapping consisted of simple chants and call-and-response rhymes over the DJ's cutting and scratching, and it became one part of an emerging cultural phenomenon called "hip-hop" (from such proto-rap chants as "Say hip, hop, you don't stop"). This term also encompassed break dancing, graffiti art and new styles of language and fashion favored by "B-boys" (from "beat-boy" or "breakboy"), best depicted in Charlie Ahearn's 1982 film *Wild Style*. Rap proved the most lasting of hip-hop's components. The first rap on record was the Sugar Hill Gang's 1979 single "Rapper's Delight," which became a Top Forty pop hit. Soon rappers like Kurtis

Public Enemy, the rap revolutionaries who replaced boasting and joking with activism.

Blow and such groups as Grandmaster Flash and the Furious Five were recording regularly. Though rap was initially built on turntable manipulations, most of these early records featured a live band playing figures based on familiar disco beats.

In 1982 Grandmaster Flash's group released ''The Message,'' a harrowing portrayal of inner-city despair with the refrain ''It's like a jungle sometimes / It makes me wonder / How I keep from going under'' and moved rap toward a new emphasis on social commentary. Though plenty of bad imitations followed, this same consciousness ran through rap's first classic album, *Run-D.M.C.* (1984). The trio from Queens not only wrote some of rap's sharpest rhymes, but it added a harder-edged delivery and stripped the backing tracks down to minimalist, crunching beats.

Where rappers before Run-D.M.C. wore outrageous costumes and concentrated on fantasy boasting, these middle-class rappers approached the ghetto itself as an outlaw fantasy. Being ''real'' or ''hard'' was the new credo, with no musical or verbal concessions to pop convention. Seventeen-year-old, million-selling L.L. Cool J was the most prominent of this next wave. His performance of ''I Can't Live Without My Radio'' in the 1985 movie *Krush Groove* heralded the arrival of a major new star. His debut, *Radio,* was so spare that the production credit read ''Reduced by Rick Rubin'' (Rubin was the cofounder of Def Jam Records), and with his omnipresent Kangol cap, L.L. represented the archetypal B-boy. By 1991 he had four platinum albums, and with two Top Twenty pop singles from that year's *Mama Said Knock You Out* and a spectacular perform-

Grandmaster Flash in 1982: "It's like a jungle sometimes/It makes me wonder/How I keep from going under."

ance backed by an acoustic band on *MTV Unplugged,* L.L. had become rap's first real pop superstar.

After that mid-Eighties burst of creativity, things quickly slowed down. Break dancing had become a national fad, turning up in television commercials and cheap exploitation movies. The street kids who originated and nurtured "breaking" turned away when they sensed it had been co-opted by the mainstream, and it appeared that rap might suffer the same fate.

Meanwhile, more traditional R&B was suffering a similar stagnation. Despite (or perhaps because of) the genre-destroying breakthroughs of Michael Jackson and Prince, black pop was reverting to familiar formulas. The dominant figure was former studio vocalist Luther Vandross, whose classically emotive romantic crooning proved to be the decade's most lasting sound. Vandross rose from singing backup for such pop stars as David Bowie to fronting a post-disco vocal trio to finding his own smooth sound. His hits alternated between such gorgeous, mid-tempo pop-tinged songs as "Give Me the Reason" or "Stop to Love" and bravura ballads, most notably a showstopping rendition of "A House

Is Not a Home." Vandross spawned such best-selling "love man" clones as Freddie Jackson and James Ingram.

The most influential black female voice of the Eighties belonged to Anita Baker. Her sultry, jazz-inflected records, sometimes called "retronuevo" for their blend of the new and the nostalgic, epitomized the mellow, ultra-classy black radio format named "Quiet Storm" (after a Smokey Robinson song). This sound won many older, more affluent listeners back to black stations but was anathema to the new, hip-hop-bred generation. ("When the quiet storm comes on, I fall asleep," Public Enemy's Chuck D rapped in the tellingly titled "How to Kill a Radio Consultant").

In the summer of 1986 Run-D.M.C. saved the day for rap with its *Raising Hell* album. The record included a collaboration with Aerosmith on a remake of the hard-rock group's 1977 hit "Walk This Way." By making the beat slam harder and adding Run-D.M.C.'s trademark crisp, aggressive delivery, the song touched a nerve with teenagers nationwide and climbed to Number Four on the pop charts.

Propelled by the single, *Raising Hell* sold 3 million

copies. Rap had arrived in Middle America. This assault on suburbia was confirmed when the Beastie Boys, three bratty white ex-punks, released *Licensed to Ill* in 1987, which, powered by the irresistible frat-raver "(You Gotta) Fight for Your Right (to Party!)," sold even better than *Raising Hell*. The Beasties' album also introduced the sound of sampling to a wide audience. New technology made it possible to replace the DJ's old cutting techniques with the more precise computerized isolation of snippets from existing records. These bits could be reconstructed into new patterns or collages, and sampling rapidly became rap's dominant creative practice.

Meanwhile, rap's sound continued to diversify, and its geographic base began to grow. It was becoming both more established and more controversial. Boogie Down Productions, from the South Bronx, was an early example of "gangsta rap," which focused on the hard realities of violence and rage in urban life. By 1989, though, the group was leading the "Stop the Violence" movement after its DJ, Scott LaRock, was shot dead trying to stop a street argument. Philadelphia's DJ Jazzy Jeff and the Fresh Prince brought a lighthearted pop attitude to rap, scoring big with their 1988 smash "Parents Just Don't Understand." In Los Angeles Ice-T ("the pusher, the player, the pimp-gangsta, high-roller, dead prez folder") put the West Coast on the map with his unblinking depictions of gang life. Queen Latifah's debut, *All Hail the Queen,* came out in 1989 and heralded a new era of strong, outspoken female rappers striking back at the genre's too-frequent woman-bashing.

Most important was Public Enemy. Beginning with *Yo! Bum Rush the Show* (1987), these Long Islanders became the most influential group in rap by replacing boasting and joking with activism. PE stated that its goal was to help create

Run-D.M.C. and the Beastie Boys: bringing rap to white folks and rock & roll to blacks.

Luther Vandross: His classic romantic crooning proved to be one of R&B's most lasting sounds.

five thousand new leaders for the black community. *It Takes a Nation of Millions to Hold Us Back* (1988) remains rap's masterpiece, a blazing amalgam of dense, insistent noise, black nationalist sloganeering and visionary street analysis. In 1989, after a scandal erupted following anti-Semitic remarks made by the group's "Minister of Information" Professor Griff, Public Enemy temporarily disbanded, only to reunite and dismiss Griff from the fold.

In the meantime, Harlem-born wunderkind Teddy Riley began experimenting with mergers of hip-hop beats and traditional R&B singing. Keith Sweat's "I Want Her" (1987) and Johnny Kemp's "Just Got Paid" (1988), both produced by Riley, brought this new fusion to the charts. In a *Village Voice* cover story on Riley, his sound was given a name befitting its

Queen Latifah: An outspoken female rapper striking back at female-bashing.

swagger and freshness: New Jack Swing. By the turn of the decade, additional artists including Riley's own group Guy, Bell Biv DeVoe and Bobby Brown— whose strutting, thunderous "My Prerogative" was one of the biggest singles of 1989—were making New Jack Swing the unchallenged ruling style of black pop. When Michael Jackson wanted to update his sound for *Dangerous* (1991), he called on Riley to replace his longtime producer Quincy Jones.

Gangsta rap bum-rushed the hip-hop world in 1989 when the Los Angeles group N.W.A. (Niggas with Attitude) released *Straight Outta Compton*. The group claimed that its graphic, lurid streetscapes were simply reports from the urban front lines, but many said that they were glamorizing the criminal life. A track from *Compton* titled "Fuck tha Police" even drew the attention of the FBI, who sent a warning letter to N.W.A's record label. So many new gangstas appeared on the block that again rap risked sinking into self-parody and stagnation, but into the breach jumped De La Soul with the *3 Feet High and Rising* album. The teenage trio from Long Island sampled Steely Dan and Johnny Cash, sported a multicolored "Afro-centric" look and projected a gentle, sometimes goofy image unlike any rappers before them. De La Soul reminded everybody that rap's real musical revolution was the fact that it could sound like anything it wanted to.

The biggest story of 1990 was the obscenity trial of Miami's 2 Live Crew. The group had sold a million copies of the locker-room sex rhymes collection *As Nasty As They Wanna Be* when Charles Freeman, a Fort Lauderdale, Florida, record store owner, was arrested for selling the album. Freeman was found guilty, but when the group itself was brought to trial, it was acquitted. Though the notoriety drove *Nasty*'s sales through the roof, the arrest made a strong impression on the rap community, where using the unexpurgated language of the street is an essential component of many records' power. Suddenly Middle America was aware of rap, though the image was a dubious one; the genre was being defined by its most lurid extremes in such high-profile places as a *Newsweek* cover story titled "Rap Rage."

Rap continued its commercial explosion into the Nineties. M.C. Hammer's innocuous dance-rap album *Please Hammer Don't Hurt 'Em* sold 15 million copies, and the simplistic rhymes and samples of white rapper Vanilla Ice sold another 8 million. *Yo! MTV Raps* debuted on the cable video channel in

Teddy Riley: The man who invented New Jack Swing, the unchallenged ruling style of black pop in the Nineties.

August 1989 and quickly became the station's highest-rated program. Rap's final breakthrough, however, may have been in June 1991, when N.W.A's second album, the brutal, often misogynistic *Efil4-zaggin* (''Niggaz 4 Life'' backward), entered *Billboard*'s pop chart at Number Two, knocking Paula Abdul out of the top spot the following week and moving a million copies in fifteen days. Public Enemy's stunning *Apocalypse 91: The Enemy Strikes Black*, released in October, enjoyed similarly spectacular sales, and the controversial, sometimes racist second album, *Death Certificate*, by former N.W.A rapper and lyricist Ice Cube also debuted in the Number Two slot.

Rap's triumph has been its ability to reinvent itself whenever the need was there. Public Enemy's Chuck D describes rap as ''black America's CNN,'' a way for a national community without access to the mainstream media to communicate and share its politics, styles and language. The exceptional talents of such artists as Teddy Riley and Luther Vandross are undeniable, but ultimately rap has continued to matter to its audience in a way that other pop styles, black and white, long ago ceased to do.

DISCOGRAPHY

ALBUMS
Rap

Beastie Boys: *Licensed to Ill* (Def Jam; r☆2, ☆1, 1986). *Paul's Boutique* (Capitol; r☆24, ☆14, 1989). *Check Your Head* (Capitol; r☆37, ☆10, 1992). **Boogie Down Productions:** *Criminal Minded* (B Boy; r☆73, 1987). *By All Means Necessary* (Jive; r☆8, ☆75, 1988). *Ghetto Music: The Blueprint of Hip Hop* (Jive; r☆7, ☆36, 1989). *Edutainment* (Jive; r☆9, ☆32, 1990). *Live Hardcore Worldwide* (Jive; r☆25, 1991). *Sex and Violence* (Columbia; r☆20, ☆42, 1992). **De La Soul:** *3 Feet High & Rising* (Tommy Boy; r☆1, ☆24, 1989). *De La Soul Is Dead* (Tommy Boy; r☆24, ☆26, 1991). **Hammer:** *Please Hammer Don't Hurt 'Em* (Capitol; r☆1, ☆1, 1990). *Too Legit to Quit* (Capitol; r☆5, ☆2, 1991). **Ice Cube:** *AmeriKKKa's Most Wanted* (Priority; r☆6, ☆19, 1990). *Kill at Will* (EP) (Priority; r☆5, ☆34, 1990). *Death Certificate* (Priority; r☆1, ☆2, 1991). **Ice-T:** *Rhyme Pays* (Sire; r☆26, ☆93, 1987). *Power* (Sire; r☆6, ☆35, 1988). *Freedom of Speech* (Sire; r☆11, ☆37, 1989). *Original Gangster (O.G.)* (Sire; r☆9, ☆15, 1991). **DJ Jazzy Jeff and the Fresh Prince:** *Rock the House* (Jive/RCA; r☆24, ☆95, 1987). *He's the DJ, I'm the Rapper* (Jive/RCA; r☆5, ☆4, 1988). *And in This Corner . . .* (Jive/RCA; r☆19, ☆39, 1989). *Homebase* (Jive; r☆5, ☆12, 1991). **L. L. Cool J:** *Radio* (Def Jam; r☆6, 1985). *Bigger and Deffer* (Def Jam; r☆1, ☆3, 1987). *Walking with a Panther* (Def Jam; r☆1, ☆6, 1989). *Mama Said Knock You Out* (Def Jam; r☆2, ☆16, 1990). **N.W.A:** *N.W.A and the Posse* (Ruthless; r☆39, 1988). *Straight Outta Compton* (Ruthless; r☆9, ☆37, 1989). *100 Miles and Runnin'* (EP) (Ruthless; r☆10, ☆27, 1990). *Efil4zaggin* (Ruthless; r☆2, ☆1, 1991). **Public Enemy:** *Yo! Bum Rush the Show* (Def Jam; r☆28, 1987). *It Takes a Nation of Millions to Hold Us Back* (Def Jam; r☆1, ☆42, 1988). *Fear of a Black Planet* (Def Jam; r☆3, ☆10, 1990). *Apocalypse '91: The Enemy Strikes Black* (Def Jam; r☆1, ☆4, 1991). **Queen Latifah:** *All Hail the Queen* (Tommy Boy; r☆6, ☆124, 1989). *Nature of a Sista'* (Tommy Boy; r☆36, ☆117, 1991). **Run-D.M.C.:** *Run-D.M.C.* (Profile; 1984). *King of Rock* (Profile; r☆12, ☆52, 1985). *Raising Hell* (Profile; r☆1, ☆3, 1986). *Tougher Than Leather* (Profile; r☆2, ☆9, 1988). *Back from Hell* (Profile; r☆16, ☆81, 1990). *Greatest Hits 1983–1991* (Profile; r☆75, ☆199, 1991). **Anthologies:** *Rap's Greatest Hits* (Priority; 1986). *Street Jams: Hip-Hop from the Top, Parts 1–2* (Rhino; 1992). *Street Jams: Electric Funk, Parts 1–2* (Rhino; 1992). *West Coast Rap: The First Dynasty, Volumes 1–3* (Rhino; 1992).

Soul and New Jack Swing

Anita Baker: *Rapture* (Elektra; ☆1, 1986). *Giving You the Best That I Got* (Elektra; r☆1, ☆1, 1988). **Luther Vandross:** *Never Too Much* (Epic; ☆19, 1981). *Forever, for Always, for Love* (Epic; ☆20, 1982). *Busy Body* (Epic; ☆32, 1983). *The Night I Fell in Love* (Epic; r☆1, ☆19, 1985). *Give Me the Reason* (Epic; ☆14, 1986). *Any Love* (Epic; r☆1, ☆9, 1988). *The Best of Luther Vandross—The Best of Love* (Epic; r☆2, ☆26, 1989). *Power of Love* (Epic; r☆1, ☆7, 1991).

Albums Produced by Teddy Riley

Bobby Brown: *Don't Be Cruel* (MCA; r☆1, 1988). *Dance! . . . Ya Know It!* (MCA; r☆7, ☆9, 1989). **Guy:** *Guy* (Uptown/MCA; r☆1, ☆27, 1988). ☆16, 1991). *The Future* (MCA) r☆1, ☆16, 1990. **Heavy D. and the Boyz:** *Livin' Large* (Uptown/MCA; r☆10, ☆177, 1987). **Kool Moe Dee:** *Kool Moe Dee* (Jive; r☆20, ☆80, 1986). *How Ye Like Me Now* (Jive; r☆4, ☆37, 1987). *Knowledge Is King* (Jive; r☆2, ☆25, 1989). **Keith Sweat:** *Make It Last Forever* (Vintertainment; r☆1, ☆15, 1987).

(Chart positions compiled from Joel Whitburn's *Record Research*, based on *Billboard*'s LPs chart, unless otherwise indicated; r☆ = position on *Billboard*'s Rhythm & Blues chart.)

Niggaz With Attitude *(from left):* Ice Cube, Dr. Dre, Eazy-E, Yella, M.C. Ren.

Grateful acknowledgment is made to the following for permission to reprint previously published material:

THE VILLAGE VOICE: ''Elton John'' by Robert Christgau originally appeared in a different version in *The Village Voice* as ''Elton John, the Little Hooker that Could,'' November 24, 1975. Copyright © 1975 by The Village Voice, Inc.

THE REAL PAPER: ''Sexy, Safe and Out of Sync/On the Road with Al Green'' by Robert Christgau. Reprinted from *The Real Paper*, March 26, 1975. Copyright © 1975 by *The Real Paper*, Cambridge, Mass.

SIMON AND SCHUSTER, INC.: Selected quotes from the book *Elvis Presley: A Biography* by Jerry Hopkins. Copyright © 1971 by Jerry Hopkins. These selections appear in the chapter ''Elvis Presley'' by Peter Guralnick.

STRAIGHT ARROW PUBLISHERS, INC.: ''Otis Redding'' by Jon Landau. Reprinted from *It's Too Late to Stop Now: A Rock & Roll Journal*. Copyright © 1972 by Jon Landau. Originally printed in *Eye* magazine.

ROCK BEGINS: "Run Old Jeremiah" traditional. RHYTHM AND GOSPEL: "Baby, Don't Do It" by Lowman Pauling Copyright © 1952 Fort Knox/Trio Music. "Work with Me Annie" by Henry Ballard Copyright © 1954 Fort Knox/Trio Music. "Annie Had a Baby" by Syd Nathan, Louis Manna and Henry Glover Copyright © 1954 Fort Knox/Trio Music. "Annie's Answer" by Al Smith and Bobby Prince Copyright © 1954 Arc Music. ELVIS PRESLEY: "Good Rockin' Tonight" by Roy Brown Copyright © 1948 Fort Knox/Trio Music. "Hound Dog" by Jerry Leiber and Mike Stoller Copyright © 1953 Duchess Music Corp. THE SOUND OF NEW ORLEANS: "Junker's Blues" by Jack Dupree Copyright © 1959 Duchess Music Corp./Elvis Presley Music/ MCA Music. "The Fat Man" by Antoine Domino and Dave Bartholomew Copyright © 1950 EMI Music Publishing. "Let the Good Times Roll" by Leonard Lee Copyright © 1956 Atlantic Music. "Sea Cruise" by Huey Smith Copyright © 1967 Cotillion Music/Warner-Tamerlane Publishing Corp. "Mother-in-Law" by Allen Toussaint Copyright © 1961 EMI Music Publishing. "I Like It Like That" by Chris Kenner Copyright © 1961 Longitude Music. "Ya Ya" by Lee Dorsey and Morgan Robinson Copyright © 1961 Longitude Music. FATS DOMINO: "The Fat Man" by Antoine Domino and Dave Bartholomew Copyright © 1950 EMI Music Publishing. "Goin' Home" by Antoine Domino and Alvin E. Lee Copyright © 1956 EMI Music Publishing. LITTLE RICHARD: "Tutti-Frutti" by Richard Penniman, Dave LaBostrie and Joel Lubin Copyright © 1955 Hal Leonard Publishing. "Ain't That Good News" by Raymond Taylor Copyright © 1953 Duchess Music. "Long Tall Sally" by Entoris Johnson, Richard Penniman and Robert Blackwell Copyright © 1956 Hal Leonard Publishing. "I'm Quittin' Show Business" by Richard Penniman copyright information unavailable. CHUCK BERRY: "School Day" by Chuck Berry Copyright © 1957 Isalee Music Publishing Corp. "It Hurts Me Too" by Elmore James and Bobby Robertson Copyright © 1965 Isalee Music Publishing Corp. "Tulane" by Chuck Berry Copyright © 1970 Isalee Music Publishing Corp. "Have Mercy Judge" by Chuck Berry Copyright © 1970 Isalee Music Publishing Corp. ROCKABILLY: "Women Love" by Jack Rhodes Copyright © 1957 Fort Knox/Trio Music.

JERRY LEE LEWIS: "Whole Lot of Shakin' Goin' On" by Dave Williams Copyright © Rosarita Music Inc. Pic Music Corp. "Little Queenie" by Chuck Berry Copyright © 1956 Arc Music Corp. BUDDY HOLLY: "American Pie" by Don McLean Copyright © 1971 Mayday Music Inc./Yahweh Tunes Inc. "Rock Around with Ollie Vee" by Sonny Curtis Copyright © 1957 Warner-Unichappell Music Inc. "Peggy Sue" by Buddy Holly, Norman Petty and Charles Hardin Copyright © 1957 MPL Communications. "Not Fade Away" by Norman Petty and Charles Hardin Copyright © 1957 MPL Communications. "Take Your Time" by Buddy Holly and Norman Petty Copyright © 1958 MPL Communications. "I'm Gonna Love You Too" by Joe Maudlin, Niki Sullivan and Norman Petty Copyright © 1957 MPL Communications. "Well All Right" by Buddy Holly, Jerry Allison, Norman Petty and Joe Maudlin Copyright © 1958 MPL Communications. "You're the One" by Buddy Holly, Slim Corbin and Waylon Jennings Copyright © 1961 Peer Music. "Barbara Ann" by Fred Fassert Copyright © 1961 Longitude Music Co. DOO-WOP: "I Love You So" by Viola Ethel Watkins and William R. Davis Copyright © 1953. SAM COOKE: "Were You There When They Crucified My Lord?" traditional. BRILL BUILDING POP: "Up on the Roof" by Carole King and Gerry Goffin Copyright © 1963 EMI Music Publishing. ROY ORBISON: "Bye Bye Love" by Felicia Bryant and Boudleaux Bryant Copyright © 1957 House of Bryant Publications. PHIL SPECTOR: "Black Pearl" by Phil Spector, Toni White and Irwin Levin Copyright © 1969 Irving Music. THE GIRL GROUPS: "Beachwood 4-5789" by George Gordy, William Stevenson and Marvin Gaye Copyright © 1962 Jobete Music Co. "Da Doo Ron Ron" by Phil Spector, Ellie Greenwich and Jeff Barry Copyright © 1963 Abkco Music Inc. "A Fine Fine Boy" by Phil Spector, William Stevenson and Marvin Gaye Copyright © 1962 Jobete Music Co. THE BEACH BOYS: "In My Room" by Brian Wilson and Gary Usher Copyright © 1964 Irving Music Inc. "I Get Around" by Brian Wilson Copyright © 1964 Irving Music Inc. "Don't Worry Baby" by Brian Wilson and Roger Christian Copyright © 1964 Irving Music Inc. "When I Grow Up (to Be a Man)" by Brian Wilson Copyright © 1964 Irving Music Inc. "That's Not Me" by Brian

(Page ii) Michael Ochs Archives; (2) John Goddard Collection; (4) Country Music Foundation Library; (5) Country Music Foundation Library; (6) From the film *Black Delta Religion*, Center for Southern Folklore, Bill Ferris, photographer; (7) Popsie/NY; (8) *left*, Michael Ochs Archives; Popsie/NY; (10) *top*, Peacock Records; Popsie/NY; (11) Popsie/NY; (12) Michael Ochs Archives; (13) *left and center*, Michael Ochs Archives; *top*, Popsie/NY; (14) *top*, Michael Ochs Archives; Popsie/NY; (15) Popsie/NY; (18) Peacock Records; (19) *top*, Popsie/NY; Michael Ochs Archives; (20) John Goddard Collection; (23) *Sepia* magazine; (24) *right*, John Edwards Memorial Foundation; (25) Nashville *Banner*, Bill Goodman, photographer; (26) Arthur Wertheimer; (27) *left*, RCA; Popsie/NY; (29) Arthur Wertheimer; (31) Frank Edwards/Vista Photo Features; (35) *top*, Charlyn Zlotnik; Herb Ritts; (39) Michael Ochs Archives; (40) John Messina; (41) Greg Shaw/"Who Put the Bomp"; (42) Michael Ochs Archives; (43) Greg Shaw/"Who Put the Bomp"; (44) *left*, RCA; Sidney Smith; (45) *left*, The Fred Lewis Collection; Ren Deaton; (46) C. Alicino/LGI; (49) John Goddard Collection; (50) Imperial Records; (51) *Phonograph Record* magazine; (53) S. Granitz/Retna; (54) *Sepia* magazine; (56) *Sepia* magazine; (57) *Sepia* magazine; (58) *Sepia* magazine; (61) Michael Ochs Archives; (63) Janus Records; (64) Annie Leibovitz; (65) Columbia Pictures Industries, Inc; (66) Michael Ochs

Archives; (68) Michael Ochs Archives; (69) Michael Ochs Archives; (70) *left*, Michael Ochs Archives; *Phonograph Record* magazine; (71) *top*, Michael Ochs Archives; Fred Lewis; (76) *top left*, Donald Petri Collection; UPI; (78) Baron Wolman; (81) *left*, Courtesy Acuff-Rose Artist Corp.; *top right*, Courtesy The Everly Brothers; *right center*, Courtesy Acuff-Rose Artist Corp.; Michael Ochs Archives; (82) *Phonograph Record* Magazine; (83) Courtesy The Everly Brothers; (86) The Buddy Holly Memorial Society; (87) The Buddy Holly Memorial Society; (89) The Buddy Holly Memorial Society; (90) The Buddy Holly Memorial Society; (91) The Buddy Holly Memorial Society; (93) Michael Ochs Archives; (94) Michael Ochs Archives; (95) *top*, *Record Exchanger*; *bottom*, Donald Petri Collection; Michael Ochs Archives; (96) *left*, *Record Exchanger*; *top*, Michael Ochs Archives; John Goddard Collection; (97) Michael Ochs Archives; (98) Michael Ochs Archives; (99) *bottom*, *Sepia* magazine; Michael Ochs Archives; (104) Popsie/NY; (105) Popsie/NY; (108) Michael Ochs Archives; (109) Popsie/NY; (110) Michael Ochs Archives; (111) Michael Ochs Archives; (114) Neal Peters Collection; (116) Neal Peters Collection; (117) Neal Peters Collection; (118) Rex Features Ltd.; (119) *left bottom*, Bettmann Archive; *top right*, Perry Henzell; Paramount Pictures Corporation; (120) *top*, Columbia Pictures Industries, Inc.; (123) *left*, Michael Ochs Archives; ABC Television;

(125) Popsie/NY; (126) *left*, Michael Ochs Archives; Popsie/NY; (128) Popsie/NY; (132) Don Paulsen; (133) Michael Ochs Archives; (136) RCA Records; (137) Wide World Photos; (140) John Goddard; (141) *left*, Popsie/NY; Michael Ochs Archives; (144) Popsie/NY; (146) Courtesy Don Kirshner; (147) Leiber/Stoller Collection; (148) Popsie/NY; (149) Popsie/NY; (150) *top*, Courtesy Don Kirshner; Popsie/NY; (154) Acuff-Rose Artist Corp.; (155) Acuff-Rose Artist Corp.; (156) Ann Summa/Onyx; (160) *top*, Popsie/NY; Michael Ochs Archives; (161) Michael Ochs Archives; (165) Don Paulsen; (166) Capricorn Records; (167) John Goddard; (168) Michael Ochs Archives; (169) Peter Freed; (172) *left*, Michael Ochs Archives; *Sepia* magazine; (173) Columbia Records; (174) *Sepia* magazine; (175) Joe McEwen Collection; (178) Michael Ochs Archives; (180) *top*, Vince Aletti Collection; Lenny Kaye Collection; (181) The Christmas Album; (182) The Christmas Album; (184) Michael Ochs Archives; (185) Michael Ochs Archives; (187) Baron Wolman; (190) Michael Ochs Archives; (191) Original Sound Records; (193) Annie Leibovitz; (195) Capitol Records; (196) Earl Leaf; (200) Michael Ochs Archives; (202) *top*, Greg Shaw/"Who Put the Bomp"; Michael Ochs Archives; (204) *left*, Greg Shaw/"Who Put the Bomp"; *center and top*, David Bieber/Bieber Archives; (206) *left*, Greg Shaw/"Who Put the Bomp"; *top*, Michael Ochs Archives; (207) Pop-

sie/NY; (218) *left,* Photo Trends; (224) Ebet Roberts; (226) M. Putland/Retna; (228) M. Putland/Retna; (231) Bob Gruen/Star File; (232) P. Figen/Retna; (234) Warner Bros. Records; (236) J. Atashian/Retna; (239) *top,* Ethan Russell; (240) Popsie/NY; (242) Peter Webb; (244) Dennis Zentek; (248) Annie Leibovitz; (249) Bob Gruen/Star File; (250) Bob Gruen/Star File; (253) R.P. Fitzgerald/LGI; (254) *left,* Joe McEwen Collection; (255) *right,* Michael Ochs Archives; (258) Will van Overbeek; (261) *left,* Popsie/NY; *Sepia* magazine; (262) Fred Lewis; (263) *left,* Don Paulsen; (264) *top,* Fred Lewis; (267) Fred Lewis; (268) Phillip Rauls; (269) *top,* Don Paulsen; Vince Aletti Collection; (273) *left,* Fred Lewis; (274) Capricorn Records; (275) Capricorn Records; (278) Popsie/NY; (279) Michael Ochs Archives; (280) Michael Ochs Archives; (281) Michael Ochs Archives; (282) Michael Ochs Archives; (283) Vinc Aletti Collection; (284) *left,* Vince Alletti Collection; Michael Ochs Archives; (285) Michael Ochs Archives; (286) *left,* Michael Ochs Archives; *Sepia* magazine; (288) *right,* Michael Ochs Archives; (289) Motown; (296) Popsie/NY; (300) *left,* Michael Ochs Archives; Grinnell A. Talbot; (301) Alice Ochs; (302) *right,* Michael Zagaris; (304) Alice Ochs; (306) Lynn Goldsmith/LGI; (307) Mike Guastella/Star File; (310) Michael Ochs Archives; (314) Baron Wolman; (315) Atlantic Records; (316) *top,* Atlantic Records; (318) C. Steiner/Retna; (321) Ebet Roberts; (322) Chuck Pulin/Star File; (325) Chris Buck; (326) *bottom,* Henry Diltz; (328) Ed Caraeff; (329) R. Reed for Edie Baskin/Onyx; (333) *right, Sepia* magazine; (335) *top,* Vince Aletti Collection; (336) *Sepia* magazine; (337) *Sepia* magazine; (340) Promotions Consolidated; (341) *left,* Promotions Consolidated; Michael Ochs Archives; (342) Michael Ochs Archives; (344) *top,* Robert Stigwood; Don Paulsen; (345) *left,* Annie Leibovitz; Ray Flerlage; (346) Ebet Roberts; (347) Deborah Feingold/Outline; (349) Gerard Malanga; (350) Gerard Malanga; (351) Michael Zagaris; (353) Waring Abbott; (354) Waring Abbott; (358) Michael Ochs Archives; (359) Michael Ochs Archives; (360) Michael Ochs Archives; (364) Herb Greene; (365) Baron Wolman; (366) *left,* Baron Wolman; Columbia Records; (367) Baron Wolman; (368) *top,* Bob Altman; (369) Annie Leibovitz; (371) Michael Ochs Archives; (372) Baron Wolman; (373) Michael Ochs Archives; (374) Jay Blakesberg; (375) Jay Blakesberg; (376)

Jay Blakesberg; (379) Baron Wolman; (380) Herb Greene; (381) Annie Leibovitz; (383) Lou Mack; (384) Herb Greene; (386) Lou Mack; (389) Elektra Records; (390) *left,* Joel Brodsky; Elektra Records; (393) Chuck Pulin/Star File; (396) *top,* Michael Ochs Archives; *bottom, Phonograph Record* magazine; (400) *center,* Bob Gruen; (402) Wide World Photos; (404) G. Gershoff/Retna; (406) L. Viti/Retna; (409) *left,* Robert Stigwood; Atlantic Records; (410) *left,* David Melhado; Atlantic Records; (413) *left,* Ed Caraeff; Courtesy James Allen Hendrix; (414) Eric Hayes; (415) Jimi Hendrix Archives; (417) *left,* Paul Takakjian; Tom Black; (420) David Bieber Archives; (421) *left,* Columbia Records; *top right,* Robert Stigwood; The Greg Geller Collection; (422) *left,* Michael Ochs Archives; (424) G. Gershoff/Retna; (426) *top,* Nick Rock/Star File; David Bieber Archives; (427) David Bieber Archives; (430) *left,* Capitol Records; Baron Wolman; (431) Art Usherson; (432) *top,* Baron Wolman; Capitol Records; (433) Baron Wolman; (434) Baron Wolman; (436) Charles Gatewood; (438) Annie Leibovitz; (440) Don Paulsen; (443) *left,* Popsie/NY; Michael Ochs Archives; (444) *left,* Annie Leibovitz; David Gahr; (445) Warner Bros. Records; (446) Robert Teese/Star File; (449) Baron Wolman; (451) Warner Bros. Records; (453) *left,* Richard E. Aaron; (456) Neal Preston; (458) Chuck Pulin/Star File; (460) Annie Leibovitz; (461) *top,* Bill Richert/Photo Reserve; (464) Neil Zlozower; (466) Lynn Goldsmith/LGI; (467) Laura Levine; (469) Ebet Roberts; (471) Ebet Roberts; (472) Neil Zlozower; (475) *top,* John Grissom; John Messina; (476) Baron Wolman; (478) *top,* Lisa Seifert/Star File; Bob Gruen/Star File; (479) Ebet Roberts; (481) Ebet Roberts; (482) Annie Leibovitz; (484) Norman Seeff; (485) Peter Simon; (486) Michael Ochs Archives; (487) Annie Leibovitz; (490) A.J. Barratt/Retna; (496) Baron Wolman; (497) Neal Preston; (498) David Bieber Archives; (501) *left,* Baron Wolman; Jann Wenner; (502) *bottom,* Columbia Records; (503) Ray Flerage; (504) Annie Leibovitz; (506) Chris Buck; (507) Annie Leibovitz; (508) *left,* Kate Simon; Rick Hardman; (509) Wide World Photos; (511) Charles Gatewood; (512) *right,* David Gest & Associates; (513) Richard Gersh Associates; (514) Richard Gersh Associates; (516) *left,* Columbia Records; (518) Michael Ochs Archives; (522) *center,* Bruce W. Talamon; (523) Thomas S. England; (528) *bottom right,* Annie Leibovitz; Helen Walters; (529) Annie Leibo-

vitz; (530) Jeff Slocomb/Outline; (534) Andy Kent; (536) Ebet Roberts; (539) Lisa Seifert/Star File; (540) *left,* Annie Leibovitz; Susan Titelman; (543) Annie Leibovitz; (544) Bonnie Schiffman; (545) Richard E. Aaron; (546) Michael Grecco/Outline; (547) *top,* Popsie/NY; Christopher Makos; (548) Rick Beban; (550) Paul Natkin/Photo Reserve; (552) Michael Zagaris; (553) Bob Gruen; (554) Bob Gruen; (555) *top,* Roberta Bayley; David Godlis; (556) Jack Mitchell/Outline; (558) Allan Tannenbaum; (559) Allan Tannenbaum; (563) Allan Tannenbaum; (564) Ron Galella; (566) Neal Preston; (567) Dagmar; (568) Ron Galella; (570) Neil Bogart; (574) *bottom,* Ann Summa; (576) *top,* Laura Levine; (577) Laura Levine; (578) *top,* Gary Pearlson; Elliot Gilbert; (580) Jim Houghton; (582) *left,* Anton Corbijn; Larry Williams; (583) Chuck Pulin/Star File; (584) *top,* Lynn Goldsmith/LGI; S. Speller/Retna; (585) Lara Rossignol/Onyx; (587) Peter Simon; (588) Peter Simon; (589) Peter Simon; (590) Michael Dobo; (591) Peter Simon; (592) Jack Beshears; (595) Bob Gruen; (596) Richard Young; (598) Bob Gruen; (599) Richard Young; (600) Larry Williams; (602) Bob Gruen; (603) Bob Gruen; (604) *left,* Richard Young; Bob Gruen; (606) Bob Gruen; (608) Lynn Goldsmith/LGI; (610) Lynn Goldsmith/LGI; (612) Neil Zlozower; (613) R. Matheu/Retna; (615) Laura Levine; (616) Leo Regan/Rex Features Ltd.; (618) Waring Abbott; (620) Jeff Albertson; (621) Mary Alfieri; (623) David Gahr; (624) *left,* A. Gallo/Retna; Dominick Conde/Star File; (627) T. Mottram/Retna; (629) Lester Glassner/Neal Peters Collection; (630) Laura Levine; (631) Lynn Goldsmith/LGI; (633) Ebet Roberts; (634) Ebet Roberts; (635) Vinnie Zuffante/Star File; (636) Anton Corbijn; (638) Anton Corbijn; (641–646) MTV Networks; (648) L. Baker/Retna; (650) Star File; (651) F. Costello/Retna; (652) Richard Young/Rex Features Ltd.; (653) Rex Features Ltd.; (654) Herb Ritts; (657) Laura Levine; (658) I. McKell/Retna; (659) Patty Beaudet; (660) MTV Networks; (661) F. Micelotta/Retna; (664) Waring Abbott; (666) Ebet Roberts; (667) Laura Levine; (669) Bernard Matussiere/Elektra; (670) Elektra Nonesuch; (672) Chris Cuffaro; (674) Laura Levine; (675) Ebet Roberts; (676) Pat Blashill; (678) Laura Levine; (680) Laura Levine; (683) Chris Buck; (684) Laura Levine; (685) Laura Levine; (686) Kristine Larsen; (687) Ebet Roberts; (688) Kristine Larsen; (689) Darin Pappas/Shooting Start/Ruthless-Priority

LESTER BANGS was an editor at *Creem* for five years. He wrote about rock from 1969—when his first reviews appeared in ROLLING STONE—to his death in 1982, at the age of thirty-three. He is the author of *Blondie* (Simon & Schuster/Delilah) and *Psychotic Reactions and Carburetor Dung* (Knopf/Vintage), a collection of essays.

TOM CARSON has written for *L.A. Weekly,* the *Village Voice,* ROLLING STONE and other publications.

ROBERT CHRISTGAU is chief music critic of the *Village Voice,* where he is a senior editor. He also writes regularly for *Playboy* and *Video Review.* He is the author of *Rock Albums of the '70s* (Da Capo) and *Christgau's Record Guide: The '80s* (Pantheon). In 1987 he won a Guggenheim Fellowship to study popular music as a world-historical phenomenon and eventually will write one or several books on the subject.

NIK COHN was born in London and grew up in Northern Ireland. He is the writer who spawned *Saturday Night Fever* and is the author of several books on rock and popular culture, including *Awopbopaloobop Alopbamboom, Ball the Wall* and *Rock Dreams* (with Guy Peelaert). He now lives in Shelter Island, New York.

J. D. CONSIDINE is the pop music critic at the *Baltimore Sun* and writes regularly for ROLLING STONE and *Musician.* His work has also appeared in a variety of music publications, an appalling number of which are no longer in business. He is a coauthor of *The Rolling Stone Album Guide* (Random House).

JONATHAN COTT is the author of *Dylan* (Rolling Stone Press/Doubleday), *Conversations with Glenn Gould* (Little, Brown) and two collections of interviews: *Forever Young* (Random House) and *Visions and Voices* (Doubleday). He is currently a contributing editor of ROLLING STONE.

ANTHONY DeCURTIS is a senior features editor at ROLLING STONE, where he oversees the record review section, and the pop music critic for *Weekend All Things Considered* on National Public Radio. He edited *Present Tense: Rock & Roll and Culture* (Duke University Press, 1992), and his liner notes for the Eric Clapton retrospective *Crossroads* won a Grammy in 1988. He holds a Ph.D. in American literature from Indiana University.

CHUCK EDDY is the author of *Stairway to Hell: The 500 Greatest Heavy Metal Albums in the Universe* (Harmony) and is presently working on *Pour ''Sugar Sugar'' on Me: A Misguided Tour Through Pop Muzik History as Suggested by Def Leppard's 'Hysteria' Album.* He has contributed to ROLLING STONE, the *Village Voice, Spin, Creem, Entertainment Weekly, Request, BAM, Graffiti, L.A. Weekly,* the *Philadelphia Inquirer, Playboy, Radio On, Swellsville, Sucks* and the U.S. Army Signal Corps. He has a journalism degree from the University of Missouri but has never used it.

KEN EMERSON is the op-ed editor of New York *Newsday.* He has written about popular music for the *New York Times,* ROLLING STONE, the *Boston Phoenix,* and elsewhere and is working on a book about Stephen Foster.

PAUL EVANS, a freelance writer, is a coauthor of *The* ROLLING STONE *Album Guide* (Random House) and is a frequent contributor to ROLLING STONE. His fiction has been published in the *South Atlantic Quarterly* and *Puerto del Sol.* He lives in Atlanta.

JIM FARBER is pop music critic of the New York *Daily News.* For six years he has written a regular music-video column for the paper; for four he has contributed to ROLLING STONE. In addition, his work has appeared in the *Village Voice, Connoisseur, New York, Premiere* and many other publications.

BILL FLANAGAN is editor of *Musician* magazine and the author of *Written in My Soul,* a book of conversations with great singer-songwriters. He has written for the *Boston Globe,* the *Boston Phoenix,* the *Real Paper,* ROLLING STONE, *Spy* and many other magazines and newspapers.

DAVID FRICKE is a senior writer at ROLLING STONE. He also contributes to the *New York Times* and is the American correspondent for the British music weekly *Melody Maker*.

HOLLY GEORGE-WARREN is the coauthor of *Musicians in Tune: Seventy-five Contemporary Musicians Discuss the Creative Process* (Fireside/Simon & Schuster, 1992). She has contributed to a number of books about rock & roll, and her writing has appeared in ROLLING STONE, *Musician, Option* and *Guitar World,* among other publications.

RUSSELL GERSTEN is currently a professor of educational research and special education at the University of Oregon in Eugene. Throughout the Seventies he wrote extensively about soul music for ROLLING STONE, the *Boston Phoenix,* the *Real Paper* and the *Village Voice.* He interviewed and wrote profiles of most of the major artists of the era, including Al Green, Gladys Knight, Bobby Bland, Esther Phillips and Chaka Khan.

PETER GURALNICK is author of a trilogy of books on American roots: *Feel Like Going Home, Lost Highway* and *Sweet Soul Music* (all published by HarperCollins). He has published a novel, *Nighthawk Blues,* as well as the critical biographical study *Searching for Robert Johnson* (Dutton). He is currently working on a biography of Elvis Presley to be published by Morrow in 1994.

BARRY HANSEN is familiar to fans of his syndicated radio program of "mad music and crazy comedy" as Dr. Demento. He has written for ROLLING STONE, *Hit Parader, Billboard* and other periodicals. He compiled the original Specialty Records reissue series and many other albums, including *Dr. Demento's 20th Anniversary Collection* on Rhino. He holds an M.A. in folk music from UCLA and has taught a course there on the development of rock.

JAMES HENKE has been an editor at ROLLING STONE since 1977. Currently the magazine's music editor, he has interviewed numerous artists over the years, including U2, Bruce Springsteen and Eric Clapton. He is also the author of *Human Rights Now!,* a journal of the 1988 Amnesty International tour.

STEPHEN HOLDEN is a music, theater and film critic for the *New York Times* and has reviewed records for ROLLING STONE for more than twenty years.

ALLAN KOZINN is a music critic for the *New York Times.*

JON LANDAU is the author of *It's Too Late to Stop Now* (Straight Arrow). He has written extensively about rock in the *Boston Phoenix, Crawdaddy* and ROLLING STONE, where he was an associate editor for many years. More recently, he has been working as a record producer and artist manager.

ALAN LIGHT is an associate editor at ROLLING STONE, where he writes on a regular basis. His work also has appeared in *Vogue,* the *South Atlantic Quarterly* and the *World Book Encyclopedia,* among other publications. A 1988 graduate of Yale University, he majored in American studies with a concentration in American popular music. He wrote his senior thesis on the Beastie Boys.

GREIL MARCUS is the author of *Dead Elvis: A Chronicle of Cultural Obsession* (Doubleday, 1991), *Mystery Train: Images of America in Rock 'n' Roll Music* (Dutton, 1975) and *Lipstick Traces: A Secret History of the 20th Century* (Harvard, 1989), and the editor of Lester Bangs's *Psychotic Reactions and Carburetor Dung* (Knopf, 1987). He is a contributing editor of ROLLING STONE.

DAVE MARSH edits *Rock & Roll Confidential* and has written and edited many books on popular music, including best-selling biographies of Bruce Springsteen and the Who. A *Playboy* music critic, he frequently lectures and writes about the relationship of music, politics and censorship.

JOE McEWEN is currently vice president of A&R at Sire Records.

DAISANN McLANE first got interested in world music in 1980, when she left the staff of ROLLING STONE and became a producer and performer of calypso music in Trinidad. She writes frequently about international sounds and other culturally related topics for the *New York Times,* the *Village Voice, Vogue* and other publications and contributes a column, "The Global Beat," to ROLLING STONE.

DON McLEESE is the pop music critic at the *Austin American Statesman* and a frequent contributor to ROLLING STONE and other music publications. He was formerly the pop music critic at the *Chicago Sun Times.*

JIM MILLER edited the first two editions of *The* ROLLING STONE *Illustrated History of Rock & Roll* and is the author of *Democracy Is in the Streets: From Port Huron to the Siege of Chicago* (Simon & Schuster, 1987) and a forthcoming biographical study of the French philosopher Michel Foucault.

JOHN MORTHLAND is a freelance writer who lives in Austin, Texas. He is the author of *The Best of Country Music* (Doubleday, 1984).

PAUL NELSON has written about music for ROLLING STONE, the *Village Voice,* the *New York Times, Circus, Penthouse, Creem,* the *Real Paper* and the *Little Sandy Review,* which he cofounded in 1961.

ROBERT PALMER is a former chief pop music critic for the *New York Times* and a frequent contributor to ROLLING STONE and other publications. His documentary films include *The World According to John Coltrane,* which he wrote and codirected, and *Deep Blues* (based on his award-winning book of the same name), a tour of Mississippi juke joints for which he served as writer and musical director.

JOE NICK PATOSKI is a senior editor at *Texas Monthly* magazine. He has written about music and popular culture for ROLLING STONE, *Creem, Country Music, Mother Jones* and other magazines and contributed passages to *Honky Tonkin': A Travel Guide to American Music* (East Woods Press, 1980). He has also managed several rock bands and worked as a DJ in Austin and Dallas–Fort Worth.

CHARLES PERRY worked for ROLLING STONE in San Francisco, then became a freelance writer specializing in food and food history and moved to Los Angeles. Today he is a staff writer at the *Los Angeles Times* and a contributor to the forthcoming *Oxford Companion to Food.* His book *The Haight-Ashbury: A History* was published by Rolling Stone Press/Simon & Schuster in 1984.

PARKE PUTERBAUGH is a contributing editor and former senior editor for ROLLING STONE. He is also a regular contributor to *Stereo Review.* His writing has appeared in numerous other magazines and newspapers, and he has annotated twenty albums for Rhino Records. He is coauthor of a series of travel books published by McGraw-Hill and is currently pursuing a master's degree in environmental management and policy at the University of North Carolina.

KIT RACHLIS is the former arts editor of the *Boston Phoenix* and former executive editor of the *Village Voice*. He is currently editor of *L.A. Weekly*.

CARRIE RICKEY, currently film critic for the *Philadelphia Inquirer*, previously reviewed movies for the *Boston Herald* and the *Village Voice* and has contributed to a variety of publications ranging from *Artforum* to the *Wall Street Journal*.

JOHN ROCKWELL, European cultural correspondent and classical recordings reviewer for the *New York Times*, has taught cultural history at Princeton University and new American music at Brooklyn College. He is the author of *All American Music: Composition in the Late Twentieth Century* (Knopf, 1983), which was nominated for a National Book Critics Circle award, and *Sinatra: An American Classic* (Rolling Stone Press/Random House, 1984).

BUD SCOPPA, author of *The Byrds* (Scholastic, 1971) and *The Rock People* (Scholastic, 1972), has spent the last two decades alternating between rock journalism and more gainful employment with several record labels. In the latter capacity, he was involved in the careers of the New York Dolls, the Tubes, the Bus Boys and other less well remembered bands. Before becoming vice president of artist development at BMG-owned Zoo Entertainment in 1990, Scoppa edited a succession of music magazines.

GREG SHAW was one of the first rock critics; between 1965 and 1979 he wrote for dozens of magazines and was editor-publisher of many, including *Mojo-Navigator*, *Phonograph Record* and *BOMP*. In the mid-Seventies BOMP also became a record company, a pioneer in the punk–new wave movement, and since then Shaw has devoted himself to making what he likes to think of as ''underground'' records in the Sixties tradition. He has also compiled reissues for various labels, written several books of arcane lore and is best known to many for the more than 100 albums of obscure Sixties garage music assembled and annotated under the titles *Pebbles*.

TOM SINCLAIR, a native New Yorker, writes about pop music for ROLLING STONE, the *Village Voice* and *The New York Times*. He is the author of the children's fantasy novel *Tales of a Wandering Warthog* (Albert Whitman, 1985).

TOM SMUCKER grew up in the Chicagoland area and has lived for more than twenty years in New York City, where he has worked almost as long for the telephone company.

JOHN SWENSON, a syndicated columnist for United Press International and Reuters, has been a ROLLING STONE contributor for seventeen years. Swenson has written or edited thirteen books, including *The* ROLLING STONE *Jazz Record Guide* and the first two editions of *The* ROLLING STONE *Record Guide*, which he coedited with Dave Marsh.

KEN TUCKER is the television critic for *Entertainment Weekly* and the rock critic for National Public Radio's *Fresh Air*. He is a coauthor of *Rock of Ages: The* ROLLING STONE *History of Rock & Roll*. His work has appeared in ROLLING STONE, the *New York Times*, the *Village Voice*, *L.A. Weekly*, *Vogue* and the *Philadelphia Inquirer*.

ED WARD has written about popular music since 1965. A coauthor of *Rock of Ages: The* ROLLING STONE *History of Rock & Roll*, he can be heard on National Public Radio's *Fresh Air* and is a contributing editor of the Austin *Chronicle*. He is also International Coordinator of the South by Southwest Music and Media Conference and is currently at work on a book about Chess Records for Pharos Books. He lives in Austin, Texas.

ELLEN WILLIS has written about feminism, cultural politics, movies and music for the *Village Voice*, ROLLING STONE, the *New Yorker* and other publications. The second edition of her collection of essays, *Beginning to See the Light*, and a new collection, *No More Nice Girls*, will be published by Wesleyan University Press in 1992. She teaches journalism at New York University.

LANGDON WINNER is a political theorist who specializes in social and political issues generated by modern technological change. He is the author of *Autonomous Technology*. He has written rock criticism for *The Atlantic Monthly*, ROLLING STONE and other publications. He was also artistic and technical consultant to the film *Koyaanisqatsi: Life Out of Balance* (1983) and is currently a visiting research scholar at the Center for Technology and Culture in Oslo, Norway. He is writing a book on the politics of design.

INDEX

ACKNOWLEDGMENTS

The discographies supplementing almost every chapter of this book were compiled from Joel Whitburn's *Record Research* books, including *Top Pop Singles 1955–1990, Top Pop Albums 1955–1985, Top R&B Singles 1942–1988,* and yearly anthologies (1985–1991) of the charts, all of which are are based on *Billboard* magazine's weekly charts. Many thanks to Gary Stewart, Ted Myers, James Austin and the staff at Rhino for their expert advice regarding anthologies, collections and rock & roll minutiae. Kudos also go to Roger Steffens, founding editor of *The Beat,* the international bimonthly reggae and world beat magazine, for his expertise in updating the discography for "Reggae," which was originally compiled by Bud Kliment (who also compiled the original discography for "The Sound of New York"). We also appreciate the research assistance given by Bob George and Jon Hafter of the Archives of Contemporary Music (ARC). In addition, thanks to Lynn Snyder and to John Lagana, Steve Futterman, Amy Kaplan, Wook Kim and Paul La Rocca of ROLLING STONE, as well as Dennis Ambrose and Jonathan Karp of Random House.